The Directory of International Sources of Business Information

Sarah Ball

Pitman Publishing
128 Long Acre, London WC2E 9AN

A Longman Group Company
First published in Great Britain in 1989

British Library Cataloguing in Publication Data
Ball, Sarah
The directory of international sources of business information.
1.Business information-Directories
I.Title
338.'0025

ISBN 0 273 03047 7

Photoset in 8/9pt Palatino by
Land & Unwin (Data Sciences) Limited, Bugbrooke, Northants
Printed in Great Britain at The Bath Press, Avon

LIST OF CONTENTS

Preface

Compiling a directory can often start as a rash promise, and end up as a labour of love, seemingly with no end in sight! Publication dates bring the project to a conclusion, although the process of checking and cross-referencing, and endeavouring to keep information up-to-date in a rapidly changing arena is never ending.

The fact that this labour of love ever saw the light of day is due in no small measure to all the organisations including embassies, chambers of commerce and stock exchanges who provided me with information. I am also indebted to the database hosts who checked and returned the database descriptions which I had prepared, and completed the questionnaire about their service, which I used to compile the Database Host Services Chart. I would like to thank the European Commission organisation, ECHO, for allowing me to use information taken from their database Brokersguide, the Federation Internationale des Bourses de Valeurs, and British Telecom International for allowing the reproduction of tables and statistics, and for providing valuable advice.

Marie McDonnell typed the bulk of the manuscript with extreme efficiency and accuracy, and I cannot thank her enough for all her assistance. I would also like to thank the friends who assisted with some of the typing and compilation, and my husband for cooking and washing up solo for the last 6 months.

Despite all efforts, I am fully aware that no directory can be completely up to date, and errors and omissions do occur. All suggestions and corrections will be gratefully received, and should be sent to me c/o Pitman Publishing.

Sarah Ball
August 1988

Foreword

This directory has become available just in time to meet a rapidly expanding need for information in the field of international investment. A few years ago, only specialists dealt in "foreign" shares, loans etc, now this is increasingly becoming the mainstream of business. The creation of a single internal market within the European Communities is just one major development that is driving this process.

One of the problems that globalisation raises is that accounting information differs dramatically from country to country. This Directory tries to solve some of the problems caused by international differences in the availability, location and presentation of financial information. This foreword will refer to the major differences in the valuation and measurement rules that underlie the reported accounting figures. There are differences in degrees of "fairness", conservatism, use of income smoothing, influence of tax-based provisions etc. As an illustration of the differences, let us examine two and take in the context of Europe: the valuation of fixed assets, and consolidation.

Valuation of Fixed Assets

There is great international variation in the predominant basis of valuation and the degree to which there is experimentation with different disclosures. In a country with detailed legal rules and a coincidence of tax and commercial accounting it must be expected that the predominant valuation system will be one that involves as little judgement as possible. Flexibility and judgement would make it difficult for auditors to determine whether the law had been obeyed and they might lead to arbitrary taxation demands. Thus, in a country such as the Federal Republic of Germany, it seems surprising that the required method of valuation is a strict form of historical cost.

At the other extreme is the Netherlands. Some Dutch companies (eg Philips) have published replacement cost financial statements since the early 1950s. Although this remains minority practice, many Dutch companies partially or supplementarily use replacement costs.

In between these two extremes, UK "rules" allow a chaotic state of affairs where some companies revalue, some of the time, using a variety of methods. This is the story for most of the English-speaking world, except that the USA and Canada keep to historical cost in the main financial statements; this is because of the influence of the SEC.

In France, Spain and Italy, where there is much government influence, there have also been inflation and interest in efficient equity capital markets. Governments and stock exchange bodies in these countries have appreciated the effects of inflation on historical cost accounting and have required revaluations. For example, after four years of significant inflation, the revaluation of assets was thought to be necessary in France in 1978. Because of the link with taxation and law, and because of an absence of a strong and innovatory body of accountants, revaluation had to be done uniformly or not at all. Thus, French revaluation was done compulsorily using government indices. It was tax-exempt and has led to subsequent annual depreciation and adjustments for tax purposes. This process is sufficiently ungainly that it has not happened since 1978, and it is now of negligible benefit because the resulting aggregate asset figures in balance sheets are neither cost nor current.

Consolidation

The prevalence of consolidation has varied dramatically among EEC countries. Most practices seem to have first enjoyed widespread adoption in the USA: for example, the normal acquisition method, the equity method and the pooling of interests/merger method. There are examples of consolidation at least as far back as the 1890s and it was widespread practice by the early 1920s.

In the UK and the Netherlands, consolidation was also practised well before the Second World

War. However, in most of continental Europe, consolidation is either a recent development or still very rare. In Germany, consolidation was made obligatory by the 1965 *Aktiengesetz* for public companies. However, foreign subsidiaries did not need to be (and generally were not) consolidated, and the use of the equity method for associated companies was not allowed. Further, there were important differences from Anglo-American practice in the use of an economic (rather than a legal) basis for "the group", and a yearly calculation of "differences arising on consolidation" based on book values rather than a once-for-all calculation of goodwill based on fair values. The Federal Republic of Germany implemented *EEC*'s Seventh Directive in 1985, thus removing most of these differences, at least from 1990 year-ends.

In France, before 1985 there was no law on consolidation. Thus, consolidation had been rare. Naturally, in a country where there is no tradition of professional accounting measurement standards, in cases where there were no law or tax requirements, practice has been very varied. In 1985, a law was passed to require listed companies to publish consolidated financial statements. Other companies must follow by 1990. In Belgium and Spain, until the 1980s, consolidation was very rare. In Italy, it has been rare even for listed companies.

The results of lack of consolidation in these many *EEC* countries is that outside investors or lenders (particularly foreigners) have grossly inadequate information, even about larger listed groups. However, the stock exchange bodies and governments of most *EEC* countries have begun to take actions to require listed or public companies to consolidate. This is designed to make their domestic capital markets more efficient and to internationalise the flows of capital. In addition, the Seventh Directive of the *EEC* requires consolidation rules by 1990.

The conclusion of this discussion is that, although this timely and remarkably useful Directory should greatly enhance one's ability to access information internationally, great care will still be needed in interpreting company accounts.

Christopher Nobes
Deloitte Professor of Accounting
University of Reading
August 1988

1 Introduction

This directory covers business information sources with the primary focus on companies, markets, finance, securities and economics. It aims to assist the business researcher or analyst to locate sources of information in Europe, USA, Canada and the Far East. These secondary sources of information are important in providing regular market and competitor intelligence, as well as supplementing primary market research (*ie* original or field research).

The information industry is a vital part of the world economy, and it is growing rapidly. In the UK it accounts for over 6 per cent of *GNP*. It embraces the media, computer services, video products, on-line and off-line data services. Computer services are growing at the rate of 20 per cent per annum in the UK. To illustrate the growth in just one of these areas - in 1980 the number of publicly accessible databases was just 400; by 1988 this figure had risen to 4000. These databases are offered by a rapidly expanding list of producers. In 1980, there were just 221 database producers, today there are around 1700. Most of the growth in this sector has come from business and financial databases, and this growth is forecast to continue.

Growth in on-line databases is likely to take place in conjunction with other media such as CD-ROM (Compact Disc-Read Only Memory). This is a system that stores large amounts of information on Compact Disc. There are various sizes of disc, which typically can store at least 500 megabytes of information. CD-ROM can be an expensive system to subscribe to, but can make good economic sense for users who wish to access large amounts of information where frequent updating is not a priority. On-line databases are likely to remain pre-eminent where up to the minute information is essential; they can also offer financial advantages for users who only need to access information on a less frequent basis. What sort of information do these on-line databases offer ? Well, the vast number available gives some indication of the choice of information on offer. For instance, the full text of company balance sheets together with profit and loss statements; trade statistics for the *EC* on a product by product basis; overseas trade opportunities and business contacts worldwide can be obtained, and if you are looking for international conferences and trade fairs, then an on-line database can be a good place to start.

It is partly against this background of rapid developments in international on-line databases that this directory has been prepared. It aims to enable the reader to select the right on-line databases for their requirements, by providing a detailed description of 660 different services offered by 149 hosts and 384 producers worldwide.

Information under one roof

There is a wealth of useful business information that is available, if you know where to look for it, and an extremely sophisticated range of products and services which assist us in identifying this information, including other business directories. However, they can often have limiting factors, either in their geographic coverage, or in the type of information source which they cover. For instance, there are good sources of information about trade associations that do not cover databases, and vice versa. To find relevant and up to date information, it is sometimes necessary to search through many sources, some of which are not easily accessible. This directory has attempted to cut across both geographic and information source boundaries. It covers a large number of countries, including all 12 *EC* countries, and a selection of 11 major industry sectors. For each country there are addresses of major banks, stockbrokers, stock exchanges, sources of advice on trade and investment, trade associations and business publications. The industry chapter provides a selection of trade associations worldwide, specialist directories, journals and market research reports.

One advantage of having a lot of information sources available 'under one roof ' is that it may well reveal that a particular piece of information, a market research report say, can be obtained on-line as well as in hard copy. The speed with which you need the information may justify the extra costs which you can incur by accessing information online. There is also a lot of valuable information which is free of charge, for example tax and investment guides produced by accountancy firms, economic and investment reports produced by banks, and export and trade information produced by government organisations such as the British Overseas Trade Board. There is no point in paying over the odds for information that is free!

The arrival of 1992

1992 is an exciting prospect with a potential single European market of over 320 million consumers. The single market will bring new opportunities but also increased competition. All of this means that we need more facts about the market, our competitors, and specifically how *EC* policy and legislation will impact on our business.

This directory aims to meet some of these needs by identifying sources of information on European markets, companies and *EC* legislation. Databases in chapter 6 include services offered by hosts in Germany, Spain, Italy, France, Denmark and other *EC* countries, who are establishing agents and offices overseas, but who are still relatively unknown outside their own countries. Chapter 6 also includes descriptions of the databases made available by ECHO, the European Community host organisation, and several European Community 1992 databases. These databases are being established to provide up to date information on company law and taxation, environment, specific industry sectors and many other areas drawing on *EC* official documentation such as the Official Journal and Directives. A number of international accountancy firms have been setting up *EC* databases as part of a wider range of services which they offer to companies who want assistance in preparing for 1992. Other specialist sources of advice are listed in chapter 2 ie the *Euro-Info* centres. These are multi-purpose information offices, situated in specific areas throughout the *EC*, and intended to assist small and medium-size enterprises (*SMEs*). They provide Community information (legislation, aids, grants etc), and have access to the Community databases. Chapter 2 also contains details of information brokers in Europe, who will access public databases and other published material on your behalf, for a fee.

How to use the directory

The best way of explaining how to use the directory is to use an example of a typical research requirement. A reader may want to find out as much information as possible about a French electronics company, perhaps because the company is a potential acquisition candidate or competitor. The way to use the directory is as follows:

If the information is required urgently
- Go to chapter 6 (On-line databases)
- Go to Section I (Company Finance and Profile)
- Look under the subheading France to find a list of French company databases
- Use the summary matrix in chapter 5 to see if more than one host offers the service
- Read the description of the database to see if it covers the type of information which you are looking for (eg balance sheet or profit and loss data etc)
- Access direct if you have signed up with the host, or go through an information broker (listed in chapter 2)
- Supplement information gathered from financial databases with press items on the company obtained from one of the news databases (see section V).

If information is less urgent
- Consult chapter 3 (Country data sources) -*France*
- Look up French company directories in the relevant section, and consult the directory in a library (unless you decide to buy it)
- You should be able to obtain basic details such as the size of the company and it's address from a directory. If the company is large and publicly quoted, you can contact the company direct and ask them to send a copy of their accounts.
- Consult the journals and periodicals section in chapter 3, as these may be worth consulting for articles on the company, and some provide annual rankings of French companies.
- If you need further advice a French Chamber of Commerce or trade section of a French embassy may be able to help (contact details in chapter 3).

Extra background information
- Consult chapter 4 (Industry data sources)-*Electronics*
- Look under the subheading for trade associations

- Contact a French trade association to see if they have prepared any recent reports on the French electronics sector
- Look under the subheading for directories , and consult the directories which look relevant to your requirements (eg some provide statistics on market size in different countries, or basic profile details on major European electronics companies).
- Look under the subheading for market research reports, to see if there is a report listed which covers the particular aspect of the industry which the company you are investigating is involved in.

There are various charts in the directory which have been produced to summarise and cross-reference information. The Summary Matrix of major database hosts in chapter 5 is aimed at the reader who wants to go on line for the first time and needs to select the host who covers the most comprehensive range of relevant databases. If you already have access to several hosts and need to quickly identify a database's subject and country coverage, the Database Country Coverage and Subject Area summary chart (appendix 3) will be useful. The Database Host Services chart in chapter 5 provides additional information about telecommunications access, extra charges, help facilities including help-line telephone numbers and the language(s) which services are provided in. The chart on timescale criteria in chapter 1, shows the time it takes to get company information from different countries in Europe.

Information Caveats

In the course of getting enthusiastic about the mass of valuable international business information which exists, it is as well at the same time to be aware of certain caveats.

- Published and on-line sources are often in the language of the country of origin. However, this is generally less of a problem when accessing predominantly financial or statistical data, and, there are brokers who offer an interpreting service (eg. Science Reference Library, London's Japanese Information Service).
- There are variations in the extent of information available and also the quality of information in different countries. Scandinavian countries, particularly Sweden, have traditionally been very open and offer excellent financial and economic information. In contrast, for other European countries such as Spain, company information is much less accessible.
- In the case of company financial information, you should be aware of the differences that exist between overseas countries in their financial reporting regulations and practices, which can make direct comparisons between companies misleading. *EC* Directives are attempting to address this problem in Europe, but it will remain an issue for the financial analyst for some time.

The tables which follow illustrate the difference between countries in terms of the number of domestic companies listed on the stock exchange, and the definitions of legal types of company. It is worth noting that there are differences in the registration procedures between countries. In a number of countries, such as France, Italy and Spain, regional filing of accounts with chambers of commerce or '*Registre du Commerce*' rather than central filing is the legal requirement, and these accounts are available either by written application or through online databases. Hopefully, these caveats will not deter the researcher who seeks to access international information, but act as a reminder that how you interpret the information is just as important as the ability to access it.

Good information is an essential basis for good decisions. As markets extend into Europe and beyond, the businesses which have a competitive advantage will be those who know how to get the most value from all the information which is available, bearing in mind *Naisbitt's* quote "we are drowning in information but starved of knowledge". I hope that this directory will give some initial pointers as to where to go for information available overseas and will give the reader the advantage of saying: "I know where we can get that information. I know how much it will cost. I know how long it will take to reach us"

Accessing Information According to Timescale Criteria

This chart summarises the process of accessing company information according to timescale criteria. The degree of urgency for information will often dictate the method or source of information which you will use. For example company information required within the hour can be obtained from on-line sources. Company accounts for UK companies required the same day can be obtained in the UK by visiting a Companies Registration Office, or through Credit Report Agencies. Microfiche on companies worldwide can be obtained the same day or within two days through organisations such as Bechtel or CIFAR (Center for International Finance and Research.)

The speed with which company accounts or credit reports can be accessed in different countries is dictated by local conditions and the availability of public records. There is not space to list timings for a large number of countries, but this chart lists the time it takes to get reports from countries in the EC, which have been quoted by some of the major credit agencies in the UK. In certain countries such as the Republic of Ireland accounts are only available for publicly quoted companies. If time is not pressing, it is possible to obtain accounts from publicly quoted companies by contacting them directly. The chart, Listed Companies-The International Picture in this section will give you an idea as to the number of publicly quoted companies in the EC and other countries worldwide.

Useful addresses:

Centre for International Financial Analysis and Research Inc (CIFAR)
601 Ewing Street
Princeton NJ 08540
USA
Tel: (010 1) 609-9210910
Telex: 382045

Bechtel Information Services
SEC Express
15740 Shady Grove Road
Gaithersburg
Maryland 20877-1454
Tel: (010 1) 301-7381507
Affiliates of Bechtel: Canada c/o The Globe & Mail
Japan c/o Maruzen co ltd
Europe c/o Information Publications International/Gower
London c/o Financial Times Business Information

EEC Company Legal Forms and Registration System

This chart provides titles and capital requirements for public, private and certain less common legal forms of company. It also indicates whether there is a centralised or decentralised method of company registration. The chart covers only EEC countries, due to the current degree of interest in these countries.

The reason for providing the chart is to assist the company researcher to distinguish public and private companies in Europe when looking at company accounts, credit reports, directories etc. The registration system has been included to point researchers in the right direction when they want to access accounts directly from the country's registry offices.

Listed Companies – The International Picture

This chart lists 38 Stock Exchanges worldwide in descending order of size according to the number of listed companies. As the number of listed companies is not an indicator as to size in market value terms, the equity value of shares of domestic companies is also included. The degree of internationalisation of markets is indicated by the column which shows the percentage of domestic companies listed on each exchange. Individual exchanges rather than countries are listed, and the last column shows how many exchanges exist in each country.

This chart can be used as a guide to the relative size of markets for countries included in this directory (together with a number of additional countries). There is inevitably some degree of overlap where companies are listed on more than one exchange, eg a number of companies listed on the Irish Exchange in Dublin are also listed on the London Stock Exchange. It was therefore not appropiate to total figures in the first two columns.

Accessing Information According to Timescale Criteria

Within the hour

Viewdata Services / Videotex Services / Teletext Services	Online Databases Subscription Services or Pay As You Go		CDROM	Information Brokers
PRESTEL	TELECOM GOLD	DUN & BRADSTREET	Large number of services now available on CDROM e.g.	UK examples:
ICC	DATASTREAM	TEXTLINE		London Business School.
CCN/GUARDIAN	DIALOG	WEFA	CIFAR foreign annual reports service.	Financial Times Business Information Service.
TOPIC	ICC	DRI		
MINITEL	DATASTAR	ADP	Standard and Poor's Corporations.	(Information provided within the hour depending on exact nature of enquiry).
CEEFAX	KOMPASS	MEAD		
BILDSCHIRMTEXT (BTX)	Real Time Stock Market Services	BRS	European Kompass	
	EXTEL	ORBIT		

Same day

Business Specialist or Local Library	Chambers of Commerce Embassies Trade Commissions Trade Associations	Company Accounts and Credit Report Services	UK Companies Registration Offices
Visit and access: Company Annual Reports Extel Cards (Company Summary Reports) McCarthy Cards (Press Cutting Service) Market Research Reports (e.g. Keynote, Jordans) Directories: Moodys Standard & Poors Thomas Register Trade Journals F & S Europe and International Indexes.	Contact by telephone or personal visit. Some organisations have libraries available for the use of researchers and enquirers by appointment. Government Departments UK – Department of Trade and Industry Banks Stockbrokers	**Dun & Bradstreet** UK Company Accounts (24 hours max.) UK Credit Report (1 – 7 days) **Jordans** UK Company Accounts (1 day) UK Credit Reports (1 – 7 days) **Infocheck** UK Company Accounts (1 day) **ICC** UK Company Accounts (24 hours maximum, depending on time of order) **CCN/Guardian** Shareholder lists for UK public companies (1 day) UK Annual Report (24 hours) UK Credit Report (1 day) **Bechtel SEC Express (USA)** USA and CIFAR Foreign Annual Reports. Full text on microfiche or hardcopy. Fastest service via courier or facsimile.	Visit in person to conduct a company search. Annual reports can be ordered and collected same day on microfiche or hardcopy. Offices in: ★ Cardiff ★ London ★ Edinburgh Tele-Index Service.

European Company Accounts and Credit Report Services
UK Credit-Rating Agencies' Credit Reports

	CCN/Guardian Superexpress	Infocheck Fastest Service	ICC Priority Express Telex	Dun & Bradstreet Priority Service	UK Companies Registration Offices
	DAYS	HOURS	HOURS	HOURS	
Belgium	2	24	72	48	
Denmark	2	48	72	48	
France	2	24	72	48	
Germany	2	24	72	48	
Greece	2	24	72	48	
Ireland, Rep. of	2	3–5 days	7 days	48	
Italy	2	24	72	48	
Luxembourg	2	72	72	48	
Netherlands	2	24	72	48	
Portugal	2	24	72	48	
Spain	2	24	72	48	
UK	1	4	24	24	3 days (postal search)

On Demand International Annual Reports Services

BECHTEL SEC/EXPRESS

– Large collection of reports filed with the SEC (USA) available.
– Holds reports on 5000 major non-USA companies.
– Distributors in Canada, UK, Europe, Japan, Asia, Australia
– Copies sent hardcopy or fiche.

CIFAR

– Holds reports on 5000 major non-USA companies.
– Next day delivery service in the USA. standing order or 'as needed' basis.

Up To 4 Weeks

European Company Accounts and Credit Report Agencies

CCN/Guardian	Jordans		ICC		Other Sources
Accounts available for most European countries from 3 – 4 days to 4 – 6 weeks depending on countries requested.	Accounts fastest service	Days	Business reports available for most European countries within 3 to 4 weeks.		*Contact public companies direct to request copy of annual report.
	Belgium	10			
Express credit reports available in 5 days. Standard report in 8 – 10 days.	Denmark	14	Express telex reports available in 5 to 10 working days.		*Write to overseas organisations e.g. company registration offices, Chambers of Commerce.
	France	14	Accounts usually take up to 28 days for delivery.		
	Germany	14			
Dun & Bradstreet	Greece	21	Fastest Service	Days	*Contact banks and stockbrokers for investment research, Eurobond prospectuses and other sources of company information.
Accounts available for most European countries. Timing depends on local conditions and availability.	Ireland, Rep. of	10–15	Belgium	30	
	Italy	30	Denmark	30	
Preliminary credit report for new investigations can take 7 – 10 days. Normal Service reports take 5 – 10 days.	Luxembourg	20	France	30	
	Netherlands	10	N. Ireland	14	
	Portugal	14	Italy	30	
Scandinavian countries e.g. Denmark and Sweden can take 10 – 20 days.	Spain	14	Netherlands	30	
	UK	1–2			
Variety of delivery methods available e.g. telephone, telex, mail or printout on own terminal depending on type and speed of service requested.	Credit Reports vary by Country – average 3 to 10 days. Republic of Ireland – accounts available for PLCs only.				

Note

Timings quoted for agency services should be treated as an approximate guide only. Speed of service depends on whether the company requires initial investigation, information requires updating or current information is already on file. Services are subject to local conditions and the availability to the public of company accounts and records.

EEC Company Legal Forms and Registration System

	Public	Private	Registration
Belgium	Societe Anonyme (SA)	Societe de Personnes a Responsibilite Limitee (SPRL)	No centralised system
	Naambze Vennootschap (NV)	Personen vennootschap met beperkte gans aansprakeliskheid (PVBA)	
	Minimum capital requirement of BFr 1.25m fully paid up	Minimum share capital of BFr 750 000, one third paid up	Companies register at their local commercial court

Other (Less Common)
Societe en commandite par actions (SCA) – Limited partner with share capital
Commanditaire Vennootschap op aandelen (CVA) – Limited partnership without share captital
Societe en Commandite Simple (SCS or EVC) – Limited partnership with share capital

	Public	Private	Registration
Denmark	Aktieselskab (A/S)	Anpartsselskab (ApS)	Centralised company register
	Minimum capital requirement of DKr 300 000, at least one third paid up	Minimum capital requirement of DKr 80 000	'Aktieselskabsr Registret'

Other (Less Common)
Kommanditaktieselskab (KA/S) – Limited partnership
Kommanditselskab (K/S) – Limited partnership
Interessentskab (I/S) – General partnership

	Public	Private	Registration
France	Societe Anonyme (SA)	Societe a Responsibilite Limitee (SARL)	No centralised system
	Minimum share capital requirement of FF 250 000	Minimum share capital requirement of FF 50 000	Companies register with a 'local Registre du Commerce'

Other (Less Common)
Societe en Commandite par Actions (SCA) – Partnership limited by shares
Groupement d'Interet Economique (GIE) – Joint venture

	Public	Private	Registration
Germany (Federal Republic of)	Aktiengesellschaft (AG) (or Corporation. Can be public or private)	Gesellschaft mit Beschrankter Haftung (GmbH) Limited liability	No centralised system
	Miminum share capital requirement of DM 100 000. At least 25% fully paid up	Minimum share capital requirement of DM 50 000	Companies submit reports to local commercial registers and Federal Gazette

Other (Less Common)
Kommanditgesellschaft auf Aktien (KGaA) – Partnership limited by shares
GmbH & Co KG – Limited liability/limited partnership
Offene Handelsgesellschaft (OHG) – General Partnership

	Public	Private	Registration
Greece	Anonymos Eteria (AE) (or Corporation. Can be public or private)	Eteria Periorismenis Efthinis (EPE) Limited liability partnership	AEs file reports with the Ministry of Commerce
	Minimum capital requirement of Dr 5 million fully paid up	Minimum capital requirement of Dr 200 000	EPEs register with local court

Other (Less Common)
Eterorrythmos Kata Metochas Eteria (EKME) – Limited partnership

	Public	Private	Registration
Ireland (Republic of)	Public Limited Company (PLC)	Private Limited Company (Ltd)	Centralised company registration office in Dublin
	Minimum share capital of I£ 30000, 25% fully paid up for all companies		
Italy	Societa per Azioni (SpA)	Societa a Responsibilita Limitata (SRL)	No centralised system
	Minimum capital of Lire 200 million	Limited liability company. Minimum capital of Lire 20 million	Companies submit reports to a Local Registrar of Business Entreprises

Other (Less Common)
Societa in Accomandita per Azioni (SAA) – Limited partnership

	Public	Private	Registration
Luxembourg	Societe Anonyme (SA) (or Corporation)	Societe a Responsibilite Limitee (SARL) Private Limited	Accounts filed with the Luxembourg or Diekirch Commercial Courts
	Minimum issued share capital of BFr 1.25 million, 25% fully subscribed.	Minimum share capital of BFr 500 000 fully paid up. Maximum 40 shareholders	

Other (Less Common)
Societe en Commandite par Actions (SCA) – Limited partnership with shares
Societe en Commandite Simple (SECS) – Limited partnership without shares
Societe en Nom Collectif – General partnership
Holding Companies – Mainly SAs

	Public	Private	Registration
Netherlands	Naamloze Venootschap (NV) (or Corporation)	Besloten Venootschap (BV) Private limited liability	No centralised system
	Minimum share capital of FL 100 000 fully paid up	Minimum share capital of FL 40 000 fully subscribed	Companies register with their local Chamber of Commerce

Other (Less Common)
Commanditaire Venootschap (CV) – Limited partnership
Commanditaire Venotschap op Aandelen (CVOA) – Limited partnership with shares
Coopertieve Verenigingen (CV) – Cooperative Societes

	Public	Private	Registration
Portugal	Sociedade Anomina de Responsabilidade Limitada (SARL) (or Corporation)	Sociedade por Quotas de Responsabilidade Limitada (Lda) Private Limited	No centralised system
	Minimum capital of Ecs 5 million, 10% fully paid up	Minimum capital of Esc 400 000, at least 50% fully paid up	Company records are filed with a local Registrar 'Registo Comercial'

Other (Less Common)
Empresa Publica (EP) – State owned
Cooperativa de Responsabilidade Limitada (CRL)

	Public	Private	Registration
Spain	Sociedad Anomina (SA) (or Corporation)	Sociedad de Responsibilidad Limitada (SL) Limited liability	No centralised system
	Miminum capital requirement Pts 10 million will be introduced in 1989. 25% capital must be subscribed and paid up. Foreign capital must be fully paid up.	Maximum capital of Pts 50 million Maximum shareholders 50	Companies register with their provincial Mercantile registry

Other (Less Common)
Sociedad Colectivas – General partnership (No limited liability)
Sociedad Cooperativas – Cooperative society
Sociedad Comanditaria – Limited partnership

	Public	Private	Registration
UK	Public Limited Company (PLC)	Private Limited Company (Limited or Ltd)	Centralised company registration system
	Minimum capital requirement of £50 000, 25% of nominal value and all premium value must be fully paid up		Companies House in Cardiff, London and Edinburgh

Note: Currently no minimum capital requirement for SA companies in Spain.
Situation in Spain and other countries will change as legislation is introduced implementing EEC Directives

Listed Companies – The International Picture (1986)

Stock Exchange	Total listed companies	$ billion Market value of equity shares of domestic companies	% of domestic companies	Number of Stock Exchanges per country
London (UK)	2685	473	78	7
Bombay (India)	1890	6	100	14
New York (USA)	1575	2129	96	9
Tokyo (Japan)	1551	1784	97	8
Australian	1193	94	97	6
Toronto (Canada)	1085	185	95	5
Osaka (Japan)	1050	1549	100	
American (USA)	796	70	94	
Paris (France)	677	153	71	7
Germany (Fed Republic)	673	258	73	8
Johannesburg (South Africa)	562	103	95	1
Istanbul (Turkey)	545	1	100	1
Amsterdam (Netherlands)	509	84	52	1
New Zealand	469	22	72	1
Luxembourg	421	26	60	1
Korea	355	14	100	1
Zurich (Switzerland)	339	129	43	7
Brussels (Belgium)	331	37	58	4
Geneva (Switzerland)	329	123	37	
Barcelona (Spain)	324	46	100	4
Singapore	317	17	38	1
Madrid	312	49	100	
Basle (Switzerland)	294	111	35	
Kuala Lumpur (Malaysia)	287	15	79	1
Copenhagen (Denmark)	281	17	98	1
Hong Kong	253	54	98	1
Mexico	235	6	100	1
Italy	184	140	100	10
Stockholm (Sweden)	161	63	96	1
Oslo (Norway)	155	10	96	10
Taiwan	130	21	99	1
Greece	114	1	100	1
Vienna (Austria)	113	7	65	1
Thailand	98	3	100	1
Helsinki (Finland)	52	12	94	1
Irish (Republic)	48	6	100	1
Lisbon (Portugal)	40	1	100	2
Indonesia	24	81	75	1

NOTES

1   Only official exchanges are included.

2   1986 figures used due to availabilty of statistics for each country for this year and the need for consistency. Many of the figures quoted for listed companies have increased since this date.

3   Bombay market value statistic is based on the value of the top 25 listed companies. It is important to note that less than a third of total listed companies are actively traded, and only between 300 and 400 are blue chip. Major shareholders and financial institutions account for 80% of total equity, and so the major share of stock is not available to the public at large.

4   Frankfurt Stock Exchange is the dominant exchange in Germany. Freiverkeher companies are included in domestic and foreign companies.

5   Milan Stock Exchange is the major exchange in Italy.

6   Luxembourg and Vienna data includes investment funds.

7   London data includes some companies that only have fixed interest securities listed. Irish companies are included as non-domestic.

8   Irish Republic figures represent companies quoted on the Irish Exchange in Dublin. Banks, third market and unlisted companies are not included. Less than half of these companies are listed on the London Stock Exchange.

9   Indonesian foreign companies include 18 foreign joint stock companies.

10   Istanbul Stock Exchange market value is based on the top 50 companies actively traded in the senior market.

11   Mexican figures include companies that listed debentures in the capital market.
12   Market values are translated to US$ using 1986 year end exchange rates (Source IMF).
Source: Federation International des Bourses de Valeurs Rapport 1986.
        Data from individual exchanges obtained for the following:
        Bombay
        Istanbul
        Taiwan
        Greece
        Thailand
        Irish Republic
        Lisbon
        Indonesia

2 European Business Information Brokers and Euro-Info Centres

The first part of this chapter lists business information brokers in Austria, Belgium, Luxembourg, Denmark, Finland, France, Federal Republic of Germany, Italy, Netherlands, Spain, Sweden, Switzerland, and the UK. These are either individuals, companies or organisations based in the EEC, which offer fee-based services and access publicly available databases. These services may be of particular interest to readers who would like to access information from the databases described in this directory, but do not want to do the searching themselves, either due to investment or time constraints.

Details provided are: name of organisation (CN), Department (DT), contact name (CP), address, hosts (HOST) and databases (DB) accessed, subject areas covered (CT), languages spoken (LA), telephone (TEL), facsimile (FAX) and telex number (TX) (where available), and a description of the brokers main services (C D).

Most of the contact details listed below are a subset of the database BROKERSGUIDE which is available free of charge on the host ECHO. It is updated every month. ECHO is an organisation working under contract for DGX111/B "Information Industries" in Luxembourg to help to improve the European information market. This database is described in more detail in Chapter 6.

Austria

CN	Infotrade
CP	Christian Hoeck
	Heiligenstaedterstr 29
	1190 Vienna
HOST	Dialog; Data-Star; News Net; Genios; STN; Telesystemes;
DB	CA Search; Chemical Business Newsbase; BDI; Hoppendstedt; D&B; Investext; Dow Jones; APS Review; Standard & Poors; Energyline
CT	Business; companies; corporations; chemistry; investment; innovation; research and development; energy
LA	German; English; Italian; Finnish
TEL	(010 43) 222-317075/ 317076
CD	General information broking; information analysis

Belgium

CN	Bibliotheque Royale Albert 1er
DT	Centre Nationale de Documentation Scientifique et Technique
CP	Mr H de Jaeger Blvd de L'Empereur 4 1000 Brussels
HOST	ESA-IRS; Inka
DB	Inka-math; Inka-mathdi; Inspec
CT	Science; engineering; technology; industry; business; medicine; pharmacy; agronomy; chemistry; metallurgy; food products; textiles; mathematics; physics; information science; system-analysis; electronics
LA	French; Dutch
TEL	(010 32) 2-5195660
TX	21157

CN	Bureau Marcel van Dijk
CP	Mr Georges van Slype Ave Loiuse 409 1050 Brussels
CT	Science; technology; economics; business; marketing; law; medicine;
LA	French; Dutch
TEL	(010 32) 2-6486697

Denmark

CN	Alborg Universitetsbibliotek
DT	Public Services Dept
CP	Mr Bill Stevenson Langagervej 4 9200 Alborg 0
HOST	Alba; Aramis; Biblioteksdata; Blaise-Line; Byggdok; Dansk Byplanlaboratorium; Datacentralen; Data-Star; Datasolve; DIALOG; Dimdi; ESA-IRS; Nordisk BDI-Indeks; NSI; Polinfo; Recku; Pergamon Orbit Infoline; SOL; UBO; Studsvik; Danmark Statistik; ECHO; IP Sharp
DB	Dianeguide

CD Polinfo is the research department of the Politikens newspapers, the main national daily in Denmark. Polinfo produces a database called Poltxt which contains articles from the Danish press, and features political and current events

CN Studstrup & Ostgaard
DT Systematic Information
CP Mr Jens Ove Skjaerbaek
    Sofiendalsvej 5
    9100 Alborg
HOST ECHO; DIALOG; ESA-IRS; Data-Star; Bonnierdata; Infoline
DB Predicasts
CT Architecture; information science; energy; electronics; pharmacology; sport; law; ecology; technology; standards; agriculture; business
LA Danish; English; German
TEL (010 45) 8-188133
FAX (010 45) 8-186732
TX 69896 DENCON DK
CD SDI, advising, document delivery, fee based services

Finland

CN Helsingin Kauppakorkeakoulun Kirjasto
    Runeberginkatu 22-24
    00100 Helsinki 10
CT Economics; business; management
LA Finnish
TEL (010 358) 0-4313425
TX 122220 ECON

CN Infotrend
CP Mrs Lea Pihkala
    Box 40
    00971 Helsinki
HOST Easynet
DB Comp.

CT Business; enviornment; fisheries; information science; social sciences; technology; transportation; natural resources; surveying; planning
LA Danish; English
TEL (010 45) 8-158522/4007
TX 69790 AUB DK

CN Handelshoejskolen I Arhus
DT Biblioteket
CP Mr Hugo Frederiksen
    Fuglesangsalle 4
    8210 Arhus V
HOST Kompass Online
DB Kompass Denmark/Norway/Sweden/Federal Republic of Germany
CT Management; business; finance; economics; marketing; statistics; language; linguistics
LA Danish; English; French; German; Spanish
TEL (010 45) 6-155588
FAX (010 45) 6-150188
CD SDI, document delivery

CN Polinfo Politikens Informationsvirksomhed
CP Mr Johs C Johansen
    37 Raadhuspladsen
    1585 Copenhagen V
HOST Retsinfo
CT Biography; business; current affairs; economics; government; industrial relations; information; labour; legislation; newspapers; politics; public affairs;
LA Danish; English; Swedish; German
TEL (010 45) 1-118511
FAX (010 45) 1-154117
TX 22341

CT Engineering; business; medicine; patents; products
LA English; Swedish; Finnish
FAX (010 358) 0-3431206
CD Fee based information service, on-line information

CN Lappeenrannan Teknillisen Korkeakoulun Kirjasto
    Pl 20
    53851 Lappeenranta 85
CT Engineering; chemistry; physics; mathematics; business; management; information technology
LA Finnish
TEL (010 358) 53-27570
FAX (010 358) 53-29852
TX 58290 LTKKSF

France

CN Arist Alsace Agence Regionale d'Information Scientifique
CP Mrs Ursula Debrun
    2, Rue Brulee
    67000 Strasbourg
HOST Questel; G Cam Serveur; Kompass Online; DIALOG; Pergamon Orbit Infoline; Fiz Technik; STN; Data-Star; ESA-IRS
DB Pascal; INPI; WPI; Grappe; Ialine; Cetim; Predicasts; EDF-DOC; CAS;
CT Surveying; evolution; business; patents; general; commerce; industry; marketing; industrial relations; documentation; companies; technology; information
LA German; French; English
TEL (010 33) 222396
TX 870999

CD Industrial information service with 4 services: rapid information delivery, studies on the art of technology, diversification help, technology offers and new products, surveying

CN Bureau Marcel van Dijk
106 Bis Rue de Rennes
75006 Paris
CT Science; technology; economics; business; marketing; law; medicine
LA French
TEL (010 33) 1-5445300

CN Information on Demand
CP Mrs Isabelle Rozwadowska
24 Rue des Ecoles
75240 Paris
HOST DIALOG; ESA-IRS; Infoline; Mead Data Central;
DB Nexis
CT Business; patents; technology
LA French
TEL (010 33) 1-3294465

Germany, Federal Republic of

CN AGI Information Management Consultants
CP Mr Ulrich Weigel
Sonnenbuehlstr 71
7750 Konstanz
HOST Data-Star; Dimdi; GID; GBI; ECHO; GENIOS
DB Bliss; BEFO; BG-BDI; HB; WW; Predicasts
CT Companies; marketing; management; products; law; business; computers; statistics; social sciences; medicine
LA German
TEL (010 49) 7531-57217
TX 4931591
MX GEO1: AGI-Konstanz

CD Counselling on information systems, retrieval and database software, information market research, SDI, document delivery, representative of Fiz Technik
CN Bitt Schleswig-Holstein
DT Beratungsstelle fur Innovation und Technologie-Transfer EV
CP Mr Hinrich Knust
Lorentzendamm 22
2300 Kiel 1
HOST Data-Star; Fiz Technik; GENIOS; STN
DB Creditreform; Doma; Energy; Hope; Inspec; Medi; Patdpa; Predicasts;
CT Business; companies; science; technology; engineering; patents
LA German; English
TEL (010 49) 431-51304
CD Technologie-Boerse, Forschungskatalog Schleswig-Holstein

CN Le Courrier
CP Mr Dietmar Hannebohn
Sodener Str 1
6380 Bad Homburg
CT Marketing; business; finance; communications; management
LA German; English; French
TEL (010 49) 69-521176
FAX (010 49) 69-520433
TX 413814

CN Exit Datenbankdienste
DT Informationsvermittlung
CP Mr Dietmar Krause
Graf Von Staufenberg Str 19
4800 Bielefeld 1
HOST Data-Star; Dimdi; DIALOG; Ecodata; Fiz Technik; ECHO; ESA-IRS; GBI; GENIOS; Inka; Juris; Mead Data Central; Infoline; Questel; STN
DB Ruralnet

CT Business; medicine; science; technology; marketing; enviornment; hardware; software; company information; patents
CN Entwicklungszentrum fur Zerspanungstechnik
DT Fachinformationsstelle Technik und Wirtschaft
CP Mr Hartmut Lutschewitz
An Den Stegmatten 7
7630 LAHR
HOST Data-Star; DIALOG; GBI; ESA-IRS; Fiz Technik; GENIOS; GID; Questel; Pergamon Orbit Infoline; STN; Dimdi; ECHO; BRS; BIS; Scimmelpfeng; Deutsches Patentamt; EPO; Edicline; Juris
DB WPI
CT Social sciences; patents; law; economics; science; engineering; management; business; pollution; technology
LA German
TEL (010 49) 7821-5802-0
FAX (010 49) 7821-5802-59
TX 754911 WKHL D
CD Information broking, SDI, document delivery, on-line training, counselling on terminal installation, translation service

CN Fachinformation Kern
CP Mr Frank-Peter Kern
Postfach 510130
4400 Muenster
HOST Ecodata
DB Eurodicautom
CT Business; data processing; military science; risks; defence; law; technology; telephone; management; telecommunications
LA German; English
TEL (010 49) 2501-58111
TX 0505-990021 FPK SO

CD Specialises in communications and data security, SDI, document delivery, translations, producer of databases on communication security, market analysis, consulting, seminars

CN GBI Gesellschaft fur Betriebswirtschaftliche Information

CP Mr Mueller-Bader Alte Muenchener Str 43 A 8000 Munich 40

HOST GBI; Fiz Technik; GENIOS

CT Economics; business; finance; accountancy; administration; data processing; taxation; psychology; sociology; politics

LA German; English

TEL (010 49) 89-9505519

CN Hessische Landesentwicklungs-und Treuhandgesellschaft mbh

DT Informationsvermittlungsstelle

CP Mr Wolf-Martin Ahrend Abraham-Lincoln-Strasse 38-42 6200 Wiesbaden

HOST Deutsche Mailbox

DB Busi

CT Patents; technology; engineering; business

LA English; German

TEL (010 49) 6121-774299

FAX (010 49) 6121-774265

TX 4186 127 HLTD

CD The HLT Group is engaged in regional economic development, and they have been building up an information exchange service in Hessen. Main areas covered are technical information, engineering, electronics, patents and business information

CN IHK Industrie-und Handelskammer Hannover-Hildesheim

DT Informationsvermittlung

CP Mr Matthias Ritter Schiffgraben 49 3000 Hannover

HOST STN; Data-Star; GENIOS; Pergamon Orbit Infoline; Fiz Technik

DB Inspec; Comp; Doma; Hope; Dechema; Busi; VWWW; Energy; Metadex; Patdpa; Dianeguide; Brokersguide

CT Business; commerce; companies; economics; energy; engineering; exports; patents; physics; technology

LA English; German

TEL (010 49) 511-3107244

FAX (010 49) 511-3107333

TX 922769 IHK H

CD Consulting for inventors, firms and other persons in our district area concerning innovations, products, subsidy possibilities, cooperation with other firms or universities etc

CN Dr Klaus und Carin Hoeck Informationsmakler

CP K und C Hoeck Alter Postweg 23 4292 Rhede

HOST GENIOS; DIALOG; ESA-IRS; Fiz Technik; Datasolve; Juris; STN; Data-Star; Infoline; GBI; ECHO

DB Creditreform; HB; WW; Genios Operator; Bliss; Brokersguide; Dianeguide;

CT German and international law; business; economics; technical and applied sciences; reporting; on-line consulting

LA German; English; Dutch

TEL (010 49) 2872-6268/ 6278

TX 051933524 GEONET G

CN Mis Muenchner Informations-Service

CP Mrs Isa Hoppenstedt & Mr Peter Mueller-Bader Pariser Str 42 8000 Munich 80

HOST Newsnet

DB Predicasts; Bliss; Hope; KBE; Doma; ZDE; BDI; HB; WW; Creitreform

CT Accounting; advertising; business; companies; exports; management; marketing; products; market research; sales; training

LA German; English; French

TEL (010 49) 89-4484611/ 4482804

CD This service has been founded by GBI Gesellschaft fur Betriebswirtschaftliche Information, and Verlag Hoppenstedt

CN Seidel & Bonin

DT Information

CP Mr Guenther Bonin Friedensstr 3A 8034 Germering

HOST Fiz Technik; STN; Data-Star; ESA-IRS; Juris; Edicline

DB Titus

CT Law; engineering; textiles; building; tourism; economics; business

LA German; English; French; Italian; Turkish

TEL (010 49) 89-8414781

TX 522 760 CLOG D

CD Access electronic databases, research, interviews, set up studies

CN WTFK Wissenschaftliche und Technische Fachkommunikation Juergen Beling

CP	Mr Juergen Beling
	PO Box 1265
	5500 Trier
HOST	Data-Star; Fiz Technik; STN; DIALOG; BRS; Edicline; GENIOS
DB	Prodis
CT	Behavioural sciences; business; vocational training; management; personnel; psychology; technology; technical education; social sciences
LA	English; German
TEL	(010 49) 6585-770
TX	051933521 DMBOX G
CD	Consultancy for scientists, researchers, and business clients. Focus on human resources, human behaviour in organisational settings, social sciences and crossfile searching

Italy

CN	Consortium Genova Ricerche
CP	Mr Mauro Ricci
	Via dell'Acciaio 139
	16152 Genova
HOST	DIALOG; ESA-IRS; ECHO; Data-Star; Pergamon; Cerved; Easynet
DB	NTIS; Compendex; Inspec; Pascal; Chemabs; Predicasts; Enrep; Ismed; Enviorline; EI Engineering Meetings
CT	Business; commerce; companies; electrical power; electrical engineering; energy; engineering; finance; trade; patents
LA	English; Italian
TEL	(010 39) 10-608511
FAX	(010 39) 10-603801
TX	281048

CD	Creation of a new scientific information enviornment, promotion of services and facilities, implementation of joint research projects, development of specific technological capabilities
CN	On-Line SAS
CP	Mr Giovanni Furente
	Via Liberta 218/A
	80055 Portici NA
HOST	Questel
DB	Comp
CT	Law; information science; engineering; enviornment; business; patents; management
LA	English; French; Italian
TEL	(010 39) 81-7755574/7755566
CD	Information brokerage, database design and training, counselling
CN	Stel-Ervizi Telematii
CP	Rosario Vargiu
	Via del Canneto 34
	09134 Cagliari
HOST	Cerved; Sear; ESA-IRS; Dimdi; Pergamon; DIALOG; Infotap
CT	Business; marketing; companies; medicine; patents; engineering; information sciences; agriculture
LA	Italian; English; French
TEL	(010 39) 70-520958
FAX	(010 39) 70-520959
TX	335215
CD	Information brokerage; database design and implementation; value added network international cooperation
CN	Stel-Servizi Telematica
DT	Settore Banche Dati
CP	Mr Bruna Vidalli
	Via del Canneto 34
	09134 Cagliari
HOST	Dimdi; ESA-IRS; PGE; Italguire

DB	Lex
CT	Information science; engineering; enviornment; business; social sciences; medicine
LA	Italian; English; French
TEL	(010 39) 70-520959
CD	Consultancy, research and other activities
CN	Systel SRL
DT	Information Engineering Dept
CP	Mr Guidotti Stefano
	CSO Duca Degli
	Abruzzi 18
	10129 Turin
HOST	DIALOG; Data-Star; IP Sharp; Pergamon Infoline; SDC-Orbit; ESA-IRS; Questel; G Cam Seveur; Profile; STN; ECHO
DB	WPI-L; Inpadoc; Predicasts; Japio; ABI-Inform; SITC; BIS Infomat;
CT	Business; commerce; companies; finance; industry; information; management; marketing; patents; planning; products; statistics; surveying; technology
LA	Italy; English; French
TEL	(010 39) 11-5612303
FAX	(010 39) 11-511825
CD	Industrial information service for innovation in technology, markets, and management. Aims to offer services, products and tools for strategic management

Luxembourg

CN	Seib Software Engineer
	Information Broker
	2A Cite J F Kennedy
	7234 Helmsange
	Grand Duchy of Luxembourg

HOST ECHO; DIALOG; Data-Star; Fiz Technik; GENIOS; Ecodata; Infoline; Creditreform; GBI; Cerved; Schimmelpfeng

DB Brokersguide; Euristote; Dianeguide; VC; Dun & Bradstreet; ICC; ISIS; EK-BDI; Infocheck; ICP; VC-Online

CT Business; company data

LA German; English; French

TEL (010 352) 337021

CD Consultancy, business and patent databases

Netherlands

CN Cobidoc BV

CP Mr Peter Rosenbrand St Antoniesbreestraat 16 1011 HB Amsterdam

HOST STN; Datasolve; GENIOS; ESA; Dimdi

CT Chemistry; engineering; biomedicine; business

LA Dutch; English; German

TEL (010 31) 20-223955

TX 18766

CD Advising on the choice of databases/ hosts and/or software and hardware required. Advice on the creation of internal databases, hire of training facilities and organisation of seminars

CN Exportbevorderings- en Voorlichting- sdienst

CP Mr R A J Van Loen Bezuidenhoutseweg 151 2594 AG Den Haag

HOST ECHO; DIALOG; Data-Star; Belindis

DB TED

CT Economics; business; industry; energy; companies; products; countries

LA Dutch; English; French; German

TEL (010 31) 70-798933

TX 31099

CD SDI, document delivery (paper or microfiche)

CN Infotech Research

CP Mr H N Wevers Trumanstede 93-20 4463 We Goes

HOST DIALOG; Questel; ESA-IRS; Pergamon Orbit Infoline

DB CAS

CT Patents; business; chemistry; technology

LA Dutch; English; French; German

TEL (010 31) 1100-20365

TX 26401 INTX NL

CD SDI, document delivery, translation service, sale of datacommunication equipment and software

CN MIC-Multimedia Information Consultants

DT Information Consultants

CP Mr Bart van der Lugt Joan Muyskenweg 22 1096 CJ Amsterdam

HOST STN; Fiz Technik; Pergamon Orbit Infoline; DIALOG; Data-Star; ESA-IRS; Questel; Dimdi; IP Sharp; ECHO; Datacentralen; Belindis; Kompass Online; Edicline; Control Data; GID; Ivev; GENIOS; GCI; Viditel; Profile

DB Predicasts; Compendex; Inspec; NTIS; Biosis Chemabs; Marketing Data MKBDOC; SITC; Dun & Bradstreet; Profile

CT Applied science; business; commerce; companies; economics; exports; imports; finance; genetic engineering; marketing; public affairs; science; technology

LA Dutch; English; French; German

TEL (010 31) 20-947745

FAX (010 31) 20-929453

TX 10743 ETG NL

CD Specialists in information consultancy eg data on markets, new products, processes, technology, companies

CN Nederlandse Organisatie voor Toegepast Natuurwetenschappelijk Onderzoek

DT Centrum voor Informatie en Documentatie, CID TNO

CP Mr Charles L Citroen Schemakerstr 97, PO Box 36 2600 AA Delft

HOST ESA-IRS; Questel; DIALOG; Dimdi; Data-Star; STN

CT Engineering; technology; economics; management; chemistry; patents; enviornment; energy; marketing; business

LA Dutch; English; French; German

TEL (010 31) 15-569330

FAX (010 31) 15-616812

TX 38071 ZPTNO NL

CD Specialised service for medium and small industry, document delivery

CN NMB Bank

DT Business Information Center HG 03-02

CP Mr J A Agasi PO Box 1800 1000 BV Amsterdam

HOST DPA

DB INVE

CT Economics; business; companies; marketing; management; trade; exports

LA	Dutch; English; German; French
TEL	(010 31) 20-5638742
FAX	(010 31) 20-5638744
TX	15786 NMBAD
CD	NMB is one of the main commercial banks in the Netherlands. It has a special department for non-banking services, which deals with export promotion, and the transfer of business information, both internally and directly to customers

CN	Quanta Data
CP	Mr W P A de Kort
	Spoorstr 2
	3740 AG Baarn
HOST	Datasolve; Data-Star; DIALOG; Dun & Bradstreet; ECHO; ESA-IRS; Infoline; RCC
CT	Business; finance; statistics; products; patents; science; technology; marketing
LA	Dutch; English; German
TEL	(010 31) 2154-20851
FAX	(010 31) 2154-17772
CD	SDI, document delivery, marketing consultancy

Spain

CN	Dun & Bradstreet
CP	Mrs Isabel Adell Lorens
	Avda Diagonal 652
	08034 Barcelona
HOST	Dun & Bradstreet
CT	Economics; business; marketing
LA	Spanish; English
TEL	(010 34) 3-2050015/ 2040398
FAX	(010 34) 3-2051669
TX	54633/54123 DUNBA E

CN	Generalitat Valenciana Impiva
DT	Instituto de la Mediana y Pequena - Industria Valenciana

CP	Mr Fernando Palop Marro
	Placa del Pais Valencia 6
	46002 Valencia
HOST	Data-Star; DIALOG; ESA-IRS; RPI
CT	Technology; economics; business
LA	Spanish
TEL	(010 34) 6-3510100
FAX	(010 34) 6-3514064
CD	Impiva provides support to Valencia's small and medium sized enterprises with a whole package of services in fields such as information delivery, technology training and marketing advice

CN	Instituto Vasco de Estudios E Investigacion, Ikerketarako Euscal Institutoa
DT	Mrs Ana-Isabel Gonzalez
	Avda de la Libertad 20
	20004 San Sebastian-Guipuzcoa
HOST	Baratz; Blaise-Line; DIALOG; ESA-IRS; IP Sharp; Questel: Pergamon Orbit Infoline
CT	Commerce; business; banking; marketing; accountancy; education; linguistics
LA	Spanish
TEL	(010 34) 43-4266-10/11

CN	Universidad de Zaragoza
DT	Servicio de Informacion y Documentacion
CP	Mr Pedro-Manuel Aguado Benedi
	Edificio Geologicas - Ciudad Universitaria
	50009 Zaragoza
HOST	DIALOG; Dimdi; ESA-IRS; Infoline; Questel; Ibertex
DB	Medlars; CAS; NASA; Index Medicus

CT	Science; agriculture; medicine; education; psychiatry; energy; telecommunications; business; computers
LA	Spanish; English
TEL	(010 34) 87-450186/ 353862
TX	58198 EDUCI E
CD	SDI, document delivery (articles and theses)

Sweden

CN	Update Scandinavia
CP	Mrs Maria Vahlgreen Wall
	PO Box 53120
	40015 Goeteborg
HOST	TESS
CT	Economics; business
LA	Swedish
TEL	(010 46) 31-178390

CN	Interfact/SVP
CP	Mr Sven Hamrefors
	Kungsgatan 29
	10386 Stockholm
CT	Business; marketing; law; economics; technology
LA	Swedish
TEL	(010 46) 8-145545
TX	15924

Switzerland

CN	Ecole Polytechnique Federal de Lausanne, Bibliotheque Central
DT	Service Recherche Documentaire Automatisee
CP	Mrs C Mercier
	1015 Lausanne
HOST	Telesystems Questel
CT	Science; technology; humanities; business
LA	French
TEL	(010 41) 21-471111
TX	26456

UK

CN	A R Partnership
DT	Information Research Service

CP	Mr Peter B Rowland 11 Market Hill Saffron Walden Essex CB10 1HQ
HOST	Blaise-Line; Data-solve; ECHO; Finsbury; Kompass On-line; Prestel; Telecom Gold
DB	AP News; EKOL; ICCF; Kompass; Mideast; Newsearch; Newsline; Textline; UPI News; Washington Post
CT	Business; current affairs; companies; finance; investigations; markets; products; research;
LA	English
TEL	799-25673/25570
FAX	799-28456
TX	94620 CWEASY G (Quote reference no 19010710)
CD	IRS specialises in searches for business, obtaining suppliers or manufacturers, market opportunities, report format as required

CN	Datasearch Business Information
CP	Mr Paul Dolan 11 Kingsmead Square Bath BA1 2AB
HOST	Predicast
DB	Textline; PTSP; Jordans; Pira; Rapra; ICCF; CCN; BIS Infomat; World Reporter
CT	Business; products; industry; marketing; companies
LA	English; French; Dutch; German; Italian
TEL	225-60526
FAX	225-60688
TX	449212 LANTEL G
CD	Specialists in corporate and related information, full annual reports service

CN	Financial Times Business Information Bracken House 10 Canon Street London EC4P 4BY
HOST	Various
DB	All major business databases
LA	English
TF	01-248 8000
TX	8811506
CD	Provides a wide range of business information services including online searching

CN	Glasgow University Library
DT	Computer Search Service
CP	Mr Robin Adams Hillhead Street Glasgow G12 8QE
HOST	DIALOG; Data-Star; ECHO; ESA-IRS; Blaise-Line; Questel; BRS; Pergamon Orbit Infoline; Datasolve; Wilsonline; NLM
DB	Medline; Biosis; Inspec; PSYC; ERIC; World Reporter; SOCA; PAIS; TED; COMP
CT	Engineering; biology; business; medicine; vetinary medicine; education
LA	English
TEL	41-3304283
TX	777070
CD	This service is available to individuals and companies holding special reader membership on payment of a fee. In addition to accessing technical and research databases, patent searching and business information is provided

CN	Global Access
CP	Mr Jonathan Lavy 78 New Bond Street London W14 9DB
HOST	DIALOG; Finsbury; IP Sharp
DB	Textline; The Information Bank

CT	Economics; business; marketing; products; companies; law; technology; art; education
LA	English
TEL	01-499 6660

CN	Information Unlimited
CP	Mr Roy Jenkins 114 Harrogate Street Bradford BD3 OLE
HOST	Data-Star; DIALOG; ECHO; ESA-IRS; Fiz Technik; Infoline; Inka; Pergamon Orbit Infoline
CT	Business; patents; politics; technology
LA	English
TEL	274- 638877

CN	Kingston Polytechnic Library
CP	R James Penrhyn Road Kingston KT1 2EE
HOST	DIALOG; Orbit; Infoline; ESA-IRS; Scimp; Profile; Kompass; Wilsonline; Questel; STN; Blaise-Line
DB	Chemabs; Inspec; World Reporter; ABI Inform; McCarthy; Biosis; Medline; Eric; Georef; Geoarchive
CT	Biology; chemistry; business; management; computing; electronics; earth sciences

CN	LBS Information Service London Business School Sussex Place Regent's Park London NW1 4SA
HOST	Various
DB	All major business databases
TF	01-724 2300
TX	27461 a/b LBSKOXG
CD	Offers a comprehensive range of research and library facilities, including on-line searching

CN   Rapra Technology
DT   Information and Lib-
      rary Services
CP   Mr Rien van den
      Hondel
      Shawbury
      Shrewsbury SY4 4NP
HOST Data-Star; DIALOG;
      ESA-IRS; Infoline;
      STN
DB   Rapra; Raptn; Comp;
      Pascal; NTIS; ICCF
CT   Polymers; Rubber
      technology; econo-
      mics; technology;
      commerce; chemistry;
      business; companies;
      plastics
LA   English; German;
      French; Dutch; Ita-
      lian; Japanese; Rus-
      sian; Hungarian;
      Polish
TEL   939-250383
TX   35134
CD   Consultancy specialis-
      ing in rubbers and
      plastics, producer of
      the Rapra database,
      document delivery
      and translation ser-
      vice

CN   Science Reference Lib-
      rary
      Business Information
      Service
      The British Library
      25 Southampton
      Building
      Chancery Lane
      London WC2A 1AW
HOST Various
DB   All major business
      databases
LA   English
TEL   01-323 7979
TX   266959
CDEL Provides on-line sear-
      ching in the areas of
      science and technolo-
      gy, business, patents
      and trademarks, and
      Japanese information.
      Access to over 100
      databases around the
      world

CN   SVP United Kingdom
CP   Lord McIntosh
      12 Argyll Street
      London W1V 1A5

HOST Data-Star; DIALOG;
      Infoline; Questel;
      Finsbury
CT   Business; marketing;
      products; companies;
      statistics
LA   English
TEL   01-734-9272
FAX   01-734 9934
TX   28929
CD   Business information
      on all subjects for re-
      tainer clients worl-
      dwide

Euro-Info Centres

These centres are funded by
the European Commission,
and have been set up to provide information to
businesses about European
Commission policies and
proposals, particularly with
the needs of small and
medium-sized businesses in
mind. These centres have access to the EC databases. At
present there is a network of
38 centres throughout the
EEC, including 4 in the UK.
This number could grow to
200 in the next 2 to 3 years

Belgium

Bureau Economique de la Pro-
vince de Namur
Palais des Expositions
Av Sergent Vrithoff 2
5000 Namur
Tel: (010 32) 81-735209

Kamervan Koophandel en Nijverheid
Markgravestraat 12
2000 Antwerp
Tel: (010 32) 3-2336732

Denmark

Arhus Amtskommune
Haslegardvaenget 18-20
8210 Arhus
Tel: (010 45) 6-150318

Odensen Erhvervsrad
Norregade 51
5000 Odense C
Tel: (010 45) 9-126121

France

Bordeaux

Comite d'Expansion
Aquitaine
Place de la Bourse 2
33076 Bordeaux Cedex
Tel: (010 33) 56-526547/529894

Lorraine

Region Lorraine
Place St Clement 1
BP 1004
57036 Metz Cedex 1
Tel: (010 33) 40-446008

Lyon

Rue de la Republique 16
69289 Lyon Cedex 02
Tel: (010 33) 56-526547/529894

Nantes

Chambre de Commerce et
d'Industrie de Nantes
Centredes Salorges
BP 718
44027 Nantes Cedex 04
Tel: (010 33) 40-446008

Strasbourg

Chambre de Commerce et
d'Industrie de Strasbourg et
du Bas-Rhin
10 Place Gutenberg
67081 Strasbourg Cedex
Tel: (010 33) 88-321255

Germany (Federal Republic of)

DHKT
Johanniterstrasse 1
Haus des Deutschen Han-
werks
5300 Bonn 1
Tel: (010 49) 228-5451

DIHT
Adenauer Allee 148
Postfach 1446
5300 Bonn 1
Tel: (010 49) 228-1040

Handwerkskammer (DHKT)
Heilbronner Strasse 43
Postfach 2621
7000 Stuttgart 1
Tel: (010 49) 71-125941

Industrie und Handelskammerd
Martin Luther Strasse 12
8400 Regensburg
Tel: (010 49) 71-125941

RKW
Heilwigstrasse 33
2000 Hamburg 20
Tel: (010 49) 40-4602087

Zenit
Dohne 54
4330 Molheim
Tel: (010 49) 20-830004

Greece

Association of Industries of
Northern Greece/Chamber of
Commerce of Northern
Greece
Place Morihovo 1
54653 Thessaloniki
Tel: (010 30) 31-539817/539682

Eommex
Rue Xenias 16
11528 Athens
Tel: (010 30) 1-3625630

Ireland (Republic of)

Irish Export Board
Merrion Hall
PO Box 203
Strand Road
Sanymount
Dublin 4
Tel: (0001) 695011

One Stop Shop
The Granary
Michael Street
Limerick
Tel: (00061) 40777

Italy

Ass della Provincia di Bologna
Via San Domenico 4
40124 Bologna
Tel: (010 39) 51-529611

Camera di Commercio Industria Artigianato e Agricoltura
di Milano
Via Merivigli 9/b
20123 Milan
Tel: (010 39) 2-85151

Camera di Commercio Industria Artigianato e Agricoltura
di Napoli
Corso Meridionale 58
80143 Naples
Tel: (010 39) 81-285322

Confartigianatoic NA CLAAI/CASA
Via Milano 18
25126 Brescia
Tel: (010 39) 30-289051

Confindustria
Viale dell'Astronomia 30
00144 Rome
Tel: (010 39) 6-59031

Luxembourg

Chambre de Commerce/Chambre des Metiers/ Federation des Industriels
Rue Alcide de Gasperi 7-BP
1503
2981 Luxembourg
Tel: (010 352) 435853

Netherlands

CIMK-RIMK
Dalsteindreef - BP 112
1112 XC Dimen-Zuid
Tel: (010 31) 20-901071

Induma/Bom/Liof
Prins Hendriklann 21a
PO Box 995
5700 AZ Helmond
Tel: (010 31) 49-2034035

Portugal

Associaco Industrial Portuense
Exponsor
4100 Porto
Tel: (010 351) 2-684814/673220

Banco de Fomento Nacional
Av Casal Ribeiro 59
1000 Lisbon
Tel: (010 351) 1-561071/562021

Spain

Camera Oficial de Comercio,
Industria y Navegacion
AV de Recalde 50
48008 Bilbao
Tel: (010 34) 4-4445054

CIDEM
Av Diagonal 403, 1
08008 Barcelona
Tel: (010 34) 3-2172008

Confederacion de Empresarios de Andalucia
Avda San Francisco Javier s/n
Edificio Sevilla 2-9
41005 Seville
Tel: (010 34) 54-642013

Confederacion Espanola de
Organizaciones Empresariales
Diego de Leon 50
28006 Madrid
Tel: (010 34) 1-4508048

IMPI - INFE
Paseo de la Castellana 141-2
28046 Madrid
Tel: (010 34) 1-4508048

UK

London

Centre for European Business
Information
Department of Employment
Small Firms Service
Ebury Bridge House
2-18 Ebury Bridge Road
London SW1W 8QD
Tel: 01-730 8115

Birmingham

European Business Centre
Birmingham Chamber of In-
dustry & Commerce
75 Harbourne Road
Birmingham B15 3DH
Tel: 021-4546171

Newcastle

North of England Euroin-
focentre
Newcastle Polytechnic Lib-
rary
Ellison Building
Ellison Place
Newcastle upon Tyne NE1
8ST
Tel: 091-2615131

Glasgow

Strathclyde Euroinfocentre
Scottish Development
Agency
25 Bothwell Street
Glasgow G2 6NR
Tel: 041-2210999

3 Country Data Sources

Austria

Sources of Economic, Stock Market Information and Investment Research Services

Banks

Central Bank
Oesterreichische
Nationalbank
Otto Wagner Platz 3
1090 Vienna
Tel: (010 43) 222-43600
Telex: 114669

Austrian Banks in London
Creditanstalt-Bankverein
29 Gresham Street
London EC2V 7AH
Tel: 01-822 2600

Die Erst Osterreichische
Spar-Casse-Bank/First
Austrian Bank
68 Cornhill
London EC3V 3LB
Tel: 01-929 4699

Girozentrale & Bank der
Osterreichischen Sparkassen
68 Cornhill
London EC3V 3QE
Tel: 01-929 2345

GZB-Vienna
2 Throgmorton Avenue
London EC2N 2AP
Tel: 01-256 5885

Osterreichische Landerbank
Scotia House
Finsbury Square
London EC2A 1PL
Tel: 01-588 4085

Zentralsparkasse &
Kommerzialbank, Wien
85 Gracechurch Street
London EC3V OAA
Tel: 01-621 1522

Major Austrian Banks
Bank Fur Arbeit und
Wirtschaft AG
Seitzergasse 28
1010 Vienna
Tel: (010 43) 222-66290
Telex: 115311

Central Wechsel- und
Creditbank AG
Zweigniederlassung Wien
Kartnerstrasse 43
1015 Vienna
Tel: (010 43) 222-532661
Telex: 113684

Creditanstalt-Bankverein
(Commercial Bank)
Schottengasse 6
1010 Vienna
Tel: (010 43) 222-66220
Telex: 133030

Die Erste Osterreichische
Sparcasse-Bank
Graben 21
1010 Vienna
Tel: (010 43) 222-66180
Telex: 115818

Genossenschaftliche
Zentralbank AG
Herrengasse 1
Schauflergasse 2
1010 Vienna
Tel: (010 43) 222-66620
Telex: 135415

Girozentrale und Bank der
Osterreichischen Sparkassen
AG
(Central Bank of the Austrian
Savings Banks)
Schubertring 5
1010 Vienna
Tel: (010 43) 222-72940
Telex: 132591

Osterreichische Kontrollbank
AG
Am Hof 4
1010 Vienna
Tel: (010 43) 222-66270
Telex: 132824

Osterreichische Landerbank
AG
(Commercial Bank)
Am Hof 2
1010 Vienna
Tel: (010 43) 222-66240
Telex: 115561

Volksbank Wien
Mitte-Wiener
Genossenschaftsbank
RGMBH
Siebensterngasse 21
PO Box 62
1071 Vienna
Tel: (010 43) 222-936639
Telex: 133384 vb wm a

Zentralsparkasse und
Kommerzialbank Wien
Vordere Zollamtsstrasse 13
1030 Vienna
Tel: (010 43) 222-72920
Telex: 133615

Stockbrokers
Wiener BorseKammer
(Vienna Stock Exchange)
Wipplingerstrasse 34
1011 Vienna

Members – Banks and Brokers

Banks

Allgemeine Sparkasse
4020 Linz an der Donau
Promenade 11-13
Tel: (010 43) 732-2391
Telex: 021778

Bank fur Arbeit und
Wirtschaft AG
1011 Wien
Seitzergasse 2-4
Tel: (010 43) 222-53453-0
Telex: 115311

Bank fur Handel und
Industrie AG
8010 Graz
Herrengasse 28
Tel: (010 43) 316-71687
Telex: 031298

Bank fur Karnten und
Steiermark AG
9020 Klagenfurt
Dr-Authur-Lemisch-Platz 5
Tel: (010 43) 4222-511555-0
Telex: 422174

Bank fur Oberosterreich und
Salzburg
4020 Linz an der Donau
Untere Donaulande 28
Tel: (010 43) 732-2802-0
Telex: 021316/021032

Bank fur Tirol und Vorarlberg
AG
6010 Innsbruck
Erler Strasse 5-9
Tel: (010 43) 5222-36641
Telex: 533535

Bank fur Wirtschaft und Freie
Berufe AG
1072 Wien
Zieglergasse 5
Tel: (010 43) 222-961546-0
Telex: 132346

Bank Gebrud Butmann Nfg
AG
1010 Wien
Schwarzenbergplatz 16
Tel: (010 43) 222-657636
Telex: 136506

Bank Winter & Co AG
1010 Wien
Singerstrasse 10
Tel: (010 43) 222-515040
Telex: 112462

Bankhaus Berger & Comp
5020 Salzburg
Rathausplatz 4
Tel: (010 43) 6222-841551
Telex: 633612

Bankhaus Carl Spangler & Co
5024 Salzburg
Schwarzstrasse 1
Tel: (010 43) 662-72571-0
Telex: 633629

Bankhaus Krentschker & Co
8010 Graz Am Eisernen Tor
(Bismarckplatz) 3
Tel: (010 43) 316-75561
Telex: 031411

Bankhaus Rossier AG
1015 Wien
Karntner Ring 17
Tel: (010 43) 222-5129696-0
Telex: 131815

Bankhaus Schelhammer &
Schattera
1010 Wien
Goldschmiedgasse 3
Tel: (010 43) 222-534340
Telex: 112323

Bankkommanditgesellschaft
Antoni, Hacker & Co
1013 Wien
Hohenstaufengasse 4
Tel: (010 43) 222-5335621
Telex: 114183

Central Wechsel- und
Creditbank Actiengesellschaft
1015 Wien
Karntner Strasse 43
Tel: (010 43) 222-51566-0
Telex: 113684

Centro Internationale
Handelsbank AG
1015 Wien
Tegetthoffstrasse 1
Tel: (010 43) 222-51520-0
Telex: 136990

Chase Manhattan Bank
(Austria) AG
1010 Wien
Parkring 12a
Tel: (010 43) 222-51589
Telex: 112570

Citibank (Austria)
Aktiengesellschaft
1015 Wien
Lothringerstrasse 7
Tel: (010 43) 222-756534-0
Telex: 112105

Constantia Privatbank AG
1010 Wien
Opernring 17
Tel: (010 43) 222-58875-0
Telex: 112667

Creditanstalt-Bankverein
1010 Wien
Schottengasse 6-8
Tel: (010 43) 222-53131-0
Telex: 114261

Die Erste Osterreichische
Spar-Casse-Bank
1010 Wien
Graben 21
Tel: (010 43) 222-53100-0
Telex: 115818

Dornbirner Sparkasse
6850 Dornbirn
Bahnhofstrasse 2
Tel: (010 43) 5572-64551
Telex: 059358

Dorotheum Auktions-
Versatz- und
Bank-Gesellschaft mbH
1010 Wien
Dorotheergasse 17
Tel: (010 43) 222-51560-0
Telex: 132230

Elsassische Bank AG
1015 Wien
Schwarzenbergplatz 1
Tel: (010 43) 222-725103
Telex: 133766

Foco Bank (Austria) AG
1010 Wien
Rathausstrasse 20
Tel: (010 43) 222-436161-0
Telex: 114911

Genossenschaftliche
Zentralbank AG
1010 Wien
Herrengasse 1
Schauflergasse 2
Tel: (010 43) 222-6662-0
Telex: 135415

Girozentrale und Bank der
Osterreichischen Sparkassen
AG
1010 Wien
Schubertring 5
Tel: (010 43) 222-7294-0
Telex: 113195

Hypothekenbank des Landes
Vorarlberg
6900 Bregenz
Hypo-Passage 1
Tel: (010 43) 5574-22745
Telex: 057634

Karntner Landes- und
Hypothekenbank
9020 Klagenfurt
Domgasse 5
Tel: (010 43) 4222-512600-0
Telex: 422438

Karntner Sparkasse
9020 Klagenfurt
Neuer Platz 14
Tel: (010 43) 4222-512655-0
Telex: 422391

Kathrein & Co
Bankaktiengesellschaft
1010 Wien
Wipplingerstrasse 25
Tel: (010 43) 222-53451
Telex: 114123/115243

Landerbank-Exportbank AG
1010 Wien
Karntner Ring 5
Tel: (010 43) 222-51411-0
Telex: 133468

Landes-Hypothekenbank
Burgenland
7000 Eisenstadt
Neusiedler Strasse 33
Tel: (010 43) 2682-3205
Telex: 17725

Landes-Hypothekenbank
Niederosterreich
1010 Wien
Wipplingerstrasse 2
Tel: (010 43) 222-53155-0
Telex: 134750

Landes-Hypothekenbank
Steiermark
8010 Graz
Radetzkystrasse 15-17
Tel: (010 43) 316-75576
Telex: 031385

Landes-Hypothekenbank
Tirol
6020 Innsbruck
Meraner Strasse 8
Tel: (010 43) 5222-36601-0
Telex: 053899

Meinl Bank AG
1015 Wien
Karntner Ring 2
Tel: (010 43) 222-654731
Telex: 132256

Oberosterreichische
Landes-Hypothekenbank
4020 Linz
Landstrasse 38
Tel: (010 43) 732-272851-0
Telex: 21239

Oesterreichische
Kontrollbank AG
1010 Wien
Am Hof 4
Tel: (010 43) 222-53127-0
Telex: 132824

Oesterreichische
Nationalbank
1090 Wien
Otto-Wagner-Platz 3
Tel: (010 43) 222-4360-0
Telex: 114775

Osterreichische
Investitionskredit AG
1013 Wien
Renngasse 10
Tel: (010 43) 222-53135-0
Telex: 114495

Osterreichische Landerbank
Aktiengesellschaft
1010 Wien
Am Hof 2
Tel: (010 43) 222-53124-0
Telex: 114016

Osterreichische
Postsparkasse
1018 Wien
Georg-Coch-Platz 2
Tel: (010 43) 222-51400
Telex: 116341

Osterreichische
Verkehrskreditbank AG
1081 Wien
Auerspergstrasse 17
Tel: (010 43) 222-427648
Telex: 115965

Osterreichische
Volksbanken-
Aktiengesellschaft
1090 Wien
Peregringasse 3
Tel: (010 43) 222-3134-0
Telex: 114084

Osterreichisches
Credit-Institut AG
1010 Wien
Herrengasse 12
Tel: (010 43) 222-53130-0
Telex: 134880

Pfandbriefstelle der
Osterreichischen
Landes-Hypothekenbanken
10400 Wien
Brucknerstrasse 8
Tel: (010 43) 222-658732-0
Telex: 132582

Raiffeisenlandesbank
Niederosterreich- Wien reg
Genossenschaft mbH
1020 Wien
Hollandstrasse 2
Tel: (010 43) 222-2636-0
Telex: 116762

Raiffeisenverbank Salzburg
reg Genossenschaft mbH
5020 Salzburg
Schwarzstrasse 13-15
Tel: (010 43) 662-71561
Telex: 631095

Salzburger
Landes-Hypothekenbank
5020 Salzburg
Residenzplatz 7
Tel: (010 43) 662-843521-0
Telex: 632602

Salzburger Sparkasse
5020 Salzburg
Alter markt 3
Tel: (010 43) 662-843571
Telex: 3622320

Sanpaolo Bank (Austria) AG
1011 Wien
Rotenturmstrasse 5-9
Tel: (010 43) 222-5353601-0
Telex: 114266

Schoeller & Co
Bankaktiengesellschaft
1010 Wien
Renngasse 1-3
Tel: (010 43) 222-53471-0
Telex: 114219

Sparkasse Braunau am Inn
5280 Braunau am Inn
Tel: (010 43) 7722-2371
Telex: 02775523

Sparkasse Innsbruck-Hall
Tiroler Sparkasse
6021 Innsbruck
Sparkassenplatz 1
Erler Strasse 8
Tel: (010 43) 5222-28761-0
Telex: 053324

Standard Chartered Bank
(Austria) AG
1010 Wien
Karntner Ring 10
Tel: (010 43) 222-653394/5
Telex: 133608

Steiermarkische Bank
Gesellschaft mbH
8010 Graz
Hauptplatz
Rathaus
Tel: (010 43) 316-7032-0
Telex: 031930

Steiermarkische Sparkasse
8011 Graz
Sparkassenplatz 4
Tel: (010 43) 316-7033-0
Telex: 031280/032629

Tiroler Handels- und
Gewerbebank reg
Genossenschaft mbH
6020 Innsbruck
Sillgasse 19
Tel: (010 43) 5222-765-0
Telex: 053574

Volksbank Wien,
Hietzing-Purkersdorf reg
Genossenschaft mbH
1140 Wien
Hutteldorfer Strasse 110
Tel: (010 43) 222-923266
Telex: 132995

Volkskreditbank
Aktiengesellschaft
4020 Linz
Rudigierstrasse 5-7
Tel: (010 43) 732-2784560
Telex: 022282
Teletex: 3732328

Welser Volksbank reg
Genossenschaft mbH
4601 Wien
Pfarrgasse 5
Tel: (010 43) 7242-6987
Telex: 025520

Wiener
Landes-Hypothekenbank
1015 Wien
Operngasse 6
Tel: (010 43) 222-5121538
Telex: 3222130

Zentralesparkasse und
Kommerzialbank, Wien
1030 Wien
Vordere Zollamtsstrasse 13
Tel: (010 43) 222-7292-0
Telex: 131251

Sources of General Background Information, Industry Sector Information and Trade Contacts

UK Addresses

Austrian Embassy and
Consular Section
18 Belgrave Mews
London SW1X 8HU
Tel: 01-235 3731
Cultural Section:
28 Rutland Gate
London SW7
Tel: 01-584 8653

Austrian Trade Commission
(The)
1 Hyde Park Gate
London SW7
Tel: 01-584 4411

Addresses in Austria

Austrian Chambers of
Commerce are autonomous
bodies, and decisions are
made by democratic elected
representatives. There are
two central organisations and
nine regional chambers. The
Foreign Trade Department
provides advice to exporters.

Bundeskammer der
Gewerblichen Wirtshaft
(Federal Economic Chamber)
Stubenring 12
1010 Vienna
Tel: (010 43) 222-65050
Telex: 32222138

Bundeskamer der
Gewerblichen Wirtschaft
HA-Aussenhandel (Foreign
Trade Department)
Wiedner Haupstrasse 63
1045 Vienna
Tel: (010 43) 222-65050

Regional Chambers

Kammer Burgenland
Ing Julius Raab-Strasse 1
7000 Eisenstadt
Kammer Karnten
Bahnhofstrasse 40-42
9021 Klagenfurt
Tel: (010 43) 4222-575550
Telex: 422439

Kammer Niederosterreich
Herrengasse 10
1014 Vienna
Kammer Oberosterreich
Hessenplatz 3
4010 Linz
Tel: (010 43) 732-78444
Telex: 21230

Kammer Salzburg
Julius Raab-Platz
5027 Salzburg
Tel: (010 43) 622-715710
Telex: 633633

Kammer Steiermark
Korblergasse 111-113
8010 Graz
Tel: (010 43) 3166010

Kammer Tirol
Mainhardstrasse 12-14
Postfach 570
6012 Innsbruck
Tel: (010 43) 5222-356510

Kammer Voralberg
Wichnergasse 9
6800 Feldkirch

Kammer Wien
Stubenring 8-10
1010 Vienna

Embassies/Councils

Amerikanische
Handelskammer in
Osterreich
Turkenstr. 9
1090 Vienna
Tel: (010 43) 222-315751
Promotes trade and
commerce between Austria
and the USA

British Council
Schenkenstrasse 4
1010 Vienna

British Embassy
Reisnerstrasse 40
1030 Vienna
Tel: (010 43) 222-731575/9
Telex: 133410 BRITEM A

British Trade Council in
Austria
Mollwaldplatz 1/12
1040 Vienna
Tel: (010 43) 222-654363

Sources of Investment and Trade Advice, Assistance and Information

The following organisations
in Austria can be contacted
for advice and information on
investment and foreign trade:

Amt der
Oberosterreichischen
Landesregierung-Abteilung
Gewerbe
Alstadt 30
4020 Linz
Tel: (010 43) 732-7200
Provincial government
organisation. Encourages
external investment in the
province of Upper Austria

Amt der Tiroler
Landesregierung-
Informationstelle fur
Betriebsneugrundungen
Altes Landhaus
6020 Innsbruck
Tel: (010 43) 5222-28701
Provincial government
organisation. Encourages
external investment in the
Tirol province

Amt der Vorarlberger
Landesregierung-Allgemeine
Wirtschaftsgelegenleiten
Montfortstr 4
6900 Bregenz
Tel: (010 43) 5574-23841
Provincial government
organisation. Encourages
external investment in the
province

Burgenland

Burgenlandische Industrie-
und Betriebsansiedlung
GmbH
Neusiedlerstrasse 33
7000 Eisenstadt
Tel: (010 43) 2682-4595

Carinthia

Karntner Betribsansiedlungs-
und Beteiligungs GmbH
Domgasse 3
9020 Klagenfurt

Lower Austria

Niederosterreichische
Raumordnumgs-
Betriebsansiedlungs- und
Strukturverbes –serungs
GmbH
Stallburggasse 4
1010 Vienna
Tel: (010 43) 222-523131

Salzburg

Salzburg Betriebsansied-
lungsgesellschaft
Julius-Raab-Platz 1
5027 Salzburg
Tel: (010 43) 662-71571
Telex: 633633

Styria

Steirermarkesche Gesellschaft
fur Betriebserweiterungen
und Betriebsansiedlungen
Radetzkystr 1
8010 Graz

Vienna

Federal Economic Chamber of
Austria
Wiedner Haupstrasse 63
1045 Vienna
Tel: (010 43) 222-6505
Telex: 3222138 BWK

Ministry for Commerce and
Foreign Trade
Stubenring 12
1010 Vienna

Ministry of Trade and
Industry
Export/Import Licensing
Office
Landstrasser Haupstrasse
55-57
1030 Vienna
Tel: (010 43) 222-725641-0

Osterreichische Exportfonds
Gottfried-Keller-Gasse 1
1030 Vienna
Tel: (010 43) 222-731213
Telex: 132846
Provides financing for export
companies

Wiener Betriebsansiedlungs
GmbH
Windmuhlgasse 26
1060 Vienna
Tel: (010 43) 222-570226

Professional Associations

Accountancy

Institut Osterreichischer
Wirtschaftsprufer
1030 Wien
Schwarzenbergplatz 8
Vienna

Banking

Verband Oesterreichischer
Banken und Bankiers
(Austrian Bankers
Association)
Borsegasse 11
1010 Vienna

Insurance

Verband der
Versicherungsunt-
ernehmungen Osterreich
(Confederation of Insurance
Companies in Austria)
3 Schwarzengergplatz 7
1030 Vienna
Tel: (010 43) 222-757651
Telex: 133289 OEVVA

VOVM
(Professional Association for
Insurance Brokers)
Eschenbachgasse 11
1010 Vienna
Tel: (010 43) 222-573632

Marketing

Verband der Marktforscher
Osterreichs
c/o Wiener Stadtische
Schottenring 30
Ringturm
1010 Vienna
Tel: (010 43) 222-6339/1101
Telex: 135140

Trade Associations

General Industry

Association of Austrian
Industrialists
Vereinigung Osterreichischer
Industrieller
Schwarzenbergplatz 4
1030 Vienna

Sektionsgeschaftsstelle:
Wiedner Haupststrasse 63
Postfach 330
1045 Vienna
Tel: (010 43) 222-6505

Chem Industrie
Postfach 325
WIED

Elektroindustrie
Rathausplatz 8
1010 Vienna
Tel: (010 43) 222-437237

Glasindustrie
Postfach 328
WIED
Tel: (010 43) 2735-3428

Metallindustrie
Postfach 338
WIED
Tel: (010 43) 2735-3445

Papierindustrie
Gumpendorfer str 6
1061 Vienna
Teletext: 32213492
Telefax: 58886-264 DW

Papier u Pappe Verarb Ind
Brucknerstrasse 8
1040 Vienna
Telefax: 655382 DW

Stein-u Keramische Industrie
Postfach 329
WIED
Tel: (010 43) 2735-3531

Textilindustrie
Rudolfsplatz 12
1010 Vienna
Fax: 5333726 DW

Company Financial and Product Information

Directories

Austrian Commercial
Directory
Published by
Jupiter Verlag
Robertgasse 2
1020 Vienna
Alphabetical and classified
lists of 50 000 firms in Austria,
includes details of products,
owners, executives, etc.

Directory of American
Business in Austria
American Chamber of
Commerce
9 Turkenstrasse
1090 Vienna

Herold Austrian Export
Directory
Published by
Bundeskammer der
Gewerblichen Wirtschaft
Abteilung fur handelspolitik
u Aussenhandel
(Ministry for Commerce and
Foreign Trade)
Wiedner Haupstr 63
1040 Vienna

Osterreichs 10 000 Grosste
Unternehmen
(Austria's 10 000 largest
companies)
Produced by
D & B – Schimmelpfeng
Gesellschaft mbH
Opernring 3-5
1015 Vienna
Published every September.
Provides addresses, products
or services, names of parent
company, decision makers,
number of employees and
sales figures

Verlag Herold Vereineigte
Anzeigen-Gesellschaft mbH
Wipplingerstrasse 14
1010 Vienna
Directory of exporters,
importers and other firms
engaged in foreign trade,
listed alphabetically.
Addresses, telephone and
telex numbers and products
are identified. English
translation provided. There is
also a list of registered firms at
the back of the directory

Economic and Market Statistical Data

Market Research Organisations

Dr Fessel und GFK
Gesellschaft fur Konsum-,
Markt- und Absatzforschung
Franz-Josefs Kai 47
1010 Vienna
Tel: (010 43) 222-53496-0

Gallup Institut
Schlagergasse 6
1090 Vienna
Tel: (010 43) 222-429292

IFES – Institut fur Empirische
Sozialforschung GmbH
Ramergasse 38
105 Vienna
Tel: (010 43) 222-555651

IMAS-Institut
Ferrogasse 42
1180 Vienna
Tel: (010 43) 222-478971

Info-Institut fur Markt und
Meinungsforschung
Mariahilferstrasse 99
1060 Vienna
Tel: (010 43) 222-565695/99
Telex: 133259
Parent company: Research
International

Institut fur
Grundlagenforschung
Furbergstrasse 14
5020 Salzburg
Tel: (010 43) 662-881320
Telex: 134271

AC Nielsen Company
Concordiaplatz 2
1010 Vienna
Tel: (010 43) 222-53497
Telex: 114469
Parent company: AC Nielsen
(USA)

Osterreichisches Gallup
Institut
Schlagergasse 6
1090 Vienna
Tel: (010 43) 222-429292
Telex: 76363
Institute is affiliated to the
Gallup organisation

Organisations Providing Economic and Statistical Data

Abteilung fur Handelspolitik
und Aussenhandel
(Ministry for Commerce and
Foreign Trade)
Stubenring 12
1010 Vienna

Abteilung fur Statistik und
Dokumentation der
Bundeskammer der
Gewerblichen Wirtschaft
(Statistical Department of the
Federal Economic Chamber)
Wiedner Haupstrasse 63
1045 Vienna
Provides economic
forecasting and market
research

Kammer fur Arbeiter und
Angestellte fur Wien
Prinz-Engen-Strasse 20-22
1040 Vienna
Tel: (010 43) 222-50165-0
Provides online database
services

Nationalokonomische
Gesellschaft
Institut fur
Wirtschaftswissenschaften
der universitat Wien
(Austrian Economic
Association)
Liechtensteinstr 13
1090 Vienna
Publishes Empirica 2 times
per annum

Osterreichisches Institut fur
Wirtschaftsforschung Arsenal
Objekt 20
Postfach 91
1103 Vienna
Tel: (010 43) 222-782601
Provides online database
services

Osterreichisches
Normungsinstitut – ON
(Austrian Standards Institute)
Heinstr 38
1021 Vienna
Tel: (010 43) 222-267535
Telex: 115960
Publishes ONORM 10 times
per annum. Responsible for
the establishment of Austrian
standards in all fields

Osterreichische Statistische
Gesellschaft
(Austrian Statistical Society)
Hintere Zollamtstrasse 2b
1033 Vienna
Tel: (010 43) 222-6628-0

Osterreichisches Statistisches
Zentralamt
(Austrian Central Statistical
Office)
Hintere Zollamtstrasse 2b
1033 Vienna
Tel: (010 43) 222-71128
Telex: 0132600
Publishes Statistiches
Handbuch fur die Republik
Osterreich (annual),
Statistiches Jahrbuch
Osterreichischer Stadte
(annual). Both contain the
latest statistics and historical
series on a wide range of
subjects. This office also
provides an online database
service. (See Chapter 6)

Osterreichistes
Wirtschaftsbund – OWB
(Austrian Economic League)
Falkestr 3
1010 Vienna
Tel: (010 43) 222-527631
Telex: 12023
Publishes Wirtschaftsbund in
Aktion and other documents

Wiener Borsekammer
(Vienna Stock Exchange)
Financal statistics provided in
the annual report, Annual
Facts Sheet, Daily Official
List, Official Gazette, and
Daily Quotation Sheet for the
Semi-Official Market

Publications

Directories

Dienstleistungs und
Behorden
Compass 1987/88
Published by Compass-Verlag
1013 Vienna 1
Wipplingstrasse 32
Directory of service and
manufacturing companies
with basic details provided
such as address and
telephone number

Finanz-Compass
Published by Compass-Verlag
Address as above
Directory of Austrian banks
and other financial
institutions.

Handels-Compass Osterreich
1987/88
Published by Compass-Verlag
Address as above
20 000 firms listed, with an
alphabetical index and
catagorised under industry
headings

Industrie-Compass
Published by Compass-Verlag
Address as above

Major Newspapers
Die Presse
Daily

Kurier
Daily

Neue Kronenzeitung
Daily

Wiener Zeitung
Daily

Journals and Periodicals
A3 Eco
Covers news and articles on
the economy and industry.
Monthly

Amtliches Kursblatt der
Wiener Borse
Official quotations on the
Vienna Stock Exchange. Daily

Austria Exports
Publisher's address
Hoher Markt 12
1010 Vienna
Quarterly

CASH
Published by Manstien
Verlag, Vienna. Provides
market and product reports
and includes company
profiles. Monthly (11 per
annum)

Contact News
Published by A
Henhapel-Marketing Center,
Salzburg

Industrie
Published by Signum Verlag,
Vienna
Covers all aspects of the
economy, including markets,
company and financial news.
Weekly

INI – Industrie Report
International
Published by Technopress,
Vienna
Covers company, product,
market news. 7 published per
annum

Trend
Covers economic, financial,
company and market news.
Monthly

Wiener Handelskammer
Published by the Vienna
Chamber of Commerce

Wirtschaft (Die) (The
Economy)
Published by Osterreichischer
Wirtschaftsverlag GmbH,
Vienna
Provides national and
regional economic data, and
regular company profiles plus
other business information.
Weekly

Belgium (and Luxembourg)

Sources of Economic, Stock Market Information and Investment Research Services

Banks

Central Bank
Banque Nationale de Belgique
SA
Boulevard de Berlaimont No 5
1000 Brussels
Tel: (010 32) 2-2194600
Telex: 21355

Belgian Banks in London
ASLK-CGER Bank
22 Eastcheap
London EC3M 1EU
Tel: 01-929 5942

Banque Belge
(General Bank)
4 Bishopsgate
London EC2N 4AD
Tel: 01-283 1080

Banque Bruxelles Lambert
SA, Bank Brussel Lambert NV
St Helen's
1 Undershaft
London EC3P 3EY
Tel: 01-283 3361

Kredietbank
Level 7
400 Basinghall Street
London EC2V 5DE
Tel: 01-638 5812

Major Belgian Banks
ASLK-CGER Bank
(Algemene Spaar – en
Lijfrentekas Caisse Generale
d'Epargne et de Retraite)
PO Box 1436
48 Wolvengracht
1000 Brussels
and
48 Rue du Fosse-aux-Loups
1000 Brussels
Tel: (010 32) 2-2136111
Telex: 26860; 61189 CGEASK
B

Banque Brussels Lambert SA
Avenue Marnix 24
1050 Brussels
Tel: (010 32) 2-5173271
Telex: 26392

Banque Degroof
44 Rue de l'Industrie
1040 Brussels
Tel: (010 32) 2-2338511
Telex: 21317

Credit Communal de
Belgique
(Gemeentekrediet Van Belgie)
Boulevard Pacheco 44
1000 Brussels
Tel: (010 32) 2-2144111
Telex: 25068 CCBEM B; 26354
CREGEM B

Generale Bank
Montagne du Parc 3
1000 Brussels
Tel: (010 32) 2-5162111
Telex: 21283

Kredietbank NV
Arenbergstraat 7
1000 Brussels
Tel: (010 32) 2-5174742
Telex: 21207

Societe National de Credit a
l'Industrie
(Nationale Maatschappij voor
Krediet aan de Nijverheid)
Avenue de l'Astronomie 14
1030 Brussels
Tel: (010 32) 2-2141211
Telex: 25996

Stockbrokers

There are four stock
exchanges in Belgium. The
Brussels exchange handles
over 90 per cent of total
securities transactions.

Bourse de Fonds Publics de
Liege
Boulevard d'Avroy 3/022-4000
Liege
Tel: (010 32) 41-232797

Commission de la Bourse de
Bruxelles
Palais de la Bourse
1000 Brussels
Tel: (010 32) 515-5110
Telex: 21374

Fondsen-en Wisselbeurs van
Antwerpen
Korte Klarenstraat 1-2000
Antwerp
Tel: (010 32) 3-2338016

Fondsen-en Wisslebeurs van
Gent
Kouter 29-9000
Gent
Tel: (010 32) 91-259678

Principal Members of the Brussels Stock Exchange (as at end 1987)

Brokers

Busschaert & Co VEG
Lippenslaan 166
8300 Knokke-Heist
Tel: (010 32) 50-603796

Philippe et Yves de Coster
SNC
Rue des Fripiers 15/17
1000 Brussels
Tel: (010 32) 2-5116318
Telex: 62206

De Ferm en Cie VGN
Kiekenmarkt 33, Bus 4
1000 Brussels
Tel: (010 32) 2-5115388

De Laet & Co VGN
Lange Gasthuisstraat 27
2000 Antwerp
Tel: (010 32) 3-2317937
Telex: 31638

Delen & Co VEG
Jan Van Rijswijcklaan 282
2020 Antwerp
Tel: (010 32) 3-2161461
Telex: 35047

De Posson et Cie SCS
World Trade Center 1
19th Floor
Box 45
Boulevard E Jacqmain 162
1210 Brussels
Tel: (010 32) 2-2185300
Telex: 22868

Dewaay Sebille Servais Cie
SCS
Tour Philips
5th Floor
Boulevard Anspach 1
Box 10
1000 Brussels
Tel: (010 32) 2-2130711
Telex: 21325

R Eeckhoudt et Cie SCS
Rue Chene au Corbeau 85
1338 Couture St Germain
Rue de Bouvy 24
7100 La Louviere
Tel: (010 32) 64-223531

E Goethels
Priester Daensplein 4
9300 Aalst
Tel: (010 32) 53-214923

M Goffin & Cie SCS
Place du Champ de Mars 2
Box 2
1050 Brussels
Tel: (010 32) 2-5117184
Telex: 21251

Nedee en Co GCV
Koningsstraat 146
5, 5, 6 de Verdieping
1000 Brussels
Tel: (010 32) 2-2121711
Telex: 62898

Peterbroeck, Van
Campenhout et Cie
Place Sainte Gudule 19
1000 Brussels
Tel: (010 32) 2-2130511
Telex: 21353

Puissant Baeyens, Poswick et
Cie SCS
Rue Ravenstein 36
Box 15
1000 Brussels
Tel: (010 32) 2-5104511
Telex: 21351

Reyers, Timmermans & Cie
SCS
Rue d'Arlon 39/41
Box 10
1040 Brussels
Tel: (010 32) 2-2300209
Telex: 25736

Smeets de Ridder, Verbaet
VEG
Frankrijklei 119
2018 Antwerp
Tel: (010 32) 3-2339000
Telex: 71466

Van de Put & Co VGN
Mechelsesteenweg 203
2018 Antwerp
Tel: (010 32) 3-2309819
Telex: 33183

Vanderborght-Van Elslande
& Cie, SCS
Rue d'Assaut 3-5
Box 3
1000 Brussels
Tel: (010 32) 2-5136994
Telex: 65843

Vander Elst SNC
Rue des Fripiers 24
Box 1
1000 Brussels
Tel: (010 32) 2-2171758
Telex 21671

Van Moer, Santerre et Cie
SCS
Boulevard Anspach 111-115
Box 7
1000 Brussels
Tel: (010 32) 2-5120127
Telex: 21669

Verhaegen, Goossens, de
Roeck & Co VEG
Rue Marche aux Poulets 33
5th Floor
1000 Brussels
Tel: (010 32) 2-5116480
Telex: 32309

Viatour, Guillaume et Cie SCS
Rue des Pierres 51
1000 Brussels
Tel: (010 32) 2-5131532

Banks
Banque Bruxelles Lambert SA
Avenue Marnix 24
1050 Brussels
Tel: (010 32) 2-7382111
Telex: 21421

Banque Degroof
44 Rue de l'Industrie
1040 Brussels
Tel: (010 32) 2-2338511

Caisse Privee Banque
Rue d'Edimbourg 26
1050 Brussels
Tel: (010 32) 2-5137530

Generale Bank
Montagne du Park 3
1000 Brussels
Tel: (010 32) 2-5162111
Telex: 21283

Kredietbank NV
Arebergstraat 7
1000 Brussels
Tel: (010 32) 2-5174111
Telex: 24078

Luxembourg
Societe de la Bourse de
Luxembourg SA
(Luxembourg Stock
Exchange)
Case Postale No 165
2011 Luxembourg
Tel: (010 352) 4779361
Fax: (010 352) 4722050
Telex: 2559 STOEX LU

Members (as at end 1987)
Banco di Roma International
SA
25c Boulevard Royal
2449 Luxembourg
Tel: (010 352) 4779081

Banque Continentale du
Luxembourg SA
2 Boulevard Emmanuel
Servais
2635 Luxembourg
Tel: (010 352) 474491

Banque Generale du
Luxembourg SA
27 Avenue Monterey
2163 Luxembourg
Tel: (010 352) 47991

Banque Indosuez
Luxembourg SA
39 Allee Scheffer
2320 Luxembourg
Tel: (010 352) 47671

Banque de Luxembourg SA
80 Place de la Gare
1616 Luxembourg
Tel: (010 352) 499241

Banque Paribas
(Luxembourg) SA
10 Boulevard Royal
2449 Luxembourg
Tel: (010 352) 4771911

Caisse d'Epargne de l'etat
1 Place de Metz
1930 Luxembourg
Tel: (010 352) 470401

Compagnie Finaciere
Europeene SA
35 Rue Notre Dame
2240 Luxembourg
Tel: (010 352) 41925

Credit Europeen SA
52 Route d'Esch
1470 Luxembourg
Tel: (010 352) 449911

Credit Industarial d'Alsace et
de Lorraine
103 Grand-Rue
1661 Luxembourg
Tel: (010 352) 499231

Credit Lyonnais
26a Boulevard Royal
2449 Luxembourg
Tel: (010 352) 4768311

Credit Suisse (Luxembourg)
SA
23 Avenue Monterey
2163 Luxembourg
Tel: (010 352) 20265

Den Norske Creditbank
(Luxembourg) SA
27 Boulevard Prince Henri
1724 Luxembourg
Tel: (010 352) 21101

Dewaay Luxembourg SA
18 Boulevard Royal
2449 Luxembourg
Tel: (010 352) 29391

Kredietbank SA
Luxembourgeoise
43 Boulevard Royal
2449 Luxembourg
Tel: (010 352) 47971

Merrill Lynch Europe SA
68-70 Boulevard de la
Petrusse
2320 Luxembourg
Tel: (010 352) 495159

Prudential Bache Securities
(Luxembourg) Inc
20 Rue de l'Eau
2449 Luxembourg
Tel: (010 352) 462121

Societe Europeene de Banque
SA
16 Rue des Bains
1212 Luxembourg
Tel: (010 352) 461411

Societe Generale Alsacienne
de Banque
15 Avenue Emile Reuter
2420 Luxembourg
Tel: (010 352) 23982

Trade Development Bank
(Luxembourg) SA
34 Avenuede la Porte-Heure
2227 Luxembourg
Tel: (010 352) 41823

Van Moer, Santerre
Luxembourg SA
43 Boulevard Prince Henri
1724 Luxembourg
Tel: (010 352) 41160

Sources of General Background Information, Industry Sector Information and Trade Contacts

UK Addresses
Belgian Embassy
103 Eaton Square
London SW1W 9AB
Tel: 01-235 5422
Telex: 918258

Belgo-Luxembourg Chamber
of Commerce in Great Britain
36-37 Piccadilly
London W1V OPL
Tel: 01-434 1815
Telex: 8953411

Addresses in Belgium
Belgium has a Chamber of
Commerce in every main
town and industrial area.
Some of the main chambers
are:

Antwerp-Kamer van
Koophandel and Nijverheid
van Antwerpen
Markgravestraat 12
2000 Antwerp
Tel: (010 32) 3-2322220
Telex: 71536

Belgian Chamber of
Commerce and Industry
112 Rue de Treves
1040 Brussels

Bruges-Kamer voor Handel
en Nijverheid voor het
Noorden
Van Westvlaanderen
Ezelstraat 25
8000 Bruges
Tel: (010 32) 50-333696
Telex: 81282

Chambre de Commerce de
Bruxelles
Avenue Louise 500
1050 Brussels
Tel: (010 32) 2-6485002
Telex: 22082

Chambre de Commerce et
d'Industrie de Charleroi
1A Boulevard General Michel
6000 Charleroi
Tel: (010 32) 71-321160
Telex: 51624

Chambre de Commerce et
d'Industrie de Namur
Residence Paola
Avenue 6
Bovesse 117
5100 Jambes-les-Namur
Tel: (010 32) 81-304937

Chambre de Commerce et
d'Industrie du Tournaisis
9B Placette aux Oignons
7500 Tournai
Tel: (010 32) 69-221121

Kamor voor Handel en
Nijverheid van Oostende
Langestraat 69
8400 Oostende
Tel: (010 32) 59-501936
Telex: 82057

Kramer van Koophandel and
Nijverheid van het Gewest
Ghent
Building Lieven Bauwens
15 Martelaarslaan
9000 Ghent
Tel: (010 32) 91-253307
Telex: 11871

British Commercial Representatives
British Chamber of
Commerce for Belgium and
Luxembourg
Rue Joseph II 30
1040 Brussels
Tel: (010 32) 3-2190787/88
Telex: 22703 BRITEM B

British Consulates-General
Lange Klarenstraat 24
2000 Antwerp

British Council
Avenue Galilee 5
1030 Brussels

British Embassy
Commercial Department
Britannia House
Rue Joseph II 28
1040 Brussels
Tel: (010 32) 3-2179000
Telex: 22703 BRITEM B

Sources of Investment and Trade Advice, Assistance and Information

There are a number of
investment and tax incentives
available to companies
considering setting up
business in Belgium. National
contacts for further advice are
listed below.

Ministry of Economic Affairs
Directions des
Investissements Prives
Etranges
23 Square De Meeus
1040 Brussels
Tel: (010 32) 2-5111930
Telex: 61932 ECOEXT
or your nearest Belgian
consulate or embassy

Regional information
City of Hasselt
Groenplein
3500 Hasselt
Tel: (010 32) 11-225961
Telex: 38062

Flanders Investment
Opportunities Council (FIOC)
Treirstraat 100
1040 Brussels
Tel: (010 32) 2-2301225
Telex: 62292

Ministry of External Relations
Government of Flanders
10th Floor
Galileilaan 5
1030 Brussels
Tel: (010 32) 2-2175800
Telex: 26990 EXTBET

Luxembourg

Board of Economic
Development
Ministry of the Economy
19-21 Boulevard Royal
PO Box 97
2010 Luxembourg
Tel: (010 352) 4794231
Telex: 3464 ECOLU

Ministry of Foreign Affairs
6 Rue de la Congregation
2910 Luxembourg
Tel: (010 352) 478261
Telex: 1702 AFETRLU

National Credit and
Investment Company
3 rue de la Congregation
1352 Luxembourg
Tel: (010 352) 478299/478305

Luxembourg Chamber of
Commerce
7 rue Alcide de Gasperi
1615 Luxembourg
Tel: (010 352) 435853
Telex: 2784 SIDLUX

Luxembourg Federation of
Industry
7 Rue Alcide de Gasperi
1615 Luxembourg
Tel: (010 352) 435366/67
Telex: SIDHEX LU

Professional Associations

Accountancy

College National des
Experts-Compatables de
Belgique
49 Rue du Congres
Brussels 1000

Institut des Reviseurs
d'Enterprises
Avenue Manix 22
Brussels 1050

Banking

Association Belge des
Banques/Belgische
Vereniging der Banken
(Association for privately
owned banks)
Rue Ravenstein 36
Box 5
1000 Brussels
Tel: (010 32) 2-5125868

Association des Caisses
d'Epargne Privees
(Private Savings Banks)
34-35 Place de Jambline de
Meux
1040 Brussels
Tel: (010 32) 2-7349909
Telex: 63186

Consultancy

Association Belge des
Conseils en Organisation et
Gestion (ASCOBEL)
Rue Ravenstein 3
1000 Brussels
Tel: (010 32) 2-5115294

Insurance

Cerde des Assureurs de
Belgique
AG Group
Boulevard Emile Jacqmain 53
1000 Brussels
Tel: (010 32) 2-2148387

Koninklijke Vereniging Van
Belgische Aktuarissen
(Royal Association of Belgian
Actuaries)
6 Kongres Straat
1000 Brussels

Union Professionelle des
Enterprises d'Assurances
Insurance House
Square de Meeus 29
1040 Brussels

Trade Associations

General industry

Federation Nationale de
Chambres de Commerce et
l'Industrie de Belgique
40 rue du Congres
1000 Brussels

Association des Fabricants de
Pates, Papiers et Cartonns de
Belgique 'Cobelpa' (Pulp,
paper and cardboard
manufacturers)
Rue d'Arlon 39-41
1040 Brussels
Tel: (010 32) 2-2307020

Comit de la Siderurgie Belge
(Iron and Steel Board)
Rue Montoyer 47
1040 Brussels
Tel: (010 32) 2-5133820

Confederation des Brasseries
de Belgique (Breweries)
Maison des Brasseurs
Grande Place 10
1000 Brussels
Tel: (010 32)
2-5114987/5122696

Confederation Nationale de la
Construction (Construction)
Rue du Lombard 34-42
1000 Brussels
Tel: (010 32) 2-5136532

Confederation Profesionnelle
du Sucre et de ses Derives
(Sugar and its Derivatives)
Avenue de Tervueren 182
1150 Brussels
Tel: (010 32) 2-7710130

Confederation de la
Recuperation (Salvage)
Place du Samedi 13
Bte 5 et 6
1000 Brussels
Tel: (010 32) 2-2179993

Federation Belge des
Enterprises de Distribution
'Fedis' (Distribution)
Rue Saint-Bernard 60
1060 Brussels
Tel: (010 32) 2-5373060

Federation Belge des
Enterprises de la
Transformation de Bois
'Febelbois'
(Woodwork)
Rue Royale 109-111
1000 Brussels
Tel: (010 32) 2-2176365

Federation Belge de
l'Industrie de la Chaussure
'Febic' (Footwear industry)
Rue F Bossaerts 53
1030 Brussels
Tel: (010 32) 2-7352701

Federation Belge des
Industries Graphiques
'Febelgra' (Printing industry)
Rue Belliard 20
Bte 16
1040 Brussels
Tel: (010 32)
2-5123638/5121492

Federation Belge des
Industries de l'Habillement
(Clothing)
Rue Montover 24
1000 Brussels
Tel: (010 32) 2-2308890

Federation
Belgo-luxembourgeoise des
Industries du Tabac 'Fedetab'
(Tobacco)
Avenue de Tervueren 270-272
Bte 20
1150 Brussels
Tel: (010 32) 2-7625720

Federation Charbonniere de
Belgique (Coal)
Avenue des Arts 21
Bte 10
1040 Brussels
Tel: (010 32) 2-2303740

Federation des Enterprises de
l'Industrie de Fabrications
Metalliques, Mecaniques,
Electriques et de la
Transformation des Matieres
Plastiques 'Fabrimetal'
(Metallurgical and plastics
engineering)
Rue des Drapiers 21
1050 Brussels
Tel: (010 32) 2-5102311

Federation des Enterprises de
Metaux non ferreux (Non
ferrous metals)
Rue Montoyer 47
1040 Brussels
Tel: (010 32) 2-5138634

Federation de l'Industrie du
Beton (Concrete)
Boulevard A Reyers 207-209
1040 Brussels
Tel: (010 32) 2-7358015

Federation de l'Industrie
Cimentiere (Cement)
Rue Cesar Franck 46
1050 Brussels
Tel: (010 32) 2-6499850

Federation de l'Industrie
Textile Belge 'Febeltex'
(Textiles)
rue Montoyer 24
1000 Brussels
Tel: (010 32) 2-2309330

Federation de l'Industrie du
Verre (Glass industry)
Rue Montoyer 47
1040 Brussels
Tel: (010 32) 2-5133820

Federation des Industries
agricoles et alimentaires
(Agricultural and Foodstuffs)
Avenue de Cortenberg 172
1040 Brussels
Tel: (010 32) 2-7358170

Federation des Industries
Chimiques de Belgique 'FIC'
(Chemicals)
Square Marie-Louise 49-51
1040 Brussels
Tel: (010 32) 2-2304090

Federation des Industries
Transormatrices de Papier et
Carton 'Fetra'
(Paper and cardboard
processors)
Chaussee de Waterloo 715
Bte 25
1180 Brussels
Tel: (010 32) 2-3441962

Federation Petroliere Belge
(Oil Federation)
Rue de la Science 4
1040 Brussels
Tel: (010 32) 2-5123003

Groupement National de
l'Industrie de la Terre cuite
(Brick industry)
Rue des Poissonniers 13
Bte 22
1000 Brussels
Tel: (010 32) 2-5112581

Groupement des Sablieres
(Sand quarries)
Quellinstraat 49
2018 Antwerpen
Tel: (010 32) 3-2236683

Incobel (International
Construction Belgium)
(Construction)
Rue de Lombard 34-42
1000 Brussels
Tel: (010 32) 2-5136532

Union Professionnelle
d'Agents Fabricants et
Importateurs exclusifs
d'objets d'art et de cadeaux
(UPAFI) (Antiques)
Rue Valere Broeckaert 64
1090 Brussels
Tel: (010 32) 2-4784321

Union Professionnelle des
Producteurs de Fibres-Ciment
(Cement)
WTC
Boulevard E Jacqmain 162
Bte 37
1210 Brussels
Tel: (010 32) 2-2192980

Union des Producteurs Belges
de Chaux, Calcaires,
Dolomies et Produits
connexes (Lime, limestone
and related products)
Rue du Trone 61
1050 Brussels
Tel: (010 32) 2-5116173

Union de la Tannerie et de la
Megisserie belges 'Unitan'
(Union of the Tanning
Industry)
Rue Th De Cuyper 161
Bte 32
1200 Brussels
Tel: (010 32) 2-7713206

Company Financial and Product Information

Directories
Belgium and Luxembourg's 10 000 Largest Companies and their Financial Figures
Published by Dun & Bradstreet, Brussels
Directory includes a ranking of the top 100 companies according to a number of criteria. The bulk of the directory is a listing of companies in alphabetical order, with basic details including sales, SIC code and subsidiary companies. Banks and insurance companies are included as well as industrial concerns

Kompass
Belgium/Luxembourg
Published by Kompass Belgium SA
The 1986/87 edition covered 22 000 Belgium and 1600 Luxembourg companies. It also includes a trade mark index

Economic and Market Statistical Data

Market Research Organisations
Aspemar SA
Avenue des Arts 2
Boite 16
1040 Brussels
Tel: (010 32) 2-2191100
Telex: 65409 ASMAR B

Ted Bates SA
Boulevard St Michel 47
1040 Brussels
Telex: 21738

Dechy Univas SA
Avenue Brugmanlaan 78-80
1060 Brussels
Telex: 25022 DECHY B

Dimarso-Gallup Belgium
54 rue des Colonies
Boite 3
1000 Brussels
Tel: (010 32) 2-2192408
Telex: 64577 DIMARSO B
Affiliated to the Gallup organisation

Marketing Unit SA
Avenue Louise 430
Box 10
1050 Brussels
Tel: (010 32) 2-6488010
Telex: 61054
Second largest market research company in Belgium

Martsteller International
Avenue Louise 225
Bte 5
1050 Brussels
Telex: 23255

A C Nielsen Company (Belgium) SA
Avenue des Arts 56
1040 Brussels
Tel: (010 32) 2-5112296
Telex: 21794

SA Suma Research International
14 rue Berkmans
1060 Brussels
Tel: (010 32) 2-5372008
Telex: 21541 UNIL B

Sobemap SA
5 Place du Champ de Mars
Boite 40
1050 Brussels
Tel: (010 32) 2-5125990
Telex: 23709
Part of Metra International Group

J Walter Thompson Company SA
Park Seny-Rue Charles Lemaire 1
1160 Brussels
Telex: 23673 JWTBRU B

Organisations Providing Economic and Statistical Data
Banque National de Belgique SA
Boulevard de Berlaimont 5
1000 Brussels
Publications: Bulletin de Documentation et Statistique
Bank's annual report provides useful financial and economic statistics

Institut Belge de l'Information et de Documentation
3 Rue Montoyer
1040 Brussels
Produces a publication entitled Belgium: Basic Statistics

Institut National de Statistique
44 Rue de Louvain
1000 Brussels
Tel: (010 32) 2-5139650
Main source of official statistics in Belgium
Publications: Annuaire Statistique de la Belgique
Statistiques Industrielles
General census publications
Bulletin de Statistique

Ministere des Affaires Economiques
23 Square de Meeus
1040 Brussels
Tel: (010 32) 2-5111930
Fax: (010 32) 2-5140389
Telex: 61932 ECOEXT
Publications: Lettre de Conjoncture (monthly)
L'Economie Belge

Ministere de l'Agriculture, Administration de la Recherche Agronomique, Institut Economique Agricole (IEA)
Manhattan Center
21 Etage
Avenue du Boulevard 21
1210 Brussels
Tel: (010 32) 2-2117635/36
Publishes a comprehensive statistical series on agriculture

Office Belge du Commerce
Exterieur
World Trade Centre
Boulevard Emile Jacqmain 162
1000 Brussels
Publishes details of trade
opportunities in its daily
bulletins. This is the official
foreign trade promotion office
of the Ministry of Foreign
Commerce

Secretariat General de l'Union
Economiqe Benelux
181 Rue de la Loi
Brussels
Publishes: Benelux Bulletin
Trimertriel de Statistique

Luxembourg
Luxembourg Federation of
Industry
7 Rue Alcide de Gasperi
1615 Luxembourg
Tel: (010 352) 435366/67
Telex: SIDHEX LU

Ministrere de l'Economie
Nationale et de l'Energie
19-21 Boulevard Royal
PO Box 97
2010 Luxembourg
Tel: (010 352) 4794231
Telex: 3464 ECOLU
Publishes Bulletin du Statec

Publications

Belgium

Major Newspapers
Agence Economique et
Financiere (AGEFI)
Business and financial daily

La Cote Libre
Financial daily

L'Echo de la Bourse (AGEFI)
(AGEFI)
Business and financial daily

De Financieel Ekonomische
Tijd
Dutch financial daily

Informateur Economique et
Financier
Daily

La Libre Belgique
Daily paper, contains a
business section

De Standard
Daily paper, contains a
business section

Journals and Periodicals
Belgian Business
Covers general commercial
and financial news. Monthly

La Bourse de Bruxelles
Financial information.
Monthly

Bulletin de la Chambre de
Commerce de Bruxelles
Bulletin produced by the
Brussels Chamber of
Commerce. Monthly

Bulletin Commercial Belge
Official journal covering
foreign trade. Monthly

Entreprende
Covers news and current
topics related to trade and
business. Produced by the
Brussels Chamber of
Commerce. Monthly

Indicateur
Publicitaire/Reklameguids
Covers advertising media.
Monthly

Information Bancaires et
Financieres
Covers banking and finance.
6 issues per annum

Le Marche Hebdomadaire
Marketing publication.
Weekly

Prospects
Provides company profiles
and a monthly review of a
particular sector of the
economy. Monthly

Telexinvest
Provides investment adivce
on the Belgian Stock Market.
Weekly

Test-Achats/Test-Aankoop
Provides investment advice
on the Belgian Stock Market.
Weekly

Trends-Tendances
Financial and statistical
information. Twice monthly

Vraag en Aanbod
Covers financial and
company news. Weekly

Luxembourg

Major Newspapers
Journal
Daily

Luxembourg Wort
Daily

Republican Lorraine
Daily

Tageblatt
Daily

Journals and Periodicals
Echo de l'Industrie
Produced by the Federation of
Industries. Covers economic,
industrial news and company
profiles. Monthly

Canada

Sources of Economic, Stock Market Information and Investment Research Services

Banks

Central Bank
Bank of Canada
234 Wellington Street
Ottawa KIA OG9
Tel: (010 1) 613-7828111
Telex: 053 4241

Canadian Banks in London
Bank of Montreal
9 Queen Victoria Street
London EC4N 4XN
Tel: 01-236 1010

Bank of Nova Scotia
Scotia House
33 Finsbury Square
London EC2A 1BB
Tel: 01-638 5644

Canadian Imperial Bank of
Commerce
Cottons Centre
Cottons Lane
London SE1 2QL
Tel: 01-234 6000

Laurentian Bank of Canada
(UK)
10 Foster Lane
London EC2V 6HH
Tel: 01-606 9910

National Bank of Canada
Princes House
95 Gresham Street
London EC2V 7LU
Tel: 01-726 6581

Orion Royal Bank
(Royal Bank of Canada
Subsidiary)
1 London Wall
London EC2
Tel: 01-600 6222

Royal Bank of Canada
(Branch)
99 Bishipsgate
London EC2
Tel: 01-920 9212

Royal Trust Bank
Royal Trust House
48-50 Cannon Street
London EC4N 6LD
Tel: 01-236 6044

Toronto Dominion Bank
Triton Court
14-18 Finsbury Square
London EC2A 1DB
Tel: 01-920 0272

**Security Houses in
London**
Bank of Montreal Capital
Markets
9 Queen Victoria Street
London EC4N 4XN
Tel: 01-236 1010
Telex 889068

Burns Fry
Staple Hall
Stone House Court
Houndsditch
London EC3A 7AU
Tel: 01-283 3040
Telex 884645

CIBC
55 Bishopsgate
London EC2N 3NN
Tel: 01-588 0800
Telex: 888229

Dominion Securities
16 St Helens Place
London EC3A 6ER
Tel: 01-628 4266

Guaranty Trust Co of Canada
(UK)
65-66 Queen Street
London EC4R 1EB
Tel: 01-248 4888
Telex: 883713

Levesque Beaubien
10 Finsbury Square
London EC2A 1AD
Tel: 01-588 6771
Telex: 8813911

McLeod, Young, Weir
International
3 Finsbury Square
London EC2A 1AD
Tel: 01-256 5656
Telex: 889283

Merrill Lynch Canada
27 Finsbury Square
London EC2A 1AQ
Tel: 01-382 8000
Telex: 8811047

Midland Doherty
2 London Wall Buildings
London EC2M 5PP
Tel: 01-638 3441
Telex: 885506

Nesbitt Thomson
Roman House
Wood Street
London EC2Y 5BA
Tel: 01-628 4488
Telex 888536

Richardson Greenshields of
Canada
Lowndes House
1-9 City Road
London EC1Y 1BH
Tel: 01-638 8831
Telex: 887439

Toronto-Dominion
International
Triton Court
14-18 Finsbury Square
London EC2A 1DB
Tel: 01-920 0272
Telex: 886142

Wood Gundy
30 Finsbury Square
London EC2A 1SB
Tel: 01-628 4030
Telex: 886752

Major Canadian Banks
Bank of Montreal
129 St James Street
Montreal
Quebec H2Y 1L6
Canada
Tel: (010 1) 514-8777110
Telex: 05267661

Bank of Nova Scotia
44 King Street West
Toronto
Ontario M5H 1H1
Tel: (010 1) 416-8666161

Canadian Imperial Bank of
Commerce
Commerce Court
Toronto
Ontario M5L 1A2
Tel: (010 1) 416-9802211
Telex: 065 24116

National Bank of Canada
600 de la Gauchetiere Street,
West
Montreal
Quebec H3B 4L2
Tel: (010 1) 514-3944000
Telex: 0525181

Royal Bank of Canada (The)
1 Place Ville Marie
Montreal
Quebec
Tel: (010 1) 514-3977000
Telex: 055 61286

Toronto-Dominion (The)
Toronto Dominion Centre
55 King Street West and Bay
Street
Toronto
Ontario M5K 1AZ
Tel: (010 1) 416-9828222
Telex: 065 24267

Stockbrokers

There are five exchanges in
Canda: Vancouver, Toronto,
Montreal, Alberta and
Winnipeg. Montreal, Toronto
and Vancouver are the three
major stock exchanges.
Toronto accounts for about 75
per cent of total traded value.

Vancouver Stock Exchange
Stock Exchange Tower
PO Box 10333
609 Granville Street
Vancouver BC V7Y 1H1
Tel: (010 1) 604-6893334
Telex: 04-55480

Members (49 as at December 1987)

Brink, Hudson & Lefever Ltd
(V)
1500 Park Place
666 Burrard Street
Vancouver BC V6C 3C4
Tel: (010 1) 604-6880133
Telex: 04-53141

Alfred Bunting & Co Limited
PO Box 49332, Bentall Centre
3314-1055 Dunsmuir Street
Vancouver BC VX 1L4
Tel: (010 1) 604-6820791

Burns Fry Limited
3300 Park Place
666 Burrard Street
Vancouver BC V6C 3X8
Tel: (010 1) 604-6855181

Canarim Investment
Corporation Ltd (V)
Stock Exchange Tower
PO Box 1033
2200-609 Granville Street
Vancouver BC VY 1H2
Tel: (010 1) 604-6888151
Telex: 04-54495

Chisholm (Hector M) & Co
Limited
Suite 300
330 Bay Street
Toronto
Ontario M5H 3T5
Tel: (010 1) 416-3624731
Telex: 06-23249

Davidson Partners Limited
900-980 Hornby Street
Vancouver BC V6B 3G6
Tel: (010 1) 604-6696797

Dean Witter Reynolds
(Canada) Inc
PO Box 11560
650 West Georgia Street
Vancouver BC V6B 4N8
Tel: (010 1) 604-6876776

Dominick & Dominick
Securities Inc
Suite 4010 Royal Trust Tower
PO Box 272
Toronto Dominion Centre
Toronto
Ontario M5K 115
Tel: (010 1) 416-3630201

Dominion Securities Inc
2100 Bell Park
666 Burrard Street
Vancouver BC V6C 3B1
Tel: (010 1) 604-6623400

First Canada Securities
International Limited
PO Box 49345
1124-1055 Drummond Street
Vancouver BC VX 1L4
Tel: (010 1) 604-6859188

First Marathon Securities
Limited
2010-1040 West Georgia Street
Vancouver BC V6W 4H1
Tel: (010 1) 604-6826351

Gardiner Group Stockbrokers
Inc
425-744 West Hastings Street
Vancouver BC V6C 1A5
Tel: (010 1) 604-6627176

Geoffrion, Leclerc Inc
1000-789 West Pender Street
Vancouver BC V6C 1H2
Tel: (010 1) 604-6826433

Georgia Pacific Securities
Corporation (V)
16th Floor Two Bentall Centre
Vancouver BC VX 1S6
Tel: (010 1) 604-6881800
Telex: 04-54398

Gordon Capital Corporation
1010-999 West Hastings Street
Vancouver BC V6C 2W2
Tel: (010 1) 604-6699555
Telex: 065-24076

Green Line Investor Services
Inc
430 West Pender Street
Vancouver BC V6C 1G9
Tel: (010 1) 604-6543710

Haywood Securities Inc (V)
11th Floor, Commerce Place
400 Burrard Street
Vancouver BC N6C 3A6
Tel: (010 1) 604-6431100

Jefferson Securities Inc (V)
1660-1140 West Pender Street
Vancouver BC V6E 4G1
Tel: (010 1) 604-6889773

Jones, Gable & Company
Limited
400-700 West Pender Street
Vancouver BC V6C 1C1
Tel: (010 1) 604-6851481

WD Latimer & Co Limited
PO Box 96, Suite 2508
Toronto Dominion Bank
Tower
Toronto
Ontario M5K 1G8
Tel: (010 1) 416-3635631
Telex: 06-22285

Levesque, Beaubien Inc
Montreal Trust Centre
7th Floor
510 Burrard Street
Vancouver BC V6C 2J6
Tel: (010 1) 604-6432800

William E Lewis (V)
630 Columbia Street
New Westminster BC V3M
1A5
Tel: (010 1) 604-5264466

Loewen Ondaatje
McCutcheon & Company
Limited
Suite 1610, Grosvenor Bldg
1040 West Georgia Street
Vancouver BC V6E 4H1
Tel: (010 1) 604-6886701

Majendie Securities Ltd (V)
Suite 1650, Daon Centre
999 West Hastings Street
Vancouver BC V6C 2W2
Tel: (010 1) 604-6826446

McDermid St Lawrence
Limited (V)
1000-601 West Hastings Street
Vancouver BC V6B 5E2
Tel: (010 1) 604-6541111
Telex: 04-54491

McLeod Young Weir Limited
Stock Exchange Tower
PO Box 10342
1100-609 Granville Street
Vancouver BC VY 1H6
Tel: (010 1) 604-6617400,
7317744

McNeil, Mantha, Inc
501-889 West Pender Street
Vancouver BC V6C 3B2
Tel: (010 1) 604-6871334

Merit Investment Corporation
1500-625 Howe Street
Vancouver BC V6C 2T6
Tel: (010 1) 604-6874800

Merrill Lynch Canada Inc
600-666 Burrard Street
Vancouver BC V6C 2A5
Tel: (010 1) 604-6823311
Telex: 04-55166

Midland Doherty Limited
11th Floor, Three Bentall
Centre
595 Burrard Street, PO Box
49020
Vancouver BC VX 1C3
Tel: (010 1) 604-6882111
Telex: 04-53146

Nesbitt Thomson Deacon Inc
Suite 1900, Park Place
666 Burrard Street
Vancouver BC V6C 2X3
Tel: (010 1) 604-6697424
Telex: 04-52351

Nesbitt Thomson Deacon
Limited
Suite 1900, Park Place
666 Burrard Street
Vancouver BC V6C 2X3
Tel: (010 1) 604-6697424

Odlum Brown Limited (V)
Suite 1800-609
Granville Street
Vancouver BC VY 1A3
Tel: (010 1) 604-6691600
Telex: 04-508811

CM Oliver & Company
Limited (V)
2nd Floor
550 West Pender Street
Vancouver BC V6C 1B5
Tel: (010 1) 604-6849211
Telex: 04-51215

Osler Inc
Third Floor, Grosvenor
Building
1040 West Georgia Street
Vancouver BC V6E 4H1
Tel: (010 1) 604-6610300
Telex: 04-507507

Pacific International Securities
Inc (V)
PO Box 10012, Pacific Centre
1500-700 West Georgia Street
Vancouver BC VY 1G1
Tel: (010 1) 604-6692174
Telex: 04-507666

Paine Webber (BC) Limited
(V)
Suite 1115-595
Howe Street
Vancouver BC V6C 3C7
Tel: (010 1) 604-6894445

Pemberton Securities Inc (V)
2400-666 Burrard Street
Vancouver BC V6C 3C7
Tel: (010 1) 604-6888411
Telex: 04-54331

Peters & Co Limited
200 Sun Life Plaza, North
Tower
140 Avenue SW
Calgary, Alberta T2P 3M3
Tel: (010 1) 403-2614850
Telex: 038-22890

Prudential-Bache Securities
Canada Ltd
Stock Exchange Tower, PO
Box 10341
909-609 Granville Street
Vancouver BC VY 1H4
Tel: (010 1) 604-6898441

Richardson Greenshields of
Canada Limited
500-1066 West Hastings Street
PO Box 129, Station A
Vancouver BC V6C 3X1
Tel: (010 1) 604-6821751 or
604-6893324
Telex: 04-53145

Tasse & Associates Limited
Suite 1200-630, Dorchester
Blvd West
Montreal
Quebec H3B 1S6
Tel: (010 1) 514-8792100
Telex: 055-61249

Union Securities Ltd (V)
1300-409 Granville Street
Vancouver BC V6C 1T2
Tel: (010 1) 604-6872201
Telex: 04-508500

Walwyn Stodgell Cochran
Murray Limited
21st Floor, Royal Centre
PO Box 11171
1055 West Georgia Street
Vancouver BC V6E 3P1
Tel: (010 1) 604-6696262
Telex: 04-54472

West Coast Securities Ltd (V)
400-815 West Hastings Street
Vancouver BC V6C 3G9
Tel: (010 1) 604-6811286
Telex: 04-508738

Wolverton & Company Ltd
(V)
PO Box 10115
801 West Georgia Street
Vancouver BC VY 1I5
Tel: (010 1) 604-6883477
Telex: 04-54460

Wood Gundy Inc
2100-885 West Georgia Street
Vancouver BC V6C 3E8
Tel: (010 1) 604-6872699

Yorkton Securities Inc
1400 Stock Exchange Tower
609 Granville Street
PO Box 10350
Vancouver BC VY 1G5
Tel: (010 1) 604-6697752

Toronto Stock Exchange
The Exchange Tower
2 First Canadian Place
Toronto, Ontario M5X 1J2
Tel: (010 1) 416-9474700
Telex: 062-17759

Members (as at 30.9.88)
Alfred Bunting & Co Limited
130 Adelaide Street West
Suite 3000
Toronto M5H 3V4
Tel: (010 1) 416-3643293

Andras Research Capital Inc
7th Floor
2 First Canadian Place
Box 449
Toronto M5X 1J7
Tel: (010 1) 416-8607600

Arachnae Securities Ltd
Buttonville Airport
Markham
Toronto L3P 3J9
Tel: (010 1) 416-4777150

Begg Securities Ltd
90 Adelaide Street West
2nd Floor
Toronto M5H 1P6
Tel: (010 1) 416-8691721

R Brant Securities Ltd
Suite 301
4 King Street West
Toronto M5H 1B6
Tel: (010 1) 416-8651090

Brault Guy O'Brien Inc
Suite 1410
P O Box 29
65 Queen Street West
Toronto M5H 2M5
Tel: (010 1) 416-8691373

Brawley Cathers Ltd
11 King Street West
Toronto M5H 1A7
Tel: (010 1) 416-3635821

L A Brenzel Securities Ltd
10 Temperance Street
Toronto M5H 1Y4
Tel: (010 1) 416-8631655

Brink Hudson & Lefever Ltd
1500 Park Place
666 Burrard Street
Vancouver
British Columbia V6C 3C4
Tel: (010 1) 604-6880133

Brockhouse & Cooper Inc
Suite 2750
800 Dorchester Boulevard
West
Montreal
Quebec H3B 1X9
Tel: (010 1) 514-8711250

Brown Baldwin Nisker
Limited
19th Floor
390 Bay Street
Toronto M5H 2Y2
Tel: (010 1) 416-9472700

Burns Fry Limited
Suite 5000
PO Box 150
First Canadian Place
Toronto M5X 1H3
Tel: (010 1) 416-3654000

Caldwell Securities Ltd
55 University Avenue
Suite 430
Toronto M5J 2H7
Tel: (010 1) 416-8627755

Canarim Investment
Corporation Ltd
2 First Canadian Place
36th floor
P O Box 27
Toronto M5X 1A9
Tel: (010 1) 416-8691900

Capital Group Securities Ltd
Suite 1810
141 Adelaide Street West
Toronto M5H 3L5
Tel: (010 1) 416-8607800

Cassels Blaikie & Co Ltd
33 Yonge Street
Suite 200
Toronto M5E 1S8
Tel: (010 1) 416-3626531

Charlton Securities Ltd
3600 First Canadian Centre
350-7th Avenue SW
Calgary, Alberta T2P 3N9
Tel: (010 1) 403-2625542

Chisholm (Hector M) & Co
Ltd
330 Bay Street
Suite 300
Toronto M5H 3T5
Tel: (010 1) 416-3624731

Connor Clark & Company
Ltd
20 Queen Street West
Suite 2812
Toronto M5H 3R3
Tel: (010 1) 416-5968714

Davidson Partners Ltd
P O Box 122
First Canadian Place
Toronto M5X 1E9
Tel: (010 1) 416-9823300

Dean Witter Reynolds
(Canada) Inc
Suite 200
Guardian of Canada Tower
181 University Avenue
Toronto M5H 3M7
Tel: (010 1) 416-3698900

Deacon Morgan McEwan
Easson Ltd
Suite 1330
North Tower
Royal Bank Plaza
Box 72
Toronto M5H 2J2
Tel: (010 1) 416-8650303

Dominick & Dominick
Securities Inc
PO Box 272
Royal Trust Tower
Toronto-Dominion Centre
Toronto M5K 1J5
Tel: (010 1) 416-3630201

Dominion Securities Inc
PO Box 21
Commerce Court South
Toronto M5L 1A7
Tel: (010 1) 416-8644000

First Canada Securities
International Ltd
Standard Life Centre
121 King Street West
P O Box 117
Toronto M5H 3T9
Tel: (010 1) 416-9477200

First Marathon Securities Ltd
2 First Canadian Place
The Exchange Tower
Suite 3100
Toronto M5X 1J9
Tel: (010 1) 416-8693707

Fraser Gingman & Co Ltd
199 Bay Street
Toronto M5J 1L4
Tel: (010 1) 416-3643125

Gardiner Group Stockbrokers
Inc
330 Bay Street
10th floor
Toronto M5H 2S8
Tel: (010 1) 416-3698400

Geoffrion Leclerc & Co Ltd
PO Box 175
Royal Bank Plaza
Toronto M5J 2J4
Tel: (010 1) 416-8651060

Geoffrion Leclerc Inc
5 Place Ville Marie
Suite 900
Montreal, Quebec
Toronto H3B 2G2
Tel: (010 1) 514-8719000

Geoffrion Leclerc Ltd
60 Yonge Street
Suite 1200
Toronto M5E 1S1
Tel: (010 1) 416-3640264

Gordon Capital Corporation
Suite 5401
PO Box 67
Toronto-Dominion Centre
Toronto M5K 1E7
Tel: (010 1) 416-3649393

Green Line Investor Services
Inc
17th Floor
Royal Trust Tower
PO Box 1
Toronto-Dominion Centre
Toronto M5K 1A2
Tel: (010 1) 416-9827980

Haywood Securities Inc
11th Floor
Commerce Place
400 Burrard Street
Vancouver
British Columbia V6C 3A6
Tel: (010 1) 604-6431100

Jones Gable & Company Ltd
110 Yonge Street
Toronto M5C 1T6
Tel: (010 1) 416-3625454

Kingwest and Company
33 Yonge Street
Suite 1220
Toronto M5E 1S9
Tel: (010 1) 416-3641503

Lafferty Harwood & Partners
Ltd
500 St Jacques Street
Suite 600
Montreal
Quebec H2Y 3R3
Tel: (010 1) 514-8453166

W D Latimer Co Ltd
PO Box 96
Toronto-Dominion Centre
Toronto M5K 1G8
Tel: (010 1) 416-3635631

Levesque Beaubien Inc
121 King Street West
Suite 600
Toronto M5H 3T9
Tel: (010 1) 416-8657400

Loewen Ondaatje
McCutcheon & Company Ltd
7 King Street East
20th Floor
Toronto M5C 1A2
Tel: (010 1) 416-8697211

MacDougall MacDougall &
Mactier Inc
First Canadian Place
PO Box 11
Toronto M5X 1A9
Tel: (010 1) 416-9770663

J D Mack Ltd
PO Box 2052
1204 Purdy's Wharf
1959 Upper Water Street
Halifax, Nova Scotia B3J 2Z1
Tel: (010 1) 902-4200077

Maison Placements Canada
Inc
130 Adelaide Street West
Suite 906
Toronto M5H 3P5
Tel: (010 1) 416-9476040

Majendie Securities Ltd
347 Bay Street
Suite 904
Toronto M5H 2R7
Tel: (010 1) 416-3661980

McCarthy Securities Ltd
55 Yonge Street
Suite 606
Toronto M5E 1J4
Tel: (010 1) 416-8629160

McConnell & Co Ltd
390 Bay Street
Suite 1400
Toronto M5H 2Y2
Tel: (010 1) 416-3644461

McDermid St Lawrence Ltd
401 Bay Street
Suite 2315
Toronto M5H 2Y4
Tel: (010 1) 416-3683811

McLean McCarthy Ltd
Suite 1300
11 King Street West
Toronto M5H 1A3
Tel: (010 1) 416-3682751

McLeod Young Weir Ltd
PO Box 433
Commercial Union Tower
Toronto-Dominion Centre
Toronto M5K 1M2
Tel: (010 1) 416-8637411

McNeil Mantha Inc
Standard Life Centre
Suite 1010, PO Box 110
121 King Street West
Toronto M5H 3T9
Tel: (010 1) 416-3692500

Merit Investment Corporation
155 University Avenue
Suite 400
Toronto M5H 2Z5
Tel: (010 1) 416-8676000

Merrill Lynch Canada Inc
Merrill Lynch Canada Tower
200 King Street West
Toronto M5H 3W3
Tel: (010 1) 416-5866000

Midland Doherty Ltd
Standard Life Tower
121 King Street West
Toronto M5H 3W6
Tel: (010 1) 416-3697400

Moss Lawson & Co Ltd
48 Yonge Street
Toronto M5E 1G7
Tel: (010 1) 416-8642700

Nesbitt Thomson Deacon Inc
150 King Street West
Suite 1900
Sun Life Tower
Sun Life Centre
Toronto M5H 3W2
Tel: (010 1) 416-5863600

Nesbitt Thomson Deacon Ltd
The Exchange Tower
2 First Canadian Place
PO Box 414
Toronto M5X 1J4
Tel: (010 1) 416-3656000

Odlum Brown Ltd
8 King Street East
Toronto M5C 1B5
Tel: (010 1) 416-3638443

Osler Inc
120 Adelaide Street West
Suite 700
Toronto M5H 1T1
Tel: (010 1) 416-8652000

Ouimet Hubbs Inc
330 University Avenue
Suite 507
Toronto M5G 1R8
Tel: (010 1) 416-9771100

Pemberton Houston
Willoughby Bell
Gouinlock Inc
Suite 1010
PO Box 110
1 First Canadian Place
Toronto M5X 1B6
Tel: (010 1) 416-8693690

Peters & Co Ltd
200 Sun Life Plaza
North Tower
140-4th Avenue SW
Calgary, Alberta T2P 3M3
Tel: (010 1) 403-2614850

Pollitt Legault & Co Inc
Suite 1500
11 King Street West
Toronto M5H 1A7
Tel: (010 1) 416-3653313

Pope & Company
15 Duncan Street
Toronto M5H 3P9
Tel: (010 1) 416-5935535

Prudential-Bache Securities
Canada Ltd
4th Floor
33 Yonge Street
Toronto M5E 1V7
Tel: (010 1) 416-8603000

Rasmussen Sharp & Co Ltd
Suite 2408
1010 Sherbrooke Street West
Montreal, Quebec H3A 2R7
Tel: (010 1) 514-2842420

Richardson Greenshields of
Canada
130 Adelaide Street West
Toronto M5H 1T8
Tel: (010 1) 416-8603400

Scotia Bond Company Ltd
Suite 1100
1809 Barrington Street
PO Box 666
Halifax, Nova Scotia B3J 2T3
Toronto
Tel: (010 1) 902-4256900

Security Trading Inc
Suite 4706
Manulife Centre
44 Charles Street West
Toronto M4Y 1R8
Tel: (010 1) 416-9612048

Sprott Securities Ltd
1 University Avenue
Suite 702
Toronto M5J 2PI
Tel: (010 1) 416-3627485

Standard Securities Ltd
Suite 1202, Metropolitan
1 University Avenue
Toronto M5J 2P1
Tel: (010 1) 416-3635911

Tasse & Associates Ltd
181 University Avenue
Suite 1118
Toronto M5H 3M7
Tel: (010 1) 416-8686200

Thomson Kernaghan & Co
Ltd
365 Bay Street
Toronto M5H 2V2
Tel: (010 1) 416-8608800

Walwyn Stodgell Cochran
Murray Ltd
Suite 800
70 University Avenue
Toronto M5J 2M5
Tel: (010 1) 416-5916000

Wood Gundy Inc
PO Box 274
Royal Trust Tower
Toronto-Dominion Centre
Toronto M5K 1M7
Tel: (010 1) 416-8698100

Yorkton Securities Inc
Suite 2700
PO Box 379
1 First Canadian Place
Toronto M5X 1J8
Tel: (010 1) 416-8643500

Addresses of Canada's three other exchanges

Montreal Exchange
Stock Exchange Tower
800 Victoria Square
Montreal
Quebec H4Z 1A9
Tel: (010 1) 514-8712424

Alberta Stock Exchange
64300 5th Avenue South West
Calgary
Alberta P2P 3C4
Tel: (010 1) 403-2627791

Winnipeg Stock Exchange
955/167 Lombard Avenue
Winnipeg
Manitoba R3B 3V3
Tel: (010 1) 204-9428431

**Sources of General
Background Information,
Industry Sector
Information and Trade
Contacts**

UK Addresses
Canada High Commission
Macdonald House
1 Grosvenor Square
London W1X OAB
Tel: 01-629 9492
Telex: 261592
Immigration Section and
Consular and Passport
Section:
Macdonald House
38 Grosvenor Street
London W1X OAA
Tel: 01-409 2071 (Immigration)
01-629 9492 (Consular and
Passport)
Press Information and
Cultural, Tourism and Public
Archives Sections:
Canada House
Trafalgar Square
London SW1Y 5BJ
Tel: 01-629 9492

Canada-United Kingdom
Chamber of Commerce
3 Regent's Street
London SW1Y 4NZ
Tel: 01-930 7711

British High Commission
80 Elgin Street
Ottawa
Ontario K1P 5K7
Tel: (010 1) 613-2371530
Telex: 0533318 UKREP OTT

Addresses in Canada

**Chambers of Commerce
in Major Canadian Cities**
Alberta Chamber of
Commerce
800, 10179 105 Street
Edmonton, Alberta T5J 1ES

Atlantic Provinces Chamber
of Commerce
14 Church Street
Moncton, New Brunswick
E1C 4Y9

British Columbia Chamber of
Commerce
801, 1199 W Pender Street
Vancouver BC V6E 2P4

Canadian Chamber of
Commerce
200 Elgin Street
Ottowa
Ontario K2P 2J7
Tel: (010 1) 613-2384000
Telex: 0533051

Manitoba Chamber of
Commerce
403, 93 Lombard Avenue E
Winnipeg, Manitoba R3B 3B1

Ontario Chamber of
Commerce
2323 Yonge Street, 5th Floor
Toronto, Ontario M4P 2C9

Quebec Chamber of
Commerce
500 St-Francois Xavier
Montreal, Quebec H2Y 2T6

Saskatchewan Chamber of
Commerce
2314 11th Avenue
203 Regina, Saskatchewan
S4P OK1

**Sources of Investment
and Trade Advice,
Assistance and
Information**

Canadian Chamber of
Commerce
(Head Office)
55 Metcalfe Street
Suite 1160
Ottawa
Ontario K1P 6N4
Tel: (010 1) 613-2384000

Canadian Exporter's
Association
Suite 250
99 Bank Street
Ottawa
Ontario
K1P 6B9
Tel: (010 1) 613-2388888
Telex: 0534888

Canadian Importers
Association Inc
World Trade Centre
60 Harbour Street
Toronto
Ontario M5J 1B7
Tel: (010 1) 416-8620002

Canadian Manufacturers
Association (The)
One Yonge Street
Toronto
Ontario M5E 1J9
Tel: (010 1) 416-3637261
Assists members with export,
market and trade advice

Government of Ontario
Business Development
Branch
Ontario House
21 Knightsbridge
London SW1X 7LY
Tel: 01-245 1222

Trade Development Bureau
c/o Department of External
Affairs
125 Sussex Drive
Ottawa
Ontario K1A OG2
Tel: (010 1) 613-9926941
Provides advice and
assistance to Canadian
exporters

Alberta
Alberta Economic
Development and Trade
14th Floor
Sterling Place
9940-106th Street
Edmonton
Alberta TSK 2P6
Tel: (010 1) 403-4274809
Telex: 0372197

British Columbia (BC)
Ministry of Economic
Development
British Columbia Enterprise
Centre
PO Box 19
750 Pacific Boulevard South
Vancouver BCV6B 5E7
Tel: (010 1) 604-6604567

Manitoba
Manitoba Industry Trade and
Technology
155 Carlton Street
Winnipeg R3C 3H8
Tel: (010 1) 204-9452466

Winnipeg Business
Development Corporation
509-167 Lombard Avenue
Winnipeg R3B OV3
Tel: (010 1) 204-9448686

NB
Dept of Commerce and
Technology
Box 6000
Kredericton
NB E3B 5H1
Tel: (010 1) 506-4532873

New Foundland
Government of New
Foundland and Labrador
Department of Development
and Tourism
PO Box 4750
St John's, New Foundland
AIC 5T7
Tel: (010 1) 709-5765600
Telex: 0164949 DIDSNF

NS
Dept of Development
Box 519
Halifax
NS B3J 2R7
Tel: (010 1) 902-4248920
Telex: 01922548

Ontario
Export Development
Corporation
151 O'Connor Street
Box 655
Ottowa
Ontario K1P 5T9
Tel: (010 1) 613-5982500
Telex: 0534136

Investment Canada
240 Sparks Street
Box 2800
Stn D
Ottawa
Ontario K1P 6A5
Tel: (010 1) 613-9959449
Telex: 0534450

Ministry of Trade and
Industry
Trade Research Section
Hearst Block
900 Bay St
Toronto
Ontario M7A 2E6
Tel: (010 1) 416-9653570

Reference Canada
Supply & Services Canada
Place du Portage 111
Ottawa
Ontario K1A 0S5
Tel: (010 1) 819-9946166
Operates telephone referral
service across the country

PEI
PEI Development Agency
West Royalty Industrial Park
Charlottetown PECIE 1BO
Tel: (010 1) 902-5664222

Quebec
Ministere de l'Industrie et du
Commerce
710 Place d'Youville
Quebec QC GIR 4Y4
Tel: (010 1) 418-6435045
Telex: 0513330

Saskatchewan
Saskatchewan Economic
Development and Trade
Trade Development Division
3rd Floor, Bank of Montreal
Blds
2103-11th Avenue
Regina, Sask S4P 3V7
Tel: (010 1) 306-7872232
Telex: 0712675

Professional
Associations

Accountancy
Canadian Institute of
Chartered Accountants
150 Bloor Street West
Toronto, Ontario M5S 2Y2
Tel: (010 1) 416-9621242
Telex: 06-22835

Certified General
Accountants Association of
Canada
740-1176 W Georgia St
Vancouver BC V6E 4A2
Tel: (010 1) 604-6693555

Banking
Canadian Bankers
Association
PO Box 348
2 First Canadian Place
600 Toronto
Ontario M5X IE1
Tel: (010 1) 416-3626092
Telex: 06-234 02

Consultancy
Canadian Association of
Management Consultants
Suite 303
45 Charles Street E
Toronto
Ontario M4Y 1S2
Tel: (010 1) 416-9639172

Institute of Management
Consultants of British
Columbia
600-890 West Pender Street
Vancouver BC V6C 1J9

Insurance
L'Institut d'Assurances du
Canada
(Life Assurance Institute of
Canada)
481 University Avenue
Toronto
Ontario M5G 2E9
Tel: (010 1) 416-5911572

L'Institut d'Assurance-Vie du
Canada
(Insurance Institute of
Canada)
Suite 2500
20 Queen Street West
Toronto
Ontario M5H 3S2
Tel: (010 1) 416-9772221

Marketing

Canadian Association of
Market Research
Organisations (CAMRO)
69 Sherbourne Street
Suite 222
Toronto
Ontario M5A 3X7
Tel: (010 1) 416-3641223

Trade Associations

General Industry

Canadian Manufacturers
Association (The)
1 Yonge Street
Toronto
Ontario M5E 1J9
Tel: (010 1) 416-3637261
Telex: 06524693
Contact for list of members

Association of Canadian
Publishers
260 King Street East
Toronto
Ontario M5A 1K3
Tel: (010 1) 416-3611408

Association of Canadian
Venture Capital Companies
Alta-Can Telecom Inc
Floor 26H
411 1st Street SE
Calgary
Alberta T2G 4Y5
Tel: (010 1) 403-2318535

Canadian Association of Data
and Professional Service
Organisations
280 Albert Street
#804 Ottawa
Ontario KIP 5G8
Tel: (010 1) 613-2303524

Canadian Chemical
Producers' Association
#805, 350 Sparks Street
Ottawa
Ontario K1R 7S8
Tel: (010 1) 613-2376215

Canadian Construction
Association
2nd Floor
85 Albert Street
Ottawa
Ontario KIP 6A4
Tel: (010 1) 613-2369455
Telex: 0534436

Canadian Electrical
Manufacturers
Representatives Association
Box 294
Kleinburg
Ontario LOJ ICO
Tel: (010 1) 416-8931689

Canadian Forestry
Association
185 Somerset Street West
#203 Ottawa
Ontario K2P OJZ
Tel: (010 1) 613-2321815

Council of Forest Industries of
British Columbia
1500/1055 West Hastings
Street
Vancouver BC V6E 2HI
Tel: (010 1) 604-6840211
Telex: 04507752

Federation of Engineering
and Scientific Associations
72 Carlton Street
Toronto
Ontario M5B 1L6
Tel: (010 1) 416-9227612

Mining Association of British
Columbia
PO Box 12540
1066 West Hastings Street
Vancouver BC V6E 3X1
Tel: (010 1) 604-6814321
Fax: (010 1) 604-6815305

Company Financial and Product Information

Directories

Blue Book of Canadian
Business
Published by The Blue Book
of Canadian Business,
Toronto
Basic reference guide to
Canadian companies,
includes profiles and listings
of over 2500 of the largest
companies operating in
Canada

Canadian Key Business
Directory (The)
Published by Dun and
Bradstreet Canada Ltd
This is a reference source for
approximately 20 000
Canadian companies
providing details which
include the names of chief
executives

Canadian Reference Book
(The)
Produced by Dun and
Bradstreet Canada Ltd,
Toronto
This is a credit rating guide
based on the Dunn and
Bradstreet Canadian
Company database,
Dunserve II

Canadian Trade Index (The)
Published by the Canadian
Manufacturers Association,
Toronto
A comprehensive directory of
manufacturing companies in
Canada. A classified list of
products manufactured in
Canada is provided, together
with a geographic list of
manufacturers and details of
service organisations

Financial Post Corporation
Service
Published by Maclean Hunter
Ltd
Provides in-depth
information for about 650 top
public companies. A booklet
is provided for each company
which provides performance
statistics going back over
several years. These booklets
are revised annually and
updated by quarterly
supplements

Financial Post Survey of
Industrials (The)
Published by Maclean Hunter
Ltd
This directory covers
approximately 1200 public
companies and provides
summarised financial
information for the previous
five years

Mergers and Acquisitions in Canada
Published by Harris-Bentley, Ontario
This is a loose-leaf service consisting of an annual binder and monthly updates. It is a useful source of data on mergers and acquisitions which also provides analyses of data

Survey of Industrials
Published by the Financial Post
Information Service, Maclean Hunter, Toronto
Directory of all Canadian public listed and unlisted industrial companies. Provides addresses, stock symbols, financial data and subsidiary information

Economic and Market Statistical Data

Market Research Organisations
ABM Research Ltd
17 Madison Avenue
Toronto
Ontario M5R 2S2
Tel: (010 1) 416-9615511
Member of CAMRO

Burke International Research Ltd
2900 Warden Avenue, Suite 230
Scarborough
Ontario M1W 2SB
Tel: (010 1) 416-4977400
Member of AMA, PMRS

Canada Market Research Ltd
1235 Bay Street
Toronto
Ontario M5R 3K4
Tel: (010 1) 416-9649222
Telex: 06526 129BUSCLUB
Member of AMA, ESOMAR, MRA, MRS, PMRS, WAPOR

Canadian Facts
1075 Bay Street
Toronto
Ontario M5S 2X5
Tel: (010 1) 416-9245751
Donald Monk
Parent Co: SK/CF Inc
Member of CAMRO

Canadian Gallup Poll Ltd (The)
45 Charles Street E
Toronto
Ontario M4Y 1S2
Tel: (010 1) 416-9612811
Fax: (010 1) 416-9613662
Telex: 0622361 GALLUPOLL

Centre de Recherche Contemporaines Ltd
2021 Union Avenue
Suite 850
Montreal
Quebec H3A 2S9
Tel: (010 1) 514-2849360
Parent Co: Contemporary Research Centre Ltd

Cogem International Inc
1420 Sherbrooke West
Montreal
Quebec H3G 1K5
Tel: (010 1) 514-8459221
Fax: (010 1) 514-845 0553
Subsidiaries: Cogem Research Inc, Telecom Evaluation Techniques Inc, Logem Marketing SA
Member of AMA, PMRS

Consumer Contact
2450 Victoria Park Avenue
Willowdale
Ontario M2J 4A2
Tel: (010 1) 416-4936111
Fax: (010 1) 416-4930176
Member of MRS, PMRS

Creative Research Group Ltd (The)
188 Eglinton Avenue East
Suite 701
Toronto
Ontario M4P 2X7
Tel: (010 1) 416-4849500
Subsidiaries: Groupe Innova Inc, Montreal, Quebec
Decision Marketing, Montreal, Quebec
Member of AAPOR, CAMRO, PMRS

Market Facts of Canada Ltd
1240 Bay Street
Toronto
Ontario M5R 3L9
Tel: (010 1) 416-9646262
Telex: 06 217 698
Subsidiaries: Joint ownership with Market Facts Inc, Chicago, USA
Member of AMA, CAMRO, PMRS

Starch Research Services Ltd
301 Donlands Avenue
Toronto
Ontario M4J 3RB
Tel: (010 1) 416-4251824
Fax: (010 1) 416-446 6173
Telex: 06-986391 TOR

Thompson Lightstone & Company Ltd
1027 Yonge Street
Suite 100
Toronto
Ontario M4W 2K9
Tel: (010 1) 416-9221140
Subsidiaries: Thompson Lightstone & Co Inc, USA, Marketing Systems Inc, Information Systems Inc
Member of PMRS

Organisations Providing Economic and Statistical Data
Canadian Department of Finance
Publications available from:
The Canadian Government Printing Centre
Ottawa
Ontario K1A OS9
Tel: (010 1) 613-9926985
Telex: 0533335 FINTB OTT
Produces the 'Quarterly Economic Review' which provides short-term data, and an annual statistical issue covering longer-term trends

Conference Board of Canada (The)
25 McArthur Avenue
Suite 100
Ottawa
Ontario K1L 6R3
Produces two quarterly forecasts, which covers Canada and the provinces. Publications include the 'Canadian Business Review' (quarterly periodical) which regularly summarises the forecasts of about eighteen other institutions. The Conference Board runs an internal database called 'AERIC'. Other publications include 'Consumer Attitudes and Buying Intentions', 'Business Attitudes and Investment Spending Intentions' (Quarterly) and Consumer Markets Update

Economic Council of Canada (The)
PO Box 527
Station B
Ottawa
Ontario K1P 5V6
Tel: (010 1) 613-9931253
This is a federal government agency. Publications include an annual review and the quarterly 'Au Courant' which provides summaries of economic forecasts

MicroMedia Ltd
158 Pearl Street
Toronto
Ontario M5H 1L3
Offers a complete collection of Statistics Canada publications on microfile. Also publishes 'Canadian Business Index' which is the primary tool to retrieve information from Canada's main business periodicals and financial newspapers

Royal Bank of Canada
Head Office
Economics Department
Montreal
Publishes Econoscope which provides industry and economic reviews and forecasts. Other major Canadian banks publish economic reviews

Statistics Canada
R H Coats Building
Ottawa
Ontario K1A OT6
Tel: (010 1) 613-9908116
Telex: 0533585
This is a federal government agency and is the single most important source of statistical data on all aspects of Canadian commerce, the economy and industries. It publishes about 600 statistical series every year, and is responsible for the Canadian Census. Major publications include:

Canadian Statistical Review. Monthly
Statistics Canada Daily
Quarterly Economic Survey
Market Research Handbook. Annual
The Market Research Handbook provides comprehensive economic product and demographic statistics from a cross section of other Statistics Canada publications.
Statistics Canada also produces the CANSIM economic online database which is available for public use (see database chapter). There are also Bureaus of Statistics in 11 Canadian states

Publications

Directories
Browning Directory of Canadian Business Information (The)
Published by Browning and Associates
Reference book providing a review of Canadian business information sources. Lists directories, market surveys, statistical reports

Canadian Almanac & Directory
Published by Copp Clark Pitman Ltd, Toronto
Distributed in Canada by Carswell/Methuen and in the USA by the Gale Research Company
Directory of over 1250 pages in 1988
Contains comprehensive information on most aspects of Canadian life. Provides contact details of cultural, government, legal, financial, educational and business institutions throughout Canada

Export Canada
The Marketing Directory for Canadian Export
Published by Canex Enterprises Inc, Surrey, BC
Provides background details on Canada's economy and industries. Main section provides addresses and other details of companies under sector headings. Covers industrial and service companies

Quick Canadian Facts
Published by Canes Enterprises Inc, Surrey, BC
Canada-UK Chamber of Commerce, London Yearbook
List of members by company, individually and UN classification

Major Newspapers
The Financial Times of Canada
Daily (Toronto)

The Gazette
Daily (Montreal)

Globe and Mail (Report on Business)
Daily (Toronto)

Le Journal de Montreal
Daily (Montreal)

Le Journal de Quebec
Daily (Quebec)

Toronto Star
Daily

Journals and Periodicals

Les Affaires
Publisher's address: Ste 903,
465 St Jean St, Montreal
Business journal. Weekly

Business Journal
Publisher's address: 3 First
Canadian Place, Box 60,
Toronto.
Published 10 times per
annum

Canadian Business
Published by CB Media Ltd,
Toronto. Produces a ranking
of the top 500 companies each
summer. Monthly

Financial Post (The) (or
Money-Wise magazine)
Published by Maclean Hunter
Ltd, Toronto. Publishes a
ranking of Canada's top 500
companies annually. Weekly
journal

Financial Times of Canada
Publisher's address: 920
Yonge Street, Toronto,
Ontario M4W 3L5. Weekly

Globe and Mail Report on
Business. Daily

Globe and Mail Report on
Business Magazine
Published by The Globe and
Mail, Toronto. Publish a
ranking of top 1000 Canadian
companies around June each
year. Monthly

Revenue Commerce
Published by Review
Commerce, Montreal.
Monthly

Small Business
Published by Maclean Hunter
Ltd. 10 times per annum

Toronto Business
Published by Zanny Ltd
Unionville, Ontario. Monthly

Trade and Commerce
Published by Sanford Evans
Communications Ltd,
Manitoba. Monthly

China

Sources of Economic, Stock Market Information and Investment Research Services

Banks

Central Bank

People's Bank of China
17 Xijiaomin Xiang
Beijing
Tel: (010 86) 1-653431
Telex: 22254

Hong Kong Branch:
2A Des Voeux Road
Central Hong Kong

Chinese Banks in London

Bank of China
8-10 Mansion House Place
London EC4N 8BL
Tel: 01-626 8301
Telex: 886935; 8812913

Branch in Manchester:
67-69 Mosley Street
Manchester M2 3JB
Tel: 061-236 8302
Telex: 669167 BKCHIM G

Branch in Glasgow:
450 Sauchiehall Street
Glasgow G2 3JD
Tel: 041-332 3354
Telex: 779784 BKCHIG G

Major Chinese Banks

Bank of China
(State Bank)
Bank of China Building
410 Fuchengmen Nei Dajie
Beijing
Tel: (010 86) 1-668941
Telex: 22254; 22289

Bank of Communications
(Commercial Bank)
200 Jiang XI Road (M)
Shanghai
Tel: (010 86) 21-213400
Telex: 33438 BOCM CN

China and South Sea Bank
Ltd
(Commercial Bank)
Beijing
International Division:
22-26 Bonham Strand East
Hong Kong
Tel: (010 86) 5-429429
Telex: 73384 CASB HX

China State Bank Ltd
Registered Office Address:
Beijing, China

Main Hong Kong Branch:
China State Bank Building
39-41 Des Voeux Road
Central Hong Kong
Tel: (010 86) 5-8419333
Telex: 73410 Khwab Hx

Kincheng Banking
Corporation
(Commercial Bank)
Registered Office Address:
Beijing

Hong Kong Branch:
51-57 Des Voeux Road
Central Hong Kong
Tel: (010 85) 5-8430222
Telex: 73405 KCBK HX

Kwantung Provincial Bank
17 Hsi Chiao Min Hsiang
Beijing

Main Hong Kong Branch:
1st-3rd Floor
Euro Trade Centre
13/14 Connaught Road
Central Hong Kong
Tel: (010 85) 5-8410410
Telex: 83654 PROVL HX

National Commercial Bank
Ltd
(Commercial Bank)
(Chekiang Hsing Yieh Bank)
Registered Office Address:
Beijing, China

Main Office Address:
1-3 Wyndham Street
Hong Kong
Tel: (010 85) 5-8432888
Telex: HX 83491

Sin Hua Trust Savings and
Commercial Bank Ltd
c/o Bank of China
23 Zhongshan Dong Yi Lu
Beijing
Tel: (010 85) 5-8420668
Telex: 73416 SINHU HX

Yien Yieh Commercial Bank
Ltd
(Commercial Bank)
Registered Office Address:
Beijing, China
Hong Kong Main Branch:
242 Des Voeux Road
Central Hong Kong
Tel: (010 85) 5-411601
Telex: 83542

A Selection of Foreign Banks in China

Barclays Bank International
Representative Office
West 2
23 Qianmen Avenue East
Beijing
Tel: (010 86) 1-552417
Telex: 22589 BARPK CN

Chartered Bank
Box 2135/4th Floor
185 Yuan Ming Yuan Lu
Shanghai
Tel: (010 86) 21-214245
Telex: 33067 CHRBK CN

Hong Kong and Shanghai
Bank
185 Yuan Ming Yuan Lu
Shanghai
Tel: (010 86) 21-216030
Telex: 33058

Midland Bank Group
Representative Office
11th Floor
CITIC Building
Jianguomenwai
Beijing
Tel: (010 86) 1-504410

Sources of General Background Information, Industry Sector Information and Trade Contacts

UK Addresses

Embassy of the People's
Republic of China (The)
49 Portland Place
London W1N 3AG
Tel: 01-636 5637 (Consular
Section)
01-636 8980 (Administrative
Office)
01-636 1835 (Visa Section)
Telex: 23851 CHINA G

Commercial Office of the
Embassy of the People's
Republic of China (The)
56-60 Lancaster Gate
London W2 3NG
Tel: 01-723 6647 (Commercial
Counsellor)
01-262 1817 (Transport, Oil,
Chemicals)
01-262 3911 (Foodstuffs,
Cereals)
Telex: 896440 CLEFSL G

Consulate General of the
People's Republic of China
(The)
Denison House
Denison Road
Manchester M14 5RX
Tel: 01-224 7478 (Consul
General)

Representative Offices of China National Import and Export Corporations

China Aviation
Administration of China
(CAAC)
153 Auckland Road
Upper Norwood
London SE19 2RH
Tel: 01-771 4052/7331
Telex: 263276 CAAC UK

China National Aeronautical
Technology Import and
Export Corporation
12 Lower Merton Rise
London NW3 3RA
Tel: 01-586 8349/8340
Telex: 266865 CATIL G

China National Arts and
Crafts Import Export
Corporation
56-60 Lancaster Gate
London W2 3NG
Tel: 01-723 8109
Telex: 23440 CHIRT G

China National Machinery
and Equipment Import Export
Corporation
56-60 Lancaster Gate
London W2 3NG
Telex: 291723 CMECLO G

China National Metals &
Mineral Import Export
Corporation
78-82 St Helens Gardens
London W10 6LH
Tel: 01-968 3928/3932
Telex: 296824 MIMET G

China National Native
Produce & Animal
By-Products Import Export
Corporation
68 St Helens Gardens
London W10 6LH
Tel: 01-968 4805/4251/4250
Telex: 265772 TUHSU G

China National Offshore Oil
Corporation
International House
1 St Katherine's Way
London E1 9UN
Tel: 01-488 2400 Ext 2119
Telex: 884671 WTC LDN G

China National Oil
Development Corporation
56-60 Lancaster Gate
London W2 3NG
Tel: 01-724 4571
Telex: 296329 CNCDCL G

China National Publications
Import and Export
Corporation
335 City Road
London EC1
Tel: 01-278 1775/1833

China National Technical
Import Corporation
23 Collingham Road
Tel: 01-373 7729
Telex: 929972 CNTUIK G

China National Tourist Office
4 Glentworth Street
London NW1
Tel: 01-935 9427/8/9
Telex: 291221

China Ocean Shipping
Company (COSCO)
52 Chepstow Villas
London W11
Tel: 01-229 2640/3004
Telex: CHSHIP G

Civil Aviation Supply
Corporation
153 Auckland Road
London SE19 2RH
Tel: 01-771 5956
Telex: 263276 CAAC UK

Fujan Foreign Trade
Corporation
56-60 Lancaster House
London W2 3NG
Tel: 01-402 9607
Telex: 264474 FTCLDN G

Minmetals (UK) Ltd
64 St Helens Garden
London W10 6LH
Tel: 01-960 6147/6149/7234
Telex: 885175 MIMET G

People's Insurance of China
(The)
100 Fenchurch Street
London EC3M 5LQ
Tel: 01-488 9696
Telex: 8814239

Sinochem (UK) Ltd
(Subsidiary of China National
Chemicals Import and Export
Corporation)
2nd Floor
Kingsbury House
15/17 King Street
London SW1Y 6QU
Telex: 928265 SNCHEM G

Sundry Import and Export Co
Ltd
76 St Helens Gardens
London W10 6LH
Tel: 01-968 3842/3
Telex: 9419310 SUNRY G

Addresses in China

Commercial Counsellor
British Embassy
11 Guang Hua Lu
Jian Guo Men Wai
Beijing (Peking)
Tel: (010 86) 1-521961/2/3/4/5
Telex: 22191 PRDRMN CN

Consul-General
British Consulate-General
244 Yong Fu Lu
Shanghai
Tel: (010 86) 21-374569
Telex: 33476 BRIT CN

Sources of Investment and Trade Advice, Assistance and Information

China is a predominantly
state trading country and the
bulk of trade is handled by
state trading corporations. A
number of these corporations
have established
representative offices in
London. Advice on exporting
goods to China can be
obtained from the relevant
representative office or the
commercial section of the
Chinese Embassy in London.
Advice and assistance for
those seeking representation
overseas can also be sought
from overseas trading
companies with offices in the
UK, China and Hong Kong,
eg Jardine Matheson, Inchape
Ltd, Wogen Resources Ltd.
Investment in China has been
mainly in the form of Chinese
foreign joint ventures, which
are being encouraged through
a range of tax and other
incentives. Advice in the UK
can be sought in the first
instance from:
Department of Trade and
Industry
Room 309
1 Victoria Street
London SW1H OET
Tel: 01-215 5252/4729
Telex: 8811074 DTIHQ G
The Department produces a
useful information pack
including addresses of main
trading corporations in China

Centre for Market and Trade
Development
International Trade Research
Institute
Ministry of Foreign Economic
Relations and Trade
2 Dongchangan Jie
Beijing
Telex: 22168 MFTPC CN
Offers agency, advertising
and market development
services to foreign companies

China Council for the
Promotion of International
Trade (CCPIT)
2 Qianmen Dongdajie
14th Floor
POB 6200
Beijing
Tel: (010 86) 1-688355 and
863869
Telex: 22305 CITIC CN
Cable: COMTRADE BEIJING

Beijing Branch:
Beijing Hotel Central Building
Room 7107
Beijing
Tel: (010 86) 1-552231 Ext 7107
Telex: BFTCC-F CN
Cable: BJCCPIT 8571 BEIJING

Shanghai Branch:
27 Zhongshan Dong Yi Lu
Shanghai
Tel: (010 86) 21-210723
Telex: 33064 SIMEX CN
Cable: COMTRADE 1289
SHANGHAI

China Exhibition Agency
25A Dongsi Shitiao
Beijing
Tel: (010 86) 1-444627

China Export Bases
Development Corporation
28 Donghou Xiang
Andingmenwai
Beijing
Telex: 22168 MFTPK CN

Fujian Branch:
1 Shangbin Lu
Fuzhou
Tel: (010 86) 1-34068

Shanghai Branch:
27 Zhongshan Dong Yi Lu
Shanghai
Tel: (010 86) 21-214617
Cable: SHCEDEC
SHANGHAI

China National Chartering
Corporation (SINOCHART)
Import Building
Erligou
Xijiao
Beijing
Tel: (010 86) 1-890931
Telex: 22153

China National Foreign Trade
Advertising Association
2 Dongchangau Jie
Beijing

China Trade Unit
British Trade Commission
PO Box 528
Hong Kong
Tel: (010 852) 5-230176
Telex: 73031 73031 UKTRADE
HX

Chinese Export Commodities
Fair
Guangzhou Foreign Trade
Centre
Guangzhou Customs
Administration
Xi Changan Jie
Beijing
Tel: (010 86)
20-556105/5579984
(010 86) 20-30848/32622
(Executive Office)

Foreign Exchange Control
Bureau
17 Xijiaomin Xiang
Beijing
Tel: (010 86) 1-338521/336304
(exchange rates)

Foreign Trade Bureau
190 Chaoyangmennei Dajie
Beijing
Tel: (010 86) 1-554808
Telex: 22470 BFTCC CN
Cable: 8571 BEIJING

Foreign Trade Economic and
Trade Arbitration
Commission (FETAC)
1 Fuxingmenwai
Beijing
Tel: (010 86) 1-868961

Sino-British Trade Council
(The)
5th Floor
Abford House
15 Wilton Road
London SW1V ILT
Tel: 01-828 5176/7
Telex: 24489 SBTC G

48 Group of British Traders
with China (The)
84/86 Rosebery Avenue
London EC1R 5RR
Tel: 01-837 2223/4
Telex: 298681 COMSER G

State Bureau of Foreign
Experts Affairs
Beijing
Tel: (010 86) 890621/892845

Beijing
Beijing Advertising
Corporation
190 Chaoyangmennei Dajie
Beijing
Tel: (010 86) 1-554986
Telex: BFTCC-C CN
Cable: ADVERCORP 7011
BEIJING

International Advertising
Department:
Xuanwumen Hotel
6th Floor
Beijing
Tel: (010 86) 1-341903 Ext 575

Beijing Economic
Development Corporation
1 Dong Dajie
Chongmenwai
POB 6201
Beijing
Tel: (010 86) 1-753680
Telex: 22337

Beijing Exhibition Centre
Xizhimenwai Dajie
Beijing
Tel: (010 86) 1-890611

Beijing Exhibition Service
Building No 1
Beijing Exhibition Centre
West
Beijing
Tel: (010 86) 1-890541 Ext 487

Beijing Foreign Trade
Corporation
Building 17
Yongandongli
Jiaoguomenwai
Beijing
Tel: (010 86) 1-595182
Telex: 22470

Beijing General
Administration of Customs of
the PRC
2 Xi Changan Jie
Beijing
Tel: (010 86) 1-556106

Beijing Import and Export
Control Committee
People's Court Building
Wangfujing Dajie
Nan Kou
Beijing
Tel: (010 86) 1-551836 Ext 336

Guangzhou
Guangdong Committee for
Economic Relations with
Foreign Countries
Dongfeng San Lu
Gaungzhou
Tel: (010 86) 20-30950

Guangdong Exhibition
Service Company
774 Dongfeng Wu Lu
8th Floor
Guangzhou
Tel: (010 86) 20-75793
Telex: 44088

Guangdong Foreign Trade
Development Corporation
774 Dongfeng Wu Lu
8th Floor
Guangzhou
Tel: (010 86) 20-775090
Telex: 44388 GDFTC CN

Guangdong Production
Information Service
Jiaochang Bei Lu
Guangzhou
Tel: (010 86) 20-24440

Permanent Hall for
Negotiation and Exhibition of
Xinjiang Export
Guangzhou Foreign Trade
Centre
Hall No 6
2nd Floor
Renmin Bei Lu
Guangzhou
Tel: (010 86) 20-62290
Telex: 44155

Shanghai
Shanghai Foreign Trade
Bureau
74 Dianchi Lu
Room 316
Shanghai
Tel: (010 86) 21-213103 Ext 71
Cable: 0981 SHANGHAI

Shanghai Foreign Trade
Corporation
27 Zhongshan Dong Yi Lu
Shanghai
Tel: (010 86) 21-217350
Telex: 33034

Government Ministries

Ministry of Chemical Industry
Liupukang
Deshengmenwai
Beijing
Tel: (010 86) 1-446561

Ministry of Coal Industry
Xingua Road
Andingmenwai
Beijing
Tel: (010 86) 1-555891

Ministry of Commerce
45 Fuxingmenwai
Beijing
Tel: (010 86) 668581

Ministry of Electronics
Industry
South Sanlihe Street
Fuxingmenwai
Beijing
Tel: (010 86) 1-868451

Ministry of Foreign Affairs
Chaoyangmennei Dajie
Beijing
Tel: (010 86)
1-555831/552190/550257

Ministry of Foreign Economic
Relations and Trade
2 Dongchangan Jie
Beijing
Tel: (010 86) 1-553031
Telex: 22168

Ministry of Light Industry
12 Dongchangan Jie
Beijing
Tel: (010 86) 1-556687

Ministry of Machine Building
Industry
Fuxingmenwai
Beijing
Tel: (010 86) 1-867008
Telex: 22341

Ministry of Metallurgical
Industry
46 Dongsi Xi Dajie
Beijing
Tel: (010 86) 1-557031

Ministry of Petroleum
Industry
Yuetan Nan Jie
Beijing
Tel: (010 86) 1-444631

Ministry of Textile Industry
12 Dongchangen Jie
Beijing
Tel: (010 86) 1-556831

Investment and Trust Corporations

Bank of China Trust
Company and Consultancy
Department
17 Xijiaomin Xiang
Beijing
Tel: (010 86) 653431 Ext 339
Telex: 22254 BCHO CN
Cable: 6892 BEIJING

Beijing Trust and Investment
Co
1 Baiguang Lu
Beijing
Tel: (010 86) 363429
Telex: 22491 BOCC CN

China International Economic
Consultants Inc
10 Tuyuguan Lu
Beijing
Tel: (010 86) 1-753480
Telex: 20049 CIECC CN

China International Trust and
Investment Corporation
(CITIC)
2 Qianmen Dongdajie
14th Floor
POB 6200
Beijing
Tel: (010 86) 1-757181
Telex: 22305

China Trade Consultants and
Technical Service Corporation
28 Donghou Xiang
Andingmenwai
Beijing
Tel: (010 86) 1-462912
Telex: 22506
Cable: 6319 CONSULTEC

Guangdong Trust and
Investment Corporation
4 Qiaoguang
POB 41
Gaungzhou
Tel: (010 86) 20-61112
Telex: 44122

Hubei International Trust and
Investment Corporation
48 Jiang Han No 1 Road
Wuhan
Hubei
Tel: (010 86) 1-25766
Telex: 40110 HBEXT CN

Kowin China Investments Ltd
UK address:
The Old Deanery
Dean's Court
London EC4V 5AA
Tel: 01-248 5514
Telex: 8955123
Fax: 01-248 4712

KCIL is part of the Kowin
Group of companies with
offices in London, Los
Angeles, Hong Kong, Beijing
and Xian. Specialises in
providing services for
companies interested in doing
business in the PRC. Advice
and assistance offered in
conjunction with Coopers &
Lybrand.

Shanghai Investment and
Trust Co
33 Zhonghan Dong Yi Lu
POB 252
Shanghai
Tel: (010 86) 21-211819

State Commissions

State Economic Commission
38 Yuetan Nan Jie
Xichengqu
Beijing
Tel: (010 86) 1-868521

State Planning Commission
38 Sanlihe
Fuxingmenwai
Beijing
Tel: (010 86) 1-868521

State Scientific and
Technological Commission
52 Sanlihe
Fuxingmenwai
Beijing
Tel: (010 86) 868361

Trade Associations

All China Federation of
Industry and Commerce
93 Beiheyan Dajie
Beijing
Tel: (010 86) 1-554321
Telex: 22044

Beijing Federation of Industry
and Commerce
89 Donganmen Nan Jie
Beijing
Tel: (010 86) 1-557725

Shanghai Federation of
Industry and Commerce
893 Huashan Lu
Shanghai
Tel: (010 86) 21-376376

State Administration for
Industry and Commerce
10 Sanlihe
Dong Lu
Xichengqu
Beijing
Tel: (010 86) 1-863031
Cable: 2092

Major Trading Corporations in China

Chemicals

China National Chemicals
Import and Export
Corporation
Erligou
Xijiao
Beijing
Tel: (010 86) 1-890931/891179
Telex: 2243

Investment

China International Trust and
Investment Corporation
2 Qianmen Dong Dajie
14th Floor
PO Box 6200
Beijing
Tel: (010 86) 1-757181/753600
Telex: 22305 CITIC CN

Instruments

China National Instruments
Import and Export
Corporation
Erligou
Beijing
Tel: (010 86) 1-890931
Telex: 22242

Machinery

China National Machinery
Import and Export
Corporation
Erligou
Beijing
Tel: (010 86) 1-890931
Telex: 22242

Metals/Minerals

China National Metals and
Minerals Import and Export
Corporation
Erligou
Beijing
Tel: (010 86) 1-890931/892376
Telex: 22241

Oil

China National Offshore Oil
Corporation
PO Box 2118
Beijing
Tel: (010 86) 1-550231
Telex: 22186 EQUIP CN

Shipping

China Ocean Shipping
Agency
Dong Changan Jie
Beijing
Tel: (010 86) 1-553424
Telex: 22264

Others

China National Light
Industrial Products Import
and Export Corporation
Donganmen Dajie
Beijing
Tel: (010 86) 1-555680
Telex: 22282

China National Technical
Import Corp
Erligou
Beijing
Tel: (010 86) 1-890931/892116
Telex: 22244

Company Financial and Product Information

Directories

Annals of China's Enterprise
Register
Published by the China Look
Publishing House, edited by
the State Administration for
Industry and Commerce of
the PRC Register of
enterprises. Provides details
of the addresses, telephone
numbers, number of
branches, nature of business,
chairman and president's
names. Written in Chinese
and English

China Directory
Published by Radiopress Inc,
Tokyo, Japan
Lists banks, corporations,
government organisations
and others. Information
includes addresses, telephone
numbers and names of
directors.

China Directory of Industry
and Commerce and Economic
(The)
Published by Xinhua
Publishing House, Beijing,
China
Also available from Science
Books International Inc,
Boston, USA
Annual

China Phone Book and
Address Directory (The)
Published by the China
Phone Book Co Ltd, Hong
Kong
Annual, published in October

Organisations Providing Economic and Statistical Data

Business International, China
Division, Hong Kong
Publishes the twice monthly
Business China, and the
China Atlas which provides
economic and statistical data
in chart form

China Statistical Information
and Consultancy Centre
38 Yuetan Nan Jie, Beijing

China Trade Information
Centre (CTIC)
POB 443
Spring Gardens
Manchester M60 1HF
Tel: 061-228 0420
Telex: MANCIC 665273

Economic Information
Agency
342 Hennesy Rd
10th-11th Floor
Hong Kong
Tel: (010 852) 5-738216
Telex: 60647 EICC HX
Cable: 7289 Hong Kong

State Statistical Bureau
38 Yuetan Nan Jie
Xichengqu
Beijing
Tel: (010 86) 1-868521
Produces the Statistical
Yearbook of China. Available
from Economic and
Consultancy Co, 12th Floor,
342 Henessy Road, Hong
Kong

World Bank (The)
Publishes studies of the
Chinese economy including
China, Long-Term
Development Issues and
Options (1985)

Major banks in China and
Hong Kong provide economic
and statistical data. Hong
Kong Bank China Services
Ltd, Hong Kong.
Publishes Laws of China
Relating to Commerce
(3-volume loose leaf set)

Xinhua News Agency
57 Xuanwumen W St
Beijing
Tel: (010 86) 667064
Telex: 22316

Overseas Offices

France
148 rue Petit Leroy
Chevilly-Larue
94150 Rungis
Telex: 204398

Hong Kong
5 Sharp Street West
Wan Sui
Hong Kong

United Kingdom
76 Chancery Lane
London WC2
Tel: 01-242 2759

United States
115 West 66th Street
New York
NY 10023
Telex: 424465

2000 South Street
Washington DC 20008
Telex: 904200

Xinhau Publishing House
publishes Chinese economic
and state statistical data.

Publications

Directories
China Hand
Investing, Licensing and
Trading in the PRC
Published by Business
International Asia/Pacific Ltd,
Hong Kong
Reference source to China's
laws and operating
conditions. Loose-leaf binder,
subscription service with
quarterly updates

China Official Annual Report
Published by Kingsway
International Publications
Ltd, Hong Kong

Directory of Chinese Foreign
Trade
Published by the Longman
Group Ltd in association with
the China Council for the
Promotion of International
Trade, Beijing

Major Newspapers
Beijing Ribao
Chinese. Daily

China Daily
English

Guangming Ribao
Chines. Daily

Renmin Ribao
Chinese. People's Daily

Wenhiui Bao
Chinese. Daily (Shanghai)

Journals and Periodicals
Beijing Review
Publisher's address: PO Box
399, Beijing 37
Available in English, French
and German. Weekly

British Industry in Chinese
Published by the Sino-British
Trade Council, London.
Quarterly

China Business Report
Published by the National
Council for US-China Trade,
USA. Every two months

China Economic News
Published by the Economic
Information and Consultancy
Co, Hong Kong. Weekly

China Economic Weekly
UK edition available from the
Anglo-Chinese Development
Corp, Bath

China Reconstructs
Distributed by the China
International Book Trading
Corporation (Guoji Shudan),
Beijing. Monthly

China's Foreign Trade
Distributed by the China
International Book Trading
Corporation (Guoji Shudian),
Beijing. Monthly

Far Eastern Economic Review
Publisher's address: GPO 47,
Hong Kong. Monthly

International Trade News
Published by Ministry of
Foreign Economic Relations
and Trade, Beijing
Includes foreign advertising.
Contact the Director of
Advertising, International
Trade News for further details

Denmark

Sources of Economic, Stock Market Information and Investment Research Services

Banks

Central Bank
Denmarks Nationalbanken
Havnegade 5
1093 Copenhagen K
Denmark
Tel: (010 45) 1-141411
Telex: 27051

Danish Banks in London
Andelsbanken Danebank
2 Throgmorton Avenue
London EC2N 2AP
Tel: 01-256 5764

Copenhagen Handelsbank
20 Canon Street
London EC4M 6GB
Tel: 01-236 5000

Den Danske Bank
44 Bishopsgate
London EC2N 4AJ
Tel: 01-628 3090

Hellerup Bank
4 Old Park Lane
London W1Y 3LJ
Tel: 01-727 0554

Jyske Bank
119-120 Chancery Lane
London WC2A 1HU
Tel: 01-831 2778

London Interstate Bank
(Sparekassen SDS Subsidiary)
140 London Wall
London EC2Y 5DN
Tel: 01-606 8899

Privatbanken
107 Cheapside
London EC2V 6DA
Tel: 01-726 6000

Provinsbanken
Park House
16 Finsbury Circus
London EC2M 7DJ
Tel: 01-374 0665

Major Danish Banks
Andelsbanken Danebank
Staunings Plads 1-3
1643 Copenhagen V
Tel: (010 45) 1-145114

Copenhagen Handelsbank
Investment Banking Division
Analysis & Information
Holmens Kanal 2
1091 Copenhagen K
Tel: (010 45) 1-128600/138600
Telex: 12186

Den Danske Bank
Holmens Kanal 12
1092 Copenhagen K
Tel: (010 45) 1-156500
Telex: 27000

Jyske Bank SA
Vestergade 8-16
8600 Silkeborg
Denmark
Tel: (010 45) 6-821122
Telex: 63231

Privatbanken
Borsgade 4
1249 Copenhagen K
Tel: (010 45) 1-141411

Provinsbanken A/S
Kannikegade 4-6
8100 Aarhus C
Tel: (010 45) 6-122522
Telex: 64403; 64692

Sparekassen SDS
8 Kongens Nytorv
1050 Copenhagen
Tel: (010 45) 1-131339
Telex: 15475 sdsfd dk

Stockbrokers

Copenhagen Stock Exchange
Kobenhavns Fondsbors
Nikolaj Plads 6
Post Box 1040
1007 Copenhagen K
Tel: (010 45) 1-933366
Telex: 16496 costex dk
(Copenhagen Stock Exchange
is the only Stock Exchange in
Denmark)

Members (as at 10 February 1988)
Benzon & Benzon
Ved Straden 20
1061 Copenhagen K
Tel: (010 45)
1-937444/931555/932555

Bjornskov & Co
Abenra 10
1124 Copenhagen K
Tel: (010 45) 1-143214

BMS Broker
Amaliegade 5 C
Postbox 2259
1019 Copenhagen K
Tel: (010 45) 1-936012

I S Hahns Enka
Nyhavn 12
1051 Copenhagen K
Tel: (010 45) 1-140099

R Henriques jr
Nikolaj Plads 2
1067 Copenhagen K
Tel: (010 45) 1-125252

Alfred Horwitz & Co
Pilestraede 52
Postbox 122
1004 Copenhagen K
Tel: (010 45) 1-930032

Leif Jensen & Co
Snaregade 10
Postbox 2054
1012 Copenhagen K
Tel: (010 45) 1-323600

Rued Jorgensen
Skt Annae Plads 10
1250 Copenhagen K
Tel: (010 45) 1-152515

Ludvig Kalckar
Vimmelskaftet 43
1161 Copenhagen K
Tel: (010 45) 1-125312

O Rye Kristiansen
Ved Stranden 10
1061 Copenhagen K
Tel: (010 45) 1-320078

Lannung & Co
Kronprinsessegade 2
1306 Copenhagen K
Tel: (010 45) 1-145533

H C Moller
St Kirkestraede 1,1
Postbox 2063
1013 Copenhagen K
Tel: (010 45) 1-910511

Erik Mollers Eftf
Gothersgade 101
1123 Copenhagen K
Tel: (010 45) 1-150545

Holger Morville
Knud Hertel & Co
Frederiksberggade 26
1459 Copenhagen K
Tel: (010 45) 1-121975

L Pedersen
Gammeltorv 22
1457 Copenhagen K
Tel: (010 45) 1-937200

Hugo Petersen
Bredgade 6
1260 Copenhagen K
Tel: (010 45) 1-121208

Aage Petersen-Hinrichsen
Gammeltorv 8
1457 Copenhagen K
Tel: (010 45) 1-114311

Aage Philip
Hauser Plads 18
1127 Copenhagen K
Tel: (010 45) 1-110905

Gudme Raaschou
Ostergade 13
1100 Copenhagen K
Tel: (010 45) 1-131970

Olaf Samson
Nikolaj Plade 5
1067 Copenhagen K
Tel: (010 45) 1-147411

ScanBroker
Amagertorv 33
1160 Copenhagen K
Tel: (010 45) 1-935800

Johs Steffensens Eftf
Pilestraede 40 B
1112 Copenhagen K
Tel: (010 45) 1-155353

Per Storhaug
Frederiksberggade 25
1459 Copenhagen K
Tel: (010 45) 1-148633

Sundberg & Co
Hojbro Plads 21
1200 Copenhagen K
Tel: (010 45) 1-112282

Thestrup & Thestrup
Frederiksborggade 4
1360 Copenhagen K
Tel: (010 45) 1-133070

Brdr Trier
Hojbro Plads 6
1200 Copenhagen K
Tel: (010 45) 1-112210

A Vollmond & Co
Amaliegade 35
1256 Copenhagen K
Tel: (010 45) 1-120312

Flemming G Wulff
Radhusstraede 6
1466 Copenhagen K
Tel: (010 45) 1-114623

Sources of General Background Information, Industry Sector Information and Trade Contact

UK Addresses
Danish Chamber of
Commerce
55 Sloane Street
London SW1X 9SR
Tel: 01-235 1255
Telex: 28103 AMBDK G

Danish Embassy
Address and telephone
number as above

Addresses in Denmark
Danish Chamber of
Commerce
Grosserer-Societet Borsen
1217 Copenhagen K
Tel: (010 45) 1-155320
Telex: 19520
Denmark has only one
centralised Chamber of
Commerce. The Chamber
provides information to
Danish and foreign importers
and exporters, which includes
information on tarriffs and
trading regulations

British Embassy
Commercial Department
36-40 Kastelsvej
2100 Copenhagen
Tel: (010 45) 1-264600
Telex: 27106 BRIEMB DK

Sources of Investment and Trade Advice, Assistance and Information

For those interested in setting
up a business in Denmark it is
advisable to make initial
contact with the Ministry of
Foreign Affairs followed by
the Directorate of Regional
Development

Information Office for Foreign
Investment in Denmark
25 Sondergade
8600 Silkeborg
Tel: (010 45) 6-825655
Telex: 63346 DANREG
This office provides
information on specific
investment questions,
including location of new
industries and assistance in
establishing contact with local
authorities

The Association of
Commercial Agents
Danmark Agentforening
Borsen
1217 Copenhagen K
Tel: (010 45) 1-144941

Danish Employers
Ferderation
113 Vester Voldgade
1503 Copenhagen V
Tel: (010 45) 1-943000

Danish Federation of Trade
Unions
12 Rosenorns Alle
1634 Copenhagen V
Tel: (010 45) 1-353541
Telex: 16170

Danish Industrial Research
and Development Fund
135 Tagensvej
2200 Copenhagen N
Tel: (010 45) 1-851066

Directorate of Customs (The)
44 Amaliegade
1256 Copenhagen K
Tel: (010 45) 1-157300

Directorate for Regional
Development
25 Sondergade
8600 Silkeborg
Tel: (010 45) 6-825655
Telex: 63346 danreg

Export Credit Council (The)
Codanhus
60 Gl Kongevej
1850 Frederiksberg C
Tel: (010 45) 1-313825
Telex: 22910

Export Promotion Council
(The)
2 Prinsesse Maries Alle
1908 Frederiksberg C
Tel: (010 45) 1-231444
Telex: 22910

Industrial Mortgage Fund
17 Nyropsgade
1602 Copenhagen V
Tel: (010 45) 1-148000
Telex: 48002

Institute for Industrial
Finance
17 Nyropsgade
1602 Copenhagen V
Tel: (010 45) 1-131321
Telex: 15070

Ministry of Foreign Affairs
2 Asiatisk Plads
1448 Copenhagen K
Tel: (010 45) 1-920000
Telex: 31292 ETR DK

Ministry of the Government
12 Slotsholmsgade
1216 Copenhagen K
Tel: (010 45) 1-127688
Telex: 22373 SOFART

Ministry of Industry
12 Slotsholmsgade
1216 Copenhagen K
Tel: (010 45) 1-923350
Telex: 22373 INDUMI DK

Monopolies Control
Authority
49 Norregade
1165 Copenhagen K
Tel: (010 45) 1-121908
Telex: 16708

Register of Companies (The)
Aktieselskabs-Registeret
4 Nygade
1164 Copenhagen K
Tel: (010 45) 1-124280

Technology Board (The)
38 Tagensvej
2200 Copenhagen N

Technology Institute (The)
Postboks 141
2630 Tastrup
Tel: (010 45) 2-996611
Telex: 33416 TIDK

Professional Associations

Accountancy

Foreningen af
Statsautoriserede Revisorer
(Association of State
Authorised Public
Accountants)
Kronprinsessegade 8
1306 Copenhagen

Foreningen af Registrerede
Revisorer
FRR-Huset
Flintholm Alle 8
Postboks 90
2000 Frederiksberg

Banking

Den Danske Bankforening
(Danish Bankers Association)
Amaliegade 7
1256 Copenhagen K
Tel: (010 45) 1-120200
Telex: 16102

Consultancy

Den Danske Sammenslutning
AF Konsulenter (DSKV)
I Virksomhedledelse
Rygaards Alle 131A
2900 Hellerup
Tel: (010 45) 1-181711
Telex: 15324

Insurance

Assurandor-stet
(Danish Insurance
Association)
Amaliegade 10
1256 Copenhagen K
Tel: (010 45) 1-137555
Fax: (010 45) 1-112353

Forsikringsoplysningen
(Danish Insurance
Information Service)
Amaliegade 10
1256 Copenhagen K
Tel: (010 45) 1-137555
Fax: (010 45) 1-112353

Trade Associations

General Industry

Industriraadet
H C Andersens Boulevard
1596 Copenhagen
Tel: (010 45) 1-152233
Telex: 9112217 iraad dk

Association of Commercial
Agents of Denmark
Borsen
1217 Copenhagen K
Tel: (010 45) 1-144941

Beklaedningsindustriens
Sammenslutning
(Association of Danish
Clothing Industries)
Puggaardsgade 17
1573 Copenhagen V
Tel: (010 45) 1-154321

British Import Union
Borsbygningen
1217 Copenhagen K
Tel: (010 45) 1-136349

Danmarks Elektriske
Materielkontrol (DEMKO)
Lyskaer 8
Postboks 514
2730 Herlev
Tel: (010 45) 2-947266

Danmarks
Fiskeeksportorforening
(Danish Fish Exporters'
Association)
Noore Voldgade 88
1358 Copenhagen K
Tel: (010 45) 1-138580

Dansk Designrad
(Danish Design Council)
Industriens Hus
H C Andersens Boulevard 18
1553 Copenhagen V
Tel: (010 45) 1-146688

Dansk Ingeniorforening
(Danish Society of Chemical,
Civil Electrical and
Mechanical Engineers)
Vester Farimagsgade 31
1606 Copenhagen V
Tel: (010 45) 1-156565

Dansk Teknisk
Oplysningstjeneste
(Danish Technical
Information Services)
H C Andersens Boulevard 18
1553 Copenhagen V
Tel: (010 45) 1-139111

Electronikfabrikant-
foreningen i Danmark
(Association of Electronic
Manufacturers in Denmark)
Borsen
1217 Copenhagen K

Entreprenorforeningen
(Danish General Contractors'
Association)
Norre Voldgade 106
1358 Copenhagen K
Tel: (010 45) 1-138801

Foreningen af Jernskibs- og
Maskinbyggerier i Danmark
(Association of Danish
Shipbuilders)
Store Kongensdage 128
1264 Copenhagen K
Tel: (010 45) 1-132416

Foreningen af Raadgivende
Ingeniorer
(Association of Danish
Consulting Engineers)
Esplanaden 34
1263 Copenhagen K
Tel: (010 45) 1-113737

Haandvaerksraadet
(Danish Handicrafts Council)
Amaliegade 15
1256 Copenhagen K
Tel: (010 45) 1-123676

Ingenior-Sammenslutningen
(Society of Engineers of
Denmark)
Domus Technica
Ved Stranden 18
1061 Copenhagen K
Tel: (010 45) 1-121311

Jern-og Metalindustriens
Sammenslutning
(Federation of Danish
Engineering and
Metalworking Industries)
Norre Voldgade 34
1358 Copenhagen K
Tel: (010 45) 1-122278

Landbrugsraadet
(The Agricultural Council)
Axelborg
Axeltorv 3
1609 Copenhagen V
Tel: (010 45) 1-145672

Landsforeningen Dansk
Arbejde
(National Association for the
Promotion of Danish
Enterprise)
Vesterbrogade 24
1620 Copenhagen V
Tel: (010 45) 1-225222

MEFA – Foreningen of
Danske Medicinfabr
(Association of the Danish
Pharmaceutical Industry)
Landemaerket 25
1119 Copenhagen K
Tel: (010 45) 1-111270

Mobelfabrikanforeningen i
Danmark
(Danish Furniture
Manufacturers' Association)
Hellerupvej 8
2900 Hellerup
Tel: (010 45) 1-629838

Plast-Sammenslutningen
(Plastics Industry Federation)
Radhuspladsen 55
1550 Copenhagen V
Tel: (010 45) 1-133022

Textilfabrikantforeningen
(Federation of Danish Textile
Industries)
Smalegade 14
2000 Copenhagen F
Tel: (010 45) 1-107711

*Company Financial and
Product Information*

Directories
Danmarks Storste
Virksomheder
(Denmark's 10 000 largest
companies)
Published by AS Okonomisk
Literatur, Copenhagen
Ranks companies by sales and
provides other financial
details, number of employees
and shareholder details

Greens Handbogen om
Dansk Erhvervsliv
(Handbook of Danish Trade)
Published annually by
Borsens Forlog, Copenhagen
Covers companies with A/S
status. 3 volumes. Volume 1
covers company financial and
shareholder details, auditors
and senior executives and
bankers are identified.
Volume 2 includes a study of
holding companies. Volume 3
is a directory of directors

Kompass Denmark
Published annually by
Forlaget Kompass Danmark
Covers basic company and
product details for over 15 000
companies. The 26th edition
was published in July 1986

Kraks Legat: The Export
Directory of Denmark
Published by Krak,
Copenhagen
Covers exporting firms and
their products

Kraks Vejviser
Published by Krak,
Copenhagen
Volume 1 provides a guide to
products and services offered
by over 73 000 active Danish
firms. Volume 2 provides
names and addresses, names
of bankers, etc. Volume 3 is a
list of all businesses registered
with the companies
registration office. Volume 4
is a 'Municipal Yearbook'.
Volume 5 is a street directory

Scandinavia's 5000 Largest
Companies
Produced by ELC
International, London
Includes the 100 largest
Danish companies. Provides
basic financial data, employee
numbers and financial ratios

Economic and Market Statistical Data

Market Research Organisations

AIM AS
Aldersrogade 6A
2100 Copenhagen O
Tel: (010 45) 1-295566
Telex: 15378 AIM DK

Elmark & Christensen
Marketing APS
Nyhavn 12
1051 Copenhagen K
Tel: (010 45) 1-141740
Telex: 16600 FOTEX DK

Gallup Markedanalyse AIS
Gamnel Vartov Vej 6
2900 Hellerup
Copenhagen
Tel: (010 45) 1-298800
Telex: 15180 GALLUP DK
Part of the Gallup
organisation

IFH Research International
Godthabsvej 187
2720 Copenhagen Vanlose
Tel: (010 45) 1-866677
Telex: 22988
Parent company is Research
International

Observa AS
Staktoften 20
2950 Vedbaeck
Tel: (010 45) 2-891511
Telex: 373310

Scan-Test
Vognmagergade 11
1148 Copenhagen
Tel: (010 45) 1-151925
Telex: 16053

Organisations Providing Economic and Statistical Data

Danmarks Statistik
(Danish Bureau of Statistics)
Sejrogade 11
2100 Copenhagen O
Tel: (010 45) 1-298222
Telex: 16236 DASTAT DK
Danmarks Statistik is the
central source for the
collection and processing of
Danish statistics. It is a very
useful source of industry
statistics.
Publications include: Monthly
Review of Statistics
Statistik Arbog (Statistical
Yearbook)
Statistik Tiarsoversigt
(Statistical 10 Year Review)
Manedsstatistik over
Udenrigshandelen (Monthly
bulletin of external trade)

Andelsbanken Danebank
Publications include the
Quarterly Observer

Copenhagen Stock Exchange
Provides financial statistics
and analysis in its monthly,
half yearly and annual reports

Den Danske Bank
Produces useful economic
publications such as Denmark
Basic Figures and Denmark in
Brief
Other large banks and
stockbrokers provide stock
market and economic
research reports to clients

Det Ookonomiske Raad
(Economic Council)
Kampmannsgade
1604 Copenhagen V
Tel: (010 45) 1-135128

Ministry of Economic Affairs
The Economic Secretariat
Slotsholmgade 12
1216 Copenhagen K
Tel: (010 45) 1-121197
Telex: 22373 SOFART
Publications: Danish
Economic Survey
The Ministry of Industry
(same address) publishes a
useful booklet, Investment in
Denmark

Ministry of Foreign Affairs
Publications Service of the
Foreign Trade Relations
Department
Asiatisk Plads 2
1448 Copenhagen K
Tel: (101 45) 1-920000
Publishes Denmark Review

Organisation of Stockbrokers
in Denmark
Ostergade 17
1100 Copenhagen K
Tel: (010 45) 1-155320
Produces stock market
statistics and research reports

Privatbanken
Publishes Danish Company
Research, Danish Investment
Research

Publications

Directories

Kongeriget Danmarks
Handels Kalender
(Kingdom of Denmark Trade
Directory)
Published by Kongeriget
Denmarks Handels-Kalender
Nygade 5
1164 Copenhagen 4
Alphabetical and classified
listing of Danish companies,
Danish embassies and
consulates, plus an index of
Danish industrial laws

Major Newspapers

Aktuelt
Daily and Sunday

Berlingske Tidende
Daily and Sunday

Borsen
Industrial and business
paper. Daily

BT
Daily

Ekstra Bladet
Daily

Information
Industrial newspaper. Daily

Journals and Periodicals

Agenten
Import and export agents, 6
issues per annum

Audio Visuelle Media
Published by AVM/Audio
Visuel Marketing APS,
Copenhagen
Covers news and reports on
all aspects of electronic
media. 11 issues per annum

Danish Export Information
Published by J C Bladforlag,
Brandelev
Covers trade contacts,
company and product
information. Quarterly

Dansk Handelsblad
Covers retailing, new product
information, company
profiles and marketing
reports. Weekly

Dansk Industri
Published by Industriradet
(Federation of Danish
Industries), Copenhagen
Provides financial and
company news. 11 issues per
annum

Detail-Bladet
Published by Erhvervs-Bladet
A/S
Provides product
information, company
profiles and trade news.
Monthly

Erhvervs-Avisen
Published by ST-Specialblade
AS
Covers trade and industry
news weekly

Erhvervs-Bladet
Covers commercial and
industry news. Free
distribution. Daily

Finanstidende
Financial news. Weekly

Lederskals og Lonsomhed
Business Journal
8 issues per annum

Maneds Borsen
Business journal. Monthly

Official List
Published by the Copenhagen
Stock Exchange. Provides
price information for each
security from the previous
day's quotation. Daily

Penge og Privatkonomi
Monthly

Revision og Regnskabsvaesen
Accountancy journal.
Monthly

Udenrigsministeriets
Tidsskript
Published by the Danish
Ministry of Foreign Affairs.
Monthly

Finland

Sources of Economic, Stock Market Information and Investment Research Services

Banks

Central Bank

Bank of Finland
Snellmaninaukio
00170 Helsinki
Finland
Tel: (010 358) 0-1831
Telex: 121224 SPFB SF

Finnish Banks in London

Kansallis-Osake-Pankki
(K-O-P)
80 Bishopsgate
London EC2N 4AH
Tel: 01-256 7575

Postipankki (UK) Ltd
10/12 Little Trinity Lane
London EC4V 2AA
Tel: 01-236 5030

Skopbank
The Old Deanery
Dean's Court
London EC4V 5AA
Tel: 01-236 4060

Union Bank of Finland
46 Cannon Street
London EC4N 6JJ
Tel: 01-248 3333

Major Finnish Banks

Helsingin Osakepankki
Bank of Helsinki
Aleksanterinkatu 17
0100 Helsinki 10
Tel: (010 358) 0-16201

Kansallis-Osake-Pankki
(K-O-P)
PO Box 10
Aleksanterinkatu 42
00100 Helsinki 10
Tel: (010 358) 0-1631
Telex: 124702

Osuuspankkien
Keskuspankki Oy (Okobank)
Arkadiankatu 23
00100 Helsinki 10
Tel: (010 358) 0-4041
Telex: 124714 OKOHE SF

Peruspankki Oy
Passivuorenkatu 4-6
00530 Helsinki
Tel: (010 358) 0-718300
Telex: 122948

Postipankki
Unioninkatu 20
00007 Helsinki 7
Tel: (010 358) 0-1641
Telex: 123687

Skopbank
Aleksanterinkatu 46
00100 Helsinki 46
Tel: (010 358) 0-13341
Telex: 122284

Union Bank of Finland Ltd
(Suomen Yhdyspankki
Oy-Foreningsbanken i
Finland Ab)
Aleksanterinkatu 30
00100 Helsinki 10
Tel: (010 358) 0-1651
Telex: 124407

Stockbrokers

The Helsinki Stock Exchange
PO Box 429 (Fabianinkatu 14)
00101 Helsinki
Finland
Tel: (010 358) 0-624161
Telex: 123460 HESE SF

Members (as at February 1988)

Arctos Securities Oy
Mannerheimintie 14B
00100 Helsinki
Tel: (010 358) 0-644722
Fax: (010 358) 0-604165
Telex: 126271

BBL Securities Oy
Etelaranta 4B
00130 Helsinki
Tel: (010 358) 0-177656
Fax: (010 358) 0-636682
Telex: 125533 JGSO SF

Banking House Keitele &
Tommila Ltd
Iso Roobertinkatu 20 – 22A 8
00120 Helsinki
Tel: (010 358) 0-602939
Fax: (010 358) 0-175100

Bensow Oy Ab
Etelaesplanadi 22A
00130 Helsinki
Tel: (010 358) 0-61261
Fax: (010 358) 0-601048
Telex: 124419 BENHO SF

Bond & Stock Oy
Fredrikinkatu 33B
00120 Helsinki
Tel: (010 358) 0-647412
Telex: 122814 SIGGO SF
Fax: (010 358) 0-647948

Citibank Oy
Aleksanterinkatu 48A
00100 Helsinki
Tel: (010 358) 0-651400
Fax: (010 358) 0-651194
Telex: 121984 CBHKI SF

Evli Securities Ltd
Mikonkatu 8A
00100 Helsinki
Tel: (010 358) 0-634306
Fax: (010 358) 0-7634382
Telex: 123927 EVLI SF

Finanssimeklarit Oy
Aleksanterinkatu 15A, 3krs
00100 Helsinki
Tel: (010 358) 0-659055
Fax: (010 358) 0-656493

Helsinki Bankers Corporation
Pohjoisesplanadi 25A
00100 Helsinki
Tel: (010 358) 0-174811
Telex: 125858 BRADE SF

L Hiisi Oy
Karkitie 5 – 7
00330 Helsinki
Tel: (010 358) 0-488059
Fax: (010 358) 0-488059

Independent Brokers Ltd
Unioninkatu 12
000130 Helsinki
Tel: (010 358) 0-625833
Fax: (010 358) 0-632565

Kansallis-Osake-Pankki
Aleksanterinkatu 42
00100 Helsinki
Tel: (010 358) 0-1631
Fax: (010 358) 0-656271
Telex: 124702 KOPF SF

H Kuningas & Co Ab Oy
Mannerheimintie 14A
00100 Helsinki
Tel: (010 358) 0-607887
Fax: (010 358) 0-605708
Telex: 123175 FERTE SF

Labour Savings Bank of
Finland (The)
Siltasaarenkatu 12
00530 Helsinki
Tel: (010 358) 0-73181
Fax: (010 358) 0-7318470
Telex: 122759

Lamy Inc Investment Bankers
Bulevardi 14
00120 Helsinki
Tel: (010 358) 0-640036
Fax: (010 358) 0-640038
Telex: 125858 BRADE SF

Midland Montagu
Osakepankki
Etelaesplanadi 22A
00130 Helsinki
Tel: (010 358) 0-601766
Fax: (010 358) 0-603479
Telex: 124210

Okobank Osuuspankkien
Keskuspankki
Arkadiankatu 23
00100 Helsinki
Tel: (010 358) 0-4041
Fax: (010 358) 0-4042298
Telex: 121475 OKOHE SF

Pankkiiriliike Ane Gyllenberg
Oy
Keskuskatu 3
00100 Helsinki
Tel: (010 358) 0-175399
Fax: (010 358) 0-175569

Pankkiirilijke Og Pro Value
Ab
Kluuvikatu 1 D,4 krs
00100 Helsinki
Tel: (010 358) 0-177544

Postipankki
Unioninkatu 20
00007 Helsinki
Tel: (010 358) 0-1641
Fax: (010 358) 0-174258
Telex: 121428 PSPPO SF

Savings Bank of Helsinki
Mannerheimintie 14
00100 Helsinki
Tel: (010 358) 0-60921
Fax: (010 358) 0-6092356
Telex: 123269 HSB SF

Erik Selin Ab Oy
Kasarmikatu 28A
00130 Helsinki
Tel: (010 358) 0-171212
Fax: (010 358) 0-602102
Telex: 124497 SELF SF

Skopbank
Aleksanterinkatu 46
00100 Helsinki
Tel: (010 358) 0-13341
Fax: (010 358) 0-1725674
Telex: 122284 SKOP SF

Unitas Ltd
Bulevardi 1A
00100 Helsinki
Tel: (010 358) 0-12301
Fax: (010 358) 0-1230337
Telex: 125811

United Bankers Ab Oy
Aleksanterinkatu 21A
00170 Helsinki
Tel: (010 358) 0-171466
Fax: (010 358) 0-657857
Telex: 126047 UNIBA SF

Sources of General Background Information, Industry Sector Information and Trade Contacts

UK Addresses
Finnish Embassy
38 Chesham Place
London SW1X 8HW
Tel: 01-235 9531
Telex: 24786

Commercial Section
30-35 Pall Mall
London SW1Y 5JG
Tel: 01-839 7262
Telex: 262360 finntr g

Addresses in Finland
There are twenty-two regional chambers of commerce in Finland. These are independent and self-financing. Approximately 90 per cent of Finnish business volume is represented by members of the chambers. The Central Chamber of Commerce deals with the foreign trade activities of the regional chambers. Foreign enquiries made to regional chambers are usually referred to the Foreign Trade Department of the Central Chamber of Commerce. Chambers get involved in export procedures via the issue of certificates of origin and other official trade documentation.

Central Chamber of
Commerce in Finland
Fabianinkatu 14
PB 1000
00101 Helsinki
Tel: (010 358) 0-650133
Telex: 121394

British Embassy
Uudenmaankatu 16-20
00120 Helsinki 12
Tel: (010 358) 0-647922
Telex: 121122 UKHKI SF

British Council
Etela Esplanadi 22
00130 Helsinki 13
Tel: (010 358) 0-640505

Helsinki Chamber of
Commerce
Kalevankatu 12
00100 Helsinki 10
Tel: (010 358) 0-644601

Sources of Investment and Trade Advice, Assistance and Information

The Central agency for trade promotion in Finland is the Finnish Foreign Trade Association, which also acts as the home liaison office of the commercial secretaries for Finnish embassies abroad. This is the primary source for foreign businessmen seeking information or advice and buying or selling opportunities.

Finnfacts Institute
Yrjonkatu 13
00120 Helsinki 12
Tel: (010 358) 0-171596
Telex: 121640 FACTS SF
This institute provides background information on Finland to help develop Finland's trading partnerships. It is maintained jointly by the employers' organisation, industrial organisations, banks, and other organisations.
UK address:
Stanhope House
Stanhope Place
London W2
Tel: 01-723 3444

Finnish Foreign Trade Association
Arkadiankatu 4-6B
00100 Helsinki 10
Tel: (010 358) 0-6941122
Telex: 121969 TRADE SF
Publishes Finnish Trade Review annually

Kauppa ja Teollisuusministerio
(Ministry of Trade and Industry)
Commission for Foreign Investments
Aleksanterinkatu 10
00170 Helsinki 17
Tel: (010 358) 0-1601

Lisenssivirasto (Licence Board)
Hakaniemenkatu 2
00530 Helsinki 53
Tel: (010 358) 0-7061

Tullihallitus (Board of Customs)
Erottajankatu 2
00120 Helsinki 12
Tel: (010 358) 0-6141
Publishes Ulkomaankauppa Kuukausijulkaisu. Foreign Trade Monthly Bulletin

Ulkomaankaupan Agenttijliitto
(Finnish Foreign Trade Agents Federation)
Mannerheimintie 72A
00260 Helsinki 26
Tel: (010 358) 0-446768

Professional Associations

Accountancy
KHT Yhdistys-Foreningen
CGR
Fredrikinkatu 61A
00100 Helsinki 10

Banking
Central Union of the Cooperative Banks (The)
Dagmarinkatu 14
00100 Helsinki 10
Tel: (010 358) 0-4041
Telex: 121475

Finnish Bankers' Association (The)
000100 Helsinki 13
Tel: (010 358) 0-6948422
Telex: 121839

Finnish Savings Bank Association (The)
Pohjoiseplanadi 35A
00100 Helsinki 10
Tel: (010 358) 0-13341
Telex: 125768

Consultancy
Finnish Association of Consulting Engineers (The)
(SNIL – affiliated to FIDIC)
Pohjantie 12A
02100 Espoo 10
Tel: (010 358) 0-460122

Finnish Association of Consulting Firms (SKOL) (The)
Pohjantie 12A
02100 Espoo 10
Tel: (010 358) 0-460122

Insurance
Suomen Vakuutusyhtioiden Keskusliitto
(Federation of Finnish Insurance Companies)
Bulevardi 28
00120 Helsinki
Tel: (010 358) 0-19251
Telex: 123511 VAKES SF

Trade Associations

General Industry
Confederation of Finnish Indstries
Etelaranta 10
00130 Helsinki 13
Tel: (010 358) 0-661665

Central Association of Finnish Clothing Industries (VATEVA)
Fredrikinkatu 41C
Helsinki
Tel: (010 358) 0-641014

Central Association of Finnish Forest Industries
Etelaesplanadi 2
Helsinki
Tel: (010 358) 0-171596

Central Association of Footwear Manufacturers
Vuorikatu 4A 7
Helsinki
Tel: (010 358) 0-170211

Central Federation of the Technical Wholesale Trade (TTK)
Ratakatu 1a B7
Helsinki
Tel: (010 358) 0-648897

Chemical Industry Federation
Fabianinkatu 7B
Helsinki
Tel: (010 358) 0-170300

Federation of Finnish
Electrical and Electronics
Industries
Etelaranta 8
Helsinki
Tel: (010 358) 0-179922

Federation of Finnish Metal
and Engineering Industries
Etelaranta 10
Helsinki
Tel: (010 358) 0-170922

Finnish Association of Freight
Forwarders
Et Makasiinikatu 4
Helsinki
Tel: (010 358) 0-175606

Finnish Cooperative
Wholesale Society (SOK)
Vilhonkatu 7
Helsinki
Tel: (010 358) 0-1881

Finnish Retail Federation
(VKL)
Mannerheimintie 76B
Helsinki
Tel: (010 358) 0-441128

Finnish Wholesalers' and
Importers' Association (STL)
Mannerheimintie 76A
Helsinki
Tel: (010 358) 0-441651

Company Financial and Product Information

Directories

Mista Mitakin Saa
(Who Supplies What in
Finland)
Published by Sininen Kirja
Oy, Helsinki
Directory of Finnish
manufacturing companies in
Finland and their products

Scandinavia's 5000 Largest
Companies
Produced by ELC
International, London
Provides rankings and basic
financial company data,
employee numbers and
financial ratios

Economic and Market Statistical Data

Market Research Organisations

Makrotest Finland Oy
Kasarmikatu 28a
00130 Helsinki 13
Tel: (010 358) 0-658933
Telex: 123739 MTF SF
Member of the Makrotest
group (UK)

Marketindex
Markkinaindeksi Oy
Tietajantie 14
02130 Espoo
Tel: (010 358) 0-4554422
Telex: 124264 INDEX SF

M-Tietokeskus Oy
Bernhardinkata 7a
00130 Helsinki
Tel: (010 358) 0-177488
Telex: 121394 MARKETDATA
SF

Suomen Gallup Oy
Lautenasaarentie 28-30
00200 Helsinki 20
Tel: (010 358) 0-6923125
Telex: 122253 RADAR SF
Affiliated to the Gallup
organisation

Taloustutkimus Oy
Susitie 11
00800 Helsinki 80
Tel: (010 358) 0-7556511
Telex: 121394

Organisations Providing Economic and Statistical Data

Central Statistical Office
PO Box 504
Annakatu 44
00101 Helsinki
Tel: (010 358) 0-17314
Telex: 1002111
Contact Statistics Library and
Archives
Produces a number of
comprehensive statistical
publications including
Statistical Yearbook of
Finland covering domestic
and foreign statistics. Also the
CSO publishes a monthly and
quarterly Bulletin of Statistics,
Statistical Surveys and
Studies of the CSO, and
Official Statistics of Finland
(OSF)

Elinkeinoelaman
Tutkinmuslaitos
Naringslivets
Forskningsinstitut (ETLA)
(Finnish Research Institute)
Lonnrotinkatu 4B
00120 Helsinki
Produces a number of useful
economic and industrial
reports including Suhdanne
(Economic Prospects), and a
study done in cooperation
with other Scandinavian
research institutes entitled
Growth Policies in a Nordic
Perspective

Ministry of Finance
Economics Department
Aleksanterinkatu 3D
00170 Helsinki 17
General Department
Kirkkokatu 14
00170 Helsinki 17
Tel: (010 358) 0-1601
Publishes National Budget
Report providing a useful
survey of the state of the
Finnish economy

Larger Finnish banks publish
statistical data on the
economy. Financial statistics
are obtainable from
publications produced by the
Bank of Finland including the
Monthly Bulletin.

Publications

Directories

Finnish Consulting Service
Published by the Finnish
Foreign Trade Association,
Helsinki

Sinnen Kirja
The Blue Book – Directory of
the Economic Life of Finland
Published by Sininen Kirja Oy
Topeliuksenkatu 33A 9
00250 Helsinki 25

Major Newspapers

Helsingen Sanomat
(Publishes a stock exchange
list providing official prices,
etc)
Daily

Kauppalehti
(Publishes a stock exchange
list providing official prices,
etc)
Daily

Journals and Periodicals

Finnish Trade Review
Published by the Finnish
Foreign Trade Association
Arkadiankatu 4-6B
PO Box 908
00101 Helsinki
Covers industry, company
and product news. 8 issues
per annum

Forum for Ekonomi och
Teknik
Published by Forlags Ab
Forum for Ekonomi och
Teknik, Mannerheimv 18
00100 Helsinki
Covers features on
economics, finance,
companies and stock market
news. Fortnightly

Mark Markkinoinnin
Ammattilehti
Published by Suomen
Markkinointiliitto
(Finnish Marketing
Federation), Helsinki
Covers marketing topics.
Available wth an English
summary and briefing. 10
issues per annum

Suomen Tukkukauppa
Published by Finnish
Wholesalers and Importers
Association, Helsinki
Covers news and articles on
the Finnish wholesale and
import trade. 10 issues per
annum

Talouselama
Published by Talouselama
Oy, Helsinki
Covers all aspects of Finnish
business, including company
surveys. Weekly

France

*Sources of Economic,
Stock Market
Information, and
Investment Research
Services*

Banks

Central Bank

Banque de France
1 Rue de la Vrilliere
75001 Paris
Tel: (010 33) 1-2615672
Telex: 220932

**Selection of French Banks
in London**

A1 Saudi Banque
52-60 Cannon Street
London EC4N 6AN
Tel: 01-236 6533

BA11
1 London Bridge
London SE1
Tel: 01-378 7070

Banque Francaise du
Commerce
Exterieur
Morgan House
1 Angel Court
London EC2R 7HU
Tel: 01-726 4020

Banque Indosuez
52-62 Bishopsgate
London EC2N 4AR
Tel: 01-638 3600

Banque Internationale pour
l'Afrique Occidentale
41 Eastcheap
London EC3M 1HX
Tel: 01-626 9898

Banque de la Mediterranee –
France
93 Park Lane
London W1Y 3TA
Tel: 01-499 8181

Banque Nationale de Paris
8-13 King William Street
London EC4P 4HS
Tel: 01-626 5678

Banque Paribas
68 Lombard Street
London EC3V 9EH

Banque Worms
15 St Swithins Lane
London EC4N 8AN
Tel: 01-626 6121

Caisse Centrale de Credit
Agricole
Condor House
14 St Paul's Churchyard
London EC4M 8BD
Tel: 01-248 1400

CIC Group
74 London Wall
London EC2M 5NE
Tel: 01-638 5700

Credit Commercial de France
Peninsular House
36 Monument Street
London EC3R 8LJ
Tel: 01-623 1131

Credit Lyonnais
84-94 Queen Victoria Street
London EC4P 4LX
Tel: 01-634 8000

Credit du Nord
10 Old Jewry
London EC2R 8DU
Tel: 01-606 0621

Societe Generale
PO Box 513
60 Gracechurch Street
London EC3V OHD
Tel: 01-626 5400

Societe Generale Merchant
Bank
PO Box 61
60 Gracechurch Street
London EC3V OET
Tel: 01-626 5622

Securities Houses in London

Banque Paribas Capital
Markets
33 Wigmore Street
London W1H OBN
Tel: 01-355 2000

BNP Capital Markets
8-13 King William Street
London EC4N 7DN
Tel: 01-283 7535

Credit Commercial de France
(Securities)
7th Floor
Peninsular House
36 Monument Street
London EC3R 8LJ
Tel: 01-623 3117

Louise Dreyfus Securities
65 Kingsway
London WC2B 6TD
Tel: 01-242 1077

Major French Banks

Banque Francaise du
Commerce Exterieur
Boulevard Haussmann 21
75427 Paris
Tel: (010 33) 1-2474747
Telex: 660370

Banque Indosuez
Boulevard Haussmann 96
75008 Paris
Tel: (010 33) 1-5612020
Telex: 650409

Banque Nationale de Paris SA
16 Boulevard des Italiens
75009 Paris
Tel: (010 33) 1-42444546
Telex: 280605

Banque Parisbas
Rue d'Antin 3
75002 Paris
Tel: (010 33) 1-2981234
Telex: 210041

Caisse Centrale des Banques
Populaires
Montmarte 115
75002 Paris
Tel: (010 33) 1-2961515
Telex: 210993

Compagnie Financiere de
Credit Industriel et
Commercial (CIC Group)
Rue de la Victoire 66
75009 Paris
Tel: (010 33) 1-42808080
Telex: 290692

Credit Agricole
Boulevard Pasteur 91-93
75015 Paris
Tel: (010 33) 1-3235202
Telex: 204670

Credit Lyonnais SA
Boulevard des Italiens 19
75002 Paris
Tel: (010 33) 1-2957000
Telex: 612400

Societe Generale
Boulevard Haussmann 29
75009 Paris
Tel: (010 33) 2982000
Telex: 290842

Stockbrokers

There are seven exchanges in
France. The Paris Stock
Exchange handles over 95 per
cent of total transactions.

Palais de la Bourse
(Paris Stock Exchange)
4 Place de la Bourse
75080 Paris
Tel: (010 33) 1-40268590
Telex: 230844 SYNAGEN

Palais de la Bourse
2 Place Gabriel
33075 Bordeaux
Tel: (010 33) 56-447091

Palais de la Bourse
Place du Theatre
59040 Lille
Tel: (010 33) 20-556820

Palais de la Bourse
BP 400
13215 Marseille
Tel: (010 33) 91-907032

Palais de la Bourse
BP 815
54011 Nancy
Tel: (010 33) 8-3365697

Palais de la Bourse
15 Place du Commerce
44000 Nantes
Tel: (010 33) 40-484196

Palais du Commerce
Place de la Bourse
69829 Lyon
Tel: (010 33) 7-8425471

Members of the Paris Stock Exchange (as at February 1987)

Auboyneau-Labouret-Ollivier
23 Boulevard Poissonniere
75002 Paris
Tel: (010 33) 1-42332180

Bacot Allain
13 Rue la Fayette
75009 Paris
Tel: (010 33) 1-40163030

Baudoin
60 Rue de Provence
75009 Paris
Tel: (010 33) 1-42806930

Boscher
28 Rue Drout
75009 Paris
Tel: (010 33) 1-42471340

Du Bouzet
10 Cite Rougement
75009 Paris
Tel: (010 33) 1-47709940

Buisson
92 Rue de Richelieu
75002 Paris
Tel: (010 33) 1-40204020

Chaussier
63 Rue Sainte-Anne
75002 Paris
Tel: (010 33) 1-42615119

Cheuvreaux de Virieu
2 Rue de Choiseul
75002 Paris
Tel: (010 33) 1-42618008

De Cholet-Dupont
3 Rue de Gramont
75002 Paris
Tel: (010 33) 1-42618322

De Compiegne-Augustin
Normand
92 Rue de Richelieu
75002 Paris
Tel: (010 33) 1-42966616

Courcoux-Bouvet
5 Rue Gaillon
75002 Paris
Tel: (010 33) 1-42664826

Delahaye-Ripault
178 Rue Montmarte
75002 Paris
Tel: (010 33) 1-42961092

Ducatel-Duval
4 Rue de la Bourse
75002 Paris
Tel: (010 33) 1-42618128

Dufour-Koller-Lacarriere
21 Rue de Choiseul
75002 Paris
Tel: (010 33) 1-42660230

Dupont-Denant
42 Rue N des Victoires
75002 Paris
Tel: (010 33) 1-42334463

Faunchier Magnan-Durant
des Aulnois
75 Rue de Richelieu
75002 Paris
Tel: (010 33) 1-42603540

A Ferri – B Ferri – C Germe
53 Rue Vivienne
75002 Paris
Tel: (010 33) 1-40263755

Francoise Dufour-Kervern
116 Rue Reaumur
75002 Paris
Tel: (010 33) 1-42364460

Gorgeu-Perquel-Krucker
11 Rue des Filles St Thomas
75002 Paris
Tel: (010 33) 1-42974651

Goy-Hauvette
142 Rue Montmarte
75002 Paris
Tel: (010 33) 1-42334456

Hamant-Carmignac
19 Rue le Pelletier
75009 Paris
Tel: (010 33) 1-48245800

Hayaux du Tilly
19 Rue de Provence
75009 Paris
Tel: (010 33) 1-42468276

de Lavandeyra
27 Rue de la Miichodiere
75002 Paris
Tel: (010 33) 1-47423909

J M Legrand – P Legrand
36 Rue Laffite
75009 Paris
Tel: (010 33) 1-47707290

Magnin-Cordelle
89 Rue la Boetie
75008 Paris
Tel: (010 33) 1-45631313

Massonaud-de Fontenay
25 Rue de Choiseul
75002 Paris
Tel: (010 33) 1-47426540

Meeschaert-Rousselle
16 Boulevard Montmarte
75009 Paris
Tel: (010 33) 1-42467264

Melendes
10 Rue du Quartre-Septembre
75002 Paris
Tel: (010 33) 1-42966022

Meunier-de la Fourniere
Michelez-le Febvre
40 Rue n d des Victoires
75002 Paris
Tel: (010 33) 1-42336196

Michel
7 Rue de la Bourse
75002 Paris
Tel: (010 33) 1-42615260

Nivard-Flornoy
20 Boulevard Montmarte
75009 Paris
Tel: (010 33) 1-42468282

Nouailhetas
8 Rue Vivienne
75002 Paris
Tel: (010 33) 1-42615362

P Oddo – P Oddo
31 Rue Saint-Augustin
75002 Paris
Tel: (010 33) 1-47422176

Philippe
3 Rue Taitbout
75009 Paris
Tel: (010 33) 1-42467295

Pinatton
8 Rue Auber
75009 Paris
Tel: (010 33) 1-42669331

Puget-Mahe
7 Rue Drouot
75009 Paris
Tel: (010 33) 1-42469234

Rondeleux
20 Rue Drouot
75009 Paris
Tel: (010 33) 1-42468281

Saintouin-Roulet
36 Rue du Louvre
75001 Paris
Tel: (010 33) 1-40260017

Schelcher-Prince
5 & 7 Rue Saint-Augustin
75002 Paris
Tel: (010 33) 1-42961616

Sellier-Suchet-Poupon
12 Rue d'Uzes
75002 Paris
Tel: (010 33) 1-42335101

J Soulie
3 Rue Rossini
75009 Paris
Tel: (010 33) 1-42464695

Y Soulie
3 Rue Rossini
75009 Paris
Tel: (010 33) 1-42469220

Tuffier-Ravier-PY
8 Rue Saint-Fiacre
75001 Paris
Tel: (010 33) 1-42615485

Wargny
9 Rue du Quartre-Septembre
75002 Paris
Tel: (010 33) 1-42966083

Wolff-Goirand
10 Rue d'Uzes
75002 Paris
Tel: (010 33) 1-45089640

Members of the Bordeaux Stock Exchange

Bentejac
62 Cours de l'Intendance
33000 Bordeaux
Tel: (010 33) 56526272

Champeil
11 Place des Quinconces
33000 Bordeaux
Tel: (010 33) 56522595

A Ferri – B Ferri – C Germe
16 Cours du Chapeau-Rouge
33000 Bordeaux
Tel: (010 33) 56485477

Lostie de Kerhor
6 bis, rue Blanc-Dutrouilh
33000 Bordeaux
Tel: (010 33) 56522122

Members of the Lille Stock Exchange

Dubly-Denoyelle
50 Boulevard de la Liberte
59012 Lille Cedex
Tel: (010 33) 20549394

Dubus
122 Rue de l'Hopital Militaire
59800 Lille Cedex
Tel: (010 33) 20570975

Dupont
120 Rue de l'Hopital Militaire
598000 Lille Cedex
Tel: (010 33) 20570757

Members of the Lyon Stock Exchange

Brac de la Perriere
12 Rue de la Republique
69002 Lyon
Tel: (010 33) 78283799

Delore
2 Place de la Bourse
69002 Lyon
Tel: (010 33) 78421220

J & S Girardet
50 Rue du Pt Edouard Herriot
69002 Lyon
Tel: (010 33) 78425595

Gorgeu-Perquel-Krucker
41 Rue de la Bourse
69002 Lyon
Tel: (010 33) 78381303

R & J P Michaux
3 Rue du President Carnot
69289 Lyon Cedex 02
Tel: (010 33) 78427192

Richard
45 Rue de la Bourse
69002 Lyon
Tel: (010 33) 78420583

Sellier-Suchet-Poupon
32 Rue de la Republique
69002 Lyon
Tel: (010 33) 78425781

Wolff-Goivand
9 Rue Grenette
69002 Lyon
Tel: (010 33) 78425118

Members of the Marseille Stock Exchange

Blisson Bonnasse
39b Rue Grigan
13286 Marseille Cedex 6
Tel: (010 33) 91549106

J F A Buisson
54 Rue Paradis
13006 Marseille
Tel: (010 33) 91331009

Ducatel-Duval
18 Rue Grignan
13001 Marseille
Tel: (010 33) 91331357

Meeschaert-Rousselle
21 Rue Grignan
13291 Marseille Cedex 2
Tel: (010 33) 91333330

Members of the Nancy Stock Exchange

J F A Buisson
57 Rue Saint-Jean
5400 Nancy
Tel: (010 33) 83351785

Douilhet
62 Rue Stanislas – BP 220
54004 Nancy Cedex
Tel: (010 33) 83371901

Kempf
10 Rue Saint-Dizier – BP 518
54008 Nancy Cedex
Tel: (010 33) 83365630

Tuffier – Ravier – PY
21 Rue de la Revinelle – BP 355
54007 Nancy Cedex
Tel: (010 33) 83321201

Members of the Nantes Stock Exchange

Boscher
15 Boulevard Gabriel
Guist'hau
4400 Nantes
Tel: (010 33) 40200700

De Champsavin
8 Rue de Gorges – Place Royale
44014 Nantes Cedex
Tel: (010 33) 40484102

Meunier – de la Fourniere –
Michelez – le Febvre
22 Rue Crebillon
4400 Nantes
Tel: (010 33) 40893476

De Portzamparc
11 Rue Lafayette – BP 374
44012 Nantes Cedex
Tel: (010 33) 40481618

Sources of General Background Information, Industry Sector Information and Trade Contacts

UK Addresses

French Chamber of
Commerce
2nd Floor
Knightsbridge House
197 Knightsbridge
London SW1
Tel: 01-225 5250

French Embassy (Commercial
Department)
21-24 Grosvenor Place
London W1
Tel: 01-235 7080
Embassy has a commercial
library which houses French
publications, statistical
sources, etc.

Addresses in France
There are twenty-two
principal regional chambers
of commerce in France, six
offices of the Paris Chamber
of Commerce and one central
organisation.
Central Organisation:
Assemblee Permanente des
Chambres de Commerce et
d'Industrie
45 avenue d'Iena
75116 Paris
Tel: (010 33) 1-47230111

Main Paris Office
Chamber de Commerce et
d'Industrie de Paris
27 avenue Friedland
75382 Paris Cedex 08
Tel: (010 33) 1-45619900
Telex: 650100

Other Main Chambers of Commerce
International Chamber of
Commerce
38 Cours Albert-1er
Paris
Tel: (010 33) 42618597

Chambre de Commerce et
d'Industrie de Bordeaux
12 Place de la Bourse
33076 Bordeaux
Tel: (010 33) 56909128
Telex: 541048

Chambre de Commerce et
d'Industrie de Boulogne
Quai Gambetta
62204 Boulogne-sur-Mer
Tel: (010 33) 21339292
Telex: 110013

Chambre de Commerce et
d'Industrie de Grenoble
6 Boulevard Gambetta
38028 Grenoble
Tel: (010 33) 76472036
Telex: 320824

Chambre de Commerce et
d'Industrie de Lyon
Palais du Commerce
20 Rue de la Bourse
69289 Lyon
Tel: (010 33) 78381010
Telex: 310828

Chambre de Commerce et
d'Industrie de Marseille
Palais de la Bourse
13222 Marseille
Tel: (010 33) 91919151
Telex: 410091

Chambre de Commerce et
d'Industrie de Nice
20 Boulevard Carabacel
06007 Nice
Tel: (010 33) 93559155
Telex: 460041

Chambre de Commerce et
d'Industrie d'Orleans et du
Loiret
23 Place du Martoi
45044 Orleans
Tel: (010 33) 38620840
Telex: 760912

Chambre de Commerce et
d'Industrie de Rouen
34 Rue Bouquet
76000 Rouen
Tel: (010 33) 35984728
Telex: 770036

Chambre de Commerce et
d'Industrie de Toulouse
2 Rou d'Alsace-Lorraine
31002 Toulouse
Tel: (010 33) 61252100
Telex: 531877

British Embassy
35 Rue de Faubourg St
Honore
75383 Paris Cedex 08
Tel: (010 33) 1-42669142
Telex: 650264 INFORM

Sources of Investment and Trade Advice, Assistance and Information

One of the main points of
contact in France for
information and advice on
setting up a business in
France is DATAR. This is a
government agency which
can provide detailed
information on France
including financial incentives,
joint venture partners, and
appropriate locations as well
as general background
information on France.

Delegation a l'Amenagement
du Territoire et a l'Action
Regionale (DATAR)
Head Office:
1 avenue Charles Floquet
75007 Paris
Tel: (010 33) 1-47836120
Telex: 200970

UK Office:
21-24 Grosvenor Place
London SW1X 7HU
Tel: 01-235 5148
Telex: 28657

USA Offices:
610 Fifth Avenue
New York
NY 10020
Tel: (010 1) 212-7579340
Telex: 235026

Midwest:
401 North Michigan Ave
Suite 3045
Chicago III 560611
Tel: (010 1) 312-6611640

Southern:
2727 Allen Parkway
Suite 811
Houston
Texas 77019
Tel: (010 1) 713-5261565

Western:
1801 Avenue of the Stars
Suite 410
Los Angeles
California 90067
Tel: (010 1) 213-8790352

Loire
Association pour le
Development Industriel de la
Loire (ADIL)
2 Rue du Coin
4200 Saint-Etienne
(Mark for the attention of
ADIL, Saint-Etienne)
Tel: (010 33) 77332190
Fax: (010 33) 77338627

Nord-Pas-de-Calais
Association pour le
Renouveau Industriel du
Nord-Pas-de-Calais (ARI)
16 Residence Breteuil
Parc Saint Maur
59000 Lille
Tel: (010 33) 20559882
Fax: (010 33) 20553815
Telex: 120936

Paris
Association Bureaux Province
20 Rue de la Tremoille
75008 Paris
Tel: (010 33) 1-7239380

Rhone Alps
Association pour le
Developpement Economique
de la Region Lyonnaise
20 rue de la Bourse
69289 Lyon Cedex 1
Tel: (010 33) 78381010
Fax: (010 33) 78385346
Telex: 310828

Sud Ouest
District del'agglomeration de
Montpellier
14 rue Mercel de Serres
34000 Montpellier
Tel: (010 33) 67521819
Telex: 490531F DUAMF

Other Organisations
ANIT (Public Information
Service)
8 Avenue de l'Opera
75001 Paris
Tel: (010 33) 1-2603738

Centre Francais du
Commerce Exterieur
(French Centre for Foreign
Trade)
10 Avenue d'Iena
75116 Paris
Tel: (010 33) 1-7236123
Telex: 611934

Direction Generale des
Douanes et Droits Indirects
(Customs and Excise
Directorate)
8 rue de la Tour-des-Dames
75436 Paris
Tel: (010 33) 1-42806722

Direction Generale des Impot
Centre des Non-Residents
9 Rue d'Uzes
75094 Paris

Droits Indirects (Division des
Autorisations Commerciales
Importations)
8 Rue de la Tour-des-Dames
75009 Paris
Tel: (010 33) 1-2806722

Ministere du Commerce de
l'Artisanat et du Tourisme
(Ministry of Commerce, Small
Business and Tourism)
Administration Centrale
80 Rue de Lille
75007 Paris
Tel: (010 33) 1-45562424

Ministere du Commerce
Exterieur
(Ministry of Foreign Trade)
41 quai Branly
75007 Paris
Tel: (010 33) 1-45507111
Telex: 250832/200994

Ministere de l'Economie et
des Finances
Direction des Relations
Economiques Exterieurs
41 Qaui Branly
75700 Paris
Tel: (010 33) 1-5559220

Ministere des Relations
Exterieures
(Ministry of Foreign Affairs)
37 Quai d'Orsay
75000 Paris
Tel: (010 33) 1-45559540

Professional Associations

Accountancy
Compagnie Nationale des
Commissaires aux Comptes
6 rue de l'Amiral de Coligny
75001 Paris

Ordre des Expets
Compatables et des
Compatables Agrees
109 Boulevard Malesherbes
75008 Paris

Banking
Association Francaise des
Banques
18 Rue la Fayette
75009 Paris
Tel: (010 33) 1-2469259
Telex: 660282

Consultancy
Chambre Syndicale des
Societes d'Études et de
Conseils (SYNTEC)
3 rue Leon Bonnat
75016 Paris
Tel: (010 33) 1-5244353
Telex: 612938 F

Federation Europeane des
Associations de Conseils en
Organisation (FEACO)
(The European Federation of
Management Consulting
Associations)
c/o SYNTEC (address as
above)
Represents 740 consulting
firms in Europe, 70 of which
employ over 100 consultants.
Total of 20 000 individual
consultants represented in
1987

Insurance
Comite Europeen des
Assurances (CEA)
3 Rue Meyerbeer
75009 Paris Cedex 02
Tel: (010 33) 1-42479464
Telex: 641901 F

Federation Francaise des Stes
d'Assurances (FFSA)
(French Federation of
Insurance Companies)
26 Boulevard Haussman
75009 Paris
Tel: (010 33) 1-42479000
Telex: 640477 F

Syndicat des Cies Francaises
de Reassurances
(French Reinsurance
Companies Association)
34-36 Boulevard de Courceiles
75017 Paris
Tel: (010 33) 1-42278682
Telex: 650493

L'Union Syndicate des Ste
Etranges d'Assurances
2 rue Pigalle
75009 Paris
Tel: (010 33) 1-45479000

Trade Associations

Agro-alimentaire (Agronomic food production)
Association Nationale des
Industries Agro-alimentaires
(ANIA)
52 rue du
Faubourg-Saint-Honore
75008 Paris
Tel: (010 33) 1-42664014

Ameublement (Furniture)
Union Nationale des
Industries Francaises de
l'Ambeublement (UNIFA)
28 bis avenue Daumesnil
75012 Paris
Tel: (010 33) 1-46286861

Automobiles et cycles (Cars and cycles)
Chambre Syndicale des
Constructeurs d'Automobiles
2 rue de Presbourg
75008 Paris
Tel: (010 33) 1-47235405

Chambre Syndicale Nationale
du Cycle et du Motorcycle
9 rue Lesueur
75016 Paris
Tel: (010 33) 1-45003136

Batiment et travaux publics (Buildings and public works)
Federation Nationale du
Batement
33 avenue Kleber
75784 Paris Cedex 16
Tel: (010 33) 1-47201020

Syndicat des Entrepreneurs
Francais Internationaux
(SEFI)
3 rue de Berrl
75008 Paris
Tel: (010 33) 1-45631114

Chimiques (Chemical Industries)
Union des Industries
Chimiques
64 avenue Marceau
75008 Paris
Tel: (010 33)
1-47205603/47207075

Construction et equipement electriques, electronique (Electronics)
Federation des Industries
Electriques et Electroniques
(FIEE)
17 rue Hamelin
75016 Paris
Tel: (010 33) 1-45051427

Groupement des Industries
de Materiels d'Equipement
Electrique et de l'Electonique
Industrielle Associee
(GIMELEC)
11-17 rue Hamelin
75783 Paris Cedex 16
Tel: (010 33) 1-45051472

Construction et reparation navale (Naval construction and repairs)
Chambre Syndicale des
Constructeurs de Navires et
de Machines Marines
47 rue de Monceau
75008 Paris
Tel: (010 33) 1-45619911

Syndicat National des
Industries de la Reparation
Navale
47 rue de Monceau
75008 Paris
Tel: (010 33) 1-45619911

Couture, habillement (Fashion, clothing)
Chambre Syndicale de la
Couture Parisienne
100-102
Faubourg-Saint-Honore
75008 Paris
Tel: (010 33)
1-42656444/42669207

Federation Francaise de la
Couture et du Pret-a-Porter
des Couturiers
110-102
Faubourg-Saint-Honore
75008 Paris
Tel: (010 33)
1-42666444/42669207

Union des Industries de
l'Habillement
8 rue de Richelieu
75001 Paris
Tel: (010 33) 1-42962415

Edition (Publishing)
Syndicat National de l'Edition
Hotel du Cercle de la Librairie
117 boulevard Saint-Germain
75279 Paris Cedex 06
Tel: (010 33) 1-43292101

Electrometallurgie et electrochimie (Electrometallurgy and electrochemistry)
Chambre Syndicale de
l'Electrometallurgie et de
l'Ectrochimie
33 rue de Lisbonne
75008 Paris
Tel: (010 33) 1-45610663

Electronique (Electronics)
Groupement des Industries
Electroniques (GIEL)
11-17 rue Hamelin
75783 Paris Cedex 16
Tel: (010 33) 1-45051427

Ferroviaires (industries) (Railways)
Federation des Industries
Ferroviaires
12 rue Bixio
75007 Paris
Tel: (010 33) 1-45561353

Fonderie et industries connexes (Foundrys)
Syndicat General des
Fondeurs de France et
Industries Connexes
2 rue de Bassano
75783 Paris Cedex 16
Tel: (010 33) 1-47235550

Materiaux de construction (Construction equipment)
Union Nationale des
Industries de Carrieres et
Materiaux de Construction
(UNICEM)
3 rue Alfred-Roll
75849 Paris Cedex 17
Tel: (010 33) 1-47660364

Matieres plastiques (Plastics)
Syndicat Professionnel des
Producteurs de Matieres
Plastiques
65 rue de Prony
75017 Paris
Tel: (010 33) 1-47631259

Mecaniques (industries) (Mechanical)
Federation des Industries
Mecaniques et
Transformatrices des Metaux
11 avenue Hoche
75382 Paris Cedex 08
Tel: (010 33) 1-45630200

Metallurgie – Mines (Metallurgical industry)
Federation des Chambres
Syndicales des Minerais
30 avenue de Messine
75008 Paris
Tel: (010 33) 1-45630266

Union des Industries
Metallurgiques et Minieres
(UIMM)
56 avenue de Wagram
75017 Paris
Tel: (010 33) 1-47665115

Metiers d'art
Confederation Francaise des
Metiers d'Art
8 rue Saint-Claude
75003 Paris
Tel: (010 33) 1-42784805

Nucleaire (industrie) (Nuclear)
Association Technique pour
l'Energie Nucleaire 'ATEN'
26 rue de Clichy
75009 Paris
Tel: (010 33) 1-45260103

Groupe Intersyndical de
l'Industrie Nucleaire (GIIN)
15 rue Beaujon
75008 Paris
Tel: (010 33) 1-42673068

Papiers cartons (Paper and cardboard)
Confederation Francaise de
l'Industrie des Papiers,
Cartons et Cellulose
(COPACEL)
154 boulevard Haussmann
75008 Paris
Tel: (010 33) 1-45627055

Parfumerie (Perfume and toiletries)
Federation Francaise de
l'Industrie des Produits de
Pargumerie, de Beaute et de
Toilette
8 place du General-Catroux
75017 Paris
Tel: (010 33) 1-47665101

Syndicat Francais de la
Parfumerie
8 place du General-Catroux
75017 Paris
Tel: (010 33) 1-47665101

Petrole (Oil industry)
Union des Chambres
Syndicales de l'Industrie du
Petrole
16 avenue Kleber
75116 Paris
Tel: (010 33) 1-45021120

Siderurgie (Iron and steel industry)
Chambre Syndicale de la
Siderurgie Francaise
5 bis rue de Madrid
75008 Paris
BP 707-08
75367
Tel: (010 33) 1-45228300

Sports et loisirs (Sports and leisure)
Federation Francaise des
Industries des Sports et des
Loisirs (FIFAS)
22 rue de Dunkerque
75101 Paris
Tel: (010 33) 1-42801250

Textiles
Union des Industries Textiles
10 rue d'Anjou
75008 Paris
Tel: (010 33) 1-42661111

Transports
Federation Nationale des
Transports Routiers
2 avenue Velasquez
75008 Paris
Tel: (010 33) 1-45631600

Union des Federations de
Transport (UFT)
68 rue Cardinet
75017 Paris
Tel: (010 33) 1-47664968

Organisations de Consommateurs (Consumers organisations)
Federation Natonale des
Cooperatives de
Consommateurs
27-33 quai Le Gallo
92100 Boulogne-Billancourt
Tel: (010 33) 1-46049178

Organisation Generale des
Consommateurs (ORGECO)
3 rue de Provence
75009 Paris
Tel: (010 33) 1-42460833

Union Federale des
Consommateurs
14 rue Froment
75011 Paris
Tel: (010 33) 1-48071900

Company Financial and Product Information

Directories
Annuaire Bancaire
Produced by DAFSA, Paris
Directory of French and
foreign banks operating in
France

Annuaire des Societes et des Administrateurs
Produced by DAFSA, Paris
Covers 1200 companies, usually those quoted on the Bourse or foreign stock exchanges

Carnet de Nouvel Economiste
Produced by Nouvel Economiste
Major executives, names, addresses and telephone numbers provided of many major French firms

France 30 000
Produced by Dun & Bradstreet
Top 30 000 French companies covered
A 1988 edition is available. Includes company trade names, location, directors' names, industry sector code

French Company Handbook
Produced by International Business Development and the International Herald Tribune
Covers 83 companies in detail. Written in English

Informations Internationales
Produced by DAFSA, Paris
Covers 1000 multinational French companies. Includes financial results, subsidiaries and affiliates, balance sheets, income statements, capital and stock exchange data

Kompass, France
Produced by SNEI
Also 19 Kompass Regionaux corresponding to the regional structure of France. Covers 58000 companies (1987 edition)

Liaisons Financieres
Produced by DAFSA, Paris
Directory of corporate links and shareholders

Repertoire Generale alphabetique des Valuers Cotees et non Cotees
Covers stocks both quoted and unquoted

Repertoire Generale alphabetique des Valuers Mobilieres Francaises et Etrangeres non Cotees en France
Covers stocks and shares, transferable securities (unquoted) in France

Economic and Market Statistical Data

Market Research Organisations

Burke Marketing Research Sarl
159 rue Nationale
75640 Paris Cedex 13
Tel: (010 33) 1-45841115
Telex: 202031
Parent company: Burke International Research GmbH

Claude Suquet et Associates (CSA)
6 Rue du Quartre Septembre
92310 Issy les Moulineaux
Tel: (010 33) 1-45581186
Telex: 205165 IRDMISI F

Cofremca
14 rue Milton
75009 Paris
Tel: (010 33) 1-42857148

DAFSA
7 Rue Bergere
75009 Paris
Tel: (010 33)1-42332123
See Chapter six for details of DAFSA's online information services

GIRA France
10 rue des Ternes
57017 Paris
Tel: (010 33) 1-4574290
Telex: 27556
Parent company GIRA (Switzerland)

Motivaction SA
12 rue Mansart
78000 Versailles
Tel: (010 33) 1-39550077
Telex: 696053
Parent company Motivaction International

MV2 Conseil
41 avenue du General Leclerc
92100 Boulogne
Tel: (010 33) 1-46203434
Telex: 202573
Member of the World Trade Group of market research companies

SOFEMA
6 rue de la Republique
78100 St Germain-en-Laye
Tel: (010 33) 1-39731420
Telex: 697843

SOFRES
16-18 rue Barbes
92129 Montrouge
Tel: (010 33) 1-46571300
Telex: 200601
Parent company: Banque de Paris et des Pays-Bas

TMO Consultants
22 rue de Quartre Septembre
75002 Paris
Tel: (010 33) 1-47423481
Telex: 280518
NB: One of the ten largest market research companies in France. Member of the INRA, International market research organisation

Organisations Providing Economic and Statistical Data

Institut National de la
Statistique et des Etudes
Economiques (INSEE)
Tour Gamma A
195 Rue de Bercy
75582 Paris Cedex 12
Produces and publishes
periodicals, statistical series,
economic forecasts, reports
and provides online
databases.
Publications can be obtained
direct from INSEE or from
Observatoires Economiques
Regionaux (Regional
Economic Observatories).
There are 22 such
observatories in France and
their addresses are listed in
INSEE's publications
catalogue.
Main INSEE statistical
publications include:

Bulletin Mensuel de
Statistique. Monthly
Provides the most up to date,
weekly, monthly and
quarterly statistical series

Extraits et Tableaux des
Comptes Nationaux. Annual
Contains extracts from French
National accounts

Tendances de la Conjoncture.
8 issues per annum
Provides French economic
series

Direction Nationale des
Statistiques de Commerce
Exterieur
(Directorate for Foreign Trade
Statistics)
192 Rue St Honore
75056 Paris
Tel: (010 33) 1-42603300
Telex: 230061 DOUSTAT

Ministere de l'Economie et
des Finances
41 Quai Branly
75700 Paris
Tel: (010 33) 1-5559220
Produces economic and
financial statistics.
Publications include:
Economic et Prevision.
Quarterly
Statistiques et Etudes
Financieres. Monthly
Notes Bleues. Weekly

Bank of France
Produces economic and
financial statistics
Publications:
Bulletin Trimestriel de la
Banque de France. Quarterly
Compte Rendu. Annual
Report

Enquete Mansuelle de
Conjoncture. Monthly
Provides economic analysis of
French industries'
performance
Statistiques Monetaires
Mensuelles. Monthly

Many other large banks and
brokers produce economic,
financial and stock market
statistics and analysis.
Institutions with strong
research capability include
the Banque Paribas, Banque
Indosuez, Credit Commercial
de France and brokers
Messchaert-Rouselle,
Cheuvreux-de Virieu and De
Lavandeyre.

Bourse de Paris
(Paris Stock Exchange)
Publications include:
Graphiques de la Bourse de
Paris. Fortnightly
Stock Exchange charts
Statistiques Mensuelles de la
Bourse de Paris. Monthly
Statistics of Stock Market
activity and prices
Annee Boursiere. Annual
report
Contains figures and statistics
on stock market activity
during the year

Publications

Directories
Annuaire de Paris et Region
Ile de France
Published by Cie de
Documentation, Paris
A business and industry trade
directory in the Paris region

Annuaire de la Press et de la
Publicite
Published by ADP, Paris
A French Willings and
Directory of Directories

France Export
Published by the Centre
Francais du Commerce
Exterieur, Paris
A directory of French
exporting firms

Qui Represente qui en France
Published by SNEI, Paris
A directory of agents in
France who represent
manufacturers worldwide

Reportoire Francais du
Commerce Exterieur
Published by Union Francaise
d'Annivaires Professionnels
(UFAP), Trappes
Foreign trade directory

Major Newspapers
AGEFI
Daily

Les Echos
Daily

Le Figaro
Daily and Sunday
supplement

Le Monde
Daily

Journals and Periodicals
Analyse Financiere
Produced by the French
Society of Financial analysts.
Quarterly

Bulletin des Indices de cours
Indices of French stocks
published by the Chambre
Syndicale. Daily

Cahiers Francais
Covers social, political and
economic issues. 5 issues per
annum

Cinquante Million de
Consommateurs
Produced by the National
Consumer Association.
Monthly

Cote Officielle (Daily Official
List)
Official quoted list of stock
market prices and decisions
and notices relating to
takeover bids, mergers and
block trading. Produced by
the Chambre Syndicale. Daily

L'Expansion
Business and economic
trends, annual ranking of top
1000 French companies.
Fortnightly

Le Monde – Dossiers et
Documents
Contains most important Le
Monde articles of the month.
Monthly

Moniteur du Commerce
International
Monitor of international
trade. Weekly.

Le Nouvel Economiste
Business and economic
surveys. Annual ranking of
the top 5000 French and
European companies. Weekly

L'Usine Nouvelle
Covers all aspects of industry
and commerce. Weekly

Valeurs Actuelles
Provides financial and
company profile information.
Weekly

La Vie Francaise
Covers business, economics,
finance and market reports.
Weekly

Germany, Federal Republic of

Sources of Economic, Stock Market Information and Investment Research Services

Banks

Central Bank
Deutsche Bundesbank
Wilhelm-Epstein-Str 14
6000 Frankfurt 50
Tel: (010 49) 69-158-1
Telex: 414431

German Banks in London
Badische Kommunale
Landesbank
Princes House
95 Gresham Street
London EC2V 7NA
Tel: 01-606 0391
Telex: 888423

Bank fur Gemeinwirtschaft
33 Lombard Street
London EC3V 9BS
Tel: 01-283 1090
Telex: 887628

Bayerische Hypotheken-&
Wechsel-Bank
Bucklersbury House
3 Queen Victoria Street
London EC4N 8HA
Tel: 01-248 4252
Telex: 894624

Bayerische Landesbank
Girozentrale
33 King Street
London EC2V 8EE
Tel: 01-726 6022
Telex: 886437

Bayerische Vereinsbank
1 Royal Exchange Buildings
London EC3V 3LD
Tel: 01-626 1301
Telex: 889196

Berliner Bank
Berliner House
81-82 Gracechurch Street
London EC3V ODS
Tel: 01-929 4060
Telex: 884131

Berliner Handels-&
Frankfurter Bank
61 Queen Street
London EC4R 1AE
Tel: 01-634 2300
Telex: 887047

Bremer Landesbank
20 Ironmonger Lane
London EC2V 8BQ
Tel: 01-600 5981
Telex: 8811626

Commerzbank
10-11 Austin Friars
London EC2N 2HE
Tel: 01-638 5895
Telex: 8954308

Deutsche Bank
6 Bishopsgate
London EC2P 2AT
Tel: 01-283 4600
Telex: 889287

Deutsche Schiffahrtsbank
Grocers Hall
Princes Street
London EC2R 8AQ
Tel: 01-726 6791
Telex: 889205

DG Bank Deutsche
Genossenschaftsbank
6 Milk Street
London EC2V 8DY
Tel: 01-726 6791
Telex: 886647

Dresdner Bank
8 Frederick Place
London EC2R 8AT
Tel: 01-606 7030
Telex: 885540

Hessische Landesbank
Girozentrale
8 Moorgate
London EC2R 6DD
Tel: 01-726 4554
Telex: 887511

Landesbank Stuttgart
Aldermary House
10-15 Queen Street
London EC4N 1TT
Tel: 01-236 2609
Telex: 8814275

London & Continental
Bankers
2 Throgmorton Avenue
London EC2N 2AP
Tel: 01-638 6111
(Joint Venture bank 76%
German)

Nord/LB/Norddeutsche
Landesbank Girozentrale
20 Ironmonger Lane
London EC2V 8EY
Tel: 01-600 1721
Telex: 884882

Westdeutsche Landesbank
Girozentrale
41 Moorgate
London EC2R 6AE
Tel: 01-638 6141
Telex: 887984

**Securities Houses in
London**
BHF Capital Markets
61 Queen Street
London EC4R 1AE
Tel: 01-329 4168

Deutsche Bank Capital
Markets
150 Leadenhall Street
London EC3V 4RJ
Tel: 01-283 0933

Major German Banks
Bank fur Gemeinwirtschaft
AG
Theaterplatz 2
6000 Frankfurt/Main 11
Tel: (010 49) 69-2580
Telex: 4122154 (International
Department)

Bayerische Hypotheken-und
Wechsel-Bank
Aktiengesellschaft
Theaterstrasse 11
8000 Munich 2

Arabellastrasse 12
8000 Munich 81
Tel: (010 49) 89-2366-1 &
89-9244-0
Telex: 52865-0 (General)

Bayerische Landesbank
Girozentrale
20 Brienner Strasse
8000 Munich 2
Tel: (010 49) 89-217101
Telex: 52862-70 (Foreign
Department)

Bayerische Vereinsbank AG
1 & 14
Kardinal-Faulhaber-Strasse
8000 Munich
Tel: (010 49) 89-21321
Telex: 528610 (Foreign
Department)

Commerzbank
Head Office
32-36 Neue Mainzer Strasse
6000 Frankfurt 1
Tel: (010 49) 69-13621
Telex: 4152530

Deutsche
Genossenschaftsbank (DG
Bank)
PO Box 100651
Am Platz der Republik
6000 Frankfurt/Main 1
Tel: (010 49) 69-744701
Telex: 412291

Deutsche
Girozentrale-Deutsche
Kommunalbank
Registered Offices:
10 Taunusanlage
6000 Frankfurt/Main 1
Tel: (010 49) 69-2693-0
Telex: 414168

32 Kurfurstendamm
1000 Berlin 15
Tel: (010 49) 30-8812096
Telex: 183353

Dresdner Bank AG
PO Box 110661
Jurgen-Panto-Platz 1
6000 Frankfurt/Main 11
Tel: (010 49) 69-2630
Telex: 415240

Kreditanstalt fur
Wiederaufbau (KFW)
Palmengartenstrasse 5-9
Postfach 11 11 41
6000 Frankfurt/Main 11
Tel: (010 49) 69-7431-0
Telex: 411352 KWFM D

Norddeutsche Landesbank
Girozentrale
1 Georgsplatz 3000
Hanover 1
Tel: (010 49) 511-1030
Telex: 9216-20 (General)

Westdeutsche Landesbank
Girozentrale
15 Herzogstrasse
4000 Dusseldorf
Tel: (010 49) 211-826-01
Telex: 858 2605

Stockbrokers
There are eight stock
exchanges in the Federal
Republic. The largest is
Frankfurt, and the other
exchanges are Dusseldorf,
Hamburg, Munich, Berlin,
Bremen, Hanover and
Stuttgart

Frankfurter Wertpapierborse
(Frankfurt Stock Exchange)
Borsenplatz 6
6000 Frankfurt 1
Tel: (010 49) 69-2197371
Telex: 411412

**Members (Banks and
Brokers – over 100
member firms)**
ACDA-BANK
Aktiengesellschaft
Allgemeine Deutsche
Credit-Anstalt
Hauptverwaltung
Frankfurt/Main
Lindenstrasse 1
6000 Frankfurt 1
Tel: (010 49) 69-7438-1

ADIG Allgemeine Deutsche
Investment-Gesellschaft mbH
Zweigniederlassung
Frankfurt/Main
Mainzer Landstrasse 5
6000 Frankfurt 1
Tel: (010 49) 69-256005-0

Allgemeine Hypothekenbank
Aktiengesellschaft
Bockenheimer Landstrasse 25
6000 Frankfurt 1
Tel: (010 49) 69-7179-0

American Express Bank
GmbH
Theodor-Heuss-Allee 80
6000 Frankfurt 90
Tel: (010 49) 69-79301-1

Amro Handelsbank AG
Hochstrasse 2
6000 Frankfurt 1
Tel: (010 49) 69-293047-48

Arab Banking Corporation,
Daus & Co GmbH
Niedenau 13-19
6000 Frankfurt 1
Tel: (010 49) 69-71403-0

Baden-Wurttembergische
Bank Aktiengesellschaft
Kleiner Schlossplatz 11
7000 Stuttgart 1
Tel: (010 49) 69-711-2094-0

Bankhaus H Aufhauser
Zweigniederlassung
Frankfurt/Main
Kaiserhofstrasse 16
6000 Frankfurt 1
Tel: (010 49) 69-281629

Borsenstrasse 19
6000 Frankfurt 1 (Borsenburo)
Tel: (010 49) 69-288266

Badische Kommunale
Landesbank-Girozentrale
Augusta-Anlage 33
6800 Mannheim 1
Tel: (010 49) 69-621-458-01

Grosse Bockenheimer Str 21
6000 Frankfurt 1
Tel: (010 49) 69-287341-43

Banco di Sicilia
Niederlassung
Frankfurt/Main
Bockenheimer Landstrasse
13-15
6000 Frankfurt 1
Tel: (010 49) 69-7122-0

Banco Exterior – Deutschland
SA
Zweigniederlassung
Frankfurt
Grosse Gallusstrasse 1-7
6000 Frankfurt 1
Tel: (010 49) 69-1330-0

Bank CIC-Union Europeene
AG
Westendstrasse 24
6000 Frankfurt 1
Tel: (010 49) 69-7160-0

Bankers Trust GmbH
Bockenheimer Landstrasse 39
6000 Frankfurt 1
Tel: (010 49) 69-7132-1

Bank fur Gemeinwirtschaft
Aktiengesellschaft
Theaterplatz 2
6000 Frankfurt 1
Tel: (010 49) 69-258-0

Bank in Liechtenstein
(Frankfurt) GmbH
Mainzer Landstrasse 5
6000 Frankfurt 1
Tel: (010 49) 69-256020

Bank of America
National Trust and Savings
Asssociation
Filiale Frankfurt/Main
Mainzer Landstrasse 46
6000 Frankfurt 1
Tel: (010 49) 69-712800

Bank of Tokyo (Deutschland)
Aktiengesellschaft
Wiesenhuttenstrasse 10
6000 Frankfurt 1
Tel: (010 49) 69-2576-0

Bankhaus Gebruder
Bethmann
Bethmannstrasse 7-9
6000 Frankfurt 1
Tel: (010 49) 69-2545-1

Bankhaus Hermann Lampe
KG
Alter Markt 3
4800 Bielefeld 1
Tel: (010 49) 69-521-582-1

Banque Nationale de Paris SA
& Co (Deutschland) OHG
Niederlassung
Frankfurt/Main
Bockenheimer Landstrasse 22
6000 Frankfurt 1
Tel: (010 49) 69-7193-0

Banque Paribas (Deutschland)
OHG
Kaiserstrasse 10
6000 Frankfurt 1
Tel: (010 49) 69-29909-0

Banque Paribas Capital
Markets GmbH
Bockenheimer Landstrasse
51-53
Frankfurt 1
Tel: (010 49) 69-727783

Barclays Bank plc
Filiale Frankfurt/Main
Frankfurt Branch
Bockenheimer Landstrasse
38-40
6000 Frankfurt 1
Tel: (010 49) 69-714080

Bayerische Hypotheken- und
Wechsel-Bank
Aktiengesellschaft
Borsenburo Frankfurt/Main
Kleiner Hirschgraben 16
6000 Frankfurt 1
Tel: (010 49) 69-298080

Bayerische Landesbank
Girozentrale
Borsenburo Frankfurt/Main
Ulmenstrasse 37
6000 Frankfurt 1
Tel: (010 49) 69-720801

Bayerische Vereinsbank
Aktiengesellschaft
Borsenabteilung
Frankfurt/Main
Bleidenstrasse 6-10
6000 Frankfurt 1
Tel: (010 49) 69-2174-1

Joh Berenberg Gossler & Co
Zweigniederlassung
Frankfurt/Main
Niedenau 61-63
6000 Frankfurt 17
Tel: (010 49) 69-720261

Berliner Bank
Aktiengesellschaft
Niederlassung
Frankfurt/Main
Bockenheimer Anlage 2
6000 Frankfurt 1
Tel: (010 49) 69-1506-1

Berliner Handels- und
Frankfurter Bank KGaA
(BHF-Bank)
Bockenheimer Landstrasse 10
6000 Frankfurt 1
Tel: (010 49) 69-718-0

Chemical Bank
Aktiengesellschaft
Ulmenstrasse 30
6000 Frankfurt 17
Tel: (010 49) 69-720431

Citibank Aktiengesellschaft
Neue Mainzer Strasse 75
6000 Frankfurt 1
Tel: (010 49) 69-1366-0

Commerzbank
Aktiengesellschaft
Neue Mainzer Strasse 32-36
6000 Frankfurt 1
Tel: (010 49) 69-1362-1

Conrad Hinrich Donner Bank
Zweigniederlassung
Frankfurt/Main
Grosse Gallusstrasse 18
6000 Frankfurt 1
Tel: (010 49) 69-287444

Credit Lyonnais SA & Co
(Deutschland) OHG
Neue Mainzer Strasse 69-75
6000 Frankfurt 1
Tel: (010 49) 69-29906-0

Daiwa Europe (Deutschland)
GmbH
Frankfurter Buro Center 6 OG
Mainzer Landstrasse 46
6000 Frankfurt 1
Tel: (010 49) 69-720316

Degussa Bank GmbH
Weissfrauenstrasse 9
6000 Frankfurt 1
Tel: (010 49) 69-218-02

Delbruck & Co Privatbankiers
Zweigniederlassung
Neue Mainzer Strasse 75
6000 Frankfurt 1
Tel: (010 49) 69-1331-0

Deutsche Bank
Aktiengesellschaft
Taunusanlage 12
6000 Frankfurt 1
Tel: (010 49) 69-7150-0

Deutsche Bank
Aktiengesellschaft
Filiale Mannheim
P 7 10-15
6800 Mannheim 1
Tel: (010 49) 69-621-1691

Deutsche Bau- und
Bodenbank
Aktiengesellschaft
Taunusanlage 8
6000 Frankfurt 1
Tel: (010 49) 69-2557-0

Deutsche Bundesbank
Wilhelm-Epstein-Strasse 14
6000 Frankfurt 50
Tel: (010 49) 69-158-1

Deutsche
Centralbodenkredit-
Aktiengesellschaft
Geschaftsstelle
Frankfurt/Main
Kirchnerstrasse 6-8
6000 Frankfurt 1
Tel: (010 49) 69-287259

Deutsche
Girozentrale-Deutsche
Kommunalbank
Taunusanlage 10
6000 Frankfurt 1
Tel: (010 49) 69-2693-0

Deutsche Hypothekenbank
Frankfurt-Bremen
Aktiengesellschaft
Taunusanlage 9
6000 Frankfurt 1
Tel: (010 49) 69-2548-0

DEKA Deutsche
Kapitalanlagegesellschaft
mbH
Mainzer Landstrasse 37
6000 Frankfurt 11
Tel: (010 49) 69-2546-0

Deutsche Pfandbriefanstalt
Korperschaft des offentlichen
Rechts
Paulinenstrasse 15
6200 Frankfurt 1
Tel: (010 49) 69-6121-3480

Deutsche Siedlungs- und
Landesrentenbank
Kennedyalle 62-70
5300 Bonn 2
Tel: (010 49) 69-228-889-215

Deutsche
Verkehrs-Kredit-Bank
Aktiengesellschaft
Untermainkai 23-25
6000 Frankfurt 1
Tel: (010 49) 69-2648-1

Deutsche Westminster Bank
Aktiengesellschaft
National Westminster Haus
Mainzer Landstrasse 49
6000 Frankfurt 1
Tel: (010 49) 69-2554-0

Deutsch-Schweizerische Bank
Aktiengesellschaft
Liebfrauenberg 37
6000 Frankfurt 1
Tel: (010 49) 69-13641

Deutsch-Skandinavische
Bank Aktiengesellschaft
Alte Rothofstrasse 8
6000 Frankfurt 1
Tel: (010 49) 69-2983-0

DG Bank Deutsche
Genossenschaftsbank
Am Platz der Republik
6000 Frankfurt 1
Tel: (010 49) 69-7447-0

DIT Deutscher
Investment-Trust
Gesellschaft fur
Wertpapieranlagen mbH
Mainzer Landstrasse 11-13
6000 Frankfurt 1
Tel: (010 49) 69-2644-0

Dresdner Bank
Aktiengesellschaft
Jurgen-Ponto-Platz 1
6000 Frankfurt 1
Tel: (010 49) 69-263-1

Dresdner Bank
Aktiengesellschaft in
Mannheim
P 2 12
6800 Mannheim 1
Tel: (010 49) 69-621-179-1

Dresdner Investment
Management
Kapitalanlagegesellschaft
mbH
Mainzer Landstrasse 11-13
6000 Frankfurt 1
Tel: (010 49) 69-2604-0

DWS Deutsche Gesellschaft
fur Wertpapiersparen mnH
Gruneburgweg 113-115
6000 Frankfurt 1
Tel: (010 49) 69-719090

Frankfurter Bankgesellschaft
Gegrundet 1899
Aktiengesellschaft
Freiherr-vom-Stein-Strasse 65
6000 Frankfurt 1
Tel: (010 49) 69-7198-0

Frankfurter Hypothekenbank
Aktiengesellschaft
Junghofstrasse 5-7
6000 Frankfurt 1
Tel: (010 49) 69-29898-0

Frankfurter Sparkasse von
1822
(Polytechnische Gesellschaft)
Neue Mainzer Strasse 49-53
6000 Frankfurt 1
Tel: (010 49) 69-2641-0

Frankfurter Volksbank eG
Borsenstrasse 1
6000 Frankfurt 1
Tel: (010 49) 69-2172-0

Frankfurt-Trust
Investment-Gesellschaft mbH
Wiesenau 1
6000 Frankfurt 1
Tel: (010 49) 69-728042-45

Heinrich Gontard & Co KG
Luginsland 1
6000 Frankfurt 1
Tel: (010 49) 69-281068

Grunelius & Co
Untermainkai 26
6000 Frankfurt 16
Tel: (010 49) 69-234141

Georg Hauck & Sohn
Bankiers KGaA
Kaiserstrasse 24
6000 Frankfurt 1
Tel: (010 49) 69-2161-1

Hessische Landesbank –
Girozentrale
Junghofstrasse 18-26
6000 Frankfurt 1
Tel: (010 49) 69-13201

Industriebank von Japan
(Deutschland)
Aktiengesellschaft
Niedenau 13-19
6000 Frankfurt 1
Tel: (010 49) 69-714050

Industriekreditbank
Aktiengesellschaft –
Deutsche Industriebank
Karl-Theodor-Strasse 6
Ecke Breite Strasse
4000 Dusseldorf 1
Tel: (010 49) 69-211-82210

Istituto Bancario San Paolo di
Torino
Filiale Frankfurt am Main
Schillerstrasse 26
6000 Frankfurt 1
Tel: (010 49) 69-2160-0

Kreditanstalt fur
Wiederaufbau
Palmengartenstrasse 5-9
6000 Frankfurt 1
Tel: (010 49) 69-7431-0

Landesbank Rheinland-Pfalz
– Girozentrale
Grosse Bleiche 54-56
6500 Mainz 1
Tel: (010 49) 69-6131-13-0

Landesgirokasse offentliche
Bank und Landessparkasse
Konigstrasse 3-5
7000 Stuttgart 1
Tel: (010 49) 711-2061-1

Landeszentralbank in Hessen
Hauptverwaltung der
Deutschen Bundesbank
Neue Mainzer Strasse 47
6000 Frankfurt 1
Tel: (010 49) 69-2561-1

Landwirtschaftliche
Rentenbank
Hochstrasse 2
6000 Frankfurt 1
Tel: (010 49) 69-2107-0

Lombardkasse
Aktiengesellschaft
Biebergasse 6-10
6000 Frankfurt 1
Tel: (010 49) 69-299001-0

Mainzer Volksbank eG
Neubrunnenstrasse 2
6500 Mainz 1
Tel: (010 49) 69-6131-148-0

Merck Finck & Co OHG
Neue Mainzer Strasse 55
6000 Frankfurt 1
Tel: (010 49) 69-2564-0

Metallbank GmbH
Reuterweg 14
6000 Frankfurt 1
Tel: (010 49) 69-159-0, 2671,
3006, 3301, 3414

B Metzler seel Sohn & Co
Grobe Gallusstrasse 18
6000 Frankfurt 1
Tel: (010 49) 69-2104-0

Morgan Guaranty GmbH
Mainzer Lanstrasse 46
6000 Frankfurt 1
Tel: (010 49) 69-7124150

Morgan Guaranty Trust
Company of New York
Zweigniederlassung
Frankfurt/Main
Mainzer Landstrasse 46
6000 Frankfurt 1
Tel: (010 49) 69-7124-0
Zentrale, 722154
Borsenabteilung

Morgan Stanley GmbH
Gruneburgweg 102
6000 Frankfurt 1
Tel: (010 49) 69-152060

Nassauische Sparkasse
Rheinstrabe 42/44
6200 Wiesbaden
Zeil 127
6000 Frankfurt 1
Tel: (010 49) 69-06121-364-1
Wiesbaden, 1307-1 Frankfurt,
1307251
Borsenabteilung
Zentrale Wertapaierabteilung

Nomura Europe GmbH
Hamburg Allee 2-10
6000 Frankfurt 90
Tel: (010 49) 69-794004-0

Nord/LB
Norddeutsche Landesbank
Girozentrale
Georgplatz 1,3000 Hannover
1
Tel: (010 49) 511-103-0,
103-2133/4

Sal Oppenheim jr & Cie
Privatbankiers seit 1789
Bockenheimer Landstrasse 20
6000 Frankfurt 17
Tel: (010 49) 69-7134-0

Ost-West Handelsbank
Aktiengesellschaft
Stephanstrasse 1
6000 Frankfurt 1
Tel: (010 49) 69-2168-0
Geldhandel

Pfalzische Hypothekenbank
Aktiengesellschaft
An der Rheinschanze 1
6700 Ludwigshafen/Rhein
Tel: (010 49) 621-5997-312
Borse direkt
Telefax: 5997-295

Nikko Securities Co
(Deutschland) GmbH (The)
Mainzer Landstrasse 46
(Frankfurter Buro Center)
6000 Frankfurt 1
Tel: (010 49) 69-720041

Rheinhyp
Rheinische Hypothekenbank
Aktiengesellschaft
Taunustor 3
6000 Frankfurt 1
Tel: (010 49) 69-2382-1

Royal Bank of Canada
Aktiengesellschaft vorm
Burgardt
Nottebohm Bank
AG (The)
Gutleutstrasse 85
6000 Frankfurt 1
Tel: (010 49) 69-273070

Salomon Brothers AG
Grobe Gallusstrasse 10-14
6000 Frankfurt 1
Tel: (010 49) 69-20241

Schroder, Munchmeyer,
Hengst & Co
Friedensstrasse 6-10
6000 Frankfurt 1
Tel: (010 49) 69-2179-0

Schweizerische
Bankgesellschaft
(Deutschland)
Aktiengesellschaft
Bockenheimer Landstrasse 23
6000 Frankfurt 17
Tel: (010 49) 69-7143-1

Schweizerische Kreditanstalt
(Deutschland) AG
Kaiserstrasse 30
6000 Frankfurt 1
Tel: (010 49) 69-2691-1

Schweizerische Kreditanstalt
(Deutschland) AG
Kaiserstrasse 30
Ulmenstrasse 30
6000 Frankfurt 1
Tel: (010 49) 69-71401-0
Allgemein, 724130-3
Borsenhandel

SGZ Bank
Sudwestdeutsche
Genossenschafts-Zentralbank
AG
Bockenheimer Analge 46
6000 Frankfurt 1
Tel: (010 49) 69-7139-0

Societe Generale – Elsassische
Bank & Co
Mainzer Landstrasse 36
6000 Frankfurt 1
Tel: (010 49) 69-7174-0

Stadtsparkasse Frankfurt am
Main
Hasengasse 4
6000 Frankfurt 1
Tel: (010 49) 69-2170-305

Tokai Bank Ltd (The)
Filiale Frankfurt/Main
Bockenheimer Landstrasse
51-53
6000 Frankfurt 17
Tel: (010 49) 69-717246

Trinkaus & Burkhardt KGaA
Niederlassung
Frankfurt/Main
Guiollettstrasse 24
6000 Frankfurt 1
Tel: (010 49) 69-71903-0

Union-Investment-
Gesellschaft mbH
Mainzer Landstrasse 47
6000 Frankfurt 1
Tel: (010 49) 69-2567-1

Vereins und Westbank AG
Hauptfiliale Frankfurt
Grobe Gallusstrasse 18
Tel: (010 49) 69-290031

Warburg-Brinckmann, Wirtz
& Co
Bankhaus M M
Niederlassung
Frankfurt/Main
Liegigstrasse 6
6000 Frankfurt 1
Tel: (010 49) 69-71006-0;
7100614 wahrend der
Borsenzeit

Westdeutsche Landesbank
Girozentrale
Taunusanlage 3
6000 Frankfurt 1
Tel: (010 49) 69-2579-1

Wiesbadener Volksbank eG
Friedrichstrasse 20
6200 Wiesbaden 1
Tel: (010 49) 6121-267-0

Wurttembergische
Kommunale Landesbank –
Girozentrale –
Lautenschlagerstrasse 20
7000 Stuttgart 1
Buro: Goethestrasse 2
6000 Frankfurt 1
Tel: (010 49) 711-2049-0
Stuttgart
(010 49) 69-28096406 Frankfurt

Yamaichi International
(Deutschland) GmbH
Feuerbachstrasse 26
6000 Frankfurt 1
Tel: (010 49) 69-71020

Sources of General Background Information, Industry Sector Information and Trade Contacts

UK Addresses
German Chamber of Industry
and Commerce in the UK
12-13 Suffolk Street
London SW1Y 4HG
Tel: 01-930 7251

Embassy of the Federal
Republic of Germany
23 Belgrave Square
London SW1X 8PZ
Tel: 01-235 5033

Addresses in the Federal Republic of Germany
British Embassy
Friedrich-Ebert-Allee 77
5300 Bonn 1
Tel: (010 49) 228-234061
Telex: 886887 BRINF D

Deutscher Industrie-und
Handelstag (DIHT)
(Federation of German
Chambers of Industry and
Commerce)
Adenaueralle 148
5300 Bonn
Tel: (010 49) 228-104-0
Telex: 886805 dihtd

There are a large number of
regional chambers of
commerce. Some of the main
ones are listed here:

Industrie-und
Handelskammer Bonn
Bonner Talweg 17
5300 Bonn
Tel: (010 49) 228-22840
Telex: 8869306

Industrie-und
Handelskammer
Frankfurt/Main
Borsenplatz
6000 Frankfurt/Main 1
Tel: (010 49) 611-21971
Telex: 411255

Industrie-und
Handelskammer zu Kolm
Unter Sachsenhausen 10-26
5000 Cologne 1
Tel: (010 49) 221-16401
Telex: 8881400

Sources of Investment and Trade Advice, Assistance and Information

Germany does not have a
central organisation which
offers assistance with inward
investment. There is a
Government department in
each of the eleven federal
states which assists
companies interested in
setting up overseas.

Federal Ministry for Regional
Planning, Building and Urban
Development
Deichmanns Aue
PO Box 250001
5300 Bonn 2
Tel: (010 49) 228-3371
Telex: 0885462

Federal Office for Trade and
Industry
Frankfurter Str 29-31
6236 Eschborn 1
Tel: (010 49) 6196 4041
Telex: 0415603 BAGEWI

Federation of all German
Employers' Association
Gustav-Heinemann-Ufer 72
5000 Cologne
Tel: (010 49) 221-37950
Telex: 8881466

Federation of German
Industries
Gustav-Heinmann-Ufer 84-88
PO Box 510548
5000 Cologne 51
Tel: (010 49) 221-3708-1
Telex: 8882601

Ministry of Foreign Trade of
the GDR
Unter den Linden 44/60
1080 Berlin
Tel: (010 49) 30-230
Telex: 1152361

Baden-Wurttemberg
Ministry of Economic Affairs
and Technology
Theodor-Heuss-Strasse 4
7000 Stuttgart 1
Tel: (010 49) 711 123 2382
Telex: 723931

Stiftung Aussenwirtschaft
Baden-Wurttemberg
Trade and Investment Office
Scloss Str 25
7000 Stuttgart 1
Tel: (010 49) 711-227879
Fax: (010 49) 711-2278722
Telex: (17) 7111141

Bavaria
Bavarian Ministry of
Economics
Industrial Location Advisory
Service
Prinzregertenstr 28 28
8000 Munich 22
Tel: (010 49) 89-21622642
Fax: (010 49) 89-21622760
Telex: 523759

Berlin
Berlin Economic
Development Corporation
Budapester Str 1
1000 Berlin 30
Tel: (010 49) 30-2636213

Bremen
Wirtschaftsforderung-
sgesellschaft Der Freien Han-
sestadt Bremen GmbH
Rembertiring 2
2800 Bremen 1
Tel: (010 49) 421-328275
Telex: 245079

Hamburg
Hamburg Business
Development Corp
Hamburger Str 11
2000 Hamburg 76
Tel: (010 49) 40-2270190
Fax: (010 49) 40-227 0190
Telex: 2165 210 HWFN

Hessen
The HLT Group
Box 3107
Abraham Lincoln Str 38-42
HLT Building
6200 Wiesbaden
Tel: (010 49) 6121-7741
Fax: (010 49) 6121-774265
Telex: 4186127

Lower Saxony
Niedersachsiches
Ministerium fur Wirtschaft,
Technologie und Verkehr
Friedrichswall 1
3000 Hannover 1
Tel: (010 49) 511-1206526
Fax: (010 49) 511-1206430
Telex: 923530

North-Rhine Westphalia
Economic Development
Corporation for North-Rhine
Westphalia
Kavalleriestrasse 8-10
4000 Dusseldorf 1
Tel: (010 49) 211-130000
Telex: 8587 830

Rhineland-Palatinate
Rheinland-Pfalzische
Gesellschaft fur
Wirtschaftsforderung mbH
Erthalstr 1
6500 Mainz
Tel: (010 49) 6131-632066
Telex: 4187643

Saarland
Saarland Economic
Development Unit
Bismark Strasse 39-41
6600 Saarbrucken
Tel: (010 49) 681-687990

Schleswig-Holstein
Economy Development
Company of
Schleswig-Holstein
Lorentzendamm 43
2300 Kiel 1
Tel: (010 49) 431-51446

*Professional
Associations*

Accountancy
Institut der Wirtschaftsprufer
in Deutschlande eV
Tersteegenstrasse 14
4000 Dusseldorf 30

Wirtschaftspruferkammer
Tersteegenstrasse 14
4000 Dusseldorf 30

Banking
Bundesverband Deutscher
Banken eV
(Federal Association of
German Banks)
Mohrenstrasse 35/41
PO Box 100246
5000 Cologne

Consultancy
Bunsverband Deutscher
Unternehemsberater BDU eV
Friedrich-Wilhelm-Strasse 2
5300 Bonn 1
Tel: (010 49) 228-238055
Telex: 8869494 BDU D

Insurance
Gesamtverband der
Deutschen
Vericherungswirtschaft eV
(GDV)
(German Insurance
Association)
Ebertplatz 1
5000 Cologne 1
Tel: (010 49) 221-7764-0
Telex: 08 8852 55

Trade Associations

General Industry
Federation of German
Industries
Gustav-Heinemann-Ufer
84-88
5000 Cologne 51

Bundesverband Druck eV
Biebricher Allee 79
Postf 1869
6200 Wiesbaden 1

Bundersverband der
Pharmazeutischen Industrie
eV
Karlstr 19-21
Postf 11 02 51
6000 Frankfurt/Main 1

Bundersvereinigung der
Deutschen
Ernahrungsindustrie eV
(BVE)
Rheinallee 18
5300 Bonn 2

Gesamtverband der
Deutschen
Aluminiumindindustrie in
der Wirtschaftsvereinigung
Metalle eV
Postf 87 06
4000 Dusseldorf 1

Gesamtverband der
Deutschen
Schwermetallindustrie
Tersteegenstr 28
4000 Dusseldorf 30

Gesamtverband der
Textilindustrie in der
Bundesrepublik Deutschland
– Gesamttextil – eV
Schaumainkai 87
Haus der Textilindustrie
6000 Frankfurt/Main 70

Verband der
Automobilindustrie eV
Westendstr 61
Postf 17 05 63
6000 Frankfurt/Main 1

Verband der Chemischen
Industrie eV
Karlstr 19-21
6000 Frankfurt
Main 1
Postf 11 19 43
6000 Frankfurt/Main 11

Zentralverband
Elektrotechnik – und –
Elektronikindustrie (ZVEI) eV
Stresemannallee 19
Postf 70 12 61
6000 Frankfurt/Main 70

Company Financial and Product Information

Directories

British Firms in Germany
Produced by the British
Chamber of Commerce
Cologne
Covers the majority of British
companies with subsidiaries,
representatives or branches in
Germany

Deutsch Amerikanische
Geschatfsbeziehunger
German American Business
Contacts
Produced by Verlag
Hoppenstedt, Darmstadt
Covers company details such
as addresses, turnover, etc
and provides an alphabetical
listing of American associate
companies with the names of
German company
connections

Deutsches Borsenadressbuch
fur Banken, Handel und
Industrie
German Exchange Directory
for Banks, Trade and Industry
Produced by Herausgegeben
vom Verlag, Deutsches
Borsenadressbuch, Hamburg
Mainly in German, although
many of the headings are in
English and French. Covers
German chambers of
commerce overseas, German
stock exchanges, companies
which are traded on the
bourses of Germany,
Luxembourg, Switzerland
and Austria, banks
worldwide plus insurance
and commodity exchanges

German Subsidiary
Companies in the United
Kingdom
Produced by the German
Chamber of London Industry
and Commerce in the UK.
Provides an alphabetical
listing of firms and their
German parent connections

Grossen 500 (Die)
Produced by Herman
Luchterhand Verlag,
Neuwied
Looseleaf company directory
covering the top 500
companies and a ranking of
top banks and finance
houses. Financial data and
ownership data is provided

Handbuch der deutschen
Aktiengesellschaften
(Handbook of German Public
Limited Companies)
Published by Hoppendstedt
Provides information on
approximately 2300 quoted
and unquoted public limited
companies whose shares are
traded on German stock
exchanges officially or in
regulated unofficial dealing.
Reports are issued in booklet
form on a weekly basis

Handbuch der Gross –
unternehmen
Produced by Hoppenstedt
The 1987 (34th edition) covers
nearly 22 000 German
companies with at least 100
employees, capital of over
DM 500 000 or a turnover
exceeding DM 10 million.
Provides financial and
shareholder information, plus
a register of firms according to
their industry sector and
product sections

Hoppenstedt Charts
Charts containing stock
exchange names, ticker
symbols, prices for securities
in Germany, USA and other
major economies

Hoppenstedt Borsenfuhrer
(Hoppenstedt's Stock Guide)
Analysis of the most
important quoted German
public limited companies.
Quarterly

Kompass Deutschland
Produced by Kompass
Deutschland Verlags u
Vertriebsges mbH
1987/88 edition covers 34 000
companies. Provides
company details plus product
information

Mittelstansische
Unternnehemen
Covers mainly medium sized
companies. Approximately
21 500 companies with
between 20-100 staff or
turnover between DM 2-10
million. A classified index in
the English edition is
provided

Nicht Notierten Deutchen
Aktiengesellschaften (Die)
Produced by Hoppenstedt
Provides detailed information
on the leading German AGs,
including financial details. 2
volumes

Sailing Aktienfuhrer
(Sailing Share Guide)
Published by Hoppenstedt
Contains reports on the 485
German and 176 foreign
public limited companies
listed for trading and
regulated unofficial dealings
on German stock exchanges.
Annual

Seibt Export Directory of
Germany
Produced by Seibt-Verlag, Dr
Artur Seibt GmbH

Wer Gehort zu Wem – Who
Owns Whom
Produced every three years
by Commerzbank
Provides details on the
shareholders and the size of
their shareholding in 10 000
companies. Both foreign and
German shareholders are
included

Economic and Market Statistical Data

Market Research Organisations

Arbeitskreis Deutscher Markforschungsinstitut
Burgschmietstrasse 2
8500 Nuremberg
Tel: (010 49) 911-395-1

Basis Research GmbH
Bockenheimer Landstrasse 98
6000 Frankfurt/Main
Tel: (010 49) 69-747941
Telex: 0414950 PRSVC D
Parent company: J Walter
Thompson Group/MRB

Roland Berger & Partner
GmbH
Arabellastrasse 33
8000 Munich 81
Tel: (010 49) 89-9223-0
Telex: 522761
Parent company: Roland
Berger International

Burke International Markt
furschungsgesellschaft
Friedrich Ebert Anlage 44
6000 Frankfurt 1
Tel: (010 49) 69-154050
Telex: 4189202
Parent company: Burke
Research Services Group
Member of ESOMAR

Contact – Census GmbH
Lyonerstrasse 11A
6000 Frankfurt/Main 71
Tel: (010 49) 611-666841
Telex: 13255
Parent company: GFK
Nurnberg

Emnid Institut GmbH & Co
Bodelschwingstrasse 23-25a
4800 Bielefeld 1
Tel: (010 49) 521-26001/0
Telex: 932833 EMNID D
Member of the Gallup
organisation

Field Research Schreiber
GmbH
Strotheweg 82-84a
Postfach 1165
4531 Lotte
Tel: (010 49) 541-125091
Telex: 94937

GFK Nurnberg
Burgschmietstrasse 2
8500 Nuremberg
Tel: (010 49) 911-395-1
Telex: 622028
Parent company: GFK GmbH
One of the world's leading
market research organisations
Member of ADM, ESOMAR

IFAK – Institut GmbH & Co
Georg-Ohm Strasse 1
Postfach 631223
6204 Taunusstein 1
Tel: (010 49) 6128-71071
Telex: 4182732
Member of ADM, BVM,
ESOMAR

IVE GmbH Research
International
Grindelberg 5
2000 Hamburg 13
Tel: (010 49) 40-441190
Telex: 2161901
Parent company: Research
International

Marplan
Forschungsgesellschaft
GmbH
Marktplatz 9
6050 Offenbach
Tel: (010 49) 69-80591
Telex: 4152642 MATP D
Parent company: Research
International

AC Nielsen Co GmbH
Ludwig-Laudmann Strasse
405
6000 Frankfurt/Main 90
Tel: (010 49) 69-79380
Telex: 412031
Parent company: AC Nielsen
(USA)

Prognos AG
Unter Sachsenhausen 37
5000 Cologne 1
Tel: (010 49) 221-16027-0
Telefax: (010 49) 221-133822
Parent company: Coopers &
Lybrand
Branches of Prognos in Basle,
Switzerland and California,
USA

Prognos AG
Nurnberger Strasse 68/69
1000 Berlin 30
Tel: (010 49) 30-2112099

Organisations Providing Economic and Statistical Data

Deutsche Bundesbank
Issues monthly and annual
reports. Publishes monthly
financial statistics in
Monatsberichte der
Deutscher Bundesbank

Deutsche Delegation der
Arbeitsgemeinschaft der
Deutschen Wertpapierborsen
2000 Hamburg 11
Tel: (010 49) 40-367444
Publishes financial
information on individual
stock exchanges.

IFO Institut fuer
Wirtschaftsforschung
Postchingerstr 5
Postfach 86 04 60
8000 Munich 86
Research Institute provides
economic analysis and
forecasts of GNP and its
components in the Federal
Republic of Germany

W Kohlhammer GmbH
(Government Publisher)
Bahnofsplatz 2
Stuttgart/Mainz 6500 42
Publishes: Survey of German
Federal Statistics
Economy and Statistics

Statistisches Bundesamt
Verlag W Kohlhammer
GmbH
Philipp-Reis-Strasse 3
Postfach 42 11 20
6500 Mainz 42
Tel: (010 49) 6121-752405
Publishes a wide range of
economic statistics covering
different industrial sectors in
Germany, import and export
data. Publications include
Aktienmarkte, a monthly
publication covering share
markets. One of the main
sources of statistics is
Statisches Jahrbuch fuer die
Bundesrepublik Deutschland
(The Federal Republic
Statistical Yearbook). Another
important source is Wirtschaft
und Statistik (official monthly
statistical report)

Government departments,
such as the Ministry of
Economics, publish a variety
of statistical and economic
publications.

Large commercial banks, eg
Deutsche Bank, Dresdner,
Commerzbank, Deutsche
Bundesbank, provide
extensive investment research
services and statistical data on
German stock exchanges.

Publications

Directories
Addresses Foreign Trade of
the GDR
Published by the Chamber of
Foreign Trade of the GDR
Provides addresses of
centralised trade authorities,
foreign trade enterprises,
GDR embassies abroad and
other information relevant to
German trade

Anschriften fuer die
Aussenwirtschaft
(Guide to Foreign Trade)
Published by Deutscher
Wirtschaftsdienst, Cologne
Loose-leaf book with monthly
supplements. Lists diplomatic
foreign missions in Germany
and German diplomatic
missions abroad plus other
organisations and official
bodies relevant to foreign
commerce

Taschenbuch des
Oeffentlichen Lebens
(Handbook of Public and
Private Institutions)
Published by Festland Verlag
Bonn, Bonn
Lists public and private
institutions of economic and
political importance in the
Federal Republic of Germany
and Berlin

Verband Behorden
Organisationer der Wirtschaft
Published by Verlag
Hoppenstedt, Darmstadt
Lists over 13 000 government
trade agencies, trade
associations and other
organisations in Germany

Major Newspapers
Berliner Morgenpost (Berlin)
Daily

Frankfurter Allgemeine
Zeitung (Frankfurt/Main)
Daily. Financial pages and
economic reports provided.

Handelsblatt
Daily

Munchner Merkur (Munich)
Daily

Tagesspiegel (Der) (Berlin)
Daily

Welt (Die) (Bonn)
Daily

Westdeutsche Allgemeine
(Essen)
Daily

Journals and Periodicals
Absatzwirtschaft (Die)
Published by Handelsblatt
GmbH, Dusseldorf
Covers advertising and
marketing. Monthly

Berlin Wirtschaft (Die)
Published by Industrie-und
Handelskammer zu Berlin,
Berlin
Covers local, national and
foreign trade, the economy
and finance, trade fairs, etc.
Fortnightly

dfz Wirtschaftsmagazin
Published by Deutscher
Fachverlag GmbH, Frankfurt,
Main
Covers retailing, wholesaling
and marketing. Monthly

Made in Europe
Published by Made in Europe
Marketing Organisation
Gmbh & Co KG,
Frankfurt/Main
Covers general consumer
products. Monthly

Manager Magazine and
Capital
Both published by WestlB,
Dusseldorf
Financial magazines
particularly relevant to the
needs of foreign investors.
Monthly

Markt & Wirtschaft
Published by IHK zu Koln,
Cologne
Covers regional trade and
industries. Monthly

Welthandel
Published by HPB
Welthandel-Verlag GmbH,
Hamburg
Covers international contacts
and trade. Bimonthly

Wirtschaftswoche
Covers stock prices and
general economic topics.
Weekly

For further listings of publications you can consult Stammleitfaden fuer Presse und Werbung, Media Daten, and Benn's Press Directory (International).

Greece

Sources of Economic, Stock Market Information and Investment Research Services

Banks

Central Bank
Banque de Grece
(Bank of Greece)
PO Box 105
21 Venizelos Avenue
10250 Athens
Tel: (010 30) 1-3201111
Telex: 215102

Greek Banks in London
Bank of Crete
8 Moorgate
London EC2R 6DD
Tel: 01-606 7971

National Bank of Greece
City Branch
50 St Mary's Avenue
London EC3
Tel: 01-626 3222

204/208 Tottenham Court Road
London W1P 9LA
Tel: 01-637 0876

6-28 Queensway
London W2 3RX
Tel: 01-229 1413

Banks in Greece
Agricultural Bank of Greece
23 Panepistimiou Street
10564 Athens
Tel: (010 30) 1-3230521-27
Telex: 215810

Commercial Bank of Greece
PO Box 16
11 Sophocleous Street
10235 Athens
Tel: (010 30) 1-3210911
Telex: 216545-9

Credit Bank
40 Stadiou Street
10252 Athens
Tel: (010 30) 1-3245111
Telex: 218691

Ergobank SA
36 Panepistimiou Street
10679 Athens
Tel: (010 30) 1-3601011-9
Telex: 218826 ERBA GR

National Bank of Greece SA
86 Eolou Street
Cotzia Square
10232 Athens
Tel: (010 30) 1-3210-411
Telex: 021-4931/8

Stockbrokers
Athens Stock Exchange (The)
10 Sophocleous Street
10559 Athens
Tel: (010 30) 1-3211301
Telex: 215820 BURS GR

Members (32 as at May 1988)
Caramanof A
4 Sophocleous
Tel: (010 30) 1-3213925

Catsoulis G
9 Aristidou
Tel: (010 30) 1-3213947

Chrissochoides G
8 Sophocleous
Tel: (010 30) 1-3213913

Cointalexis P
7-9 Sophocleous
Tel: (010 30) 1-3217196

Comninos N
7-9 Sophocleous
Tel: (010 30) 1-3218847

Depolas L
9 Aristidou
Tel: (010 30) 1-3213286

Devletoglou N
5 Sophocleous
Tel: (010 30) 1-3244615

Giannopoulos A
7-9 Sophocleous
Tel: (010 30) 1-3219188

Gravanis D
8 Sophocleous
Tel: (010 30) 1-3218158

Hadellis E
7-9 Sophocleous
Tel: (010 30) 1-3213920

Hadjelias B
7-9 Sophocleous
Tel: (010 30) 1-3213303

Hadjelias M
7-9 Sophocleous
Tel: (010 30) 1-3213303

Kotzambassis A
41 Stadiou
Tel: (010 30) 1-3211801

Kyranis M
9 Aristidou
Tel: (010 30) 1-3218723

Lavrentakis S
9 Aristidou
Tel: (010 30) 1-3218662

Manouilides A
1 Sophocleous
Tel: (010 30) 1-3217806

Mavrikis J
10 Sophocleous
Tel: (010 30) 1-3213949

Pantelakis J
9 Aristidou
Tel: (010 30) 1-3218577

Pantelides E
1 Sophocleous
Tel: (010 30) 1-3214214

Pantelides P
4 Sophocleous
Tel: (010 30) 1-3215777

Pededekas C
5 Sophocleous
Tel: (010 30) 1-3211424

Pervanas G
7-9 Sophocleous
Tel: (010 30) 1-3251875

Petropoulakis E
8 Sophocleous
Tel: (010 30) 1-3213937

Portalakis Z
1a Pesmazoglou
Tel: (010 30) 1-3214830

Raymondos P
10 Sophocleous
Tel: (010 30) 1-3213880

Sarros N
7-9 Sophocleous
Tel: (010 30) 1-3219963

Siafakas A
9 Aristidou
Tel: (010 30) 1-3242221

Sotiriadis T
6 Aristidou
Tel: (010 30) 1-3222166

Theodorides C
6 Aristidou
Tel: (010 30) 1-3226321

Tsekouras D
1 Permazoglou
Tel: (010 30) 1-3215275

Tzemos P
5 Sophocleous
Tel: (010 30) 1-3219441

Voilis P
7-9 Sophocleous
Tel: (010 30) 1-3241280

Sources of General Background Information, Industry Sector Information and Trade Contacts

UK Addresses
Embassy of Greece
11a Holland Park
London W11 3TP
Tel: 01-727 8040

Greek Embassy
National Tourist Organisation
195 Regent Street
London W1
Tel: 01-734 5997

Addresses in Greece
American-Hellenic Chamber
of Commerce
17 Valaoritou
10671 Athens
Tel: (010 30) 1-3618385
Telex: 223063 ANCH GR
and
Hellenic-American Chamber
of Commerce in New York
29 Broadway Str
New York
NY 10006
Tel: (010 1) 212-9438594

Athens Chamber of
Commerce and Industry
7-9 Academias Street
10671 Athens
Tel: (010 30) 1-3624280
Telex: 215707 EBEA GR

British Embassy
1 Ploutarchou Street
139 Athens
Information Department:
2 Karageorgi Servias
Syndagma Square
125 Athens
Tel: (010 30) 1-7236211

British Hellenic Chamber of
Commerce
4 Valaoritou Street
10675 Athens
Tel: (010 30) 1-3620168

Chamber of Small and
Medium Sized Industries
18 Academias Street
10559 Athens
Tel: (010 30) 1-3630253
Telex: 210976 VEA
and
27 Aristotelous
54624 Thessaloniki
Tel: (010 30) 31-275255
Offices also in Agrinio, Chios,
Drama, Ionnina, Iraklion,
Kalamata, Kavala, Kerkyra,
Komotini, Larissa, Mitilini,
Patra, Pireas, Samos and
Volos.

Economic Chamber of
Commerce
188 Sygrou Avenue
17671 Athens
Tel: (010 30) 1-9523348
Telex: 218355 OEE GR

International Chamber of
Commerce
27 Kanigos
10682 Athens
Tel: (010 30) 1-3610879

Professional Chamber of
Athens
44 Panepistimiou 1
10679 Athens
Tel: (010 30) 1-3601651

Technical Chamber of Greece
4 Karageorgi Servias
10248 Athens
Tel: (010 30) 1-3244842
Telex: 218374 TEE GR

Union of Chamber of
Commerce and Industry in
Greece
7-9 Akadimias
10671 Athens
Tel: (010 30) 1-3624060
Telex: 215707 EBEA GR

Sources of Investment and Trade Advice, Assistance and Information

Athens Chamber of
Commerce
7-9 Academias Street
Athens
Tel: (010 30) 1-3602411

Customs and Excise Office
6 Marni Street
Athens
Tel: (010 30) 1-5223910

Directorate of Foreign
Commerce
Ministry of Commerce
Pl Kaningos
10181 Athens
Tel: (010 30) 1-3628368
Telex: 215282 YPEM GR

Greek Export Promotion
Organisation
1 Mitropoleos
10557 Athens
Tel: (010 30) 1-3247010
Telex: 220201 HOPE GR

Hellenic Industrial
Development Bank (ETBA)
18 Panepistimiou Street
10672 Athens
Tel: (010 30) 1-3237981
Telex: 215203 ETVA GR

Ministry of Foreign Affairs
(Foreign Trade Department)
Leoforos Vass Sophias 5
1067 Athens
Tel: (010 30) 1-3601281
Telex: 216593

National Tourist Organisation
2 Amerikis
10564 Athens
Tel: (010 30) 1-3234727
Telex: 215832 GRTA GR

Company Financial and Product Information

Directories
Greek Export Directory
Published by the Athens
Chamber of Commerce and
Industry
Provides a list of Greek
exporters. Written in Greek,
English, French and German

Hellenic Export Directory
Who is Who Business
Directory
Published by Compu-Type
SA, Athens
Provides entries for Greek
companies grouped by
product area. Information
provided is address,
telephone, telex and product
details

ICAP Financial Directory of
Greek Companies (The)
Published by ICAP Hellas SA,
Athens
The 1987 edition contained
12000 active enterprises
classified by industry sector.
It contains information on
products, financial services,
agents and importers. Details
on companies includes
financial data, number of
employees and lines of
business

Products of Greece
Published by Link
International Ltd, Athens
Provides a listing of over 1500
Greek companies and their
products and services

Yearbook of the Athens Stock
Exchange
Published by the Athens
Stock Exchange
Provides an alphabetical list
of Greek companies, together
with their address, number of
employees, directors, activity
and brief financial details.
Companies are grouped by
industry sector

Professional Associations

Banking
Hellenic Banks Association
Stadiou 10
133 Athens
Tel: (010 30) 1-3233278
Telex: 223743

Marketing
Hellenic Institute of
Marketing
Vas Sofias 27
10774 Athens
Tel: (010 30) 1-7235545-6
Telex: HMA 8812

Trade Associations

General Industry
General Confederation of
Small and Medium Sized
Businesses and Craftsmen of
Greece
Tzortz St Quaning's Square 10
Athens
Tel: (010 30) 1-3616600

Hellenic Organisation of
Small and Medium Size
Industries and Handicrafts
Xenias & Evrou
11528 Athens
Tel: (010 30) 1-7701101
Telex: 218819 HMIH GR

Syndesmos Ellinon
Viomichanon (SEV)
Federation of Greek
Industries
Xenofontos 5
118 Athens
Tel: (010 30) 1-3237325
Telex: 216247

Association of the Greek
Cement Industry
Plateia Karitsi 10
10561 Athens
Tel: (010 30) 1-3237636

Enosis Eisagogeon Chimikon
Proionton
(Importers of Chemical
Products)
Ymittou 20
18540 Peiraia
Tel: (010 30) 1-4179708

Enosis Ellinon Efopliston
(Union of Greek Shipowners)
Sotiros 12
Athens
Tel: (010 30) 1-4117919

Enosis Ellinon
Sidiroviomichanon
(Greek Iron and Steel Union)
Pl Loudovikou Meg
Athens
Tel: (010 30) 1-4178412

Enosis Panellinos
Viomichanon
Khostoyfantourgon
(Panhellenic Union of Textile
Manufacturers)
Xenofantos 5
118 Athens
Tel: (010 30) 1-3232046

Hellenic Aerosol Association
Souri Street
Peristeri
Athens
Tel: (010 30) 1-5741411

Hellenic Association of
Ready-Made Clothes
Manufacturers
Voulis 7
10562 Athens
Tel: (010 30) 1-3223979

Panellinios Omospondia
Somateion Engatastaton
Ilektrologon
(Electrical Contractors
Association)
Pl Eleftherias 2
10553 Athens
Tel: (010 30) 1-3211630

Panellinios Syndesmos
Viomichanon Keramopoion
(Ceramics Association)
Marni 8
103 Athens

Shipping Chamber of Greece
Akti Miaouli 85
18538 Piraieus
Tel: (010 30) 1-4118811
Telex: 212857

Syndesmos Anonymon
Etairon Kai (EPE)
(Companies Association)
Panepistimiou 16
Athens
Tel: (010 30) 1-3620274

Syndesmos Eisagoger
Anitprosopon Aftokiniton
(Motor Vehicle Industry and
Wholesale Association)
Logoninitzi 42
Athens
Tel: (010 30) 1-35798

Syndesmos Ergolabon
Ilektrikon Ergo
(Electrical Contractors
Association)
Pl Eleftherias 2
Athens
Tel: (010 30) 1-3210040

Syndesmos Etairon Emborias
Petrelaioeidon en Elladi
(Motor Vehicle Retail
Association)
Phetidos 4
Athens
Tel: (010 30) 1-7245172

Economic and Market Statistical Data

Market Research Organisations

EMRB (Hellas) Ltd
20 Voukourestiou Street
10671 Athens
Tel: (010 30) 1-3625807
Telex: 216768 SPRC GR
Parent company: MRB
International (JWT, London)

ICAP Hellas SA
64 Vas Sophias Avenue
11528 Athens
Tel: (010 30) 1-7247884
Telex: 215668
Parent company: Credit
Bank, Athens

KEME – Marketing Research
Centre Hellas Ltd
24 Hippodamou Street
Pangrati
11635 Athens
Tel: (010 30) 1-7018082
Telex: 218602
Parent company: MEMRB Ltd
(Middle Eastern Marketing
Research Bureau), Cyprus

Marketing Analysis Ltd
10 Dimitressa
11528 Athens
Tel: (010 30) 1-7239622
Telex: 218344 IBS GR

Market Research Centre Ltd
(The)
10 Georgoula Street
Psychiko
11524 Athens
Tel: (010 30) 1-6922767
Telex: 218446

Metrix Research Centre SA
105-107 Vas Sofias Avenue
11521 Athens
Tel: (010 30) 1-6440661
Telex: 218807 LEOU GR
Parent company: JN Leoussis
Advertising SA

AC Nielsen Hellas Ltd
2 Harokopou Street
17671 Kallithea
Athens
Tel: (010 30) 1-9588771
Telex: 219098
Parent company: AC Nielsen
Company (USA)

Research International Hellas
25 Alexandroupoleos Street
11527 Athens
Tel: (010 30) 1-7753001
Telex: 215668
Parent company: Research
International

Organisations Providing Economic and Statistical Data

Athens Stock Exchange
Stock market statistics are
available in the Stock Market
Year Book, Gazette of Stock
Market Prices and the Annual
Bulletin.

Bank of Greece
Athens
Publishes a monthly statistical
bulletin

Commercial Bank of Greece
11 Sophocleous Street
10235 Athens
Publishes Commercial Bank
of Greece: Economic Bulletin,
quarterly. Free of charge

National Investment
Company
(Part of the National Bank of
Greece)
Kouleniou 1
10559 Athens
Tel: (010 30) 1-3228536
Telex: 214931
Provides stock market
statistics

National Statistical Service of
Greece
14-16 Lycourgou Street
12 Athens
Tel: (010 30) 1-3249-302
Telex: 21674 ESYE GR
This organisation comes
under the Ministry of
National Economy and
consists of the Central
Statistical Survey, statistical
services of each Ministry, and
fifty statistical field offices
located in capital towns of
each department of Greece.
The library of the NSS holds
all the publications of the
service and of other Greek
organisations. Statistical
publications are also available
in Greek embassies overseas.
Publications include:
Statistical Yearbook of Greece
Concise Statistical Yearbook
Monthly Statistical Bulletin
Annual Industrial Survey
Foreign Trade of Greece

Publications

Directories
American-Hellenic Chamber
of Commerce Business
Directory
Published by the
American-Hellenic Chamber
of Commerce, Athens.
Provides an alphabetical list
of members and USA firms
established or represented in
Greece

British-Hellenic Chamber of
Commerce Business Directory
of Members
Published by the
British-Hellenic Chamber of
Commerce, Athens
Provides an alphabetical
listing of over 7000 member
companies with details of
products, addresses, names
of directors etc

Greek Shipping Directory
Published by Greek Shipping
Publications Co Ltd, Piraeus
Provides full details of all
Greek vessels and a listing of
shipowning companies,
managers and agents in
Piraeus, London and New
York

Major Newspapers
Akropolis
Daily

Avriani
Daily

Dimoprasiaka Nea o Kosmos
Daily

Eleftheri Ora
Daily

Emporikon Vima
Daily

Ephimeris Diakirixeon
Daily

Ephimeris Dimoprasion Kai
Pleistiriasmon
Daily

Express
Daily

Geniki Dimoprasion
Daily

Icho Ton Dimoprasion
Daily

Imerissia
Daily

Kathimerini
Daily

Kerdos
Daily

Naftemboriki
Daily

Nea Imerissia Ephimeris
Diakirixeon & Dimoprassion
Daily

Ta Nea
Daily

Journals and Periodicals
Broker (The)
Published by Akti Posidonos
1 Dimosthenous Piraeus
Monthly

Business and Finance
Publisher's address: 10
Fokidos Street, 608 Athens

Deltion
Published by the Greek
Chamber of Commerce.
Monthly

Economikos Tachydromos
Publisher's address: 3
Christou Lada, 10237 Athens.
Weekly

Economotechniki
Financial Journal
Publisher's address: 44 Koilis
Street, 309 Athens

Ellinikes Ependyseis
Investment Journal
Publisher's address: 7 Paleon
Patrou, Germanou Street,
Athens

Greece's Weekly
Publisher's address: 10
Fokiodos Street, 11526
Athens. Weekly

Greek-American Trade
Published by the
American-Hellenic Chamber
of Commerce, 17 Valaoritou
Street, Athens. Monthly

Trapeziki Economotechniki
Epitheorissis
Publisher's address: 44
Omirou Street, Athens.
Banking journal. Monthly

Viomihaniki Epitheorissis
Publisher's address: 4
Zalokosta Street, 10671
Athens.
Financial journal. Monthly

Hong Kong

Sources of Economic, Stock Market Information, and Investment Research Services

Banks

Central Bank
There is no central bank in
Hong Kong. The
Commissioner of Banking is
appointed to exercise general
supervision and control over
banks.
Commissioner of Banking
9th Floor
Queensway Government
Offices
66 Queensway
Tel: (010 852) 5-8622671

Hong Kong Banks in London
British Bank of the Middle
East
(Hong Kong & Shanghai
Banking Corp Branch)
Falcon House
Curzon Street
London W1Y 8AA
Tel: 01-493 8331

Hong Kong & Shanghai
Banking Corp
PO Box 199
99 Bishopgate
London EC2P 2LA
Tel: 01-638 2366
Telex: 885945 HSBCLO

James Capel Bankers
(Hong Kong & Shanghai
Banking Corp Branch)
7 Devonshire Square
London EC2M 4HN
Tel: 01-626 0566

Overseas Trust Bank
37 Mincing Lane
London EC3R 7BQ
Tel: 01-626 4167

Shanghai Commercial Bank
5 Bow Churchyard
London EC4M 9DH
Tel: 01-248 8291

Securities Houses in London

McIntosh Hamson Hoare
Govett
Pacific House
4 Broadgate
London EC2M 7LE
Tel: 01-374 7911

Major Hong Kong Banks

Bank of Credit and Commerce
Hong Kong Ltd
5/F1 Admiralty Centre
Tower 1
18 Harcourt Road
Tel: (010 852) 5-8226228

Bank of East Asia Ltd
PO Box 31
10 Des Voeux Road Central
Tel: (010 852) 5-8423200
Telex: 73017 HX

Dao Heng Bank Ltd
7-19 Bonham Strand East
Tel: (010 852) 5-447141

Far East Bank Ltd
16 Fl
Far East Consortium Building
121 Des Voeux Road Central
Tel: (010 852) 5-455222
    and
99-103 Queen's Road Central
Tel: (010 852) 5-455166

Hang Lung Bank Ltd
GPO Box 9572
3rd Floor
United Centre
95 Queensway
Tel: (010 852) 5-283300
Telex: 73755 HX; 73092 HX

Hang Seng Bank Ltd
GPO Box 2985
77 Des Voeux Road Central
Tel: (010 852) 5-8255111
Telex: 73311; 73323; 75225;
63030

Hong Kong and the Shanghai
Banking Corporation (The)
(Head Office)
1 Queen's Road Central
Tel: (010 852) 5-8221111
Telex: 73201 HKBG HX

Hua Chiao Commercial Bank
Ltd
88-98 Des Voeux Road Central
Hua Chiao Commercial
Building
Tel: (010 852) 5-429888
Telex: 83502 HCCB HX

Ka Wah Bank Ltd (The)
232 Des Voeux Central
Tel: (010 852) 5-457131
Telex: 74636 HWBNK HX
(General)

Liu Chong Hing Bank Ltd
GPO Box 2535
24 Des Voeux Road Central
Tel: (010 852) 5-8417417
Telex: HX 75700

Nanyang Commercial Bank
Ltd
Nanyang Commercial Bank
Building
151 Des Voeux Road Central
Tel: (010 852) 5-8520888
Telex: 73412 NANHO HX

Overseas Trust Bank Ltd
OTB Building
160 Gloucester Road
Tel: (010 852) 5-766657
Telex: 74545 Octob Hx
(General office)

Shanghai Commercial Bank
Ltd
12 Queen's Road Central
Tel: (010 852) 5-8415415
Telex: HX 73390

Sin Hua Trust Savings and
Commercial Bank Ltd
2-8 Wellington Street Central
Tel: (010 852) 5-213377

Standard Chartered Bank (CI)
Ltd
9/Fl Gloucester Tower
Tel: (010 852)
5-243037/8444283

Wing Lung Bank Ltd
45 Des Voeux Road Central
Tel: (010 852) 5-8268333
Telex: HX 73360; HX 73661

Wing on Bank Ltd
22 Des Voeux Road Central
Tel: (010 852) 5-251261

Stockbrokers

Stock Exchange

Most of the leading dealers in
Hong Kong are branches of
major international broking
firms. The list of brokers
below therefore features these
brokers plus a few of the large
Chinese brokers. Sung Hung
Kai Securities is one of the
largest Chinese firms and
James Capel and Vickers da
Costa are two of the largest
foreign brokers in terms of
volume of business.

Stock Exchange of Hong
Kong Ltd
Exchange Square
Tel: (010 852) 5-221122
Fax: (010 852) 5-8104475
Telex: 86839 STOEX HX

Hong Kong Futures Exchange
Ltd
Hutchison House
Harcourt Road
Tel: (010 852) 5-251005
Telex: 65236 HKFE HX

Principal Brokers (605 active registered brokers in 1986)

American Stockbrokers in Hong Kong
Bache Halsey Stuart (Hong Kong) Ltd
Shell House
9th Floor
24 Queens Road Central
Tel: (010 852) 5-229051

Kidder Peabody and Company Ltd
1707 Connaught Centre
Central
Tel: (010 852) 5-249291

Loeb, Rhoades, Hong Kong Ltd
401 Lane Crawford House
14 Des Voeux Road
Central
Tel: (010 852) 5-243030

Merrill Lynch, Pierce, Fenner and Smith
St George's Building
15th Floor
2 Ice House Street
Tel: (010 852) 5-249351

Shearson Hayden Stone Far East Ltd
St George's Building
7th Floor
2 Ice House Street
Tel: (010 852) 5-257261

White, Weld and Company Inc
2403 Connaught Centre
Connaught Road
Central
Tel: (010 852) 5-231046

Other Foreign Stockbrokers in Hong Kong
Astaire and Company Far East (British)
901 Hutchison House
10 Harcourt Road
Tel: (010 852) 5-230160

Bain and Company (Australian)
1501 Gammon House
Harcourt Road
Tel: (010 852) 5-255221

James Capel (Far East) Ltd (British)
South China Building
6th Floor
1-3 Wyndham Street
Tel: (010 852) 5-237156

W I Carr Sons and Company (Overseas) Ltd (British)
St George's Building
8th Floor
2 Ice House Street
Tel: (010 852) 5-255361

Cazenove and Company (Far East) (British)
808 Hutchison House
10 Harcourt Road
Tel: (010 852) 5-264211

Daiwa Securities International (Hong Kong) Ltd (Japanese)
Hang Chong Building
12th Floor
5 Queens Road
Central
Tel: (010 852) 5-250121

Hoare and Govett (Far East) Ltd (British)
3401 Connaught Centre
Connaught Road
Central
Tel: (010 852) 5-256291

Nikko Securities Company (Asia) Ltd (Japanese)
St George's Building
19th Floor
2 Ice House Street
Tel: (010 852) 5-248011

Nomura International (Hong Kong) Ltd (Japanese)
1412 Connaught Centre
Connaught Road
Central
Tel: (010 852) 5-255171

Richardson Securities of Canada (Pacific) Ltd (Canadian)
Bank of Canton Building
6th Floor
6 Des Voeux Road
Central
Tel: (010 852) 5-258211

Rowe and Pitman (Far East) Ltd (British)
1415 Connaught Centre
Connaught Road
Central
Tel: (010 852) 5-224123

Vickers da Costa and Company (Hong Kong) Ltd (British)
1211 Connaught Centre
Connaught Road
Central
Tel: (010 852) 5-251362

Yamaichi International (Hong Kong) Ltd (Japanese)
910 Hutchison House
10 Harcourt Road
Tel: (010 852) 5-248014

Chinese Brokers
Chin Tung Securities Ltd
Bank of America Tower
Central

Mok Ying Kie
Hong Kong Diamond Exchange Building

Sung Hung Kai Securities Ltd
3rd Floor
Admiralty Centre
18 Harcourt Road

Tung Shing Securities Co
5th Floor Bank of East Asia Building
10 Des Voeux Road
Central

R Yu and Co
Room 1102-1103 Yu To Sang Building
37 Queen's Road
Central

Sources of General Background Information, Industry Sector Information and Trade Contacts

UK Addresses

Hong Kong Trade
Development Council
8 St James's Square
London SW1Y 4JZ
Tel: 01-930 7955
Telex: 916923 CONLON G

Hong Kong Government
Office
6 Grafton Street
London W1X 3LB
Tel: 01-499 9821
Telex: 05128404 HKGOVTG

Addresses in Hong Kong

American Chamber of
Commerce
Swine House
10/F Central
Tel: (010 852) 5-260165
Telex: 83664 AMCC

British Chamber of
Commerce
6th Floor
8 Queen's Road
Central
Tel: (010 852) 5-8108118

Canadian Chamber of
Commerce
11th Floor
Tower 1
Exchange Square
Tel: (010 852) 5-244711
Telex: 76216 PVHK HX

Chinese General Chamber of
Commerce
Chinese General Chamber of
Commerce Building 7/F
24-25 Connaught Road
Central
Tel: (010 852) 5-256385
Cable: CHICHACOM

Chinese Manufacturers'
Association of Hong Kong
(The)
CMA Building
64-66 Connaught Road
Central
Tel: (010 852) 5-456166
Telex: 63526 MAFTS HX

Hong Kong General Chamber
of Commerce
United Centre 22/F
95 Queensway
Tel: (010 852) 5-299229
Telex: 83535 TRIND HX

Hong Kong Japanese
Chamber of Commerce and
Industry
38th Floor
Hennessy Centre
500 Hennessy Road
Causeways Bay
Tel: (010 852) 5-776252

Indian Chamber of
Commerce
69 Wyndham Street 2/F
Tel: (010 852) 5-233877
Telex: 64993 INCHA HX

Kowloon Chamber of
Commerce
3/F
KCC Building
2 Liberty Avenue
Kowloon
Tel: (010 852) 3-7600393
Cable: KOWCHAM

Swedish Chamber of
Commerce (The)
3607 Gloucester Tower
The Landmark
11 Pedder Street
Central
Tel: (010 852) 5-250349
Telex: 85946

Sources of Investment and Trade Advice, Assistance and Information

Foreign compaies wishing to
establish a place of business
in Hong Kong should get in
contact with the Registrar of
Companies, Companies
Registry

Business Registration Office
Inland Revenue Department
3/F Windsor House
311 Gloucester Road
Causeway Bay
Tel: (010 852) 5-8943143

Chinese Manufacturers
Association
CMA Building
64-66 Connaught Road
Central
CMA Building
3rd and 4th Floors
Tel: (010 852) 5-456166
Telex: 63526 MAFTS HX
Provides a trade enquiry
service. Acts as a match
maker in bringing together
overseas investors and Hong
Kong industrialists in various
types of joint ventures and
cooperative programmes.

Commissioner of Banking
Room 1604
Hang Chong Building
5 Queen's Road Central
Tel: (010 852) 5-222606

Commissioner for Labour
(The)
Labour Department
16th Floor
Harbour Building
38 Pier Road
Central
Tel: (010 852) 5-8524090

Companies Registry
13-14th Floor
Queensway Government
Offices
66 Queensway
Tel: (010 852) 5-8622604

Department of Customs and
Excise
Department of Industry
Department of Trade
Ocean Centre
5 Canton Road
Kowloon
Tel: (010 852) 3-7222333

Hong Kong Export Credit
Insurance Corporation
South Seas Centre
Tower 1
2/F
75 Mody Road
Tsimshatsui East
Kowloon
Tel: (010 852) 3-7233883
Telex: 56200 HKXC HX
Assists exporters in Hong
Kong to sell to overseas
buyers on credit terms

Hong Kong Exporters
Association
Room 920
Star House
3 Salisbury Road
Tsimshatsui
Kowloon
Tel: (010 852) 3-699851
Set up to protect and develop
Hong Kong's export trade
and improve the quality
standards of local products

Hong Kong Industrial Estates
Corporation
Suite 107 Estate Centre
19 Dai Cheong Street
Taipo Industrial Estate
Tel: (010 852) 0-6531183
Cables: INDESTATES
Independent statutory body
which assists in providing
land and prebuilt standard
factories for new industrial
development in Hong Kong

Hong Kong Productivity
Council and Productivity
Centre
12/F World Commerce Centre
Harbour City
11 Canton Road
Tsimshatsui
Kowloon
Tel: (010 852) 3-7235656
Telex: 32842 HKPC HX
Specialises in production
management services for
interested overseas investors

Hong Kong Standards and
Testing Centre
10 Dai Wang Street
Tai Po Industrial Estate
Tai Po
New Territories
Tel: (010 852) 0-6530021

Hong Kong Trade
Development Council
(Head Office)
29th (Suite 2904) 30th, 31st
and 32/F
Great Eagle Centre
23 Harbour Road
Tel: (010 852) 5-8334333
Telex: 73595 CONHK HX
Council has overseas offices
in Amsterdam, Barcelona,
Frankfurt, Hamburg,
London, Milan, Paris,
Stockholm, Vienna and
Zurich. Offers a free trade
enquiry service and has a
Management Information
Services section

Hong Kong Trade Fair Ltd
Room 4306
China Resources Building
Harbour Road
Wanchai
Tel: (010 852) 5-736211

Immigration Department
Mirror Tower
61 Mody Road
Tsimshatsui East
Kowloon
Tel: (010 852) 3-7333111
Telex: 45656

Insurance Division
Registrar General's
Department
12th Floor
Queensway Government
Office
Queensway
Tel: (010 852) 5-8622565

Urban Services Dept
12/F Central Government
Offices
West Wing
Tel: (010 852) 5-95578

Professional Associations

Accountancy
Hong Kong Society of
Accountants
17th Floor
Belgian House
77-79 Gloucester Road
Wanchai

Banking
Hong Kong Association of
Banks
Prince's Building
Room 525
5 Ice House Street
PO Box 11391
General Post Office
Tel: (010 852) 5-211288/9
Telex: 71716 HKAB HX

Insurance
Fire, Marine & Accident
Insurance Associations of
Hong Kong
Room 504
9 Ice House Street
Tel: (010 852) 5-228289
Telex: LOWEBINGHAMS HX

Trade Associations

Chinese Manufacturers'
Association of Hong Kong
(The)
CMA Building
64-66 Connaught Road
Central
Tel: (010 852) 5-456166
Telex: 63526 MAFTS HX
Represents manufacturers
and traders of all sizes.
Member of the International
Chamber of Commerce.
Active in promoting
industrial and trade
development

Federation of Hong Kong
Industries
Hankow Centre
Room 408
5-15 Hankow Road
Tsimshatsui
Kowloon
Tel: (010 852) 3-7242855
Telex: 30101 FHKI HX
Represents all sectors of the
manufacturing industry in
Hong Kong. Set up in 1960 to
promote and protect the
interests of Hong Kong
industry

Hong Kong Tourist
Association
35th Floor
Connaught Centre
Tel: (010 852) 3-7225555
(Telephone information
service available in many
languages)

Company Financial and Product Information

Directories

Business Directory of Hong Kong
Published by Current Publications Ltd. Annually lists manufacturing and service firms. Provides details of their address, products, senior executives and in some cases their bank. It also lists addresses for trade associations, chambers of commerce and government bodies

Dun's Guide
Ratings of Hong Kong Businesses
Published by Dun & Bradstreet (Hong Kong) Ltd
Companies listed alphabetically. Provides indicators as to companies' financial and credit strength

Hong Kong Enterprises
Published by Hong Kong Trade Development Council
Provides a guide to new products, manufacturers and their addresses

Key European Businesses in Hong Kong
Published by Dun & Bradstreet (Hong Kong) Ltd
Covers 500 companies where the parent or ultimate holding company is in one of 16 European countries. Provides details of companies' addresses, telephone, telex, business sector, senior management, paid up capital and name of parent company

Economic and Market Statistical Data

Market Research Organisations

AGB McNair Hong Kong Ltd
16/F CC Wu Building
302-308 Hennessy Road
Wanchai
Tel: (010 852) 5-737760
Fax: (010 852) 5-732247
Telex: 563685
Parent company: AGB Research Plc
Subsidiaries: Hong Kong Adex
Int Affiliation: AGB

Consumer Search Hong Kong Ltd
12/F Wanchai Commercial Centre
200 Johnston Road
Wanchai
Tel: (010 852) 5-8916687
Telex: 64505 TSICL HX

Executive Surveys Ltd,
Marketing Services China Ltd
1B Perfect Building
28 Sharp St West
Wanchai
Tel: (010 852) 5-741418
Telex: 65122 HX for Min

International Research Associates (Hong Kong) Ltd
13/F Easey Commercial Building
853 Hennessy Road
Wanchai
Tel: (010 852) 5-8933421
Fax: (010 852) 5-8919346
Telex: 72085 FSANA FX
Subsidiaries: Frank Small Associates
Int Affiliation: INRA

Frank Small Associates Ltd
16/F Easey Commercial Building
253 Hennessy Road
Wanchai
Tel: (010 852) 5-8911175
Fax: (010 852) 5-8919346
Telex: 72085 FSANA FX
Parent company: Frank Small Associates (Aust) Pty Ltd
Subsidiaries: International Research Associates (Hong Kong) Ltd

Marketing Decision Research Co Ltd
21st Floor
114-120 Lockhart Road
Wanchai
Tel: (010 852) 5-202350
Telex: 63099 WELKY HX

Survey Research Hong Kong Ltd
19/F Centre Point
181-185 Gloucester Road
Wanchai
Tel: (010 852) 5-732296
Fax: (010 852) 5-8916242
Telex: 65122 SRH HX
Cable: SUREACH
Subsidiaries: Hong Kong Media Research Ltd
Int Affiliation: AGB Research Plc

Walmsley Research Ltd
4310 China Resources Building
26 Harbour Road
Wanchai
Tel: (010 852) 5-755778
Fax: (010 852) 5-755154
Telex: 74159 WACO HX
One of Hong Kong's longest established and largest independent research agencies

Wesley Chemicals Hong Kong Limited
1902-3 Hang Seng Bank North Point Building
339 King's Road
Tel: (010 852) 5-660292/662226
Telex: 72138 WESLY HX
Cable: WESLEYCHEM

Organisations Providing Economic and Statistical Data

Census and Statistics Department
Kai Tak Commercial Building
317 Des Voeux Road Central
Tel: (010 852) 5-455678
Publishes Hong Kong Trade Statistics (2 volumes).
Monthly

Publications available locally from the Government Publications Centre Post Office Building Connaught Place Orders for local and overseas mailings should be addressed to: Director of Information Services Department Information Services Department Beaconsfield House

Industrial Promotion Office Hong Kong Government Office 6 Grafton Street London W1X 3LB UK Tel: 01-499 9821 Telex: 051 28404 HKGOVTG

Monetary Statistics Unit Monetary Affairs Branch 24th Floor Admiralty Centre Tower 11 18 Harcourt Road Tel: (010 852) 5-290125 Publishes consolidated monetary statistics

Hong Kong Government produces: Annual Budget Papers, Annual Reports of the Government of Hong Kong (available from Her Majesty's Stationery Office, UK), Report on the Survey of Overseas Investment in Hong Kong's Manufacturing Industries 1987

Large stockbroking firms and major banks such as Hong Kong and Shanghai Bank, Hang Seng Bank and the Standard Chartered Bank, produce statistics and reports on the Hong Kong stock market and local economy

Publications

Directories
AA's Far East Businessman's Directory
Publisher's address:
PO Box 1623
Hong Kong

All Asia Guide
Publisher's address:
181-185 Gloucester Road
Centre Point
Hong Kong
Annual

Asian Press and Media Directory
Publisher's address:
1303 World Trade Centre
Causeway Bay
Hong Kong

Business Directory of Hong Kong
Published by Current Publications Ltd
Hong Kong

China Phone Book and Address Directory
Published by The China Phone Book Company, Hong Kong.
Annual

Chinese Buyers Guide to British Industry
(Chinese Language)
Publisher's address:
CTPS
PO Box 4013
Hong Kong
or
CTPS
10 Elm Road
Wanstead
London E11 2JE
UK

Far East Economic Review Yearbook
Publisher's address:
181-185 Gloucester Road
GPO Box 160
Centre Point
Hong Kong
Annual

Hong Kong Shipping Guide
Produced by Hang Seng Bank Ltd
GPO Box 2985
77 Des Voeux Road
Central
Hong Kong

Hong Kong Trade Directory
Publisher's address:
44-66 South Ealing Road
London W5 4QA
Tel: 01-567 4410

International Business Directory for China
(Chinese language)
Publisher's address:
GPO Box 3724
342 Hennessy Road
Hong Kong

Journals and Periodicals

Major Business Newspapers
Asian Wall Street Journal
English. Daily. Provides stock market information

Financial Daily
Chinese. Daily. Provides stock market information

Hong Kong Economic Journal
Chinese. Daily. Provides stock market information

Hong Kong Standard
English. Daily. Provides stock market information

International Herald Tribune
English. Daily

South China Morning Post
English. Daily. Provides stock market information

Periodicals
Asian Business
Published by Far East Trade Press Ltd, Hong Kong
Monthly

Asian Finance
Publisher's address:
Suite 9B
Hyde Centre
223 Gloucester Road
Hong Kong
Telex: 83013 AFNDC

China Economic News
Publisher's address:
Hennessy Road
Hong Kong
Weekly

China Trade Report
Publisher's address:
406-409 Marina House
PO Box 160
Hong Kong

Export/Import Finance
Review
Publisher's address:
2 Wellington Street
16th Floor
Hong Kong
Monthly

Far Eastern Economic Review
Publisher's address:
181-185 Gloucester Road
GPO Box 160
Centre Point
Hong Kong
Provides economic, business
and political coverage

Hong Kong Apparel
Published by the Hong Kong
Trade Development Council.
Quarterly

Hong Kong Business Today
Publisher's address:
1204 San Toi Building
130-136 Connaught Road
Central
Hong Kong
Monthly

Hong Kong Enterprise
Published by the Hong Kong
Trade Development Council.
Features product news.
Monthly

Hong Kong Government
Gazette
Published by Government
Printing Dept, Hong Kong.
Weekly

Hong Kong Profile
Published by: Eurasia Media
Co Ltd, Hong Kong.
Monthly

Hong Kong Stock Exchange
Monthly Gazette
Published by: The Hong
Kong Stock Exchange

Hong Kong Toys
Published by the Hong Kong
Trade Development Council.
Annual.

Hong Kong Trader
Published by the Hong Kong
Trade Development Council.
Bimonthly. Provides news
and views of the territory.

India

Sources of Economic, Stock Market Information and Investment Research Services

Banks

Central Bank
Reserve Bank of India
PO Box 1007
Bombay 400023
Tel: (010 91) 22-295602
Telex: 115673

Indian Banks in London
Bank of Baroda
31-32 King Street
London EC2V 8EN
Tel: 01-606 8888

Bank of India
16 Finsbury Circus
London EC2M 7DJ
Tel: 01-628 3156

Canara Bank
14 Moor Lane
London EC2Y 9DJ
Tel: 01-628 2187

State Bank of India
State Bank House
London EC2P 2JP
Tel: 01-600 6444

Syndicate Bank
2a Eastcheap
London EC3M 1AA
Tel: 01-626 9681

Ucobank
Finsbury House
23 Finsbury Circus
London EC2M 7UY
Tel: 01-256 7435

Major Indian Banks
Bank of Baroda
(State Bank)
Central Office
3 Walchand Hirachand Marg
PO Box 10046
Ballard Pier
Bombay 400038
Tel: (010 91) 22-260341
(Central Office)
Telex: 011-75119

Bank of India
(Commercial Bank)
Express Towers
Nariman Point
Bombay 400021
Tel: (010 91) 22-2023020
Telex: 2281; 2983

Canara Bank
(Commercial Bank)
112 Jayachamarajendra Road
PO Box 6648
Bangalore 560002
Tel: (010 91)
812-221581/220490/221790
Telex: 845205; 8458075

Indian Overseas Bank
(State Bank)
PO Box 3765
762 Anna Salai
Madras 600002
Tel: (010 91)
44-81970/82041/82051
Telex: 041-6123 IOBF IN

Industrial Development Bank
of India
Narim Bhavan
227 Vinay K Shah Marg
Nariman Point
Bombay 400021
Tel: (010 91) 22-2027012
Telex: 0112193

Punjab National Bank
(Commercial Bank)
7 Bhikaji Cama Place
Africa Avenue
New Delhi 110066
Tel: (010 91) 11-602303 (Head
Office)
Telex: 61906; 61614

State Bank of India
Backbay Reclamation
Bombay 400021
Tel: (010 91) 22-293196
Telex: 011-2995

Syndicate Bank
(State Bank)
PO Box 1
Manipal – 576 199
Karnataka State
Tel: (010 91) PBX 8261
Telex: 847201/2/3

UCO Bank
(State Bank)
10 Bradbourne Road
Calcutta 1
Tel: (010 91) 33-260120/260280
Telex: 021-5019 UCOG IN;
021-4323 UCOF IN

Stockbrokers

Stock Exchanges
There are 14 stock exchanges
in India. The largest are
Calcutta, Bombay, Delhi and
Madras in terms of company
listings and market
capitalisation. The Bombay
exchange accounts for the
major share of total market
capitalisation in India.

Ahmedabad Stock Exchange
Association Ltd (The)
Manek Chowk
Ahmedabad-380 001
Tel: (010 91) 272-367149/36788

Bangalore Stock Exchange Ltd
M Block
1st Floor
Unity Buildings
J C Road
Bangalore-560 002
Tel: (010 91) 812-227238
(Office)

Stock Exchange, Bombay
(The)
Phiroze Jeejeebhoy Towers
Dalal Street
Bombay-400 023
Tel: (010 91) 22-272720/272523
Telex: 011-5925 STEX IN

Calcutta Stock Exchange
Association Ltd (The)
7 Lyons Range
Calcutta-700
Tel: (010 91) 33-229366/221641

Cochin Stock Exchange Ltd
37/1003 T D Road
Ernakulam
Cochin-682 011

Delhi Stock Exchange
Association Ltd (The)
3 & 4/4B Asaf Ali Road
New Delhi-110 002
Tel: (010 91) 11-271302/279000

Gauhati Stock Exchange Ltd
(The)
Saraf Building-Annex A T
Road
Gauhati-781 001 (Assam)

Hyderabad Stock Exchange
Ltd (The)
5-1-711/712 Bank Street
Hyderabad-500 001

Kanara Stock Exchange (The)
Mangalore-575 001

Ludhiana Stock Exchange Ltd
Lajpath Rai Market
Clock Tower
Ludhiana-141 008
Tel: (010 91) 161-39318/9

Madhya Pradesh Stock
Exchange Ltd
67 Bada Sarafa
Indore-452 002
Tel: (010 91) 731-32366

Madras Stock Exchange Ltd
11 Second Line Beach
Madras-600 001
Tel: (010 91) 44-512237/510845

Pune Stock Exchange Ltd
III Floor
Maharashtra Banking
Building
Baji Rao Road
Pune-411 002
Tel: (010 91)
212-441679/470584

Uttar Pradesh Stock Exchange
Association Ltd (The)
14/76 Civil Lines
Kanpur-208 001
Tel: (010 91) 512-49815

List of Members of the Bombay Stock Exchange (selection of firms only – 408 active members as at June 1987)

Ahmedabad
M/S Champaklal Bhailal
Choksi
2252/2 Mahurat Pole
Manke Chowk
Ahmedabad
Tel: (010 91)
272-364024/366130

Bangalore
M/S M Nanjappaiah Jahgirdar
205 K Kamraj Road
Bangalore-560 042

Bombay
M/s Bhupendra Champaklal
Devidas
Bhupen Chambers
Dalal Street
Fort
Bombay-400 021
Tel: (010 91) 22-230169/230113

M/s Chimanlal Manaklal
11 Raja Bahadur Motilal
Mansion
45 Tamarind Street
Fort
Bombay-400 023
Tel: (010 91) 22-274755

M/s Jamnadas Morarjee & Co
Stock Exchange Plaza
2nd Floor
Dalal Street
Bombay-400 023
Tel: (010 91) 22-244077

Anantrai Amershi Parekh
Table No 28
4th Floor
West Wing
c/o Stock Exchange
Tel: (010 91) 22-270013

Mrs Monica Mahesh Patel
3rd Floor
27 Cama Building
24/26 Dalal Street
Bombay
Tel: (010 91) 22-272392

M/s D S Purbhoodas & Co
1107 P J Towers
Dalal Street
Fort
Bombay-400 023
Tel: (010 91) 22-241441

Calcutta
M/S Manoj Dhupelai & Co
Nilhat House
6th Floor
11 R N Mukherjee Road
Calcutta-700 001
Tel: (010 91) 33-247021/245940

M/S Place Siddons & Gough
Pvt Ltd
6 Lyons Range
Calcutta-700 001
Tel: (010 91) 33-227391/225391

Madras
M/S Paterson & Co
Vanguard House
48 Second Line Beach
Madras-600 001
Tel: (010 91) 44-22332/24771

M/S Venkataraman & Co
78 Dr Rangachari Road
Mylapore
Madras-600 004
Tel: (010 91) 44-71723/72762

New Delhi
M/S Amritlal Bajaj & Co
606 Kailash Building
26 Kasturba Gandhi Marg
New Delhi-110 001
Tel: (010 91) 11-44537/46431

M/S Harish Bhasin & Co
Raja Ram Bhasin & Co
Jeevan Mansion
8/4 Deshbandhy Road
New Delhi-110 055
Tel: (010 91) 11-528365/527359

Sources of General Background Information, Industry Sector Information and Trade Contacts

UK Addresses
Indian Chamber of
Commerce in Great Britain
124 Middlesex Street
London E1 7HY
Tel: 01-247 8078

Office of the High
Commissioner for India
India House
Aldwych
London WC2B 4NA
Tel: 01-836 8484

Addresses in India
Federation of Indian
Chambers of Commerce and
Industry
Federation House
Tansen House
Tansen Marg
New Delhi-110 001
Tel: (010 91) 11-344124/324992
Telex: 2546

Major State Chambers of Commerce

Ahmedabad (Capital of Gujarat State)
Gujarat Chamber of
Commerce and Industry
Gujarat Chamber Building
Ranchodlal Road
Ahmedabad-380 009

Andhra Pradesh State
Cocanada Chamber of
Commerce
Commercial Road
Kakinada
Andhra Pradesh

Bombay (Capital of Maharashtra State)
Belgo-Indian Chamber of
Commerce and Industry
Taj Building
210 Dr D Naroji Road
Bombay-400 001

Bombay Chamber of
Commerce and Industry
Mackinnon Mackenzie
Building
Ballard Estate
Bombay-400 038
Tel: (010 91) 22-264681
Telex: 0112671

Indian Merchants' Chamber
76 Veer Nariman Road
Bombay-400 020

Indo-American Chamber of
Commerce
1-C Vulcan Insurance
Building Veer Nariman Road
Bombay-400 020

Indo-German Chamber of
Commerce
Vulcan Insurance Building
Veer Nariman Road
Bombay-400 001

Italian Chamber of Commerce
Vaswani Mansions
D Vachha Road
Bombay-400 001

Maharashtra Chamber of
Commerce
12 Rampart Row
Bombay-400 001

Calcutta (State Capital of West Bengal)
Bengal Chamber of
Commerce and Industry
PO Box 280
Royal Exchange 6
Netaji Subhas Road
Calcutta-700 001

Bengal National Chamber of
Commerce
P11
Mission Row Extension
Calcutta

Bharat Chamber of
Commerce
8 Old Court House Street
Calcutta

Indian Chamber of
Commerce
India Exchange
India Exchange Place
Calcutta-700 001

Karnataka State
Federation of Karnataka
Chambers of Commerce and
Industry
Kempegowda Road
Bangalore

Kerala (State in South West India)
Calicut and Malibar Chamber
of Commerce
Chamber House
Cherooty Road
Calicut-673 032

Cochin Chamber of
Commerce and Industry
Aerodrome Road
Cochin 3

Travancore Chamber of
Commerce
Alleppey
Kerala

Madras (Capital of Tamil Nadu)
Andhra Chamber of
Commerce
2272/2 Angappa
Nick Street
Madras

Hindustani Chamber of
Commerce
Hindustani Chamber
Building
8 Kondy Chetty Street
Madras-600 001

Madras Chamber of
Commerce and Industry
Dave House Annexe
41 Kasturi
Ranga Road
Alwarpet
Madras-600 018
Tel: (010 91) 44-451452
Telex: 41536

Southern India Chamber of
Commerce and Industry
Indian Chamber Buidlings
Esplanade
Madras

New Delhi (Indian Capital)
Associated Chambers of
Commerce and Industry
Allahabad Bank Building
17 Parliament Street
New Delhi-110 001
Tel: (010 91) 11-310704
Telex: 2537

Punjab, Haryana & Delhi
Chamber of Commerce and
Industry
Phelps Building
PHD House
412 Siri Institutional Area
New Delhi-110 016

Uttar Pradesh State
Merchants Chamber of Uttar
Pradesh
15/57 Civil Lines
Kanpur

Upper Indian Chamber of
Commerce
PO Box 63
Kanpur

UK Commercial Representatives

Bombay
Deputy High Commissioner
British High Commissioner
PO Box 815
Bombay-400 023
Tel: (010 91) 22-274874
Telex: 011-2850

Calcutta
Deputy High Commissioner
British High Commissioner
PO Box 9073
Calcutta-700 071
Tel: (010 91) 33-445171/5
Telex: 041-7169

Madras
Deputy High Commission
24 Anderson Road
Madras 600006
Tel: (010 91) 44-473136
Telex: 041-7169

New Delhi
Counsellor (Economic and
Commercial)
British High Commission in
India
Chanakyapuri
New Delhi-110 021
Tel: (010 91) 11-601371
Telex: 3165125 BHC IN

*Sources of Investment
and Trade Advice,
Assistance and
Information*

The Indian Investment Centre
is the main source of advice in
India for prospective
investors. This is a
government organisation. It is
advisable for UK inquirers to
obtain a copy of the note on
investment and collaboration
in Indian industry from the
Overseas Trade Division of
the Department of Trade and
Industry. This contains
information on the various
controls surrounding foreign
investment and licensing
arrangements.

Indian Investment Centre
Jeevan Vihar Building
Parliament Street
New Delhi-110 001
and
263 Regent Street
London W1
Tel: 01-492 8488
and
445 Park Avenue
New York
NY 10022
Tel: (010 1) 212-7533600

Employers' Federation of
India (The)
148 Mahatma Gandhi Road
Army and Navy Building
Bombay-400 001

Ministry of Commerce
Udyog Bhavan
New Delhi-110 011

Ministry of External Affairs
South Block
New Delhi-110 001

Ministry of Finance
North Block
New Delhi-110 001

Ministry of Industry
North Block
New Delhi-110 001

Ministry of Law, Justice and
Company Affairs
Shastri Bevan
New Delhi-110 001

Ministry of Planning
Yojana Bhavan
Parliament Street
New Delhi-110 001

Trade Development
Authority
Bank of Baroda Building
16 Parliament Square
New Delhi-110 001

Selection of Export Promotion Councils

Federation of Indian Export
Organisations
Allahabad Bank Building
17 Parliament Street
New Delhi-110 001

Bombay

Basic Chemicals,
Pharmaceuticals and
Cosmetic Soaps
Export Promotion Council
7 Cooperage Road
Bombay-400 039

Cotton Textiles Export
Promotion Council
Engineering Centre
9 Mathew Road
Bombay-400 004

Gem and Jewellery Export
Promotion Council
D-15 Commerce Centre
Tardeo Road
Bombay-400 034

Plastics and Linoleums Export
Promotion Council
Tulsiani Chambers
Nariman Point
Bombay-400 021

Silk and Rayon Textiles
Export Promotion Council
Resham Bhavan 78
Veer Nariman Road
Bombay-400 020

Wool and Woollens Export
Promotion Council
Churchgate Chambers
New Marine Lines
Bombay-400 020

Calcutta

Shellac Export Promotion
Council
14/1B Ezra Road
Calcutta-700 001

Tea Board of India
14 Brabourne Road
Calcutta-700001

Cochin

Cashew Export Promotion
Council
World Trade Centre
Mahatma Gandhi Road
Ernakulam
Cochin-682 016

Marine Products Export
Development Authority
Mahatma Gandhi Road
Ernakulam
Cochin-682 016

Spices Export Promotion
Council
World Trade Centre
Mahatma Gandhi Road
Ernakulam
Cochin-682 016

Kanpur

Export Promotion Council for
Finished Leather, Leather
Manufacturers
PO Box 198
15/46 Civil Lines
Kanpur-208 001

Madras

Handloom Export Promotion
Council
123 Mount Road
Madras-600 006

Leather Export Promotion
Council
Marble Hall
3/38 Vepery High Road
Madras-600 003

Tobacco Export Promotion
Council
123-C Mount Road
Madras-600 006

New Delhi

Processed Food Export
Promotion Council
R-15 ND South Extension Part
II
New Delhi-110 049

Sports Goods Export
Promotion Council
1/E6 Jhandewala Extension
New Delhi 110 055

Professional Associations

Accountancy

Institute of Chartered
Accountants of India
PO Box 7100
Indraprastha Marg
New Delhi-110 002

Institute of Cost and Works
Accountants of India
Cost Accountants' Hall
12 Sudder Street
Calcutta-700 016

Banking

Foreign Exchange Dealers'
Association of India
Maker Tower F
PO Box No 238
Cuffee Parade
Bombay-400 005

Indian Banks' Association
Stadium House
6th Floor
Block 3
81-83 Veer Nariman Road
Churchgate
Bombay-400 020
Tel: (010 91) 22-222365
Telex: 011-5146 IBA

Consultancy
Management Consultants'
Association of India
6th Floor
Eucharistic Congress Building
No 1115 Convent Street
Bombay-400 039

Insurance
Indian Insurance Companies'
Association
Co-operative Insurance
Building
Sir P Mehta Road
Fort
Bombay-400 001

Marketing
Indian Market Research
Bureau
Esplanade Mansions
Mahatma Ghandi Road
Bombay-400 023
Telex: 011-3555

Institute of Marketing and
Management
62-F Sujan Singh Park
New Delhi-110 003
Tel: (010 91) 11-699224
Telex: 31-3643

Trade Associations

Bombay – Trade
Federations
Advertising Agencies
Association of India
111-A Mahatma Gandhi Road
Fort
Bombay-400 001

All India Association of
Industries
Wakefield House
11 Sprott Road
Ballard Estate
Bombay-400 001

All India Automobile and
Ancillary Industries
Association
80 Dr A B Road
Worli
Bombay-400 018

All India Exporters
Association
Janmabhoomi Chambers
J Vima Marg
Fort Street
Bombay-400 001

All India Federation of Master
Printers
101 Worli Sea Face Road
Worli
Bombay-400 018

All India Footwear and
Rubber Goods Manufacturers
Association
Nirmal
3rd Floor
241 Backbay Reclamation
Nariman Point
Bombay-400 020

All India Glass Merchants
Association
166 Abdul Rehman Street
Bombay-400 003

All India Importers
Association
Churchgate House
32 Veer Nariman Road
Bombay-400 020

All India Instrument
Manufacturers and Dealers
Association
A-32
Navyug Nivas
Dr D Bhadkamkar Road
Bombay-400 007

All India Non-ferrous Metal
Industries Association
Liberty Building
Marine Lines
Bombay-400 020

All India Plastics
Manufacturers Association
3rd Floor
Jahangir Building
133 Mahatma Gandhi Road
Bombay-400 001

All India Radio and
Electronics Manufacturers
and Merchants Association
Sukh Sagar
Hughes Road
Opera House
Bombay-400 007

All India Wool Trade
Federation (The)
PO Box 1061
Bombay

Association of Indian
Automobile Manufacturers
Army and Navy Building
Mahatma Gandhi Road
Fort
Bombay-400 001

Association of Indian
Industries
4th Floor
Co-operative Insurance
Building
Sir Pherozshah Mehta Road
Fort
Bombay-400 001

Audit Bureau of Circulation
Ltd
Wakefield House
4th Floor
Ballard Estate
Bombay-400 001

Automobile Dealers
Association of Maharashtra
Ltd
c/o Bombay Chamber of
Commerce and Industry
Mackinnon Mackenzie
Building
Ballard Estate
Bombay-400 001

Federation of Bombay Retail
Cloth Dealers Association
24/30
1st Marine Street
Bombay-400 002

Federation of Electricity
Undertaking of India
Electric House
Colaba
Bombay-400 005

Federation of Paper Traders
Association of India
54 Sutar Chawl
Bombay-400 002

Federation of Woollen
Manufacturers in India
J K Building
Dougall Road
Ballard Estate
Bombay-400 038

Indian Cotton Mills
Federation (The)
Elphinstone Building
Veer Nariman Road
PO Box 1051
Bombay

Indian Electrical
Manufacturers Association
35 Himgiri
Pedder Road
Bombay-26

Indian Rubber Industries
Association
12 Rampart Row
Fort
Bombay-400 001

Indian Woollen Mills
Federation
Churchgate Chambers
New Marine Lines
Bombay-400 020

Iron, Steel and Hardware
Merchants and
Manufacturers Chamber of
India
403 Loha Bhawan
Frere Road
Bombay-400 009

Delhi

Federation of Indian Export
Organisations
17 Parliament Street
New Delhi-1

Indian Chemical
Manufacturers Association
Sira Vithaldas Chambers
6th Floor
16 Apollo Street
Bombay-400 001

Indian Engineering
Association (Western Region)
Mackinnon Mackenzie
Building
Ballard Estate
Bombay-400 001

Indian National Committee
International Chamber of
Commerce
Federation House
New Delhi-1

Textile Association (India)
Regd (The) (Bombay branch)
72-A Shivaji Park Cr Road
Bombay-400 028

Trade Mark Owners
Association of India
Army and Navy Building
Mahatma Ghandi Road
Bombay-400 001

Company Financial and Product Information

Directories

Directory of 15 000 Indian
manufacturers, exporters,
suppliers
Published by Business
Explorer, New Delhi, 6th
Edition 1985/86
Provides address and product
details for companies
throughout India. Companies
are grouped by industry and
products

Kothari's Industrial Directory
of India
Published by Kothari
Enterprises, Madras, 35th
Edition 1986
Contains detailed financial
figures for over 200
companies. Corporate units
are classified under one of 15
industry headings. Also
general information provided
on the Indian economy, and
government policies.
Company coverage includes
financial service institutions

Economic and Market Statistical Data

Market Research Organisations

Choice Consultants
101 Manju Mahal
Pali Mahal
Pali Hill
Bombay-400 050
Tel: (010 91) 22-540042
Member of ESOMAR

Domestic Research Bureau
PO Box 10032
Bombay-400 001
Tel: (010 91) 22-221222
Telex: 2323 HLHO IN
Parent company: Hindustan
Lever Ltd
Member of ESOMAR, MRS

Indian Market Research
Bureau
Esplanade Mansions
1st Floor
Mahatma Gandhi Road
Bombay-400 01
Tel: (010 91) 22-242623
Parent company: Hindustani
Thompson Associates Ltd
Member of ESOMAR

Institute of Marketing and
Management
62.F Sujan Singh Park
New Delhi-110 003
Tel: (010 91) 11-699224
Telex: 313643 IMM IN

Marg Marketing and Research
Group PVT Ltd
201 Dalamal Towers
Nariman Point
Bombay-400 021
Tel: (010 91) 22-223293
Telex: 0116897
Member of ESOMAR and
MRS

MRAS Marketing Research &
Advisory Services PVT Ltd
803 Embassy Centre
Nariman Point
Bombay-400 021
Tel: (010 91) 22-231222
Telex: 112117 APGO IN
Member of ESOMAR and
MRS

Organisations Providing Economic and Statistical Data

Central Statistical
Organisation
Manager of Publications
New Delhi 6
Publications include:
Estimates of National
Product, Savings and Capital
Formation. Annual
Monthly Abstract of Statistics

Corporate Investment
Research & Consultancy
Bureau (CIRCON)
802-C Arjun Nagar
Kotla Mubarakpur
New Delhi-110 003
Provides research statistics on
the Indian stock market.
Weekly review is available on
subscription

Ministry of Finance
North Block
New Delhi-110 001
Publishes an annual economic
survey. Other government
reports include:
Budget of the Central
Government. Annual
Five Year Plans

Reserve Bank of India
PO Box 1007
Bombay-400 023
Publishes a number of reports
which provide Indian
financial and economic
statistics, including Reserve
Bank of India Bulletin
(monthly) and Report on
Currency and Finance
(annual)

Major banks with merchant
banking divisions such as the
State Bank of India, and
foreign banks produce
economic and stock market
data

Directorate of Economics and
Statistics
Madhya Pradesh
Publishes a bulletin of
statistics annually

Publications

Directories
All India Telephone Directory
Published by Indian Export
Trade Journal, Bombay
Classified by trades,
professions, etc

Bombay Chamber of
Commerce and Industry
Directory of Members

CompJournal, Bombay
Classified by trades,
professions, etc

Bombay Chamber of
Commerce and Industry
Directory of Members

Computer Directory of India
(The)
Published by Constellate
Consultants Ltd, New Delhi
Listings of systems, suppliers
and computer installations

Indian Export Yearbook
Published by M/S Sales
Overseas, New Delhi
Covers importers, exporters,
manufacturers, Indian
agents, government trade
offices in India and abroad

Indian Industrial Directory
(Thapar's) 14th Edition 1987
Published by Thapar
International Industrial
Services, Bombay.
This is a major reference
source for Indian business.
Over 150 000 addresses of
Indian joint stock companies
are classified by industry
sector and state. It also lists
useful government and trade
association addresses,
together with lists of
members of associations
Punjab Haryana & Delhi
Chamber of Commerce and
Industry: Directory of
Members
Available from The Chamber,
PHD House, New Delhi-110
016

Times of India (The)
Directory and Yearbook

Major Newspapers
Daily Milap
Daily

Economic Times
English. Daily

Financial Express
English

Hindustan
Hindi

Indian Express
English

National Herald
English

Statesman (The)
English. Daily

Sunday Statesman
Weekly

Sunday Standard
Weekly

Times of India
English. Daily and weekly
(Sunday)

Times Weekly
Sunday

Journals and Periodicals
Business India
Publisher's address: Wadia
Building, 17/19 Dalal Street,
Bombay
Fortnightly

Business World. Fortnightly
Business Standard. Daily
Publisher's address: 145
Atlanta, 209 Ceremonial Blvd,
Nariman Point, Bombay

Commerce
Publisher's address: NKM
International House, 178
Backbay Reclamation,
Bombay
Weekly

Indian Management
Publisher's address:
Institutional Area, Lodhi
Road, New Delhi-3
Monthly

Ireland, Republic of

Sources of Economic, Stock Market Information, and Investment Research Services

Banks

Central Bank
Central Bank of Ireland
(Banc Ceannais na Eireann)
559 Dame Street
Dublin 2
Tel: (0001) 716666
Telex: 31041

Irish Banks In London
Allied Irish Banks
12 Old Jewry
London EC2R 8DP
Tel: 01-606 3070

Bank of Ireland
36 Queen Street
London EC4R 1BN
Tel: 01-329 4500

Major Irish Banks
Allied Irish Banks Ltd
Bank Centre
Ballsbridge
Dublin 4
Tel: (0001) 600311
Telex: 25232

Bank of Ireland
Lower Baggott Street
Dublin 2
Tel: (0001) 785744
Telex: 25573

Investment Bank of Ireland
91 Pembroke Road
Dublin 4
Tel: (0001) 686433
Telex: 25505

Stockbrokers
Irish Stock Exchange (The)
28 Anglesea Street
Dublin 2
Tel: (0001) 778808
Fax: (0001) 776045
Telex: 93437

Allied Irish Securities Ltd
3 College Green
Dublin 2
Tel: (0001) 796777

Beale, Sheffield & Co
15 South Mall
Cork
Tel: (010 353) 21 270828
Telex: 75811

Bloxham, Maguire
9/12 Fleet Street
Dublin 2
Tel: (0001) 776653
Telex: 935662
12 Marlboro Street
Cork
Tel: (010 353) 21 270697
Telex: 76158
46 Cecil St
Limerick
Tel: (010 353) 61-44065
Telex: 70707

Butler & Briscoe
3 College Green
Dublin 2
Tel: (0001) 777348
Telex: 25282
7 Lower Rowe Street
Wexford
Tel: (010 353) 53-22187

Campbell O'Connor & Co
8 Cope Street
Dublin 2
Tel: (0001) 77-1773

J & E Davy
Davy House
49 Dawson Street
Dublin 2
Tel: (0001) 797788
Telex: 93968

Doak & Co
3-5 Suffolk Street
Dublin 2
Tel: (0001) 770952

Goodbody James Capel
5 College Green
Dublin 2
Tel: (0001) 793888
Telex: 93719

McCaw, Fleming & Judd,
Incorporating
M W O'Reilly & Co
Aston House
Aston's Place
Dublin 2
Tel: (0001) 776941
Telex: 93915

W & R Morrogh
74 South Mall
Cork
Tel: (010 353) 21 277581
Fax: (021) 277581
Telex: 76145

National City Dillon &
Waldron Ltd
Ferry House
48/53 Lower Mount Street
Dublin 2
Tel: (0001) 612944
Telex: 30262

O'Brien & Toole
2 College Street
Dublin 2
Tel: (0001) 778797

Porter & Irvine
18/19 College Green
Dublin 2
Tel: (0001) 793715/793582
Telex: 24448

Riada & Co
28/29 Grafton Street
Dublin 2
Tel: (0001) 791411
Telex: 90546

Solomons, Abrahamson & Co
Bank of Ireland Chambers
1-3 Westmoreland Street
Dublin 2
Tel: (0001) 778264

Stokes & Kelly, Bruce, Symes
& Wilson, Incorporating
Cusack & Hinton, A.H. Hines
& Co
Moore, Gamble, Carnegie &
Co
24 Anglesea Street
Dublin 2
Tel: (0001) 770572

*Sources of General
Background Information,
Industry Sector
Information and Trade
Contacts*

UK Addresses
Irish Embassy
17 Grosvenor Place
London SW1X 7HR
Tel: 01-235 2171
Passport Office: 01-245 9033

Irish Export Board
Ireland House
150-151 New Bond Street
London WlY OHD
Tel: 01-491 3660

Irish Industrial Development
Authority
548 Davies Street
London W1
Tel: 01-629 5941

Addresses in the
Republic of Ireland
Chambers of Commerce exist
in all main Irish towns and
industrial areas. Some of the
main Chambers are listed
below:

Chambers of Commerce of
Ireland
7 Clare Street
Dublin 2
The CCI represents over 50
Chambers throughout
Ireland. Its main objectives
are to provide Irish business
and encourage foreign trade
and investment.

Cork Chamber of Commerce
Fitzgerald House
Summer Hill
Cork
Tel: (010 353) 21-509044
Telex: 26159

Dublin Chamber of
Commerce
7 Clare Street
Dublin 2
Tel: (0001) 764291
Telex: 90716
Fax: (0001 766043)

Dundalk Chamber of
Commerce
14 The Crescent
Dundalk
Tel: (010 353) 42-34224

Limerick Chamber of
Commerce
96 O'Connell Street
Limerick
Tel: (010 353) 61-45180

Waterford Chamber of
Commerce
George's Street
Waterford
Tel: (010 353) 51-72639

Embassies
British Embassy
33 Merrion Road
Dublin 4
Tel: (0001) 695211
Telex: 25296 UKDB EI

*Sources of Investment
and Trade Advice,
Assistance and
Information*

Contact should be made
initially with the Industrial
Development Authority, the
organisation responsible for
promoting industrial
development in Ireland.
Ireland offers substantial
concessions to foreign
companies bringing
employment particularly to
the more rural areas. Contact
the IDA for full details. The
IDA has a regional office in
Ireland and nineteen overseas
offices in Europe, the USA,
Australia and the Far East.

Federated Union of
Employers
Baggot Bridge House
84/86 Lower Baggot Street
Dublin 2
Tel: (0001) 601011
Telex: 93806

Foras Aisegnng Saothair
(FOS)
PO Box 456
Upper Baggot Street
Dublin 4
Tel: (0001) 685777
Telex: 93313 AnCO EI
FOS is the result of the
amalgamation of AnCO and
the National Manpower
Training Board.

Industrial Development
Authority (IDA)
Wilton Park House
Wilton Place
Dublin 2
Tel: (0001) 686633
688444
602244
Telex: 24525
Fax: (0001) 603703

Institute for Industrial
Research & Standards
Glasrevin
Dublin 9
Tel: (0001) 370101
Fax: (0001) 379620
Telex: 32501

Irish Export Board
Merrion Hall
Strand Road
Sandymount
Dublin 2
Tel: (0001) 695011

National Board for Science &
Technology (The)
Shelbourne House
Shelbourne Road
Dublin 4
Tel: (0001) 683311
Telex: 30327 NBST EI

National Microelectronics
Research Centre
Lee Maltings, Prospect Row
Cork
Tel: (010 353) 21-276871
Telex: UK 265871 MONREF G
Ref EIM 240

Professional Associations

Accountancy

Chartered Institute of
Management Accountants
(The)
44 Upper Mount Street
Dublin 2
Tel: (0001) 761721

Institute of Certified Public
Accountants in Ireland
22 Upper Fitzwilliam Street
Dublin 2
Tel: (0001) 767353

Institute of Chartered
Accountants in Ireland
87-89 Pembroke Road
Ballsbridge
Dublin 4
Tel: (0001) 680 400
Fax: (0001) 680842
Telex: 30567

Institute of Management
Accountants
11 Hume Street
Dublin 2
Tel: (0001) 763042
Fax: (0001) 614631
Telex: 75148

Institute of Taxation in
Ireland
15 Fitzwilliam Square
Dublin 2
Tel: (0001) 688181

Banking

Institute of Bankers In Ireland
(The)
Nassau House
Nassau Street
Dublin 2
Tel: (0001) 793311
Telex: 25843

Irish Bank Officials
Association
93 St Stephens Green
Dublin 2
Tel: (0001) 722255
Telex: 90746 IBOA EI

Irish Building Societies
Association
Adelaide House
19-20 Adelaide Road
Dublin 2
Tel: (0001) 784833
Fax: (0001) 784029
Telex: 30232

Consultancy

Association of Consultancy
Engineers in Ireland
51 Northumberland Road
Dublin 4
Tel: (0001) 600374

Association of Management
Consultants Organisations
(AMCO)
Confederation House
Kildare Street
Dublin 2
Tel: (0001) 779801

Institute of Management
Consultants in Ireland
1 Stokes Place
St Stephens Green
Dublin 2
Tel: (0001) 735566

Marketing

Marketing Institute of Ireland
Ltd (The)
12 Fitzwilliam Place
Dublin 2
Tel: (0001) 685176

Marketing Society (The)
c/o Michael Caraher
Guiness Group Sales
157 Thomas Street
Dublin 8
Tel: (0001) 757911

Trade Associations

General Industry

Confederation of Irish
Industry
Confederation House
Kildare Street
Dublin
Tel: (0001) 779801
Fax: (0001) 777823
Telex: 93502

AECI (Association of
Electrical Contractors Ireland)
McKinley House
16 Main Street
Blackrock
Co Dublin
Tel: (0001) 886499

Association of Woollen &
Worsted Manufacturers of
Ireland
Confederation House
Kildare Street
Dublin 2
Tel: (0001) 779801

Booksellers Association of GB
and Ireland
Book House Ireland
65 Middle Abbey Street
Dublin 1
Tel: (0001) 730108

Chartered Institute of
Building
c/o Federation House
Canal Road
Dublin 6
Tel: (0001) 977487

Construction Industry
Federation (The)
Federation House
Canal Road
Dublin 6
Tel: (0001) 977487

Electrical Industries
Federation of Ireland (EIFI)
c/o 1A South Brown Street
Dublin 8
Tel: (0001) 531002

Federation of Irish Chemical
Industries
13 Fitzwilliam Square
Dublin 2
Tel: (0001) 765116/7
Telex: 33212

Federation of Trade
Associations (The)
127 Lower Baggot Street
Dublin 2
Tel: (0001) 765078

Institute of Chemical
Engineers (The)
(Irish Branch)
Attn D. O'Callaghan
c/o Jacobs International Ltd.,
Merrion Road
Dublin 4
Tel: (0001) 695666

Institute of Electrical
Engineers (The)
(Irish Branch)
6 Tivoli Close
Dun Loaghaire
Co Dublin

Institute of Engineers of
Ireland (The)
22 Clyde Road
Dublin 4
Tel: (0001) 684341

Institute of Petroleum (Irish
Branch)
c/o Bill Lynch Shipping
Services Ltd.,
Old Harbour Office
North Wall Extension
Tel: (0001) 732299
Telex: 33576

Irish Association of
Distributive Trades Ltd
Rock House
Main Street
Blackrock
Co Dublin
Tel: (0001) 887584
Telex: 90521

Irish Business Equipment
Trade Association (IBETA)
59 Merrion Square South
Dublin 2
Tel: (0001) 761679

Irish Computer Society
Dundrum Castle
Balinteer Road
Dundrum
Dublin 16
Tel: (0001) 982692

Irish Dairy Industries
Association
Confederation House
Kildare Street
Dublin 2
Tel: (0001) 779801
Fax: (0001) 777823
Telex: 93502

Irish Farmers Association
Irish Farm Centre
Naas Road
Bluebell
Dublin 12
Tel: (0001) 501166
Telex: 30211

Irish Printing Federation
Baggott Bridge House
84/86 Lower Baggott Street
Dublin 2
Tel: (0001) 601011
Telex: 24593

Pharmaceutical Society of
Ireland
37 Northumberland Road
Dublin 4
Tel: (0001) 600699

Retail Grocery, Dairy & Allied
Trades Association
(RGDATA)
Rock House
Main Street
Blackrock
Co Dublin
Tel: (0001) 88313
Telex: 90521

Society of the Irish Motor
Industry (The)
5 Upper Pembroke Street
Dublin 2
Tel: (0001) 761690

Trade & Professional
Publishers Association
32 Upper George Street
Dun Laoghaire
Co Dublin
Tel: (0001) 800470

Company Financial and Product Information

Directories
Business and Finance Top 800
Part of the periodical
'Business and Finance'
published by Belenos
Publications Ltd, Dublin
League table of 750 leading
Irish companies, ranked by
turnover, and 50 financial
institutions, ranked by assets.
Details provided include
profit, number of employees
and name of client executive.
More detail including market
capitalisation is provided for
quoted companies

Irish Kompass Register of
Industry and Commerce
Published by Kompass
Ireland
Register gives detailed
information on over 5000 Irish
companies, geographically
arranged. Products and
service classifications are
provided for over 20 000 items
in English, French and
German

Overseas Companies in
Ireland
Produced by the Industrial
Development Authority,
Dublin
Directory listing grant aided
foreign firms in Ireland. Basic
details such as address,
telephone number and name
of parent company are
provided for each firm listed

Times 1000
Published by Times Books, 16
Golden Square, London W1R
4BN
Data is supplied by Extel
Financial
Contains a ranking of the top
20 companies in Ireland,
ranked by turnover. Details
provided include turnover,
capital employed, profit and
main activity

Economic and Market Statistical Data

Market Research Organisations

Altwood Research of Ireland Ltd
15 Adelaide Street
Dun Laoghaire
Co Dublin
Tel: (0001) 804761
Fax: (0001) 841008
Telex 90789
(Specialises in grocery products)

Cygnet Marketing Consultants
Enterprise House
Plassey Technological Park
Castletroy
Limerick
Tel: (010 353) 61-338177
Fax: (010 353) 61-338065
Telex: 70182
(Specialises in industrial and technical products and services)

Dale Parry Market Research Ltd
99 Upper Rathmines Road
Dublin 6
Tel: (0001) 974182
Telex: 90148

Eukon Associates
41 Fitzwilliam Place
Dublin 2
Tel: (0001) 766736
Telex: 32798

ICR Limited
Irish Consumer Research
24 Ely Place
Dublin 2
Tel: (0001) 764961

Irish Marketing Surveys Ltd
19-21 Upper Pembroke Street
Dublin 2
Tel: (0001) 761196
Telex: 30617
(Largest market research company in Ireland)

Landsdowne Market Research
12 Hatch Street
Dublin 2
Tel: (0001) 613483
Fax: (0001) 613479
Telex: 30617

Market Research Bureau of Ireland Ltd
43 Northumberland Avenue
Dun Laoghaire
Co Dublin
Tel: (0001) 804661

A C Nielsen of Ireland Ltd
36 Merrion Square
Dublin 2
Tel: (0001) 765112
Telex: 93734

SUS Research Ltd.,
(Socio-Economic Research & Consultancy)
9 Northumberland Road
Dublin 4
Tel: (0001) 608055
Telex: UK 265871 MONREF G

Ulster Marketing Surveys Ltd
115 University Street
Belfast BT7 1HP
Tel: (0232) 84-231060/9
(Largest local market research company in Northern Ireland)

Organisations Providing Economic and Statistical Data

Central Statistics Office
St Stephen's Green House
Dublin 2
Tel: (0001) 767531
Fax: (0001) 682221
and
Ardee Road
Rathmines
Dublin 6
Tel: (0001) 977144
Fax: (0001) 972360
This is the major source of official statistics in Ireland. Publications include:
Retail Sales Index. Monthly
Census of Distribution (1987 census scheduled)
Business of Advertising Agencies. Annual
Estimated numbers and expenditures of visitors to Ireland and Irish visitors abroad. Annual
The CSO collects, compiles, analyses and publishes social and economic statistics for Ireland. It also occasionally undertakes special surveys

Irish Stock Exchange (The)
Publishes a number of publications which provide financial and stock market statistics. These include the following:
Daily Official List
The Handbook of Irish Securities
The Irish Smaller Companies Market
Stock Exchange Fact Book. Quarterly
Stock Exchange Fact Sheet. Monthly
Equity Actuary List. Annual

Department of Industry &
Commerce
Kildare Street
Dublin 2
Tel: (0001) 614444
Fax: (0001) 762654
Telex: 93478
(Government Publications
GPO Arcade
Dublin 1)
Various government
publications available from
the address above which
provide economic and trade
statistics for Ireland:
Trade statistics of Ireland.
Monthly
Irish Statistical Bulletin.
Quarterly

Confederation of Irish
Industry
Publishes economic statistics
in Economic Review,
Business Forecast,
Newsletter. Weekly

Institute of Bankers
Publishes financial statistics
in the Irish Banking Review

Institute of Public
Administration
57/61 Landsdowne Road
Dublin 4
Tel: (0001) 686233
Publishes a large number of
books in the field of
administration, economics,
law and related disciplines

Publications

Directories
Administration Yearbook and
Diary
Published by the Institute of
Public Administration,
Dublin
Provides addresses and other
details on companies in
Ireland, financial institutions,
trade and professional
associations. It also covers a
separate section for Northern
Ireland and institutions of the
European Community.
Financial and economic
statistics are provided at the
back the book.

Irish Export Directory
Published for the Irish Export
Board by Jemma Publications
Ltd., Dublin.
Comprises three parts, an
alphabetical products index,
classified list of suppliers and
an alphabetical list of
suppliers. There is also a list
of Irish Embassies overseas at
the front of the directory

Irish Exporter Yearbook and
Diary
Published by Jude
Publications, Dublin
Contains a chart of Ireland's
top 100 exporters, details of
shipping lines and agents,
Irish diplomatic
representation abroad and
features covering relevant
topics for traders.

Major Newspapers
Irish Independent. Daily
Irish Press. Daily
Irish News. Daily
Irish Times. Daily
Sunday Press. Weekly
Sunday World. Weekly

Journals and Periodicals
Accountancy Ireland
Published by the Institute of
Chartered Accountants in
Ireland
Fortnightly

Business & Finance
Published by Belenos
Publications
Covers business, finance and
market news and includes
company profiles. Weekly

Business Forecast
Published by the
Confederation of Irish
Industry. Monthly

Economic Review
Published by the
Confederation of Irish
Industry. Quarterly

Finance
Published by Fintel
Publications, Dublin.
Monthly (subscription only)

Industry and Commerce
Published by Jude
Publications, Dublin
Produced by the Chambers of
Commerce of Ireland. Covers
business and industry news.
Monthly

Irish Banking Review
Published by the Irish
Bankers' Federation.
Monthly.

Irish Business
Published by Bedstone Ltd
Dublin

Irish Business Equipment
Journal
Publisher's address:
Callaghan House, 13/16 Dame
St, Dublin
Tel: (0001) – 710044

Irish Exporter
Published by Jude
Publications
Official Journal of the Irish
Exporters Association.
Monthly

Management
Published by Jemma
Publications Ltd. Monthly

Thoms Commercial Directory
of Ireland
Published by Thom's
Directories Ltd., Dublin.
Provides details of
government departments,
state sponsored boards and
companies, professional
associations. Also gives a
detailed street directory for
Cork, a directory of
companies and Who's Who in
Ireland

Trade Links Journal
Published by Libra House
Ltd, Dublin
Covers trade developments in
Europe. Bi-monthly

Italy

Sources of Economic, Stock Market Information and Investment Research Services

Banks

Central Bank
Banca D'Italia
Via Nazionale 91
00184 Rome
Tel: (010 39) 6-47921
Telex: 610021

Italian Banks in London
Banca Commerciale Italiana
42 Gresham Street
London EC2V 7LA
Tel: 01-600 8651

Banca D'Italia
39 King Street
London EC2V 8JJ
Tel: 01-606 4201

Banca Nazionale dell
Agricoltura SpA
85 Gracechurch Street
London EC3V 0AR
Tel: 01-623 2773; 01-283 7381

Banca Nazionale del Lavoro
33-35 Cornhill
London EC3V 3QD
Tel: 01-623 4222

Banca Populare de Milano
52-54 Gracechurch Street
London EC3V 0EH
Tel: 01-623 9431; 01-623 5979

Banca Populare di Novara
43 London Wall
London EC2M 5TB
Tel: 01-628 0237

Banco di Napoli
1 Moorgate
London EC2R 5TB
Tel: 01-726 4131

Banco di Roma
81-87 Gresham Street
London EC2V 7NQ

Banco di Santo Spirito
21-23 Ironmonger Lane
London EC2V 8EY
Tel: 01-726 2651

Banco di Sicilia
99 Bishopsgate
London EC2P 2LA
Tel: 01-638 0201

Cariplo
6 Lombard Street
London EC3V 9AA
Tel: 01-283 3166

Cassa di Risparmio
di Firenze
di Genova e Imperia
di Torino
di Verona, Vicenza e Belluno
Wax Chandlers Hall
Gresham Street
London EC2V 7AD

Credito Italiano
17 Moorgate
London EC2R 6HX
Tel: 01-606 9011

Instituto Bancario San Paolo
di Torino
9 St Paul's Churchyard
London EC4M 8AB
Tel: 01-236 2311

ItaB Bank
20 Cannon Street
London EC4M 6XD
Tel: 01-236 7464
(Joint venture bank)

Italian International Bank
122 Leadenhall Street
London EC2V 4PT
Tel: 01-623 8700

Montei dei Paschi di Siena
Tel: 01-623 3847

Major Italian Banks
Banca Commerciale Italiana
Piazza della Scala 6
20121 Milan
Tel: (010 39) 2-88501

Banca Nazionale
dell'Agricoltura
Via Salaria 231
00199 Rome
Tel: (010 39) 2-85881

Banca Nazionale del Lavoro
Via Veneto 119
00187 Rome
Tel: (010 39) 6-47021

Banco di Napoli
Via Toledo 177
80132 Naples
Tel: (010 39) 81-7911111

Banco di Roma
Viale Tupini 180
00144 Rome
Tel: (010 39) 6-54451

Cassa di Risparmio di Roma
Via Marco Minghetti 17
00187 Rome
Tel: (010 39) 6-87071

Credito Italiano
Piazza Cordusio 2
20123 Milan
Tel: (010 39) 2-88621

Stockbrokers
There are ten stock exchanges in Italy. Milan accounts for over 90 per cent of total equity volume in Italy. The other nine exchanges in descending order of importance are: Rome, Turin, Genoa, Bologna, Florence, Naples, Palermo, Trieste and Venice.

Borse Valori di Milano
(Milan Stock Exchange)
Piazza Degli Affari 6
20123 Milan
Tel: (010 39) 2-85344632
Telex: 321430 MICOMB 1

Members (125 as at February 1988)
Adorno dr Giovanni
Via Leopardi, 9
Tel: (010 39) 2-4988841

Agnese dr Savino
Via Nirone, 8
Tel: (010 39) 2-85971
Fax: (010 39) 2-8597248
Telex: 321154 PASTOR 1

Albanese dr Vittorio
V S Orsola, 13
Tel: (010 39) 2-8900946

Albertini dr Alberto
Via Borromei, 5
Tel: (010 39) 2-85731
Fax: (010 39) 2-8058006
Telex: 334079 ALBERT 1

Albertini dr Isidoro
v.Borromei, 5
Tel: (010 39) 2-85731
Fax: (010 39) 2-8058006
Telex: 334079 ALBERT 1

Aletti dr Urbano
Via S Spirito, 14
Tel: (010 39) 2-77121
Fax: (010 39) 2-784664
Telex: 350104 ALETTI 1

Allara rag Teobaldo
Via Carducci, 12
Tel: (010 39) 2-862328

Aloisio de Gaspari dr G
Via pr M Teresa, 11
Tel: (010 39) 2-807643; 8053580
Telex: (010 39) 2-321185
ALODEG 1

Arnaboldi dr Renzo
Via dei Piatti 1/3
Tel: (010 39) 2-808107
Fax: (010 39) 2-8693392

Azzoni dr Paolo
Via Borromei, 5
Tel: (010 39) 2-85731
Telex: 334079 ALBERT 1
Fax: (010 39) 2-8058006

Baroffio dr Giorgio
F Buonaparte, 53
Tel: (010 39) 2-877635
Telex: 8690424

Belloni dr Leonardo
Via della Posta, 8
Tel: (010 39) 2-809566
Fax: (010 39) 2-876267
Telex: 315553 BELL 1

Belloni dr. Maurizio
Via dei Piatti 1/3
Tel: (010 39) 2-808107
Fax: (010 39) 2-8693392

Belloni Santino
Via della Posta, 8
Tel: (010 39) 2-809566
Telex: 315553 BELL 1
Fax: (010 39) 2-876267

Bergancini dr Giancarlo
Via pr M Teresa, 7
Tel: (010 39) 2-878526

Bereri dr Riccardo Maria
Via Dante 7
Tel: (010 39) 2-89010000
Fax: (010 39) 2-98010079

Berti dr Lorenzo
Via Meravigli 18
Tel: (010 39) 2-8056540/41

Bertolini dr Patrizio
Via Nirone 8
Tel: (010 39) 2-85971; 8057366
Fax: (010 39) 2-8597248
Telex: 321154 PASTOR I

Biasci Giorgio
Via Meravigli, 4
Tel: (010 39) 2-8056555

Boffa dr Massimo
Via della Posta, 10
Tel: (010 39) 2-8057145
Fax: (010 39) 2-8057161
Telex: 322269 BOSOL I

Borroni dr Paolo
Via Brisa 7
Tel: (010 39) 2-865131

Bottazi dr Bruno
Via S Prospero 4
Tel: (010 39) 2-806169

Brioschi dr Davide
Via F Buonaparte, 76
Tel: (010 39) 2-809971
Telex: 350316 BRIDAV 1

Brocca dr Franco
Via Meravigli, 14
Tel: (010 39) 2-867551

Buffa dr Ezio
Via Nirone, 8
Tel: (010 39) 2-85971
Fax: (010 39) 2-8597248
Telex: 321154

Campisi dr ing G Franco
VG Negri, 8
Tel: (010 39) 2-8690231/2/3/4/5

Capelli rag. Carlo
Via Olmetto, 1
Tel: (010 39) 2-809516
Telex: 340082 CAPASS 1

Capelli dr Claudio
Via Olmetto, 1
Tel: (010 39) 2-809516
Telex: 340082 CAPASS 1

Capra Leone
Piazza Cordusio 2
Tel: (010 39) 2-865027

Ceresole dr Giuseppe
Via Meravigli,16
Tel: (010 39) 2-809139
Fax: (010 39) 2-874872

Cerutti Giancario
VG Negri, 10
Tel: (010 39) 2-867282
Telex: 3200039 CERMEN 1

Chiesa dr giuseppe
Via Dogana. 3
Tel: (010 39) 2-8692950

Colomba dr Nicola
CSo Magnenta, 60
Tel: (010 39) 2-4818445

Combi dr Giorgio
Via Torino, 2
Tel: (010 39) 2-809981
Telex: 334063 LEOMI 1

Combi dr Vincenzo
VG Casati, 1
Tel: (010 39) 2-874063/874065

Compstella dr Aldo
Via Meravigli 4
Tel: (010 39) 2-878366

Fumagalli dr Ettore
Via Maravigli 16
Tel: (010 39) 2-801545/6/7/8
Telex: 325494 FUSOL I

Gaudenzi dr Leonida
VS Vittore al T 3
Tel: (010 39) 2-8057172
Telex: 316337 GAULEO

Giussani dr Francesco
Via Torino, 15
Tel: (010 39) 2-804898

Imperato dr Alessandro
Via Turati, 6
Tel: (010 39) 2-6572491

Inttroini dr France
Via Meravigli 18
Tel: (010 39) 2-8056540

Ioppolo dr Giuseppe
Via Copernico, 49
Tel: (010 39) 2-6882752

Kuster rag. Giuliano
p.Borromeo, 12
Tel: (010 39) 2-800341

Lanella dr Lodovico
Via Meravigli, 3
Tel: (010 39) 2-865341
Telex: 334047

Legnani dr Giorgio
Via Camperio, 9
Tel: (010 39) 2-871491

Legnani dr Giuliano
Via Dell' Ambrosiana, 22
Tel: (010 39) 2-8692437

Leonzio dr Dario
Via Torino, 2
Tel: (010 39) 2-809981
Telex: 332063 LEOMI 1

Lesma dr Aldo
Piazza Affari, 3
Tel: (010 39) 2-8693366

Lombardi dr Angelo
VSM Segreta, 6
Tel: (010 39) 2-867633

Lunatici dr Luciano
Via Nirone 10
Tel: (010 39) 2-801095
Telex: 334509 LUNA 1

Mach di Palmstein dr
Amedeo
Via Brisa.3
Tel: (010 39) 2-872391

Malacarne Almonte
Via pr M Teresa,11
Tel: (010 39) 2-8052044

Marioni dr Franco
Via Borromei, 1/A
Tel: (010 39) 2-8051832

Martini dr Giacomo
Via Pantano 2
Tel: (010 39) 2-8693894

Matturi dr Gianluigi
Via C Cantu 1
Tel: (010 39) 2-801515
Fax: (010 39) 2-860545
Telex: 335602 MTTGLG

Matturi rag. Vincenzo
VC Cantu 1

Mazza Midana dr Guido
Via Meravigli, 16
Tel: (010 39) 2-809029

Menicatti dr Aldo
Via S Orsola, 13
Tel: (010 39) 2-8900946
Fax: (010 39) 2-874641
Telex: 353259 TEDMI

Milla dr Giovanni Luigi
VV Hugo 1
Tel: (010 39) 2-4980841 (10 lines)
Telex: 325287 MILLAG

Mortari dr Piero
VSM Segreta, 6
Tel: (010 39) 2-878472
Fax: (010 39) 2-876839

Murchio dr Giorgio
Via Camperio 9
Tel: (010 39) 2-809869
(010 39) 2-867724

Nattino dr Angelo
Via Meravigli, 12
Tel: (010 39) 2-876821

Nicolini Angelo
Via G Negri 8
Tel: (010 39) 2-8690231

Oriani rag. Luciano
Piazza Affari, 3
Tel: (010 39) 2-8693366

Panigada Walter
Via Borromei 11
Tel: (010 39) 2-874450

Pastorino dr Carlo
Via Nirone 8
Tel: (010 39) 2-85971
Fax: (010 39) 2-8597248
Telex: 321154 PASTOR 1

Pedercini dr Luigi
Via della Posta 8
Tel: (010 39) 2-809566
Fax: (010 39) 2-876267
Telex: 315553 BELL 1

Pellizzoni rag Dario
Via della Posta 10
Tel: (010 39) 2-8057145/6/7/8
Telex: 322269 BOSOL 1

Pirovano dr Alberto
Via Nerino 9
Tel: (010 39) 2-801171/2/3/4
Telex: 314112 MANCEN 1

Piva dr Pier Paolo
Via Torino 2
Tel: (010 39) 2-809981
Telex: 334063 LEOMI 1

Raimondi dr Valter
Via C Cantu 1
Tel: (010 39) 2-8056418
Telex: 335602

Rampini dr Roberto
Via pr M Teresa 11
Tel: (010 39) 2-807643
Telex: 321185 ALODEG

Reposi dr Franco
C Porta Romano 3
Tel: (010 39) 2-862958
Fax: (010 39) 2-879859

Sersale dr Maria Teresa
V Cardinal Federico 1
Tel: (010 39) 2-878654
Fax: (010 39) 2-865316

Sozzi dr Gianangelo
Foro Buonaparte 76
Tel: (010 39) 2-809971
Fax: (010 39) 2-860457
Telex: 350316 BRIDAV I

Tedeschi dr Roberto
VS Orsola 13
Tel: (010 39) 2-8900946
Fax: (010 39) 2-874641
Telex: 353259 TEDMI

Zaffaroni dr Mario Vittorio
Via del Bollo 4
Tel: (010 39) 2-862651/5

Member Banks
Banca Commerciale Italiana
Piazza della Scala 6
20121 Milan
Tel: (010 39) 2-88501
Telex: 310080

Banco di Roma
Piazzo Tommaso Edison 1
20123 Milan
Tel: (010 39) 2-88631
Telex: 616184 BRMI I

Banca Nazionale
Dell'Agricoltura
Piazza Fontana 4
20122 Milan
Tel: (010 39) 2-88941
Telex: 320210

Banca Nazionale del Lavoro
Piazza San Fedele 3
20100 Milan
Tel: (010 39) 2-88841
Telex: 310101

Banca Populare di Milano
Scarl
Piazza Filippo Meda 2-4
20121 Milan
Tel: (010 39) 2-77001
Telex: 320003

Cassa Di Risparmio Delle
Provincie
Lombarde (Cariplo)
Via Monte di Pieta
20121 Milan
Tel: (010 39) 2-88661
Telex: 313010

Credito Italiano
Piazza Cordusio 2
20123 Milan
Tel: (010 39) 2-88621
Telex: 312401

Instituto Bancario San Paolo
di Torino
Via Broletto 9-11
20121 Milan
Tel: (010 39) 2-88081
Telex: 334230

Sources of General Background Information, Industry Sector Information and Trade Contacts

UK Addresses
Italian Chamber of Commerce
for Great Britain
Walmar House
296 Regent Street
London W1R 6AE
Tel: 01-637 3153

Italian Consultate General
38 Eaton Place
London SW1
Tel: 01-235 9371

Italian Embassy
Commercial Office
14 Three Kings Yard
London W1Y 2GH
Tel: 01-629 8200
Telex: 23520

Italian Trade Centre
37 Sackville Street
London W1
Tel: 01-734 2412
Telex: 24870

Addresses in Italy
There are approximately 95
Italian chambers of commerce
in Italy. A selection of these
are listed below. Company
records which are held by
each chamber are mounted on
an online database provided
by Cerved – see Chapter six
for further details.

American Chamber of
Commerce in Italy
12 via Agnello
20121 Milan
Tel: (010 39) 2-807955

British Chamber of
Commerce for Italy
Via Tarchetti 1/3
20121 Milan
Tel: (010 39) 2-6595860
Telex: 610512

Camera di Commercio
Industria Artigianato &
Agricottura
Piazza Mercanzia 4
40125 Bologna
Tel: (010 39) 51-267681
Telex: 510240 PALAF

Addresses of other Chambers of Commerce in Italy
Corso Meridionale 58
80143 Naples
Tel: (010 39) 81-285322

Corso Porta Nuova 96
37122 Verona
Tel: (010 39) 45-591077
Telex: 480096 CAMVER

Piazza della Borsa 14
34121 Trieste
Tel: (010 39) 40-60445
Telex: 460165 CDCTS

Via de Burro 147
00186 Rome
Tel: (010 39) 6-6794541
Telex: 616376 CAROMA

Via E Amari II
90139 Palermo
Tel: (010 39) 91-58922
Telex: 910216 CAMCO

Via Garibaldi 4
16124 Genova
Tel: (010 39) 10-2094
Telex: 270623 CELIG

Via Meravigli 9/b
20123 Milan
Tel: (010 39) 2-85151
Telex: 312482 COMCAM

Via Parini 16
22100 Como
Tel: (010 39) 31-25611
Telex: 380547 CAMCO

Via S Francesco da Paola 24
10123 Turin
Tel: (010 39) 11-57161
Telex: 221247 CCTO

Confederazione Generale
Italiana del Commercio e
del Turismo (Confcommercio)
(General Confederation of
Italian Commerce)
Piazza GC Belli 2
00153 Rome
Tel: (010 39) 6-58661
Telex: 614217 CONFCO 1

Unione Italiana delle Camere
di Commercio
Industria Artigianato e
Agricultura
(Association of Chambers of
Commerce in Italy)
Piazza Sallustio 21
00187 Rome
Tel: (010 39) 6-479961
47041

Embassies

British Embassy
Via XX Settembre
90A
00187 Rome
Tel: (010 39) 6-4755441
Telex: 610049

Sources of Investment and Trade Advice, Assistance and Information

Istituto per l'Assistenza allo
Sviluppo del
Mezzogiorno (IASM)
Viale Pilsudski 124
00197 Rome
This is a government agency
which is in charge of assisting
the development of southern
Italy and the islands

Istituto Mobiliaire Italiano
(IMI)
Viale dell'Arte 25
00144 Rome
This is a government-owned
organisation which has set up
an investment information
office, and provides
medium-term credit

Istituto Nazionale per il
Commercio Esterol (ICE)
21 via Liszt
00100 Rome
Tel: (010 39) 6-59921
Italian government agency for
the promotion of foreign
trade

Istituto per la Ricostrazione
Industriale (IRI)
Via Vittorio Vereto 85
00187 Rome
Tel: (010 39) 6-47271

Ministry of Foreign Trade
Viale America
00144 Rome
Tel: (010 39) 6-5993

Ministry of Industry,
Commerce & Crafts
Via Molise 2
00187 Rome
Tel: (010 39) 6-4705

Professional Associations

Accountancy

Consiglio Nazionale dei
Dottori Commercialisti
Via Poli 29
Rome 00187

Banking

Associazione Bancaria Italiana
Piazza del Gesu 49
00186 Rome
Tel: (010 39) 6-67671
Telex: 680212

Associazione Nazionale
Aziende Ordinarie di Credito
Via A Boita 8
Casella Postale N1803
20100 Milan

Consultancy

Associazione Fra Societa E
Studi di Consulenza di
Direzione ed Organizzazione
Aziendale (ASCSCO)
Via San Paolo 10
20121 Milan
Tel: (010 39) 2-796157

Insurance

Consorzio Italiano di
Assicurazioni Aeronautiche
Via dei Giuochi Istmici 40
(PO Box 6317, 00100
Rome-Prati)
00194 Rome
Tel: (010 39) 6-365831
Telex: 610348

Istituto Italiano degli Attuari
(Italian Institute of Actuaries)
Via del Corea 3
00186 Rome
Tel: (010 39) 6-3606051

Sindacato Nazionale Agenti
di Assicurazione
(National Insurance Agents'
Association)
Via Lanzone 2
20123 Milan
Tel: (010 39) 2-864461

Marketing

Associazione Italiana per gli
Studi di Marketing
Via Olmetto 3
20123 Milan
Tel: (010 39) 2-863293

Trade Associations

General Industry

Confederazione Generale
dell'Industria Italiana
(Confindustria)
(General Confederation of
Italian Industry)
Viale dell'Astronomia 30
00144 Rome
Tel: (010 39) 6-59031
Telex: 613230 CONFIN I
Produces an online database
of Italian companies. See
Chapter six

Confederazione Cooperative
Italiane
Bg S Spirito 78
00193 Rome
Tel: (010 39) 6-6565604

Agriculture

Confederazione Generale
dell'Agricoltura Italian
Corso Vittorio Emanuele 11
101-00186 Rome
Tel: (010 39) 6-65121

Building and Building Materials

Associazione dell'Industria
Italia del Cemento, del
Fibro-Cemento, della Calce e
del Gesso
Via di S Teresa 23
00198 Rome
Tel: (010 39) 6-864314

Associazione Italiana Tecnico
Economica del Cemento
(AITEC)
Via di S Teresa 23
00198 Rome
Tel: (010 39) 6-864714
Telex: 611321 AITEC I

Associazione Nazionale
Costruttori Edili (ANCE)
Via Guattani 16
00161 Rome
Tel: (010 39) 6-84881
Telex: 626846 ANCE I

Federceramica
Piazza del Liberty 8
20121 Milan
Tel: (010 39) 2-790725/793780
Telex: 32825 FEDECE I

Associazione Nazionale degli
Industriali del Laterizl
(ANDIL)
Via A Torlonia 15
00161 Rome
Tel: (010 39) 6-861376
Telex 623602 ANDIL I

Associazione Nazionale
Industrie Refrattari (ANIR)
Via alla Porta degli Archi 3/18
16121 Genoa
Tel: (010 39) 10-540000

Associazione Nazionale
Produttori di Argille Espanse
(AN-PAE)
Via Vittoria Colonna 2
20149 Milan
Tel: (010 39) 2-4987628

Associazione Nazionale del
Produttori di Piastrelle di
Ceramica
(Assopiastrelle)
Viale San Giorgio 2
41049 Sassuolo (MO)
Tel: (010 39) 59-805900
Telex: 511050 ASSCER I

Chemicals &
Pharmaceuticals

Associazione Italiana
Ospedalita Privata (AIOP)
Via Lucrezio Caro 67
00193 Roma
Tel: (010 39) 6-311073/310034

Associazione Nazionale
dell'Industria Farmaceutica
(Farmindutria)
Piazza di Pietra 34
00186 Rome
Tel: (010 39) 6-650981
Telex: 614281 FARMIN I

Federchimica – Federazione
Nazionale dell'Industria
Chimica
Via Accademia 33
20131 Milan
Tel: (010 39) 2-63621
Telex: 332488 FECHIM I

Clothing

Associazione Italiana degli
Industriali dell'Abbigliamento
Foro Bunonaparte 70
20121 Milan
Tel: (010 39) 2-809016
Telex: 333594 INDABB I

Associazione Italiana della
Pellicceria
Presidenza: Corso Venezia 47
20121 Milan
Tel: (010 39) 2-7750

Direzione: Lungotevere degli
Anguillara 9
00153 Rome
Tel: (010 39) 6-5810854

Associazione Italiana
Produttori Maglierie e
Calzetterie
Via della Moscova 33
20121 Milan
Tel: (010 39) 2-6571641
Telex: 312587 UNATEX I

Electrical Engineering

Associazione Nazionale
Industrie
Elettroteciche ed
Elettroniche (ANIE)
Via A Algardi 2
20148 Milan
Tel: (010 39) 2-32641
Telex: 321616 ANIE l

Engineering

Associazione Costruttori
Italiani di Macchinario per
l'Industria.
Tessile (ACIMIT)
Via Tevere 1
20123 Milan
Tel: (010 39) 2-4988125
Telex: 334651 ACIMIT I

Associazione Costruttori
Italiani Macchine e Accessori
per la
Lvorazione del Legno
(ACIMALL)
Centro Commerciale Milano
Fiori
1 Strada – Palazzo F3
20094 Assago (MI)
Tel: (010 39) 2-8242101
Telex: 341267 ACIMAL I

Associazione Costruttori
Italiani Macchine Grafiche,
Cartotecniche ed Affini
(ACIMGA)
Via Bertani, 10
20154 Milan
Tel: (010 39) 2-3495144
Telex: 333518 ACIMGA I

Associazione Costruttori
Macchine, Attrezzature per
Ufficio e
per il Trattamento delle
Informazioni (ASSINFORM)
Via Larga 23
20122 Milan
Tel: (010 39) 2-878941
Telex: 324643 ASSINF I

Associazione Industrie
Aerospaziali (AIA)
Via Nazionale 200
00184 Rome
Tel: (010 39) 6-460247
Telex: 680440 AVIOAS I

Associazione Nazionale
Industria Meccanica Varia ed
Affine
(ANIMA)
Piazza Diaz 2
20123 Milan
Tel: (010 39) 2-809006
Telex: 310392 ANIMA I

Associazione Nazionale fra
Industrie Automobilistiche
(ANFIA)
Corso Galileo Ferraris 61
10128 Turin
Tel: (010 39) 11-5761
Telex: 221334 ANFIA I

Food and Drink

Associazione degli Industriali
della Birra e del Malto
Via Savoia, 29
00198 Rome
Tel: (010 39) 6-865161
Telex: 614486 ASSBIR I

Associazione degli Industriali
Mugnai e Pastai d'Italia
Via dei Crociferi 44
00187 Rome
Tel: (010 39) 6-6785409
Telex: 621487 MOLPAS I

Associazione Industrie
Dolciarie Italiane (AIDI)
Via Barnaba Oriani 92
00197 Rome
Tel: (010 39) 6-875735
Telex: 611551 ASSDOL I

Associazione Industrie Risiere
Italiane
Via Bernardino da Feltre 6
27100 Pavia
Tel: (010 39) 382-24241
Telex: 320082 ASSIND I

Associazione Italiana
Industriali Prodotti
Alimentari
(AIIPA)
Via Pietro Verri 8
20121 Milan
Tel: (010 39) 2-796645
Telex: 330881 AIIPA I

Associazione Italiana
Lattiero-Casearia
Via Pietro Verri 8
20121 Milan
Tel: (010 39) 2-700621

Associazione Italiana tra gli
Industriali delle Acque e
Bevande
Gassate (ABG)
Via Pietro Verri 8
20121 Milan
Tel: (010 39) 2-796645

Associazione Nazionale
Industriali Distillatori di
Alcoli e di
Acquaviti
Via Barberini 86
00187 Rome
Tel: (010 39) 6-4740851
Telex: 721406 DISTIL I

Associazione Nazionale fra gll
Industriali dello Zucchero
dell'Alcool e del Lievito
Via Bartolomeo Bosco 57/4
16121 Genoa
Tel: (010 39) 10-565491

Federazione Italiana
Industriali Produttori
Esportatori ed
Importatori di Vini,
Acquaviti, Liquori, Sciroppi,
Aceti ed Affini
(Federvini)
Via Mentana 2/B
00185 Rome
Tel: (010 39) 6-4740700
Telex: 612506 FEDVIN I

Unione Industriali Pastai
Italiani (UNIPI)
Via Po 102
00198 Rome
Tel: (010 39) 6-853291
Telex: 611540 UNIPI I

Unione Nazionale
deli'Avicoltura (UNA)
Via Pasubio 4
00195 Rome
Tel: (010 39) 6-316397
Telex: 620304 UNA I

Unione Nazionale Industriali
Bevande Gassate (UNIBG) V
le
Tel: (010 39) 6-5924668

Metal Industry
Associazione fra i Costruttori
in Acciaio
Italiani (ACAI)
Via F Turati 38
20121 Milan
Tel: (010 39) 2-6599002

Associazione Industrie
Siderurgiche
Italiane (ASSIDER)
Piazza Velasca 8
20122 Milan
Tel: (010 39) 2-860351
Telex: 311438 ASIDER I

Associazione Nazionale delle
Fonderie
(ASSOFOND)
Via Rismondo 78
27100 Pavia
Tel: (010 39) 382-38402
Telex: 326344 AFOND I

Associazione Nazionale
Industrie Metalli
Ferrosi (ASSOMET)
Via Bazzoni 12
20123 Milan
Tel: (010 39) 2-4985523
Telex: 312031 ASSMET I

Associazione Produttori
Italiani di Ferroleghe
ed Affini (ASSO FERLEGHE)
Via Finocchiaro Aprile 14
20124 Milan
Tel: (010 39) 2-6590081
Telex: 335604 FERLEG I

Industrie Siderurgiche
Associate (ISA)
Via Gustavo Fara 39
20124 Milan
Tel: (010 39) 2-6709336
Telex: 332666 ISA I

Mines and Quarries
Associazione dell'Industria
Marmifera Italiana e delle
Industrie
Affini
Via Nizza 59
00198 Rome
Tel: (010 39) 6-860959

Associazione Mineraria
Italiana
Via Cola di Rienzo 297
00192 Rome
Tel: (010 39) 6-352261
Telex: 622264 ASSIMIN I

Associazione Nazionale
Estratrtori Produttori Lapidel
Affini
(ANEPLA)
Sede Centro direzionale
Milanofiori
Strada 4 – Pal, A2
20094 Assago (Milan)
Tel: (010 39) 2-8244191

Unione Generale degli
Industriali Apuani del Marmo
ed Affini
((UGIMA)
Via Sette Luglio, 16 bis
54033 Carrara
Tel: (010 39) 585-70396

Paper, Cardboard and Paper Processing
Associazione Italiana fra gli
Industriali
della Carta, Cartoni e Paste
per Carta
(Assocarta)
Corso Italia 6
Piano 11
20122 Milan
Tel: (010 39) 2-804146
Telex: 320572 CARTAM I

Associazione Nazionale
Italiana Industrie
Grafiche Cartotecniche e
Trasformatrici
Piazza Conciliazione 1
20123 Milan
Tel: (010 39) 2-4981051
Telex: 331674 Gracar l

Public Utilities

Electricity
Unione Nazionale Aziende
Auto Produttrici e
Consumatrici di
Energia Elettrica (UNAPACE)
Via Paraguay 2
00198 Rome
Tel: (010 39) 6-864602
Telex: 616387 UNAPACE I

Gas
Associazione Nazionale
Industriali Gas (ANIG)
Via Alessandro Torlonia 15
00161 Rome
Tel: (010 39) 6-8125242

Petrol
Unione Petrolifera
Viale Civilta del Lavoro 38
00144 Rome
Tel: (010 39)
6-5914841/5915743
Telex: 611455 UNPETR I

Water
Associazione Nazionale fra gli
Industriali degii Acquedotti
(ANFIDA)
c/o Acquedotto Nicolay SpA
Piazza della Vittoria 11
16121 Genoa
Tel: (010 39) 10-587441

Publishing
Associazione del Fonografici
Italiani (AFI)
Via Vittor Pisani 22
20124 Milan
Tel: (010 39) 2-652636
2-6598773

Associazione Italiana Editori
(AIE)
Via delle Erbe 2
20121 Milan
Tel: (010 39) 2-8059244

Rubber
Associazione Nacionale fra
Industrie
della Gomma, Cavi Elettrici
ed Affini
(Assogomma)
Via S Vittore 36
20123 Milan
Tel: (010 39) 2-4988168
Telex: 335175 ASSGOM I

Textiles

Cotton
Associazione Cotoniera
Italiana
Via Borgonuovo 11
20121 Milan
Tel: (010 39) 2-802142
Telex: 312479 ACOTEZ I

Hemp
Associazione Nazionale del
Lino della Canapa e delle
Fibre
Dure
Via della Moscova 33
20121 Milan
Tel: (010 39) 2-6559613
Telex: 312587 UNATEX I (per
Linocanapiera)

Silk and Rayon
Associazione Serica Italiana
Via Odescalchi 17
22100 Como
Tel: (010 39) 31-260360

Associazione Italiana del
Torcitori della Seta e del Fill
Artificialie Sintetici
Via della Moscova 33
20121 Milano
Tel: (010 39) 2-6571641
Telex: 312587 UNATEX I

Wool
Associazione dell'Industria
Laniera Italiana
Via Borgonuovo 11
20121 Milan
Tel: (010 39) 2-808641/4

Transport and Communication
Confederazione Generale del
Traffico e dei Transporti
Via Panama 62
00198 Rome
Tel: (010 39) 6-855576

Federazione Nazionale
Ausiliari del Traffico e
Transporti Complementari
(AUSITRA)
Via D A Azuni 9
00196 Rome
Tel: (010 39) 6-3602900

Company Financial and Product Information

Directories
Annuario Generale Italiano
Published by Guida Monaci
SpA, Rome
Directory of official bodies,
trade associations and
companies. Each entry
provides the name, address,
telephone, telex number,
executives names, main
activities, branches and
principal subsidiaries of the
company or organisation. It
comes in three volumes;
indexes are in English,
French, German and Spanish

Dun's 2000
Produced by Dun &
Bradstreet, Kosmos SpA,
Milan
1987 edition covered 2790
companies. Companies are
ranked by sales. Other data
provided includes the chief
executive's name, activity,
percentage of turnover
exported, number of
employees and the
company's equity capital

Kompass Italia
Produced by Divisione
Kompass del Gruppo
Editoriale Fabbri SpA.
1986 edition covered 30 000
companies. It also includes
embassies in Italy, official
bodies, trade associations,
foreign companies and their
agents in Italy

Le Principali Societa Italiane Produced by Mediobanca. Covers industrial companies with a turnover of over Lire 150 billion. Companies are ranked by sales and other key financial figures are provided. A ranking is also provided for financial service companies including banks and insurance companies

Economic and Market Statistical Data

Market Research Organisations

A&R – Analisi & Ricerche
Corso Porta Romana 54
20122 Milan
Tel: (010 39) 2-8693065
Telex: 311250
Member of AISM, ESOMAR

AGB Italia SpA
Via Serbelloni 4
20122 Milan
Tel: (010 39) 2-7742
Telex: 325 264
Parent company: AGB Research Plc
Affiliated to: Europanel
Member of AISM, ESOMAR

Burke Marketing Research
Corso Vercelli 25
20144 Milan
Tel: (010 39) 2-4988261
Telex: 313445 BURKE I
Fax: (010 39) 2-4985983
Parent company: Burke International
Member of AISM, ESOMAR

CER Research International
Via Tito Speri 8
20154 Milan
Tel: (010 39) 2-653663
Telex: 314141
Parent company: Research International
Member of AISM, ESOMAR, MRS

CIRM Market Research SrL
Via Lodovico Mangini 1
20129 Milan
Tel: (010 39) 2-5400988
Fax: (010 39) 2-5459774
Affiliated to: Global Market Research Ltd
Member of AISM, ESOMAR

CRA SAS Consulenti Di Marketing e Ricercatori Ass
Via Le Bianca Maria 37
20122 Milan
Tel: (010 39) 2-784709
Fax: (010 39) 2-782266

Databank SpA
Direzione Commerciale
Corso Italia 8
20122 Milan
Tel: (010 39) 2-8052855
Telex: 324217 DTBK 1

Demoskopea SrL
Via Nino Bixio 4
20129 Milan
Tel: (010 39) 2-221051
Telex: 313103 DEMOS I
Member of AISM

Due Sigma SrL
Via Ippolito Nievo 28/A
2015 Milan
Tel: (010 39) 2-4980635
Member of ESOMAR

Image Marketing Research SrL
Via Paolo Sarpi 56
20154 Milan
Tel: (010 39) 2-3450581
Member of ESOMAR Research Institute

Mesomark SrL
Viale Carso 1
00195 Rome
Tel: (010 39) 6-3599366
Telex: 620238 ROME
Member of ESOMAR Research Institute

A C Nielsen
Via Dante 7
20123 Milan
Tel: (010 39) 2-85621
Telex: 3340591

Pragma SrL
Via Salaria 298/A
00195 Rome
Tel: (010 39) 6-868018
Telex: 625412
Member of AISM, ASSARIM, ESOMAR

Recom International SrL
Corso Buenos Aires 77a
20124 Milan
Tel: (010 39) 2-6704212
Fax: (010 39) 2-6700734
Member of AISM, ESOMAR

RM Ricerche di Mercato
Via Reggio 6
43100 Parma
Tel: (010 39) 521-772410
Member of ESOMAR

Roland Berger and Partner SrL
Via Cerve 13
20121 Milan
Tel: (010 39) 2-793714
Telex: 313845
Parent company: Roland Berger & Partner GmbH
Member of ASSCO, ESOMAR

Organisations Providing Economic and Statistical Data

CER – Centro Europa Ricerche
Via L Luciani 1
00197 Rome
Tel: (010 39) 6-3609449
3619090

Istituto Centrale di Statistica (ISTAT)
Via C Balbo 16
00100 Rome
Tel: (010 39) 6-4673
Source of official statistics for Italy
Publications available from ISTAT include the following:
Annuario Statistico Italiano
Bolletino Mensile di Statistica
Indicatori Mensili
Statistica Mensile del Commercio con l'Estero

Milan Stock Exchange provides statistics on the Italian stock market. Publications produced in English include the following:
Annual Report
The performance of listed shares
The Stock Exchange Monthly Report

Prometeia
Via S Vitale 15
40125 Bologna
Tel: (010 39) 51-268883

Most large Italian banks and brokers provide economic and financial information. The Banco d'Italia produces a Bollettino Economico, and Annual Report

Publications

Directories
American Chamber of Commerce for Italy
Publishes a directory which lists over 7350 US companies which are active in the es

American Chamber of Commerce for Italy
Publishes a directory which lists over 7350 US companies which are active in the es

American Chamber of Commerce for Italy
Publishes a directory which lists over 7350 US companies which are active in the Italian market. It also lists 2700 member firms. It provides details on branches, agents, distributors and licensees

British Chamber of Commerce for Italy
Publishes a directory of British member companies grouped by business classification

(Le) Camera di Commercio Industria Artgianato e Agricoltura en Italia
Published by Union Camere, Rome
Directory of Italian Chambers of Commerce

Major Newspapers
Corriere dello Sera
Daily

Il Fiorino
Daily

La Gazzette del Matino
Daily

Il Giornale d'Italia
Daily

Italia Oggi
Daily

Il Messaggero
Daily

La Repubblica
Daily

Il Sole 24 Ore
Daily

La Stampa
Daily

Il Tempo
Daily

Journals and Periodicals
Avvisatore
Publisher's address: Viale della Liberta 135,
90143 Palermo
Economics. Daily

L'Azione Commerciale
Publisher's address: Via Teatro Dolfin 4
33100 Treviso
Covers commerce, retailing and tourism. Weekly

Economics e Tributi
Publisher's address: Via P Lomazzo 52
20154 Milan
Fortnightly

Espansione
Publisher's address: 20090
Segrate
Milan
Economics, trade and industry. Monthly

Europa Domani
Published by Stampa Economica SrL
Covers economics, finance, trade and industry. Monthly

Li Giornale del Commercio e Turismo
Publisher's address: Piazza Gioacchino
Belli 2
00153 Rome
Commerce. Weekly

L'Impresa
Publisher's address: Via Paolo Lomazzo 52
20154 Milan
Management. 6 issues per annum

Largo Consumo
Published by Editoriale Largo Consumo SrL
Covers industry, product, company profiles and market reports. Monthly

Made in Italy
Published by Rivista del Commercio Estero
Covers trade, product, company information and business contacts. Bi-monthly

Il Mondo
Publisher's address: Via Solferino 28
20121 Milan
Weekly

Mondo Economico
Publisher's address: Via P Lomazzo 52
20154 Milan
Business. Weekly

Tempo Economico
Published by Fratelli Pini Editoro SrL
Covers economic news, finance and marketing. Monthly

Japan

Sources of Economic, Stock Market Information and Investment Research Services

Banks

Central Bank
Bank of Japan (Nippon
Ginko)
2-2-1 Hongoku-cho
Nihonbashi
Chuo-Ku
Tokyo
Tel: (010 81) 3-279-1111
Telegrams: Totsukuni
Telex: J22763

Japanese Banks in London
Ashikaga Bank
Level 9
City Tower
40 Basinghall St
London EC2V 5DE
Tel: 01-236 1286
Telex: 892816

Bank of Fukuoka
Bow Bells House
Bread St
London EC4M 9BQ
Tel: 01-236 2288
Telex: 893817

Bank of Hiroshima
18 King William St
London EC4N 7BR
Tel: 01-623 2442
Telex: 8814908

Bank of Japan
27-32 Old Jewry
London EC2R 8EY
Tel: 01-606 2454
Telex: 884517

Bank of Kyoto
52 Cornhill
London EC3V 3PH
Tel: 01-626 6897
Telex: 933044

Bank of Tokyo
20-24 Moorgate
London EC2R 6DH
Tel:01-638 1271
Telex: 884811

Bank of Tokyo International
(Bank of Tokyo)
20-24 Moorgate
London EC2R 6DH
Tel: 01-628 3000
Telex: 883254

Bank of Yokohama
40 Basinghall St
London EC2V 5DE
Tel: 01-628 9973
Telex: 887995

Chiba Bank
12th Floor
Winchester House
77 London Wall
London EC2N 1BE
Tel: 01-638 2406
Telex: 884193

Chuo Trust & Banking
Woolgate House
Coleman St
London EC2R 5AT
Tel: 01-726 6050
Telex: 8812700

Dai-Ichi Kangyo Bank
P & O Bldg
Leadenhall St
London EC3V 4PA
Tel: 01-283 0929
Telex: 884042

Daiwa Bank
St Helen's
1 Undershaft
London EC3A 8JJ
Tel: 01-623 8200
Telex: 886569

Export-Import Bank of Japan
2nd Floor
Warnford Court
Throgmorton St
London EC2N 2AT
Tel: 01-638 0175
Telex: 8952604

Fuji Bank
25-31 Moorgate
London EC2R 6HQ
Tel: 01-628 4477
Telex: 886317

Hokkaido Takushoku Bank
31-45 Gresham St
London EC2V 7ED
Tel: 01-606 8961
Telex: 884353

Hokuriku Bank
10 Throgmorton Avenue
London EC2M 2DL
Tel: 01-628 7699
Telex: 894095

Hyogo Sogo Bank
2F Phoenix House
18 King William St
London EC4N 7BR
Tel: 01-623 7602
Telex: 265474

Industrial Bank of Japan
Bucklersbury House
Walbrook
London EC4N 8BR
Tel: 01-236 3266
Telex: 885393

IBJ International
(Industrial Bank of Japan)
Bucklersbury House
3 Queen Victoria St
London EC4N 8HR
Tel: 01-236 1090
Telex: 925621

Iyo Bank
Level 6
City Tower
40 Basinghall St
London EC2V 5DE
Tel: 01-588 2791
Telex: 949011

Japan Development Bank
P & O Building
122-138 Leadenhall St
London EC3V 4PT
Tel: 01-623 0172
Telex: 888907

Japan International Bank
107 Cheapside
London EC2V 6BR
Tel: 01-600 0931
(Joint Venture Bank)

Joyo Bank
103 Cannon St
London EC4N 5BB
Tel: 01-623 2033
Telex: 8956812

Kyowa Bank
93-95 Gresham St
London EC2V 7NA
Tel: 01-606 9231
Telex: 883317

Long-Term Credit Bank of
Japan
18 King William St
London EC4N 7BR
Tel: 01-623 9511
Telex: 885305

Mitsubishi Bank
1 King St
London EC2V 8LQ
Tel: 01-606 6644
Telex: 8958931

Mitsubishi Trust & Banking
Corp
33 Lombard St
London EC3V 9AJ
Tel: 01-929 2323
Telex: 945777

Mitsui Bank
34-35 King St
London EC2V 8ES
Tel: 01-606 0611
Telex: 888519

Mitsui Trust and Banking
99 Bishopsgate
London EC2M 3XD
Tel: 01-638 0841
Telex: 888679

Nippon Credit Bank
City Tower
40 Basinghall St
London EC2V 5DE
Tel: 01-638 6411
Telex: 893273

Nippon Credit International
(Nippon Credit Bank)
City Tower
40 Basinghall St
London EC2V 5DE
Tel: 01-638 6911
Telex: 947861

Nippon Trust Bank
22 Lovat Lane
London EC3R 8EB
Tel: 01-929 2916
Telex: 267188

Nomura International
Finance
(Nomura Securities)
Nomura House
24 Monument Fr
London EC3R 8AJ
Tel: 01-929 2366
Telex: 9413063

Norinchukin Bank
6th Floor
131 Finsbury Pvt
London EC2A 1AY
Tel: 01-588 6589
Telex: 892698

Norinchukin International
(Norinchukin Bank)
6th Floor
131 Finsbury Pvt
London EC2A 1AY
Tel: 01-588 6593
Telex: 936122

Saitama Bank
30 Cannon St
London EC4M 6XH
Tel: 01-248 9421
Telex: 886400

Sanwa Bank
Commercial Union Bldg
1 Undershaft
London EC3A 8LA
Tel: 01-283 5252
Telex: 888350

Seventy-Seven Bank
7th Floor
Northgate House
20-24 Moorgate
London EC2R 6DH
Tel: 01-628 5506
Telex: 933055

Shoko Chukin Bank
Bow Bells House
Bread St
London EC4M 9BQ
Tel: 01-236 2805
Telex: 893813

Sumitomo Bank
Temple Court
11 Queen Victoria St
London EC4N 4TA
Tel: 01-236 7400
Telex: 887667

Sumitomo Trust & Banking
62-63 Threadneedle St
London EC2R 8BR
Tel: 01-628 5621
Telex: 888924

Taiyo Kobe Bank
16-17th Floor
Commercial Union Bldg
1 Underschaft
London EC3A 8TB
Tel: 01-621 1430
Telex: 886349

Tokai Bank
P & O Building
Leadenhall St
London EC3V 4RD
Tel: 01-283 8500
Telex: 887375

Toyo Trust and Banking
5th Floor
Bucklersbury House
83 Cannon St
London EC4N 8AJ
Tel: 01-236 4020
Telex: 885619

Yasuda Trust & Banking
1 Liverpool St
London EC2M 7NH
Tel: 01-628 5721
Telex: 922040

Zenshinren Bank
103 Cannon St
London EC4N 5AD
Tel: 01-621 1763
Telex:

Securities Houses in London
A selection of some of the
largest firms represented in
London

Bank of Tokyo Capital
Markets
20 Moorgate
London EC2R 6DH
Tel: 01-628 3000

Dai-Ichi Europe
Durrant House
8-13 Chiswell Street
London EC1Y 4TQ
Tel: 01-588 4872

Daiwa Europe
5 King William St
London EC4N 7AX
Tel: 01-548 8080

Fuji International Finance
101 Moorgate
London EC2M 6TQ
Tel: 01-638 1421

Kokusai Europe
52-54 Gracechurch St
London EC3
Tel: 01-626 2291

Nikko Securities Co (Europe)
Nikko House
17 Godliman St
London EC4V 5BD
Tel: 01-248 9811

Nomura International
Nomura House
24 Monument St
London EC3R 8AJ
Tel: 01-283 8811

Mitsubishi Finance
International
1 King St
London EC2V 8EB
Tel: 01-726 4500

Mitsui Finance International
3 London Wall Building
London Wall
London EC2M 5PP
Tel: 01-588 4672

New Japan Securities Europe
4 Fenchurch St
London EC3M 3AL
Tel: 01-626 7855

Sanwa International
PO Box 245
1 Undershaft
London EC3A 8BR
Tel: 01-623 7991

Sumitomo Finance
International
107 Cheapside
London EC2V 6HA
Tel: 01-600 0161

Tokai International
Mercury House
Triton Court
14 Finsbury Square
London EC2A 1DR
Tel: 01-638 6030

Yaimaichi International
(Europe)
Finsbury Court
111-117 Finsbury Pavement
London EC2A 1EQ
Tel: 01-638 5599

Major Japanese Banks

Dai-Ichi Kangyo Bank Ltd
1-5 Uchisaiwaicho 1-chome
Chiyoda-ku
Tokyo 100
Tel: (010 81) 3-5961111
Fax: (010 81) 3-5962585
Telex: J 22315

Daiwa Bank Ltd (The)
21 Bingomachi 2-chome
Higashi-ku
Osaka 541
Tel: (010 81) 6-2711221
Telex: J 63284 DAIBANK

Fuji Bank Ltd
1-5-5 Otemachi
Chiyoda-ku
Tokyo 100
Tel: (010 81) 3-2162211
Fax: (010 81) 3-2144150
Telex: J 22722

Industrial Bank of Japan (The)
3-3 Marunouchi 1-chome
Chiyoda-ku
Tokyo 100
Tel: (010 81) 3-2141111
Telex: J 22325

Long Term Credit Bank of
Japan Ltd
2-4 Otemachi 1-chome
Chiyoda-ku
Tokyo 100
Tel: (010 81) 3-2115111
Telex: J 24308

Mitsibushi Trust and Banking
4-5 Marunouchi 1-chome
Tokyo 100
Tel: (010 81) 3-2121211
Telex: J 24259

Mitsubishi Bank Ltd
7-1 Marunouchi 2-chome
Chiyoda-ku
Tokyo 100
Tel: (010 81) 3-2401111
Telex: J 22358

Mitsui Bank Ltd
1-2 Yaraku-cho 1-chome
Chiyoda-ku
Tokyo 100
Tel: (010 81) 3-5011111
Telex: J 22378

Nippon Credit Bank Ltd
13-10 Kudan-Kita 1-chome
Chiyoda-ku
Tokyo 102
Tel: (010 81) 3-2631111
Telex: J 26921

Sanwa Bank Ltd
10 Fushimimachi 4-chome
Higashi-ku
Osaka 541
Tel: (010 81) 6-2022281
Telex: 63234

Sumitomo Bank Ltd
Head Office
3-2 Marunouchi 1-chome
Chiyoda-ku
Tokyo
Tel: (010 81) 3-2825111
Telex: J 63266

Sumitomo Trust and Banking
Corporation
15 Kitahama 5-chome
Higashi-ku
Osaka 541
Tel: (010 81) 6-2202121
Telex: J 63775

Tokai Bank Ltd
21-24 Nishiki 3-chome
Naka-ku
Nagoya
Tel: (010 81) 52-2111111
Telex: J 59612

Toyo Trust and Banking Co
Ltd (The)
4-3 Marunouchi 1-chome
Chiyoda-ku
Tokyo 100
Tel: (010 81) 3-2872211
Telex: 2224925

Yasuda Trust and Banking Co
Ltd
2-1 Yaesu 1-chome
Chuo-ku
Tokyo
Tel: (010 81) 3-2788111
Telex: 2223828

Stockbrokers

Japan has 8 stock markets.
Tokyo handles over 80 per
cent of trading volume
followed by Osaka, Nagoya,
Kyoto, Hiroshima, Fukuota,
Niigata and Sapparo.

Tokyo Stock Exchange
2-1-1
Nishombashi-Kayaba-cho
Chuo-ku
Tokyo 103
Tel: (010 81) 3-6660141
Telex: 02522759 TKOSE J

Osaka Securities Exchange
2-1 Kitahama
Higashi-ku
Osaka 541
Tel: (010 81) 6-2031151
Telex: 05225118 OSASE J

Chiyoda Securities
2-15 Nihombashi-Muromachi
3-chome
Chuo-ku
Tokyo 103
Tel: (010 81) 3-2712311

Cosmo Securities
16-10 Nihombashi 1-chome
Chuo-ku
Tokyo 103
Tel: (010 81) 3-2724611

Daiichi Securities
6-2 Nihombashi-Muromachi
1-chome
Chuo-ku
Tokyo 103
Tel: (010 81) 3-2442600

Daiwa Securities
6-4 Otemachi 2-chome
Chiyoda-ku
Tokyo 100
Tel: (010 81) 3-2432111

Ichiyoshi Securities
14-1 Hacchobori 2-chome
Chuo-ku
Tokyo 104
Tel: (010 81) 3-5556200

Izumi Securities
17-24
Shinkawa 1-chome
Chuo-ku
Tokyo 104
Tel: (010 81) 3-5554811

Kaisei Securities
13-2 Nihombashi-Kabuto-cho
Chuo-ku
Tokyo 103
Tel: (010 81) 3-6661431

Kokusai Securities
26-2 Nishi-Shinjuku 1-chome
Shinjuku-ku
Tokyo 163
Tel: (010 81) 3-3487211

Kosai Securities
Nihon Building
6-2 Otemachi 2-chome
Tokyo 100
Tel: (010 81) 3-2460811

Maruman Securities
1-10 Nihombashi 2-chome
Chuo-ku
Tokyo 103
Tel: (010 81) 3-2720640

Marusan Securities
5-2 Nihombashi 2-chome
Chuo-ku
Tokyo 103
Tel: (010 81) 3-2725211

Meiko Securities
14-1 Nihombashi-Koami-cho
Chuo-ku
Tokyo 103
Tel: (010 81) 3-6668091

Mito Securities
13-5 Nihombashi
3-chome
Chuo-ku
Tokyo 103
Tel: (010 81) 3-2746111

National Securities
6-7 Nihombashi-Kabuto-cho
Chuo-ku
Tokyo 103
Tel: (010 81) 3-6660321

New Japan Securities
6-20 Kyobashi 1-chome
Chuo-ku
Tokyo 104
Tel: (010 81) 3-5611111

Nikko Securities
3-1 Marunouchi 3-chome
Chiyoda-ku
Tokyo 100
Tel: (010 81) 3-2832211

Nippon Kangyo Kakumaru
Securities
6-1 Marunouchi 1-chome
Tokyo 100
Tel: (010 81) 3-2867111

Nomura Securities
9-1 Nihombashi 1-chome
Chuo-ku
Tokyo 103
Tel: (010 81) 3-2111811

Okasan Securities
17-6 Nihombashi 1-chome
Chuo-ku
Tokyo 103
Tel: (010 81) 3-2722211

Sanyo Securities
8-1 Nihombashi-Kayaba-cho
1-chome, Chuo-ku
Tokyo 103
Tel: (010 81) 3-6661233

Taiheiyo Securities
17-10 Kyobashi 1-chome
Chuo-ku
Tokyo 104
Tel: (010 81) 3-5664511

Takagi Securities
12-11 Nihombashi 1-chome
Chuo-ku
Tokyo 103
Tel: (010 81) 3-2813231

Tokyo Securities
7-3 Marunouchi 2-chome
Chiyoda-ku
Tokyo 100
Tel: (010 81) 3-2143211

Towa Securities
16-7 Nihombashi 1-chome
Chuo-ku
Tokyo 103
Tel: (010 81) 3-2781511

Toyo Securities
20-5 Nihombashi 1-chome
Chuo-ku
Tokyo 103
Tel: (010 81) 3-2740211

Universal Securities
4-2 Marunouchi 3-chome
Chuo-ku
Tokyo 100
Tel: (010 81) 3-2843511

Wako Securities
6-1 Nihombashi-Koami-cho
Chuo-ku
Tokyo 103
Tel: (010 81) 3-6678111

Yamaichi Securities
4-1 Yaesu 2-chome
Tokyo 104
Tel: (010 81) 3-2763181

Yamatane Securities
7-12 Nihombashi-Kabuto-cho
Chuo-ku
Tokyo 103
Tel: (010 81) 3-6693211

Note: The companies listed
above are 'integrated
securities companies' ie they
have been granted a licence
by the Minister of Finance to
carry out all four catagories of
business: dealing, brokerage,
underwriting and selling, and
have a minimum capital stock
of 3 billion yen

Sources of General Background Information, Industry Sector Information and Trade Contacts

UK Addresses

Anglo-Japanese Economic
Institute (The)
Room 1-6 2nd Floor
314-322 Regent Street
London W1R 5AD
Tel: 01-637 7872

Exports to Japan Unit
British Overseas Trade Board
Department of Trade and
Industry
1 Victoria Street
London SW1
Tel: 01-215 4804

Japan Association
Regis House
43-46 King William Street
London EC4R 9BE
Tel: 01-623 5320

Japan Business Policy Unit
School of Industrial and
Business Studies
University of Warwick
Coventry CV4 7AL

Japanese Chamber of
Commerce and Industry
Room 506
Chronicle House
72-78 Fleet Street
London EC4Y 1HY
Tel: 01-353 8166
Fax: 01-583 5286

The Japanese Embassy
46 Grosvenor Street
London W1X OBA
Tel: 01 493 6030

Japan Information Centre
(Japanese Embassy)
9 Grosvenor Square
London W1X 9LB
Tel: 01-493 6030

Japanese Information Service
British Library
25 Southampton Buildings
London WC2A 1AW
Tel: 01-323 7925
Fax: 01-323 7930
(Information service in the
field of science, technology
and business)

Japan Research Centre
School of Oriental and
African Studies
Malet Street
London WC1E 7HP
Tel: 01-637 2388

JETRO (Japan Trade Centre)
Leconfield House
Curzon Street
London W1Y 7FB
Tel: 01-493 7226

Library of Japanese Science
and Technology
24 Duke Street
Whitley Bay
Northumberland NE26 3PP
Tel: 091-2533479

Addresses in Japan

American Chamber of
Commerce in Japan
7th Floor
Fukide No 2 Building
1-21 Toranomon 4-chome
Minato-ku
Tokyo 105
Tel: (010 81) 3-4335381
Fax: (010 81) 3-4361446
Telex: 2425104 KYLE J

Australian Chamber of
Commerce in Japan
CPO Box 1096
Tokyo 10091
Tel: (010 81) 3-2017861

British Chamber of
Commerce in Japan
3rd Floor
Kowa Building No 16
9-20 Akasaka 1-chome
Minato-ku
Tokyo 107
Tel: (010 81) 3-5051734
Fax: (010 81) 3-5052680

British Embassy
1 Ichiban-cho
Chiyoda-ku
Tokyo 102
Tel: (010 81) 3-2655511
Fax: (010 81) 3-2655580
Telex: J22755 PRODOME
(International)

Canadian Chamber of
Commerce in Japan
3rd Floor CCCJ Bldg
8-8 Azabu Juban 2-chome
Minato-ku
Tokyo 106
Tel: (010 81) 3-4532640
Fax: (010 81) 3-4532662

French Chamber of
Commerce and Industry in
Japan
6th Floor Banque Indosuez
Bldg
1-2 Akaska 1-chome
Minato-ku
Tokyo 107
Tel: (010 81) 3-5870061
Fax: (010 81) 3-5870104
Telex: J32383 CCIFJ

German Chamber of
Commerce and Industry in
Japan
7th Floor Akasaska Tokyu
Bldg
14-3 Nagata-cho 2-chome
Chiyoda-ku
Tokyo 100
Fax: (010 81) 3-5931350
Telex: J26229 GERHAKA

Japan Chamber of Commerce
and Industry
(Nihon Shoko Kaigisho)
2-2 Marunouchi 3-chome
Chiyoda-ku
Tokyo 100
Tel: (010 81) 3-2837851
Telex: 2224920 JPNCCI J
Contact direct for list of
members

Organisations Providing Trade and Investment Advice, Assistance and Information

Bank of Japan
Foreign Department
(see Central Bank)

Far East Trade Service Center
3rd Floor Nagai International
Bldg
12-19, Shibuya 2-chome
Shibuya-ku
Tokyo 150
Tel: (010 81) 3-4079711
Fax: (010 81) 3-4079715
Telex: 2423591 FETS J

Japan Development Bank
Foreign Department
9-1 Otemachi 1-chome
Chiyoda-ku
Tokyo 100
Tel: (010 81) 3-2703211

Japan External Trade
Association (JETRO)
2-5 Toranomon 2-chome
Minato-ku
Tokyo 105
Tel: (010 81) 3-5825522
Fax: (010 81) 3-5870219
Telex: J24378
JETRO provides a wide range
of services which includes
trade information, research
on economic and trade
trends, supporting economic
cooperation between Japan
and other countries. It has a
head office, four main offices
and twenty-six additional
offices in Japan, plus
branches worlwide

Japan Federation of Prefectual
Trade Promotion Agencies
Kokusai Kaunko Kaikan Bldg
8-3 Marunouchi 1-chome
Chiyoda-ku
Tokyo 100
Tel: (010 81) 3-2136870

Japan Foreign Trade Council,
Inc
6th Floor, World Trade Centre
Bldg
4-1 Hamamatsu-cho 2-chome
Minato-ku
Tokyo 105
Tel: (010 81) 3-4355952

Japan Regional Cooperation
Toranomon Mitsui Bldg
8-1 Kasumigaseki
3-chome
Chiyoda-ku
Tokyo 100
Tel: (010 81) 3-5015211
Provides information on
industrial location etc.

Manufactured Imports
Promotion Organization
(MIPRO)
6th Floor, World Import Mart
Bldg
1-3 Higashi Ikebukuro
3-chome
Toshima-ku
Tokyo 170
Tel: (010 81) 3-9882791
Fax: (010 81) 3-9881629

Ministry of International
Trade and Industry
3-1 Kasumigasek, 1-chome
Chiyoda-ku
Tokyo 100
Tel: (010 81) 3-5011511

Professional Associations

Accountancy
The Japanese Institute of
Certified Public Accountants
18-3 Hongo 5-chome
Bunkyo-ku
Tokyo 113
Tel: (010 81) 3-8151451

Banking
The Federation of Bankers
Associations of Japan
1-3-1 Marunochi
Chiyoda-ku
Tokyo
Tel: (010 81) 3-2163761
Telex: 26830

Consulting
Association of Management
Consultants in Japan
1-38 Shibakouen 3-chome
Minato-ku
Tokyo 105
Tel: (010 81) 3-4362085

Japan Institute of
Management and
Administration
Ichigaya Hoso Bldg 1-5
Kudankita 4-chome
Chiyoda-ku
Tokyo 102
Tel: (010 81) 3-2611145

Insurance
Life Insurance Association of
Japan
3rd Floor
Shinkokusai Building 4-1
3-chome
Marunouchi
Chiyoda-ku
Tokyo 100
Tel: (010 81) 3-2862734

Songai Hoken Jigyo
Kenkyujyo
(Non-life Insurance Institute
of Japan)
3-chome
Kanda-Surugdai
Chiyoda-ku
Tokyo
Tel: (010 81) 3-2555511

Marketing
Japan Marketing Association
(The)
Wako Bldg
4-8-5 Ropponpi, 4-chome
Minato-ku
Tokyo
Tel: (010 81) 3-4035101
Fax: (010 81) 3-4035106

Japan Marketing Research
Association (JMRA)
No 20 Sankyo Bldg
11-5 Iidabashi 3-chome
Chiyoda-ku
Tokyo 101
Tel: (010 81) 3-2653677

Trade Associations

All Japan Lead Pipe and Sheet
Industrial Association
Murakami Tatemono Bldg
11-1 Shinbashi 2-chome
Minato-ku
Tokyo
Tel: (010 81) 3-5010502

All Japan Machinist Hand
Tool Manufacturers
Association
Kikai Shinko Kaikan 5-8
Shibakoen 3-chome
Minatoku
Tokyo
Tel: (010 81) 3-4322007

Communications Industries
Association of Japan
Annex Sankei Bldg
7-2 Otemachi 1-chome
Chiyoda-ku
Tokyo
Tel: (010 81) 3-2313156

Electronic Industries
Association of Japan
Tosho Bldg 2-2
Marunouchi 3-chome
Chiyoda-ku
Tokyo
Tel: (010 81) 3-2112765

Federation of Pharmaceutical
Manufacturers' Association of
Japan (The)
9 Nihonbashi Hon-cho
2-chome
Chuo-ku
Tokyo
Tel: (010 81) 3-2700581

Japan Aluminium Federation
Nihombashi Asahi Seimei
Bldg
1-3 Nihonbashi 2-chome
Chuo-ku
Tokyo
Tel: (010 81) 3-2744551

Japan Automobile
Manufacturers Association
Inc
Otemachi Bldg 6-1
Otemachi 1-chome
Chiyoda-ku
Tokyo
Tel: (010 81) 3-2165771

Japan Chemical Industry
Association
2-6 Kasumigaseki 3-chome
Chiyoda-ku
Tokyo
Tel: (010 81) 3-5800751

Japan Iron and Steel
Federation (The)
Keidanren Kaikan Bldg
9-4 Otemachi
1-chome
Chiyoda-ku
Tokyo
Tel: (010 81) 3-2793611

Japan Machinery Federation
(The)
Kikai Shinko Bldg
5-8 Shibakoen 3-chome
Minato-ku
Tokyo
Tel: (010 81) 3-4345381

Japan Paper Association
Kami Pulp Kaikan Bldg 9-11
Ginza 3-chome
Chuo-ku
Tokyo
Tel: (010 81) 3-5432411

Japan Petrochemical Industry
Association
Iino Bldg
1-1 Uchisaiwai-cho 2-chome
Chiyoda-ku
Tokyo
Tel: (010 81) 3-5012151

Japan Plastics Industry
Federation
Tokyo Club Bldg
2-6 Kasumigaseki 3-chome
Chiyoda-ku
Tokyo
Tel: (010 81) 3-5800771

Japan Printers' Association
Nihon Insatsu Kaikan 16-8
Shintomi 1-chome
Chuo-ku
Tokyo
Tel: (010 81) 3-5512223-5

Japan Textile Council
9 Nihonbashi Hon-cho
3-chome
Chuo-ku
Tokyo
Tel: (010 81) 3-2417801

Japan Textile Machinery
Association
Kikai Shinkoen 3-chome
Minatoku
Tokyo
Tel: (010 81) 3-4343821

Company Financial and Product Information

2000 Importers of Japan
Published by the Japan
External Trade Association
(JETRO)
Contains over 2000 company
entries and 100 product
categories cross referenced

Buyers Guide of Tokyo
Published by the Foreign
Trade Association, Tokyo.
Provides details of Japanese
companies and indicates
products exported and
countries of destination

Diamond's Japan Business
Directory
Published by Diamond Lead
Co Ltd, Tokyo
Contains company financial
and product information.
Trade names and brand
names are also provided
together with a general
review of industries

Directory of Foreign Capital
Affiliated Enterprises in Japan
Published by Business
Intercommunications Inc,
Tokyo
Provides names of investors,
foreign capital ratios and
other relevant details

Industrial Groupings in Japan
Published by Dodwell
Marketing Consultants
This directory provides
shareholder and general
financial details on the major
industrial groups in Japan

Japan Chemical Directory
Published by The Chemical
Daily Co Ltd, Tokyo

Japan Companies:
Consolidated Data
Published by Japan Economic
Journal, Tokyo

Japan Company Handbook
Published by Tokyo Keijai
Shinposha Ltd, Tokyo (The
Oriental Economist).
Provides background and
financial details for the latest 2
years, for Japanese companies

Japan Electronic Buyers'
Guide
Published by Dempa
Publications, Inc

Japan Telephone Book,
Yellow Pages
Published by Japan Yellow
Pages Ltd
Classified list of companies

Japan Times Directory
Published by Japan Times Ltd
Provides contact details for
Japanese companies and
organisations

Japan Trade Directory
Published by the Japan
External Trade Association
(JETRO)
Provides addresses, annual
sales and capital figures,
together with a list of
products exported and
imported for each company
listed

Economic and Market Statistical Data

Market Research Organisations

Dentsu Research Ltd
23-17 Shinkawa 1-chome
Tokyo 104
Tel: (010 81) 3-5538311
Fax: (010 81) 3-5538326
Parent company: Dentsu Inc

Japan Market Research
Bureau, Inc
Fujita Bldg
2-13-2 Kami-Osaki
Shinagawa-ku
Tokyo 141
Tel: (010 81) 3-4734029
Parent company: MRB Group

Marketing Center Co Ltd
30-6 Jingumae 4-chome
Shibuya-ku
Tokyo 150
Tel: (010 81) 3-4023121
Fax: (010 81) 3-4039737

Marketing Intelligence
Corporation
14-11 Yato 2-chome
Tanashi-shi
Tokyo 188
Tel: (010 81) 424-231111
Fax: (010 81) 424-225721
Telex: 2822545 MICJ

Nippon Research Center Ltd
Daini-Nagaoka Bldg
2-8-5 Hatchobori
Chuo-ku
Tokyo 104
Tel: (010 81) 3-5522415
Fax: (010 81) 3-5530024
Telex: 02224052 NIPRES
Affiliated to Gallup
International Research
One of the largest research
companies in Japan covering
consumer markets.

Tokyo Research Consultants
Co Ltd
Nishiyama-Kogyo-Nibancha
Bldg
5 Nibancho
Chiyoda-ku
Tokyo 102
Tel: (010 81) 3-2344351
Fax: (010 81) 3-2344345
Parent company: Marketing
Research Services Inc

Yano Research Institute
2-10-1 Nihonbashi Hamacho
Chuo-ku
Tokyo 103
Tel: (010 81) 3-6679188
Fax: (010 81) 3-6670269
Telex: 2522278 YANO J
Parent company: Yano
Research Institute (USA) Ltd

Organisations Providing Economic and Statistical Data

Bank of Japan (The)
Research and Statistics
Department
Produces the Economic
Statistics Annual, provides
financial statistics, national
accounts and other economic
data

Bank of Tokyo (The)
Economic Research Division
Produces a number of
economic and financial
reports including the monthly
Tokyo Financial Review.
Other large Japanese banks
publish stock market research
and economic statistics. For
example the Industrial Bank
of Japan produces the IBJ
Monthly Report, and the
Japanese Finance and
Industry Quarterly Survey

Economic Research
Association
15-10 Ginza 3-chome
Chuo-ku
Tokyo 104
Tel: (010 81) 3-5423331

Dai-Ichi Kangyo Bank
Produces the DKB Economic
Report

Institute for Economic and
Financial Research
Toranomon NN Bldg
21-17 Toranomon 1-chome
Minato-ku
Tokyo 105
Tel: (010 81) 3-5084568

Institute for Financial Affairs
Inc
19 Minamimoto-machi
Shinjuku-ku
Tokyo 160
Tel: (010 81) 3-3581161
Fax: (010 81) 3-3577416
Telex: J23749 IFFAI

Institute of Foreign Exchange
and Trade Research (The)
4 Nihonbashi Hongokucho
3-chome
Chuo-ku
Tokyo 103
Tel: (010 81) 3-2417721

Institute of Statistical
Research
18-16 Shinbashi 1-chome
Minato-ku
Tokyo 105
Tel: (010 81) 3-5918496

International Trade and
Industry Research Institute
8-9 Ginza 2-chome
Chuo-ku
Tokyo 104
Tel: (010 81) 3-5353051

Japan Federation of Economic
Organizations (Keidanren)
Keidanren Kaikan 9-4
Otemachi 1-chome
Chiyoda-ku
Tokyo
Tel: (010 81) 3-2791411

Japanese Information Center
of Science and Technology
(JICST)
5-2 Nagata-cho 2-chome
Chiyoda-ku
Tokyo 100
Tel: (010 81) 3-5816411
Fax: (010 81) 3-5933375
Telex: 2223604 JICST J

Japan Institute for Economic
Research
Entsuji-Gadelius Bldg
2-39 Akasaka
5-chome
Minato-ku
Tokyo 107
Tel: (010 81) 3-5840571

Japan Institute for Social and
Economic Affairs
(Kezai Koho Center)
6-1 Otemachi 1-chome
Tokyo 100
Tel: (010 81) 3-2011416
Fax: (010 81) 3-2011418
Telex: 2225452 KKCTOK J
Private, non profit
organization. Works in
cooperation with the Japan
Federation of Economic
Organizations. Produces a
number of publications
including Japan Update and
Japan Information Resources
in the USA

Japan Securities Research
Institute
5-8 Nihonbashi
Kayabacho 1-chome
Chuo-ku
Tokyo 103
Tel: (010 81) 3-6690737

Kansai Economic Federation
Nakanoshima-Center Bldg
2-27 Nakanoshima 6-chome
Kita-ku
Osaka
Tel: (010 81) 6-4410101

Ministry of International
Trade and Industry
Produces a number of
publications covering trade
and industry including
statistics on Japanese industry
sectors

Research Bureau
Economic Planning Agency
3-1-1 Kasumigaseki
Chiyoda-ku
Tokyo 100
Publishes a number of major
sources of statistics such as
the Statistical Handbook of
Japan; Economic Survey of
Japan

Research Institute on the
National Economy
Aoyama Tower Bldg
24-15 Minami Aoyama
2-chome
Minato-ku
Tokyo 107
Tel: (010 81) 3-4035271

Tokyo Stock Exchange
Publications include:
Annual Statistics Report
Monthly Statistics Report
A Profile of the TSE
Tokyo Stock Exchange Fact
Book
Key Statistics for the
Securities Market and
Economy in Japan
Stock market research is also
provided by the large
securities houses such as
Daiwa Securities, Nikko
Securities, Nomura
Securities, and Yaimaichi
Securities

World Economic Information
Services
World Trade Center Bldg
4-1 Hamatsucho 2-chome
Minato-ku
Tokyo 105
Tel: (010 81) 3-4355731

Publications

Directories
Japan Business Publications
in English
Produced by the British
Library, Business Information
Service.
Provides a listing of the
British Library's holdings.
Lists sources of statistics,
market information, industry
surveys, plus trade and
business journals

Japan Directory
Published by Japan Press Ltd,
Tokyo
Consists of two volumes.
Provides contact details for
Japanese companies, service
organizations, embassies and
associations

Japan Directory of
Professional Associations
Published by Japan
Publications Guide Service,
Tokyo

Japanese Addresses in the UK
Published by the
Anglo-Japanese Economic
Institute, London.
Provides addresses of
Japanese banks, associations,
and companies in the UK

Standard Trade Index of
Japan (STI) (The)
Published by the Japan
Chamber of Commerce and
Industry, Tokyo.
Provides addresses and
telephone numbers for a wide
range of organizations in
Japan, including economic,
government and trade
associations

Major Newspapers
Tokyo:

Akahata
Daily

Asahi Evening News
Daily. English

Asian Wall Street Journal
Daily

Business Japan
Daily

Daily Yomiuri
Daily. English

Dempa Shimbun
Daily

Japan Times
Daily. English

Mainichi Shimbun
Daily

Nihon Keizai Shimbun
Daily

Nihon Kogyo Shimbun
Daily

Nikkei Ryutsu Shimbun
Daily

Nikkei Sangyo Shimbun
Daily

Seikyo Shimbun
Daily

Tokyo Shimbun
Daily

Tokyo Times
Daily

Yomiuri Shimbun
Daily

Journals and Periodicals
Asahi Business
Publisher's address:
Chuo-ku, Tsukiji 7-8-5,
Tokyo. Weekly

Bulletin of the
Anglo-Japanese Economic
Institute, London
Bi-monthly

Business Japan
Published by Nikkan Kogyo
Shinbunsha. Monthly

Dentsu Japan Marketing
Published by Dentsu Inc,
Tokyo
Bi-monthly

Diamond. Weekly
Diamond Report. Weekly
Diamond Harvard Business. 6
issues per annum
Publisher's address for the
above 3 journals: 1-4-2
Kasumigaseiki, Chiyoda-ku,
Tokyo 100

Digest of Japanese Industry
and Technology
Published by Japan Trade and
Industry Publicity Inc.
Monthly

Economic Journal
Published by Nihon Keizai
Tsushin Sha, Tokyo.
Fortnightly

Far Eastern Economic Review
Weekly

Japan Commerce and
Industry
Published by the Japan
Chamber of Commerce and
Industry. Monthly

Japan Economic Journal
Published by Japan Economic
Journal. Weekly

Kaikei Journal
Published by Daiichi Hoki
Shuppan, Tokyo. Monthly

News from MITI
Published by the Ministry of
International Trade and
Industry, Tokyo
Monthly

Nikkei Business
Published by Nikkei
McGraw-Hill Co, Tokyo.
Fortnightly

Oriental Economist
Published by the Oriental
Economist, Tokyo. Monthly

Tokyo Business Today
Published by the Oriental
Economist, Tokyo. Monthly

Tokyo Money
Published by Dia
International Corporation,
Tokyo. Monthly

Trade Times
Published by the Trade Times
Ltd in association with the
Japan Machinery Exporters
Association, Tokyo

World Traders
Published by the World Trade
Centre of Japan Inc, Tokyo.
Quarterly

Korea, Republic of

Sources of Economic,
Stock Market
Information, and
Investment Research
Services

Banks

Central Bank
Bank of Korea
110, 3-ka
Namdaemoon Ro
Chung-ku
Seoul 100
Tel: (010 82) 2-77107/7785011
Telex: 24711; 24712

Korean Banks in London
Bank of Korea
Plantation House
31-35 Fenchurch Street
London EC3M 3DX
Tel: 01-626 8321

Bank of Seoul
107 Cheapside
London EC2V 6DT
Tel: 01-606 3050

Cho Hung Bank
Plantation House
31-35 Fenchurch Street
London EC3M 3DX
Tel: 01-623 7791

Commercial Bank of Korea
72-73 Basinghall Street
London EC2V 5DX
Tel: 01-606 3871

Export-Import Bank of Korea
Plantation House
31-35 Fenchurch Street
London EC3M 3DX
Tel: 01-623 1831

Korea Development Bank
(Address as above)

Korea Exchange Bank
1, Old Jewry
London EC2R 8DU
Tel: 01-606 0191

Korea First Bank
80 Cannon Street
London EC4N 6HH
Tel: 01-626 9264

Major Korean Banks
Bank of Seoul
10-1 Namdaemun-ro
2-ka Chung-ku
Seoul
Tel: (010 82) 2-77160
Telex: K23311-5

Cho Hung Bank
14, 1-ka
Namdaemun-ro
Chung-ku
Seoul
Tel: (010 82) 2-7332000
Telex: K23321/5

Commercial Bank of Korea
111-1, 2-ka
Namdaemun-ro
Chung-ku
Seoul
Tel: (010 82) 2-77130/287271
Telex: K24611/6

Export-Import Bank of Korea
PO Box YPO 641
Seoul
Tel: (010 82) 2-7841021

Hanil Bank
CPO Box 1033
130 Namdaemun-ro
2-ka, Chung-ku
Seoul
Tel: (010 82) 2-77120
Telex: K23823/31

Korea Development Bank
(The)
CPO Box 28
10-2, Kwanchol-dong
Chongno-ku
Seoul
Tel: (010 82) 2-7332121
Telex: K27463

Korea Exchange Bank
181, Ulchiro 2-ka
Chung-ku
Seoul 100
Tel: (010 82) 2-77146
Telex: 23141/5

Korea First Bank
100 Kongpyung-dong
Chongno-ku
Seoul 110
Tel: (010 82) 2-7330070
Telex: K23685

Stockbrokers
The Korea Stock Exchange in
Seoul is the only exchange in
Korea

Korea Stock Exchange
33, Yoido-dong
Youngdeungpo-ku
Seoul 150-010
Tel: (010 82) 2-7833371
Telex: K28384 KOSTEX

Members (as at February 1988)
Bookook
34-2 Yoido-dong
Youngdeungpo-ku
Seoul 150-010
Tel: (010 82) 2-7841010

Coryo
25-5, 1-ka Chungmuro
Jung-ku
Seoul 100
Tel: (010 82) 2-77136

Daehan
44-31 Yoido-dong
Youngdeungpo-ku
Seoul 150-010
Tel: (010 82) 2-7851661-9

Daewoo
34-3 Yoido-dong
Youngdeungpo-ku
Seoul 150-010
Tel: (010 82) 2-7843311/8851

Daeyu
25-15 Yoido-dong
Youngdeungpo-ku
Seoul 150-010
Tel: (010 82) 2-7827201

Daishin
34-8 Yoido-dong
Youngdeungpo-ku
Seoul 150-010
Tel: (010 82) 2-7841711/1811

Dongnam
34 Yoido-dong
Youngdeungpo-ku
Seoul 150-010
Tel: (010 82) 2-7835351/9

Dongbang
809-10 Yeogsam-dong
Gangnam-ku
Seoul 135-080
Tel: (010 82) 2-5532256

Dongsuh
34-1 Yoido-dong
Youngdeungpo-ku
Seoul 150-010
Tel: (010 82) 2-7847233

Hanheung
111 Da-dong
Jung-ku
Seoul 100-180
Tel: (010 82) 2-7571661

Hanil
51 Sokong-dong
Jung-ku
Seoul 100-070
Tel: (010 82) 2-7778315/9

Hanshin
44-1 Yoido-dong
Youngdeungpo-ku
Seoul 150-010
Tel: (010 82) 2-7843911/4911

Hanyang
34-11 Yoido-dong
Youngdeungpo-ku
Seoul 150-010
Tel: (010 82) 2-7852211

Hyundai
77 Mugyo-dong
Jung-ku
Seoul 100-170
Tel: (010 82) 2-7576511/21

Korea First
44-11 Yoido-dong
Youngdeungpo-ku
Seoul 150-010
Tel: (010 82) 2-7847233

Kunsul
59-20, 1-ka
Myung-dong
Jung-ku
Seoul 100-021
Tel: (010 82) 2-7766134/6

Lucky
83-5 Yoido-dong
Youngdeungpo-ku
Seoul 150-010
Tel: (010 82) 2-7847111/7751

Seoul
59-1, 1-ka
Myung-dong
Jung-ku
Seoul 100-021
Tel: (010 82) 2-7541300

Shinhan
31-2, 2-ka
Myung-dong
Jung-ku
Seoul 100-170
Tel: (010 82) 2-7771851/5

Shinyoung
34-8 Yoido-dong
Youngdeungpo-ku
Seoul 150-010
Tel: (010 82) 2-7843701

Sinheung
6, 2-ka
Ulchiro
Jung-ku
Seoul 100-192
Tel: (010 82) 2-7768260/9

Ssangyong
198, 2-ka
Ulchiro
Jung-ku
Seoul 100-192
Tel: (010 82) 2-77112

Taepyong
35-2 Yoido-dong
Youngdeungpo-ku
Seoul 150-010
Tel: (010 82) 2-7854991

Tongyang
6, 2-ka
Ulchiro
Jung-ku
Seoul 100-192
Tel: (010 82) 2-77151

Yuhwa
35-2 Yoido-dong
Youngdeungpo-ku
Seoul 150-010
Tel: (010 82) 2-7857951

Sources of General Background Information, Industry Sector Information and Trade Contacts

UK Addresses
Korea Trade Advisory Group
Overseas Trade Division
Department of Trade and
Industry
1, Victoria Street
London SW1H 0ET
Tel: 01-215 3352

Korea Trade Centre
Vincent House
Vincent Square
London SW1P 2NB
Tel: 01-834 5082
Fax: 01-630 5233
Telex: 22375 KOTRA G

Korean Embassy
4 Palace Gate
London W8
Tel: 01-581 0247

Addresses in Korea
American Chamber of
Commerce in Korea
307 Chosun Hotel
87-1 Sokong dong
Chung-ku
Seoul
Tel: (010 82) 2-7523061
Telex: 242560

British Chamber of
Commerce
23rd Floor
Daewoo Building
54 Namdaemunno
5-ga, Chung-ku
Seoul
Tel: (010 82) 2-7543680-9
Telex: K24480

Japanese External Trade
Organization (JETRO)
Taepyongro 1-ga
Chung-gu
Seoul
Tel: (010 82) 2-7398657
Telex: JETROSK K24461

Korea Chamber of Commerce
and Industry
45 Namdaemunno 4-ga
Chung-gu
Seoul
Tel: (010 82) 2-7570757
Telex: CHAMBER K25728

Seoul Chamber
(Addresses as above)

British Commercial
Counsellor
British Embassy
4 Chung-Dong
Chung-ku
Seoul
Tel: (010 82) 2-7257341
Telex: 27320 PRODOM K

Sources of Investment and Trade Advice, Assistance and Information

Foreign firms are allowed to set up Korean subsidiaries, but are not permitted to import on their own account. Finding a reliable agent is essential when doing business in Korea. Enquirers in the UK can contact the British Overseas Trade Board Advisory Group for initial advice.

Association of Foreign Trading Agents of Korea (AFTAK) (The)
45-14 Yoido-dong
Yungdungpo-ku
Seoul
Tel: (010 82) 2-7822206
Telex: KOFFER K23540

Economic Planning Board (EPD) (The)
82-1 Sejong-ro
Chongro-ku
Seoul

Korea Employers' Federation
43-1, Tohwa 2-dong
Mapo-ku
Seoul
Tel: (010 82) 2-7128261
Cable: KOEMPLOY SEOUL

Korea-US Economic Council, Inc
10-1 Hoehyon-dong
2-ga, Chung-ku
Seoul
Tel: (010 82) 2-7555496
Telex: KOTRASO K24265
Provides information and policy guidance to American business people seeking opportunities and contacts in Korea.

Korea Foreign Traders Association
Korean World Trade Centre
CPO Box 117
10-1, 2-ka
Hoehyon-dong
Chung-ku
Seoul
Fax: (010 82) 2-7541337
Telex: 24265 KOTRASO

Korean Trade Promotion Corporation
CPO Box 1621
10-1, 2-ka
Hoehyon-dong
Chung-ku
Seoul
Tel: (010 82) 2-7534180/9
Telex: 23659/27326

Ministry of Finance
Foreign Investment
Promotion Division
Istchumgang-dong
Kwachomshi
Kyonggido
Tel: (010 82) 2-5039276

Ministry of Trade and Industry (MTI)
77-6 Sejong-ro
Chongro-ku
Seoul

Professional Associations

Accountancy
Korean Institute of Certified Public Accountants
46-22 Susong-dong
Chongro-ku
Seoul
Tel: (010 82) 2-7378761

Banking
Korea Federation of Banks
4, 1-ka Myong-dong
Chung-ku
Seoul 100
Tel: (010 82) 2-7545414

Consultancy
Korea Consultants International
65-228 Hangangno 3-ka
Yongsan-ku
Seoul
Tel: (010 82) 2-7347771
Telex: KOCONST K23218

Korea Management Association
45-1 Tohwa-dong
Mapo-ku
Seoul
Tel: (010 82) 2-7199518

Insurance
Korea Non-Life Insurance Association
6th Floor
KRIC Building
80 Susong-dong
Chongro-ku
Seoul
Tel: (010 82) 2-7394161

Life Association of Korea
60-1 Chungmuro 3-ka
Chung-ku
Seoul

Marketing
Korea Marketing Association
45 Namdaemunno 4-ka
Chung-ku
Seoul
Tel: (010 82) 2-752875
Telex: DONGACO K28359

Trade Associations

General Industry
Federation of Korean Industries (The)
28-1 Youido-dong
Yongdungpo-ku
Seoul
Tel: (010 82) 2-7830821
Telex: FEKOIS K25544

Agriculture and Fishery Development Corporation
65-228 Hangangno 3-ka
Yongsan-ku
Seoul
Tel: (010 82) 2-7928201
Telex: AAFDC K23297

Electronic Industries Association of Korea
648, Yoksam-dong
Kangnam-ku
Seoul
Tel: (010 82) 2-5530941

Korea Advanced Institute of Science and Technology
39-1 Hawolgok-dong
Songbuk-ku
Seoul
Tel: (010 82) 2-9678801
Fax: (010 82) 2-9634013
Telex: KISTROK K27380

Korea Auto Industies Corp
Association
35-4 Youido-dong
Yongdungpo-ku
Seoul
Tel: (010 82) 2-7848261
Telex: KAIASK K22373

Korea Computers
Cooperative
427-5 Kongdok-dong
Mapo-ku
Seoul
Tel: (010 82) 2-7126990

Korea Consumer Goods
Exporters Association
10-1, Hoehyon-dong, 2-ka
Chung-ku
Seoul
Tel: (010 82) 2-7573161
Fax: (010 82) 2-7550782

Korea Electronic Industries
Cooperative
813-5 Pangbae-dong
Kangnam-ku
Seoul
Tel: (010 82) 2-5332309

Korean Federation of Textile
Industries
10-1 Hoehyon-dong 2-ka
Chung-ku
Seoul
Tel: (010 82) 2-7780821
Telex: KOFOTI K22677

Korean Foods Industry
Association Inc
1174-4 Socho-dong
Kangnam-ku
Seoul
Tel: (010 82) 2-5855052

Korea Metal Industry
Cooperative
13-31 Youido-dong
Yongdungpo-ku
Seoul
Tel: (010 82) 2-7837811

Korea Paper Manufacturers'
Association
76-28 Hannam-dong
Yongsan-ku
Seoul
Tel: (010 82) 2-7985861
Telex: KPASSO K25921

Korea Pharmaceutical
Industry Association
19-20 Kwanchol-dong
Chongno-ku
Seoul
Tel: (010 82) 2-7342401

Korea Telecommunication
Industry Cooperative
Room 910, Hanam Building
44-27 Youido-dong
Yongdungpo-ku
Seoul
Tel: (010 82) 2-7843621

Company Financial and Product Information

Korea Directory (1988)
Published by the Korea
Directory Company, Seoul
Contains address, telephone,
telex, fax numbers and names
of top executives for Korean
firms and organisations.
Covers manufacturing and
service organisations,
including banks, insurance
companies and trade agents

Korea Yellow Pages
Published by Korea Yellow
Pages Ltd, Seoul
Covers over 18 000 firms.
Provides addresses,
telephone numbers, and lists
trade fairs and exhibitions

Korean Business Directory
Published by the Korean
Chamber of Commerce and
Industry
Contains listings of
commodities, firms, financing
and service companies, and
economic organisations

Korean Trade Directory
Published by Korean Traders
Association, Seoul
Includes a listing of exporters
and importers by
commodities, and foreign
firms established in Korea

Economic and Market Statistical Data

Market Research Organisations

Hankook Research Company
5-6 F1 Sungho Building
Yeogsam-dong
Gangnam-ku
Seoul
Tel: (010 82) 2-5629731/3
Fax: (010 82) 2-5543027
Telex: K23989 HANR

Korea Survey (Gallup) Polls
Ltd
221 Sajik-dong
Chong-ro
Seoul
Tel: (010 82) 2-7368448
Fax: (010 82) 2-7399696
Telex: K25053 KIPOMIP

AC Nielsen Company (Korea
Branch)
10th Floor, Namkyung
Building
8-2 Samsung-dong
Kangnam-ku
Seoul
Tel: (010 82) 2-5461181
Telex: K26168 NIELKOR

Oricom Inc
105-7 Nonhyun-dong
Kangnam-ku
Seoul
Tel: (010 82) 2-5103114
Fax: (010 82) 2-5423966

Frank Small & Associates Ltd
(Seoul Branch)
Namsan Mansion
Suite 1001
726-74 Hannam-dong
Yongsan-ku
Seoul
Tel: (010 82) 2-7932998
Fax: (010 82) 2-5338089
Telex: FSAKOR K32260
Seoul Marketing Survey
237-12 Kongdeok-dong
Mapo-ku
Seoul
Tel: (010 82) 2-7155130
Telex: K29775

Organisations Providing Economic and Statistical Data

Bank of Korea (see banks section for address) produces a range of financial and economic statistical data. Publications include the following:
Economic Statistics Yearbook
Monthly Statistical Bulletin
Quarterly Economic Review
Other large Korean banks publish economic and financial statistics. For example, the Korean Development Bank produces the KDB Report (monthly)

Economic Planning Board, (National Bureau of Statistics) (see Investment section for address) publishes the following:
Economic Bulletin. Monthly
Korea Statistical Yearbook
Major Statistics of the Korean Economy
Monthly Statistics of Korea

Korea Development Institute
270-41 Chongnyangni-dong
Tongdaemun-ku
Seoul
Tel: (010 82) 2-9678811
Produces 'Quarterly Economic Outlook'

Korea Listed Companies Association
33 Youido-dong
Yongdungpo-ku
Seoul
Tel: (010 82) 2-7836501

Korea Securities Dealers Association (KSDA)
34 Youido-dong
Yongdungpo-ku
Seoul
Tel: (010 82) 2-7835391
Publishes 'Securities Market in Korea'

Korea Stock Exchange (see Stockbrokers section for address) produces a fact book which contains detailed statistics on the Korean stock market

Korea Trade Office (KOTRA) (see Investment section for address), is a government organisation which produces statistics on Korean trade, and economics

Lucky Research Institute
HQ: 20 Yoido-dong
Yongdungpo-ku
Seoul 150
Tel: (010 82) 2-7871114
Provides statistics on the Korean stock market in a daily and monthly report. It also provides company analysis

Office of Customs Administration
71 Nonhyon-dong
Gangnam-ku
Seoul
Tel: (010 82) 2-5427141
Publishes 'Monthly Foreign Trade Statistics'

Publications

Directories

American Chamber of Commerce in Korea Membership Directory
Lists members and provides addresses and telephone numbers

Association of Foreign Trading Agents of Korea, Directory
Provides details of main items traded and suppliers

Korea Annual
Published by the Hapdong News Agency, Seoul

Major Newspapers

Chosun Ilbo
Daily and weekly editions

Dong-A Ilbo
Oriental daily news

Han-Joong Daily News
Daily

Hyundae Economics Daily

Joong-Ang
Daily

Korean Commercial Press Report
Daily

Korean Economic Daily
English. Daily

Korea Herald
English. Daily

Korea Times
English. Daily

KOTRA Marketing News
Daily

Maeil Kyungje Shinmun
Daily. Economic coverage

Seoul Kyungje Shinmun
Daily. Economic coverage

Journals and Periodicals

Asia Wall Street Journal
Publisher's address:
Room 302, 111
Chunghak-dong,
Chongro-ku, Seoul

Business Korea
Publisher's address:
Yoido, PO Box 273, Seoul 150

Electronic Times
Monthly

Far Eastern Economic Review
Publisher's address:
KPO Box 244, Seoul

Korean Business Review
Publisher's address:
Samilro Building
10, Kwanchul-dong,
Chongro-ku, Seoul
Weekly

Naeway Business Journal
Daily

News Review
Publisher's address:
1-12, 3-ga Haehyon-dong,
Chung-ku, Seoul
Weekly

Malaysia

Sources of Economic, Stock Market Information, and Investment Research Services

Banks

Central Bank
Bank Negara Malaysia
PO Box 10922
50929 Kuala Lumpur
Tel: (010 60) 3-2988044
Telex: 3201

Malaysian Banks in London
Bank Bumiputra Malaysia
Berhad
36-38 Leadenhall Street
London EC3A 1AP
Tel: 01-488 2021

Malayan Banking Berhad
74 Coleman Street
London EC2R 5BN
Tel: 01-638 0561

Major Malaysian Banks
Arab Malaysian Merchant
Bank Berhad
22nd Floor
Bangunan Arab-Malaysian
55 Jalan Raja Chulan
PO Box 10233
50708 Kuala Lumpur
Tel: (010 60) 3-922155
Telex: 31167; 31169 ABMAL
MA

Bank Bumiputra Malaysia
Berhad
Menara Bumiputra
Jalan Melaka
PO Box 10407
50100 Kuala Lumpur
Tel: (010 60) 3-2988011;
2919199

Development and
Commercial Bank Berhad
Wisma On Tai
161B Jalan Ampang
PO Box 10145
50907 Kuala Lumpur
Tel: (010 60) 3-2617177
Telex: MA 31032 DC BANK

Malayan Banking Berhad
100 Jalan Tun Perak
50050 Kuala Lumpur
Tel: (010 60) 3-2308833
Telex: MA 30438

Malayan United Bank Berhad
21st Floor
Mui Plaza
Jalan P Ramlee
50250 Kuala Lumpur
Tel: (010 60) 3-2411533
Telex: MA 32590 MUBHO;
MA 30714 MUBBFX

Perwira Habib Bank Malaysia
Berhad
3rd Floor
Wisma SPK
Jalan Sultan Ismail
PO Box 10459
50915 Kuala Lumpur
Tel: (010 60) 3-2432000
Telex: MA 30448 NABIB

Public Bank Berhad
(Commercial bank)
Bangunan Public Bank
6 Jalan Sultan Sulaiman
5000 Kuala Lumpur
Tel: (010 60) 3-2741788
Telex: MA 30584 (General)

Sabah Bank Berhad
Tower A, Zone 2
Jalan Tuaran
88990 Kota Vinabalu
Sabah
Tel: (010 60) 88-218911
Telex: SBB MA 80294

Southern Bank Berhad
PO Box 12281
49 Jalan Hang Lekiu
50772 Kuala Lumpur
Tel: (010 60) 3-2300222;
2387900

United Asian Bank Berhad
PO Box 10753
Menara UAB
6 Jalan Tun Perak
50724 Kuala Lumpur
Tel: (010 60) 3-2931722
Telex: 31144 UNISIA MA
(General)

United Malayan Banking
Corporation Berhad
Bangunan UMBC
Jalan Sultan Sulaiman
PO Box 12006
50935 Kuala Lumpur
Tel: (010 60) 3-2309866
Telex: MA 30483; MA 30662

Wah Tat Bank Berhad
Head Office: No 15 Jalan Bank
PO Box 87
96007 Sibu
Sarawak
East Malaysia
Tel: (010 60) 84-336733
Telex: MA72024 WAHTAT

Stockbrokers
Kuala Lumpur Stock
Exchange (The)
3rd Floor, Block C
Damansara Centre
Damansara Heights
50490 Kuala Lumpur
Tel: (010 60) 3-2546433
Telex: 30241 KLSE MA

Kuala Lumpur Members (143 members including 53 member companies 1988)
Arab-Malaysian Securities
SDN.BHD
15th Floor, Bangunan
Arab-Malaysian
55 Jalan Raja Chulan
50200 Kuala Lumpur
Tel: (010 60) 3-2382788
General office
Fax: 2383162
Telex: AMSEC MA 31796

BBMB Securities SDN BHD
Box 36, Bangunan MAS, Suite
2.1
2nd Floor, Jalan Sultan Ismail
50250 Kuala Lumpur
Tel: (010 60) 3-2619900
Fax: 2613087
Telex: MA 21335

Charles Bradburne & Co
(1930) SDN BHD
2nd Floor, President House
Jalan Sultan Ismail
50250 Kuala Lumpur
Tel: (010 60) 3-2485411;
2485431
Cables: TALLYHO
Telex: CEEBEE MA 33186

Cimb Securities SDN BHD
Lot No 22.02, 2nd Floor
Menara Promet
Jalan Sultan Ismail
PO Box 10126
50704 Kuala Lumpur
Tel: (010 60) 3-2422088 (20
lines)
Cables: LOWSEC
Telex: MA 30991

H A Securities SDN BHD
1st Floor, Wisma On-Tai
161B Jalan Ampang
50450 Kuala Lumpur
Tel: (010 60) 3-2617666
Fax: (010 60) 3-2618062
Cables: HASEC Kuala
Lumpur
Telex: AZAM MA 21314

K & N Kenanga SDN BHD
8th Floor, Pernas
International Building
801 Jalan Sultan Ismail
50250 Kuala Lumpur
Tel: (010 60) 3-2613066 (5
lines)
Cables: KENSTOCK Kuala
Lumpur
Telex: KEN MA 31070

Leong & Co SDN BHD
12th Floor, Wisma
Hamzah-Kwong Hing
1 Leboh Ampang
50100 Kuala Lumpur
Tel: (010 60) 3-2305022
(Administration)
 (010 60) 3-2325611 (Trading)
Fax: (010 60) 3-2321589
Cables: SHAREBOND
Telex: MA 31363 SHABON

Malayan Traders & Co SDN
BHD
6th Floor, Menara Tun Razak
Jalan Raja Laut, PO Box 10310
50710 Kuala Lumpur
Tel: (010 60) 3-2935088 (6
lines)
Fax: (010 60) 3-2923478
Cables: ACORN Kuala
Lumpur

Mayban Securities Sendirian
Berhad
30th Floor, Menara Maybank
100 Jalan Tun Perak
50050 Kuala Lumpur
Tel: (010 60) 3-2323822;
2323833
Fax: (ISD):2323660
Telex: MAYSEC MA 20294

Noone & Co SDN BHD
10th Floor, Bena Towers
No 160, Jalan Ampang
PO Box 10190
50450 Kuala Lumpur
Tel: (010 60) 3-2618055;
2618157
Telegrams: HINOON
Telex: HOLD MA 31186

OSK & Parners SDN BHD
10th Floor, Plaza MBF
Jalan Ampang
50450 Kuala Lumpur
Tel: (010 60) 3-2619200
Fax: (010 60) 3-2618254
Telex: MA 30272
Telegrams: 'DOCK'

Othman & Ng SDN BHD
19th & 20th Floor, UBN
Tower
Jalan P Ramlee
50250 Kuala Lumpur
Tel: (010 60) 3-2321277
Fax: (010 60) 3-2322369
Telex: ONSED MA 30848

P B Securities SDN BHD
Lot 264, 2nd Floor
Wisma HLA
Jalan Raja Chulan
50200 Kuala Lumpur
Tel: (010 60) 3-2413011
Fax: (010 60) 3-2431951
Cables: GEPESEC Kuala
Lumpur
Telex: GP MA 31072

Rashid Hussain Securities
SDN BHD
10th Floor, Menara Tun Razak
Jalan Raja Laut, PO Box 12699
50786 Kuala Lumpur
Tel: (010 60) 3-2934166
Fax: (010 60) 3-2936182
Cables: REZEKI KUALA
LUMPUR
Telex: RHSSB MA 31790 RHS
MA 31791

Seagroatt & Campbell SDN
BHD
Wisma Hamzah-Kwong Hing
7th Floor
No 1 Leboh Ampang
PO Box 10790
50100 Kuala Lumpur
Tel: (010 60) 3-2327122;
2327103/8
Cables: SECAM, Kuala
Lumpur
Telex: MA 32816 SEAGRO

UMBC Securities SDB BHD
21st Floor, Bangunan UMBC
Jalan Sultan Sulaiman
5000 Kuala Lumpur
Tel: (010 60) 3-2749288;
2749778
Fax: (010 60) 3-2749907
(Administration)
Telex: MA 20289 USECSB
(Administration)

Zalik Securities SDN BHD
9th Floor, Menara Apera-ULG
84 Jalan Raja Chulan
50200 Kuala Lumpur
Tel: (010 60) 3-2616544;
3-2616584
 3-2616581; 3-2616591
Telex: MA 31097

Member Companies in Selangor

Kajang
Apex Securities SDN BHD
3rd Floor, Wisma Apex
145A-C Jalan Bukit, PO Box 16
43007 Kajang, Selangor
Tel: (010 60) 3-8332214
Fax: (010 60) 3-8362135
Telex: CHLICK MA 31617

Klang
Klang Securities SDN
22A Jalan Yeo Guan Hup
41000 Kelang, Selangor
Tel: (010 60) 3-3325725

Petaling Jaya
Halim Securities SDN BHD
4th Floor, Menara MPPJ
Jalan Tengah
46770 Petaling Jaya
PO Box 561, 46300 Selangor
Tel: (010 60) 3-7555777;
7555008
Fax: (010 60) 3-7554612
Telex: MA 36007

Mohaiyani Securities SDN
54 Jalan SS21/35
47400 Damansara Utama
Petaling Jaya, Selangor
Tel: (010 60) 3-7197345;
7197353
Telex: MOSEC MA 37476

Shah Alam
A T Securities SDN BHD
Tingkat 1, Kompleks PKNS
40000 Shah Alam, Selangor
Tel: (010 60) 3-5594900
Fax: (010 60) 3-5599682
Telex: AT SSB MA 39863

**Member Companies in
Johore**

Batu Pahat
Koh & Lee Securities SDN
3A, 4A, 5A (1st Floor)
Jalan Fatimah
83000 Batu Pahat, Johore
Tel: (010 60) 7-442282
Telex: MA DHSB 60303
Cables: SAHAM BATU
PAHAT

Johore Bahru
Eng Securities SDN
Suites 1001, 1003 and 1005
10th Floor
Merlin Inn Tower, Jalan
Meldrum
80000 Johore Baru, Johore
Tel: (010 60) 7-226211/5
Cables: ENGSEC
JOHOREBARU

Hamid & Chua Securities
SDN
4th Floor, Wisma Great
Oriental
23 Jalan Meldrum, PO Box 762
80000 Johore Baru
Tel: (010 60) 7-230422/28
Cables: JOHORESEC Johore
Bahru
Telex: CHUA MA 60645

Muar
Aliah & Company Securities
SDN BHD
2nd Floor, 16-17 Jalan
Maharani
P O Box 106
84007 Muar, Johore
Tel: (010 60) 6-923332
Telex: AASEC MA 60414

**Member Companies in
Kedah**

Alor Setar
Alor Setar Securities SDN
2nd Floor, Wisma AIA
999 Jalan Teluk Wanjah
05200 Alor Setar, Kedah
Tel: (010 60) 4-717088; 717089
Telex: ASSEC MA 42024

**Member Companies in
Kelantan**

Kota Bharu
Lee & Kee Securities SDN
BHD
5503 Jalan Sri Maha Raja
PO Box 204, 15720 Kota Bharu
Kelantan
Tel: (010 60) 9-782798; 718299
Cables: LEESAHAM

**Member Companies in
Malacca**
Chuaco Securities (Melaka)
SDN
Lot 9 & 10, 1st Floor
Bangunan Tabong Haji
Jalan Bandar Kaba
PO Box 209
95740 Melaka
Tel: (010 60) 6-228044; 228135
Cables: RUTIN, MALACCA
Telex: CHUACO MA 62855

Malacca Traders SDN BHD
171 Jalan Bunga Raya
PO Box 248
75750 Melaka
Tel: (010 60) 6-222322; 222372
Cables: MACATRA

Syarikat Tan Chow & Loh
Securities SDN
19-21 Lorong Hang Jebat
PO Box 93, 75710 Melaka
Tel: (010 60) 6-225211; 225414
Cables: KNIGHTS

**Member Companies in
Negeri Sembilan**
Kimara Securities SDN
49 Jalan Yam Tuan
70000 Seremban
Tel: (010 60) 6-727701
Telex: KIMARA MA 63989

Seremban Securities SDN
BHD
Tingkat 3, 22 & 23, Jalan Dato
Bandar Tunggal, PO Box 238
70720 Seremban, Negeri
Sembilan
Tel: (010 60) 6-723131/4;
723137
Telex: CTSEC MA 63951

**Member Companies in
Pahang**

Kuantan
WK Securities SDN
3rd Floor, Bangunan Asia Life
34-40 Jalan Telok Sisek
25000 Kuantan, Pahang
Tel: (010 60) 9-528111 (5 lines)

**Member Companies in
Penang**
AA Anthony & Co SDN
9 Beach Street, PO Box 245
10730 Pulau Pinang
Tel: (010 60) 4-624301; 624302
(General)
Cables: ANTHO, PENANG
Telex: AAACOS MA 40891

Hwang & Yusoff Securities
SDN BHD
Levels 2 & 3, Wisma Sri
Pinang
60 Green Hall
10200 Penang
Tel: (010 60) 4-376996
Fax: (010 60) 4-379597
Telex: HANDY MA 40709
 HWANG MA 40949
Cables: SOUTHSTOCK,
Penang

Syarikat Soon Theam SDN
1st Floor, 2 Penang Street
10200 Penang
Tel: (010 60) 4-622361
Cables: YUREKA, Penang

Thong & Oh Securities SDN
BHD
Wisma Sri Pinang
Level 6, 60 Green Hall
10200 Penang
Tel: (010 60) 4-375481
Fax: (010 60) 4-375741
Cables: TOSECURE
Telex: THONGO MA 40675

United Traders Securities
SDN
6th Floor, Wisma Manilal
3 Penang Street, 10200
Penang
Tel: (010 60) 4-615954; 617864
(Trading)
 4-613679 (Administration)
Telex: UNTRAD MA 40834
Cables: STOSHA

Yusoff & Chan SDN
2nd Floor, 64 Bishop Street
10200 Penang
Tel: (010 60) 4-614166
Fax: (010 60) 4-622299
Telex: YUSSEC MA 40323

**Member Companies in
Perak**

Ipoh
Botly & Co SDN BHD
2nd Floor, Wisma Nanyang
Siang Pau
224-226, Jalan Sultan Iskandar
30000 Ipoh
Tel: (010 60) 5-545715; 536614
Cables: TRANSFER, Ipoh

C S Securities Sendirian
Berhad
189 Jalan Sultan Iskandar
30000 Ipoh
Tel: (010 65) 5-508233
Fax: (010 60) 5-507242
Cables: SECURE, Ipoh
Telex: CSSEC MA 44151

Kin Khoon & Co SDN BHD
23 & 25, Wisma Kota Emas
Jalan Dato Tahwil Azhar
PO Box 421, 30910 Ipoh
Tel: (010 65) 5-543311
Cables: KINSHARE, Ipoh
Telex: MA 44184 KINCO

Perak Traders & Co SDN
BHD
Bangunan Chinese Chamber
of Commerce
37 Jalan Bandar Raya, 30000
Ipoh
Tel: (010 65) 5-515711; 515117
Cables: SHARE, Ipoh
Telex: PEKTRA MA 44549

RNA Securities SDN
73-75 Clarke Street, 30000
Ipoh
Tel: (010 65) 5-537633/666
Telex: RNASEC MA 44325

Y K Fung Securities SDN
BHD
65 Clarke Street
30300 Ipoh
Tel: (010 65) 5-519591
Cables: FUNGSEC, Ipoh
Telex: YKFUNG MA 44179

Yew Securities SDN BHD
Level 2, Wisma U-Meng
Jalan Bandaraya, 30000 Ipoh
Tel: (010 65) 5-512122
Telegram: SECURITY Ipoh
Telex: MA 44129

Taiping
Nadzri & Ng Securities SDN
BHD
1st & 2nd Floors
18-20 Jalan Taming Sari
34300 Taiping, Perak
Tel: (010 65) 5-831390; 821192
Telex: UNTUNG MA 44315

**Sources of General
Background Information,
Industry Sector
Information and Trade
Contacts**

UK Addresses
Malaysian Trade Commission
(The)
17 Curzon Street
London W1Y 7FE
Tel: 01-499 7388
 01-499 5908
Telex: 265193 MTCLON G

Malaysian High Commission
Commercial Section
45 Belgrave Square
London SW1X 8QT
Tel: 01-235 8033

Customs Department
17 Curzon Street
London W1Y 7FE
Tel: 01-493 3826

Addresses in Malaysia
Associated Chinese
Chambers of Commerce and
Industry of Malaysia
c/o Chinese Assembly Hall
1 Jalan Maharajalela
50150 Kuala Lumpur
Tel: (010 60) 3-2320473;
2383287
Telex: MA 32995 KLSCC

Associated Indian Chambers
of Commerce and
Industry of Malaysia
Wisma UOA
36 Jalan Ampang
PO Box 12564
50450 Kuala Lumpur
Tel: (010 60) 3-23887917
Telex: MA 33526 SICC

British High Commission
13th Floor
Wisma Damansara
Jalan Semantan
50490 Kuala Lumpur
Tel: (010 60) 3-2541533
Telex: 30245

Malay Chamber of Commerce
& Industry of Malaysia
Tingkat 17
Plaza Pekeliling
2 Jalan Tun Razak
50400 Kuala Lumpur
Tel: (010 60) 3-2928522;
2928501
Telex: MA 30954 DEWANA

Malaysian International
Chamber of Commerce
and Industry
Tingkat 10
Wisma Damansara
Jalan Semantan
PO Box 10192
50706 Kuala Lumpur
Tel: (010 60) 3-2542117;
2541690
Telex: MA 32120 COMER

National Chamber of
Commerce and Industry of
Malaysia
17th Floor
Plaza Pekeliling
Jalan Tun Razak
Kuala Lumpur
Tel: (010 60) 3-2989873;
2989871
Telex: MA 33642 NACCI

Sabah Chamber of Commerce
Bangunan Central
Jalan Sagunting
88000 Kota Kinabulu
Tel: (010 60) 88-54913

United Chamber of Sarawek
Chamber of Commerce, c/o
Ernst and Whinney
Room 301, 3rd Floor
Wisma Bukit Mata
Jalan Tuanku Abdul Rahman
93100 Kuching
Sarawek

Sources of Investment and Trade Advice, Assistance and Information

The Malaysian Government
welcomes foreign investment
in the manufacturing sector.
It is government policy to
encourage projects to be
undertaken on a joint-venture
basis. The main Malaysian
organisations to contact for
advice on trading or investing
in Malaysia are the Malaysian
Export Trade Centre and
Malaysian Industrial
Development Authority.

Advertising Standards
Authority of Malaysia
c/o Coopers and Lybrand
Hong Kong Bank Building
Leboh Pasar
Kuala Lumpur

Director General of
Immigration
Administration Headquarters
2nd Floor Bangunan Bukota
Jalan Pantai Baru
59200 Kuala Lumpur
Tel: (010 60) 3-7578155

Federal Land Development
Authority (FELDA)
FELDA Headquarters, Jalan
Perumahan Gurney
54000 Kuala Lumpur
Tel: (010 60) 3-2935066
Telex: MA 32159

Industrial Relations
Department
Police Co-operative Building,
5th Floor
Jalan Sulaiman, 50000 Kuala
Lumpur
Tel: (010 60) 3-2380329

Inland Revenue Department
Blocks 11 & 8A
Government Offices Complex
Jalan Duta, 50600 Kuala
Lumpur
Tel: (010 60) 3-2547055;
2546066

Malaysian Export Trade
Centre
International Trade Division
Ministry of Trade and
Industry
Ground Floor, Wisma PKNS
Jalan Raja Laut
50350 Kuala Lumpur
Tel: (010 60) 3-2928122
Telex: MA 33721 MEXPO

Malaysian Industrial
Development Authority
(MIDA) Offices
The Director-General
Malaysian Industrial
Development Authority
3rd-6th Floors, Wisma
Damansara
Jalan Semantan, PO Box
10618
50720 Kuala Lumpur
Tel: (010 60) 3-2543633
Cables: FIDAMAL
Telex: MIDA MA 30752

MIDA Regional Office
Room No 5, 7th Floor
Kompleks Tun Abdul Razak
Jalan Wong Ah Fook
80720 Johore Bahru
Johor
Tel: (010 60) 7-220550

MIDA Regional Office
LKPM Wilayah Utara
8th Floor, Wisma PKNK
Jalan Sultan Badlishah
05720 Alor Setar
Kedah
Tel: (010 60) 4-723978

MIDA Regional Office
5th Floor, Bangunan PKINK
Jalan Tengku Maharani
15500 Kota Bharu
Kelantan
Tel: (010 60) 9-783151

MIDA Regional Office
5th Floor, Bangunan Asia Life
Jalan Telok Sisek, PO Box 178
25720 Kuantan
Pahang
Tel: (010 60) 9-522243

MIDA Regional Office
1st Floor (Tower Block)
Bangunan Wisma Wan
Mohamed
Jalan Kelab, PO Box 210
30720 Ipoh
Perak
Tel: (010 60) 5-513036; 513833

Malaysian Trade Union
Congress
19 Jalan Barat
46200 Petaling Jaya
PO Box 38
46700 Kuala Lumpur
Tel: (010 60) 3-7560224/5

Ministry of Finance
Block 9
Khazanah Malaysia
Jalan Duta
50592 Kuala Lumpur
Tel: (010 60) 3-2546066;
2540011

Perbadanan Nasional BHD
(PERNAS)
Menara Tun Razak
Jalan Raja Laut
PO Box 10493
50714 Kuala Lumpur
Tel: (010 60) 3-2935177

Registrar of Companies
Tingkat 16-20
Bangunan Kuwasa
Jalan Raja Laut
50350 Kuala Lumpur
Tel: (010 60) 3-2933733

Sarawak Economic
Development Corporation
PO Box 400
93902 Kuching
Tel: (010 60) 82-416777
Telex: 70063

Tourist Development
Corporation Malaysia
45 Jalan Tun Ismail
50480 Kuala Lumpur
Tel: (010 60) 3-2935188
Telex: 30093

Professional Associations

Accountancy

Institut Akauntan Malaysia
c/o Malaysian Association of
Certified Public Accountants
No 15 Jalan Medan Tuanku
50300 Kuala Lumpur
Malaysia

Banking

Association of Banks in
Malaysia (The)
23rd Floor
West Wing
Bangunan
Dato Zainal
Jalan Meleka
Kuala Lumpur
Tel: (010 60) 3-2922143

Institute of Bankers, Malaysia
Level 5
The Amoda
22 Jalan Imbi
55100 Kuala Lumpur
Tel: (010 60) 3-2426722

Insurance

General Insurance
Association of Malaysia
3rd Floor, Wisma PIAM
150 Jalan Tun Sambanthan
50470 Kuala Lumpur
Tel: (010 60) 3-2747395

National Association of
Malaysian Life Insurance
Agents (NAMLIA)
Hwa Li Building, 4th Floor
63/65 Jalan Ampang
50450 Kuala Lumpur
Tel: (010 60) 3-2303032

Trade Associations

Association of Natural Rubber
Producing Countries (The)
2nd Floor
Wisma Getah Asli 1
148 Jalan Ampang
Kuala Lumpur
Tel: (010 60) 3-2481735;
2488716

Automotive Federation of
Malaysia/
Malaysian Motor Vehicles
Assemblers Association
c/o Amim Holding SDN BHD
Batu Tiga Industrial Estate
Jalan Sesiku
4000 Shah Alam
Selangor
Tel: (010 60) 3-2435576

Federal Agricultural
Marketing Authority
5th-8th Floors, Bangunan
KUWASA
Jalan Raja Laut
50350 Kuala Lumpur
Tel: (010 60) 3-2932622;
2932626

Federation of Malaysian
Manufacturers
17th Floor, West Wing
Wisma Sime Darby
Jalan Raja Laut
PO Box 12194
50350 Kuala Lumpur
Tel: (010 60) 3-2931244
Telex: MA 32437 FMM

Federation of Malaya Timber
Exporters Association
c/o Hew & Company
3rd Floor, Straits Trading
Building
Leboh Pasar Besar
Kuala Lumpur
Tel: (010 60) 3-2986266

Federation of Rubber Trade
Associations of Malaysia
138 Jalan Bandar
50000 Kuala Lumpur
Tel: (010 60) 3-2384006

Fisheries Development
Authority
Tingkat 7, Wisma PKNS
Jalan Raja Laut
50628 Kuala Lumpur
Tel: (010 60) 3-2924044

Furniture Manufacturers and
Traders Federation of
Malaysia (The)
75-1 Jalan Mega Mandung
Kompleks Bandar, Batu 5
Jalan Kelang, Kuala Lumpur
Tel: (010 60) 3-7825708

Malayan Edible Oil Mfrs
Association
134-1 Jalan Brickfield
Kuala Lumpur
Tel: (010 60) 3-2747420

Malaysian Association of
Malay Exporters
c/o Rosdin Corporation SDN
BHD
35 Mezzanine Floor, KL
Hilton
Jalan Sultan Ismail
50250 Kuala Lumpur
Tel: (010 60) 3-2480255
Telex: MA 30763

Malaysian Automotive
Component Parts
Manufacturers Association
c/o Malaysian Sheet Glass
BHD
Batu 13 Sungei Buloh
4700 Sungei Buloh
Selangor
Tel: (010 60) 3-6561001

Malaysian Garment
Manufacturers Association
(The)
9B Jalan Lengkongan Brunei
Pudu
Kuala Lumpur
Tel: (010 60) 3-2422491

Malaysian International
Shipping Corporation Berhad
Wisma MISC, Jalan Conley
PO Box 10371
50712 Kuala Lumpur
Tel: (010 60) 3-2428088

Malaysian Oil Palm Growers
Council of Malaysia
3rd Floor
Wisma Getah Asli l
148 Jalan Ampang
Kuala Lumpur
Tel: (010 60) 3-2425088

Malaysian Plastics
Manufacturers Association
37 Jalan 20/14
Paramount Garden
Petaling Jaya
Selangor
Tel: (010 60) 3-7763027

Malaysian Plywood
Manufacturers Association
(The)
36 & 36A Jalan Telawi,
Bangsar Baru
Kuala Lumpur
Tel: (010 60) 3-2548062;
2543357

Malaysian Rubber Research &
Development Board
Bangunan Getah Asli
148 Jalan Ampang
PO Box 10508
50716 Kuala Lumpur
Tel: (010 60) 3-2484422;
2484690

Malaysian Timber Industry
Board
5th Floor
Bgn Sateras
Jalan Ampang
PO Box 10887
50728 Kuala Lumpur
Tel: (010 60) 3-2486233;
2484791

North Borneo Timber
Producers Association
Block XLI, Jalan Tiga
Sandakan
Tel: (010 60) 89-2137787

Palm Oil Refiners Association
of Malaysia
10th Floor, Room 1006
Wisma MPI
Jalan Raja Chulan
Kuala Lumpur
Tel: (010 60) 3-2488916;
2488893

Palm Oil Registration and
Licensing Authority (PORLA)
4th Floor, Block B
Damansara Office Complex
Jalan Dungan
PO Box 12184
50770 Kuala Lumpur
Tel: (010 60) 3-2547122

Persatuan Bank Dalam
Malaysia
23rd Floor, West Wing
Bangunan Datuk Zainal
Jalan Melaka
Kuala Lumpur
Tel: (010 60) 3-2922143;
2922243

Sarawak Manufacturers
Association
23 Jalan Ang Cheng Ho
Kuching
Tel: (010 60) 82-24682

Selangor Chinese Textile
General Goods
Merchant Association
59B Jalan Sultan
Kuala Lumpur
Tel: (010 60) 3-2384170

Timber Association of Sabah
Bandar Ramai Ramai
Sandakan
Tel: (010 60) 89-43847

Timber Exporters Association
of Sarawak
81 Kampung Nyabor Road
Sibu
Tel: (010 60) 84-333317

Timber Trade Federation of
Malaysia
c/o Rothmans International
Snooker Centre
5th Floor Wisma HLA
Jalan Raja Chulan
50200 Kuala Lumpur
Tel: (010 60) 3-2486605/6

Tin Industry Research &
Development Board
9th Floor Ming Building
Jalan Bukit Nanas
PO Box 12560
50782 Kuala Lumpur
Tel: (010 60) 3-2328461

Company Financial and Product Information

Directories

Annual Companies
Handbook
Published by the Kuala
Lumpur Stock Exchange
264 companies are listed
under broad categories.
Details provided include
address, registrars, auditors,
summary accounts

Directory of Registered
Companies in Malaysia
Published by Focusworld
SDN BHD, Kuala Lumpur
Includes information on over
150 000 licensed businesses

Kompass Malaysia
Published by Berita Kompass
SDN BHD
Volume I contains listing of
companies by products and
services. Also covers agencies
and trademarks.
Volume II contains basic
company facts. Entries are
arranged by states and by
alphabetical order.

Economic and Market Statistical Data

Market Research Organisations

Datasearch (Malaysia) SDN
BHD
6th Floor Wisma Lianseng
126 Jalan Bukit Bin Tang
55100 Kuala Lumpur
Tel: (010 60) 3-2412462;
243048arch (Malaysia) SDN
Frank Small and Associates
Malaysia
10 Jalan Ipoh
51200 Kuala Lumpur
Tel: (010 60) 3-2921166
Telex: MA31778 FSAKUL
Parent company: Frank Small
& Associates (Aust.) pty
Member of MRS

Omsearch (Malaysia) SDN
BHD
392C, 3rd Floor
Jalan Pudu
Kuala Lumpur 55100
PO Box 6126
Kuala Lumpur 55710
Tel: (010 60) 3-2425714;
2425796
Telex: MA 32488 CCSM
Member of MRS

P A Consulting Services SDN
BHD
Wisma Gerah Asli II
5th Floor
148, Jalan Ampang
50450 Kuala Lumpur
Tel: (010 60) 3-2612322;
2612360
Telex: MA 30233
Parent company: PA
International

Stochastic Marketing SDN
BHD
91M, SS 21/37 Damansara
Utama
Petaling Jaya
Selangor
Tel: (010 60) 3-7194278
Fax: (010 60) 3-7197685

Survey Research Malaysia
SDN BHD
63-C Jalan Lok Yew
55200 Kuala Lumpur
PO Box 12231
50943 Kuala Lumpur
Tel: (010 60) 3-2486122
Telex: ESAREM MA 30077
Affiliated to Survey Research
Group Ltd/AGB
Member of AMA, MRS

Organisations Providing Economic and Statistical Data

Bank Negara
PO Box 10922
50929 Kuala Lumpur
Produces Annual Reports,
plus a 'Quarterly Economic
Review'

Department of Statistics
Wisma Statistik
Jalan Cenderasari
50514 Kuala Lumpur
Tel: (010 60) 3-2922133
Publishes an annual statistical
bulletin
Publishes industrial statistics
in an Industrial Survey and
many
other sources of economic
statistics

Malaysian Industrial
Development Authority
Produces a number of useful
publications which provide
economic, labour, and
industrial statistics plus
statistics on the size of
overseas investment by
companies in Malaysia.
Publications include:
Annual Report
Directory of Approved
Companies
Malaysia, Investment in the
Manufacturing Sector
Malaysia, Manpower for
Industry
Brief on the Industrial Master
Plan (IMP)
Malaysia, Infrastructure for
Industry
Malaysia Industrial Digest
This digest includes a list of
projects, ie investments and
joint ventures approved by
the Ministry of Trade and
Industry

Ministry of Finance
Block 9
Khazanah Malaysia
Jalan Duta
5092 Kuala Lumpur
Produces annual Economic
Reports. Government
economic statistics
can also be found in the Five
Year Plans, 'Fifth Malaysia
Plan 1986-90'

Ministry of Labour
Research and Planning
Division
Tingkat 1-3 (Level 2-4)
Block B
Jalan Satu
Pusat Bandar Damansara
Damansara Heights
50532 Kuala Lumpur
Tel: (010 60) 3-2424088
Details on employment,
manpower development,
labour market, wages,
collective bargaining,
conditions of employment are
available in the following
publications produced by the
Ministry of Labour:
Benefits Workers enjoy under
various labour laws in
Malaysia
The Labour Indicators
Labour and Manpower
Report
Occupational Wages Survey
(major source of statistics on
employment and wage rates)
Wages and Employment
practices in the
manufacturing sector

Stock Exchange (Kuala
Lumpur)
Publications are available
providing statistics on the
Malaysian stock market.
These include:
Annual Companies
Handbook
KLSE Annual Report
KLSE Daily Closing Indices
KLSE Weekly Turnover and
Value Daily Diary
Listing Manual
KLSE Weekly Turnover and
Value Facts sheet

Major banks and brokers
provide statistics on the
Malaysian economy and stock
market, eg Rashid Hussain
Securities, Bank Negara
Malaysia.

Publications

Directories
Information Malaysia
Published by Belai Berita
Kuala Lumpur. Annual

Malaysia - A Foreigners
Guide
Published by Hornbill Books,
Kuala Lumpur
Reference book providing
information on Malaysian
business practices, culture,
travel, education

New Straits Times Annual
Published by Belai Berita,
Kuala Lumpur
Available in English

New Straits Times Directory
Published by Belai Berita,
Kuala Lumpur

Who's Who in the Malaysian
Chinese Community
Published by Budayamas
SDN, Kuala Lumpur

Major Newspapers
Berita Harian
Malay. Daily

Berita Minggu
Malay. Daily

Daily Times
(main local financial
newspaper)
English. Daily

Malay Mail
English. Daily

Malayan Thung Pau
Chinese. Daily

New Straits Times
English. Daily

New Sunday Times
English. Weekly

Star (The)
English. Daily

Sunday Mail
English. Weekly

Utusan Malaysia
Daily

Utusan Zaman
Weekly

Journals and Periodicals
Asian Trade and Industry
Publishers address:
PO Box 836
Kuala Lumpur
Monthly

Asiaweek
Published by Asiaweek Ltd,
Hong Kong
One of the main local
business journals
Weekly

Far Eastern Economic Review
Published by FEER, Hong
Kong
Weekly

Investors Digest
One of the main financial
journals.
Published by the Kuala
Lumpur Stock Exchange.
Monthly

Malaysian Business
Publishers: Belai Berita, Kuala
Lumpur
One of the main business
journals
English. Bi-monthly

Malaysian Digest
Published by the Ministry of
Foreign Affairs
Kuala Lumpur
Political journal. Monthly

Malaysian Government
Gazette
Publishers: Government
Printing Dept
Kuala Lumpur

Puspa Niaga
Publishers: Balai Berita, Kuala
Lumpur
Published 6 times per annum

Sarawak by the Week.
Weekly
Pedoman Ra'ayat. Monthly
Published by the Malaysian
Information Office,
Kuching

Sarawak Gazette
Published by Government
Printing Office,
Kuching
English. Monthly

Netherlands

Sources of Economic, Stock Market Information and Investment Research Services

Banks

Central Bank
De Nederlandsche Bank NV
PO Box 98
Westeinde 1
1000 AB Amsterdam
Tel: (010 31) 20-5249111
Telex: 11355

Dutch Banks in London
Algemene Bank Nederland
61 Threadneedle Street
London EC2P 2HH
Tel: 01-628 4272

Amsterdam-Rotterdam Bank
NV
101 Moorgate
London EC2M 6SB
Tel: 01-638 2700

Bank Mees and Hope NV
Princes House
95 Gresham Street
London EC2V 7NA
Tel: 01-606 4022

Credit Lyonnais Bank
Nederland
41-43 Madox Street
London W1R OBS
Tel: 01-499 6343

EBC Amro Bank
(Subsidiary of
Amsterdam-Rotterdam Bank)
10 Devonshire Square
London EC2M 4HS
Tel: 01-621 0101

F Van Lanschot International
1 Finsbury Square
London EC2M 4HS
Tel: 01-588 2783

Nederlandsche
Middenstandsbank
2 Copthall Avenue
London EC2R 7BD
Tel: 01-628 5311

Pierson, Helding, Pierson
(Stockbrokers)
Level 15
City Tower
40 Basinghall Street
London EC2V 5DE
Tel: 01-628 5091

Rabobank Nederland
63 Mark Lane
London EC3R 7NE
Tel: 01-488 2311

UBAF Bank
30 Gresham Street
London EC2V 7LP
Tel: 01-606 7777
(Joint venture bank – 50%
Dutch)

Major Dutch Banks
Algemene Bank NV
(Commercial bank)
Vijzelstraat 32
1000 EG Amsterdam
Tel: (010 31) 20-299111
Telex: 11417

Amsterdam-Rotterdam Bank
NV
(Commercial bank)
Herengracht 595
1017 CE Amsterdam
and
Coolsingel 119
Rotterdam
Tel: (010 31) 10-289393
Telex: 11006

De Nationale
Investeringsbank NV
(National Investment Bank)
Carnegieplein 4
2517 HJ The Hague
Tel: (010 31) 70-425425

Nederlandse Credietbank NV
(Commercial bank)
Herengracht 458
1017 Amsterdam
Tel: (010 31) 20-5569111
Telex: 14385

Nederlandsche
Middentstandsbank NV
(Commercial bank)
Eduard van Beinumstraat 2
1077 XT Amsterdam
Tel: (010 31) 20-5439111
Telex: 11402
Postbank NV
Haarlemmerweg 506
1014 BL Amsterdam
Tel: (010 31) 20-5849111
Telex: 10102 PSTB NL

Rabobank
(Commercial bank)
Croeselaan 18
3521 CB Utrecht
Tel: (010 31) 30-909111
Telex: 40200

Stockbrokers

Amsterdam Stock Exchange
Amsterdamse Effectenbeurs
Beursplein 5
PO Box 19163
1000 GD Amsterdam
Tel: (010 31) 20-239711
Telex: 12302 EFBEU NL

Members in Amsterdam (as at November 1987)
Algemene Bank Nederland
NV
Vijzelstraat 32
1017 HL
Tel: (010 31) 20-299111

Amsterdam-Rotterdam Bank
NV
Foppingadreef 22
1102 BS
Tel: (010 31) 20-289393

Amstgeld NV
Paleisstraat 1
1012 RB
Tel: (010 31) 20-236438

Bangert & Co BV (J Frederik)
Kerkstraat 363
1017 HW
Tel: (010 31) 20-262251

Bank der Bondsspaarbanken
NV
Singel 236
1016 AB
Tel: (010 31) 20-221066

Bank Van Der Hoop Offers
NV
Keizersgracht 497
1017 DM
Tel: (010 31) 20-5501501

Bank Itec NV
Westeinde 26
1017 ZP
Tel: (010 31) 20-5502311

Bank Mees & Hope NV
Herengracht 548
1017 CG
Tel: (010 31) 20-5279111

Bank Mendes Gans NV
Herengracht 619
1017 CE
Tel: (010 31) 20-238181

Banque Paribas Nederland
NV
Herengracht 539-543
1017 BW
Tel: (010 31) 20-5204911

Banque de Suez Nederland
NV
Herengracht 320-324
1016 CE
Tel: (010 31) 20-229726

Barclays de Zoete Wedd
Nederland NV
Weteringschans 109
1017 SB
Tel: (010 31) 20-268630

Bary & Co NV (H Albert DE)
Herengracht 450
1017 CA
Tel: (010 31) 20-5554911

Beaufort & Kraaijenhagen NV
(DE)
Dam 4
1012 NP
Tel: (010 31) 20-263011

Bond Center Amsterdam BV
NZ Voorburgwal 100
1012 SG
Tel: (010 31) 20-265535

Brand NV (DW)
Keizersgracht 215
1016 DT
Tel: (010 31) 20-264164

Broekman's Commissiebank
BV
Rokin 9-15
1012 KK
Tel: (010 31) 20-238926

Citco Bank Nederland NV
Strawinskylaan 1725
1077 XX
Tel: (010 31) 20-622411

Citicorp Investment Bank
(The Netherland) NV
Herengracht 545-549
1017 BW
Tel: (010 31) 20-5515911

CLN Oyens & van Eeghen
NV
Herengracht 197
1016 BE
Tel: (010 31) 20-5579411

Cooperatieve Centrale
Raiffeisen-boerenleenbank
BA (Rabobank Nederland)
NZ Voorburgwal 162-170
1012 SJ
Tel: (010 31) 20-240825

'S-Gravenhage
Nationale Investeringsbank
NV (DE)
Carnegieplein 4
2517 KH
Tel: (010 31) 70-425425

Nutsspaarbank TE
'S-Gravenhage (Stitching)
Jan Hendrikstraat 4
2512 GL
Tel: (010 31) 70-120911

Philipse & Co BV
Emmapark 10
2592 ET
Tel: (010 31) 70-854103

Staal Bankiers NV
Lange Houtstraat 4-8
2511 CW
Tel: (010 31) 70-469480

Groningen
Noordnederlands
Effectenkantoor BV
Westerkade 16
9718 AS
Tel: (010 31) 50-145345

Haarlem
Nutsspaarbank West
Nederland (Stichting)
Fonteinlaan 5
2012 JG
Tel: (010 31) 23-185185

S'Hertogenbosch
Lanschot Bankiers NV (F Van)
Hoge Steenweg 27-31
5211 JN
Tel: (010 31) 73-153911

Lentjes & Drossaerts NV
Verwerstraat 29
5211
Tel: (010 31) 73-818818

Joure
Intereffekt Commissionairs
BV
Sewei 2
8501 SP
Tel: (010 31) 5138-4845

Leeuwarden
Friesland Bank BA
(Cooperatieve Vereniging)
Zuiderstraat 1
8911 BN
Tel: (010 31) 5100-443123

Maastricht
Spaarbank Limburg
(Stichting)
Markt 17-18
6211 CJ
Tel: (010 31) 43-296666

Rotterdam
Bank van der Hoop Offers NV
Westersingel 88
3015 LC
Tel: (010 31) 10-4363688

Credit Lyonnais Bank
Nederland NV
Coolsingel 63
3012 AB
Tel: (010 31) 10-4695911

Mulco NV
heer Bokelweg 133
3032 AD
Tel: (010 31) 10-4650711

Rotterdam BV
(Effectenkantoor)
Beursplein 37
3011 AA
Tel: (010 31) 10-4051234

Utrecht
Centrale Volksbank (Stichting
Spaarbank)
Maliebaan 15
3581 CB
Tel: (010 31) 30-344211

Crediet-en Effectenbank NV
Herculesplein 5
3584 AA
Tel: (010 31) 30-560911

Rabobank Nederland
(Cooperatieve Centrale
Raiffeisen-Boerenleenbank
BA)
Croeselaan 18
3521 CB
Tel: (010 31) 30-909111

Verenigde Spaarbank NV
Koningin Wilhelminalaan 7-9
3527 LA
Tel: (010 31) 30-959911

Wageningen
Gelders-Utrechtse Spaarbank
(Stichting)
Plantsoen 25
6701 AS
Tel: (010 31) 8370-97111

Wormerveer
Aten Effecten BV (Cornelis)
Zaanweg 75
1521 DN
Tel: (010 31) 75-283951

Sources of General Background Information, Industry Sector Information and Trade Contacts

UK Addresses
Netherlands – British
Chamber of Commerce
The Dutch House
307-308 High Holborn
London WC1V 7LS
Tel: 01-405 1358

Royal Netherlands Embassy
38 Hyde Park Gate
London SW7 5DP
Tel: 01-584 5040

Addresses in the Netherlands
There are eight main regional
chambers of commerce in the
Netherlands:

Kamer van Koophandel en
Fabrieken voor Amsterdam
Koningin Wilhelminaplein 13
1062 HH Amsterdam
Tel: (010 31) 20-172882
Telex: 18888

Kamer van Koophandel en
Fabrieken voor s'Gravenhage
Alexander Gogelweg 16
The Hague
Tel: (010 31) 70-795795
Telex: 33003

Kamer van Koophandel en
Fabrieken voor Haarlem en
Omstreken
Postbus 73
Nassauplein 4-6
2011 PG Haarlem
Tel: (010 31) 23-319017
Telex: 41567

Kamer van Koophandel en
Fabrieken voor Midden
Gelderland
6800 KZ Nieuwe Plein IB
6811 KN Arnhem
Tel: (010 31) 85-516969
Telex: 45276

Kamer van Koophandel en
Fabrieken voor Noordelijk
Overijssel
Postbus 630
Weeshuisstraat 27
8011 TZ Zwolle
Tel: (010 31) 38-218047
Telex: 42281

Kamer van Koophandel en
Fabrieken voor Rotterdam
Postbus 30025
Coolsingel 58
3001 DA Rotterdam
Tel: (010 31) 10-4145022
Telex: 23760

Kamer van Koophandel en
Fabrieken voor Tilburg en
Omstreken
Reitseplein 1
5037 AA Tilburg
Postbus 90154
5000 LG
Tel: (010 31) 13-654122
Telex: 52384

Kamer van Koophandel en
Fabrieken voor Utrecht en
Omstreken
Postbus 48
Waterstraat 47
3500 AA Utrecht
Tel: (010 31) 30-331412
Telex: 47730

Sources of Investment and Trade Advice, Assistance and Information

The Netherlands has a
complex system of grants and
subsidies. Incentives to
investors can be general,
regional or special. One of the
first points of enquiry for
potential investors is the
Netherlands Foreign
Investment Agency who
provide assistance from the
preliminary research stage
through to implementation.
The NFIA is a division of the
Ministry of Economic Affairs,
responsible for the promotion
and development of new and
existing foreign business.
Services are free of charge and
confidential.

Netherlands Foreign
Investment Agency
Bezuidenhoutseweg 91
PO Box 20101
2500 EC
The Hague
Tel: (010 31) 70-796322
Fax: (010 31) 70-317079
Telex: 31099 ECZA
The NFIA operates through
its own offices, as well as
embassies and chambers of
commerce:

USA

Los Angeles Office
11755 Wilshire Boulevard
Los Angeles
CA 90025
Tel: (010 1) 213-477 8288
Fax: (010 1) 213-312 0771
Contact: Mr I De Jong

New York Office
One Rockerfeller Plaza
New York
NY 10020
Tel: (010 1) 212-246 1434
Fax: (010 1) 212-246 9769
Telex: 125240 INDCOM NL
NYK

San Francisco Office
601 California Street
San Francisco
CA 94108
Tel: (010 1) 415-981 2586
Fax: (010 1) 415-981 2586
Telex: 797688 NIC SF
Contact: Mr A H D M Roosen

Japan

Royal Netherlands Embassy
Denmark House
6th Floor
4-17-35 Minami-Aoyama
Minato-ku
Tokyo 107
Tel: (010 81) 3-4034263/4
Fax: (010 81) 3-4034230
Telex: 29475 NEDIC JA

Korea

Royal Netherlands Embassy
Kyobo Building
14th Floor
1 Chongno 1-KA
Chogno-ku
Seoul
Tel: (010 82) 2-7321924
Fax: (010 82) 2-7321925
Telex: K23624 HOLLAND

Europe

Office for Europe
91 Bezuidenhoutseweg
PO Box 20101
2500 EC
The Hague
Tel: (010 31) 70-797029
Fax: (010 31) 70-796322
Telex: 31099 ECZA NL

Taipei Office
The Netherlands Council for
Trade Promotion
Netherlands Foreign
Investment Section
Room B
5th Floor
Artist Construction Building
687 Min Sheng East Road
Taipei 10591
Taiwan
Tel: (010 886) 2-7135760
Fax: (010 886) 2-7130194
Telex: 28774 NCHTPE

Holland International
Distribution Centre
Koopmanstraat 1, 2288
Rijswijk
Netherlands
Address for correspondence:
POB 1069
2280 CB Rijswijk
Netherlands
Tel: (010 31) 70-907881
Fax: (010 31) 70-906363

The Holland International
Distribution Centre is the
national agency for transport
and physical distribution. It
assists and advises companies
worldwide

Regional Sources of Advice

Amsterdam
City of Amsterdam City Hall
(The)
OZ Voorburgwal 197
1012 EX Amsterdam
Tel: (010 31) 20-5522201
Fax: (010 31) 20-5523426
Telex: 16575

Flevoland
Province of Flevoland (The)
PO Box 55
8200 AB Lelystad
Tel: (010 31) 3200-70411
Fax: (010 31) 3200-72590
Telex: 70638

Gelderland
Gelderland Development
Authority (The)
PO Box 206
6800 LT Arnhem
Tel: (010 31) 85-511334
Fax: (via KvK) (010 31)
85-516901
Telex: 45808 GOM GL

The Hague
City of the Hague City Hall
(The)
Burg de Monchyplein 14
2585 BD The Hague
Tel: (010 31) 70-123911
Fax: (010 31) 70-608677
Telex: 31455 VRLGV

Limburg
Limburg Investment Bank
(The)
PO Box 800
6200 AV Maastricht
Tel: (010 31) 43-280280
Fax: (010 31) 43-280200
Telex: 56706

North Brabant
North Brabant Development
Authority (The)
Postbus 3089
5203 DB 's-Hertogenbosch
Tel: (010 31) 73-408240
Fax: (010 31) 73-423557
Telex: 50050 LIEVE NL

Province of North Brabant
Provinciehuis (The)
Brabantlann 1
5216 TV's Hertogenbosch
Tel: (010 31) 73-812187
Fax: (010 31) 73-141115
Telex: 50796 PBNL NL

North Holland
Northern Development
Authority (The)
PO Box 424
9700 AK Groningen
Tel: (010 31) 50-267826
Fax: (010 31) 50-261475
Telex: 53917

Province of North Holland
(The)
p/a ETD for North Holland
PO Box 3007
2001 DA Haarlam
Tel: (010 31) 23-319199

Overijssel
Overijssel Development
Authority (The)
Burg van Royensingel 12
8000 AN Zwolle
Tel: (010 31) 38-214722
Fax: (010 31) 38-225802
Telex: 42493

Rotterdam
City of Rotterdam City Hall
(The)
Coolsingel 40
3011 AD
Rotterdam
Tel: (010 31) 10-4172512
Fax: (010 31) 10-4173512
Telex: 26437 ROTDM NL

South Holland
Province of South Holland
(The)
Koningskade 1/2
2596 AA
The Hague
Tel: (010 31) 70-117057
Fax: (010 31) 70-117090
Telex: 31088 CBKZH

Utrecht
Province of Utrecht (The)
PO Box 18100
3510 CC Utrecht
Tel: (010 31) 30-589111
Fax: (010 31) 30-522564
Telex: 70306

Zeeland
Province of Zeeland (The)
p/a Acquisitiegroep Zeeland
St Pieterstraat 42
4331 EW Middelburg
Tel: (010 31) 1180-31011
Fax: (010 31) 1180-311592
Telex: 37786

Ministerie van Economische
Zaken
Industrial Commissioner for
Western Europe
Postbus 20101
2500 EC Den Haag
Tel: (010 31) 70-797029
Telex: 31099

Ministrie van Fainancien
Casauriestraat 32
2511 VB Den Haag
Tel: (010 31) 70-767767
Telex: 33141

Ministerie van Sociale Zaken
en Werkgelegenheid
Externe Betrekkingen
Zeestraat 73
2518 AA Den Haag
Tel: (010 31) 70-715911
Telex: 32226

Professional Associations

Accountancy
Nederlands Institut van
Registeraccountants
Mensinge 2
1008 AD Amsterdam

Banking
Nederlandse
Bankiersvereniging
(Netherlands Bankers
Association)
Keizersgracht 706
Postbus 19870
1000 GW Amsterdam

Vereniging Van
Deviezenbanken
(Association of Foreign
Exchange Banks)
Keizergracht 706
Postbus 19870
1000 GW Amsterdam

Consultancy
Raad van
Organisatie-Adviesbureaus
(ROA)
Koningslaan 34
PO Box 5451
1007 AL Amsterdam
Tel: (010 31) 20-739551
Telex: 17141 WISRA NL

Insurance
Nederlandse Vereniging van
Makelaars in Assurantien en
Assurantieadviseurs (NVA)
(Dutch Association of
Insurance Brokers and
Insurance Intermediaries)
Koningin Wilhelminalaan 12
3818 HP Amersfoot
Tel: (010 31) 20-631414
Telex: 76275

Verbond van Verzekeraars in
Nederland
(Union of Insurers in the
Netherlands)
Groothertoginnelaan 8
2517 EG The Hague
Tel: (010 31) 70-614731
Telex: 34053

Trade Associations

Algemene Nederlandse Bond
van Groenten – en Fruit
Exporteurs
Bezuidenhoutseweg 82
Postbus 90410
2509 LK 's-Gravenhage
Tel: (010 31) 70-850100
Telex: 31147 VAKBL NL

Bloemenbureau Holland
Verbeekstraat 11
Postbus 9324
2300 PH Leiden
Tel: (010 31) 71-312031
Telex: 30264 WFTC NL

Bond van
Bloembollenhandelaren
Weersteinstraat 12
Postbus 170
2180 AD Hillegom
Tel: (010 31) 2520-18544
Telex: 41512 BOLEX NL

Bond van Coop
Zuivelverkoopverenigingen
Volmerlaan 7
Postbus 5831
2280 HV Rijswijk ZH
Tel: (010 31) 70-997422
Telex: 34328 FNZ NL

Bureau Teppema BV
Wassenaarsweg 80
Postbus 90606
2509 LP 's-Gravenhage
Tel: (010 31) 70-264251
Telex: 32576 ECON NL

Centraal Bureau van de
Tuinbouwveilingen in
Nederland
Javastraat 80
Postbus 80509
2508 GM 's-Gravenhage
Tel: (010 31) 70-46974
Telex: 31085 CBT NL

Centraal Verkoopkantoor
Zuurkool BV
Oudervaart 36
Postbus 14
1749 ZG Warmenhuizen
Tel: (010 31) 2269-1541

Contactgroep van
Werkgevers in de
Metaalindustrie (CWM)
Jongkindstraat 20
Postbus 1598
3000 BN Rotterdam
Tel: (010 31) 10-360000
Telex: 23203 CWM NL

Cooperatieve Vereniging
Centraal Brouwerij Kantoor
UA
Herengracht 282
Postbus 3462
1001 AG Amsterdam
Tel: (010 31) 20-252251
Telex: 14088 CENEB NL

Dutch Exporters of Computer
Services (DECS)
Doornstraat 25
Postbus 82257
2508 EG 's-Gravenhage
Tel: (010 31) 70-524499

Dutch Furniture Export
Organization (DUFEX)
Westerhoutparkt 10
2012 JM Haarlem
Postbus 100
2100 AC Heemstede
Tel: (010 31) 23-319137
Telex: 41661 CBM NL

Export Council van de
Koninklijke Nederlandse
Uitgeversbond
Keizersgracht 391
1016 EJ Amsterdam
Tel: (010 31) 20-267736

Federatie Nederlandse
Wolindustrie en Wolhandel
(FENEWOL)
De Schutterij 16
Postbus 518
3900 AM Veenendaal
Tel: (010 31) 8385-24352
Telex: 37216 TECO NL

Federatie van Nederlandse
Handelaren in Granen
Zaden en Peulvruchten (Fed
GZP)
Posthoornstraat 21
Postbus 202
3000 AE Rotterdam
Tel: (010 31) 10-139270
Telex: 21486 GVG NL

Het Nederlands Zuivelbureau
Volmerlaan 7
Postbus 30
2280 AA Rijswijk ZH
Tel: (010 31) 70-953395
Telex: 33411 NZB NL

Holland Cheese Exporters
Association
Sir Winston Churchilllaan 275
2288 EA Rijswijk ZH
Tel: (010 31) 70-409911

Holland Herring Fisheries
Association
Westhavenkade 63
Postbus 12
3130 AA Vlaardingen
Tel: (010 31) 10-346034
Telex: 21310 WKSV NL

Koninklijke Algemene
Vereniging voor
Bloembollencultuur
Parklaan 5
Postbus 175
2180 AD Hillegom
Tel: (010 31) 2520-15254
Telex: 41030 IBC NL

Nat Coop Aan – en
Verkoopvereniging voor
Land – en Tuinbouw GA
CEBECO-HANDELSRAAD
Blaak 31
Postbus 182
3000 AD Rotterdam
Tel: (010 31) 10-544911
Telex: 21398 CBCO NL

Nederlandse Bond van
Handelaren in Vee
Assauplein 12
Postbus 85814
2508 CM 's-Gravenhage
Tel: (010 31) 70-469621
Telex: 31503 BHV NL

Nederlandse Cacao – en
Cacaoproduktenvereniging
Nijenburg 75
1081 GE Amsterdam
Tel: (010 31) 20-444802
Telex: 11950 NECOA NL

Nederlandse Federatie voor
de Handel in
Pootaardappelen (NFP)
Van Stolkweg 31
Postbus 80537
2508 GM 's-Gravenhage
Tel: (010 31) 70-512461
Telex: 31423 VBNA NL

Nederlands Instituut voor
Afzetbevordering van
Akkerbouwprodukten
(NIVVA)
Stadhoudersplantsoen 12
Postbus 17337
2502 CH 's-Gravenhage
Tel: (010 31) 70-652830
Telex: 34500 NIVAA NL

Nederlandse Vereniging van
Carrosseriebedrijven
(FOCWA)
Oranjelaan 2
Postbus 1050
2340 BB Oegstgeest
Tel: (010 31) 71-153821

Nederlandse Vereniging van
Fabrikanten van
Geconserveerde Melk
Laan van Meerdervoort 20
Postbus 85868
2508 CN 's-Gravenhage
Tel: (010 31) 70-650769
Telex: 31563 NVFGM NL

Nederlandse Vereniging van
Kaasexporteurs
Laan van Meerdervoort 18
Postbus 85810
2508 CM 's-Gravenhage
Tel: (010 31) 70-604812/3
Telex: 34087 GEMZU NL

Nederlandse Vereniging voor
Handel en Industrie op het
gebied van Scheepsbouw en
Watersport (HISWA)
Gebouw Metropool
Weesperstraat 93
1018 VN Amsterdam
Tel: (010 31) 20-221307
Telex: 14428 HISWA NL

Nederlandse Vereniging voor
de Specerijhandel
Herengracht 462
Postbus 3699
1001 AL Amsterdam
Tel: (010 31) 20-249090
Telex: 10280 AMPRO NL

Orde van Nederlandse
RaadgevendeIngenieurs
ONRI
Javastraat 44
2585 AP 's-Gravenhage
Tel: (010 31) 70-630756

Stichting Afzetbevordering
Nederlandse Eiprodukten
Groenedijk 78
3311 DC Dordrecht
Tel 78-138325

Stichting ter Bevordering van
de Uitvoer van Gebruiksvee
en Slachtvee
Nassauplein 12
Postbus 85814
2508 CM 's-Gravenhage
Tel: (010 31) 70-469621
Telex: 31503 BHV NL

Stichting Centraal College
van Samenwerkende
Oranisaties op het Gebied van
het Bouwwezen 'Cencobouw'
Benoordenhoutseweg 21
Postbus 90603
2509 LP 's-Gravenhage
Tel: (010 31) 70-262021
Telex: 32227 AVBB NL

Stichting Gemeenschappelijk
Zuivelsecretariaat
Laan van Meerdervoort 18
Postbus 85810
2508 CM 's-Gravenhage
Tel: (010 31) 70-604812/3
Telex: 34087 GEMZU NL

Stichting Mikrocentrum
Kruisstraat 74
Postbus 359
5600 AJ Eindhoven
Tel: (010 31) 40-432503
Telex: 59337 MIKRO NL

Stichting Nederlandse
Apparaten voor de
Procesindustrie NAP
Vlietweg 14
Postbus 443
2260 AK Leidschendam
Tel: (010 31) 70-200400
Telex: 31320 VNCI NL

Stichting Tabakverwerkende
Industrie
Bilderdijklaan 23
Postbus 309
5600 AH Eindhoven
Tel: (010 31) 40-116130

Stichting Voorlichtingsbureau
Vlees
Vleeswaren en
Vleesconserven
Sir Winston Churchilllaan 275
2288 EA Rijswijk ZH
Tel: (010 31) 70-409922
Telex: VEVLE NL

Vereniging de Nederlands
IJer – en Staalproducerende
Industarie (NIJSI)
Vondellaan 10
1942 LJ Beverwijk
Postbus 10000
1970 CA IJmuiden
Tel: (010 31) 2510-94661
Telex: 35211 HOVS NL

Vereniging der Nederlandse
Groenten – en
Fruitverwerkende Industrie
Terweepark 2
Postbus 177
2300 AD Leiden
Tel: (010 31) 10-176214
Telex: 39286

Vereniging Nederlandse
Kerftakindustrie
Plaszoom 362
Postbus 4262
3006 AG Rotterdam
Tel: (010 31) 10-526100
Telex: 24215 VNK NL

Vereniging van
Bloemeneilingen in
Nederland
Verbeekstraat 11
Postbus 9324
2300 PH Leiden
Tel: (010 31) 71-312031
Telex: 30265 VBN NL

Vereniging van Confectie – en
Tricotage Ondernemingen
(FENECON)
Confectiecentrum 2.08.02
Koningin Wilhaminaplein 13
1062 HH Amsterdam
Tel: (010 31) 20-156811
Telex: 15749 KLEDO NL

Vereniging van Fabrikanten
en Groothandelaren in
Boterconcentraten
Laan van Meerdervoort 18
Postbus 85810
2508 CM 's-Gravenhage
Tel: (010 31) 70-604812/3
Telex: 34087 GEMZU NL

Vereniging van Fabrikanten
van Banket, Beschuit, Biscuit,
koek en annverwante
produkten Verbisco
Raamweg 44
2596 HN 's-Gravenhage
Tel: (010 31) 70-460643

Vereniging van
Groothandelaren in Boter
Laan van Meerdervoort 18
Postbus 85810
2508 CM 's-Gravenhage
Tel: (010 31) 70-604812/3
Telex: 34087 GEMZU NL

Vereniging van Nederlandse
Aannemers met Belangen in
het Buitenland (NABU)
Mesdagstraat 118
Postbus 90611
2509 LP 's-Gravenhage
Tel: (010 31) 70-244472
Telex: 32564 NIVAG NL

Vereniging van Nederlandse
Eiproduktenfabrikanten
Groenedijk 78
3311 DC Dordrecht
Tel: (010 31) 78-138325

Vereniging van Nederlandse
Exporteurs van Aardappelen
(VENEXA)
Van Stolkweg 31
2585 JN s'Gravenhage
Tel: (010 31) 70-512461
Telex: 31423 VBNA NL

Vereniging van Nederlandse
Koffiebranders en
Theepakkers
Max Havelaarlaan 317
1183 LT Amstelveen
Tel 20-456856
Telex: 18765 VRIES NL

Vereniging van Nederlandse
Papier – en Karonfabrieken
Julianastraat 30
Postbus 3009
2001 DA Haarlem
Tel: (010 31) 23-319125
Telex: 41069 PAPER NL

Vereniging van Nederlandse
Visconservenfabrikanten
Treubstraat 17
Postbus 72
2280 AB Rijswijk
Tel: (010 31) 30-949383
Telex: 32490 PROVI NL

Vereniging van de
Nederlandse Chemische
Industrie
Vlietweg 14
P 443
2260 AK Leidschendam
Tel: (010 31) 70-209233
Telex: 31320 VNCI NL

Vereniging van de
Nederlandse
Pluimveeverwerkende
industrie NEPLUVI
Ultrechtseweg 31
3704 HA Zeist
Tel: (010 31) 3403-61634

Vereniging van Verf – en
Drukinktfabrikanten
Groot Haesebroekseweg 1
Postbus 71
2240 AB
Wassenaar
Tel: (010 31) 1751-78044

Vereniging voor de
Aardappelverwerkende
Industrie (VAVI)
Van Stolkweg 31
2585 JN 's-Gravenhage
Tel: (010 31) 70-512461
Telex: 31423 VBNA NL

Vereniging voor de Metaal –
en de Elektrotechnische
Industrie (FME)
Bredewater 20
Postbus 190
2700 AD Zoetermeer
Tel: (010 31) 79-531100
Telex: 32157 FME NL

Vereniging voor de
Nederlandse Vleeswaren
Industrie
Wagenaarweg 14
Postbus 87936
2508 DH 's-Gravenhage
Tel: (010 31) 70-547311
Telex: 34416 VNV NL

Company Financial and Product Information

Directories
Bankenboekje (Banking
Directory)
Published by Nederlands
Institut voor Het Bank-en
Effectenbedrif, Amsterdam
Provides addresses, financial
figures and identifies
shareholders and associate
companies

Inkoop-en
Aanbestedingsregister voor
Rijks Gemeente-instellingen
Published by Uitgave:
Uitgeversmaatschappij Vewe
BV, Mijdrecht
Directory of Dutch
companies, grouped by
product or service

Kompass Nederlands
Published by Kompass
Nederlands BV
Provides address and product
details for 24 000 companies
1987/88 23rd edition

Nederlands ABC Voor
Handel en Industrie
Published by ABC Voor
Handel en Industrie, Haarlem
Provides particulars of over
22 000 producers, exporters,
importers and agents
grouped by industry sector
and product group

Nederlands Ondernemingen
en hun Financiale Kenmerken
(Dutch Companies and their
Financial Characteristics)
Produced by Dun and
Bradstreet BV, Rotterdam
Largest section of this
directory covers industrial
companies. Details include
sales ranking, capital, number
of employees plus financial
ratios. League tables are also
provided for service
companies, banks and
insurance companies

Economic and Market Statistical Data

Market Research Organisations
AGB Dongen BV
Mgr Schaepmanlaan 55
5103 BB Dongen
Tel: (010 31) 1623-14950
Telex: 54582
Parent company: AGB
Research plc (UK)

Centrum BV
Plantage Gebouw
Plantage Middenlaan 62
1018 DH Amsterdam
Tel: (010 31) 20-244211
Telex: 15727 CENTR NL
Parent company: Centrum
Groep BV (Amsterdam)

Interview BV
Overtoom 519-521
1054 LH Amsterdam
Tel: (010 31) 20-834411
Telex: 11029

Nederlandse Institut voor de
Publieke Opinie en het
Marktonderzoek – NIPO BV
Barentszplein 7
1013 NJ Amsterdam
Tel: (010 31) 20-248844
Telex: 14614
Undertakes wide range of
market and industrial
research. Founding member
of Gallup International

Nederlandse Stichting voor
Statistiek NV (NSS)
Bankaplein La
2585 EV The Hague
Tel: (010 31) 70-528528
Telex: 32167
Parent company: Produce
Studies (UK)

A C Nielsen (Netherlands) BV
Amsteldijk 66
1079 LH Amsterdam
Tel: (010 31) 20-444972
Telex: 112659
Parent company: A C Nielsen

SVP Sijthoff BC
PO Box 16050
2500 The Hague
Tel: (010 31) 70-190575
Telex: 32695 SYNFONL
Parent company: VP
International (Switzerland)
and Sisthoff Pers BV
(Netherlands)
Note: Information broker

Organisations Providing Economic and Statistical Data

Central Bureau voor de
Statistiek (CBS)
Prinses Beatrixlaan
Postbus 59
2270 AZ Voorburg
Tel: (010 31) 70-694341
Telex: 32692 CBS NL
National Statistical Office
provides economic
demographic and social
statistics and analysis.
Publishes Statistical Yearbook
of the Netherlands and other
major statistical publications.

Contactgroep
Exportdeskundigen CGE
Villa Sonnenbergh
Utrechtseweg 27
6862 AB Oosterbeek

Economisch Instituut voor het
Midden – en Kleinbedrijf
Italee laan 33
2711 CA Zoetermeer
Tel: (010 31) 79-413634
National research institution
which specialises in small to
medium sized
enterprises

Export Service Centrum ESC
Nieuwe Plein 3
Postbus 400
6800 AK Arnhem

Foreign Trade Statistics Office
Kloosterwes 1
POB 4481
6401 CZ Heerlen
Tel: (010 31) 45-736666
Telex: 56724

Stichting het Nederlands
Economische
Instituut – NEI (Netherlands
Economic Institute)
Burgemeester Oudlaan 50
3062 PA Rotterdam
Tel: (010 31) 10-525511
Telex: 25490
Publications include:
Economisch Statistische
Berichten
Foundation of Empirical
Economic research series,
plus various reports and
books

Stichting Nederlandse Export
Combinatie NEC
Huizen Neclenburgh
Soesterberrgsestraat 158
3768 MD Soest

Publications

Directories

GIDS – bij de Officiele
Prijscourant van de
Amsterdamse Effectenbeurs
(Guide to official prices
quoted on the Amsterdam
Stock Exchan- bij de Officiele
Prijscourant van de
Amsterdamse Effectenbeurs
(Guide to official prices
quoted on the Amsterdam
Stock Exchange)
Published by JH de Bussy,
Amsterdam

Hollands Exports Directory
Series
Published by ABC voor
Handel en Industrie CV,
Haarlem

Netherlands-British Trade
Directory
Published by the
Netherlands-British Chamber
of Commerce, London

Pyttersen's Nederlandse
Almanak
(Guide to Dutch public and
private institutions)
Published by Utigvey van
Loghum Slaterus, Deventer

Major Newspapers

De Courant Nieuws van de
Dag
Daily

De Telgraaf
Daily

De Volksrant
Daily

Economisch Dagblad
Daily

Het Financieel Dagblad
Daily

Het Financieel Economisch
Daily

NRC Handelsblad
Daily

Journals and Periodicals

Bedrifjfsdocumentaire
Publisher's address:
PO Box 34
2501 AG The Hague
Management journal. 10
issues per annum

De Accountant
Publisher's address:
PO Box 7984
1008 AD Amsterdam
11 issues per annum

Beleggers Belangen
Publisher's address:
1160118
1012 SH Amsterdam
Investment journal. Weekly

Economisch Statistische
Berichten (ESB)
Publisher's address:
PO Box 4224
3006 AE Rotterdam
Weekly

FEM – Financial Economisch
Magazine
Publisher's address:
Spuistraat 110-112
1012 VA Amsterdam
Fortnightly

Officiele Prijscourant
Produced by the Amsterdam
Stock Exchange Committee
Contains official
announcements, prices of
traded securities. Daily

Norway

Sources of Economic, Stock Market Information and Investment Research Services

Banks

Central Bank
Norges Bank (Bank of
Norway)
Postboks 1179 Sentrum
0107 Oslo 1
Tel: (010 47) 2-316000
Telex: 71369 N BANK N

Norwegian Banks in London
Bergen Bank
Shackleton House
4 Battlebridge Lane
London SE1 2HP
Tel: 01-357 6373

Christiania Bank
9 King Street
London EC2V 8EA
Tel: 01-726 6213

Den Norske Creditbank
20 St Dunstans's Hill
London EC3R 8HY
Tel: 01-621 1111

Union Bank of Norway
20 Swithins Lane
London EC4N 8AD
Tel: 01-623 3192

Major Norwegian Banks
A/S Forretningsbanken
Sondregate 10
PO Box 236
7001 Trondheim
Tel: (010 47) 7-9000
Telex: 55050

Bergen Bank
Torvalmenning 2
PO Box 826
5001 Bergen
and
Kirkegaten 23-25
PO Box 1170
Oslo 1
Tel: (010 47) 2-317100
Telex: 42018

Bergens Skillingsbank A/S
Radsluplass 4
5001 Bergen
Tel: (010 47) 5-310050
Telex: 42082

Christiania Bank og
Kreditkasse
Stortovet 7
PO Box 1166
0107 Oslo 1
Tel: (010 47) 2-485000
Telex: 71043

Den Norske Creditbank
(Commercial Bank)
Kirkegaten 21
Oslo 1
Tel: (010 47) 2-481050
Telex: 18290

Fellesbanken
(Union Bank of Norway)
Bankplassen 4
Oslo
Tel: (010 47) 2-412120
Telex: 71369

Rogalandsbanken AS
Haakon VII Gate
PO Box 209
4001 Stavanger
Tel: (010 47) 4-526080

Sparebanken ABC
(Union Bank of Finland)
Postboks 1172 Sentrum
Kirkegaten 14-18
0107 Oslo 1
Tel: (010 47) 2-319050
Telex: 19558

Stockbrokers
There are ten exchanges in
Norway. Oslo is by far the
most active and international
followed by Bergen and
Trondheim. The other nine
exchanges have little or no
activity. These are:
Fredrikstad, Drammen,
Kristiansand, Stavanger,
Haugesund, Alesund and
Kristiansund.

Oslo Bors
(Oslo Stock Exchange)
Tollbugt 2
Box 460
0105 Oslo 1
Tel: (010 47) 2-423880
Telex: 77242 BOERS N

Bergen Bors
(Bergen Stock Exchange)
Olav Kyrresgt 11
5000 Bergen
Tel: (010 47) 5-316569

Trondheim Stock Exchange
Dronningens gt 12
7000 Trondheim
Tel: (010 47) 7-512200

Members of the Oslo Stock Exchange (banks and brokers) (as at February 1988)

Astor Fonds A/S
Postboks 9501 Egertorget
0128 Oslo 1
Grensen 12
Tel: (010 47) 2-335320
Fax: (010 47) 2-336915
Telex: 72004

Bergen Bank A/S
Postboks 1170 Sentrum
0107 Oslo 1
Kirkegt 19
Tel: (010 47) 2-400550
Fax: (010 47) 2-419508
Telex: 71069
Telegram: Bergenbank

BFP Securities A/S
Postboks 7218 Homansbyen
0307 Oslo 3
Parkveien 35
Tel: (010 47) 2-445510
Fax: (010 47) 2-448477
Telex: 79349 BFP N

Bodd Fonds A/S
Postboks 1866 Vika
0124 Oslo 1
Stranden 3
Tel: (010 47) 2-426813
Fax: (010 47) 2-360556
Telex: 77029

Gunnar Bohn & Co A/S
Postboks 588 Sentrum
0106 Oslo 1
Langkaia 1
Tel: (010 47) 2-414050
Fax: (010 47) 2-619564
Telex: 76790
Telegram: Bonfonds

Christiania Bank of
Kreditkasse
Postboks 1166 Sentrum
0107 Oslo 1
Skippergt 40
Tel: (010 47) 2-485000
Fax: (010 47) 2-568650
Telex: 76833
Telegram: Kreditkassen

Citibank A/S
Postboks 1481 Vika
0116 Oslo 1
Tordenskioldsgt 8-10
Tel: (010 47) 2-426720
Fax: (010 47) 2-426796
Telex: 19570

Den Norske Creditbank
Postboks 1171 Sentrum
0107 Oslo 1
Kirkegt 24
Tel: (010 47) 2-481050; 481502
Fax: (010 47) 2-482875
Telex: 78175
Telegram: DNCF O

Elcon Securities A/S
Postboks 624 Sentrum
0106 Oslo 1
Langkaia 1
Tel: (010 47) 2-421044
Fax: (010 47) 2-418961
Telex: 76883

Finanshuset A/S
Postboks 653 Sentrum
0106 Oslo 1
Ovre Slottsgt 10
Tel: (010 47) 2-335480
Fax: (010 47) 2-203332
Telex: 77584

Fokus Bank A/S
Postboks 9525 Egertorget
0128 Oslo 1
Akersgt 41
Tel: (010 47) 2-429360
Fax: (010 47) 2-411046
Telex: 71119

Fondsfinans A/S
Postboks 1782 Vika
0122 Oslo 1
Haakon VII's gt 6
Tel: (010 47) 2-415970
Fax: (010 47) 2-425426
Telex: 19159
Telegram: Fonds n

Forenede Fonds A/S
Postboks 1974 Vika
0125 Oslo 1
Klingenberggt 4
Tel: (010 47) 2-418095
Fax: (010 47) 2-332135
Telex: 71649
Telegram: Bonds N

Invest Securities A/S
Postboks 1243 Vika
0110 Oslo 1
Tel: (010 47) 2-421545
Fax: (010 47) 2-423733
Telex: 74753

N A Jensen & Co A/S
Postboks 267 Sentrum
0103 Oslo 1
Radhusgt 23 V
Tel: (010 47) 2-202092
Fax: (010 47) 2-360032
Telex: 19234

Jotun Fonds A/S
Postboks 1444 Vika
0115 Oslo 1
Universitetsgt 22/24
(Jotunhuset)
Tel: (010 47) 2-429300
Fax: (010 47) 2-619592
Telex: 78624 STOCK N

Carl Kierulf & C A/S
Postboks 236 Sentrum
0103 Oslo 1
Langkaia 1
Tel: (010 47) 2-421942
Fax: (010 47) 2-422415
Telex: 78154
Telegram: Kierulfco

Nevi Fonds A/S
Postboks 458 Sentrum
0105 Oslo 1
Dronningensgt 8 A
5 etg
Tel: (010 47) 2-635030
Fax: (010 47) 2-635100
Telex: 74416 NEVIF N

NordBroking A/S
Postboks 1213 Vika
0110 Oslo 1
Rosenkrantzgt 21
Tel: (010 47) 2-334510
Fax: (010 47) 2-417541
Telex: 77386
Telegram: Nordbank

Norse Partners A/S
Postboks 1770 Vika
0122 Oslo 1
Kronprinsesse Marthas pl 1
6 etg
Tel: (010 47) 2-335152
Fax: (010 47) 2-419737
Telex: 78534 NORSE N

Orkla Finans (Fondsmegling)
A/S
Postboks 8274 Hammersborg
0129 Oslo 1
Teatergt 9
Tel: (010 47) 2-207040
Fax: (010 47) 2-203689
Telex: 79562 OAFIN N

Oslo Finans A/S
Postboks 1543 Vika
0117 Oslo 1
Stranden 3
Tel: (010 47) 2-418220
Fax: (010 47) 2-410466
Telex: 76728

Pre Fonds A/S
Postboks 1434 Vika
0115 Oslo 1
Tordenskioldsgt 3
Tel: (010 47) 2-422160
Fax: (010 47) 2-360413
Telex: 79664 VERDI N

Scanfonds A/S
Postboks 691 Sentrum
0106 Oslo 1
Kongensgt 31
Tel: (010 47) 2-428555
Fax: (010 47) 2-428697
Telex: 74992

S-Fonds A/S
Postboks 387 Sentrum
0102 Oslo 1
Langkaia 1 A VIII
Tel: (010 47) 2-427210
Fax: (010 47) 2-360040

Sparenbanken ABC
Postboks 1172 Sentrum
0107 Oslo 1
Kirkegaten 14-18
Tel: (010 47) 2-319050
Fax: (010 47) 2-318609
Telex: 19558

Sparenbanken Vest
Fred Olsens gt 3
0152 Oslo 1
Tel: (010 47) 2-334910
Fax: (010 47) 2-336700

Stavanger
Fondsmeglerforretning A/S
(Stafonds)
Postboks 1604 Vika
0119 Oslo 1
Stranden 3
Tel: (010 47) 2-422158
Fax: (010 47) 4-427476

Stock-Invest A/S
Postboks 684 Sentrum
0106 Oslo 1
Rosenkrantzgt 9
Tel: (010 47) 2-551111
Fax: (010 47) 2-425855
Telex: 74944 STINV-N

Sundal Collier Montagu A/S
Postboks 825 Sentrum
0104 Oslo 1
Langkaia 1
Tel: (010 47) 2-420460
Fax: (010 47) 2-420095/363327
Telex: 74490

Tennant Fonds A/S
Postboks 297 Sentrum
0103 Oslo 1
Jernbanetorget 2
Tel: (010 47) 2-334280
Fax: (010 47) 2-336388
Telex: 71258

Fearnley Finans (Fonds) A/S
Postboks 1158 Sentrum
0107 Oslo 1
Radhusgt 27
Tel: (010 47) 2-417000
Fax: (010 47) 2-411273
Telex: 78000 FTANK

Members of the Bergen Stock Exchange
Bergen Bank A/S
Postboks 826
5001 Bergen
Tel: (010 47) 5-211000
Fax: (010 47) 5-211152
Telex: 42018
Telegram: Bergenbank

A/S Bergens Skillingsbank
Postboks 892/3
5001 Bergen
Radstuplass 4
5000 Bergen
Tel: (010 47) 5-310050
Fax: (010 47) 5-327467
Telex: 42082

Den Norske Creditbank
Bradbenken 1
Postboks 4040
5023 Bergen
Tel: (010 47) 5-320050
Fax: (010 47) 5-328171
Telex: 42049
Telegram: Creditbank

Fokus Bank A/S
Postboks 1162
5001 Bergen
Rastuplass 2/3
5000 Bergen
Tel: (010 47) 5-218600
Fax: (010 47) 5-318339
Telex: 42045
Telegram: Vestlandsbanken

Libra Fonds A/S
Postboks 500
5011 Bergen
Verftsgt 2 C
5011 Bergen
Tel: (010 47) 5-321710
Fax: (010 47) 5-153040
Telex: 40124

S-Fonds A/S
Postboks 451
5001 Bergen
Vaskerelvvn 39
5000 Bergen
Tel: (010 47) 5-317575
Fax: (010 47) 5-232055
Telex: 2421 441020

Sparebanken Vest avd Bergen
Postboks 854
5001 Bergen
Tel: (010 47) 5-318050
Fax: (010 47) 5-217410
Telex: 42249
Telegram: Sparebanken

Members of the Drammen Stock Exchange
Drammens Bors
Bragernes Torg 13
3000 Drammen

Fokus Bank A/S
Postboks 54
3001 Drammen
Bragernes Torg 2
3000 Drammen
Tel: (010 47) 3-836790
Fax: (010 47) 3-836766
Telex: 76308
Telegram: Buskerudbank

Sparebanken Buskerud
Postboks 1122
5001 Drammen
Tel: (010 47) 3-836780
Fax: (010 47) 3-891418
Telex: 18932

Members of the Haugesund Stock Exchange
Bergen Bank A/S
Postboks 23
5501 Haugesund
Haraldsgt 125
5500 Haugesund
Tel: (010 47) 4-722022
Fax: (010 47) 4-727430
Telegram: Bergenbank

Haugesund Sparenbank
Fondsavdelingen
Postboks 203
5501 Haugesund
Haraldsgt 115
5500 Haugesund
Tel: (010 47) 4-729000
Fax: (010 47) 4-726142
Telex: 42911

Members of the Kristiansand Stock Exchange
Kristiansands Bors
Storkaien 10
6501 Kristiansand N

Sorlandsbanken A/S
Postboks 202
4601 Kristiansand S
Markensgt
11 og 16
4600 Kristiansand S
Tel: (010 47) 42-29745; 21080
Fax: (010 47) 42-20044
Telex: 21355

Sandefjord
Den Norske Creditbank
Postboks 220
3201 Sandefjord
Radhusgt 13
3200 Sandefjord
Tel: (010 47) 34-67000; 67310
Fax: (010 47) 34-67957
Telex: 21995

Members of the Stavanger Stock Exchange
Stavanger Handelskammer
Handelens Hus
Postboks 182
4001 Stavanger

Rogalandsbanken A/S
Fondsavdeling
Postboks 289
4001 Stavanger
Lars Hertervigsgt 5
4000 Stavanger
Tel: (010 47) 4-535027
Fax: (010 47) 4-567355

Sparebanken Rogaland
Postboks 218
4001 Stavanger
Domkirkeplassen 1
4000 Stavanger
Tel: (010 47) 4-533000/533560
Fax: (010 47) 4-531864
Telex: 33016
Telegram: Sparebanken

Stavanger
Fondsmeglerforretning A/S
Postboks 163
4001 Stavanger
Langmannsgt 5
4000 Stavanger
Tel: (010 47) 4-520011
Fax: (010 47) 4-523031
Telex: 73710

Tromso
Sparebanken Nord
Postboks 853
9000 Tromso
Sjogt 8
9000 Tromso
Tel: (010 47) 83-57011/86020
Fax: (010 47) 83-88684
Telex: 64170

Members of the Trondheim Stock Exchange
Trondheim Bors
Dronningensgt 12
7000 Trondheim

DnC Trondelag
Postboks 2233
7001 Trondheim
Olav Trygvassonsgt 39-41
7000 Trondheim
Tel: (010 47) 7-513611
Fax: (010 47) 7-532689
Telex: 55026

Fokus Bank A/S
Postboks 6090
7003 Trondheim
Sondre gt 10
7000 Trondheim
Tel: (010 47) 7-882011
Fax: (010 47) 7-534565
Telex: 55050
Telegram: Forretningsbank

Midt-Norge Fonds A/S
Postboks 744
7001 Trondheim
Olav Trygvassonsgt 35
7000 Trondheim
Tel: (010 47) 7-514430
Telex: 55177

Sparebanken Midt-Norge
Postboks 701
7001 Trondheim
Kongensgt 4
7000 Trondheim
Tel: (010 47) 7-585111
Fax: (010 47) 7-585044
Telex: 55177
Telegram: Sparebank

Tronder Finans Fonds A/S
Postboks 2086
7001 Trondheim
Munkegt 64
7000 Trondheim
Tel: (010 47) 7-528240
Fax: (010 47) 7-531892
Telex: 75730 TFINA

Tonsberg
Sparebanken Vestfold
Fondsavd
Postboks 214
3101 Tonsberg
Tel: (010 47) 33-77100
Fax: (010 47) 33-16108
Telex: 70372

Members of the Alesund Stock Exchange
Sunnmorsbanken A/S
Postboks 124
6001 Alesund
Korsegt 8
6000 Alesund
Tel: (010 47) 71-24776
Fax: (010 47) 71-20063/24896
Telex: 42301

Sources of General Background Information, Industry Sector Information and Trade Contacts

UK Addresses

Norwegian Chamber of
Commerce (The), London
Norway House
21-24 Cockspur Street
London SW1Y 5BN
Tel: 01-930 0181
Telex: 917294 NORCC G

Export Council of Norway
(The)
Norway Trade Centre
20 Pall Mall
London SWIY 5NE
Tel: 01-839 6261/7
Telex: 265635 EXNOR IDN

Royal Norwegian Embassy
25 Belgrave Square
London SW1X 8QD
Tel: 01-235 7151
Commercial Division:
20 Pall Mall
London SW1Y 5NE
Tel: 01-839 6261
Consular Division:
25 Belgrave Square
London SW1X 8QD
Tel: 01-235 7151

Addresses in Norway

Norwegian Chambers of Commerce

Arendal Handelskammer
Postboks 197
4801 Arendal
Tel: (010 47) 41-25000

Bergens Handelskammer
Postboks 832
5001 Bergen
Tel: (010 47) 5-316569

Drammens Handelskammer
Postboks 75
3001 Drammen
Tel: (010 47) 3-832459

Haugesunds Handelskammer
Postboks 185
5501 Haugesund
Tel: (010 47) 47-22466

Kristiansands
Handelskammer
Postboks 291
4601 Kristiansand S
Tel: (010 47) 42-25167

Lofoten Handelskammer
Postboks 82
8341 Stamsund
Tel: (010 47) 88-89100
Fax: (010 47) 88-89228
Telex: 64011

Oslo Handelskammer
Drammensveien 30
0255 Oslo 2
Tel: (010 47) 2-557400
Fax: (010 47) 2-558953

Rana Handelskammer
(Ole Tobias Olsensgt 23)
Postboks 70
8601 Mo
Tel: (010 47) 87-50455

Sarpsborg Handelskammer
Postboks 305
1701 Sarsborg
Tel: (010 47) 31-57100

Skiens Handelskammer
Postboks 655
3701 Skien
Tel: (010 47) 35-20524

Stavanger Handelskammer
Postboks 182
4001 Stavanger
Tel: (010 47) 4-536035

Troms Handelskammer
Postboks 2801
9001 Tromso
Tel: (010 47) 83-55133

Trondheim Handelskammer
Postboks 11
7001 Trondheim
Tel: (010 47) 7-512200

British Commercial Representative in Norway:

Commercial Department
British Embassy
Thomas Heftyesgate 8
0264 Oslo 2
Tel: (010 47) 2-552400
Telex: 71575
British Business Forum (c/o
British Embassy).
Membership open to
individuals or companies who
engage in two-way trade or
inward investment into the
UK

Sources of Investment and Trade Advice, Assistance and Information

The organisations listed
below or your local
Norwegian Chamber of
Commerce can be contacted
for initial advice and
information on joint ventures,
and production under licence
and franchises.

British Council
Fridtjof Nansensplass 5
4th Floor
0160 Oslo 1
Tel: (010 47) 2-426848

Finansdepartementet
(Ministry of Finance)
Akersgate 42 (Block G)
Oslo 1
Tel: (010 47) 2-119090
Telex: 72095 fdep n

Handelsdepartementet
(Ministry of Trade)
Victoria Terrasse 7
Oslo 2
Tel: (010 47) 2-314050

Industridepartementet
(Ministry of Industry)
Akersgate 42 (Block Y)
Oslo 1
Tel: (010 47) 2-119090

Norges Eksportrad
(Export Council of Norway)
Drammensveien 40
Oslo
Tel: (010 47) 2-437700

Oslo Import og Export
Agenters Forening
(Oslo Import and Export
Agents' Association)
Postboks 2302 Solli
Drammensveien 30
Oslo 2

Utenriksdepartementet
(Ministry of Foreign Affairs)
7 Juniplass 1
Oslo 1
Tel: (010 47) 2-204170

Professional Associations

Accountancy
Norges Registrerte Revisorers
Forening
Gyldenloves-gate 44
0260 Oslo 2

Norges Statsautoriserte
Revisorers Forening
Uranienborg Terrasse 9
0351 Oslo 3

Banking
Den Norske Bankforening
(Norwegian Bankers
Association)
Postboks 1489
Oslo 5

Association of Norwegian
Savings Banks (The)
Universitetsgaten 8
0164 Oslo 1

Consultancy
Norsk Foreining Av
Radgivere I Bedriftsledelse
(NFRB)
c/o Norconsult
Kjorboveien 20
1300 Sandvika
Tel: (010 47) 2-545330
Telex: 72075

Raadfivende Ingeniorenes
Forening
(Consulting Engineers
Association)
Akersgt 35a
Oslo 1
Tel: (010 47) 2-333240

Insurance
Norges Forsikringsforbund
(Association of Norwegian
Insurance Companies)
Forsikringens Hus
Hansteensgaten 2
Postboks 2473 Solli
0202 Oslo 2

Trade Associations

General Industry
Norges Handelsstands
Forbund
(Federation of Norwegian
Commercial Associations)
Postboks 2483 Solli
Oslo 2

Norges Industriforbund
(Federation of Norwegian
Industries)
Norges Industriforbund
Drammensveien 40
Oslo 2

Canning
De Norske Hermetikfabrikers
Landsforening
(Norwegian Canners
Association)
Alex kiellendsg-2
4000 Stavanger
Tel: (010 47) 4-529044

Construction
Norges Byggmesterforbund
(Association of Norwegian
Engineering Industries)
St Olavs gt 23
Oslo 2
Tel: (010 47) 2-115017

Electrics and Electronics
Norges
Elektrohandlerforbund
(Norwegian Electrical Goods
Handlers Association)
Storgata 14
Oslo 1
Tel: (010 47) 2-422047

Norsk Elektrolevarandorers
Forening
(Norwegian Electrical Goods
Suppliers Association)
Haakon VII's gate 2
Tel: (010 47) 2-421305

Engineering
Medaniske Verksteders
Landsforening
(Federation of Norwegian
engineering industries)
Oscarsgt 20
Postboks 7072-H
Oslo 3

Norges Ingeniorganisasjon
(Norwegian Engineers
Association)
Prof Dahls g 18
Oslo 3
Tel: (010 47) 2-449942

Estate Agents
Norges
Eiendomsmeglerforbund
(Norwegian Association of
Estate Agents)
Storg 5
Postboks 362 Sentrum
Oslo 1
Tel: (010 47) 2-416889

Forestry
Det Norske Skogselskab
(Norwegian Forestry Society)
Wergetv 23B
Oslo 1

Glass
Glassbransjeforbundet i
Norge
(Glass Trade Association in
Norway)
Kr Augustsgate 7B
Oslo 1
Tel: (010 47) 2-111465

Plastics
Norsk Plastforening
(Norwegian Plastics
Association)
Rosenkrantz gate 17
Oslo 1
Tel: (010 47) 2-413012

Shipping
Norges Rederforbund
(Norwegian Shipowners
Federation)
Raadhusg 25
Oslo 1

Skibsbyggerienes
Landforening
(Norwegian National
Shipbuilders Association)
Oscars g 20
Oslo 3
Tel: (010 47) 2-465820

Textiles
Tekstilfabrikkenes Forening
(Norwegian Textile
Manufacturers Association)
Postboks 488 Sentrum
Oslo 1

Tekstilfabrikkenes Konsulent
– og Opplysningskontor
(Textile Manufacturers
Consulting and Information
Office)
Prinsens gate 2
Oslo 1
Tel: (010 47) 2-426930

Tobacco
Tobaksfabrikernes
Landsforening AV 1901
(Norwegian Tobacco Factories
Association)
Fr Nansenspl 9
Oslo 1

Wholesale
Fetevaregrossistenes
Lansforening
(Norwegian Wholesale
Provision Merchants
Association)
Drammensvn 30
Oslo 2

Company Financial and Product Information

Directories
Norge Kompass
Published by Kompass Norge
A/S, Oslo
Provides basic details on
Norwegian companies
including addresses and
products manufactured.
Annual

Norges Storste Bedrifter
(Norway's Largest
Companies)
Published by Okonomisk
Literatur A/S, Oslo
Available from ELC
International, London
Contains financial
information on the 8000
largest companies in Norway
Details provided for the 100
largest companies include
their sales, profit, export and
employees

Economic and Market Statistical Data

Market Research Organisations
Gallup – NOI
Huitfeldtsgate 51
Postboks 2306
0201 Oslo 2
Tel: (010 47) 2-115900
Telex: 71205
Parent company: Norsk
Opinionsinstitutt AS

Norges Markedsdata
Drammensvejen 154
Postboks 1
Skoyen
Oslo 2
Tel: (010 47) 2-554270
Telex: 72560
Parent company: A C Nielsen
Co (USA)

Scan-Fact AS
Oevre Slottsgatan 25
0128 Oslo 1
Tel: (010 47) 2-111054
Telex: 81017

Organisations Providing Economic and Statistical Data
Statistisk Sentralbyraa
Skipperg 15
0152 Oslo 1
Tel: (010 47) 2-413820
This is the Norwegian
government central statistical
office, which is the best
source of information for
economic and industry data
in Norway. Statistisk
Sentralbyraa publish and sell
a great many statistical and
other industry information
booklets. Publications
include:
Manedsstatiskk over
Utenrikshandelen
Monthly bulletin of external
trade
Statistisk Arbok: Statistical
Yearbook of Norway
Statisk Manedshefte:
Monthly Bulletin of Statistics
Economic Survey of Norway

Bergen Bank
Produces a booklet entitled
Norway – a Brief Business
Guide and a number of other
publications providing
economic and stock market
statistics

Christiania Bank
Publishes:
Economic Review
Establishing Business in
Norway
and other economic and
investment research items

Den Norske Creditbank
Publishes:
Figures in a Nutshell
DNC Monthly Surveys of
Trade, Industry and Finance
DNC Bors Guide
DNC Economy and Policy

Other Norwegian banks, such
as Sparebanken ABC,
produce statistical
information on the economy
and stockmarket

Norges Fondsmeglerforbund
(Norwegian Stockbrokers'
Association)
Tollbugaten 2
Oslo 1
Tel: (010 47) 2-411975

Publications

Directories

Norwegian Chamber of
Commerce in London
Yearbook and Directory of
Members
Lists details of members, their
names, addresses, telex and
telephone numbers

Norwegian Companies with
UK Subsidiaries
Produced by the Export
Council of Norway, London
Lists addresses and telephone
numbers of Norwegian
parent companies and their
UK subsidiaries

Norwegian Petroleum
Published by Norwegian
Information

Major Newspapers

Adresseavisen
Daily

Aftenposten
Daily

Arbeiderbladet
Daily

Bergens Tidende
Daily

Dagbladet
Daily

Stavanger Aftenblad
Daily

VG – Verdens Gang
Daily

Journals and Periodicals

Byranytt
Published by the Norwegian
Association of Advertising
Agencies.
Covers advertising and
marketing. Monthly

Eksport Aktuelt
Published by the Export
Council of Norway, Oslo
Covers trade, company news
and market reports. 20 issues
per annum

Farmand
Published by A/S Farmand,
Oslo
Covers economics, finance,
marketing and politics.
Weekly

Koeffbladet in
Published by Koeff-Gruppen
A/S
Covers retail, company
information, new products,
etc. Monthly

Naeringsrevyen
Published by Schibsted
Fagpresse A/S, Oslo
Covers trade and industry,
politics, economics. Monthly

Oekonomisk Rapport
Published by A/S Hjemmet,
Oslo
Covers finance, trade and
industry. Fortnightly

Portugal

Sources of Economic, Stock Market Information and Investment Research Services

Banks

Central Bank

Banco de Portugal
Rua de Comercio, 148
1100 Lisbon
Tel: (010 351) 1-362931
Fax: (010 351) 1-364843
Telex: 16554

Portuguese Banks in London

Anglo Portuguese Bank Ltd
21 Great Winchester Street
London EC2N 2HH
Tel: 01-588 7575

Banco Espirito Santo &
Comercial de Lisboa
4 Fenchurch Street
London EC3M 3AT
Tel: 01-283 5381

Banco Nacional Ultramarino
1 Royal Exchange Avenue
London EC3V 3LT
Tel: 01-283 5535

Banco Pinto and Sotto Mayor
5th Floor
10 Philpott Lane
London EC3M 8AA
Tel: 01-626 5021

Banco Portugues de Atlantico
77 Gracechurch Street
London EC3V OBQ
Tel: 01-626 1711

Banco Totta and Acores
68 Cannon Street
London EC4N 6AQ
Tel: 01-236 1515

Major Portuguese Banks

Banco Espirito Santo e
Comercial
Av dos Aliados 45
4000 Porto
Tel: (010 351) 1-320031
Telex: 22368

Banco Nacional Ultramarino
24 Rua Augusta
PO Box 2069
1102 Lisbon Cedex
Tel: (010 351) 1-369981/9
Telex: 12187

Banco Pinto & Sotto Mayor
International Division:
Rua Mouzinho da Silveira
26-6 A
1200 Lisbon
Tel: (010 351) 1-572198
Telex: 12516
Head Office:
28 Rua do Ouro
1103 Lisbon Codex
Tel: (010 351) 1-370261
Telex: 12516

Banco Portugues do Atlantico
Rua Aurea 110-116
1100 Lisbon
Tel: (010 351) 1-361321
Telex: 42944

Banco Totta & Acores
Rua Aurea 88
1100 Lisbon
Tel: (010 351) 1-369421
Telex: 12266

Caixa Geral de Depositos
Largo do Calhariz
1109 Lisbon Codex
Tel: (010 351) 1-371181
Telex: 42547

Stockbrokers
The two stock exchanges in
Portugal are located in Lisbon
and Oporto.

Bolsa de Valores de Lisboa
(Lisbon Stock Exchange)
Praca de Comercio
1100 Lisbon
Tel: (010 351) 1-879416/879417
Telex: 44751 BVLISB P

Bolsa de Valores do Oporto
(Oporto Stock Exchange)
Palacio de Bolsa
4000 Oporto

Members of the Lisbon
Stock Exchange
Pedro Reis Fernandes
Caldeira
Rua de S Juliao 138
1100 Lisbon
Tel: (010 351) 1-326619
Fax: (010 351) 1-326619
Telex: 44562 CALDEI P

Judite Marina Fernandes
Correia
Av Duarte Pacheco –
Complexo Amoreiras
Torre 1
8 andar – Salas 9, 10 & 11
1000 Lisbon
Tel: (010 351) 1-653141

Jose Alberto Taveira Marques
Av de Republica 9-6
1000 Lisbon
Tel: (010 351) 1-570892
Fax: (010 351) 1-570841
Telex: 64543 TAVAMR P

Luis Leitao Ricciardi
Rua dos Fanqueiros No 14
1400 Lisbon

Eduardo V Roquette Ricciardi
Rua dos Fanqueiros 26a 28
1100 Lisbon
Tel: (010 351) 1-876333
Fax: (010 351) 1-864922
Telex: 15344 RICCMA P

Riccardo Serrao Franco
Schedel
Rua da Prata, 185-2
1100 Lisbon
Tel: (010 351) 1-326642
Fax: (010 351) 1-326658
Telex: 14846 SOHL P

Abilio Agostinho de Sousa
Rua da Prata 48
1100 Lisbon
Tel: (010 351) 1-878303
Fax: (010 351) 1-878422
Telex: 12974 ABILIS P

Sources of General
Background Information,
Industry Sector
Information and Trade
Contacts

UK Addresses
Portuguese Chamber of
Commerce and Industry in
the UK
New Bond Street House
1-5 New Bond Street
London W1Y 9PE
Tel: 01-493 9973
Telex: 918089 ICEP G

Consulate General
Silver City House
62 Brompton Road
London SW3 1BJ
Tel: 01-581 8722

Portuguese Embassy
11 Belgrave Square
London SW1X 8PP
Tel: 01-235 5331
Telex: 28484

Portuguese Embassy Trade
Office
1-5 New Bond Street
London W1Y 9PE
Tel: 01-493 0212

Addresses in Portugal
British Consulate
HM Consul, Oporto
Avenida de Boavista 3072
4100 Oporto Codex
Tel: (010 351) 1-684789
Telex: 26647 UKOPO P

British Consulate
Rue de Santa Isabel
21-1 Esq
8500 Portimao
Tel: (010 351) 082-23071

British Embassy
First Secretary (Commercial)
Rua de S Domingos A Lapa
35-39
1296 Lisbon
Tel: (010 351) 1-61191/5
Telex: 12278 PROLIS P

British Institute in Portugal
Rua de Luis Fernandes
Lisbon
Tel: (010 351) 1-369208

Camera de Comercio
Americana
155,5-ED Esterf
1000 Lisbon
Tel: (010 351) 1-572561/80

Camera de Comercio e
Industria da Madeira
41 Av Arriaga
9000 Funchal
Tel: (010 351) 91-30137/38/39

Camera de Comercio Luso
Britanica
British Portuguese Chamber
of Commerce (The)
8 Rue de Estrela
PO Box 2190
Lisbon
Tel: (010 351) 1-661586
Telex: 12787 BRICHA P

Other offices:
Rua Sa do Bandeira 784-2-E-f
Oporto
Rua Mayor Reins Gomes 13
9000 Funchal
Madeira
The British Portuguese
Chamber of Commerce
promotes Anglo-Portuguese
trade relations and provides a
number of trade-related
services to members.

Camara de Comercio
Portuguesa
Portuguese Chamber of
Industry and Commerce
(The)
Rua das Portas de Santo
Antao 89
1100 Lisbon
Tel: (010 351) 1-327179/323472
Telex: 13441 ACL-CCP
Offers various services
including the preparation of
economic and market studies.
Provides legal, tax and
customs information for
Portuguese companies and
foreign importers and
exporters. This is a central
chamber with two branch
offices, in Porto and Ponta
Delgada.

Camara do Comercio
International
Delegacao Nacional
Portuguesa
Rua das Portas de Santos
Antao 89
1100 Lisbon
Tel: (010 351) 1-363304
Fax: (010 351) 1-324304
Telex: 13441 ACL-CCP

Sources of Investment and Trade Advice, Assistance and Information

The Foreign Investment
Institute and ICEP
(Government Trade Office)
are two of the main
organisations in Portugal
concerned with trade and
investment. The Foreign
Investment Institute gives
official approval to foreign
investment in Portugal.
Information is available on
location, legal and
employment issues. It also
promotes the setting up of
joint ventures with foreign
companies.

Associacao Comercial e
Industrial de Coimbra
Av sa da Bandeira 90/2
3000 Coimbra
Tel: (010 351) 39-22843/33631
Telex: 52207 ACIC P

Associacao Industrial
Portuense
Av da Boavista 2671
4100 Porto
Tel: (010 351) 2-672257/672275
Telex: 25492 AIRPORT P

Associacao Industrial
Portuguesa (AIP)
Praca das Industrias
1300 Lisbon
Tel: (010 351) 1-644161/645341
Telex: 15650 AIPFIL P

Banco de Fomento Nacional
Av Casel Ribeiro 59
1000 Lisbon
Tel: (010 351) 1-522279/523419
Telex: 64752 FOBANC P

Confederacao da Industria
Portuguesa (CIP)
Av 5 de Outubro 35/1 PTA
1000 Lisbon
Tel: (010 351) 1-547454
Telex: 13564 CIP P

Direccao Geral do Comercio
Externo
Av da Republica 79
1600 Lisbon
Tel: (010 351) 1-771911/763437
Telex: 13418 COMEXT P

Foreign Investment Institute
(IIE)
Av da Liberdade 258-4 PTA
1200 Lisbon
Tel: (010 351) 1-570607
Telex: 14712 IFIPOR P

Instituto de Apoio as
Paquenas e Medias Empresas
(IAPMEI)
Rua Rodrigo da Fonseca 73
1200 Lisbon
Tel: (010 351) 1-560251/560372
Telex: 15657 IAPMEI P

Instituto do Comercio Externo
(ICEP)
Av 5 de Outubro 101
1000 Lisbon
Tel: (010 351) 1-730103
Telex: 16486 ICEP P

Instituto de Comercio Externo
de Portugal (ICEP)
R Julio Dinis 748-8
4000 Porto
Tel: (010 351) 2-65055
Telex: 22413 ICPOR P
ICEP is the Portuguese
Government Trade Office and
is concerned with promoting
Portuguese exports. It has
offices in Portugal and
overseas.

Instituto do Emprego e da
Formacao Profissional (IEFP)
Av Jose Malhoa 11
1000 Lisbon
Tel: (010 351) 1-7265123
Telex: 63186 IEFPSC P

Ministry of Foreign Affairs
Largo do Rilvas
1354 Lisbon
Tel: (010 351) 1-601028

Regional information is
available from the following
two commissions:
Commission for the
Coordination of the Alentejo
Region
Rua da Misericordia 9
7000 Evora
Tel: (010 351) 66-24093/24094

Commission for the
Coordination of the Algarve
Region
Praca da Liberdade 2
8000 Faro
Tel: (010 351) 89-22646
Fax: (010 351) 89-83411
Telex: 56110 CCRALC P

Professional Associations

Accountancy
Associacao Portuguesa de
Contabilistas
Rua dos Douradores 20/1
1100 Lisbon

Camara dos Revisores Oficiais
de Contas
Av 5 de Outubro 114/2
O Esq
Lisbon

Sociedade Portuguesa de
Contabilidade
Rue Barata Salgueiro 1/2 Esq
1100 Lisbon

Banking

Associacao Portuguesa de
Bancos
Campo Grande 28/12C
1700 Lisbon
Tel: (010 351) 1-779857

Consulting

Associacao Portuguesa de
Projectistats e Consultores
(APPC)
Av Antonio Augusto Aguiar
126/7
1000 Lisbon
Tel: (010 351) 1-520476

Insurance

Associacao Portuguesa de
Seguros (APS)
(Portuguese Insurers
Association)
Av Jose Malhoa
Lote 1674/5
5th Floor
1000 Lisbon
Tel: (010 351) 1-2484477
Telex: 43196 APS P

Marketing

Sociedade Portuguesa de
Comercializacao (SPC)
Av Elias Garcia 172/2 Esq
Lisbon
Tel: (010 351) 1-774457

Trade Associations

Adhesives

Associacao de Industrias de
Colas Aprestos e Produtos
Similares
Av Guerra Junqueiro 8/2e
1000 Lisbon
Tel: (010 351) 1-894502

Chemicals and Pharmaceuticals

Associacao de Grossistas de
Productos Quimicos e
Farmaceuticos
Av Antonio Aug Aguiar 118
Lisbon 1

Associacao Portuguesa das
Empresas Industriais de
Productos Quimicos
Av D Carlos 1-45-3
Lisbon 2
Tel: (010 351) 1-606796
Telex: 18721

Drink

Associacao dos Exportadores
de Vinho do Porto
Palacio da Associacao
Comercial
R de Ferreira Borges
4000 Oporto
Tel: (010 351) 2-25191
Telex: 22159 ASCOM P

Machine Tools

Associacao Nacional da
Industria de Moldes
(CEFAMOL)
Av do Vidreiro 21-3 DH
2430 Marinha Grande
Tel: (010 351) 44-53229

Centro de Cooperacao dos
Industriais de Maquinas
Ferramentas (CIMAF)
Rua Manuel Pinto de
Azevedo 439
4100 Oporto
Tel: (010 351) 2-675071
Telex: 23118 CIMNOR P

Metals – Production and Transformation

Associacao Portuguesa de
Fundicao
Rua do Campo Alegre 672-2
Esq
4100 Oporto
Tel: (010 351) 2-690675
Telex: 27180 APF P

Mineral Products

Gabinete de Apoio a Industria
Vidreira
Largo de Andaluz 16-1 Dto
1000 Lisbon
Tel: (010 351) 1-549810

Printing and Publishing

Editorial Verbo
Rua Carlos Testa 1
1000 Lisbon

Textiles

Federacao Nacional das
Empresas Texteis (FNET)
Rua Goncalo Cristovao 96-1
4000 Porto Codex
Tel: (010 351) 2-317961
Telex: 22812

Tourism/Catering

Association Portugaise des
Agents de Voyages et
Tourisme
Rue Duque de Palmela 2-1 DT
Lisbon
Tel: (010 351) 1-558641
Telex: 14339 APAVT P

Uniao de Associacoes da
Industria Hoteleira e
Similares do Centro-sul de
Portugal
Av Duque de Avila 75
Lisbon 1
Tel: (010 351) 1-576979/577060

Union des Associations de
l'Industria et Similaires du
Nord du Portugal
Rua Fernandez Tomas 235
Oporto

Company Financial and Product Information

Directories

Anuario Comercial de
Portugal
Produced by Empresa Publica
dos Jornais Noticias e Capital
(EPNC), Lisbon. Lists
companies and products.
Information on companies
consists of addresses and
telephone numbers

Camara de Comercio
Luso-Britanica
Produced by the
Portuguese-British Chamber
of Commerce
Provides a classified list of
companies involved in
various sectors of the
Portuguese economy. Details
include their addresses,
telephone and telex numbers

Principais Empresas de Portugal
Produced by Dun & Bradstreet, Lisbon
1986 edition covered 3500 industrial and commercial companies. The main section provides a company ranking by sales. It provides the names of directors, main activity, SIC codes and other items. It also provides a series of league tables covering companies in the financial services sector, and a directory of directors

Economic and Market Statistical Data

Market Research Organisations

IEM
Apartado 2012
1101 Lisbon
Tel: (010 351) 1-684106
Telex: 12151
Parent company: Research International

Marktest
Rua de S Jose 183-2
1100 Lisbon
Tel: (010 351) 1-323212
Telex: 15322 MKTLQ P

AC Nielsen
Rua Rosa Aranjo 34.4
1200 Lisbon
Tel: (010 351) 1-554412
Telex: 12748
Parent company: AC Nielsen Company (USA)

Norma
Av 5 Outubro 122
1000 Lisbon
Tel: (010 351) 1-767604/8
Telex: 62550 NORMAG P
Affiliated to the Gallup organisation

Quantum-Estudos de Mercado Lda
Rua Ferreira Lapa 32-6
1100 Lisbon
Tel: (010 351) 1-541757
Telex: 42395 REDORB P

Organisations Providing Economic and Statistical Data

Banco de Portugal
Av da Republica 65-10
1094 Lisbon Codex
Publishes:
Banco de Portugal: Report of the Board of Directors (includes statistical, financial and economic data)
Indicadores Economicos: Portugal
(Economic Indicators: Portugal)

Bolsa de Valores de Lisboa
(Lisbon Stock Exchange)
Provides a databank (S11B) covering all listed and most unlisted companies. Other publications provide detailed financial and stock market information.
Annual Report
Daily official list (available on subscription)
General Information on the Lisbon Stock Exchange
Financial information on listed companies (balance sheet of past three years)
Statistical Information on the Securities Market. Monthly Provides turnover, indexes, prices and characteristics of listed securities.

Instituto do Comercio Externo (ICEP)
Publishes:
Comercio Externo Portugues
(Portugal's Foreign Trade)

Instituto Nacional de Estatistica
(National Statistical Institute)
Av Antonia Jose de Almeida 5
1078 Lisbon
Tel: (010 351) 1-802080
Telex: 43719 PC DINE; 63738 P
This is the main source of statistical information for continental Portugal, the Azores, and Madeira. The library has a large stock of statistical publications, and is open to the public.
Publications include:
Anuario Estatistico
(Statistical Yearbook)
Boletim Mensal de Estatistica
(Monthly Bulletin of Statistics)
Estatistica Industriais
(Industrial Statistics)
Indices de Producao Industrial
(Indexes of Industrial Production)
Estatisticas do Comercio Externo
(Statistics of Foreign Trade)
Boletim Mensal das Estatisticas do Comercio Externo
(Monthly Bulletin of Foreign Trade Statistics)

Publications

General Directories

Camara de Comercio Luso-Britanica
(British Portuguese Chamber of Commerce)
Directory
Provides details of member companies grouped by industry/product sector

Export Directory of Portugal
Published by Interprodo Lda, Lisbon
Contains details of trade and export services, travel agencies, exporters, general merchants, and provides general background information.

Portugal Exporter
Published by Empresa Publica
dos Jornais Noticias e Capital
(EPNC)
Contains details of
Portuguese exporters,
catagorised under product
headings. Also provides
details of services offered by
official commercial
organisations such as the
Instituto do Comercio Externo
(ICEP)

Top Export
Published by Jovitur Lda,
Lisbon
Directory of Portuguese
exporters.

Major Newspapers
A Capital
Daily

O Comercio do Porto
Daily

Correio dos Acores
Daily

Correio de Manha
Daily

O Dia
Daily

Diario de Coimbra
Daily

Diario de Lisboa
Daily

Diario de Noticias
Daily

Diario Popular
Daily

Expresso
Weekly

Jornal de Noticias
Daily

O Jornal
Weekly

O Pais
Weekly

O Semanario
Weekly

A Tarde
Daily

Tempo
Weekly

Journals and Periodicals
Actualidade Economica
Publisher's address: R Palma
288-2 Sala-2, 1100 Lisbon

AIP Informacao
Publisher's address:
Praca das Industrias
1399 Lisbon Codex
Monthly (Free)

Algarve
Publisher's address:
Rua de Alportel 25-29, Faro
Weekly

Algarve News
Published by Travel Press
Europe Ltd, Lagos, Algarve
Covers local and national
news. Fortnightly

Anglo-Portuguese News
Published by APN, Monte
Estoril
Covers full news and general
features for foreign residents.
Weekly

Barcelense
Publisher's address:
Rua Barjona Freitas 2628,
Barcelos
Weekly

Boletim de Informandes
Publisher's address: R
Correeiros 15-3, 1100 Lisbon
Covers news on tenders, and
general commerce. Bi-weekly

British Chamber of
Commerce Journal
Monthly

Confidencial Negocios
Publisher's address: R
Navegantes 16 r/c A, 2750
Cascais
Covers economy, f Commerce
Journal
Monthly

Confidencial Negocios
Publisher's address: R
Navegantes 16 r/c A, 2750
Cascais
Covers economy, f Commerce
Journal
Monthly

Confidencial Negocios
Publisher's address: R
Navegantes 16 r/c A, 2750
Cascais
Covers economy, finance and
business. Fortnightly

Diario da Republica
Publishes annual reports of
Portuguese companies

Economia e Desenvolvimento
Publisher's: Pr Luis Canoes
36-4 E, 1200 Lisbon
Covers economy and
development

Expresso
Publisher's address: Rua
Duque de Palmela 37, Lisbon
Weekly newspaper

Jornal Portugues de
Economica e Finanias
Publisher's address: R
Fanqueiros 65-26, 1100 Lisbon
Covers Portuguese economy
and finance

Newsletter
Published by Associacao
Industrial Portuguesa, Lisbon
Covers industry and
commerce

O Pais
Publisher's address:
Rua D Pedro V 7, Lisbon
Weekly

Revista de Contabilidade e
Comercio
Published by Jose Henriques
Garcia, Oporto
Covers commerce and trade.
Quarterly

Revista Mensal da Camara da
Comercio Luso-Britanica
Publisher's address:
8 Rua da Estrela, Lisbon
Covers commerce and trade.
Monthly

Singapore

Sources of Economic, Stock Market Information, and Investment Research Services

Banks

Central Bank
Monetary Authority of
Singapore
PO Box 4456
Maxwell Road
Singapore 9001
Tel: (010 65) 2255577
Telex: 21382 ORCHD RS
Cable: MONETARY

Singapore Banks in London
Development Bank of
Singapore
19-21 Moorgate
London EC2R 6BU
Tel: 01-628 8541

Overseas-Chinese Banking
Corporation
111 Cannon Street
London EC4N 5AS
Tel: 01-626 8391

Overseas Union Bank Ltd
61-62 Coleman Street
London EC2P 2EU
Tel: 01-628 0361

United Overseas Bank Ltd
19 Great Winchester Street
London EC2N 2BH
Tel: 01-628 3504

Major Banks in Singapore
Bank of Singapore
Tong Eng Building
101 Cecil Street 01-02
Singapore 0106
Tel: (010 65) 2239266
Telex: 27149 BOS LTD RS

Chung Khiaw Bank
10 Anson Road
01-01 International Plaze
Singapore 0207
Tel: (010 65) 2228622
Telex: 22027

Development Bank of
Singapore
DBS Building
6 Shenton Way
Singapore 0106
Tel: (010 65) 2201111
Telex: 24455

Far Eastern Bank
156 Cecil Street
Far Eastern Bank Building
PO Box 2950
Singapore 0106
Tel: (010 65) 2219055
Telex: 23029

Four Seas Communications
Bank
19-25 Cecil Street
Singapore 0104
Tel: (010 65) 2249898
Telex: 23670

Industrial and Commercial
Bank
ICB Building
2 Shenton Way
Singapore 0106
Tel: (010 65) 2211711
Telex: 21112

International Bank of
Singapore
01-02 Shell Tower
50 Raffles Place
Singapore 0104
Tel: (010 65) 2234488
Telex: 23579

Lee Wah Bank
01-093 Robina House
1 Shenton Way
Singapore 0106
Tel: (010 65) 2258844
Telex: 21529

Overseas-Chinese Banking
Corporation
OCBC Centre
65 Chulia Street
Singapore 0104

Stockbrokers
Stock Exchange of Singapore
Ltd
1 Raffles Place
24-00
OUB Centre
Singapore 0104
Maxwell Road
PO Box 2306
Singapore 9043
Tel: (010 65) 5353788
Telex: RS 21853

Members (27 as at February 1988)
Alliance Securities (Pte)
156 Cecil Street
08-01/08
Far Easter Bank Building
Singapore 0106
Tel: (010 65) 2225466

Associated Asian Securities
(Pte) Ltd *
10 Anson Road
14-03
International Plaza
Singapore 0207
Tel: (010 65) 2210488

J Ballas & Co Pte Ltd
06-01
Straits Trading Building
9 Battery Road
Singapore 0104
Tel: (010 65) 5358111

BT Brokerage & Associates
Pte Ltd
50 Raffles Place
21-03/04
Shell Tower
Singapore 0104
Tel: (010 65) 2249233

Cathay Securities Pte Ltd
04-11/17
2 Shenton Way
ICB Building
Singapore 0106
Tel: (010 65) 2220442/3

City Securities (Pte) *
3 Philip Street
07-01/02
Matterhorn Building
Singapore 0104
Tel: (010 65) 53300355

DBS Securities Singapore Pte
Ltd
6 Shenton Way
06-27
DBS Building
Singapore 0106
Tel: (010 65) 2259677/65

Fraser Roach & Co Pte Ltd
10 Collyer Quay
27-01
Ocean Building
Singapore 0104
Tel: (010 65) 5359455

G K Goh (Stockbrokers) Pte
Ltd
21 Collyer Quay
08-00
Hong Kong Bank Building
Singapore 0104
Tel: (010 65) 2251228

Grand Orient Securities Pte
07-00
MNB Building
50 Robinson Road
Singapore 0106
Tel: (010 65) 2209811

Hoare Govett Summit
Securities Pte Ltd
65 Chulia Street
22-01
OCBC Centre
Singapore 0104
Tel: (010 65) 5333388

Kay Hian Pte Ltd
1 Bonham Street
22-01
UOB Building
Singapore 0104
Tel: (010 65) 5332936/5353036

Kim Eng Securities (Pte) Ltd
5 Shenton Way
13-00
UIC Building
Singapore 016
Tel: (010 65) 2209090/2209575

Lee & Co (Stock and Share
Brokers) Pte Ltd
14 Robinson Road
11-01/02
Far East Finance Building
Singapore 0104
Tel: (010 65) 2244921

Lim & Tan (Pte)
10 Collyer Quay
12-04 to 09
Ocean Building
Singapore 0104
Tel: (010 65) 5330595

Morgan Grenfell Asia &
Partners Securities Pte Ltd
65 Chulia Street
26-01
OCBC Centre
Singapore 0104
Tel: (010 65) 5331818

OCB Securities Pte Ltd
18 Church Street
06-00
OCBC Centre South
Singapore 0104
Tel: (010 65) 5352882

Ong & Co Pte Ltd
76 Shenton Way
06-00
Ong Building
Singapore 0207
Tel: (010 65) 2239466

OUB Securities Pte Ltd
50 Collyer Quay
01-01
Overseas Union House
Singapore 0104
Tel: (010 65) 2251166

Pacific Union Co (Pte)
Shenton House
18-01
3 Shenton Way
Singapore 0106
Tel: (010 65) 2207211

Paul Morgan & Associates
(Securities) Pte Ltd
11 Collyer Quay
18-01
The Arcade
Singapore 0104
Tel: (010 65) 2219991 (8 lines)

Phillip Securities (Pte)
95 South Bridge Road
11-17
South Bridge Centre
Singapore 0105
Tel: (010 65) 336001 (5 lines)

J M Sassoon & Co (Pte) Ltd
1 Raffles Place
44-00
OUB Centre
Singapore 0104
Tel: (010 65) 53528888/66

Tat Lee Securities Pte Ltd
63 Market Street
12-06/07
Tat Lee Bank Building
Singapore 0104
Tel: (010 65) 5339666

Tsang & Ong Stockbrokers
(Pte) Ltd
16-00
The Arcade
11 Collyer Quay
Singapore 0104
Tel: (010 65) 2245877

UOB Securities Pte Ltd
1 Bonham Street
11-00
UOB Building
Singapore 0104
Tel: (010 65) 5356868

**Approved Overseas
Representative Office**
Sun Hung Kai Securities Pte
Ltd
20 Collyer Quay
18-01
Tung Centre
Singapore 0104
Tel: (010 65) 2241688

* Non-trading members

*Sources of General
Background Information,
Industry Sector
Information and Trade
Contacts*

UK Addresses
Singapore Economic
Development Board
International House
World Trade Centre
London E1
Tel: 01-481 4308

Singapore High Commission
2 Wilton Crescent
London SW1X 8RW
Tel: 01-235 8315

Singapore High Commission
Students Department and
Consular Section
5 Chesham Street
London SW1
Tel: 01-235 9067
Telex: 262564 SHCIUK G

Addresses in Singapore

American Business Council
354 Orchard Road
10-12
Shaw House
Singapore 0923
Tel: (010 65) 2350077
Telex: RS 50296 ABCSIN

British Business Association
3rd Storey
Inchape House
450/452 Alexandra Road
Singapore 0511
Tel: (010 65) 4754192
Telex: RS 21400 BORNEO

British High Commission
Tanglin Road
Singapore 1024
Tel: (010 65) 4739333
Telex: RS 21218 UK REP

Japanese Chamber of
Commerce and Industry
79 Robinson Road
24-04
CPF Building
Singapore 0106
Tel: (010 65) 2210541

Singapore Chinese Chamber
of Commerce and Industry
Chinese Chamber of
Commerce and Industry
Building
47 Hill Street
09-00
Singapore 0617
Tel: (010 65) 3378381
Telex: RS 33714 SCCC 1

Singapore Federation of
Chambers of Commerce and
Industry
47 Hill Street
03-01
Chinese Chamber of
Commerce and Industry
Building
Singapore 0617
Tel: (010 65) 3389761
Telex: RS 26228 SFCC 1

Singapore Indian Chamber of
Commerce
101 Cecil Street
23-01
Tong Eng Building
Singapore 0106
Tel: (010 65) 2222505
Telex: RS 22336 SINDCC

Singapore International
Chamber of Commerce
6 Raffles Quay
05-00
Denmárk House
Singapore 0104
Tel: (010 65) 2241255/2241256
Telex: RS 25235 INTCHAM

Singapore Malay Chamber of
Commerce
10 Anson Road
20-01
International Plaza
Singapore 0207
Tel: (010 65) 2211066
Tel: (010 65) 2230347
Telex: RS 25521 SMCC

Sources of Investment and Trade Advice, Assistance and Information

The four main government
agencies which potential
investors or traders can
contact in Singapore are the
Singapore Trade
Development Board, the Port
of Singapore Authority, the
Civil Aviation Authority and
the Customs and Exise
Department.
   The Singapore Trade
Development Board's services
include chanelling trade
enquiries to Singapore
suppliers, providing
assistance and information on
setting up trading or
distribution operations in
Singapore, providing
information on trade
regulations, statistics and
market development
information.

Civil Aviation Authority of
Singapore
PO Box 1
Singapore Changi Airport
Singapore 9181
Tel: (010 65) 5421122
Telex: RS 21231 AVIATEL

Construction Industry
Development Board
133 Cecil Street
09-01/02
Keck Seng Tower
Singapore 0106
Tel: (010 65) 2256711
Telex: RS20818 CONDEB

Customs and Excise
Department
Maxwell Road
Customs House
Singapore 0106
Tel: (010 65) 2223511
Telex: RS 28817 SINCUS

Export Credit Insurance
Corporation of Singapore Ltd
3702/3 DBS Building
Singapore 0106

Housing and Development
Board
National Development
Building
Maxwell Road
Singapore 0106
Tel: (010 65) 2251212/4444
Telex: RS 22020

Immigration Department
South Bridge Centre
South Bridge Road
08-26
Singapore 0105
Tel: (010 65) 5322877

Ministry of National
Development
National Development
Building
Maxwell Road
Singapore 0106
Tel: (010 65) 2221211
Telex: RS 34369

Monetary Authority of
Singapore (The)
10 Shenton Way
MAS Building
Singapore 0207
Tel: (010 65) 2255577
Telex: RS 28174 ORCHID

National Computer Board
NCB Building
71 Science Park Drive
Singapore 0511
Tel: (010 65) 7782211
Telex: NCB RS 38610
or:
US Office:
National Computer Board of
Singapore
55 Wheeler Street
Cambridge
Mass 02138
Tel: (010 1) 617-4979392
Telex: 710-3201382

National Productivity Board
NPB Building
Bukit Merah Central
Singapore 0315
Tel: (010 65) 2786666
Telex: RS 36047 SINNPB

Port of Singapore Authority
PSA Building
460 Alexandra Road
Singapore 0511
Tel: (010 65) 2747111
Telex: RS 21507 PORT

Singapore Department of
Trade
Suite 201
2nd Floor
World Trade Centre
Telok Blangah Road
Singapore
Tel: (010 65) 2719388
Telex: RS 28617

Singapore Economic
Development Board
EDB Head Office
250 North Bridge Road
24-00
Raffles City Tower
Singapore 0617
Tel: (010 65) 3362288
Telex: RS 26233 SINEDB
UK Office:
Singapore Economic
Development Board
Entableture Floor
International House
World Trade Centre
1 St Katharines Way
London EL9
Tel: 01-481 0745
Telex: 888674 SEDB UK 6
US Office:
55 East 59th Street
New York
NY 1022
Tel: (010 1) 212-4212200
Telex: 421848 TDB NY

Singapore Institute of
Standards and Industrial
Research (SISIR)
179 River Valley Road
Singapore 0617
Tel: (010 65) 3360933
Telex: RS 28499 SISIR

Singapore Trade
Development Board
Head Office:
1 Maritime Square
03-01
World Trade Centre
Telok Blangah Road
Singapore 0409
Tel: (010 65) 2719388
Telex: RS 28617/28170
TRADEV
Overseas centres exist in
Europe, the USA and Japan

Professional Associations

Accountancy
Singapore Society of
Accountants
(Statutory Accounting Body)
Registered and
Administrative Office:
15 Beach Road
05-03/06
Beach Centre
Singapore 0718
Tel: (010 65) 3367020

Banking
Association of Banks in
Singapore (The)
Level 2
PIL Building
140 Cecil Street
Singapore 0106
Tel: (010 65) 2244300
Telex: 20533

Insurance
General Insurance
Association of Singapore
150 Cecil Street
07-01/04 Wing on Life
Building
Singapore 0106

Life Insurance Association
80 Marine Parade
15-00 Parkway Parade
Singapore 1544

Singapore Insurance Brokers
Maxwell Road
PO Box 405
Singapore 9008

Trade Associations

Association of Electronic
Industries in Singapore (The)
6001 Beach Road
08-07
Golden Mile Tower
Singapore 0719

Rubber Association of
Singapore
14 Collyer Quay
13-00
Singapore Rubber House
Singapore 0104
Tel: (010 65) 5353333
Telex: RS 20554 AB RASING

Singapore Association of
Shipbuilders and Repairers
1 Maritime Square
09-50
World Trade Centre
Singapore 0409

Singapore Association of Ship
Suppliers
10 Anson Road
11-02
International Plaza
Singapore 0207
Tel: (010 65) 2201205

Singapore Building Materials
Suppliers Association
490C Jln Besar
Singapore 0820
Tel: (010 65) 2984660

Singapore Contractors
Association Ltd
Construction House
1 Bt Merah Lane 2
Singapore 0315
Tel: (010 65) 2789577
Telex: RS 22406 SCAL

Singapore Freight Forwarders
Association
6001 Beach Road
11-07/08
Golden Mile Tower
Singapore 0719
Tel: (010 65) 2964645

Singapore Manufacturers'
Association
1 Maritime Square
02-18
World Trade Centre
Singapore 0409
Tel: (010 65) 2785211
Telex: RS 24992 SMA

Company Financial and Product Information

Directories
Singapore Electronics
Manufacturers Directory
Published by: Times Trade
Directories Pte Ltd
Provides basic details on
electronic manufacturers in
Singapore, including address,
year established, manager or
name of director, staff figures,
main banker, products and
services offered

Singapore Manufacturers and
Products Directory
Published by: Department of
Statistics, Singapore
Produced every two years.
Contains latest information
on existing and new firms
with an index of products and
industrial services.
Information is taken from the
census of Industrial
Production. Information for
each company includes
address, telephone and telex
number, source of main
capital (country of origin),
principal products and
number of employees

Economic and Market Statistical Data

Market Research Organisations
Acorn Marketing and
Research Consultants Pte Ltd
75 Tanglin Road
03-00
Singapore 1024
Tel: (010 65) 7336565
Telex: RS 56610 ACORNS
Member of MRS

Applied Research
Corporation
303 Tanglin Road
Singapore 1024
Tel: (010 65) 4795011
Telex: RS 38806 uniarc
Parent company: National
University of Singapore

Frank Small and Associates
(SEA) Pte Ltd
510 Thomson Road
SLF Complex
15-03
Singapore 1129
Tel: (010 65) 2589911
Telex: RS 50317 FSASIN
Parent company: Frank Small
& Associates (Aust) Pty Ltd

PA Consultancy Services Pte
Ltd
11 Dhoby Ghaut
10-10
Cathay Building
Singapore 0922
Tel: (010 65) 3360911
Telex: PERSAD RS 23193
Parent company: PA
International

Survey Research Singapore
432 Balestier Road
Public Mansion 02-436
Singapore
Tel: (010 65) 2528596
Telex: RS 24546
Parent company: AGB Pacific
(One of Singapore's largest
research agencies)

Trade Protection Associates
(Pte) Ltd
140 Robinson Road
03-03 Chow House
Singapore 0106
Tel: (010 65) 2228172/2228247
Telex: RS 22867 TPA
Note: Serves mainly overseas
clients. Provides commercial
status reports on companies
in Singapore, Malaysia and
Indonesia as well as market
studies.

Organisations Providing Economic and Statistical Data
Department of Statistics
5th Storey
Fullerton Building
Singapore 0104
Tel: (010 65) 5336121
Telex: STATS RS 20826
Produces the major series of
demographic, economic and
social statistics on Singapore.
Publications include:
Monthly Digest of Statistics
Covers demography, labour,
GDP by industry, industrial
production, trade, finance,
transport and prices

Singapore Statistical News
Monthly bulletin

Singapore Trade Statistics
Provides monthly and annual
figures on imports and
exports

Yearbook of Statistics
Provides statistical series on
demographic, economic and
social characteristics of
Singapore

Report on the Census of
Industrial Production
Provides principal statistics
by major industry group

Economic Development
Board
1 Maritime Square
10-40
World Trade Centre
Telok Blangah Road
Singapore 0409
Tel: (010 65) 2710844
Telex: SINEDB RS 26233

Ministry of Trade and
Industry
CPF Building
79 Robinson Road
40-00
Singapore 0106
Tel: (010 65) 2229666
Telex: MTI RS 24702
Publishes an annual
Economic Survey of
Singapore. This covers
manufacturing, trade,
productivity, prices, plus
monetary and financial
developments, with useful
summary tables at the back of
the report

Singapore Stock Exchange
Provides statistics on the
Singapore Stock Market.
Publications include:
Securities Market in
Singapore (book)
Company Statex Service:
Weekly updating service.
This service provides financial
reports of companies listed on
the exchange

Singapore Tourist Promotion
Board
Raffles City Tower
36-04
250 North Bridge Road
Singapore 0617
Research Department
publishes a statistical report
on visitor arrivals to
Singapore (monthly) plus an
annual version

Publications

Directories
Export Lines
(The Directory of Singapore
Goods and Services)
Published by: Times Trade
Directories PTE Ltd,
Singapore
Covers companies
categorised by product and
service area, and a useful
introduction covering general
economic and trade
information

Singapore Exports and
Services Showcase
Published by: Haghey and
Hoyle Private Ltd, Singapore
Lists manufacturers who
export goods from Singapore.
An index is provided to
enable users to establish who
makes a particular product or
provides a particular service.
Plus there is a useful
Singapore convention and
exhibition calendar

Times Business Directory of
Singapore
(107th Edition 1987)
Published by Times
Periodicals Pte Ltd, Singapore
Comprehensive directory
providing company listings in
alphabetical order, companies
classified by sector or by
product brand names.
Addresses of government
bodies and trade associations
are also provided

Trade Link
Published by: The Singapore
Manufacturers' Association
(SMA)
Covers a wide range of
manufacturing sectors, and
lists companies under each
sector heading. Also provides
notes of guidance on how to
do business in Singapore,
plus manufacturing statistics,
ie value added, number of
establishments, etc.

Major Newspapers
Berita Harian
Malay. Daily

Berita Minggu
Malay. Weekly

Business Times
English. Daily

Shin Min Daily News
Daily

Straits Times (The)
English. Daily

Journals and Periodicals
Asia Research Bulletin
Published by Straits Times
Press, Singapore

Business Opportunities
Publisher's address:
PO Box 503
Marine Parade Post Office
Singapore 9144

Economic Bulletin
Published by: Singapore
Chamber of Commerce
This covers domestic trade
news, trade fairs, financial
and industrial developments.
Special report in the August
1987 issue included the
Business Times' Top 100 list
of companies in terms of
market capitalisation and
shareholders' funds.
Contains a listing at the back
of Singapore and foreign
company registrations and a
trade enquiry register

Far Eastern Technical Review
Publisher's address:
Alain Charles House
27 Wilfred Street
London SW1E 6PR

Singapore Business
Published by: Times
Periodicals Pte Ltd
(subsidiary of The Straits
Times Press Ltd), Times
Centre, Singapore
Regular features include news
on the corporate scene, new
companies, new products,
key economic and financial
indicators. Monthly

Singapore Manufacturer
(The)
Published by the Singapore
Manufacturers Association
and the Times Publishing
Group
News on companies,
products, new developments,
etc. Quarterly

Singapore Stock Exchange
Journal
Published by the Stock
Exchange of Singapore Ltd

Spain

Sources of Economic, Stock Market Information and Investment Research Services

Banks

Central Bank
Banco de Espana
Alcala 50
28014 Madrid
Tel: (010 34) 1-4469055
Telex: 27783

Spanish Banks in London
Banca March
Peek House
20 Eastcheap
London EC3M 1EB
Tel: 01-623 1554
Telex: 8814952

Banco Central
Triton Court
Finsbury Square
London EC2A 1AB
Tel: 01-588 0181
Telex: 8812997

Banco de Bilbao
100 Cannon Street
London EC4N 6EH
Tel: 01-623 3060
Telex: 8811693

Banco de Credito &
Inversiones
31 Palace Street
London SW1E 5HW
Tel: 01-834 7487

Banco de Sabadell
27 Wood Street
London EC2V 7AL
Tel: 01-726 8481
Telex: 8814314

Banco de Santander
10 Moorgate
London EC2R 6LB
Tel: 01-606 7766
Telex: 8812851

Banco de Vizcaya
58-60 Moorgate
London EC2R 6BN
Tel: 01-920 0121
Telex: 893461

Banco Espanol de Credito
Estates House
66 Gresham Street
London EC2V 7BB
Tel: 01-606 4883
Telex: 8811360

Banco Exterior UK
60 London Wall
London EC2P 2JB
Tel: 01-628 8714
Telex: 886820

Banco Hispano Americano
15 Austin Friars
London EC2N 2DJ
Tel: 01-628 4499
Telex: 8813971

Banco Pastor
3 Burne House
88-89 High Holborn
London WC1V 6LS
Tel: 01-242 0478
Telex: 27425

Banco Urquijo Union
15 Austin Friars
London EC2N 2DJ
Tel: 01-628 4499
Telex: 8813971

Caja de Ahorros de Bilbao
Suite 100
Warnford Court
London EC2N 2AT
Tel: 01-628 0441
Telex: 887607

Caja de Ahorros de Galicia
125 Kensington High Street
London W8 5SF
Tel: 01-938 1805
Telex: 919284

Confederation Espanola de
Cajas de Ahorros
(CECA)
16 Waterloo Place
London SW1Y 4AR
Tel: 01-925 2560
Telex: 296984

Major Banks in Spain
Banco Atlantico SA
Diagonal 407 bis
Barcelona
Tel: (010 34) 1-2371240
Telex: 52267

Banco de Bilbao
Paseo de la Castellana 81
28046 Madrid
Tel: (010 34) 1-5826000
Telex: 44458

Banco Central
Calle de Alcala
28014 Madrid
Tel: (010 34) 1-2328820
Telex: 43402

Banco de Espanol de Credito
(Banesto)
Paseo de la Castellana 7
Madrid
Tel: (010 34) 1-4191708
Telex: 27755

Banco Exterior de Espana
Carrera de San Jeronimo 36
Madrid
Tel: (010 34) 1-4294477
Telex: 27741

Banco Hispano Americano
Plaza de Canaleja 1
Madrid
Tel: (010 34) 1-2224660
Telex: 44404

Banco Internacional de
Comercio
Carrera de San Jeronimo 28
Madrid 14
Tel: (010 34) 1-4292693
Telex: 23914

Banco Popular Espanol
Valazquez 34
28001 Madrid
Tel: (010 34) 1-4319010
Telex: 22511

Banco de Santander
Paseo de Pereda 9-12
Santander
Tel: (010 34) 42-221200
Telex: 35883

Banco de Vizcaya
Gran Via 1
48001 Bilbao
Tel: (010 34) 4-4166400
Telex: 32040

Caixa de Barcelona
Avenida Diagonal 530
08006 Barcelona
Tel: (010 34) 3-2016666
Telex: 97214; 97824

Caja de Madrid
Plaza de Celenque No 2
28013 Madrid
Tel: (010 34) 1-4453200
Telex: 23090; 46655

Stockbrokers
Madrid Stock Exchange
Bolsa de Madrid
1 Plaza de la Lealtad
Madrid 28014
Tel: (010 34) 1-2214790
Telex: 27619 BOLMDE

**Members (85) as at
February 1987**
(Listed in descending order
according to length of
membership)
Jesus Maria Agurruza
Aztarain
Ruiz de Alarcon 13
Tel: (010 34) 1-2328530

Adolfo Pries y Bertran
Avda de Alfonso XIII 188
Tel: (010 34) 1-2599204

Antonio Sanz de Bremond y
Mira
Goya 47-7
Tel: (010 34) 1-4314480

Pedro Francisco Ojalvo
Manzanares
Academia 8
Tel: (010 34) 1-4672699

Jose Manuel Nunez-Lagos
Moreno
Jose Ortega y Gasset 29
Tel: (010 34) 1-4351210

Enrique Jose de Benito y
Rodriguez
Plaza de la Lealtad 2
Tel: (010 34) 1-4485600

Manuel de la Concha y
Lopez-Isla
Velazquez 150
Tel: (010 34) 1-2628704

Fernando Aquilar Garelly
Goya 15
Tel: (010 34) 4316883

Juan Jesus Roldan Fernandez
Velazquez 71
Tel: (010 34) 1-2765719

Rafael Boulet Sirvent
Montalban 10-4
Tel: (010 34) 2323783

Adolfo Ruiz de Velasco y del
Valle
Nunez de Balboa 71-1 B
Tel: (010 34) 1-4316163

Javier Molina Alcaraz
Antonio Maura 18
Tel: (010 34) 1-5212001

Jesus Fernandez Amatriain
Montalban 5
Tel: (010 34) 1-5220190

Juan Monjardin Losada
Antonio Maura 9
Tel: (010 34) 1-2311901

Jaime de Aguilar y Otermin
Goya 47-7
Tel: (010 34) 1-4314480

Francisco Javier Ramos
Gascon
Villalar 6-3 izda
Tel: (010 34) 1-4317781

Pablo de la Nuez de la Torre
Antonio Maura 5-4 dcha
Tel: (010 34) 1-2318609

Juan de Arteaga y Piet
Alberto Alcocer 7
Tel: (010 34) 1-2501207

Carlos Fernandez Gonzalez
Eduardo Dato 23
Tel: (010 34) 1-4194945

Valentin Garcia Martinez
Barquillo 13-3
Tel: (010 34) 1-5215079

Esteban Helguero Uribe
Claudio Coello 125-2
Tel: (010 34) 1-2753912

Luis Felipe Martinez-Gil
Lopez
Velazquez 11-4 izda
Tel: (010 34) 1-4311975

Carlos Javier Torres Diz
Juan de Mena 11-4
Tel: (010 34) 1-2324110

Miguel Cerezo Fernandez
Castellana 164
Tel: (010 34) 1-4581200

Jose Maria Otamendi
Aranguren
Antonia Maura 18
Tel: (010 34) 1-2310704

Francisco Fernandez Flores
Goya 47-7
Tel: (010 34) 1-4314480

Jose Luis Contreras Gongora
Castello 25-4 E
Tel: (010 34) 1-4310178

Antonio Garcia Pons
Nunez de Balboa 30-1 D
Tel: (010 34) 1-4111249

Luis J Ques Cardell
Orense 66-9 B
Tel: (010 34) 1-2709032

Joaquin Pulido Cordero
Francisco Gervas 14-7 B
Tel: (010 34) 1-2703901

Jaime Sanchez Gonzalez
Avda Ramon y Cajal 95
Tel: (010 34) 1-4137278

Felipe Gomez-Acebo y
Muriedas
P de la Habana 12-2
Tel: (010 34) 1-4137278

Jose Antonio Sanz Castaneda
Antonio Maura 5-2 izda
Tel: (010 34) 1-5212929

Jose Fernandez
Alvarez-Castellanos
Marques de la Ensenada 2-4
Tel: (010 34) 1-4192803

Felipe Jesus Carrion Herrero
Alfonso XI 7
Tel: (010 34) 1-2326847

Jose Luis Perez Gomez
Alcala 67
Tel: (010 34) 1-2763117

Luis Manuel Gonzalez
Martinez
Castello 117 Apt 533-536
Tel: (010 34) 1-4115513

Juan Lazcano Bilbao
Antonio Maura 10-4 dcha
Tel: (010 34) 1-5224710

Alfonso Corona de la Torre
Antonio Maura 7-5
Tel: (010 34) 1-2313407

Miguel Angel Liobera Lies
Casada del Alisal 7
Tel: (010 34) 1-2281601

Pedro Guerrero Guerrero
Villanueva 16
Tel: (010 34) 1-4313996

Ignacio Garralda Ruiz de
Velasco
Plaza de la Lealtad 3-4
Tel: (010 34) 1-4701212

Jose Maria Baldasano
Supervielle
Plaza de Salamanca 2
Tel: (010 34) 1-4353765

Jose Fernando Usera Cano
P de la Castellana 52
Tel: (010 34) 1-4162011

Francisco Gonzalez
Rodriguez
Antonio Maura 9-2 dcha
Tel: (010 34) 1-4646013

Jose Antonio Aguirre
Rodriguez
Conde de Aranda 5-4 izq
Tel: (010 34) 1-4351063

Ricardo Defarges Ibanez
Goya 39-1
Tel: (010 34) 1-2750038

Vicente Santana Aparicio
Antonio Maura 7-1 izda
Tel: (010 34) 1-5228350

Emilio Vinas Barba
Antonio Maura 7-1 izda
Tel: (010 34) 1-5228350

Victor Morales Montoto
P de la Castellana 100
Tel: (010 34) 1-411504510

Luis Usera Cano
Jorge Juan 30
Tel: (010 34) 1-4315543

Joaquin Osuna Costa
P de Recoletos 21-3 dcha
Tel: (010 34) 1-5218350

Pedro Rodriguez-Ponga
Salamanca
Jorge Juan 28
Tel: (010 34) 1-4311408

Carlos Jose Entrena Palomero
Principe de Vergara 9-3
Tel: (010 34) 1-4357353

Jose Maria Gonzalez de Leon
Santos
Jorge Juan 28
Tel: (010 34) 1-4311408

Francisco Contreras Gongora
Juan de Mena 10
Tel: (010 34) 1-5229184

Ramon Acin Ferrer
Antonio Maura 5
Tel: (010 34) 1-5214781

Rafael Martinez Monche
Goya 7-2 dcha
Tel: (010 34) 1-4355009

Juan Jori Cardona
Pza de las Cortes 4-2
Tel: (010 34) 1-4292409

Jose Antonio Villaverde Beato
Ruiz de Alarcon 13
Tel: (010 34) 1-2328530

Vicente Garcia de Juan
Goya 47-3
Tel: (010 34) 1-2769702

Juan Ignacio Garmendia
Miangolarra
Zurbano 56-2-3
Tel: (010 34) 1-4198350

Dna Iluminada Garcia Diaz
Serrano 116
Tel: (010 34) 1-4117740

Pedro Dominguez Sors
Ayala 17-1
Tel: (010 34) 1-4318427

Enrique Tevar del Olmo
Alcala 95-7 dcha
Tel: (010 34) 1-4355205

Miguel Navarro Tarraga
Alala 17-1
Tel: (010 34) 1-2767306

Rafael Monjo Carrio
Serrano 116
Tel: (010 34) 1-4117501

Ricardo Arveras Carrasco
Antonio Maura 11
Tel: (010 34) 1-4793612

Jose Emilio Canseco Canseco
Antonio Maura 11-1
Tel: (010 34) 1-2327547

Francisco Cotti Urcelay
Alfonso XII 42
Tel: (010 34) 1-4671249

Juan Carlos Ureta Domingo
P de la Castellana 52
Tel: (010 34) 1-4162011

Jose Enrique Cachon Blanco
Orfila 3
Tel: (010 34) 1-4190231

Manuel Vargas-Suniga de
Juanes
Pza Marques Salamanca 10
Tel: (010 34) 1-2756150

Pedro de Elizalde y Aymerich
Pza de las Cortes 5
Tel: (010 34) 1-4292875

Jose Miguel Garcia Lombardia
P de Recoletos 14
Tel: (010 34) 1-4313341

Antonio Morenes Giles
Conde de Aranda 1
Tel: (010 34) 1-4316625

Carlos Jose Cabezas
Velazquez
Jorge Juan 16-2 D
Tel: (010 34) 1-4351608

Jesus Roa Martinez
Velazquez 53
Tel: (010 34) 1-4353041

Dna Julia Sanz Lopez
Antonio Maura 5-2
Tel: (010 34) 1-5212929

Manuel Pizarro Moreno
Antonio Maura 6-4 izda
Tel: (010 34) 1-5211189

Emilio Recoder de Casso
Antonio Mauro 6-4 izda
Tel: (010 34) 1-5211189

Jose Gregorio Juncos
Martinez
Goya 23
Tel: (010 34) 1-4354908

Alberto Bravo Olaciregui
Serrano 7-3 dcha
Tel: (010 34) 1-2767807

Federico Garayalde Nino
Antonio Maura 20-3 dcha
Tel: (010 34) 1-5219319

Carmelo Lacaci de la Pena
P de Reoletos 14
Tel: (010 34) 1-4313341

Valencia Stock Exchange
Bolsa Oficial de Comercio de
Valencia
Pascual y Genis 19
46002 Valencia
Tel: (010 34) 6-3529965
(010 34) 6-3521487
Telex: 62880

Members
Francisco Trullenque Sanjuan
Felix Pizcueta 13 2
Tel: (010 34) 6-3520801

Jose Luis Jimenez Portilo
Pceta Queroi 11 11
Tel: (010 34) 6-3533526/7

Jose Maldonado Chiarri
Embajador Vich 3
Tel: (010 34) 6-3525737

Joaquin Maldonado Chiarri
Embajador Vich 3
Tel: (010 34) 6-3525737

Martin Perez Bellod
Joaquin Costa 55
Tel: (010 34) 6-3349459

Carlos Samper Reig
Perez Pujol 5
Tel: (010 34) 6-3516659

Jose Leach Albert
Colon 58 1
Tel: (010 34) 6-3510625

Juan Piquer Pascaul
R Gcia Sanchiz 1
Tel: (010 34) 6-3514085

Jose Samper Reig
Salva 4 Entresuelo
Tel: (010 34) 6-3510892

Luis Francisco Roux Camacho
Pl del Ayuntamiento 5 7 21
Tel: (010 34) 6-3521728

Federico Die Cortes (1)
Felix Pizcueta 13-2
Tel: (010 34) 6-3520801

Andres de la Fuente
O'Connor
Comedias 8
Tel: (010 34) 6-3315446

Antonio Lopez Selles
Poeta Quintana 5
Tel: (010 34) 6-3515398

Barcelona Stock Exchange
Bolsa de Barcelona
Paseo Isabel 11 No 1
08003 Barcelona
Tel: (010 34) 3-3196200
Telex: 54601; 54131

Colegio de Agentes de
Cambio y Bolsa
(Stockbrokers Association)
(address as above)

Members (a selection)
Fco Javier Aguirre de la Hoz
Paseo de Gracia 55-57 8 2
08007 Barcelona
Tel: (010 34) 3-2153820
Fax: (010 34) 3-2152571

Miguel Alvarez Angel
Paseo de Gracia 42 4 2
08007 Barcelona
Tel: (010 34) 3-3027002
Telex: 54022
Fax: (010 34) 3-3173995

Rafael Bartolome Laborda
Diagonal 468 8 A y B
08006 Barcelona
Tel: (010 34) 3-2187172

Fernando Bautista Perez
Corcega 270 4 2
08008 Barcelona
Tel: (010 34) 3-2374904
Fax: (010 34) 3-2375128

Carmen Boulet Alonso
Diputacion 279
08007 Barcelona
Tel: (010 34) 3-3012418

Miguel Angel Buitrago Novoa
Diagonal 427 bis 6 5
08036 Barcelona
Tel: (010 34) 3-2005005

Ana Carreras Cruells
Provenza 300 pral 1
08037 Barcelona
Tel: (010 34) 3-2160108

Angelo Fco Carretero Martin
Pja Valeri Serra 11-13 1 1
08011 Barcelona
Tel: (010 34) 3-3232538
Angelo Jesus Carretero
Ramirez
Balmes 200 5 2
08006 Barcelona
Tel: (010 34) 3-2381011

Enrique de la Concha
Lopez-Isla
Roselton 246 4 2
08008 Barcelona
Tel: (010 34) 3-2153688

Isabel Estape Tous
Diagonal 442 entl 2
08037 Barcelona
Tel: (010 34) 3-2172562
Fax: (010 34) 3-2172662

Salvador Farres Reig
Diagonal 534 9
08006 Barcelona
Tel: (010 34) 3-2001766

Fernando Gispert Estrada
Paseo de Gracia 25 3
08008 Barcelona
Tel: (010 34) 3-3018148
Telex: 98413
Fax: (010 34) 3-3021787

Agustin Iranzo Reig
Diputacion 256 5 1
08007 Barcelona
Tel: (010 34) 3-3176143

Ignacio Martinez-Echeverria
Ortega
Paseo de Gracia 47
08007 Barcelona
Tel: (010 34) 3-2156161

Pedro Lecuona Ortuzar
Paseo de Gracia 97 4 2
08007 Barcelona
Tel: (010 34) 3-2152817

Salvador Miras Gomez
Lauria 118 4 2
08037 Barcelona
Tel: (010 34) 3-2581807
Telex: 98983

Francisco Palop Tordera
Diagonal 468 7 8
08036 Barcelona
Tel: (010 34) 3-2180612
Fax: (010 34) 3-2380452

Ignacio de la Mora Leblanc
Paseo de Gracia 54 3 D
08007 Barcelona
Tel: (010 34) 3-2159828
Telex: 99597
Fax: (010 34) 3-2151226

Manuel Richi Alberti
Gran Via 617
08007 Barcelona
Tel: (010 34) 3-3176617
Fax: (010 34) 3-3179836

Javier Martinez Monche
Paseo de Gracia 42 3 1
08007 Barcelona
Tel: (010 34) 3-3022623

Jose Serna Masia
Diagonal 423-425 1 2
08036 Barcelona
Tel: (010 34) 3-2002944
Fax; (010 34) 3-2002018

Jaime Ruiz Cabrero
Balmes 177 pral 1
08006 Barcelona
Tel: (010 34) 3-2186054

Enrique Viola Tarragona
Paseo de Gracia 55
08007 Barcelona
Tel: (010 34) 3-2159094
Telex: 97009
Fax: (010 34) 3-2150495

Bilbao Stock Exchange
Bolsa de Bilbao
Jose Maria Olabarri 1
48001 Bilbao
Tel: (010 34) 4-4157411
Telex: 32709 BOLBI

Sources of General Background Information, Industry Sector Information and Trade Contacts

UK Addresses
Spanish Chamber of
Commerce in Great Britain
(Camara Oficial de Comercio
de Espana en Gran Bretana)
5 Cavendish Square
London W1M ODP
Tel: 01-637 9061
Telex: 8811583

Spanish Embassy
24 Belgrave Square
London SW1X 8QA
Tel: 01-235 5555
Telex: 261333

Commercial Section
22 Manchester Square
London SW1M 5AP
Tel: 01-486 0101
Telex: 266406

Spanish Consulate General
20 Draycott Place
London SW3 2SB
Tel: 01-581 5921

Addresses in Spain
There are approximately 85
Chambers of Commerce in
Spain. The Consejo Superior
de Cameras Oficiales de
Comercio, Industria y
Navegacion is the
central organisation of the
Chambers of Commerce,
Industry and Navigation of
Spain.

Consejo Superior de Camaras
Oficiales de Comercio
Industria y Navegacion
Claudio Coello 19 1
Madrid 1
Tel: (010 34) 1-2753400

A selection of regional Chambers
Camera oficial de Comercio y
Industria de Madrid
Huertas 13
Madrid
or
Plaza de la Independencia 1
(Service Office)
Tel: (010 34) 1-4293193
Telex: 27307; 22034 COIME

Camera Oficial de Comercio y
Industria de Barcelona
San Antonio 39/41
Tarrasa
Tel: (010 34) 3-7842111
Telex: 56137 COCIT E

Camera Oficial de Comercio,
Industria y Navegacion de
Barcelona
Casa Lonja del Mar
Paseo Isabel II 1
Barcelona
Tel: (010 34) 4-3192421

Ancha 11-13 (Service Office)
Barcelona
Tel: (010 34) 4-3023462

British Chamber of
Commerce
Marques de Valdeiglesias 3
28004 Madrid 4
Tel: (010 34) 1-2219622

British Embassy
Calle de Fernando el Santo 16
28010 Madrid 4
Tel: (010 34) 1-4190200
Telex: 27656

United Kingdom
Consulates-General
Edificio Torre de Barcelona
Diagonal 477 (13th Floor)
Apartado de Correos 12111
Barcelona 36
Tel: (010 34) 3-3222151
Telex: 52799 BRBAR E
and
Alameda de Urquijo 2-3
Bilbao 8
Tel: (010 34)
4-4157600/4157711
Telex: 32446 BRBIL E

Sources of Investment and Trade Advice, Assistance and Information

The Directorate of Regional
Economic Incentives advises
investors on all aspects of
setting up business in Spain,
including advice on
incentives. It also puts people
in touch with other Spanish
government organisations
involved in this area. SEPS is
the state agency which
develops land, industrial
building, technology, parks
and other areas throughout
Spain.

Bank of Industrial Credit
Carrera San Jeronimo 40
Madrid 14
Tel: (010 34) 1-4296068

Directorate of Regional
Economic Incentives
Ministerio de Economia y
Hacienda
Paseo de la Castellana
147-PTA 11
Madrid 16
Tel: (010 34) 1-1-5710271

Empresa Nacional de
Innovacion SA
Plaza de Salamanca 8
Madrid 6
Tel: (010 34) 1-4014004

Instituto Nacional de
Industria
Plaza de Salamanca 8
Madrid 6
Tel: (010 34) 1-4014004

Ministerio de Industria y
Energia
General Technical Secretariat
Paseo de la Castellana 160
Madrid 16
Tel: (010 34) 1-2596148

Sociedad Estatal de
Promocion y Equipamiento
del Suelo (SEPES)
Paseo de la Castellana 91
28026 Madrid
Tel: (010 34) 1-4565015

Regional contacts

Andalucia
Institute for the Promotion of
Industry in Andalucia
Avda de la Rep Argentina 24
41011 Sevilla
Tel: (010 34) 54-275302

Aragon
Corporation for Industrial
Promotion
Pza de los Sitios 7
50001 Zarazoga
Tel: (010 34) 76-388115

Asturias
Regional Corporation for
Promotion
Gil de Jaz 10
33004 Oviedo
Tel: (010 34) 85-257234

Cantabria
CINDE
Vargas 53
39003 Santander
Tel: (010 34) 42-370819

Castilla-Leon
Entidad de Promocion
Empresarial
Crta de Rueda km 3,500,47008
Valladolid
Tel: (010 34) 83-279000

Castilla-La Mancha
Corporation for Regional
Development
Marques de Mendigorria 1
45003 Toleda
Tel; (010 34) 25-224948

Cataluna
CIDEM
Paseo de Gracia 105
08008 Barcelona
Tel: (010 34) 3-2373645

Extremedura
Department of Industry and
Energy
Camilo Jose Cela 2
Merida (Badajoz)
Tel: (010 34) 24-310162

Galicia
SITEGA
Monelos s/n Edif Servicios
Multiples
15008 La Coruna
Tel: (010 34) 81-297222

Madrid
General Bureau of Promotion
Garcia de Paredas 65
28010 Madrid
Tel: (010 34) 1-4422455

Navarra
Diputacion Foral de Navarra
Avda de Carlos III 2
31002 Pamplona
Tel: (010 34) 48-227100

Pais Vasco
DENAC (Desarrollo de
Nuevas Actividades SA)
Plaza de Espana 4
48001 Bilbao (Vizcaya)
Tel: (010 34) 4-4248645

Valencia
Institute for the Small and
Medium-sized Enterprises of
Valencia
Plaza del Pais Valenciano 6
46002 Valencia
Tel: (010 34) 6-3510100

Professional Associations

Accountancy
Instituto de Censores Jurados
de Cuentas de Espana
Calle General Arrando 9
28010 Madrid

Banking
Asociacion Espanola de Banca
CAEB
Velazquez 64-66
28006 Madrid

Confederation Espanola de
Cajas de Ahorros CECA
(Confederation of Spanish
Savings Banks)
Alcala 27
28014 Madrid

Consejo Superior Bancario
CSB
(Central Committee of
Spanish Banking)
Jose Abascal No 57
28003 Madrid

Consultancy
Asociacion-Espanola de
Empresas de Ingenieria y
Consultoras (ASEINCO)
Claudio Coello 86 4
28006 Madrid
Tel: (010 34) 1-4312380
Telex: 45265

Insurance
Direccion General de Seguros
Paseo de la Castellana 44
Madrid

Marketing
Asociacion Espanola de
Estudios de Mercado
(AEDEMO)
Marketing y Opinion
Urgel 152 Atico 2a
08036 Barcelona
Tel: (010 34) 3-2538509

Asociacion Nacional de
Empresas de Investigacion de
Mercados y de la Opinion
Publica
Breton de los Herreros 21 2
dcha
28003 Madrid
Tel: (010 34) 1-4413953

Trade Associations

Books and Publications
Asociacion Espanola de
Publicidad Exterior (AEP)
Alberto Alcocer 40
28016 Madrid
Tel: (010 34) 1-2505028

Federacion Nacional de
Industrias Graficas
Barquillo 11
28004 Madrid
Tel: (010 34) 1-2229084

PUBLIEXPORT
Unidad de Exportadores de
Publicaciones
Paseo de la Castellana 166
28046 Madrid
Tel: (010 34) 1-4586591

Servicios de Comercio
Exterior del Producto Grafico
Barquillo 11
28004 Madrid
Tel: (010 34) 1-2227249

Electronics, Plastics, Chemicals
Asociacion Espanola de
Fabricantes de Pinturas
(ASEFAPI)
Juan Ramon Jimenez 2
28036 Madrid
Tel: (010 34) 1-2593796

Asociacion Espanola de
Industrias de Plasticos
(ANAIP)
Raimundo Fernandez
Villaverde 57
28003 Madrid
Tel: (010 34) 1-2344526

Asociacion Espanola de
Productores de Fibras
Quimicas
Diagonal 520
08029 Barcelona
Tel: (010 34) 3-2096577

Asociacion de Fabricantes de
Perfumeria y Afines
(STAMPA)
San Bernardo 23
28015 Madrid
Tel: (0101 34) 1-2421616

Asociacion Nacional de
Fabricantes de Fertilizantes
(ANFE)
Serrano 27
28001 Madrid
Tel: (010 34) 1-4350802

Asociacion Nacional de
Industrias Electronicas
(ANIEL)
Principe de Vergara 74
28006 Madrid
Tel: (010 34) 1-4111661

Federacion del Sector
Quimico
Lauria 44
Barcelona
Tel: (010 34) 3-3176908

Foodstuffs of Animal Origin
Asociacion de Exportadores
de Bacalao Seco y Salado
Barquillo 38
28004 Madrid
Tel: (010 34) 1-4193445

Asociacion de Exportadores
de Mejillones y Ostras
Jacometrezo 4
28013 Madrid
Tel: (010 34) 1-2229289

Asociacion de Exportadores
de Pescado y Cafalopodos
Congelados (AEPYCE)
Diego de Leon 44
28006 Madrid
Tel: (010 34) 1-4113156

Asociacion de Mayoristas de
Exportadores-Importadores
de
Pescado y Marisco Fresco y
Congelado
Muelle de Palloza s/n
Puerto Pesquero
La Coruna
Tel: (010 34) 81-294665

Federacion Nacional de
Asociaciones de Fabricantes
de Conservas
Semiconservas y Salazones de
Pescado y Mariscos
Areal 152
Pontevedra
Tel: (010 34) 86-212398

Grupo Exportador de
Conservas de Pescado
Carretera del Rincon 18
Las Palmas de Gran Canaria
Tel: (010 34) 28-263928

Foodstuffs of Vegetable Origin

Agrupacion Espanola de
Exportadores de Aceite de
Oliva (GRUPEX)
Jose Abascal 40
28003 Madrid
Tel: (010 34) 1-4468812

Asociacion de Empresarios de
Comercio al por Mayor
y Exportadores de Frutas,
Hortalizas e Industrias Afines
Avenida de Malaga 1
41004 Seville
Tel: (010 34) 54-231015

Footwear, Leather Goods, Furnishings

Asociacion Espanola de
Modelistas del Calzado
(AMEC)
Jose Maria Peman 17
Elda
03012 Alicante
Tel: (010 34) 65-380581

Asociacion de Fabricantes de
Calzado del Norte de Espana
(AFACNOR)
San Blas 2
Arnedo
26006 Logrono
Tel: (010 34) 41-381332

Consejo Espanol de la Piel
Nunez de Balboa 116
28006 Madrid
Tel: (010 34) 1-2627001

Federacion Espanol de
Fabricantes de Marroquineria
Articulos de Viaje y Afines
Velazquez 4
28001 Madrid
Tel: (010 34) 1-2766103

Federacion de Industrias del
Calzado Espanol (FICE)
Nunez de Balboa 116
28006 Madrid
Tel: (010 34) 1-2627001

Metallurgy, Siderometallurgy, Machinery & Tools

Asociacion Espanola de
Fabricantes de Herramientas
de Corte (AFEC)
Principe de Vergara 74
28006 Madrid
Tel: (010 34) 1-2621651

Comite Espanol Importador
de Maquinaria para la Madera
Trafalgar 4
08010 Barcelona
Tel: (010 34) 3-3179586

Asociacion Nacional de
Construcciones Metalicas y
Calderia (SERCOMETAL)
Principe de Vergara 74
28006 Madrid
Tel: (010 34) 1-2625416

Asociacion Nacional de
Fabricantes de Componentes
y Accesorios de Maquinas y
Herramientas (ACOMHE)
Aguirre Miramon 2
20002 San Sebastian
Tel: (010 34) 43-272100

Asociacion Nacional de
Fabricantes Exportadores de
Cuchilleria (FEXCU)
Principe de Vergara 74
28006 Madrid
Tel: (010 340 1-4113329

Asociacion Nacional de
Fabricantes de Maquinaria y
Equipos
para Ganaderia y Avicultura
(AMEGA)
Casanova 118-120
08036 Barcelona
Tel: (010 34) 3-2543300

Asociacion Nacional de
Industrias del Cobre
(UNICOBRE)
Jose Abascal 47
28003 Madrid
Tel: (010 34) 1-4423521

Miscellaneous

Asociacion de Exportadores
Asturianos (EXPORASTUR)
Gil de Jaz 10
33004 Oviedo
Tel: (010 34) 85-250799

Asociacion Espanola de
Exportadores de Joyeria
Plateria y Relojeria
Casanova 118-120
08036 Barcelona
Tel: (010 34) 3-2543300

Asociacion Espanola de
Fabricantes de Pequenos
Electrodomesticos
Rocafor 241-243
08029 Barcelona
Tel: (010 34) 3-2309903

Asociacion Espanola de
Fabricantes Exportadores de
Articulos
Instrumentos y Aparatos de
Medicina (AFEDEMIC)
Londres 16
28028 Madrid
Tel: (010 34) 1-2560004

Agrupacion de Fabricantes de
Cemento de Espana
(OFICEMEN)
Velazques 23
28001 Madrid
Tel: (010 34) 1-4029300

Asociacion Espanola de
Empresas Constructoras de
Actividad Internacional
(AECI)
Serrano 174
28002 Madrid
Tel: (010 34) 1-2629201

Asociacion Espanola de
Joyeros y Plateros
Principe de Vergara 74
28006 Madrid
Tel: (010 34) 1-4113813

Asociacion de Fabricantes de
Equipos de Climatizacion
Francisco Silvela 69
28028 Madrid
Tel: (010 34) 1-4027383

Asociacion Nacional de
Fabricantes de
Electrodomesticos (ANFEL)
de Linea Blanca
Principe Vergara 74
28006 Madrid
Tel: (010 34) 1-2627506

Asociacion Nacional de
Fabricantes de Mobilario de
Oficina (ASFAMO)
Principe Vergara 74
28006 Madrid
Tel: (010 34) 1-2627506

Asociacion Nacional de
Normalizacion de Bienes de
Equipo (BEQUINOR)
Principe de Vergara 74
28006 Madrid
Tel: (010 34) 1-4112756

Federacion de Asociaciones
de Armadores de Buques
(FECCOM)
de Pesca Fresca en Aguas de
la CEE
Lagasca 40
28001 Madrid
Tel: (010 34) 1-4032648

Asociacion Nacional de
Fabricantes de Papel Carton
Alcala 85
28009 Madrid
Tel: (010 34) 1-2763003

Agrupacion Empresarial de la
Industria Zoosanitaria
(VETERINDUSTRIA)
Zurbano 34
28010 Madrid
Tel: (010 34) 1-4100238

Asociacion de Empresas
Refinadoras de Petroleo
(ASERPETROL)
Maria de Molina 37
28006 Madrid
Tel: (010 34) 1-2627950

Asociacion Espanola de
Anticuarios
Velayos 12
28035 Madrid
Tel: (010 34) 1-2272057

Federacion Espanola de
Marketing
Princesa 1
28008 Madrid
Tel: (010 34) 1-2423788

Asociacion de Corresponsales
de Prensa Extranjera
Pinar 5
28006 Madrid
Tel: (010 34) 1-2612904

Asociacion Medicas
Villanueva 11
28001 Madrid
Tel: (010 34) 1-4317780

Asociacion Nacional de
Armadores de Buques
Congeladores de Cefalopodos
(ANACEF)
Luis Morate 6
Las Palmas de Gran Canaria
Tel: (010 34) 28-272650

Asociacion Nacional de
Armadores de Buques
Congeladores de Pesca de
Merluza (ANAMER)
Edificio Vendedores
Pto Pesquero
Pontevedra
Tel: (010 34) 86-420 422

Federacion Nacional de
Empresas de Instrumentacion
Cientifica
Medica, Tecnic y Dental
(FENN)
Fernandez de la Hoz 52
28010 Madrid
Tel: (010 34) 1-419 7017

Asociacion de Exportadores
de Control de Calidad
Gran Via 29
28013 Madrid
Tel: (010 34) 1-2227759

Textiles and their Manufacturers

Federacion Espanola de
Empresas de la Confeccion
Peligros 2
Madrid
Tel: (010 34) 1-2227552

Federacion Nacional de la
Industria Textil Lanera
San Quirico 30
08020 Sabadell
Barcelona
Tel: (010 34) 3-7259311

Tourism

Agrupacion Hotelera de las
Zonas Turisticas de Espana
(ZONTUR)
Gremio Toneleros 54
Poligono La Victoria
07009 Palma de Mallorca
Tel: (010 34) 71-204000

Federacion Espanola de
Asociaciones de Agencias de
Viaje
Plaza Pio XII 3
07012 Palma de Mallorca
Tel: (010 34) 71-222244

Toys, Giftware & Games

Asociacion Empresarial de
Articulos de Regalo
Alcala 155
28009 Madrid
Tel: (010 34) 1-2759425

Asociacion Empresarial de
Juegos Automatizados
(ASEJU)
Diego de Leon 28
28006 Madrid
Tel: (010 34) 1-4311819

Asociacion Espanola de
Fabricantes de Juguetes
O'Donnell 4
28009 Madrid
Tel: (010 34) 1-2754975

Transport Equipment

Asociacion Espanola de
Fabricantes de Automoviles,
Camiones, Tractores y sus
Motores (ANFAC)
Fray Bernardino Sahagun 24
28036 Madrid
Tel: (010 34) 1-4577881

Asociacion Nacional de
Constructores de
Motocicletas,
Ciclomotores y Bicicletas
(SERMOTO)
Principe Vergara 74
28006 Madrid
Tel: (010 34) 1-4557978

Asociacion de Transporte
Internacional (ASTIC)
Orense 36
28020 Madrid
Tel: (010 34) 1-4557978

Wines

Federacion de Empresas
Vinicolas y Bebidas
Alcoholicas (FEVIBA)
Plaza de Sevilla 45
11006 Jerez
Cadiz
Tel: (010 34) 56-334516

Federacion Nacional de
Criadores y Exportadores de
Vinos
Martires Concepcionistas 18
28006 Madrid
Tel: (010 34) 1-4012191

Grupo Exportadores de Vino
de Rioja
Gran Via Juan Carlos 1 – 14
26002 Logrono
Tel: (010 34) 41-222837

Company Financial and Product Information

Directories

Camara de Comercio en
Espana
(British Chamber of
Commerce in Spain Members
Directory)
Contains listing of member
companies, which includes
addresses, telephone
numbers and industry
classification codes

Duns 15 000 Principales
Empresas Espanolas
Produced by Dun and
Bradstreet SL, Madrid
Contains two main sections;
one shows the distribution of
larger companies against
criteria of province and
activity, sales band, number
of employees and sectors; the
second section provides basic
details on companies,
including sales, number of
employees and name of the
chief executive

Kompass Espana
Produced by Kompass
Comercial Destribuidora SA
Covers 24 000 companies.
Includes a listing of foreign
firms and agents in Spain

Las 2000 Mayores Empresas
Espanolas
Produced by Fomento de la
Produccion, Barcelona
Contains ranking of 2095
Spanish companies, and
covers around forty industry
sectors. A series of league
tables makes up the bulk of
this directory

Economic and Market Statistical Data

Market Research Organisations

Alef, Gabinete de Estudios
Economicos y Sociales SA
Calle Cinca 19
28002 Madrid
Tel: (010 34) 1-4576408

Aryo SA
Corazon de Maria 6
28002 Madrid
Tel: (010 34) 1-4135814

Data SA
General Oraa 70
28006 Madrid
Tel: (010 34) 1-2612857
Telex: 48681 SADT E

Emopublica SA
Capitan Haya 56
28020 Madrid
Tel: (010 34) 1-2705099

Indecsa Research
International
Tambre 33
28002 Madrid
Tel: (010 34) 1-4113003
Telex: 41547 INDES E
Parent company: Research
International (UK)

Instituto Gallup SA
C Fortuny 14
28010 Madrid
Tel: (010 34) 1-4104345
Telex: 42221 IGOP E
Member of the Gallup
Organisation

A C Nielsen Co
Luchana 23-6
PO Box 10149
28010 Madrid
Tel: (010 34) 1-4473762
Telex: 46278
Parent company: A C Nielsen
Company (USA)

Sofemasa
Torre de Madrid 14
28013 Madrid
Tel: (010 34) 1-2489697
Telex: 45637
Parent company: Metra
Group (UK)

Organisations Providing Economic and Statistical Data

Instituto Nacional de
Estadistica
Paseo de la Castellana 183
28046 Madrid
Tel: (010 34) 1-2799300
Telex: 43247 ESTD E
This is the main source of
official statistical data in Spain
Publications include the
following:

Boletin de Estadistica.
Published 6 times per annum
Provides data on major
sectors, employment, and
prices

Espana: Annuario
Estadistico. Annual
Yearbook providing data on
all main topics, including
balance of payments, trade,
employment and industrial
and service sectors in Spain

Direccion General de Aduanas e Impuestos Especiales
Servicio de Estadistica
Guzman el Bueno 137
28071 Madrid
Tel: (010 34) 1-2543200
Telex: 23058 ADUMA E
Publications include:
Estadistica del Comercio Exterior. Comercio por Productos y Precios.
Comercio por Paises (Foreign Trade Statistics by products, prices and by country).
Annual
Informe Mensual Sobre el Comercio Exterior. Annual

Ministerio de Economia y Hacienda
Almagro 34
28010 Madrid
Tel: (010 34) 1-4103143
Contact Servicio de Publicaciones at the above address for a publications list

Ministerio de Economia y Hacienda
Secretaria de Estado de Comercia Espanola
Paseo de la Castellana 162
Planta 16
28046 Madrid
Publications include:
Boletin Economico de Information Comercial Espanola
This weekly publication contains news items on the economy, trade and statistics on industrial production

Ministerio de Industria y Energia
Paseo de la Castellana 160
Madrid 16
Tel: (010 34) 1-5710271
Publishes statistics on Spanish industries

Various large Spanish banks produce publications on the Spanish economy and stock market. Some examples are listed below:

Banco de Bilbao: Informes Economicos. Annual
Situacion. Monthly

Banco Central: Boletin Informativo

Banco de Espana: Informes Anuales. Annual

Banco Hispano Americano (Ltd), London, publishes a bi-monthly newsletter on the Spanish economy and stockmarket

Madrid Stock Exchange publications include a Daily Official List, Annual Report and Studies Service

Barcelona Stock Exchange produces similar publications, including the Year Book of the Barcelona Stock Exchange and Financial Bulletin.

Publications

Directories
Ibar-Anuario Comercial Iberoamericano
(Spanish-American Commercial Directory)
Published by Ibar, Madrid, every 3 years. Contains 4 parts. Part 1 lists banks, insurance companies, transit agents and 5000 headings covering Spanish exports

Prodei: Directory of Spanish Industry, Export and Import. Annual
Produced by Editado por Prodei, Madrid
Directory of commodities and products which Spain imports and exports. Lists trade marks in alphabetical order and Spanish importers and exporting firms

Major Newspapers
El Alcazar
Daily

Cinco Dias
Economic. Daily

Diario 16
Daily

Iberian Daily Sun
English. Daily

El Pais
Daily

Journals and Periodicals
Actualidad Economica
Published by Punto Editorial SA, Madrid
Covers economy, industry, trade and finance. Weekly

Boletin Servex
Published by Banco de Bilbao, Servicio de Estudios, Bilbao
Covers foreign trade. Fortnightly

Campana
Published by Ediciones Campana SA, Madrid
Covers marketing and advertising. Fortnightly

Comercio e Industria
Publisher's address: Huertas 13, 28012 Madrid
Covers trade and industry. Fortnightly

Los Domingos de ABC
Publisher's address: Calle de Servano 61, 28006 Madrid
Weekly

Economia y Finanzas Espanolas
Publisher's address: Antonio Acuna 11, 28009 Madrid
Covers banking, finance, industry sector analysis and trade. Monthly

Nueva Empresa
Published by Comunicar SA, Madrid.
Covers the economy, industry sectors and includes company surveys Fortnightly

El Pais Semanal
Publisher's address: Miguel Yuste 40
28037
Madrid
Weekly

Situacion
Published by Banco de Bilbao
Covers trade, industry and the economy. Quarterly
(Available in English and Spanish)

Sri Lanka

*Sources of Economic,
Stock Market
Information and
Investment Research
Services*

Banks

Central Bank
Central Bank of Sri Lanka
34-36 Janadhipathi Mawatha
Colombo 1
Sri Lanka
Tel: (010 94) 1-21191; 27325;
29938; 20863
Telex: 21176; 21290; 21627

Sri Lankan Banks in London
Bank of Ceylon
22-24 City Road
London EC1Y 2AJ
Tel: 01-256 7545

Major Banks in Sri Lanka
The two state-owned banks,
the Bank of Ceylon and the
People's Bank dominate the
banking business in Sri
Lanka. The Bank of Ceylon
has over 200 branches in Sri
Lanka. The People's Bank has
over 300 branches.

American Express Bank
Limited
45 Janadhipathi Mawatha
Colombo 1
Tel: (010 94) 1-31288

Bank of America
324 Galle Road
Colombo 3
Tel: (010 94) 1-575080

Bank of Credit and Commerce
International (Overseas)
Limited
21-23 Upper Chatham Street
Colombo 1
Tel: (010 94) 1-545840

Banque de l'
Indochine et de Suez
Ceylinco House
Janadhipathi Mawatha
Colombo 1

Banque Indosuez
1st Floor
Ceylinco House
Colombo 1
Tel: (010 94) 1-36181

Citibank NA
1st Floor
Iceland Building
Galle Face
Colombo 3
Tel: (010 94) 1-549061

Commercial Bank of Ceylon
Limited
21 Bristol Street
Colombo 1
Tel: (010 94) 1-549888

Grindlays Bank Limited
37 York Street
Colombo 1
Tel: (010 94) 1-546150

Hatton National Bank Limited
10 RA de Mel Mawatha
Colombo 3
Tel: (010 94) 1-21885/6/7
Telex: 22152 HATNBK CE

Hong Kong and Shanghai
Banking Corporation
24 Sir Baron Jayatilaka
Mawatha
Colombo 1
Tel: (010 94) 1-25435
Telex: 21152 HSBC CE

National Savings Bank
Savings House
225 Galle Road
Colombo 3
Tel: (010 94) 1-573008

People's Bank
75 Sir Chittampalam A
Gardiner Mawatha
Colombo 2
Tel: (010 94) 1-27841
Telex: 21143 (International
Division)
Telegram: Janabank

Standard Chartered Bank
(The)
Janadhipathi Mawatha
Colombo 1

State Bank of India
16 Sir Baron Jayatilaka
Mawatha
Colombo 1
Tel: (010 94) 1-26133

Stockbrokers
Colombo Securities Exchange
(Gte) Ltd (The)
(Companies Registration
Office)
Mackinons Building
2nd Floor
York Street
Colombo 1
Tel: (010 94) 1-546581; 545279;
545280
Telex: 21124 MACKINON CE

Members (as at February 1988)
Bartleet & Co Ltd
Standard Chartered Bank
Building
Janadhipathi Mawatha
Colombo 1
Tel: (010 94) 1-22331/2/3/4/5

City Investment Services (Pvt)
Ltd
York Arcade Building
No 27/4/1 York Arcade Road
Colombo 1
Tel: (010 94) 1-546901; 26287

Forbes & Walker Ltd
29 Braybrooke St
Colombo 2
Tel: (010 94) 1-27961

JB Stockbrokers & Financial
Services (Pvt) Ltd
150 St Joseph Street
Colombo 14
Tel: (010 94) 1-549191/2/3

Mercantile Stock Brokers Ltd
55 Janadhipathi Mawatha
Colombo 1
Tel: (010 94) 1-2661.1/2-9

Serendib Trust Services Ltd
34 WAD Ramanayake
Mawatha
Colombo 2
Tel: (010 94) 1-25213/4/5

Somerville & Co Ltd
137 Vauxhall St
Colombo 2
Tel: (010 94) 1-29201

Sources of General Background Information, Industry Sector Information and Trade Contacts

UK Addresses

High Commission for the
Democratic Socialist Republic
of Sri Lanka
13 Hyde Park Gardens
London W2 2LU
Tel: 01-262 1841 (general)
01-262 3996 (trade and
commercial)
Telex: 25844

Addresses in Sri Lanka

The Federation represents all
the chambers in the island
and maintains close contact
with the government on trade
and industry policy.

Federation of Chambers of
Commerce and Industry
20 First Floor
Galle Face Court 2
Colombo 1
Tel: (010 94) 1-23158

The Ceylon Chamber of
Commerce is the only trade
chamber to include members
from all sections of the
business and trade
community. Its annual report
provides a useful overview of
commercial events over the
last year.
It can provide information on
companies in Sri Lanka

Ceylon Chamber of
Commerce
PO Box 274
127 Lower Chatham Street
Colombo 1
Tel: (010 94) 1-21745
1-21191
Telex: 21193

National Chamber of
Commerce of Sri Lanka
PO Box 1375
2/F YMBA Building
Main Street
Colombo 1
Tel: (010 94) 1-25271

National Chamber of
Industries
PO Box 1775
1/F 20 Galle Face Courts 2
Colombo 3
Tel: (010 94) 1-29038

Sri Lanka Chamber of Small
Industries
12 Rotunda Gardens
Colombo 3
Tel: (010 94) 1-549692

British High Commission
First Secretary (Commercial
and Economic)
190 Galle Road
Kollupitiya
Colombo 3
Tel: (010 94) 1-27611
Telex: 21101 UKREPCE
Postal address:
British High Commission
PO Box 1433
Colombo

Sources of Investment and Trade Advice, Assistance and Information

A comprehensive range of
assistance and incentives is
offered to foreign investors
through the Foreign
Investment Advisory Council
and the Greater Colombo
Economic Commission.

Authority for non-Free trade
zone projects:

Foreign Investment Advisory
Council
International Economic
Cooperation Division
Ministry of Finance and
Planning
1/F Room 120 Galle Face
Secretariat
Colombo 1
Tel: (010 94) 1-26286
Telex: 21409 FINMIN CE

Authority for Free Trade Zone
projects:

Greater Colombo Economic
Commission
14 Sir Baron Jayatillaka
Mawatha
PO Box 1768
Colombo 1
Tel: (010 94) 1-34403
Telex: 21332 ECONCOM CE

Colombo Plan (for
Cooperative Economic and
Social Development in Asia
and the Pacific)
12 Melbourne Avenue
PO Box 596
Colombo 1

Companies Registration
Office
Ceylon Security Exchange Ltd
Stock Market Trading Floor
Mackinons Building
2nd Floor
Colombo 1
Tel: (010 94) 1-29881
Telex: 21124 MACKINON CE

Department of Commerce
4th Floor
Rakshana Mandiraya
Vauxhall Street
Colombo 2

Export Promotion Council of
Ceylon
5 Charlemont Road
Colombo

Sri Lanka Export
Development Board
310 Galle Road
Colombo 3
Tel: (010 94) 1-573044
Telex: 21457 EXDEV CE

Sri Lanka Importers,
Exporters and Manufacturers
Association
26 Reclamation Road
PO Box 1050
Colombo

Sri Lanka National Council
International Chamber of
Commerce
17A Airfield Place
Colombo 3

Sri Lanka State Trading
Corporation
68/70 York Street
PO Box 263
Colombo
Tel: (010 94) 1-25167/8

Trade and Shipping
Information Service
PO Box 1525
31 Galle Face Courts 2
Colombo 3

Trade Associations

Export Trade Associations
affiliated to the Chamber
(Addresses available from the
Ceylon Chamber of
Commerce)

Coconut Products Exporters
Association

Coir Fibre Exporters
Association

Colombo Rubbers Traders'
Association

Colombo Tea Traders
Association

Sri Lanka Apparel Exporters
Association

Sri Lanka Association of
Producers & Exporters of
Spices and other Produce

Sri Lanka Gem Traders
Association

Other Associations affiliated
to the Chamber:

Association of Principal
Agents of the National
Insurance Corporation

Business Council

Ceylon Association of
Manufacturers

Ceylon Association of
Steamer Agents

Ceylon Engineering Traders'
Association

Colombo Brokers' Association

Colombo Motor Traders'
Association

Commercial Banks'
Association

Hire Purchase & Finance
Association of Sri Lanka

Pesticides Association of Sri
Lanka

Sri Lanka (Ceylon) Tourist
Association

Sri Lanka Pharmaceutical
Manufacturers' Association

Tourist Hotels Association of
Sri Lanka

Company Financial and Product Information

Directories
Ferguson's Ceylon Directory
Published by the Associated
Newspapers of Ceylon Ltd,
Colombo

Handbook of Rupee
Companies
Produced by the Colombo
Brokers Association
Lists companies registered in
Sri Lanka and quoted on the
share market

Sri Lanka Chamber of
Commerce
Directory of Garment
Manufacturers and Exporters
Produced by the Sri Lanka
Chamber of Commerce,
Colombo

Economic and Market Statistical Data

Market Research Organisations
Economist Intelligence Unit
(The)
5A Longden Terrace
Colombo 7

Grant Kenyon and Eckhardt
(Lanka Ltd)
Grant House
101 Galle Road
Colombo 4

Lanka Marketfacts (Pvt) Ltd
7A Charles Terrace
Off Alfred Place
Colombo 3
Tel: (010 94) 1-575218
Telex: 21545 KENECK CE
Parent company: Grant Bozell
Jacobs Kenyon & Eckhardt

Lanka Market Research
Bureau Ltd
23 Glenaber Place
Colombo 4
Tel: (010 94) 1-581357; 500437
Telex: 21971
Parent company: MRB Group
Ltd, UK

Masters Advertising and
Marketing Consultants
177 Inner Flower Road
Colombo 7

Vision Limited
17, 1/1 Chartered Bank
Building
Colombo 1

Wicks Advertising &
Marketing Ltd
736 Maradana Road
Colombo 10

Organisations Providing Economic and Statistical Data
Agrarian Research and
Training Institute
114 Wijerama Mathawa
Colombo 7
Tel: (010 94) 1-598539

Census and Statistics
Department
6 Albert Crescent
Colombo 7
Tel: (010 94) 1-92988

Statistics Department
Central Bank of Sri Lanka
Janadipathi Mawatha
Colombo 1
Publishes Central Bank of
Ceylon Bulletin. Monthly;
Economy and Social Practices
of Sri Lanka; Annual Report

Ceylon Institute of Scientific and Industrial Research
363 Baudhaloka Mawatha
Colombo 7
Tel: (010 94) 1-93807

Marga Institute
61 Isipathana Mawatha
Colombo 5
Tel: (010 94) 1-585186

Ministry of Plan Implementation
Publications Bureau
PO Box 500
Secretariat Building
Colombo
Publishes Statistical Abstract of the Democratic Socialist Republic of Sri Lanka annually

Sri Lanka Customs Department
Colombo
Publishes External Trade Statistics bi-annually

Publications

Directories
Ceylon Chamber of Commerce
Annual
Register of Members
Published by the Ceylon Chamber of Commerce, Colombo

Asia and Pacific
Published by the World of Information, Essex, UK
Contains information on Sri Lanka

Asia Yearbook
Published by the Far Eastern Economic Review, Hong Kong
Contains information on Sri Lanka

Foreign Economic Trends and their Implications for the United States: Sri Lanka
Annual
Prepared by the American Embassy, Colombo
Published by US Department of Commerce, USA
Contains information on the economy of Sri Lanka

Market Profiles for Asia and Oceania (Overseas Business Reports)
Published by US Department of Commerce, USA

Major Newspapers

Colombo
Ceylon Daily Mirror
English. Daily

Ceylon Daily News
English. Daily

Ceylon Observer
English. Daily

Dawasa
Sinhalese. Daily

Dinpathi
Tamil. Daily

Island (The)
English/Sinhalese. Daily

Lanka Guardian
Daily

Sun
English. Daily

Sunday Mirror
Weekly

Sunday Times
Weekly

Journals and Periodicals
Business Lanka
Published by Trade and Shipping Information Service of the Ministry of Trade and Shipping
Contains news on local industry and the economy.
Quarterly

Ceylon Commerce
Published by Ceylon National Chamber of Commerce, Colombo
Monthly

Ceylon Government Gazette
Published by the Government Press, Colombo. Weekly

Ceylon Trade Journal
Published by Ceylon National Chamber of Commerce.
Quarterly

Industrial Ceylon
Published by Ceylon National Chamber of Industries.
Quarterly

Sweden

Sources of Economic, Stock Market Information and Investment Research Services

Banks

Central Bank
Sveriges Riksbank
Box 16283
10325 Stockholm
Sweden
Tel: (010 46) 8-787000
Telex: 19150

Swedish Banks in London
Arbuthnot Latham Bank
(Subsidiary of Nordbanken)
133 Finsbury Pavement
London EC2A 1AY
Tel: 01-628 9876

Enskilda Securities/Skandinaviska
(Subsidiary of Skandinaviska Enskilda Banken)
26 Finsbury Square
London EC2A 1DS
Tel: 01-638-3500

Gotabanken
Gota House
70 Cannon Street
London EC4N 6AE
Tel: 01-248 2266

Nordic Representatives
(Joint Venture bank)
22 Eastcheap
London EC3M 1EM
Tel: 01-929 7972

PK English Trust
(Subsidiary of PK Banken)
4 Fore Street
London EC2
Tel: 01-920 9120

Svenska Handelsbanken
(Subsidiary)
17 Devonshire Square
London EC2M
Tel: 01-377 8040

SwedBank/Sparbankernas
Bank
(Representative Office)
The Old Deanery
Dean's Court
London EC4V 5AA
Tel: 01-236 4060

Securities Houses in London
Carnegie International
1 Farringdon Street
London EC4M 7LH
Tel: 01-489 1999

Gota Securities
Gota House
70 Cannon Street
London EC4N 6AE
Tel: 01-248 2266

Svenska & Co
14 Devonshire Row
London EC2M 4RH
Tel: 01-377 6066

Major Swedish Banks
Forsta Sparbanken
Hamngatan 31
10331 Stockholm
Tel: (010 46) 8-7690000
Telex: 17588

Gotabanken
Sveavagen 14
10377 Stockholm
Tel: (010 46) 8-7904000
Telex: 19240 (General
enquiries)

Post-och Kreditbanken (PK
Banken)
Hamngatan 12
10371 Stockholm
Tel: (010 46) 8-7818000
Telex: 19310 (International
Division)

Nordbanken
Regeringsgatan 38
PO Box 7133
10387 Stockholm
Tel: (010 46) 8-7963000
Telex: 17616

Skandinaviska Enskilda
Banken (SE Banken)
Kungstradgardsgatan 8
10640 Stockholm
Tel: (010 46) 8-221900 (Head
Office and SEB International)
Telex: 16600 ESSEBH S

Skanska Banken
10 Sodergatan
20540 Malmo
Tel: (010 46) 40 351000
Telex: 33209 (General Office)

Sparbankernas Bank
(Swedbank)
Brunkebergstorg 8
10534 Stockholm
Tel: (010 46) 8-222320
Telex: 12826

Svenska Handelsbanken
Blasieholmstorg 11
10328 Stockholm
Tel: (010 46) 8-7691000
Telex: 11090 HANDST S

Stockbrokers

Stockholm Fondbors (Stock
Exchange)
Kallergrand 2
Box 1256
11182 Stockholm
Tel: (010 46) 8-143160
Telex: 13551 BOURSES

Members of Stockholm Stock Exchange

Banks
Bohusbanken
Box 7094
10387 Stockholm
Tel: (010 46) 8-7967030

Foreningsbankernas Bank
Box 5844
10248 Stockholm
Tel: (010 46) 8-7823000

Forsta Sparbanken
10331 Stockholm
Tel: (010 46) 8-7690000

Gotabanken
10377 Stockholm
Tel: (010 46) 8-7904000

Nordbanken
Box 7133
10387 Stockholm
Tel: (010 46) 8-79630000

Ostgota Enskilda Bank
Box 7523
10392 Stockholm
Tel: (010 46) 8-7960400

PKBanken
10371 Stockholm
Tel: (010 46) 8-7818000

Skandinaviska Enskilda
Banken
10640 Stockholm
Tel: (010 46) 8-7635000

Skanska Banken
Box 7405
10391 Stockholm
Tel: (010 46) 8-7238100

Skaraborgsbanken
Box 7832
10398 Stockholm
Tel: (010 46) 8-7895600

Sparbankernas Bank
10534 Stockholm
Tel: (010 46) 8-7901000

Svenska Hankelsbanken
10328 Stockholm
Tel: (010 46) 8-7691000

Wermlandsbanken
Box 7443
10391 Stockholm
Tel: (010 46) 8-7900100

Stockbrokers
Aragon Securities
Fondkommission AB
Box 7254
10389 Stockholm
Tel: (010 46) 8-140110

Aros Fondkommission AB
Nybrokajen 15
11148 Stockholm
Tel: (010 46) 8-72346000

Alfred Berg Fondkommission
AB
Box 16200
10324 Stockholm
Tel: (010 46) 8-7235800

B&B Fondkommission AB
Box 7214
10388 Stockholm
Tel: (010 46) 8-245740

Carnegie Fondkommission
AB
Box 16080
10322 Stockholm
Tel: (010 46) 8-247800

Consensus Fondkommission
AB
Box 7774
10396 Stockholm
Tel: (010 46) 8-7890700

Hagglof & Ponsbach
Fondkommission AB
10336 Stockholm
Tel: (010 46) 8-7910200

Sven Hagstromer
Fondkommission AB
Box 2265
10316 Stockholm
Tel: (010 46) 8-7233600

Nordia Fondkommission AB
Box 7124
10387 Stockholm
Tel: (010 46) 8-248030

Merchant, Grundstrom &
Partners Fondkommission AB
Box 5016
10241 Stockholm
Tel: (010 46) 8-7913500

Montagu Fondkommission
AB
Box 7615
10394 Stockholm
Tel: (010 46) 8-145900

E Ohman Jor
Fondkommission AB
Box 7415
10391 Stockholm
Tel: (010 46) 8-141770

Penningmarknadsmaklarna
PM Fondkommission AB
Box 7128
10387 Stockholm
Tel: (010 46) 8-249700

Persson & Co
Fondkommission AB
Box 7362
10390 Stockholm
Tel: (010 46) 8-7916800

Stockholm Fondkommission
AB
Box 7487
10392 Stockholm
Tel: (010 46) 8-110525

United Brokers
Fondkommission AB
Box 5853
10248 Stockholm
Tel: (010 46) 8-117470

Sources of General Background Information, Industry Sector Information and Trade Contacts

UK Addresses
Swedish Chamber of
Commerce
72-73 Welbeck Street
London W1M 7HA
Tel: 01-486 4545
Fax: 01-935 5487
Telex: 22620

Swedish Embassy
11 Montagu Place
London W1H 2AL
Tel: 01-724 2101
Fax: 01-724 4174
Telex: 28249

Swedish Trade Council
73 Welbeck Street
London W1M 7HA
Tel: 01-935 9601
Telex: 22620

Addresses in Sweden
Stockholm Chamber of
Commerce
Vastra Tradgardsgatan 9
Box 16050
10322 Stockholm
Tel: (010 46) 8-231200

Federation of Swedish
Chamber of Commerce
Jakobs Torg 3
Box 16050
10322 Stockholm
Tel: (010 46) 8-231200

British-Swedish Chamber of
Commerce in Sweden
Ann-Christin Geinhoff
Pehrsson (Director)
Grevgatan 34
Box 5512
11485 Stockholm
Telex No and ASWBK: 054
10838

Counsellor (Commercial and
Economic)
British Embassy
Skarpogatan 6-8
115 27 Stockholm
Tel: (010 46) 8-670140
Telex: 19340 BRITEMB S

Sources of Investment and Trade Advice, Assistance and Information

Sveriges Handelsgenters
Forbund
(Federation of Swedish
Commercial Agents)
Hantverkargatan 46
11221 Stockholm
Tel: (010 46) 8-540975

Standardiserings-
kommisionen i Sverige (SIS)
(Swedish Standards Institute)
Tegnergatan 11
10366 Stockholm
Tel: (010 46) 8-237250

Sveriges Exportrad
(Swedish Trade Council)
Artillerig 42
11485 Stockholm

Foretagareforbundet
(The Company Association)
Odengatan 87
11322 Stockholm

A Selection of Regional Development Funds
Handelns Arbetsgivareorg
(HAO)
(Swedish Employers
Confederation)
Birger Jarlsgatan 53
Box 1720
11187 Stockholm
Tel: (010 46) 8-7627700

Malmohus Ian
Studentgatan 4
Box 4245
20313 Malmo
Tel: (010 46) 40-100780

Riksskatteverket
(National Tax Board)
Tritonvagen 21
17194 Solna
Tel: (010 46) 8-7648000

Stockholms Ian
Dalagatan 100
Box 23135
10435 Stockholm
Tel: (010 46) 8-151400

Uppsala Ian
Sturegatan 1
Box 2046
75002 Uppsala
Tel: (010 46) 18-100320

Professional Associations

Accountancy
Foreningen Auktoriserade
Revisorer FAR
(Authorised Public
Accountants Association)
Nortullsgatan 6
Box 6417
11382 Stockholm
Tel: (010 46) 8-234130

Svenska Revisorsamfundet
(Swedish Society of
Accountants)
Radmansgatan 18
11425 Stockholm

Banks
Svenska Bankforeningen
(Swedish Bankers
Association)
Box 7603
10394 Stockholm
Tel: (010 46) 8-243300

Svenska
Sparbanksforeningen
(Swedish Savings Bank
Association)
Box 16426
10327 Stockholm

Computing
Svenska Dataforeningen
(Swedish Data Processing
Association)
Larsbergsvagen 42
18138 Lidingo

Svenska Samfundet for
Informationsbehandling
(Swedish Society for
Information Processing)
Box 22114
10422 Stockholm

Consultancy
Svenska
Organisationskonsulenters
Forening (SOK)
Skepporgatan 22
11452 Stockholm
Tel: (010 46) 8-7836611

Insurance
Forsakringsbolagens
Riksforbund
(Association of Insurance
Companies)
Tegeluddsvagen 100
11587 Stockholm
Tel: (010 46) 8-7837000

SACO/SR
(Confederation of
Professional Associations)
Lilla Nygatan 14
10315 Stockholm
Tel: (010 46) 8-225200

Marketing
Swedish Market Research
Society
M-Gruppen
Box 17048
10462 Stockholm

Sveriges Marknadsforbund
(Swedish Marketing
Federation)
Ludvigsbergsgatan 20
11726 Stockholm
Tel: (010 46) 8-680855

Trade Associations

Sveriges Industriforbund
(Federation of Swedish
Industries)
Storgatan 19
Box 5501
11485 Stockholm
Tel: (010 46) 8-7838000

In line with the increasingly
important cooperation among
the Nordic countries and their
industries, the Federation
works closely with the
industrial federations in
Denmark, Finland, Norway
and Iceland. It also cooperates
with international bodies
including the BIAC, CEIF,
ICC and UNICE.
Subsidiaries include:
Naringslivets Ekonomifakta
AB (an information company
run jointly by the Federation
and the Swedish Employers
Confederation – SAF)
AB Industribyran
Institutet for Utlandsk Ratt
AB (Swedish Foreign Law
Institute)
AB Skatteinformation (Tax
Information)

Members of the Federation of Swedish Industries
Association of Swedish
Bakers (The)
Hovslagargatan 5
11148 Stockholm

Association of Swedish
Chemical Industries
Box 5501
11485 Stockholm

Association of the Swedish
Prefabricated Concrete
Industries (The)
Box 1270
17124 Solna

Association of the Swedish
Ready-Made Clothing
Industry (The)
Box 16133
10323 Stockholm

Federation of Swedish Food
Industries
Box 5501
11485 Stockholm

General Department of the
Federation of Swedish
Industries (The)
Box 5501
11485 Stockholm

National Association of the
Swedish Joinery Factories
Kaptensgatan 15
11457 Stockholm

National Association of
Swedish Wooden House
Manufacturers (The)
Box 14085
10440 Stockholm

National Federation of
Swedish Sawmills and
Swedish Wood Exporters'
Association (The)
Box 26083
10041 Stockholm

Swedish Association of
Mechanical, Electrical and
Electronical Engineering
Industries
Box 5506
11485 Stockholm

Swedish Brick and Tile
Manufacturers' Association
Box 5873
10248 Stockholm

Swedish Construction
Federation (The)
Box 27308
10254 Stockholm

Swedish Electrical
Manufacturers' Association
Box 5501
11485 Stockholm

Swedish Federation of
Graphic Art Industries (The)
Box 16383
10327 Stockholm

Swedish Flour Milling
Association (The)
Olof Palmes Gata 20B
11137 Stockholm

Swedish Furniture
Manufacturers' Association
Box 14012
10440 Stockholm

Swedish Iron and Steel Works
General Association
Box 1721
11187 Stockholm

Swedish Mining Association
(The)
Box 5501
11485 Stockholm

Swedish Plywood
Manufacturers' Association
(The)
Villagatan 1
11432 Stockholm

Swedish Pulp and Paper
Association (The)
Villagatan 1
11432 Stockholm

Swedish Shipbuilders'
Association (The)
Eriksberg
Box 8008
40277 Goteborg

Swedish Shoe Manufacturers'
Association (The)
Box 16105
10332 Stockholm

Swedish Tanners Association
(The)
Box 16105
10323 Stockholm

Swedish Wallboard
Manufacturers' Association
(The)
Villagatan 1
11432 Stockholm

Textile Council (The)
Box 16133
10323 Stockholm

Other Trade and Industrial Associations

Grafiska Industriforbundet
(Printers Trade's Federation)
Blasieholmsgatan 4A
Box 16383
10327 Stockholm
Tel: (010 46) 8-7626800

Sveriges Grossistforbund
(Federation of Wholesalers
and Importers)
Grevgatan 34
Box 5512
11485 Stockholm
Tel: (010 46) 8-6635280

Sveriges Kopmannaforbund
(Retail Federation)
Kungsgatan 19
10561 Stockholm
Tel: (010 46) 8-7915300

Swedish National Board for
Technical Development
Box 43200
10072 Stockholm

Company Financial and Product Information

Directories

Adri De Ridder
(Access to the Stock Market)
Published by The Federation
of Swedish Industries,
Stockholm
Studies primary markets in
Sweden and the UK

ELC Europe's Largest
Companies
Published by ELC
International, London
Covers Swedish
manufacturing and service
companies, and provides
information in the form of
company rankings, basic
financial information and
addresses

Kompass Sweden and
Sveriges Handelskalender
Published by Bonniers
Foretagsinformation,
Stockholm
Kompass is provided in two
volumes. It covers enterprises
of all kinds engaged in
production and service
activities. It includes
wholesalers, banks and
insurance companies

Svensk Industrikalender
(Swedish Industrial
Directory)
Published annually by The
Federation of Swedish
Industries, Stockholm
Covers major Swedish
manufacturers

Svensk
Inrikeshandelskalender
(Domestic trade directory)
Published by Nordik
Handelsreklam AB,
Gothenburg

Sveriges Storsta Foretag
(Sweden's 1000 Biggest
Companies)
Published by Liber
Laronmedel AB, Stockholm
Provides tables for turnover,
share capital, and employees
covering the largest
companies in Sweden

The Swedish Companies Act
1975
Published by The Federation
of Swedish Industries,
Stockholm
Contains all amendments to
the 1975 Act prior to January 1
1986

Swedish Export Directory
Published annually by The
Swedish Trade Council,
Stockholm

Telefonkatalogen (Telephone
Directories)
Swedish telephone directories
are very informative as they
provide information on the
company's main business,
and identify branch offices,
principals and departments,
etc

*Economic and Market
Statistical Data*

**Market Research
Organisations**
Burke Marketing Research AB
Box 14093
40020 Goteborg
Tel: (010 46) 31-830280

GEK Marknadsforskning AB
Box 87
22100 Lund
Tel: (010 46) 46-181600
Telex: 32270 GFKS S
Parent company: GFK
Nurnberg (West Germany)

Institutet for
Marknadsundersokningar AB
(IMU)
Virebergsvagen 19
Box 1367
17127 Solna
Tel: (010 46) 8- 7340030
Telex: 19467
Parent Company: Testologen
AB

Interfact/SVP AB
Kungsgatan 36
Box 75188
10430 Stockholm
Tel: (010 46) 8-145545
Telex: 15924 INFACT S
Parent company: Svenska
Dagbladet AB
Note: Information brokers

AB Marketing Bo Jonsson
Box 510
16215 Vallingby
Tel: (010 46) 8-380035
Telex: 14310 ABM S
Parent company:
Marketindex OY (Finland)

AC Nielsen
Storholmsgatan 11
Skarholmen
Tel: (010 46) 8-7405060
Telex: 11277 NIELSEN N
Parent company: AC Nielsen
Company (US)

SIFO
Angermannagatan 174
Box 131
16212 Vallingby 1
Tel: (010 46) 8-879370
Telex: 17795 SIFO S
Note: affiliated to the Gallup
organisation

Testologen-IMU
Box 2050
19102 Sollentuna
Tel: (010 46) 8-35960

**Organisations Providing
Economic and Statistical
Data**
Statistika Centralbyran
(The Central Bureau of
Statistics)
Karlavagen 100
11581 Stockholm
Tel: (010 46) 8-7834000
This is the major source for
statistical reports. Swedish
sources are often more
detailed and up to date than
international sources.
Publications from Statistika
Centralbyran include:
Series of the Official Statistics
of Sweden (SOS)
Historical Statistics of Sweden
Statistical Abstract of Sweden
(summarised statistics)
Monthly Digest of Swedish
Statistics (most important
source of short term statistics)
Year books, annual reports,
etc
Forecasting Information
(contains manpower reports)
Statistical Reports (series
covering sixteen subgroups
eg housing and construction,
credit market, transport)

Affarsvarlden (publishers of
economic data)
Box 1234
11182 Stockholm

Ekonomiska
Forskningsinstitutet vid
Handelshogskolan
(Economic Research Institute
of Stockholm School of
Economics)
Sveavagen 65
Box 6501
11383 Stockholm
Tel: (010 46) 8-7360120

Handelns Utredningsinstitut
(Retail Research Institute)
Box 27267
10253 Stockholm
Tel: (010 46) 8-630195

Industriens
Utredningsinstitut
(The Swedish Industrial
Institute for Economic and
Social Research)
Grevgatan 34
11453 Stockholm
Tel: (010 46) 8-7838000

Konjunkturinstitutet
(The National Institute of
Economic Research)
Nygatan 1
Box 1228
11182 Stockholm
Tel: (010 46) 8-240740

Studieforbundet Naringsliv
och Samhalle
(Industrial Council for Social
and Economic Studies)
Skoldungagatan 2
11427 Stockholm
Tel: (010 46) 8-232520

Svenska Institutet (publishers
of economic data)
Box 7437
Kungstradgarden
10391 Stockholm

Publications

Directories
Foretagskatalogen
Publisher's address:
Norrlandsgatan 21
Box 7850
10394 Stockholm
Nationwide directory of
companies and institutions

M Kalendern (The Swedish
Technical Directory)
Published by Fournir,
Stockholm
Covers manufacturers under
seperate headings such as
steel, metals, etc. Also covers
wholesalers and agents under
different product headings,
and suppliers

Sveriges Statskalender
Lists government officials,
institutions and agencies,
official organisations, etc.
Published annually

Taxeringskalendern
Published annually by
Kalenderforlaget, Solna
Personal incomes directory

Vem ar Det (Who's Who)
Published by Nordstedt and
Soners Forlag AB
Contains approximately
10000 biographies

Major Newspapers
Aftonbladet
Daily

Arbetarbladet
Daily

Arbetet
Daily

Barometern
Daily

Dagens Nyheter
Daily

Expressen
Daily

Goteborgs-Posten
Daily

Sundsvalls Tidning
Daily

Svenska Dagbladet
Daily

Journals and Periodicals
Affarsvarlden
Financial journal. Weekly

Aktuellt om Fusioner
Published by SPK (Statens
pris-och Kartell-namnd),
Stockholm
Company information
including merger and
acquisitions information.
Four issues per annum

Cooperative Technical
Research
Published by The Swedish
National Board for Technical
Development (STU),
Stockholm
Free of charge

Energy Technology
Published by The STU,
Stockholm
Free of charge

Facts Sheets
Published by Svenska
Institutet
Contains information on
Swedish industry, economy,
taxes, foreign trade,
education and research

INFO
Published by The Swedish
Advertisers Association,
Stockholm
Covers advertising,
marketing and public
relations. Monthly

Monthly Statistical Digest
Published by Allman
Manadsstatistik

New Knowledge, New
Technology, New Products
Published by The STU,
Stockholm
Free of charge

Nytt Fran Industriforbundet
Published by The Federation
of Swedish Industries
Fortnightly

SIP Newsletters
Weekly newsletter covering
current affairs, trade and
industry, science and
technology
Published in English

Svensk Handel
Published by Sveriges
Grossistforbund, Stockholm
Covers news on products,
and companies involved in
wholesaling and importing.
Appears as monthly annex to
daily newspaper Dagens
Industri

Sweden Now
Published by
Ingenjorsforlaget AB,
Stockholm
Covers Swedish trade and
industry, company profiles,
and products Provided in a
number of languages
including English. Bimonthly

Swedish Business Report
Published by Affarsvarlden
Publication covering mainly
company news. Fortnightly

Swedish Economy (The)
Published quarterly by The
Institute of Economic
Research
(Konjunkturinstitutet)

Viewpoint
Published by The Federation
of Swedish Industries
Summary of economic and
industrial news

Veckans Affarer
Published by Affarsforlaget,
Stockholm
Covers trade and industry.
Weekly

Switzerland

Sources of Economic, Stock Market Information and Investment Research Services

Banks

Central Bank
Banque Nationale Suisse
15 Borsenstrasse
8022 Zurich
Tel: (010 41) 1-2213750
Telex: 812400

Swiss Banks in London
Banca del Gottardo
Salisbury House
Finsbury Circus
London EC2M 5QQ
Tel: 01-382 9873
Telex: 925361

Banca della Svizzera Italiana
Windsor House
39 King St
London EC2V 8DQ
Tel: 01-600 5745
Telex: 884821

Bank Julius Baer
Bevis Marks House
Bevis Marks
London EC3A 7NE
Tel: 01-623 4211
Telex: 887272

Bank Oppenheim Pierson
(Schweiz)
Level 15
City Tower
40 Basinghall Street
London EC2V 5DE
Tel: 01-628 7839
Telex: 885119

Banque Intercommerciale de
Gestion
1 Great Cumberland Place
London W1H 7AL
Tel: 01-491 1066
Telex: 883605

Banque de la Mediterranee
Suisse
93 Park Lane
London W1Y 3TA
Tel: 01-499 8181
Telex: 8811404

Banque Scandinave en Suisse
10 Hill Street
London W1X 7FU
Tel: 01-629 3634
Telex: 886642

Credit Suisse
24 Bishopsgate
London EC2N 4DN
Tel: 01-623 3488
Telex: 887322

Credit Suisse First Boston
(Financial Credit Suisse First
Boston)
24 Great Titchfield Street
London W1P 7AA
Tel: 01-332 4000
Telex: 892131

Discount Bank & Trust
34 Grosvenor Square
London W1A 4QP
Tel: 01-629 0801
Telex: 894032

Habib Bank AG Zurich
92 Moorgate
London EC2P 2EX
Tel: 01-638 1391
Telex: 888056

Handelsbank NW
1 Finsbury Square
London EC2A 1AD
Tel: 01-374 0565
Telex: 885477

Ingeba International
Co-operative Bank
20 Copthall Avenue
London EC2R 7JD
Tel: 01-638 1511
Telex: 88659

Overland Trust Bank
101 Cannon Street
London EC4N 5AD
Tel: 01-283 2931
Telex: 8812591

Swiss Bank Corp
99 Gresham Street
London EC2P 2BR
Tel: 01-606 4000
Telex: 887434

Swiss Bank Corp
International
(Swiss Bank Corp)
Three Keys House
130 Wood Street
London EC2V 6AQ
Tel: 01-600 0844
Telex: 889381

Swiss Cantobank
(International)
5th Floor
Moor House
London Wall
London EC2Y 5ET
Tel: 01-920 9696
Telex: 8813560

Swiss Volksbank
48-54 Moorgate
London EC2R 6EL
Tel: 01-628 7777
Telex: 917777

Trade Development Bank
24 Grafton Street
London W1A 2HL
Tel: 01-491 2211
Telex: 887358

Union Bank of Switzerland
122 Leadenhall Street
London EC3V 4PA
Tel: 01-929 4111
Telex: 887341

United Overseas Bank
103 Mount St
London W1Y 5HE
Tel: 01-491 1530
Telex: 25119

Security Houses
GIBA International
20 Copthall Avenue
London EC2R 7EE
Tel: 01-588 9329

Lombard Odier International
Portfolio Management
Norfolk House
13 Southampton Place
London WC1A 2AJ
Tel: 01-831 2350

Sarasin (UK)
Sarasin House
5-6 St Andrew's Hill
London EC4V 5BY
Tel: 01-236 0212

UBS (Securities)
Stock Exchange Building
Old Bond Street
London EC2N 1EY
Tel: 01-588 6666

Major Swiss Banks
Bank Leu AG
Bahnhofstrasse 32
8001 Zurich
Tel: (010 41) 1-2191111
Telex: 812174

Banque Contonale de Berne
(Kantonalbank von Berne)
8 Place Federale
3001 Berne
Switzerland
Tel: (010 41) 31-222701
Telex: 911122 (General)

Banque Nationale Suisse
Borsenstrasse 15
8022 Zurich
Tel: (010 41) 1-2213750
Telex: 813530

Schweizerischer Bankverein
(Swiss Bank Corporation)
Registered Office:
Aeschenvorstadt 1
Basle
General Management:
Aeschenplatz 6
Basle
Tel: (010 41) 61 202020

Schweizerischer Kreditanstalt
(Credit Suisse)
Paradaplatz 8
8021 Zurich
Tel: (010 41) 1-2151111
Telex: 812412

Schweizerischer
Bankgesellschaft
(Union Bank of Switzerland)
45 Bahnhofstrasse
8021 Zurich
Tel: (010 41) 1-2341111

Schweizerische Volksbank
Bundesgasse 26
3011 Berne
Tel: (010 41) 31-328111
Telex: 911156

Zurcher Kantolbank
Bahnhofstrasse 9
Box 4039
8022 Zurich
Tel: (010 41) 1-2201111
Telex: 812140

Stockbrokers
Securities trading takes place
in seven major cities in
Switzerland. The largest
exchanges are in Basle,
Geneva and Zurich.

Stock Exchanges
Zurich Stock Exchange
Bleicherweg 5
8021 Zurich
Tel: (010 41) 1-2111470

Association des Bourses
Suisses
Zurcher Effektenborse
(Zurich Stock Exchange
Association)
Bleicherweg 5
8021 Zurich
Tel: (010 41) 1-2292111
Telex: 813065

Basle Stock Exchange
Aeschenplatz 7
4002 Basle
Tel: (010 41) 61-251150

Geneva Stock Exchange
10 Rue Petitot
1211 Geneva 11
Tel: (010 41) 1-280684

Bourse Suisse de Commerce
Postfachs 7075
Bahnhofquai 7
8023 Zurich
Tel: (010 41) 1-2112870

Bourse des Cereales de Zurich
Seefeldstr 7
8008 Zurich
Tel: (010 41) 1-475880

Bourse des Cereales et
Produits Agricoles de Berne
Postfach 2407
3001 Berne
Tel: (010 41) 31-254655

Bourse de Lausanne
Rue Mauborget 9
1003 Lausanne
Tel: (010 41) 21-227827

Bourse de Neuchatel
c/o Banque Cantonale
Neuchateloise-4
Place Pury-Neuchatel
Tel: (010 41) 38-254714

St Galler Effektenborse
9000 St Gallen

Licences to trade in securities
on the Zurich Stock Exchange
have been issued to 24 banks.
178 other firms hold licences
to engage in the securities
trade outside the Stock
Exchange. The 24 banks listed
below make up the
membership of the Zurich
Stock Exchange Association.

Allgemeine Elsassische
Bankgesellschaft, Sogenal
Strassburg, Filiale Zurick
Bleicherwes 1
8001 Zurich
Tel: (010 41) 1-2207111

Amro Bank und Finanz
Bleicherwes 21
8022 Zurich
Tel: (010 41) 1-2025995

Banca della Svizzera Italiana,
Filiale Zurich
Bleicherwes 37
8022 Zurich
Tel: (010 41) 1-2058111

Bank Cantrade AG
Bleicherwesg 30
8038 Zurich
Tel: (010 41) 1-4816100

Bank Hofmann AG
Talsrasse 27
8022 Zurich
Tel: (010 41) 1-2115760
Telex: 812133

Bank Julius Baer & Co AG
Bahnofstrasse 36
8022 Zurich
Tel: (010 41) 1-2285111
Telex: 812154

Bank Leu AG
Bahnhofstrasse 32
8001 Zurich
Tel: (010 41) 1-2191111
Telex: 812174

Bank Oppenheim Pierson
(Schweiz) AG
Uraniastrasse 28
8022 Zurich
Tel: (010 41) 1-2116333

Bank Rinderknecht AG
Bahnhofstrasse 28a
8022 Zurich
Tel: (010 41) 1-2111552

Bank J Vantobel & Co AG
Bahnhofstrasse 3
8022 Zurich
Tel: (010 41) 1-2118270
(010 41) 1-4887111

Handelsbank NW
Talstrasse 59
8022 Zurich
Tel: (010 41) 1-2145111

Maerki, Baumann & Co AG
Dreikonigstrasse 8
8022 Zurich
Tel: (010 41) 1-2022684

Overland Trust Banca,
Lugano
Zweigniederlassung Zurich
Todistrasse 17
8022 Zurich
Tel: (010 41) 1-2013111

Privatbank und
Kerwaltungsgesellschaft
Banengasse 29
8022 Zurich
Tel: (010 41) 1-2289111

Rahn und Bodmer
Talstrasse 15
8022 Zurich
Tel: (010 41) 1-2113939

Rud, Blass & Cie
Inhaber Blass & Cie
Bankgeschaft
Talacker 21
8039 Zurich
Tel: (010 41) 1-2114910

Ruegg Bank AG
Waagsasse 5
8022 Zurich
Tel: (010 41) 1-2116267

A Sarasin & Cie Basle
Zweigniederlassung Zurich
Talstrasse 66
8022 Zurich
Tel: (010 41) 1-2114656
Telex: 813008

Schweizerische
Bankgesellschaft
(Union Bank of Switzerland)
45 Bahnhofstrasse
8021 Zurich
Tel: (010 41) 1-2341111

Schweizerische Bankverein
(Swiss Bank Corporation)
Paradeplatz 6
8021 Zurich
Tel: (010 41) 1-2231111
Telex: 813471

Schweizerische Depositen
und Kreditbank
Lowenstrasse 49
8021 Zurich
Tel: (010) 411-2116790
Telex: 812364

Schweizerische Kreditanstalt
(Credit Suisse)
Paradeplatz 8
8021 Zurich
Tel: (010 41) 1-2151111
Telex: 812412 or 813512

Schweizerische Volksbank
(Swiss Volksbank)
Bahnhofstrasse 53
8021 Zurich
Tel: (010 41) 1-2281111
Telex: 812575

Zurcher Kantonalbank
Bahnhofstrasse 9
8022 Zurich
Tel: (010 41) 1-2201111
Telex: 812281

**Foreign Exchange and
Money Brokers**
Astley & Pearce SA
Talacker 41
8001 Zurich
Tel: (010 41) 1-2211770
Telex: 812051

Cofep SA
Via S Balestra 27
6900 Lugano
Tel: (010 41) 91-228901
Telex: 73331

Cosmorex SA Geneve
65 rue du Rhone
1211 Geneva 3
Tel: (010 41) 22-357651
Telex: 23811

Cosmorex Zurich AG
Postfach
8021 Zurich
Tel: (010 41) 1-2110950
Telex: 813391

Courtiner SA
9 rue de la Croiz-d'Or
1211 Geneve 3
Tel: (010 41) 22-286222
Telex: 423855

Dagues-Bie & Cie SA
15 rue du Jeu-de-l'Arc
1207 Geneve
Tel: (010 41) 22-354770
Telex: 27161

Finex AG
Dufourstrasse 101
8008 Zurich
Tel: (010 41) 1-2511850
Telex: 57115

Interacor AG
Am Schanzergraben 23
8039 Zurich
Tel: (010 41) 1-2023411
Telex: 815599

Interchange SA
Rue de la Gare
1110 Morges
Tel: (010 41) 21-723041
Telex: 458270

Rp Martin Bierbaum AG
Munstergasse 21
8001 Zurich
Tel: (010 41) 1-474060
Telex: 815133

Sihaco, Siemers, Hass & Co
Forchstr 239
8032 Zurich
Tel: (010 41) 1-551771
Telex: 55310

Tullett & Tokyo Forex Ltd
Tiechestrasse 39
8037 Zurich
Tel: (010 41) 1-3636343
Telex: 815275

Velcor SA
45-47 rue de Lausanne
1211 Geneve 1
Tel: (010 41) 22-311250
Telex: 289213

Sources of General Background Information, Industry Sector Information and Trade Contacts

UK Addresses
Embassy of Switzerland
16-18 Montagu Place
London W1H 2BQ
Tel: 01-723 0701

No Swiss Chamber of Commerce exists in the UK. Trade and commercial enquiries should be made to the embassy.

Addresses in Switzerland
SHIV Schweizerischer
Handels-und
Industrie-Verein
USCI Union Suisse du
Commerce et de l'Industrie
Borsenstr 26
8001 Zurich
Tel: (010 41) 1-2212707

Swiss Cantonal Chambers of Commerce:
Aargauische Industrie und
Handelskammer
Entfelderstrasse 11
5001 Aarau
Tel: (010 41) 64-255577

Basler Handelskammer
St Albansgraben 8
4001 Basle
Tel: (010 41) 61-231888

Berner Handelskammer
Gutenbergstrasse 1
3001 Berne
Tel: (010 41) 31-261711

Berner Handelskammer Buro
Biel
Hugistrasse 2
2501 Biel
Tel: (010 41) 32-224681

Bundner Handels und
Industrieverein
Poststrasse 43
7002 Chur
Tel: (010 41) 81-224745

Camera di Commercio
dell'Industria e
dell'Artigianato
Corso Elvezia 16
6901 Lugano
Tel: (010 41) 91-235031

Chambre de Commerce et
d'Industrie du Jura
Chemin de la Perche 2
2900 Porrentruy
Tel: (010 41) 66-662465

Chambre de Commerce et
d'Industries de Geneve
Boulevard du Theatre 4
1211 Geneve
Tel: (010 41) 22-215333

Chambre Fribourgeoise du
Commerce
Rue de la Banque 1
1700 Fribourg
Tel: (010 41) 37-225655

Chambre Neuchateloise du
Commerce et de l'Industrie
Rue de la Serre 4
2000 Neuchatel
Tel: (010 41) 38-257541

Chambre Valaisanne de
Commerce
Rue de la Blancherie 2
1950 Sion
Tel: (010 41) 27-227575

Chambre Vaud du Commerce
et de l'Industrie
Avenue d'Ouchy 47
1000 Lausanne 13
Tel: (010 41) 21-277291
Telex: 25405

Glarner Handelskammer
Spielhof 14a
8750 Glarus
Tel: (010 41) 58-611173
Telex: 875573

Handelskammer Winterthur
Postfach 78
8402 Winterthur
Tel: (010 41) 52-221717

Kaufmannisches Directorium
Handelskammer St Gallen
Gallusstrasse 16
9001 St Gallen
Tel: (010 41) 71-231515

Solothurnische
Handelskammer
Westbahnhofstrasse 6
4500 Solothurn
Tel: (010 41) 65-222324

Thurgauische
Handelskammer
Bahnofstrasse 10
8570 Weinfelden
Tel: (010 41) 72-221919

Zentralschw Handelskammer
Kapellplatz 2
6002 Luzern
Tel: (010 41) 41-516865

Zurcher Handelskammer
Bleicherweg 5
8001 Zurich
Tel: (010 41) 1-2210742

British-Swiss Chamber of
Commerce in Switzerland
(The)
Freiestr 155
8032 Zurich
Tel: (010 41) 1-553131
Telex: 916219

Sources of Investment and Trade Advice, Assistance and Information

Association Suisse de Defense
des Investisseurs (ASDI)
Postfach 3413
4002 Basle
Tel: (010 41) 61-496736

Association Suisse des
Agents-representants
Rosenweg 6
8962 Bergdietikon
Tel: (010 41) 1-7402855
Telex: 825217

Delegation du Commerce
Centralbahnstr 9
4010 Basle
Tel: (010 41) 61-223385

Department Federal des
Affaires Etrangeres (DFAE)
Bundeshaus-West
3003 Berne
Tel: (010 41) 31-612111
Secretariat General:
Eigerstr 73
3003 Berne
Tel: (010 41) 31-612111

Federal Office for Labour and
Industry
Department of Industry
Mattenhofstrasse 5
3003 Berne
Tel: (010 41) 31-612871

Contact the above office for
federal information and
contact names in Cantonal
Economic Development
Offices.

Federation Suisse des
Importateurs et du Commerce
de Gros (VSIG)
Centralbahnstrasse 9
4010 Basle
Tel: (010 41) 61-223385

Office Suisse d'Expansion
Commerciale (OSEC)
Stampfenbachstr 85
8035 Zurich
Tel: (010 41) 1-3632250
Telex: 817272

Societe pour le Developpment
de l'Economie Suisse
Mainaustr 30
8034 Zurich
Tel: (010 41) 1-2519256
and
Rue de Candolle 20
1211 Geneve 3
Tel: (010 41) 22-203811
and
Spitalgasse 4
3001 Berne
Tel: (010 41) 31-226296
and
Corso Elvezia 16
6900 Lugano
Tel: (010 41) 91-228212

Societe Suisse des Employes
de Commerce (SSEC)
Hans Huber-Str 4
8027 Zurich 2
Tel: (010 41) 1-2024710

Swiss Exporting Consultants
(SWEYCO)
c/o OSEC, BP 1128
Avant-Poste 4
1001 Lausanne
Tel: (010 41) 21-203231
Telex: 455425

Professional Associations

Accountancy
Swiss Institute of Auditing
Firms and Certified
Accountants
Linmatquai 120
8001 Zurich

Banking
Association of Foreign Banks
in Switzerland
Kurhausstrasse 28
8032 Zurich

Association Suisse des
Banquiers
(Swiss Bankers Association)
Aeschenplatz 7
Postfach 4182
4002 Basle
Tel: (010 41) 61-235888

Associations Suisse des
Banques de Credit et
Etablissements de
Financment
Stauffach erstr 35
8004 Zurich
Tel: (010 41) 1-2427587

Consultancy
Association Suisse des
Conseils en Organisation et
Gestion (ASCO)
Forchstrasse 95
8032 Zurich
Tel: (010 41) 1-536420

Financial Analysts
Associations Suisse des
Analystes Financiers
Rue Adrien-Lachenal 26
Case Postale 968
1211 Geneve 3

Insurance
Association Suisse
d'Assurances
Schweizerischer
Versicherungsverband
(Swiss Insurance Association)
Richard Wagner-Strasse 6
8002 Zurich
Tel: (010 41) 1-2024826

Marketing
Groupement Romand du
Marketing (GREM)
2 Avenue Agassiz
1001 Lausanne
Tel: (010 41) 21-202811
Telex: 25730

Konferenz Schweizerischer
Markt und
Meinungsforschungs
Institute/
Conference des Instituts
Suisses d'Etude de Marche et
d'Opinion
Analyses Economiques et
Sociales SA
Route de Vallaire 149
1024 Ecublens/Lausanne
Tel: (010 41) 21-354142
Telex: 25847

Schweizerische Gesellschaft
fur Marketing
Bleicherweg 21
Postfach 1057
8022 Zurich
Tel: (010 41) 1-2023425

Verband Schweizerischer
Marktforscher/
Association Suisse des
Specialistes en Etude de
Marche
c/o IHA Institut fur
Marktanalysen AG
Obermattweg 9
6052 Hergiswil/NW
Tel: (010 41) 41-950111
Telex: 866291

Trade Associations

Association Suisse des
Droguistes (Chemicals and
Drugs)
Langfeldweg 119
2501 Biel
Tel: (010 41) 32-425051

Association Suisse pour
l'Energie Atomique (ASPEA)
(Energy)
Monbijoustr 5
3001 Berne
Tel: (010 41) 31-225882
Telex: 912110

Association Suisse de
l'Industrie de l'Habillement
(ASIH) (Clothing)
Utoquai 37
8008 Zurich
Tel: (010 41) 1-2525334
Telex: 58166

Association Suisse des
Industriels de l'Aluminium
(Aluminium)
Dufourstr 31
8024 Zurich
Tel: (010 41) 1-2512952

Association Suisse de
l'Organisation de Bureaux
(Office Equipment)
Rudishaldenstr 28
8800 Thalwil
Tel: (010 41) 1-720/6206783

Association Suisse des
Societes de Services
Informatiques (Computing)
Badensrstr 551
Tel: (010 41) 1-4924294
Telex: 822537

Chambre Textile Suisse
(Textiles)
Beethovenstr 20
8022 Zurich
Tel: (010 41) 1-2015755
Telex: 816601

Groupe de l'Industrie Suisse
de la Construction
(Construction)
Talacker 50
Postfach 4406
8021 Zurich
Tel: (010 41) 1-2117750

Informationsstelle fur
Electricitatsanwendung
Baihnhogplatz 9
8023 Zurich
Tel: (010 41) 1-2110355
Telex: 814262

Societe Suisse des Industries
Chimiques (Chemicals and
Drugs)
Nordstrasse 15
8035 Zurich
Tel: (010 41) 1-3631030
Telex: 817028

Company Financial and Product Information

Directories

Banques Etrangeres en Suisse
Published by Publications
Bancaires, Petit-Lancy
Listing of details for foreign
banks in Switzerland. Also
publish Establissements
Bancaires en Suisse. Both
publications are updated
annually

Kompass-Schweiz/Suisse
Liechtenstein
Last edition 1987/88
Published by Kompass
Schweiz Verlag AG, Zurich
Swiss companies listed with
basic details grouped under
product and service industry
classifications. Also listing of
trade marks, trade names and
agencies

Swiss Financial Year Book
Seventh edition 1986/87
Edited by Elvetica Edizioni
SA, Chiasso
Contains extensive
information on 50 major
companies (quoted on Stock
Exchange), 494 banks, 112
finance companies, 111
insurance companies and 7
Swiss Stock Exchanges

Economic and Market Statistical Data

Market Research Organisations

AES Analyses Economiques
et Sociales SA
Route de Vallaire 149
1024 Ecublens
Lausanne
Tel: (010 41) 21-354142
Telex: 25847 AESSA CH
Cable: AESSA
Int affiliation: INRA (Europe),
IMD
Member of Esomar, Silk,
VSMF

D & S Institut fur Markt-und
Kommumikationforschung
AG
Hegibachstrasse 68
8032 Zurich
Tel: (010 41) 1-553211
Fax: (010 41) 1-537315
Member of Esomar, Silk,
VSMF

DemoSCOPE
Marktforschungsinstitut AG
Klusenstrasse 18
6043 Adligenswil
Tel: (010 41) 41-301188
Telex: 862807
Cable: SCOP
Fax: (010 41) 41-316294
Subsidiaries: Scope,
Psychologische
Marktforschung und test
labor AG, Zurich, DataScope,
Datenverarbeitung in
Markt-und Sozialforschung
AG
Int affiliation: IRIS
Member of Esomar, Silk,
VSMF

GIRA SA
178 Route de Collex
1239 Collex
Geneva
Tel: (010 41) 22-741010
Telex: 27556
Subsidiaries: Gira France,
Gira UK, Gira Spain
Member of Esomar, EVAF

IHA Institut for
Marktanalysen AG
Obermattweg 9
6052 Hergiswil
Tel: (010 41) 41-950111
Telex: 866291
Fax: (010 41) 41-953714
Parent company: ATAG
Allgemeine Treuhand AG
Subsidiaries: GFM, IFG,
Interfield AG, Institut Irniger
AG, I
G Handelsforschung
Int affiliation: Europanel
Member of Silk

Institute for Market Research
(IMR AG)
Wiesenstrasse 7
8008 Zurich
Tel: (010 41) 1-479260
Telex: 57143 IMR CH
Parent company: Fides Trust
Company
Member of Esomar, Silk,
VSMF

Isopublic Swiss Institute for
Public Opinion
Witikonerstrasse 297
8053 Zurich
Tel: (010 41) 537272
Telex: 56153 ISOPU CH
Int affiliation: Gallup
International
Member of Esomar, Silk,
VSMF

Link Intermarket Data Ltd
Spannortstr 7/9
6003 Lucerne
Tel: (010 41) 41-447373
Telex: 862844
Fax: (010) 41 41-449816
Parent company: Link
Marketing Services
Member of Esomar, MRS,
Silk, VSMF

Marketing Group SA (The)
11 Rue des Moraines
1227 Carouge
Geneva
Tel: (010 41) 22-427930
Telex: 423329
Cable: Merchgroup Gen
Parent company: The
Marketing Group Inc
Subsidiaries: The Marketing
Group France SARL, TMG
Italia SRL, TMG Iberica SA

MIS Trend & MIS Crealyse
3 Pont Bessieres
1005 Lausanne
Tel: (010 41) 21-209503
Fax: (010 41) 21-228846
Member of ASSEM, Esomar,
Silk

AC Nielsen SA
PO Box 3967
6002 Lucerne
Tel: (010 41) 41-303333
Telex: 78240
Parent company: AC Nielsen
Company USA
Member of Esomar, Silk

Prognos AG
Steinengraben 42
4011 Basle
Tel: (010 41) 61-223700
Telex: 963323 PROG CH
Fax: (010 41) 61-224069
Parent company: Coopers &
Lybrand

P Robert et Associes SA
International Marketing
Research
Avenue de Lonay 19
1110 Morges
Tel: (010 41) 21-710654
Telex: 458203
Cable: PRA CH
Parent company: Data-A SA
Member of Esomar, Grem,
Silk, VSMF, Wapor

Organisations Providing Economic and Statistical Data

AGEFI
Societe de l'Agence
Economique et Financiere
Rue de Geneve 7
Case Postale 2113
1002 Lausanne
Tel: (010 41) 21-200316
Telex: 450211

Agence Telegraphique Suisse
SA
(Economic publishers)
Langgasstr 7
3001 Berne

Associated Press (The)
(Economic publishers)
Bahnhofplatz 10b
3001 Berne

Bundesmat fur Statistik
(Office Federal de la
Statistique/Federal Office for
Statistics)
Hallwylstr 15
3003 Berne
Tel: (010 41) 31-618660

Eidgenossisches
Volkswistschaftsdepartment
(Federal Department for
Public Economy)
Bundeshaus Ost
3003 Berne
Tel: (010 41) 31-612111

Statisches Amt des Kantons
Zurich
Hirschengraben 56
8090 Zurich
Tel: (010 41) 1-474900

Zurich Stock Exchange
Bleicherweg 5
8021 Zurich
Produces a statistical monthly
report plus other publications
including:
The Zurich Stock Exchange
available in English
Quotations Sheet
Legal Handbook of the Zurich
Stock Exchange

Publications

Directories

Der Schweizerische
Einkaufsfuhrer (Swiss Guide
of Buyers)
21st edition 1987
Published by CJ Bucher Ltd,
Lucerne
UK Agent Kempse Publishing
Group, London
Alphabetical listing of Swiss
suppliers and products Plus a
listing of banks,
transportation companies,
international forwarding
agencies and travel offices

Schweizer Jahrbuch des
Offentlichen Lebens
Annuaire Suisse de la Vie
Publique 1987/88
Published by Verlag Schwabe
& Co AG, Basle
An extremely comprehensive
guide to government,
economic and trade
organisations in Switzerland.
Addresses, telephone and
telex numbers provided

Schweizer PR &
Medien-Verzeichnis
(Swiss PR and Media
Directory)
Published by Edition Renteria
SA, Zurich
15th edition 1988
Useful guide to public
relations agencies and their
publishers. Names of editors,
directors etc are provided

Schweizerisches
Ragionenbuch
Annuaire Suisse du Registre
du Commerce
Official Register of Swiss
Chambers of Commerce
Published by Orell Fussli
Informationswerke, Zurich

Swiss Export Directory
Products and Services of
Switzerland
Produced by the Swiss Office
for the the Development of
Trade (SODT),
Zurich
Available direct from the
above or from your local
Swiss Embassy or Chamber of
Commerce.
Major source directory for
information on 8500 Swiss
companies, 10 000 products
and services in Switzerland
and 7000 trade marks.
Companies listed by major
industrial activity. Also useful
addresses provided on
foreign embassies and
chambers of commerce in
Switzerland

Swiss and Liechtenstein
Who's Who (The)
Published by Verlag
Worthsee

Swiss Stock Guide
Published by The Union Bank
of Switzerland
Philips and Drew Global
Research Group, Zurich

Major Newspapers

Allgemeines Industrie-und
Wirtschaftsblatt
Daily
An English version of the
above newspaper, Swiss
Business will be available
(published in conjunction
with the Swiss Office for the
Development of Trade)

Le Matin
Daily

Neue Zurcher Zeitung (NZZ)
Daily

Schweizerische
Handelszeitung
Daily. Major financial
newspaper

La Suisse
Daily

24 Heures
Daily
One of the major business
papers

Journals and Periodicals

Auslandmarkte
Published by Schweiz
Zentrale fur
Handelsforderung, Lausanne
Monthly

Aussenwirtschafts
The Swiss Review of
International Economic
Relations
Published by the Schweiz
Institut fur
Aussenwirtschafts, St Gallen
Four times per annum

Die Wirtschaftspraxis
VAV-Information
Organ des Schweizerischen
Verbandes akademischer
Volks-und
Betriebswirtschafter VAV,
Zurich
Four times per annum

Finanz und Wirtschaft
Publisher's address:
Weberstr 8-10
Postfach 8021 Zurich
Twice a week

Schweizerische
Handels-Zeitung
Publisher's address:
Bleicherweg 20
Postfach 8039 Zurich
Financial newspaper
Weekly

Swiss Export
Publisher's address:
Hintere Hauptgasse 9
4800 Zofingen
Four times per annum

Swiss Quality Products
Guide to Swiss economy and
business opportunities
Publisher's address:
13 bis Chemin Chantemerle
1010 Lausanne

Swiss Review of World
Affairs
Published by Neue Zurcher
Zeitung (NZZ), Zurich
Monthly

Switzerland Your Partner
Published by The Office
Swisse d'Expansion
Commerciale (OSEC),
Lausanne

Taiwan

Sources of Economic, Stock Market Information and Investment Research Services

Banks

Central Bank
Central Bank of China
2 Roosevelt Road
Section 1
Taipei 107
Tel: (010 886) 2-3936161

Taiwanese Banks in London
First Commercial Bank
2 South Place
London EC2M 2RB
Tel: 01-628 2612
Telex: 897237

Major Banks in Taiwan
Bank of Communications Co
Ltd
91 Heng Yang Road
Taipie 10003
Tel: (010 886) 2-3613000
Telex: 11341 CHAOTUNG

Bank of Taiwan
120 Chungking South Road
Section 1
Taipei 10036
Tel: (010 886) 2-314 7377/7388
Telex: 11201; 11202; 11637;
21084; 27500; 27501

Chang Hwa Commercial
Bank Ltd
38 Section 2
Tsuyu Road
Taichung
Tel: (010 886) 2-222001/230001
Telegram: Chbank

China Development
Corporation
7th-10th Floor
Cathay Gemini Building
581 Tunhwa South Road
Taipei
Tel: (010 886) 2-7002780
Telex: 23147 CHIDELCO

City Bank of Taipei (The)
50 Section 2
Chungshan N Road
Taipei
Tel: (010 886) 2-5425656
Telex: 11722

Cooperative Bank of Taiwan
(The)
PO Box 33
77 Kuan Chien Road
Taipei 100
Tel: (010 886) 2-3118811
Telex: 23749 COOPBANK

First Commercial Bank
30 Chungking South Road
Section 1
Taipei
Tel: (010 886)
2-3111111/3613611
Telex: 11310; 11729; 11740;
11741

Hua Nan Commercial Bank
Ltd
33 Kaifeng Street
Section 1
Taipei
Tel: (010 886)
2-3619666/3713111
Telex: 11307; 11592

International Commercial
Bank of China
100 Chilin Road
Taipei 104 24
Tel: (010 886) 2-5633156
Telex: 11300 INCOBK

Land Bank of Taiwan
46 Kuan Chien Road
Taipei
Tel: (010 886) 2-3613020
Cable: 0960

Medium Business Bank of
Taiwan (The)
PO Box 109
72/74 Chung King South Road
Section 1
Taipei
Tel: (010 886)
2-3719241/3719251
Telex: 14484 MBBTBANK;
21124 MBBTBANK

Stockbrokers
Taiwan Stock Exchange
Corporation
9th Floor
City Building
85 Yen-Ping South Road
Taipei
Tel: (010 886) 2-3315434

Members (as at February 1988)
Asia Securities Co Ltd
Tel: (010 886) 2-3116391-8
Tainan Branch
Tel: (010 886) 6-2271191

Bank of Communications
Savings Department
Tel: (010 886) 2-7024775
Taichung Branch
Tel: (010 886) 4-296196-9

Bank of Taiwan Trust
Department
Tel: (010 886) 2-3710893

Central Trust of China
Banking Trust Department
Tel: (010 886) 2-33117154
Taichung Branch
Tel: (010 886) 4-238374-6
Kaohsiung Branch
Tel: (010 886) 7-2829223-5

Chang Hwa Bank Saving
Department
Tel: (010 886) 2-3315957
Taichung Branch
Tel: (010 886) 255161-5

City Bank of Taipei Trust
Department
Tel: (010 886) 2-5819948

Cooperative Bank of Taiwan
Savings Department
Tel: (010 886) 2-3118001-11
Tainan Branch
Tel: (010 886) 6-260148-50
Kaohsiung Branch
Tel: (010 886) 7-5514339
Taichung Branch
Tel: (010 886) 4-255141-4

Far East Securities Co Ltd
Tel: (010 886) 2-5511031-5
Tainan Branch
Tel: (010 886) 6-2213655

First Bank Savings
Department
Tel: (010 886) 2-3714081-3
Kaohsiung Branch
Tel: (010 886) 7-5215691-5
Taichung Branch
Tel: (010 886) 4-287111-6

First Securities Co Ltd
Tel: (010 886) 3314341

Hong Cheng Securities Ltd
Tel: (010 886) 3613485

Hwa Nan Bank Savings
Department
Tel: (010 886) 2-3718463
Kaohsiung Branch
Tel: (010 886) 7-5216021-5

Jih-Sun Securities Co Ltd
Tel: (010 886) 5512722

Jen Hsin Securities Co Ltd
Tel: (010 886) 3141141-9

Kai Ta Securities Co Ltd
Tel: (010 886) 3111612
Taichung Branch
Tel: (010 886) 4-243191-5

Land Bank of Taiwan Savings
Department
Tel: (010 886) 2-3821194
Taichung Branch
Tel: (010 886) 4-266845
Kaohsiung Branch
Tel: (010 886) 7-5515231-7
Hsin-chu Branch
Tel: (010 886) 243113-5
Chiayi Branch
Tel: (010 886) 2241150-7
Tainan Branch
Tel: (010 886) 6-2200558
Hualien Branch
Tel: (010 886) 38-351171-6

Medium Business Bank of
Taiwan Trust Department
(The)
Tel: (010 886) 2-3821675
Ping-tung Branch
Tel: (010 886) 8-347317-9
Chiayi Branch
Tel: (010 886) 2278043-5
Kaohsiung Branch
Tel: (010 886) 7-2610610-7
Taichung Branch
Tel: (010 886) 4-272981-2

Sheng Hoh Securities Co Ltd
Tel: (010 886) 3315556-9
Taichung Branch
Tel: (010 886) 4-219561-5

Shin Kuang Securities Co Ltd
Tel: (010 886) 3313121-5

Tah Hsin Securities Co Ltd
Tel: (010 886) 3619010

Ting Kong Securities Co Ltd
Tel: (010 886) 3113030

Trust Department ICBC
Tel: (010 886) 2-3311067

United World Chinese
Commercial Bank Trust
Department
Tel: (010 886) 2-3310025

Well-Phone Securities Co Ltd
Tel: (010 886) 5816111
Kaohsiung Branch
Tel: (010 886) 7-5612231-7

Yuen Ta Securities Co Ltd
Tel: (010 886) 7511212

Yung Li Securities Co Ltd
Tel: (010 886) 3111540-9

Securities Traders
Asia Trust and Investment Co
Ltd
Tel: (010 886) 2-5315678

Cathay Investment & Trust
Co Ltd
Tel: (010 886) 2-3114881

China Investment and Trust
Co
Tel: (010 886) 2-7165111

China Stock and Investment
Co
Tel: (010 886) 2-5371795-8

China United Trust &
Investment Corp
Tel: (010 886) 2-5510168

Oriental Investment Corp
Tel: (010 886) 2-3115015

Overseas Trust Corp (The)
Tel: (010 886) 2-7139911

Taiwan Development & Trust
Co
Tel: (010 886) 2-3944333

Taiwan First Investment and
Trust Co
Tel: (010 886) 2-7525353

Taiwan Securities Investment
Co
Tel: (010 886) 2-5515161

***Sources of General
Background Information,
Industry Sector
Information and Trade
Contacts***

UK Addresses
Anglo-Taiwan Trade
Committee
4th Floor
Minster House
272-274 Vauxhall Bridge Road
London SW1V 1BB
Tel: 01-828 9167
Telex: 896941 ATTIC G

The UK does not have diplomatic relations with Taiwan.

Addresses in Taiwan
Chia-I District Industrial Association
6th Floor
278 Min Chuan Road
Chai-I
Tel: (010 886) 5-2234321

General Chamber of Commerce of the Republic of China (The)
Rose Mansion
7th Floor
162 Hsin Yi Road
Section 3
Taipei
Tel: (010 886) 2-7080785
Telex: 11396 JUNGTAI

Hsinchu Hsien Chamber of Commerce
112 Chung Cheng Road
Hsinchu
Tel: (010 886) 35-222230

Hsin-Chu Industrial Society
412 Chung Hwa Road
Chu Pei Hsiang
Shin Chu Hsien
Tel: (010 886) 35-557334

Keelung Industrial Association
6th Floor
39 Shou 2nd Road
Keelung
Tel: (010 886) 32-257342

Kinmen Chamber of Commerce
35 Lane 4
Zu-Pu East Road
Chin-Chen Chen
Kinmen Hsien
Tel: (010 886) 2337 Chin-Chen

Koahsiung Chamber of Commerce
8 Chien Kuang Road
Kaohsiung
Tel: (010 886) 7-5318121

Nan Tou Hsihn Chambers of Trade
24 Min-Chuan Street
Nan Tou City
Nan Tou Hsien
Tel: (010 886)
49-222074/225151

Taichung Chamber of Commerce
3rd Floor
38 Shyh Fu Road
Taichung
Tel: (010 886) 4-2223378

Taipei Chamber of Commerce
4th Floor
78 Hwaining Street
Taipei
Tel: (010 886) 2-3811783

Taiwan Chamber of Commerce
7th Floor
13 Yung Yuan Road
Taipei
Tel: (010 886)
2-3113144/3114152
Cable: TCOC TAIPEI

Taoyuen Chamber of Commerce
5 Ren Ay Road
Taoyuen
Tel: (010 886) 33-322361

Sources of Investment and Trade Advice, Assistance and Information

In the UK the Anglo-Taiwan Trade Committee assists British companies in selling their goods and services in Taiwan. Details of export opportunities supplied by the ATTC are published regularly via the Export Intelligence Service of the British Overseas Trade Board. The ATTC maintains offices in London and Taipei. There is a worldwide network of China External Trade Development Councils, and Far East Trade Service Inc offices.

Taipei Office:
Anglo-Taiwan Trade Committee
PO Box 59632
11th Floor
China Building
36 Nanking East Road
Section 2
Taipei 10408
Tel: (010 886) 2-5214116/8
Telex: 11106 ATTIC

Government Organisations
Board of Foreign Trade (MOEA)
Head Office:
1 Hukou Street
Taipei
Tel: (010 886) 2-3510271

Council for Cultural Planning and Development
4th Floor
102 Ai-Kuo E Road
Taipei
Tel: (010 886) 2-3518030

Council for Economic Planning and Development
9th Floor
Nanking E Road
Section 2
Taipei
Tel: (010 886) 2-5513522

Government Information Office
3 Chunghsiao E Road
Section 1
Taipei
Tel: (010 886) 2-3419211

Industrial Development Bureau
109 Hankow Street
Section 1
Taipei
Tel: (010 886) 2-3317531

Industrial Development and Investment Center (IDIC)
10th Floor
Yumin Building
7 Roosevelt Road
Section 1
Taipei
Tel: (010 886) 2-3947213

International Cooperation
Department
5th Floor
277 Roosevelt Road
Section 3
Taipei
Tel: (010 886) 2-3918198

Ministry of Economic Affairs
15 Foochow Street
Taipei
Tel: (010 886) 2-3517271

Ministry of Finance
2 Aikuo W Road
Taipei
Tel: (010 886) 2-3511611

Ministry of Foreign Affairs
2 Chiehshou Road
Taipei
Tel: (010 886) 2-3119292

Overseas Chinese Affairs
Commission
30 Park Road
Taipei
Tel: (010 886) 2-3810039

Far East Trade Service Inc
offices are in Japan,
Bangladesh, India, Sri Lanka,
Australia, Kuwait, Saudi
Arabia, UAE, Austria, France,
Netherlands, Sweden,
Federal Republic of Germany,
Spain, Africa and USA.

UK Office:
Taiwan Products Promotion
Co Ltd
432-436 Grand Buildings
Trafalgar Buildings
Trafalgar Square
London WC2N 5HD

USA Office:
Far East Trade Service Inc
The Merchandise Mart
Suite 272
Chicago
Ill 60654
Tel: (010 1) 312-3219338
Telex: 253726 FAREAST TR
CGO

CETDC Inc
41 Madison Avenue
New York
NY 10010
Tel: (010 1) 212-5327055
Telex: 426299 CETDC NY

Professional Associations

Accountancy
National Federation of
Certified Accountants
Associations of the Republic
of China
10th Floor
142 Chung-Hsiao East Road
Section 4
Taipei
Taiwan

Banking
Bankers Association of the
Republic of China
8th Floor
46 Kuanchien Road
Taipei
Tel: (010 886) 2-3616019
Cable: BAROC TAIPEI

Trade Associations

General Industry
Chinese National Federation
of Industry
17th Floor
30 Chungking S Road
Section 1
Taipei
Tel: (010 886) 2-3149405/9

Chinese National Association
of General Contractors
10th Floor
Hsin-Foo Building
21 Chang-An E Road
Section 1
Taipei
Tel: (010 886) 2-5818014

Importers and Exporters
Association of Taipei
3rd Floor
65 Nanking East Road
Section 3
Taipei
Tel: (010 886) 2-5813521

Taipei Computers Association
3rd Floor
201 Fu Hsing N Road
Taipei
Tel: (010 86) 2-7132661

Taipei Industrial Association
2nd-3rd Floor
117-1 Chengsun Road
Section 1
Pan Chiao City
Taipei Hsien
Tel: (010 886) 2-9625504

Taipei Office Appliances
Association
9th Floor
386 Yun Hua S Road
Taipei
Tel: (010 886) 2-7719287

Taiwan Association of
Machinery Industry
3rd Floor
110 Hwai Ning Street
Taipei
Tel: (010 886) 2-3813722

Taiwan Electrical Appliance
Manufacturers Association
7th Floor
315-317 Sung Chiang Road
Taipei
Tel: (010 886) 2-5410122

Taiwan Electrical Engineering
Association
11th Floor
76 Sung Chiang Road
Taipei
Tel: (010 886) 2-5719238

Taiwan Food Industrial
Association
6th Floor
10 Chungking S Road
Section 1
Taipei
Tel: (010 886) 2-3719848

Taiwan Importers and
Exporters Association
14th Floor
2 Fu Shing N Road
Taipei
Tel: (010 886) 2-7731155

Taiwan Paper Industry
Association
5th Floor
Taize Building
20 Pa Teh Road
Section 3
Taipei
Tel: (010 886) 2-7526352

Taiwan Plastics Industry
Association (The)
7th Floor
162 Chang An E Road
Section 2
Taipei
Tel: (010 886) 2-7719111

Company Financial and Product Information

Directories
Kompass Taiwan
Published by Kompass
Taiwan Ltd, Taipei
Directory listing companies
and products

Taiwan Business Directory
Published by China Credit
Information Service Ltd,
Taipei
Provides details of
manufacturing and service
companies, industrial
associations, government
organisations and foreign
trade offices in Taiwan

Taiwan Buyers Guide 1986/87
Published by China
Productivity Center, Taipei
Directory of manufacturers,
exporters and importers and
service organisations in
Taiwan

Top 500 Taiwan Companies
Published by China Credit
Information Service Ltd,
Taipei
Ranking of top 500 and
second 500 industrial
companies in Taiwan. Also
ranks service companies
(approximately 1500 listings
in total)

Economic and Market Statistical Data

Market Research Organisations
Columbia Associates Ltd
285 Nanking E Road
Section 3
4th Floor
Taipei
Tel: (010 886) 2-7132731
Telex: 10451 CLUMBA

Gaynor Associates
International
10th Floor
311 Nanking East Road
Section 3
Taipei 10566
Tel: (010 886) 2-7135201
Telex; 21317 GEICO
Parent company: Gaynor
Associates International HK

Professional Research
Organisation Ltd (PRO) Ltd
4F, 8-1, Lane 69
Sung Chiang Road
Taipei
Tel: (010 886) 2-5971192
Telex: 13162 CHVO

Frank Small and Associates
Ltd (Taiwan Branch)
125 Nanking East Road
Section 2
8/F-1
Taipei
Tel: (010 886) 2-5414128
Telex: 25141 FSATW
Parent company: Frank Small
& Associates (Aust) Pty

Survey Research Asia Pacific
Ltd (Taiwan Branch)
GPO Box 11955
Taipei 100
Tel: (010 886)
2-7816078/7729278
Telex: 20420 SURAP
Parent company: Survey
Research Asia Pacific Ltd

Organisations Providing Economic and Statistical Data
Stock market research in
Taiwan is limited. Local
research is provided by
brokers such as Asia Securites
Ltd and Yung Li Securities,
but brokers' monthly
publications are usually in
Chinese.

Taiwan Stock Exchange
Provides financial statistics in
the TSE annual report and
fact books.

Publications

Directories
Directory of Taiwan
Published by China News.
Annual

Importers of the Republic of
China
Exporters of the Republic of
China
Published by China External
Trade Development Council,
Taipei
Lists export commodities and
suppliers. Provides general
information and useful
addresses in Taiwan

Taiwan Who's Who in
Business
Publisher's address:
PO Box 46
167 Taipei
Annual

Taiwan Yellow Pages
Published by Taiwan Yellow
Pages Corp, Taipei

Major Newspapers

Taipei
Central Daily News
Chinese. Daily

China News
English. Daily

China Post
English. Daily

China Times
Chinese. Daily

Commercial Times
Daily

Economic Daily News
Chinese. Daily

Mandarin Daily News

Min Tsu Evening News

United Daily News

Journals and Periodicals
Free China Journal
Weekly

Free China Review
English. Monthly

Free China Weekly
English

Sinorama
English

Publisher's address for above
periodicals:
3-1 Chung Hsiao E Road
Section 1
Taipei

ECO
Publisher's address:
5-2 Alley 16
Lane 72
Pateh Road
Section 4
Taipei
News magazine in English.
Monthly

Taiwan Trade
Publisher's address:
11F1
50 Nanking E Road
Section 4
Taipei
Monthly

Trade Opportunities in
Taiwan
Publisher's address:
10F1 201 Tun Hwa N Road
Taipei

Trade Winds
Publisher's address:
132 Hsin Yi Road
Section 2
POB 7-179 Taipei
Business magazine in English

Thailand

Sources of Economic, Stock Market Information, and Investment Research Services

Banks

Central Bank
Bank of Thailand
PO Box 154
273 Bang Khunprom
Bangkok 10200
Tel: (010 66) 2-2823322
Telex: 72012/3

Thai Banks in London
Bangkok Bank
61 St Mary Avenue
London EC3A 8BY
Tel: 01-929 4422

Siam Commercial Bank
1 Founders Court
3/F Lothbury
London EC2R 7DB
Tel: 01-606 7596

Thai Farmers Bank
80 Cannon Street
London EC4N 6HH
Tel: 01-623 4975

Major Thai Banks
Bangkok Bank Ltd
333 Silom Road
Bangkok 10500
Tel: (010 66) 2-2343333
Telex: 82638; 82670; 82906;
72011

Bangkok Bank of Commerce
Ltd
171 Suriwong Road
Bangkok 10500
Tel: (010 66) 2-2342931;
2355040
Telex: TH 82525; TH 20644

Bangkok Metropolitan Bank
Ltd
Suan Mali
Bangkok
Tel: (010 66) 2-2230561
Telex: 82281; 81153; 87383

Bank of Ayudhya Ltd
PO Box 491
550 Ploenchit Road
Bangkok
Tel: (010 66) 2-2528171;
2528391
Telex: TH 72003; TH 82334

First Bangkok City Bank
20 Yukhon
2 Suan Mali
Bangkok 10100
Tel: (010 66) 2-2230500-19
Telex: 72000; 82018; 84120

Krung Thai Bank Ltd
35 Sukhumvit Road
Bangkok 10110
or
PO Box 44
Bangkok Mailing Centre
Bangkok 1000
Tel: (010 66) 2-2512111
Telex: 81179; 82079; 82331 KT
BANK TH

Siam City Bank Ltd
PO Box 488
Bangkok Mail Center
1101 New Petchburi Road
Bangkok 1000
Tel: (010 66) 2-2530200
(International Division)
Telex: 82477 NAKONBK TH

Siam Commercial Bank Ltd
PO Box 15
1060 Petchaburi Road
Bangkok 10400
Tel: (010 66) 2-2513114
Telex: 82876 SIAMCOM TH;
20492 SIAMBNK TH

Thai Farmers Bank Ltd
400 Phahon Yothin Avenue
Bangkok 10400
Tel: (010 66) 2-2701122;
2701133
Telex: 81159 FARMERS TH

Thai Military Bank Ltd
34 Phayathai Road
Bangkok 10400
Tel: (010 66) 2-2460020;
International Dept 2457760
Telex: 82324; 87697; 87698;
87900 MILITBK TH

Stockbrokers
The Securities Exchange of
Thailand (SET) in Bangkok is
the only Stock Exchange in
Thailand. There are
approximately 29 member
securities companies who are
all licensed by the Ministry of
Finance.

Stock Exchange
Securities Exchange of
Thailand
Sinthon Building 2nd Floor
132 Wireless Road
Bangkok 10500
Tel: (010 66) 2-2522710-12
Telex: 84063 CHASEFX TH
(SET)

Members (a selection of the larger brokers in 1987)
Adkinson Securities Ltd
Sinthon Building
132 Wireless Road
Bangkok 10500
Tel: (010 66) 2-2500665-9

Asia Credit Ltd
320 Rama 4 Road
Bangkok 10500
Tel: (010 66) 2-2351477-506

Ayudhya Investment and
Trust Co Ltd
7th Floor, Bank of Ayudhya
Building
550 Ploenchit Road
Bangkok 10500
Tel: (010 66) 2527251-5

Bangkok First Investment &
Trust Ltd
300 Silom Road
Bangkok 10500
Tel: (010 66) 2-2334160

Bara Investment and
Securities Co Ltd
968 Rama 4 Road
Bangkok 10500
Tel: (010 66) 2-2332534

Book Club Finance and
Securities Co Ltd (The)
8th Floor, Siam Commercial
Bank Building
1060 New Petchburi Road
Bangkok 10400
Tel: (010 66) 2-2519756-60

Cathay Trust Co Ltd
Cathay Trust Building
1016 Rama 4 Road
Bangkok 10500
Tel: (010 66) 2-2330421-9

Dynamic Eastern Finance Co
Ltd
459-471 Asoke-Din Daeng
Road
Phyathai
Bangkok 10310
Tel: (010 66) 2-2455010-4

General Finance & Securities
Co Ltd
62 Soi Langsuan
Ploenchit Road
Bangkok 10500
Tel: (010 66) 2-2513141-50

International Finance and
Consultants Co Ltd
44 Sathorn Nua Road
(opposite to YMCA)
Bangkok 10500
Tel: (010 66) 2-2350851

International Trust and
Finance Co Ltd
Kong Boonma Building
697-701 Silom Road
Bangkok 10500
Tel: (010 66) 2-2347002-6

Kiatnakin Finance &
Securities Co Ltd
78 Bush Lane
New Road
Bangkok 10500
Tel: (010 66) 2-2336460-9

Mithai Europartners Finance
and Securities Co Ltd
7th Floor, Silom Building
197/1 Silom Road
Bangkok 10500
Tel: (010 66) 2-2336554-5

Multi-Credit Corporation of
Thailand Ltd
6th Floor, Kian Gwan House
140 Wireless Road
Bangkok 10500
Tel: (010 66) 2-2529830-44

National Finance and
Securities Co Ltd
4th Floor (Room 422)
Siam Centre
965 Rama 1 Road
Bangkok 10500
Tel: (010 66) 2-2519460

Nava Finance and Securities
Co Ltd
34 Phyathai Road
Bangkok 10400
Tel: (010 66) 2-2826770-6

Phatra Thanakit Co Ltd
Phatra Thanakit Building
183 Sukhumvit Road, Soi
13-15
Bangkok 10110
Tel: (010 66) 2-2521191

Poonpipat Finance and
Securities Co Ltd
17th Floor, Sathorn Thani
Building
90 46-48 North Sathorn Road
Bangkok 10500
Tel: (010 66) 2-2340661

Siam Industrial Credit Co Ltd
(The)
Siam Industrial Credit
Building
130 Wireless Road
Bangkok 10500
Tel: (010 66) 2-2513173-4

Thai Finance Co Ltd
Sinthon Building
132 Wireless Road
Bangkok 10500
Tel: (010 66) 2-2500353-6

Thai Financial Syndicate Ltd
16 Plabplachai Road
Bangkok 10500
Tel: (010 66) 2-2230724

Thai Financial Trust Co Ltd
1426/13-17 Krung Kasem
Road
Bangkok 10100
Tel: (010 66) 2-2231321-40

Thai Overseas Trust Co Ltd
335 New Road
Bangkok 10100
Tel: (010 66) 2-2214191-5

Thai Securities Co Ltd
7th Floor, Boonmitr Building
138 Silom Road
Bangkok 10500
Tel: (010 66) 2-2339885-93

Union Asia Finance Ltd
Roamsermikij Building
136 Silom Road
Bangkok 10500
Tel: (010 66) 2-2354900-9

Sources of General Background Information, Industry Sector Information and Trade Contacts

UK Addresses
Offices of the Commercial
Counsellor
Royal Thai Embassy
9 Stafford Street
London W1H 4RT
Tel: 01-493 5749
Telex: 298706 THAITR G
Cable: THAITRADE
LONDON

Royal Thai Embassy
29-30 Queen's Gate
London SW7 5JB
Tel: 01-589 0173
01-589 2857 Visa Section
01-589 7266 Economic &
Financial Counsellor

Office of the Information
Attache
28 Prince's Gate
London SW7 1QF
Tel: 01-584 5421

Addresses in Thailand

Chambers of Commerce
Board of Trade of Thailand
150 Rajbopit Road
Bangkok 10200
Tel: (010 66) 2-22100555;
2211827; 2219350
Telex: 84309 BOT TH
Cable: TRADEBOARD
BANGKOK

Thai Chamber of Commerce
150 Rajbopit Road
Bangkok 10200
Tel: (010 66) 2-2216532-4;
2213351; 2211753; 2213863
Telex: 72093 TCC TH

American Chamber of
Commerce in Thailand
7th Floor, Kian Gwan Bldg
140 Wireless Road
Bangkok 10500
Tel: (010 66) 2-2511605;
2519266-7

Australian-Thai Chamber of
Commerce
17th Floor, Ocean Insurance
Bldg
163 Surawong Road
Bangkok 10500
Tel: (010 66) 2-2334476
Telex: 82505 PFIZER TH

British Chamber of
Commerce
6th Floor, Bangkok Insurance
Bldg
302 Silom Road
Bangkok 10500
Tel: (010 66) 2-2341140-69 Ext
335

Chambre de Commerce
Franco-Thai
9th Floor, Kian Gwan Bldg
140 Wireless Road
Bangkok 10500
Tel: (010 66) 2-2519385-6
Telex: 21005 FTCC TH

German-Thai Chamber of
Commerce
6th Floor, 699 Silom Road
Kongboonma Bldg
Bangkok 10500
Tel: (010 66) 2-2362396;
2364711
Telex: 82836 GTCC TH

India-Thai Chamber of
Commerce
13 Soi Attakarnprasit
Sathorn Tai Road
Bangkok 10120
Tel: (010 66) 2-2861506;
2861961

Japanese Chamber of
Commerce Bangkok
15th Floor, Amarin Tower
Bldg
500 Ploenchit Road
Bangkok 10500
Tel: (010 66) 2-2569170-3

Thai-Chinese Chamber of
Commerce
233 Sathorn Tai Road
Bangkok 10120
Tel: (010 66) 2-2112365-69

Thai-Italian Chamber of
Commerce
3rd Floor, Turismo Thai Bldg
511 Sri Ayudhya Road
Bangkok 10400
Tel: (010 66) 2-2471558
Telex: 84070 TURISMO TH
ATTN TICC
Fax: 66-2-2463993

Thai-Korean Chamber of
Commerce
8th Floor
Kongboonma Bldg
699 Silorn Road
Bangkok 10500
Tel: (010 66) 2-2331322-3
Telex: 82335 MOOGONG TH

UK
British Embassy
Wireless Road
Bangkok
Tel: (010 66) 2-2527161/9

USA
American Embassy
95 Wireless Road
Bangkok
Tel: (010 66) 2-2525040

Sources of Investment and Trade Advice, Assistance and Information

The government body
responsible for encouraging
overseas investment in
Thailand is the Board of
Investment (BOI).

Board of Trade of Thailand
150 Rajbophit Road
Bangkok
Tel: (010 66) 2-2219350
Telex: 84309

Department of Export
Promotion
22/77 Ratchadaphisek Road
Bang Klen
Bangkok 10900
Tel: (010 66) 2-5115066/77
Telex: 82354 DEPGREL TH

Department of Foreign Trade
Thanon Sanam Chai
Bangkok 10200
Tel: (010 66) 2-223141481-5
Telex: 72277 DEPFORT TH

Export Service Centre
Department of Commercial
Relations
Ministry of Commerce
22/77 Rachadaphissk Road
Bangkok 10900
Tel: (010 66) 2-5515066/77

Ministry of Commerce
Thanon Sanam Chai
Bangkok 10200
Tel: (010 66)
2-2220827/2239551
(010 66) 2-2210835/2210877
Telex: 82389 MINOMER TH

Office of the Board of
Investment
16th-17th Floor
Thai Farmers Bank Building
400 Phaholyothin Road
Bangkok 10400
Tel: (010 66)
2-2701400/2701410
Telex: 82542 TH; 81159 TH

Professional Associations

Accounting
Institute of Certified
Accountants and Auditors of
Thailand
c/o Office of the Auditor
General
of Thailand
Grand Palace
Bangkok 10200

Banking
Thai Bankers' Association
(The)
Sathorn Thani Building
90 North Sathorn Road
Bangkok

Insurance
General Insurance
Association
223 Soi Ruamruedee
Wireless Road
Bangkok 10500
Tel: (010 66) 2-2514120

Insurance Brokers
Association
64 Silom Road
Bangkok
Tel: (010 66) 2-2330901

Thai Life Assurance
Association
3611 Soi Sapan Ku
Rama 1V Road
Bangkok 10120
Tel: (010 66) 2-2860897

Management
Thailand Management
Association
308 Samaggi Insurance Bldg
Silom Road
Bangkok 5
Tel: (010 66) 2-2342624

Trade Associations

General
Association of Thai Industries
294/14 Samsen Road
Tambol Dusit
Bangkok
Tel: (010 66) 2-2800951

Animal Health Products
Association
69/26 Soi Athens Theater
Phayathai Road
Bangkok 10400
Tel: (010 66) 2-2528773

Artificial Flower, Foliage and
Plant Manufacturers
Association
15/1 Moo 15 Romklao Road
Minburi
Bangkok 10510
Tel: (010 66) 2-5170805-6

Association of Chemical
Traders
2nd Floor, Siam Science
Service Bldg
4862/4-5 Rama IV Road
Prakhanong
Bangkok 10110
Tel: (010 66) 2-3919695;
3919048

Association of Domestic Tour
Operators
133/20 Rajprarob Road
Makkasan
Bangkok 10400
Tel: (010 66) 2-2452616;
2452687; 2455658

Association of Finance
Companies
3rd Floor, Sinthorn Bldg
Wireless Road
Bangkok 10500
Tel: (010 66) 2-2500129

Association of International
Trading Companies
394/14 Samsen Road
Bangkok 10300
Tel: (010 66) 2-2800951

Association of Members of
the Securities Exchange
3rd Floor, Sinthorn Bldgs
Wireless Road
Bangkok 10500
Tel: (010 66) 2-2522380 Ext 337

Association of Thai Steel
Industry
36/5-7 Soi 39
Sukhumvit Road
Bangkok 10110
Tel: (010 66) 2-3923898

Auto Gas Service Association
38/59 Laibmanamchaophaya
Road
Yannawa
Bangkok 10120
Tel: (010 66) 2-2892294

Auto Parts Manufacturers
Association
79/1 Chueaploeng Road
Bangkok 10120
Tel: (010 66) 2-2860810

Automotive Industries
Association
394/14 Samsen Road
Bangkok 10300
Tel: (010 66) 2-2800951

Bangkok Chinese Importers &
Exporters Association
869-875 Songwad Road
Bangkok 10100
Tel: (010 66) 2-2211594

Bangkok Ice Transporters
Association
1042-4 New Petchburi Road
Bangkok 10310
Tel: (010 66) 2-2517623-4

Bangkok Medical Trader
Association
1714 Krung Kasem Road
Bangkok 10100
Tel: (010 66) 2-2224339

Bangkok Motion Picture
Exhibitors Association
352 3rd Floor, Siam Theater
Bldg
Rama 1 Road
Bangkok 10500
Tel: (010 66) 2-2511735;
2512861

Bangkok Rice Millers
Association
233 Sathorn Tai Road
Bangkok 10120
Tel: (010 66) 2-2119329;
2118721

Bangkok Shipowners &
Agents Association
227 Tarua Road
Klong Toey
Bangkok 10110
Tel: (010 66) 2-2863101

Book Importers &
Distributors Association
292/15-16 Luklaung Road
Near Paris Theater
Bangkok 10300
Tel: (010 66) 2-2820583

Chinese Construction
Association
209 Nawarat Lane
Yannawa
Bangkok 10120

Coffee Manufacturers
Association
185 Soi 39
Sukhumvit Road
Bangkok 10110
Tel: (010 66) 2-3923185

Cosmetic Manufacturers
Association
1091/22-23 Soi Charurat
Makkasan
Petchburi Road
Bangkok 10400
Tel: (010 66) 2-2222559;
2239572-3

Cosmetics Association
1765 Ramkhamheang Road
Huamak
Bangkok 10240
Tel: (010 66) 2-3141415

Crops Producer and Trade
Promotion Association
32/9 Soi Aree Samphan 4
Rama VI Road
Samsen Nai
Bangkok 10400

Department Stores
Association
Central Department Store
Bldg
306 Silom Road
Bangkok 10500
Tel: (010 66) 2-2336930-9;
2354430-9

Druggists Association
2452 New Petchburi Road
Ekamai
Bangkok 10310
Tel: (010 66) 2-3144981

Electric Appliances Trade
Association
Room 205, 2nd Floor
Rama Theatre Bldg
Rama IV Road
Bangkok 10500
Tel: (010 66) 2-2331790

Fire Extinguisher
Manufacturers and Traders
Association
103 Soi Susarn
Silom Road
Bangkok 10500
Tel: (010 66) 2-2812353;
2817310

Formed Glass Dealers
Association
102 Chula Soi 16
Phyathai Road
Bangkok 10500
Tel: (010 66) 2-2524281

General Insurance
Association
223 Soi Raumrudee
Wireless Road
Bangkok 10500
Tel: (010 66) 2-2514120;
2514132

Glassware Products
Association
645/40 Soi Metro Shopping
Centre
Petchburi Road
Bangkok 10400
Tel: (010 66) 2-2513818

Housing Business Association
104/11-13 Phaholyothin Road
Bangkhen
Bangkok 10900
Tel: (010 66) 2-5210991;
5215357

Ice Wholesalers Association
1042-44 Petchburi Road
Pratunam
Bangkok 10400
Tel: (010 66) 2-2517623-4

Insurance Brokers
Association
2nd Floor, HLR Bldg
285 Convent Road
Bangkok 10500
Tel: (010 66) 2-2347680-6

International Phonogram &
Videogram of Thai Producers
Association
11th Floor, Rahdamri Arcade
95 Rahdamri Road
Bangkok 10500
Tel: (010 66) 2-2514186

Jewellers' Association
42/1 Soi Panumas
Ban Moh Road
Bangkok 10200
Tel: (010 66) 2-2214465

Jute Bag Traders Association
219-221 Songsawad Road
Bangkok 10100
Tel: (010 66) 2-2345615

Leather Association
2-4 Soi Phaisingto
Rama IV Road
Prakhanong
Bangkok 10110
Tel: (010 66) 2-2501658-9

Lighter Owners Association
Thailand
1138/12-13 Ratchadapisek
Road
Bangkok 10120
Tel: (010 66) 2-2842827-9

Motor Coach Operators
Association
1032/36-7 Soi Ruamsirimit
Phaholyothin Road
Bangkhen
Bangkok 10900
Tel: (010 66) 2-2792762

Oil Traders Association
603/4-6 Nakhon Chaisri Road
Dusit
Bangkok 10300
Tel: (010 66) 2-2410771

Palm Oil Refiners Association
212 Soi Yotse
Bamrungmeung Road
Bangkok 10100

Pharmaceutical Products
Association
75 Sukhumvit 42 Road
Prakhanong
Bangkok 10110
Tel: (010 66) 2-3918204

Photographic Dealers
Association
96-98 Chula Soi
6 Rama IV Road
Bangkok 10500
Tel: (010 66) 2-2154271

Press Distributors Association
194/17-18 Petchburi Road
Phayathai
Bangkok 10400
Tel: (010 66) 2-2802963-4

Radio, Television & Sound
System Traders Association
119 Charasmaung Road
Bangkok 10500
Tel: (010 66) 2-2514894;
2518250

Real Estate Association
662 Rama IV Road
Bangkok 10500
Tel: (010 66) 2-2334980 Ext 117

Rice Exporters Association
37 Soi Ngamduplee
Rama IV Road
Yannawa
Bangkok 10120
Tel: (010 66) 2-2863258;
2865279; 2865105

Road Transport Operators
Association
37/1-2 Sukhumvit Soi 51
Prakhanong
Bangkok 10110
Tel: (010 66) 2-3910422 Ext 31

Sawmills Association
101/1 Amnuaysongkram Road
Bangkok 10110
Tel: (010 66) 2-2434754-5

Siam International Mining
Association
204/3 Visudhikasat Road
Bangkok 10200
Tel: (010 66) 2-2823373;
2820534; 2825214

Small Industries Association
174/1 Soi Watmai Amatarot
Visudhikasat Road
Bangkok 10200
Tel: (010 66) 2-2818695

Society of Thai Weights and
Measures Manufacturing
265/177-178 Soi Thaveevatana
Sathupradit Road
Bangkok 10120
Tel: (010 66) 2-2842042

Southeast Asia Cattle
Breeders & Traders
Association
294 Viphavadirangsit Road
Lamlukka
Patumtanee Province 12150
Tel: (010 66) 2-5236662-3

Sports Goods Trade
Association
80/2-4 Chareonphol Square
Rama I Road
Bangkok 10500
Tel: (010 66) 2-2141546;
2141942

Stevedoring Employer
Association
4th Floor, Manorome Bldg
Rama IV Road
Bangkok 10110
Tel: (010 66) 2-2493656

Sugar Dealers Association
298/134 Luklaung Road
Bangkok 10100
Tel: (010 66) 2-2236923

Tanning Industry Association
4174-6 Soi Kluaynamthai
Rama IV Road
Bangkok 10110
Tel: (010 66) 2-3912182;
3927947

Tea Merchants Association
7th Floor
Suankwangtung Flat
70 Rama IV Road
Bangkok 10100
Tel: (010 66) 2-2220748;
2214511; 2216416 Ext 709

Thai Agricultural Merchants
Association
582-584 Anuwongse Road
Bangkok 10100
Tel: (010 66) 2-2220301

Thai Aquaculture
Development and Exporting
Association
1575 Chareon Nakorn Road
Klongsarn
Bangkok 10500
Tel: (010 66) 2-4371262;
4377866

Thai Bankers Association
14th Floor, Sathorn Thani
Bldg
90 Sathorn Nua Road
Bangkok 10500
Tel: (010 66) 2-2341818

Thai Barge Operators
Association
713/57
Liabmeanamchoaphaya Road
Sathupradit
Yannawa
Bangkok 10120
Tel: (010 66) 2-2843070;
2847172

Thai Battery Trade
Association
3669/3-4 Rama IV Road
Prakhanong
Bangkok 10110
Tel: (010 66) 2-3918991;
3924985

Thai-Chinese Promotion of
Investment and Trade
Association
15th Floor, Asoke Tower Bldg
219/48-51 Sukhumvit 21 Road
Bangkok 10110
Tel: (010 66) 2-2512059

Thai Coffee Exporters
Association
1298 Songwad Road
Bangkok 10100
Tel: (010 66) 2-2211264

Thai Contractors Association
110 Wireless Road
Bangkok 10500
Tel: (010 66) 2-2510697;
2522953; 2522591

Thai Convention Promotion
Association
15th Floor, Room 1509/2
Bangkok Bank Bldg
333 Silom Road
Bangkok 10500
Tel: (010 66) 2-2350731-2

Thai Electrical Contractors
Association
235/3-5 Soi 21
Sukhumvit Road
Prakhanong
Bangkok 10110
Tel: (010 66) 2-2583872

Thai Feed Mill Association
117/1 Sukhumvit 55 Road
Prakhanong
Bangkok 10110
Tel: (010 66) 2-3913425

Thai Fertiliser and
Agricultural Marketing
Association
148-150 Chakrapetch Road
Wangburapa
Bangkok 10200
Tel: (010 66) 2-2219241;
2218807

Thai Fertiliser Producers
Trade Association
787 Soi Kingchand
Chand Road
Yannawa
Bangkok 10120
Tel: (010 66) 2-2110774;
2114616

Thai Finance & Security
Association
312/203 Silom Road
Bangkok 10500
Tel: (010 66) 2-2335856

Thai Fishery and Frozen
Products Association
312/2-3 Silom Road
Bangkok 10500
Tel: (010 66) 2-2536769

Thai Fishmeal Producers
Association
189 Intamara Soi 33
Suttisarn Road
Bangkok 10400
Tel: (010 66) 2-2773330

Thai Food Processors'
Association
888/95 11th Floor
Mahatun Plaza Bldg
Pioenchit Road
Bangkok 10300
Tel: (010 66) 2-2536791-4

Thai Fruits and Vegetables
Exporters Association
298/14 Pitsanuloke Road
Bangkok 10300
Tel: (010 66) 2-2819268

Thai Furniture Industry
Association
5th Floor, HHL Bldg
485 Convent Road
Bangkok 10500
Tel: (010 66) 2-2355830;
2355834

Thai Garment Manufacturers'
Association
968, 4th Floor
U Chuliang Bldg
Rama IV Road
Bangkok 10500
Tel: (010 66) 2-2342948;
2354222-3

Thai Gem Exporters
Association
277/1-2 Rama I Road
Bangkok 10500
Tel: (010 66) 2-2142641-4

Thai Glass Traders
Association
110-112 Chaokhumrop Road
Pomprab
Bangkok 10100
Tel: (010 66) 2-2215255

Thai Handicraft Promotion
Association
Thai Handicraft Promotion
Division
4th Floor, Room 423
Ministry of Industry Bldg
Rama VI Road
Bangkok 10400
Tel: (010 66) 2-2824149 Ext 221

Thai Hardware Association
132/37-9 Tanuratana 2 Road
Yannawa
Bangkok 10120
Tel: (010 66) 2-2868590;
2862667

Thai Ice Manufacturers Trade
Association
308 Soi Suwannaram
Charansanitwong Road
Bangkok 10700

Thai Jute Association
52/3 Thai Laithong Bldg
Surawong Road
Bangkok 10500
Tel: (010 66) 2-2342623;
2349024; 2330871

Thai Jute Mill Association
283 Sriboonruang 1 Bldg
Silom Road
Bangkok 10500
Tel: (010 66) 2-2341438-9;
2337000 Ext 14

Thai Life Assurance
Association
36/1 Soi Saphanku
Rama IV Road
Bangkok 10120
Tel: (010 66) 2-2860897;
2863105; 2863107

Thai Magnetic Tape and
Record Traders Association
2000/45 Soi Watvorajanyawas
New Road
Bangkok 10120
Tel: (010 66) 2-2891370

Thai Maize & Produce
Traders Association
52/17-18 Thai Laithong Bldg
Surawong Road
Bangkok 10500
Tel: (010 66) 2-2337560;
2333042; 2344387

Thai Merchant Association
150 Rajbopit Road
Bangkok 10200
Tel: (010 66) 2-2213300;
2226092

Thai Mining Association
120/3 Soi Saladaeng
Silom Road
Bangkok 10500
Tel: (010 66) 2-2333158;
2334144

Thai Orchid Exporters
Association
34/19 Moo 7
Petkasem Road
Bangkae
Bangkok 10160
Tel: (010 66) 2-4210020-5

Thai Packing Association
Industrial Service Division
Soi Klauynamthai
Rama IV Road
Bangkok 10110
Tel: (010 66) 2-3915722;
3915081 Ext 23, 24

Thai Pesticides Association
56, 9th Floor, Yada Bldg
Silom Road
Bangkok 10500
Tel: (010 66) 2-2350100-9

Thai Pharmaceutical
Manufacturers Association
2884 Rattapaitoon Bldg
New Petchburi Road
Bangkok 10310
Tel: (010 66) 2-3147461

Thai Plastic Industries
Association
3rd Floor, Mahatun Bldg
215-217 Rajawongse Road
Bangkok 10100
Tel: (010 66) 2-2236183-6 Ext
45

Thai Plywood & Veneer
Association
3rd Floor, Laemthong Bank
Bldg
289 Surawong Road
Bangkok 10500
Tel: (010 66) 2-2344123

Thai Printing Association
2 Nang Linchee Road
Yannawa
Bangkok 10120
Tel: (010 66) 2-2545568

Thai Pulp and Paper Industry
Association
394/14 Samsen Road
Bangkok 10300
Tel: (010 66) 2-2800951

Thai Rice Mills Association
81-81/1 Soi Rongnanmkhang
Talad Noi
Bangkok 10100
Tel: (010 66) 2-2359445-9

Thai Rubber Traders
Association
57 Rongmuang Soi 5
Pathumwan
Bangkok 10500
Tel: (010 66) 2-2143420

Thai Ship Builders and
Repairers Association
158/2 Sukhothai Road
Dusit
Bangkok 10300
Tel: (010 66) 2-2410686;
2410540

Thai Shipowner's Association
59 New Road
Bangkok 10120
Tel: (010 66) 2-2115339;
2115389; 2119428

Thai Shoes Industrial Trade
Association
245/40 Soi Yuthasil
Pinklao-Bangyikhan Road
Bangkok 10700

Thai Silk-Association
Industrial Service Division
Soi Klauynamthai
Rama IV Road
Bangkok 10110
Tel: (010 66) 2-3912896

Thai Soap and Detergents
Manufacturers Association
120 Silom Road
Bangkok 10500
Tel: (010 66) 2-2339693

Thai Stationery Traders
Association
1173/5 New Road
Bangrak
Bangkok 10500
Tel: (010 66) 2-2359351-2

Thai Steel Furniture
Association
357-363 Mahachai Road
Bangkok 10200
Tel: (010 66) 2-2210362;
2216998

Thai Sugar Manufacturing
Association
78 Kiatnakin Bldg
Bush Lane
New Road
Bangkok 10500
Tel: (010 66) 2-2334156;
2335858

Thai Sugar Producers
Association
8th Floor, Thai Ruam Toon
Bldg
794 Krung Kasem Road
Bangkok 10100
Tel: (010 66) 2-2822022;
2820990

Thai Synthetic Fibre
Manufacturers' Association
4th Floor, Dusit Thani Bldg
946 Rama IV Road
Bangkok 10500
Tel: (010 66) 2-2330750;
2331701-3

Thai Tailors Association
107/17-18 Rangnam Road
Bangkok 10400
Tel: (010 66) 2-2452791;
2456667

Thai Tapioca Flour Industries
Trade Association
4th Floor, Phanthip Plaza
Bldg
604/3 Petchburi Road
Bangkok 10400
Tel: (010 66) 2-2518491;
2519008; 2529933 Ext 420, 421

Thai Textile Manufacturing
Association
454-460 Sukhumvit Road
Near Washington Theatre
Bangkok 10110
Tel: (010 66) 2-2582044,
2582023

Thai Timber Exporters
Association
4th Floor, Union Insurance
Co Ltd Bldg
462/1-5 Siphaya Road
Bangkok 10500
Tel: (010 66) 2-2355105-9 Ext
34, 35

Thai Tourism Industry
Association
Narai Hotel
222 Silom Road
Bangkok 10500
Tel: (010 66) 2-2333350;
2336503-4 Ext 203

Thai Transporters Association
485/1 Sriayudhaya Road
Phayathai
Bangkok 10400
Tel: (010 66) 2-2451447

Thai Video Tape & Disc
Trader Association
120/126 Indra Trade Center
Room 3019 Rajprarop Road
Bangkok 10400
Tel: (010 66) 2-2511111;
2521111 Ext 719

Thai Weaving Industry
Association
54/87-88 KM1
Thonburi-Pakthor Road
Bangkhuntian
Bangkok 10150
Tel: (010 66) 2-4276668-9

Thailand Placement
Association
114/3 Setsiri Road
Samsen Nai
Bangkok 10400
Tel: (010 66) 2-2784312;
2796721

Thailand Shipping
Association
137-141 Tha Rua Road
Klong Toey
Bangkok 10110
Tel: (010 66) 2-2862195

Thai Industrial Promotion
Association
90/17 Rajprarop Road
Bangkok 10400
Tel: (010 66) 2-2457773

Timber Exporters & Importers
Association
144/16-17 Silom Road
Bangkok 10500
Tel: (010 66) 2-2354135-7

Timber Merchant Association
4 Yen-Agart Road
Bangkok 10120
Tel: (010 66) 2-2495565

Tinplate Container
Manufacture Association
251 Soi 21 Sukhumvit Road
Bangkok 10110
Tel: (010 66) 2-3917547

Tobacco Wholesalers
Association
185 Soi 4
Sukhumvit Road
Klong Toey
Bangkok 10110
Tel: (010 66) 2-2512966

Trade & Contracting
Promotion Association
6/1 Soi Kasemsophon
Samsen Road
Bangkok 10300
Tel: (010 66) 2-5859210

Company Financial and Product Information

Directories
Association of Thai Industries
Industrial Directory (The)
Published by Business
Information and Research Co
Ltd, Bangkok
Provides names, addresses
and identifies directors and
officials for Thai companies

Thailand's Exporters
Published by the Department
of Export Promotion, Royal
Thai Government Lists
exporters in alphabetical
order. Printed in English

Economic and Market Statistical Data

Market Research Organisations
Deemar Company Ltd
29/5 Soi Saladaeng 1
PO Box 2732
Bangkok
Tel: (010 66) 2-2344520;
2344521
Telex: 87258 DEEMAR TH
Parent company: AGB
Research plc
Affiliated to SRG and AGB
International
Member of MRS

IMRS Co Ltd (Industrial
Market Research
Services)
21/2 Soi Aree 3
Phaholyolthin Road
Bangkok 10400
Tel: (010 66) 2-2794227
Telex: 82539 THAIHAN TH

International Research
Associates (INRA) Ltd
712/4 Sukhumvit Road
Bangkok 10110
Tel: (010 66) 2-2590261-2
Telex: 87468 ABAC TH
Parent company: Starch
INRA Hooper Inc
Affiliated to INRA

Organisations Providing Economic and Statistical Data
Bank of Thailand, Bangkok
Produces a number of useful
publications which provide
economic and financial
statistics. These include
'Quarterly Bulletin',
'Economic Conditions'
(annual), Monthly Bulletin
Other large Thai banks, eg
Bangkok Bank, publish
economic reports and
bulletins.

Bangkok Post
Produces economic reviews in
June and December

Department of Business
Economics
Rajdamnoen Ave
Bangkok 10200
Tel: (010 66)
2-2817340/2817199
Telex: 72041 DEPBUSE TH

The Stock Exchange of
Thailand publishes a fact
book and annual report,
which contains financial
statistics on the Thai Stock
Market.

National Statistical Office
Lan Luang Road
Bangkok 10100
Tel: (010 66) 2-2813022
Publishes 'Quarterly Bulletin
of Statistics'

Publications

Major Newspapers

Bangkok
Ban Muang
Thai. Daily

Bangkok Post
English. Daily

Bangkok World
English. Daily

Business Post
Daily

Chia Pao Daily News
Chinese. Daily

Khao Panich
Thai Daily. (trade news)

Nation Review (The)
English. Daily

Periodicals
Bangkok Weekly
Publisher's address:
533-539 Sriayuthaya Road
Bangkok
Thai. Weekly

Business in Thailand
Publisher's address:
P O Box 1217
Bangkok 4
English. Monthly

Business Review
Publisher's address:
9/1 Soi 15
Sukhumvit Road
Bangkok
English. Weekly

Business Times
Publisher's address:
Thai Bldg
1400 Rama IV Road
Bangkok 10110
English. Weekly

Financial Post
Publisher's address:
Mansion 4
Rajdamnern Avenue
Bangkok
Weekly

Industry
Publisher's address:
156 Suriwongse Road
Bangkok
Thai/English. Monthly

Investor
Publisher's address:
Parisak Bldg
4th Floor, 138/1 Petchburi
Road
Bangkok 10400
English. Monthly

Turkey

Sources of Economic,
Stock Market
Information and
Investment Research
Services

Banks

Central Bank
Turkiye Cumhuriyet Merkez
Bankasi
(Central Bank of the Republic
of Turkey)
Ataturk Bulvari 40
Ulus
Ankara
Tel: (010 90) 4-3125200-09
Telex: 42993/42423 MBAJ TR

Turkish Banks in London
AK International Ltd
(AK Bank)
10 Finsbury Square
London EC2A 1HE
Tel: 01-628 3844

Central Bank of the Republic
of Turkey
Centric House
391 Strand
London WC2R OLT
Tel: 01-379 0548

Ottoman Bank
King William House
2A Eastcheap
London EC3M 1AA
Tel: 01-626 5932

TC Ziraat Bankasi
48 Bishopsgate
London EC2
Tel: 01-374 4554

Turkiye Garanti Bankasi
141-142 Fenchurch Street
London EC3M 6BL
Tel: 01-626 3803

Turkiye Is Bankasi
21 Aldermanbury
London EC2V 7HA
Tel: 01-606 7151

Yapi & Kredi Bankasi
Stock Exchange Building
Old Broad Street
London EC2N 1HP
Tel: 01-628 2907

Major Turkish Banks
Turk Dis Ticaret Bankasi AS
(Turkish Foreign Trade Bank)
Yildiz Posta Caddesi 54
80280 Gayrettepe
Istanbul
Tel: (010 90) 1-1724180
(general)
1-1725293 (international)
Telex: 27992 TDTB TR
(general)
27991 DISP TR (international
division)

Turk Ekonomi Bankasi AS
Istiklal Cad 284 Odakule
PO Box 640
80050 Beyoglu
Istanbul
Tel: (010 90)
1-1512121/1431672
Telex: 25358 TEBU TR
22043 TEBU TR

Turkiye Cumhuriyet
Ziraat Bankasi
(Agricultural Bank of the
Turkish Republic)
Bankalar Caddesi
No 42 Ulus
Ankara
Tel: (010 90)
4-3103747/3103819
Telex: 44004 HSBB TR

Turkiye Halk Bankasi AS
(Cooperative and State Bank)
Ilkiz Sok No 1
Sihhiye
Ankara
Tel: (010 90) 4-1335729
Telex: 44201

Turkiye Is Bankasi AS
Ataturk Bulvari 191
Kavaklidere
Ankara
Tel: (010 90) 4-1281140
Telex: 42082 TAB TR
43388 TIB TR

Turkiye Vakiflar Bankasi TAO
Ataturk Bulvari 207
Kavaklidere
Ankara
Tel: (010 90) 4-1277120
(general)
4-1266121 (foreign
department)
Telex: 44428/9

Stockbrokers

Istanbul is the only stock
exchange in Turkey. It was
inaugurated at the beginning
of 1986. Of the 545 companies
listed (July 1988), only 50 are
actively traded in the senior
market.

Istanbul Stock Exchange
(IMKB)
Gurkan Caddesi 40
Cagaloglu
Istanbul
Tel: (010 90) 1-5261990
Fax: (010 90) 1-5207111
Telex: 22748 IMKB TR

Members (77 as at June 1988)
(Selection listed below)

Investment Banks
Desiyab-Devlet Sanayi ve Isci
Yatirim Bankasi
(State Industry and Workers'
Investment Bank)
2 Tasocagi C Urfali Ishani 4/1
Mecidiyekoy
Istanbul
Tel: (010 90) 1-1666959
Fax: (010 90) 1-1660442
Telex: 42457 DSYB TR

T.Ihracat Kredi Bankasi
(State Investment Bank)
Milli Mudafaa C 20
Bakanliklar
Ankara
Tel: (010 90) 1-1171300
Fax: (010 90) 1-1257896
Telex: 42606 DYB TR

T Sinai Kalkinma Bankasi
Meclis-i Mebusan C 137
Findikli
Istanbul
Tel: (010 90) 1-1512792
Fax: (010 90) 1-1432975
Telex: 24344 TSKB TR

Commercial Banks
AdaBank
Buyukdere C 40 Mecidiyekoy
Istanbul
Tel: (010 90) 1-1726420
Fax: (010 90) 1-1726443
Telex: 27279 ADAB TR

AKbank
Bankalar C
55 Karakoy
Istanbul
Tel: (010 90) 1-1520300
Telex: 24139 AKUM TR

BNP-AK Bankasi
Tak-1 Zafer C
Vakif Han C Blok Taksim
Istanbul
Tel: (010 90) 1-1448780

Citibank
Macka
Istanbul
Tel: (010 90) 1-1485640
Fax: (010 90) 1-1415014
Telex: 26277 CITI TR

Standard Chartered Bank
Nispetiye C 38k: 1 1.Levent
Istanbul
Tel: (010 90) 1-1700492
Fax: (010 90) 1-1722271
Telex: 26862 SCHB TR

T Ticaret Bankasi
Nuruosmaniye C
81 Cagaloglu
Istanbul
Tel: (010 90) 1-5276471
Fax: (010 90) 1-5214781
Telex: 23479 TIFO TR

Turk Ekonomi Bankasi
Odakule Is Merkezi K: 13
Bayoglu
Istanbul
Tel: (010 90) 1-1512121
Fax: (010 90) 1-1496558
Telex: 25358 TEBU TR

Yapi Kredi Bankasi
Halaskargazi C 85/2
Osmanbay
Istanbul
Tel: (010 90) 1-1412355
Fax: (010 90) 1-1489004
Telex: 24718 YAGE TR

Brokerage Houses
Acar Securities
Buyukdere C 108/1 Oyak
Ishani K: 6 Esentepe
Istanbul
Tel: (010 90) 1-1751300

Bogazici Securities Inc
Cumhuriyet C Merkez Apt
165/1 Harbiye
Istanbul
Tel: (010 90) 1-1416456
Telex: 27806 BMD TR

Derbosa Securities Inc
Dervisoglu S Dervis Han 14
Sirkeci
Istanbul
Tel: (010 90) 1-5228313
Fax: (010 90) 1-5121110
Telex: 27920 DEV TR

Naci Bakir Securities Inc
Buyukdere C 18/A Sisli
Istanbul
Tel: (010 90) 1-1484230
Fax: (010 90) 1-1411680
Telex: 26386 YULA TR

Setat Securities Trading Inc
Ergenekon C
100/A Ferlikoy
Istanbul
Tel: (010 90) 1-1310505
Fax: (010 90) 1-1403061
Telex: 27401 HELD TR

Vatirim Finansman
Investment and Finances Inc
Buyukdere C Tatko Binasi
127/4 Gayrettepe
Istanbul
Tel: (010 90) 1-1754480
Telex: 20346 YFAS TR
Fax: (010 90) 1-1724448

Sources of General Background Information, Industry Sector Information and Trade Contacts

UK Addresses
British Chamber of
Commerce of Turkey
(UK Liaison Officer)
69 Cannon Street
London EC4M 5AB
Tel: 01-248 4444

Turkish-British Chamber of
Commerce and Industry in
the UK
Avon House
360-366 Oxford Street
London W1N 9HA
Tel: 01-499 4265

Turkish Embassy
Commercial Counseller
43 Belgrave Square
London SW1 8PA
Tel: 01-235 4233 (commercial
section)
01-235 4991
Fax: 01-235 2207
Telex: 919643 TROFIS G

Addresses in Turkey
Adana Chamber of
Commerce
Abidinpasa Caddesi
Adana
Tel: (010 90)
711-12404/13779/13417
Telex: 62187 ASO TR

Ankara Chamber of
Commerce
Sehit Tegmen Kalmaz
Caddesi 20
Ankara
Tel: (010 90)
1-3104145/3243260
Telex: 42029 ODAL TR

British Chamber of
Commerce of Turkey (Inc)
PO Box 190
Karakoy
Istanbul
Tel: (010 90) 1-1490658

British Consulate-General
Consul (Commercial)
Tepebasi
Beyoglu
Istanbul
Tel: (010 90) 4-1447540
Telex: 24122 BRITAIN IST
and
Modern Tercume Burosu
Ankara
Tel: (010 90)
4-1178122/1181470

British Embassy
First Secretary (Economic and
Commercial)
Sehit Ersan Caddesi 46A
Cankaya
Ankara
Tel: (010 90) 4-274310
Fax: (010 90) 4-1683214
Telex: 42320 PROD TR

Business Language and
Translation Services
Turk Argus Ajans
Istanbul
Tel: (010 90)
1-1441634/1498466

Istanbul Chamber of
Commerce
PO Box 377
Ragip Gumuspala CAd
Eminonu
Istanbul
Tel: (010 90)
1-5205100/5266215
Telex: 23682 ODA TR

Istanbul and Marmara Region
Maritime Chamber of
Commerce
80050 Beyoglu
Istanbul
Tel: (010 90) 1-1435495
Telex: 24727 DTO TR

Izmir Chamber of Commerce
and Industry
Ataturk Cad 126
Izmit
Tel: (010 90) 211-255576/16000
Telex: 52331

Union of Chambers of
Commerce, Industry,
Maritime Commerce and
Commodity Exchanges of
Turkey
Ataturk Bulvari No 149
Bankanliklar
Ankara
Tel: (010 90) 4-177700
Telex: 46011/2

Sources of Investment Advice, Assistance and Information

Export Promotion Center
Undersecretariat for Treasury
and Foreign Trade
Mithatpasa Cad No 60 Kizilay
Ankara
Tel: (010 90) 4-1172223
Telex: 42228 IGM TR

Foreign Investment
Department
State Planning Organisation
Necati Bay Caddesi 110
Ankara
Tel: (010 90) 4-2290071
Telex: 42110

Foreign Trade Association of
Turkey
Otim Binasi
A Blok Kat 4
Besiktas
Istanbul
Tel: (010 90) 1-1723828
Telex: 26689 FTAT TR

IGEME
(Export Promotion Research
Centre)
Mithatpasa CAd No 60
Kizilay
Ankara
Tel: (010 90) 4-172223
Telex: 42-28 IGM TR

Istanbul Textile and Apparel
Exporters Union
Maya Sokak
Maya Ham 10/1
Gayrettepe
Istanbul
Tel: (010 90) 1-1743030
Fax: (010 90)
1-1743040/1663305
Telex: 25955 IIM TR

Ministry of Foreign Affairs
Ankara
Telex: 42203 SAFA TR

Ministry of Industry and
Commerce
Ankara
Telex: 42598 STBA TR

YASED
(Association for Foreign
Capital Coordination)
OTIM
Ihlamur Serfi Sarayn
Besihtas
Istanbul

Professional Associations

Accountancy

Turkiye Muhasebe Uzmanlari
Dernegi
PO Box 508
Karakoy
Istanbul

Banking

Turkiye Bankalar Birligi
Mithatpasa Caddesi 12
Yenisehir
Ankara

Trade Associations

General Secretariat of Antalya
Exporters Union
Ihracatacilar Birligi Genel
Sekreterligi Antalya
Telex: 56128 anta tr
Fax: (010 90) 311-25468

General Secretariat of
Exporters Unions of Agri for
Live Animals and Animal
Products
Agri Ili Canli Hayvan Madde
ve Mahsulleri
Ihracatci Birlikleri Genel
Sekreterligi Agri

General Secretariat of
Exporters Union of the
Eastern Provinces for Live
Animals and Animal Products
Dogu Vilayetleri Canli
Hayvan Madde ve Mahsulleri
Ihracatcilari Birligi Genel
Sekreterligi Kars
Tel: (010 90) 0211-1428

General Secretariat of
Exporters Unions of Erzurum
for Live Animals and Animal
Products
Erzurum Ili Canli Hayvan
Madde ve Mahsulleri
Ihracatci Birlikleri Genel
Sekreterligi Erzurum

General Secretariat of
Exporters Union of Igdir for
Live Animals, Cotton, Wool,
Fleece, Fresh Fruits and
Vegetables
Igdir Canli Hayvan, Pamuk,
Yun, Yapagi, Yas Sebze ve
Meyve
Ihracatcilari Birligi Genel
Sekretarligi Igdir

General Secretariat of
Exporters Union of South
Eastern Anatolia for Live
Animals and Animal Products
Hurriyet Cad Dr Ibrahim
Soylemez Sok No 4 Gaziantep
Tel: (010 90) 851-22411
Fax: (010 90) 851-30613
Telex: 69170 690 45 GIB TR

General Secretariat of
Exporters Union of Van
District for Live Animals and
Animal Products
Van Ili ve Cevresi Canli
Hayvan Madde ve Mahsulleri
Ihracatcilari Birligi Genel
Sekreterligi Van

General Secreteriat of
Hazelnut Exporters Union of
the Black Sea Region
Arifbey Cad No 18 Giresun
Tel: (010 90) 0511-1338 2426
Fax: (010 90) 0511-1103
Telex: 82475 FIN TR

General Secretariat of Izmir
Exporters Unions
1375 Sok No 25 Kat 3
Alsancak Izmir
Tel: (010 90) 51-218699/218696
Fax: (010 90) 51-216560
Telex: 52192 IZIB TR
53138 EXUN TR

General Secretariat of Istanbul
Exporters Unions
Rihtim Cad Ihracatcilar Birligi
Ishani Karakoy Istanbul
Tel: (010 90) 1-1455612
Fax: (010 90) 1-1455611
Telex: 24557 BUK TR
25490 IIB TR

General Secretariat of Mersin
Exporters Unions
Uray Cad Icel
Tel: (010 90) 741-15710
Fax: (010 90) 741-23325
Telex: 67121 MIB TR
67306 IIB TR

General Secretariat of Tobacco Exporters union of Aegean Region
Akdeniz Cad No 5 Kat 4/407
Izmir
Tel: (010 90) 51-254321/140558
Telex: 52692 EGTU TR

General Secretariat of Turkish Metal Exporters Union
Cumhuriyet Cad Itir Apt No 295 Kat 5 Daire 10
Harbiye
Istanbul
Tel: (010 90) 1-1413046/7
Telex: 24427 MADE TR

Company Financial and Product Information

Directories

Major Companies of Turkey Directory
Published by Poyraz Yayincilik As
Istanbul
Lists over 1000 major companies in Turkey. Details provided include addresses, names of officials, products and trade names. Also provides information on Turkish markets and over 800 products and services. Written in English. Annual

Izmir Export Catalogue
Published by Izmir Ticaret Odasi, Izmir
Classified lists of exporters and their products

General Exporters-Importers Directory
Published by AGT Research Development and Information Corp, Istanbul.
Provides over 6400 listings of manufacturers, importers, exporters and foreign trade agencies. Information provided includes names, addresses and telephone numbers

Adres Kitabi
(Trade Directory of Istanbul)
Published by Istanbul Odasi, Istanbul
Lists exporters, importers, building contractors and commission agents

Turkey Industry and Trade Directory
Published by AGT Research Development & Information Corp, Istanbul
Provides over 14 500 listings of producers, foreign trade investment service companies, representatives and wholesalers in Turkey. Arranged under main product group headings

Clothing and Textile Catalog
Published by AGT Research Development and Information Cort, Istanbul.
Provides names and addresses of 2300 listings of companies in the Turkish textile industry

Economic and Market Statistical Data

Market Research Organisations

G and A Baker Ltd Research Unit
Cumhuriyet Cad No 16
K-Han Apt
Elmadag
Istanbul
Tel: (010 90) 1-1312765
Telex: 27869 UNIT TR
Affiliated to Research International

PEVA Piyasa Etvo Danisma ve Arastirma Tic Ltd
Beyoglu Istiklal Cad Imam Sok No 1
Istanbul
Tel: (010 90) 1456647/1494011
Telex: 25069 BEYG X TR
Affiliated to INRA

PIAR Marketing Research Company Ltd
Gazeteciler Mah Saglam Fikir Sok No 19
80300 Esentepe
Istanbul
Tel: (010 90) 1-1675566
Telex: 30139 TYP TR
Affiliated to Gallup Intenational

Organisations Providing Economic and Statistical Data

Devlet Istatistik Enstitusu
(State Institute of Statistics)
Necati Bey Caddesi
114 Ankara
Tel: (010 90) 4-236330
This is the main source of official statistics in Turkey. The Institute is responsible for collection and compilation of economic and social statistical data. It also conducts statistical surveys and produces the annual census. The research library of the institute is open to the public. Publications include:
Turkiye Istatistik Yilligi
(Statistical Yearbook of Turkey)
Turkiye Istatistik cep Yilligi
(Statistical Pocketbook of Turkey)
Aylik Istatistik
(Monthly Bulletin of Statistics)
Aylik Ekonomik Gostergeler
(Monthly Economic Indicators)
Yillik Imalat Sanayii Anvket Sonuclari
(Annual Survey of the Manufacturing Industry)

Ministry of Industry and Commerce
General Secretariat of Foreign Trade
Publishes a quarterly publication providing trade statistics, Foreign Trade of Turkey

State Planning Organisation
Produces five year plans
which include historic and
forecast economic statistics

Turkiye Is Bankasi AS
Ataturk Bulvari 191
Ankara
Publishes:
Economic Indicators of
Turkey. Annual
Review of Economic
Conditions. Quarterly
Bi-monthly Review
Economic Report. Annual

Turkiye Cumhuriyet Merkez
Bankasi
(Central Bank of the Republic
of Turkey)
Ataturk Bulvari 40
Ulus
Ankara
Publishes the Quarterly
Statistical Survey and a
Monthly Bulletin

Turkish Industrialists and
Businessmen's Association
(TUSIAD)
Cumhuriyet Caddesi
Ferah Apt
2339-10 Harbiye
Istanbul
Publishes The Turkish
Economy

Publications

Directories
Europa Yearbook
Published by Europa Ltd,
London.
Includes a section on Turkey.
Provides facts and statistics
and lists of addresses of
Turkish government offices,
embassies and trade
organisations.

Major Newspapers
Adalet
Daily

Ankara Ekspres
Daily

Ankara Ticaret Gazetesi
Daily

Ekonomide Egemenlik
Daily

Is ve Ekonomi
Daily

Milliyet
Daily

Ticaret
Daily

Turkish Daily News
Daily (English)

Turkish Daily News
International
Weekly

Turkiye Iktisat Gatzetesi
Daily

Periodicals
Banka ve Ekonomik Yorumlar
Publisher's address:
Cagalogu
Catalcesme Sok 17 Kat 4
Istanbul
Banking journal

Ekonomi ve Politika
Publisher's address:
Ataturk Bulvari 199/A44
Kavaklikere
Ankara
Weekly

Istanbul Ticaret Odasi
Mecmuasi
Journal of the Istanbul
Chamber of Commerce.
Quarterly

Middle East Review
Publisher's address:
Necatiby Cad 57/5
Ankara
Monthly

Near East Briefing
Publisher's address:
Olungar Sok 2/1
Bakanliklar
Ankara
International business.
Quarterly

Nokta
Published by Gelisim
Yayinlari
Buyukdere Cad
Sanayii Sok No 221
1 Levent
Istanbul
News magazine. Weekly

Tekstil & Teknik
Published by Enver Oren,
Istanbul
Journal of the textile industry
in Turkey. Monthly

Ticaret-Export Turkey
Publisher's address:
Gazi Bulvari No 18
Izmir
Quarterly by subscription

Trade Journal
Published by the British
Chamber of Commerce of
Turkey Association, Istanbul.
Monthly

Turkey Economic News
Digest
Publisher's address:
Karanfil Sok 56
Ankara
Monthly

UK

Sources of Economic, Stock Market Information and Investment Research Services

Bank

Central Bank
Bank of England
Threadneedle Street
London EC2R 8AH
Tel: 01-601 4444
Telex: 885001

Major UK Banks
Bank of Scotland
The Mound
Edinburgh EH1 1Y2
Tel: 031-442 7777
Telex: 72275

Barclay's Bank plc
54 Lombard Street
London EC3P 3AH
Tel: 01-626 1567
Telex: 884970; 887591

Clydesdale Bank plc
30 St Vincent Place
Glasgow G1 2HL
Tel: 041-248 7070
Telex: 77135

Coutts & Co
440 Strand
London WC2R OQS
Tel: 01-379 6262
Telex: 883421

Gerrard & National Holdings
plc
33 Lombard Street
London EC3V 9BQ
Tel: 01-623 9981
Telex: 883589

Hambros Bank Ltd
41 Bishopsgate
London EC2P 2AA
Tel: 01-588 2851
Telex: 883851
Fax: 01-638 0480

Hill Samuel & Co Ltd
100 Wood Street
London EC2P 2AJ
Tel: 01-628 8011
Telex: 888822

Kleinwort Benson Ltd
20 Fenchurch Street
London EC3P 3DB
Tel: 01-623 8000
Telex: 888531

Lloyds Bank plc
71 Lombard Street
London EC3P 3BS
Tel: 01-626 1500
Telex: 888301

Midland Bank plc
Poultry
London EC2P 2BX
Tel: 01-260 8000
Telex: 8811822

Samuel Montague & Co Ltd
10 Lower Thames Street
London EC3R 6AE
Tel: 01-260 9000
Telex: 887213 SMCO

Morgan Grenfell & Co Ltd
23 Great Winchester Street
London EC2P 2AX
Tel: 01-588 4545
Telex: 8953511

National Westminster Bank
plc
41 Lothbury
London EC2P 2BP
Tel: 01-726 1000
Telex: 888388

Royal Bank of Scotland plc
(The)
PO Box 31
42 St Andrew's Square
Edinburgh EH2 2YE
Tel: 031-556 8555
Telex: 72230

J Henry Schroder Wagg & Co
Ltd
120 Cheapside
London EC2V 6DS
Tel: 01-382 6000
Telex: 885029

Standard Chartered Bank
38 Bishopsgate
London EC2N 4DE
Tel: 01-280 7500
Telex: 885951

Ulster Bank Ltd
47 Donegall Place
PO Box 232
Belfast BT1 5AU
Tel: 084-220222
Telex: 747334

S G Warburg
33 King William Street
London EC4R 9AS
Tel: 01-280 2222
Telex: 22941 SGWLON G

Stockbrokers
There are six Stock Exchanges
in the UK and the Republic of
Ireland which make up the
Associated Stock Exchange,
seven if you include the two
exchanges which form
Midlands and Western
seperately.

London
International Stock Exchange
(The)
Throgmorton Street
London EC2N 1HP
Tel: 01-588 2355
Telex: 886557

Irish
International Stock Exchange
(The)
28 Anglesea Street
Dublin 2
Tel: 0001-778808
Telex: 4537

Midlands & Western
International Stock Exchange
(The)
Margaret Street
Birmingham B3 3JL
Tel: 021-236 9181
Telex: 338397

International Stock Exchange
(The)
St Nicholas Street
Bristol BS1 1TH
Tel: 0272-24541

Northern
International Stock Exchange
(The)
76 King Street
Manchester
Tel: 061-833 0931
Telex: 667093

Northern Ireland
International Stock Exchange
(The)
Northern Bank House
10 High Street
Belfast BT1 2BP
Tel: 0232-21094
Telex: 747050

Scotland
International Stock Exchange
(The)
Stock Exchange House
PO Box 141
69 St George's Place
Glasgow G2 1BU
Tel: 041-221 7060

A Selection of Members
Astaire & Co
117 Bishopsgate
London EC2M 3TD
Tel: 01-283 2081

Buckmaster & Moore
The Stock Exchange
London EC2P 2JT

James Capel & Co
Winchester House
100 Old Broad Street
London EC2N 1BQ
Tel: 01-588 6010
Telex: 888866

Capel-Cure Myers
Bath House
Holborn Viaduct
London EC1A 2EU
Tel: 01-236 5080
Telex: 886653

Cazenove & Co
12 Tokenhouse Yard
London EC2R 7AN
Tel: 01-588 2828
Telex: 886758

T C Coombes & Co
5-7 Ireland Yard
London EC4V 5EE
Tel: 01-248 2033
Telex: 883237

De Zoete & Bevan
25 Finsbury Circus
London EC2M 7EE
Tel: 01-588 4141
Telex: 883179

Fielding, Newson-Smith & Co
Garrard House
31 Gresham Street
London EC2V 7DX
Tel: 01-606 7711
Telex: 883395

J M Finn & Co
Salisbury House
London Wall
London EC2M 5TA
Tel: 01-628 9688
Telex: 887281

Panmure Gordon & Co
9 Moorfields Highwalk
London EC2Y 9DS
Tel: 01-638 4010
Telex: 883832

W Greenwell & Co
Bow Bells House
Broad Street
London EC4M 9EL
Tel: 01-236 2040
Telex: 883006

Grievson, Grant & Co
Barrington House
59 Gresham Street
London EC2P 2DS
Tel: 01-606 4433
Telex: 887336

Henderson Crosthwaite & Co
194-200 Bishopsgate
London EC2M 4LL
Tel: 01-283 8577
Telex: 883924

Hoare Govett Ltd
Heron House
319-325 High Holborn
London WC1V 7PB
Tel: 01-404 0344
Telex: 885474

Kitcat & Aitken
The Stock Exchange
London EC2N 1HB
Tel: 01-588 6280
Telex: 888297

Laing & Cruickshank Inc
McAnally, Montgomery & Co
Piercy House
London EC2R 7BE
Tel: 01-588 2800
Telex: 888397

Laurie, Milbank & Co
72-73 Basinghall Street
London EC2V 5DP
Tel: 01-606 6622
Telex: 8954681

L Messel & Co
Winchester House
100 Old Broad Street
London EC2P 2HX
Tel: 01-606 4411
Telex: 884591

Mullens & Co
15 Moorgate
London EC2R 6AN
Tel: 01-638 4121
Telex: 888279

Pember & Boyle
PO Box 435
30 Finsbury Circus
London EC2P 2HB
Tel: 01-638 6242
Telex: 888626

Phillips & Drew
120 Moorgate
London EC2M 6XP
Tel: 01-628 4444
Telex: 291163

Quilter Goodison & Co
Garrard House
31-45 Gresham Street
London EC2V 7LH
Tel: 01-600 4177
Telex: 883719

Rowe & Pitman
City-Gate House
39-45 Finsbury Square
London EC2A 1JA
Tel: 01-606 1066
Telex: 883427

E B Savory Milln & Co
3 London Wall Buildings
London EC2M 5PU
Tel: 01-638 1212
Telex: 887289

Scott, Goff, Layton & Co
Salisbury House
London Wall
London EC2M 5SX
Tel: 01-628 4433
Telex: 886594

Scrimgeour, Vickers & Co
20 Copthall Avenue
London EC2R 7JS
Tel: 01-600 7595
Telex: 885171

Simon & Coates
1 London Wall Buildings
London EC2M 5PT
Tel: 01-588 3644
Telex: 885128

Strauss, Turnbull & Co
3 Moorgate Place
London EC2R 6HR
Tel: 01-638 5699
Telex: 883201

Vickers Da Costa Ltd
Regis House
King William Street
London EC4R 9AR
Tel: 01-623 2494
Telex: 886004

Williams De Broe Hill Chaplin
& Co
PO Box 515
Pinners Hall
Austin Friars
London EC2P 2HS
Tel: 01-588 7511
Telex: 887084

Wood, MacKenzie & Co
62-63 Threadneedle Street
London EC2R 8HP
Tel: 01-600 3600
Telex: 883369

Sources of General Background Information, Industry Sector Information and Trade Contacts

There are over 200 Chambers
of Commerce throughout the
UK. A small selection of the
main chambers is provided
below:

Birmingham Chamber of
Industry and Commerce
PO Box 360
75 Harborne Road
Edgbaston
Birmingham B15 3DH
Tel: 021-454 6171
Telex: 338024

Bolton Chamber of
Commerce and Industry
Silverwell House
Silverwell Street
Bolton BL1 1PX
Tel: 0204-33896
Fax: 0204-361780
Telex: 635109 CHAMCOM G

Cardiff Chamber of
Commerce and Industry
101-108 The Exchange
Mount Stuart Square
Cardiff CF1 6RD
Tel: 0222-481648
Telex: 497492 CHAMCOM G

Edinburgh Chamber of
Commerce and
Manufacturers
3 Randolph Crescent
Edinburgh EH3 7UD
Tel: 031-225 5851
Telex: 72465 CHAMCOM G

Glasgow Chamber of
Commerce and
Manufacturers
30 George Square
Glasgow G2 1EQ
Tel: 041-204 2121
Fax: 041-204 2121
Telex: 777967

London Chamber of
Commerce and Industry
69 Cannon Street
London EC4N 5AB
Tel: 01-248 4444
Fax: 01-489 0391
Telex: 888941

Manchester Chamber of
Commerce and Industry
56 Oxford Street
Manchester M60 7HJ
Tel: 061-236 3210
Fax: 061-236 4160
Telex: 667822 CHAMCOM G

Merseyside Chamber of
Commerce and Industry
Number One
Old Hall Street
Liverpool L3 9HG
Tel: 051-227 1234
Fax: 051-2360121
Telex: 627110 CHAMCOM G

Northern Ireland Chamber of
Commerce and Industry
Chamber of Commerce
House
22 Great Victoria Street
Belfast BT2 7BJ
Tel: 0232-244113
Telex: 747538 BELCOM G

Sheffield Chamber of
Commerce and
Manufacturers
33 Earl Street
Sheffield S1 3FX
Tel: 0742-730114
Fax: 0742-766644
Telex: 547676 CHAMCO G

Welsh Office
Industry Department
New Crown Buildings
Cathays Park
Cardiff CF1 3NQ
Tel: 0222-825097
Telex: 498228

Sources of Investment and Trade Advice, Assistance and Information

British Overseas Trade Board
(BOTB)
1 Victoria Street
London SW1H OET
Tel: 01-215 5336 (Export to
Europe)
Telex: 8811074

The BOTB assists and advises
British exporters, and advises
the Government on matters of
overseas trade. Regional
offices exist in Bristol,
Birmingham, Cambridge,
Cardiff, Glasgow, Leeds,
Liverpool, Manchester,
Nottingham,
Newcastle-upon-Tyne,
Reading and Northern
Ireland.
A number of services are
offered including the Product
Data Store, located at the
address above, where free
information is available on
particular products and
industries. The Export
Intelligence Service provides
news of export opportunities
to companies in the UK.

Customs and Excise
Department
New King Beam House
22 Upper Ground
London SE1 9PJ
Tel: 01-620 1313
Fax: 01-382 5570

Department of Trade and Industry (The)
1-19 Victoria Street
London SW1H OET
Tel: 01-215 7877 (general switchboard)
The DTI Enterprise initiative offers British business a valuable range of information and resources. Initiatives cover the following areas:
The Single Market (special 1992 hot-line on 01-200-1992)
The Consultancy Initiatives
The Marketing Initiative
The Design Initiative
The Quality Initiative
The Manufacturing Initiative
The Business Planning Initiative
The Financial and Information Initiative
The Regional Initiative
The Export Initiative
The Research and Technology Initiative
The Business and Education Initiative
Support services (overseas market data, patent information, small firms service)

Foreign and Commonwealth Office
Downing Street
London SW1A 2AL
Tel: 01-233 3000
Telex: 297711

Industrial Development Board for Northern Ireland
IDB House
64 Chichester Street
Belfast BT1 4JX
Tel: 0232-233233
Telex: 747025

Scottish Export Office
Industry Department of Scotland
Alhambra House
45 Waterloo Street
Glasgow G2 6AT
Tel: 041-248 2855
Telex: 777883

Welsh Office Industry Dept
Crown Building
Cathays Park
Cardiff CF1 3NQ
Tel: 0222 825111
Telex: 498228

Professional Associations

Accountancy
Chartered Institute of Management Accountants (The)
63 Portland Place
London W1N 4AB
Tel: 01-637 2311
Fax: 01-631 5309

Institute of Chartered Accountants in England and Wales
PO Box 433
Chartered Accountants' Hall
Moorgate Place
London EC2P 2BJ
Tel: 01-628 7060
Telex: 88443

Institute of Chartered Accountants of Scotland (The)
27 Queen Street
Edinburgh EH2 1LA
Tel: 031-225 5673
Telex: 727530

Banking
British Bankers' Associations (The)
10 Lombard Street
London EC3V 9EL
Tel: 01-623 4001
Telex: 888364

Insurance
Association of British Insurers
Aldermary House
Queen Street
London EC4N ITT
Tel: 01-248 4477
Fax: 01-489 1120
Telex: 937035

Trade Associations

There are hundreds of trade associations in the UK. A full listing can be found in directories published by CBD Publications. The Macmillan Directory of Business Information Sources provides a useful listing of trade associations and organisations which provide industry information. This directory is organised by industry sector (Standard Industrial Classification codes).
A small selection of associations and institutions are listed below.

Aluminium Federation Ltd
Broadway House
Calthorpe Road
Fiveways
Birmingham B15 1TN
Tel: 021-455 0311

Association of the British Pharmaceutical Industry
12 Whitehall
London SW1A 2DY
Tel: 01-930 3477

British Adhesives and Sealants Association
2a High Street
Hythe
Southampton SO4 6YW
Tel: 0703-842765

British Equipment Trade Association
8 Southampton Place
London WC1A 2EF
Tel: 01-405 6233

British Independent Steel Producers Association
5 Cromwell Road
London SW7 2HX
Tel: 01-581 0231

British Ports Association
Commonwealth House
1-19 New Oxford Street
London WC1A 1DZ
Tel: 01-242 1200

British Retailers Association
Commonwealth House
19 New Oxford Street
London WC1A 1PA
Tel: 01-404 0955

British Rubber Manufacturers
Association
90 Tottenham Court Road
London W1P OBR
Tel: 01-580 2794

British Safety Council
62 Chancellors Road
London W6 9RS
Tel: 01-741 1231

British Security Industry
Association
PO Box 85
46 Gillingham Street
London SW1V 1HY
Tel: 01-630 5183

British Standards Institution
2 Park Street
London W1A 2BS
Tel: 01-629 9000

British Stationery & Office
Products Association
6 Wimpole Street
London W1M 8AS
Tel: 01-637 7692

British Textile Machinery
Association
220-224 The Royal Exchange
Manchester M2 7BX
Tel: 061-834 2991

British Tourist Authority
4 Bromwells Road
London SW4 OBJ
Tel: 01-622 3256

British Toy and Hobby
Manufacturers' Association
80 Camberwell Road
London SE5 OEG
Tel: 01-701 7271

British Woodworking
Federation
82 New Cavendish Street
London W1M 8AD
Tel: 01-580 5588

British Wool Marketing Board
Oak Mills
Station Road
Clayton
Bradford
Tel: 0274-882091

Chemical Industries
Association
Alembic House
Albert Embankment
London SE1 7TU
Tel: 01-735 3001

Federation of Wholesale and
Industrial Distributors
Panton House
25-27 Haymarket
London SW1Y 4EN
Tel: 01-930 2002

Iron and Steel Statistics
Bureau
NLA Tower
12 Addiscombe Road
Croydon CR9 3JH
Tel: 01-686 9050

Lighting Industry Federation
Swan House
207 Balham High Road
London SW17 7BQ
Tel: 01-675 5432

Paint Research Association
Waldegrave Road
Teddington TW11 8LD
Tel: 01-977 4427

Plastics and Rubber Institute
11 Hobart Place
London SW1H OHL
Tel: 01-245 9555

Radio, Electrical and
Television Retailers'
Association
Retra House
57-61 Newington Causeway
London SE1 6BE
Tel: 01-403 1463

Company Financial and Product Information

Directories

Alphabetical Index of
Companies
Published by the Department
of Trade and Industry,
Companies House, Crown
Way, Maindy, Cardiff
Listing of all companies
registered in England, Wales,
Scotland and Northern
Ireland. Available with or
without daily updates.
Monthly

A-Z of UK Brank Leaders
Published by Euromonitor
Publications Ltd, London
Provides details of over 500
companies in the UK with
main brands and financial
data

Crawfords Directory of City
Connections
Published by the Economist
Publications Ltd, London
Provides details of the
financial advisers of over 5000
UK listed, USM and major
unlisted companies

CRO Directory of Companies
Produced by the Company
Registration Office. The CRO
for England and Wales has an
office in Cardiff and London.
There is also an office in
Edinburgh (covering
Scotland) and Belfast
(covering Northern Ireland).
Provides notification of recent
annual returns and accounts
and other company details

Extel Card Service
Produced by Extel Financial
Ltd, London
Not strictly a directory but
provides directory type
summary financial and
background information on
UK quoted and unquoted
companies

Extel Handbook of Market
Leaders
Published by Extel Financial
Ltd, London
Covers over 700 companies
listed in the FT actuaries
index

ICC Financial Surveys and
Company Directories
Published by ICC Information
Group Ltd, London.
Over 200 volumes, providing
ranking and financial details
for up to 1000 companies per
industry sector

Kelly's Manufacturers and
Merchants Directory
Published by Kelly's
Directories, East Grinstead
Covers 82 000 UK
manufacturers, wholesalers
and firms. Provides product
and contact details

Key British Enterprises
Produced by Dun &
Bradstreet Ltd, London
Provides financial and
background information on
the top 20 000 UK firms.

Kompass Register of British
Industry and Commerce
(also UK Kompass
Management Register UK
Trade Names)
Published by Kompass
Publishers, East Grinstead
Kompass Register is provided
in four volumes and covers
35000 companies, their
products and financial data

Macmillan's Unquoted
Companies
Published by Macmillan
Publishers Ltd
Covers 10 000 unquoted
companies. Provides financial
and trading details

Sell's Directory of Product
Services
Published by Sell's
Publications Ltd, Epsom
Lists 65 000 firms; 10 000 trade
names

Stock Exchange Official
Yearbook
Published by the Stock
Exchange, London
Provides financial and
background details for over
2000 quoted UK companies

The Times 1000
Published by Times Books
Ltd, London
Directory provides a ranking
of UK's top 1000 companies.
Financial and trading details
are provided. Also covers
financial institutions

Economic and Market Statistical Data

Market Research Organisations

AGB Financial Market
Research Ltd
410-420 Rayners Lane
Pinner
Middlesex HA5 5HG
Tel: 01-429 2000
Parent company: AGB
Research plc

Audits of Great Britain Ltd
AGB Research Centre
West Gate
London W5 1UA
Tel: 01-997 8484
Telex: 262251 AGB-G

BIS Marketing Research Ltd
Barry House
20-22 Worple Road
London SW19 4DH
Tel: 01-947 7411
Telex: 8813024

BJM Research Partners Group
Ltd
Lynton House
7-12 Tavistock Square
London WC1H 9QJ
Tel: 01-388 3191
Telex: 21328 BJMARMG

British Market Research
Bureau Ltd
53 The Mall
Ealing
London W5 3TE
Tel: 01-567 3060
Fax: 01-840 1655
Telex: 935526 MRBG

Burke Marketing Research
Ltd
Station House
Harrow Road
Wembley
Middlesex HA9 6DE
Tel: 01-903 1399
Telex: 923755 IPORES G

Business Decisions Ltd
24-30 Great Titchfield St
London W1P 7AD
Tel: 01-580 8061
Telex: 943763 CROCOM G

IFT Marketing Research Ltd
Ruxley Towers
Ruxley Ridge
Claygate
Esher
Surrey KT10 OUG
Tel: 0372-67311
Telex: 929993 EWPRO
Parent company: Gordon
Simmons Research Group

Independent Research
Bureau Ltd
101-111 High Road
London E18 2QP
Tel: 01-505 9211
Telex: 892181 DIAL G

Industrial Research Bureau
(IRB)
27 Greenholm Road
London SE9 1UQ
Tel: 01-850 0607
Telex: 8951761 BECK G

Makrotest Ltd
Sinclair House
The Avenue
London W13 8NT
Tel: 01-998 7733
Telex: 934821 MKRTST G

Market & Opinion Research
International (MORI)
32 Old Queen Street
London SW1H 9HP
Tel: 01-222 0232
Fax: 01-222 1653
Telex: 295230 MORI G

Marplan Ltd
5-13 Great Suffolk Street
London SE1 ONF
Tel: 01-928 1200

MAS Survey Ltd
25 Wellington Street
London WC2E 7DW
Tel: 01-240 2861

AC Nielsen Company Ltd
Nielsen House
London Road
Headington
Oxford OX3 9RX
Tel: 0865-64851
Telex: 83136 NIELOX G

NOP Market Research Ltd
Tower House
Southampton Street
London WC2E 7HN
Tel: 01-836 1511
Telex: 8953744 NOPRES G

Social Surveys (Gallup Poll)
Ltd
202 Finchley Road
London NW3 6BL
Tel: 01-794 0461

Taylor Nelson & Associates
Ltd
44-46 Upper High Street
Epsom
Surrey KT17 4QS
Tel: 03727-29688
Telex: 291561 VIASOS G

Organisations Providing Economic and Statistical Data

City University Business
School
Produce a publication called
Economic Review. Quarterly

Department of Trade and
Industry
Business Statistical Office
BSO Library
Government Buildings
Cardiff Road
Newport
Gwent NP9 1XG
Tel: 0633-222973
The DTI produce the Business
Monitor Series, which
provide data on industries
compiled from individual
companies returns within
each sector. These are
quarterly, monthly and
annual and can be ordered
from the address above or
through the HMSO (Her
Majesty's Stationery Office)
The DTI also publishes a
weekly magazine, British
Business, which provides
regular up-to-date statistics,
including direct investment
data, news items and trade
articles
Other publications:
Family Expenditure Survey
General Household Survey
National Income and
Expenditure (Blue Book)
Overseas Trade Statistics
Financial Statistics
Economic Progress Report
Economic Trends
Annual Abstract of Statistics
Monthly Digest of Statistics
Regional Trends
Social Trends

Department of Trade and
Industry (The)
Statistics and Market
Intelligence Library
1 Victoria Street
London SW1H OET
Tel: 01-215 5444
Provides access to trade
statistics and general
statistical publications from
all over the world

Department of Trade and
Industry
Offices in Scotland, Wales
and Northern Ireland:

Scottish Office
New St Andrew's House
Edinburgh EH1 3SX
Tel: 031-5568400

Welsh Office
Crown Building
Cathays Park
Cardiff CF1 3NQ
Tel: 0222-825111 Ext 825065
(Economic statistics)

Northern Ireland
Department of Economic
Development
Massey Avenue
Belfast BT4 2JP
Tel: 0232-233233

Press and Information Service
(The)
Central Office of Information
Great George Street
London SW1P 3AQ
Tel: 01-233 3000
Publishes Government
Statistics: A Brief Guide to
Sources, which provides
details of UK official statistical
publications.

HMSO Bookshop
49 High Holborn
London WC1V 6HB
Tel: 01-211 5656
UK Government publications
can be obtained from the
above address. One of the
most comprehensive sources
of information on official
publications available from
the HMSO is the CSO Guide
to Official Statistics.

Sources for Further Information on Government Statistics:

Sources of Unofficial UK
Statistics
D Mort and L Siddall
Published by Gower
Publishing Ltd, Aldershot,
Hants

Sources of Statistics and
Market Information
Produced by The Statistics
and Market Information
Ingelligence Library, London

Liverpool Macroeconomic
Research Ltd
Department of Economic and
Business Studies
University of Liverpool
PO Box 147
Liverpool L69 3BX
Tel: 051-709 6002
Publishes the Quarterly
Economic Bulletin, which
provides economic forecasts

London Business School
Sussex Place
Regents Park
London NW1 4SA
Tel: 01-262 5050
Centre for Economic
Forecasting
Publishes Economic Outlook.
This is available three times
per annum and provides
economic forecasts for the UK

National Institute of
Economic and Social Research
2 Dean Trench Street
London SW1P 3HE
Tel: 01-222 7665
Publish the National Institute
Economic Review.
Quarterly

Publications

Directories

Current British Directories
Published by CBD Research
Ltd, Kent, UK

Directory of British
Associations
Published by CBD Research
Ltd, Kent, UK
Provides information on
national associations,
societies, institutes and
similar organisations which
have a voluntary membership
in all fields of activity.
Coverage includes Scotland
and the Republic of Ireland

Government and Industry
A Business Guide to
Westminster, Whitehall and
Brussels
Published by Kluwer
Provides information and
contact details on Parliament,
Government, the Civil Service
and EC institutions

The Top 3000 Directories and
Annuals
Published by Alan Armstrong
& Associates Ltd, London
Provides listings of directories
covering both UK and
international information

Major Newspapers

Daily Express

Daily Mail

Daily Mirror

Daily Telegraph

Financial Times

Guardian (The)

Independent (The)

London Evening Standard
(The)

Times (The)

Observer (The)
Weekly

Sunday Express
Weekly

Sunday Telegraph
Weekly

Sunday Times
Weekly

Journals and Periodicals

Accountant (The)
Published by Lafferty
Publications Ltd, London.
Monthly

Accounting Age
Published by VNU Business
Publications, London.
Weekly

British Business
Published by the Department
of Trade and Industry,
London. Weekly

Business
Published by Business People
Publications Ltd, London.
Monthly

Business Information Review
Published by Headland Press,
Cleveland. Quarterly

Campaign
Paper serving the advertising
industry

Director
Published by Director
Publications Ltd, London.
Monthly

Economist (The)
Published by Economist
Newspapers Ltd, London
Provides UK and overseas
political and business news.
Weekly

Financial Weekly
Published by Financial
Weekly Ltd
Provides financial and general
business news

Investors's Chronicle
Published by FT Business
Information Ltd
Provides company data and
financial analysis. Weekly

Management Today
Published by Management
Publications Ltd, London

Money Management &
Unitholder
Published by FT Business
Information Ltd. Monthly

Money Observer
Published by the Observer
Ltd. Monthly

Money Week
Published by EMAP Business
& Computer Publications Ltd.
Weekly

For details of other business journals available consult Benn's Media Directory, published by Benn Information Services Ltd; Willings Press Guide published by British Media Publications; British Rate and Data (BRAD) published by British Rate and Data, London. BRAD is published every month, providing up-to-date information on press sources. Willings and Benn's directories are published annually and give details of newspapers, journals and publishers in the UK and overseas.

USA

Sources of Economic, Stock Market Information and Investment Research Services

Banks

Central Bank
Federal Reserve System
Board of Governors
Twentieth Street and
Constitution Avenue
North West Washington DC
20551

American Banks in London
Bank of America
25 Cannon Street
London EC4P 4HN
Tel: 01-634 4000

Bankers' Trust
Dashwood House
69 Old Broad Street
London EC2P 2EE
Tel: 01-726 4141

Chase Manhattan Bank
Woolgate House
Coleman Street
London EC2P 2HD
Tel: 01-726 5000

Citibank
PO Box 78
336 Strand
London WC2R 1HB
Tel: 01-240 1222

Citicorp Investment Bank
(Subsidiary of Citicorp)
335 Strand
London WC2R 1LS
Tel: 01-836 1230

Continental Illinois National
Bank and Trust
Co of Chicago
162 Queen Victoria Street
London EC4V 4BS
Tel: 01-236 7444

First National Bank of
Chicago
First Chicago House
90 Long Acre
Covent Garden
London WC2E 9RB
Tel: 01-240 7240

Manufacturers Hanover
(Subsidiary of Manufacturers
Hanover Trust)
7 Princes Street
London EC2P 2EN
Tel: 01-600 4585

Manufacturers Hanover Trust
7 Princes Street
London EC2P 2LR
Tel: 01-600 5666

Morgan Guaranty Trust
County of New York
1 Angel Court
London EC2R 7AE
Tel: 01-600 2300

Security Pacific National Bank
4 Broadgate
London EC2M 7LE
Tel: 01-588 0303

Security Houses in London
Bear, Stearns International
9 Devonshire Square
London EC2M 4YL
Tel: 01-626 5656
Telex: 8811424

Brown Brothers Harriman &
Co
Prince Rupert House
64 Queen Street
London EC4R 1AD
Tel: 01-248 2077
Telex: 8954033

Dean Witter Capital Markets
Internation
56 Leadenhall Street
London EC3A 2BH
Tel: 01-480 8500
Telex: 8956201

Dean Witter Reynolds Inc
56 Leadenhall Street
London EC3A 2BH
Tel: 01-480 8500
Telex: 8956201

Dillon, Read
Devonshire House
Mayfair Place
London W1X 5FH
Tel: 01-493 1239
Telex: 8811055

Dominick & Dominick
8 Little Trinity Lane
London EC4V 2AA
Tel: 01-236 6851
Telex: 885473

Donaldson, Lufkin and
Jenrette International
Jupiter House
Triton Court
14 Finsbury Square
London EC2A 1BR
Tel: 01-638 5822
Telex: 8811356

Drexel Burnham Lambert
Winchester House
77 London Wall
London EC2N 1BE
Tel: 01-920 9797
Telex: 884448

Eberstadt Fleming
25 Copthall Avenue
London EC2R 7DR
Tel: 01-374 0961
Telex: 297451

Fahnestock & Co
Roman House
Wood Street
London EC2Y 5BA
Tel: 01-588 5892
Telex: 888358

First Boston Corp
24 Great Titchfield Street
London W1P 7AA
Tel: 01-322 4500
Telex: 884211

First Interstate Capital
Markets
First Interstate House
6 Agar Street
London WC2H 4HN
Tel: 01-379 5915
Telex: 947161

First National Boston
39 Victoria Street
London SW1
Tel: 01-799 3333
Telex: 886705

Gintel & Co
31-35 Fenchurch Street
London EC3M 3DX
Tel: 01-626 5522
Telex: 8952472

Goldman Sachs International
Corp
5 Old Bailey
London EC4M 7AH
Tel: 01-248 6464
Telex: 887902

Hambrecht & Quist
International
8 Queen Street
London EC4N 1SP
Tel: 01-248 6306
Telex: 8812303

EF Hutton & Co (London)
EF Hutton & Co (Securities)
152-156 Upper Thames Street
London EC4R 3UH
Tel: 01-623 0800
Telex: 884735

Jesup & Lamont International
Pembroke House
40 City Road
London EC1Y 2AX
Tel: 01-253 3810
Telex: 24423

Kidder, Peabody Securities
Kidder, Peabody
International
Kidder, Peabody & Co
107 Cheapside
London EC2V 6DD
Tel: 01-480 8200
Telex: 884694

Kitcat Aitken & Safran
71 Queen Victoria Street
London EC4V 4DE
Tel: 01-588 8981
Telex: 888297

Mabon Nugent International
3rd Floor
Lloyds Chambers
1 Portsoken Street
London E1 8DS
Tel: 01-488 9291
Telex: 8952807

Mellon Securities
6 Devonshire Square
London EC2M 4LB
Tel: 01-220 7073
Telex: 8812182

Merrill Lynch Europe
27 Finsbury Square
London EC2A 1AQ
Tel: 01-382 8000
Telex: 8811047

Morgan Guaranty
30 Throgmorton Street
London EC2N 2NT
Tel: 01-600 7545
Telex: 8954804

Morgan Stanley International
Kingsley House
1 Wimpole Street
London W1M 7AA
Tel: 01-709 3000
Telex: 8812564

Oppenheimer & Co
Stockley House
130 Wilton Road
London SW1V 1LQ
Tel: 01-834 8088
Telex: 915152

Paine Webber International
1 Finsbury Avenue
London EC2M 2PA
Tel: 01-377 0055
Telex: 297361

Prudential-Bache Securities
(UK)
9 Devonshire Square
London EC2M 4HP
Tel: 01-283 9166
Telex: 8956411

LF Rothschild & Co
International
Parkgate
21 Tothill Street
London SW1H 9LL
Tel: 01-222 1212
Telex: 922922

Salomon Brothers
International
Victoria Plaza
111 Buckingham Palace Road
London SW1W OSB
Tel: 01-721 2000
Telex: 886441

Shearson Lehman Brothers
International
1 Broadgate
London EC2M 7HA
Tel: 01-601 0111
Telex: 888881

Smith Barney & Co
Brewers Hall
Aldermanbury Square
London EC2V 7HR
Tel: 01-600 5633
Telex: 886595

Smith Barney, Harris Upham
International
18 Finsbury Circus
London EC2M 7AQ
Tel: 01-588 6040
Telex: 893486

Swiss American Securities
24 Bishopsgate
London EC2N 4BQ
Tel: 01-283 2284
Telex: 928291

Thomson McKinnon
Securities
Greenly House
40 Dukes Place
London EC3A 5HJ
Tel: 01-626 1511
Telex: 884562

Tucker Anthony & RL Day
15 St Helen's Place
London EC3A 6DE
Tel: 01-588 1451
Telex: 886306

Wertheim Securities
55 London Wall
London EC2M 5TP
Tel: 01-638 8243
Telex: 8813511

Wertheim Schroeder
International
120 Cheapside
London EC2V 6DS
Tel: 01-600 0256
Telex: 8812025

Major American Banks

Bank of America
Bank of America Center
555 California Street
San Francisco
California 94104
Tel: (010 1) 415-622 3456
Telex: RCA 27248

Bank of Boston
767 Fifth Avenue
New York NY 10153
Tel: (010 1) 212-350 0300
Telex: 420676

Bankers Trust Company
16 Wall Street
New York NY 10005
Tel: (010 1) 212-775 2500
Telex: ITT 420066

Chase Manhattan Bank (The)
1 Chase Manhattan Plaza
New York NY 10081
Tel: (010 1) 212-552 2222
Telex: RCA 232163

Citibank NA
399 Park Avenue
New York NY 10022
Tel: (010 1) 212-559 1000
Telex: 347

Continental Illinois National
Bank and Trust Company of
Chicago
231 South LaSalle Street
Chicago
IL 60697
Tel: (010 1) 312-828 2345
Telex: 025233

First National Bank of Boston
(The)
100 Federal Street
Boston
Mass 02110
Tel: (010 1) 617-434 2200
Telex: 940581

First National Bank of
Chicago (The)
1 First National Plaza
Chicago
IL 60670
Tel: (010 1) 312-732 5965
Telex: 4330253

Manufacturers Hanover Trust
Co
270 Park Avenue
New York
NY 10017
Tel: (010 1) 212-286 6000
Telex: 232337

Morgan Guaranty Trust
Company of New York
23 Wall Street
New York
NY 10015
Tel: (010 1) 212-483 2323
Telex: TWX 710-581-4040

Stockbrokers

The nine main Stock
Exchanges in the USA are the
American, Boston,
Cincinnati, Midwest, New
York, Pacific, Philadelphia,
Intermountain and Spokane
Stock Exchanges.

American Stock Exchange
86 Trinity Place
New York NY 10006
Tel: (010 1) 212-3061000
Telex: 129297

New York Stock Exchange
11 Wall Street
New York NY 10005
Tel: (010 1) 212-656 3000

National Association of
Securities Dealers Inc
1735 K Street NW
Washington DC 20006
Tel: (010 1) 202-728 8000

Selection of Major Brokers

Henry Ansbacher Inc
277 Park Avenue
New York NY 10172
Tel: (010 1) 212-688 5544

Bear, Stearns & Co
55 Water Street
New York NY 10041
Tel: (010 1) 212-952 5000

Standford C Bernstein & Co
Inc
767 Fifth Avenue
New York NY 10153
Tel: (010 1) 212-486 5800

Alex Brown & Sons Inc
63 Wall Street
New York NY 10005
Tel: (010 1) 212-747 0960

Brown Brothers Harriman &
Co
59 Wall Street
New York NY 10005
Tel: (010 1) 212-483 1818

Dean Witter Reynolds Inc
130 Liberty Street
New York NY 10006
Tel: (010 1) 212-524 2222

Dillon Read & Co Inc
535 Madison Avenue
New York NY 10022
Tel: (010 1) 212-906 7000

Donaldson, Lufkin & Jenrette
Securities Corp
140 Broadway
New York NY 10005
Tel: (010 1) 212-902 2000

Drexel Burnham Lambert Inc
60 Broad Street
New York NY 10004
Tel: (010 1) 212-480 6000

First Boston Corporation
(The)
Park Avenue Plaza
New York NY 10055
Tel: (010 1) 212-909 2000

Goldman, Sachs & Co
85 Broad Street
New York NY 10004
Tel: (010 1) 212-902 1000

EF Hutton & Co Inc
1 Battery Park Plaza
New York NY 10004
Tel: (010 1) 212-742 5000

Kidder, Peabody & Co Inc
10 Hanover Square
New York NY 10005
Tel: (010 1) 212-747 2000

Merrill Lynch Capital Markets
1 Liberty Plaza
165 Broadway
New York NY 10080
Tel: (010 1) 212-637 7455

Morgan Stanley & Co Inc
1251 Avenue of the Americas
New York NY 10020
Tel: (010 1) 212-974 4000

Oppenheimer & Co Inc
1 New York Plaza
New York NY 10004
Tel: (010 1) 212-825 4000

Paine Webber Inc
140 Broadway
New York NY 10005
Tel: (010 1) 212-437 2121

Prudential-Bache Securities
100 Gold Street
New York NY 10292
Tel: (010 1) 212-791 1000

LF Rothschild, Unterberg,
Towbin
55 Water Street
New York NY 10041
Tel: (010 1) 212-425 3300

Salomon Brothers Inc
1 New York Plaza
New York NY 10004
Tel: (010 1) 212-747 7000

Shearson Lehman Brothers
Inc
2 World Trade Centre
New York NY 10048
Tel: (010 1) 212-321 6000

Smith Barney, Harris Upham
& Co Inc
1345 Avenue of the Americas
New York NY 10105
Tel: (010 1) 212-399 6000

Sources of General Background Information, Industry Sector Information and Trade Contacts

UK Addresses

British American Chamber of
Commerce (The)
19 Stratford Place
Suite 311
London W1N 9AF
Tel: 01-491 3361
Fax: 01-493 8280
Telex: 291429 NETNYN G

American Embassy
Grosvenor Square
London W1A 1AE
Tel: 01-499 9000

American Embassy
US International Marketing
Centre
(address as above)
Tel: 01-629 4304

American Embassy
US Information Service
55/56 Upper Brook Street
London W1A 2LH
Tel: 01-499 9000

American Chamber of
Commerce (UK)
75 Brook Street
London W1Y 2EB
Tel: 01-493 0381
Telex: 23675 AMCHAM G

Addresses in the USA

British American Chamber of
Commerce (The)
275 Madison Avenue
New York NY 10016
Tel: (010 1) 212-889 0680
Fax: (010 1) 212-683 0621

British Embassy (The)
3100 Mass Avenue NW
Washington DC 20008
Tel: (010 1) 202-4621340
Fax: (010 1) 202-8984255

US Chamber of Commerce
(The)
1615 H St NW
16th Floor
Washington DC 20062
Tel: (010 1) 202-463 5478
Telex: 248302

Professional Associations

Accountancy
American Accounting
Association
653 S Orange Avenue
Sarasota
FL 33577

American Institute of
Certified Public Accountants
1211 Avenue of the Americas
New York NY 10019

National Association of
Accountants
919 Third Avenue
New York NY 10022

Banking
American Bankers
Association
1120 Connecticut Avenue NW
Washington DC 20036
Tel: (010 1) 202-467 4000
Telex: 892787

American Institute of Banking
1120 Connecticut Avenue NW
Washington DC 20036

Consultancy
Association of Management
Consulting Firms (The)
(ACME)
230 Park Avenue
New York NY 10169
Tel: (010 1) 212-697 9693

Insurance
American Insurance
Association
85 John Street
New York NY 10038
Tel: (010 1) 212-669 0533

Insurance Information
Institute
110 William Street
New York NY 10038
Tel: (010 1) 212-644 2100

Marketing

American Advertising
Federation
1225 Connecticut Avenue NW
Washington DC 20036

American Marketing
Association
222 South Riverside Plaza
Suite 606
Chicago IL 60606

Marketing Research
Association
111 East Wacker Drive
Suite 600
Chicago IL 60601

Trade Associations

American Apparel
Manufacturers Association
1611 North Kent Street
Arlington
VA 22209

American Automobile
Association
8111 Gatehouse
Falls Church VA 22042

American Imported
Automobile Dealers
Association
1220 19th Street NW
Washington DC 20036

American Paper Institute
216 Madison Avenue
New York NY 10016

American Petroleum Institute
2101 L St NW
Washington DC 20037

American Society of
Mechanical Engineers
345 E 47th Street
New York NY 10017

American Textile
Manufacturers Institute
400 S Tryon St
Suite 2124
Charlotte
NC 28285

American Wood Council
1619 Massachusetts Avenue
NW
Washington DC 20036

Associated Builders and
Contractors
444 N Capital St
Washington DC 20001

Association of Home
Appliance Manufacturers
20 N Wacker Drive
Chicago
IL 60606

Chemical Marketing Research
Association
139 Chestnut Avenue
Staten Island
New York NY 10305

Chemical Specialities
Manufacturing Associations
1001 Connecticut Avenue
Washington DC 20036

Electronic Industries
Association
2001 Eye St NW
Washington DC 20006

Food Marketing Institute
1750 K St NW
Washington DC 20006

International
Communications Association
Box 836
Austin TX 77401

Metallurgical Society
345 E 47th Street
New York NY 10017

Mining and Metallurgical
Society of America
230 Park Avenue
Rm 1352
New York NY 10017

National Association of
Electric Companies
1140 Connecticut Avenue NW
Washington DC 20036

National Association of
Furniture Manufacturers
8401 Connecticut Avenue
Suite 911
Washington DC 20015

National Association of Real
Estate Brokers
1025 Vermont Avenue NW
Suite 1111
Washington DC 20005

National Association of Retail
Grocers of the US
Sunrise Valley
Dr Reston VA 22090

Society of Cable Television
Engineers
1523 O St NW
Washington DC 20005

Company Financial and Product Information

Directories
America's Corporate Families
and International Affiliates
Published by Dun &
Bradstreet

Billion Dollar Directory –
America's Corporate Families
Published by Dun &
Bradstreet

Dun's Business Rankings
Published by Dun's
Marketing Services, NJ
Provides ranking for the top
7500 US companies

MacRae's Blue Book
Published by MacRae's, New
York
Provides directory details for
original equipment market
companies

Million Dollar Directory
Published by Dun's
Marketing Services, NJ
Provides directory details for
over 160 000 US businesses

Moody's Public Utility Manual and News Reports
Moody's Municipal and Government News Reports
Moody's Bank and Finance Manual and News Reports
Moody's Industrial Manual and News Reports
Moody's International Manual and News Reports
Moody's Industry Review
Published by Moody's Investors' Service

Reference Book of Corporate Management
America's Corporate Leaders
Published by Dun & Bradstreet

Standard & Poor's Register of Corporations
Published by Standard and Poor's
Consists of 3 volumes. Covers over 45 000 corporations. Provides financial details and names of executives

Thomas Register of American Manufacturers, Thomas Register Catalog File
Published by Thomas Publishing Company, New York
Covers over 1 350 000 companies

US & Canadian Reference Books
Published by Dun & Bradstreet

Ward's Business Directory
Published by Information Access Company, Belmont CA
Three volumes. Covers the largest US public and private companies. Also includes major international companies

Economic and Market Statistical Data

Market Research Organisations

Burke International Research
800 Broadway
Cincinnati
OH 45202
Tel: (010 1) 513-3818898

Business Research Associates
Suite 2013
215 Park Avenue South
New York NY 10013
Tel: (010 1) 212-3539051
Telex: 382026 BUSRES UD
Fax: (010 1) 212-3539063

Business Science International Inc (BSI)
270 Sylvan Avenue
Englewood Cliffs NJ 07632
Tel: (010 1) 201-8710999

CRC Information Systems Inc
435 Hudson Street
New York NY 10014
Tel: (010 1) 212-6205678

Crossley Surveys
275 Madison Avenue
New York NY 10016
Tel: (010 1) 212-6929320

Custom Research Inc
10301 Wayzata Boulevard
PO Box 26695
Minneapolis
MN 554260695
Tel: (010 1) 612-5420800
Divisions include: Custom Research International, Custom Research Telephone

Data Development Corporation
600 Third Avenue
New York NY 10016
Tel: (010 1) 212-8672440

Full Line Research Inc
315 Walt Whitman Road
Huntington Station
New York NY 11746
Tel: (010 1) 516-4231216

Gallup Organisation Inc (The)
53 Bank Street
Princeton NJ 08542
Tel: (010 1) 609-9249600

Harvey Research Organisation Inc
1400 Temple Building
Rochester NY 14604
Tel: (010 1) 716-2324268

Heller Research Corp (The)
358 Main Street
Port Washington
NY 11050
Tel: (010 1) 516-8834521
(010 1) 212-7320960

Lieberman Research Inc
1140 Avenue of the Americas
New York NY 10036
Tel: (010 1) 212-3061800

Prognos AG
3000 Sand hill Road
Building 1-230
Menlo Park
California 94025
Tel: (010 1) 415-8549833
Fax: (010 1) 415-8549837

Research International
205 Lexington Avenue
New York NY 10016
Tel: (010 1) 212-6792500

Russell Marketing Research Inc
152 East 71st Street
New York NY 10021
Tel: (010 1) 212-8793350

Sherman Group Inc (The)
10 Village Square
Glen Cove NY 11542
Tel: (010 1) 516-6761410

Daniel Yankelovich Group Inc (The)
1350 Avenue of the Americas
New York NY 10019
Tel: (010 1) 212-2471313

Organisations Providing Economic and Statistical Data

Bureau of the Census
Washington DC
Publishes Statistical Abstract of the United States

Bureau of Economic Analysis
US Department of Commerce
14th Street between
Constitution Avenue and E St
NW
Washington DC 20230
Tel: (010 1) 202 377 3263
Main publications are the
Business Conditions Digest,
Business Statistics, Survey of
Current Business

Bureau of Industrial
Economics
Department of Commerce
Washington DC
Publishes US Industrial
Outlook

Council of Economic Advisors
Executive Office of the
President
Publishes Economic
Indicators

Economics Statistics Bureau
of Washington
Washington DC
Publishes the Handbook of
Basic Economics Statistics

NASDAQ produces a fact
book providing financial
statistics

New York Stock Exchange
Publishes Fact Book,
Common Stocks Listed,
Common Stocks Indexes

US Federal Government
Statistics can be traced using
the Congressional
Information Service,
American Statistics Index

Publications

Directories
ACME Inc – The Association
of Management Consulting
Firms
Directory of members
ACME, New York
Provides information on
ACME and a directory of
member US consulting firms

American Association of
Exportes
ACME, New York
Provides information on
ACME and a directory of
member US consulting firms

American Association of
Exportes
ACME, New York
Provides information on
ACME and a directory of
member US consulting firms

American Association of
Exporters and Importers
Membership Directory
Published by the American
Association of Exporters and
Importers, New York

American Export Register
Published by Thomas
International Publications
Company, New York

American Library Directory
Provides listings of US and
Canadian libraries
Published by Bowker
Publishing Company, Ann
Arbor

Consultants and Consulting
Organisations Directory
Published by Gale Research
Company, Detroit

Directory of Directories
Published by Gale Research
Company, Detroit
Provides details of over 10 000
directory titles

Directory of Special Libraries
and Information Centres
Published by Gale Research
Company, Detroit

Encyclopedia of Business
Information Sources
Published by Gale Research
Company, Detroit
Covers many types of
information sources including
electronic, print and
organisational sources

Encyclopedia of
Governmental Advisory
Organisations
Published by Gale Research
Company, Detroit

Federal Database Finder
Published by Information
USA, Washington DC
Directory of free and
fee-based databases available
from the US federal
government

Federal Statistical Directory:
The Guide to Personnel and
Data Sources
Published by Oryx Press,
Phoenix, Arizona

Federal Yellow Book
Published by Graham and
Trotman
Directory of USA federal
government departments and
independent agencies

National Directory of State
Agencies
Published by National
Standards Association,
Bethesda, MD

Official Export Guide
Published by North American
Publishing Company,
Philadelphia

Research Services Directory
Published by Gale Research
Company, Detroit
Guide to over 3400 firms,
laboratories and individuals
in the private sector providing
contract or fee based research
services

Major Newspapers

New York
Daily News
Daily

Journal of Commerce
Daily

New York City Tribune
Daily

New York Post
Daily

New York Times
Daily

New York Times Magazine
Weekly

Wall Street Journal (The)
Daily

World
Daily

Survey of Current Business
Published by the Bureau of
Economic Analysis,
Washington DC. Monthly

Wall Street Journal Magazine
Publisher's address:
22 Cortland Street
New York NY 10007

Journals and Periodicals

Barrons
Published by Dow-Jones
Finance and investment
newspaper, providing
company reviews and stock
market statistics. Weekly

Business Week
Published by McGraw Hill
Leading US business
magazine. Provides
company, industry and
economic news. Weekly

Forbes
Published by Forbes Inc
Covers features on
companies, industries, and
finance. Fortnightly

Fortune
Published by Time Inc
Covers the US economy,
marketing, industry, business
policy and corporate profiles.
Provides an annual ranking of
US manufacturing and service
companies. Monthly

Harvard Business Review
Academic business magazine.
Covers business theory and
strategy amongst other areas.
Bi-monthly

Institutional Investor
Published by Capital Cities
Comms Inc, New York.
Monthly

Money
Published by Time Inc, New
York. Monthly

Moody's Handbook of
Common Stocks
Published by Moody's.
Monthly

4 Industry Data Sources

Chemicals

Trade Associations

International

International Association of
Chemical Expertise
1 rue Gabriel-Vicaire
75003 Paris
France
Tel: (010 33) 1-48875363

International Centre for
Chemical Studies
Univerza Edvarda
Kardeljaljubljani
Trg Osvodboditve 11
Ljublijana
Yugoslavia

Europe

Conseil Europeen des
Federations de l'Industrie
Chimique (CCEFIC)
Avenue Louise
Bte 71
1050 Brussels
Belgium
Tel: (010 32) 2-6402095
Telex: 62444 CEFIC B
Fax: (010 32) 2-6401981

Austria

Fachverband der Chemischen
Industrie Osterreichs (FCIO)
Wiedner Haupstrasse, 63
Postfach 325
1045 Vienna
Tel: (010 43) 1-22265050
Telex: 111871 BUK A

Belgium

Federation des Industries
Chimiques de Belgique (FIC)
Square Marie-Louise, 49
1040 Brusse Is
Tel: (010 32) 2-2304090
Telex: 23167 FECHIM B

Denmark

Foreningen af Danske
Kemiske Industries (FDKI)
Okesmosen – 9
OK-2840 Holle Copenhagen
Tel: (010 45) 2-424088

Ireland, Republic of

Federation of Irish Chemical
Industries (FICI)
13 Fitzwilliam Square
Dublin 2
Tel: (0001) 765116
Telex: 33212 FICI EI

Finland

Chemical Industry Federation
of Finland
Hietaniemen Katu 2
PL 359
00101 Helsinki
Tel: (010 358) 0-447122
Telex: 124890 KKLRX SF
Fax: (010 358) 0-447960

France

Union des Industries
Chimiques (UIC)
Avenue Marceau, 64
75008 Paris
Tel: (010 33) 1-47205603
Telex: 630611 CHIMUNI F
Fax: (010 33) 1-47204869

Germany, Federal Republic of

Verband der Chemischen
Industrie e. V (VCI)
Karlserasse, 21
Postfach 11 1943
6000 Frankfurt 11
Tel: (010 49) 69-22561
Telex: 411372 VCIF D
Fax: (010 49) 69-2556471

Italy

Federazione Nazionale
dell'Industria Chimica
(Federchimica)
Via Academia 33
20131 Milan
Tel: (010 39) 2-63621
Telex: 332488 FECHIM
Fax: (010 39) 2-8135800764

Netherlands

Vereniging Van de
Nederlandse Chemische
Industrie (VNCI)
Vlietwey, 14
2260 AK Leidschendam
Tel: (010 31) 70-209233
Telex: 31320 VNCI NL

Norway

Norjes Kjemiske
Industrigruppe (NKI)
Drammensveien, 40
POB 2435 solli
N 0202 Oslo 2
Tel: (010 47) 2-437000
Telex: 71434 NORIN N
Fax: (010 47) 2-390108

Portugal

Associacao Purtuguesa das
Empresas Industrias de
Produc Quimicos (APEIPQ)
Avenida D Carlos 1-45-3
Lisbon 2
Tel: (010 351) 1-606796
Telex: 18721 APEIPQ

Spain

Federacion Empresarial de la
Industria Quimica Espanola
(FEIQUE)
Hermosilla 31-1 dcha
28001 Madrid
Tel: (010 34) 1-4317964
Telex: 45960 FEIQ E

Sweden

Sveriges Kemoka
Industrikontor (SKI)
Storgaran, 19
Box 5501
11485 Stockholm
Tel: (010 46) 8-7838000
Telex: 19990 SWED IND S
Fax: (010 46) 8-636323

Switzerland

Schweizerische Gesellschaft
fur Chemische Industrie
(SGCI/SSIC)
Nordstrasse, 15
Postfach 328
8035 Zurich
Tel: (010 41) 1-3631030
Telex: 52872 CHIMICH

UK

Chemical Industries
Association Ltd
Kings Buildings
Smith Square
London SW1P 3JJ
Tel: 01-834 3399
Telex: 916672
Fax: 01-834-4469

USA

Chemical Manufacturers
Association (CMA)
2501 M Street NW
Washington DC 20037
Tel: (010 1) 202-6590060
Telex. WVT 89617 CMA WSH

Synthetic Organic Chemical
Manufacturers Association,
Inc
1330 Connecticut Avenue W
Suite 300
Washington DC 20036
Tel: (010 1) 202-6590060

Australia

Australian Chemical Industry
Council (ACIC)
130 Albert Road
South Melbourne
Victoria 3205
Tel: (010 61) 3-6996299
Telex: 37754 ACIC AA
Fax: (010 61) 3-6996717

Canada

Canadian Manufacturers of
Chemicals Association
Suite 710
116 Street
Ottawa
Ontario K1P 563

New Zealand

New Zealand Chemical
Industry Council, Inc
PO Box 27-189
8th Floor, Cumberland House
235-237 Willis Street
Wellington
Tel: (010 64) 4-842607

South America

Argentina

Camara de la Industria
Quimica Y Petroquimica
14th Floor
Avenida Leandro N Alem
Buenos Aires
Tel: (010 54) 1-3117732
(010 54) 1-3130944

Brazil

Associacao Brasileira da
Industria Quimica ede
Produtos Derivados
(ABIQUIM)
Rua Santo Antonio, 184-17/18
Andaris
01314 Sao Paulo SP
Tel: (010 55) 11-373481
Telex: 31460 ABIQ BR

South East Asia

India

Indian Chemical
Manufacturers Association
India Exchange Place
Calcutta 700 001
Tel: (010 91) 33-204136
Telex: 217432 ISMA IN

Japan

Japan Chemical Industry
Association
Tokyo Club Building, 4th
Floor
2-6 Kasumiga seki: 3 Chome
Chiyoda Ku
Tokyo
Tel: (010 81) 3-5800751
Telex: 23557 JCIA J
Fax: (010 81) 3-5800764

Directories

International

Chemical Company Profiles
Covers Africa, Asia,
Australasia, Western Europe
IPC Industrial Press
London
UK

Chemical Plant Contractor
Profiles
Chemical Intelligence
Services
London
UK

Chemical Research Faculties –
an international directory
American Chemical Society
Washington DC
USA

Directory of World Chemical
Producers
Chemical Information
Services
Oceanside, New York
USA

Facts and Figures about the
World's Biggest Paint
Manufacturers
KC Luyber, Amsterdam
Netherlands

World Chemistry Industry
Yearbook, 1987
Chemical Industries
Association
London
UK

Worldwide Petrochemical
Directory
Pennwell Publishing
Oklahoma
USA

Europe

Annual Review of the
Chemical Industry
United Nations (covers
Europe)
HMSO Books
London
UK

Chemfacts
Surveys of products and
producers in
Belgium, Germany, France.
Italy, Netherlands,
Portugal, Scandinavia, Spain
and the UK
Chemical Intelligence
Services
London
UK

Chemical Sources Europe
Chemical Services Europe
Mountain Lakes, New Jersey
USA

Directory of Chemical
Producers, Western Europe
SRI International
California
USA

Directory of West European
Chemical Producers
Chemical Information
Services
New York

European Chemical Buyers
Guide
IPC Business Press
London
UK

Austria
Handbuch der Chemischen
Industrie
Osterreichs
Fachverband der Chemischen
Industrie
Osterreichs
Vienna

France
Butane – Propane
Guide Repertoire
JAM
Paris

France – Plastiques: annuaire
officel des plastiques
Creations editions et
Productions Publicitaires
Paris

Guide du Syndicat Generale
des Commerces et Industries
du Caoutchouc et des
Plastiques
APROCAP
Paris

Syndicat National du
Caoutchouc, des Plastiques et
des Industries qui s'y
Rattachent (Annual)
Michael Bongrand SA
Paris

**Germany, Federal
Republic of**
Firmerhandbuch Chemische
Industrie
(Information on
manufacturers and
wholesalers,
plus products)
Editors: Verband der
Chemischen Industrie
Publishers: Egon Verlag
Dusseldorf

Kunststoffe – Plastics
Bezugsquellervegister
Vogt-Schild AG
Solothurn

Netherlands
Handboek voor de
Nederlandse Chemische
Industrie
Samson
Alphen a/d Rijn

Spain
Guia Catalogo Plasticos
Espanoles
Guide Catalogue of Spanish
Plastics
Agrupacion Nacional de
Plasticos

Plastico Espanoles
Asociacion Espanola de
Industriales de Plasticos
Madrid

Scandinavia
Buyers Guide to Plastics
Foreningen Sveriges
Plastfabrikanter
Stockholm

Index of Chemical
Manufacturers in Finland
Kemian Keskushitto
Helsinki

Skandinavisk Plastindustri
Okonomisk Literatur, A/S
Oslo

Sweden's Chemical Industry
A directory of manufacturers
and products
Kemikontoret
Stockholm

Australia
Australian Plastics and
Rubbers Buyers Guide
IPC Business Press
Sydney

UK
British Association for
Chemical Specialities
Directory of members,
products and services
Chemical Industries
Association
London

British Chemical Engineering
Contractors Association
Directory of the BCECA
London

British Plastics Federation
Buyers Guide
London

Buyers Guide to Plastics
Materials and Machinery and
Equipment for the Plastics
Industry
British Plastics Federation
London

Chemical Industry Directory
and Who's Who
Benn Business Information
Services
Tonbridge
Kent

Directory of Consulting
Practices in Chemical and
Related
Subjects
Royal Institute of Chemistry
London

EOACS: Equipment Selector
and Classified Directory for
the Chemical, Food and
Allied Process Industries
EDACS Data Ltd
Bournemouth

Financial Times Industrial
Companies: Chemicals
Longman Group
London

Institution of Chemical
Engineers: List of Consultants
Institution of Chemical
Engineers
Rugby

Plastics in Building: Index of
Applications and Suppliers
British Plastics Federation
London

Plastics Industry Directory
Maclaren
London

Where to Buy Chemicals and
Chemical Plant
Where to Buy
London

USA
Chem Sources USA
Directories Publishing Co
Flemington, NJ

Chem Suppliers Directory
de Gruyter
Berlin, New York

Chemical Guide to the United
States (7th edition)
Noyes Park Ridge, NJ

Chemical Week: Buyers
Guide
McGraw-Hill
New York

OPD Chemical Buyers
Directory
Schnell Publishing Co
New York

Plastics: Desk-top Data Bank
Cordura
San Diego, California

Canada
Canadian Plastics Directory
and Buyers' Guide
Southam
Don Mills, Ontario

Israel
Israel Chemical Industry:
Background and
Development
Ministry of Industry
Jerusalem

Israel Plastics Manufacturers
Directory
Israel Periodicals Co
Tel Aviv

South East Asia

India
Indian Chemical Directory,
11th edition
Technical Press Publications
Bombay

Indian Plastics Guide
Astra
Bombay

Japan
JC Chemicals Guide
The Chemical Daily Co
Tokyo

Market Research Reports

This section lists recently
published market research
reports which cover various
aspects of the chemical
industry. Details provided are
title of report, publisher, year
of publication, price and
geographic coverage.

Adhesives
Key Note Publications Ltd
(UK)
1988
£105
UK

Antioxidants
The Freedonia Group Inc
(USA)
1988
$800
USA

Antioxidants: Markets,
Materials
Business Communications Co
(USA)
1987
$1750
USA

Biotechnology Products
Key Note Publications Ltd
(UK)
1988
£105
UK

Britain's Plastics Industry
Jordan & Sons Ltd (UK)
1987
£125
UK

Catalysts
The Freedonia Group Inc
(USA)
1988
$800
USA

Chem-Facts: Polyethylene
Chemical Intelligence
Services (UK)
1987
Price on request
Worldwide

Chem-Facts: Polypropylene
Chemical Intelligence
Services (UK)
1988
Price on request
Worldwide

Chem-Facts: United Kingdom

Chemical Intelligence
Services (UK)
1987
Price on request
UK

Chem-Facts: West Germany
Chemical Intelligence
Services (UK)
1988
Price on request
West Germany

Chemical Manufacturers and
Distributors
ICC Financial Surveys (UK)
1987
£185
UK

Chemical Process Economics
Chem Systems International
Ltd (UK)
1988
£7,500
Worldwide

Chemicals – Process
Evaluation and Chem
Systems
International Ltd (UK)
Annually
$26,000
Worldwide

Chemicals for the Detergent
Industry
Business Communications Co
(USA)
1987
$1750
USA

Chemicals for the
Semiconductor Industry
Business Communications Co
(USA)
1988
$1750
USA

Custom Chemical Synthesis
IAL Consultants Ltd (UK)
1987
£95
France

Dry Batteries
Key Note Publications Ltd
(UK)
1987
£105
UK

Dyes & Organic Pigments
The Freedonia Group Inc
(USA)
1988
$800
USA

Electronic Chemicals
IAL Consultants Ltd (UK)
1987
£1125
UK

Electronic Chemicals
IAL Consultants Ltd (UK)
1988
£1125
France

Ethylene Oxide & Derivatives
The Freedonia Group Inc
(USA)
1988
$800
USA

European Market for
Industrial Cleaning
Chemicals
Industrial Market Research
Ltd (UK)
1987
Price on request
Europe

Fertilizer Outlook
The Freedonia Group Inc
(USA)
1988
$1700
USA

Future for Plastic Pipe
Systems in Construction and
Civil Engineering
Corporate Development
Consultants Ltd (UK)
1988
£5500
W Europe. UK

Household Cleaning Products

Key Note Publications Ltd
(UK)
1988
£105
UK

Industrial and Institutional
Cleaners
Business Trend Analysts
(USA)
1987
$695
USA

Metal Finishing Chemicals
The Freedonia Group (USA)
1988
$800
USA

Mineral and Fibre Re-inforced
Thermoplastic
Corporate Development
Consultants Ltd (UK)
1987
£5000
W Europe

Oil Field Chemicals
The Freedonia Group Inc
(USA)
1988
$800
USA

Photographic Chemicals
The Freedonia Group Inc
(USA)
1988
$800
USA

Plastic Additives
The Freedonia Group Inc
(USA)
1988
$1700
USA

Plastics Processing
Key Note Publications Ltd
(UK)
1987
£105
UK

Speciality Agricultural
Chemicals
Business Communications Co
(USA)
1987
$1950
USA

Structural and Specialty
Adhesives
Business Communications Co
(USA)
1988
$1750
USA

Water Treatment Chemicals
IAL Consultants Ltd (UK)
1987
£200
UK

Periodicals and Journals

International & Pan European

Analytical Chemistry
Chemic Arlagen & Verfahren Europe
Chemical and Engineering News
Chemical Industry
Chemical Products International
Chemical Week
Chemical Plants & Processing
Chemische Industrie International
Computer Applications in the Laboratory (CAL)
CPI Purchasing
European Chemical News
European Plastics News
Hydrocarbon Processing International Edition
International Lab-Deck
International Labmatic
Journal of the Chemical Society
Laboratory Products Technololgy
Manufacturing Chemist & Aerosol News
UK Direct Information Service
UK Lab-Deck

Belgium

Bulletin des Societies Chimiques Belges
Chemie Magazine Chimie Magazine

Denmark

Archiv for Pharmaci og Chemi
Dansk Kemi (Chemical Industry)
Farg och Lack Scandinavia
Plast Nyt
Plast Panorama Scandinavia (Plastics)
Plastics

Finland

Kemia-Kemi (Chemical Industry)
Kemikalikauppias (Cosmetics & Perfumery)

France

L'Actualite Chimique
Analusis (Chemicals)
Annales de Chimie

Biochimie
Bulletin de la Societe Chimique de France
Chimie Catalogue des Achats
Chimie Magazine
Informations Chimie
Porphyre

Germany, Federal Republic

Aerosol Report (German, French, English)
Angwandte Chemie (Chemical)
CAL-Computeranwendung im Labor
Chemical Plants & Processing (English/German)
Chemie Anlagen und Verfahren (Chemical Industry)
Chemie-Ingenieur Technik (Chemical Engineers)
Chemie in Unserer Zeit (Chemistry)
Chemie-Technik
Chemiker Industrie
CLB
Die Chemische Produktion
Europa-chemie (Chemicals)
G-I-T (Laboratory Equipment)
Labo (Chemicals Industry)
Labo Cards
Die Makromolekulave Chemie
Nachrichten aus Chemie und Technik (Chemistry)
Verfahrenstechnik
Werkstoffe und Korrosion

Italy

La Chimica e L'Industria
Chimica Oggi
ICP – Rivisti dell'Industria Chimica
L'Industria della Gomma
Interplastics
Macplas
Materie Plastiche ed Elastomeri
Plast – Rivista delle Materie Plastiche
Poliplasti e Plastici Rinforzati
Seleplast
Technologie Chimiche

Netherlands

Analytica Chimica Acta (Chemistry)
Biochimica et Biophysica Acta (Chemistry)

Chemisch Weckblad (Chemicals)
Chemisch Weckblad Magazine
Chempress (Chemical/Metal Trade)
Clinica Chimica Acta
Desalination
Nederlands Chemische Industrie
Plastica (Plastics)
Thermochimica Acta
Trends in Analytical Chemistry

Spain

Afinidad (Chemical)
Caucho
Ingeniera Quimica
Quimica e Industria
Revista de Plasticos Modernos

Sweden

Acta Chemica Scandinavica
Farg och Lach Scandinavia
Gummi Nyt
Kemisk Tidskrift (Chemicals)
Cellulosa (Supplement to KT)
Plast Nordica
Plastforum Scandinavia

Switzerland

Chemische Rundschau
Chimia/Chemie Report
Kunststoffe-Plastics
Swiss-Chem
Swiss Plastics
Synthetic

UK

Analyst (The)
Analytical Proceedings
British Journal of Pharmaceutical Practice
British Polymer Journal
Chemical Communications
Chemical Engineer
Chemical Engineer Diary & Institution News
Chemical Engineering Abstracts
Chemical Hazards in Industry
Chemist & Druggist
Chemistry in Britain
Chemistry & Industry
Chemistry International
European Chemical News
Fertiliser International
Industrial Chemistry Bulletin
Journal of Chemical Research

Journal of Chemical
Technology & Biotechnology
Journal of Clinical & Hospital
Pharmacy
Journal of Labelled
Compounds & Radio
Pharmaceuticals
Labdeck
Laboratory Products
Technology
Manufacturing Chemist
Minilab
Modern Chemist
Nitrogen
OTC Index
OTC Medication
Pesticide Science
Pharmaceutical Business
News
Pharmaceutical Journal (The)
Pharmaceutical Medicine
Pharmacy International
Pharmacy Today
Phosphorus & Potassium
Polymer
Practical Biotechnology
Process Biochemistry
Process Economics
International
Process Engineering
Process Equipment News
Processing
Scrip-World Pharmaceutical
News
Speciality Chemicals
Sulphur
What's New in Processing
Where to Buy Chemical &
Chemical Plant

Canada

Canadian Chemical,
Pharmaceutical & Product
Directory
Canadian Process Equipment
& Control News
Chemical Buyers Guide
Chemistry in Canada
Process Industries in Canada

USA

American Chemical Society
Lab Guide
American Chemical Society
Research Journals
Butane-Propane News
CEC – The Process Industry
Catalogue
Chemical Abstracts
Chemical Business
Chemical Engineering
Chemical Engineering

Catalog
Chemical Engineering News
Chemical Engineering
Progress
Chemical Equipment
Chemical Industry Product
News
Chemical Marketing Reporter
Chemical Processing
Chemical Products
International
Chemical Purchasing
Chemical Review (American
Chemical Society)
Chemical Week
Chemtech (Chemical
Technology)
CPI Purchasing
Farm Chemicals
Industrial Chemical News
Inorganic Chemistry
(American Chemical Society)
International Journal of
Chemical Kinetics
International Journal of
Quantum Chemistry
Journal of the American
Chemical Society
Journal of Applied Polymer
Science
Journal of Chemical
Education
Journal of Chemical
Information & Computer
Sciences
(American Chemical Society)
Journal of Histochemistry &
Cyto Chemistry
Journal of Medical Chemistry
Journal of Organic Chemistry
Journal of Physical Chemistry
Journal of Polymer Science
Organic Chemistry
SCI Quest
Soap, Cosmetics, Chemical
Specialities

Asia

India

Chemical Age of India
Chemical Engineering World
Chemical Industry News
Chemical Life
Chemical Times (The)
India Chemical Engineer
India Chemical Manufacturer

Japan

Bulletin of the Chemical
Society of Japan
Chemical Engineering

Chemistry Letters
Fine Chemical
Gomu Seihin Tokei Geppo
Kagaku Kogyo
Kagaku Koji
Kagaku Kyoiku
Japan Plastics Age (English)
Journal of Chemical
Engineering
Kagaku Kogaku
Kagaku Keizai
Kagaku to Kogyo
Kinzoku
Kinzoku Jihyo
Nihon Gomu Shi
Nihon Kinzoku Gakka i Shi
Plastic Age

People's Republic of China

Huaxue Xuebao (Acta
Chimica Sinica)
(in Chinese, but with English
abstracts and a table of
contents in English published
by Science Press, 137
Chaoyangmennei St, Beijing)
Huaxue Tongbao (Chemistry
Bulletin)
(in Chinese, no English
abstracts)
Fexi Huaxue (Analytical
Chemistry)

Australia

Australasian Corrosion
Engineering
Australian Chemical
Engineering
Chemical Engineering in
Australia
Chemistry in Australia
PACE – Thomson's Process &
Control Engineering

Government Publications

UK Government Statistics

British Business Quarterly
Article 'Activity in the
Chemicals Industry'
Coverage includes indices of
production, sales, imports,
exports, and average earnings

Indicators of Industrial
Activity (OECD)
Industrial Short Term Trends
(Eurostat)
Monthly Digest of Statistics

UK National Accounts
Annual Abstract of Statistics
Digest of Welsh Statistics
Northern Ireland Annual
Abstract of Statistics
Process Industries Investment
Forecasts (WEDO)
Scottish Abstract Statistics

Adhesive Film, Cloth and Foil
Business Monitor: PQ 2569

Chemical Treatment of Oils and Fats
Business Monitor: PQ 2563

Dyestuffs and Pigments
Business Monitor: PQ 2516

Essential Oils and Flavouring Materials
Business Monitor: PQ 2564

Explosives
Census of Production
Reports: PA 256

Fertilisers
Annual Abstract of Statistics
Business Monitor: PQ 2513
Census of Production
Reports: PA 251
Monthly Digest of Statistics

Formulated Adhesives and Sealants
Business Monitor: PQ 2562
Census of Production
Reports: PA 256

Formulated Pesticides
Business Monitor: PQ 2568
Census of Production
Reports: PA 256

Inorganic Chemicals
Annual Abstract of Statistics
Business Monitor: PQ 2511
Monthly Digest of Statistics

Miscellaneous Chemical Products for Industrial Use
Business Monitor PQ 2567
Census of Production
Reports: PA 256

Organic Chemicals
Annual Abstract of Statistics
Business Monitor : PQ 2512

Census of Production
Reports: PA 251
Monthly Digest of Statistics

Paints, Varnishes and Painter's Fillings
Business Monitor: PQ 2551

Perfumers, Cosmetics and Toilet Preparations
Business Monitor: PQ 2582
Census of Production
Reports: PA 258

Pharmaceutical Products
Business Monitor: PQ 2570
Census of Production
Reports: PA 257

Photographic Materials and Chemicals
Business Monitor: PQ 2591
Census of Production
Reports: PA 259

Polishes and Miscellaneous Chemical Products
Business Monitor: PQ 2599

Printing Ink
Business Monitor: PQ 2552

Soap and Synthetic Detergents
Business Monitor: PQ 2581
Census of Production
Reports: PA 258
Monthly Digest of Statistics

Synthetic Resins and Plastics Materials
Annual Abstract of Statistics
Business Monitor: PQ 2514
Census of Production
Reports: PA 251
Monthly Digest of Statistics

Synthetic Rubber
Annual Abstract of Statistics
Business Monitor: PQ 2515
Census of Production
Reports: PA 251
Monthly Digest of Statistics
Rubber Statistical Bulletin

Computers

Trade Associations

Europe
European Association of
Manufacturers of Business
Machines and Data
Processing Equipment
(EUROBIT)
PO Box 710109
Lyoner Strasse 28
6000 Frankfurt am Main 71
Germany, Federal Republic of

European Computer
Manufacturers Association
(ECMA)
114 rue du Rhone
1204 Geneva
Switzerland

France
Federation des Industries et
du Commerce
des Equipments de Bureau et
d'Informatique
(FICOB)
6 Place de Valois
75001 Paris

Syndicat National des
Fabricants
d'Ensembles d'Informatique
Bureautique
et de leurs Applications
Telematiques
(SFIB)
4 Place de Valois
75001 Paris

Germany, Federal Republic of
Fachgemeinschaft Buro-und
Informationstechnik im
VDMA
Lyoner Strasse 18
Postfach 71 08 64 6000
Frankfurt/Main 71

Italy
ASSINFORM
Via Larga 23
20122 Milano
(Associazione Costruttori
Machine, Attrezzature
per Ufficio e per il
Trattamento delle
Informazioni)

Netherlands
Nederlands Genootschap
voor Commicatie Technieken
(NGCT)
Postbus 9272 3506 GG
Utrecht
(plus telecoms)

UK
Computing Services
Association
Hanover House
73/74 High Holborn
London WC1V 6LE
Tel: 01-405 2171

National Computing Centre
(The)
Head Office:
Oxford Road
Manchester M1 7ED
Tel: 061-228 6333
London:
11 New Fetter Lane
London EC4A 1PU
Tel: 01-353 4875

Business Equipment Trade
Association
8 Southampton Place
London WC1
Tel: 01-405 6233

British Computer Society
13 Mansfield Street
London W1M 0BP
Tel: 01-637 0471

Computer Services Associations in Europe

Austria
Verband Osterreichischer
Softward Industrie
c/o Dataservise
Landstrasse Haupstrasse 5
1030 Vienna
Tel: (010 39) 43222-7543265
Telex: 111890

Belgium
INSEA
Rue des Drapiers 21
1050 Brussels
Tel: (010 32) 2-5102311
Fax: (010 32) 2-5102301
Telex: 21078

Denmark
ESF EDB
Systemleverandorernes
Forening Att.ESFDENM
Admiralgade 15
1066 Copenhagen K Tel: (010
45) 1-931660
Telex: 16600 FOTEX DK

Finland
TIPAL RY
PL 555
00101 Helsinki
Tel: (010 358) 0-524288
Fax: (3580) 529119

France
Syntec Informatique
3 Rue Leon Bonnat
75016 Paris
Tel: (010 33) 1-45244353
Fax: (010 33) 1-42882684

Germany, Federal Republic of
Bundesverband Deutscher
Unternehmensberater (BDU)
Friedrich-Wilhelm Strasse 2
5300 Bonn
Tel: (010 49) 228-8055/6/7/8
Fax: (010 49) 228-230625
Telex: 8869494

Ireland, Republic of
Information and Computing
Services Association (ICSA)
Confederation House
Kildare Street
Dublin 2
Tel: 0001-779801
Fax: 0001-777823
Telex: 93502

Italy
Associazione Nazionale
Aziende Servize Informatica E
Telematica
(ANASIN)
Via Santa Tecla 4
20122 Milan
Tel: (010 39) 2-870768
Fax: (010 39) 2-874259

Netherlands
Vereniging Computer Service
Software Bureaus (COSSO)
Koningslaan 34
Postbus 5451
1007 AL Amsterdam
Tel: (010 31) 20-5738777
Telex: 17141

Norway
Norske Datasentralers
Landsforbund
c/o A/L Landbruksdata
Box 3671, Gamlebyen
0135 Oslo 1
Tel: (010 47) 2-673782
Fax: (010 47) 2-197511

Portugal
Associacao Portuguesa Das
Empresas de Servicios de
Informatica (APESI)
c/o Time-Sharing SARL
Rua Almeida Brandao 24a
1200 Lisbon
Tel: (010 351) 1-603181
Telex: 15823

Spain
Asociacion Espanola
Empresas Informatica
(SEDISI)
Diagonal 618 3 A
08021 Barcelona
Tel: (010 34) 3-2099022

Sweden
Dataserviceforetagens
Branschorganisation (SEBRO)
Box 4049
102 61 Stockholm
Tel: (010 46) 8-422450

Switzerland
GES Swiss Computer Services
Association
Badenerstrasse 551
8048 Zurich
Tel: (010 41) 1-4924294
Fax: (010 41) 1-4926774
Telex: 822537 COMPCH

Turkey
Bilgi Islem Hizmetleri Dernegi
(TUSCA)
c/o Sebim
Kemeralti Cad
Balkan Han no 69 Kat 4
Karakoy
Istanbul
Tel: (010 90) 1-1524342
Telex: 38133 DAK TR

UK
Computing Services
Association
Hanover House
73/74 High Holborn
London WC1V 6LE
Tel: 01-405 2171
Fax: 01-405 4119
Telex: 263224

Directories

International
CAD International Directory
Butterworth & Co
Sevenoaks
Kent
UK

Computers and Computing
Information Sources
Directory
Gale Research Co
Detroit
USA

Computer Graphics World
Buyers Guide, 1987
Computer Graphics World
Littleton, MA
USA

Electronics Research Centres,
1986
(World Directory of
organisations and
programmes)
Longman Group
Harlow
Essex
UK

International Directory of
Information Products on CD
ROM (The), 1987
Alan Armstrong & Associates
London
UK

UK
A-Z of Financial Technology
Suppliers (The), 1987/88,
Banking
Technology
Alphabetical listing of
principal financial technology
suppliers with
details of their companies,
products and customers.
Electronic services offered by
main banking institutions.
Listing of management
consultants in the financial
technology
field

Audio Visual and
Microcomputer Handbook
Kogan Place Ltd
London

Britain's Data
Communication Equipment
Suppliers
Jordan Information Services
London

British Computer Services
Jordan Information Services
London

Computer Users Yearbook
VNU Business Publications
London
Vol 1 Equipment
Vol 2 Services
Vol 3 Directory of Computer
Installations

Computer Users Yearbook,
Who's Who (The), 1987
VNU Business Publications
London
Directory of 'top people' in
the computer industry –
users;
service providers and many
actuaries; educators and
directors of
associations and institutes

Computing Services
Association Official Reference
Book
Sterling Publications
London

CRI Directory of Expert
Systems
Learned Information
Oxford

DataCommunications Book
(The)
VNU Business Publications
London

Dial 87 – Computing
(Hardware, peripherals,
recruitment, training,
consumables)
Dial Industry Publications
East Grinstead, Sussex

Dial Industry – Electrical,
Electronics, Computers
Instrumentation
Dial Industry Publications
East Grinstead, Sussex

Directory of Electronics,
Instruments and Computers
(Buyers Guide)
Morgan Grampian Books
Publishing Co
London

Educational Software
Directory
RR Bowker Ltd
Sevenoaks, Kent

IBM PC Guide
Beacon Publications
Wellingborough,
Northamptonshire

ICL Guide (The)
Beacon Publications
Wellingborough,
Northamptonshire

Information Technology in
the UK
Blackwell Scientific
Publications
Oxford
List of associations, councils,
societies

Information Technology,
Computer and
Communications Hardware
Index,
1987
Technical Indexes Ltd
Bracknell, Berkshire
Guide to manufacturers and
their products

M & E Educational Software
Directory
Pitman Publishing
London

Microsystems Hardware
Directory, 1988 (Annual)
NCC Microsystems Centre
London

Microsystems Software
Directory, 1988
NCC Microsystems Centre
London

Microsystems Training
Directory, 1988
NCC Microsystems Centre
London

PC Yearbook, 1988
VNU Business Publications
London

Software Users Yearbook
(The), 1987
VNU Business Publications
London
Directory of software,
services and suppliers

Europe
Investment in Computer
Services, 1988
Green & Co (Brokers)
London
Profile of the computer
services industry

France
Industries Electriques et
Electroniques Francais
FIEE (Federation of Industries
Electriques et Electroniques)
Buyers Guide
SACEL
Paris
Lists Fench exporters of
electrical and electronic
products

**Germany, Federal
Republic of**
Made in Europe – Technical
Equipment Catalogue
Annual Buyers Guide
Made in Europe Marketing
Organisation GmBH
Frankfurt/Main

Norway
Index for Electronikk
(Electronic buyers guide)
AS Okonomisk Literatur

Kommunikassions – Guiden
(Communications Guide)
AS Okonomisk Literatur
Lists producers, agents etc

Spain
Secartys Catalogue –
Electronics from Spain
Secartys
Barcelona

Switzerland
Datapro Directory of
Microcomputer Software
Datapro Services SA
Lausanne

Datapro Directory of Small
Computers
Datapro Services SA
Lausanne

Datapro Manufacturing
Automation Services
(updated monthly)
Datapro Services SA
Lausanne

USA
Business Software Directory
Information Sources Inc
Glenview, IL

Computer Publishers and
Publications
Published by Communication
Trends
Distributed by Gale Research
Co
Detroit, MI

Computer Peripherals Review
GML Information Service
Lexington, MA

Computer Review
GML Information Service
Lexington, MA

Computer Terminals Review
GML Information Service
Lexington, MA

Computers and People
Berkeley Enterprises Inc
Newtonville, MA
Directory and buyers guide
Listing of 3500 companies
offering hardware and
software products
and services

Datacommunications Product
Directory (mainly US market)
Architecture Technology
Corp
Minneapolis, MN
(Available from Online
Publications, Pinner, Middx)

Directory of Computer
Software
US Department of Commerce
National Technical
Information Service
Product Management
Springfield, VA

Directory of Consultants in
Computer Systems
Research Publications
Lake Bluff, IL
(Available from Gale
Research)

Directory of Top Computer
Executives
Applied Computer Research
Phoenix, AZ

S Klein Directory of
Computer Graphics
Suppliers, 1987
Technology Business
Communications
Sudbury, MA

Robotics CAD/CAM Market
Place
RR Bowker Co
(Xerox information company)
New York

Robotics Industry Directory
Technical Database Corp
Conroe, Texas
Also produces:
Computer Vision Directory
Industrial Censor Directory
Programmable Controllers
Directory
CAM Directory
CAD Directory
Engineering/Scientific
Software Directory

CAD/CAM Software
Directory

Software Directory (Annual)
ICP (International Computer
Programmes)
Indianapolis, IN
Microcomputer Series
Mainframe and
Minicomputer Series
(also available from ICP,
London)

Canada
Browning Database Review
(The)
Browning and Associates
Toronto
Overview of databases

CEE Electronics Directory and
Buyers Guide
Maclean Hunter Ltd
London
Listing of worldwide
electronic companies, and
products available to
Canadian users

Asia
Apeed Asian and Pacific
Electrical and Electronic
Directory
Intercontinental Marketing
Corp
Tokyo
Covers 15 countries

Apeed Computer and
Communications Directory,
1985/86
Intercontinental Marketing
Corp
Tokyo

Asian Computer Directory
Computer Publications Ltd
Hong Kong

Far East Computer Guide
Covers products and services
in the Far East
Beacon Publications
Wellingborough,
Northamptonshire
UK

China
China Electronics and
Electrical Products
Croner Publications
New Malden, Surrey

India
Computer Directory of India
(The)
Constellate Consultants Ltd
New Delhi
Details of computer systems,
suppliers etc.

Japan
High-Tech Start-up Ventures
in Japan
Japan Economic Journal
Tokyo

High Technology Robot
Market in Japan (The)
Intercontinental Marketing
Company
Tokyo
Manufacturers' data, market
trends etc

Japanese Business Directory
'Diamonds'
Diamond Lead Co
Tokyo
Includes communications
companies
1000 plus listings of Japanese
companies

Japanese R & D Centers: Data
Processing and
Telecommunications
Eurogestion
Tokyo

Personal Computer Systems
in Japan
Major company profiles
Intercontinental Marketing
Corp
Tokyo

Taiwan
Annual Taiwan Electronics
Buyers Guide
Trade Winds
Taiwan

New Zealand
Computer Book (The)
Suppliers Directory
Fourth Estate Periodicals
Wellington

Market Research Reports

This section lists recently
published market research
reports which cover various
aspects of the computer
industry. Details provided
below are title of report,
publisher, year of publication,
price and geographic
coverage.

80386 In-Depth Report
Romtec plc (UK)
1987
£995
Worldwide

Annual Market Review (UK
business micro market)
Romtec plc (UK)
Annually
£695
UK

Bar Code Markets: Key
Growth Areas in Service
Industries
International Resource
Development Inc (USA)
1987
$1650
USA

BOSS (British Office Systems
Service)
Wharton Information
Systems (UK)
1988
£500
UK

Buying Motivations for DTP
Systems in the UK
Romtec plc (UK)
1988
£875
UK

CAD/CAM/CAE Industry:
New Market Opportunities
Venture Development
Corporation (USA)
1987
$1850
USA

Computers in Banking
Market Intelligence Research
Company (USA)
1988
Price on request
USA

Computing Services Industry
1986-1996
Coopers & Lybrand (UK)
1986
£28.75
UK

DAT: The Emerging US
Market for
Consumer/Professional
Audio and
Computer Storage
Venture Development
Corporation (USA)
1988
$2250
USA

Desktop Publishing
The Freedonia Group Inc
(USA)
1988
$800
USA

Desktop Publishing Systems –
The Next Phase
International Planning
Information (USA)
1988
$1295
USA

Electronic Document
Interchange Market – US and
International
International Resource
Development Inc (USA)
1987
$2100
Worldwide

European Markets for PCs
and SBSs
Romtec plc (UK)
1988
£995
Europe

Expert Systems in Banking
International Planning
Information (USA)
1988
$885
USA

Color Printer Markets
International Resource
Development Inc (USA)
1987
$1850
USA

Computer-Aided Software
Engineering
Business Technology
Research Inc. (USA)
1988
$1950
USA

Computer-Aided Software
Engineering: Commercial
Strategies
Ovum Ltd. (UK)
1987
£385
US & Europe

Computer/Office Automation
Manufacturers & Distribution
Strategies
Yano Research Institute
(Japan)
1987
Price on request

Computer Security Markets
International Resource
Development Inc (USA)
1987
$1850
USA

Computer Software in
Banking
Market Intelligence Research
Company (USA)
1988
Price on request
USA

Computer Terminals
Specialists in Business
Information Inc (USA)
1987
$325
USA

Computers for Artificial
Intelligence:
Technology Assessment and
Forecast; 2nd edition
Technical Insights, Inc (USA)
1987
$285
USA

Expert Systems in Banking
and Securities
Ovum Ltd (UK)
1988
£465
US & Europe

Expert Systems Markets &
Suppliers
International Planning
Information (USA)
1988
$735
USA

Expert Systems Markets and
Suppliers
Ovum Ltd (UK)
1988
£385
US & Europe

Home Computers/Software
Key Note Publications (UK)
1987
£105
UK

Impact of Parallel Processing
on High Performance
Computing (The)
International Planning
Information (USA)
1988
$1485
USA

Intelligent Sensors: The
Merging of Electronics and
Sensing
Technical Insights, Inc (USA)
1988
$1000
USA

Introduction to Computers in
Shops
RMDP Ltd (UK)
1985
£75
Worldwide

Market Analysis and
Projections Microcomputer
Hardware and Software
1987-1992
Romtec plc (UK)
1988
£995
UK

Market for 3.5-Inch Disk
Drives (The)
Venture Development
Corporation (USA)
1988
$2250
USA

Market for Computer
Equipment (The)
Middle East Marketing
Research Bureau (Cyprus)
1985
$2900
Saudi Arabia

Market for Industrial
Computers (The)
Business Trend Analysts
(USA)
1987
$1750
USA

Microcomputer Graphics
Markets
Market Intelligence Research
Company (USA)
1988
Price on request
USA

Microcomputers
Key Note Publications (UK)
1987
£105
UK

Networking Computers
Wharton Information
Systems (UK)
1988
£950
UK

Neurocomputing: The
Technology, The Players, The
Potential
Technical Insights, Inc (USA)
1987
$1350
USA

New Wave of Computer
Software (The)
Business Communications Co
(USA)
1987
$1750
USA

New Wave of Computer
Software, Analysis and
Forecasts
Business Communications Inc
(USA)
1987
$1750
USA

OASIS (Office Automation
Systems Information Service)
Wharton Information
Systems (UK)
1988
£5000
Europe

OEM Market Review 1988
Romtec plc (UK)
1988
£495
UK

Office Software
Key Note Publications (UK)
1987
£105
UK

On Line Databases
Key Note Publications (UK)
1987
£105
UK

Optical Disk Document
Storage and Retrieval Systems
International Resource
Development Inc (USA)
1987
$2100
USA

Outlook for the European
Computer Office Automation
and Software Markets
MSRA Inc (USA)
1987
$450
Europe

Personal Computer Local
Area Networks: Markets &
Strategies to 1993
Probe Research Inc (USA)
1988
$3395
USA

Personal Computers (Market
Direction Reports)
Euromonitor Publications Ltd
(UK)
Every six months
£975
USA/Europe

Personal Computers in UK
Offices
Wharton Information
Systems (UK)
1987
£500
UK

Personal Computers: UK
Marketing Strategies for
Industry (UK)
1988
£55
UK

Personal Computing
Market Assessment
Publications (UK)
1988
£350
UK

Speech Processing:
Techonolgy, Applications and
Markets
Business Technology
Research Inc (USA)
1988
$1950
USA

Strategic Planning For
Computer Integrated
Manufacturing
International Planning
Information (USA)
1988
$525
USA

Tempest Secure Computing
Equipment & Markets
International Resource
Development Inc (USA)
1987
$2100
USA

UK Business Micro
Marketplace 1987-1992
Romtec plc (UK)
1988
£995
UK

UK Computer Distribution
Channels: Structure, Trends
& Performance
Romtec plc (UK)
1987
£1095
UK

UK Desktop Publishing
Market (The)
Romtec plc (UK)
1988
£995
UK

UK Monitors Market (The):
Structure and Future Trends
Romtec plc (UK)
Updated Annually
£950
UK

US CAE/CAD/CAM Markets
Business Trend Analysts
(USA)
1987
$1750
USA

US Forecast 1984-1993: Vol. 1
– Microcomputer Hardware
Romtec plc (UK)
1988
£1200
USA

US Forecast 1984-1993: Vol. 2
– Peripherals
Romtec plc (UK)
1988
£1200
USA

US Laptop Computer
Industry (The)
Venture Development
Corporation (USA)
1987
$2250
USA

US Market for Document
Scanners (The)
Venture Development
Corporation (USA)
1987
$2250
USA

Video & Graphic Presentation
Systems
International Planning
Information (USA)
1988
$995
USA

Word Processors
Key Note Publications (UK)
1987
£105
UK

Periodicals and Journals

See Electronics and
Telecommunication
sections

Government
Publications

UK Government
Statistics

Computer Services
British Business HMSO
(Weekly Magazine)
Production Statistics
Business Monitor Series
(HMSO)
BMPQ 3301 and 3302

Business Monitor Series cover
sales by UK based
manufacturers. However,
very few high technology
products are included, such
as for example CAD/CAM,
industrial robots. More
detailed analytical
information on particular
sectors is only available
through one-off surveys and
reports commissioned by
government departments or
related bodies.

Overseas Trade Statistics

High Technology Sector
Official Sources in the
EEC

France
FIEE (Federation des
Industries Electriques et
Electroniques)
Supplies data to the SESSI.

SESSI (Service d'Etude des
Strategies et des Statistique
Industrielles)
Publications: Annuaire de
Statistique Industrielle.
Bulletin Mensuel de
Statistique Industrielle

Italy
Institute Centrale de Statistica
Publications: Annuario di
Statistiche Industriali

Germany, Federal
Republic of
Statistisches Bundesamt
(Federal Statistical Office)
Publications: Systematisches
Guttervereichnis fur
Produktionsstatkstiken
(Subject index)
Produktion im
Produzierended Gewerbe des
In-und
Auslandes (covers
manufacturing industry)

Electronics

Trade Associations

Europe
European Committee of
Manufacturers of Electrical
Domestic Equipment,
(CECED)
via G Donizetti 30
20122 Milan
Italy
Tel: (010 39) 2-5456351

European Electronic
Component Manufacturers
Association, (EECA)
Avenue Louise 430 (Boite 12)
1050 Brussels
Belgium
Tel: (010 32) 2-6475011

Electronic Capital Goods
Associations in the EEC

Members of the Conference of Radio & Electronic Equipment Associations (ECREEA)

ANIE
via G Caccinj 1
00198 Rome
Italy

EFFD, Boersen
1217 Copenhagen K
Denmark

FABRIMETAL
Rue des Drapiers 21
1050 Brussels
Belgium

FME
Bredewater 20
Postbus 190
2700 Ad Zoetermeer
Netherlands

SPER
11 Rue Hamelin
Paris XV1eme
France

ZVEI
6000 Frankfurt (Main) 70
Stresemannallee 19
Federal Republic of Germany

Members of the European Electronic Component Manufacturers Association

Belgium
Fabrimetal
Rue des Drapiers 21
1050 Brussels
Tel: (010 32) 2-5112370
Telex: 21078

France
Syndicat des Industries de
Tubes Electroniques et
Semiconducteurs (SITELESC)
Syndicat des Industries de
Composants Electroniques
Passifs (SYCEP)
11 Rue Hamelin
75783 Paris Cedex 16
Tel: (010 33) 1-5051427
Telex: 611045

Germany, Federal Republic of
Fachverband Bauelemente
Elektronik
FV 23 IM ZVEI
Zentralverband der
Elektrotechnischen
Industrie EV
BlumenstraBe 6
8500 Nurnberg
Tel: (010 49) 911-204916
Telex: 626078

Italy
Associazione Nazionale
Industrie Elettrotecniche ed
Elettroniche (ANIE)
Gruppo 29
Componenti Elettronici
Via Algardi 2
20148 Milan
Tel: (010 39) 2-3264
Telex: 321616

Netherlands
Groep Fabrieken van Aktieve
en Passieve Elektronische
Bouwelementen (FAPEL)
Bredewater 20
2715 CA Zoetermeer
Tel: (010 31) 79-219221
Telex: 32157

Spain
ANIEL
Principe de Vergara 74 (4th
Planta)
Madrid 6
Tel: (010 34) 1-4111661
Telex: 43908

UK
Electronic Components
Industry Federation (ECIF)
7/8 Saville Row
London W1X 1AF
Tel: 01-437 4127
Telex: 8954834

Other National Associations

France
Federation des Industries
Electriques et Electroniques
(FIEE)
11 rue Hamelin
75783 Paris Cedex 16

Groupement des Industries
Electroniques (GIEL)
11, rue Hamelin
75783 PARIS Cedex 16

Germany, Federal Republic of
Zentralverband der
Elektrotechnischen Industrie
ev (ZVEI)
P O Box 700969
Stresemannallee 19
6000 Frankfurt am Main 70

Ireland, Republic of
Electronic Industry
Federation of Ireland (EIFI)
16 Main Street
Blackrock
Co Dublin

Electro-Technical Council of
Ireland (ECTI)
Ballymun Road
Dublin 9

Italy
Associazione Nazionale
Industrie Elettrotechnich ed
Elettroniche (ANIE)
Via G Caccini 1
00198 Rome

Portugal
Gremio Nacional dos
Industriais de Electricidade
Avenida de Republica
44-50
1000 Lisbon

UK
Association of Control
Manufacturers
8 Leicester Street
London WC2H 7BN

Association of Manufacturers
of Domestic Electrical
Appliances
AMDEA House
593 Hitchin Road
Stopsley
Luton LU2 7UN

British Electrical Systems
Association
Granville Chambers
2 Radford Street
Stone
Staffordshire ST15 8DA

British Radio and Electronic
Manufacturers Association
Landseer House
19 Charing Cross Road
London WC2H 0ES

Electric Cable Makers
Confederation
56 Palace Road
East Molesey
Surrey KT8 9DW

Electrical Contractors
Association
ESCA House
34 Palace Court
London W2 4HY

Electrical Installation
Equipment Manufacturers
Association
8 Leicester Street
London WC2H 7BN

Electronic Engineering
Association
Leicester House
8 Leicester Street
London WC2 7BN

Institute of Electrical
Engineers
2 Savoy Place
London WC2R 0BL

Lighting Industry Federation
Swan House
207 Balham High Road
London SW17 7BQ

Microwave Association
16A The Broadway
London SW19 1RF

National Electronics Council
Room 211
Savoy Hill House
Savoy Hill
London WC2R 0BV

Sira Ltd
South Hill
Chislehurst
Kent BR7 5EH
(Sira is an independent
centre. It supplies research
and development and
technology services.)

USA
Electronics Industries
Association
2001 Eye Street NW
Washington DC 20006
Marketing Services
Department produces the
Electronics Market Data Book

Directories

International
Electrical World Directory of
Electric Utilities
McGraw-Hill
New York
USA

Electronics Research Centres
– World Directory of
Organizations and
Programmes
Longman Group
Harlow, Essex
UK

Mackintosh Yearbook of
International Electronics Data
(Annual)
Coverage: Far East, Japan,
Canada, USA, Australia
BEP Data Services
Luton
UK

Profile of Worldwide
Semiconductor Industry
BEP Data Services
Luton
UK

Semi Custom Integrated
Circuits Yearbook
BEP Data Services
Luton
UK

World Electronics Companies
File
(Looseleaf)
BEP Data Services
Luton
UK

Yearbook of Electronics
Import/Export Data
BEP Data Services
Luton
UK
Covers: Europe, US and
Japan

World Electronics Data
Yearbook
BEP Data Services
Luton
UK
Covers: W Europe (Volume I)
US, Asia, Japan, Pacific
(Volume 2)
Europe
European Consumer
Electronics Directory (The)
Euromonitor Publications
London
UK

European Electronic
Component Distributor
Directory (Biannual)
BEP Data Services
Luton
UK
Covers 14 European countries

Mackintosh European
Electronic Companies File
BEP Data Services
Luton
UK

Mackintosh Yearbook of West
European Electronics Data
BEP Data Services
Luton
UK

World Electronics Data
Yearbook – Volume 1
BEP Data Services
Luton
UK

UK
BEAMA Handbook
British Electrical and Allied
Manufacturers Association
London

Desktop Publishing Directory
and Buyers Guide
Spicer & Pegler
London

Dial Industry: Electrical,
Electronics, Computers,
Instrumentation
Dial Industry Publications
East Grinstead, Sussex

Directory of Electronics,
Instruments and Computers
Morgan Grampion
London

Distributor Survey
ES Publications
New Malden, Surrey
Lists distributors of electronic
components

Electrical and Electronic
Trades Year Book
IPC Electrical – Electronic
Press
London

Electrical and Electronics
Trades Directory
Peter Peregrinus
Stevenage

Electrical Wholesalers
Federation Year Book
Electrical Wholesalers
Association
London

Electrical Supply Handbook
The Electrical Times
London

Electroheat Directory
British National Committee
for Electroheat
London

Electro Medical Trade
Association Products
Directory
Electro Medical Trade
Association
Guildford, Surrey

Electronic Components
Industry Federation
Handbook
ECIF
London

Electronic Engineering
Association Product Directory
Electronic Engineering
Association
London

Electronic Engineering Index
Technical Indexes Ltd
Bracknell, Berkshire
Supplier and product guide

Electronic Publishing
Handbook
Online Publications
Pinner, Middlesex

Electronics Engineers
Reference Book
Butterworth
Sevenoaks, Kent
Covers sources of
information, and major
electronics companies

FT Industrial Companies:
Electronics
Longman Group
Harlow, Essex

Institution of Electrical
Engineers, Year book and list
of members
IEE
London

France
AVCD L'Annuaire de
L'Audiovisuel Paris
SEPP
Paris

Federation des Industries
Electriques et Electroniques
Handbook (Annual)
Directory covering 25 member
trade associations
FIEE
Paris

USA
Electrical Appliance and
Utilization Equipment List
Underwriters Laboratories
Chicago, IL

Electrical Construction
Materials Directory
Underwriters Laboratories
Chicago, IL

Electronic Buyers Guide
McGraw-Hill
New York

Electronic Design's Gold Book
Hayden
Rochell Park, New Jersey

Electronic Engineers Master
Tech Publishers
New York

Electronic Industry
Telephone Directory
Harris Publishing (USA)
Available from BEP Data
Services

Electronic News Financial
Fact Book and Directory 1987
Fairchild Publications
New York

Surface Mounting Directory
D Brown Associates (USA)
Available from BEP Data
Services

Sweets Catalog File
Products for Engineering
Electrical and Related
Products
McGraw-Hill
New York

Who's Who in Electronics
Lists US manufacturers and
distributors
B Klein
Florida

Asia
Apeed Asian and Pacific
Electrical and Electronic
Directory
Covers 19 countries
Intercontinental Marketing
Corporation
Tokyo
Japan

Asian Electrical and
Electronics Trades Directory
Allied Trading Company,
Tokyo
Japan

Indian Electronics Directory
Elcina
New Delhi
India

Japan Electronics Almanac
1987
Dempa Publications Inc
Tokyo
Japan

Japanese Measuring
Instruments
Japan Measuring Instruments
Federation
Tokyo
Japan

Key players in the Japanese
Electronics Industry
Dodwell Marketing
Consultants
Tokyo
Japan

Mechanical and Electronic
Industries Yearbook of China
Economic Information
Agency
Hong Kong

Membership List: Electronic
Industries Association of
Japan
EIAJ
Tokyo
Japan

World Electronics Data
Yearbook – Volume 2
USA, Asia, Japan, Pacific
BEP Data Services
Luton
UK

Australia
Australian Electronics
Directory
Technical Indexes (Aust) Pty
Ltd
East Cheltenham
Victoria

Market Research Reports

This section lists recently
published market research
reports which cover various
aspects of the electronics
industry. Details provided
below are title of report,
publisher, year of publication,
price and geographic
coverage.

Analytical Instruments
The Freedonia Group Inc
(USA)
1988
$800
USA

Asia-Pacific Board Assembly
Industry 1987
BEP Data Services (UK)
1987
Price on request
Asia

Automatic Product/People
Identification Systems,
Hardware, Software
Business Communications Co
(USA)
1988
$2250
USA

Automotive Electronics
Market in Japan 1987
Yano Research Institute
(Japan)
1987
Price on request
Japan

Britain's Access Control
Industry
Jordan & Sons Ltd (UK)
1988
£125
UK

Britain's Top 500 Electronics
Companies
Jordan & Sons Ltd (UK)
1988
£125
UK

Computer Peripherals Market
in Japan
Yano Research Institute
(Japan)
1986
Price on request
Japan

Consumer Electronics
Euromonitor Publications Ltd
(UK)
Updated every 6 months
£975
USA, Europe

Consumer Electronics in
Western Europe
Euromonitor Publications Ltd
(UK)
1986
£275
Europe

Consumer Electronics
Market Assessment
Publications (UK)
1987
£375
UK

Defense Electronics
The Freedonia Group Inc
(USA)
1988
$1700
USA

Domestic Electrical
Apppliances
Euromonitor Publications Ltd
(UK)
Updated every 6 months
£975
USA, Europe

Electronic Banking
Post News (UK)
1986
£149
Worldwide

Electronic Banking
The Freedonia Group Inc
(USA)
1988
$800
USA

Electronic Component
Distributors
Key Note Publications (UK)
1987
£105
UK

Electronic Component
Manufacturers
Key Note Publications (UK)
1987
£105
UK

Electronic Home (The)
Business Communications Co
(USA)
1987
$1600
USA

Electronic Image Processing
(EIP)
Prognos AG (Switzerland)
1986
25.000 SFrs
USA, Japan, Western Europe

Electronic Instruments for
Clinical-Chemical Analysis
Databank Spa (Italy)
1988
£1400
Italy

Electronic Instruments for
Laboratory Measurements
Databank Spa (Italy)
1988
£1400
Italy

Electronic R&D Centers in
Japan – 1988
International Planning
Information (USA)
1988
$495
Japan

European Electronic
Companies File
BEP Data Services (UK)
1987
Price on request
Europe

Europecast – Active and
Passive Component Markets
1987-1990
International Planning
Information (USA)
1988
$490 each, all four $1,750
Europe

International Passive
Components, Production and
Trade
Survey Force Ltd (UK)
1988
£300
Worldwide

Japanese Electronics: Has the
Strategy for Dominance
Failed ?
MSRA Inc (USA)
1987
$795
Japan

Keyboard Industry (The), 3rd
Edition
Venture Development
Corporation (USA)
1988
$3950
USA

Korean Electronics: The New
Rising Sun
MSRA Inc (USA)
1987
$195
Korea

Lighting Equipment
Key Note Publications (UK)
1987
£105
UK

Market Share in Japan
Yano Research Institute
Japan

Marketing & Product Trends
in the Electronic Typewriter
MSRA Inc (USA)
1987
$995
Worldwide

Medical Electronic Equipment
Key Note Publications (UK)
1988
£105
UK

N Ireland Electrical
Appliances
Ulster Marketing Surveys Ltd
(N Ireland)
1988
£150
N Ireland

NEC 1988: The Drive for The
Top
Domicity Ltd (Canada)
1988
US $1495
Japan, USA, Canada

Optoelectronics
The Freedonia Group Inc
(USA)
1988
$800
USA

Power Protection Industry
(The): Strategic Issues
Redefine the Competitive
Arena
Venture Development
Corporation (USA)
1988
$4250
USA

Printed Circuits
Key Note Publications (UK)
1988
£105
UK

Profile of the European
Connector Industry
BEP Data Services
1987
Price on request
Europe

Profile of the Worldwide
Capacitor Industry (1988/89)
BEP Data Services (UK)
1988
Price on request
Worldwide

Profile of the Worldwide
Semiconductor Industry
(1987/1988)
BEP Data Services (UK)
1987
Price on request
Worldwide

Prospects for the Printed
Circuit Board Industry (1987)
Yano Research Institute
(Japan)
1987
Price on request
Japan

Report on Semiconductor
User Industries in Japan
Yano Research Institute
Japan

Scientific Instruments
Key Note Publications (UK)
1987
£105
UK

Semiconductor Subcontract
Assembly Industry
BEP Data Services (UK)
1988
Price on request
Worldwide

Semicustom IC Yearbook
BEP Data Services (UK)
1988
Price on request
Worldwide

Small Electrical Appliances in
Europe
Euromonitor Publications Ltd
(UK)
1986
£275
Europe (W)

Smart Card (The)
Post News (UK)
1986
£134
Worldwide

Status of the Semiconductor
Industry (1988)
International Planning
Information (USA)
1988
$370
USA

Strategic Reference (The):
High Tech Companies in
Japan
Yano Research Institute
1987
Japan

Structure of the Japanese
Electronics Industry (The),
2nd edition
Dodwell & Co (Japan)
1988 (Dec)
Y60,000
Japan

Superconductive Materials &
Devices
Business Technology
Research Inc (USA)
1987
$1,950
USA

Switching Power Supply
Industry: The Changing
Nature of OEM Demand,
Technology and Competition
Venture Development
Corporation (USA)
1988
$3,490
USA

Toshiba: A Competitive
Analysis
Domicity Ltd (Canada)
1987
US$1,195
Japan, USA, Canada

Videotex
Key Note Publications (UK)
1987
£105
UK

VLSI Through 1995 – Market
Analysis and Trends
International Planning
Information (USA)
1988
$1,995
USA

White Goods in Europe
Euromonitor Publications Ltd
(UK)
1987
£275
Europe

Who's Who in Electronics
BEP Data Services (UK)
Annual
Price on request
USA

World Electronics Companies
File
BEP Data Services (UK)
Annual
Price on request
Worldwide

Worldwide Laser Markets
International Resource
Development Inc (USA)
1987
$1850
Worldwide

Yearbook of World
Electronics Data, 1988: Vol 1 –
W.Europe,
Vol 2 – America, Japan
International Planning
Information (USA)
1988
$625 (Vol 1) $975 (Vol 2)
Europe, USA, Japan, Asia
Pacific

Yearbook of World
Electronics Data: Vol 1 – W
Europe, Vol 2 – America,
Japan, Asia
BEP Data Services (UK)
Annual
Price on request
Worldwide

Periodicals and Journals

International and
Pan-European
ACE International
All about Personal Computers

Byte (PCs)
Communication Systems
Worldwide
Computer Network
Computer Product News
Computerworld
ECE International
Electrical Review
International
Electronics Week
Information Technology
Intelligence
Information World Review
Integrated Circuits
International
Journal of Semicustom
Integrated Circuits
Microelectronics Journal

Europe

Austria
A3 – Volt
Comparing
Elektro Journal
Elektro Radio Hander
Elektro Wirtschaft
Elektronik Report
Oesterreichische Elektro
Wirtshaft
Oesterreichische Zeitscrift fur
Elektrizitats Wirtshaft

Belgium
BNB Mensuel/Maandblad
Belgian Video
Computer Organ Inform
Computer Product News
Data Careers
Data News
Electra
Electronic Product News
International Business
Equipment
Personal Computer and
Software
Videodoc

Denmark
Aktuel Data/EDB
Aktuel Elektronik
Computerworld Denmark
Data Nytt
Electra
Elektronik Information
Elektronik Nyt
Installations Nyt
Nordisk Data Nytt
PC World Denmark

Finland
Elektroniikkauutiset
IDEA
Mikro
Sahko – Electricity in Finland
Sahkourakoitsaija (Electrical)
Tietoviikko (Computers)

France (Computers)
Bureau et Informatique
Commodore Magazine
Decision Informatique
Distributique
Logiciels et Services
Micro Systems
Micro Verte
Minis et Micros
Le Monde Informatique
OPC (IBM)
Ordi (IBM)
Ordinateurs
Pom's (Apple)
Ressources Temps Reel
Ol Digest
Ol Hebdo
Ol Mensuel

Germany, Federal Republic of (Computers)
BIT
CAD/CAM
CAD/CAM Report
CAE Journal
Computerbrief
Computer Business
Computer Magazin
Computerwoche
Die Computer-Zeitung
EDV & Handwerk
Der Informatiker
Infowelt
Kompatibel (IBM)
MC-Die Mikrocomputer Zeitschrift
Mega Y
Microbit
Mini-Micro Magazin
Online

Italy (Computers)
Applicando (Apple)
Automazione Oggi
Bit (Consumer)
Chip
Commodore
Compuscoula
Computer
Computerworld Italia
Data Manager
EG Computer
L'Informatica

Informatica 70
Linea EDP
MC Microcomputer
Micro & Personal Computer
Office Automation
PC Magazine
Sinclair Computer
Sistemi & Automazione
Telecommunicazioni Oggi
Zerauno

Netherlands
AG Report
De Automatisering – Gids
Cadcam
Chip/Micromix
Comma's
Computable
Computer World Benelux
Computer World Netherlands
Databus (Micro)
Dossier Commodore
Electra
Electronica Top International
Elektronika Hobbie
Elektrotechniek/Elektronica
Het Elektrotechnisch Vakblad
Elektuur
Informatie (Computers)
PC +
PC World Benelux
Personal Computer
Radio Bulletin

Spain
Actualidad Electronica
Anales de Mecanica y Electricidad
BIT
Chip
Computerworld Espana
Electra
Electronica Hoy
Elektor
Eurofach Electronica
Informatica y Automatica
Micros
Mundo Electronico
El Periodico Informatico
Tu Micro Commodore
Tu Micro Personal
ZX

Sweden
Computer Buyers Guide
Computer Sweden
Computer World Focus
Datateknik (Computer Technology)
Datavarlden (Computer World)
Datornytt med Maskin-och

programvara
Elteknik med Aktuell
Elektronik (Electro industries)
Industrielle Datateknik
Modern Elektronik
Nypekuik
Svenska PC World
Tidskriften ERA

Switzerland
Bulletin SEV
Bureaux et Systems
Computer Forum
Computerworld Schweiz
Electronique
Elektrotechnik
Informatique et Bureautique
Journal des Telecommunications
Neue Technik
Output (Computers)
Sysdata
Unterhaltungs Elektronik

Canada
CIPS Review
Canadian Data Systems
Communication Systems
Computer Data
Computerworld Canada
Computing Canada
Data Products News
EIC
Electronic Procurement Index for Canada
Electronic Products and Technology
Electronics and Communications
Electronics Today
PC World Canada
Software Canada

Major Canadian Publishers
Maclean-Hunter Ltd
777 Bay Street, Toronto

Southam Inc
150 Bloor Street West
Suite 900, Toronto

Plesman Publishing
2 Lansing Square, Suite 703
Toronto)

Australia
Australasian Computerworld
Australian Audio Visual Book
Australian Computer Bulletin
Australian Computer Journal
Australian Electronics

Bulletin
Australian Electronics
Engineering
Australian Micro Computer
Australian Personal
Computer
COMDEC
Computerworld Australia
Data Trend (EDP Manual)
Electronics News
Monitor (Electronics)
Pacific Computer Weekly
What's New in Computing
What's New in Electronics

Asia
Asia Computer Weekly
Asian Computer Monthly
Asian Computerworld
Asian Sources Electronics
Asian Sources
Electronics/Components
Australasian Computerworld
Communications
International – South East
Asia edition
Computer Asia
Far East Computer Guide
International Electronics for
China
Japan Electronics Today
News
Micro-Asia

China (Technical – Published outside China in English)
China Computerworld
China Technical Review
Computer China
Communications Today
Data Communications
(McGraw-Hill, Hong Kong)
Defence Review (Chinese)
Electronics Bulletin (Chinese)
Electronics News for China
Engineering News Record
(Chinese)
China Computer Monthly
China Computerworld
Conmilit (defence)
Process Automation
Instrumentation
US/China Construction
Report – Western Technology
and management

Hong Kong
Asian Computer Directory
Asian Computer Monthly
China Tech

Computer Decision
Electronic Technology

India
Dataquest
Electrical India
Electricity and Electronics
Electronic Digest
Electronic Engineer
Indian Electrical Contractor
and Trader

Japan
Aski (PCs)
Bit
Computerworld Japan
Data Tsushin
Dempa Shimbun
Denki Gakkai Zasshi
Denki Kyokai Zasshi
Denki Shimbun
Denshi Gagaku
Electronics Digest
Journal & Electronic
Engineering
New Electronic Products
nki Kyokai Zasshi
Denki Shimbun
Denshi Gagaku
Electronics Digest
Journal & Electronic
Engineering
New Electronic Products
nki Kyokai Zasshi
Denki Shimbun
Denshi Gagaku
Electronics Digest
Journal & Electronic
Engineering
New Electronic Products
nki Kyokai Zasshi
Denki Shimbun
Denshi Gagaku
Electronics Digest
Journal & Electronic
Engineering
New Electronic Products
Nikkei Electronics
Nikkei High Tech Report
(Benn Publications, UK)
PC World

Government Publications

UK Official Sources

General Statistics
Business Monitor PA 1000
Covers engineering volume
indices of sales and orders
British Business
Monthly Digest of Statistics
United Kingdom National
Accounts
Family Expenditure Survey
(Available from HMSO –
annual)

Alarms and Signalling Equipment
Business monitor: PQ 3433
Census of Production
Reports: PA 343

Basic Electrical Equipment
Business Monitor: PQ 3420
Census or Production
Reports: PA 342

Batteries and Accumulators
Business Monitors: PQ 3432
Census of Production
Reports: PA 343

Components, other than Active Components, Mainly for Electronic Equipment
Business Monitor: PQ 3444
Census of Production
Reports: PA 344

Domestic Electrical Appliances
Business Monitor: PQ 3460
Statistics for the Domestic
Electrical Appliance Industry
(Association
of Manufacturers of Domestic
Electrical Appliances)
Census of Production
Reports: PA 346

Electrical Equipment for Motor Vehicles, Cycles and Aircraft
Business Monitor: PQ 3434
Census of Production
Reports: PA 343

Electrical Instruments and Control Systems
Business Monitor: PQ 3442
Census of Production
Reports: PA 344

Electric Lamps and Lighting Equipment etc
Business Monitor: PQ 3470
Census of Production
Reports: PA 347

Electronic Consumer Goods and Miscellaneous Equipment
Business Monitor: PQ 3454
Census of Production
Reports: PA 345

Electronic Sub-Assemblies and Active Components
Business Monitor: PQ 3453
Census of Production
Reports: PA 345

Gramophone Records and Pre-Recorded Tapes
Business Monitor: PQ 3452
Census of Production
Reports: PA 345

Insulated Wires and Cables
Business Monitor: PQ 3410

Measuring Checking and Precision Instruments and Apparatus
Business Monitor: PQ 3710
Census of Production
Reports: PA 371

Medical and Surgical Equipment and Orthapaedic Appliances
Business Monitor: PQ 3720
Census of Production
Reports: PA 372

Miscellaneous Electrical Equipment for Industrial Use
Business Monitor: PQ 3435
Census of Production
Reports: PA 343

Office Machinery; Electronic Data Processing Equipment
Business Monitors PQ 3301 and PQ3302
Census of Production
Reports: PA 330

Radio and Electronic Capital Goods
Business Monitor: PQ 3443
Census of Production
Reports: PA 344

Spectacles and Unmounted Lenses: Optical Precision Instruments
Business Monitor: PQ 3731/3732
Census of Production
Reports: PA 373

Telegraph and Telephone Equipment
Business Monitor: PQ 3441
Census of Production
Reports: PA 344

Financial Services

Trade Associations

International Banking Associations

Commercial Banks
Federation Bancaire de la Communaute Europeenne
Avenue de Tervuren 168 (Bte)
1150 Brussels
Belgium
Tel: (010 32) 2-7710094
Telex: 23516

Federacion Latinoamericana de Bancos (Felaban)
Carrera 9-,9. 91-10
Apartado Aereo 091959-114
Bogota
Colombia
Tel: (010 57) 1-2361707/236131

ASEAN Bankers Association
c/o Bank Bumi Daya
Jalan Kebon Sirih 66
Jakarta
Indonesia

Arab Bankers Association
1/2 Hanover Street
London
W1R 9WB
UK

European Banks Advisory Committee
c/o European Banks International Co
Avenue Louise 61
1050 Brussels
Belgium
Tel: (010 32) 2-5386240

West African Bankers Association
c/o West African Clearing House
Freetown
Sierra Leone
West Africa

Savings Banks
Institut International des Caisses d'Epargne
1-3 Rue Albert-Gos
1206 Geneva
Switzerland
Tel: (010 41) 22-477466

Groupement des Caisses d'Epargne de la CEE
Square E Plasky 92-94
1040 Brussels
Belgium
Tel: (010 32) 2-7368047

Nordic Delegation of Central Savings Bank Organisations
Pohjoisesplanadi 35A
Postbox 47
00101 Helsinki 10
Finland
Tel: (010 358) 0-18271

Confederation Internationale du Credit Populaire
c/o Chambre Syndicale de Banques Populaires
131 Avenue de Wagram
75847 Paris
France
Tel: (010 33) 1-7631250/2673848
Telex: 290457

Co-operative Banks
Groupement des
Cooperatives d'Epargne et de
Credit de la CEE
Rue de la Science 23-25 (Bte 9)
1040 Brussels
Belgium
Tel: (010 32) 2-2301124

Confederation Internationale
du Credit Agricole
Beethovenstrasse 24
8002 Zurich
Switzerland
Tel: (010 41) 1-2016848

Mortgage Institutions
International Union of
Building Societies and
Savings Associations
20 N Wacker Drive
Suite 2267
Chicago
Illinois
USA 60606
Tel: (010 1) 312-7266676
Telex: 9102213834

European Federation of
Building Societies
3 Saville Row
London W1X 1AF
UK
Tel: 01-437 0655

European Community
Mortgage Federation
14 Avenue de la Joyeuse
Entree
(Bte 2)
1040 Brussels
Belgium
Tel: (010 32) 2-2302551
Telex: 26047

Credit Unions
World Council of Credit
Unions
PO Box 391
Home Office
5810 Mineral Point Road
Madison
Wisconsin 53701
USA
Tel: (010 1) 608-2317130
Telex: 467 918

Asian Confederation of Credit
Unions (ACCU)
PO Box 24-171
Bangkok 10240
Thailand
Tel: (010 66) 2-3776781
Telex: 81023/20458

Finance House
European Federation of
Finance Houses
(EUROFINAS)
Avenue de Tervuren 267
(Bte 10)
1150 Brussels
Belgium
Tel: (010 32) 2-7712107

Insurance Association
International Office of
Assurance and Reinsurance
Brokers (BIPAR)
40 Avenue Albert Elisabeth
1200 Brussels
Belgium
Tel: (010 32) 2-7333522

Austria

Commercial Bank
Verband Osterreicher Banken
und Bankiers
Borsegasse 11
1010 Vienna
Tel: (010 43) 222-661771
Telex: 132824

Savings Banks
Girozentrale und Bank der
Osterreichischen Sparkassen
Schubertring 5
1011 Vienna
Tel: (010 43) 222-72940
Telex: 133006

Hauptverband der
Osterreichischen Sparkassen
Postfach 256
Grimmelshausengasse 1
1030 Vienna
Tel: (010 43) 222-734581
Telex: 1 31823

Oesterreichische
Volksbanken
Peregringasse 3
1090 Vienna
Tel: (010 43) 222-31340
Telex: 134206/114233

Co-operative Banks
Genossenschaftliche
Zentralbank (GZB)
Herrengasse 1
1010 Vienna
Tel: (010 43) 222-66620
Telex: 76795

Osterreichischer
Genossenschaftsverband
Postfach 157
Schottengasse 10
1013 Vienna
Tel: (010 43) 222-312641
Telex: 1 14268

Osterreichischer
Raiffeisenverband
Hollandstrasse 2
1020 Vienna
Tel: (010 43) 222-26360
Telex: 116769

Mortgage Institution
Arbeitsgemeinschaft
Osterreichischer
Bausparkassen
Alpenstrasse 70
5020 Salzburg

Finance House
Interessengemeinschaft der
Osterreichischen
Finanzierungsbanken
Hanuschgasse 1
1015 Vienna
Tel: (010 43) 222-573657
Telex: 111 543

Insurance Association
Verband der Versicherung-
sunternehmungen
Osterreich

Belgium

Commercial Bank
Association Belge des
Banques
Rue Ravenstein 36 (Bte 5)
1000 Brussels
Tel: (010 32) 2-5125868
Telex: 25575

Savings Bank
Association des Caisses
d'Epargne Privees
Avenue des Arts 13-14 (Bte 1)
1040 Brussels
Tel: (010 32)
2-2196941/2194314
Telex: 63186

Mortgage Institution
Association Belge des
Entreprises Hypothecaires
Avenue de la Joyeuse Entree
12
(Boite 4)
1040 Brussels
Tel: (010 32) 2-2310793
Telex: 26047

Finance House
Groupement des Activites du
Credit
(Bte 11)
Avenue de Broqueville 302
1200 Brussels
Tel: (010 32) 2-7705485

Insurance Associations
Comite Belge des Assureurs
Incendie ASBL
Union Professionnelle des
Entreprises d'Assurances
(UPEA)

Cyprus

Commercial Bank
Cyprus Commercial Banks
Association
PO Box 1657
Nicosia

Insurance Association
Insurance Association of
Cyprus

Denmark

Commercial Bank
Danish Bankers Association
7 Amaliegade
1256 Copenhagen K
Tel: (010 45) 1-120200
Telex: 16102

Savings Bank
Association of the Danish
Savings Bank
62-64 Koebmagergade
1150 Copenhagen K
Tel: (010 45) 1-151811
Telex: 15965

Mortgage Institution
Council of Danish Mortgage
Credit Institutes
Vesterborgade 4 A
1620 Copenhagen V
Tel: (010 45) 1-124811

Finance House
Byggeriets Realredifond
Gammel Kongevej 74
1845 Copenhagen V

Insurance Association
Assurandor Societetet

Finland

Commercial Banks
Finnish Bankers' Association
(The)
Fabianinkatu 8
00130 Helsinki
Tel: (010 358) 0-177521
Telex: 121839

Joint Delegation of the Banks
(The)
Lonnrotinkatu 13
00120 Helsinki 12
Tel: (010 358) 0-645031

Savings Bank
Finnish Savings Banks'
Association (The)
Pohjoisesplanadi 35 A
00100 Helsinki
Tel: (010 358) 0-18271
Telex: 125786

Co-operative Bank
Central Association of the
Co-operative Banks (The)
Arkadiankatu 23
PL 308
00101 Helsinki
Tel: (010 358) 0-4041
Telex: 124714

Finance House
Finnish Finance Houses
Association (The)
c/o The Finnish Bankers'
Association
Fabianinkatu 8
00100 Helsinki
Tel: (010 358) 0-177521
Telex: 121839

Insurance Association
Suomen Vakuutusyhtioiden
Keskusliitto

France

All Banks
Association Francaise des
Etablissements de Credit
36 rue Taitbout
75009 Paris

Private Bank
Office de Co-ordination
Banquaire et Financiere
66 Rue Chaussee d'Antin
75009 Paris
Tel: (010 33) 1-2854613

Commercial Bank
Association Francaise des
Banques
18 Rue Lafayette
75009 Paris
Tel: (010 33) 1-2469259
Telex: 660282

Savings Banks
Caisse Nationale d'Epargne
3 Rue St Jean Baptiste de la
Salle
75293 Paris Cedex 06
Tel: (010 33) 1-5307777
Telex: 250 356

Centre National des Caisses
d'Epargne et de Prevoyance
5 Rue Masseran
75007 Paris
Tel: (010 33) 1-5675527
Telex: 200668

Co-operative Banks
Caisse Nationale de Credit
Agricole
91 Boulevard Pasteur
75015 Paris
Tel: (010 33) 1-3235202
Telex: 250971

Chambre Syndicale des
Banques Populaires
131 Avenue Wagram
75847 Paris Cedex 17
France
Tel: (010 33) 1-7631250
Telex: 290457

Confederation Nationale de
Credit Mutuel
88-90 Rue Cardinet
75017 Paris
Tel: (010 33) 1-7660151
Telex: 640373

Federation National du Credit
Agricole
48 Rue la Boetie
75008 Paris
Tel: (010 33) 1-5630300

Mortgage Institution
Union d'Epargne et de Credit
pour le Financement
Immobilier
51 Boulevard des Dames
13242 Marseille-Cedex 1

Postal Bank
Cheques Postaux
16 Rue Favorites
75015 Paris
Tel: (010 33) 1-5307777
Telex: 250300

Finance House
Association Professionnelle
des Etablissements Financiers
12 Avenue d'Eylau
75116 Paris
Tel: (010 33) 1-5536425
Telex: 660 870

Insurance Associations
Assemblee Pleniere des
Societes d'Assurances contre
l'Incendie et les Risques
Divers

Association Generale des
Societes d'Assurances contre
les Accidents
Comite Europeen des
Assurances –
(Not a national association –
umbrella for most European
insurance associations)

Federation Francaise des
Societes d'Assurances (FFSA)

Groupement Technique de la
Branche Accidents et Risques
Divers

Reunion des Societes
d'Assurances sur la Vie

**Germany, Federal
Republic of**

Commercial Banks
Bundesverband Deutscher
Banken
Mohrenstrasse 35-41
5000 Koln 1
Tel: (010 49) 221-16631
Telex: 8882730

Verband Der
Gemeinwirtschaftlichen
Geshaftsbanken
Berliner Freiheit 36
5300 Bonn
Tel: (010 49) 228-631566
Telex: 886810

Verband Offentlicher Banken
Am Fronhof 10
5300 Bonn 2
Tel: (010 49) 228-820040
Telex: 885707

Savings Bank
Deutscher Sparkassen und
Giroverband
Simrockstrasse 4
5300 Bonn 1
Tel: (010 49) 228-2041
Telex: 886709

Co-operative Bank
Bundesverband der
Deutschen Volksbanken und
Raiffeisenbanken
Heussallee 5
5300 Bonn 1
Tel: (010 49) 228-5091
Telex: 886779

Mortgage Institutions
Bundesgeschaeftsstelle der
Landesbausparkassen
Simrockstrasse 4-18
5300 Bonn 1
Tel: (010 49) 228-2041
Telex: 886709

Verband Deutscher
Hypothekenbanken
Holbeinstrasse 17
5300 Bonn 2
Tel: (010 49) 228-372026
Telex: 885677

Verband der Privaten
Bausparkassen
Dottendorferstrasse 82
5300 Bonn 1
Tel: (010 49) 228-239041
Telex: 886834

Finance House
Bankefachverband
Konsumenten und
gewerbliche Spezialkredite
(BKG)
Bonn-Center, H I 1104
Bundeskanzlerplatz
5300 Bonn 1
Tel: (010 49) 228-214038
Telex: 88 64 53

Insurance Associations
Gesamtverband der
Deutschen
Versicherungswirtschaft eV

Verband der
Lebensversicherung-
sunternehmen eV

Greece

All Banks
Hellenic Banks Association
10 Stadiou Street
105 64 Athens
Tel: (010 30) 1-3233278
Telex: 223743

Insurance Associations
Association of Insurance
Companies Operating in
Greece

Insurers Union of Greece

Iceland

Commercial Bank
Samband Islenzkra
Vidskiptabanka
Landsbanki Islands
Austurstraeti 11
Reykjavik

Insurance Association
Association of Icelandic
Insurance Companies

Ireland, Republic of

All Banks
Irish Bankers Federation
(The)
Nassau House
Nassau Street
Dublin 2
Tel: (0001) 715311
Telex: 25843

Commercial Bank

Irish Banks Standing
Committee
Nassau House
Nassau Street
Dublin 2
Tel: 0001 715311
Telex: 25843

Savings Bank

Association of Trustee
Savings Banks
The Administration Centre
Douglas
Cork
Tel: (010 353) 21-931301

Mortgage Institution

Irish Building Societies
Association (The)
Adelaide House
19/20 Adelaide Road
Dublin 2
Tel: (0001) 784833
Telex: 30232

Credit Union

Irish League of Credit Unions
Castleside Drive
Rathfarnham
Dublin 14
Tel: (0001) 908911

Finance House

Irish Finance Houses
Association Limited
Fitzwilton House
Wilton Place
Dublin 2
Tel: (0001) 760306/682222
Telex: 24258

Insurance Association

Insurance Institute of Ireland
32 Nassau Street
Dublin 2
Tel: (0001) 772753

Italy

Commercial Bank

Associazione Bancaria Italiana
Piazza del Gesu 49
00186 Rome
Tel: (010 39) 6-67671
Telex: 680212

Savings Bank

Associazione fra le Casse di
Risparmio Italiane
Luzzotti fra le Bache Popolari
Viale di Villa Grazioli 23
00198 Rome
Tel: (010 39) 6-853693
Telex: 680204

Co-operative Banks

Associazione Nazionale Luigi
Luzzotti fra le Banche
Popolari
Via Montevideo no 18
Rome
Tel: (010 39) 6-852051
Telex: 612575

Associazione Tecnica delle
Banche Popolari Italiane
Via Nazionale 230
00184 Rome
Tel: (010 39) 6-464444
Telex: 613533

Credit Unions

Assicredito
Via Paisiello
500198 Rome
Tel: (010 39) 6-858041

Associazione Nazionale
Aziende Ordinarie di Credito
Via Brennero 1
Milan
Tel: (010 39) 2-4988235
Telex: 334355

Insurance Associations

Associazione Nazionale fra le
Imprese Assicuratrici (ANIA)

Concordato Italiano Incendio

Ufficio Centrale Italiano

Luxembourg

All Banks

Association des Banques et
Banquiers
23 Avenue Monterey
2163 Luxembourg
Tel: (010 352) 29501
Telex: 1701

Insurance Association

Assocation des Compagnies
d'assurances agrees au
Grand-Duche de Luxembourg
(ACA)

Netherlands

Commercial Bank

Nederlande
Bankiersvereniging
Keizersgracht 706
1017 EW Amsterdam
Tel: (010 31) 20-230281

Savings Bank

Nederlandse Spaarbankbond
Postbus 3861
1001 AR Amsterdam
Tel: (010 31) 20-221066

Co-operative Bank

Co-operative Centrale
Raiffeisen-Boerenleenbank
Postbus 8098
3503 SE Utrecht
Tel: (010 31) 30-909111
Telex: 40200

Mortgage Institution

Nederlandse Vereniging van
Hypotheekbanken
Postbus 95374
2509 CJ s'Gravenhage
Tel: (010 31) 70-858048

Finance House

Vereniging van Financier-
ingsondernemingen in
Nederland
Postbus 456
1400 al Bussum
Tel: (010 31) 2159-33753
Telex: 43458

Insurance Associations

Nederlandse Vereniging van
Levensverzekeraars NVL

Verbond van Verzekeraars in
Nederland

Vereniging van
Branassuradeuren in
Nederland

Norway

Commercial Bank

Norwegian Bankers'
Association (The)
Dronning Maudsgate 15
0250 Oslo 2
Tel: (010 47) 2-411830
Telex: 17218

Savings Bank
Sparebankforeningen i Norge
PO Box 6772
St Olavsplass
Oslo 1
Tel: (010 47) 2-110075

Insurance Associations
Norges Forsikringsforbund
Skadeforsikringsselskapenes
Forening

Spain

Commercial Banks
Asociacion Espanola de Banca
Privada (AEB)
Velazquez, 64-66 Planta 6
28006 Madrid
Tel: (010 34) 1-4460011
Telex: 45359

Consejo Superior Bancario
Jose Abascal 57
28003 Madrid
Tel: (010 34) 1-4410611
Telex: 22 937

Junta Provincial de Banca de
Barcelona
Plaza de Catalana 17
Barcelona

Savings Bank
Confederacion Espanola de
Cajas de Ahorros (CECA)
Alcala 27
28014 Madrid
Tel: (010 34) 1-2327810
Telex: 22355

Mortgage Institution
Banco Hipotecario de Espana
Avenida Calvo Sotelo 10
Madrid

Finance Houses
Asociacion Espanola de
Financiadores
Almirante 1
3 Madrid 4
Tel: (010 34)
1-2211020/2211028/2211029

Asociacion Nacional de
Entidades de Financiacion
(ASNEF)
Paseo de la Castellana 128-5
28046 Madrid
Tel: (010 34) 1-4115465
Telex: 46784

Insurance Associations
Sindicato Nacional del Seguro

Union Espanola de Entidades
Aseguradoras,
Reaseguradoras Y de
Capitalizacion (UNESPA)

Sweden

Commercial Banks
Swedish Bankers' Association
(Svenska Bankfoereningen)
Box 7603
103 94 Stockholm
Tel: (010 46) 8-243300
Telex: 10427

Banco Provinsbankernas
Centrala Organisation
Kungsgatan 26
POB 3533
103 69 Stockholm

Savings Bank
Swedish Savings Banks'
Association (The) (Svenska
Sparbanksfoereningen)
Box 16426
103 27 Stockholm
Tel: (010 46) 8-141020
Telex: 11834

Co-operative Bank
Federation of Swedish
Co-operative Banks (Sveriges
Foeringsbankers
Foerbund)
Box 30144
104 25 Stockholm
Tel: (010 46) 8-7377500

Finance House
Swedish Association of
Finance Houses (The)
(Finansbolagens Foerening)
Box 45110
104 30 Stockholm
Tel: (010 46) 8-144875
Telex: 12123

Insurance Associations
Svenska Forsakringsbolags
Riksforbund

Svenska Livforsakringsbolags
Riksforbund

Switzerland

All Banks
Schweizerische
Bankierveenigung
Aeschenvorstadt 4
Postfach 4182
4002 Basle
Tel: (010 41) 61-235888
Telex: 63248

Commercial Banks
Verband Schweizerischer
Kantonalbanken
Spiegelgasse 1
Postfach 2243
4001 Basle
Tel: (010 41) 61-251616

Vereinigung Schweizerischer
Privatbankiers
Lowenstrasse 40
8023 Zurich
Tel: (010 41) 1-2213535

Savings Bank
Verband Schweizerischer
Regionalbanken und
Sparkassen
Bahnhofplatz 10
Postfach 2469
3001 Berne
Tel: (010 41) 31-228646

Co-operative Banks
Federation Vaudoise des
Caisses de Credit Mutuel
1261 Bassins
Tel: (010 41) 663115

Schweizer Verband der
Raiffeisenkassen
Vadianstrasse 17
9001 St Gallen
Tel: (010 41) 71-219111

Finance House
Verband Schweizerischer
Kreditbanken und
Finanzierungsinstitute
c/o Dr W Haefelin
Stauffacherstrasse 35
8004 Zurich
Tel: (010 41) 1-2427587

Insurance Associations
Schweizerischer
Versicherungsverband/
Association Suisse
d'Assurances

Union Suisse des Assureurs Prives Vie (UPAV)/ Schweizerische Vereinigung Privater Lebensversicherer (VPL)

Turkey

Commercial Bank
Turkiye Bankalar Birligi
Mithatpasa Caddesi 12
Yenisehir
Ankara

Insurance Association
Turkiye Sigorta ve Reasurans
Sirketlesi Birligi

UK
British Bankers' Association
10 Lombard Street
London EC3V 9EL
Tel: 01-623 4001
Telex: 888 364

Chartered Institute of Bankers
(The)
10 Lombard Street
London EC3V 9EL
Tel: 01-623 3531
Librarian: Mrs Paula Jiks

Northern Ireland Bankers'
Association
Fountain House
19 Donegall Place
Belfast BT1 5AB
Tel: 0232-227551

Committee of London
Clearing Bankers
10 Lombard Street
London EC3V 9AP
Tel: 01-283 8866

Committee of Scottish
Clearing Bankers
19 Rutland Square
Edinburgh EH1 2DD
Tel: 031-229 1326

Foreign Banks Association
c/o Banque Belge
4 Bishopsgate
London EC2N 2AD
Tel: 01-283 1080

Association of Consortium
Banks
c/o International Mexican
Bank Ltd
29 Gresham Street
London EC2V 7ES
Tel: 01-600 0880

Mortgage Institution
Building Societies Association
3 Saville Row
London W1
Tel: 01-437 0655

Credit Unions
Association of British Credit
Unions
PO Box 135
Credit Union Centre
High Street
Skelmersdale
Lancs WN8 8A 6P
Tel: 0695-31444

Association of British Factors
Moor House
London Wall
London EC2Y 5HE
Tel: 01-638 4090

Finance Houses
Finance Houses Association
18 Upper Grosvenor Street
London W1X 9PB
Tel: 01-491 2783

Consumer Credit Trade
Association (The)
3 Berners Street
London W1E 4JZ
Tel: 01-636 7564

Equipment Leasing
Association Ltd
18 Upper Grosvenor Street
London W1X 9PB
Tel: 01-491 2783

Insurance Associations
Association of British Insurers
Aldermary House
Queen Street
London EC4N 1TT
Tel: 01-248 4477

British Insurance Brokers
Association
130 Fenchurch Street
London EC3M 5DJ
Tel: 01-623 9043

Other Activities
Financial Intermediaries,
Managers and Brokers
Regulatory Organisation
(FIMBRA)
22 Great Tower Street
London EC3R 5AQ
Tel: 01-929 2711

Issuing Houses Association
Granite House
101 Cannon Street
London EC4V 5BA
Tel: 01-283 7334

National Association of Estate
Agents
Arban House
21 Jury Street
Warwick CV34 4EH
Tel: 0926-496800

National Association of
Pension Funds
12-18 Grosvenor Gardens
London SW1W 0DH
Tel: 01-730 0585

Sterling Brokers Association
(The)
c/o Butler Till Ltd
Adelaide House
London Bridge
London EC4

Yugoslavia

Commercial Bank
Udruzenje Banaka Jugoslavije
Masarikova 5/IX
11001 Belgrade
Tel: (010 38) 11-684797

Insurance Association
Udruzenje Osiguravajucih
Organizacija Jugoslavije

Australia

Commercial Bank
Australian Bankers
Association
360 Collins Street
Melbourne
Victoria 3000
Tel: (010 61) 3-679131
Telex: 22806

Mortgage Institutions
Australian Association of
Permanent Building Societies
8 Thessiger Court
Deakin ACT
Australia 2600
Tel: (010 61) 62-811588
Telex: 62408

Australian Council of
Co-operative Housing
Societies (The)
7th Floor
390 Little Collins Street
Melbourne
Victoria 3000

Credit Union
Australian Federation of
Credit Unions Ltd
8th Floor
500 George Street
Sydney
NSW 2000
Tel: (010 61) 2-2647526
Telex: 23803

Finance House
Australian Finance
Conference Ltd
17th Floor
388 George Street
Sydney
NSW 2000
Tel: (010 61) 2-2315877
Telex: 23719

Cash Management Institution
Cash Management Trust
Association
5th Floor
93 York Street
Sydney
NSW 2000
Tel: (010 61) 2-2997888
Telex: 27113

Insurance Associations
Insurance Council of
Australia Limited (The)

Life Insurance Federation of
Australia (The)

New Zealand

Commercial Bank
NZ Bankers Association
PO Box 3043
Wellington
Tel: (010 64) 4-728838

Savings Bank
Associated Trustee Banks
Databank House
PO Box 2260
00644 Wellington
Telex: 60881

Mortgage Institution
Building Societies Association
(NZ) Inc
7th Floor
Kelvin Chambers
16 The Terrace
PO Box 10-053
Wellington

Credit Union
New Zealand Credit Union
League
Box 585
Hamilton
Tel: (010 64) 71-392082
Telex: 21215

USA

All Banks
Association of Reserve City
Bankers
1710 Rhode Island Avenue
NW
Washington DC 20036
Tel: (010 1) 202-2965709

Bank Marketing Association
309 W Washington Street
Chicago
Illinois 60606
Tel: (010 1) 312-7821442

Consumer Bankers
Association
1300 North 17th Street
Suite 1200
Arlington
Virginia 22209
Tel: (010 1) 703-2761750

Electronic Funds Transfer
Association
1029 Vermont Avenue NW
Suite 800
Washington DC 20005
Tel: (010 1) 202-7833555

Independent Bankers
Association of America
1625 Massachusetts Avenue
NW
Suite 202
Washington DC 20036
Tel: (010 1) 202-3328980

National Bankers Association
122 C Street NW
Suite 240
Washington DC 20001
Tel: (010 1) 202-7833200

Western Independent
Bankers
11 Embarcadero West
Oakland
California 94607
Tel: (010 1) 415-8395992

Commercial Banks
American Bankers
Association
1120 Connecticut Avenue NW
Washington DC 20036
Tel: (010 1) 202-4674000
Telex: 892787

Association of Bank Holding
Companies
730 15th Street NW
Washington DC 20005
Tel: (010 1) 202-3931158

Savings Banks
American League of Financial
Institutions
1511 K Street NW
Washington DC 20006
Tel: (010 1) 202-6285624

National Council of Savings
Institutions
1101 15th Street NW
Suite 400
Washington DC 20005
Tel: (010 1) 202-3310270

United States League of
Savings Institutions
111 E Wacker Drive
Chicago
Illinois 60601
Tel: (010 1) 312-6443100
Telex: 9102215144

Mortgage Institution

Mortgage Bankers
Association
1125 15th Street NW
Washington DC 20005
Tel: (010 1) 202-8616500

Credit Unions

Credit Union National
Association
5710 Mineral Point Road
Box 431
Madison
Wisconsin 53701
Tel: (010 1) 608-2314000
Telex: 265446

National Association of
Federal Credit Unions
1111 N 19th Street
Suite 700
Arlington
Virginia 22209
Tel: (010 1) 703-5224770

Finance House

American Financial Services
Association
1101 14th Street NW
Washington DC 20005
Tel: (010 1) 202-2890400

Mutual Fund

Investment Company
Institute
1600 M Street NW
Washington DC 20036
Tel: (010 1) 202-2937700

Insurance Associations

Alliance of American Insurers
American Council of Life
Insurance (The)
American Insurance
Association
Insurance Information
Institute
Life Offices Management
Association

Canada

Commercial Banks

Canadian Bankers
Association
PO Box 348
2 First Canadian Place
Toronto M5X 1E1
Tel: (010 1) 416-3626092
Telex: 06-234 02

Associations des Banquiers
Canadiens
Suite 720
1801 Ave McGill College
Montreal
Quebec H3A 2N4

Savings Banks

La Federation des Caisses
Populaires Acaisennes
PO Box 920
Caraquet
New Brunswick E0B 1KO
Tel: (010 1) 506-7273478

La Confederation des Caisses
Populaires et d'Economie
Desjardins du Quebec
100 Avenue des
Commandeurs
Levis
Quebec G6V 7N5
Tel: (010 1) 418-8352323
Telex: 6513533

Trust Bank

Trust Companies Association
of Canada
7th Floor
335 Bay Street
Toronto M5H 2R3
Tel: (010 1) 416-3641207

Co-operative Bank

Canadian Co-operative Credit
Society
300 The East Mall
Islington
Ontario M9B 6B7
Tel: (010 1) 416-2321262
Telex: 06-967677

Insurance Associations

Canadian Life & Health
Insurance Association (The)
Insurance Bureau of Canada

Hong Kong

All Banks

Hong Kong Association of
Banks
Prince's Building
Room 525
PO Box 11391
General Post Office
Tel: (010 852) 5-211288

Credit Union

Credit Union League of Hong
Kong
603 Jade Mansion
40 Waterloo Road
Kowloon
Tel: (010 852) 3-856982

Insurance Associations

Accident Insurance
Association of Hong Kong
Fire Insurance Association of
Hong Kong
Insurance Council of Hong
Kong
Life Insurance Council of
Hong Kong

India

Commercial Bank

Indian Bank's Association
Stadium House
6th Floor, Block 3
81-83 Veer Nariman Road
Churgata
Bombay 400 020
Tel: (010 91) 22-2365
Telex: 0115146 IBA

Insurance Association

Insurance Association of
India
Calcutta Regional Committee
(Tariff Advisory Committee)
Madras Regional Committee
(Tariff Advisory Committee)
Tariff Advisory Committee
(Bombay)
Tariff Advisory Committee
(General Insurance)

Indonesia

Commercial Bank

Indonesian National Private
Banks Association
Jalan Sindanglaya 1
Jakarta
Tel: (010 62) 21-351170

Insurance Association

Dewan Asuransi Indonesia

Japan

All Banks
Federation of Bankers'
Association of Japan
(Tokyo Bankers' Association
Inc)
1-3-1 Marunouchi
Chiyoda-Ku
Tokyo
Tel: (010 81) 3-2163761
Telex: 26830

Commercial Banks
Regional Banks Association of
Japan (The)
3-1-2 Uchikanda
Chiyoda-Ku
Tokyo
Tel: (010 81) 3-2525171

Trust Company Association
of Japan
2-6-2 Otemachi
Chiyoda-Ku
Tokyo

Savings Banks
National Association of Sogo
Banks
5 Sanban-Cho
Chiyoda-Ku
Tokyo
Tel: (010 81) 3-2622181
Telex: 232 2011

Co-operative Banks
National Association of
Shinkin Banks (The)
3-8-1 Kyobashi
Chuo-Ku
Tokyo
Tel: (010 81) 3-5634111

National Central Society of
Credit Co-Operations
1-9-1 Kyobashi
Chuo-Ku
Tokyo
Tel: (010 81) 3-5672451

Insurance Associations
Foreign Non-Life Insurance
Association of Japan
Japan Institute of Life Insura
.nce
Life Insurance Association of
Japan (The)
Marine and Fire Insurance
Association of Japan (The)

Korea, Republic of

Commercial Bank
Bankers' Association of Korea
4,1-ka Myong-Dong
Chung-Ku
Seoul 100
Tel: (010 82) 2-7767165

Insurance Associations
Korea Non-Life Insurance
Association
Life Insurance Association of
Korea (The)

Malaysia

Commercial Bank
Association of Banks in
Malaysia (The)
23rd Floor
West Wing
Bangunan
Dato Zainal
Kuala Lumpur
Tel: (010 60) 3-922143/243

Finance House
Association of Finance
Companies of Malaysia
The Bang Dato' Zainal
Kuala Lumpur
Tel: (010 60) 3-925455

Insurance Associations
General Insurance
Association of Malaysia
Life Insurance Association of
Malaysia

Pakistan

Commercial Bank
Pakistan Banks' Association
National Bank of Pakistan
Building
POB 4937
1.1 Chundrigar Road
Karachi 2
Tel: (010 92) 21-236686

Insurance Association
Insurance Association of
Pakistan

Philippines

Commercial Banks
Bankers' Association of the
Philippines
Room S-314, 3rd Floor
Secretariat Building
CCP Complex
Roxas Boulevard
Manila

Insurance Association
Insurance & Surety
Association of the Philippines
(The)

Singapore

Commercial Bank
Association of Banks in
Singapore (The)
Level 2, PIL Building
140 Cecil Street
Singapore 0106
Tel: (010 65) 2244300
Telex: 20533

Insurance Associations
General Association of
Singapore
Life Insurance Association

Taiwan

Commercial Bank
Bankers Association of the
Republic of China
8th Floor
46 Kuanchien Road
Taipei

Insurance Association
Taipei Insurance Association

Thailand

Commercial Bank
Thai Bankers' Association
(The)
Sathorn Thani Building
90 North Sathorn Road
Bangkok

Insurance Association
General Insurance
Association of Thailand (The)

Note: Insurance Associations
If you wish to contact specific
associations, addresses can be
obtained from:

Association of British Insurers
(The)
London
UK
Tel: 01-248 4477

Directories

International
Balance of Payments
EC Publications office
HMSO Books
London
UK
Covers the EEC, USA and
Japan

Bankers Almanac and Year
Book
Thomas Skinner Directories
East Grinstead, Sussex
UK
(Also available from IPC
Business Press, New York)

Bankers Almanac World
Ranking
Thomas Skinner Directories
East Grinstead, Sussex
UK

Bank Register
Euromoney Publications
London
UK
Directory of the world's major
financial institutions

Business Line Finance
Euromonitor Publications
London
UK

Commodities Future Trading
Mansell
London
UK
(Distribution Management
Services)
A guide to information
sources and computerised
services.

Commodity Yearbook
Turret-Wheatland
Rickmansworth
Herts
UK
Includes analysis and
forecasts

Directory of Financial Futures
Exchanges
Macmillan Publications Co
Basingstoke
Hants
UK
Directory of members and
players

Directory of World Stock
Exchanges
New York Stock Exchange
USA

Euromarket Directory
Euromoney Publications
London
UK
Directory of borrowers in
international markets

Eurostudy Annual
Eurostudy Publications
London
UK
Database on Euromarkets

Finance Directory
International
Sterling Publications
London
UK

Financial Directories of the
World
Vallancey International
Guernsey
A guide to the information
sources in finance,
economics, employment,
property and law

GT Guide to World Equity
Markets (The)
Euromoney Publications
London
UK
Description of the equity
market in 36 markets

Guide to World Commodity
Markets
Kogan Page
London
UK

Hambro Euromoney Guide
(The)
Euromoney Publications
London
UK

International Business
Lawyers Index and Industrial
Property (The)
Datapress
Geneva
Switzerland

International Financial
Directory (The)
Euromoney Publications
London
UK
Merger of Merrill Lynch's
Euromoney Directory and
Bank Register

International Insurance
Industry Guide
Coopers and Lybrand
London
UK
Detailed information on
regulatory, accounting and
taxation practices overseas

Merrill Lynch Euromoney
Publications
Euromoney Publications
London
UK
Worldwide bank directory

Moodys Bank and Finance
Manual and News Report
Moodys Investor Service
c/o Dun and Bradstreet
London
UK

Polks World Bank Directory
Polk
Nashville
Tennessee
USA

Sources of World Financial
and Banking Information
Gower Publishers
Farnborough
UK

Traders Directory of Foreign
Exchange Futures and
Options Dealers
Euromoney Publications
London
UK

Who Owns What in World
Banking
FT Business Information Ltd
London
UK

Who's Who in International
Banking
International Trader
Publications Co Ltd
London
UK

World Currency Yearbook
Covers 145 currencies

World Financial System (The)
Longman Group
Harlow, Essex
UK
A comprehensive reference
source

World Insurance, FT
International Yearbook
Financial Times Business
Publications
London
UK
1160 company entries in 81
countries

Worldwide Directory: Foreign
Exchange, Futures and
Options Dealers
Euromoney Publications
London
UK

Europe
Major Financial Institutions of
Continental Europe
Graham and Trotman
London
UK

Allied Dunbar Investment
Guide
Longman Group
Harlow, Essex
UK

Allied Hambro Pensions
Guide 1987
Long $man Group
Harlow, Essex
UK

Association of Certified
Accountants Directory
London
UK

Beckets Directory to the City
of London
Becket Publications
London
UK

British Insurance Industry – A
Statistical Review (The)
Kluwer Publications Ltd
Brentford, Middlesex
UK

Building Societies Fact Book
Building Societies Association
UK

Building Societies Fact File
Longman Group
Harlow, Essex
UK

Company Pension Benefits
Monks Publications
Debden Green
Saffron Walden, Essex
UK

Compendium of Building
Society Statistics
Building Societies Association
UK

Crawford's City Changes
Economist Publications
London
UK
(annual subscription service)

Crawford's Corporate
Finance
Economist Publications
London
UK
Sources of business finance in
the UK

Crawfords Directory of
Market Makers in UK Equities
Economist Publications
London
UK
Details of shares traded by
UK's 32 registered market
makers

Crawford's Investment
Research Index
Economist Publications
London
UK
Guide to UK investor
relations

Dealers in Securities and
Authorised Trust Schemes
HMSO
London
UK

Directory of City Connections
Crawford Publications
Economist Publications
London
UK

Directory of Dealing Room
Systems and Services
Kogan Page/First Market
Intelligence
London
UK

Dun and Bradstreet Register
Dun and Bradstreet
London
UK
Details on companies and
credit ratings. Also available
on microfiche. Five volumes

Extel Capital Gains Tax
Service
Extel Statistical Services Ltd
London
UK

Extel Handbook of Market
Leaders
Extel Statistical Services Ltd
London
UK

Extel Issuing House Year
Book
Extel Statistical Services Ltd
London
UK

Extel Prospectuses and New
Issues fiche service
Extel Statistical Services Ltd
London
UK
(12 issues per annum)

Extel Register of Registrars
Extel Statistical Services Ltd
London
UK
Directory of professional
registrars and companies

Extel USM Handbook
Extel Statistical Services Ltd
London
UK
Published every January and
July

Financial Reporting – A
Survey of UK Published
Accounts
Institute of Chartered
Accountants
London
UK

Financial Services Guide
Beacon Publications
Wellingborough,
Northamptonshire
UK

Gilt-Edged Market (The)
Wedd Durlacher Mordaunt &
Co
London
UK

Guide to Financial Times (FT)
Statistics
Financial Times Business
Information
London
UK

Institute of Actuaries Year
Book (The)
Institute of Actuaries
Alden Press
Oxford
UK

Institute of Chartered
Accountants in England and
Wales (The)
The Institute of Chartered
Accountants
London
UK
List of members and firms

Institute of Cost and
Management Accountants
(The)
The Institute of Cost and
Management Accountants
London
UK
List of members

Insurance Directory and Year
Book (The)
Buckley Press
Brentford, Middlesex
UK

Insurance Register (UK)
City Financial Insurance
Publications
Brentford, Middlesex
UK

Investment Trust Year Book
and Who's Who
Macmillan Publishers
London
UK

London Commodity
Exchange
The London Commodity
Exchange Ltd
London
UK
List of exchange members

Longman USM Directory
Longman Group
Harlow, Essex
UK

Official Sources of Finance
and Aid for Industry in the
UK
National Westminster Bank
plc
Commercial Information,
Market Intelligence
Department
London
UK

Stock Exchange (The)
London Stock Exchange
UK
Register of firms and
members

Sunday Telegraph Business
Finance Directory
Graham and Trotman
London
UK

Sunday Telegraph UK
Finance Directory
Graham and Trotman
London
UK

Survey of Insurance Brokers
Directory of registered limited
company insurance brokers

Unit Trust Yearbook
Financial Times Business
Information
London
UK

Venture Capital Report Guide
to Venture Capital in the UK
Venture Capital Report Ltd
Henley-on-Thames
UK

Wharton Annual
Pergamon Books Ltd
Oxford
UK
Forecasts and market trends

Netherlands
Bankenboekje
Nederlands Institu voor het
Bank – en Effectenbedrijif
Amsterdam

Switzerland
Swiss Stock Guide
Union Bank of Switzerland
Zurich

USA
Corporate Finance Bluebook
National Register Publishing
Co Inc
Wilmette, IL
Lists key financial
decision-makers in US
corporations

Corporate Finance
Sourcebook
National Register Publishing
Co Inc
Wilmette, IL
Lists financial specialists and
firms

Moody's Bank and Finance
Manual and News Reports
1987
Moody's Investor Service
c/o Dun and Bradstreet
London
Covers up to 7 years of the
latest financial accounts,
details of US companies'
capital structure including
bond ratings.
Includes banks, trust
companies, savings and loan
associations (volume 1).
Insurance, finance, real
estate, investment companies
(volume 2).
Unit Investment Trusts
(volume 3).

Asia
Asia Banking Almanac
Asiamedia Co Ltd
Hong Kong

Bankers Handbook for Asia
Asian Finance Publications
Hong Kong

Middle East
Arab Banking and F inance
Handbook
Falcon Publishing
Manama
Bahrain

MEED – Middle East
Directory
MEED Group Ltd
London
UK

Market Research Reports and Publishers

This section lists recently
published market research
reports which cover
various aspects of the
Financial Services sector.
Details provided below
are title of report, publisher,
year of publication, price and
geographic
coverage.

Accountants & Survey
Databank Ltd (UK)
1988
£1500
UK

Advanced Banking
Euromonitor Publications Ltd
(UK)
1987
£235
UK

Attitudes of Mortgage
Intermediaries (The)
Janet Levin Associates (UK)
1988
£1750
UK

Banking Monitor
Executive Surveys Ltd (Hong
Kong)
1987
Price on request
Hong Kong

Banques de Marches (Les)
Eurostaf Dafsa (France)
1987
FF9.300
Europe

British Merchant Banks (3rd
Edition)
Databank Ltd (UK)
1988
£1400
UK

Building Societies
Key Note Publications Ltd
(UK)
1987
£105
UK

Business Capital Sources
B Klein Publications (USA)
1988
$35
USA

Business Ratio Report:
Finance Houses
ICC Business Ratios (UK)
Annual
£165
UK

Business Ratio Report:
Insurance Broke ,rs
ICC Business Ratios (UK)
Annual
£165
UK

Business Ratio Report: Unit
Trust Managers
ICC Business Ratios (UK)
Annual
£165
UK

Car Finance Decision (The)
Janet Levin Associates (UK)
1987
£200
UK

City Financial Insurance
Register
Kluwer Publishing Ltd (UK)
1987
£45
UK

Commercial Paper
Euromoney plc (UK)
1987
£75 (UK), $125 (US)
Worldwide

Commodity Brokers
ICC Financial Surveys (UK)
1988
£145
UK

Compendium of Building
Society Statistics, 7th edition
The Building Societies
Association (UK)
1988
£25
UK

Consumer Banking in the
United States
The Economist Publications
(UK)
1987
£150 (UK & Europe),$220 (N
America), £153 (ROW)
USA

Consumer Credit & Loans
Market Assessment
Publications (UK)
1987
£200
UK

Consumer Finance: Market
Segmentation Study
Campbell Keegan Ltd (UK)
1986
Price on request
UK

Consumer Savings
Mintel Publications Ltd (UK)
1988
£550
UK

Corporate Credit Card Market
(The)
Industrial Market Research
Ltd (UK)
1988
Price on request
UK

Corporate Financial Advisory
Services
Databank Spa (Italy)
1988
£1400
Italy

Corporate Loans
DRI/New York (USA)
1987
Price on request
USA

Corporate Venturing
National Economic
Development Office (UK)
1987
£5.00
UK

Corporate Venturing News
Venture Economics Inc (USA)
1988
$345
Worldwide

Credit & Charge Cards
Euromonitor Publication [s
Ltd (UK)
Updated every 6 months
£975
Europe/USA

Credit Card Decision (The)
Janet Levin Associates (UK)
1987
£500
UK

Credit Card Industry: A
Strategic Market Analysis
(The)
Business Communications Co
(USA)
1988
$2150
USA

Credit Cards
Key Note Publications Ltd
(UK)
1987
£105
UK

Customer Service Index
Market Facts of Canada Ltd
(Canada)
Annual
Price on request
Canada

Debt Collecting & Factoring
Key Note Publications Ltd
(UK)
1987
£105
UK

Electronic Banking in the
1990s – ATMs, POS
Terminals, Debit Cards,
Home Banking
Business Communications Co
(USA)
1988
$2450
USA

Electronic Banking in the
1990s – Services, Structure,
Branches, Productivity,
Software
Business Communications Co
(USA)
1988
$2450
USA

Electronic Developments in
Consumer Banking
Mintel Publications Ltd (UK)
1987
£495
UK

EuroCommercial Paper
Euromoney plc (UK)
1987
£75 (UK), $125 (US)
Worldwide

European Investment Banks
Databank Ltd (UK)
1988
£1400
Europe

Expanding Financial Centres:
Hong Kong
The Economist Publications
(UK)
1987
£95 (UK & Europe), $155 (N
America), £98 (ROW)
Hong Kong

Expanding Financial Centres:
Singapore
The Economist Publications
(UK)
1987
£95 (UK & Europe), $155 (N
America), £98 (ROW)
Singapore

External Capital for Small
Firms – Recent Developments
National Economic
Development Office (UK)
1986
£3.50
UK

Finance for the Homemaker –
Special Report
Mintel Publications Ltd (UK)
1987
£495
UK

Financial Aspects of
Industrial Restructuring
National Economic
Development Office (UK)
1986
£5.00
UK

Financial Institutions
Providing Medium and Long
Term Credit to Industry
Databank Spa (Italy)
1988
£1400
Italy

Financial Research Survey
NOP Market Research Ltd
(UK)
1987
Price on request
UK

Financial Services Guide
Matrix Publishing Group Ltd
(UK)
1988
£22.50
UK

Finding Money for Your
Business
Confederation of British
Industry (UK)
1987
£3.50
UK

Guide to European Venture
Capital Sources, 2nd edition
Venture Economics Ltd (UK)
1988
£95
Europe

House Purchase Decision
(The)
Janet Levin Associates (UK)
1987
£950
UK

Household Flow of Funds
Survey (The)
Market Facts of Canada Ltd
(Canada)
Annual
Price on request
Canada

Instalment Credit and
Finance
ICC Financial Surveys (UK)
1988
£145
UK

Insurance
Market Assessment
Publications (UK)
1987
£200
UK

Insurance & Banking Guide
Matrix Publishing Group Ltd
(UK)
1988
£20
Middle East

Insurance Brokers
Key Note Publications Ltd
(UK)
1988
£105
UK

Insurance Brokers – London
and South
ICC Financial Surveys (UK)
1987
£185
UK

Insurance Brokers – Midlands
and North
ICC Financial Surveys (UK)
1987
£185
UK

Insurance Brokers' Monitor
Taylor, Nelson Financial Ltd
(UK)
Quarterly
£3000 per quarter
UK

Insurance Buyer's Guide
(The)
Kluwer Publishing Ltd (UK)
1988
£15
UK

Insurance Companies
Databank Spa (Italy)
1988
£1400
Italy

Insurance Companies
Key Note Publications Ltd
(UK)
1987
£105
UK

Insurance Guide
Matrix Publishing Group Ltd
(UK)
1987
£11
Asia

International Housing
Finance Factbook 1987
The Building Societies
Association (UK)
1987
£8.00
Worldwide

International Tax Summaries:
A Guide for Planning and
Decisions
John Wiley & Sons Ltd (UK)
1988
£75/$115
Worldwide

Japanese Investment Banks in
Europe
Databank Ltd (UK)
1988
£1400
Europe

Latest Innovations in the US
Mortgage Market
The Economist Publications
(UK)
1987
£138 (UK & Europe), $240 (N
America), : £141 (ROW)
USA

Lending to Small Firms – A
Study of Appraisal and
Monitoring Methods:
Literature Survey
National Economic
Development Office (UK)
1986
£5.00
UK

Lending to Small Firms –
Study of Appraisal &
Monitoring Methods
National Economic
Development Office (UK)
1986
£5.00
UK

Loan Decision (The)
Janet Levin Associates (UK)
1988
£950
UK

Marketing of Financial
Services
The Scottish Council for
Development and Industry
(Scotland)
1985
£45
Scotland

Merchant Banking
Databank Spa (Italy)
1988
£1400
Italy

Merger & Acquisition Source
Book
B Klein Publications (USA)
1987
$185
USA

Mergers & Acquisitions in
Canada
Venture Economics Canada,
Ltd (Canada)
1988
$Can225
Canada

Mutual Fund Industry (The)
Packaged Facts (USA)
1986
$495
USA

N Ireland Financial Monitor
Ulster Marketing Surveys Ltd
(N Ireland)
Annually
£2000
N Ireland

New Wealth & The Individual
Mintel Publications Ltd (UK)
1987
£550
UK

Pensions – Special Report
Mintel Publications Ltd (UK)
1988
£550
UK

Permanent Health Insurance
Kluwer Publishing Ltd (UK)
1988
£14.95
UK

Personal Finance Market
(The)
Jordan and Sons Ltd (UK)
1987
£85
UK

Personal Financial Services
Euromonitor Publications Ltd
(UK)
1988
£325
UK

Plastic Cards
Euromonitor Publications Ltd
(UK)
1987
£235
UK

Pratts Guide to Venture
Capital Sources, 12th edition
Venture Economics Inc (USA)
1988
$125
Canada, USA

Projecting Prepayment Rates
for Mortgage Backed
Securities
DRI/New York (USA)
1988
Price on request
USA

Promoting Growth in Venture
Capital
Corporate Development
Consultants Ltd (UK)
1987
£5850
UK

Property Finance
Market Assessment
Publications (UK)
1987
£275
UK

Retail Banking
Databank Ltd (UK)
1988
£1400
UK

Retail Banks: Profiles of the
Major Companies
Databank Spa (Italy)
1988
£1400
Italy

Savings & Investments
Market Assessment
Publications (UK)
1987
£275
UK

Savings Decision (The)
Janet Levin Associates (UK)
1988
£950
UK

Savings War (The)
Kluwer Publishing Ltd (UK)
1988
£75
UK

Secteur Bancaire en Europe
(Le) (2 volumes)
Eurostaf Dafsa (France)
1988
FF18.600
Europe

Small Business Investment
Companies
B Klein Publications (USA)
1988
$35
USA

Societes de Credit-Bail
Immobilier (Les)
Eurostaf Dafsa (France)
1987
FF7.000
France

Stockbrokers
Databank Spa (Italy)
1988
£1400
Italy

Study of the Rural Banking
and Finance Market
AgriMark Consultants Pty
Ltd (Australia)
1987
Price on request
Australia

Terms & Conditions of
Venture Capital Partnerships
Venture Economics Inc (USA)
1987
$495
USA

Trends in UK Buy-Outs
Venture Economics Ltd (UK)
1987
£495
UK

Trends in Venture Capital
Venture Economics Inc (USA)
1988
$925
USA

UK Financial Institutions
Key Note Publications Ltd
(UK)
1988
£105
UK

US Investment Banks in
Europe (2nd Edition)
Databank Ltd (UK)
1988
£1400
Europe

Venture Capital
Venture Economics Canada,
Ltd (Canada)
1988
$Can 295
Canada

Venture Capital Investors
Service
Venture Economics Inc (USA)
1988
£195
UK

Venture Capital:
Opportunities and
Considerations for Investors
Venture Economics Inc (USA)
1987
$1800
USA

Venture Capital Valuation
Methods
Venture Economics Ltd (UK)
1987
£170
UK

Venture Capital Yearbook
Venture Economics Inc (USA)
1988
$125
USA

Periodicals and Journals

International/Pan-European/USA

Agefi International Financial
Review
Banking Technology
Banking World
British Business
Building Societies (BSA)
European Bulletin
Business America
Corporate Finance
Euromoney
Financial Services
International
Forbes
Fortune International
Institutional Investor
International
International Accounting
Bulletin
International Tax Report
Investment International
Investors Alert
Journal of Commerce
Re Report
Retail Banker International
Review (The) – Insurance
Worldwide
Wall Street Journal
What Investment
International
World Accounting Report
(FT)
World of Banking
World Information Courier
World Trade Information

Europe

Austria

Austria Offert
Austrian Technology Report
Borsen Kurier
Buro Report
IW- Neue Internationale
Wirtschaft
Konsum Osterreich
Profil
Salzburger Wirtschaft
Trend
Wiener Wirtschaft die
Wirtschaft

Zeitschrift fur
Nationalukonomie
Zeitschrift fur Verwaltung

Belgium

Belgian Business
Bourse – Revue
Commerce in Belgium
Doc Umentatilon
Commerciale et Comptable
L'Echo des Tirages
Les Europeens
L'Eventail
Guide Fiscal Permanent
Intermediaire/Intermediair
Mercure
De Middenstand
Trends and Trends
Tendances
De Verzekeringswereld

Denmark

Agenten
Dansk Industrie
Denmark Review
Finanstidende
Lederskab og Lonsomhed
Maneds Borsen
Revision og Regnskabsvaesen
Spare Kassen

Finland

Fakta
Finnfacts
Finnish Business Report
Forsakring Stidning
(Insurance)
Kaupparteknikko
Saastopankki (Savings Banks)
Vakuutussanomat
(Insurance)

France

Annuaire Desfosses
L'Argus (Insurance)
Argus International
L'Assurance Francais ie
Banque
Bilans Hebdomadaires
Journal des Finances
Mieux Vivre
Revenue Fiduciaire
La Revue Francaise
Tribune des Assurances
La Vie Francaise

Germany, Federal Republic of

Der Bankkaufmann (Banking)
Der Betrieb
Betriebswirtschafts-Magazin
Bild Post

Creditreform (Taxation)
DM
Frankfurter Borsenbriefe
Geldinstitute (Banking)
Gesichertes Leben
(Insurance)
Neue Wirtschafts-Briefe
(Taxation)
Steurwarte (Taxation)
Versicherungsbetriebe
(Insurance)
Die Versicherungs-Praxis
Wertpapier (Investment)
Zeitschrift fur des Gesamte
Kreditwesen

Ireland, Republic of
Accountancy Ireland
Business and Finance
Institute of Bankers in Ireland
Journal
Irish Banking Magazine
Irish Banking Review
Quarterly Review (Central
Bank)

Italy
L'Azione Commerciale
Giornale delle Assicurazioni
(Insurance)
Mondo Economico
Successo
Tempo Economico

Netherlands
De Accountant
Accountant-Adviseur
Assurantie Magazine
(Insurance)
Bankpraet (Banking)
Beleggers Belangen
(Investment)
De Beursbengel (Commerce
and Insurance)
Financiele Economisch
Magazine (FEM)
Financiele Koerier
Handelsbelangen (Commerce
and Finance)
Imago (Insurance)
Investors Alert (Stock Market)
De Makelaar
Vraagbaak voor het
Assuratiewezen (Insurance)

Norway
Skatt og Budsjett (Taxpayers)
Sko
Storkjokken

Spain
Actualidad Economica
Banca Espanola
Comercio e Industria
Economia y Finanzas
Espanolas
El Financiero
Finanzas
El Mundo Financiero
Relaciones Financieras

Sweden
Affars Ekonomi-Management
NU
Affarsvarlden
Aktiespararen (Shareholders)
Foreningsbankerna
(Cooperative Banks)
Foretagsekonomi
(Accountants/Auditors)
Forsakringstidningen
(Insurance)
Information
Privata Affarer (Private
Investors)
Sparbankerna (Banking)
Sunt Fornuft (Taxpayers)
Svensk Handelstidning

UK
Accountancy
Accountancy Age
Accounting and Business
Research
Banker (The)
Banking FINTAC Report
Bank of England Bulletin
Banking Technology
Banking World
British Tax Review
BSA Bulletin
Building Society News
Business Week
Crawfords Directory of City
Changes
Economist (The)
Electronic Banking and
Finance
Euromoney
Financial Weekly
Institutional Investor
Insurance Age
Insurance Weekly
Investors Chronicle
Journal of Retail Banking
Leasing Digest
Managerial Finance
Money Management
Pensions
Pensions World
Retail Banker International

Middle East
Arab Banking and Finance
Arab Business Report
Arabian Insurance Guide
Middle East Review

Canada
Business and Finance in
Ontario
Canadian Banker and ICB
Review
Canadian Insurance
Corporate Insurance in
Canada
Finance
Journal of Commerce
Money-Wise Magazine
Pensions and Benefits
Revue Commerce

Asia
Asian Banking
Asian Finance
Asian Finance Young
Executive
Asian Money Manager
Far Eastern Economic Review

China
China Investment Guide
China Trade Magazine
China Trader
China's Foreign Trade

Hong Kong
Asiabanking
Business Asia
Financial Chronicle
Hong Kong Business Today

India
Capital
Economic Age
Indian Banking

Australia
ANZ Bank Business
Indicators
Australian Accountant
Australian Financial Review
Australian Stock Exchange
Journal
Bankers Magazine of
Australia
Bulletin (The)
Business Review Weekly
Chartered Accountant in
Australia
Personal Investment
Taxation in Australia

Government Publications

UK Official Statistics

General Industry
Annual Abstract of Statistics
Bank of England Quarterly
Bulletin
Financial Statistics
(HMSO publication)
Mainly quarterly data
providing summary capital
and financial transaction
accounts classified by major
groupings of companies and
institutions.
Northern Ireland Annual
Abstract of Statistics
Scottish Abstract of Statistics
United Kingdom National
Accounts

Banking Sector
Annual Abstract of Statistics
Bank of England Quarterly
Bulletin
Bank of England Report and
Accounts
Bank Return (Bank of
England, weekly)
British Business
Business Monitor: SDM6
SDQ7
Economic Trends (HMSO)
Financial Statistics (HMSO)

Building Societies
Building Society Yearbook
Press Notice (Buiding
Societies Association,
monthly)

Insurance Companies
Annual Report of the British
Insurance Association
British Business
Business Monitor: MA16
MQ5
Insurance Business Annual
Report
(HMSO publication)
Insurance Facts and Figures
(available from the British
Insurance Association)
Life Assurance in the United
Kingdom

Unit Trusts
Annual Abstract of Statistics
Financial Statistics
Press Release (Unit Trust
Association, monthly)
Unit Trust Yearbook (The)
Northern Business
Information (USA)

Food & Drink

Trade Associations

Europe

Belgium
Federation des industries
agricoles et alimentaires (FIA)
172 avenue de Cortenbergh
1040 Brussels
Tel: (010 32) 2-358170
Telex: 26 246 FIA B

Denmark
Industriraadet (Federation of
Danish Industries)
Aldersrogade 20
2200
Copenhagen N
Tel: (010 45) 2-836611
Telex: 22993 IRAAD DK

France
Association nationale des
industries agricoles et
alimentaires (ANIAA)
52 rue de Faubourg St Honore
75008 Paris
Tel: (010 33) 1-2664014
Telex: 641 784 ANIAA

Germany, Federal Republic of
Bundesvereinigung der
Deutschen
Ernahrungsindustrie eV
Rheinallee 13
53000 Bonn
Tel: (010 49) 228-351011
Telex: 885 697 NAEHR D

Ireland, Republic of
Food Drink & Tobacco
Federation of Ireland
Confederation House
Kildare Street
Dublin 2
Tel: (0001) 779801
Telex: 4711 CII EI

Italy
Confederazione generale
dell'industria italiana –
Confidustria (Confederation
of Italian Industries)
Viale dell'Astronomia 30
Casella postale 2444
00144 Rome
Tel: (010 39) 6-59031
Telex: 63162 CONF INDU

Netherlands
Commissie voor de
Nederlandse voedsel – en
agrarische industrie (VAI)
Prinses Beatrixlaan 5
Postbus 2110
2509 AB The Hague
Tel: (010 31) 70-814171
Telex: 32146 VNO NL

Sweden
Sveriges Industriforbund
(Federation of Swedish
Industries)
Storgatan 19
Box 5501
114 85 Stockholm

Sveriges Kottgrossister (Meat)
Box 142
182 12 Danderyd

UK
Food & Drink Federation
(The)
6 Catherine St
London, WC2B 5JJ
Tel: 01-836 2460
Telex: 299 388 fdfg
Fax: 01 836 0580

USA
American Bakers Association
2020 K St NW
Washington DC 20006
Tel: (010 1) 202-2965800

American Dairy Association
6300 N River Road
Rosemont
IL 60018
Tel: (010 1) 312-6961860

American Meat Institute
PO Box 3556
Arlington
VA 22209
Tel: (010 1) 703-8411030

National Licences Beverage
Association
1025 Vermont Avenue NW
Suite 601
Washington DC 20036
Tel: (010 1) 202-7379118

United Fresh Fruit &
Vegetable Association
1019 19th Street NW
Washington DC 20036
Tel: (010 1) 202-4662400

Asia

Japan
Food and Nutrition
Association
(Eiyo Shokuryo Kyokai)
Sin Kokusai Bldg
4-1, Marunouchi 3-chome
Chiyoda-ku
Tokyo
Tel: (010 81) 3-2644131

Japan Dairy Products
Association
(Nihon Nyuseihin Kyokai)
Nyugyo Kaikan
3-13, Kioi-cho
Chiyoda-ku
Tokyo
Tel: (010 81) 3-2644131

Japan Spirits & Liquor Makers
Association
(Nihon yoshu shuzo kamiai)
Koura Bldg
1-6 Nihonbashi kayaba-cho
1-chome
Chuo-ku
Tokyo
Tel: (010 83) 3-6684621-2

Directories

International
International Brewers
Directory and Soft Drink
Guide
Verlag fur Internationale
Wirtschaftsliteratur
Zurich
Switzerland

International Sugar Economic
Yearbook and Directory
FO Licht
Ratzeburg

UKER's International Tea &
Coffee Buyers' Guide
Tea Coffee Trade Journal Co
Whitestone
New York
USA

World Directory of Food &
Drink Manufacturing
Companies
Agra-Canadian Publications
London
UK

Europe

France
Guide Ria Des Fournisseurs
de L'Industrie Alimentaire
Editions Sepaic
Paris

Les Principaux Groupes de
L'Industrie Alimentaire
Francaise
APRIA
Paris

UK
Binstad's Directory of Food
Trade Marks and Brand
Names
Food Trade Press
Kent

Bottler's Yearbook
Wallington
Surrey

Brewery Manual and Who's
Who in British Brewing
Northwood Publications
London

British Frozen Food
Federation (Yearbook)
The Federation
Grantham

Buyer's Guide to the Meat
Industry
Thomson Magazines
London

Companies in the Food
Industry
Institute of Grocery
Distribution
Watford

Dial Industry, Food catering,
drink & tobacco
Dial Industry
East Grinstead

Food & Drink Trade Yearbook
and Diary (The)
British Independent Grocers
Association
Farnborough
Hants

Food Industry Directory
Newman Books
London

Food Manufacture
Morgan-Grampian
London

Food Trades Directory and
Food Buyers Yearbook
Newman Books
London

Foodbrokers and
Merchandisers Directory
Institute of Grocery
Distribution
Watford

Freezer Centres Directory
Institute of Grocery
Distribution
Watford

Frozen & Chilled Foods
Yearbook
Retail Journals Ltd
London

Institute of Brewing
(List of Members)
Institute of Brewing
London

Sugar Industry Buyers Guide
International Sugar Journal
High Wycombe

UK Drinks Manual (The)
MDS Beverage Publications
Newquay

USA
Candy Industry Buying Guide
Magazines for Industry
New York

Chilton's Food Engineering
Master
Chilton
Radnor PA

Prepared Foods
(Buyers Guide)
Gorman
Chicago

Quick Frozen Foods: directory
of frozen food processors
Harcourt Brace Jovanovitch
New York

Market Research Reports

This section lists recently
published market research
reports which cover various
aspects of the food and drink
industry. Details provided
below are title of report,
publisher, year of publication,
price and geographic
coverage.

Alcoholic Drinks
Euromonitor Publications Ltd
(UK)
1988
£375
UK

Aperitifs
Key Note Publications (UK)
1988
£105
UK

Bakery & Cereal Products
Market Assessment
Publications (UK)
1987
£250
UK

Beer
Databank Spa (Italy)
1988
£1400
Italy

Beverage Industry: Markets,
Players, Packaging Trends
Business Communications Co
(USA)
1987
$1500
USA

Beverages Category Report
Marketing Intelligence Service
Ltd (USA)
Monthly
$1000/yr (12 issues)
USA, Canada, Europe, Japan

Biscuits and Pastry Products
(Factory Produced)
Databank Spa (Italy)
1988
£1400
Italy

Bread and Bread Substitutes
(Factory Produced)
Databank Spa (Italy)
1988
£1400
Italy

Breakfast Cereals
Key Note Publications (UK)
1988
£105
UK

Britain's Catering Industry
Jordan & Sons Ltd (UK)
1988
£125
UK

Business Ratio Report:
Bakeries
ICC Business Ratios (UK)
Annual
£165
UK

Business Ratio Report:
Brewers
ICC Business Ratios (UK)
Annual
£165
UK

Business Ratio Report:
Confectionery
ICC Business Ratios (UK)
Annual
£165
UK

Business Ratio Report: Dairy
Products
ICC Business Ratios (UK)
Annual
£165
UK

Business Ratio Report:
Distillers
ICC Business Ratios (UK)
Annual
£165
UK

Business Ratio Report: Food
Ingredients
ICC Business Ratios (UK)
Annual
£165
UK

Business Ratio Report: Food
Processors (Intermediate)
ICC Business Ratios (UK)
Annual
£165
UK

Business Ratio Report: Food
Processors (Major)
ICC Business Ratios (UK)
Annual
£165
UK

Business Ratio Report: Wine &
Spirits Merchants
ICC Business Ratios (UK)
Annual
£165
UK

Candy Market (The)
Packaged Facts (USA)
1988
$1350
USA

Canned Foods
Market Assessment
Publications (UK)
1987
£250
UK

Cheese Market (The)
Find/SVP (USA)
1988
$1295
USA

Cheese Market (The)
Business Trend Analysts
(USA)
1988
$750
USA, Canada

Chilled Foods
Market Assessment
Publications (UK)
1987
£250
UK

Chilled Foods & Ready Meals
Euromonitor Publications Ltd
(UK)
1987
£255
UK

Cider
Key Note Publications (UK)
1988
£105
UK

Confectionery Monitor
Gordon Simmons Research
Ltd (UK)
Continuous
On request
UK

Convenience & Prepared
Foods
Euromonitor Publications
Ltd(UK)
1987
£325
UK

DOC, High Quality Wines
Databank Spa (Italy)
1988
£1400
Italy

Delicatessen Foods: UK
Marketing Strategies for
Industry (UK)
1988
£55
UK

Distillers (White Spirits)
Key Note Publications (UK)
1988
£105
UK

Drinks Industry in Turkey
(The)
Walker Marketing (UK)
1988
£1000
Turkey

EEC Dairy Market Report,
1987
in conjunction with ZMP,
Bonn
Agra Europe (UK)
1987
£50
Europe

Ethnic Foods: UK
Marketing Strategies for
Industry (UK)
1988
£55
UK

European Dairy Conference,
1987 papers
Agra Europe (UK)
1988
£78
Europe

European Drinking Habits
Key Note Publications (UK)
1988
£285
Europe

European Fruit and Vegetable
Markets and Trade
Agra Europe (UK)
1987
£78
Europe

Family Food and Drink Panel
Taylor, Nelson Food & Drink
Ltd (UK)
Annual
£15,000-£20,000
UK

Fast Food: UK
Marketing Strategies for
Industry (UK)
1988
£55
UK

Fish & Fish Products
Market Assessment
Publications (UK)
1987
£200
UK

Fish Retailing
Key Note Publications (UK)
1988
£105
UK

Flavourings & Fragrances
Euromonitor Publications Ltd
(UK)
1987
£325
UK

Flour Milling
Databank Spa (Italy)
1988
£1400
Italy

Food Additives
The Freedonia Group Inc
(USA)
1988
$1700
USA

Food and Beverage
Containers
Business Trend Analysts
(USA)
1988
$895
USA, Canada

Food Company Performances
Institute of Grocery
Distribution (UK)
1987
£90 (non-members)
UK

Food Expenditure
Institute of Grocery
Distribution (UK)
1987
£90 (non-members)
UK

Food Industry in Turkey (The)
Walker Marketing (UK)
1987
£800
Turkey

Food Manufacturing: An
Economic Review
Institute of Grocery
Distribution (UK)
1987
£60 (non-members)
UK

Food Retailing 1987
Institute of Grocery
Distribution (UK)
1987
£160 (non-members)
UK

Food Service Fact Book
Technomic Inc (USA)
1988
On request
USA

Foods Category Report
Marketing Intelligence Service
Ltd(USA)
Monthly
$1000/yr (12 issues)
USA, Canada, Europe, Japan

Fortified Wine
Market Assessment
Publications (UK)
1987
£200
UK

Freezer Centres: UK
Marketing Strategies for
Industry (UK)
1988
£55
UK

Frozen Food: UK
Marketing Strategies for
Industry (UK)
1988
£55
UK

Health & Diet Foods
Market Assessment
Publications (UK)
1987
£235
UK

Hot Drinks
Key Note Publications (UK)
1988
£105
UK

Ice Cream Market (The)
Find/SVP (USA)
1988
$1295
USA

Ice-cream Production
Databank Spa (Italy)
1988
£1400
Italy

Image of Manufacturers
Among Key Grocery Accounts

Gordon Simmons Research
Ltd (UK)
Continuous
£3750
UK

Image-Radars: Beer
Fessel
GFK (Austria)
1987
AS 29,000
Austria

Image-Radars: Coffee
Fessel
GFK (Austria)
1987
AS 29,000
Austria

Image-Radars: Mineral Water
Fessel
GFK (Austria)
1987
AS 34,000
Austria

Image-Radars: Sparkling
Wine
Fessel
GFK (Austria)
1987
AS 29,000
Austria

Impact of Information
Technology and Systems on
the Food
Industry
Technomic Inc (USA)
1988
On request
USA

L'industrie Mondiale des
Boissons Non Alcoolisees
Eurostaf Dafsa (France)
1987
FF8.900
Worldwide

International Food and Drink
Monitor
Taylor, Nelson Food & Drink
Ltd (UK)
Annual
SFr 80,000
Worldwide

Italian Foods Market (The)
Packaged Facts (USA)
1988
$1350
USA

Liquid Packaging
Corporate Development
Consultants Ltd (UK)
1988
£6000
W Europe

Management Compensation
(in the food industry)
Food Marketing Institute
(USA)
Annually
On request
USA

Market for Bakery Products
(The)
Business Trend Analysts
(USA)
1988
$795
USA

Market Profile: Bacon
Specialists in Business
Information Inc (USA)
1987
$325
USA

Market Profile: Cheese
Specialists in Business
Information Inc(USA)
1987
$350
USA

Market Profile: Wine and
Brandy
Specialists in Business
Information Inc (USA)
1987
$325
USA

Market Profile: Yogurt
Specialists in Business
Information Inc (USA)
1987
$350
USA

Markets for Microwavable
Foods (The)
Business Trend Analysts
(USA)
1988
$750
USA

Mass Merchandised 'Healthy'
Food
Business Communications Co
(USA)
1987
$1500
USA

Meat and Meat Products
Key Note Publications (UK)
1988
£105
UK

Mexican Foods Market (The)
Packaged Facts (USA)
1988
$995
USA

Microwaveable Foods Market
Find/SVP (USA)
1988
$1295
USA

New Products in Grocers 1988
KAE Development Ltd (UK)
1988
£350
UK

Nutritional Standards and
Awareness (5 volumes)
(single volumes also available)

Fessel
GFK (Austria)
1987
AS 54,000
Austria

Outlook for the Foodservice
Distributor into the 1990's –
Implications to Suppliers
Technomic Inc (USA)
1988
On request
USA

Own Brands
Key Note Publications (UK)
1988
£105
UK

Pasta Market (The)
Find/SVP (USA)
1988
$1295
USA

Pasta Products
Databank Spa (Italy)
1988
£1400
Italy

Prepared Takeout Foods
Find/SVP (USA)
1988
$1295
USA

Processed Fruits and
Vegetables
Business Trend Analysts
(USA)
1988
$795
USA

Rice Milling
Databank Spa (Italy)
1988
£1400
Italy

Saudi Arabian Market for
Food Processing Equipment
Middle East Marketing
Research Bureau (Cyprus)
1986
$3000
Saudi Arabia

Soft Drink Niche Markets
Packaged Facts (USA)
1988
$1150
USA

Soft Drinks
Market Assessment
Publications (UK)
1987
£250
UK

Sparkling Wines
Databank Spa (Italy)
1988
£1400
Italy

Spirits & Liqueurs
Market Assessment
Publications (UK)
1987
£300
UK

Table Wines
Databank Spa (Italy)
1988
£700
Italy

Trends
(in the food industry)
Food Marketing Institute
(USA)
Annually
On request
USA

US Hot Beverage Market (The)
Business Trend Analysts
(USA)
1988
$750
USA

US Processed Meat Industry
(The)
Business Trend Analysts
(USA)
1988
$795
USA

Wine
Market Assessment
Publications (UK)
1987
£185
UK

Periodicals and Journals

International & Pan European
Beverage World International
Coffee International
Drinks International
Food Engineering
International
Food Europe (English,
French, German, Italian)

Food World News
International Drinks Bulletin
Made in Europe – World Food
& Drink
North European Dairy Journal
Preserved Milk
Quick Frozen Foods
International
World Directory of Food &
Drink Manufacturing
Companies
World Food & Drink Report
World New Products (Food &
Drink Industry)

Europe

Austria
Back Journal (Bakery)
Fachzeitung fur den
Lebensmittelhandel (Food
Trade)

Belgium
La Boucherie Belge/De
Belgische Beenhouweriji
(Meat)
L'Epicier/De Kruidenier
(Grocery Trade)

Finland
Kauppa ja Koti (Independent
Grocers' Stores)
Kauppias (Grocery Retailers)
Leipuri (Bakers &
Confectioners)
Lihalehti (Butchers)

France
Agro-Industries
Amphitryon
Bacchus International
Bios (Brewing)
Boissons de France
Bonne Table de Tourisme
La Boucherie Francaise
La Boulangerie Francaise
Le Boulanger-Patissier
Confiseur-Glacier
Le Cafetier Resaurateur
Parisien
Charcuterie et Gastronomie
Collectivities Express
La Confiserie
Cuisine et Vins de France
L'Epicerie Francaise
Equip Hotel
France Laitiere
L'Hotelier
L'Hotellerie
L'Hotellerie Madame

L'Industrie Hoteliere
Industries Alimentaires et
Agricoles (Food)
Libre Service Actualises
Logis et Auberges de France
Neid L'Information des Vins
et Spiritueux (Wines & Spirits)
Neo Restauration
Revue Generale de
L'Hotellerie
Revue Laitiere Francaise
Revue Technique des Hotels
et Restaurants
Revue du Vin de France
Revue Vinicole Internationale
(Wines & Spirits)
La Sucrerie Francaise
Toute l'Alimentation
Toutes les Nouvelles de
l'Hotellerie et du Tourisme
La Vie des Metiers

Germany, Federal Republic of
Allgemeine Backer Zeitung
(Bakers)
Allgemeine Fleischer-Zeitung
(Butchers)
Back Journal (Bakers)
Back Zeitung (Bakers)
Bako Informationen (Bakers)
Die Bar
Der Biergrosshandel
Brauei Journal (Brewing)
Brauindustrie (Brewing)
Brauwelt (Breweries)
Brauwelt International
(English)
Brot & Backwaren (Bakers)
DEI Die Ernahrungsindustrie
(Food beverages & tobacco)
DBZ Wickruf (Bakery)
Deutsche Getranke –
Wirtschaft
Deutsche Lebensmittel
Rundschau (Food)
Das Erfrischungsgetrank
(Mineral Waters)
Fast Food Praxis
Feinkost Revue
(Delicatessens)
Fleisch Lebensmittel Markt
(Butchers)
Die Fleischerei (Butchery
Trade and Industry)
Die Fleischwirtschaft
(Butchers)
Flussiges Obst (Beverages)
GV Grossverbraucher
GV Praxis (Food & Deep
Freeze)

Getranke Industrie (Liscensed
Trade)
Getranke Markt (Marketing &
Engineering in Beverages)
Getranke Revue (Licensed
Trade)
Gordian (Food Technology)
Kakoa & Zucker (Cocoa &
Sugar)
Die Kleinbrennerei (Distillers)
Konditorei und Cafe (Bakers
and Confectioners)
Lebensmittel Praxis
Lebensmittel-Technik
Lebensmittel-Zeitung
Der Minerabrunnen (Mineral
Waters)
Neve Fleischer Zeitung
(Butchers)
Snack
Susswaren (Confectionery)
Tageszeitung fur Brauerei
(Brewing)
Die Weinwirtschaft/Markt
Die Weinwirtschaft/Technic
Zukerindustrie (Sugar)

Ireland, Republic of
Catering & Licensing Review
Checkout (Food Trade)
Food Progress
Irish Bakery World
Irish Meat Journal
Retail News (Food Trade)
Shelf (Food)
Vintner's World

Italy
Industrie Alimentari (Food)
Industrie delle Bevande
(Drinks)
Pasticceria Internazionale
(Confectionery, Ice Cream)
Tecnica Molittoria (Millers,
Bakers)

Netherlands
De Bakker (Bakery)
Bakkerswereld (Bakers)
De Banketbakkerij (Bakers,
Confectioners)
Consudel (Confectionery)
Drankendetail (Wines)
Drankengids (Wines & Spirits)
Food Magazine (Retail)
Food Press
Levensmiddelenmarkt
(Grocery)
Maandblad Suikerunic (Sugar
Trade)
Missets Distrifood (Wholesale
& Retail)

Moderne Voeding (Health Food)
S en L (Grocery Trade)
De Slager (Butchery Trade)
Vlees & Vleeswaren (Meat)

Spain
Alimaq
Alimentacion, Equipos y Technologia
Alimentaria
Carnica 2000 (Meat)
Cervaza y Malta
El Comestible
La Confiteria Espanola (Confectionery)
Dulcypas
Heladaria Internacional (Ice Cream)
Molineria y Panaderia (Baking & Milling)
Panorama Panadero
Vida Apicola (Honey)

Sweden
Brod Konditorn (Bakers & Confectioners)
Fri Kopenskap (Food Stores)
ICA – Nyheteroch Debatt (Grocery Trades)
Kottbranschen (Meat Trades)
Livs (Retail Grocery)
Livsmedelsteknik (Food Manufacturing)
Supermarket (Food Trades)

Switzerland
Alimenta
Backer-Konditor-Zeitung
Braueri und Getranke-Rundschau
Candis
Der Confiseur
Food Engineering International
Lebensmittel Technologies
Lebensmittel Wissenschaft & Technologie
Metzger & Wurster
Schweizer-Brauerei-Rundschau (Brewing)
Schweizerische-Metzger-Zeitung (Butcher)
Schweizerische Milch-Zeitung
Schweizerische-Wirte-Zeitung
Swiss Food
Union Helvetia

UK
A la Carte
Bakers' Review

Baking Today
Bartender International
Brewer (The)
Brewers' Guardian
Brewing & Distilling International
British Baker
British Food Journal
British Hotelier & Restaurateur Bulletin (The)
CMM/Confectionery Manufacture & Marketing
Cash & Carry Caterer
Cash & Carry Wholesaler
Caterer & Hotelkeeper
Catering
Catering Business (The)
Catering & Licensing Review
Catering South West
Catering Update
Chef
Chef & Brewer Mirror
Confectionery Production
La Cuisine
Decanter
Drinks International
Drinks Marketing
FMS Magazine
Fish Products
Fish Trader
Flavour & Fragrance Journal
Food & Cookery Review
Food & Drink
Food & Drugs Industry Bulletin
Food Europe
Food Flavourings, Ingredients Packaging & Processing
Food Manufacture
Food Marketing
Food Packer International
Food Processing
Food Production
Food Trade Review
Food World News
Free House Monthly
Friers Catering Advertiser
Frozen & Chilled Foods
Frozen Food Management
Frozen Food World
Fruit Trades Journal
Golf Club Steward
Good Food Retailing
Grapevine
Harper's Wine & Spirit Gazette
Home Brew Supplier
Hospitality
Hotel & Catering Technology
Hotels & Restaurants International

ITC
Ice Cream & Frozen Confectionery
Industrial Caterer
Innkeeper
International Beverage News
International Sugar Journal
International Travel Catering
Journal of Food Technology
Journal of the Institute of Brewing
Licensed Catering
Licensee
MTJ Products
Meat Industry
Meat Trader Viewpoint
Meat Trades Journal
Members Only
Middle East Food Trade & Catering Equipment
Morning Advertiser & Licensed Restaurateur
Popular Foodservice
Pub Caterer
Pub, Club & Wine Bar
Pub Leader
Publican
Retail Fruit Trade Review
SMM-Snack Food Manufacture & Marketing
Scottish Club Monthly
Scottish Licensed Trade Guardian
Scottish Licensed Trade News
Seafood International
Soft Drinks Trade Journal
Sugar Cane
Ulster Licensed Trade News
Wales Caterer's Guide
What Wine?
Whats Brewing
Wholefood Magazine
Wine Bar
Wine Butler
Wine & Spirit
Winepress
World Sugar Journal

Canada
L'Alimentation au Quebec
Bakers' Journal
Barrique et Marmite
Beverage Alcohol Reporter
Canadian Beverage Review
Canadian Grocer
Canadian Institute of Food Science & Technology Journal
L'Epicier (The Grocer)
Food in Canada
Mmon Marche
Modern Dairy
Super Fare

Western Grocer
Wine & Dine
Wine Tidings

USA
All About Beer
Bakers Digest
Bakery Production &
Marketing
Baking Industry Magazine
Bar Business
Better Nutrition
Beverage Bulletin
Beverage Industry
Beverage Industry News
Beverage Media
Beverage Retailer Weekly
Beverage World
Beverages
Bon Appetit
Brewers Bulletin
Brewers Digest
CFI-Commercial Food Service
Candy Marketer
Candy & Snack Industry
Catering Today
Chocolatier – the Magazine for
Gourmet Chocolate Lovers
Confectioner
Cooking for Profit
Dairy Field
Dairy Foods
Fast Service
Food Engineering
Food & Equipment Product
News
Food Management
Food Merchants Advocate
Food Product Development
Food Production/Managment
Food Sanitation
Foodservice Distributor
Salesman
Foodservice Equipment
Specialist
Food Service Marketing
Foodservice Technology
International (Kitchen
Planning)
Food Technology
Food Trade News
Food & Wine
Fresh Baked
Frozen Food Age
Gourmet – The Magazine of
Good Living
Grocers Spotlight
Grocery Communication
Health Foods Retailing
Liquor Store
Manufacturing Confectioner
Marketing

Meat Processing International
Milling & Baking News
Modern Brewery Age
Modern Brewery Age Blue
Book
Modern Grocer
Monthly Magazine of Food &
Wine
National Provisioner (Meat
Trade)
Quick Frozen Foods
International
Snack Food
Tea & Coffee Trade Journal
World Coffee & Tea
World Food & Drink Report

Asia

India
Food & Beverages
Indian Hotelier & Caterer

Japan
New Food Industry
Sho Kudo
Shokuhin
Shokuhin Kaihatsu
Shokuhin Kogyo
Shokuhin Nippon
Shokukin to Kagaku
Skoku no Kagaku

Government Publications

UK Official Sources

General Statistics
Annual Abstract of Statistics
Digest of Welsh Statistics
MAFF Food Facts
Monthly Digest of Statistics
Northern Ireland Annual
Abstract of Statistics
Scottish Abstract of Statistics
United Kingdom National
Accounts
Welsh Agricultural Statistics

Animal & Poultry Foods
Agricultural Statistics in
Scotland
Agricultural Statistics in the
United Kingdom
Annual Abstract of Statistics
Census of Production
Reports: PA 422
Monthly Digest of Statistics
Output and Utilisation of
Farm Produce in the United
Kingdom

Scottish Abstract of Statistics
Statistical Information Notice
(MAFF)

Bacon Curing, Meat and Fish Products
Annual Abstract of Statistics
Business Monitors: PQ 4122
and 4150
Census of Production
Reports: PA 412 and PA 415
Monthly Digest of Statistics
Statistical Information Notice
– UK Slaughtering Statistics
(MAFF)

Biscuits
Annual Abstract of Statistics
Business Monitor: PQ 4197
Census of Production
Reports: PA 419
Monthly Digest of Statistics
Scottish Abstract of Statistics

Bread and Flour Confectionery
Business Monitor: PQ 4196
Census of Production
Reports: PA 419

Cocoa, Chocolate, Sugar and Confectionery
Annual Abstract of Statistics
Census of Production
Reports: PA 421
Cocoa Market Report
Monthly Digest of Statistics

Food Consumption
Annual Abstract of Statistics
Annual Review of Agriculture
Digest of Welsh Statistics
Family Expenditure Survey
MAFF Food Facts
Northern Ireland Family
Expenditure Survey
Regional Trends
Sea Fisheries Statistical Tables
Supplies Bulletin
United Kingdom Imports and
Exports of Fish
United Kingdom National
Accounts

Food Industries (Other)
Annual Abstract of Statistics
Business Monitor: PQ 4115
(Margarine)
PQ 4239 (Starch and
Miscellaneous)

Census of Production
Reports: PA 411 and 423
Monthly Digest of Statistics
Statistical Information Notice
(MAFF)

Fruit and Vegetable Products

Annual Abstract of Statistics
Business Monitor: PQ 4147
Census of Production
Reports: PA 414
Monthly Digest of Statistics
Statistical Information Notice
(MAFF)

Grain Milling

Agricultural Statistics United Kingdom
Annual Abstract of Statistics
Census of Production
Reports: PA 416
Monthly Digest of Statistics
Output and Utilisation of Farm Produce in the United Kingdom
Scottish Abstract of Statistics
Scottish Agricultural Economics

Milk and Milk Products

Annual Abstract of Statistics
Business Monitor: PQ 4213 (Ice Cream)
Census of Production
Reports: PA 413 and PA 421
Digest of Welsh Statisics
Monthly Digest of Statistics
Northern Ireland Annual Abstract of Statistics
Output and Utilisation of Farm Produce in the United Kingdom
Scottish Agricultural Economics
Statistical Information Notice (MAFF)

Sugar

Annual Abstract of Statistics
Census of Production
Reports: PA 420
Monthly Digest of Statistics

Vegetable and Animal Oils and Fats

Annual Abstract of Statistics
Business Monitor: PQ 4116
Census of Production
Reports: PA 411

Monthly Digest of Statistics
Statistical Information Notice
(MAFF)

Metals

Trade Associations

International

Association Internationale
pour la Promotion du
Silicium Metal
c/o Franco Trisconi
Via ai Ronchi Casa Ferrini
CH 6592 S Antonino/Ti
Switzerland
Tel: (010 41) 92-741841
Telex: 846 448

Association des Pays
Exportateurs de Mineral de
Fer
14 Chemin Auguste Vilbert
CH 1218 Grand Saconnex
Geneva
Switzerland
Tel: (010 41) 22-82955
Telex: 289 443

Arab Iron & Steel Union
BP No 4
Cheraga (Alger)
Algeria
Tel: (010 213) 781579-80
Telex: 52553

ASM Europe
BP 4809
75424 Paris Cedex 09
France

Battery Council International
111 East Wacker Drive
Chicago
IL 60601
USA
Tel: (010 1) 312-6446610
Telex: 254073

Bismuth Institute Information
Centre
47 Rue de Ligne
1000 Brussels
Belgium
Tel: (010 32) 2-2186040
Telex: 62162 BISMUT

Bureau International de la
Recuperation
Place du Samedi 13
Bte 4
1000 Brussels
Belgium
Tel:(010 32)2-2178251
Telex: 61965

Cadmium Association
34 Berkeley Square
London W1X 6AJ
UK
Tel: 01-499 8425
Telex: 261286

Chromium Association
30 Blvd Haussmann
5008 Paris
France
Tel: 010 33)1-43875365
Telex: 290515

Cipek
39 Rue de la Bienfaisance
75008 Paris
France
Tel: (010 33)42250024
Telex: 649077.

Club des Marchands de Fer
de la CECA
Rue de la Bonte 4
Bte 1
11050 Brussels
Belgium
Tel: (010 32) 2-5374343

Cobalt Development Institute
Ravenstein 3
1000 Brussels
Belgium

Cobalt Development Institute
95 High Street
Slough SL1 1DH
UK
Tel: 0753-38735
Telex: 847466

Comite des Associations
Europeennes de Fonderie
2 Rue de Bassano
75783 Paris
France
Tel: (010 33)47235550
Telex: 620 617

Comite International pour le
Developpement et L'Étude de
la ConstructionTubulaire
81 Rue des Belles Feuilles
75116 Paris
France
Tel: (010 33)50219 00
Telex: 611906

Comite de Liason du Negoce
des Metaux Non-Ferreux
de la CCE
Place du Samedi 13
1000 Brussels
Belgium

Commission de Federations
et Syndicats Nationaux
des Enterprises de
Recuperation de Ferrailles de
Marche Commun
Place du Samedi 13
1000 Brussels
Belgium
Tel: (010 32)2179993

Council of Mining and
Metallurgical Institutions
44 Portland Place
London W1N 4BR
UK
Tel: 01-580 3802
Telex: 261410

Eurofer
5 Square de Meeus
1040 Brussels
Belgium
Tel: (010 32) 2-5129830
Telex: 62112

European Aluminium
Association
Konigsallee 30
PO Box 1207
4000 Dusseldorf 1
West Germany
Tel: (010 49) 211-80871
Telex: 8587 407

European Coil Coating
Association
4th Floor
Rue Montoyer 47
1040 Brussels
Belgium
Tel: (010 32) 2-5136052
Telex: 20689

European Independent
Steelworks Association
205 Rue Belliard
Boite 18
1040 Brussels
Belgium
Tel: (010 32) 2-2307962
Telex: 65138 EISA

European Zinc Institute
PO Box 2126
5600 CC Eindhoven
Netherlands
Tel: (010 31) 40-122497
Telex: 51860

Federation Internationale des
Associations de Negociants
en Aciers,
Tubes et Metaux
64 St Alban-Anlage
Postfach
4006 Basle
Switzeraland
Tel: (010 41) 61-421730
Telex: 963895

Federation des Reclamineurs
de la CECA (Federal)
47 Rue Montoyer
1040 Brussels
Belgium
Tel: (010 32) 2-5133820
Telex: 21287

Institut des Producteurs de
Ferro-Alliages d'Europe
Occidentale
4 Chemin des Trois-Rois
CP 3030
CH 1002 Lausanne
Switzerland
Tel: (010 41) 21-238832
Telex: 25951 FIRO CH
Fax: (010 41)21-223653

Instituto Latinoamericano del
Fierro y el Acero
Casilla 16065
Santiago 9
Chile
Tel: (010 56)2-2237581
Telex: 340348 ILAFFA CK

International Bauxite
Association
63-67 Knutsford Boulevard
PO Box 551
Kingston 5
Jamaica
West Indies
Tel: (010 1 809) 9264535/7
Telex: 2428 ITNBAJA

International Copper
Research Association
708 Third Avenue
New York
NY 10017
USA
Tel: (010 1) 212-6979355
Telex: 62934

International Iron & Steel
Institute
Rue Col Bourg 120
1140 Brussels
Belgium
Tel: (010 32) 2-7359075
Telex: 22639

International Lead Zinc
Research Organisation
292 Madison Avenue
New York
NY 1001
USA
Tel:(010 1)212-5322373
Telex: 148320

International Lead & Zinc
Study Group
Metro House
58 St James's Street
London SW1A 1LD
UK
Tel: 01-499 9373
Telex: 299819

International Magnesium
Association
Lancaster Building
Suite 400
7927 Jones Branch Drive
McLean
VA 22102
USA
Tel: (010 1) 703-4428888
Telex: 7108330313
Fax: (010 1)703-8939340

International Pig Iron
Secretatiat
Breite Strasse 69
Postfach 6709
4000 Dusseldorf
West Germany
Telex: (010 49) 211-08582286

International Precious Metals
Institute
Government Building
ABE Airport
Allentown
PA 18103
USA
Tel:(010 1) 215-2661570

International Primary
Aluminium Institute
New Zealand House
Haymarket
London SW1Y 4TE
UK
Tel: 01-930 0582-9
Telex: 917837

International Rebars
Exporters & Producers
Association
c/o Celsa
Apartado des Correos 4
San Andreas de la Barca
Barcelona
Spain

International Steel Trade
Association'Ballards'
Valley Road
Kenley
Surrey CR2 5DJ
UK
Tel: 01-668 4416

International Tin Council
Haymarket House
1 Oxendon Street
London SW1Y 4EQ
UK
Tel: 01-930 0451
Telex: 918939

International Tin Research
Institute
Kingston Lane
Uxbridge
Middlesex UB8 3PJ
UK
Tel: 0895-72406

International Tube
Association
PO Box 84
Leamington Spa
Warwickshire CV32 5FX
UK
Tel: 0926-34137
Telex: 312548 INTRAS G
Fax: 0926 314755

International Wrought
Copper Council
6 Bathurst Street
Sussex Square
London W2 2SD
UK
Tel: 01-723 7465
Telex: 23556
Fax: 01 724 0308

Manganese Centre
17 Avenue Hoche
75008 Paris
France
Tel: (010 33) 1-45630634

Minor Metals Traders
Association
69 Cannon St
London EC4N 5AB
UK
Tel: 01-248 4444
Telex: 888941

Nickel Development Institute
Suite 1200
7 King Street East
Toronto
Ontario M5C 1A2
Canada
Tel:(010 1) 416-3628850
Telex: 06218565

Non-Ferrous Metals
Information Centre
47 Rue Montoyer
1040 Brussels
Belgium
Tel: (010 32) 2-5138634
Telex: 22077
Fax: (010 32) 2-5117553

Organisation of European
Aluminium Smelters
Graf-Aldof Strasse 18
PO Box 200 840
4000 Dusseldorf
West Germany
Tel: (010 49) 211-320672
Telex: 8582508

Scandinavian Copper
Development Association
PO Box 191
2600 Glostrup
Denmark
Tel: (010 45) 452961644
Telex: 33513

Scandinavian Lead Zinc
Association
Kungstensgatan 38
113 59 Stockholm
Sweden

Selenium Tellurinium
Development Association Inc
PO Box 3096
Darien
CT 06820
USA
Tel: (010 1) 203-6550470

South East Asia Iron & Steel
Institute
PO Box 7759
Airmail Distribution Center
Manila International Airport
Passay City
Philippines
Tel: (010 63) 6732161/6732069
Telex: 66396 SEASI PN; 29084
SEASI PH

Tantalum-Niobium
International Study Center
40 Rue Washington
1050 Brussels
Belgium
Tel: (010 32) 2-6495158
Telex: 65080 INAC B
Fax: (010 32) 2-6493269

Uranium Institute
12th Floor
Bowater House
68 Knightsbridge
London SW1X 7LT
UK
Tel: 01-225 0303
Telex: 917611
Fax: 225 0308

World Bureau of Metal
Statistics
41 Doughty Street
London WC1N 2LF
UK
Tel: 01-405 2771
Telex: 298970

Zinc & Lead Asian Services
124 Exhibition Street
Melbourne
Victoria 3000
Australia
Tel: (010 61) 3-6541611
Telex: 38806

Europe

France
Association Syndicale des
Marchands de Fers de France
91 Rue de Piromensnil
75008 Paris
Tel:
(010 33) 1-45619944
Telex: 560680

Centre d'Information Cuivre,
Laitons, Alliages
58 Rue de Lisbonne
750008 Paris
Tel:(010 33) 1-42252567
Telex: 660610

Centre d'Information du
Plomb
1 Avenue Albert Einstein
BP 106
78191 Trappes Cedex
Tel: (010 33) 1-30620583
Telex: 696745

Centre de Recherches du Fer
Blanc
Chaussee d'Europe
Boite Postale 135
57103 Thionville Cedex
Tel: (010 33) 82344533

Centre Technique du Zinc
34 Rue Collange
92307 Levallois-Perret
Tel: (010 33) 47394740
Telex: 611843

Chambre Syndicale du
Commerce International des
Metaux et Minerais
31 Avenue
Pierre-ler-de-Serbie
75784 Paris Cedex 16
Tel: (010 33) 1-472361-69-58
(Ext 504, 445, 443)
Telex: 611059

Chambre Syndicale des Mines
de Fer de France
56 Avenue de Wagram
75854 Paris Cedex 17
Tel: (010 33) 1-40542024
Telex: 280676

Chambre Syndicale des
Producteurs de Fer-Blanc et
de Fer
Noir
5 Rue Paul Cezanne
75008 Paris
Tel: (010 33) 1-4563110
Telex: A 280172

Chambre Syndicale de la
Siderurgie Francaise
5 bis, Rue de Madrid
75379 Paris Cedex 08
Tel: (010 33) 1-45228300
Telex: 650392

Chambre Syndicale du Zinc et
du Cadmium
34 Rue Collange
92307 Levallois-Perret
Tel: (010 33) 47394740
Telex : 611843

Federation des Chambres
Syndicales des Minerais et
des Metaux Non-Ferraux
30 Avenue de Messine
75008 Paris
Tel: (010 33) 1-45630266
Telex: 650438

Office Technique pour
l'Utilisation de l'Acler
5 bis, Rue de Madrid
75379 Paris Cedex 08
Tel: (010 33) 1-45228300
Telex: 650392

Syndicat General des
Fondeurs de France et
Industries Connexes
2 Rue de Bassano
75783 Paris Cedex 16
Tel:
(010 33) 1-7235550
Telex: 620617 SYGEFON F

Syndicat National du
Commerce des Produits
Siderurgiques
65 Avenue Victor-Hugo
75116 Paris
Tel: (010 33) 1-45007250
Telex: 620868

Syndicat National du
Profilage des Produits Plats
en Acier
25 Rue d'Astorg
75008 Paris
Tel: (010 33) 1-42669370
Telex: 29319

Germany, Federal Republic of
Aluminium-Zentrale eV
Konigsallee 30
PO Box 1207
4000 Dusseldorf 1
Tel:(010 49) 211-320821
Telex: 8587407
Fax: (010 49) 211-132567

Ausschuss fur
Pulvermetallurgie,
Gemeinschaftsausschuss des
Vereins Deutscher
Eisenhutteleute, des Vereins
Deutscher Ingenieure, der
Deutschen Gesellschaft
fur Metallkunde, des
Fachverbandes
Pulvermetallurgie und der
Deutschen
Keramischen Gesellschaft
Postfach 921
5800 Hagen 1
Tel: (010 49) 2331-51041
Telex: 823806

Beratung Feuerverzinken
Hochstrasse 113
Postfach 1020
5800 Hagen 1
Tel: (010 49) 2331-25041
Telex: 0823814

Beratungsstelle fur
Stahlverwendung
Kasernenstrasse 36
Postfach 1611
4000 Dusseldorf
Tel: (010 49) 211-829-1
Telex: 08582286

Blelberatung eV
Tersteegenstrasse 28
4000 Dusseldorf 30
(Postfach 8706 Dusseldorf 1)
Tel: (010 49) 211-34458
Telex: 08584721

Bundesverband der
Deutschen Schrottwirtschaft
eV
Graf-Adolf-Strasse 12
4000 Dusseldorf 1
Tel: (010 49) 211-320335/36

Bundesverband Deutscher
Stahlhandel eV
Graf-Adolf-Platz 12
4000 Dusseldorf
Tel: (010 49) 211-30094
Telex: 8587760

Deutsche Gesellschaft fur
Metallkunde
Adenauerallee 21
6370 Oberusel
Tel: (010 49) 6171-4081

Deutscher Giessereiverband
Sohnstrasse 70
Postfach 87 09
4000 Dusseldorf 1
Tel: (010 49) 211-68711

Deutscher Schrottverband eV
Brabanter Strasse 8
Postfach 270341
5000 Cologne 1
Tel: (010 49) 221-253069
Telex: 8881610 RECY

Edelstahlhadels-Vereinigung
eV
Breite Strasse 69
Postfach 28 07
4000 Dusseldorf 1
Tel: (010 49) 211-8291
Telex: 8584482

Fachverband
Aluminiumhalbzeug-
Verband, im Verband der
Aluminium
Verabeitenden Industrie eV
Tersteegenstrasse 28
Postfach 8706
4000 Dusseldorf 1
Tel: (010 49) 211-454710
Telex: 08584721
Fax: (010 49) 211-4547111

Fachverband
Ferrolegierungen, Stahl-und
Leichtmetallveredler eV
Friedrichstrasse 29
Postfach 3024
000 Dusseldorf 1
Tel: (010 49) 211-661414

Fachverband
Pulvermetallurgie
Goldene Pforte 1
5800 Hagen 1
Tel: (010 49) 2331-51041
Telex: 823806

Gemeinschaftsausschuss
Verzinken eV
Beethovenstrasse 12
4000 Dusseldorf 1
Tel: (010 49) 211-661568

Gesamtverband der
Deutschen
Aluminiumindustrie
Tersteegenstrasse 28
PO Box 8706
4000 Dusseldorf
Tel: (010 49) 211-454710
Telex: 08584721

Geschaftsfuhrung des
Vereins Deutscher
Giessereifachleute
Haus der Giesserei-Industrie
Sohnstrasse 70
Postfach 82 25
4000 Dusseldorf 1
Tel: (010 49) 211-68711
Telex: 8586885

Gesellschaft Deutscher
Metallhutten und Bergleute
eV
Paul-Ernst-Strasse 10
POB 210
3392 Clausthal-Zellerfeld
Tel: (010 49) 5323-3438
Telex: 953828 TUCLZ D

Roheisenverband Breite
Strasse 69
4000 Dusseldorf 1
Tel: (010 49) 211-829-1
Telex: 08582286

Stahl-Service Arbeitskreis
Stixchesstrasse 136-150
Postfach 10 06 80
5090 Leverkusen
Tel: (010 49) 214-36214
Telex: 8510804

Stahlrohrverband eV
Tersteegenstrasse 3
4000 Dusseldorf
Tel: (010 49) 211-434754
Telex: 08584791
Fax: (010 49) 211-434757

Unternehmensverband
Saarbergbau
Mainzer Strasse 95
Postfach 361
6600 Saarbrucken 3
Tel: (010 49) 681-4051
Telex: 4221240
Fax: (010 49) 405-4205

Verband der Aluminium
verabeitenden Industrie eV
Schumannstrasse 46
6000 Frankfurt/Main 1
Tel: (010 49) 69-748024
Telex: 411717

Verband der Deutschen
Feuerverzinkungsindustrie
eV
Sohnstrasse 70
4000 Dusseldorf 1
Tel: (010 49) 211-67900

Verband Deutscher
Druckgiessereien
Postfach 8706
4000 Dusseldorf 1
Tel: (010 49) 211-45471-0
Telex: 8 584721

Verein Deutscher
Eisenhuttenleute
Sohnstrasse 65
Postfach 82 09
4000 Dusseldorf 1
Tel: (010 49) 211-67070
Telex: 8 582 512 STE D
Fax: (010 49) 211-6707310

Vereinigung Deutscher
Schmeizhutten
Graf Adolf Strasse 18
4000 Dusseldorf 1
Tel: (010 49) 211-320672
Telex: 858 2508

Wirtschaftsverband Eisen,
Blech und Metall
Verarbeitende Industrie eV
Kaiserwerther Strasse 135
Postfach 321 230
4000 Dusseldorf 30
Tel: (010 49) 211-454930
Telex: 08 584 985

Wirtschaftsverband
Grosshandel Metallhalbzeug
eV
Heilsbachstrasse 25
Postfach 14 03 62
5300 Bonn
Tel: (010 49) 228-645761-3
Telex: 8869622

Wirtschaftsvereinigung
Eisen- und Stahlindustrie
Breite Strasse 69
Postfach 8705
4000 Dusseldorf 1
Tel: (010 49) 211-8291
Telex: 8 58 22 86

Wirtschaftsvereinigung
Metalle eV
Tersteegenstrasse 28
PO Box 8706
4000 Dusseldorf
Tel (010 49) 211-454710
Telex: 08584721
Fax: (010 49) 211-45471-11

Zentrale fur
Gussverwendung
Sohnstrasse 70
Postfach 87 09 27
4000 Dusseldorf 1
Tel: (010 49) 211-68711
Telex: 08586885

Zinkberatung eV
Freidrich-Ebert-Strasse 37/39
4000 Dusseldorf 1
Tel: (010 49) 211-350867

UK
Aluminium Coatings
Association, Aluminium
Extruders Association,
Aluminium Federation, and
the Aluminium Rolled
Products
Manufacturers Association
Broadway House
Calthorpe Road
Five Ways
Birmingham B15 1TN
Tel: 012-455 0311
Telex: BIRCOM-G 338 024

Aluminium Stockholders
Association
32-36 Station Road
Gerrards Cross
Bucks
Tel: 0753-888427
Telex: 848531

Association of British Mining
Equipment Companies
Grosvenor Gardens House
35 Grosvenor Gardens
London SW1 0BS
Tel: 01-828 2966
Telex: 911124

Association of Bronze and
Brass Founders
136 Hagley Road
Edgbaston
Birmingham B16 9PN
Tel: 021-454 4141
Telex: 336993

Association of Light Alloy
Refiners Ltd
313 The Linen Hall
162-168 Regent Street
London W1R 5TB
Tel: 01-437 9969

British Association for
Brazing and Soldering
c/o BNF Metals Technology
Centre
Grove Laboratories
Denchworth Road
Wantage
Oxon OX12 9BJ
Tel: 023-572992
Telex: 837166

British Bronze and Brass Ingot
Manufacturers Association
136 Hagley Road
Edgbaston
Birmingham B16 9PN
Tel: 021-454 4141
Telex: 336993

British Constructional
Steelwork Association Ltd
35 Old Queen Street
London SW1H 9HZ
Tel: 01-222 2254
Telex: 27523
Fax: 01-222 3026

British Forging Industry
Association
245 Grove Lane
Handsworth
Birmingham B20 2HB
Tel: 021-554 3311

British Foundry Association
8th Floor, Bridge House
121 Smallbrook
Queensway
Birmingham B5 4JP
Tel: 021-643 3377
Fax: 021-643 5064

British Hardmetal Association
Light Trades House
3 Melbourne Avenue
Sheffield S10 2QJ
Tel: 0742-663 084
Telex: 547676 CHAMCO G

British Independent Steel
Producers Association
5 Cromwell Road
London SW7 2HX
Tel: 01-581 0231-5
Telex: 262134
Fax: 01-589 4009

British Investment Casting
Trade Association
Royton House
George Road
Edgbaston
Birmingham B15 1NU
Tel: 021-455 8872
Telex: 335394

British Lead Manufacturers
Association
St Andrews House
22 High Street
Epsom
Surrey KT19 8AH
Tel: 03727-43976
Telex: 948 104 BRIDGE G
Fax: 03727-43210

British Metal Castings
Council
8th Floor
Bridge House
121 Smallbrook
Queensway
Birmingham B5 4JP
Tel: 021-643 3377
Fax: 021-643 5064

British Metallurgical Plant
Constructors Association
162-8 Regent Street
London W1R 5TB
Tel: 01-734 3031
Telex: 28905

British Non-Ferrous Metals
Federation
Crest House
7 Highfield Road
Edgbaston
Birmingham B15 3ED
Tel: 021-454 7766
Telex: 339161

British Powder Metal
Federation
Ashton Court
67A Compton Road
Wolverhampton WV3 9QZ
Tel: 0902-28987

British Reinforcement
Manufacturers Association
15 Tooks Court
London EC4A 1LA
Tel: 01-831 7581
Telex: 297510 VALOCK G

British Scrap Federation
16 High Street
Brampton
Huntingdon
Cambs PE18 8TU
Tel: 0480-55249
Telex: 32546

British Secondary Metals
Association
Park House
25 Park Road
Runcorn
Cheshire WA7 4SS
Tel: 092-8572400
Telex: 629034 EDWILL G

British Welded Steel Tube
Association
38 Pamela Road
Northfield
Birmingham B31 2QG
Tel: 021-477 9465

China Clay Association
John Keay House
St Austell PL25 4DJ
Tel: 0726-74482

Coal Preparation Plant
Association
Fountain Precinct
1 Balm Green
Sheffield S1 3AF
Tel: 0742-766789
Telex: 54170
Fax: 0742-766213

Cold Rolled Sections
Association
Centre City Tower
7 Hill Street
Birmingham B5 4UU
Tel: 021-643 5494
Telex: 339420

Copper Development
Association
Orchard House
Mutton Lane
Potters Bar
Herts EN6 3AP
Tel: 0707-50711
Telex: 27711

Copper Smelters and Refiners
Association
Crest House
7 Highfield Road
Edgbaston
Birmingham B15 3ED
Tel: 021-454 7766
Telex: 339161

Ductile Iron Producers
Association
8th Floor
Bridge House
121 Smallbrook
Queensway
Birmingham B5 4JP
Tel: 021-643 3377
Fax: 021-643 5064

Ferro Alloys & Metal
Producers Association
c/o Peat Marwick, Mitchell &
Co
The Fountain Precinct
1 Balm Green
Sheffield S11 3AF
Tel: 0742-766789
Telex: 54170
Fax: 0742-766213

Lead Contractors Association,
Lead Development
Association
34 Berkeley Square
London W1X 6AJ
Tel: 01-499 8422
Telex: 261286

Lead Smelters & Refiners
Association
St Andrews House
22 High Street
Epsom
Surrey KT19 8AH
Tel: 03727-43976
Telex: 948104 BRIDGE G
Fax: 03727-43210

Light Metal Founders
Association
136 Hagley Road
Edgbaston
Birmingham B16 9PN
Tel: 021-454 4141
Telex: 336993 HEATH G

Metal Finishing Association
27 Frederick Street
Birmingham B1 3HJ
Tel: 021-236 2657-9
Telex: 334003 BIJGIF

Metal Packaging
Manufacturers Association
Elm House
19 Elmshott Lane
Chippenham
Slough
Berks SL1 5QS
Tel: 06286-5203

Metalforming Machinery
Makers Association Ltd
Queensway House
2 Queensway
Redhill
Surrey RH1 1QS
Tel: 0737-68611
Telex: 948669 TOPJNL G

Mining Association of the
United Kingdom
6 St James's Square
London SW1Y 4LD
Tel: 01-930 2399
Telex: 24639

National Federation of Clay
Industries
Federation House
Station Road
Stoke-on-Trent ST4 2SA
Tel: 0782-747256
Telex: 367446

National Metal Trades
Federation
Fleming House
Renfrew Street
Glasgow G3 6TG
Tel: 041-332 0826
Telex: 779433

Primary Tungsten
Association
280 Earls Court Road
London SW5 9AS
Tel: 01-373 7413
Telex: 889 077

Process Plant Association
Leicester House
8 Leicester Street
London WC2H 7BN
Tel: 01-437 0678
Telex: 263 536 ELECT G
Fax: 01-437 4901

Red Lead & Litharge
Manufacturers Association
St Andrews House
22 High Street
Epsom
Surrey KT19 8AH
Tel: 03727-43976
Telex: 948 104 BRIDGE G
Fax: 03727-43210

Stainless Steel Fabricators'
Association
14 Knoll
Road
Dorking
Surrey RH4 3FW
Tel: 0306-884079

Steel Castings Research &
Trade Association
5 East Bank Road
Sheffield S2 3PT
Tel: 0742-28647
Telex: 54281

Zinc Alloy Die Casters
Association
Zinc Development
Association
34 Berkeley Square
London W1X 6AJ
Tel: 01-499 6636
Telex: 261286

USA

American Copper Council
10 W 33rd Street
New York
NY 10001
Tel:(010 1) 212-7142249

American Institute for
Imported Steel Inc
11 West 42nd Street
New York
NY 10036
Tel: (010 1) 212-9211765
Telex: 961 613
Fax: (010 1) 212-3025758

American Iron Ore
Association
915 Rockerfeller Bldg
614 Superior Avenue NW
Cleveland
OH 44113-1306
Tel: (010 1) 216-2418261

American Metal Importers
Association
PO Box 97
Demerest
NJ 07626

American Wire Producers
Association
Suite 700
1101 Connecticut Avenue NW
Washington DC 20036
Tel: (010 1) 202-8571155
Telex: 89582

Association of Brass & Bronze
Ingot Manufacturers
PO Box 91741
Cleveland
OH 44101
Tel: (010 1) 216-4592100

Association of Industrial
Metalizers, Coaters &
Laminators
61 Blue Ridge Road
Wilton
CT 06897
Tel: (010 1) 203-7625611

Association of Iron & Steel
Engineers
Suite 2350
Three Gateway Center
Pittsburgh
PA 15222
Tel: (010 1) 412-2816323

Cast Metals Federation
455 State Street
Des Plaines
IL 60016
Tel: (010 1) 312-2972430

Coal Exporters Association of
the United States Inc
The Coal Building
1130 17th Street NW
Washington DC 20036
Tel: (010 1) 202-4632639
Telex: TWX 710 822 1167

Copper & Brass Servicenter
Association Inc
Adams Building
Suite 109
251 West Dekalb Pike
King of Prussia
PA 19406
Tel: (010 1) 215-2656658

Copper Development
Association Inc
Greenwich Office Park 2
PO Box 1840
Greenwich
CT 06836
Tel: (010 1) 203-6258210
Telex: 643784

Forging Industry Association
55 Public Square
Cleveland
OH 44113
Tel: (010 1) 216-781626!0

Foundry Equipment &
Materials Association
1133 15th Street NW
Suite 1000
Washington DC 20005
Tel: (010 1) 202-4299440

Independent Zinc Alloyers
Association
Suite 603
1000 16th Street NW
Washington DC 20036
Tel: (010 1) 202-7850558
Fax: (010 1) 202-7850210

Lead Industries Association
Inc
292 Madison Avenue
New York
NY 10017
Tel: (010 1) 212-5784750

Lead-Zinc Producers
Committee
1320 19th NW
Suite 600
Washington DC 20036
Tel: (010 1) 202-4667720
Telex: 710 822 0015
Fax: (010 1) 202-4662710

Metal Powder Industries
Federation
105 College Road East
Princeton
NJ 08540
Tel:(010 1) 609-4527700
Telex: TWX 510 685 2516

Missouri Limestone
Producers Association
PO Box 1725
124 E Capitol
Jefferson City
MO 65102
Tel: (010 1)314-6350208

National Association of
Aluminium Distributors
1900 Arch Street
Philadelphia
PA 19103
Tel: (010 1)215-5643484

National Association of Metal
Finishers
111 E Wacker Drive
Chicago
IL 60601
Tel: (010 1)312-6446610

National Association of
Recycling Industries Inc
330 Madison Avenue
New York
NY 10017
Tel: (010 1)212-8677330

National Association of Steel
Pipe Distributors Inc
1726 Augusta
Suite 102
Houston
TX 77057
Tel: (010 1)713-7816405

National Coil Coaters
Association
1900 Arch Street
Philadelphia
PA 19103
Tel: (010 1)215-5643484

National Steel Producers
Association
1055 Thomas Jefferson Street
NW
Washington DC 20007
Tel: (010 1)202-3421160

Refractory Metals Association
105 College Road East
Princeton
NJ 08540
Tel: (010 1)609-4527700
Telex: TWX 510 685 2516

Silver Users Association Inc
Suite 404
1717 K Street NW
Washington DC 20006
Tel: (010 1)202-7853050

Steel Bar Mills Association
1221 Locust Street
Suite 405
St Louis
MO 63103
Tel: (010 1)314-2312011

Titanium Development
Association
1 West Monument Avenue
Suite 510
PO Box 2307
Dayton
OH 45401
Tel: (010 1) 513-2238432

West Coast Metal Importers
Association
450 Wilshire Blvd
Suite 408
Los Angeles
CA 90010
Tel: (010 1) 213-3874595

Asia

Japan

Aluminium Products
Association
13-13 Akasaka 2-chome
Minato-ku
Tokyo
Tel:(010 81) 3-5837502

Cold Rolled Steel Strip
Association of Japan
Zenkoku Nenryo Kaikan
Building
12-15 Ginza 8-chome
Chuo-ku
Tokyo
Tel: (010 81) 3-5415711

Japan Aluminium Federation
Nihonbashi Asahi Seimei
Building
1-3 Nihonbashi 2-chome
Chuo-ku
Tokyo 103
Tel: (010 81) 3-2744551
Telex: 0222 3074 jalf j
Fax: (010 81) 3-2743179

Japan Brass Makers
Association
No 12-22 Tsukiji 1-chome
Chuo-ku
Tokyo
Tel: (010 81) 3-5426551
Telex: 23793

Japan Copper Development
Association
Konwa Building
12-22 Tsukiji 1-chome
Chuo-ku
Tokyo 104
Tel: (010 81) 3-5426631-3
Telex: 23793

Japan Ferro-Alloy Association
Tokyo Kurabu Building
No 2-6 Kasumigaseki 3-chome
Chiyoda-ku
Tokyo
Tel: (010 81) 3-5800841-4
Fax: (010 81) 3-5800845

Japan Iron & Steel Exporters
Association
3-2-10 Nihonbashi Kayabacho
Chuo-ku
Tokyo 103
Tel: (010 81) 3-6694811
Telex: 025 23607

Japan Iron & Steel Federation
Keidanren Kaikan
9-4 Otemachi 1-chome
Chiyoda-ku
Tokyo 100
Tel: (010 81) 3-2793611
Telex: 222 4210
Fax: (010 81) 3-2450144

Japan Lead Zinc
Development Association
New Hibiya Building
3-6 Uchisaiwaicho 1-chome
Chiyoda-ku
Tokyo
Tel: (010 81) 3-5035796

Japan Light Metal Association
Nihonbashi Asahiseimei
Building
1-3 Nihonbashi 2-chome
Chuo-ku
Tokyo
Tel: (010 81) 3-2733041
Fax: (010 81) 3-2132918

Japan Non-Ferrous Metal
Exporters Association
6F Konwa Building
12-22 Tsukiji 1-chome
Chuo-ku
Tokyo 104
Tel: (010 81) 3-5426551

Japan Stainless Steel
Association
Tekko Kaikan Building
2-10 Nihonbashi Kayabacho
3-chome
Chuo-ku
Tokyo 103
Tel: (010 81) 3-6694431

Japanese Electric Wire &
Cable Makers Association
Konwa Building
12-22 Tsukiji 1-chome
Chuo-ku
Tokyo 104
Tel: (010 81) 3-5426031

Non-Integrated Steel
Producers Association
c/o Japan Iron & Steel
Federation
Keidanren Kaikan
9-4 Otemachi 1-chome
Chiyoda-ku
Tokyo 100
Tel: (010 81) 3-2411921
Telex: 222 4210

Welded Pipe Association
3F Saito Building
No 7 Takara-machi 3-chome
Chuo-ku
Tokyo 104
Tel: (010 81) 3-5617334

Directories

International
International Zinc and
Galvanising Survey
Metal Bulletin Journals Ltd
Surrey
UK

Iron and Steel Works of the
World
Metal Bulleting Books Ltd
London
UK

Metal Traders of the World
Metal Bulletin Books Ltd
Surrey
UK

Metallurgical Plantmakers of
the World
Metal Bulletin Books Ltd
Surrey
UK

Non Ferrous Metal Works of
the World
Metal Bulletin Books Ltd
Surrey
UK

Stainless Steel; An
International Survey of
Stainless Steel Industry
Metal Bulletin Books Ltd
Surrey
UK

Steel Traders of the World
Metal Bulletin Books Ltd
Surrey
UK

Who's Who in Steel
Metal Bulletin Books Ltd
Surrey
UK

World Coal Industry Report
and Directory
Institute of Ecology
University of Georgia
USA

World Directory and
Handbook of Metals
Engineers' Digest
London
UK

World Mines Register
Miller Freeman Publications
San Francisco
USA

Europe

France
Federation des Chambres
Syndicates de Minerais et des
Metaux
Non Ferreux (Annuaire)
Paris

Federation des Industries
Mechaniques et
Transformatrius des
Metaux (Annuaire)
Paris

Societe de L'Industrie
Minerale (Annuaire)
Saint Etienne

Germany, Federal Republic of
Aluminum Lieferuerzeichnis
Aluminum-Verlag
Dusseldorf

Die Eisen, Bech und Metall
Verabeitende Industrie,
Stahlverformung und Ihre
Helfer
Industriesch
av-verlagsgesellschaft
Darmstadt

Die Eisen,
Stahl-und-Ne-metal-Industrie
und Ihre Helfer
Industriesch au
verlagsgesellschaft
Darmstadt

Metall
Metall-Verlag
Berlin

Yearly Buyer's Guide for the
World Metal Branch From
Ore Extraction to Metal
Finishing
Riederer-Verlag
Stuttgart

Sweden
Svensk Metal &
Maskinkalender
Fournir
Stockholm

UK
British Non-Ferrous Metals
Federation Directory
British Non-Ferrous Metals
Federation
Birmingham

Dial Industry – Metals, Metal
Working
IPC Business Prices
Information Services
East Grinstead

Fab Guide: Welding and
Metal Fabrication
Welding and Metal
Fabrication
London

Ferro-Alloy Directory
Metal Bulletin Books Ltd
Surrey

Ferro-Alloys Survey
Metal Bulletin Books Ltd
Surrey

Financial Times Mining
International Yearbook
Longman
London

Stainless Steel Directory
Modern Metals Publications

USA
Metal Distribution
Fairchild
New York

Metal Progress Heat Treating
Buyer's Guide and Directory
American Society for Metals
Metals Park
Ohio

Canada
Financial Post Survey of
Mines and Energy Resources
(The)
Maclean Hunter

Asia
SEAISI
Directory of Iron and Steel
Works in Member Countries
SEAISI
Singapore

India
Handbook of Indigeneously
Manufactured Machinery,
Equipment and
Explosives For Use in Mines
Indian Bureau of Mines
Nagpur

Australia
Register of Australian Mining
Lodestone Press
Leederville
WA

Middle East

Israel
Israel Metal Industry
Directory
Ministry of Commerce and
Industry
Jerusalem

Market Research Reports

This section lists recently
published market research
reports which cover various
aspects of the metals
industry. Details provided
below are title of report,
publisher, year of publication,
price and geographic
coverage.

Aluminium, 3rd edition
Roskill Information Services
(UK)
1988
£590/$1150
Worldwide

Arsenic, 6th edition
Roskill Information Services
Ltd (UK)
1988
£380/$760
Worldwide

Business Ratio Reports: Drop
Forgers
ICC Business Ratios (UK)
Annual
£165
UK

Business Ratio Reports: Iron
Founders
ICC Business Ratios (UK)
Annual
£165
UK

Business Ratio Report: Metal
Finishers
ICC Business Ratios (UK)
Annual
£165
UK

Business Ratio Report:
Mining & Quarrying
ICC Business Ratios (UK)
Annual
£165
UK

Business Ratio Report: Non
Ferrous Founders
ICC Business Ratios (UK)
Annual
£165
UK

Business Ratio Report: Spring
Manufacturers
ICC Business Ratios (UK)
Annual
£165
UK

Business Ratio Report: Waste
& Scrap
ICC Business Ratios (UK)
Annual
£165
UK

Cadmium, 6th edition
Roskill Information Services
Ltd (UK)
1988
$410/$845
Worldwide

Chromium, 6th edition
Roskill Information Services
Ltd (UK)
1988
£510/$1020
Worldwide

Competition in the Alumina
Market: Costs, Prices and
Profits to 1995
Commodities Research Unit
Ltd (UK)
1987
£10,900
Worldwide

Copper, 4th edition
Roskill Information Services
Ltd (UK)
1988
£565/$1150
Worldwide

Electric Steel Sheet
Consumption to 2000
Commodities Research Unit
Ltd (UK)
1988
£6500
Worldwide

Engineering Ceramics, 3rd
edition
Roskill Information Services
Ltd (UK)
1988
£340/$680
Worldwide

Forgings
The Freedonia Group Inc
(USA)
1988
$1700
USA

Hot Forging and Pressing of
Steel Products
Databank Spa (Italy)
1988
£700
Italy

Metal Finishers
ICC Financial Surveys (UK)
1988
£165
UK

Powder Metal Products
The Freedonia Group Inc
(USA)
1988
$800
USA

Powder Metallurgy
Business Communications Co
(USA)
1987
$1950
USA

Primary Aluminium Smelting
Costs 1984-89
Commodities Research Unit
Ltd (UK)
1987
£4250
Worldwide

Rhenium, 4th edition
Roskill Information Services
Ltd (UK)
1988
£360/$720
Worldwide

Shearson Lehman Brothers
Annual Reviews
(seven reviews covering all
major individual metals)
Metal Bulletin plc (UK)
Annual
£100/$150
Worldwide

Silicon Metal into the 1990s
Commodities Research Unit
Ltd (UK)
1987
£5500
Worldwide

Special Steels
Databank Spa (Italy)
1988
£1400
Italy

Specialty Metals (1985)
Business Communications Co
(USA)
1988
$2450
USA

Stainless Steel Consumption
to 2000: Opportunities for
Stainless Steel and Alleoy
Metal Producers
Commodities
Research Unit Ltd (UK)
1987
£5900
Worldwide

Steel Mill Products
The Freedonia Group Inc
(USA)
1988
$800
USA

Steel Pipes, Welded and
Seamless
Databank Spa (Italy)
1988
£1400
Italy

Steel Production
Databank Spa (Italy)
1988
£1400
Italy

Steel and Alloy Steel Wires
and Wire Products
Databank Spa (Italy)
1988
£700
Italy

Threats and Opportunities in
Copper and Copper Alloy
Strip, Sheet and Plate Vol 1 –
Western Europe, Vol 2 – East
Asia
Commodities Research Unit
Ltd (UK)
1987
£8000 per vol, £13,250 for 2
vols
Worldwide

Wolff's Guide to the London
Metal Exchange – 3rd edition
Metal Bulletin plc (UK)
1987
£38
UK

World Aluminium – A Metal
Bulletin Databook
Metal Bulletin plc (UK)
1987
£48.50
Worldwide

World Aluminium Capacity
Handbook, 1985-1996
Metal Bulletin plc (UK)
1987
£220
Worldwide

World Stainless Steel
Statistics 1987
Metal Bulletin plc (UK)
1987
£152/$364/DM758
Worldwide

Zinc Smelting: An Industry in
Transition
Commodities Research Unit
Ltd (UK)
1988
£12,000
Worldwide

Periodicals and Journals

International
Annual Bulletin of Steel
Statistics for Europe
Foundry Trade Journal
International
International Journal of
Fatigue
International Journal of
Refractory and Hard Metals
International Metals Review
International Steel Statistics
International Zinc and
Galvinizing Survey
Iron and Steel Works of the
World
Metallurgical Plantmakers of
the World
New Materials International
Non-Ferrous Metal Works of
the World
Quarterly Bulletin of Steel
Statistics for Europe
Statistics of World Trade in
Steel
Steel Times International
Steel Traders of the World
Tin International
Tube International
World Aluminium – A Metal
Bulletin Databook
World Copper Databook
World Metal Statistics
World Steel Trade
World Trade Steel

Europe

Austria
Metall

Belgium
L'Usine Industrial Digest –
Het Bedrijf Industrial Digest

Denmark
Jern-og Maskinindustrien

France
Fonderie-Fondeur D'Aujourd
Hui
Metaux Deformation
Le Trefile

Germany, Federal Republic of
Aluminium
Bander Bleche Rohre
Blech Rohre Profile
Der Buchsenmacher
Draht
Drahtwelt
Materialprufung
Metall
Metalloberflache
MPT-Metallurgical Plant and
Technology
Der Praktiker
Praktische Metallographie
Schweissen & Schneiden
Wire
Zeitschrift fur Metallkunde
Zeitschriften-und
Bucherschau Stahl und Eisen

Italy
Fonderia Interfaccia
Il Filo Metallico
La Metallurgia Italiana
Trattamenti e Finitura

Netherlands
Bouwen met Staal
Metaal en Kunststof
Metaal en Techniek
Toeleveren & Uitbesteden

Portugal
Maquinas E Metais

Spain
Alambre
Simet

Switzerland
Journal of the Less Common
Metals
Journal of Organometallic
Chemistry
Synthetic Metals

UK
Alloys Index
Aluminium Industry
Anti-Corrosion
BCIRA Journal

British Corrosion Journal
Foundry Trade Journal
Foundry Worker
Heat Treatment of Metals
Industrial Corrosion
Journal of Constructional
Steel Research
Lead Abstracts
Materials Science and
Technology
Metal Bulletin
Metal Bulletin Monthly
Metal Bulletin Prices and Data
Metal Construction
Metal Industry News
Metals Abstracts
Metals Abstracts Index
Metals and Materials
Non-Ferrous Alert
Powder Metallurgy
Refractories Journal
Stainless Steel Industry
Steel Castings Abstracts
Steel News
Steel Times
Trading in Metals
Welding Institute Research
Bulletin
Welding Review
Wire
Zinc Abstracts

USA
Foundry Management and
Technology
Metal Progress
Metals Week
Metalworking News
Precision Metal
Products Finishing
Welding Design and
Fabrication
Welding Distributor (The)

Canada
Metalworking Production and
Purchasing

Australia
Castings Magazine
Steel Construction
Steel Fabrication Journal

*Government
Publications*

UK Official Sources

**Metal Manufacturers:
General Statistics**
Annual Abstract of Statistics
British Business
Digest of Welsh Statistics
Monthly Digest of Statistics
Northern Ireland Annual
Abstract of Statistics
Scottish Abstract of Statistics
United Kingdom National
Accounts

**Forging, Pressing and
Stamping**
Annual Abstract of Statistics
Business Monitor: PQ3120
Census of Production
Reports: PA 224
Census of Production
Reports: PA 312
Monthly Statistical Bulletin
United Kingdom Mineral
Statistics

Iron Castings etc
Annual Abstract of Statistics
Annual Statistics of the British
Steel Corporation
Business Monitor PQ 3111
Census of Production
Reports: PA 311
Iron Foundries Press Notice
Iron and Steel Industry –
Annual Statistics

Iron and Steel
Census of Production
Reports: PA 221 and PA 222
Economic Trends
Monthly Digest of Statistics
Overseas Trade Statistics
Press Notice: Steel Industry
Statistics
UK Exports of Iron and Steel

**Non-Ferrous Metal
Foundries**
Business Monitor: PQ 3112

**Steel Wire and Steel
Products**
Business Monitor: PQ 2234
Census of Production
Reports: PA 223

Motor Vehicles

Trade Associations

International
Organisation Internationale
des Constructeurs
d'Automobiles (OICA)
4 Rue de Berri
75008 Paris
France
Tel: (010 33) 1-43590013
Telex: BPICA 290012F

Comite de Liason de la
Construction Automobile
5 Square de Meeus
1040 Brussels
Belgium
Tel: (010 32) 2-5127930

Europe

Austria
Fachverband der
Fahrzeugindustrie
Osterreichs
Weidner Haupstrasse 63
1045 Vienna 4
Tel: (010 43) 1-6505/4803

Belgium
Chambre Syndicale du
Commerce Automobile de
Belgique
Boulevard de la Woluwe 46,
Bte 6
1200 Brussels
Tel: (010 32) 2-7710085
Telex: 63191

Fabrimetal
Rue des Drapiers 21
1050 Brussels
Tel: (010 32) 2-5112370
Telex: 21078B

Federation des Associations
de l'Industrie et du
Commerce de
l'Automobile
Boulevard de la Woluwe 46,
Bte 6
1200 Brussels
Tel: (010 32) 2-7710085
Telex: 63191

Federation Belge des
Industries de l'Automobile et
du Cycle
Boulevard de la Woluwe 46,
Bte 6
1200 Brussels
Tel: (010 32) 2-7710085

Salon de l'Automobile de la
Moto et du Cycle
Boulevard de la Woluwe 46,
Bte 6
1200 Brussels
Tel: (010 32) 2-7710085

Denmark
Automobil-Importorernes
Sammenslutning
Ryvangs Alle 68
2900 Hellerup
Tel: (010 45) 1-623999

Danmarks
Automobil-Forhandler-
Forening
Alhambravej 5
1826 Frederiksberg C
Tel: (010 45) 1-314555

Forenede Danske Motorejere
Blegdamavej 124
2100 Copenhagen 0
Tel: (010 45) 1-382112

Finland
Autoalan Keskuslitto RY
Yrjonkatu 14-B
00120 Helsinki 12

Autolitto RY
Fabianink 14
00100 Helsinki 10

Autonosatukkukauppiaat
Mannerheimintie 76
00250 Helsinki
Tel: (010 358) 0-493901

Autotuojat RY
Annankatu 31-33 D 59
00100 Helsinki 10
Tel: (010 358) 0-605102

France

Chambre Syndicale du
Commerce et de la Reparation
Automobile (CSNCRA)
6 Rue Leonard de Vinci
75116 Paris
Tel: (010 33) 1-5021910
Telex: 611538

Chambre Syndicale des
Constructeurs d'Automobiles
(CSCA)
2 Rue de Presbourg
75008 Paris
Tel: (010 33)
1-7235405/7235427
Telex: 610446F

Chambre Syndicale des
Importateurs d'Automobiles,
Cycles et Motocycles
33 Avenue de Wagram
75008 Paris
Tel: (010 33) 1-7665165

Federation des Industries des
Equipements pour Vehicules
(FIEV)
112-114 Avenue Charles de
Gaulle
92522 Neuilly sur Seine
Tel: (010 33) 46370636

Federation des Syndicats de la
Distribution Automobile
(FEDA)
10 Rue Pergolese
75782 Paris Cedex 16
Tel: (010 33) 1-5003971
Telex: 2607171

Union Technique de
l'Automobile, du Cycle et du
Motocycle (UTAC)
157 Rue le Courbe
75017 Paris
Tel: (010 33) 1-8425390
Telex: 692775 UTAC

Germany, Federal Republic of

Deutsche
Automobil-Treuhand GmbH
Hohenzollernstr 10
Stuttgart-S

Verband der
Automobilindustrie eV (VDA)
Postfach 170563
Westendstrasse 61
6000 Frankfurt am Main 17
Tel: (010 49) 69-75701
Telex: 411293

Verband der Importeure von
Kraftfahrzeugen eV (VDIK)
Postfach 2414
Heuchelheimer Strasse 19
6380 Bad Homburg vdh
Tel: (010 49) 6172-32071
Telex: 415883

Verband der
Kraftfahrzeugteile und
Zweirad-Grosshandler eV
Postfach 1680
Oberstrasse 36-42
4030 Ratingen

Ireland, Republic of

Automobile Association
23 Suffolk Street
Dublin

Royal Irish Automobile Club
34 Dawson Street
Dublin

Society of Irish Motor
Industry
5 Upper Pembroke Street
Dublin
Tel: (0001) 761690/766332

Italy

Associazione Industrie dei
Tranporti Automobilistici
Via Regina Elena 11
Rome

Associazione Nazionale
Ausiliari del Traffico e dei
Trasporti
Complimentari
Piazza Mignanelli 3
Rome

Associazione Nazionale fra
Industrie Automobilistiche
Corso Galileo Ferraris 61
10128 Turin
Tel: (010 39) 11-5761

Unione Nazionale
Rappresentanti Autoveicoli
Esteri
(Importers Association)
Via G Aureliana 2
Rome
Tel: (010 39) 6-480751

Netherlands

Nederlands Vereniging de
Rijwiel en
Automobiel-Industrie RA
Europaplein 2
1078 GZ Amsterdam
Tel: (010 31) 20-440944
Telex: 12100

Norway

Automobildel-og
Rekvisita-Grossistenes
Forening
Norges Grossistforbund
Drammensveien 30
Oslo 2
Tel: (010 47) 2-567390

Automobilgrossistenes
Landsforening
H Heyerdahisgate 1
Oslo
Tel: (010 47) 2-414872

Automobilforhandlernes
Landsforbund
O Slottsgt 14
Oslo

Automobilimportorenes
Landsforening (BIL)
Hauchsgt 1
Oslo 1
Tel: (010 47) 2-202006

Autoriserte
Automobilforhandleres
Forening
Akersgaten 43
Oslo

Norges Bilbransjeforbund
Bogstadveien 46
Oslo

Opplysningsradet for
Veitrafikken
Professor Dahisgate 10355
Oslo 3

Portugal

AFIA
Rua do Crasto 190
4100 Porto

Associacao Do Comercio
Automovel de Portugal
(ACAP)
Rua da Palmeria 6
1294 Lisbon
Tel: (010 351) 1-370048
Delegacao do Norte:
Rue de Santa Catarina 693-4
Porto
Tel: (010 351) 2-25606

Associacao dos Industriais de
Montagem de Automoveis
Rua de Palmeira 6
1200 Lisbon

Spain
Agrupacion Nacional de
Fabricantes de Automoviles y
Camiones
Fray Bernardino, Sahagun 24
Madrid 16
Tel: (010 34) 1-4577881

Aniacam (Vehicle Importers)
Cea Bermudez 14 1C
28003 Madrid
Tel: (010 34) 1-2544896

Asociacon de Importadores y
Exportadores de Madrid
Ferraz 16
Madrid
Tel: (010 34) 1-474212

Servicio Tecnico Comercial de
Fabricantes de Equipos y
Componentes para
Automocion (Sernauto)
Castello 120
Madrid 6

Sweden
Bilindustriforeningen (BIL)
(Association of Swedish
Automotive Manufacturers
and Wholesalers)
Box 5514
Storgatan 19
11485 Stockholm
Tel: (010 46) 8-7838000
Telex: 11923

Motorbranschens
Riksforbund
(The National Swedish
Association for Motor Retail
Trades and Repair)
Karlavagen 14a
Box 5611
11486 Stockholm

Switzerland
Association Suisse des
Negociants en Gros de
Branches de Vehicules a
Moteur
Fachstrasse 6
8942 Oberrieden

Autogewerbe Verband der
Schweiz
Mittelstrasse 32
Berne

Chambre Syndicale Suisse de
l'Automobile et Branches
Annexes
Postfach 112
1218 Grand Sacconex Genf
Geneva 4
Tel: (010 41) 22-981111
Telex: 422784

Union des Industriels en
Carrosserie
Wulfingerstrasse 147
8407 Winterthur

Turkey
Otomotiv Sanayii Dernegi
Akdogan Sok 30
Besiktas
Istanbul

Turkiye Turing ve Otomobil
Kurumu
Sisli Meydan
Istanbul

UK
Institute of the Motor
Industry
Fairshares
Brickendon
Herts SG13 8PG
Tel: 099286-521

Motor Agents Association
201 Great Portland Street
London W1N 6AB
Tel: 01-580 9122

Motor Industry Research
Association
Watling Street
Nuneaton
Warwickshire CV10 7U
Tel: 0203-348541

Society of Motor
Manufacturers and Traders
Forbes House
Halkin Street
London SW1X 7DS
Tel: 01-235 7000
Contact: W S Cottrell, Senior
External Trade Executive
(Car registration statistics UK,
international market research
conducted for car
manufacturers and traders)

USA
American Automobile
Association
8111 Gatehouse Road
Falls Church
VA 22047

American Trucking
Association
2200 Mill Road
Alexandria
VA 22314

Automotive Parts and
Accessories Association Inc
5100 Forbes Boulevard
Lanham
MD 20706

Automotive Service Industry
Association
444 N Michigan Avenue
Chicago
IL 60611-3975

Motor and Equipment
Manufacturers' Association
300 Sylvan Avenue
Englewood Cliffs
NJ 07632

Motor Vehicle Manufacturers'
Association of the US Inc
300 New Center Building
Detroit
MI 48202
and
1620 Eye Street NW
Suite 1000
Washington DC 20006

National Automobile Dealers
Association
8400 Westpark Drive
Maclean
VA 22102

Society of Automotive
Engineers Inc
400 Commonwealth Drive
Warrendale
PA 15096

Speciality Equipment Market
Association
11540 E Slauson Avenue
Whittier
California 90607

Canada

Automotive Industries
Association of Canada
1272 Wellington Street
Ottawa
Ontario K1Y 3A7

Automotive Parts
Manufacturers Association
(Canada)
55 York Street
Toronto
Ontario M5J 1RJ

Canadian Automobile
Association
150 Gloucester Street
Ottawa 4
Ontario

Federation of Automobile
Dealer Associations of
Canada
2221 Yonge Street
Toronto 7
Ontario

Motor Vehicle Manufacturers
Association
25 Adelaide Street
E Toronto
Ontario M5C 1Y7

Motor Vehicle Safety
Association 1901
50 Hillboro Avenue
Toronto 5
Ontario

Africa

Kenya

Royal East African
Automobile Association
c/o PO Box 87
Nairobi
Kenya

South Africa

Automobile Association of
South Africa
AA House
De Villiers Street
PO Box 596
Johannesburg

Motor Industries Federation
1st Floor, Harland House
17 Loveday Street
17 Johannesburg

National Association of
Automobile Manufacturers of
South Africa (NAAMSA)
PO Box 40611
Arcadia 0007
Pretoria 0002

Royal Automobile Club of
South Africa
National Mutual Buildings
Church Square
Cape Town

Asia

Hong Kong

John B P Byrne & Co
Secretaries
Motor Traders Association of
Hong Kong
Hopewell Centre 41/F
183 Queen's Road East

India

Association of Indian
Automobile Manufacturers
Army and Navy Building
3rd Floor, Mahatma Gandhi
Road
Fort, Bombay 1

Automotive Component
Manufacturers Association
80 Dr Annie Besant Road
Worli, Bombay 400 018

Federation of All India
Automobile Spare Parts
Dealers Associations
3620/21 Netaji Subhash Marg
Daryaganj
Delhi 6

Federation of Automobile
Dealers Associations
534 Sardar Vallabhdhai Patel
Road
Bombay 400 007

Indian Institute of Road
Transport
Best House
PO Box 192
Fort, Bombay 400 001

Indonesia

Gaakindo (Association of
Automobile Agents and
Assemblers)
Gedung Cikini Baru Lt
iv/410 Jalan Cikini Raya
95 Jakarta

Japan

Japan Auto-Body Industries
Association
Kishimoto Building 2-1
2-chome
Marunouchi
Chiyoda-ku
Tokyo

Japan Auto Parts Industries
Association
16-15 Takanawa
1-chome
Minato-ku
Tokyo 108

Japan Automobile Dealers
Association
107 5-7-17 Minami Aoyama
Minato-ku
Tokyo

Japan Automobile
Manufacturers Association
Inc
Otemachi Building
6-1 Otemachi, 1-chome
Chiyoda-ku
Tokyo 100

Japan Automotive Machinery
and Tool Manufacturers
Association
Kikai-Shinko-Kaikan No 304
5-8
3-chome
Shibakoen
Minato-ku
Tokyo 105

Japan Motor Industrial
Federation, Inc
Otemachi Buiding
6-1 Otemachi, 1-chome
Chiyoda-ku
Tokyo 100

Society of Automotive
Engineers of Japan Inc
10-2 Gobancho
Chiyoda-ku
Tokyo 102

Korea, Republic of
Korea Auto Industries Corp
Association
1638-3 Seucho-Dong
Kangnam-Gu
Seoul 135
Tel: (010 82) 2-5870014/18
Telex: K22373

Malaysia
Malaysian Motor Assemblers
Association
c/o Borneo Motors (M) SDN
BHD
76-78 Jalan Ampang
Kuala Lumpur

Pakistan
Pakistan Automobile
Corporation Ltd
6th Floor, PNSC Building,
M Khan Road
Karachi

Pakistan Automobile Spare
Parts Importers-Dealers
Association
1-8/4 Rimpa Plaza
Karachi

Philippines
Automotive Manufacturers
Institute Inc
5th Floor ITC Building
337 Buendia Avenue
Extension
Makati
Manila

Bus Operators Association
Room 313, Anita Building
Quezon Avenue
Quezon City

Consolidated Automotive
Parts Producers Association
Inc
8th Floor, RFM Building
Pioneer
Pasig Manila

Philippine Automotive
Association (PAA)
Room 208 Far East Bank
Building
Buendia Avenue
Corner Pasong Tamo
Makati
Manila

Philippine Automotive Parts
Producers Association Inc
328 Rizal Avenue Extension
Calcoocan City
Manila

Philippine Motor Association
(PMA)
4077 R Magsaysay Boulevard,
Sta Mesa
Manila

Singapore
Motor Traders Association of
Singapore
c/o Inchape House, 10th Floor
450 Alexandra Road
Singapore 5

The Singapore Cycle & Motor
Traders Association
184a King George's Avenue
Block 803
Singapore 0820

Thailand
Association of Thai
Industries, Automobile Club
(The)
7th Floor, Suriyothai Building
260 Paholyothin Road
Bangkok

Thai Automobile Parts
Manufacturers Association
No 5 Vip Havadee Rangsit,
Dingdang Don Muang,
Bangkok

**Australia and New
Zealand**

Australia
Most states have branch
offices of the following
organisations:

Australian Automobile
Chamber of Commerce
464 St Kilda Road
Melbourne VIC 3004

Australian British Trade
Association (The)
PO Box 141
Manuka
ACT 2603

Australian Road Federation
582 St Kilda Road
Melbourne VIC 3004

Federal Chamber of
Automotive Industries
Canberra House
Marcus Clarke Street
Canberra ACT 2601

Federation of Automotive
Products Manufacturers
8th Floor, Canberra House
Marcus Clarke Street
Canberra ACT 2601

National Automobile Dealers
Association
464 St Kilda Road
Melbourne VIC 3004

New Zealand
Associated Motor Importers
and Distributors of New
Zealand Inc
PO Box 490
Wellington 1

British Trade Association of
New Zealand Inc
PO Box 11-363
Commerce House
126 Wakefield Street
Wellington

Federated Road Transport
Organisation of NZ Inc
PO Box 1778
Wellington

Motor Vehicles
Manufacturers Association
PO Box 390
Wellington 1

New Zealand Automobile
Association Inc
PO Box 1824
Wellington

New Zealand Automotive
and Cycle Wholesalers
Association Inc
PO Box 3178
Wellington

New Zealand Motor Body
Builders Association
PO Box 1087
Wellington

New Zealand Motor Trade
Association Inc
PO Box 9244
Wellington

New Zealand Motor Trade
Federation
PO Box 857
Wellington

New Zealand Road
Federation
PO Box 1778
Wellington

New Zealand Tractor &
Industrial Equipment
Importers Association
PO Box 390
Wellington

South and Central America

Argentina
Asociacion de Fabricas de
Automotores (ADEFA)
Marcelo T de Alvear 636
5 Piso
Buenos Aires

Asociacion de Fabricantes de
Conjuntos Importantes para
la Mecanizacion
del Agro y del Transporte
(AFCIMAT)
Reconquista 379
Of 206/7 Buenos Aires

Camera de la Industria
Automotriz (CIA)
Viamonte 1167
5 Pico
Of 20/21 Buenos Aires

Camara Industrial Fabricantes
de Automotres, Repuestos,
Accesorios y
Afines (CIFARA)
Uruguay 766
Planta Baja
Of 3 Buenos Aires

Brazil
Associaco Nacional de
Maquinas, Veiculos,
Accessorios e Pecas
131 Av Rio Branco
Rio de Janeiro DF

Sindicato Nacional da
Industria de Pecas para
Automoveis e Similares
Viaduto dona Paulina 80 4.0
andar cj
01595 Sao Paulo

Sinicato Nacional da Industria
de Tractores, Caminhoes,
Automoveis e Veiculos
Similares (ANFAVEA)
Avda, Indianopolis 496

Chile
Asociacion de Importadores
de Automoviles (ACCIA)
Teatinos 248
Santiago

Colombia
Acolfa (Asociacion
Colombiana de Fabricantes de
Auto Partes)
Carrera 7a No 33-49 Oficina
301
PB 6188 Bogota

Associacao Nacional de
Importadores de Vehiculos
Automotores Andemos
Ed H Faux
Av Jimenez 7-25
Bogota

Federacion Metalurgica
Colombiana (Fedmetal)
Carrrera 7a No 13-65
Piso 3
Bogota

Mexico
Asociacion Mexicana de la
Industria Automotriz (AC)
Avenida Benjamin Franklin
132
Mexico 18 DF

Asociacion Nacional de
Fabricantes de Productos
Automotrices AC
Av Ejercito Nacional 533-302
Mexico 5 DF

Camara Nacional de la
Industria de Transformacion
Av San Antonio 256
Mexico 18 DF

Peru
Asociacion de Plantas de la
Industria Automotriz (APIA)
El Rosario 343
Lima 18

Venezuela
Asociacion de Distribuidores
de Automotores y
Maquinarias (ADAM)
Av Los Chorros No 21
Residencias Ina-Iona Sebucan
Apartado 3925
Caracas

Camera de Fabricantes
Venezolanos de Productos
Automotrices (FAVENDPA)
Puente Anauco, Edif
Camera de Industriales Piso 7
San Bernadino
Caracas

Camara de la Industria de
Vehiculos Automotores
(CIVA)
Centro Ciudad Comercial
Tamanaco
Nivel C-2
Mezzanina 1
Ofic 4 Urb
Chuao-Caracas

Canidra (Importers and
Distributors)
Av Este 2 No 215, Edif
Camera de Comercio de
Caracas,
Piso 5
Ofic 4, Apartado 5538
Los Caobos

Directories

Europe

Belgium
Catalogue General de
l'Industrie et du Commerce
Automobile de Belgique
Comaubel
Brussels
Belgium

France

Bottin de l'Auto, du Cycle et
de la Moto
Societe Didot-Bottin
Paris

Federation des Industries des
Equipment pour Vehicules
(List of producers and
products)
Federation des Industries des
Equipment pour Vehicles
Neuilly-sur-Seine

Federation des Syndicates de
la Distribution Automobile
(List of members)

Germany, Federal Republic of

Hersteller-Nochweis der
Deutschen
Automobilindustrie
Verband der
Automobilindustrie
Frankfurt/Main

UK

Autotrade Directory
Morgan-Grampian
London

Commercial Vehicle and PSV
Buyers Guide
Kogan Page
London

Motor Trader Handbook
IPC Transport Press
London

SMMT Buyers Guide to the
Motor Industry of Great
Britain (The)
SMMT
London

Society of Motor
Manufacturers and Traders
List of Members
SMMT
London

USA

Ward's Automotive Yearbook
Wards
Detroit, MI

Canada

Automotive Service Data
Book
Maclean Hunter
Toronto

Asia

Japan

Guide to the Motor Industry
of Japan
Japan Motor Industrial
Federation
Tokyo

Market Research Reports

This section lists recently
published market research
reports which cover various
aspects of the automotive
industry. Details provided
below are title of report,
publisher, year of publication,
price and geographic
coverage.

4WD Segment (The)
Fessel
GFK (Austria)
1988
AS 12,000
Austria

Automotive Aftermarket
The Freedonia Group Inc
(USA)
1988
$1700
USA

Autoparts
Key Note Publications (UK)
1987
£105
UK

Brazilian Motor Industry:
Change and Opportunity
(The)
The Economist Intelligence
Unit (UK)
1987
£85 (UK & Europe), $160 (N
America), £88 (ROW)
Brazil

CVT in Automobiles
The Freedonia Group Inc
(USA)
1987
$800
Worldwide

Car Aftermarket (The)
Euromonitor Publications Ltd
(UK)
1987
£275
UK

Car Drivers and Media Using
Fessel
GFK (Austria)
1988
AS 30 000
Austria

Car Finance
Mintel (Australia)
1986
Price on request
Australia

Car Guarantees and Buying
Decision
Fessel
GFK (Austria)
1988
AS 15 000
Austria

Car Market Information
System
Fessel
GFK (Austria)
1988
AS 36 000
Austria

Car Rental
Euromonitor Publications Ltd
(UK)
Updated every six months
£975
Europe, USA

Commercial Vehicles
Databank Spa (Italy)
1988
£1400
Italy

Diesel Cars 1972-1990
Euromonitor Publications Ltd
(UK)
1986
£275
Europe

Electrical and Electronic
Automotive Equipment
Databank Spa (Italy)
1988
£1400
Italy

European Emissions Control
and Automotive Fuel Use
DRI Europe Ltd (UK)
1986
Price on request
Europe

European Trucks Forecast
Report
DRI Europe Ltd (UK)
Twice yearly
Price on request
Europe

Financial Status Report:
European Vehicle
Manufacturers
DRI Europe Ltd (UK)
1986
Price on request
Europe

Image-Radars: Fuel Makes
Fessel
GFK (Austria)
1988
AS 50 000
Austria

Joint Ventures and
Agreements in the West
European Motor Industry
The Economist Intelligence
Unit (UK)
1987
£85 (UK & Europe), $160 (N
America), £88 (ROW)
Europe

Motor Distributors
Key Note Publications (UK)
1987
£105
UK

Motorcycles
Databank Spa (Italy)
1988
£1400
Italy

N Ireland Car Market
Ulster Marketing Surveys Ltd
(N Ireland)
1988
£430
N Ireland

OEM Automotive Electronics
The Freedonia Group Inc
(USA)
1988
$1700
N America

Passenger Cars
Databank Spa (Italy)
1988
£1400
Italy

South Korean Motor Industry
(The)
The Economist Intelligence
Unit (UK)
1987
£125 (UK & Europe), $225 (N
America), £128 (ROW)
S Korea

Statistical Yearbooks
Vols 1 & 2
Automotive Industry Data
(UK)
Annually
£80 each
Europe

Structure of the Japanese
Auto Parts Industry (The)
3rd edition
Dodwell & Co (Japan)
1986
£400
Japan

Unification of the EC Market
by 1992: The Impact on the
Automotive
Industry
DRI Europe Ltd (UK)
1988
Price on request
Europe

Vehicle Leasing & Hire
Key Note Publications (UK)
1987
£105
UK

Vehicular Lighting
The Freedonia Group Inc
(USA)
1988
$800
N America

Women's Role in Car Buying
Decision
Fessel
GFK (Austria)
1987
AS 12 000
Austria

World Automotive Forecast
Report
DRI Europe Ltd (UK)
Twice yearly
Price on request
Worldwide

World Autos, Light Trucks &
Vans
The Freedonia Group Inc
(USA)
1987
$1700
Worldwide

Periodicals and Journals

International and Pan European

ACE International (Motor
Industry)
Automobile International
Automotion Industries
International
Automotion Industry Data
Automovil Internacional
(Spanish)
European Motor Business
L'Information du Vehicle
International Vehicle News
(Manufacturer & Supply)
Motor Engines
World Car

Europe

Austria
Der Fahrzeughandel (Auto
Trade)

Belgium
L'Auto Journal
Auto-Moto-Revve (Trade)
Car Belgium
Comaubel Catalogue
Generale/Algemen Katalogus

Fegarbel-Revve (Trade)
Le Moniteur de
l'Automobile/DL Autogido
Motor
Royal Auto/KACB Revve

Denmark
Aktuel Bilsport – Auto –
Orientering
Auto-Auisen-Autig
(Workshops & Dealers)
Auto Nyt (Motor Trade)
Bil og Motor (Motor Trades)
Bilen Motor og Sport
(Motoring)
Motor (Car Owners)
Motor Bladet
Motor Magasinet (Motor
Trade & Service Stations)
Motor Sevice og Autoeknisk
Tidsskrift

Finland
Aja (Motoring)
Auto ja Liikenne (Motoring)
Diesel-lehti (Auto/Diesel
Engineering)
Moottori
Suomen Autolenti (Motor
Trade)
Tekniikan Maailma (Popular
Mechanics)
Tuulilasi (Motoring,
Motorbikes, Caravans)
Vauhdin

France
L'Action Automobile et
Touristique
Argues de l'Automobile
Auto Helodo
Auto Journal
Automobiliste (Vintage Cars)
L'Automobils
Auto Moto
Auto Verte
CRA Infos
E Chappement
L'Equipe (Moteurs) Rubrique
Automobile
L'Expert Automobile
Le Fanauto (Vintage Cars)
France Auto
L'Information du Vehicule
(English, French)
Ingenieurs du l'Automobile
Moto Journal
Moto Revue
Moto Verte
L'Officiel du l'Automobile
Revue Technique Automobile
Revue Technique Cavrosseric

Revue Technique Diesel
Sport – Auto

Germany, Federal Republic of
ACE Lenkrad (Motoring)
ADAC Motor-Welt
(Motoring)
ATZ – Automobil Technische
Zeitschrift (Automobile
Engineering)
Auto Bild
Auto Fachmann (Trade)
Autohaus (Trade)
Automobil-Industrie
Auto Motor und Sport
Auto/Motor & Zubehor
Auto & Reise (Motoring)
Auto und Verkehr
Auto Zeitung
Christophorus (Porsche –
German, English, French)
Fahrzeug und Karosserie
(Carriage Building)
Gute Fahrt (VW Motoring)
KF2 – Betrieb
Kraftfahzeuguermieter (Car
Hire)
Krafthand (Motor Trade)
Markt fur Klassische
Automobile und Motorrader
MO (Motorcycles)
MT2 Motortechnische
Zeitschrift
Das Motorad (Motor Cycles)
Motor Klassik
Taukstelle

Ireland, Republic of
Auto Ireland
Irish Automotive Aftermarket
Irish Garage
Irish Motor Industry
Motoring Life
Private Motorist

Italy
ATA (Professional)
Auto & Design
Autocapital
Auto (Motoring)
L'Automobile
Automobilismo
Automondo
Autorama (Motoring)
Autoservice (Garages)
Garage e Officina
Genti Motori
Ilustratofiat
Motitalia
La Moto
Motociclismo

Motocross
Motor
Motosprint
Quattro route (Automobiles)
Starter
Tuttomoto (Motorcycles)

Netherlands
De Auto
Auto & Motor Technick
Auto-Info
Auto Toeruit (Touring)
Autovisie
het Bovagblad
Motovisie (Motorcycles)

Norway
Motor
Motorforeven
Motorliv

Spain
Auto Hebdu
Automecanica
Automovil
Autopista
Auto Revisita
Moto Verde (Motorcycling)
Motociclismo
Que Automovil Compro?
SEAT-86
SoloAuto
Solo Moto Actual
(Motorcycling)

Sweden
Alt on MC (Motoring)
Cykel-och Mopednytt (Cycle
& Moped Riders)
MC-Nytt (Motoring Cycling)
Motor (Motoring)
Motorbranschen (Motor
Dealers)
Motorforearen (Motoring)
Start & Speed (Motor Sports
& Dealers)
Det Suenska Motormagasinet
(Motor Trade)
Teknikens Varld

Switzerland
ACS Au
to (Motoring) (French &
German)
Auto-Ilustrierte
Automobil Revve
Auto-Technik (Professional)
Carrossier (Professional)
Moto
Revve Automobil
Schweizer Auto-Gwerbe

UK
Accessories, Components
and Equipment International
Autocar
Automobile (Veteran Cars)
Automotive Commercial
Refinisher
Autoparts & Accessory
Retailer
Autotrade
Autoworld
Business Car
Car
Car Accessory Trader
Car Buyer
Car Choice
Car Fleet Management
Car Mechanics
Car Parts & Accessories
Civil Service Motoring
Company Car
Cycle & Motorcyle Trade
Monthly
Disabled Driver (The)
Executive Car
Garage & Automobile Retailer
Garage Equipment News &
Component Review
Glass's Guide to Commercial
Vehicle Valves
Glass's Guide to Used Car
Valves
Glass's Guide to Used Motor
Cycle Valves
London Motorist
MTE – Motor Trade Executive
Motor
Motor Caravan Magazine
Motor Industry Management
Motor Marketing Weekly
Motor Trader
Motorcycle Dealer
Motorcycle Trader
Motoring News
Motoring Weekly
Motorist
Motorist Digest
Motorists' Guide to New &
Used Car Prices
New Car Prices & Information
Parkers Car Price Guide
Service Station
Toyota Today
Tyres & Accessories
Used Car Prices &
Information
What Car?
Workshop Equipment News
Your Car Magazine

Canada
Alberta Motorist
Auto Hebdo (French/English)
Auto Trader Magazine
L'Automobile
Automotive Retailer
Canadian Automobile Trade
Cycle Canada
Manitoba Motorist
Moto Journal (French)
Motor in Canada
Motorcycle Dealer & Trade
Saskatchewan Motorist
Service Station & Garage
Management

USA
American Clean Car
(Carwash Operators)
American Motorcyclist
Automobile Body Repair
News
Automobile Chain Store
Automobile Cooling Journal
Automobile Design &
Development
Automobile Engineering
Automobile Fleet
Automotile Industries
Automobile Industries
International
Automobile International
(English & Spanish)
Automobile Marketing
Automotive News
Automotive Rebuilder
Autoweek
Car Care News
Car & Driver
Cars
Cars & Trucks (Retail
Management)
Commercial Car Journal
Counterman (sales people in
automobile aftermarket)
Cycle (Motorcycling)
Diesel Equipment
Superintendent
Import Car
International Motorcycle
Trade Journal
International Vehicle News
Modcon Cycle
Motor
Motor Age
Motor Service (Repairs)
Motor Tread
Motorcycle Dealer News
Motorcycle Industry
Motorcycle Industry Business
Journal
Motorcycle Industry Shopper

Motorcycle Product News
Motorcyclist
Motor land
Off-Road (Recreational
Vehicles)
Popular Mechanics
RU Business (Recreational
Vehicles)
Road & Track
Solidarity (United Auto
Workers)
Southern Automotive Journal
Speed & Custom Dealer
(Automotive)
Super Customs & Hot Rods
(Customised American Cars)
Super Service Station
Superauto Illustrated (Deluxe
Foreign Cars)
Ward's Auto World

Asia

Hong Kong
Auto Magazine

India
Auto Guide
Automobile Reporter
Motor (Tamil)
Scooter Guide
Upper India Motorist
Wheel Fare

Japan
Auto Bi
Auto Sport
Auto Technic
Car & Driver
Car Graphic
Car Styling
Car Top
Driver
Motor Car
Motor Fan
Motor Fan Graphity
Motor Life
Motor Magazine
Motor Mainichi
Motor Rider
Motor Road
Motor Vehicle
Motorcyclist
Shinsha Album

Australia
Australasian Dirt Bike
Australasian Motor Cycle
News
Automobile Engineer
Modern Motor
Motor Manual

Motor Trade Journal
Motoring Reporter
Refinisher
SAE-Australia (Automotive
Engineers)
Tasmanian Motor News
VACC Journal (Victorian
Automobile Chamber of
Commerce)
WAACC's Motor Industry
Wheels

Government
Publications

UK Official Statistics
Annual Abstract of Statistics
Annual Vehicle Census in GB
Basic Road Statistics
Business Monitor: MM1
MM2
(Motor vehicle registrations)
Department of Transport
Press Notices
Digest of Welsh Statistics
Monthly Digest of Statistics
Motor Industry in Great
Britain (The)
Motor Industry of Great
Britain (The) (SMMT-Society
of Motor Manufacturers and
Traders)
Northern Ireland Annual
Abstract of Statistics
Regional Trends
Scottish Transport Statistics
Survey of the Transport of
Goods by Road
Transport Statistics Great
Britain

Pharmaceuticals

Trade Associations

Europe

Austria
Osterreichische
Apothekerkammer
Spitalgasse 31
1094 Vienna 1X

Osterreichischer
Apothekerverband
Spitalgasse 31
1094 Vienna 1X

Belgium
Association Pharmaceutique
Belge
11 rue Archimede
1040 Brussels

Czechoslovakia
Czechoslovak Pharmaceutical
Association
Dlouha 15
11000 Prague 1

Denmark
Danmarks Apotakerforsning
Hammerichsgade 14
1611 Copenhagen

Dansk Farmaceutforening
Toldbogade 36
Copenhagen 1253

Finland
Finnish Pharmaceutical
Society, Pieni
Roobertinkatu 14 C
00120 Helsinki 12

France
Conseil National de l'Ordre
des Pharmacians
4 avenue Ruysdael
75008 Paris

Germany, East
Pharmezeutische Gesellschaft
der Deutschen
Demokratischen Republik
Grosse Seestrasse 4
1120 Berlin

Germany, Federal
Republic of
Asbeitagemeinschaft der
Berufsvartretungen
Deutscher Apotheker
Beethovenplatz 1-3
6000 Frankfurt am Main 97

Deutscho Pharmazeutische
Gesellschaft
Frankfurter Strasse 250
Darmstadt

Gibraltar
Gibraltar Pharmaceutical
Society
Calpe Pharmacy
PO Box 89

Greece
Greek Pharmaceutical
Association Emm.
Benakis 30
Athens 142

Panhellenic Pharmaceutical
Association
1 rue Chalcocondyli
Athens 141

Hungary
Hungarian Pharmaceutical
Association
Hogyes Endre E.14
1092 Budapest

Iceland
Islands Farmaceutforening
Oldugotu 4
PO Box 316
Reykjavik

Italy
Federazione Ordini
Farmacisti Italiani
Via Palestro 75
00185 Rome

Luxembourg
Union Nationale des
Pharmaciens
Luxembourgeois
17 Rue de Gibraltar
Luxembourg

Malta
Chamber of Pharmacists
Federation of Professional
Bodies
1 Wilga St
Paceville

Netherlands
Koninklijke Nederlandse
Maatschaddij ter Bevordering
der Pharmacia
11 Alexanderstraat
The Hague 2541

Northern Ireland
Pharmaceutical Society of
Northern Ireland
73 University Street
Belfast BT7 1HL

Norway
Norges Apotekerforening
Arbiens Gate 3
Oslo 2

Norsk Farmaceutisk Selskap
Sorligt 8
Oslo 5

Poland
Polskie Towarzysto
Farmaceutycno
Ul.Dluga 16
00-238 Warsaw

Portugal
Pharmaceutical Society of
Portugal
18 rua da Sociedade
Farmaceutica
Lisbon 1

Scotland
Scottish Pharmaceutical
Federation
135 Buchanan Street
Glasgow G1 2JQ

Spain
Consejo General de Colegios
Oficiales de Farmaceuticos
Villaneuva 11
Madrid 1

Sweden
Sveriges Farmaceutforbund
Bryggargartan 10
Box 613
101 28 Stockholm

Switzerland
Schweizerischer
Apothekerverein
Postfach 3006
3000 Berne 7

Societe Suisse de Pharmacie
Marktgasse
Postfach 3006
3000 Berne 7

Turkey
Turkish Pharmaceutical
Association
Halaskargazi CD 287/8
Osmanbey
Istanbul

UK
National Pharmaceutical
Association
40-42 St Peter's Street
St Albans
Herts AL1 3NP

Pharmaceutical Society of
Great Britain
Secretariat:
S Southwell, FPS
1 Lambeth High Street
London SE1 7JN
Tel: 01-735 9141

Yugoslavia
Union des Societes
Pharmaceutiques de
Yugoslavia
12/1 Mose Pijade
Belgrade 11000

Australia
Pharmaceutical Association of
Australia
10th Floor, Canberra House
Marcus Clarke St
Canberra City
(PO Box 456)

Pharmaceutical Society of
Queensland
4 Wickham Street
Petrie Bight
Brisbane 4000
Queensland

Pharmacy Board of
Queensland
42 George Street
Brisbane 4000
Queensland

Pharmacy Guild of Australia
(The)
14 Thesiger Court
PO Box 36
Deakin
ACT 2600

New Zealand
Pharmaceutical Society of
New Zealand
Pharmacy House
124 Dixon Street
PO Box 11-640
Cambridge Terrace
Wellington 1

USA
American Pharmaceutical
Association
2215 Constitution Avenue
NW
Washington DC 20037

National Pharmaceutical
Association
College of Pharmacy
PO Box 934
Howard University
Washington DC 20059

National Pharmaceutical
Council
Suite 468
1030 Fifteenth Street NW
Washington DC 20005

Asia

China
Pharmaceutical Society of the
Republic of China (The)
c/o 1 Jen-Ai Rd, 1st Section
Taipei
Taiwan

Hong Kong
Pharmaceutical Society of
Hong Kong
PO Box 1298

India
Indian Pharmaceutical
Association
Kalina
Santacruz (East)
Bombay 400-098

Japan
Pharmaceutical Society of
Japan
12-15501 Shibuya 2-chome
Shibuya-ku
Tokyo 150

Korea
Pharmaceutical Association of
Korea
Pharmacist Building
18-13 Kwan-Chul-Dong
Chong-Ro-Ku
Seoul

Malaysia
Malaysian Pharmaceutical
Society
PO Box 158
Petaling Jaya
W Malaysia

Pakistan
Pharmaceutical Society of
Pakistan
129 Wazir Mansion
Nicol Road
Karachi

Singapore
Pharmaceutical Society of
Singapore
PO Box 70

Sri Lanka
Pharmaceutical Society of Sri
Lanka
c/o Department of Pharmacy
Faculty of Medicine
University of Colombo
Colombo 8

Thailand
Pharmaceutical Association of
Thailand (The)
Pharmacy Building
(Chulalonghorn University)
Phyathai Road
Bangkok 10500

Other Countries

Argentina
Associacion Farmaceutica y
Bioquimica Argentina
Bartolome Mitre 2041
1039 Buenos Aires

Ecuador
Federacion Farmaceutica dà
Guyas,
Apartado 3407
Guayaquill

Egypt
Pharmaceutical Society of
Egypt
Dar El Hekma
42 Kasr El-Aini St
Cairo

El Salvador
Union Farmaceutica de El
Salvador
Club Farmaceutico
San Salvador

Fiji
Phamaceutical Society of Fiji
PO Box 368
109 Cumming St
Suva

Gambia
Gambia Pharmaceutical
Association
PO Box 35
Bathurst
The Gambia
West Africa

Ghana
Pharmaceutical Society of
Ghana
PO Box 2133
Accra

Iran
Iranian Pharmaceutical
Association
No 215
Koorish Building
Aryamehr Avenue
Tehran

Iraq
Iraq Pharmaceutical
Association
Ma'ari St
Entrance of Mansour City
Baghdad

Israel
Pharmaceutical Association of
Israel
PO Box 29594
Tel-Aviv

Jamaica
Pharmaceutical Society of
Jamaica
41 Lady Musgrove Road
Kingston 10

Jordan
Jordan Pharmaceutical
Association
PO Box 1124
Amman

Kenya
Pharmaceutical Society of
Kenya
PO Box 44290
Nairobi

Mauritius
Societe Pharmaceutique de
I'lle Maurice
PO Box 17
Rose Hill

Philippines
Philippine Pharmaceutical
Association
10th Floor
Cardinal Building
Cor Herran & F Agoncillo Sts
Ermita
Manila

South Africa
Pharmaceutical Society of
South Africa (The)
PO Box 31360
Braamfontein, 2017
Johannesburg

Directories

International
Annual Register of
Pharmaceutical Chemists
Pharmaceutical Press
London
UK

Cosmetics International
Directory
Cosmetics International
London
UK

Martindale – The Extra
Pharmacopoeia
Pharmaceutical Press
London
UK
(Also available online)

Pharmaceutical Trademark
Directory
IMS World Publications
London
UK
Covers 36 world markets

Pharmacology and
Pharmacologists: an
International Directory
Oxford University Press
Oxford
UK

World Directory of
Pharmaceutical
Manufacturers
IMS World Publications
London
UK
Covers 2500 companies and
43 countries

World Pharmaceutical
Directory
Unlisted Drugs
Chatham
New York
USA

World Pharmaceuticals
Introductions
IMS World Publications
Chatham
New York
USA

Europe

France

Catalogue Generale de
l'Industrie Pharmaceutique
Edition et documentation
Paris

Spain

Annual Drug Data Report
J R Prous SA
Barcelona
Available online

UK

Association of the British
Pharmaceutical Industry
Directory of Members and
Associated Companies
ABPI
London

British National Formulary
Pharmaceutical Press
London

British Pharmaceutical
Industry
Jordan Information Services
London
Covers 187 companies

Chemist and Druggist
Yearbook and Directory
Benn Business Information
Services
Tonbridge Wells, Kent

Drugs Handbook
Macmillan Press
Basingstoke, Hants

EBL Guide (The): UK
Directory of Pharmaceutical
and Related Products
Edwin Burgess Ltd
Publications Division
Princes Risborough
Bucks

Medicines and Poisons Guide
Pharmaceutical Press
London

Pharmaceutical Codex
Pharmaceutical Press
London

Pharmaceutical Handbook
Reference Manual
Pharmaceutical Press
London

Proprietary Articles Trade
Association Reference Book
Sterling Publications Ltd
London

USA

American Drug Index
Harper and Row
London

CTFA Membership Directory
Cosmetic, Toiletry and
Fragrance Association
Washington DC

PMD Pharmaceuticals
Marketers Directory
Fisher-Stevens
Clifton, New Jersey

Who's Who in the Cosmetic
Industry

Asia

India

Indian Pharmaceutical Guide
Pamposh Publications
New Delhi

Japan

Japanese Drug Directory
Covers drugs in Japan and
overseas
Japan Pharmaceutical Traders
Association
Tokyo

Pharmaceutical
Manufacturers of Japan
Yakugyo Jiho Co Ltd
c/o Maruzen Co Ltd
Tokyo

Market Research Reports

This section lists recently
published market research
reports which cover
various aspects of the
pharmaceutical industry.
Details provided below are
title of report, publisher, year
of publication, price and
geographic
coverage.

Analgesics
Euromonitor Publications Ltd
Updated every 6 months
£975
Europe/USA

Anti-Cancer Drugs
Theta Corporation (USA)
1986
$600
USA

Biotechnology Health Care
The Freedonia Group Inc
(USA)
1988
$800
USA

Britain's Pharmaceutical
Industry
Jordan & Sons Ltd (UK)
1986
£150
UK

Britain's Pharmaceutical
Industry – Financial Update
Jordan & Sons Ltd (UK)
1987
£150
UK

Business Ratio Report:
Pharmaceutical
Manufacturers
ICC Business Ratios (UK)
Annual
£165
UK

Chemist Goods
Databank Spa (Italy)
1988
£700
Italy

China's Pharmaceutical
Opportunities
PJB Publications Ltd (UK)
1987
£95/$187/DM 343
China

Company Profiles (various)
PJB Publications Ltd (UK)
Various
Price on request
Worldwide

Cough and Cold Preparations
Specialists in Business
Information Inc (USA)
1987
$325
USA

Cough and Cold Remedies
Euromonitor Publications Ltd
(UK)
Updated every 6 months
£975
Europe/USA

Dermatological Preparations
Specialists in Business
Information Inc (USA)
1987
$325
USA

Diagnostic Reagents & Tests
Kits
The Freedonia Group Inc
(USA)
1988
$800
USA

Digestive Remedies
Euromonitor Publications Ltd
(UK)
Updated every 6 months
£975
Europe, USA

Drug & Pharmaceutical
Packaging
The Freedonia Group Inc
(USA)
1987
$800
USA

Emerging New Compounds
PJB Publications Ltd (UK)
1987
£30/$59/DM 108
Worldwide

Ethical Pharmaceutical
Markets
Theta Corporation (USA)
1987
$750
USA

Good Clinical Practice in
Europe
PJB Publications Ltd (UK)
1988
£80/$158/DM 289
Europe

Home Medicare
Market Assessment
Publications (UK)
1987
£275
UK

L'industrie Pharmaceutique
dans le Monde
Eurostaf Dafsa (France)
1988
FF9.300
Worldwide

International Company Image
Study Among GPs
Martin-Hamblin Research
(UK)
1988
Price on request
Europe

Japanese Pharmaceutical
Challenge (The)
PJB Publications Ltd (UK)
1987
£95/$187/DM 343
Japan

Japanese Pharmaceutical
Issues 1988
PJB Publications Ltd (UK)
1988
£90/$178/DM 320
Japan

Japanese Pharmaceutical
Market: How to Take the
Hurdle (The)
Prognos AG (Switzerland)
1987
SFrs 15.000
Japan

Medicated Skincare
Euromonitor Publications Ltd
(UK)
Updated every 6 months
£975
Europe/USA

New Focus on
Pharmaceuticals
National Economic
Development Office (UK)
1986
£20
UK

Nonprescription
Contraceptives
Packaged Facts (USA)
1988
$1250
USA

Nonprescription Drugs
Business Trend Analysts
(USA)
1988
$850
USA

OTC Cold, Nasal & Cough
Remedies
Packaged Facts (USA)
1988
$1150
USA

OTC Pharmaceuticals
Key Note Publications Ltd
(UK)
1988
£105
UK

Ophthalmic Goods: UK
Marketing Strategies for
Industry (UK)
1988
£55
UK

Parallel Imports and EEC Law
PJB Publications Ltd (UK)
1988
£85/$168/DM 306
Europe

Pharmaceutical Company
Image Study Among General
Practitioners
Martin-Hamblin Research
(UK)
1988
Price on request
UK

Pharmaceutical Company
League Tables
PJB Publications Ltd (UK)
1987
£105
Worldwide

Pharmaceutical
Manufacturers and
Distributors
ICC Financial Surveys (UK)
1987
£145
UK

Pharmaceutical Products
Worldwide: A Market
Analysis
PJB Publications Ltd (UK)
1987
£350
Worldwide

Pharmaceuticals
Databank Spa (Italy)
1988
£700
Italy

Pharmaceuticals – Focus on
R&D
National Economic
Development Office (UK)
1987
£7.50
UK

Pharmaprojects
PJB Publications Ltd (UK)
Constantly updated
Price on request
Worldwide

Prescribed Pharmaceuticals
Key Note Publications Ltd
(UK)
1988
£105
UK

Prescription Pharmaceuticals
and OTC Health Care
Products
Databank Spa (Italy)
1988
£1400
Italy

Promotion Monitor
Merlin Ltd (UK)
3 times per year
£2250
Jordan, Syria

Promotion Monitor
Merlin Ltd (UK)
3 times per year
£3300
Egypt

Promotion Monitor
Merlin Ltd (UK)
3 times per year
£3000
Saudia Arabia

Promotion Monitor
Merlin Ltd (UK)
3 times per year
£2250
Kuwait, UAE

Promotion Monitor
Merlin Ltd (UK)
3 times per year
£3500
Pakistan

Promotion Monitor
Merlin Ltd (UK)
3 times per year
Price on request
Middle East

Prospects & Strategies for the
Pharmaceutical Industry
(1987)
Yano Research Institute
(Japan)
1987
Price on request
Japan

Scrip Yearbook
PJB Publications Ltd (UK)
1988
£75
Worldwide

Success Strategies for the
Changing Pharmaceutical
Industry
The Wilkerson Group, Inc
(USA)
1987
$26,500
USA

UK OTC Healthcare Report
(The)
Euromonitor Publications Ltd
(UK)
1987
£975
UK

Understanding
Pharmaceuticals in the EEC
PJB Publications Ltd (UK)
1987
£80/$158/DM 289
Europe

Vitamins and Minerals
Market (The)
Packaged Facts (USA)
1988
$1250
USA

Vitamins and Nutrients
Specialists in Business
Information Inc (USA)
1987
$325
USA

Vitamins and Nutrients
Business Trend Analysts
(USA)
1988
$750
USA

Vitamins and Tonics
Euromonitor Publications Ltd
(UK)
Updated every 6 months
£975
Europe, USA

World Drug Market Manual
(Vol 1)
IMS International (UK)
1988
Price on request
Worldwide

Yearbook of the
Medical/Pharmaceutical
Industry (1987)
Yano Research Institute
(Japan)
1987
Price on request
Japan

Periodicals and Journals

International and
Pan-European
Scrip World Pharmaceutical
News
World Pharmaceutical
Introductions

Europe

Austria
Die Apotheke (Pharmacists)
Osterreichische
Drogisten-Zeitung
(Pharmacists)

Belgium
Annales Pharmaceutiques
Belges
Journal de Pharmacie de
Belgique

Denmark
Archiv for Pharmaciogkemi
(Pharmacists)
Industria Farmaceuten
(Industrial pharmacy,
medicine etc)
Laboremus (Pharmaceutical
chemists)

Finland
Semina (Phamarcy)

France
Les Actualities
Pharmaceutiques
Annales de Pharmaceutique
Francaise
L'Industrie Pharmaceutique
Le Pharmacien de France

**Germany, Federal
Republic of**
Apotheken-Praxis
(Pharmacists)
Der Apotheker
Arzneitmitlel Forschung
Die Pharmazeutische.
Industrie

Ireland, Republic of
Irish Pharmacy Journal
MIMS (Ireland)

Italy
Collegamento (Pharmacists)
L'Informatore Farmaceutico
Notiziario Medico
Farmaceutico
Panorama Farmaceutico

Netherlands
Arts en Wereld
De Drogist
Pharmacy International

Spain
El Farmaceutico

Sweden
Apoteksteknikern
(Pharmaceutical chemists)
Farmaceutisk Tidskrift
Svensk Farmaceutisk Tidskrift

Switzerland
Journal Suisse de Pharmacie
Swiss Pharma

UK
British Journal of
Pharmaceutical Practice
Chemist and Druggist
Journal of Clinical and
Hospital Pharmacy
Journal of Labelled
Compounds and Radio
Pharmaceuticals
OTC Index
OTC Medication
Pharmaceutical Business
News
Pharmaceutical Journal (The)
Pharmaceutical Medicine
Pharmacy International
Pharmacy Today
Scrip – World Pharmaceutical
News

USA
American Druggist
American Pharmacy
Current Prescribing
Drug and Cosmetic Industry
Drug Topics: The News
Magazine for Today's
Pharmacies
Journal of the American
Pharmaceutical Association
Journal of Continuing
Education in Pharmacy

Journal of Pharmaceutical
Sciences
New Price Report (Price
listings for drug stores)
Pharmaceutical and Cosmetic
Equipment
Pharmaceutical Executive
Pharmaceutical Technology
Pharmacy Times
RX Magazine

Canada
Canadian Pharmaceutical
Journal
Drug Merchandising
Le Pharmacien
Quebec Pharmacie

Australasia

Australia
Australian Journal of Hospital
Pharmacy
People and Drugs Magazine

Asia

India
Eastern Pharmacist
Indian Journal of Hospital
Pharmacy (The)

Japan
Iyaku Journal
Kokusai Iyakuhin Joho
Yakuji

Government
Publications

UK Official Statistics
Business Monitor: PQ 2570
Census of Production
Reports: PA 257
(Available from HMSO)

Printing & Publishing

Trade Associations

International

INTERGRAF (International
Confederation for Printing &
Allied Industries) aisbl
Square Marie-Louise 18 Bte
25-27
1040 Brussels
Belgium
Tel: (010 32)2-2308646
Telex: 64 393
EUROGF B

Europe

Austria

Hauptverband der
graphischen
Unternehmungen
Oesterreichs
Grunangergasse 4
1010
Vienna
Tel: (010 43) 222-526609

Verband Industrieller
Buchbinder
Brucknerstrasse 8
1040
Vienna
Tel: (010 43) 222-655382

Belgium

FEBELGRA
Rue Belliard 20, bte 16
1040 Brussels
Tel: (010 32) 2-5123638
Fax: (010 32) 2-5135676
Telex: 26854 ABEJOU

Denmark

Dansk Provins
Bogtrykkerforening
Bogtrykkernes Hus
Helgavej 26
5100 Odense
Tel: (010 45) 9-130601

Grafiske Organisationer (GO)
Landemaerket 11
Postfach 2210
1018 Copenhagen K
Tel: (010 45) 1-156040
Fax: (010 45)1-140788

Finland

Graafinen Keskusliitto
Lonnrotinkatu 11A
00120 Helsinki 12
Tel: (010 358) 0-602911
Fax: (010 358) 0-603527

France

Federation Francaise de
l'Imprimerie et des Industries
Graphiques
115 Boulevard Saint Germain
75006 Paris
Tel: (010 33) 1-46342115

Germany, Federal Republic of

Bundesverband Druck eV
Biebricher Allee 79
Postfach 1869
6200 Wiesbaden 1
Tel: (010 49) 6121-803111
Fax: (010 49) 6121-803113
Telex: 418 6888 BVD

Norway

Grafiske Bedrifters
Lansforening
Akersgaten 16
0158 Oslo 1
Tel: (010 47) 2-412180
Fax: (010 47) 2-363498

Spain

Federacion Nacional de
Industrias Graficas
Barquillo 11, 4 D
Madrid 4
Tel: (010 34) 1-5227249

Sweden

Sveriges Grafiska
Arbetsgivare – och
Industriorganisationer
Blasieholmsgatan 4A
Box 16 383
103 27 Stockholm
Tel: (010 46) 8-7626000

Switzerland

Schweizerischer Verband
Graphischer Unternehmen
(Association suisse des arts
graphiques)
Carmenstrasse 6
Postfach 39
8030 Zurich 30
Tel: (010 41) 1-2521440
Fax: (010 41) 1-2521743

Secretariat Romand
48 av General Guisan
1009 Pully
Tel: (010 41) 21-280107
Fax: (010 41) 21-295118

Verband der Schweizer
Druckindustrie
(Association de l'Industrie
Graphique Suisse)
Schosshaldenstrasse 20
3000 Berne 32
Tel: (010 41) 31-431511

Verein der Buchbindereien
der Schweiz – Federation
Suisse de la Reliure
Post fach 2618
3001 Berne
Tel: (010 41) 31-257364
Fax: (010 41) 31-257364

UK

British Printing Industries
Federation
11 Bedford Row
London WC1R 4DX
Tel: 01-242 6904

USA

Printing Industries of
America
1730 North Lynn Street
Arlington, Virginia 22209

Asia

Hong Kong

Hong Kong Printers
Association (The)
48-50 Johnston Road
Hong Kong

India

All India Federation of Master
Printers
E-14 South Extn Part II
New Delhi 110049

Indonesia

Indonesian Master Printers
Association
23 Jalan Letjen Haryono MT
Jakarta Selatan

Philippines

Printing Industries
Association of the Philippines
Cheers Executive Center
1240 Gral Luna Street
Ermita
Manila

Singapore

Singapore Master Printers
Association
04-02 Association Building
68 Lorong 16 Geylang
Singapore 1439

Australia

Printing & Allied Trades
Employers' Federation of
Australia
Lithgow Street 77
St Leonards
PO Box 58
New South Wales 2065
Tel: (010 61) 2-4382777

Directories

International

Benn's International Media
Directory
Benn Publications
Tonbridge
Kent
UK

International Authors and
Writers Who's Who (The)
International Biographical
Centre
Cambridge
UK

International Book Trade
Directory
Bowker
London
UK

International Literary Market
Place
Bowker
London
UK

Europe

France

Annuaire Gutenberg
Technorama
Paris

UK

5001 Hard-To-Find Publishers
and their Addresses
Alan Armstrong and
Associates
London

BRAD
British Rate and Data
Directories and Annuals
Mclean-Hunter
London

Benn's Press Directory
Benn Publications
Tonbridge
Kent

Book and Periodical
Publishers
ICC Business Ratios
London

British Printer Dataguide
Mclean-Hunter
London

Cassell's Directory of
Publishing
Cassell
London

Directory of Book Publishers
and Wholesalers
Booksellers' Association of
Great Britain and Ireland
London

Member and Products Index
British Federation of Printing
Machinery and Supply
London

Printing Trades Directory
Printing Trades Journal
London

Publishing and Bookselling
Directory (The)
Hamilton House
Brixworth,
Northampton

USA

MIMP: Magazine Industry
Market Place
Bowker
New York

Printing Trades Directory
Bowker
New York

Market Research Reports

This section lists recently
published market research
reports which cover various
aspects of the printing and
publishing industry. Details
provided below are title of
report, publisher, year of
publication, price and
geographic coverage.

Blue Book Marketing
Information Reports
AF Lewis & Co Inc (USA)
Quarterly
$185 (annually)
USA/Canada

Book Publishing
Key Note Publications (UK)
1987
£105
UK

Book Publishing
Databank SA (Spain)
1988 (Oct)
£1600
Spain

Book Publishing
Databank Spa (Italy)
1988
£1400
Italy

Britain's Book Publishing
Industry
Jordan & Sons Ltd (UK)
1988
£125
UK

Britain's Magazine Publishing
Industry
Jordan & Sons Ltd (UK)
1987
£125
UK

Britain's Newpaper Industry
Jordan & Sons Ltd (UK)
1987
£125
UK

Business Press
Key Note Publications (UK)
1988
£105
UK

Business Ratio Report: Book
Publishers
ICC Business Ratios (UK)
Annual
£165
UK

Business Ratio Report:
Booksellers
ICC Business Ratios (UK)
Annual
£165
UK

Business Ratio Report:
Newspaper Publishers
ICC Business Ratios (UK)
Annual
£165
UK

Business Ratio Report:
Periodical Publishers
ICC Business Ratios (UK)
Annual
£165
UK

Business Ratio Report:
Printers (Intermediate)
ICC Business Ratios (UK)
Annual
£165
UK

Business Ratio Report:
Printers (Major)
ICC Business Ratios (UK)
Annual
£165
UK

Commercial Printing
Key Note Publications (UK)
1988
£105
UK

Consumer Magazines
Key Note Publications (UK)
1987
£105
UK

Electronic Image Processing
in the Graphics Industry
Prognos AG (Switzerland)
1986
SFrs 7.500
Worldwide

Greeting Cards
Key Note Publications (UK)
1988
£105
UK

Image Processing: The
European Market
Wharton Information
Systems (UK)
1987
£850
Europe

Ink Jet Printing: Printing
Industry Applications and
Impacts
Gorham International Inc
(USA)
1985
$2800
USA

Media Market 2000
Prognos AG (Switzerland)
1987
Price on request
W Germany

Newspaper and Periodical
Publishing
Databank Spa (Italy)
1988
£1400
Italy

Newspaper Publishers
ICC Financial Surveys (UK)
1988
£125
UK

Newspapers
Key Note Publications (UK)
1988
£105
UK

Printers – London and South
ICC Financial Surveys (UK)
1988
£185
UK

Printers – Midlands and
North and Scotland
ICC Financial Surveys (UK)
1988
£165
UK

Printing Technology 2000
Prognos AG (Switzerland)
1987
SFrs 7.500
Worldwide

Printing and Papeterie Works
Databank Spa (Italy)
1988
£700
Italy

Publishing Books
Databank Ltd (UK)
1988 (Oct)
£1400
UK

Publishing Newspapers &
Magazines
Databank Ltd (UK)
1988
£1400
UK

Reprography & Graphic
Communications
Diamond Research Corp.
(USA)
Monthly
$295 per year
USA, Europe, Japan

Specialty Papers & Films:
Imaging Media
Diamond Research Corp
(USA)
1988
$1595
USA

Synthetic Papers, Current
Use of and Potential Use for
Synthetic Paper
Corporate Development
Consultants Ltd (UK)
1987
£1200
UK

Text Processing & Desk Top
Publishing
Wharton Information
Systems (UK)
1987
£850
Europe

UK Pre-Press Market (The)
Industrial Market Research
Ltd. (UK)
1987
Price on request UK

Women's Magazines
Key Note Publications (UK)
1987
£105
UK

Periodicals and Journals

International and
Pan-European
Export Graphics USA
Plan & Print
Printlink International
World Wide Printer

Europe

Austria
Graphische Revue
Osterreichs (Printing)

Denmark
Bogrtykk-erns Distriktsblade
(Printers)
Danske Presse (Newspaper
Publishers)
Media Scandinavia (Press
Directory)

Finland
Faktori (Printing)
Kirjapainotaito-Graefikko
(Printing)
Paikallishehdisto (Newspaper
Publishers)
Sanomalehtein Litto (Press
Guide)

France
Annuaire 4000 Imprimerieres
Francaise (Printers)
Caractere (Printing)
La France Graphique
(Printing)
L'Imprimerie Francaise
(Printing)

L'Imprimerie Nouvelle
(Printing)
Transaction (Paper &
Printing)

Germany, Federal
Republic of
Druckprint
Der Druckspiegel
Druckwelt
EPI-Export Polygraph
International
Infografik (Graphic Data
Processing)
Offset Praxix (Printing)
Der Polygraph (Printing)
Polygraph Addressbuch

Ireland, Republic of
Irish Printer

Italy
Annuciatore Poligrafico
(Printing)
L'Editore (Publishing)
Linea Grafica (Printing)
Il Poligrafico Italiano
(Printing)

Netherlands
Repro en Druk

Norway
Dagspressen (Daily Press)
Norsk Aviskatalog (Press
Guide)
Norsk Faktortidende
(Printing)

Spain
Graficas (Printing/Paper)
Press Graph (Printing)

Sweden
Grafia (Graphic & Printing
Industries)
Grafiskt Forum med Nordisk
Bogtryckarekonst (Graphic
Industries)

Switzerland
Druck-Industrie (Printing)
TM-Typographische
Monatsblatter (Printing)

UK
British Printer
Bookseller (The)
Commercial Printer
Information Service
Graphic Reproduction
Ink & Print

Inplant & Instant Printer
Newspaper Report
Offset Printing &
Reprographics
Print
Print Advertiser
Print Buyer
Print Link International
Print Media Service
Printing World
Printshop
Production Journal
Professional Printer
Publisher (The)
Reproduction
Reprographics & In-Plant
Advertiser
Reprographics Information
Service
SOGAT Journal

USA

Publishing
Editor & Publisher
Editor & Publisher
International Year Book
Editor & Publisher Market
Guide
Magazine Design &
Production
Magazine Industry Market
Place
Publishers Auxillary
Publishers Weekly
Technology Watch – for the
Graphic Arts & Information
Industries

Printing
American Printer
EP&P Electronic Printing &
Publishing
Export Grafics/Export
Graficas (Printing – English,
Spanish)
Fine Print
Flexo
Graphic Arts (Spanish –
Printing Trades)
Graphic Arts Monthly
Graphic Arts Monthly Buyers
Guide
Graphics Today
In-Plant Printer
In-Plant Reproductions
(Printing)
Ligature, the Typographic
Communication Journal
New England Printer &
Lithographer
Plan & Print
Print (Graphic Arts)

Printing & Graphic Arts
Executive
Printing Impressions
(Graphic Arts)
Printing Views
Swap or Buy
(Printing/typesetting
Machinery)
Typeworld
Typographical Journal
World-wide Printer

Canada
Canadian Printer & Publisher
Canadian Publishers
Directory
Quill & Quire (Books)

Asia

Hong Kong
Asian Press & Media
Directory

India
Paper Printpack India
Paperprintpack Times
Printing Times
Publishing Today

Japan
Nihon Dokusho Shimbun
(Books & Magazines)
Shinbun Keikei (Newspaper
Management)
Shinkan News (New
Publication News)
Shinkan Tenbo (New
Publication News)
Shuppan Geppo (Publication
Reports)
Shuppan Joho (Publication
Information)
Shuppan News (Publication
News)

Australia
Australian Books in Print
Australian Bookseller &
Publisher
Australian Printer
Australian Small Offset
Printer
Printers' News

Government Publications

UK Official Sources

General Statistics
Annual Abstract of Statistics
British Business
Digest of Welsh Statistics
Family Expenditure Survey
General Statistics
Monthly Digest of Statistics
Northern Ireland Annual
Abstract of Statistics
Scottish Abstract of Statistics
United Kingdom National
Accounts
Welsh Economic Trends

Miscellaneous Paper & Board Products
Business Monitor: PQ 4728 &
PQ 4725
Census of Production
Reports: PA 472

Packaging Products & Board
Annual Abstract of Statistics
Business Monitor: PQ 4725 &
PQ 4728
Census of Production
Reports: PA 472

Packaging Products, Paper and Pulp
Annual Abstract of Statistics
Business Monitor: PQ 4724
Census of Production
Reports: PA 472

Printing & Publishing
Annual Report of the Press
Council
Audit Bureau of Circulation
British Rate & Data (BRAD) –
contains circulation data for
newspapers and periodicals
Business Monitor: PQ 4751
(Newspapers)
PQ 4752 (Periodicals)
PQ 4753 (Books)
PQ 4754 (Miscellaneous)
Monthly Circulation Review:
gives newspaper circulation
by class, eg daily, Sunday etc
Census of Production
Reports: PA 475

Pulp, Paper & Board
Annual Abstract of Statistics
Annual Statistics:
Confederation Europeene de
l'Industrie des Pates, Papiers
et Cartons (CEPAC)
Business Monitor:PQ 4710
Census of Production
Reports: PA 471
Monthly Digest of Statistics
Pulp and Paper Industry
(The) (OECD)
Scottish Abstract of Statistics
Yearbook of Forest Products
(Food and Agriculture
Organisation)

Telecommunications

Trade Associations/ Organisations

International
International Institute of
Communications
Tavistock House South
Tavistock Square
London WC1H 9LF
USA

International Institute:
Information and
Communication
3940 Cote des Neiges
Suite D-3
Montreal
Quebec
Canada H3H 1W2

International
Telecommunication Union
(ITU)
Headquarters
Place des Nations
1211 Geneva 20
Switzerland

International
Telecommunications User
Group (INTUG)
18 Westminster Palace
Gardens
Artillery Row
London SW1P 1RR
UK

International
Telecommunications Satellite
Organisation (INTELSAT)
3400 International Drive NW
Washington DC 20008-3098
USA

Pacific Telecommunications
Council
1110 University Avenue Suite
308
Honolulu
Haiwaii 96826
USA

Society for Worldwide
Interbank
Financial Telecommunication
(SWIFT)
Avenue Ernest Solvay 81
1310 La Hulpe
Belgium

Europe
European Computer
Manufacturers Association
(ECMA)
114 rue du Rhone
1204 Geneva
Switzerland

European Conference of
Associations of
Telecommunication Cables,
Industries (EUROTELCAB)
Secretary
56 Palace Road
East Molesey
Surrey KT8 9DW
UK

European Conference of Posts
and Telecommunications
Administrations (The)
(CEPT)
Liaison office:
Seilerstrasse 22
Case Postale 1283
3001 Berne
Switzerland
Secretariat:
Direction Generale des Postes
et des Telegraphes
1530 Copenhagen
V Denmark
(Represents 26
administrations)

European Network for
Scientific and Technical
Information (Euronet Diane)
B Mahon
177 Route d'Esch
1471 Luxembourg

European
Telecommunications and
Professional Electronics
Industry (ECTEL) (Joint
Conference)
Secretary General
Mr W Weiss
c/o ZVEI
Stresemannallee 19
Postfach 70 09 69
6000 Frankfurt/Main 70
W Germany

Assistant secretary General
c/o TEMA
Leicester House
8 Leicester Street
London WC2H 7BN
UK

European
Telecommunications Satellite
Organisation (EUTELSAT)
Andrea Caruso
Tour Marie Montparnasse
33 Avenue du Maine
75755 Paris Cedex 15
France

Belgium
Conseil Professionel Mondial
des Postes et Telecoms
C Damen
Rue de Treves 33
1040 Brussels

Denmark
Nordiske Teleansattes
Samarbeidsorgan (NTS)
Grudntrigsvej 25
1864 Frederiksberg C

Finland
Nordic Cooperation on
Telecomms
Pekka Tarjanne
Post-Och Telestyrelsen
Postbox 1001 SF 00101
Helsinki 10

France
Association Francaise des
Utilisateurs du Telephone et
des
Telecommunications
(AFUTT)
BP 1,92430 Marnes-la
Coquette

Industries Francaises du
Telephone du Telegraphe et
de leurs
Applications Telematiques
(SI3T)
64 Rue de Monceau
75008 Paris

Syndicat National des
Installateurs en
Telecommunications (SNIT)
5 Rue Hamelin
75116 Paris

Germany, Federal Republic of
Bundesverband
Vertriebsunternehmen Buro
Organisations – und
Kommunikationstechnik
Dietrich-Bonhoeffer-Strasse 4
6380 Bad Homburg

Fachverband Informations –
und –
Kommunikationstechnik des
ZVEI
Stresemannallee 19
Postfach 70 09 69
6000 Frankfurt/Main
(Manufacturers of
Telecommunication
Equipment)

Norway
Nordisk Tele Union NTTF
Torggt 17 V11
Oslo 1

Skandinavisk Telegraf og
Telefon
Foderasjon
Norsk Telegraf – Of
Telefonfarbund
Torggt 17
Oslo

Switzerland
Centre for Telecomms
Development
DH K Westendorf
c/o ITU Place des Nations
1211 Geneva 20

Postal Telegraph and Telephone International (PTT 1)
Stefon Nedzynski
Avenue du Lignon 36
1219 Geneva

UK
Association of Viewdata Information Providers Ltd
27 Cockspur Street
London SW1Y 5BN

British Approvals Board for Telecommunications
Mark House
9-11 Queens Road
Hersham
Walton-on-Thames
Surrey KT12 5NA

British Computer Society (The)
13 Mansfield Street
London W1M 0BP

British Facsimile Industry Consultative Committee
9 London Road
Newbury
Berks RG13 1JL

Eurodata Foundation (The)
54 Fetter Lane
London EC4
Undertakes market research and publications activities for European Post and Telecommunications Administrations

Federation of Communication Services
PO Box 442
London SE19 3LZ
Serves the mobile communications industry

Independent Telecommunications Suppliers Association
1 West Ruislip Station
Ruislip
Middlesex HA4 7DW

Information Technology Users' Standards Association
Centre Point
103 New Oxford Street
London WC1A 1DU
Supported by the NCC, DTI, Central Computer and Telecommunications Agency and the British Standards Institution

Institute of Scientific Technical Communications
17 Bluebridge Avenue
Brookmans Park
Hatfield
Herts AL9 7RY

Institution of Electrical Engineers
Savoy Place
London WC2R 0BL

International Press Telecommunications Council
Studio House
Hen and Chickens Court
184 Fleet Street
London EC4A 2DA

Telecom Dealers Association
17 Jessica Road
London SW18 2QL

Telecommunication Engineering and Manufacturing Association (TEMA)
Leicester House
8 Leicester Street
London WC2H 7BN
TEMA is the primary trade association for the telecomms manufacturing industry in the UK

Telecommunications Managers Association (TMA)
40 Chatsworth Parade
Petts Wood
Orpington
Kent BR5 1RW
Branch of the Institute of Administrative Management. Role of the TMA is to represent the views of business users on telecommunications issues in the UK

Telecommunications Users' Association
34 Grand Avenue
London N10
TUA is comprised of a group of over 400 independent companies, formed to represent their interests in telecommunications

Telephone Cable Makers' Association
56 Palace Road
East Molesey
Surrey KT8 9DW

Videotex Industry Association
102-108 Clerkenwell Road
London EC1M 5SA

US
Alternative Carrier Telecomms Association (ACTA)
8465 Clover Leaf Drive
McLean
VA 22102
Publication: ACTA Monthly Report

Association of Independent Television Stations (Broadcasting) (INTV)
1200 18th St
NW Suite 502
Washington DC 20036
Tel: (010 1) 202-8871970

Association of Data Processing Service Organisations (ADAPSO)
1300 N 17th Street, Suite 300
Arlington
VA 22209
Tel: (010 1) 703-5225055

Association of Long Distance Telephone Companies (Communications) (ALTEL)
115 D Street, SE, Suite G-6
Washington DC 20003
Tel: (010 1) 202-5469022

Cellular Communications Industry Association (CCIA)
1150 17th Street, NW, Suite 607
Washington DC 20036
Tel: (010 1) 202-7850081

Electronic Industries
Association
2001 Eye Street NW
Washington DC 2006
Tel: (010 1) 202-4574900

Inter-American Telecomms
Conference (CITEL)
c/o OAS
1889 F St NW
Washington DC 20006
Publication: CITEL Bulletin,
Semi-annual

International Association of
Satellite Users and Suppliers
(Communications) (IASUS)
PO Box DD
McLean
VA 22101
Tel: (010 1) 703-7592094

International
Communications
Associations (ICA)
12750 Merit Dr, Suite 828
LB-89
Dallas
TX 75251
Tel: (010 1) 214-2333890

International PBX
Telecommunicators
(Communications) (IPC)
c/o Murlie Walthall
2412 Lamberts Avenue
Richmond
VA 23234
Tel: (010 1) 804-2319065

International
Tele/Conferencing
Association
(Communications) (IT/CA)
1299 Woodside Drive, #101
McLean
VA 22102
Tel: (010 1) 703-5566115

Land Mobile
Communications Council
(LMCC)
1150 17th Street, NW, Suite
1000
Washington DC 20036
Tel: (010 1) 202-4571138

Manufacturers' Radio
Frequency Advisory
Committee
(Broadcasting) (MRFAC)
6269 Leesburg Pike, Suite 304
Falls Church
VA 22044
Tel: (010 1) 703-5327459

National Association of
Broadcasters (Broadcasting)
(NAB)
1771 N St, NW,
Washington DC 20036
Tel: (010 1) 202-2933500

National Cable Television
Association (Broadcasting)
(NCTA)
1724 Massachusetts Avenue
NW
Washington DC 20036
Tel: (010 1) 202-7753550

National Satellite Cable
Association (NSCA)
World Centre Building, #702
918 16th Street, NW
Washington DC 20006
Tel: (010 1) 202-6592928

National Association of
Cellular Agents (Telecomms)
NACA
1716 Woodhead Street
Houston
TX 77019
Publication: Cellular Agent
(Newsletter)

National Association of
Satellite Equipment
Manufacturers
(Communications) (NASEM)
PO Box 470300
7955 East 50th Street
Tulsa
OK 74145
Tel: (010 1) 918-4960386

North American
Telecommunications
Association (NATA)
c/o Millie McOwen
2000 M St, NW, Suite 550
Washington DC 20036
Tel: (010 1) 202-2969800

Public Service Satellite
Consortium
(Communications) (PSSC)
1660 L Street, NW, Suite 910
Washington DC 20036
Tel: (010 1) 202-3311154

Society for Private and
Commercial Earth Stations
(Communications) (SPACE)
c/o Chuck Hewitt
709 Pendleton Street
Alexandria
VA 22314
Tel: (010 1) 703-5496990

Society of
Telecommunications
Consultants (STC)
One Rockefeller Plaza, Suite
1410
New York
NY 10020
Tel: (010 1) 212-5823909

Telecommunications Dealers
Association (TDAO)
PO Box 27297
Cincinnati
OH 45227
Tel: (010 1) 513-6312165

US Telecommunications
Suppliers Association
(USTSA)
333 N Michigan Avenue,
Suite 1618
Chicago
IL 60601
Tel: (010 1) 312-7828597

United States Telephone
Association
(Communications) (USTA)
1801 K Street, NW, Suite 1201
Washington DC 20006
Tel: (010 1) 202-8721200

Videotex Industry
Association (Data Processing)
(VIA)
1901 N Ft Myer Drive, Suite
200
Rosslyn
VA 22209
Tel: (010 1) 703-5220883

Canada

Canadian Business
Telecommunications Alliance
67 Yonge Street
Suite 1102
Toronto
Ontario M5E 1J8

Canadian Independent
Telephone Association
Box 8077/ PO 41
London
Ontario N6G 2BO

Electrical and Electronic
Manufacturers Association of
Canada (EEMAC)
One Yonge Street
Suite 1608
Toronto
Ontario M5E 1R1

Ontario Telephone
Association
103 Ontario Street
Box 2257
Bracebridge
Ontario POB 1CJ

Quebec Telephone
Association
3232 Belanger Street
East Montreal
Quebec H1Y 1B7

Telecomm Canada
410 Laurier Avenue West
PO Box CP 2410
Station D
Ottawa
Ontario K1P 6H5

Teleconferencing Association
of Canada
c/o MacDonald &
Dettemingborough
111 King Street
E Toronto
Ontario M5C 1G6

South America

Asociacion de Empresas
Estatales de
Telecomunicaciones de
Acuerdo
Subregional Andino
Calle San Ignacio
No 969 y Jonas Guerrero
Casilla 6042
Quito

Centre of Telecomms for the
Third World
Dr C Pablo Roberts
Apartado 7981
San Jose
Costa Rica

Asia

Japan

Communications Industry
Association of Japan
Sankei Building
Annex 7-2
1-Chome, Ohte-Machi
Chiyoda Ku
Tokyo 100

Japan Telecommunication
Industries Federation (JTIF)
Toranomon Kotohira Kaikan
Building
1-2-8 Toranomon
Minato-Ku
Tokyo 105

Thailand

Asia-Pacific Telecommunity
Office Compound of the
Communications Authority of
Thailand
New Road
Bangkok 10500
Established 1979 by an
intergovernmental agreement
under the auspices of
the UN Economic and Social
Commission for Asia and
Pacific.
Member nations: 20 countries
including most countries in
Asia and Australia

Directories

International

Data Reports on International
Telecommunications
Datapro SA
Lausanne
Switzerland

International Directory of
Telecommunications
Longman Group
Harlow
Essex
UK
Market trends, companies,
statistics

MacKintosh Yearbook of
International Electronics Data
B.E.P Data Services
Luton
Contains data on
telecommunications

Marconi International
Register
Telegraphic cable and radio
45 000 firms worldwide listed

Mercury International
Telecommunications
Directory
Mercury
London
UK

Telefax International
Telex – Verlag – Jaeger
Waldmann GmBH
Darmstadt
Lists subscribers worldwide

Yearbook of Common Carrier
Telecommunication Statistics
(annual)
International
Telecommunications Union
(ITU)
Geneva
Switzerland

Europe

Eurodata Foundation
Voicebook
Eurodata Foundation
London
UK
Focus on voice
communication services and
equipment

Eurodata Foundation
Yearbook
Eurodata Foundation
London
UK
Contains details on data and
text communication services
and equipment
provided by European PTTS.
Includes tarrifs

Eurofax – The West European
Fax Directory
Northcote House Publications
Ltd
Plymouth
UK
Office reference book

Mackintosh Yearbook of West
European Electronics Data
BEP Data Services
Luton
UK
Contains data on
telecommunications

British Telecom
BT Fax: The Official UK
directory
British Telecom
London
UK

Communications
Macmillan Press
Basingstoke
UK
Guide to telecommunication
organisations

Communications
Management Yearbook
EMAP Business and
Computer Publications Ltd
London
UK

Communications Users'
Yearbook, 1988
NCC
Manor House Press Ltd
London
UK

Datacomms Book, 1987
Guide to equipment, services
etc
VNU Publications
London
UK

Telecomms Products and
Services Directory
Telecommunications Press
London
UK

Telecommunications Users
Handbook, 1986/87
Telecommunications Press
London
UK

UK Facsimilie Directory
British Telecom
London
UK

Netherlands
Fibre Optics Sourcebook
Elsevier Applied Science
Publishers
Barking, Essex
UK

US
Fax Directory
USA, Canada, Mexico
Dial-a-fax directories
Burlington, VT

How to find information
about companies in
Telecommunications, Data
Processing and Office
Automation
Washington Researchers
Publishing
Washington DC

Interactive Cable TV
Handbook (The)
Phillips Publishing Inc
Bethesda, MD

PBX System Guide
The Marketing Programs and
Services Group
Gaithersburg, MD

Telecom Fact Book
Television Digest Inc
Washington DC

Telecommunications
Sourcebook
North American
Telecommunications
Association (NATA)
Washington DC

Telecommunications Systems
and Services Directory
Gale Research
Detroit, MI

Telephony's Directory and
Buyers Guide
Lists products, suppliers,
associations
Telephony Publishing Corp
Chicago, IL
(also available from
Telephony, Chelmsford,
Essex)

Market Research Reports

This section lists recently
published market research
reports which cover various
aspects of the
telecommunications industry.
Details provided below are
title of report, publisher, year
of publication, price and
geographic coverage.

AT&T: A Strategic Analysis:
1987 edition
Northern Business
Information (USA)
1987
$1975
USA

Alcatel: A Strategic Analysis
Northern Business
Information (USA)
1987
$1975
USA

Analysis of Business
Telecommunications Buying
Policies of the Top
250 Companies in Europe
Systems Dynamics Ltd (UK)
1988 (Dec)
£19,600
Europe

Analysis of the Latest Product
Market & Marketing Trends
in the
Dynamic Facsimile Industry
MSRA Inc (USA)
1987
$995
Worldwide

Business Ratio Report:
Telecommunications Industry
ICC Business Ratios (UK)
Annual
£165
UK

Cellular Telecommunications
Markets
Market Intelligence Research
Company (USA)
1988
Price on request
USA

Central Office Equipment
Market: 1988 edition
Northern Business
Information (USA)
1988
$1975
USA

Centrex Market
Opportunities : 1988 edition
Northern Business
Information (USA)
1988
$2500
USA

Centrex vs PBX vs Key: The
Under-100 Line Markets
Probe Research Inc (USA)
1988
$2750
USA

Choosing a PABX or Key
Telephone System
Systems Dynamics Ltd (UK)
Regular updates
£90
UK

Customer Premises Telecom
Equipment & The Regional
Bell Companies
International Resource
Development Inc (USA)
1987
$985
USA

DOJ Proposals and the Huber
Report
Probe Research Inc (USA)
1987
$895
USA

Data, Text & Voice
Encryption Worldwide
Markets
International Resource
Development Inc (USA)
1987
$1850
Worldwide

Database of Products
Conforming to the MAP
Specification
System Dynamics Ltd (UK)
Regular updates
£150
Worldwide

Digital Cross Connect
Systems: Strategies and
Markets to 1992
Probe Research Inc (USA)
1987
$2795
USA

Distribution Channels for
Telecom Products
Market Intelligence Research
Company (USA)
1987
Price on request
USA

Dossier: World Telecom
Markets
Northern Business
Information (USA)
Annually
$22,500
Worldwide

EEC Telecoms Market
Outlook
Telecommunications Industry
Research (TIR) (UK)
1988
£225 (Europe) $440 (ROW)
Europe
(Individual country studies
also available)

European Market for Private
Switching Systems (The) –
PABXs and KTSs
System Dynamics Ltd (UK)
1988
£14,000
Europe

Factory Communications
Through 1991: Industrial
Local Area Networks, MAP,
CIM, and Beyond
Venture Development
Corporation (USA)
1987
$4950 (Part I), $4950 (Part II),
$8750 (I & II)
USA

Fiber Optics and Video:
Telcos vs. Cable Operators in
the Battle to Fiber
the Home
Probe Research Inc (USA)
1988
$3395
USA

IBM/ROLM
Telecommunications
Strategies and Directions: The
Next Five Years
Probe Research Inc (USA)
1987
$3750
USA

ISDN and Its Impact on
Consumer Premise
Equipment
Business Communications Co
(USA)
1987
$1950
USA

ISDN: Customer Premises
Equipment
Ovum Ltd (UK)
1987
£465
US & Europe

ISDN: European Initiatives in
the Context of World
Developments
Systems Dynamics Ltd (UK)
1986
£180
Europe

ISDN Strategies
Market Intelligence Research
Company (USA)
1988
Price on request
USA

Incoming Call Processing
Equipment & Software
International Resource
Development Inc (USA)
1987
$1850
USA

L'industrie Mondiale des
Telecommunications
Eurostaf Dafsa (France)
1987
FF8.900
Worldwide

International Fiber Optics
The Freedonia Group Inc
(USA)
1988
$1700
Worldwide

International
Telecommunications: Market,
Production and Trade
Globe Book Services (UK)
1986
£225
Worldwide

Key Telephone Systems
Market: 1988
Northern Business
Information (USA)
1988
$1975
USA

LAN Media: How Much,
What Kind, Where?
Business Communications Co
(USA)
1988
$2250
USA

Market for Satellite Earth
Stations (The)
BEP Data Services (UK)
1987
Price on request
Australia, South Pacific

Modernising China's
Telecommunications:
Implications for International
Firms
The Economist Publications
(UK)
1987
£330 (UK & Europe), $500 (N
America), £333 (ROW)
China

NYNEX: The Future of an
RBOC
Probe Research Inc (USA)
1988
$6595
USA

Network Management
Hardware & Software
Markets
International Resource
Development Inc (USA)
1988
$2300
UK

Network Management
Systems: Pressures, Products,
Predictions
Business Communications Co
(USA)
1988
$1950
USA

ONA & Gateways:
Implementation Strategies,
Emerging Markets
Probe Research Inc (USA)
1988
$2750
USA

ONA and CEI: The Strategic
and Market Implications
Probe Research Inc (USA)
1987
$2750
USA

Outlook for TI Services and
Equipment (The)
Business Communications Co
(USA)
1988
$2250
USA

PBX and Related Markets:
1988 edition
Northern Business
Information (USA)
1988
$1975
USA

Packet Switching Services &
Equipment
International Resource
Development Inc (USA)
1987
$1850
Worldwide

Pay Phones and
Pay-As-You-Go Calling
Business Communications Co
(USA)
1987
$1750
USA

Personal Telecommunications
Euromonitor Publications Ltd
(UK)
1988
£325
UK

Pocket Pagers
The Freedonia Group Inc
(USA)
1988
$800
USA

Private Payphone Markets
Market Intelligence Research
Company (USA)
1987
Price on request
USA

Private Telecommunications
Networks – Equipment &
Service Markets
International Resource
Development Inc (USA)
1987
$1,850
USA

Satellite Communications
Services & Equipment
Markets, US
International Resource
Development Inc (USA)
1987
$2300
USA

Satellite Transmission
Business Communications Co
(USA)
1987
$1750
Worldwide

Telecommunications (Market
and Industry Profile)
ICC Business Ratios (UK)
Annual
£165
UK

Telecommunications – Special
Report
Mintel Publications Ltd (UK)
1987
£1100
UK

Telecommunications
Equipment
Databank Spa (Italy)
1988
£1400
Italy

Telecommunications
Equipment
The Freedonia Group Inc
(USA)
1988
$1700
USA

Telecommunications
Equipment (Manufacturers
and Distributors)
Key Note Publications (UK)
1987
£105
UK

Telecommunications
Equipment Industry 1986
Yano Research Institute Ltd
(Japan)
1986
Japan

Telecommunications in
Europe
Key Note Publications (UK)
1988
£285
Europe

Telecommunications in
Retailing, 1986-91
RMDP Ltd (UK)
1986
£195
UK

Telecommunications:
International
Telecommunications
Markets, Production
& Trade
Survey Force Ltd
1988
£300
Worldwide

Telecommunications: the
Opportunities of Competition
Ovum Ltd (UK)
1987
£675
US, UK, Japan

Telematica 1988 – Business
Telephone Markets
Logica Consultancy Ltd (UK)
1988
£8000
Europe

Telematica 1988 – Data
Connection Markets
Logica Consultancy Ltd (UK)
1988 (Dec)
£8000
Europe

Telematica 1988 – Electronic
Mail Markets
Logica Consultancy Ltd (UK)
1988 (Nov)
£8000
Europe

Telematica 1988 – Local Area
Network Markets
Logica Consultancy Ltd (UK)
1988 (Oct)
£10,000
Europe

Telematica 1988 – PBX
Markets
Logica Consultancy Ltd (UK)
1988 (Sept)
£8000
Europe

Telematica 1988 – Wide Area
Network Markets
Logica Consultancy Ltd (UK)
1988
£8000
Europe

Telephone Bypass:
Developments, Opportunities
Business Communications Co
(USA)
1987
$1750
USA

Telephony-NBI Survey of
Corporate America, Vol 1
Northern Business
Information (USA)
1987
$1975
USA

Telephony-NBI Survey of
Corporate America, Vol 2
Northern Business
Information (USA)
1987
$7500
USA

Tracking of International
Developments in Electronic
Messaging and VANS (The)
Systems Dynamics Ltd (UK)
Annually
£19,600/annum
Worldwide

Transmission Equipment
Market: 1988 Edition
Northern Business
Information (USA)
1988
$1975
USA

UK Telecommunications
Market Opportunities
International Resource
Development (USA)
1987
$1650
UK

US Cellular Mobile Telephone
Industry (The)
Venture Development
Corporation (USA)
1988
$4950
USA

US Facsimile Industry (The):
The Prospects for an End User
Based Renaissance
Venture Development
Corporation (USA)
1987
$4950
USA

US Telecom Market:
Entrepreneurial
Opportunities
Market Intelligence Research
Company (USA)
1987
Price on request
USA

US Voice Mail/Voice
Response Industry (The), 2nd
edition
Venture Development
Corporation (USA)
1988
$2950
USA

World PBX, Centrex and Key
System Markets: 1988 Report
Northern Business
Information (USA)
1988
$1975
Worldwide

World Public Switching
Market: 1988 edition
Northern Business
Information (USA)
1988
$1975
Worldwide

Worldwide Office
Automation: Markets, Trade
& Production
Survey Force Ltd (UK)
1988
£300
Worldwide

X400 Markets: The Users
Decide
Ovum Ltd (UK)
1988
£465
US & Europe

Periodicals and Journals

Note: Many of the
telecommunications
periodicals and journals listed
under country headings have
international as well as
national coverage

International
Communication Systems
Worldwide
Communications Engineering
International
Communications
International
Data Communications
Datamation
Inter Media
International Business
Equipment
INTUG News (International
Telecommunications User
Group)
Journal des
Telecommunications
Mackintosh European
Electronics Company Bulletin
Telecommunications Dollar
Telecommunication Journal
Telecommunications Policy

Europe

France
La Lettre 2000
Messages
Mesures
Le Monde Informatique
Radio-REF
Telecom France (French PTT)

Germany, Federal Republic of
Archiv fur das Post-und
Fernmeldewesen
EEE-Elektronik-Technologie/
Elektronik-Andwendungen/
Eltronik-Marketing
ETZ-Elektronische Zeitschrift
IFO Institut Fur
Wirtschaftsforschung
(Publishes telecomms reports)
Nachrichtentechnik
Elektronik
NTZ Nachrichtenische
Zeitschrift
RV Deckers Verlag G Shenk
GMBH
(Publishes a monthly
telecomms report)
Siemens Telecom Report
ZPF-Zeitschrift fur das
Post-und Fernmeldewesen

Italy
Millecanali
Rassegna Postelgrafonica
Sistemi Di
Telecommunicazioni

Portugal
Electricidade
Revista Nacional de
Telematica

Spain
CQ Radio Amateur
Eurofach Electronica
Revista T

Switzerland
PTT-Zeitschrift-Revue des
PTT-Rivista PTT

UK
Business Computing and
Communications
Cellular Today
Comms Monthly
Communicate
Communications
Communications Engineering
International

Communications
International
Communications
Management
Communications Systems
Worldwide
Computer Communications
Data Communication
Datamation
EFT International
Fintech New Media Markets
Fintech Telecom Markets
Information Processing and
Management
International
Communications Report
Network
Oftel News
Prestel Directory and
Magazine (Videotex)
Telecom Today
Telecomms Monthly
Telecomms Regulation
Review
Telecommunications News
Telecommunications Policy
Telematics and Infomatics

USA
Bell Telephone Magazine
Business Communications
Review
Cellular Radio News
Communications
International
Communications News
Communications Week
Computers in the Telephone
Industry
Connections
CPE Strategies
Data Communications
Electronic Business
Electronic Engineering Times
Electronic News
Electronics
FCC Week
Fiber/Laser News
Fiber Optics &
Communications
High Technology
Insights: The Information
Age
Interactive Cable TV
Handbook (The)
Interconnection
International Networks
Journal of
Telecommunications
LAN (Local Area Networks)
Long Distance Letter
MIS Week

Mobile Phone News
NATA Reports (North
American
Telecommunications
Association)
Personal Communications
Perspective on AT & T
Products & Marketing
Radio Communications
Report
Report on AT & T (The)
Report on Telco Marketing
(The)
Satellite Week
Signal (Armed Forces
Communications &
Electronics Association)
Sound & Communications
Specialized Mobile Radio
News
Telecom Strategy Letter (The)
Telecom Times & Trends
Telecom Trade Reporter
Telecommunications
Telecommunications Product
Review
Telecommunications
Products & Technology
Telecommunications Week
Teleconnect
Telephone Bypass News
Telephone Engineer &
Management (TEAM)
Telephone News
Telephony
(see also the Annual
Telephony Directory and
Buyers' Guide)
Telocator
This Month in
Telecommunications
Trends in Communications
Regulation
View Text
Voice Processing

Asia

India
Indian Journal of Radio and
Space Physics

Government Publications

UK Government Statistics

Postal Services
Annual Abstract of Statistics
(HMSO)
Post Office Report and
Accounts

Prices
European Marketing Data
and Statistics
Euromonitor (Annual)

Telecomms Equipment
Business Monitor: BM PQ
3441
British Telecommunications
and Mitel 1986 (Cmnd 9715)
(Data on sales of PABX
equipment)
(both available from HMSO)

Telecomms Industry
Business Monitor: PQ 3441
(available from HMSO)

Telegrams
Annual Abstracts of Statistics
(Covers numbers of UK and
foreign telex connections)
British Telecom (BT Centre,
81 Newgate St, London EC1A
7AJ)

Telephones
British Telecom
Supplementary Report
(supplement to annual report)
European Marketing Data
and Statistics Family
Expenditure Survey
Report (HMSO)
General Household Survey
(HMSO)
Regional Trends (HMing Data
and Statistics Family
Expenditure Survey
Report (HMSO)
General Household Survey
(HMSO)
Regional Trends (HMSO)
Siemens International
Telephone Statistics
Social Trends (HMSO)
United Nations International
Trade Statistics

United Nations Statistical
Yearbook
United Nations Yearbook of
Industrial Statistics

Wires and Cables
Business Monitor: PQ 3410

Textiles

Trade Associations

International
International Textile
Manufacturers Federation
Am Schanzengraben 29
Postfach CH – 8039 Zurich
Switzerland
Tel: (010 41)
1-2017080/2017747
Telex: 56798
Fax: (010 41) 1-2017134

Europe

Austria
Verein der Baumwollspinner
und Weber Oesterreichs
Rudolfsplatz 12
1013 Vienna
Tel: (010 43) 1-639751
Telex: 114125 OETEX

Belgium
Federation Belge de
l'Industrie du Coton et des
Fibres Chimiques (FEBEC)
Building Lieven Bauwens
Martelaarsaan 39
9000 Ghent
Tel: (010 32) 91-253597/253211
Telex: 22380 EUROTEX (via
Comitextil)

Denmark
Textilindustrien
(Federation of Danish Textile
Industries)
Bredgade 41
7400 Herning
Tel: (010 45) 7-121366
Telex: 621991 JYTEX
Fax: (010 45) 7-122350 texin

Finland
Puuvillatehtaitten Yhdistys
Bomullsfabrikernas Forening
(Finnish Cotton Textile
Industry Association)
Etelaranta 10
00130 Helsinki 13
Tel: (010 358) 0-31541/661561
Telex: 125854 TEXOR SF

France
Syndicat General de
l'Industrie Cotonniere
Francaise
3 Av Ruysdael
BP 724-08
75367 Paris Cedex 08
Tel: (010 33) 1-42679723
Telex: 640324 SYNCO

**Germany, Federal
Republic of**
Bremer Baumwollborse
Wachtstrasse 17-24
PO Box 10 67 27
2800 Bremen 1
Tel: (010 49) 421-321901
Telex: 244632 BAUMW

Industrieverband Garne eV
(Natur – und
Chemiefasergarne)
Schaumainkai 87
6000 Frankfurt/Main 70
Tel: (010 49) 69-6313055-57
Telex: 411463 GARNE

Industrieverband Gewebe aus
Baumwolle und anderen
Farsen eV
Schaumainkai 87
6000 Frankfurt/Main 70
Tel: (010 49) 69-6313026-27
Telex: 411691 IVGEW

Greece
Union des Industriels
Cotoniers de Grece
5 rue Xenofontos
Athens
Tel: (010 30)
1-3234775/3224429

Italy
Associazione Cotoniera
Italiana
11 Via Borgonuovo
20121 Milan
Tel: ((010 39) 2-8692142
Telex: 312479 ACOTEX

Netherlands
Textielverening KRL
PO Box 518
3900 AM Veenendaal
Tel: (010 31) 8385-24352
Telex: 37216 TECO

Norway
Tekstilfabrikkenes Forening
Postboks 488 Sentrum
0105 Oslo 1
Tel: ((010 47) 2-426930
Telex: 17562 TEFO

Portugal
Associacao Nacional das
Industrias Texteis
Algodoeiras e Fibras
Rua Goncalo Cristovao 96-1-2
Porto
Tel: (010 351) 31-7961-64
Telex: 22812 ANITAF

Spain
Asociacion Industrial Textil
de Proceso Algodonero
(AITPA)
Granvia 670
08010 Barcelona
Tel: (010 34) 3-3189200
Telex: 54408 SECEA

Sweden
Textilradet
Blasieholmsgatan 5
Box 16133
10323 Stockholm
Tel: (010 46) 8-236890
Telex: 11550 SVERTEX

Switzerland
Industrieverband Textil (IVT)
Beethovenstrasse 20
Postfach 4838
8022 Zurich
Tel: (010 41) 2015755
Telex: 816610 IVT

Vereinigung Schweizerischer
Rohlbaumwoll-Vertreter
Klosbachstrasse 48
Postfach
8032 Zurich
Tel: (010 41) 1-2517077
Telex: 815162 DAEN

Turkey
Turkiye Tekstil Sanayii
Isverenleri Sendikasi
Besiktas Akaretler
Visnezade Cami Maydani
Efe Apt D10
Istanbul
Tel: (010 90)
1-601405-09/1600056
Telex: 26422 TIS

UK
British Textile Employers'
Association (The)
Reedham House
31 King Street West
Manchester M3 2PF
Tel: 061-834 7871-73
Telex: 666737 BTEA

Liverpool Cotton Association
(The)
620 Cotton Exchange Bldg
Edmund Street
Liverpool L3 9LH
Tel: 051-2366041
Telex: 627849 COTTEX

USA
AMCOT
PO Box 259
Bakersfield
California 93302
Tel: (010 1) 805-3275961
Telex: 682412

American Cotton Shippers
Association (ASCA)
Mezzanine – Suite 1
Cotton Exchange Bldg
PO Box 3366
Memphis
Tennessee 38173
Tel: (010 1) 901-5252272
Telex: 53972

American Textile
Manufacturers Institute. Inc
(ATMI)
1101 Connecticut Ave NW
Suite 300
Washington DC 20036
Tel: (010 1) 202-8620500
Telex: 7108229489 (TWX)
ATMI

Africa
Federation de l'Industrie
Textile Africaine et Malgache
(FITAM)
2 Avenue Hoche
75008 Paris
France
Tel: (010 33) 1-42275196
Telex: 650860 FIDAFRI

Tunisia
Federation Nationale de
Textile (FENATEX)
5 rue Charles de Gaulle
Tunis
Tel: (010 216) 1-245191/255303
Telex: 13982 UTICA

Asia

India
Indian Cotton Mills'
Federation (The)
Textile Center PB 1449
34 P D'Mello Road
Poona Street
Bombay 400 009
Tel: (010 91) 22-862043-47
Telex: 1175426 ICMF

Japan
The Japan Cotton Traders'
Association
8-2 Utsubo-Honmachi
1-chome, Nishi-ku
Osaka 550
Tel: (010 81) 6-4416931
Telex: 05242177 JCTA

Japan Spinners' Association
Mengyo Kaikan Building
8 Bingo-machi, 3-chome
Higashi-ku
Osaka 541
Tel: (010 81) 6-2318431
Telex: 5222230 SPINAS

Korea
Spinners and Weavers
Association of Korea
43-8 Kwanchul-dong
Chongro-ku
KPO Box 398
Seoul 110
Tel: (010 82) 2-2355741/8
Telex: 25986 SWAKOR

Malaysia
Malaysian Textile
Manufacturers' Association
3rd Floor, TO18-TO20
Sungei Wang Plaza
Jalan Bukit Bintang
SWP Box 594
Kuala Lumpur 55100
Tel: (010 60)
3-2486454/2486587
Telex: 30528 MTMA

Pakistan
All Pakistan Textile Mills
Association
Principal Office
Muhammadi House
II Chundrigar Road
PO Box No 5446
Karachi 2
Tel: (010 92) 21-234989/225541
Telex: 25037 APTMA

Singapore
Singapore Textile and
Garment Manufacturers'
Association
30-B Seah Street
Singapore 0718
Tel: (010 65) 3372022
Telex: 39585 STGMA

Taiwan
Taiwan Textile Federation
22 Ai Kuo East Road
Taipei
Tel: (010 886) 2-3417251
Telex: 23143 TTFROC

Australia
Textile Clothing and
Footwear Council of Australia
Limited (The)
7th Floor
99 Queen Street
Melbourne
Victoria 3000
Tel: (010 61) 3-679671
Telex: 151795 TECLOF

Middle East

Egypt
Chamber of Spinning and
Weaving Industry
43 Cherif Street
PO Box 251
Cairo
Tel: (010 20)
2-746932/748238/748319
Telex: 92624 PERTX UN

Israel
Manufacturers' Association of
Israel (Textile Department)
29 Hamered Street
PO Box 50022
61 500 Tel Aviv
Tel: (010 972) 3-650121
Telex: 342651 MAIS IL

South America

Argentina
Federacion de Industrias
Textiles Argentinas (FITA)
Av Leandro N Alem 1067
Piso 8
Buenos Aries
Tel: (010 54)
1-310499/310599/316899
Telex: 21749 UNIAR

Directories

International
Deskbook of World Fibers
Lennox-Kerr
New York
USA

International Directory: The
Nonwoven Fabrics Industry
INDA
New York
USA

International Silk Association
L'Association Internationale
de la Soie
Lyon
France

Europe

Germany, Federal
Republic of
Die Textil-Industrie und Ihre
Heffer
Industrieschau-
Verlagsgesellschaft
Darmstadt

Italy
Annuario dell 'Industria
Italiana della Magliera e Della
Calzetteria (Yearbook of the
Italian Knitting Industry)

Macchine Italiana ed
Accessorie per L'Industria
Tessile
(Italian Machines and
Accessories for the Textile
Industry)

Assoc Costruttori Italiana di
Macchinario per L'Industria
Tessile, Milan

Portugal
Guia-Mor Textil/Calcado
Guiao
Lisbon

Sweden
Svensk Textil &
Bekladnaaskalender
Fournir
Stockholm

Switzerland
Handbuch der
Schweizerischen Textil,
Bekleidungs und
Lederwirtschaft
Verlag fur Wirtschaftsliteratur
Zurich

Switzerland Textile
Machinery
Swiss Association of
Machinery Manufacturers,
Textile Machinery Group
Zurich

UK
British Textile Machinery
Association – Members and
their Products Directory
British Textile Machinery
Association

Buyers Guide to UK
Furnishing Fabric
Manufacturers/Cotton and
Allied Textiles
National Economic
Development Office

Directory of British Clothing
and Textile Importers
Trade Research Publications
Berkhamstead

Hards Clothing Industry
Yearbook
United Trade Press
London

Index to Textile Auxiliaries
Industrial Press
Manchester

Liverpool Cotton Association:
Directory
Liverpool Cotton Association
Liverpool

Textile Month Deskbook of
UK Agents
Textile Business Press
London

USA
Davison's Knit Goods Trade
Davison Publishing Company
Ridgewood, New Jersey

Davison's Salesman's Book: A
Directory of Mills and Dyers
in the United States and
Canada
Davison Publishing Company
Ridgewood, New Jersey

Davison's Textile Blue Book
Davison Publishing Company
Ridgewood, New Jersey

Asia

India
Worral's Textile and
Engineering Directory
Commerce Publications
Bombay

Australia
Textile and Apparel Index of
Australia (The)
Textile Index of Australia
North Manly, NSW

Market Research Reports

This section lists recently
published market research
reports which cover various
aspects of the textile industry.
Details provided are title of
report, publisher, year of
publication, price and
geographic coverage.

Business Ratio Report: Cotton
and Man-Made Fibre
Processors
ICC Business Ratios (UK)
Annual
£165
UK

Business Ratio Report: Dyers
& Finishers
ICC Business Ratios (UK)
Annual
£165
UK

Business Ratio Report: Textile
Machinery Industry
ICC Business Ratios (UK)
Annual
£165
UK

Business Ratio Report: Wool
ICC Business Ratios (UK)
Annual
£165
UK

Carpets
Key Note Publications Ltd
(UK)
1987
£105
UK

Carpets and Rugs
The Freedonia Group Inc
(USA)
1988
$1700
USA

Cotton Spinning and
Doubling
Databank Spa (Italy)
1988
£1400
Italy

Cotton and Man-Made Fibre
Manufactucurers and
Distributors
ICC Financial Surveys (UK)
1988
£165
UK

Demand for, and Supply of,
Textiles in Western Europe
Prognos AG (Switzerland)
1986
SFrs 25.000
Europe

Man-Made Fibre Industry in
W Europe (The): A New
Structure, A New Strength
The Economist Intelligence
Unit (UK
1987
£150 (UK & Europe), $270 (N
America), £153 (ROW)
Europe

Fibres
Key Note Publications Ltd
(UK)
1987
£105
UK

Home Furnishings
Key Note Publications Ltd
(UK)
1988
£105
UK

Household Textiles: UK
Marketing Strategies for
Industry (UK)
1987
£55
UK

Lifting the Barriers to Trade
National Economic
Development Office (UK)
1986
£9.50
Worldwide

Narrow Fabric Manufacturers
and Distributors
ICC Financial Surveys (UK)
1988
£165
UK

Nonwoven Fabrics
Specialists in Business
Information Inc (USA)
1987
$325
USA

Sewing and Knitting Products

Databank Spa (Italy)
1988
£700
Italy

Silk Weaving
Databank Spa (Italy)
1988
£700
Italy

Textile Fibers
The Freedonia Group Inc
(USA)
1988
$800
USA

Wool Combing, Synthetic
Fibre Processing
Databank Spa (Italy)
1988
£700
Italy

Woollen Textiles For Clothing
Databank Spa (Italy)
1988
£1400
Italy

Woollen Yarns For Industry
Databank Spa (Italy)
1988
£1400
Italy

Periodicals and Journals

International &
Pan-European
Carpet Manufacturer
International
Fiber Producer
International Dyer
International Textile Bulletin
International Textiles
Leather
Leather Guide
Nonwovens Yearbook
Schuh Technik
Tekstil & Teknik
Textile Horizons
Textile Praxis International
Textile World
WST English Knitting
WST International

Europe

Austria
Osterreichische
Textil-Mitteilungen (Textiles)
Osterreichische
Textil-Zeitung

Belgium
Confectie
De Tex-Textilis
Texbel
Texpress
Textile Magazine

Denmark
Teknisk Tidskrifft for Textil og
Beklaedning
Textil

Finland
Nykytekstiili (Textiles &
Clothing)
Tekstiiliehti (Textile Industry)
Teski (Textile Dealers)

France
L'industrie Textile
(Equipment)
Journal du Textile
L'Officiel des Textiles

Germany, Federal
Republic of
Bekleidung und Wasche
Chemiefasern Textil Industrie
Haustex (Textiles)
Heimtex (Carpets)
Melliand (Textile Machinery)
Peiz International (Furs)
Textilberetrieb (Textile
Industry)
Textil-Mitteilungen
Textil Praxis International
Textil Wirtschaft Accessories
Textilwirtschaft
WST International (Knitting
Machinery)
WST Wirkerei & Strickerei
Technik

Ireland, Republic of
Futura (Textiles & Leather)

Italy
Arredo Tessile Complementi
(Household Textiles)
Confezione
GAP-Italia
Laniera
Selezione Tessile
La Sposa
Tex Home
Textilia

Netherlands
International Textiles
Texpress

Spain
Confeccion Industrial
Ingenieria Textil
NINS
Pinker-Moda
Revisita Linca Espanola
Tecnica del Punto
Tecnica Textil International

Sweden
Habit (Textiles & Clothing)
Textil Branchen (Textile Trades)

Switzerland
Internationales Textil Bulletin
Mittex
Textil Revue
Textil Veredlung
Textiles Suisses
Textiles Suisses Interieurs

UK
BTMA Directory
British Clothing Manufacturer Bulletin (The)
Clothing Machinery Times
Cotton Outlook
Courtaulds News
Drapers' Record
Fabrics International
Fur Review
Home Textiles Review
International Dyer, Textile Printer, Bleacher & Finisher
Journal of the Society of Dyers & Colourists
Knitting & Haberdashery Review
Knitting International
Manufacturing Clothier
Sewing Machine Times
Shuttle
Textile Forecast
Textile Horizons
Textile Month
Trader (The)
Wool Record

Canada
Canadian Apparel Manufacturer
Canadian Textile Directory
Canadian Textile Journal

USA
American Dyestuff Reporter
American Fabrics & Fashions
America's Textiles
Apparel World
Bobbin/Bobina
Carpet & Rug Industry

Fiber World
Geotechnical Fabrics Report
Home Fashions Textiles
Homesewing Trade News
Impressions: the magazine for the imprinted sportswear industry
Industrial Fabric Products Review
Knitting Times
Modern Knitting Management
Modern Textiles
Needle's Eye
Textile Chemist & Colorist
Textile Panamericanos
Textile Products & Processes
Textile World

Asia

China, People's Republic of
China Textile
Textile World

Hong Kong
Textile Asia

India
Clothing Journal
Garments India
Indian Silk
Indian Textile Journal (The)
Textile Industry of India
Textile Industry Trade Journal
Textile News
Textile Trends

Japan
Colour Design
Nihon Seni Shimbun
Seni
Seni Kako
Seni Kagaku
Seni Tokei Geppo
Senikai
Senken Shimbun (Fashion Trade)

Australia
Australian Leather Journal, Boot & Shoe Recorder
Clothing & Allied Trades Union Journal
Domestic Textiles & Wallcoverings Trade
Ragtrader
Textile & Apparel Manufacturer
Textile Journal of Australia

Government Publications

UK Official Sources

Textiles: General Statistics
Annual Abstract of Statistics
British Business
Digest of Welsh Statistics
Monthly Digest of Statistics
Northern Ireland Annual Abstracts of Statistics
Quarterly Statistical Review
Scottish Abstracts of Statistics
United Kingdom National Accounts
Welsh Economic Trends

Carpets
British Business
Business Monitor: PQ 4384
Business Monitor: PQ 4385
Carpet Annual (covers production, exports, and imports of carpets for major trading countries)
Monthly Digest of Statistics

Clothing and Footwear
Annual Abstract of Statistics
British Business
Business Monitor: PQ 4531
PQ 4532
PQ 4533
PQ 4534
PQ 4535
PQ 4536
PQ 4537
PQ 4538
PQ 4539
PQ 4510

Census of Production Reports: PA 453
PA 451
Monthly Digest of Statistics
United Kingdom National Accounts

Leather
Business Monitor: PQ 4410
Business Monitor: PQ 4420
Census of Production Reports: PA 441
Census of Production Reports: PA 442

Made-up Textiles
Business Monitor: PQ 4557
Business Monitor: PQ 4385

Production of Man-made Fibres
Annual Abstract of Statistics
British Business
Business Monitor: PQ2600
Census of Production
Reports: PA 260
Monthly Digest of Statistics
Textile Month (published by
Textile Business Press Ltd)
Wool Record (includes trade
data and international wool
prices)

Spinning and Doubling of Cotton
Annual Abstract of Statistics
British Business
Business Monitor: PQ 4321
Business Monitor: PQ 4336
Census of Production
Reports: PA432
Monthly Digest of Statistics
Weekly Raw Cotton Circular
(provides daily world future
market quotations, world
spot market quotations and
other market data)

Textile Finishing
Business Monitor: PQ 4370
Census of Production
Reports: PA437

Weaving of Cotton, Silk, Man-made Fibres
Annual Abstract of Statistics
Business Monitor: PQ 4322
Census of Production
Reports: PA432
Monthly Digest of Statistics
Trade Review of the Cotton
and Allied Industries

Woollen and Worsted
British Business
Business Monitor: PQ 4310
Monthly Bulletin of Statistics
Monthly Digest of Statistics
National Wool Textile Export
Corporation Statistical
Bulletin (includes data on
EEC trade)

5 On-line Databases — Background

Introduction

On-line databases in this chapter refers to information in computerised form. This information may be in the form of indexed references to source material, statistics and prices, or the full text of documents such as market reports or journal articles. On-line retrieval of information is the process of accessing a remote computer through a telephone line from a terminal in your home or office.

Hosts are organisations which mount databases on a computer and offer them to the public on behalf of the database producer. Producers usually receive a royalty or licence fee, although users are normally charged a combined host and royalty fee per connect hour together with print charges.

Hosts have been selected for inclusion on the basis of the wide range of services offered, or where they have been identified as offering particulary relevant or unique information services. The same database may be offered by a number of different hosts, and you will find between two to ten hosts listed for a number of databases in this chapter.

In order to standardise terms which refer to online and offline print charges, online type and offline print is used. These are terms used by DIALOG which is the largest host represented. Print charges have been quoted at the maximum rate, ie for a standard or full reference, and it is important to note that cheaper rates may be available for a short reference.

Methods of charging users for accessing online information services varies between hosts, some offer subscription services, although most of the hosts in this directory offer pay as you go services. Prices quoted in this chapter can be used to help you choose the cheapest service by comparing the connect hour charges. However other factors which you should take into consideration are exchange rates, discounts and print charges.

Structure
This directory lists all of the main database files and services available online under thirteen different subject areas. Under each main subject heading databases are listed alphabetically. A description of each file is provided, together with the price per connect hour and print charges. All databases listed are in English unless otherwise specified.

The subject areas covered are as follows:

Section I	Company Finance and Profile
Section II	General Management/Who's Who
Section III	Marketing
Section IV	Economics
Section V	News and Current Affairs
Section VI	Overseas Trade Opportunities
Section VII	Specialist Industry Databases
Section VIII	Science and Technology
Section IX	Industry Wide Databases
Section X	Securities
Section XI	Accountancy and Tax
Section XII	Bibliographic
Section XIII	EEC

Choosing a Database Host
The first step you need to take is to identify which hosts provide the most useful databases, and at the most reasonable cost. Other factors which need to be taken into account are the availability of training courses, helplines and other support services, the quality of manuals and other user aids, and the ease of use in terms of searching and accessing the results of your search.

Demonstrations are usually offered by host organisations, and it is useful to ask all the questions you need with the benefit of seeing the service in action before you commit yourself. Certain hosts also offer the facility of free online time to enable you to test the service before signing up.

Once you do decide to sign a contract with a host you will be issued with a password which gives you access to the sevice, and which you will type onto the terminal in order to 'log on'. The other password which you will require is the Network User Identity (NUI) which gives you access to the national telecommunications network.

Choosing Equipment

The basic equipment required for searching online databases is a terminal, telephone line, modem, printer and communications software. It is advisable to check with the host as to exactly what equipment is required to access their service. Some online services such as Datastream and Textline offer the facility of a dedicated terminal, which can be leased or rented. There are a wide range of modems on the market, and advice in the UK on what equipment to buy is available in the section which follows this introduction on sources of further advice and information.

Cost Considerations

Summary

Set Up Costs
personnel time
cost of manuals
NUI (network user identifier), connection charge (PSS-NUI for UK users), terminal and communications equipment (eg software, modem)

Ongoing Costs
connect time charges and/or subscriptions
printing and administrative charges
telecommunication charges
operator costs (including cost of training)
administrative overheads
equipment rental (if applicable)

Direct Costs

Hosts Charges
The average on-line connection cost per hour is £50. Some hosts such as Data-Star and Dimdi charge a separate royalty/licence fee, whereas others such as DIALOG and ESA-IRS include these in the per hour rate. The majority of hosts in this chapter charge on a per use rather than a subscription basis (see host summary chart for details). Dun & Bradstreet charge a subscription fee which is calculated on a volume-related sliding scale.

In terms of print charges, off-line prints often work out cheaper than on-line prints. This involves a request to the host computer to send a print out of the results of your search. You may also find it useful to have regular updates sent to you through an SDI service (selective disseminated information).

Telecommunications Charges
There are a number of different ways of accessing hosts' computers, which include using the Datel service, where data is transmitted over the public voice telephone network (PSTN), or using a dedicated data communications network such as the Public Data Network (PDN) in the UK. The International Packet Switching Service (IPSS) allows customers of the PDN to access hosts located overseas and is currently connected to over 100 networks in more than 70 countries.

IPSS call charges contain two elements – duration and volume. An IPSS call to the USA or Canada costs 3.75p per 30 seconds (£4.50 per hour) and 2.25p per 5 data segments transferred (£4.50 per kilosegment). One segment can contain between 1 and 64 characters, although the average number of characters per segment when carrying out on-line database access is 45. The charges for IPSS calls to Europe are 1.5p per 30 seconds (£1.80 per hour) and 0.9p per 5 segments (£1.80 per kilosegment). Call charges for all other countries outside Europe and North America are 4.5p per 30 seconds (£5.40 per hour) and 2.7p per 5 segments (£5.40 per kilosegment).

IPSS is a cost-effective service for information retrieval. As a guide assuming that 10 A4 pages (containing 20,000 characters) were transmitted during a 15 minute call to a US database, the call charges would be £3.13.

If you wish to have dial up access to the Public Data Network you will need to obtain a Network User Identity (NUI). This allows you to dial into the local Packet Switching Exchange via the telephone network. The charge in the UK for an NUI is £40 (one-off), plus a quarterly rental charge of £10. If you also need to receive incoming calls it may be worth considering having a dedicated data line connection to the local exchange. Charges for such a service are £700 (one-off) plus £350 quarterly rental. For both types of access you will also need a terminal, modem and telephone line.

Some of the largest hosts offer access through their own private networks, for example Dun & Bradstreet's DunsNet, IDC's IDCNET, DIALOG's DIALNET, ESA/IRS ESANET, and BRS BRSNET.

Telecommunication charges will need to be added to the standard search charges which you see quoted in this chapter, and these obviously vary according to which network you use.

Searching

Searching methods vary between different databases and hosts. The usual method for accessing information is entering keywords and constructing search terms. Training and the use of cheap or free online training files help users to carry out a search in the quickest and cheapest way possible. It is also useful to be familiar with the hardcopy version of the database in the case of, for example, a directory, as you can anticipate the type of information which is available.

A database host may have a number of files which could all potentially meet your requirements when you are carrying out a particular search. Rather than accessing each one in turn it is faster and cheaper to cross search between files, where the host offers this service. The major hosts listed in this directory such as DIALOG and Data-Star all offer this facility.

There are also a number of on-line directories of databases, such as the service offered by Cuadra Associates, and Dundis offered by the European Community host organisation, ECHO (see Section X111, Chapter 6). These will help you to identify relevant and new databases for a given subject area.

Potential Uses and Application of Databases

Main benefits of electronic information are:

- speed of access
- wide coverage
- flexibility
- accessibility
- constant up-dating

Speed of access and constant up-dating is obviously critical in some businesses, as for example in the securities sector. Also, information in hardcopy directories is often available on line, and the on-line version contains more recent data as it is updated more frequently. Flexibility becomes an advantage when you either want to analyse economic or company financial information on line, search for companies which match certain criteria, or down load information onto your personal computer for future editing or analysis.

Companies considering using on-line databases need to conduct their own cost/benefit analysis and decide whether their particular information needs justifies the cost. However, even if the need is for basic monitoring of papers and journals, the sheer volume of material makes electronic scanning more cost effective than manual methods.

Disadvantages include:

- Information available will never fill every information need of companies and will still need to be supplemented with hardcopy material.
- Printed sources often offer advantages in terms of ease of use and cost of access.
- Some database services, eg Textline, Datastream, ICC's viewdata service are menu driven and are relatively easy to use by an inexperienced searcher. However, others such as DIALOG, and Data-Star are best accessed by users who have had the benefit of training and experience in searching techniques.
- Industry-specific databases are much stronger in some areas, eg technology than others and have some way to go before coverage can be described as comprehensive.

However, the availability of business information on line is constantly improving in terms of quantity, coverage and quality.

Applications

Setting up an Information Process

It is usually most productive for users in companies to identify the types of information which they will need on a regular basis, and develop an information profile. This can then be turned into a standard interrogation pattern, which can be used to interrogate a number of databases on a daily, weekly or monthly basis.

Setting up an Internal Marketing Database

A comprehensive information system would need to combine internal data with data obtained from secondary sources. This can form the basis of a marketing database which can be used to plan sales activities, analyse potential or existing customers, generate mail shots and contacts listings etc.

Newsletters

Internal newsletters covering competitor or industry news can be generated using on-line databases. Useful databases for this application include: Textline, the Financial Times, BIS Infomat and the wide range of other news databases which are available (see sections 111 and V).

Market Analysis

Key research questions:
- What is the total market size?
- What is the current and forecast market growth rate?
- How is the market segmented?
- What is the market potential for our products?
- What are the characteristics of our customers? (eg structure, present and future needs)

Using market research databases can be valuable as a way of identifying previous research which has been conducted in specific areas. Databases such as FINDEX and Marketing Surveys Index (see section 111) list published research, others contain forecasts, market trends and time series on different countries worldwide.

Research can be focused on specific products, and here there are a number of patent databases, including INPADOC which contains over 12 million patent documents from 50 countries. Major database providers include: MAID, DIALOG, Mead, Data-Star, Orbit, and Pergamon.

Industry Analysis

Key research questions:
- What are the key success factors in the industry?
- How attractive is the industry? (eg is it mature/slow growth or emerging and experiencing fast growth? How profitable is it?)
- How fragmented or concentrated is the industry?
- How strong is the competition in the industry?
- How are we advantaged/disadvantaged vis-a-vis our competitors?
- What is the cost of entry?
- What is the pricing structure?
- What are the distribution channel methods and requirements?

Industry size and forecast data can be obtained through the use of the economics service offered by Datastream and other major hosts, plus market databases such as Euromonitor and Maid. There are also specialist industry databases which are listed in Section VII of Chapter 6, which provide background information, technical information and news on new products.

Figures can be obtained on industry norms such as average profit margins and return on capital employed through ICC Keynote, Jordan's industry surveys, Datastream, and Industry Performance Monitor (see section 1X). It is also possible to analyse the performance of companies within particular industry sectors – either your own competitors, or all companies listed under a specific SIC code.

Company Financial Information and Profiles

Key research questions:
- How many competitors do we have? (Number, location, market share.)
- What are their strengths and weaknesses?

- What is their current strategy and is there evidence that this will change in the foreseeable future?
- How profitable are they?

Research headings
- Structure – core businesses
- – parent company, and subsidiaries
- Key personnel
- Strengths
- Weaknesses
- Market focus
- Market strategy
- International development
- Recent acquisitions
- Financial performance figures

Company information is one of the most common applications of on-line databases.

Major uses are:
- Preparing competitor profiles
- Preparing customer profiles
- Preparing acquisition, merger or agent profiles

A good deal of information can be obtained to identify the parent company, subsidiaries, and financial strength and trends, including performance comparisons against industry norms or other companies. Major database services for financial analysis of UK companies are ICC and Datastream. Dun & Bradstreet, Moody's and Standard & Poor's are major services for the analysis of US companies, and Worldscope, Datastream, Predicasts and Hoppendstedt for Europe and the Far East. These services can be supplemented by a search in newspaper and business journal databases, such as Textline and the Financial Times.

Customer Analysis
Key research questions:
- Type, location, SIC number?
- Strengths and weaknesses of customers? (Creditworthiness etc)
- What are the key buying influences?
- What benefits are our customers seeking?

Directory databases form a basis for mail shots and promotional activities, and a starting point for sales and market planning.

Suggested databases for the UK include
- ICC, McCarthy, Dun and Bradstreet
- Overseas – Kompass, Hoppendstedt, Dun & Bradstreet

Share Prices and Other Investor Services
Electronic information is essential for transmission of data covering share prices, exchange rates, traded options and other securities news. This is available through viewdata services as well as on-line services. TOPIC is the largest private viewdata system in the world, with approximately 3500 terminals in use. This is operated by the Stock Exchange of the UK and Republic of Ireland. Other major service providers are for the UK, Extel, FT, Datastream and Reuters. International coverage is provided by the above plus other major hosts such as Citicorp, IP Sharp and Quotron.

Technology, New Products
News of developments in technology and new products are contained in the specialist industry databases (Section VII, Chapter 6) and Science and Technology databases (Section VIII, Chapter 6). Typical databases in this category are Predicasts New Product Announcements, and INSPEC. Information on patents, trademarks, regulations and standards can be found in the industry-wide database section (section IX, Chapter 6). It is also worth looking at the research databases listed in section X for news of current research in the UK or overseas.

Economic Conditions
Key research questions:
- What are the basic trends and fluctuations in the economy?

- What is the forecast for growth of GDP generally and by industry sector?
- What is the forecast for inflation / unemployment / interest rates / exchange rates?

Key factors:
- Employment
- Interest rates
- Business cycles
- Fiscal / monetary policies

Databases are particularly useful for accessing economic indicators for most countries worldwide, including economic forecasts. They can also be used for sophisticated macro and micro economic modelling. Major database providers in this category are Datastream, WEFA, GE Information Services, IDC, Citicorp, and IP Sharp.

Sources of Further Information and Advice

UK
ASLIB
The Association for Information Management
Information House
26-27 Boswell Street
London WC1N 3JZ
Tel: 01-430 2671
Telex: 23667
Fax: 01-430 0514
ASLIB offers members practical advice and information on a wide range of information management areas, including on-line information retrieval methods and systems, choice of databases etc

ECHO
European Commission Host Organisation
BP 2373
1023 Luxembourg
Tel: (010 352) 488041
Offers access to a number of databases which are sponsored wholly or partly by the European Commission. These include a number of services designed to inform and assist users with searching, and the choice of software etc

EURIPA
European Information Industry Association
Secretariat
PO Box 19
Wilmslow
Cheshire SK9 2DZ
Tel: 0625-532602
This association represents companies in the information industry, including database producers and hosts. Activities include holding meetings and producing reports

Library and Information Technology Centre
Polytechnic of Central London
235 High Holborn
London WC1V 7DN
Tel: 01-430 1561
Telex: 261074 PCLITC
Offers demonstrations of micro computers and information retrieval software to small groups of visitors by appointment. The Centre also has demonstration passwords to a number of hosts and access to some or all of their databases.

International Packet Switching Service (IPSS) – Prices

The following countries are connected to PSS through IPSS:

Country	Network	DNIC	Call Charges Duration per 30 seconds	Volume per 5 segments
Antigua			I/C to UK only	
Argentina	Arpac	7222	4.50	2.70
Australia	Austpac	5052		2.70
	Data Access	5053		2.70
Austria	Radio Austria	2329		0.90
	Datex-P	2322		0.90
Bahamas	Idas		I/C to UK only	
Bahrain	Bahnet	4263	4.50	2.70
Barbados			I/C to UK only	
Belgium	DCS	2062	1.50	0.90
Bermuda	Bermudanet	3503	4.50	2.70
Brazil	Interdata	7240	4.50	2.70
	Renpac	7241	4.50	2.70
Canada	Globedat	3025	3.75	2.25
	Infoswitch	3028	3.75	2.25
	Datapac	3020	3.75	2.25
Channel Is	PSS	2342	Inland call rate	
Chile	Chilepac	7303	4.50	2.70
	Entel	7302	4.50	2.70
China P.R. of			I/C to UK only	
Colombia	Dapaq		I/C to UK only	
Costa Rica	Radiografica		I/C to UK only	
Cote de Ivoire	Sytranpac	6122	4.50	2.70
Cuba			I/C to UK only	
Denmark	Datapac 23	82/2383	1.50	0.90
Dominican Rep			I/C to UK only	
Egypt	Arento		I/C to UK only	
Finland	Datapak	2442	1.50	0.90
	Digipak	2443	1.50	0.90
France	Transpac	2080	1.50	0.90
French Antilles	Dompac	3400	4.50	2.70
French Guiana	Dompac	7420	4.50	2.70
French Polynesia	Tompac	5470	4.50	2.70
Gabon	Gabonpac	6282	4.50	2.70
Germany (Fed Rep)	Datex-P	2624	1.50	0.90
Greece	Helpac	2022	1.50	0.90
Guam			I/C to UK only	
Guatamala	Guatel		I/C to UK only	
Honduras			I/C to UK only	
Hong Kong	Datapak	4545	4.50	2.70
	Idas		4.50	2.70
Hungary	Datex-L	2160	1.50	0.90
Iceland	Icepac	2740	1.50	0.90
Indonesia	Skop	5101	4.50	2.70
Irish Rep	Eirpac	2724	1.50	0.90
Israel	Isranet	4251	4.50	2.70
Italy	Italcable	2227	1.50	0.90
	Itapac	2222	1.50	0.90
Jamaica			I/C to UK only	
Japan	Venus-P	4408	4.50	2.70
	DDX-P	4401	4.50	2.70
Kuwait			I/C to UK only	

Country	Network	DNIC	Call Charges Duration per 30 seconds	Volume per 5 segments
Luxembourg	Luxpac	2704	1.50	0.90
Malaysia	Maypac	5021	4.50	2.70
Mexico	Telepac	3340	4.50	2.70
Netherlands	Datanet 1	2041	1.50	0.90
New Caledonia	Tompac	5460	4.50	2.70
New Zealand	Pacnet	5301	4.50	2.70
Norway	Datapak	2422	1.50	0.90
Oman			I/C to UK only	
Panama	Intelpaq		I/C to UK only	
Peru			I/C to UK only	
Philippines	Etpi		I/C to UK only	
	Gmcr		I/C to UK only	
	Philcom		I/C to UK only	
Portugal	Telepac	2680	1.50	0.90
Puerto Rico			I/C to UK only	
Reunion	Dompac	6470	4.50	2.70
San Marino	X-Net SMR	2922	1.50	0.90
Singapore	Telepac	5252	4.50	2.70
South Africa	Saponet	6550	4.50	2.70
South Korea	Dacom-Net	4501	4.50	2.70
Spain	Tida	2141	1.50	0.90
	Iberpac	2145	1.50	0.90
Sweden	Datapak	2402	1.50	0.90
Switzerland	Telepac	2284	1.50	0.90
Taiwan	Udas	4877	4.50	2.70
	Pacnet	4872	4.50	2.70
Thailand	Idarc		I/C to UK only	
Trinidad	Datanett	3740	4.50	2.70
	Texdat	3745	4.50	2.70
Tunisia	Red25	6050	1.50	0.90
Turkey		2862	4.50	2.70
United Arab Emirates	Emdan	4243	4.50	2.70
USA	Accunet	3134	3.75	2.25
	Autonet	3126	3.75	2.25
	Compuserve	3132	3.75	2.25
	FTCC	3124	3.75	2.25
	Globenet	3150	3.75	2.25
	Marknet	3136	3.75	2.25
	MCII-Impacs	3104	3.75	2.25
	RCA-LSOS	3113	3.75	2.25
	ITT-UDIS	3103/3107	3.75	2.25
	SNET	3140	3.75	2.25
	Telenet	3110/3125	3.75	2.25
	TRT-Datapak	3119	3.75	2.25
	Tymnet	3106	3.75	2.25
	Wutco	3101	3.75	2.25
USSR	Iasnet	2502	1.50	0.90
Vanuatu	Viapac	5410	4.50	2.70
Virgin Is (US)			I/C to UK only	
Yugoslavia	Yupac	2201	1.50	0.90
Zimbabwe	Zimnet	6482	4.50	2.70

For further information about existing or planned international packet switching services please consult:

British Telecom International
Data Marketing Group
Room 501 Holborn Centre
120 Holborn
London EC1N 2TE
Tel: 01-492 2750
Telex: 21601 BTI G
EMAIL: GOLD 73:TIP005

Source: British Telecom International

International Packet Switching Service – National Contacts

Australia
Austpac
Telecom Australia
DNS Marketing (Austpac)
Commercial Services Department
Data Marketing Branch
8th Floor
518 Little Bourke St
Melbourne VIC 3000
Tel: (010 61) 3-6067772
Telex: DASERV AA 35683

OTC Data Access
Overseas Telecommunications Commission (A)
Box 7000, GPO
Sydney 2001
Tel: (010 61) 2-2305000
Telex: OTCOM AA20591

Austria
Radio Austria
Radio-Austria AG
Customer Services
Mr G Kmet
Renngasse 14
1010 Vienna
Tel: (010 43) 1-5337552 ex 99,86
Telex: 114731 RAA

Datex-P
Vienna:
Mr Leiner
Postdirektion
Baeckerstrasse 1
1010 Vienna
Tel: (010 43) 1-51515

Belgium
DCS
RTT Data Transmission Dept
Blvd de L'Imperatice 17-19
1000 Brussels
Tel: (010 32) 2-2131261
Telex: 29280 CDDATA

Brazil
Interdata
Arne S Freinsibler
Special Services Section
Av Marechal Floriano 99
99-12 Andar
20080 Rio de Janeiro
Tel: (010 55) 21-2168328
Telex: 2121810 EBTL BR

Renpac
Address as above

Canada
Datapac
Mr W J Enns
Datapac International
Product Manager
160 Elgin St
Ottawa Ontario
Canada K1G 3J4
(010 1) 613-5677571

Globedat
George Orsal
Marketing Dept. 17th floor
680 Ouest Rue Sherbrooke
Montreal, Quebec H35 2S4
Tel: (010 1) 514-2817981
Telex: 05-25690

Infoswitch
Mr R D Mark
Product Manager
Switched Data Service
Marketing
CNCP
Suite 1803, West Tower
3300 Bloor Street West
Toronto Ontario M8X 2WP
Tel: (010 1) 416-2326150
Telex: 06524462 CNCPMKTG ONT

Denmark
Datapak
Gesper Duus
Posts and Telegraphs Marketing Dept
Roedovrevej 241
2610 Roedovre
Tel: (010 45) 1-993665
Telex: 19791 KTASKH DK

Finland
Datapak
Mr Tauno St Jernberg
PTL-Tele
Fintelcom
PO Box 526
00101 Helsinki
Tel: (010 358) 0-7042373
Fax: (010 358) 0-7042659
Telex: 123434 TEINT SF

France
Transpac
Leased Circuit Access
Transpac
28 Eme Etage
Tour Maine Montparnasse
33 Av du Maine
75755 Paris Cedex 15
Tel: (010 33) 1-45385211
Telex: 260676

Germany (Federal Republic of)
Datex-P
Deutsche Bundespost
Fernmeldetechnisches Zentralamt
Referat Kundenberatung fuer Dateldienste
Postfach 5000
6100 Darmstadt
Tel: (010 49) 6151-834641
Teletex: 2627-6151946 FTL
Datl

Greece
Helpac
Mr Xanthopoulos
Telex-Data Transmission Division
5 Stadiou Street
GR 105562 Athens
Tel: (010 30) 1-3219599
Fax: (010 30) 1-3473299
Telex: 215482 DSSGR

Hong Kong
Datapak
Mr Robin Lau
Senior Controller, Marketing Support
Datacom Services
Hong Kong Telephone Co
PO Box 479
GPO Hong Kong
Tel: (010 852) 5-287183
Fax: (010 852) 5-8932322
Telex: 89193 DCOMS HX
For further information call
(via PSS) A94545500104

IDAS
Mr Y S Wu
Manager Sales Data Services
Text Services Division
GPO Box 597
New Mercury House
22 Fenwick St
Wanchai, Hong Kong
Tel: (010 852) 5-8621628
Fax: (010 852) 5-8612143
Telex: 83000 CWCOMHX

Indonesia
SKDP
Mr Wahyu Wi Jayadi
Sales Manager
PT Indosat, Wisma Antara
Lt.10
Jl. Merdeka Selatan 17
Jakarta 10110
Tel: (010 62) 21-376338
Telex: 44383 or 46134 INDSAT
1A

Ireland (Republic of)
Eirpac
Joe Troy
Data Services Section
Telecom Eireann
6-8 College Green
Dublin 2
Tel: 0001-778222
Telex: 91280 TXDN E1

Israel
Isranet
Marius Goldstein
BEZEQ
Customer Service and
Marketing Section
International Calls Dept
116 Derekh Petahtiova
Tel Aviv
Tel: (010 972) 3-208377
Telex: 361188 TELO IL

Italy
Itapac
Mr Andrea Macchioni
Ministero PTT (Itapac)
Direzione Centrale Servizi
Viale Europa 160
00100 Rome
Tel: (010 39) 6-54601 ex 4969
Telex: 610070 GENTEL 1

Italcable
Address as above

Japan
DDXP
Kokusai Denshin Denwa Co
Ltd (KDD)
2nd Marketing Division
Commercial Dept
Marunochi Mitsui Building
2-2 Marunochi 2-Chome
Chiyoda-Yu
Tokyo 100
Tel: (010 81) 3-2408449
Telex: 24700 KDDSALES

Venus P
Address as above

Korea
DNS
Datacommunications Corp of
Korea
Marketing Dept
Communication Division
11th Floor
The Korea Stock Exchange
Building
33 Yeoeido-Dong
Yeongdeungpo-Ku, Seoul
Tel: (010 82) 2-7833991
Telex: 28311 DACOM K

Luxembourg
Luxpac
Mr Gilbert Hoscheid
Administration des P et T
Division des Telecommunications
5 Rue de Hollerich
2999 Luxembourg
Tel: (010 352) 4991722
Telefax: (010 352) 493049
Telex: 60520 PTSAT LU

Netherlands
Datanet 1
Jolanda Rens
PTT Datacommunications
PB 3000
2500 GA The Hague
Netherlands
Tel: (010 31) 70-438611
Fax: (010 31) 70-437605
Telex: 32544 DACOM NL

New Zealand
Pacnet
Brian Mitchell
Telecom Corporation of New
Zealand
Telecom Head Office
International Operations
7-27 Waterloo Quay
Wellington
Tel: (010 64) 4-738444
Telex: 31688 TELINT

Norway
Datapak
Ms Turid Male
Ms Hjoerdis Brustad
Norwegian Telecommunications Administration
Postboks 6701
St Olavs Plass
Oslo 1
Tel: (010 47) 2-488990
Telex: 71203 GENTLN

Portugal
Telepac
Eng. Nuno Matos
CTT e TLP em Consorcio
Edificio Picoas
Av Fontes Periera de Melo 38-9
1000 Lisbon
Tel: (010 351) 1-540020 ex
1468/1469
Telex: 64200 TDATAP

Singapore
Telepac
The Divisional Manager
Singapore Telecom Data Services
31 Exeter Road
Singapore 0923
Tel: (010 65) 7343344
Fax: (010 65) 7333008
Telex: RS39555 BTS

South Africa
Saponet
The Postmaster General
Telecommunications (3K65)
Private Bag X74
0001 Pretoria
Tel: (010 27) 21-4092399
Telex: 322889

Spain
Iberpac
Mr Victor Sanz
Mr Angel Huertas
Telefonica
Departamento de Negocios
Paseo de Recoletos 37-41
28004 Madrid
Tel: (010 34) 1-4105460
Telex: 47786 CTNC E

Tida
Mr Huertas
Marketing Services and Development
CTNE
Plaza de Espana 4
Madrid 13
Tel: (010 34) 1-4105460
Telex: 47786 CTNC E

Sweden
Datapak
Swedish Telecom Data Communications
Sales Division
Gunnel Kling
10390 Stockholm
Tel: (010 46) 8-7806228
Telex: 12020 DATASTH S

Switzerland
Telepac
Mr M P Laesser
PTT Suisse
Victoriastrasse 21
3030 Berne
Tel: (010 41) 31-621111 (PTT HQ)
31-624374 (M P Laesser)
Telex: 911010 PTTCH

Taiwan
Pacnet
Mr Yen Swen
Chief of Pacnet
42 Jen A1 Road SEC 1
Taipei
Tel: (010 886) 2-3443117
Telex: 20684 PACNET

Udas
Mr C Y Chow
Chief of Business Centre
International Telecommunications Administration
31 Al-Kuo East Road
Taipei
Tel: (010 886) 2-3443771
Telex: 11127

Thailand
Idarc
Mr Santi Phanthumkomol
Commercial Division
The Communications Authority of Thailand
4th Floor, Thai Farmers Bank Building
142 Silom Road
Bangkok 10500
Tel: (010 66) 2-2331050 ex 2353
Telex: 80013 CATCOM TH

Turkey
Mr Nedret Suzme
Head of Datacommunications Group
General Directorate of PTT
Technical and Operational Dept
Ruzsarli Sokak Catalhan Mulus Ankara
Tel: (010 90) 4-3243533
Fax: (010 90) 4-3245332
Telex: 82142586

UK
PSS
PSS Customer Support
4th Floor, Tenter House
45 Moorfields
London EC2Y 9TH
Tel: 0800-282444 (National)
01-250 8045 (International)
Telex: 884769

USA
Autonet
ADP Autonet
175 Jackson Plaza
Ann Arbor
Michigan 48106
Tel: (010 1) 313-7696800

Compuserve
Compuserve Network Services
5000 Arlington Center Boulevard
Columbus
Ohio 43220
Tel: (010 1) 614-4578600

FTCC
FTCC McDonnell Douglas
90 John St
New York NY10038
Tel: (010 1) 212-6699866
Telex: 822030/82633

Globenet
Abby Braune
Tel: (010 1) 703-6584500

ITT Worldnet
Mr Peter Calistri
ITT World Communications Inc
International Operations
100 Plaza Drive
Secaucus NJ 07096
Telex: 426869 ITT-INTOPS

Marknet
USA:
Client Services
GE Information
401 No Washington St
Rockville
Maryland 20850
Tel: (010 1) 301-3404000
UK:
25-29 High St
Kingston upon Thames
Surrey KT1 1LN
Tel: 01-546 1077

MCII-Impacs
Gideon Sasson
MCI International
International Drive
Rye Brook NY 10573
Tel: (010 1) 914-9346531
Telex: 62135 MCIIENGR

RCA-LSDS
RCA Global Communications Inc
200 Centennial Avenue
Piscataway NJ 08854
Tel: (010 1) 201-8854128
Telex: 299795 RCAUR

Telenet
International Services
Telenet Communications Corporation
12490 Sunrise Valley Drive
Reston VA 22096
Tel: (010 1) 703-6895573
Telex: 258525 GTETCCUR

Tymnet

Europe:
Dominique Marchand
Tymnet Extended Services
165 Bureaux de la Colline
92213 St-Cloud Cedex
Tel: (010 33) 1-49112344

TRT
Mr John Cahill
Mr Peter Sarro
TRT International Services
1331 Pennsylvania Avenue
NW
Washington DC 20004
Tel: (010 1) 202-8792264
202-8792270
Telex: 197779

US:
Mr Keith Curtis
Tymnet
External Network Services
2070 Chain Bridge Road
Vienna VA 22180
Tel: (010 1) 703-8279110
703-3566972

Notes
This list provides contact details for 53 national networks. The International Packet Switching Service (IPSS) is connected to over 100 networks, and latest contact details for networks not included here can be obtained in the UK from the British Telecom International, Data Marketing Group. (Tel: 01-492 2742)
Fax: 01-831 9959
Telex: 21601 BTI G

Source: British Telecom International·IPSS Marketing

UK Packet Switching Exchanges

PSE	110 or 300 bit/s	1200/75 bit/s	1200 bit/s Duplex
Aberdeen	0224 642242	0224 642484	0224 642644
Belfast	0232 8281	0232 8291	0232 8201
Birmingham	021 2145139	021 2146191	021 2143061
Brighton	0273 851111	0273 852111	0273 853111
Bristol	0272 216411	0272 216511	0272 216611
Cambridge	0223 82511	0223 82411	0223 82111
Cardiff	0222 376111	0222 376171	0222 376191
Edinburgh	031 3379141	031 3379121	031 3379393
Glasgow	041 2042011	041 2042031	041 2042051
Ipswich	0473 671111	0473 672111	0473 673111
Leeds	0532 470711	0532 470611	0532 470811
Liverpool	051 2110000	051 2125127	051 2136327
London 1	01 825 9421 or 261 9421	01 407 8344	01 928 2333
London 2	01 928 9111	01 928 3399	01 928 1737
London 3	01 840 0688	01 840 1399	01 840 5500
London 4	01 680 9421	01 680 8500	01 680 7999
London 5	01 200 9000	01 200 0888	01 200 1353
London 6	01 541 0666	01 541 0222	01 541 0444
Luton	0582 8181	0582 8191	0582 8101
Maidstone	0622 885111	0622 886111	0622 887111
Manchester	061 8330242	061 8330091	061 8330631
Newcastle	091 2314171	091 2314181	091 2314161
Nottingham	0602 881311	0602 881411	0602 881511

PSE	110 or 300 bit/s	1200/75 bit/s	1200 bit/s Duplex
Portsmouth	0705 53011	0705 53911	0705 53811
Reading	0734 389111	0734 380111	0734 384111
Sheffield	0742 414171	0742 414181	0742 414191
Slough	0753 6141	0753 6131	0753 6171

This list of Packet Switching Exchanges offers a guide to the coverage available using the dial-up service to PSS. Over 90% of the business population is covered by a local or 'a' rate call. There are currently six London Packet Switching Exchanges.

Summary Matrix — Major Database Hosts

Chapter six provides descriptions of 660 databases offered by 148 hosts and 384 producers. Because of the way the chapter is organised it is not easy to see the cross section of services offered by any one host.

This chart has been produced in order to allow you to see the range of databases offered by 57 hosts which provide at least three of the databases listed in this directory. Due to space constraints it was not possible to include the full range of databases offered by each host in the directory, but the chart should give you a good idea as to who provides what, and the different strengths of hosts, eg some cover a large number of databases in different fields (DIALOG, Data-Star, ESA-IRS), whereas others offer a smaller number but are equally valuable as they specialise in certain fields (Maid in marketing, STN 1in Science and Technology).
The number of databases listed for some of the larger hosts is as follows:

DIALOG	161	STN	24
Data-Star	69	Maid	20
ESA-IRS	59	Fiz Technik	19
Orbit	42	Telesystemes Questel	19
BRS	38	GENIOS	19
IP Sharp	32	Mead	16
GE Information	29	DRI	14
PROFILE	25	Business Direction	14
Pergamon	24		

This chart can be used in conjunction with Appendix 3 which provides a summary of country coverage and subject area for each database, listed in alphabetical order.

Summary Matrix · Major Database Hosts

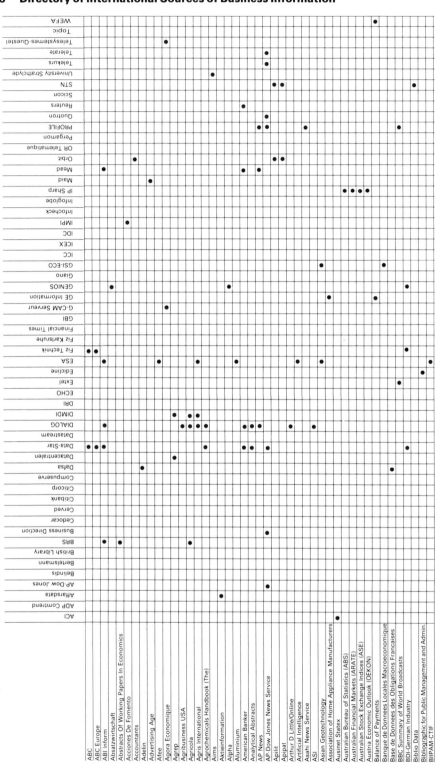

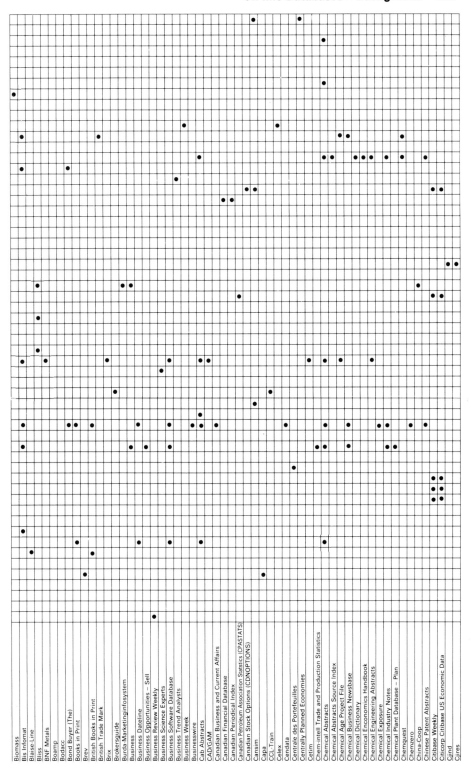

Host \ Database	Claims	Coffeeline	Commodities (Commodity)	Commodity Options (Comoptions)	Company Facts and Addresses	Compendex Plus	Compustat	Computer Database	Computerpat	Comtrend	Concursqs Publicos	Conf	Conference Papers Index	Consumer Reports	Context – Business Microcomputer	Corporate & Industry Research Reports	Corporate Affiliations	Cronos Eurostat	Cross Directory File	Cscorp	CSO UK Macroeconomic and Financial Statistics	Ctrim	Cuadra Directory of Online Databases	Current Technology Index	D&B Dun's France Marketing	D&B Dun's Market Identifiers	D&B Dun's Financial Records	D&B International Dun's Market Identifiers	D&B Million Dollar Directory	D&B-Canadian Dun's Market Identifiers	Daily and Sunday Telegraph (The)	Daily Currency Exchange Rates (Currency)	Dataeco	Dataline (Textile Service)	Datastream Company Accounts Service	Datastream Economics Services	Datastream Equity Research Services	Datastream Financial Futures Service	Datastream Fixed Interest Services	Datastream Investment Accounting Service	Datastream Traded Options Service	Datastream Valuation Services	Dati Anagraphici Di Impresse Iatliane	Dea	Defotel	Der Betrieb	Deutsche Bundesbank Data (Bundesbank)
WEFA																	●			●																											●
Topic																																															
Telesystemes-Questel																						●		●																						●	
Teletate																																															
Telekurs																																															
University Strathclyde																																															
STN				●							●						●																														
Scicon																																															
Reuters																																		●													
Quotron																																															
PROFILE																														●																	
Pergamon							●																			●																					
OR Telematique																																															
Orbit	●			●																		●																									
Mead														●																																	
Maid															●																																
IP Sharp		●	●																																								●				●
Infoglobe																																															
Infocheck																																															
IMPI													●																																		
IDC		●				●																																									
ICEX																																															
ICC																																															
GSI-ECO																	●			●																							●				
Giano																																														●	
GENIOS																																															●
GE Information																																															
G-CAM Serveur																																															
GBI																																															
Financial Times																									●																						
Fiz Karlsruhe																																															
Fiz Technik																																															
ESA				●			●																											●													
Edicline			●																																												
Extel																																															
ECHO																																															
DRI																													●																		
DIMDI																																															
DIALOG	●	●		●		●							●	●		●								●		●	●	●	●	●																	
Datastream																																			●	●	●	●	●		●	●					
Data-Star				●		●										●					●			●																							
Datacentralen																			●	●																											
Dafsa																																															
Compuserve																																															
Citicorp																																															
Citibank																																															
Cerved																																														●	
Cedocar				●																																											
Business Direction																																															
BRS				●		●								●																																	
British Library																																															
Bertelsmann																																															
Belindis																																															
AP-Dow Jones																																															
Affarsdata																																															
ADP Comtrend										●																																					
ACI																																															

DHSS Data
Dialindex
Dialog Publications
Dialog Quotes and Trading
Dianeguide
Din-German Standards and Technical Rules
Direction of Trade Statistics
Directorio de Bases de Datos
Directorio de Empresas Industriales
Directory of American Research and Technology
Disclosure
Disclosure/Spectrum Ownership
Disposiciones Legales
Dissertation Abstracts Online
Ditr (Standards and Specifications)
DMS Contract Awards
DMS Market Intelligence Reports
Doe Energy
DRI – Cost Forecasting
DRI Commodities
DRI Europe
DRI-Facs
DRI-Sec
Dun's Electronic Yellow Pages Construction
Dun's Electronic Yellow Pages Financial
Dun's Electronic Yellow Pages Manufacturers
Dun's Electronic Yellow Pages Professionals
Dun's Electronic Yellow Pages Retailers
Dun's Electronic Yellow Pages Services
Dun's Electronic Yellow Pages Wholesalers
Dun's Market Identifiers
Dundis
Eabs
EAE
Earnings Guide
Eastern Bloc Countries Economic Statistics
Ecdin Data Bank
Eclatx
Econ Base Timeseries & Forecasts
Economics Abstracts International
Economic Literature Index
Economist (The)
Economist Intelligence Unit
Economist Intelligence Unit Retail Business
EDF-DOC
Edit
EI Engineering Meetings
Einkaufs–1X1
EIS Online
EIU-International Travel & Tourism Reports
Elcom
EIU Travel & Tourism Analyst
Electric Power Database
Electric Power Industry Abstracts
Electronic Publishing Abstracts
Emis
Empresas
Encyclopedia of Associations
Endoc

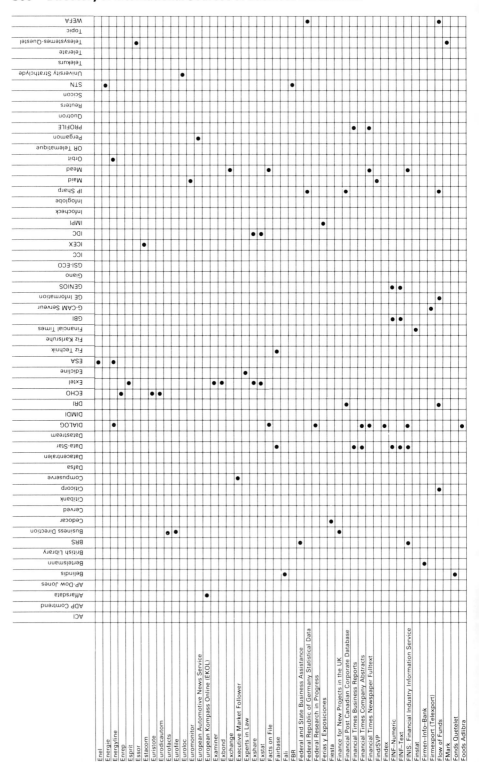

Foreign Exchange Database
Foreign Trade and Economic Abstracts
Foreign Traders Index
Forest
Forkat
Frost and Sullivan Market Research
Frost and Sullivan Political Risk
FSTA
FT Currency & Share Index
Fxbase
Fxpro
Gatt
Geld (Money)
General Electric Company (GECAST)
Genus Operator
Gestion des Valeurs Mobilieres
Global Perspective (TM) Country Outlooks
Global Report
Globe
Globe and Mail Online (The)
GPO Monthly Catalog
GPO Publications Reference File
Hadoss
Handelsblatt
Harvard Business Review
Heilbron
Henley Centre for Forecasting
Hong Kong Stock Exchange (HKSTOCK)
Hong Kong Stock Exchange Fastprice
Hoppendstedt Austria
Hoppendstedt Netherlands
Hoppenstedt Directory of German Companies
Ialine
Ibsedex
ICC British Company Directory
ICC Canadian Corporations
ICC British Company Financial Data Sheets
ICC Full Text Company Accounts
ICC Industrial Averages
ICC International Business Research
ICC Sharewatch
ICC Stockbroker Research
ICC Viewdata Service
ICCA Australian Accounting Database
Iconda
IES–DC
Imf International Financial Statistics
Index Service
Industrial Market Location
Industrial Production
Industry and International Standards
Industry Data
Industry Data Sources
Industry Performance Monitor
Infocheck
Information Service-Exchange
Informatitres

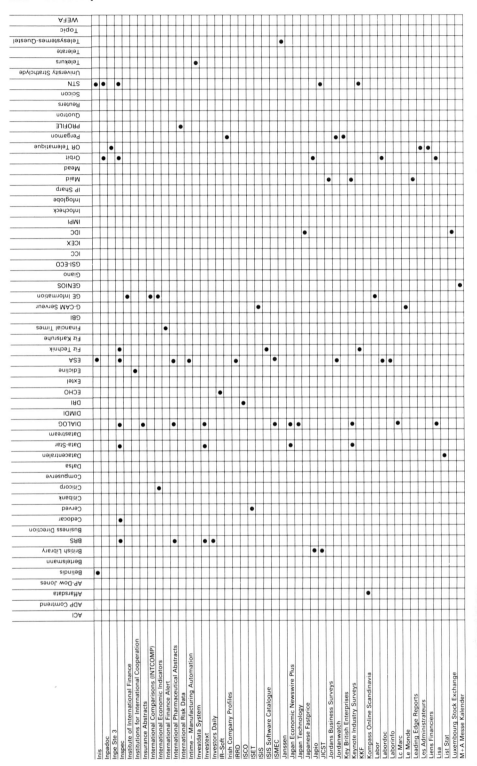

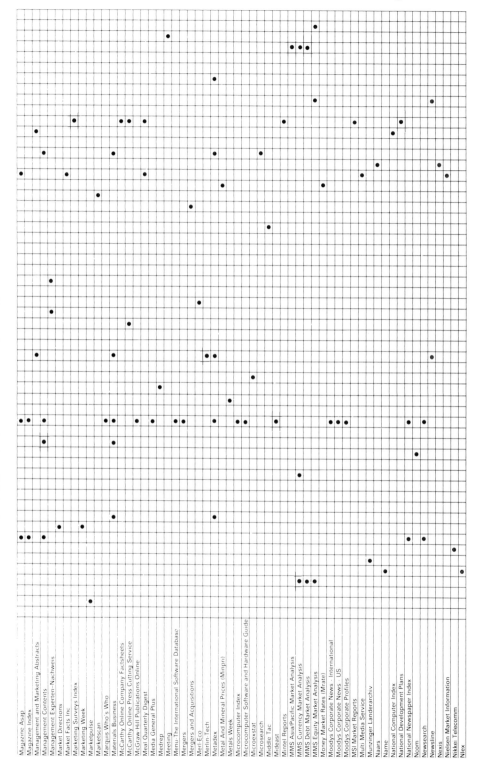

Host	Nodo	Nomura Research Institute (Nri/e)	Nordic Energy Index	Norm	North American Stock Market (Nastock)	Ntis	Nuclear Science Abstracts	Ocle East-Reference	Oecd Data	Oecd Main Economic Indicators	Oferes	Oil And Gas Journal Energy Database	Oil And Gas Journal Energy Forecasts	Online Chronicle	Orbi	Otisline	Over The Counter Information	P/E News	Pabli	Packaged Facts	Packaging Science And Technology Abstracts	Pais International	Paperchem	Pascal	Patdpa	Patos Pct Applications	Patolis	Patos European Patents	Patos German Patents	Pestdoc	Pharmaceutical News Index	Polis (UK)	Pricedata	Priceplus	Producer Price Indexes	Progno	Pts Aerospace/Defense Markets & Technology	Pts Annual Reports Abstracts	Pts F & S Indexes	Pts International Forecasts	Pts Marketing & Advertising Reference Service	Pts New Product Announcements	Pts Prompt	Pts Us Forecasts	Pts Us Time Series	Publishers, Distributors & Wholesalers	Quarterly Financial Report	Qui Decide En France
WEFA	•								•	•																																			•			
Topic																	•																															
Telesystems-Questel																								•																								
Telerate																																																
Telekurs																																																
University Strathclyde																																																
STN																									•																							
Scicon																																	•															
Reuters																																																
Quotron																																																
PROFILE																																																
Pergamon																																																
OR Telematique															✓																																	
Orbit				•													•																		•													
Mead																				•																												
Maid																			•																													
IP Sharp				•					•	•																																						
Infoglobe																																																
Infocheck																																																
IMPI																																																
IDC																																														•		
ICEX											•																																					
ICC																																																
GSI-ECO											•																																					
Giano																																																
GENIOS																																																
GE Information	•								•	•																																			•			•
G-CAM Serveur																																																•
GBI																																												•				
Financial Times																																																
Fiz Karlsruhe																																																
Fiz Technik																																																
ESA				•																	•			•									•		•													
Edicline																																																
Extel																																		•														
ECHO																		•																														
DRI											•																																					
DIMDI																				•																												
DIALOG				•	•									•			•			•	•	•	•							•							•	•	•	•	•	•	•	•	•	•	•	•
Datastream																																																
Data-Star				•													•			•																	•	•	•	•	•	•	•	•	•	•		
Datacentralen		•																																														
Dafsa																																																
Compuserve																																																
Citicorp																																																
Citibank																																																
Cerved	•																																															
Cedocar				•																																•												
Business Direction																																																
BRS				•	•															•																	•	•								•		
British Library																											•																					
Bertelsmann																										•		•	•																			
Belindis			•																			•																										
AP-Dow Jones																																																
Affarsdata																																																
ADP Comtrend																																																
ACI																																																

Quotron 800
Quotron Symbol Guide
Rapra Abstracts
Rapra Trade Names
Reference Book Of Corporate Management
Registro De Establecimientos Industriales
Remarc
Report On Business Corporate Database
Research Index
Reserve Bank Of Australia Bulletin (RBA)
Retribuzioni Operai E Apprendisti
Reuter Monitor
Reuters
Reuters Country Reports
Ringdoc
Robomatix
Ruralnet
Saatchi And Saatchi Compton Media
Sae Global Mobility
Sani
Sanp
Scan
Scan-A-Bid-Scan
Sdim2
Sdim1
Sdoe
Sec 1 National Accounts
Securities Industry
Sesame
Shops
Sibil
Sigle
Social Scisearch
Societe Generale De Banque
Spacesoft
Spearhead
Sphinx
Ssie Current Research
Standard & Poors (S&P) Marketscope
Standard & Poors Corporate Descriptions
Standard & Poors News
Standard & Poors Register Biographical
Standard & Poors Register Corporate
Standard Industrial Classification
Standard And Specifications
Standards Search
Stars
Statistiche Del Commercio Estero Dell' Italia
Statistiche Economiche
Stock Exchange Of Singapore (Singstock)
Stor-Tele
Supertech
Sveriges Handelskalander
Syce
Sydney Stock Exchange Statex Service (Statex)
Ta
Tax Notes Today

	ACI	ADP Comtrend	Affarsdata	AP-Dow Jones	Belindis	Bertelsmann	British Library	BRS	Business Direction	Cedocar	Cerved	Citibank	Citicorp	Compuserve
Ted														
Tele Inform														
Telecommunications														
Teledata														
Teledoc														
Telefirm														
Telerate														
Tend														
Textile Technology Digest														
Textile-Wirtschaft														
Textline														
Thesauri														
Thomas New Industrial Products														
Thomas Regional Industrial Suppliers														
Thomas Register Online														
Tidningsdatabasen			●											
Times Newspapers (The)														
Titus														
Tmint														
Topic														
Toronto Stock Exchange 300 Index & Stock Stat														
Touristic-Information Facts and Abstracts														
Trade And Industry Asap								●						
Trade And Industry Index														
Trade Statistic														
Transdoc														
Transin														
Trinet Company Database														
Trinet Establishment Database														
Tris														
UK Company Profile														
Ulrich's Periodicals								●						
United Nations Commodity Trade Statistics														
United Nations Industrial Statistics														
United Nations National Accounts														
United Nations Population Statistics														
United States Economic Statistics														
United States National Accounts														
United States Stock Market (Usstock)														
United States Stock Options (Usoptions)														
Unlisted Market Guide (The)														
UPI News														
US Class														
US Patents														
USA Monitor														
Vademecum														
Valordata														

	Dafsa	Datacentralen	Data-Star	Datastream	DIALOG	DIMDI	DRI	ECHO	Extel	Edicline	ESA	Fiz Technik	Fiz Karlsruhe	Financial Times
Ted								●						
Tele Inform														
Telecommunications											●			
Teledata														
Teledoc														
Telefirm														
Telerate														
Tend														
Textile Technology Digest					●									
Textile-Wirtschaft														
Textline											●			
Thesauri								●						
Thomas New Industrial Products					●									
Thomas Regional Industrial Suppliers					●									
Thomas Register Online					●									
Tidningsdatabasen														
Times Newspapers (The)														
Titus												●		
Tmint														
Topic														
Toronto Stock Exchange 300 Index & Stock Stat														
Touristic-Information Facts and Abstracts										●				
Trade And Industry Asap					●									
Trade And Industry Index					●									
Trade Statistic			●											
Transdoc											●			
Transin														
Trinet Company Database					●									
Trinet Establishment Database					●									
Tris					●									
UK Company Profile														
Ulrich's Periodicals					●						●			
United Nations Commodity Trade Statistics														
United Nations Industrial Statistics														
United Nations National Accounts														
United Nations Population Statistics														
United States Economic Statistics														
United States National Accounts														
United States Stock Market (Usstock)														
United States Stock Options (Usoptions)														
Unlisted Market Guide (The)														
UPI News					●									
US Class														
US Patents														
USA Monitor														
Vademecum														
Valordata														

	GBI	G-CAM Serveur	GE Information	GENIOS	Giano	GSI-ECO	ICC	ICEX	IDC	IMPI	Infocheck	Infoglobe	IP Sharp	Maid
Ted														
Tele Inform														
Telecommunications														
Teledata														
Teledoc														
Telefirm		●												
Telerate														
Tend						●								
Textile Technology Digest														
Textile-Wirtschaft				●										
Textline														
Thesauri														
Thomas New Industrial Products														
Thomas Regional Industrial Suppliers														
Thomas Register Online														
Tidningsdatabasen														
Times Newspapers (The)														
Titus														
Tmint														
Topic														
Toronto Stock Exchange 300 Index & Stock Stat													●	
Touristic-Information Facts and Abstracts														
Trade And Industry Asap														
Trade And Industry Index														
Trade Statistic														
Transdoc														
Transin														
Trinet Company Database														●
Trinet Establishment Database														
Tris														
UK Company Profile											●			
Ulrich's Periodicals														
United Nations Commodity Trade Statistics													●	
United Nations Industrial Statistics			●											
United Nations National Accounts			●											
United Nations Population Statistics			●											
United States Economic Statistics			●											
United States National Accounts			●											
United States Stock Market (Usstock)													●	
United States Stock Options (Usoptions)													●	
Unlisted Market Guide (The)														
UPI News														
US Class														
US Patents														
USA Monitor														●
Vademecum														
Valordata														

	Mead	Orbit	OR Telematique	Pergamon	PROFILE	Quotron	Reuters	Scicon	STN	University Strathclyde	Telekurs	Telerate	Telesystemes-Questel	Topic	WEFA
Ted					●										
Tele Inform			●												
Telecommunications															
Teledata											●				
Teledoc													●		
Telefirm															
Telerate												●			
Tend															
Textile Technology Digest															
Textile-Wirtschaft															
Textline							●								
Thesauri															
Thomas New Industrial Products															
Thomas Regional Industrial Suppliers															
Thomas Register Online															
Tidningsdatabasen															
Times Newspapers (The)					●										
Titus									●						
Tmint													●		
Topic														●	
Toronto Stock Exchange 300 Index & Stock Stat															
Touristic-Information Facts and Abstracts															
Trade And Industry Asap	●														
Trade And Industry Index															
Trade Statistic															
Transdoc															
Transin													●		
Trinet Company Database	●														
Trinet Establishment Database	●														
Tris															
UK Company Profile															
Ulrich's Periodicals															
United Nations Commodity Trade Statistics															
United Nations Industrial Statistics															
United Nations National Accounts															●
United Nations Population Statistics															
United States Economic Statistics															
United States National Accounts															
United States Stock Market (Usstock)															
United States Stock Options (Usoptions)															
Unlisted Market Guide (The)						●									
UPI News															
US Class		●													
US Patents		●													
USA Monitor															
Vademecum									●						
Valordata											●				

Database Host Services Chart

This chart provides details on support services and other details which have been considered useful either for readers who are in the process of selecting a new database host to sign up with, or for readers who have already signed up with hosts and would find the list of help-line numbers useful. Hosts often provide support facilities such as special files for cross-searching the databases which they offer, on-line news or help facilities, newsletters, and manuals. Method of payment and currency of payment are important factors if you are selecting a new service. The telecommunication networks which can be used to access services are also listed, including any private networks which a host offers.

The information which is provided in this chart is based on responses to questionnaires which were completed by hosts. In a few cases methods and currency of payment are under review and may have changed when this book is published.

Value Line Data Base-11
Vdin
Verband Der Vereine Creditreform E.V.
Videcom
Vitis-Vea
Volkswagenwerk
VTB
Washington Post Electronic Edition
Washington Presstext
Water Resources Abstracts
Weldasearch
Wharton Econometric World Forecasts
Who Inform
Who Makes Machinery
Who Owns Whom
Who Supplies What
Wirtschastswoche
World Affairs Report
World Aluminium Abstracts
World Bank Debt Tables (Wdebt)
World Bank International Business Opps
World Patents Index
World Textiles
Worldscope
WTI
ZDE
Zvei Electro-Buying Guide

Database Host Services Chart

| | User aids | | Training | | News | User guides | SDI |
Host	On-line services	On-line news	Country	Charges	letters	and manuals	Servic
ADP Comtrend	Menu lists services and file users are entitled to view.	No	U.S.A. U.K. Switzerland Holland Belgium Luxembourg France Germany	Included in installation cost.	No	User Guide for Videcom Videcom Plus, Trendsetter & Marketpulse. Marketpulse supplies a symbol guide covering over 120 000 securities	No
Agra Europe	Statistics indexed under a selection code	No	Details provided on request	Details provided on request	Twelve	User guide and code lists (free)	No
Affarsdata	No	Anslag-stavlan file	Sweden (Stockholm) International telephone courses (30 minutes). Training databases.	Free	Nyheter fran AffarsData (Monthly)	User guide (free)	No
AP–Dow Jones News Service	N/A. (All services are real time broadcast news)	No	Negligible training required		No	N/A	N/A
Belindis	No	News file	Belgium (Brussels)	Free	No	Stairs User's Manual BF 200. Other manuals prices on request	No
Bertelsmann	CROS index file (for BRS data-bases). XXXX (for German language databases)	"News"	Germany (Munich)	DM 300 plus VAT (per person/per day)	Kund-eninfo (6–10 issues per annum)	BRS/SEARCH Manual DM 62.5 Munzinger Landerarchiv Manual DM 30 PATOS Manual DM 50 "Who Supplies What?" Manual DM 30	Yes (fc paten databa only D per up plus p and pc
Blaise	Index of files available. Explain facility describes main features of each file.	"News"	U.K.	£120 (2 days) Inhouse course-prices on request	BLAISE (6 issues per annum)	User Manual £36 (UK) £39 (overseas) Prices above are for additional copies Initial documentation included in subscription charge.	Yes

Help desk contact number	Charging method	Other charges	Currency	Language	Access Days	Hours (local time)	Telecommunications networks & gateway services
(USA) (01 01) 800-5825955 (UK) 0800-525711	Subscription	Monthly rental per product	According to country of installation	English	Monday to Friday	0800 to 1830	Direct links supplied to ADP's data centres
(UK) 0892-33813	Subscription and pay as you go	None	£ Sterling	English	7 days a week	24 hours	All public networks worldwide.
(Sweden) (010 46) 87-364555	Majority pay as you go	None	SKr	Mainly Swedish (Kompass is searchable in other languages	7 days a week	24 hours	Datapak (Network user address: 2402001150) Gateway access to Data-Star and Global Report
(USA) (010 1) 212-4162313 (UK & Europe) 01-353 2906 (FDR) (01049) 69-740931 (Switzerland) (01041) 1-2512244	Subscription	None	£ Sterling (UK) DM (FDR) US $ (ROW)	English	6 days (closed Sunday)	24 hours	Dedicated PTT line
(Belgium) (010 32) 2-2336737	Pay as you go	None	BF	English, French, Dutch and Multilingual	Monday to Friday	0900 to 1800	DCS and any interconnected data network
(FDR) (010 49) 89-43189682 89-43189683	Pay as you go	Initial registration fee DM 800 (Includes 2 day's training documentation etc.)	DM	English and German	6 days (closed Sunday)	0800 to 2200 (Monday to Friday) 0800-1200 (Saturday)	All public networks Datex-P and related networks. Gateway access to BRS information Technologies, USA.
(UK) 01-323 7070 Open 0900 to 1700 Monday to Friday	Mainly used as a sub-scription service with additional pay as you go charges. BLAISE-LINE card offers some free time for payment in advance	Annual subscription £55 (UK) £65 (overseas)	£ Sterling	Multilingual	Monday to Friday	0800 to 1900	PSS, IPSS JANET (The Joint Academic Network)

Host	User aids		Training		News letters	User guides and manuals	SDI Service
	On-line services	On-line news	Country	Charges			
BRS	CROS index file FILE database information file	"News"			BRS Bulletin (Every 2 months)	BRS System Reference Users Manual plus guides	Yes $4 plus off line docum charge royalty fee and postag
Business Direction (British Telecom)			UK (3 types of courses)	£50 per person/per half day)	No	Dow Jones User Manual £15. Business Direction User Manual £15.	No Consul service can cor searche client's behalf
Butterworth Telepublishing (Markets Mead's LEXIS service in the UK and Commonwealth except Canada)	Menu screen displays different libraries	No	UK (London)	£100 (2 half day sessions)	LEXIS Brief (3 times per Annum)	One free guide per user. Additional copies £5 each	No
Cedocar	No	No	France	FF 1400 (per 1½ days per person)	SIGNAL (4 issues per annum)	Lexique FF 1000	Yes (pr varies file)
Citiservice (Prestel)	Demonstration databases available	Prestel's "What's New" facility	N/A	N/A	Citiservice Update (Quarterly)	Manuals (free to members)	No
Commodity Systems Inc.	CSI Marstet database	No	No	N/A	CSI News Journal (Monthly)	Quicktrieve User's Manual (free with subscription to CSI Data Retrieval Service)	Yes
Compu-Mark	No	No	UK (on site)	Free	No	User guides (2 available for UK service) User manual for USA service (free)	No
Data-Star	CROSS Index file	NEWS database	USA and Europe	Available on request	Data-Star News (Monthly)	Business Manual, Chemical Manual, Biomedical Manual, System Reference Manual. Teach-Yourself Diskettes available	Yes (pr varies file)

Help desk contact number	Charging method	Other charges	Currency	Language	Days	Access Hours (local time)	Telecommunications networks & gateway services
(US) (010 1) 800-3454277	Subscription and pay as you go	$75 password fee (Open access plan) or Deposit (Advance purchase plan)	US $	English	7 days	24 hours	Telenet, Tymnet, Datapac, Direct Dial.
(UK) 01-822 1322 or 01-403 6777 (Telecom Gold)	Initial Subscription fee £25. (One-off) Pay as you go for each database	Annual subscription for Dow Jones News £30.	£ Sterling	English	7 days a week	24 hours	Access via Prestel or Telecom Gold. Gateway access to Dow Jones News/ Retrieval. (Note Telecom Gold acts as a gateway to a number of other business database services).
(UK) 01-405 1311 Open 0900 to 1800 Monday to Friday (Help desks in USA and France)	Subscription Minimum monthly commitment £350	Initial registration fee £350	£ Sterling	English (90%) French (10%)	7 days a week	0700 to 1845 (1200 to 1845 Sunday)	Mainly direct dial
No	Pay as you go	None	FF	French and English		0800 to 1830	Transpac, Teletel
(UK) 04862-27431	Subscription and pay as you go	Initial registration fee £42. Quarterly fee £42 (non-professionals £120 (professionals)	£ Sterling	English		24 hours	Prestel
(USA) (010 1) 407-3928663	Subscription	Initial account fee $150 (includes software)	US $	English	7 days a week	24 hours	Tymnet, Compunet, Telenet
(USA) (010 1) 202–7377900 (UK) 01-404 4963 (Belgium) (010 32) 3-2207211	Pay as you go	None (UK) $50 software fee (USA)	£ (UK) US $ (USA)	English	7 days a week	24 hours	PSS (UK), and direct dial for local users. Telenet (USA) and direct dial for local users
(USA) (010 1) 800-2217754 (UK) 01-930 5503 Help desk service offered by other contacts in Europe	Pay as you go	None	US $ (USA customers) SFr (ROW) Note: This situation may change in 1988/89	Mainly English	7 days a week	24 hours (closed 0430 to 0600 Mondays to Fridays. 0600 to 0900 Saturdays)	Gateway access to Fiz-Technik

| Host | User aids | | | | News letters | User guides and manuals | SDI Services |
| | On-line services | On-line news | Training | | | | |
			Country	Charges			
Datastream	Menu facilities. On-line HELP pages associated with each service/data base	Yes (Series of programmes provide news on services)	Training available in all countries where service is offered	Price included in cost of service	Datastream Focus. (Quarterly)	Guides and manuals provided for each service (Included in cost of service)	Yes
DIALOG	DIALINDEX (File 411) DIALOG ONE-SEARCH (Allows cross searching)	CHRONOLOG	Training available worldwide (details on request)	Prices available on request	CHRONOLOG Monthly DIALOG Europe News (Quarterly)	Complete Guide to searching DIALOG £55 Blue sheets £30	Yes (price varies by file and number offline prints request
ESA-IRS Dialtech	Questindex	"Flash" messages displayed	Training provided by National Centres	Prices available on request	IRS Dialtech Newsletter (UK). Issued every 2-3 months	Quest User Manual Quest Mini Manual Quest Pocket Guide	Yes (price varies by file
Dun & Bradstreet		Yes	Customer Relations Consultants available. Seminars run every year	Free	Credit News (Bi-monthly)	User guides (Free)	N/A
Edicline		CSTAIRS	UK Germany Switzerland Austria	£60 per person/per day	EDIC NEWS 5 issues per annum	Database description sheets	No
Extel	No	No	UK Micro EXSTAT Courses	£250 per person: 2 days basic. £350 per person: 2 days advanced.	Update. Image. IAS News. IDD News. Topic (Quarterly)	Exshare; Exbond IAS Exstat MicroExstat Tripos Price Plus (Free)	Yes (prices vary)
Financial Times	Help facility to access information on the database	Menu of new files	UK (London) France Switzerland Germany Belgium	£50 per person per day	No	PROFILE users guide. McCarthy users guide. Financial Times Business Reports Users Guide	No

Help desk contact number	Charging method	Other charges	Currency	Language	Days	Access Hours (local time)	Telecommunications networks & gateway services
(USA) (010 1) 212-5248400 (UK) 01-251 2540 (France) (010 33) 1-49019000 (Switzerland) (010 41) 1-2410580 (FDR) (010 49) 69-726480 (Netherlands) (010 31) 10-4246666	Majority of customers pay by subscription	None	According to country responsible for support	Mainly English	7 days a week	24 hours	Leased lines Direct dial up PSS/IPSS
(USA) (010 1) 415-8583810 (UK) 0865-730275 (France) (010 33) 1-43550202 Contact Béatrice Grenet	Majority pay as you go	Initial registration fee US $25	US $. Non US customers pay in local currency where DIALOG has a distributor	Mainly English	Monday to Saturday	24 hours	Dialnet ITT Worldcom, Tymnet, Telenet, PSS/IPSS PDN Gateway Services include Dialog Quotes and Trading The official Airlines Guide (OAG)
(USA) (010 1) 415-9482326 European Centres run own help desk 01-215 6578 6577 6582	Pay as you go	None	Local	English	Monday to Friday Sunday	0630 to 2130 0930 to 2130	PDN, ESANET - ESA's private network. INIS, AGRIS, Reuter's Textline, PROFILE Information "Two way" links with Pergaman Financial Data Services.
(International Desk) 01-377 4327 (UK Customer Services) 01-377 4377	Subscription and pay as you go combined	None	Local according to country responsible for providing support	Mainly English	Monday to Friday	0700 to 2100 (UK) 0800 to 2000 (USA)	DunsNet (D & B private network) DunsNet provides access to D & B worldwide offices and the Official Airlines Guide (OAG)
(UK) 0273-813238 Also services other European countries	Pay as you go	Initial registration fee £60	£ Sterling	English and German	6 days a week	0700 to 1900	All national networks e.g. PSS, Datex-P, Tymnet, Datapac, InfoNet
(USA) (010 1) 212-5131570 (UK and Europe) 01-253 2909	Subscription	Annual Service Charge	£ Sterling Exshare also payable in SFr or US $	English	Monday to Friday	0700 to 1900 (Examiner)	Price Plus access via BT's Telecom Gold Gateway Services: Extel Earnings Guide
(UK) 01-925 2323 (UK) 0932 761444	Subscription and pay as you go	Initial registration fee £110	£ Sterling	English French German	7 days a week	0000 to 2300 Monday to Friday 1000 to 2200 Saturday to Sunday	Telecom Gold

| Host | User aids | | Training | | News letters | User guides and manuals | SDI Services |
	On-line services	On-line news	Country	Charges			
G. CAM Serveur	CROS Database listing	No	France	FF 1000 per person/per day	G. CAM Actualité 4 to 5 issues per annum	Manuals and slides available. Details on request	No
GBI	No	No	No		No	Sudok– Handbuch (Free) Betriebswirts -chaftlicher Thesaurus DM60	No
GENIOS	Info-file	News Messages	Germany	DM 125 per person/per day	GENIOS Kunden- information 6 to 8 issues per annum	GENIOS– Leitfaden Manual DM125	Yes (pri vary per file)
GE-Information Services	QDATA SEARCH Module provides information on databases	QDATA NEWS	USA Canada (other countries on request)	US $100 per person/per day	QDATA NEWS QMOD NEWS (Monthly)	QMOD Data Book (5 volume set) US $25 per volume	
ICC	N/A	News Messages	UK (other countries on request)	2 free training places for new subscribers to Viewdata	ICC Database News (Quarterly)	"ICC on DIALOG". "ICC on Data-Star" £17.50 each. User manual included in initial fee to Viewdata	No
IDC	No	News Messages	USA Canada UK Belgium Germany Japan Hong Kong	US $1000– US $1500 per day/per instructor. (Maximum of 10 per class)	No	ANALYTICS Manual (2 volumes) Database and Systems Guide US $60	Yes (pri varies p service)

Help desk contact number	Charging method	Other charges	Currency	Language	Days	Access Hours (local time)	Telecommunications networks & gateway services
(France) (010 33) 1-45387072	Pay as you go	None	FF	Mainly French Some services in English	7 days a week	0800 to 2200	Transpac. Inet 2000 (Canada) and Easynet (USA)
(FDR) (010 49) 89-14482804	Pay as you go	None	DM	German	Monday to Friday	0830 to 1700	Datex-P
(FDR) (010 49) 211-8388184-188	Pay as you go	None	DM	German English	Monday to Friday (Sat/Sun unattended service)	0730 to 2200	All national networks PSS SNA, SNI 3270-standard Btx=Bildschirmtext (Videotext). Gateway access to PROFILE, VWD Cologne, Al Balyan Arab Information Bank), IP Sharp, JURIS, FIZ Karlsruhe/STN.
(USA–Haver Analytics) (010 1) 212-9869300 (GE-Information) (010 1) 800-6388730	Option of pay as you go or subscription. Monthly minimum $50	Initial fee for new clients US$ 150 (USA) Existing clients US $50	Local (via GE-Information) US$ (via Haver Analytics)	English	7 days a week	24 hours	GEISCO or via local public data networks if GEISCO does not have local access. UK: GEISCO or PSS
(USA) (010 1) 201-4550011 (UK) 01-250 3922 UK number applicable to other European users	Pay as you go	Initial registration fee £100 for Viewdata (includes training, manuals, support)	£ Sterling	English	7 days a week	24 hours	PSS Direct dial
(USA) (010 1) 617-8954444 Customer support. (010 1) 617-8608451 Data help (010 1) 212-3066666 IDSI Customer Service (UK) 01-583 0765 (GDR) (010 49) 69-253077 (Belgium) (010 32) 2-5116864 Other contact numbers for USA and the Far East available on request.	Subscription and pay as you go. Regular online time sharing is a subscription service. ISDI is pay as you go	Monthly service charge $150	Local	English	7 days a week	24 hours	IDCNET – IDC's private network. Telenet Tymnet Gateway access offered to WEFA

| Host | User aids | | Training | | News letters | User guides and manuals | SDI Service |
	On-line services	On-line news	Country	Charges			
IMPI	SOS retrieval software available	News Service	Spain (run monthly)	Free	No	Manual available for users of SIE databases (Business Information System) Free	No
Infocheck	No	No	UK	Free (1 day)	Infocheck Newsbrief (monthly)		No
Info Globe	No	Yes. Menu driven service	Canada USA	C$180 per day/per person	Info Globe News (Bi-monthly)	News Package. Financial Package C$75 each	No
IP Sharp	Type "help" and "describe" to access menus of available databases	Individual databases and retrieval software packages have own on-line news facilities	Worldwide (provided by local offices)	Prices vary. Certain courses are free	Aviation News. Economic News. Energy News. Financial News. (8 issues per annum)	Reference guides available for every data area (eg finance), user guides for individual databases. Manuals for software packages (usually free)	Yes. (Prices vary per databa.
Jordans	No	News on screen on recently published surveys	UK or via Pergamon	Direct access clients not usually charged	Jordan Information Review (Quarterly)	Manuals for direct access clients and via Pergamon	Yes (via Pergam
Lotus Development	Menu Structure	Product News available as a menu option	Europe	2 days free with each subscription	No	Manuals provided for all data services and software (free)	No
MAID	No	News up-dates sent to customers	UK (London) USA (New York) France (Paris) Italy (Rome) Turkey Israel Portugal Spain Netherlands Belgium Denmark	Free	Report Update (Weekly)	Reference manual. User manual (Free)	No

Help desk contact number	Charging method	Other charges	Currency	Language	Access Days	Hours (local time)	Telecommunications networks & gateway services
(010 34) 91-2703302 for Spanish users only	Services are free. Users are selected according to certain criteria. (Contact IMP direct for details)	None	Ptas	Spanish	Monday to Friday	0900 to 1900 0900 to 1500 (Friday)	RTC Iberpac X.25
(UK) 01-377-8872	Subscription or pay as you go		£ Sterling	English	7 days a week	24 hours	Service can be accessed via:- Mercury Telecom Gold Kompass PROFILE Prestel Infotap
(USA) (010 1) 416-5855250	Pay as you go	Initial Registration fee C$349	C$	English	7 days a week	24 hours	Datapac Tymnet Telenet
(USA) (010 1) 800-3871558 (UK) 01-222-7033 Rest of Europe can contact their local branch or the London office.	Pay as you go	None	Local	English (some databases offer access in French or German)	7 days a week	24 hours (2 hours down time on Sunday)	IPSANET – IP Sharp's private network. PSS Austpac Maypac Datanet 1 Pacnet Datapac Telenet Datapak Telepac Datex-P Transpac DCS Tymnet Eirpac Gateway access to Dow Jones News/ Retrieval. Official Airlines Guide (OAG). (Further Services to be added in the future)
(USA) (010 1) 617-5778500 (UK) 01-253 3030 Direct Access	Pay as you go	None	£ Sterling	English	7 days a week		PDN
(USA) (010 1) 617-5778500 (UK and Europe) 0753-840281	Subscription	None	Local	English		24 hours	N/A
(USA) (010 1) 212-2453513 (UK) 01-935 6460	Subscription plus pay as you go. £4,250 p.a.	None	£ Sterling or US $	English	7 days a week	24 hours	PSS/IPSS

| Host | User aids | | Training | | News letters | User guides and manuals | SDI Service |
	On-line services	On-line news	Country	Charges			
MEAD	No	Banner Page 'Practice Library'	UK USA	US$75 per person/per day (London)	NEXIS Newsbrief (Monthly)	Reference Guide and Library Contents (free)	No
OR Telematique	On-line help facility	Yes	France	Free	Available in the near future	User Guide (free)	Yes (p varies file)
ORBIT	Database Index File DBI. Master index to all ORBIT data bases.	NEWSDOC Service	Europe	Prices available on request	Searchlight (Monthly)	ORBIT user guide US$55 Quick Reference Guide US$35 Database manuals US$15 Workbook US$115	Yes (p varies file)
Pera Otis	No	No	UK	Free half day	No	OTISLINE User manual	Curre aware servic
Pergamon	No	? News Command	UK	£90 + VAT	Update (Quarterly)	Manuals available	Yes (price vary)
PROFILE	Menu Service 22 'file groups'. On-line details of each file content	Banner messages	UK (London)	£50 + VAT per half day	Offline (Quarterly)	User Guides Training Disks	No
Telekurs	Help facilities available	Enquiry service available on line	Any country where Telekurs is represented	Costs included in system costs	No	Manuals provided free	No
Textline		News page	UK	1 day free of charge	Keywords (Quarterly)	SIC Code books. User Guides. Total Cost £50	No
Telesystems – Questel	List of databases available	Messages	Europe	Prices on request	Questel Actualities. Questel-a-Gram. (4 issues per annum)	Questel plus Manual Service plus Specialist database documentation	Yes (price vary)

Help desk contact number	Charging method	Other charges	Currency	Language	Days	Access Hours (local time)	Telecommunications networks & gateway services
(USA) (010 1) 513-8656999 (UK) 01-488 9187 UK number also covers Europe	Subscription and pay as you go	Initial registration fee US$200	US $	English	7 days a week	0710 to 1900	Access via any 1200/1200 or 1200/75 Service
(France) (010 33) 47-525184	Subscription only FF 1350 per database		FF	French (multi-lingual services in the near future)	7 days a week	24 hours	Transpac Vidéotex – Teletel
(UK) 01-993 7334 (GDR) (010 49) 6173-63025 (France) (010 33) 91-029094	Pay as you go	None	US $ (French or German users can pay in FF or DM)	English	7 days a week	24 hours Monday to Friday (except 2145 to 2215) Saturday 0000 to 1600 Sunday 1600 to 0000	Tymnet Telenet Available via PSS in near future (1988)
0664-501501 ex 548	Subscription Service	£250 + VAT per annum (Total charges)	£ Sterling	English	Monday to Friday	0830 to 1630	PSTN
01-993 7333	Pay as you go (Subscription service available if requested).	No	US $ (USA) £ Sterling (ROW)	English	Monday to Friday	24 hours	PSS, IPSS Telenet, Tymnet. Most European public networks. Gateway access to ESA-IRS; The Official Airlines Guide (OAG)
0932-787231	Mainly pay as you go	Initial Registration Fee £110	£ Sterling US $ FF	English	7 days a week	23 hours a day (Monday to Friday) 1000 to 2200 Saturday 1000 to 0000 Sunday	Datapac, Datapak, Datex-P, DCS, Iberpac, IPSS, Luxpac, PSS, Telenet, Transnet Transpac, Tymnet
(UK) 01-404 4575 (USA) (010 1) 203-3538100 (Zurich) (010 41) 1-428010	Subscription service only	For certain services	£ (UK) or local currency	National language (option of English, French, German, Italian)	7 days a week	24 hours	Access via Telekurs own network utilising Tandem and Siemens computers.
(UK) 01-324 7563 (USA) (010 1) 800-4249600	Subscription and pay as you go	No	Local currency	English	7 days a week	24 hours	PSS Direct Dial ESA-IRS offer gateway access to Textline
(UK) 0625-876711 (Rest of Europe) (010 33) 1-45826464 (USA) (010 1) 800-4249600	Pay as you go	US$115 initial fee	FF (France) US$ (ROW)	French	7 days a week	0230 to 0030	Any network linking up to Transpac i.e. IPSS, Datex-P, Telenet, Tymnet, etc.

6 On-line Databases – Descriptions

Section I Company Financial and Profile Information

International
D&B International Dun's
Market Identifiers
Dataline Service
Datastream Company
Accounts Service
Dunsdata
Dunsprint
Exchange (Mead service)
Exstat
Financial Times Company
Abstracts
Global Report
Investext
McCarthy Online Company
Fact Sheets
McCarthy Online Press Cut-
ting Service
Microexstat
Moody's Corporate News –
International
PTS F&S Indexes
PTS Promt
Textline (Service)
Who Owns Whom
Worldscope

Europe
ABC Europe
Dataline Service
Datastream Company
Accounts Service
Dunsdata
Dunsprint
European Kompass Online
Investext
Kompass Online Scandinavia
McCarthy Online Company
Factsheets
McCarthy Online Press Cut-
ting Service
Moody's Corporate News In-
ternational
PTS Promt
Who Owns Whom
Worldscope

Austria
Hoppenstedt Austria

Belgium
D&B International Dun's
Market Identifiers
Dataline Service
Dunsprint
European Kompass Online
Investext
PTS Promt
Societe Generale De Banque
(see Economics Section)
Who Owns Whom
Worldscope

Denmark
D&B International Dun's
Market Identifiers
Dataline Service
European Kompass Online
Kompass Online Scandinavia
PTS Promt
Soliditet Online Service (SOS)
Telecom
Who Owns Whom
Worldscope

Finland
Dataline Service
Datastream Company
Accounts Service
European Kompass Online
Investext
Textline (abstracts from 4 Fin-
nish publications)
Worldscope

France
Adelin
Bodacc (see Overseas Trade
Opportunities Section)
Bottin des Enterprises
Centrale des Portefeuilles
CJTRES
D&B Dun's France Marketing
D&B International Dun's
Market Identifiers
Dataline Service
Datastream Company
Accounts Service
Defotel

Delphes
Dunsprint
EAE
European Kompass Online
Essor
Firmexport
INPI STE 3
Investext
Liens Financiers
PTS Promt
Qui Decide en France
Sirene
Tele Inform
Telefirm
Who Owns Whom
Worldscope

Germany, Federal Republic of
ABC
ABC Europe
BDI-German Industry
Company Facts and
Addresses
D&B International Dun's
Market Identifiers
Dataline Service
Datastream Company
Accounts Service
Dunsprint
Einkaufs – 1*1
European Kompass Online
FINF – Numeric
FINF – Text
Firmen Info Bank
Hoppenstedt Directory of
German Companies
Investext
PTS Promt
Verband der Vereine Credit-
reform EV
Who Makes Machinery
Who Owns Whom
Who Supplies What
Worldscope
ZVEI – Electro Buying Guide

Greece
D&B Dun's International
Market Identifiers
PTS Promt
Who Owns Whom

Ireland, Republic of
Dataline Service
Dunsprint
ICC British Company
Datasheets
Irish Company Profiles
PTS Promt
Who Owns Whom

Italy
D&B International Dun's
Market Identifiers
Dataline
Dati Anagraphici di Impresse
Italiane
Dati Anagraphici di Impresse
Lombarde
DEA
Dunsprint
European Kompass Online
Investext
PTS Promt
SANI
SANP
SDOE
SIBIL
Who Owns Whom
Worldscope

Luxembourg
Dataline Service
European Kompass Online
PTS Promt
Who Owns Whom

Netherland
D&B International Dun's
Market Identifiers
Dataline Service
Datastream Company
Accounts Service
Dunsprint
European Kompass Online
Hoppendstedt Netherlands
Nexis (Dutch analysts) Ser-
vice (see Marketing Section)
PTS Promt
Who Owns Whom
Worldscope

Norway
Dataline
European Kompass Online
Kompass Online Scandinavia
Textline (includes abstracts
from 2 Norwegian publica-
tions)
Worldscope

Portugal
D&B International Dun's
Market Identifiers
Dunsprint
PTS Promt
Textline
Who Owns Whom

Spain
Camerdata
D&B International Dun's
Market Identifiers
Dataline
Directorio de Empresas In-
dustriales
Dunsprint
Empresas
European Kompass Online
Investext
Oferes
PTS Promt
Registro de Establecimientos
Industriales
Sistema de Informacion Bur-
satil
SYCE
Who Owns Whom
Worldscope

Sweden
AktieInformation (see Secur-
ities Section)
Dataline Service
European Kompass Online
Findata
Investext
Kompass Online Scandinavia
Stor-Tele
Sveriges Handelskalander
Textline (includes abstracts
from 5 Swedish publications)
Worldscope

UK
Dataline Service
Datastream Company
Accounts Service
Dun's Market Identifiers
Dunsprint
Exstat
Financial Times Company In-
formation
ICC British Company Direc-
tory
ICC British Company Finan-
cial Datasheets
ICC Full Text Company
Accounts
ICC Industrial Averages
ICC Sharewatch
ICC Stockbroker Research

ICC Viewdata Service
Infocheck
Industrial Market Location
Investext
Irish Company Profiles
Jordanwatch
Jordans Direct
Key British Enterprises
Kompass Online
McCarthy Online Company
Fact Sheets
McCarthy Online Press Cut-
ting Service
Microexstat
UK Company Profile
Who Owns Whom

Non-European Countries

USA

Public Companies
Compustat
Compustat Telecommunica-
tions (see Compustat)
Compustat Utility (see Com-
pustat)
Corporate and Industry
Analyst Research Reports
(CIRR)
Datastream Company
Accounts Service
Disclosure
Disclosure/Spectrum Own-
ership
Exchange (see Mead Service)
Global Report (see Marketing
Section)
Investext
Media General Plus
Moody's Corporate News
Moody's Corporate Profiles
NAARS (Mead Service)
PTS Annual Reports Ab-
stracts
PTS F&S Indexes
Standard & Poors – Corporate
Descriptions
Standard & Poors – News
Standard & Poors (S&P)
Marketscope
Value Line Data Base-11
Worldscope

Corporate Directories
Corporate Affiliations
D&B Dun's Financial Records
D&B Dun's Market Identifiers
D&B Million Dollar Directory
Dun's Electronic Yellow
Pages Construction

Financial
Manufacturers
Professionals
Retailers
Services
Wholesalers
Standard & Poor's Register
Corporate
Thomas Regional Industrial
Suppliers
Thomas Register Online
Trinet Company Database
Trinet Establishment Database

Australia and New Zealand

Ausinet Statex
Dunsprint
Textline (includes 3 news
sources)
Worldscope

Canada

Canadian Business and Current Affairs (see News Section)
Canadian Financial Database
Compustat
Corporate and Industry Research Reports (CIRR)
D&B Canadian Dun's Market
Identifiers
Dataline Service
Financial Post Canad ian
Corporate Database
ICC Canadian Corporations
Investext
PTS Promt
Report on Business Corporate
Database
Who Owns Whom
Worldscope

Japan

Asian Wall Street Journal (see
Textline)
Asahi News Service (see
News Section)
Dataline Service
Datastream Company
Accounts Service
Global Report (see Marketing
Section)
Investext
Japan Economic Newswire
Plus (see Economics Section)
Japan Technology (see Industry Section)
Japan Times (see Textline)
Jiji Press (see Textline)
Kyodo News (see Japan Economic Newswire Plus)
Nikkei Telecom (see Economics Section)
PTS Promt
Worldscope

India

Business Standard (see Textline)
Business World (see Textline)
Economic Times (see Textline)
Global Report (see Marketing
Section)
Investext
Times of India (see Textline)
Worldscope

Far East Other Countries

Asian Wall Street Journal (see
Textline)
Business Times (Malaysia)
(see Textline)
Business Times (Singapore)
(see Textline)

Datastream Company
Accounts Services
Far East Economic Review
(see Textline)
Global Report (see Marketing
Section)
Investext
Needs-TS (see Economics Section)
Textline
Worldscope (Hong Kong,
Malaysia, Singapore, South
Korea)

Middle East & Gulf

Arab News (see Textline)
Arab Times (see Textline)
Gulf Times (see Textline)
Mideast (see Economics Section)
Saudi Business (see Textline)
Worldscope

Africa

Textline (includes 7 news
sources)

Central and South America

Textline (includes 8 news
sources)

Australia and New Zealand

Dunsprint
Textline (includes 3 news
sources)
Worldscope

Name:	ABC
Description:	This is the on-line version of the four-language buyers' guide 'ABC-Quellenwerk fur Einkauf-Verkauf'. It contains entries for manufacturers and their products in the Federal Republic of Germany. It also contains comprehensive company information.
Language:	File ABCD is the German version File ABCE is the English version
Source:	Equivalent to the printed version
Years Covered:	Latest available
File Size:	76 000 records
Updates:	Company data: every 2 years Other data: annual
Database Producer:	ABC der Deutschen Wirtschaft Verlagsgesellschaft mbH

Available From:	FIZ Technik File ABCD and ABCE
	DM 250 per connect hour
	DM 2.3 per on-line type
	DM 2.6 per off-line print
	DM 1.3 for company address and telecom information only
	Data-Star File ABCE
	Contact direct for prices (new file)

Name:	ABC Europe
Description:	This database covers the European export industry. It contains references to products manufactured and offered for sale by about 149 000 companies in 32 European countries. Records relating to German companies (about 50 per cent) are identical with those compiled in database ABCE.
Source:	Equivalent to printed buyers' guides 'ABC der Deutschen Wirtschaft' and 'ABC Europ Production'
Years Covered:	Latest available
File Size:	149 000 records
Updates:	Quarterly
Database Producer:	ABC der Deutschen Wirtschaft Verlagsgesellschaft mbH and Europ Export Edition GmbH
Available From:	FIZ Technik File EURD
	DM 250 per connect hour
	DM 2.3 per on-line type
	DM 2.6 per off-line print
	DM 1.3 for company address and telecom information only
	Data-Star File EURO
	Contact direct for prices (new file)

Name:	Adelin
Description:	Adelin is one of the major French company databases. It provides details of the principal shareholders of major French companies and traces companies' links with subsidiaries and affiliates. Direct shareholders consist of 36 000 participants with a holding exceeding 1 per cent of the total equity capital. Indirect shareholders consist of approximately 35 000 participants who own over 10 per cent of the equity. 35 000 direct subsidiaries are listed and 26 000 firms where the main companies have an indirect shareholding.
	The total of 63 000 companies listed on this database is expected to increase to 80 000 over the next few months. It has been described by French researchers as providing accurate details and useful information on changes in the shareholders of French companies.
Source:	Equivalent to the directory 'Liaisons Financieres' produced by Dafsa-Kompass
Years Covered:	Latest available information and 5 years historic information
File Size:	36 000 direct shareholders, 35 000 indirect shareholders
Updates:	
Database Producer:	DAFSA
Available From:	DAFSA

Name:	Ausinet Statex
Description:	Ausinet Statex provides financial data on companies listed on the Sydney Stock Exchange.
Source:	Sydney Stock Exchange
Years Covered:	Current
File Size:	
Updates:	Daily
Database Producer:	ACI Computer Services
Available From:	ACI Computer Services
	A$40 per month fee
	A$150 per connect hour (share prices and financials)
	A$250 per connect hour (inquiry and analysis)

Name:	BDI-German Industry
Description:	The BDI-German Industry database is the online version of the universally known business address book 'Die Deutsche Industrie – Made in Germany'. The databank contains around 90 000 product terms and supply sources from nearly 20 000 export-oriented industrial companies in the capital goods and consumer goods industry. Details provided are company name, address and telecommunication details. Information is provided on shareholders, ownership structure and the history of the company. This information will allow you to construct a reasonably comprehensive company profile.
Language:	German
Source:	Information and reference work 'BDI-Die Deutsche Industrie / Made in Germany'
Years Covered:	Current
File Size:	Around 90 000 supply sources from approximately 20 000 companies, divided up into more than 9500 product groups (specific nomenclature)
Updates:	Currently once a year
Database Producer:	Verlag W Sachon GmbH & Co
Available From:	GENIOS File BDI
	DM 234 per connect hour
	DM 2.2 per on-line type
	DM 2.7 per off-line print
	FIZ Technik File BDID (German version)
	File BDIE (English version)
	DM 250 per connect hour
	DM 2.8 per on-line type
	DM 3.1 per off-line print
	DM 1.3 for company address and telecom information only
	Data-Star File BDIE
	Contact direct for prices (new file)

Name:	Bottin des Enterprises
Description:	Covers 350 000 French firms. Provides the following details: addresses, telephone numbers, principal executives, lines of business and names of affiliates.
Source:	Company reports
Years Covered:	
File Size:	350 000 companies
Updates:	
Database Producer:	Valscop-Duplex
Available From:	Valscop-Duplex

Name:	Camerdata
Description:	Camerdata provides basic details on approximately 1.8 million Spanish companies. Details include addresses, number of employees and line of business (4-6 digit activity codes are used). Other useful facts include the company's legal form, and the sales turnover figure for larger companies. Recently data has been added on foreign trade, so you can identify what companies export to what countries, the value and type of goods. The CCCN system is used for goods coding. This service is not directly accessible by end users but the searches are carried out on your behalf by Camerdata. Especiales Service provides mailing lists extracted from the database by user-defined criteria. Suscripciones Service provides companies selected by users' own criteria on magnetic tape or floppy disc. Updates are then supplied at regular intervals.
Source:	Data gathered by 85 local Chambers of Commerce
Years Covered:	Latest available data
File Size:	Approximately 1.8 million companies
Updates:	Annual (Camerdata)
	Continuous (Chambers of Commerce)
Database Producer:	Camerdata

Available From:	Camerdata
	Especiales Service:
	Pts 8 per address
	Pts 1 extra charge per address supplied on a sticker
	Suscripciones Service:
	Varies according to volume of information supplied

Name:	Canadian Financial Database
Description:	This database provides the full text of financial statements from major Canadian publicly held corporations and crown corporations. It enables users to check for dividends per share and earnings per share, compare the results of companies to industry standards and study the reporting patterns for the translation of foreign currency, extraordinary items, etc.
Source:	Company accounts
Years Covered:	Latest data available
File Size:	
Updates:	Annual
Database Producer:	
Available From:	Info Globe
	$349 initiation fee
	$240 per connect hour
	0.10c per key item
	0.02c per off-line print (per line)

Name:	Centrale des Portefeuilles
Description:	This database covers information on investment in French institutions. It includes the value of transferable securities, lists of shareholders and the amount of stock market capital for each institution.
Source:	
Years Covered:	
File Size:	160 000 references
Updates:	Quarterly
Database Producer:	Societe de Etudes pour le Developpement Economique et Social (SEDES)
Available From:	DAFSA
	FININFO

Name:	CJTRES
Description:	The focus of this database is on earnings data from over 4000 French industrial companies. It also provides aggregated statistics on 90 industrial sectors. Data is taken from surveys conducted every six months by the National Statistical Office.
Source:	Institut Nationale de la Statistique et des Etudes Economiques (INSEE)
Years Covered:	1967 to date
File Size:	Covers approximately 4000 companies and 90 industrial sectors
Updates:	Every 6 months
Database Producer:	INSEE
Available From:	GSI ECO

Name:	Company Facts and Address
Description:	This database covers the travel industry in the Federal Republic of Germany. It contains information on 850 companies in the tourism industry and provides details on turnover, annual report data, management, address, details of incorporations and other statistical data. The German title of this database is Firmeninformationen.
Language:	English and German
Source:	Earning reports and studies
Years Covered:	1984 to date (current information)
File Size:	2300 citations
Updates:	Twice a year
	1000 citations added per annum
Database Producer:	Edicline (UK)
Available From:	Edicline File COAD
	£60 per connect hour

Name: Compustat
Description: Compustat databases provide financial, statistical and market information
                         for different groups of U.S. publicly quoted companies. The different
                         databases are as follows:
                         Compustat Utility Data Base
                         Compustat Telecommunications
                         Compustat Business Information
                         Compustat Industrial Data Base – includes the primary, supplementary,
                         tertiary and aggregate files, Canadian, OTC and full coverage files.
Source: Annual reports filed with the SEC plus other company financial statements
Years Covered: Maximum 20 years of annual data, 48 quarters of quarterly data
File Size: Varies with each database
Updates: Varies with each database, generally weekly
Database Producer: Standard & Poor's Compustat Services Inc
Available From: Interactive Data Corporation (IDC)
                         Annual Compustat subscription fees are billed by Standard & Poor's
                         Compustat Services.
                         Compustat data accessed in timesharing is surcharged on a sliding scale, in
                         addition to Analytics sliding scale.
                         Analytics charges:
                         $250 per month plus sliding scale per access fee on a monthly basis
                         First 25 000 hits 7c per hit
                         Next 100 000 hits 5c per hit
                         Additional hits 2c per hit
                         Surcharges:
                         $50 monthly base charge plus sliding scale per access fee

Name: Corporate Affiliations
Description: This database is the on-line equivalent to the printed 'Directory of
                         Corporate Affiliations'. It is a company directory of corporate family
                         linkage. Each parent company record contains the complete corporate
                         family tree. Each affiliate company record contains the portion of the
                         corporate family tree in which that particular company fits. Key
                         information includes: company name, address and telephone number;
                         ticker symbol and stock exchange; up to 20 Standard Industrial
                         Classification (SIC) codes and descriptions; number of employees; total
                         assets; sales; net worth; names of executives and board of directors; and
                         corporate family hierarchy.
Source: Corresponds to the publication 'Directory of Corporate Affiliations'
Years Covered: Current
File Size: 42 500 records
Updates: Quarterly reloads
Database Producer: National Register Publishing Company
Available From: DIALOG File 513
                         $84 per connect hour
                         $1.25 per on-line type
                         $1.25 per off-line print
                         10c per report element
                         15c per mailing label (format 10)

Name: Corporate and Industry Research Reports Online Index
Description: CIRR provides access to company and industry research reports issued by
                         major USA and Canadian securities and institutional investment firms.
                         Reports analyse over 8000 publicly quoted companies and provide financial
                         information, charts, tables, etc. It also includes 350 special reports and a
                         special feature is the provision of research from the New York Society of
                         Security Analysis. Full text of all the reports covered are available on
                         microfiche from the producer.
Source: USA and Canadian securities and investment firms
Years Covered: 1982 to date
File Size: 8000 companies

Updates: Quarterly
Database Producer: J A Micropublishing Inc
Available From: BRS File CIRR
                       $57 per connect hour
                       94c per on-line type
                       89c per off-line print
                       SDI profile: $4

Name:	D&B – Canadian Dun's Market Identifiers
Description:	This database contains address, financial and marketing data on over 350 000 Canadian public and private companies.
Source:	Dun & Bradstreet
Years Covered:	Current
File Size:	372 766 records
Updates:	Quarterly reloads
Database Producer:	Dun & Bradstreet Canada Ltd
Available From:	DIALOG File 520
	$100 per connect hour
	$2 per on-line type
	$2 per off-line print

Name:	D&B Dun's Financial Records
Description:	Dun's Financial Records contain comprehensive financial information, company history and operations information on over 700 000 US companies and establishments. Information includes up to three years of accounts and key ratios on each company. Companies included are both private and public. A company's financial position may be compared to others in the same industry as determined by industry norm percentages.
Source:	Data is generated from D & B's information on more than 6 million companies and is the same as the data used in the Dun's Market Identifiers database (DIALOG file 516)
Years Covered:	Current data (up to 3 years historical)
File Size:	732 499 records
Updates:	Quarterly reloads
Database Producer:	Dun's Marketing Service
Available From:	DIALOG File 519 (see also File 516)
	$135 per connect hour
	$85 per on-line type
	$85 per off-line print

Name:	D&B Dun's France Marketing
Description:	This is a directory of 200 000 French companies in all sectors which have a minimum of 10 employees or a minimum annual turnover of 10 million French francs. It provides details of turnover, staff numbers, activity, SIC code, names and job titles of managers, address, parent company, legal status, year established and Dun's identifying number.
Source:	Based partially on France 30 000 Dun and Bradstreet directory
Years Covered:	
File Size:	200 000 companies
Updates:	Annual
Database Producer:	Dun and Bradstreet France
Available From:	Telesystemes-Questel File DBFM
	$92 per connect hour
	46c per on-line type
	$1.23 per off-line print

Name: D&B International Dun's Market Identifiers
Description: This database contains directory listings, supplemented with sales volume and marketing data, as well as references to parent companies, for over 500 000 leading public and private companies in 133 countries (other than the US) around the world. Companies are selected for inclusion based on size as determined by annual sales volume, national prominence and international interest (eg trading position etc). Names, addresses, SIC codes, annual sales, number of employees, type of company, Duns number, parent company and other related information is provided for each company listing.
Source: Company accounts reports and details provided by companies to D & B
Years Covered: Current data
File Size: 475 307 records
Updates: Quarterly reloads
Database Producer: Dun's Marketing Services
Available From: DIALOG File 518
                               $100 per connect hour
                               $2 per on-line type
                               $2 per off-line print

Name: D&B Dun's Market Identifiers
Description: The D&B Dun's Market Identifiers presents detailed information on more than two million US business establishments which have 10 or more employees or more than $1 million in sales. In addition D&B Dun's Market Identifiers contains records of all the establishments in the corporate family of the firms with 10 or more employees even though companies themselves may have fewer than 10 employees. D&B Dun's Market Identifiers contains current address, product, financial and marketing information for each company. Comprehensive financial information is provided for approximately 700 000 of the 2 million companies on the database. Both public and private companies are included as well as all types of commercial and industrial establishments and all product areas.
Source: Based partially on the 'Principal International Businesses' Directory'
Years Covered: Current data (up to 3 years historical data)
File Size: Approximately 2 million records
Updates: Quarterly reloads
Database Producer: Dun's Marketing Services
Available From: DIALOG File 516
                               $100 per connect hour
                               $2.5 per on-line type
                               $2.5 per off-line print
                               Pergamon Financial
                               See Dun's Market Identifiers (covers UK only)

Name: D&B Million Dollar Directory
Description: The D&B Million Dollar Directory comprises comprehensive business information on 160 000 US companies from the three-volume 'Million Dollar Directory' series. Listings are limited to companies with a net worth of half a million dollars or more and include hard to find information on businesses which are privately held as well as publicly owned companies. These business establishments may be headquarters, subsidiaries or single locations. Records contain address including country and SMSA primary and secondary SIC codes, annual sales, and number of employees. Also included are the names of individuals holding positions in 25 executive function areas, stock exchanges and the ticker symbol for public companies that import and/or export.
Source: D&B 'Million Dollar Directory'
Years Covered: Current
File Size: Approx 160 000 records as of 1987
Updates: The file is reloaded annually with current information
Database Producer: Dun's Marketing Services

Available From: DIALOG File 517
$100 per connect hour
$2 per on-line type
$2 per off-line print
Name:

Name: Dataline (Textline Service)
Description: Dataline is a company financial data and forecasting facility available
through the Textline Service. The Dataline service is divided into three
main subsections: Dataline 1, 2 and 3. Dataline 1 provides access to a large
database of company accounts displaying up to 5 years' history of financial
statements. The information is in a standardised, structured format at three
alternative levels of detail and comprises: income statement, balance
sheets, finance table and accounting ratios. (You can choose to access all of
these records.)

For companies with full accounts information disclosure, the service also
provides a sophisticated financial modelling system (Dataline 2 and
Dataline 3) that enables detailed forecasts to be derived from the projection
of key variables. Dataline 2 is an internally generated forecast, whereas
Dataline 3 is a user generated forecast that enables assumptions generated
by the user to be combined with the relationships established by the model.

The information on Dataline is based on well over 3000 trading
companies drawn from an international list and including leading concerns
in:

Australia	Ireland, Rep of	New Zealand
Austria	Italy	Norway
Belgium	Japan	Spain
Denmark	Luxembourg	Sweden
Finland	Netherlands	Switzerland
France	United Kingdom	
Germany, Federal Republic of		

Of the 3000 companies listed, 1500 are UK quoted, 500 UK unquoted, and
700 are international. The 5-year forecast facility is available for most UK
quoted companies.

The user is guided through the searches by a series of multiple choice
prompts.

Source: Information is derived from the EXSTAT database, a product of the Extel
Group Ltd
Years Covered: Last 5 years
File Size: 3000 companies
Updates: Weekly
Database Producer: Reuters
Available From: Reuters
£75 per connect hour
30p per on-line type
(10p per title 20p per abstract)
ESA-IRS File 21
£94.51 per connect hour
Printing charges are format dependant
Use ? Charges on line for price list

Name: Datastream Company Accounts Services
Description: UK:
Data is held on all UK quoted industrial companies, all UK major financial
companies, all USM quoted companies and 500 of the largest unquoted UK
companies (third market) and non-UK-owned subsidiaries. Additionally
there are presently company accounts on 83 000 UK unquoted companies
on the ICC files and this number is expanding.

Programs allow the display of financial figures for up to 5 years and
include:
Program 190 (191 for unquoted companies)

Profit and loss accounts
Balance sheet
Financing table
Accounting ratios
Company profile
   Facility to create and store own formats or expressions (eg can create own definition of accounting ratios, etc using Programme 300)
Program 130:
Shareholdings of over 5 per cent of the equity of the UK quoted companies
Directors shareholdings
Facilities are available to customers to enable them to:
carry out searches (programs 73 to 78 and 90)
conduct company performance comparisons (program 190V)
use graphics to present company accounts data (program 401)
look at z-scores on UK industrial companies (program 192)
obtain general financial news on companies (program 99A-H)
create own list of companies (program 80A)
International:
Databases cover those companies whose stocks are relatively heavily traded, although it may extend to over-the-counter companies eventually. Company accounts are available for companies in the following countries:

USA	Netherlands
Japan	France
Canada	Sweden
Germany,	Australia
Federal Republic of	Norway
By the end of 1988:	
Switzerland	Italy
Belgium	Norway
Denmark	Spain
Hong Kong	

The actual companies and countries covered is flexible, according to customer requirements. International company accounts are provided in the 190 series of programs. An international News Service is available in the company accounts program 99Z.

Source:	Filed accounts
	Annual reports
Years Covered:	Starting from 1968
File Size:	Variable
Updates:	As results published
Database Producer:	Datastream
Available From:	Datastream
	Prices vary according to services required
	Price guide
	Business research service (dial up):
	£750 per annum
	Extra charges for each access
	Company Watch Service:
	£9550 per annum
	No extra charges for programs except the ICC company accounts (191) program where usage is metered

Name:	Dati Anagraphici di Impresse Lombarde
Description:	This database provides basic information on over 14000 industrial companies in Milan and other parts of the Lombardy region. Information includes: addresses of company headquarters and branches, date incorporated, legal form, nominal capital, number of employees, products manufactured, trademarks, patents held and countries which the company trades with.

Language: Italian
Source:
Years Covered: Current
File Size: 14 000 companies
Updates:
Database Producer: Assolombardo
Available From: SIRIO

Name: Dati Avagraphici di Imprese Italiane
Description: This database provides basic details on over 350 000 Italian firms. The
                   following details are provided: company address, date incorporated, legal
                   form, number of employees and codes showing the type of products
                   manufactured.
Language: Italian
Source: Company reports and accounts
Years Covered: Latest available information
File Size: 350 000 companies
Updates:
Database Producer: Confindustria
Available From: GIANO

Name: DEA
Description: DEA provides on-line news provided by ANSA, Italy's leading news
                   agency. This database provides news on company events such as
                   purchases, disposals and press releases on annual balance sheets. Full text
                   news and abstracts are available from 1982 and abstracts only are available
                   from 1975 to 1982.
Langauge: Italian
Source: ANSA new items from Italy and the rest of the world
Years Covered: January 1975 to 1982 (abstracts only)
                   1982 to date (full text and abstracts)
File Size: Over 1 350 000 citations
Updates: Daily (with approximately 450 news items)
Database Producer: ANSA
Available From: Cerved File DEA
                   Lire 146 000 per connect hour

Name: Defotel
Description: Defotel is one of the most important company databases in France. It
                   provides information on all the companies quoted on the Paris Stock
                   Exchange plus approximately 400 unlisted companies. For each company
                   the following information is provided:
                   Financial performance and stock exchange figures
                   Accounts, including profits over the past 2 years
                   Companies' legal form
                   Details of changes in the company's capital since 1960
                   Bonds, stocks
                   Addresses, subsidiaries
                   Names of auditors
                   Products and services
                   Board members
Language: French
Source: Paris Stock Exchange
                   Company financial statements
Years Covered: 6 years' historic data for Stock Exchange
                   2 years' historic data for accounts
File Size: Over 1500 companies in total
Updates: As relevant information becomes available
Database Producer: Cote Desfosses

Available From:	Telesystemes-Questel File Defotel
	$85 per connect hour
	$1.23 per on-line type
	$7.70 per off-line print

Name:	Delphes
Description:	This database is a very important source of information covering press releases on all French companies. It also covers news items on industry sectors and products both in France and overseas. Delphes can be searched using free text, using the name of a company, product, industry sector, country or other terms.
Source:	Over 1000 French and foreign periodicals are searched on a regular basis and articles entered into the database.
Years Covered:	1975 to date
File Size:	Over 300 000 bibliographic citations
Updates:	Weekly
Database Producer:	Chambre de Commerce et d'Industrie de Paris (Paris Chamber of Commerce and Industry) Co-produced by a number of other Chambers of Commerce and organisations in France.
Available From:	Chambre de Commerce et d'Industrie de Paris (CCIP) (Paris Chamber of Commerce and Industry) FF 600 per connect hour G CAM Serveur FF 600 per connect hour Access available via Minitel in France. Contact the CCIP for a list of the other databases which they produce and distribute, and for a list of Les Centres Relais Telematiques de la CCIP-who can access these databases on your behalf.

Name:	Directorio de Empresas Industriales
Description:	This database is a directory of Spanish companies. It contains basic details such as address, location, and number of employees.
Source:	Tax licences
Years Covered:	Updated to 1986
File Size:	555 000 documents
Updates:	Periodically
Database Producer:	Sistema de Informacion Empresarial
Available From:	Instituto de la Pequena y Mediana Empresa Industrial (IMPI) Contact direct for prices

Name:	Disclosure
Description:	Disclosure provides extracts of reports filed with the US Securities and Exchange Commission (SEC) by publicly owned companies. Disclosure includes extracts of the 10-K and 10-Q financial reports, 20-F financial reports, proxy statements, management decisions and registration reports for new registrants. Disclosure provides an on-line source of information for marketing intelligence, corporate planning and development, portfolio analysis, accounting research, and corporate finance. The database also provides in-depth management information for these companies such as officers' and directors names and the chief executive's letter from annual reports (taken from the Disclosure Management file).
Source:	The primary source is the SEC which provides the original document of each report filed annually by public companies
Years Covered:	Current (up to 5 years' historical)
File Size:	30 549 records
Updates:	Weekly

Database Producer:	Disclosure Information Group
Available From:	DIALOG File 100
	$45 per connect hour
	$13 per on-line type
	$17 per off-line print
	MEAD File DISCLO
	$20 per connect hour
	$15 per search
	Dialcom Business Direction
	Part of Gateway Service to Dow Jones / News Retrieval
	£30 subscription fee per annum
	£100 per connect hour
	£24 per execution of the 'all' command
	BRS File DSCL
	$35 per connect hour
	$13 per on-line type
	$15 per off-line print

Name:	Disclosure Management
Description:	This database contains management information on over 10 000 US public companies. The information includes the Chief Executive's letter in full unedited text, list of subsidiaries, officers and directors.
	Full in-depth information can be found in Disclosure Financials.
Source:	The major source is the Securities and Exchange Commission which provides the documents as they are presented by these companies
Years Covered:	Current
File Size:	Approximately 10 931 records
Updates:	Weekly
Database Producer:	Disclosure Information Group
Available From:	DIALOG File 541
	$45 per connect hour
	$7 per on-line type
	$11 per off-line print

Name:	Disclosure / Spectrum Ownership
Description:	Disclosure / Spectrum Ownership details the common stock holdings of major institutions, corporate insiders and 5 per cent beneficial owners for approximately 5000 Disclosure Management companies. This information is derived from the filings made with the Securities and Exchange Commission on a quarterly or as required basis as ownership of stock changes. Detailed data list specific institutions and individuals, their relationship to the company, their stock holdings, and their most recent trades. Disclosure / Spectrum Ownership may be used to analyse the holdings of publicly quoted companies as an indication of market strength.
Source:	Generated from the Disclosure Management database and from 3 publications containing data produced by Computer Directions Advisors Inc: 'Spectrum 3' (Institutional Holdings), 'Spectrum 5' (5% Ownership Holdings) and 'Spectrum 6' (Ownership by Insiders)
Years Covered:	Current data
File Size:	Approx 5798 public companies
Updates:	Quarterly
Database Producer:	Disclosure Information Group
Available From:	DIALOG File 540
	$60 per connect hour
	$25 per on-line type
	$25 per off-line print
	BRS File OWNR
	$60 per connect hour
	$28 per on-line type
	$33 per off-line print

Name: Dunsdata Services
Description: Dunsdata provides information reports on companies in the UK and over
                          270 countries worldwide. Ten out of twelve EEC countries are covered
                          on line (June 1988). Reports are geared toward providing a summary of a
                          company's financial status, commercial standing and creditworthiness.
                          Company reports can include structure, capital (identifies shareholders
                          where information available), financial history, bankers, credit rating,
                          payment record, industry / company comparisons, ratios. Selected sections
                          of a report can be requested, depending on the customer's information
                          needs. As well as on line, the service is available in hard copy form, by
                          telex, facsimile, magnetic tape or over the telephone.
                              Summary information is available over the phone through computer
                          generated synthesised voice.
                              Summary of Dunsdata Services:
                          Business Information Reports
                          Payment Analysis Reports – in depth with industry comparatives
                          Duns Financial Profile – financial ratios with industry comparatives
                          Profile Plus – as above but with sophisticated computer-generated narrative
                          Duns Alert Services – comprehensive range of monitoring services
                          detailing any changes in a business
Source: Press
                          Direct contact with companies
                          Accounts files of major suppliers
                          Legal records
                          Company registration offices
Years Covered: UK back to 1981
                          Rest of Europe back to 1983/84 (subject to local data protection acts)
File Size: 15 million companies on line
Updates: Daily (UK 4 million updates)
Database Producer: Dun & Bradstreet
Available From: Dun & Bradstreet
                          Price is volume related on subscription
                          Example: UK Business Information Report
                          max £50; min £6.65

Name: Dun's Electronic Yellow Pages Construction Directory
Description: The Electronic Yellow Pages Construction Directory provides online yellow
                          page information for contractors and construction agencies. These include
                          housing contractors, industrial builders, highway construction agencies,
                          steel and concrete work contractors and listings for businesses engaged in
                          building, both residential and industrial, and related trades such as
                          plumbing, painting and electronic work. Electronic Yellow Pages records
                          include company name and address, modified 4-digit Standard Industrial
                          Classification code, telephone number, county and city population size
Source: Data is gathered from 4800 telephone books and specialised directories in
                          the USA
Years Covered: Current
File Size: 900 232 records
Updates: Quarterly reloads
Database Producer: Dun's Marketing Services
Available From: DIALOG File 507
                          $60 per connect hour
                          20c per on-line type
                          20c per off-line print

Name: Dun's Electronic Yellow Pages Manufacturers Directory
Description: Dun's Electronic Yellow Pages Manufacturers Directory provides online
                          yellow page information for manufacturing firms located in the United
                          States. All types of establishments are covered, including food products,
                          apparel, lumber, chemicals, metal, machinery, and furniture. Electronic
                          Yellow Pages records include company name and address, modified 4-
                          digit Standard Industrial Classification code, in the SIC Code range

	1850-3999, telephone number, county and city population size.
Source:	Data is gathered from state industrial listings, vertical market manufacturing directories and 4800 USA telephone books
Years Covered:	Current
File Size:	685 933 records
Updates:	Quarterly reloads
Database Producer:	Dun's Marketing Services
Available From:	DIALOG File 510
	$60 per connect hour
	20c per on-line type
	20c per off-line print

Name:	Dun's Electronic Yellow Pages Professionals Directory
Description:	Dun's Electronic Yellow Pages Professionals Directory provides online yellow page information for professionals in insurance, real estate, medicine, law, engineering and accounting. Also included are hospitals and various medical laboratories and clinics. Physicians and surgeons are listed by speciality. The database contains a full directory listing for each corporation company, firm, or individual. Electronic Yellow Pages records include company name and address, modified 4-digit Standard Industrial Classification code, telephone number, county and city population size.
Source:	Data is gathered from 4800 US telephone books and is cross-checked and qualified with over 50 specialised sources
Years Covered:	Current
File Size:	856 622 records
Updates:	Quarterly reloads
Database Producer:	Dun's Marketing Services
Available From:	DIALOG File 502
	$60 per connect hour
	20c per on-line type
	20c per off-line print

Name:	Dun's Electronic Yellow Pages Retailers Directory
Description:	Dun's Electronic Yellow Pages Retailers Directory provides on-line yellow page information for retailers located in the United States. The range of retail establishments includes lumber stores, paint stores, hardware stores, retail nurseries and garden suppliers, grocery, meat and other food stores, gasoline stations, auto and vehicle dealers, clothing stores, furniture stores, book stores, eating places, drinking places, florists, etc. A full directory listing is included for each retail establishment. In addition to the name and address, records include modified 4 digit Standard Industrial Classification code, telephone number, county and city population size.
Source:	Data is gathered from 4800 US telephone books and is cross checked and qualified with more than 50 specialised sources.
Years Covered:	Current
File Size:	2 486 569 records
Updates:	Quarterly reloads
Database Producer:	Dun's Marketing Services
Available From:	DIALOG File 504: SIC Codes 5200-5499
	File 505: SIC Codes 5500-5799
	File 506: SIC Codes 5800-5999
	$60 per connect hour
	20c per on-line type
	20c per off-line print

Name: Dun's Electronic Yellow Pages Services Directory
Description: Dun's Electronic Yellow Pages Services Directory provides online yellow
                             page information for all types of services including financial services,
                             business services, office and recreational services. A full directory listing is
                             included for establishments in over 4800 US cities. Hotels, motels,
                             laundries, barber shops, employment agencies and other rental services are
                             covered as well as any other business involved in providing a service to the
                             public. In addition to the name and address, records include a modified
                             4-digit Standard Industrial Classification code, telephone number, county
                             and city population size
Source: Data is gathered from 4800 US telephone books and is cross-checked and
                             qualified with more than 50 specialised sources
Years Covered: Current
File Size: 2 134 935 records
Updates: Quarterly reloads
Database Producer: Dun's Marketing Services
Available From: DIALOG File 508: SIC Codes 7000-7299
                             0700-0799
                             4000-4999
                             File 509: SIC Codes 7300-7999
                             $60 per connect hour
                             20c per on-line type
                             20c per off-line print

Name: Dun's Electronic Yellow Pages Wholesalers Directory
Description: Dun's Electronic Yellow Pages Wholesalers Directory provides online
                             yellow page information for wholesalers located in the USA. Wholesalers
                             included are; automotive parts, lumber and plywood, toy and hobby
                             suppliers, electrical equipment, plumbing and heating equipment, farm
                             and garden machinery, etc. A full directory listing is included for each retail
                             establishment. In addition to the name and address, records include a
                             modified 4-digit Standard Industrial Classification code, telephone
                             number, county and city population size.
Source: Data is gathered from 4800 US telephone books and is cross checked and
                             qualified with more than 50 specialised sources
Years Covered: Current
File Size: 981 070 records
Updates: Quarterly reloads
Database Producer: Dun's Marketing Services
Available From: DIALOG File 503
                             $60 per connect hour
                             20c per on-line type
                             20c per off-line print

Name: Dun's Market Identifiers
Description: This database takes up where Key British Enterprises leaves off, by offering
                             similar sales and marketing profiles on a further 200 000 UK companies.
                             Companies covered represent the most actively traded companies in the
                             country and span small, medium and large organisations involved in every
                             area of business and industry. Records include sales turnover, export sales
                             percentage, legal status, SIC codes, employees, parent name and director's
                             name. It is potentially useful for:
                             Direct mail
                             Planning and market research
                             Telesales

Source:
Years Covered: Current
File Size: 200000 companies
Updates: Monthly
Database Producer: Dun & Bradsheet (UK)
Available From:.   Pergamon Financial File DMI
                     £78 per connect hour
                     £2 per on-line type
                     72p per off-line print

Name: Dunsprint (On-line Service)
Description: On-line access to data collected and analysed by Dun and Bradstreet on
                     over 15 million companies and firms in the UK and worldwide. UK
                     database contains records of approximately 1.6 million businesses, with
                     detailed information on over 500000 of these. Full reports can be accessed
                     immediately covering any of the following areas:
                     Company's major shareholders
                     Company's main activities
                     Payment information
                     Public records
                     Legal records
                     Press coverage
                     Credit rating and appraisals
                         Besides a credit rating each record provides:
                     Address
                     Telephone number
                     Legal form
                     Lines of business
                     SIC codes
                     Names of directors or partners
                     Parent or subsidiary companies
                     Company history
                     Court judgements against it
                     3 years' profit and loss data
                     Dividends paid
                     Changes in capital structure
                     Business investigations can be ordered online
                     Other services:
                     Financial profiles – indepth financial analysis with
                     industry comparatives
                     Duns Alert Services – monitors changes
                     Payment analysis
Source: Press
                     Direct contact with companies
                     Accounts files of major suppliers
                     Legal records
                     Company registration offices
Years Covered: Up to 3 years' historic financial data
File Size: 15 million companies
Updates: Daily
Database Producer: Dun & Bradstreet
Available From: Dun & Bradstreet
                     Price for services is volume related on subscription
                     Example: UK Business Information Report
                     Max £29; min £10.45

Name: EAE
Description: This database provides information on French companies with over 20
                     employees including historical turnover figures, pre-tax profits,
                     employees, exports, investments and value added. Information is based on
                     the Ministry's annual industrial survey.

Source: Ministere du Developpment Industriel et Scientifique
Years Covered: Historic data and latest figures available
File Size:
Updates: Annual
Database Producer: Ministere de Developpment Industriel et Scientifique
Available From: GSI-ECO

Name: Einkaufs-1X1
Description: This is the online version of the printed buyers' guide 'Einkaufs-1X1 der
                         deutschen Industrie'. It contains entries for manufacturers and their
                         products in the Federal Republic of Germany
Language: German
Source: Equivalent to printed version
Years Covered: Current
File Size: 58 000 records
Updates: Quarterly
Database Producer: Deutscher Addressbuch Verlag fuer Wirtschaft
                         und Verkehr GmbH
Available From: FIZ Technik File E1X1
                         DM 250 per connect hour
                         DM 1.8 per on-line type
                         DM 2.1 per off-line print
                         DM 1.3 for company address and telecom information only
                         Data-Star File E1X1
                         Contact direct for prices (new file)

Name: Empresas
Description: A Spanish company directory
Source: Catalogues, sub-contracting exchanges, data from the companies
                         themselves
Years Covered: Latest information supplied by companies
File Size: 30 000 documents
Updates: Periodically
Database Producer: Business Information System
Available From: Instituto de la Pequena y Mediana Empresa Industrial (IMPI)
                         Contact direct for prices

Name: ESSOR
Description: ESSOR is a trade directory of industrial companies in France covering
                         businesses employing over 10 people. Information provided includes
                         names of directors and senior managers, lines of business, turnover,
                         nominal capital, number of employees and exports.
Language: French
Source: Company annual reports
Years Covered: Current (no historic data)
File Size: 76 000 firms
Updates: Annual
Database Producer: Union Francaise d'Annuaire Professionnels (UFAP)
Available From: Telesystemes-Questel File ESSOR
                         $80 per on-line connect hour
                         55c per on-line type
                         55c per off-line print

Name: European Kompass Online (EKOL)
Description: EKOL is the European version of Kompass Online. It provides details on
                         305 000 European companies in 12 major West European countries taken
                         from the European Kompass directories. Data includes company name,
                         address, telephone and telex numbers, number of employees, products
                         manufactured or distributed, imported or exported and names and job
                         titles of directors.

Facilities include direct record access, selection of companies by any of the above criteria and bulk printing of lists or labels.

The twelve countries covered are:

Belgium	Italy	Spain
Denmark	Luxembourg	Sweden
Germany, Federal	Netherlands	Switzerland
Republic of	Norway	UK
France		

Source:	European Kompass directories
Years Covered:	Current
File Size:	305 000 companies
Updates:	Weekly
Database Producer:	Kompass Online
Available From:	Kompass Online
	£90 per connect hour
	8-14p per off-line print
	Minimum charge of 500 companies per day
	NB: Users of Kompass Online database have access to EKOL with no additional charges other than connect time.
	AffarsData
	Covers 4 Kompass directories for Sweden, Norway, Denmark and the Federal Republic of Germany
	SKr 720 per connect hour

Name:	Exchange (MEAD Service)
Description:	This service offers indepth research reports on US and international companies and industries, prepared by professional research analysts at leading investment banks and brokerage firms. The date of availability of reports reflects the first month or year of substantial coverage and depends on the agreement with ea ch investment bank and brokerage firm. Also included is extracted information from SEC filings and annual reports on more than 10300 companies; full-text 10-Q and 10-K (excluding exhibits) filings for 1500 companies; plus earnings projections and presentation transcripts.
Source:	As above
Years Covered:	Varies by file. Some files go back to 1981-83 and up to the present.
File Size:	Over 10 300 US companies
Updates:	First month or year of substantial coverage. Depends on availability of documents from banks and brokers
Database Producer:	MEAD Data Central
Available From:	MEAD Data Central
	$24 per search for combined company and industry files
	$15 per search for individual files (ie by broker or type of financial report, etc)
	$15 per search for ABECOR (Association Banks of Europe Corporation Country Reports) File
	$15 per search for ENS Evans Economics, Electronic News Service

Name:	Exstat
Description:	Exstat is a database of company financial and trading information in computer-readable form. Data is compiled direct from the annual general reports and other company sources of information and covers 3500 industrial and commercial companies – British quoted and unquoted, including the USM. There is also a selection of European, Australian and Japanese companies.
Source:	Annual reports and other company sources
Years Covered:	1971 to date
File Size:	Approximately 3500 UK quoted and unquoted companies
Updates:	Weekly
Database Producer:	Extel Financial

Available From:	Extel Financial
	Contact Extel direct for prices
	Interactive Data Corporation (IDC)
	$5300 per annum or $675 per month subscription fee
	(maximum of 5 userids)
	Additional $2650 subscription fee per annum for use in DataSheet
	Additional $5300 subscription fee per annum to permit
	downloading
	Analytics charges:
	$250 per month, plus sliding scale per access fee, on
	monthly basis, 2c to 7c per hit

Name:	Financial Post Canadian Corporate Database (FPCORP)
Description:	This database provides time series of balance sheet and income account data taken from Canadian corporations' annual reports, annual and quarterly data. IP Sharp provides only annual data. Most companies listed in the Toronto Stock Exchange 300 Composite index are included
Source:	Company reports
Years Covered:	Annual data – 1959 to date
	Quarterly data – 1968 to date
File Size:	Over 100 000 time series
Updates:	Periodically as data becomes available
Database Producer:	Financial Post Information Service
Available From:	FRI Information Services Ltd
	C$6000 annual subscription payable to Financial Post
	IP Sharp
	C$4500 annual subscription payable to
	Financial Post or
	10c Cdn per item
	Data Resources Inc
	Subscription services only
	C$6000 annual subscription payable to
	Financial Post
	Information Plus

Name:	Financial Times Company Abstracts
Description:	The Financial Times Company Abstracts database covers all articles in the London and Frankfurt editions of the 'Financial Times' newspapers which refer to a company. The database therefore summarises the major part of the newspapers' contents with the main exceptions of advertisements, news summary, letters to the editor, commodity prices, world stock market, FT share information service. The database began in January 1981 as the Fintel Company Newsbase, the file was then upgraded in Summer 1982 to become the Financial Times Company Abstracts database with longer, more informative summaries of original articles and it uses the same format as the Predicasts database. All company names appearing in the original 'Financial Times' article appear in the database. Company names which are the major focus of the article appear in the body of the database abstract. Companies which are discussed in a minor way are listed at the end of the abstract with the comment 'also discussed is/are ...'. Companies which are mentioned only in passing in the article are listed at the end of the abstract, with the comment 'also mentioned is/are ...'.
Source:	London and Frankfurt editions of the 'Financial Times'
Years Covered:	1981 to date
File Size:	158 009 records
Updates:	Weekly
Database Producer:	Financial Times Electronic Publishing Ltd
	D-S Production Ltd

Available From:	Data-Star File FNTL
	£48.98 per connect hour
	51p per on-line print
	44p per off-line print
	SDI profile: £2.73
	DIALOG File 560
	$72 per connect hour
	80c per on-line type
	85c per off-line print

Name:	Findata
Description:	Findata is one of the major databases providing financial and economic data in Sweden. It is used by financial analysts as part of their basic analysis or for credit ratings and investigations. It provides annual reports on 300-400 Swedish quoted companies, and some Finnish quoted companies. 500 variables are provided per company (predefined key ratios). Company/industry analysis can be conducted.
	Currently this data is used by USA or UK clients for investigatory purposes, and is supplied in a magnetic media or hard copy. Due to the need to understand Swedish accounting rules it is more productive to allow Findata staff to conduct the investigation, supply it to you via tailor-made software and to assist in the interpretation of the figures.
Source:	Annual reports
Years Covered:	1966 to date (quoted companies only)
File Size:	300-400 Swedish companies
	500 variables per company
Updates:	As data is available
Database Producer:	Findata
Available From:	Findata
	Charges vary according to nature and size of the task
	Guide charges:
	Skr 6000 per day (investigator's time) plus computer access charge

Name:	FINF-Numeric
Description:	Annual results and commercial balance sheet figures of German industrial companies, standardised and comparable, according to BiRiLiG (the German law relating to guidelines for balance sheets).
Source:	Company reports
Years Covered:	Last four years
File Size:	1000 companies (as at Jan 1988)
Updates:	Monthly
Database Producer:	Gesellschaft fur Betriebswirtschaftliche Information mbH (GBI)
Available From:	GENIOS File FNN
	DM 120 per connect hour
	DM 30 per on-line type
	DM 30 per off-line print
	See Coin-Numeric on Data-Star

Name:	FINF-Text
Description:	Up-to-date information about companies from the German-language business press.
Source:	German-language business press
Years Covered:	Current
File Size:	6000 (as at Jan 1988)
Updates:	Monthly
Database Producer:	Gesellschaft fur Betriebswirtschaftliche Information mbFH (GBI)

Available From:	GENIOS File FITT
	DM 240 per connect hour
	DM 0.8 per on-line type
	DM 0.8 per off-line print
	See Coin-Text on Data-Star

Name:	Firmen-Info-Bank
Description:	This database provides information on about 22 000 firms in the Federal Republic of Germany, with particular reference to about 150 000 decision makers. Both public and private firms are included which meet the criteria of a minimum annual turnover of about 20 million Marks. For every firm the following information is available: name, address, telephone number, and when these can be obtained the telex number, telefax number, BTX number, trade code number as it appears in the relevant section of the German Statistics Office system of coding, programmes for production, trading and supplying of services, membership of a group of companies, affiliated companies, turnover, number of employees, legal constitution, business year capital, and year of foundation. In addition, specific information is provided relating to the companies' decision makers, classified according to their status and function within the companies' legal framework.
	Target group and potential users of this database include departments dealing with imports, market research, planning, marketing, management, journalists, advertising agencies, research institutes, unions and political associations.
Language:	German
Source:	All the information is investigated and checked by AZ Bertelsmann GmbH. The FIB data are also obtainable via BTX 3 033
Years Covered:	Current
File Size:	Approximately 22 000 companies
Updates:	Quarterly
Database Producer:	AZ Bertelsmann GmbH
Available From:	Bertelsmann File DFIB
	DM 200 per connect hour (licence fee)
	DM 78 per connect hour
	DM 0.80-DM 3 per paragraph or subparagraph on line*
	* Since the cost per document is cumulative, the final amount is dependent on the type of paragraphs or subparagraphs requested.

Name:	Guardian Online
Description:	The Guardian Online database contains public record information on every company registered in the United Kingdom. It also contains credit information and reference information collected as a result of CCN's private viewdata network, usually at local telephone call rates. The service is a straightforward menu-driven system offering a Registered Office Search, company profile, financial analysis with up to 6 years' financial information, 27 operating ratios and industry ratio analysis. There is also a Constant Review Service allowing you to monitor a company, and on-line ordering facilities.
Source:	Company registration offices
	Company financial statements
Years Covered:	Up to 6 years' historic data
File Size:	Detailed financial information available on over 70 000 companies in the UK
Updates:	
Database Producer:	CCN/Guardian
Available From:	CCN/Guardian
	If customer uses own terminal a small connection charge is payable, which includes a manual and training session. If customer requires a terminal, this can be supplied on special rental terms.

Price guide:
Registered Office Search: £1.50
Company Profile: £3
Financial Profile: £15
Full Gold Report: £20
Constant Review Service:
Up to 100 companies 25p per company per month
A number of other services are available, including
credit reports (hard copy), insolvency service, postal
and telephone enquiry services.

Name: Hoppenstedt Austria
Description: The Hoppenstedt Austria database is the on-line version of the directory
                        'Osterreich 2000'. It provides detailed descriptions of all branches and all
                        business enterprises of over 3500 major companies in Austria. Companies
                        are covered on the basis that they have a minimum turnover of 100 million
                        Austrian Schillings and/or a mimimum of 200 employees.
                           Data available includes the company's industry, legal form, bankers,
                        management, ownership, branches and foreign outlets, and a description
                        of operations.
Source: 'Osterreich 2000'
Years Covered: Latest available
File Size: Approx 3500 companies
Updates: Once a year (September)
Database Producer: Hoppenstedt Wirtschaftsdatenbank GmbH
Available From: Data-Star File HOAU
                        £97.96 per connect hour
                        65p per on-line print
                        49p per off-line print
                        DIALOG File 529 (combined with Hoppendstedt Germany)
                        $105 per connect hour
                        $2.60 per on-line type
                        $2.60 per off-line print

Name: Hoppenstedt Directory of German Companies
Description: The Hoppenstedt Germany database represents the on-line version of the
                        directory 'Handbuch der Grossunternehmen' and provides detailed
                        company descriptions of all branches and business enterprises of 36 000
                        major companies in the Federal Republic of Germany and West Berlin. The
                        reports are published according to the following Ncriteria: minimum of 20
                        employees or minimum of 2.5 million turnover. In case of doubt, the
                        inclusion of the entry depends on the economic importance of the
                        enterprise concerned. Records include company name, address, industry
                        SIC code, bankers, ownership, branches and foreign outlets, and a
                        description of operations.
Language: German and English
Source: 'Handbuch der Grossunternehmen', 'Handbuch der Mittelstaendischen
                        Unternehmen'
Years Covered: Current
File Size: 35 000 companies
                        36 520 records (DIALOG)
Updates: 3 times per annum: January, July and September
                        Quarterly reloads (DIALOG)
Database Producer: Hoppenstedt Wirtschaftsdatenbank GmbH
Available From: Data-Star File HOPE
                        £97.96 per connect hour
                        £1.43 per on-line print
                        £1.43 per off-line print
                        DIALOG File 529
                        $105 per connect hour
                        $2.6 per on-line type
                        $2.6 per off-line print

Name: Hoppenstedt Netherlands
Description: The Hoppenstedt Netherlands database is the online version of the
                          directory 'Nederlands ABC Voor Handel en Industrie'. The database
                          provides company profiles of 22000 companies in the Netherlands. The
                          basis of selection is the number of employees, whereby the number varies
                          according to the industry sector. Data Qavailable includes the company's
                          industry, bankers, names of directors and foreign business partners, capital
                          and employees.
Source: 'Nederlands ABC Voor Handel en Industrie'
Years Covered: Latest available
File Size: 22000 companies
Updates: Annual, August or September
Database Producer: ABC Voor Handel en Industrie
Available From: Data-Star File HONL/ABCN
                          £97.96 per connect hour
                          67p per on-line print
                          49p per off-line print
                          DIALOG File 529 (combined file with Hoppendstedt Germany)
                          $105 per connect hour
                          $2.60 per on-line type
                          $2.60 per off-line print

Name: ICC British Company Directory
Description: Every live limited company in Scotland, England and Wales is listed in the
                          directory. Live company records normally contain the following
                          information: registered company number, company name, registered office
                          address, accounts reference date, made-up date of annual return, date of
                          latest accounts, reference to the detailed financial data file (DIALOG file
                          562) plus dates of incorporation and other statutory document filings.
Source: Records filed at Companies Registration Offices
Years Covered: Latest information held at Registration Offices
File Size: Over 2 million companies
Updates: Daily on ICC Viewdata. Weekly updates, quarterly
                          reloads (DIALOG)
Database Producer: ICC
Available From: DIALOG File 561
                          $72 per connect hour
                          25c per on-line type
                          25c per off-line print
                          Data-Star File ICUK
                          £63.67 per connect hour
                          Print charges vary according to fields accessed
                          ICC Viewdata Service
                          £75 per connect hour
                          25p per viewdata page displayed

Name: ICC British Company Financial Datasheets
Description: This database provides access to analyses of directors' Reports and
                          Accounts for over 100000 British companies. Companies selected for
                          inclusion are of commercial significance and coverage includes quoted and
                          non-quoted public and private companies from all industrial and service
                          sectors in the UK. Full format datasheets are available for 75 per cent of
                          these companies and summary 'abridged' datasheets are available for the
                          remainder. Most of the services through which this file is available offer
                          great flexibility in searching. This service also contains entries for 92000
                          companies registered in the Republic of Ireland.
Source: Latest available published accounts held at Companies
                          House
Years Covered: Latest 4 years
File Size: Over 100000 companies
Updates: Weekly
Database Producer: ICC

Available From: ICC Viewdata Service
                       £75 per connect hour
                       25p per viewdata page displayed
                       DIALOG File 562
                       $96 per connect hour
                       $8 per on-line type (full format)
                       $8 per off-line print (full format)
                       $4 per on-line type (abridged datasheet)
                       $4 per off-line print (abridged datasheet)
                       Data-Star File ICUK
                       £63.67 per connect hour
                       £7.55 per on-line type (full format)
                       £7.55 per off-line print (full format)
                       Dialcom Business Direction
                       £138 per connect hour
                       Datastream – Programs 190 and 191
                       Offers full format companies only
                       Citibank's Global Report
                       Offers access to the top 12 000 British companies
                       Guardian (CCN Systems)

Name: ICC Canadian Corporations
Description: This database contains detailed profile, financial and performance for
                       approx 5000 top Canadian companies. These include over 1400 public
                       companies trading on the five Canadian Stock Exchanges – Toronto,
                       Montreal, Vancouver, Winnipeg and Alberta. The top 1000 public
                       companies identified in the 'Globe and Mail's Report on Buiness' magazine
                       are included. The file also covers approx 2000 subsidiaries and privately
                       held companies with over $10 million in revenue that file annual reports
                       with the Corporations Branch of Consumer and Corporate Affairs. Plus
                       major provincial and federal crown corporations.
Source: Company annual financial statements
Years Covered: Latest available information
                       Historic data for the last 5 years
File Size: 5000 companies
Updates: Weekly
Database Producer: ICC Canada Ltd
                       Micromedia Ltd
Available From: Data-Star File ICCA
                       £63.67 per connect hour
                       £6.02 per on-line type (full format)
                       £6.02 per off-line print (full format)
                       IST-Informatheque File ICC-E (English version)
                       File ICC-F (French version)
                       $120 per connect hour
                       25c per on-line type (citation)
                       $2 per STD format online
                       $10 per on-line type (MAX format)
                       Also available via Questel
                       Due to become available on Dialcom Business Direction

Name: ICC Full Text Company Accounts
Description: This file comprises the annual reports and accounts published by quoted
                       companies, typically including items such as review of the business climate
                       in which the company is operating; chairman's report; details of products;
                       forecasts; full company accounts; detailed explanations, etc. Data can be
                       sorted in a variety of ways.
                       Initially this database covers British companies listed on the London Stock
                       Exchange. Plans for development include the addition of European and
                       other overseas company accounts.
Source: Companies House
Years Covered: Latest accounts

File Size: Full text of over 2000 UK Quoted companies' annual reports. Over 5000
                            reports published by 23 leading British brokers.
Updates: Regularly
Database Producer: ICC
Available From: To be available shortly via Data-Star and DIALOG (within ICC
                            International Business Research – file 563)

Name: ICC Industrial Averages
Description: ICC calculates average performance statistics for British industries using
                            the data on individual companies in the Financial Datasheets file. Typical
                            rates of return can be accessed for any sector of industry defined by either a
                            Standard Industrial Classification (SIC) or ICC industry coding. Each sector
                            must have a minimum of 20 companies in the ICC financial Datasheets file
                            to warrant inclusion. Statistics are presented as upper, median or lower
                            quartile for all the main business ratios.
Source: ICC financial datasheets file
Years Covered: Up to 8 years' historic data
File Size: Over 100000 companies analysed
Updates: Monthly
Database Producer: ICC
Available From: ICC Viewdata Service
                            £75 per connect hour
                            25p per page displayed

Name: ICC Sharewatch
Description: This service provides details of shareholders who own 0.25 per cent and
                            above of any UK quoted company. Via Viewdata and TOPIC, it also
                            displays details of recent official notifications of shareholdings and
                            directors' trades. The ICC Viewdata service offers the ability to search on
                            'insider' name.
Source: Based on research by ICC. Primary sources are details of reportable trades
                            provided to ICC by the Stock Exchange, annual shareholder returns and
                            analyses received from company registrars
Years Covered: Current
File Size: Approx 2000 records
Updates: Continually updated
Database Producer: ICC
Available From: ICC Viewdata service
                            £75 per connect hour
                            £1 per Viewdata page displayed
                            Data-Star File ICUK
                            £63.67 per connect hour
                            Print charges vary according to fields accessed
                            Dialcom Business Direction
                            £138 per connect hour
                            Initial fee payable of £1000 (includes 5 hours' connect time)
                            ICC Sharewatch on Topic – London Stock Exchange
                            Available on a subscription basis
                            Existing TOPIC users contact ICC for details
                            Non-TOPIC users contact the Stock Exchange Sales and Marketing
                            Department on 01-588-2355 Ext 28177

Name: ICC Stockbroker Research
Description: This database contains research reports published by leading British and
                            international stockbroking firms. The file can be searched to identify
                            reports covering specific companies or industries, or reports by named
                            analysts. Either complete reports or particular sections can be retrieved and
                            printed out. As at May 1988, 31 stockbrokers were providing their reports
                            on this file. These include Philips and Drew, Citicorp, Scrimgeour Vickers
                            & Co, Morgan Grenfell Securities and Paine Webber.
Source: Stockbroker research
Years Covered: Current (file launched in Feb 1987)

File Size:	4000 reports available. Approx 500 documents added per month
Updates:	Monthly
Database Producer:	ICC
Available From:	Data-Star File ICBR
	£63.67 per connect hour
	41p per TX paragraph printed on line
	Dialcom Business Direction available Summer 1988
	DIALOG offers this service as part of ICC International Business Research (file 563)

Name:	ICC Viewdata Service
Description:	This service provides on-line access to the ICC Directory of Companies, Financial Datasheets, Industrial averages and Sharewatch databases. Special features include on-line ordering, automatic monitoring, colour graphic comparisons for measuring companies' performance against other companies or their industry sector, and on-line credit scores for around 65000 companies.
Source:	As per industrial databases
Years Covered:	Current and up to 10 years' historic financial data
File Size:	Reference data for approx 2 million companies, 100000 detailed company datasheets and 2000 shareholding records
Updates:	Daily
Database Producer:	ICC
Available From:	ICC
	£75 per connect hour
	25p per page displayed from CRO Directory, Company Datasheets and Industry Quartiles.
	£1 per page displayed from ICC Sharewatch
	NB: The page charge is only levied the first time a page is displayed during the access of a specific section of a company or industry quartile record.

Name:	Industrial Market Location
Description:	This database holds information on over 140000 UK manufacturing and warehousing establishments. It enables the searcher to target companies by such variables as industry sector, location, and employee number. It also provides details of the key decision maker and helps to identify those companies who have computing facilities, or an export/import department. This database can be used for:
	Identifying sales prospects
	Market research projects
	Creating company profiles
	Identifying key personnel
Years Covered:	Current
File Size:	140000 companies
Updates:	Six times per year
Database Producer:	Market Location Limited
Available From:	Pergamon Financial File IML
	£70 per connect hour
	£2.50 per on-line type
	£2.50 per off-line print
	7SDI profile: £5

Name:	Infocheck
Description:	Basic UK company information is provided on over 1.2 million companies. Full financial reports are provided with ratios and credit opinion for over 200000 limited companies. Searches can be done by company number, name or part name. The database is automatically updated once accounts are filed with the Registrar of Companies.
Source:	Registrar of Companies
Years Covered:	Current (up to 4 years' historic)
File Size:	1.2 million UK companies

Updates:	Over 3000 companies added each week
Database Producer:	Infocheck Ltd
Available From:	Infocheck Ltd
	Annual host fee
	300 full reports £4000
	600 full reports £5000
	1200 full reports £4500
	Infocheck offer other services:
	Company Search Services
	Company Status Reports
	Overseas Reports
	Infocheck Fiche Register
	Pergamon Financial File Check
	£70 per connect hour
	£8.50 per on-line type
	£8 per off-line print
	PROFILE
	Gateway Service
	Full report £9.50
	Basic report 50p
	Infocheck connect charge 33p
	Telecom Gold
	Contact direct for prices

Name:	INPI STE 3
Description:	This database holds the accounts and balance sheets of 400 000 French companies. This has been produced under the authority of 'L'Institut National de la Propriete Industrielle'. It is sourced from the financial reports which French companies lodge each year with the local Registre du Commerce et des Societes. The database also provides financial ratios.
	Companies in France are required to file accounts with their local Registre du Commerce. Many of these offices produce their own databases which provide company accounts on line. Company accounts from these offices can be ordered through Infogreffe. INPI provides accounts registered at all of these Registres du Commerce. Information is made available as soon as accounts have been filed.
Source:	Company accounts
Years Covered:	SAs: 1981 to date
	SARLs: 1984 to date
File Size:	400 000 French companies
Updates:	As soon as annual information is made available
Database Producer:	French National Register of Trade (Registre National du Commerce et des Societes)
Available From:	OR Telematique
	FF 1350 subscription fee per annum
	Choice of subscription options available

Name:	Investext
Description:	The Investext database provides the full text of industry and company reports generated by financial analysts of 27 leading investment banking firms in the US, Europe, Canada and Japan. Data is available on approximately 1000 of the largest US public companies, and on 500 smaller, emerging companies. Each report is divided into individual pages, each of which comprises a separate record. Reports are indexed by subject, product, company, industry, and SIC code.
	Reports contain sales and earnings forecasts, market share projections, R&D expenditures and related data.
	Non-US participants provide research on some 1000 large firms listed on stock exchanges in Japan, West Germany, Britain, France, Italy, Holland, Belgium, Switzerland, Sweden and Canada.
Source:	Investment banks worldwide
Years Covered:	From July 1982 to date

File Size:	467 633 records
Updates:	Weekly
Database Producer:	Technical Data International
Available From:	DIALOG File 545
	$96 per connect hour $4.50 per on-line type
	$4.50 per off-line print
	SDI profile: $3.50
	Data-Star File INVE
	£68.27 per connect hour
	£2.30 per on-line print (per TX paragraph)
	£2.30 per off-line print (per TX paragraph)
	BRS File INVT
	$102 per connect hour
	$4.75 per on-line type
	$4.75 per off-line print
	SDI profile: $4

Name:	Irish Company Profiles
Description:	The ICP database represents a unique source of company information on top companies in the Republic of Ireland. The database focuses specifically on the manufacturing sector and is an extremely valuable tool for anyone wishing to reach this market. Irish Company Profiles enables you to identify target companies by trade description, number of employees, trade marks or key personnel.
	This database can be useful for:
	Identifying new markets
	Preparing company profiles
	Generating mail shots
Source:	Combination of questionnaires and company visits
Years Covered:	Current
File Size:	15 000 companies
Updates:	Every 2 months
Database Producer:	Institute of Industrial Research and Standards
Available From:	Pergamon Financial File ICP
	£60 per connect hour
	50p per on-line type
	50p per off-line print

Name:	Jordan's Direct (Service)
Description:	Jordan's own system offers simple, easy to use on-line searching for locating specific companies, displaying company information and for the monitoring and ordering of Companies House information. Selection of companies is by full name, registered office number, or by keyword search. Search criteria is more limited than that which can be used with the JordanWatch file via Pergamon Infoline.
Source:	Companies House, London and Edinburgh Gazettes
Years Covered:	Current (up to 5 years' historic)
File Size:	Approximately 1.9 million UK companies
Updates:	Daily
Database Producer:	Jordan & Sons Ltd
Available From:	Jordan & Sons Ltd
	Charges reflect length of time and amount of information displayed
	Guide prices:
	£72 per connect hour; £84 from 4.7.88
	£6 per on-line type (per company, full format);
	£7 from 4.7.88
	£6 per off-line print (full company, full format);
	£7 from 4.7.88

Name:	JordanWatch
Description:	The JordanWatch database contains records for every registered British company taken from Companies House and supplemented by the 'London and Edinburgh Gazettes'. For all companies over a certain size, full accounts for up to 5 years including ratios and trends are available on line. For all smaller companies a full on-line document ordering and monitoring service enables you to request accounts to be delivered direct from Jordans and Sons the following day. In addition, you can target companies by different financial criteria and by location or industry type.

This database can be used for:

Checking the financial status of UK companies

Monitoring for changes in directors, filing or accounts etc

Identifying acquisition targets

Full searching is possible, using a range of financial or other criteria such as business sector. It is also possible to cross search, and link up with the shareholder information files.

Source:	Companies House
	'London & Edinburgh Gazettes'
Years Covered:	Up to 5 years' historic data
File Size:	Approx 1.9 million UK companies
Updates:	Weekly
Database Producer:	Jordan & Sons Ltd
Available From:	Pergamon Financial File Jordans
	£72 per connect hour
	£8.40 per on-line type
	£8.40 per off-line print
	Jordans (Direct) Education and Training File
	£20 per connect hour
	ESA-IRS File 158
	Gateway service to Pergamon
	£88.91 per connect hour
	£9.22 per on-line type
	£9.22 per off-line print
	Telecom Gold
	Contact direct for prices

Name:	Key British Enterprises
Description:	This is a directory-style database which provides information on 20 000 major British companies, which account for 90 per cent of industrial expenditure in the UK. It is ideal for generating mailing lists, creating company profiles, and marketing requirements such as sales and purchasing. Specific company details can be checked such as address, directorships or trade names. Companies can be targeted by searching on business activity, overseas markets, number of employees or turnover.

Records include the following: address, SIC codes, number of employees, company formation details, ownership, markets, trade names, branches and directors' names.

Source:	Dun & Bradstreet
Years Covered:	Current
File Size:	20 000
Updates:	Monthly
Database Producer:	Dun & Bradstreet
Available From:	Pergamon Financial File KBE
	£78 per connect hour
	£2.40 per on-line type
	72p per off-line print
	SDI profile: £5
	Dun & Bradstreet
	Data available from D&B on magnetic tape, floppy disc or mailing label print-outs.

Name: Kompass Online
Description   Kompass Online makes available the company information from
                        'Kompass', 'Kelly's', 'Directory of Directors', 'Dial Industry', 'British
                        Exports' and a number of other commercial directories in a single unified
                        file.
                             The file currently covers over 115000 UK companies with details of their
                        products and services under 45000 catagories. It also covers over 250000
                        named executives, trade names, ownership, finances and overseas agents.
                        Facilities include direct record access, selection of companies by their
                        products, size, location and over 40 other characteristics. It also enables
                        bulk printing of lists and labels.
Source: 'Kompass', 'Kelly's', 'Directory of Directors', 'Dial Industry', 'British
                        Exports'
Years Covered: Current
File Size: 115000 UK companies
Updates: Weekly
                        2000 updates per week
Database Producer: Kompass Online
Available From: Kompass Online
                        UK Companies File:
                        Prime Time (0900-1900)
                        £50 per connect hour (Search types 1 and 2)
                        £70 per connect hour (Search type 3)
                        Off-Peak (1900-2200)
                        £20 per connect hour (Search types 1 and 2)
                        £50 per connect hour (Search type 3)
                        UK Registered Companies File:
                        £30 per connect hour
                        10p per on-line type (per company)
                        50p per off-line print (per company)
                        (Minimum charge of 500 companies per day for off-line prints)
                        Telecom Gold
                        Contact direct for prices

Name: Kompass Online (Scandinavia)
Description: Affarsdata offers the Kompass directories online for Sweden, Norway,
                        Denmark and the Federal Republic of Germany. These directories contain
                        product and company information including basic company details such as
                        address, telephone and telex numbers. Users can select and search for
                        company and product information by a number of different criteria.
Language: Databases are in the native languages for Kompass Norway, Denmark and
                        the Federal Republic of Germany. They are also searchable in English
Source: Equivalent to the published Kompass directories
Years Covered: Current
File Size: 25000 products and services coded
                        85000 companies
                        (total size for all four databases)
Updates: Annual
Database Producer: Affarsdata
Available From: Affarsdata
                        SKr 720 per connect hour

Name: Liens Financiers
Description: Covers shareholders and participations of the 80000 largest French
                        companies. Also lists the subsidiaries or affiliates of major French firms
                        both in France and abroad. Sources of information are identified to enable
                        the user to refer to the original source if required.
Language: French
Source: Sources include company reports, specialist press and official notices
Years Covered: Current
File Size: 80000 companies
Updates: Daily

Database Producer: OR Telematique
Available From: OR Telematique
FF 1350 subscription fee per annum
Choice of subscription options available

Name: McCarthy Online Company Fact Sheets
Description: McCarthy Online Company Fact Sheets (MFC)
holds company fact sheets on approximately 1000 companies drawn from
UK quoted companies and the top 100 foreign companies quoted on the
London Stock Exchange. Companies covered are listed in the 'McCarthy
Users Handbook'. Information includes name of chairman, MD, directors,
auditors, registrars, address of head office, activities summary,
capitalisation and financial history (turnover, profit, earnings per share).
Source: Company accounts
Years Covered: Current (5 years' historical)
File Size: 1000 UK, 100 overseas companies
Updates:
Database Producer: McCarthy Information Ltd
Available From: PROFILE File mfc
£84 per connect hour
1p per off-line print (per line)
Minimum £2 per off-line request
Access available to all McCarthy and Profile common users files (see list
under database host notes)

Name: McCarthy Online Press Cutting Service
Description: This database (MCC) holds the full text reproduction of articles from
leading national and international business publications. They are indexed
to facilitate searches by company name, nationality, industry, source and
date of publication.
    Non-English articles are not translated. Information is usually accessible
within 72 hours of publication.
Language: Various, mainly English
Source: Over 70 international business publications including 'Euromoney',
'Fortune International', 'Investors Chronicle', 'Les Echos', 'Wall St Journal
Europe'
Years Covered: October 1985 to date
File Size: 370 000 records (as at June 1988)
Updates: Daily
Approx 15 000 records added per month
Database Producer: McCarthy Information Ltd
Available From: PROFILE File MCC
£84 per on-line connect hour
1p per off-line print (per line)
Minimum £2 per off-line request
Access available to all McCarthy and Profile common user files (see list
under database host notes)
Financial Times Electronic Publishing
£80 per connect hour
Bulk subscription:
100 hours £6230 (£62.30 per hour)
50 hours £3400 (£68.00 per hour)
25 hours £1875 (£75.00 per hour)

Name: Media General Plus
Description: This database provides detailed financial and stock-trading information on
approximately 4400 public companies.
    The data includes weekly and yearly information on high and low stock
prices and volumes, balance sheets and income statements, together with
key ratios and indexes.

Companies covered are all those that appear on the New York and American Exchanges, all National Market Companies (NADSQ) and selected OTC companies.

Summary industry information is also provided with each company record.

Source:	Information taken from forms: 10-K, 10-Q, interim results and reports and prospectuses filed with the SEC
Years Covered:	Current
File Size:	5961 records
Updates:	Weekly reloads
Database Producer:	Media General Financial Services Inc
Available From:	DIALOG File 546
	$72 per connect hour $3 per on-line type
	$4 per off-line print

Name:	MicroEXSTAT
Description:	MicroEXSTAT is a microcomputer based system comprising company financial information and a sophisticated software package developed jointly by Extel and the London Business School for detailed analysis of company accounts.

The MicroEXSTAT database is compiled from the same source as Extel Cards and currently covers over 2500 commercial and industrial companies including: companies listed on the UK Stock Exchange, the Unlisted Securities Market and the main unquoted UK companies. Approximately 700 companies from continental Europe, Japan and Australia are also covered.

Financial data available includes annual balance sheet and profit and loss account items, plus year end share prices and capital data. Background information such as industrial classification, ownership, auditors and bankers codes are also available as well as industry average figures for comparative analysis.

Using simple menu commands a variety of standard reports are available such as balance sheet, income and cash flow statements and ratio analysis. The software also enables rapid search of the companies' database according to financial criteria specified by the user.

Any of the reports produced by MicroEXSTAT can be presented for use with such software packages as Lotus 1-2-3, etc, permitting the preparation of financial forecasts.

Source:	Company annual reports and accounts
Years Covered:	Current (up to 6 years' historic data)
File Size:	Over 2500 UK companies
	700 companies from continental Europe, Japan and Australia
Updates:	Weekly
Database Producer:	Extel Financial
	London Business School
Available From:	Extel Financial
	Contact Extel direct for prices

Name:	Moody's Corporate News – International
Description:	Moddy's Corporate News contains business news and financial information on more than 3900 major corporations and institutions in 100 countries worldwide. It contains both tabular and textual records. Tabular records include data from earnings reports and balance sheets. Textual records cover business news announcements. This database offers valuable material, but it has a restricted coverage of European companies. Only the largest companies are included.
Source:	Company financial reports and announcements
Years Covered:	1983 to date
File Size:	26 279 records
Updates:	Weekly
Database Producer:	Moody's Investors Service Inc

Available From:	DIALOG File 557
	$96 per connect hour $1 per on-line type
	$1 per off-line print

Name:	Moody's Corporate News – US
Description:	This database covers business news and financial information on approximately 13 000 publicly held US corporations, including financial service institutions. The same format is used as for Moody's Corporate News International.
Source:	
Years Covered:	1983 to date
File Size:	233 675 records
Updates:	Weekly
Database Producer:	Moody's Investors Services Inc
Available From:	DIALOG File 556
	$75 per connect hour
	25c per on-line type
	25c per off-line print

Name:	Moody's Corporate Profiles
Description:	This database provides descriptive information on important publicly held US companies. It covers all companies on the New York and US Stock Exchanges, and 1300 active OTC companies. It includes 5-year financial histories, key statistics and analyses of more than 900 companies of high investor interest. Information is also provided on quarterly earnings, dividends, and other company developments.
Source:	Company financial reports
Years Covered:	Current (5 years' historic data)
File Size:	4227 records
Updates:	Weekly
Database Producer:	Moody's Investors Services Inc
Available From:	DIALOG File 555
	$60 per connect hour $4 per on-line type
	$4 per off-line print
	10c per report elements
	50c per mailing label (format 10)

Name:	NAARS (Mead Service)
Description:	NAARS provides 5 years' worth of annual reports for over 4200 US companies. It is made available as a service by agreement with the American Institute of Certified Public Accountants (AICPA). It provides accounting materials containing inter alia, the annual reports of certain public corporations plus selected accounting literature covering US financial reporting standards.
	Files:
	AR – Combined Annual Reports
	86/87 – Annual Reports
	85/86 – Annual Reports
	84/85 – Annual Reports
	83/84 – Annual Reports
	82/83 – Annual Reports
	81/82 – Annual Reports
	LIT – Authoritative accounting materials
	SLIT – Superseded literature
	ALLIT – Combined LIT and SLIT files
Source:	As above
Years Covered:	1981 to date (5 years' historic data)
File Size:	Over 4200 public companies
Updates:	Weekly
Database Producer:	American Institute of Certified Public Accountants

Available From: Mead Data Central
                     $17 per search for Combined Reports (File AR)
                     $14 per search for all other files

Name: Oferes
Description: Oferes provides basic company details on over 30 000 Spanish exporting
                     companies. Details included are: address, telephone and telex numbers,
                     number of employees, languages spoken, trademarks, product sectors,
                     value of exports and countries of destination.
Language: Spanish
Source: Company reports and information supplied by companies
                     direct to the INFE
Years Covered: Latest available
File Size: 30 000 companies
Updates: Every 2 weeks
Database Producer: Instituto Nacional de Fomento de la Exportacion (INFE)
Available From: Instituto Espanol de Comercio Exterior (ICEX)
                     (Prices available direct from ICEX)

Name: Pagine Gialle Electroniche
Description: This service is similar to the American 'Electronic Yellow Pages'. It provides
                     basic information for over 800 000 Italian companies, with fuller product
                     information for 100 000 of these. Approximately 200 000 advertisements are
                     included.
Language: Italian
Source:
Years Covered: Latest available
                     6File Size: 800 000 companies
Updates: As information becomes available
Database Producer: Seat
Available From: Sarin SpA

Name: PTS Annual Reports Abstracts
Description: Annual Reports Abstracts contains statistical tables, textual abstracts, and
                     directory-type corporate establishment records abstracted from Annual
                     Reports and 10K Reports of over 4000 publicly held corporations. Statistical
                     tables present a 5-year history of sales, profits, assets, spending and other
                     important financial data from the numeric section of company reports in as
                     much product line and geographical detail as possible. Text abstracts
                     summarise discussions about product lines, past performance, future goals
                     and strategies, and company organisation found in the text of each report.
                     Up to 80 per cent of the text of a corporate annual report is available. A
                     corporate establishment record presents major lines of business (by SIC
                     code), sales, employment, headquarter address and telephone number,
                     and stock exchange symbol. Company coverage includes all New York and
                     American Stock Exchange listed companies and the most active 800 OTC
                     (over-the-counter) companies. It also includes 800 selected companies from
                     Canada, Europe and Japan.
Source: Annual reports
Years Covered: Current
                     5 years' historical data
File Size: 208 217 records
Updates: Corporate and table records are updated quarterly and replaced annually.
                     The text abstracts are updated monthly
Database Producer: Predicasts Inc

Available From:	DIALOG File 17
	$126 per connect hour 68c per on-line type
	78c per off-line print
	Data-Star File PTAR
	£62.76 per connect hour
	29p per on-line print
	19p per off-line print
	BRS File PTSA
	$90 per connect hour
	80c per on-line type
	75c per off-line print

Name:	PTS PROMT
Description:	Predicasts PROMT (Predicasts Review of Markets and Technology) abstracts all significant information appearing in thousands of newspapers, business magazines, government reports, trade journals, bank letters and special reports throughout the world. In addition, the database covers regional business news and abstracts from corporate a nd industry research reports. The PROMT database provides the following information: acquisitions, capacities, end users, environment, international trade, market data, new products, production, regulations and technology. This information covers products and services of the following industries: chemicals, communications, computers, electronics, energy, fibers, food, instruments and equipment, metals, paper, plastics and rubber. Items are indexed by product, by type of information, geographically and by company.
Source:	Over 1200 publications including brokers' reports, journals, corporate news releases, corporate annual reports, Japanese publications and PR Newswire Service
Years Covered:	1972 to date
	1978 to date (Data-Star)
File Size:	1 435 275 records
	Information on over 120 000 companies (public and private)
Updates:	PTS PROMT: weekly, about 2400 records per update
	PTS PROMT Daily: updated daily, held for up to 5 days (then transferred to PTS PROMT)
Database Producer:	Predicasts Inc
Available From:	DIALOG
	File 16 PTS PROMT
	$126 per connect hour
	63c per on-line type
	73c per off-line print
	SDI profile: $9.95
	File 602 PTS PROMPT Daily
	$132 per connect hour
	68c per on-line type
	78c per off-line print
	Data-Star File PTSP
	£65.51 per connect hour
	34p per on-line print
	25p per off-line print
	SDI profile: £2.73
	BRS File PTSP
	$95 per connect hour
	67c per on-line type
	62c per off-line print
	SDI profile: $4

Name:	Qui Decide en France
Description:	This database provides basic information on over 80 000 companies in France and approximately 260 000 senior executives. Information includes the address, telephone, telex numbers, legal status, lines of business, current nominal capital and turnover. Each company makes up a separate document.
Language:	French
Source:	Annual directories produced by Le Groupe DPV: 'Qui Decide en France', 'Qui Decide en Region Parisienne', 'Qui Decide en Region Nord', 'Qui Decide en Region Rhone-Alpes'
Years Covered:	Current
File Size:	Approx 80 000 documents
Updates:	6 times per annum
Database Producer:	Groupe DPV
Available From:	G CAM Serveur File DCID
	FF 620 per connect hour

Name:	Registro de Establecimientos Industriales
Description:	This database is a directory of Spanish industrial companies. It contains basic financial and product details.
Source:	Registro de Establecimientos (Register of companies)
Years Covered:	1984 to date
File Size:	92 000 documents
Updates:	Periodically
Database Producer:	Sistema de Informacion Empresarial
Available From:	Instituto de la Pequena y Mediana Empresa Industrial (IMPI)
	Contact direct for prices

Name:	Report on Business Corporate Database
Description:	This database provides 300 financial data items for over 1750 Canadian companes including all active public companies traded on Canadian stock exchanges. Quarterly information is available for over 350 major Canadian corporations.
Source:	Annual or quarterly financial statements
Years Covered:	10 years' historic data
File Size:	Over 1750 companies
	300 financial data items
Updates:	Quarterly and annual
Database Producer:	
Available From:	Info Globe
	$349 initiation fee
	$150 per connect hour
	10c per data item

Name:	SANI
Description:	SANI (National Register of Firms) is the largest database on Italian businesses. It is sourced from the Register of Firms which every Chamber of Commerce is required to keep, and which by law must record every firm in its province.
	The file offers detailed information on each firm (legal status, date of founding, share capital, tax code number, industry sector, branches, number of employees, personal data on directors, etc) as well as lists of firms selected by various criteria (location, legal status, industry sector, number of employees, share capital), all of which can be combined.
Language:	Italian
Source:	Chambers of Commerce
Years Covered:	Latest data available
File Size:	Over 4 million items
Updates:	Daily

Database Producer: Cerved
                      Societa Nazionale di Informatica delle Camere di Commercio
Available From: Cerved File SANI
                      Lire 122079 per connect hour (prime time)
                      Lire 99883 per connect hour (non-prime time)

Name: SANP
Description: SANP (National Defaulters File) offers data on the protests (including
                      unpaid bank drafts, bad cheques) of both individuals and companies
                      throughout Italy over 5 years.
                          This file can máke available both data on single defaulters and variously
                      selected lists. A special feature is the procedure for finding 'new defaulters'
                      which makes it possible to identify those who have been subjected to
                      default procedure for the first time in the last 5 years.
Language: Italian
Source: Official bulletins of the Chambers of Commerce
Years Covered: Last 5 years
File Size: 25 million items (average)
Updates: Fortnightly
Database Producer: Cerved
                      Societa Nazionale di Informatica delle Camere di Commercio
Available From: Cerved File SANP
                      Lire 166471 per connect hour (prime time)
                      Lire 133177 per connect hour (non-prime time)

Name: SDOE
Description: This database contains information on Italian companies ordinarily
                      engaged in import and / or export business. The file records the following
                      data:
                      Company name, headquarters, telephone number, telex
                      Number of employees
                      Line of business
                      Average revenue for the most recent years
                      Export sales expressed in percentage of total revenue
                      Export channels used by the company
                      Products handled, identified by SIC code number
                      Trading countries
Language: Italian
Source: Chambers of Commerce
Years Covered: Latest available data
File Size: Covers over 60000 firms
Updates: Annual
Database Producer: Cerved
                      Societa Nazionale di Infomatica delle Camere di
                      Commercio
Available From: Cerved File SDOE
                      Lire 166471 per connect hour (prime time)
                      Lire 133177 per connect hour (non-prime time)

Name: SIBIL
Description: SIBIL consists of 2 sub-files:
                          SABB-BUSARL – contains the balance sheets of Italian limited companies
                      (approx 200000) for the latest 3 years as published in the official bulletin
                      ('BUSARL') of limited companies produced by the Chambers of Commerce.
                          SABRI – contains balance sheet data for the 30000 largest companies over
                      the latest 3 fiscal years. Balance sheets are reclassified by standard patterns
                      in conformity with the EEC directives. Accounts are supplemented with
                      data such as export sales, mergers and divestitures.
Language: Italian

Source:	Company financial statements
	Chambers of Commerce
	Centrale dei Bilanci conducts financial analysis of data held in SABRI
Years Covered:	Latest 3 fiscal years
File Size:	200000 limited companies, 30000 largest companies
Updates:	As records are available at Chambers of Commerce
Database Producer:	Cerved
	Societa Nazionale d'Informatica delle Camere di Commercio
Available From:	Cerved
	SABB:
	Lire 122079 per connect hour (prime time)
	Lire 99883 per connect hour (non-prime time)
	SABRI:
	Lire 126000 per connect hour (prime time)
	Lire 100000 per connect hour (non-prime time)
	Additional 50000 lire for each company balance sheet
	analysis in SABRI

Name:	Sirene
Description:	Sirene provides basic information on French firms. Data includes address, industry sector, legal status, number of salaried employees, and quarterly turnover figures. Firms covered include industrials, telecommunication, financial service, agricultural and public organisations amongst others.
Language:	French
Source:	Company accounts
Years Covered:	Current
File Size:	Approx 3.2 million firms
Updates:	Daily
Database Producer:	Institut National de la Statistique et des Etudes Economiques (INSEE)
	Ministere de l'Economie
Available From:	INSEE
	Contact direct for price and access details

Name:	Sistema de Informacion Empresarial
Description:	This database provides basic details on over 10000 Spanish companies. Details include address, telephone and telex numbers and a list of each company's products or services.
Source:	Direct from companies
Years Covered:	Latest available information
File Size:	10000 companies
Updates:	As data becomes available
Database Producer:	Instituto de la Pequena y Mediana Empresa Industrial (IMPI)
Available From:	Ministerio de Industria y Energia

Name:	Soliditet Online Service (SOS)
Description:	Soliditet Online is a factual reference database. It contains information about all joint stock companies and private companies, parent companies and subsidiaries or other affiliated companies in Denmark. Financial status and accounting figures are provided. Users can order complete accounts and reports on companies online.
Source:	Company reports
Years Covered:	Latest available
File Size:	
Updates:	
Database Producer:	Kobmandsstandsstanders Oplysningsbureau A/S
	(The information bureau of the trades association)
Available From:	Kobmandsstandsstandens Oplysningsbureau A/S
	Contact direct for prices

Name: Standard & Poor's Corporate Descriptions
Description: This database offers in-depth descriptions of approximately 11 000 publicly
                               held US corporations, including a complete corporate background, all
                               income account and balance sheet figures, and important stock and bond
                               data.
Source: Company financial reports
Years Covered: Current
File Size: 13 928 records
Updates: 2 times a week
Database Producer: Standard and Poor's Corporation
Available From: DIALOG File 133
                               $85 per connect hour
                               $3.50 per on-line type
                               $3.50 per off-line print

Name: Standard & Poor's (S&P) Marketscope
Description: This database provides concise descriptions of operations for over 4700
                               companies including background information, commentaries on future
                               prospects, earnings and dividends projections (on about 1000 companies)
                               and tables showing sales and earnings by lines of business. A statistical
                               page provides current and historical financial data including price range
                               and P/E range. Other features of the database include a commentary
                               provided 8 times daily on current market activity, S & P stock investment
                               recommendations, US interest rates and a Marketmovers facility which
                               monitors active and volatile issues throughout the day.
Source: Company annual reports and statements, US exchanges, Standard and
                               Poor's own analysts' reports and recommendations
Years Covered: Real time
File Size: 4700 companies
Updates: Varies according to type of information. Company financial data is updated
                               daily. Company descriptions are updated as new information becomes
                               available. Market commentary is updated 8 times a day. Interest rates are
                               updated 6 times a day
Database Producer: Standard & Poor's Corporation
Available From: Standard & Poor's Corporation
                               Contact direct for prices

Name: Standard & Poor's News
Description: This database contains every news story and financial update printed by
                               Standard and Poor on more than 10 000 US companies since June 1979.
                               Users can search by company name, date of record, key words or phrases.
                               Users can also segment the file to allow access to either financial records or
                               news stories. Financial records include annual report and interim earnings
                               statements in tabulated form.
Source: Major sources include:
                               Annual and interim stockholders reports
                               Company press releases
                               10-K, 10-Q and 8-K reports filed with the SEC
                               Releases from NYSE, ASE and regional exchanges
                               Leading US and Canadian newspapers
Years Covered: 1979 to date
File Size: 588 090 records
Updates: Daily (300-400 news stories added daily)
Database Producer: Standard & Poor's Corporation

Available From: DIALOG
                        File 134 and File 132 (July 1985 to date)
                        $96 per connect hour
                        25c per off-line print
                        SDI profile: $5.95
                        Standard and Poor's Corporation
                        Service available on CD ROM
                        Contact Diane Rollert for further information
                        Global Report – Citicorp Service
                        Contact Citicorp direct for prices
                        Guide:
                        £250 flat fee per month
                        Entitles user to 6 hours' access
                        £34 per hour for time used in excess of 6 hours

Name: Standard and Poor's Register – Corporate
Description: Standard and Poor's Register – Corporate provides important business
                        facts on over 45000 leading public and private US (and some non-US)
                        companies, with sales in excess of 1 million dollars. This directory file
                        includes company records for parent companies plus subsidiaries,
                        divisions, and affiliates. Records include current company address,
                        financial and marketing information, and a listing of officers and directors
                        with positions and departments. Further biographical information is
                        available for approximately 72000 of these executives in the 'Standard and
                        Poor's Register' – Biographical database (DIALOG file 526).
Source: 'Standard and Poor's Register of Corporations', Volume One
Years Covered: Current
File Size: 46238 records
Updates: Quarterly reloads
Database Producer: Standard and Poor's Corporation (USA)
Available From: DIALOG File 527
                        $84 per connect hour
                        $1.50 per on-line type
                        $1.50 per off-line print
                        20c per report element
                        25c per mailing label (format 10)

Name: Stor-Tele
Description: Stor-Tele contains yellow-page type of information for approximately 92000
                        Swedish companies. This can be a useful means of identifying location,
                        existence of subsidiaries, telephone numbers and addresses amongst other
                        details.
Source: Directories
Years Covered: Current
File Size: 92000 companies
Updates: Annual
Database Producer: Affarsdata
Available From: Affarsdata
                        SKr 720 per connect hour

Name: Sveriges Handelskalander
Description: This database contains information similar to the Kompass directories, but
                        with a broader product classification for approximately 15000 Swedish
                        companies. Company information includes address, telephone and telex
                        numbers, and a listing of products and services offered.
Source: 'Sveriges Handelskalander' directory
Years Covered: Current
File Size: 15000 companies
Updates: Annual
Database Producer: Affarsdata
Available From: Affarsdata
                        SKr 720 per connect hour

Name: SYCE
Description: SYCE provides data on Spanish exporting companies, including the value of exports, company addresses, number of employees, etc. This complements the Oferes file, and allows users to rank companies and undertake further analysis of statistics provided.
Language: Castellano and English
Source: Direccion General de Aduanas and the Oferes file
Years Covered: Latest available information
File Size: Approx 24 000 references
Updates:
Database Producer: Instituto Nacional de Fomento de la Exportacion (INFE)
Available From: Instituto Espanol de Comercio Exterior (ICEX)
                     Prices available direct from ICEX

Name: Telecom
Description: This is a full text Danish database covering financial and political news both in Denmark and overseas. It also holds the accounting figures of companies registered on the Copenhagen stock exchange, with key figures and P/E ratios. It also contains stock and share prices quoted on the stock exchange.
Source: News sources. Copenhagen stock exchange.
Years Covered: Current
File Size:
Updates: Daily
Database Producer: Borsinformation Telecom
Available From: Borsinformation Telecom
                     Contact direct for prices and access details

Name: Telefirm
Description: Telefirm provides basic information on approximately 640 000 French firms including addresses, telephone and telex numbers, legal status, names of chief executives, date of incorporation, main line of business, nominal capital and number of employees.
Source: Chambers of Commerce and industry throughout France
Years Covered: Latest available information
File Size: 640 000 firms
Updates: Weekly
Database Producer: Chambre de Commerce et d'Industrie de Paris
Available From: G CAM Serveur File FIRM
                     FF 400 per connect hour

Name: Tele Inform
Description: Tele Inform consists of two services which provide information on over 2.5 million companies in France. Tele Inform 1 provides financial information, historical turnover and profit figures. Credit ratings and credit reports are the main services of Tele Inform 1. There is also a service providing free follow up on a company, where you can be advised on all the changes that occur during one year. Tele Inform 2 provides current commercial information, including the number of employees, industry code, address, phone number and turnover.
Language: French
Source: Derived from notices in the official gazettes, company accounts, local correspondents, etc
Years Covered: Latest available data
File Size: Over 2.5 million companies
Updates: Daily
Database Producer: Groupe Galande
Available From: O R Telematique
                     FF 1350 subscription fee per annum
                     Choice of subscription options available

Name: Textline
Description: Textline is a service which consists of a large computerised store of business
                  information going back to January 1980. It provides users with either
                  abstracts or full text data about companies, industries, economics, politics
                  and the EEC from over 1500 worldwide newspapers and journals. Each
                  summary is written in English. The service is relatively easy to use, as items
                  can be retrieved by specifying a key word or phrase. It is also possible to
                  retrieve more general categories of information using a number of simple
                  indexing terms. Users can search individual sources or selected databases
                  identified either by country of origin or specialist industry sector. Either
                  way, users are guided through searches by a series of multiple choice
                  prompts. Searches are also made more effective through the use of code
                  numbers, which are accessible online. Information on a particular
                  company, for example, can be obtained by simply entering the company
                  code and specifying sources when prompted, or type 'all' if you want to
                  search the entire database.
Source: Newspapers, journals, press releases, brokers' circulars, corporate financial
                  reports.
                  Country sources:
                  UK and Western Europe (all EEC countries except Greece
                  and Luxembourg)
                  USA
                  Canada
                  Middle East
                  India and the Far East
                  Africa
                  Latin America
                  Eastern Europe and USSR
                  Australasia
                  Specialist sources:
                  Banking and finance
                  Computing and electronics
                  Property and construction
                  Marketing, media and retailing
                  Insurance and investment
                  Chemicals and engineering
                  Accountancy and taxation
                  Travel
                  Aerospace and defence
Years Covered: 1980 to date
File Size: Over 1500 source publications
Updates: Approx 5000 abstracts per week
Database Producer: Reuters
Available From: Reuters
                  £75 per connect hour
                  30p per on-line type
                  (10p per title; 20p per abstract)
                  ESA-IRS File 21
                  £94.51 per connect hour
                  Printing charges are format dependent
                  Use? Charges on-line for price list

Name: Thomas Regional Industrial Suppliers
Description: Thomas Regional Industrial Suppliers contains listings for distributors,
                  manufacturers' representatives and service organisations providing
                  industrial products and services in 14 major US industrial regions. The
                  database covers over 320 000 companies which are product and service
                  sources for over 3000 categories of products.
Source: Equivalent to the publication 'Regional Industrial
                  Purchasing Guide'
Years Covered: Current
File Size: 306 946 records

Updates:	Quarterly reloads
Database Producer:	Thomas Publishing Company Inc
Available From:	DIALOG File 537
	$84 per connect hour
	40c per on-line type
	45c per off-line print
	23c per mailing label (format 10)

Name:	Thomas Register Online
Description:	Thomas Register Online contains information on what is made in the US, where it is made and who makes it. The file covers over 133 000 US manufacturers, with over 50 000 classes of products and over 106 000 trade or brand names. The file includes the current listings for more than 1 million individual product and service sources.
Source:	Equivalent to the publication 'Thomas Register of American Manufacturers'
Years Covered:	Current
File Size:	140 734 records
Updates:	Annual reload
Database Producer:	Thomas Publishing Company Inc
Available From:	DIALOG File 535
	$100 per connect hour
	$1.50 per on-line type
	$1.50 per off-line print
	25c per mailing label (format 10)

Name:	Trinet Company Database
Description:	Trinet Company is a directory file which provides current address, financial and marketing information. The database covers top private and public companies which operate in the USA.
	Data on individual establishments are contained in a companion file, Trinet Establishment.
	The database includes HQ for all multi-establishment companies which own establishments employing 20 or more people, as well as single establishment companies with 20 or more people.
	The following information is included in each report:
	Company name
	Annual sales
	Market share statistics
	Employees by activity
	Foreign ownership (if more than 10 per cent)
	Address and telephone number
	Per cent of company sales within most sectors
	Stock trading symbol
Source:	The majority of the information comes from published annual and quarterly reports, industry and trade publications, directories, telephone interviews and US Census Bureau Statistics
Years Covered:	Current
File Size:	219 688 records
Updates:	Quarterly
Database Producer:	Trinet Inc
Available From:	DIALOG File 532
	$90 per connect hour
	$1.60 per on-line type
	$1.60 per off-line print
	MEAD File TRICO
	$20 per connect hour
	$15 cost of search
	MAID
	£4250 annual subscription
	(including training, codes etc)
	£80 per connect hour

Name: Trinet Establishment Database
Description: Trinet Establishment provides information on US companies such as
                   location, headquarters name, per cent of industry sales, industry
                   classification and employment size. It covers nearly 400 000 manufacturers
                   and non-manufacturers that employ 20 or more people.
                       See Trinet Company Database which is the directory file.
Source: Annual and quarterly reports, telephone interviews, US
                   Census Bureau Statistics
Years Covered: Current data
File Size: 373 865 records
Updates: Quarterly
Database Producer: Trinet Inc
Available From: DIALOG File 531
                   $90 per connect hour
                   50c per on-line type
                   50c per off-line type
                   MEAD File TRIEST
                   $20 per connect hour (all files)
                   $15 cost of search

Name: UK Company Profile
Description: The UK Company Profile database is claimed by its producers to be the
                   largest online database of its kind in the world with over 199 000 public and
                   private full company reports available on line.
                       The UK Company Profile consists of:
                   A Management Profile:
                   Registered office, activities, share capital and principal shareholders,
                   holding Co, directors, company secretary, register of charges, date of
                   incorporation, date of latest annual return, details of mortgages and
                   An Accounting Profile:
                   Comments on the financial performance of the company. Up to 4 years'
                   extracts from the latest accounts with up to 75 key ratios
Source: Company accounts
Years Covered: Latest 4 years
File Size: Over 199 000 company reports
Updates: The profiles are automatically updated when latest audited accounts are
                   filed
Database Producer: Infocheck
Available From: Infocheck
                   £12.50
                   VAT per report drawn off the database or requested
                   Subscription arrangements are available that could reduce the report cost to
                   £4 each

Name: Value Line Database II
Description: Value Line provides annual, quarterly and some monthly historical
                   financial statistics and ratios for over 1800 major industrial, transportation,
                   retail and utility companies. It also covers over 100 banks, insurance plus
                   savings and loans companies. The Estimates and Projections file provides
                   over 70 items of forecast data for 1600 of the companies followed in the
                   Value Line Investment Survey. This file can be purchased separately and
                   items covered include price performance indicators, proprietary
                   investment measures and projected growth rates of key financial indicators
                   for the next 3 to 5 years. The Value Line Convertible Database available
                   through timesharing enables users to update Value Line's evaluation of
                   convertible securities using the latest prices they select.
Source: Research based on data from financial exchanges and company financial
                   statements carried out by Value Line Security analysts
Years Covered: Annual data: 1955 to date
                   Quarterly data: 1963 to date
File Size: 1800 stocks
                   Over 400 data items presented for each year

Updates:	Value Line – weekly
	Estimates & Projections – all data reviewed and updated at least once a quarter
Database Producer:	Value Line Inc
Available From:	Value Line
	Value Line Data Base II: $8250 annual subscription fee per customer
	Above as an option to the E&P file: $2750 per customer
	Estimates and Projections file: $8250 per customer
	Above as an option to DBII: $2750 per customer
	Value Line Convertibles Data Base: $6600 per customer
	Also software products available
	Interactive Data Corporation (IDC)
	Plan A $6500 per annum subscription
	Plan B $2000 per quarter subscription
	Contact IDC direct for Analytics charges
	Compuserve
	Drexel Burnham Lambert
	Factset Data Systems
	Finstat (Shearson Lehman Hutton)
	Lotus Development Corp
	Randall-Helms
	Salomon Brothers (Stockfacts)
	Available to Salomon clients only. Contact Salomon
	direct for further details.
	Shaw Data Service
	Vestek Systems
	Wilshire Associates
	Zacks Investment Research

Name:	Verband der Vereine Creditreform eV
Description:	Contains financial and textual reports on approximately 320 000 German companies. Each profile includes the company name, address, telephone number, legal form, founding year, financial data management, ownership, industry codes, business description, and number of employees. The database contains current information and is updated quarterly. The intended user group includes: decision makers in the area of economics; marketing and public relations departments; and company heads and controllers.
Language:	German
Source:	All public registers, company surveys, Creditreform's own research, reports
Years Covered:	Current
File Size:	Approx 341 000 company files
Updates:	Quarterly
Database Producer:	Verband der Vereine Creditreform eV
Available From:	GENIOS File VC
	DM 291 per connect hour
	DM 16 per on-line type
	DM 16 per off-line print
	Bertelsmann File DVVC
	DM 240 per connect hour (licence fee)
	DM 78 per connect hour
	DM 5 to DM 16 per on-line type
	DM 5 to DM 16 per off-line print
	Data-Star File DVVC
	Contact direct for prices (new file)

Name:	Who Makes Machinery
Description:	This is the on-line version of the buyers' guide 'Who Makes Machinery' published by Hoppenstedt in cooperation with the German Machinery and Plant Manufacturers Association (VDMA). It contains references to products manufactured and offered for sale by about 4400 companies in Germany.
Language:	German
Source:	German Machinery and Plant Manufacturers Association (VDMA)
Years Covered:	Current
File Size:	4400 records
Updates:	Annual
Database Producer:	Hoppenstedt Wirtschaftsverlag GmbH in cooperation with Verband Deutscher Maschine und Anlagenbau (VDMA)
Available From:	FIZ Technik File VDMA
	DM 250 per connect hour
	DM 2.3 per on-line type
	DM 2.6 per off-line print
	DM 1.3 for company address and telecom info only
	Data-Star File VDME
	Contact direct for prices (new file)

Name:	Who Owns Whom
Description:	Who Owns Whom provides detailed information on the structure of corporate groups and companies on an international basis. This service builds up a file of historical information on the parentage of any one of 300 000 listed companies, so users can keep track of their movements within corporation groups. Who Owns Whom is ideal for obtaining a clear outline of ownership structure or for gaining advance warning of any possible conflict of interest. This database can be used to:
	Monitor international corporations
	Analyse geographical dependencies
	Create corporate profiles
Source:	
Years Covered:	Current
File Size:	25 000 parent companies
	275 000 subsidiary companies
Updates:	Monthly
Database Producer:	Dun & Bradstreet
Available From:	Pergamon Financial File WOW
	£125 per connect hour
	28p per off-line print
	Dun & Bradstreet
	Available on magnetic tape

Name:	Who Supplies What?
Description:	This database has two subfiles: the English version (EWLW) and German version (DWLW). Who Supplies What? (Wer Liefert Was) is the online version of the buyers' guide issued by the publishing house Wer Liefert Was. It contains references to more than 200 000 products manufactured and offered for sale by about 55 000 companies in the Federal Republic of Germany and West Berlin. Each profile includes the company name, address, where available telephone and telex number, trade name and product line. The intended user group includes individuals in the following areas: sales, retail and wholesale trade, import and export, and distribution and marketing.
Language:	English and German versions
Source:	Online equivalent to the printed version 'Who Supplies What?' ('Wer Liefert Was')
Years Covered:	Current
File Size:	55 000 records
	Approx 2500 new records added per update

Updates:	Bi-annually
Database Producer:	Bezugsquellennachweis fuer den Einkauf Wer Liefert Was? GmbH
Available From:	FIZ Technik File WLW
	DM 250 per connect hour
	DM 1.8 per on-line type
	DM 2.1 per off-line print
	DM 1.3 for company address and telecom information only
	Bertelsmann File DWLW (German version)
	File EWLW (English version)
	DM 145 per connect hour (licence fee)
	DM 78 per connect hour
	DM 1.50 per on-line type
	DM 1.50 per off-line print
	Data-Star File WLWE
	Contact direct for prices (new file)

Name:	Worldscope
Description:	Worldscope provides financial information on the world's leading industrial corporations, banks, insurance companies and financial service firms. Financial statements are presented in as close a form as possible to the original. Four standard financial statement formats are used for: industrial, bank, insurance and financial services. Users can scan across all countries for companies meeting certain criteria, eg return on equity, net income growth. Twenty four countries are included in the service. Two thousand of the companies covered are US and 2000 are from the other 23 countries. Data includes financial statements, stockholding and share price information, financial performance ratios and company specific accounting practices information. A unique feature of the service is the ability to translate financials into selected exchange rates.
	The service is provided on CD ROM, and subscription includes an optical disc drive, which plugs into IBM XT, AT or compatible computers. It is possible to transfer files to leading software packages such as Lotus 123 or to ASCII files. Software is provided to facilitate retrieval and the modelling of data.
Source:	Worldscope database
	(developed through a joint venture between Wright Investors' Service and the Center for International Financial Analysis and Research)
Years Covered:	Annual data from 1980 to date
	Monthly data from 1986 to date
File Size:	4500 companies from 24 countries
Updates:	Monthly
Database Producer:	The Center for International Financial Analysis and Research (CIFAR)
Available From:	Lotus Development (UK, USA) on CD ROM
	Basic subscription rate: £7000 per annum which includes an optical disc reader, information retrieval software, training and manuals, etc. Exact price depends on user's specific data requirements. Volume discount schedule available.
	Available on line through other hosts, eg InfoGlobe, Finstat, CompuServe.
	Real Decision Corporation distributes Worldscope on mainframe computer tape.
	UK distributor for Worldscope is NMW Computers plc, Nantwich, Cheshire
	Telesystemes-Questel is the affiliate for Compuserve in France.
	Contact distributors direct for price details.

Name:	ZVEI Electro-Buying Guide
Description:	The ZVEI database is the online version of the information and reference work 'ZVEI Elektro / Einkaufsfuhrer / Die Deutsche Elektro-Industrie'. It covers approx 16 000 product terms and producer details available from all areas of the German electro and electronics industry. About 1900 companies are named with address, stelecommunication details and the

production programme. These details are complemented by detailed corporate data, eg ownership shares, structural data, representations, and development. The combination of detailed production programme and individual corporate data can be used to construct comprehensive company profiles in the German electro and electronics industry.

Language: German
Source: Information and reference work (ZVEI) 'Elektro-Einkaufsfuhrer / Die Deutsche Elektroindustrie'
Years Covered: Current
File Size: Approx 16 000 supply sources from about 1900 companies split up into around 2500 product groups (specific nomenclature)
Updates: Annual
Database Producer: Verlag W Sachon GmbH & Co
Available From: Genios File ZVEI
                    DM 234 per connect hour
                    DM 2.2 per on-line type
                    DM 2.7 per off-line print
                    FIZ Technik File ZVEI
                    DM 250 per connect hour
                    DM 2.8 per on-line type
                    DM 3.1 per off-line print
                    DM 1.3 for company address and telecom information only
                    Data-Star File ZVEE
                    Contact direct for prices (new file)

Section II General Management

ABI/Inform
Bibliographic for Public Management and Administration
BLISS
Harvard Business Review Information Service – Exchange
ISIS
Management Contents

Management and Marketing Abstracts
SCANP
SCIMP

Who's Who

Les Administrateurs
Business Science Experts
Directory of American Research and Technology
Disclosure (see Company Section)

Kompass Online
Management Experten – Nachweis
Marquis Who's Who
Qui Decide en France (see Company Section)
Reference Book of Corporate Management
Standard & Poor's Register – Biographical
Vademecum
Who Inform

Name: ABI/Inform
Description: The ABI/Inform database is designed to meet the information needs of executives and covers all aspects of business and management. ABI/Inform stresses general decision science information which is applicable to many types of business and industries. It specifically covers banking, insurance, real estate, accounting and finance.
Source: Over 550 journals in the areas of accounting, administration, advertising, banking, data processing, economics, employee benefits, finance, insurance, international trade, labour relations, operations research, real estate, social conditions, statistics, business law, stocks and bonds, taxes and training and education
Years Covered: 1971 to date
File Size: Approx 400 000 records
Updates: Monthly or weekly
                Approx 30 000 citations added per annum

Database Producer: UMI/Data Courier
Available From: DIALOG File 15
    $105 per on-line connect hour
    80c per on-line type
    $1.30 per off-line print
    SDI profile: $9.95
    Data-Star File INFO
    £54.49 per connect hour
    33p per on-line print
    36p per off-line print
    SDI profile: £1.63
    ESA-IRS File 30
    £59.50 per connect hour
    31.5p per on-line type
    61.9p per off-line print
    SDI profile: £1.40
    MEAD File ABI (Abstracts)
    $20 per connect hour (all files)
    plus $11 per search
    BRS File INFO
    $70 per connect hour
    57c per on-line type
    67c per off-line print
    SDI profile: $4

Name: Les Administrateurs
Description: This is an on-line 'Directory of Directors', covering over 1 million business
    executives. Directors' names, current posts and brief biographical
    information is provided.
Source: Legal information
Years Covered: Current
File Size: 1 million executives
Updates: Daily
Database Producer: Groupe Galande
Available From: OR Telematique
    FF 1350 subscription fee per annum
    Choice of subscription options available

Name: Bibliographic for Public Management and Administration
Description: This is a bibliography (systematical order) of books and periodical articles in
    the fields of public management and economics. The German title of this
    database is Bibliographie zur Offentlichen Unternehmung und
    Verwaltung.
Language: German
Source: Specialist books and articles published in the Federal Republic of Germany
Years Covered: 1981 to date
File Size: 1700 citations
Updates: Twice a year
Database Producer: Nomos Datapool
    Nomos Verlagsgesellschaft mbH
Available From: Edicline File BOWI
    £60 per connect hour

Name: BLISS
Description: Betriebswirtschaftliches Literatur-Suchsystem (BLISS) is an economic
    literature search system which offers information on German and
    international economic literature. It is the main German-language literature
    bank covering economic subjects and related areas in detail.
    Subjects covered:
    Management, organisation, planning
    Information and EDP
    Marketing and trade

Material handling and logistics
Personnel and employment
Production
Controlling
Banking and insurance
Service, administration, office
Finance and investment
Economic law
Quantitative processes

Language:	German and English
Source:	Trade magazines (350 German and international publications)
	Essays (46 000)
	Dissertations and research reports (15 000)
Years Covered:	1975 to date
File Size:	93 000 records (as at Jan 1988)
Updates:	Monthly, 10 000 publications added per annum
Database Producer:	Gesellschaft fur Betriebswirtschaftliche Information mbH (GBI)
Available From:	GENIOS File BLIS
	DM 240 per connect hour
	DM 0.7 per on-line type
	DM 1.0 per off-line print
	SDI profile: DM 10
	FIZ Technik File BLISS
	DM 250 per connect hour
	DM 0.8 per on-line type
	DM 1.1 per off-line print
	SDI profile: DM 10
	GBI File BLISS
	DM 120 per connect hour
	DM 0.2 per on-line type
	DM 60 per off-line print (up to 15 titles)
	DM 180 per off-line print (up to 60 titles)

Name:	Business Science Experts
Description:	The database contains references to corporate and individual business science experts in the Federal Republic of Germany and West Berlin. Records contain the name, address, telephone number and a brief professional profile.
Language:	English and German
Source:	Producer's own studies
Years Covered:	Current
File Size:	2000 citations, 200 citations added per annum
Updates:	Quarterly
Database Producer:	Nomos Datapool
	Nomos Verlagsgesellschaft mbH
Available From:	Edicline File WEX
	£60 per connect hour

Name:	Directory of American Research and Technology
Description:	The DART database is on on-line directory of research and development capabilities of industrial organisations in the United States. It offers access to details of key personnel within the laboratories covered, as well as doctoral disciplines, R & D programmes, and number of professional staff. DART also includes 'not for profit' and privately financed organisations engaged in research projects.
	This database is potentially useful for locating personnel or companies involved in specific research, and for headhunting and research projects.
Source:	Industrial organisations
Years Covered:	Current
File Size:	11 000 records
Updates:	Annual
Database Producer:	R R Bowker Company

Available From:	Pergamon Financial File DART
	£50 per connect hour
	20p per on-line type
	35p per off-line print
	ESA-IRS File 150
	Gateway Service to Pergamon Infoline
	£67.2 per connect hour
	22.4p per on-line type
	38.5p per off-line print

Name:	Harvard Business Review
Description:	Harvard Business Review provides articles in full text or, if preferred, summaries of articles, from the 'Harvard Business Review'. It covers a complete range of strategic management subjects of interest to professional managers and researchers. Areas covered include management; business ethics; marketing; economic outlook; accounting; organisational behaviour; industry analysis; automation; international trade.
Source:	'Harvard Business Review'
Years Covered:	1976 to date (full text)
	1971 to date (citations and abstracts)
File Size:	2780 records
Updates:	Bimonthly
Database Producer:	John Wiley & Sons Inc
Available From:	DIALOG File 122
	$96 per connect hour
	$7.50 per off-line print (full text)
	20c per off-line print (citation)
	Data-Star File HBRO
	£57.24 per connect hour
	No extra charges
	BRS File HBRO
	$80 per connect hour
	37c per on-line type
	55c per off-line print
	SDI profile: $4
	MEAD File HBR
	$5 per search

Name:	Information Service – Exchange
Description:	This database covers international cooperation and institutions. Short information is given about the international exchange of management personnel, students, practicians, pupils, teachers, artists, journalists and young people.
Source:	Full text of 'Informationsdienst Austausch' (News)
Years Covered:	1978 to date
File Size:	1300 citations. 150 citations added per annum
Updates:	Monthly
Database Producer:	Nomos Datapool
	Nomos Verlagsgesellschaft mbH
Available From:	Edicline File HIZA
	£60 per connect hour

Name:	ISIS
Description:	ISIS is a bibliographic database providing 170 citations with abstracts, to literature on French and international economics, law, industry, insurance and computer science. It also provides articles on business administration, marketing and personnel management.
Language:	French
Source:	1500 periodicals, 1000 books and 1500 other documents
Years Covered:	1975 to date
File Size:	170 citations

Updates:	Weekly
	Approx 500 records added per update
Database Producer:	Chambre de Commerce et d'Industrie de Paris
Available From:	G CAM Serveur
	FF 470 per connect hour

Name:	Management Contents
Description:	Management Contents provides broad coverage of a variety of business and management-related topics including: accounting, decision science, economics, finance, government and public administration, industrial relations, management, managerial economics, marketing, operations research, personnel and production. Over 65 of the leading journals in the field of law are now available on the database.
Source:	The database summarises all articles, except book reviews and letters to the editor, from both US and foreign (English language) journals, as well as proceedings and transactions. Research reports are also indexed and abstracted
Years Covered:	1974 to date
File Size:	Approx 260 000 records
Updates:	Monthly
Database Producer:	Information Access Company
Available From:	DIALOG File 75
	$96 per connect hour
	75c per on-line type
	80c per off-line print
	SDI profile: $9.95
	Data-Star File MGMT
	£48.98 per connect hour
	25p per on-line print
	17p per off-line print
	SDI profile: £1.63
	BRS Files MGMT, MGMB (includes backfile)
	$67 per connect hour
	45c per on-line type
	40c per off-line print
	SDI profile: $4
	ORBIT Search Service File Management
	$90 per connect hour
	48c per on-line type
	55c per off-line print
	SDI profile: $5.95

Name:	Management Experten-Nachweis
Description:	This database (MANEX) contains references to approximately 2500 corporate and individual management experts in the fields of science, marketing, business and business consulting in Austria, the Federal Republic of Germany and Switzerland. Each company or individual description includes name, address, telephone number and brief professional profile.
Language:	English and German
	Covers:Austria, Federal Republic of Germany and Switzerland
Source:	
Years Covered:	Current
File Size:	2500 records (as of January 1988)
Updates:	100 records added per month
Database Producer:	Gesellschaft fur Betriebswirtschaftliche Information mbH (GBI)

Available From:	GBI File MANEX
	DM 120 per connect hour
	DM 2 per on-line type
	GENIOS File MANX
	DM 240 per connect hour
	DM 3 per on-line type
	DM 3 per off-line print

Name:	Management and Marketing Abstracts
Description:	Management and Marketing Abstracts covers all aspects of management and marketing worldwide from the theoretical and practical viewpoint. The database monitors over 200 major journals in the fields of management and marketing and contains summaries of articles, as well as reports, newspapers, books and legislative material.

This database can be useful for:

Research
Teaching
Product management
Monitoring trends
Preparing company profiles

Source:	Over 200 marketing and management journals
Years Covered:	1976 to date
File Size:	26 500
Updates:	Fortnightly
Database Producer:	Paper and Board Packaging Industries Research Association (PIRA)
Available From:	Pergamon Financial File MMA
	£70 per connect hour
	30p per on-line type
	30p per off-line print
	SDI profile: £5
	ESA-IRS File 160
	Gateway Service to Pergamon
	£79.80 per connect hour
	20.3p per on-line type
	23.1p per off-line print

Name:	Marquis Who's Who
Description:	Marquis Who's Who contains detailed biographies on nearly 101 000 individuals. Top professionals in business, sports, government, the arts, entertainment, science and technology are included in the database. Data in the records include career history, education, creative works, publications, family background, current address, political activities and affiliation, religion, and special achievements. Marquis Who's Who corresponds to the printed publications 'Marquis Who's Who in America' and 'Who's Who in Science and Technology'.
Source:	'Marquis Who's Who in America'
	'Who's Who in Science and Technology'
Years Covered:	Current
File Size:	97 250 records
Updates:	Quarterly
Database Producer:	Marquis Who's Who Inc
Available From:	DIALOG File 234
	$150 per connect hour
	$2.50 per on-line type
	$2.50 per off-line print

Name:	Reference Book of Corporate Management
Description:	This database is the online version of Dun and Bradstreet's 'Corporate Management Reference Book'. It contains the professional histories and biographical details on principal officers and directors employed by top US companies. Using RBCM, users can identify these key individuals by current employer, age or education and check on details of their military or

work histories. It can be a useful tool for the purposes of:
Headhunting
Research work
Identifying key personnel
Creating company profiles

Source:	Equivalent to the publication 'Reference Book of Corporate Management'
Years Covered:	Current
File Size:	Indivduals from over 12 000 US companies
Updates:	Annual
Database Producer:	Dun's Marketing Services (USA)
Available From:	Pergamon Financial File RBCM
	£65 per connect hour
	£1.50 per on-line type
	£1.50 per off-line print
	SDI profile: £5

Name:	SCANP
Description:	SCANP is a bibliographic database covering Scandinavian periodicals in the fields of management, economics and business. The database can be searched using keywords, author, broad subject group, language, year, names of firms and journal name.
Language:	English, Danish, German, Norwegian, Swedish
Source:	260 Scandinavian sources including journal articles and research reports
Years Covered:	1977 to date
File Size:	Approx 2000 references added per annum
Updates:	4 times per annum
Database Producer:	Arhus School of Economics
	Norwegian School of Economics
	Helsinki School of Economics
	Stockholm School of Economics
	Copenhagen School of Economics
Available From:	Helsinki School of Economics
	Annual subscription FiM 1650

Name:	SCIMP
Description:	SCIMP is a unique European management database. It provides an index to European management periodicals plus American periodicals. It covers the fields of management, business sciences and economics. The database can be searched using keywords, broad subject groups, free text, author's name, year of publication, language, company name and journal name. Languages:English, French, German, Italian, Spanish, Dutch
Source:	160 periodicals scanned
Years Covered:	1978 to date
File Size:	Approx 6000 references added per annum
Updates:	10 times per annum
Database Producer:	European Business School Librarians Group
Available From:	Helsinki School of Economics
	Annual subscription FiM 2000

Name:	Standard & Poor's Register – Biographical
Description:	Standard & Poor's Register – Biographical provides extensive personal and professional data on key executives affiliated with public and private, US and non-US companies, with sales of 1 million dollars and over. Each biographical reference provides a comprehensive profile of personal, professional, and educational details on executives and directors from the companies listed in Standard & Poor's Register – Corporate (DIALOG file 527).
Source:	Equivalent to the publication 'Standard & Poor's Register of Corporations, Directors and Executives', Volume Two
Years Covered:	Current
File Size:	71 127 records

Updates:	Biannual reload
Database Producer:	Standard & Poor's Corporation (USA)
Available From:	DIALOG File 526
	$84 per connect hour
	$1.50 per on-line type
	$1.50 per off-line print

Name:	Vademecum
Description:	Vademecum provides a reference to educational and research institutions in the Federal Republic of Germany. It contains addresses, a description of the main research activities and information on leading scientists. It is the online version of the 8th edition of 'Vademecum Deutscher Lehr-und Forschungsstatten'.
Language:	German
Source:	Questionnaires completed by educational and research institutions
Years Covered:	Current
File Size:	Over 7000 addresses
Updates:	
Database Producer:	Raabe Verlag, Stuttgart in cooperation with FIZ Karlsruhe
Available From:	STN File Vademacum
	£64 per connect hour
	20p per on-line type
	35p per off-line print

Name:	Who Inform
Description:	Who Inform (WIW) covers the Federal Republic of Germany and West Berlin. It contains company information and descriptive information in the fields of consulting, services and management. There are references to corporate and individual experts and each citation includes their name, address, phone number and a brief professional profile.
Language:	English and German
Source:	Full text of 'Handbuch der Informations und Beratungsangebote fur die Wirtschaft'
Years Covered:	1986 to date
File Size:	6300 records
	100 records added per annum
Updates:	Quarterly
Database Producer:	Ges fur Informationsmarkt-Forschung (GIF)
Available From:	Edicline File WIW
	£60 per connect hour

Section III Marketing

Market Survey Directories

Arthur D Little/Online
FINDEX
Industry Data Sources
Marketing Surveys Index

Market Surveys and Reports

Business Trend Analysts
Consumer Reports
Economist Intelligence Unit
Economist Intelligence
Unit-Retail Business

EIU International Travel & Tourism Reports
EIU Travel & Tourism Analyst
Eurofile
Euromonitor
Find/SVP
Frost and Sullivan Market Research
Henley Centre for Forecasting
ICC International Business Research
Jordans Business Surveys
Keynote Industry Surveys
Leading Edge Reports
Market Directions
Market Facts Inc
Mercatis
Mintel Reports
MSI Market Reports

Nielsen Market Information
Packaged Facts
USA Monitor

Advertising and Media

Advertising Age
Burda – MarketingInfoSystem
FTBR Media File (see FT Business Reports in Industry Section)
Genius Operator
Meal Quarterly Digest
Multi Media Service
NCOM
PTS Marketing and Advertising Reference Service
Saatchi and Saatchi Compton Media

Market Forecasts

International
Find/SVP
Frost and Sullivan Market
Research Reports
PTS International Forecasts
(see Economics Section)

Europe
Eurofacts (see Economics
Section)
Eurofile
Euromonitor
Market Directions
Mercatis
PTS International Forecasts
(see Economics Section)

UK
Keynote Industry Surveys
PTS International Forecasts
(see Economics Section)

PTS Promt (see Company
Section)

USA
Business Trend Analysts
Find/SVP
Frost and Sullivan Market
Research Reports
Industry Performance
Monitor (see Industry-wide
Section)
Packaged Facts
PTS Promt (see Company
Section)
PTS US Forecasts (see
Economics Section)

Market and Industry News

ABI/Inform (see General
Management Section)
Absatzwirtschaft

Arthur D Little/Online
BIS Infomat
Business Review Weekly
The Economist
Financial Times Business
Reports
Global Report
Globe and Mail Online
Handelsblatt
Magazine ASAP
Magazine Index
Marketing Week
McGraw Hill Publications
Online
Nexis
PTS Promt (see Company
Section)
Teleborsen
Textline (see Company
Section)
Trade and Industry ASAP
Trade and Industry Index

Name:	Absatzwirtschaft
Description:	The 'Absatzwirtschaft data bank' (ASW) is the online version of 'Absatzwirtschaft', the biggest German magazine for marketing. It contains unabridged articles with practice-oriented examples and background reports, analyses and prognoses for the following areas: Marketing (strategy, planning, conception, mix, methods, instruments) Marketing research Product policy Packing and logistics Communication Sales (distribution) Training, careers, marketing services, marketing costs and controlling Industry, market sectors and campaigns
Language:	German
Source:	The monthly issue of 'Absatzwirtschaft'
Years Covered:	January 1982 to date
File Size:	Approximately 5300 unabridged articles
Updates:	Monthly
Database Producer:	Handelsblatt GmbH, Absatzwirtschaft
Available From:	GENIOS File ASW DM 240 per connect hour DM 1 per on-line type DM 1 per off-line print SDI profile: DM 10

Name:	Advertising Age
Description:	Provides reports on the advertising and promotional activities of major USA corporations. Selected indepth market research reports are also provided in areas ranging from financial services to the automotive industry and covering distribution activity and promotional attitudes of major market players. The Advertising Age directory of the top 200 advertisers in the USA is also available.
Source:	'Advertising Age'
Years Covered:	November 1985 to date

File Size:
Updates:
Database Producer: Advertising Age
Available From: MAID
                     Annual subscription: £4250
                     (including training, codes, manuals, etc)
                     £80 per connect hour

Name: Arthur D Little/Online
Description: Arthur D Little/Online provides an index to the non-exclusive information
                    sources of Arthur D Little Inc, its divisions and subsidiaries. Providing
                    broad coverage of industries, technologies and management topics, this
                    database contains references to forecasts, planning reports and
                    development reports in the following subject areas and industries: strategic
                    planning, economic forecasts, opinion research, company assessments,
                    energy management, chemicals and related products, consumer products
                    and services, electronics, health care, telecommunications and more.
                    Announcements of meetings, seminars and forums sponsored by Arthur D
                    Little and its subsidiaries are also included. In addition to indexing and
                    availablilty of information, some records contain tables of contents, lists of
                    tables, and/or extensive executive summaries.
Source: Arthur D Little reports
Years Covered: 1977 to date
File Size: 1369 records
Updates: Bimonthly
Database Producer: Arthur D Little Inc
Available From: DIALOG File 192
                    $114 per connect hour
                    50c per on-line type (citation)
                    $100 per on-line type (full text)
                    50c per off-line print (citation)
                    $100 per off-line print (full text)

Name: Burda – MarketingInfoSystem
Description: This database (MADI) is a marketing documentation and information
                   system for advertisers. The relevant contents of a large number of
                   publications are stored in precis form (abstracts) in the following areas:
                   media, publishing houses, advertising, market research, media research,
                   products, markets, companies, documentations, studies and the theme of
                   the study (retrievable with the code FRABO).
Language: German
Source: 6 supra-national daily newspapers, more than 50 trade magazines, annual
                   publication periodicals, studies and market surveys
Years Covered: Current
File Size: Approx 18000 documents (abstracts)
Updates: Monthly
Database Producer: Burda GmbH, Abtlg Markt-Service
Available From: GENIOS File MADI
                   DM 210 per connect hour
                   DM 0.8 per on-line type
                   DM 0.8 per off-line print
                   SDI profile: DM 15

Name: Business Review Weekly (BRWE)
Description: BRWE provides references to articles from the Australian 'Business Review
                  Weekly'. It is a bibliographic database covering news items on finance,
                  industry, business, accounting, information technology and other
                  business-related areas.
Source: Corresponds to the publication 'Business Review Weekly'
Years Covered: 1983 to date
File Size:

Updates:	Weekly
	Approx 50 records added per week
Database Producer:	Australian Financial Review Information Service
Available From:	ACI Computer Services
	A$ 40 monthly fee
	A$ 150 per connect hour
	A$ 0.30 per off-line print

Name:	Business Trend Analysts
Description:	BTA business reports are available in full text through MAID and cover consumer products, electronics, food, industrial equipment and a number of other industry sectors. Each report covers market potential, pricing, company financial data, new products and a number of other market and financial facts.
Source:	Business Trent Analysts
Years Covered:	Current
File Size:	
Updates:	
Database Producer:	Business Trend Analysts
Available From:	MAID
	Annual subscription: £4250
	(including training, codes, manuals, etc)
	£80 per connect hour

Name:	Consumer Reports
Description:	Consumer Reports contains the complete text of the 11 regular monthly issues of the printed 'Consumer Reports'. Published by the non-profit Consumers Union, 'Consumer Reports' is the nation's preeminent product-test and consumer advisory publication. Consumers Union does not permit users of its material to use its name or work including the Consumer Reports database, in advertising, as endorsement of a product or service or for any other commercial purpose. 'Consumer Reports' publishes results of tests on products ranging from major purchases such as automobiles and appliances to everyday items, such as foods and cleaning supplies.
	Test reports include brand name ratings and Consumers Union recommendations. Also examined are financial services and money management organisations, health, nutrition and other medical matters, new laws affecting consumers and on product recalls.
Source:	'Consumer Reports' publication
Years Covered:	Monthly issues 1982 to date
File Size:	4575 records
Updates:	Monthly
Database Producer:	Consumers Union of the United States Inc
Available From:	DIALOG File 646
	$60 per connect hour
	50c per on-line type
	75c per off-line print

Name:	The Economist
Description:	The database contains the full text of this major business weekly journal, produced in London but distributed worldwide. It provides coverage of international political developments, economics, finance, business and company news, science and technology.
Source:	Equivalent to the published version
Years Covered:	December 1981 to date
File Size:	Approx 80 items added each week
Updates:	Weekly (usually available on the date of publication)
Database Producer:	Economist Publications

Available From:	PROFILE File ECN
	£84 per connect hour
	1p per off-line print (per line)
	Minimum £2 per off-line request

Name:	Economist Intelligence Unit
Description:	This database contains qualitative and quantitative special reports and studies analysing UK and international automotive markets. It covers production, consumption, sales, market size, market shares and recent developments. An important feature for users in the automotive industry are the International, European and Japanese Motor Surveys.
Source:	Economist Intelligence Unit Research
Years Covered:	November 1985 to date
File Size:	
Updates:	Periodically
Database Producer:	Economist Intelligence Unit
Available From:	MAID
	Annual subscription: £4250
	(including training, codes, manuals, etc)
	£80 per connect hour

Name:	Economist Intelligence Unit – Retail Business
Description:	The Economist provides a monthly series Retail Business on line, which covers the UK retail trade with emphasis on consumer goods market research, distribution patterns and sales trends, including consumer expenditure forecasts. It also provides the monthly research series 'Marketing in Europe', which covers consumer goods markets and distribution in Europe.
Source:	The Economist Publications Ltd
Years Covered:	November 1985 to date
File Size:	
Updates:	Monthly, as reports available
Database Producer:	The Economist Publications Ltd
Available From:	MAID
	Annual subcription: £4250
	(including training, codes, manuals, etc)
	£80 per connect hour

Name:	EIU International Travel and Tourism Reports
Description:	These reports are quarterly and provide data and comment on tourism markets worldwide. Twenty country reports a year survey developments, trends and forecasts for national tourism markets.
	Data covers the development of the industry; analysis of trends in tourist arrivals, expenditure, accommodation, occupancy; the role of tourism in the national economy and levels of public and private sector support; international competing destinations; overseas promotion; carriers and operators.
	This service is valuable for monitoring the industry: airlines, banks, advertising agencies, national tourism offices and international organisations.
Source:	Economist Intelligence Unit
Years Covered:	Current
File Size:	20 country reports per annum
Updates:	Annual
Database Producer:	Economist Intelligence Unit
Available From:	MAID
	Annual subscription: £4250
	(including training, codes, manuals, etc)
	£80 per connect hour

Name: EIU Travel & Tourism Analyst
Description: This is the on-line version of a monthly business information publication
                           for the international travel and tourism industry, containing reports and
                           forecasts, covering all markets and sectors of activity from aviation to
                           lodging, business and leisure travel.
                               Travel & Tourism Analyst is appropriate to industry planners, financial
                           analysts and all those monitoring the industry. Internationally, it tackles
                           areas that affect market size and operation such as travel flows,
                           expenditure patterns, demographic indicators, operator performance and
                           investment trends.
Source: Economist Intelligence Unit
Years Covered: Current
File Size:
Updates: Monthly
Database Producer: Economist Intelligence Unit
Available From: MAID
                           Annual subscription: £4250
                           (including training, codes, manuals, etc)
                           £80 per connect hour

Name: Eurofile
Description: This is an on-line directory of marketing and trade information covering
                           key European industries. The database is designed for marketing and
                           strategic planning. Twelve key consumer market sectors ranging from food
                           and drink to automotives are covered in 16 European countries. Each report
                           provides information on market sizes and trends, useful contacts, sources
                           of information and leading companies.
Source: Derived from data and information prepared for inclusion in Euromonitor's
                           industry directories
Years Covered: Statistics: 5 years
                           Company data: latest available
File Size: Contact Euromonitor for current size
Updates: New data monthly
                           Annual revision
Database Producer: Euromonitor
Available From: Dialcom Business Direction
                           £80 per connect hour

Name: Euromonitor
Description: Euromonitor contains monthly reports studying a broad range of consumer
                           goods and services and in-depth product surveys on specific national
                           markets. Market Research Great Britain contains six reports in each
                           monthly issue covering a particular product sector, and data includes
                           market size and forecasts. Market Research Europe provides a European
                           overview and in-depth product reports. All data is full text.
Source: Euromonitor
Years Covered: November 1985 to date
File Size:
Updates: Monthly
Database Producer: Euromonitor
Available From: MAID
                           Annual subscription: £4250
                           (including training, codes, manuals, etc)
                           £80 per connect hour

Name: Financial Times Business Reports
Description: This database offers on-line access to key 'Financial Times' newsletter
                           services, normally available only on subscription. The database covers four
                           main groups of newsletter:
                           FinTech:

Full text, over 7000 articles related to business aspects of new technology, including telecommunications, office automation and personal computer markets.
Media:
Over 20000 articles covering analysis of international trends, companies and technologies in the field of broadcasting, publishing, etc. Media contains the full text of 'News Media Markets and Media Monitor'.
Finance and Business:
Specialised news and comment on international finance and overseas markets. This file contains the full text of 9 newsletters which includes 'International Banking Report' and 'World Insurance Report'.
Energy:
Full text of over 7000 articles relating to key energy sectors, taken from 8 newsletters includingthe 'FT Energy Economist'.
Records are indexed by country, topic, content and trade names, plus company and personal names where appropriate.

Source:	Equivalent to the FT business newsletters
Years Covered:	Fintech: 1986 to date (1984 Data-Star)
	Media: 1986 to date (1985 Data-Star)
	Finance and Business: 1986 to date
	Energy: 1987 to date
File Size:	Over 37000 articles
Updates:	Fortnightly
Database Producer:	Financial Times Electronic Publishing
Available From:	Data-Star File FTBR
	£48.98 per connect hour
	51p per on-line print
	44p per off-line print
	PROFILE
	File ftb FTBR Busines Finance
	File fte FTBR Energy file
	File ftt FTBR Fintech file
	File ftm FTBR Media file
	£84 per connect hour
	1p per off-line print (per line)
	Minimum £2 per request

Name:	FINDEX Reports and Studies
Description:	The FINDEX (the Directory of Market Research Reports, Studies and Surveys) database indexes and describes all industry and market research reports, studies and surveys, from over 300 US and international publishers. Reports produced by investment research firms covering individual companies and industries are also included. The database provides abstracts summarising the content of each report, indexing by broad industry group and by specific industry segment of product. The purchase price of the reports is also given and the reports can be ordered from the National Standards Association via Dialorder on line. The FINDEX database is designed specifically for use by information managers, librarians, marketing researchers, market analysts, corporate planners and other executives who need to know about the existence of important analyses of markets, industries and companies.
Source:	The database corresponds to the printed directory 'FINDEX'
Years Covered:	1977 to date
File Size:	11369 records
Updates:	Quarterly reloads
Database Producer:	National Standards Association
Available From:	DIALOG File 196
	$105 per connect hour
	$1.50 per on-line type
	75c per off-line print

Name: Find/SVP
Description: Find/SVP is a leading business information and research firm. Its Market
                   and Competitor Intelligence Reports cover a variety of topical subjects and
                   are designed to assist the business executive in making strategic decisions.
                      Reports include complete market size, share and growth data, forecasts,
                   profiles of key players, rundowns on product offerings and distribution
                   channels, data on user perceptions and advertising/promotion strategies
                   and appendices. Find/SVP provides the full text of selected 'Market and
                   Competitor Intelligence Reports' exclusively on line through MAID.
Source:
Years Covered: Current
File Size:
Updates: Periodically
Database Producer: Find/SVP
Available From: MAID
                   Annual subscription: £4250
                   (including training, codes, manuals, etc)
                   £80 per connect hour

Name: Frost and Sullivan Market Research (FSFS)
Description: Frost & Sullivan Market Research (FSFS) contains detailed summaries of
                   over 200 market research reports providing in-depth analysis and forecasts
                   of technical and market trends.
                      These summaries cover a broad spectrum of industrial markets including
                   data processing, energy and power systems, chemicals and plastics,
                   communications, electronics, defence and aerospace. Studies cover world
                   markets with primary emphasis on Europe and the United States.
Source: The database contains references to the full published Frost & Sullivan
                   market research reports. Original reports may be obtained from Frost &
                   Sullivan; the report number and price information for each report is
                   recorded
Years Covered: Current reports (approx latest 2-3 years)
File Size: 608 documents (as at December 1986)
Updates: Approx 4 times per annum
Database Producer: Frost & Sullivan, London
Available From: Data-Star
                   Contact direct for prices

Name: Genius Operator
Description: The Genius Operator advertising database (Gert Richter) evaluates
                   advertisements in business press and in consumer and target-group
                   magazines, both quantitatively and qualitatively. Coverage includes
                   headline slogan, description of the illustration, shape and all media
                   technical details including insertion costs. Data gives information about the
                   activities of industry sectors and companies, product information and
                   trends. It provides a basis for marketing and advertising planning.
                      Database fields which can be searched are:
                   Advertiser
                   Branch of industry (also by SIC-code)
                   Product
                   Headline
                   Slogan
                   Description of the illustration
                   Shape
                   Where observed (medium)
                   Date of publication
Language: German
Source: All national advertising insertions of at least 0.1 page in the newspapers
                   and magazines with the highest coverage in the following categories:
                   illustrated programme, youth, sport, motor cars, hobbies, men, women,
                   living, science and technology, business
Years Covered:

File Size:	210 000 advertisements from the business and consumer press
Updates:	Monthly
Database Producer:	Genius Operator
	Advertising data bank
	Gert Richter
Available From:	GENIOS File GO
	DM 310.2 per connect hour
	DM 0.5 per on-line type
	DM 1.0 per off-line print
	SDI profile: DM 10

Name:	Global Report (Citicorp Service)
Description:	Global report is a relatively new, comprehensive business information service. The major subjects which it covers are:

Companies – news, stock quotes and background information on 10 000 publicly listed companies. Mainly US companies at present
Over 800 are non-USA companies whose securities are traded in the USA, but this number will expand
Industries – news, statistics and developments for over 100 industry sectors
Markets – news, rates, analyses, advice. Includes bonds, commodities, foreign exchange, funds and trusts, money markets, options, stocks. Foreign exchange rates are available for 170 currencies from 20 international banks and dealers. Money market rates are real time
International business – news for over 100 countries, and in-depth profiles for 24 countries including the US and Far East
Major 24 countries for whom in-depth profiles are available are:

Argentina	Hong Kong	Philippines
Australia	India	Singapore
Belgium	Italy	South Africa
Brazil	Japan	Spain
Canada	Korea	Sweden
France	Mexico	Switzerland
Germany, Federal	Netherlands	UK
Republic of	Norway	USA
Greece		

Files cover a large number of subject areas including currency (plus forecasts), economics, exchange controls, financing, politics, taxes, trade (export, import controls, etc).
Information provided falls into three basic types:
Time sensitive, updated (eg interest rates)
News (world, country and corporate)
Current reference (eg tax regulations in Brazil)
The major strengths of this service is its international country data coverage, subject range and ease of use with the help of a menu-driven system.

Source:	Major newswires and publishers around the world including:

AP-Dow Jones
Business International
Citibank
Comtex
DAFSA
Dow Jones
Financial Times Business Information
Global Analysis Systems
ICC
Kyodo
Knight-Ridder
Money Market Services
Quotron
Standard & Poors

Years Covered:
File Size:

Updates:	Real time price information
	(available 24 hours a day)
Database Producer:	Citibank NA (USA)
Available From:	Citibank NA (UK): Europe and Africa
	Global Electronic Markets
	Citibank NA (Hong Kong): Asia-Pacific
	Contact Citibank direct for fees
	Guide: £250 flat fee per month
	Entitles user to 6 hours' access
	£34 per hour for time used in excess of 6 hours

Name:	Globe and Mail Online
Description:	The 'Globe and Mail' is Canada's most respected newspaper, and one of Canada's most comprehensive sources of information. Facts are available on a number of important business areas including mergers and acquisitions, and recent trade and industry statistics. All items are fully indexed. Other news databases offered by Info Globe are The Northern Miner
	Online and Computing Canada Online.
Source:	The 'Globe and Mail' daily newspaper
Years Covered:	November 1977 to date
File Size:	
Updates:	Daily (0600 Eastern time)
Database Producer:	Info Globe
Available From:	Info Globe
	$349 initiation fee
	$180 per connect hour
	30c per article
	2c per off-line print (per line)

Name:	Handelsblatt
Description:	The Handelsblatt databank (HB) is the on-line version of 'Handelsblatt', the largest German daily newspaper for business and finance. It contains articles in unabridged text form and offers important information in a wide range of areas including:
	Economics and politics
	Money and credit
	World economy
	Companies
	Company law and !taxes
	Company notices
	New contracts
	Dividends
	Commodity markets
	Foreign markets
	Customs information
	Financial section (apart from Stock Exchange prices)
Language:	German
Source:	'Handelsblatt', published daily on Stock Exchange trading days
Years Covered:	June 1984 to date
File Size:	Approx 140 000 articles in unabridged form
Updates:	Daily
Database Producer:	Handelsblatt Verlagsgruppe GmbH
Available From:	GENIOS File HB
	DM 240& per connect hour
	DM 1 per on-line type
	DM 1 per off-line print
	SDI profile: DM 10

Name: Henley Centre for Forecasting
Description: This database consists of two files which can be searched seperately or in
                             combination. Leisure Futures covers the main sectors of leisure
                             expenditure in the UK, and includes a leisure time usage survey. Planning
                             Consumer Markets provides information to assist in market planning for
                             consumer goods in the UK.
                             Forecasts go up to 5 years.
Source: Henley Centre for Forecasting
Years Covered: Autumn 1985 to date
File Size:
Updates: Quarterly
Database Producer: Henley Centre for Forecasting
Available From: PROFILE File LF
                             File PCM
                             File HCF (both files)
                             Monthly standing charge £70 (for each of the 2 files)
                             £84 per connect hour
                             1p per off-line print (per line)
                             Minimum £2 per off-line request

Name: ICC International Business Research
Description: This database provides a major single source to business and financial
                             intelligence and is to be launched in Summer 1988. The database will
                             provide the complete text of British quoted companies' annual reports and
                             accounts. It also contains ICC's databases of 'Stockbroker Research' and
                             'Key Note' marketing information sector reports.
Source: Company annual reports, contributing stockbrokers, Key Note Publication
Years Covered: Current
File Size: N/A
Updates: Monthly
Database Producer: ICC
Available From: DIALOG File 563
                             Contact DIALOG direct for prices (new file)

Name: Industry Data Sources
Description: The Industry Data Sources database identifies and describes sources of
                             statistical and directory information on 65 major industries. The main focus
                             is on USA, Canadian and European sources. Information on industries in
                             Australia, Asia and South America is also regularly added to the database.
                             Records include a short abstract about the item plus full information
                             needed for ordering from the publisher (ie contact person, address and
                             telephone number). Entries are indexed by 9 controlled vocabularies,
                             including Standard Industrial Classification, data descriptors and country
                             designations.
Source: Market research reports, investment studies, statistical summaries, special
                             issues of trade journals, financial and economic reports, forecasts,
                             directories, yearbooks, industry newsletters, selected journal articles,
                             numeric databases, monographs, conference proceedings, dissertations
                             and other secondary reference sections
Years Covered: 1979 to date
                             International coverage was begun in July 1981
File Size: 122314 records
Updates: Monthly
Database Producer: Information Access Company
Available From: DIALOG File HARF
                             $96 per connect hour
                             60c per on-line type
                             40c per off-line print
                             SDI profile: £1.63
                             BRS File HARF
                             $62.50 per connect hour
                             13c per on-line type

33c per off-line print
SDI profile: $4
Data-Star File HARF
£47.60 per connect hour
4p per on-line print
11p per off-line print
SDI profile: £1.63

Name:	Jordans Business Surveys
Description:	Business surveys are compiled by leading industry insiders and provide profiles on key British industries. They cover market size and structure, financial and trading performance of major companies, company addresses and names of senior decision makers.
	Jordans company profiles are also available on line which cover 12000 companies in the UK with a turnover of over £5 million.
Source:	Jordans Business Surveys
Years Covered:	1985 to date
File Size:	Approx 21 industry sectors
Updates:	As reports are made available
Database Producer:	Jordan & Sons Ltd
Available From:	MAID
	Annual subscription: £4250 (including training, codes, manuals, etc)
	£80 per connect hour

Name:	Keynote Industry Surveys
Description:	Covers 120 full text research reports every year covering a wide range of UK industrial and commercial market sectors. Keynote reports provide data on the market, ie market size, trends etc, major company profiles and a section on sources of further information.
Source:	ICC
Years Covered:	November 1985 to date
File Size:	400 reports
Updates:	As annual reports are published
Database Producer:	Keynote Surveys Ltd
Available From:	MAID
	Annual subscription: £4250 (including training, codes, manuals, etc)
	£80 per connect hour
	Data-Star (ICKN)
	£100.41 per connect hour
	Soon to be available on DIALOG

Name:	Leading Edge Reports
Description:	The Leading Edge group is a department of senior analysts and project directors of Business Trend Analysts Inc, an established leader in Consumer and Industrial Research (Business Trend Analysts reports are also available on MAID). The Company, founded in 1974, specialises in off-the-shelf and proprietary research. In early 1985, the Company acquired the report operation of Predicasts Inc, the US publisher of technology-based marketing research.
	Areas covered include the following:
	CAE/CAD/CAM
	Industrial computers
	Robotics
	Chemotherapy
	Roofing and siding
	Mini mill steelmaking
	Polymeric materials in automobiles
Source:	Leading Edge
Years Covered:	Current
File Size:	
Updates:	Monthly
Database Producer:	Leading Edge group

Available From:	MAID
	Annual subscription: £4250
	(including training, codes, manuals, etc)
	£80 per connect hour

Name:	Magazine ASAP
Description:	Magazine ASAP provides complete text and indexing for over 100 publications selected from the approximately 400 publications covered in Magazine Index. The full text of each article is searchable. Full text of articles, editorials, reviews and product evaluations are available.
Source:	Over 100 American magazines
Years Covered:	1983 to date
File Size:	134 949 records
Updates:	Monthly
Database Producer:	Information Access Company
Available From:	DIALOG File 647
	$96 per connect hour
	$1 per on-line type
	$2 per off-line print
	MEAD MASAP (Groupfile)
	$20 per connect hour
	$19 per search
	BRS File MSAP
	$98 per connect hour
	$1 per on-line type
	$2 per off-line print

Name:	Magazine Index
Description:	Magazine Index provides coverage of over 435 popular American magazines supplying information on a broad range of topics including current affairs, consumer product evaluations, sports and recreation, business, environment, science and technology. In addition to general references, Magazine Index will serve businesses and government libraries with information which is often not available on other on-line databases.
Source:	Over 435 American magazines
Years Covered:	The file covers from 1959-70 and 1973 to the present. The full text of over 50 magazines from 1983 to the present is available
File Size:	509 879 records
Updates:	Monthly
Database Producer:	Information Access Company
Available From:	DIALOG File 47
	$90 per connect hour
	20c per on-line type
	40c per off-line print
	SDI profile: $10.95
	BRS File MAGS
	$93 per connect hour
	$1.20 per on-line type
	$2.25 per off-line print
	SDI profile: $4

Name:	Market Directions
Description:	This is a unique European consumer marketing database which offers over 300 original research reports covering French, Italian, UK, USA and West German markets. Currently 76 product groups are covered in the following sectors: foods, electrical appliances, household cleaning, cosmetics and toiletries, consumer electronics, healthcare, drinks, tobacco, leisure goods, automotives, hotels and catering, financial and business. Each report presents a full survey in text and tables identifying main trends, size and future outlook.
Source:	Compiled by Euromonitor's international network of market analysts and consultants

Years Covered:	10 years (5-year trends/5-year forecasts)
File Size:	380 product/country sector reports
Updates:	Monthly
Database Producer:	Euromonitor
Available From:	Dialcom Business Direction
	£80 per connect hour
	£10 per on-line type (tabular record)
	£1.50 per on-line type (text record)

Name:	Market Facts Inc
Description:	This database provides a series of special reports covering the American personal financial services sector. Reports are prepared by industry specialists such as bankers and financial product marketers. Areas covered include:
	The home equity loan market
	Home mortgages
	Savings bonds
	Credit unions
	Debit cards
Source:	Market Facts Inc research
Years Covered:	November 1985 to date
File Size:	
Updates:	Weekly
Database Producer:	Market Facts Inc
Available From:	MAID
	Annual subscription: £4250 per annum
	(including training, codes, manual, etc)
	£80 per connect hour

Name:	Marketing Surveys Index
Description:	Marketing Surveys Index is a comprehensive directory of business research on UK, European and international markets. The database contains details of published market research reports, including a brief summary of contents, keyword index and bibliographic details.
Source:	'Marketing Surveys Index' published monthly by Marketing Strategies for Industry
Years Covered:	January 1983 to date
File Size:	
Updates:	Monthly. Over 5000 updates including new reports added monthly
Database Producer:	Marketing Strategies for Industry
Available From:	PROFILE
	£84 per connect hour
	1p per off-line print (per line)
	Minimum £2 per off-line request

Name:	Marketing Week
Description:	'Marketing Week' is a weekly journal which covers the latest events in the marketing and media world. It enables you to find information on new product launches, agency accounts, news on individuals in the sector and aspects of marketing strategy.
Source:	Equivalent to the printed version
Years Covered:	Current
File Size:	
Updates:	Weekly
Database Producer:	Centaur Publications
Available From:	Dialcom Business Direction
	£102 per connect hour

Name: McGraw-Hill Publications Online
Description: This database provides the complete text for many major McGraw-Hill
                       publications including 'Business Week', 'Aviation Week & Space
                       Technology', 'Chemical Week', 'Engineering News Record', 'Electronics',
                       'Chemical Engineering', 'Data Communications', 'Nuclear Fuel', 'Inside
                       NRC', 'Nucleonics Week', with more to be added in the future. The
                       database covers not only general business but also specific industries, ie
                       aerospace, chemical processing, electronics, and construction. The
                       complete text of each article is searchable and can be retrieved online in
                       addition to being printed offline.
Source: McGraw-Hill Publications
Years Covered: 1985 to date
File Size: 77 815 records
Updates: Weekly
Database Producer: McGraw-Hill Inc
Available From: DIALOG File 624
                       $96 per connect hour
                       $1.80 per off-line print
                       SDI profile: $3.50

Name: Meal Quarterly Digest
Description: Meal Quarterly Digest is a quarterly publication from MEAL providing
                       summaries of advertising expenditure in the UK for major brands and
                       product groups by month; by quarter and during the previous 12 months.
                       All main media groups are covered. There is also an exclusive share of voice
                       analysis, showing the percentage share of total advertising spent by any
                       brand of product within a given MEAL expenditure category.
Source: Equivalent to the quarterly publication 'Meal Quarterly Digest'
Years Covered: November 1985 to date
File Size:
Updates: Quarterly
Database Producer: MEAL
Available From: MAID
                       Annual subscription: £4250
                       (including training, codes, manuals, etc)
                       £80 per connect hour
                       PROFILE File MEAL
                       £84 per connect hour
                       £65 monthly standing charge
                       1p per off-line print (per line)
                       Minimum £2 per off-line request

Name: Mercatis
Description: Mercatis is a major French marketing database covering consumer markets
                       in France. The database covers prices, sales, activities of different sectors of
                       distribution, economic and demographic data as well as medium term
                       forecasts (up to 1991) provided by SEDES. In addition it is possible to
                       compare the performance of different distribution outlets in a specific
                       market sector, and obtain turnover figures for hypermarkets, supermarkets
                       and wholesalers.
Language: French
Source: Database producers' own data and forecasts
Years Covered: Current
                       Forecasts up to 1991
File Size: N/A
Updates: Regular

Database Producer:	Public:
	INSEE, BDF
	Semi-public:
	COE, CTCO, SEDES
	Private:
	Societes de Panels, ie SECODIP, INTERCOR, NIELSEN
	Companies with an interest in commercial equipment
	Points de Vente
	IFLS
	LSA
Available From:	INSEE
	SLIGOS

Name:	Mintel Reports
Description:	This database contains the full text of each report from Mintel's four regular market research publications. These are published monthly and quarterly and are based on original commissioned research. The publications covered are 'Market Intelligence', 'Retail Intelligence', 'Leisure Intelligence', 'Personal Finance Intelligence'.
Source:	Mintel
Years Covered:	Varies by file (1982 is the earliest date)
File Size:	Varies by file
Updates:	Monthly or quarterly
Database Producer:	Mintel
Available From:	PROFILE File MMI
	MRI
	MLI
	MPF
	MINTEL (all files)
	Monthly standing charge £35
	£84 per connect hour
	1p per off-line print (per line)
	Minimum £2 per off-line reque:st

Name:	MSI Market Reports
Description:	This database contains the full text of Market Reports produced by Marketing Strategies for Industry (MSI). Reports usually cover the UK, although some cover market sectors in other European countries.
Source:	Market Report Series produced by MSI
Years Covered:	February 1987 to date
File Size:	70 reports (1987)
Updates:	Whenever new reports become available
Database Producer:	Marketing Strategies for Industry
Available From:	PROFILE File MSR
	£84 per connect hour
	1p per off-line print (per line)
	Minimum £2 per off-line request

Name:	Multi Media Service
Description:	Multi Media is a quarterly publication on line offered by BAR/LNA. It provides national advertising expenditures for over 35000 brands and products in the USA. Each brand is grouped into one of 275 product categories. Moving annual totals are provided for all brands, plus exclusive share of voice analysis.
Source:	Leading National Advertisers' (LNA) print expenditure data
	Broadcast Advertisers Reports Inc (BAR)
Years Covered:	Current
File Size:	35000 brands of products covered
Updates:	Quarterly
	Backdated to the fourth quarter 1985
Database Producer:	BAR/LNA Publishers

Available From:	MAID
	Annual subscription: £4250
	(including training, codes, manuals, etc)
	£80 per connect hour

Name:	NCOM
Description:	NCOM contains all publications on mass communication published in Scandinavia. All communication media are covered, ie press, radio, television, film and new communications technology. It also includes social communication forms, eg civic communication, business and organisational communication.
Source:	Books, dissertations, research reports, journals
Years Covered:	1975 to date
File Size:	Approx 11 000 documents
Updates:	Quarterly
	1200 documents added per annum
Database Producer:	5 national centres of NORDICOM in Denmark, Finland, Iceland, Norway and Sweden
Available From:	Datacentralen File NCOM
	DK 240 per connect hour
	DK 2 per off-line print

Name:	Nexis
Description:	Nexis is one of Mead Data Central's services. Nexis is a group of libraries covering general news and business information from over 400 international sources. Nine sub-libraries make up Mead's Nexis service:
	Nexis
	Encyclopedia Britannica
	US Government documents
	Information bank
	ASAP II
	US patents (Lexpat)
	Business abstracts
	Cobmputers and communications
	US Government and political news
	Users can search a group of files, individual files or search across the whole library. There is also a facility to allow you to search all documents in the library from 1986 to date (current file). Files in the Nexis library are combined into groups by publication type, ie newspapers, magazines, wire and newsletters. They are also grouped by subject, ie business, finance, government news and trade/technology. Most files are in one 'dtype' group and one 'subject' group.
	One of the strengths of the service is that items are in full text. Mead claims to offer the largest full-text database in the world.
Source:	Over 350 international publications
Years Covered:	Varies according to file. Most files go back to 1980-82. A few go back to 1975
File Size:	Over 32 million articles
Updates:	Varies according to publications
Database Producer:	Mead Data Central
Available From:	Mead Data Central International
	Nexis Library:
	$19 per search for group files
	$5 per search for individual files
	ASAP II Library:
	$19 per search for group files
	$5 per search for individual files
	Encyclopedia Britannia:
	$19 per search
	Government documents:
	$19 per search for combined file
	$11 per search for individual file

Information bank:
$19 per search for combined file
$5 per search for individual file
US Patent and Trademark Office:
$35 per search for utility patents
$19 per search for utility, plant and design patents
$5 other individual files
Other libraries – contact Mead direct for prices

Name:	Nielsen Market Information
Description:	This database provides details on the national annualsterling value of over 200 UK product areas monitored from seven markets:
	Grocery markets
	Confectionery in grocers
	Toiletries in grocers
	Confectionery market
	Health and beauty aids
	Off licence liquor
	Cash and carry
	Information is broken down by geographic reghion, store type and includes trend data.
Source:	Full text equivalent of the publication 'A C Nielsen Market Information Manual'
Years Covered:	1985 to date
File Size:	200 product areas
Updates:	Weekly
Database Producer:	A C Nielsen
Available From:	MAID
	Annual subcription: £4250
	(including training, codes, manuals etc)
	£80 per connect hour

Name:	Packaged Facts
Description:	Packaged Facts major business is publishing syndicated market studies. These studies, which are marketingoriented, are all on consumer products, and include not only in-depth analyses,but also forecasts and projections. In addition, all feature Packaged Facts format which is designed to provide an overview of the market on one hand, and a basic reference source of data and information on the other. In each study the following areas are covered:
	The products
	The market (size and growth, factors in future market growth, sales projections and market composition)
	The marketers (leading companies, the competitive situation, marketing trends, new product development, advertising and promotion)
	Distribution channels and the retail level (margins, co-op ads, retailer opinions, etc)
	Consumer usage (purchase habits and attitudes)
	The full text of Packaged Facts studies are available exclusively online through MAID.
Source:	Packaged Facts
Years Covered:	Current
File Size:	
Updates:	Periodically
Database Producer:	Packaged Facts
Available From:	MAID
	Annual subscription: £4250
	(including training, codes, manuals, etc)
	£80 per connect hour

Name: PTS Marketing & Advertising Reference Service
Description: PTS Marketing and Advertising Reference Service (PTS MARS) contains
                         information on the marketing and advertising of consumer goods and
                         products. This file provides data on a wide variety of goods and services
                         including the companies which provide them, the advertising agencies and
                         media used to advertise them, and the marketing strategies devised to sell
                         them. Sources include core advertising industry journals and
                         newsletters, consumer-oriented trade publications, business method
                         journals, and the advertising columns/sections of major newspapers.
Source: Over 75 sources including specialist industry journals
Years Covered: 1984 to date
File Size: 131 211 records
Updates: Weekly (Data-Star)
                         Daily (DIALOG and Predicasts)
Database Producer: Predicasts
Available From: DIALOG File 570
                         $150 per connect hour
                         58c per on-line type
                         68c per off-line print
                         SDI profile: $4.95
                         Data-Star File PTMA
                         £68.27 per connect hour
                         29p per on-line print
                         19p per off-line print
                         SDI profile: £2.73

Name: Saatchi & Saatchi Compton Media
Description: These databases include UK Media, Euromedia, Asia/Pacific and
                         Worldmedia. They cover major media developments and trends with
                         concise summaries of the key developments. They are divided into the
                         following sections:
                         Television
                         Radio
                         Cinema
                         Outdoor
                         Print
                         New Media
                         Research
Source: Saatchi &k Saatchi Compton reports
Years Covered: Current
File Size:
Updates:
Database Producer: Saatchi & Saatchi Compton
Available From: Dialcom Business Direction
                         £80 per connect hour

Name: Teleborsen
Description: This is a full-text reference database. It provides news about developments
                         in trade and industry in Denmark, financial markets and the political
                         situation.
Source: Various published sources
Years Covered: Current
File Size:
Updates:
Database Producer: Copenhmagen Handelsbank
Available From: Copenhagen Handelsbank
                         Contact direct for price and access details

Name: Trade and Industry ASAP
Description: This differs from the database Trade and Industry Index in that it offers full
                       text retrieval and is sourced from 85 journals out of the 300 journals covered
                       in Trade and Industry Index. It also includes news releases from PR
                       Newswire.
Source:
Years Covered: 1983 to date
File Size: 400 287 records
Updates: Monthly
Database Producer: Information Access Company
Available From: DIALOG File 648
                       $96 per connect hour
                       $1 per on-line type
                       $2 per off-line print
                       MEAD TIASAP (Group File)
                       $20 per connect hour
                       $19 cost of search
                       BRS File TSAP
                       $98 per connect hour
                       $1 per on-line type
                       $2 per off-line print
                       SDI profile: $4

Name: Trade and Industry Index
Description: The Trade and Industry Index database indexes over 300 business, trade
                       and industry journals. Newspapers, books and US government documents
                       are indexed selectively. The database provides in a single source, current
                       and comprehensive coverage of major trade journals and industry-related
                       periodicals representing all the Standard Industrial Classifications. Trade
                       and Industry Index provides access to the full text of PR Newswire, and
                       business and trade information from nearly 1200 additional publications.
                       Information can be found on the following broad areas: banking,
                       insurance, securities, agriculture, oil and gas, public utilities, taxation,
                       wholesale and retail trade, construction, design and manufacturing,
                       forestry and paper products.
Source: Newspaper sources include 'The Wall Srtreet Journal', 'The New York
                       Financial Section', 'American Banker' and 'Barrons'. Journal coverage
                       includes such publications as 'Advertising Age', 'Coal Age', 'BYTE',
                       'Electronic Design', 'National Underwriter', 'Oil and Gas Journal' and 'Tax
                       Advisor'.
Years Covered: 1981 to date
File Size: 2 998 803 records
Updates: Monthly
Database Producer: Information Access Company
Available From: DIALOG File 148
                       $90 per connect hour
                       20c per on-line type
                       40c per off-line print
                       SDI profile: $11.95

Name: USA Monitor
Description: USA Monitor contains full-text research reports on all major consumer and
                       retail markets in the USA. Each study presents an assessment of trends in a
                       particular product sector, a full written analysis and detailed market
                       statistics. Markets covered include cosmetics and toiletries, soft drinks,
                       tobacco, food, consumer electronics, household cleaning. Twenty-one
                       markets are covered in total.
Source: USA Monitor (registered trademark of Euromonitor Publications Ltd)
Years Covered: November 1985 to date
File Size: 21 market sectors are covered
Updates: Annually

Database Producer: Euromonitor Publications Ltd
Available From: MAID
                       Annual subscription: £4250 per annum
                       (including training, codes, manuals, etc)
                       £80 per connect hour

Section IV Economic Data and Statistics

International

Abstracts of Working Papers in Economics
AP Dow Jones News Services (see News Section)
Balance of Payments
Datastream Economics Services
Direction of Trade Statistics
DRI Cost Forecasting
Econ Base: Time Series and Forecasts
Economic Literature Index (see Bibliographic Section)
Economics Abstacts International
Fonds Quetelet
Foreign Trade and Economic Abstracts
Frost and Sullivan Political Risk Country Reports-(FSRI)
Global Perspective (TM) Country Outlooks (GPCO)
Global Report (see Marketing Section)
GLOBE (Global Lending and Overseas Banking Evaluator)
IMF International Financial Statistics
Institute of International Finance
International Comparisons (INTCOMP)
International Economic Indicators
International Risk Data
Labordoc
Laborinfo
MMS Debt Market Analysis
Munzinger Landerarchiv
National Development Plans
OECD Data
OECD Main Economic Indicators
PTS International Forecasts
Reuters Country Reports
Textline (country briefs available) (see Company Section)
Trade Statistics

United Nations Industrial Statistics
United Nations National Accounts
United Nations Population Statistics
Wharton Econometric World Forecasts
World Bank Debt Tables (WDEBT)

European

ABECOR – Association of European Banks (available via Mead's Exchange service/not listed)
Banque de Donnees Locales Macroeconomique
Cronos Eurostat
Datastream Economics Services
DRI Cost Forecasting Data Bank
DRI Europe
Eurofacts
FALI
Global Perspective (TM) Country Outlooks (GPCO)
SEC 1 National Accounts (CRONOS)
Textline (country briefs, news items etc) (see Company Section)

Austria
Austria Economic Outlook (OEKON)
ISIS (Integrated Statistical Information System)

Belgium
Global Report (see Marketing Section)
Societe Generale de Banque

Finland
FINP (see Bibliographic Section)
THES (see Bibliographic Section)

France
Agora Economique (see News Section)

Banque de Donnees Locales Macroeconomique
CJIND
CTRIM
Dataeco
DRI – Cost Forecasting Data Bank
Fonds Quetelet
Global Perspective (TM) Country Outlooks (GPCO)
Global Report (see Marketing Section)
MERL – ECO
Sphinx
TEND

Germany, Federal Republic of
Deutsche Bundesbank Data (Bundesbank)
Federal Republic of Germany Statistical Data
Global Perspective (TM) Country Outlooks (GPCO)
Global Report (see Marketing Section)
PROGNO

Italy
DRI – Cost Forecasting Data Bank
Global Perspective (TM) Country Outlooks (GPCO)
Global Report (see Marketing Section)
ISCO
ISET
Prezzi
Retribuzioni Operai e Apprendisti
Statistiche del Commercio Estero dell 'Italia
Statistiche Economiche
Superstat

Netherlands
Global Perspective (TM)
Global Report (see Marketing Section)

Norway
Global Report (see Marketing Section)

Scandinavia
Findata (see Company Section)
SCANP (see General Management Section)

Spain
Base de Datos Estadisticos Municipales
BD-INE
Cronos INE
ECOCAT
ESPAN
Estacom

Sweden
Global Perspective (TM)
Global Report (see Marketing Section)
List Stat
Statistics Sweden

Switzerland
Global Report (see Marketing Section)

UK
CSO UK Macroeconomic and Financial Statistics
Henley Centre for Forecasting (see Marketing Section)

Eastern Bloc

Centrally Planned Economies
Eastern Bloc Countries
Economic Statistics (WIIW)

Non-European Countries

USA
ASI
Cendata
Citibase Weekly (CBWeekly)
Citicorp Citibase US Economic Data (Citibase)
Flow of Funds
General Electric Company (GECAST)
Global Perspective (TM)
Country Outlooks (GPCO)
Global Report (see Marketing Section)
Labor
Producer Price Indexes
PTS US Forecasts
PTS US Time Series
Quarterly Financial Report
Survey of United States Forecasts

United States Economic Statistics
United States National Accounts
Wharton Econometric World Forecasts
Wharton Economic News (see Nexis in Marketing Section)

Central and South America
Global Perspective (TM)
Country Outlooks (GPCO)
Global Report (see Marketing Section)
(WEFA produce a number of Latin American data banks not listed here)

Australia
Australian Bureau of Statistics (ABS)
Global Perspective (TM)
Country Outlooks (GPCO)
Global Report (see Marketing Section)
Reserve Bank of Australia Bulletin (RBA)

Canada
Alberta Statistical Information System
Cansim
Global Perspective (TM)
Country Outlooks (GPCO)
Global Report (see Marketing Section)

Asia
Datastream Economics Service
Global Perspective (TM)
Country Outlooks (GPCO)
Global Report (see Marketing Section)
Japan Economic Journal (see Nexis in Marketing Section)
Japan Economic Newswire Plus
MMS Asia/Pacific Market Analysis (see Securities Section)
Nikkei Telecomm –
Macroeconomic forecasts provided for:
Japan
Korea
China
Nomura Research Institute (NRI/E)
Wharton Econometric World Forecasts

China
Global Perspective (TM)
Country Outlooks (GPCO)
Nikkei Telecomm

Hong Kong
Global Perspective (TM)
Country Outlooks (GPCO)
Global Report (see Marketing Section)

India
Global Report (see Marketing Section)

Japan
DRI Cost Forecasting Data Bank
Global Perspective (TM)
Country Outlooks (GPCO)
Global Report (see Marketing Section)
Japan Economic Journal (see Nexis in Marketing Section)
Japan Economic Newswire Plus
Needs-TS
Nikkei Telecomm
Nomura Research Institute (NRI/E)

Philippines
Global Perspective (TM)
Country Outlooks (GPCO)
Global Report (see Marketing Section)

Singapore
Global Report (see Marketing Section)
South Korea, Republic of
Global Perspective (TM)
Country Outlooks (GPCO)
Global Report (see Marketing Section)
Nikkei Telecomm

Thailand
Global Perspective (TM)
Country Outlooks (GPCO)

Middle East
Global Perspective (TM)
Country Outlooks (GPCO)
Mideast
(WEFA produce a number of Middle East data banks not listed here)

Name: Abstracts of Working Papers in Economics
Description: Contains abstracts of key economics papers issued by over 60 world
                    research organisations, including universities and government
                    organisations.
Source: Research papers
Years Covered: 1982 to date
File Size:
Updates: Monthly
Database Producer: Hal White, University of California Department ofEconomics
Available From: BRS File AWPE
                    $55 per connect hour (basic plan)
                    35c per on-line type
                    25c per off-line print

Name: Alberta Statistical Information System
Description: Contains the Alberta Bureau of Statistics database, Canada Census data
                    and unpublished government information. It also provides access to time
                    series from Cansim (see database listing). Data can be displayed in the form
                    of charts, graphs and maps.
Source: Alberta Bureau of Statistics, Canadian Census data, unpublished Canadian
                    government data
Years Covered: Varies. Generally 1976 to date
File Size: Over 50 000 time series
Updates: Varies. Monthly and annually
Database Producer: Alberta Bureau of Statistics
Available From: ACI Computer Services
                    $84 per connect hour
                    On-line type charge included in hourly rate
                    10c per off-line print (per page)

Name: ASI
Description: ASI (American Statistics Index) is a comprehensive index of the statistical
                    publications from more than 500 US federal offices or regional issuing
                    agencies. ASI provides abstracts and indexing of all federal statistical
                    publications, including non-GPO publications, which contain social,
                    economic, demographic or natural resources data. It also covers a selection
                    of their publications with scientific and technical data. Types of statistical
                    data to be found in ASI include: population and economic censuses;
                    international trade data; Consumer Price Index reports; unemployment
                    statistics; agricultural data on production, yield, prices, etc; vital statistics
                    and educational data.
Source: Us Federal Offices statistical publications
Years Covered: 1973 to date
File Size: 147 759 records
Updates: Monthly
Database Producer: Congressional Information Service Inc
Available From: DIALOG File 102
                    $90 per connect hour
                    25c per off-line print

Name: Australian Bureau of Statistics (ABS)
Description: This database covers major socio-economic time series data relating to
                    Australia. It is grouped into a number of subject areas. A selection of these
                    is listed below:
                    Balance of payments
                    Private finance
                    Public finance
                    Construction
                    National accounts
                    Wholesale prices
Source: Australian Bureau of Statistics

Years Covered:	From 1953 to date
File Size:	
Updates:	Economic and financial data are updated daily
Database Producer:	IP Sharp
Available From:	IP Sharp
	Access via 39 Magic
	Contact IP Sharp direct for prices

Name:	Austria Economic Outlook (OEKON)
Description:	This database provides economic forecasts for Austria from leading industrialists.
Source:	Vereinigung Osterreichischer Industrieller (VOE 1)
Years Covered:	From Jan 1974
File Size:	
Updates:	Quarterly
Database Producer:	IP Sharp/Vereinigung Osterreichischer Industrieller (VOE 1)
Available From:	IP Sharp
	Access via 39 Magic
	Contact IP Sharp direct for prices

Name:	Balance of Payments
Description:	BOPDATA contains data selected from the International Monetary Fund's Balance of Payments Statistics. Data covers over 25 000 series of annual historical data covering over 130 countries. Data includes all standard items from the IMF's aggregated and detailed presentations as well as a full complement of non-standard exceptional financing series. New data are loaded into BOPDATA each month, preceding publication in the 'IMF Bulletin' by up to a year.
Source:	IMF Balance of Payments Statistics
Years Covered:	1960 to date
File Size:	25 000 data series, 130 countries
Updates:	Data is updated by the second business day of each month from a tape issued by the IMF
Database Producer:	Haver Analytics Inc/IMF
Available From:	GE Information Services
	25c per data series
	or subscription options:
	$1500 per annum subscription for unlimited access to all the US databases
	$2500 per annum subscription for all US economic plus international databases
	WEFA File BOPDB
	£1600 subscription fee per annum or
	£1.60 per data series
	(only available via Interactive Data Corporation (IDC)
	when available from WEFA)

Name:	Banque de Donnees Locales Macroeconomique
Description:	This is an economic database covering France, the EEC and OEDC countries. For France, data provided includes: general statistics on revenues, employment, demography, production and price indexes, national accounts and financial statistics.
Language:	French
Source:	Statistical institutes of the EEC, OECD, national statistical services and the IMF, central French bank and French government sources
Years Covered:	1945 to date
File Size:	100 000 data series
Updates:	Periodically, as new data becomes available
Database Producer:	Institut National de la Statistique et des Etudes Economiques (INSEE)
Available From:	GSI-ECO (as a Dataeco database)
	INSEE File BDM
	(INSEE also offers a file called Banque de Donnees Locales (BDL))

Name: Base de Datos Estadisticos Municipales de Cataluna
Description: This is a Spanish economic database, covering the areas of population,
                             housing and utilities, schools, communications, transportation, business
                             and industry, financial institutions, agriculture and tourist facilities Over
                             100 annual time series are available for each of the 940 municipalities in
                             Catalonia.
Source: Spanish national statistics
Years Covered: 1975 to date
File Size: 100 annual time series
Updates: Annual
Database Producer: Consorcio de Informacion y Documentacion de Cataluna
Available From: Consorcio de Informacion y Documentacion de Cataluna

Name: BD-INE
Description: BD-INE is a Spanish economic database. It provides 45 000 time series of
                             socio-economic, demographic and business data for Spain.
Source:
Years Covered: Varies by series. Earliest data starts in 1900
File Size: 45 000 time series
Updates: Monthly
Database Producer: Instituto Nacional de Estadistica (INE)
Available From: Entel, SA

Name: CANSIM
Description: CANSIM offers comprehensive socio-economic data from Statistics
                             Canada. It is presented in time series format, including over 45 000 time
                             series. Coverage includes:
                             Government publications
                             National accounts
                             Prices and price indexes
                             Labour statistics
                             Manufacturing and primary industries
                             Capital and finance – banking and corporate financial
                             statistics, interest rates, etc
                             Construction
                             External trade
                             Population
                               The database is accessible around-the-clock, worldwide. Data can be
                             downloaded and manipulated using services offered by IP Sharp such as
                             Infomagic, Magic and Superplot. CANSIM mini base is a subset of the most
                             popular time series of the main base. Each host may provide access to both
                             the mini and main base.
Source:
Years Covered: 1946 to present
                             Some data goes back to 1914
File Size: Over 50 000 time series (main base)
                             25 000 time series (mini base)
Updates: Daily
Database Producer: Statistics Canada (CANSIM)
Available From: ACT Computer Services
                             $84 per connect hour
                             10c per off-line print charge (per page)
                             On-line print charge included in hourly rate
                             WEFA File CANSIMDB
                             £1600 subscription fee per annum or
                             £1.60 per data series
                             Analyste-Conseil Systeme Informatique
                             Canada Systems Group
                             Conference Board of Canada
                             Crowntek Communications Inc
                             DRI Information Plus
                             IP Sharp

Per series surcharge of 50c Canadian
Interactive Data Corporation (IDC)File CANSIMDB
(not available via IDC as of July 1988, but being negotiated)
Contact hosts direct for price and access details

Name:	Cendata
Description:	Cendata offers US Bureau of Census news releases and statistical data based on current economic and demographic reports. Press releases are generally narrative in form, while the 'Data' sections usually consists of tales. There are 2 separate Cendata files on DIALOG, a standard DIALOG file (file 580) and an easy-to-use menu file. Both files contain identical information, but logon procedures and search techniques differ.
Source:	US Bureau of the Census news releases and reports
Years Covered:	Current
File Size:	1918 records
Updates:	Daily
Database Producer:	US Bureau of the Census
Available From:	DIALOG File 580
	$36 connect hour
	20c per off-line print (full record)

Name:	Centrally Planned Economies
Description:	This database provides macroeconomic data on Eastern Europe and the USSR and 9000 annual time series. Areas covered include: GNP, investment and fixed capital by economy and industry sector, balance of payments, income accounts by origin sector and end use. Short-term and long-term forecasts are provided for GNP, employment, population, investment, capital stock, foreign trade plus other variables.
Source:	USA and foreign national statistical publications
Years Covered:	Earliest data from 1960
	5-year short-term, 20-year long-term forecasts
File Size:	9000 annual time series
Updates:	Twice per annum (forecast data)
	Annual (historic data)
Database Producer:	WEFA
Available From:	WEFA Files CPE, CPEMOD, CPEBASE
	£1600 subscription fee per annum
	or £1.60 per data series
	CISI Network Corporation, Uni-Coll Division

Name:	Citibase Weekly (CBWeekly)
Description:	CBWeekly provides weekly financial and US economic data compiled by Citicorp Database Service from a range of government, institutional and private sources. This database can be used to monitor the US economy from week to week, and to project monthly figures before they are released.
	It contains financial series, such as money supply, interest rates and yields; banking statistics, such as Citibank's LIBOR rates; commodity prices; financial futures and other economic indicators reported on a weekly basis, such as unemployment claims.
Source:	The Federal Reserve Board, the American Metal Market, the Commodity Research Bureau, the 'Journal of Commerce' and the 'Wall Street Journal'.
Years Covered:	Mostly 1980 to date
File Size:	Over 550 weekly time series
Updates:	Updated each weekday at approx 1800 hours in New York as data becomes available
Database Producer:	Citicorp/Haver Analytics Inc

Available From:	GE Information Services
	Subscription service only
	$130 per month subscription fee
	Citicorp
	$1560 timesharing annual subscription charge
	Timesharers: Citibank, Compuserve, GE Information Services,
	IP Sharp, Merrill Lynch, MIT and Rapidata
	Contact above direct for price and access details
	Global Report (Citibank Service)
	Guide: £250 flat fee per month
	Entitles user to 6 hours' access
	£34 per hour for time used in excess of 6 hours

Name:	Citicorp Citibase US Economic Data (Citibase)
Description:	Citibase contains data covering all aspects of the US economy gathered from over 100 government and private sources by Citicorp Database Services. Monthly, quarterly and annual time series are provided. Areas covered are: national income and product accounts, business cycle indicators, information on money supply, bank assets and reserves, credit, interest rates, industrial production, prices, wholesale and retail sales, orders and inventories, housing starts and construction, employment and earnings, productivity, capacity utilisation and capitalexpenditures. Projections taken from the American Statistical Association/National Bureau of Economic Research Joint Outlook Survey are available for 17 indicators of capital investment. The survey is conducted each quarter.
Source:	Government and private data compiled by Citicorp
Years Covered:	1946 to date
File Size:	5500 time series
Updates:	Each weekday at approximately 1800 hours in New York and as new data becomes available
Database Producer:	Citicorp/Haver Analytics Inc
Available From:	GE Information Services
	Subscription service only
	$187.50 per month subscription fee
	Citicorp
	$2250 timesharing annual subscription charge
	Timesharers: Citibank, Compuserve, GEISCO, IP Sharp, Merrill Lynch, MIT and Rapidata
	Contact above direct for price and access details
	Global Report (Citibank Service)
	Guide: £250 flat fee per month
	Entitles users to 6 hours' access
	£34 per hour for time used in excess of 6 hours
	IP Sharp
	Access via Infomagic or 39 Magic
	Contact IP Sharp direct for prices

Name:	CJIND
Description:	CJIND (Conjacture dans l'Industrie) provides 250 monthly time series of historic and forecast data on supply and demand for French industrial products. It covers 35 industrial sectors with the exception of construction and agriculture. Areas covered are: production, domestic and foreign industrial orders and demand, finished products, stocks and short term variations in sale prices.
Source:	INSEE's Monthly Business Survey
Years Covered:	
File Size:	250 time series
Updates:	Monthly
Database Producer:	Institut National de la Statistique et des Etudes Economiques (INSEE)
Available From:	GSI ECO
	Contact direct for price and access details

Name:	Cronos Eurostat
Description:	This is a comprehensive European statistical database. It consists of approximately 25 macroeconomics domains, each covering a specific subject area (eg iron and steel, energy, agriculture) which are grouped into 6 main subject areas:

General statistics
Economic and financial statistics
Energy and industrial statistics
Agriculture and fisheries
Social statistics
Foreign trade statistics
All domains are available on tape and currently only 8 are available on line. Others will be added subject to demand. The 8 domains currently available are as follows:
ICG General economic information
IC2 Eurostatus short term trends
ZPVD General statistics on developing countries
BISE Production and foreign trade by product
ZENI Energy statistics
ZPAI Agricultural products
PRAG Agricultural prices indices
SOCI Social statistics

Source:	National Statistical Offices, OECD, UNESCO, IMF, etc
Years Covered:	Most data goes back to the mid 1960s
File Size:	Over 800 000 time series as at January 1987
Updates:	Daily, biweekly, monthly, quarterly, annually
Database Producer:	Statistical Office of the European Communities
Available From:	Datacentralen File Cronos Eurostat

Access via:
DC-TIME
DK 675 per connect hour
Based on
DK 15 per minute for the first 15 minutes
DK 10 per minute for time beyond the first 15 minutes
Access via:
CRONOS
DK 15 per first access to a time series
DK 5 per reuse of a time series
DK 2 per off-line print
WEFA File CRONOS
£1600 subscription fee per annum (per bank)
or £1.60 per data series
GSI ECO

Name:	Cronos INE
Description:	Cronos INE is a Spanish economic database, providing 78 000 time series of Spanish economic, demographic and sociological statistics.
Language:	Spanish
Source:	Instituto Nacional de Estadistica (INE) (Spanish National Statistical Office)
Years Covered:	Varies by series
File Size:	78 000 time series
Updates:	Monthly
Database Producer:	Instituto Nacional de Estadistica (INE)
Available From:	Instituto Nacional de Estadistica (INE)

Name: CSO UK Macroeconomic and Financial Statistics
Description: Data corresponds to CSO publications such as 'Economic Trends',
                             'Financial Statistics', 'Monthly Digest of Statistics'. The database provides
                             about 14 000 monthly, quarterly and annual time series related to
                             economics in the UK. The file is divided into the following major
                             catagories: main economic indicators, national accounts, balance of
                             payments, index of production, producer and retail price indexes,
                             commodity flow accounts, employment and earnings, financial statistics.
Source: Data is compiled from various sources by the UK Civil Service
Years Covered: Varies by series. Some data starts from 1947
File Size: 14 000 time series
Updates: Monthly, major revisions annually
Database Producer: Central Statistical Office (CSO)
Available From: WEFA File CSODB
                             £1600 subscription fee per annum
                             £1.60 per series
                             Data Resources (DRI)
                             (part of DRI Europe database)
                             Dimensions (CSO)
                             Information Plus
                             Interactive Data Corporation (IDC) File CSODB
                             (not available as of July 1988 via IDC but being negotiated)

Name: CTRIM (Comptes Nationaux Trimestriels)
Description: Quarterly national accounts for France
Source: INSEE
Years Covered: Current
File Size:
Updates:
Database Producer: Institut National de la Statistique et des Etudes
                             Economiques (INSEE)
Available From: GSI ECO

Name: Dataeco
Description: Dataeco is a collection of databases on French and international economics
                             and finance. Databases included are:
                             CEPII CHELEM – harmonised time series on international trade
                             CEPII-Country – time series on economic indicators for France
                             CEPII-PIB – provides gross GDP (in US dollars) for 201 countries
                             CEII-POP – total population for 201 countries
                             CEII-DEM – world real and trend indexes covering 57 industrial sectors
                             CEII-BAL – balance of payments data
                             IMF
                             INSEE
                             OECD annual national income accounts
                             OECD indicators of industrial activity
                             OECD main economic indicators
                             OECD quarterly national income accounts
                             GSIDATA – contains French economic indicators and overall economic
                             trends
Source: OECD, IMF, INSEE
Years Covered: Varies by database
File Size: Varies by database
Updates: Varies by database
Database Producer: GSI ECO and others including the CEPII (Centre d'Etudes Prospectives et
                             d'Informations Internationales)
Available From: GSI ECO

Name:	Datastream Economics Services
Description:	Datastream provides an extensive economic statistics service. A database of 10 000 economic indicators is maintained for leading Western economies. This includes a macroeconomic series for each country, plus interest and exchange rates.

Over 4000 series are provided for the UK and 100-500 for each of the other 25 countries. Countries covered:

Australia	Japan	UK
Belgium	Netherlands	USA
Canada	South Africa	
France	Switzerland	
Germany, Federal Republic of		
Italy		

Extra series are provided for all OECD countries. Series can be displayed in a variety of formats including the computation of percentage and absolute changes, seasonal adjustment, rebasing facilities and regression.

Datastream also provides a UK econometric model with forecasts up to 2 years on a quarterly, semi-annual or annual basis. Forecasts can be based on either Datastream's own selected variables or on the users' own selection of variables. Forecasts cover the following items:
GDP
Personal income
Public authorities' current expenditure
Gross Domestic Fixed Capital formation
Consumers' expenditure
Overseas trade
GDP price deflators
Labour productivity and cost indices
Aggregate corporate income

Source:	IMF, OECD, official national statistics
	Commentary available on line from professional economists
Years Covered:	Start date for most series is 1970 but in many cases, particularly for the UK, the start date is much earlier
File Size:	10 000 economic indicators covering 150 countries
Updates:	Monthly, quarterly or annually according to the regularity of the publication of the series
Database Producer:	Datastream
Available From:	Datastream
	Price guide
	Business Research Service (dial up):
	£750 per annum plus extra charge for each access
	Moneywatch Service:
	£9500 per annum – no extra charge/access

Name:	Deutsche Bundesbank Data (Bundesbank)
Description:	This database provides economic and financial statistics produced and published by the Deutsche Bundesbank (Central Bank). Main areas covered are:
	Banking and securities statistics
	Currency exchange rates
	Balance of payments statistics
Source:	Deutsche Bundesbank
Years Covered:	1948 to date
File Size:	More than 11 000 time series
Updates:	Monthly, within 7-10 days after release of tape
Database Producer:	Bundesbank

Available From:	WEFA File Deutschebundesbank
	£1600 subscription fee per annum or
	£1.60 per data series
	IP Sharp
	Access via 39 Magic
	Contact IP Sharp direct for prices

Name:	Direction of Trade Statistics
Description:	IMFDOT covers the exports and imports by major trading partners for the OECD and 'Baker 15' countries. The database offers over 6500 data series which covers imports and exports for trading partners of 38 countries and aggregate regions. All series are reported in millions of US dollars.
Source:	IMF Direction of Trade Statistics
Years Covered:	1948 to date (annual data)
	January 1963 to date (monthly data for the USA and Japan)
File Size:	6500 data series
Updates:	Monthly
Database Producer:	Haver Analytics Inc/IMF
Available From:	GE Information Services
	$1 per data series
	or choice of subscription options:
	$1500 per annum subscription for unlimited access to all the international databases
	$2500 per annum subscription for all the international plus US economic databases
	WEFA File DOTDB
	£1600 subscription fee per annum or
	£1.60 per data series
	(only available via Interactive Data Corporation (IDC) when available from WEFA)

Name:	DRI-COST Forecasting Data Bank
Description:	This database covers economic data for France, Italy, UK, Japan and the Federal Republic of Germany. It provides 1800 quarterly and monthly time series for producer and wholesale price indexes, construction costs, wages and earnings. Construction cost and earnings data is provided for 46 industrial and construction sectors. Price indexes are provided for over 700 commodities.
Source:	Sources include: Statisches Bundesamt (FRG), INSEE (France), Central Bureau voor de Statistiek (Netherlands), Dept of Trade and Industry (UK), Instituto Centrale de Statistica (Italy)
Years Covered:	Varies by series
File Size:	1800 time series
Updates:	Periodically, as new data becomes available
Database Producer:	Data Resources (DRI)
	Data Products Division Headquarters
Available From:	Data Resources (DRI)
	DRI offers most of it's historical databases through two pricing options: annual subscription fee or Information Plus. The latter option does not involve an upfront fee and is more suitable for short term projects or occasional analysis.
	Contact direct for further details.

Name:	DRI Europe
Description:	DRI Europe contains economic data gathered by statistical agencies and compiled by SRI staff. It provides over 66000 weekly, monthly, quarterly, semi-annual and annual financial and economic indicators for Europe. Coverage includes national income and product accounts, industrial production by activity, wages and prices by sector, employment by sector, interest and exchange rates, and balance of payments.
Source:	Statistical agencies in Europe
Years Covered:	Current

File Size:	66 000 statistical indicators
Updates:	Varies by series
Database Producer:	Data Resources (DRI)
	Data Products Division Headquarters
Available From:	Data Resources (DRI)

DRI offers most of it's historical databases through two pricing options: annual subscription fee /or Information Plus. The latter option does not involve an upfront fee and is more suitable for short term projects or occasional analysis. Contact direct for further details.

Name:	Eastern Bloc Countries Economic Statistics (WIIW)
Description:	This database provides comprehensive national economic statistics for COMECON countries. It covers national income, production, imports and exports, government incomes and outlays, crop yields and the labour force.
Source:	The Vienna Institute for Comparative Economic Studies
Years Covered:	From 1950 to date
File Size:	
Updates:	Monthly, quarterly and annually, as data becomes available from Institute
Database Producer:	IP Sharp
Available From:	IP Sharp Associates
	Access via 39 Magic
	Contact IP Sharp direct for prices

Name:	ECOCAT
Description:	ECOCAT is a Spanish economic bibliographic database. It covers literature on the economics of Catalonia. Information is in the form of citations and abstracts.
Source:	Periodicals, catalogues, conference proceedings
Years Covered:	1980 to date
File Size:	Approx 2250 citations
Updates:	Monthly
Database Producer:	Consorcio de Informacion y Documentacion de Cataluna
Available From:	Consorcio de Informacion y Documentacion de Cataluna

Name:	Econ Base: Timeseries & Forecasts
Description:	Econ Base contains a broad range of econometric time series covering subject areas such as economics, business conditions, finance, manufacturing, household income distribution, and demographics. It contains US regional and international data, and provides forecast data on several of the series.
Source:	WEFA
Years Covered:	1984 to present
File Size:	12 000 records
Updates:	Monthly reloads
Database Producer:	WEFA
Available From:	DIALOG File 565
	$75 per connect hour
	$5 per on-line type
	$5 per off-line print
	($1 per record format 5)
	WEFA

Name:	Economics Abstracts International
Description:	Economics Abstracts International (EAI) is a bibliographic database compiled by the Documentation and Library branch of the Netherlands Foreign Trade Agency of the Dutch Ministry of Economic Affairs with the purpose of providing access to worldwide economic information for exporting companies and for all organisations interested in market trends, economic developments, management problems, and economic science.
	Subjects covered:
	Third world economic development
	European Business Forecasts

	East-West trade
	Import regulations
	Investment climates
	Economic working papers
	Cor..modity markets
	Bank reports
	Energy economics
	Business intelligence
	Chamber of commerce reports
	Foreign markets
Source:	Journal articles, monographs (books), annual reports, international periodicals, government publications, annual publications, reference works, directories, statistical sources
Years Covered:	January 1974 to date
File Size:	Approx 145000 citations
Updates:	Every two weeks
Database Producer:	Stichting Economische Publikaties
	The documents recorded in the ECAB database are available from the library of the Dutch Ministry of Economic Affairs mostly in photocopies or microfiche
Available From:	Belindis File ECAB
	BF 3000 per connect hour
	BF 10 per 10 lines displayed on line
	BF 10 per off-line print

Name:	ESPAN
Description:	ESPAN is a bibliographic database which contains statistical information on Spain going back to 1960.
	Statistics are analysed and there is a description of each of the statistical tables found in the publications which are included in the database. This service is expected to become available to the public in September 1988.
Source:	Official statistics
Years Covered:	1960 to date
File Size:	N/A
Updates:	N/A
Database Producer:	Consorci d'Informacio i Documentacio de Catalunya (CIDC)
Available From:	As above
	Contact direct for further availability details

Name:	Estacom
Description:	Estacom provides Spanish trade statistics with a focus on exports. It covers geographic distribution, the value of imports and exports, and the primary country(s) of destination or origin.
Language:	Spanish
Source:	Official custom registration documents from the 'Direccion General de Aduanas'
Years Covered:	1985 to date
File Size:	
Updates:	5 times per annum
Database Producer:	Instituto Nacional de Fomento de la Exportacion (INFE)
Available From:	Instituto Espanol de Comercio Exterior (ICEX)

Name:	Eurofacts
Description:	This is a pan-European database which covers major marketing and economic parameters, and industry data. Comparative statistical tables present data on demographics, trade, employment, production, market sizes and relevant industry data for 16 countries and 250 products within each country. Data is presented in monthly, quarterly and yearly time series.
Source:	Euromonitor researchers using data from a wide range of sources throughout Europe

Years Covered:	Last 5 years
File Size:	Approximately 700 statistical tables
Updates:	Monthly
Database Producer:	Euromonitor
Available From:	Dialcom Business Direction
	£80 per connect hour

Name:	FALI
Description:	FALI is a bibliographic database compiled by the Central Library of the Belgian Ministry of Foreign Affairs. It contains citations from about 600 periodicals.
	Subjects covered are:
	Diplomatic history
	Political science
	Home politics and political structures
	Multilateral and bilateral external relations
	European problems
	Security and defence problems
	International institutions
	Industrial and economic policy
	International economic and financial relations
	Socio-economic problems
Language:	French, Dutch, English, German, Spanish
Source:	Journal articles: 47 per cent
	Monographs: 53 per cent
Years Covered:	1981 to date
File Size:	10 000 citations
Updates:	Monthly
Database Producer:	Ministry of Foreign Affairs
	Central Library
Available From:	Belindis File FALI
	BF 1200 per connect hour
	BF 5 per 10 lines displayed on line
	BF 5 per off-line print

Name:	Federal Republic of Germany Statistical Data (Statisbund)
Description:	Statisbund contains over 20 000 time series which cover a large number of economic subject areas including labour, foreign trade, prices, national accounts, transportation and agriculture.
Source:	Official statistics
Years Covered:	From 1950 to date
File Size:	Over 20 000 time series
Updates:	Monthly
Database Producer:	IP Sharp
Available From:	WEFA
	£1600 subscription fee per annum or
	£1.60 per data series
	IP Sharp
	Access via 39 Magic
	Contact IP Sharp direct for prices

Name:	Flow of Funds
Description:	FFUNDS contains quarterly information on financial assets and liabilities by sector categorised by transaction type. Data is collected by the Federal Reserve Board for its publication 'Flow of Funds'.
	The focus is on funds raised and supplied in credit markets, and on uses and sources of funds.
	Approximately 2300 series are stored including series from the 'Flow of Funds Chart Book'. Seasonally adjusted data for total credit market debt is offered for most sectors. Over 52 financial and non-financial sectors are covered.
Source:	US Federal Reserve Board publication 'Flow of Funds'

Years Covered: 1952 to date
File Size: Approx 2300 series
    Approx 3600 series (IP Sharp)
Updates: Quarterly
Database Producer: Haver Analytics Inc/Federal Reserve Board
Available From: GE Information Services
    25c per data series or choice of subscription options:
    $1500 per annum subscription for unlimited access to all of the US economic databases or
    $2500 per annum subscription for all US economic plus international databases
    WEFA File FLOWDB
    £1600 subscription fee per annum or
    £1.60 per data series
    Citicorp
    $500 timesharing annual subscription charge
    (Citibank timesharing only)
    IP Sharp
    Provided on file USFLOW
    Access via 39 Magic
    Contact IP Sharp direct for prices
    ADP Data Services
    DRI
    Merrill Lynch

Name: Fonds Quetelet
Description: Fonds Quetelet (QLIB) is a bibliographic database compiled by the Fonds Quetelet Library. It contains worldwide information on economics.
    Subjects covered:
    Micro economics
    Management
    Economic theories
    International economics
    Econometrics
    Statistics
    Regional economics
    Law
    Labour
    Sociology
    Energy
Language: French, Dutch, English, German
Source: Journal articles: 60 per cent
    Monographs: 40 per cent
Years Covered: 1973 to date
File Size: Approximately 220000 citations (September 1986)
    Annual growth: 10000 citations
Updates: Fortnightly
Database Producer: Ministry of Economic Affairs
    Fonds Quetelet Library
    The documents recorded in the QLIB file are available at the Fonds Quetelet Library
Available From: Belindis
    BF 1500 per connect hour
    BF 4 per off-line print
    (BF 750 for manual and classification system)

Name: Foreign Trade and Economic Abstracts
Description: Foreign Trade and Economic Abstracts provides brief summaries of articles on international market trends, economic developments, particular economic climates, management problems and economic science. Abstracts point to sources of data on foreign markets, trade, investment climates, import regulations and export business. Information on energy and other

fields relevant to international trade is included as is some theoretical literature on management techniques. English language sources account for over 50 per cent of material; remaining sources are French, German and Dutch.

Language:	Summaries are written in English, French, German and Dutch. All descriptors assigned by the database producer are in English
Source:	The database covers about 1000 international journals as well as reports, reference works and government publications. A core list of about 250 journals are dealt with in depth
Years Covered:	1974 to date
File Size:	186 626 records
Updates:	Fortnightly
Database Producer:	Netherlands Foreigan Trade Agency
Available From:	DIALOG File 90
	$78 per connect hour
	25c per on-line type
	30c per off-line print
	SDI profile: $4.95
	Data-Star File IEAB
	£54.49 per connect hour
	15p per on-line print
	11p per off-line print
	SDI profile: £1.63

Name:	Frost and Sullivan Political Risk Country Reports – FSRI
Description:	Frost & Sullivan's Political Risk Country Reports assess the political and economic conditions in the 85 countries most important to international business. Every country report forecasts the 18-month and 5-year outlook for regime stability, turmoil, financial transfers, direct invecstments and export markets.
Source:	Frost & Sullivan
Years Covered:	Current information
File Size:	85 countries
Updates:	Updated as new data becomes available or conditions change
Database Producer:	Frost & Sullivan, USA
	Frost & Sullivan, UK
Available From:	Data-Star
	Contact direct for prices

Name:	General Electric Company (GECAST)
Description:	The GECAST data file contains history and forecasts for the United States economy. The files are prepared and maintained by the Economic Research and Forecasting Operation of the General Electric Company.
	Coverage includes national accounts, productivity, construction, industrial production, corporate profits, trade statistics, interest rates, plant and equipment spending, prices, government receipts and expenditures and income.
	The most current GECAST files are always named GECASTQ (quarterly) and GECASTA (annual). Previous files are also available.
Source:	GEC's Economic Research and Forecasting Operation
Years Covered:	1960 to date
	Annual forecasts for the next 10 years
	Quarterly forecasts to the end of the next calendar year
File Size:	Over 300 economic indicators are forecast
Updates:	Quarterly
Database Producer:	Haver Analytics Inc
Available From:	GE Information Services
	No data charges
	Available on user numbers beginning CCQ05 or CBQ65

Name: Global Perspective (TM) Country Outlooks (GPCO)
Description: Global Perspective Inc prepares concise country reports focusing on
                   important issues or warning signals for the short term and longer term.
                       Country outlook texts include a short-term and a medium-term scenario
                   covering overall market prospects, exchange rates, investment, and the
                   policy/polithical outlook.
                       A table of 4-year forecasts of real GDP, trade, exchange rates, consumer
                   prices, and hourly compensation supplements the text for all countries
                   except China and Hong Kong.
                       Reports are currently available for: Argentina, Australia, Brazil, Canada,
                   China, France, Germany, Hong Kong, Italy, Japan, Mexico, Netherlands,
                   Philippines, Saudi Arabia, South Korea, Sweden, Thailand, USA, UK and
                   Venezuela.
Source: Global Perspective Inc
Years Covered: 4 year foreicasts for all countries except China andHong Kong
File Size: 20 countries covered
Updates: Each country report is updated at least once a quarter
Database Producer: Global Perspective Inc/Haver Analytics Inc
Available From: GE Information Services
                   $50 per country report
                   or a subscription fee of $1920 per annum allows unlimited access

Name: GLOBE (Global Lending and Overseas Banking Evaluator)
Description: GLOBE (Global Lending and Overseas Banking Evaluator) provides
                   approximately 8000 time series of historical and forecast economic and
                   financial data for 120 countries. Users can obtain reports on current
                   assessments of conditions and risks in any of the countries covered. Data is
                   categorised under the following headings:
                   Market structure and adaptability
                   External balance and liquidity
                   Economic policy and management
                   Debt position and servicing
Source: Bank for International Settlements, Eurodata, International Monetary
                   Fund, OECD, UN, World Bank
Years Covered: Varies by series
                   Earliest data goes back to 1960
File Size: 8000 time series
Updates: Weekly
Database Producer: WEFA
Available From: WEFA File GLOBE
                   £1600 subscription charge per annum or
                   £1.60 per data series

Name: IMF International Financial Statistics
Description: The IFS database provides complete coverage of the International Monetary
                   Fund's 'International Financial Statistics'.
                       Coverage includes over 23000 series of historical data. Data includes
                   interest and exchange rates, national accounts, price and production
                   indexes, money and banking, export commodity prices, and balance of
                   payments for nearly 200 countries and regional aggregates. It contains data
                   for approximately 40 countries and regions that do not have country pages
                   in the monthly publication. Some indicators are expressed in dollars for all
                   countries to facilitate cross-country analysis. Annual data are stored for all
                   series. For variables where disaggregate data are reported, monthly or
                   quarterly values are also available.
Source: IMF publication 'International Financial Statistics'
Years Covered: 1948 to date
File Size: Over 23000 data series (GE)
                   Over 21000 data series (IP Sharp)
Updates: Second business day of each month (GE Information Services)
                   Third business day of each month (IP Sharp)
Database Producer: International Monetary Fund (IMF)

Available From:	GE Information Services
	25c per data series
	or subscription options:
	$1500 per annum subscription for unlimited access to all the international databases
	$2500 per annum subscription for access to all the international plus US economic databases
	ADP Subscription Service
	Comshare Inc
	DRI
	Merrill Lynch
	National Data Corporation
	Dimensions
	IP Sharp
	Contact IP Sharp direct for prices
	WEFA
	£1600 subscription fee per annum
	or £1.60 per data series
	$25 per connect hour
	$100 standing charge per month or hourly pricing plan
	GSI-ECO
	175 Ecus peak-time
	87.5 Ecus off-peak
	Telesystemes-Eurodial
	$100 monthly minimum charge
	Citicorp
	$2000 timesharing annual subscription charge
	(Citibank timesharing only)

Name:	Institute of International Finance
Description:	The IIF gathers statistics on the economies and debt positions of debtor countries. Approximately 50 developing countries are covered. Over 150 variables are provided on the domestic economy, trade balance, external liabilities, debt service payments, government and monetary sectors, and structural factors for each country. Projections through current year are given for most countries.
Source:	IIF
Years Covered:	Annual data from 1970
File Size:	Over 150 variables included
Updates:	
Database Producer:	Haver Analytics Inc
Available From:	GEI Information
	No data charges
	(Subscription only database – prices available direct from GE Information Services)
	Restrictions:
	Use of the database is restricted to members of the Institute of International Finance with user numbers on the CEQ68 catalog. Contact Haver Analytics for information on IIF membership

Name:	International Comparisons (INTCOMP)
Description:	INTCOMP contains international economic data adjusted to be comparable to US terms. The data comes from unpublished Bureau of Labor Statistics' documents. Data on labour force, employment, and unemployment are compiled and adjusted by the US Bureau of Labor Statistics. A set of relative GDPs, converted to common units using purchasing price parity rather than market exchange rates, are unpublished estimates from the BLS. A set of data comparing manufacturing productivity among countries is equivalent to that published in the 'Monthly Labor Review'.
Source:	Bureau of Labor Statistics (unpublished documents)

Years Covered:	Current
File Size:	
Updates:	Monthly
Database Producer:	Haver Analytics Inc/Bureau of Labor Statistics
Available From:	GE Information Services
	$1 per data series
	or subscription option options:
	$1500 per annum for unlimited access to all the international databases
	$2500 per annum subscription for access to all international plus US economic databases

Name:	International Economic Indicators
Description:	IEIDATA is offered by the Center for International Business Cycle Research at Columbia University. Data includes composite leading and coincident indexes for 15 countries and country groups. The database has nearly 300 monthly and quarterly data series. Nine countries are covered: Australia, Canada, France, Germany, Italy, Japan, Taiwan, the United Kingdom and the United States. Composite indexes of leading and coincident indicators are included for each country. These indexes were created using methods developed by the Center for International Business Cycle Research under Dr Geoffery Moore. Multi-country composite indexes are also available.
Source:	Center for International Business Cycle Research, Columbia University
Years Covered:	1948 to date
File Size:	300 data series
Updates:	Monthly
Database Producer:	Haver Analytics Inc/Center for International Business Cycle Research
Available From:	GE Information Services (via QMOD and QDATA File IEIDATA)
	$5 per series
	or subscription charge of $600 per annum for unlimited use (no charge per series)
	Citicorp
	$600 timesharing annual subscription charge
	(timeshares: Citibank, Compuserve, GE Information Services, IP Sharp, Merrill Lynch, MIT and Rapidata)

Name:	International Risk Data
Description:	This database contains detailed monthly reports and forecasts on 70 countries of significance to businesses. A further 100 countries are covered more briefly. There are also quarterly reports which provide more detailed analysis and long-term risk projections.
Source:	Control Risks Information Services
Years Covered:	
File Size:	Covers 170 countries
Updates:	Monthly
Database Producer:	Control Risks Information Services
Available From:	PROFILE File IRD
	£200 monthly standing charge
	1p per off-line print (per line)
	Minimum £2 per off-line request

Name:	ISCO
Description:	Istituto Nazionale per lo Studio della Congiuntura (ISCO) is an Italian economic database. It provides 800 monthly time series on Italian industrial production indexes, import and export indexes for prices and volume of goods, and sales and orders indexes. It also includes business outlook survey data.
Source:	Italian statistics
Years Covered:	Varies by series
File Size:	800 time series
Updates:	Periodically, as data available
Database Producer:	Data Resources (DRI)

Available From: Data Resources (DRI)
(Part of DRI Europe database)
DRI offers most of its historical databases through two pricing options: annual subscription fee or Information Plus. The latter option does not involve an upfront fee and is more suitable for short term projects or occasional analysis. Contact direct for further details.

Name: ISET
Description: ISET (Informazioni Statistiche Economiche Territoriali) provides regional economic statistical data for Italy. It contains a variety of data aggregates such as the territorial distribution of firms in a given industry, or an industry breakdown of firms in a given area. It also provides the distribution of firms by legal status or number of employees, number of firms started business or are going out of business during the 6-month period.
Source: Data is taken from Cerved's other files which are sourced from company details registered with Chambers of Commerce
Years Covered: Current
File Size: Over 1 million tables
Updates: Twice a year
Database Producer: Cerved and Societa Nazionale di Informatica delle Camere di Commercio
Available From: Cerved
Lire 122 079 per connect hour (prime time)
Lire 99 883 per connect hour (non-prime time)

Name: ISIS (Integrated Statistical Information System)
Description: ISIS (Integriertes Statistisches Informationssystem) offers comprehensive statistical data on Austria. It provides socio-economic indicators for Austria covering: demography, agriculture and forestry, regional statistics, industry and trade, foreign trade, transport and tourism, social statistxics and housing, finance and national accounts. Over 350 million time series are provided on a monthly, quarterly and annual basis. The software system for the administration and usage of this database is LASD which runs on IBM 370 compatible processors under the operating system MVS.
Source: Database producer – Austrian national statistics
Years Covered: Varies, earliest data goes back to 1869
File Size: 350 million time series
Updates: Varies by series
Database Producer: Oesterreichisches Statistisches Zentralamt
Technisch-Methodische Abteilung
Available From: Oesterreichisches Statistisches Zentralamt
Subscription required
Contact Statistical Office direct for prices and usage conditions.
(Not available through commercial hosts at present)

Name: Japan Economic Newswire Plus
Description: Japan Economic Newswire Plus contains the complete combination of all English-language newswires as reported by Kyodo News Service, Tokyo, Japan. It includes both the Japan Economic Daily (JED) and Kyodo English Language News (KENS) newswires. The file is produced by Kyodo News Service, Japan's largest news agency and a cooperative of the Japanese press. Coverage includes both general and business news from Japan, as well as international news which relates to Japan. It provides text of official statements issued by international groups such as the International Monetary Fund, GATT and OECD conferences.
Source: Compiled in Tokyo by Kyodo News Service editors utilising the services of over 2000 correspondents and additional employees in Japan and overseas news bureaus
Years Covered: 1984 to date
File Size: 52 675 records
Updates: Daily
Database Producer: Kyodo News Service

Available From:	DIALOG File 612
	$96 per connect hour
	60c per off-line print
	SDI profile: $3.95
	Data-Star File KYOP
	Contact direct for prices

Name:	Labor
Description:	Labor contains employment and earnings data by industry. The database covers monthly adjusted and unadjusted data on employment, weekly earnings and hours, hourly earnings and overtime hours for production workers by industry; measures of total employment and employment of women.
	Over 490 manufacturing and non-manufacturing industries are included and these are coded by Standard Industrial Classification. Earnings are expressed in current dollars per hour. Annual wage and employment data is provided for approximately 85 industries and aggregates.
	This includes total compensation, wages and salaries, number of employees, number of full-time equivalent employees, number of persons engaged in production, and number of hours worked by industry.
Source:	Data compiled by the Bureau of Labor Statistics for its Establishment Survey published in 'Employment and Earnings'. All other data is collected by the Commerce Department and published in the 'Survey of Current Business'.
Years Covered:	1948 to date (annual data)
	1947 to date (monthly data)
File Size:	Covers over 490 industry sectors
Updates:	Every July (annual data)
	First week of each month (monthly data)
Database Producer:	Haver Analytics Inc/Bureau of Labor Statistics
Available From:	GE Information Services
	25c per data series
	Electronic Data Systems (EDS) provides the Bureau of Labor Statistics Electronics News Release containing major US economic indicators.
	No data charges, cost is based on computer time used.
	Contact Donald Fairbairn at EDS (Maryland) for access and price details.

Name:	Labordoc
Description:	Produced by ILO in Geneva, Labordoc includes journal articles, books, conference papers, technical documents and ILO publications held in the ILO Library on labour questions worldwide. Some 75 per cent of the database represents material about particular regions and countries. The main subjects are:
	Industrial relations and labour laws
	Employment and working conditions
	Security
	Vocational training
	Labour-related aspects of economics, social development, rural development, technological change, etc.
Language:	Documents are in a multitude of languages, with English representing approximately 60 per cent, French 20 per cent and Spanish 10 per cent. Records contain searchable abstracts and index terms in English from the ILO Thesaurus
Source:	ILO Publications, plus other relevant journals, books, conference papers. Corresponds to 'International Labour Documentation Monthly' (ILO)
Years Covered:	1965 to present
File Size:	Approx 146000 records
Updates:	Approx 550 records per month
Database Producer:	Central Library and Documentation Branch, International Labour Office
	User aids and abstract bulletin are available from the above

Available From: ESA-IRS File 53
                     £66.50 per connect hour
                     14.7p per on-line type
                     25.5p per off-line print
                     SDI profile: £4.90
                     ORBIT Search Service File Labordoc
                     $110 per connect hour
                     25c per on-line type
                     50c per off-line print
                     SDI profile: $6.50

Name: Laborinfo
Description: Produced by the International Labour Office (ILO) in Geneva, Laborinfo is
                     a back-up service to the ILO quarterly 'Social and Labour Bulletin' (SLB)
                     and includes law, regulations, EC Directives, judicial decisions, collective
                     agreements, monographs, policy statements and research papers by
                     governments and intergovernmental agencies, employers' organisations
                     and trade unions. It also covers all SLB articles.
                        Laborinfo focuses on new developments and significant trends on the
                     labour scene in both industrialised and developing countries. The main
                     emphasis is on:
                     Social, economic and employment policies
                     Impact of new technologies
                     Industrial relations and collective bargaining
                     Labour legislation covering the working environment,
                     Job protection and social security
                     Strategies of multinational corporations
                     Education, training and skill requirements
Language: Documents in Laborinfo are in all major languages. Each record contains an
                     abstract in everyday English followed by searchable index terms selected
                     from the ILO Thesaurus
Source: Corresponds to the ILO quarterly 'Social and Labour Bulletin'
Years Covered: 1980 to present (some entries from 1974)
File Size: Approx 9000 records
Updates: Approx 350 records every 4 months
Database Producer: Social and Labour Bulletin Section, International Labour Office
Available From: ESA-IRS File 87
                     Also available to subscribers on com-microfiches, updated bi-annually
                     £66.50 per connect hour
                     14.7p per on-line type
                     25.5p per off-line print
                     SDI profile: £4.90

Name: List Stat
Description: List Stat is a Nordic bibliographic database which contains information on
                     the holdings of statistical publications from the world, held in the statistical
                     libraries of Denmark, Finland and Norway. The database is due to be
                     complete in 1988. Users may borrow periodicals or order photocopies from
                     all three libraries.
Source: Nordic statistical libraries
Years Covered: Current
File Size: 3200 documents (as of Feb 1987)
Updates: Quarterly
Database Producer: Danmarks Statistick – Denmark
                     Tilastokeskus – Central Statistical Office of Finland
                     Statistisk Sentralbyra – Norway
Available From: Datacentralen
                     DK 180 per connect hour
                     DK 2 per off-line print (per page)

Name: MERL-ECO
Description: This is an economic database providing statistics on French industry and
                         economics.
Source:
Years Covered: 1973 to date
File Size: 30 000 records
Updates: Monthly
                         Approx 200 records added per update
Database Producer: Merlin-Gerin Service Documentation
Available From: G CAM Serveur File MERL
                         FF 450 per connect hour

Name: Mideast
Description: The Mideast database covers aspects of life and work in the Middle Eastern
                         countries, especially business and economics as well as science, society,
                         religion, politics and law. This database includes details of business
                         opportunities in the region. It can be useful for:
                         News information
                         Current affairs and political/social situation in the Middle East
Source: Economic and current affairs publications
Years Covered: 1979 to date
File Size: 60 521
Updates: Monthly
Database Producer: Learned Information Ltd
Available From: DIALOG File 249
                         $75 per connect hour
                         30c per off-line print

Name: MMS Debt Market Analysis
Description: This database is made up of two sections:
                             The Economic Section provides commentaries, forecasts and analyses of
                         the debt markets. It provides weekly surveys of Federal Reserve open
                         market policy and operations, interest rate trends, economic indicators and
                         weekly economic surveys.
                             The Technical Section provides a technical analysis of the international
                         cash and futures markets. This includes commentary from analysts on the
                         floors of the major exchanges, yield curves, point and figure charts, trading
                         strategies and coverage of mortgages markets, gold, silver and bond
                         markets.
Source: US Federal Reserve information
                         MMS weekly economic surveys
                         Analysts from the major financial futures exchanges
Years Covered: Current
File Size:
Updates: Weekly
Database Producer: Money Market Services (MMS)
Available From: Telerate Systems Inc
                         Economic Section: $275 per month
                         Technical Section: $195 per month
                         AP-Dow Jones News/Retrieval
                         $120 per connect hour

Name: Munzinger Landerarchiv
Description: The Munzinger Record Library contains selected brief information on
                         countries throughout the world and their dependent territories and on
                         national and international organisations covering the following themes:
                         Politics (executive bodies, diplomacy, constitution and administration,
                         parties and unions, mass media, defence system)
                         The economy (currency, public finance, aid to the developing countries,
                         the economy and foreign trade, transport) Social questions and culture (the
                         population, social institutions, law and justice, religion, racial groups)
                         Geographical features, climate, general data relating to the geography of

the region, chronological table Literary information.
This database is targeted at users in the following sectors: the daily and
weekly press, radio and television, those involved in economic affairs (eg
export firms), industry, officials of all kinds and grades, publishing
companies, schools and educationalists, journalists and advertisers.

Language:	German
Source:	Online equivalent of the 'International Handbook – Countries of the World Today', published by the information service of the Munzinger Record Library
Years Covered:	Current
File Size:	Approx 11 000
Updates:	Monthly
Database Producer:	Bertelsmann Informations Service GmbH and WILA-Verlag KG
Available From:	Bertelsmann File MUNZ
	Licence fee DM 150
	DM 78 per connect hour
	DM 1 per on-line type
	DM 1 per off-line print

Name:	National Development Plans
Description:	This database contains information on the development plans of over 70 countries. The producers of the database, Metra, produce summaries of these plans in English and comment on the countries' progress against the plan targets.
Source:	Government economic and development plans
Years Covered:	Varies by country
File Size:	Covers 70 countries
Updates:	
Database Producer:	Metra Consulting Group
Available From:	PROFILE File NDP
	£84 per connect hour
	1p per off-line print (per line)
	Minimum £2 per off-line request

Name:	Needs-TS
Description:	Needs-TS is Nikkei's on-line timesharing system for economic analysis. This is a new product offered by the same producers who provide Nikkei Telecom.
	It offers data covering 5 million series and provides corporate and economic data for Japan. Company profiles are also available for China and Hong Kong, but not stock information. Needs offers users the facility to set up their own portfolio of companies which they wish to monitor. It offers a range of analytical services – from the selection of component stocks, to the selection, management and evaluation of portfolios. Users can conduct a profit and loss evaluation by industry and set up company rankings by profitability. Risk and return and stock market indicators are also available.
Source:	
Years Covered:	Current
File Size:	5 million data series
	17 000 major companies
Updates:	Daily
	Prices updated 10 times a day
Database Producer:	Nihon Keizai Shimbun
Available From:	Mitsui & Co (London or New York Branch)
	Prices vary according to specific customer requirements. Payment consists of a non-recurring initial fee and a choice of payment schedule.
	Basic fee: $1000 initial
	$250 monthly
	Data usage fee varies from $150 to $1350 per month depending on service

Name:	Nikkei Telecomm
Description:	The Nikkei Telecomm database covers the following areas:
	News
	Market today
	Stock information
	Bond information
	Foreign exchange & money
	Commodity information
	Corporate information (Japan, China & Korea)
	Major industrial indicators
	International trade indicators
	Semiconductor information
	Major economic indicators
	Macroeconomic forecasts
	The English language version of this database covers listed companies only. The Japanese version covers a larger number of Japanese language journals and includes unlisted companies.
Source:	'Nikkei News Flash'
	Top articles
	'Japan Times'
	'Tokyo Financial Review'
	'Japan Economic Journal'
	'Tradescope'
	'Speaking of Japan'
	'Japan Economic Almanac'
	'Nikkei Newsletter on Bond & Money'
	'Focus Japan'
	'Nikkei NJewsletter on Commodities'
	'Outlook for the Japanese Economy'
	'Nikkei High Tech Report'
	'Monthly Finance Review'
	'IBJ Monthly Report'
	'Tokyo Financial Letter'
Years Covered:	Current
File Size:	
Updates:	Daily (Newsfile is real time)
	Prices updated 10 times a day
Database Producer:	Nihon Keizai Shimbun Inc
Available From:	Science Reference Library
	Japanese Information Service
	$180 per connect hour (plus VAT)
	Japanese language version should be available at the library later in 1988
	Mitsui & Co (agents for Nihon Keizai Shimbun Inc)
	$450 per month
	$60 per connect hour
	or:
	research subscription (for less regular users)
	$150 per month
	$120 per connect hour
	Kokusai Information Service Co Ltd (Japan)

Name:	Nomura Research Institute (NRI/E)
Description:	The NRI/E database contains history and selected forecasts of the Japanese economy and industry. Subscription to the database includes issues of the 'Monthly Review' and the 'Quarterly Review', which discuss current economic developments.
	Coverage includes national income and product accounts, industrial production, consumer and producer prices, international trade by product category, interest rates, financial flows and the census of manufacturers.
	Each quarter, 5 quarter forecasts are entered for 38 variables including gross national expenditure, balance of payments and prices.
Source:	Nomura Research Institute

Years Covered:	Forecasts for the next 5 quarters
File Size:	Over 5000 annual, quarterly, monthly and weekly time series
Updates:	Daily
	Weekly data are updated each Monday
Database Producer:	Haver Analytics Inc/Nomura Research Institute
Available From:	GE Information Services
	Subscription service only
	$1500 subscription fee per annum
	Restrictions:
	Database available on user numbers beginning with
	CCQO1, CBQ65, CCQO5 or CEQ68
	WEFA File NRIEDB
	£1600 subscription fee per annum or
	£1.60 per data series

Name:	OECD Data
Description:	OECD Data provides information on the latest economic developments in 25 leading industrial countries. IP Sharp provides 13 different OECD databases.

OECD member countries are:

Australia	Greece	Norway
Austria	Iceland	Portugal
Belgium	Ireland,	Spain
Canada	Republic of	Sweden
Denmark	Italy	Switzerland
Finland	Japan	Turkey
France	Luxembourg	United Kingdom
Germany, Federal	Netherlands	United States
Republic of	New Zealand	

Yugoslavia participates in the work of the OECD with a special status.

Coverage:
Main economic indicators
Economic outlook
Annual and quarterly national accounts
Indicators of industrial activity
Flows and stocks of fixed capital
Labour force statistics
Business surveys and cyclical indicators
Trade
Development Assistance Committee
S J Rundt world risk analysis packageWorld Bank debt tables
Monthly statistics of foreign trade – separate
database: OECDTRA

Source:	OECD
Years Covered:	Latest available data
File Size:	25 countries covered
Updates:	Monthly, when tapes arrive from the OECD
Database Producer:	OECD
Available From:	IP Sharp
	Contact IP Sharp direct for prices
	WEFA File OECD
	£1600 subscription fee per annum or
	£1.60 per data series

Name:	OECD Main Economic Indicators
Description:	This is the on-line version of the 'Main Economic Indicators' publication. It covers all 25 OECD countries plus selected data for North America and the European Community. Approximately 6500 monthly, quarterly and annual economic time series are provided, including national income, industrial production, domestic and foreign trade and balance of payments.
Source:	Statistics provided by OECD

Years Covered:	1960 to date
File Size:	6500 time series for 25 OECD countries
Updates:	Monthly
Database Producer:	Organisation for Economic Cooperation and Development (OECD)
	Data Dissemination and Reception Unit
Available From:	WEFA File OECD
	£1600 subscription fee per annum or
	£1.60 per data series
	DAIWA Securities Research Institute
	Data Resources (DRI)
	Subscription required
	Dimensions
	Available on a per-use basis
	IP Sharp
	Access via 39 Magic
	Contact IP Sharp direct for prices
	GSI-ECO (Dataeco database)
	IBM Information Network Services – Europe
	Nomura Securities Co

Name:	Prezzi
Description:	Prezzi is an Italian economic database. It provides approximately 350000 Italian consumer prices and price indexes on family expenditures by workers and salaried emplyees.
Language:	Italian
Source:	Istituto Centrale di Statistica (ISTAT)
Years Covered:	1947 to date
File Size:	350000 indexes
Updates:	Monthly
Database Producer:	Istituto Centrale di Statistica (ISTAT)
Available From:	Istituto Centrale di Statistica (ISTAT)

Name:	Producer Price Indexes
Description:	PPIDATA consists of US producer price indexes for individual commodities and commodity groupings (PPIs) and for the net output of industries and their product (PPIs Revised) selected from the Bureau of Labor Statistics' Producer Prices and Price Indexes.
	The database covers:
	Commodity, industry output, stage-of-processing, and durability indexes
	PPI series ranging from the most aggregate commodity groupings to the most detailed (BLS 8-digit code) level; PPIR series from the industry level (4-digit SIC code) to the most detailed product (9-digit) level
	Estimated values for months in which the BLS could not report a price index
	Special series constructed by General Electric Corporate purchasing, linking old and new price indexes
	Metals price indexes covering silver, gold, aluminium, copper, nickel, lead, tin and zinc
Source:	US Bureau of Labor Statistics' Producer Prices and Price Indexes
Years Covered:	January 1970 to date
File Size:	Over 3000 monthly series of historical data
Updates:	Monthly
Database Producer:	Haver Analytics Inc/US Bureau of Labor
Available From:	GE Information Services
	25c per data series
	or subscription options:
	$1500 per annum subscription for unlimited access to all the US economic databases
	$2500 per annum subscription for all US economic plus international databases
	WEFA File WPIDB
	£1600 per annum subscription or

£1.60 per data series
Interactive Data Corporation (IDC) File WPIDB
Electronic Data Systems (EDS) provides the Bureau of Labor
Statistics Electronics News Release containing major
US economic indicators.
No data charges, cost is based on computer time used.
Contact Donald Fairbairn at EDS (Maryland) for access and price details.

Name:	PROGNO
Description:	PROGNO contains references and abstracts of business-oriented daily news and periodicals which contain forecasts and news of developments in the fields of policy, economics and society. It covers all German-language countries.
Language:	German
Source:	Daily newspapers, periodicals
Years Covered:	W 1987 to date
File Size:	3500 records
Updates:	Monthly
	200 records added per update
Database Producer:	Gesellschaft fur Betriebswirtschaftliche Information mbH (GBI)
Available From:	GBI File PROGNO
	DM 120 per connect hour
	DM 0.80 per document per on-line type

Name:	PTS International Forecasts
Description:	The Predicasts International Forecasts database contains abstracts of published forecasts with historical data for countries worldwide covering industries, products and general economics.Each record usually contains numeric data for a base year plus a short-range and long-range forecast – the years for which data are presented are those given in the original source. Predicasts aim to collect published forecasts together, and several conflicting forecasts for a particular product will often be found. Predicasts make no judgement on quality but, in addition to source details, the author or corporate source is also included where forecasts are attributed.
Source:	Published forecasts (in tabular form) taken from trade journals, business publications and newspapers.
	Information is abstracted from more than 1000 international sources
Years Covered:	1971 to date (DIALOG)
	1978 to date (Data-Star)
File Size:	666 369 records
Updates:	Quarterly and monthly
Database Producer:	Predicasts Inc
Available From:	DIALOG File 83
	$114 per connect hour
	38c per on-line type
	48c per off-line print
	Data-Star File PTFC
	£62.76 per connect hour
	20p per on-line print
	11p per off-line print

Name:	PTS US Forecasts
Description:	This database contains abstracts of published forecasts for the USA from trade journals, business and financial publications, key newspapers, government reports and special studies. Each record typically contains historical base period data, a short-term forecast and a long-term forecast. Coverage includes general economics, all industries, products and end-use data.
	See also PTS International Forecasts.
Source:	Various including journals, newspapers, reports
Years Covered:	July 1971 to date
File Size:	466 863 records

Updates:	Monthly
Database Producer:	Predicasts Inc
Available From:	DIALOG File 81
	$114 per on-line connect hour
	38c per on-line type
	48c per off-line print
	Data-Star File PTFC
	£62.76 per connect hour
	20p per on-line print
	11p per off-line print

Name:	PTS US Time Series
Description:	The Predicasts US Time Series is composed of two subfiles:

Predicasts Composites. Contains about 500 time series on the US. Time series include historical data (since 1957) and projected consensus of published forecasts through to 1990. These projections for 1985, 1990 and 1995 are made by Predicasts itself. Projections are based on a consensus of expert opinion rather than on a mathematical model and are clearly marked 'Predicasts' in the source field of the record. Coverage includes production or usage of major materials, products, energy and vehicles and other economic, demographic, industrial and product data.

Predicasts Basebook. Contains annual data from 1957 to date for about 47 000 series on US production, consumption, price, foreign trade and usage statistics for agriculture, mining, manufacturing and service industries.

Source:	Tables of statistics are derived from government and international agency sources (eg UN, FAO, OECD, etc) and special subject sources (eg International Iron and Steel Institute)
Years Covered:	1957 to date (years covered vary by record)
File Size:	45 103 records
Updates:	Quarterly
Database Producer:	Predicasts Inc
Available From:	DIALOG File 82
	$114 per connect hour
	35c per on-line type
	40c per off-line print
	Data-Star File PTTS
	£62.76 per connect hour
	20p per on-line print
	11p per off-line print

Name:	Quarterly Financial Report
Description:	The database QFR contains quarterly aggregate statistics on the financial position of US corporations by industry as reported in the 'Quarterly Financial Report'.

It provides:

Quarterly estimates of income statements and balance sheets for all manufacturing, mining and trade corporations classified into 42 groupings by industry and asset size

Data for the first, second and third quarter are made available during the following quarter. Data for the fourth quarter are released the following April.

Source:	US Government 'Quarterly Financial Report'
Years Covered:	1981 to date
File Size:	6000 time series
Updates:	Quarterly
Database Producer:	Haver Analytics Inc

Available From:	GE Information Services
	$1 per data series
	or subscription options:
	$1500 per annum for unlimited access to all the US economic databases
	$2500 per annum subscription for all US economic plus the international databases

Name:	Reserve Bank of Australia Bulletin (RBA)
Description:	This database provides financial and economic statistics produced and published by the Reserve Bank of Australia.
Source:	Reserve Bank of Australia
Years Covered:	July 1969 to date
File Size:	
Updates:	Weekly, monthly, quarterly, biannually and annually
Database Producer:	IP Sharp
Available From:	IP Sharp
	Access via 39 Magic
	Contact IP Sharp direct for prices

Name:	Retribuzioni Operai e Apprendisti
Description:	This is an Italian economics database. It provides 1800 quarterly and annual time series on wages and covers Italian industrial firms with over 50 employees. Data is aggregated by industrial sector and geographic entity.
Language:	Italian
Source:	'Quarterly Report' on employment, wages and work hours produced by the Ministry of Labour and Social Planning
Years Covered:	1978 to date
File Size:	1800 time series
Updates:	Quarterly
Database Producer:	Confindustria
Available From:	GIANO (Sistema Informatico della Confindustria)
	Access limited to Confindustria member firms

Name:	Reuters Country Reports
Description:	This service monitors political and economic developments and news in 190 countries, and is geared to the needs of businesses involved in international trade and investment. Statistics provided include key economic indicators. 50 countries are covered in more depth, and information includes industry sector profiles, structural, liquidity and policy indicators. Reuters will be adding new countries to this list and more profiles. The service is easy to use due to the menu driven features which are incorporated. Existing clients who access Reuters other services via a dedicated terminal can access the country reports service simply, using a pre-programmed keyboard.
Source:	Reuters own network of staff worldwide.
Years Covered:	Current
	Information held for 3 months
File Size:	190 countries (August 1988)
Updates:	
Database Producer:	Reuters
Available From:	Reuters
	Subscription or connect hour service
	Hourly block contract can be purchased starting at 5 hours per month.
	Contact direct for prices, equipment and further access details.

Name:	SEC I National Account (CRONOS)
Description:	SEC I provides annual series of main aggregates of national accounts according to the European system of integrated economic accounts, which is the European community version of the UN system of national accounts. Currency is national, ECUs (European Currency Units) and in purchasing power standards.

Source:	CRONOS – corresponds to the publication 'National Accounts-ESA-Aggregates'
Years Covered:	Most series begin in 1960
File Size:	
Updates:	
Database Producer:	Statistical Office of the European Community (Eurostat)
Available From:	WEFA File CRONOS
	£1600 subscription fee per annum or
	£1.60 per data series
	GSI ECO
	175 Ecus (peak time)
	87.5 Ecus (off-peak time)
	1 Ecu per series

Name:	Societe Generale de Banque
Description:	SGBD is a bibliographic database covering economics and finance. Subjects include:
	Belgian economic sectors
	Raw materials, basis materials, European and worldwide sectors
	State of economic activities and economic outlook in Belgium and on an international level
	State of economic activities and finances in the developing coutries
	Belgian economic, financial and social legislation
	EC policies and directives in the economic, financial and social fields
	International economic, financial and monetary problems
	Banking activities, techniques and products
	International capital and the credit market
	Financial management and marketing activities of companies
	Economic theories, financial analysis and portfolio management
Language:	Various
Source:	The main Belgian and foreign newspapers
	Over 1000 different Belgian and foreign periodicals
	Studies and reports by international organisations
	Publications of the Belgian Ministries, official organisations and the European Communities Banker's information bulletins
	Reports of professional unions and organisations
Years Covered:	1979 to date
File Size:	Approx 81000 references (September 1986)
	12000 citations added per annum
Updates:	Monthly
Database Producer:	Societe Generale de Banque
	Centre d'Information
	Subject to legislation and copyright, the SGB will deliver full text hard copies (reproduction) at cost price (reproduction plus possible copyright)
Available From:	Belindis File SGBD
	BF 3000 per connect hour
	BF 10 per 10 lines displayed on line
	BF 10 per off-line print
	Data-Star File SGBD
	£51.43 per connect hour
	6p per on-line print
	12p per off-line print

Name:	Sphinx
Description:	Sphinx is a French bibliographic database which provides references in the field of economics, employment, demography, commerce, industry, agriculture and urbanisation plus other related areas. This is an important part of INSEE's information service providing data at a local level.
Language:	French
Source:	Supplied by the 22 regional economic offices which make up the regional network of INSEE

Years Covered:	June 1977 to date
	INSEE publications 1970 to date
File Size:	40 000 records
Updates:	Fortnightly
	About 120 records per update
Database Producer:	Institute National de la Statistique et des Etudes Economiques (INSEE)
Available From:	G CAM Serveur File SPHX
	FF 370 per connect hour

Name:	Statistiche del Commercio Estero dell'Italia
Description:	This is an Italian economic database, providing monthly time series on Italian imports and exports. It covers 8300 products and product groups which are classified according to Italian customs codes. It provides aggregated data by country of origin and destination, and balance of trade figures for trading partners and regions.
Language:	Italian
Source:	National statistical agencies
Years Covered:	1978 to date
File Size:	8300 products and product groups
Updates:	Monthly
Database Producer:	Confindustria
Available From:	GIANO

Name:	Statistiche Economiche
Description:	This is an Italian economic database, covering over 12 000 monthly, quarterly and annual time series on Italian industrial production and plant utilisation. Data is classified and aggregated by industrial branch, class, subclass, product group, subgroup and individual products.
Language:	Italian
Source:	Isco-Mondo Economico (research organisation)
	Italian government, Central Institute of Statistics
Years Covered:	1972 to date (annual)
	1976 to date (other series)
File Size:	12 000 time series
Updates:	Annual
Database Producer:	Confindustria
Available From:	GIANO

Name:	Statistics Sweden
Description:	Two Swedish economic databases are provided through this service:
	RSDB is a regional statistical database covering education, employment, industry, income, enterprises, housing and construction amongst other areas. Material is classified by county and municipality.
	TSDB is a time series database covering the credit market, energy, foreign trade, finance, national accounts and prices and international statistics
Source:	Official statistical sources. International sources are the OECD's Foreign Trade (Series A), Main Economic Indicators (MEI), Business Surveys, Cyclical Indicators, and Indicators of Industrial Activity. Plus the IMF's International Financial Statistics
Years Covered:	1970 to date
File Size:	
Updates:	Monthly or quarterly
Database Producer:	
Available From:	Statistics Sweden
	SKr 1000 annual subscription charge
	Search options:
	Menu-driven dialogue:
	SKr 100 per matrix search cost
	SKr 10 per 100 tablecells per output

Name:	Superstat
Description:	Superstat is an Italian economic statistical database covering population, income, consumption, savings, investment and industrial production. It provides over 2000 time series and data is presented at both the provincial and municipal level. Information can also be found on the number of businesses in each of the 8093 municipalities. SARIN also offers a range of direct marketing services drawing on its databases of Italian businesses, telephone directories etc.
Language:	Italian
Source:	Italian census plus other official statistics
Years Covered:	1981 to date
	Census date from 1971
File Size:	2000 time series
Updates:	Annual
Database Producer:	SARIN SpA
Available From:	SARIN SpA
	Annual subscription: Lire 21 million plus pay as you go charges
	Flat rate charges can be negotiated according to customer requirements
	Software: SAS

Name:	Survey of United States Forecasts
Description:	USCASTS contains quarterly projections of gross national product and unemployment for the United States by 10 forecasters.
	USCASTS includes GNP in current and constant prices, the GNP deflator and unemployment for the United States.
Source:	Ten forecasters including:
	WEFA
	Data Resources Inc
	Merrill Lynch Economics Inc
	Conference Board
	GEC
Years Covered:	Forecast range varies among the forecasters
	Most extend up to 8 quarters
File Size:	N/A
Updates:	Updated as forecasts are made available
Database Producer:	Haver Analytics Inc
Available From:	GE Information Services
	No data charges

Name:	TEND
Description:	Tendences de la Conjoncture Chahier 2 (TEND) provides analysis of French national accounts, including indicators relating to the international environment, world demand and French external exchanges. It also covers:
	Total resources and uses
	Industrial production
	Wages and labour costs
	Household and enterprise incomes
	Employment
Language:	French
Source:	Analysis undertaken by INSEE
Years Covered:	
File Size:	
Updates:	
Database Producer:	Institut National de la Statistique et des Etudes Economiques (INSEE)
Available From:	GSI ECO
	60 Ecus per month (fee)
	175 Ecus per connect hour (peak time)
	87.5 Ecus per connect hour (off-peak time)

Name: Trade Statistics
Description: Tradstat holds published government import/export information on all
                    reported commodities and products (over 50 000) from 11 European
                    countries plus Japan, Brazil, Canada and the USA. UK trade breakdown by
                    port has recently been added. Monthly figures show trade details between
                    the rest of the world and Spain, France, Belgium, Netherlands, Italy,
                    Germany (Federal Republic of), UK, Brazil, Canada, USA and Japan.
                    Figures are normally available within 4-6 weeks of the month end. Annual
                    figures are provided for the above countries plus data from Austria,
                    Norway, Sweden and Switzerland. Harmonised codes are used for 1988
                    data. MNIMEXE, US, Japanese and Canadian customs product code
                    classifications are used for pre-1988 data. There are 20 report formats
                    available. Bank of England exchange rates are built into the system
Source: Obtained directly from customs offices of the reporting country
Years Covered: Current
File Size: Over 50 000 commodities and products
Updates: Updated from computer tape as soon as statistics are available from
                    customs offices
Database Producer: Data-Star
Available From: Data-Star
                    Standard rate:
                    £30 per connect hour
                    £5-£15 per on-line print (per report)
                    £5-£15 per off-line print (per report)
                    Price depends on report type and number of products
                    Regular monthly printed reports can be ordered.
                    Price per report is same as at standard rate

Name: United Nations Industrial Statistics
Description: UNIND consists of historical data by industry compiled by the United
                    Nations and published in the 'Yearbook of Industrial Statistics'. Data are
                    classified by ISIC codes up to the 4-digit level and cover mining and
                    quarrying, manufacturing, electricity, gas and water supply.
                        Data is provided covering the size of the labour force, wages and salaries,
                    quantity of electricity consumed, output, value added, gross fixed capital
                    formation and index numbers of industrial production. Data availability
                    can precede publication in the Yearbook by nearly a year.
Source: United Nations
Years Covered: 1967 to date
File Size: 17 500 annual time series are provided for over 100 countries
Updates: Database updated as figures are released from the UN
Database Producer: Haver Analytics Inc/United Nations
Available From: GE Information Services
                    25c per data series or
                    subscription options:
                    $1500 per annum for unlimited subscription access to all the international
                    databases
                    $2500 per annum subscription for all the international and US economic
                    databases

Name: United Nations National Accounts
Description: The United Nations National Accounts database (UNNA) consists of
                    national annual accounts data compiled by the United Nations and
                    published in the 'Yearbook of National Accounts'. The data are updated
                    annually from a tape supplied by the UN Statistical Office. Data for
                    centrally-planned economies are included. Detailed breakdowns are
                    provided of GNP components, covering personal consumption
                    expenditure, investment, government expenditure and trade. Data are
                    reported in national currency, in current and constant terms when

available. Exchange rates are stored in the database for conversion to dollars. Updates precede publication of the 'National Accounts Yearbook' by several months.

Source:	United Nations
Years Covered:	1950 to date
File Size:	7500 variables covering 150 countries
Updates:	Annual
Database Producer:	Haver Analytics Inc/United Nations
Available From:	GE Information Services
	25c per data series or
	subscription options:
	$1500 per annum subscription for unlimited access to all the international databases
	$2500 per annum subscription for all the international plus the US economic databases
	WEFA File UNNIADB
	£1600 subscription fee per annum or
	£1.60 per data series

Name:	United Nations Population Statistics
Description:	UNPOP contains demographic data compiled by the United Nations Population Division. Projection measurements through the year 2025 are developed using country specific fertility, mortality and migration rates for most countries. The database provides 7500 time series for 135 countries including major regions and the world. All data are annual and projections extend to 2025. Data is reported in 5-year intervals and converted to time series through logarithmic interpolation. Data includes urban, working age and total population and is broken down by sex and age group.
Source:	United Nations
Years Covered:	Annual data starts in 1950
	Projections extend to 2025
File Size:	7500 time series, 135 countries
Updates:	
Database Producer:	Haver Analytics Inc/United Nations
Available From:	GE Information Services
	25c per data series (if not an international
	database subscriber) or
	Subscription options:
	$1500 per annum subscription for unlimited access to all international databases
	$2500 per annum subscription for all the international plus US economic databases

Name:	United States Economic Statistics
Description:	This database contains key economic and financial statistics taken from US government and Federal Reserve Board press releases. It includes the major components of GNP in current and constant dollars, GNP deflators and growth rates, consumer and producer price indexes, international transactions, housing starts, value of new construction put in place, plant and equipment expenditures, industrial production, capacity utilisation, manufacturers' shipments, inventories and orders, money stock and selected interest rates.

Both seasonally adjusted and not seasonally adjusted data are available if published by the source agency. Annual values are stored for deflators and growth rates that cannot be aggregated correctly using standard QMOD aggregation methods. |
Source:	US Government
	Federal Reserve Board
Years Covered:	1946 to date
File Size:	
Updates:	Data is updated within 2 hours of releases from the source for most data series

Database Producer:	Haver Analytics Inc/US Government Federal Reserve Board
Available From:	GE Information Services
	$1 per data series

Name:	United States National Accounts
Description:	Over 5000 time series are available, most beginning in 1946 and some annual data goes back as far as 1929. Detailed breakdowns are provided of all GNP components: personal consumption expenditure, investment, government expenditure and trade. All variables are available in current dollars. Many series provide data in constant 1982 dollars and deflators. Both annual and quarterly series are available for deflators and growth rates that cannot be aggregated correctly by standard QMOD aggregation methods. Unpublished quarterly series include producers' durable equipment, change in business inventories and auto output data. Unpublished monthly series include personal consumption expenditures and sales, inventories and production data for automobiles.
Source:	Data compiled by the Bureau of Economic Analysis and published in the 'Survey of Current Business'
Years Covered:	Most series from 1946 to date
File Size:	
Updates:	Monthly
Database Producer:	Haver Analytics Inc/Bureau of Economic Analysis
Available From:	GE Information Services
	25c per data series

Name:	Wharton Econometric World Forecasts
Description:	This database provides 7000 annual time series of historical and forecast economic data for OECD countries and South Africa. Coverage includes foreign trade, GDP expenditure by use in nominal and real terms, imports and exports, balance of payments in local currency and US dollars, wages and employment, plus crude oil export data for 16 oil-producing countries.
Source:	IMF, OECD, UN and national source data
Years Covered:	1948 to date
	5-year forecasts
File Size:	7000 annual time series for 25 countries
Updates:	Quarterly
Database Producer:	WEFA
Available From:	CISI Network Corporation
	Uni-Coll Division
	WEFA
	£1600 subscription fee per annum or
	£1.60 per data series

Name:	World Bank Debt Tables (WDEBT)
Description:	WBDEBT contains data equivalent to that published in the 'World Debt Tables' on public and private external long-term debt. Projected debt service payments data provided by the External Debt Division of the World Bank are also included in the database.
	Data is provided on debt outstanding, commitments, disbursements, principal and interest repayments, net flows and transfers and total debt service. WBDEBT carries additional data not available in the 'World Debt Tables' publication:
	Differentiation of financial market creditors
	Cancellations for each country reporting
	At a global level, breakdown of various creditor sources into concessional and non-concessional lending
Source:	World Bank
Years Covered:	1970 to date
	10-year projections
File Size:	Over 20000 annual data series
Updates:	Updated throughout the year as information is released by the reporting countries

Database Producer: Haver Analytics Inc/World Bank
Available From: GE Information Services
25c per data series or subscription options:
$1500 per annum subscription for unlimited access to all the international databases
$2500 per annum subscription for all the international plus US economic databases
WEFA
£1600 subscription fee per annum or
£1.60 per data series
GSI ECO
25 Ecus fee per month
175 Ecus peak time
87.5 Ecus off-peak
IP Sharp
Access via 39 Magic
Contact IP Sharp direct for prices

Section V News and Current Affairs

Predominantly US Sources

AP Dow Jones News Services
AP News
Business Dateline
Business Week
Businesswire (see Industry Section)
Facts on File
Information Bank Library (see Nexis in Marketing Section)
National Newspaper Index
Newsearch
UPI News
Washington Post Electronic Edition
Washington Presstext

International Sources

Agora Economique

Asahi News Service
BBC Summary of World Broadcasts
BIS Infomat
Canadian Business and Current Affairs
Canadian Periodical Index
The Daily and Sunday Telegraph
The Economist (see Marketing Section)
Financial Times Newspaper Fulltext Database
The Globe and Mail Online (see Marketing Section)
Government and Political News Library (see Nexis in Marketing Section)
Japan Economic Newswire (see Economics Section)
Mideast File (see Economics Section)
Le Monde
Newsline
Nexis (see Marketing Section)
Nikkei Telecomm (see

Economics Section)
PROGNO (see Economics Section)
PTS Promt (see Company Section)
Reuters
Research Index
Textline (see Company Section)
Tidningsdatabasen
Times Newspapers (The)
VDIN
Wirtschaftswoche
World Affairs Report
World Exporter (see PROFILE Service)
World Reporter (see PROFILE Service)

Name: Agora Economique
Description: Full text of Agence France Presse news dispatches. AECO contains news items on French and international economics from the AFP economic newswire. AGRA contains news items from the AFP general newswire covering international and French news.
Source: AFP economic newswire
Years Covered: AECO and AGRA from 1983
File Size:
Updates: Daily
Database Producer: Agence France Presse

Available From: G CAM Serveur (all files)
                     FF 670 per connect hour
                     Telesystemes-Questel Files (AECO and AGRA only)
                     $100 per connect hour
                     30c per on-line type
                     30c per off-line print
                     SDI profile: $9.25 plus print charges
                     Reseaux Commerciales Informatiques SA (RCI)
                     Offers a service called Calvacom via AFP which covers various subfiles of
                     the Agence France. Presse news releases. Monthly subscription or per
                     connect hour charges. Contact direct for prices.

Name: AP-Dow Jones News Services
Description: Range of real time news services offered for the financial markets and the
                     media. All services run 24 hours a day, 6 days a week. 'Newscall' is an
                     on-line display and retrieval system for all AP-DJ's services.
                        Specialised news reports include the following:
                     Economic Report – worldwide financial, industrial and political information
                     Bankers Report – coverage of international money markets
                     Foreign Exchange Report
                     Financial Wire – news for the international equity investment community
                     Capital Markets Report – news and analysis of the Eurobond, US fixed
                     interest and financial futures market
                     International Petroleum Report – designed for buyers and sellers of oil and
                     oil products in the spot and futures markets
                     Canadian Service – news, information and statistics on Canadian business
                     and financial markets.
Source: AP-Dow Jones financial journalists stationed in key financial and business
                     centres around the world, together with the global news-gathering
                     resources of the Associated Press and Dow Jones
Years Covered: Current
File Size:
Updates: Real time
Database Producer: AP-Dow Jones News Services
Available From: Economic Report: AP-DJ Newscall
                     $736 per month
                     Fides
                     Telerate
                     Bankers Report: AP-DJ Newscall
                     $581 per month
                     Telerate
                     Foreign Exchange: AP-DJ Newscall
                     Report:$581 per month
                     Telerate
                     Financial Wire: AP-DJ Newscall
                     $736 per month
                     ADP Financial
                     Bloomberg
                     Pont Data
                     Quotron
                     Telekurs
                     Telerate
                     Wang-Shark
                     Capital Markets AP-DJ Newscall
                     Report: $581 per month
                     Bloomberg
                     Fides
                     Telerate
                     International AP-DJ Newscall
                     Petroleum Report: $406 per month
                     Telerate (Energy Service)
                     Canadian Service:AP-DJ Newscall

$388 per month
Other Charges: Display fee $40 per month
Delivery charge $65 per month
(Services delivered by other vendors pay a delivery fee to that vendor)
Gateway Services: Data-Star File DJNS
£60 per connect hour
24p per on-line type
17p per off-line print
SDI profile: £1.63
PROFILE File code dj
£84 per connect hour
1p per off-line print (per line)
Minimum £2 per off-line request

Name:	AP News
Description:	AP(Associated Press) News provides the full text of national, international and business news from the AP data stream service, available 48 hours after the data was first transmitted. AP News includes general, domestic, political, business and financial, international, Washington DC and entertainment news.
Source:	135 US and 83 overseas news bureaus
Years Covered:	July 1984 to date
File Size:	349 923 records
Updates:	DIALOG File 258 (current file) daily
	DIALOG File 259 monthly
Database Producer:	Press Association Inc
Available From:	DIALOG
	File 258, AP News (Daily)
	$84 per connect hour
	20c per on-line type
	25c per off-line print
	DIALOG
	File 259, AP News
	$84 per connect hour
	10c per on-line type
	25c per off-line print
	MEAD Associated Press Political Service
	$19 per search for all files in the service
	$5 per individual file
	PROFILE File AP
	£84 per connect hour
	1p per off-line print (per line)
	Minimum £2 per off-line request

Name:	Asahi News Service
Description:	This database is produced by a special editorial team at 'Asahi Shimbun', Tokyo's leading daily newspaper. It covers events in the Far East and Japan, and focuses on Japanese policy and international relations, trade, telecommunications, electronics, medicine, pharmaceuticals and agriculture. The full text of each daily newswire transmission is carried.
Source:	'Asahi Shimbun'
Years Covered:	2 August 1982 to date
File Size:	7 to 8 items added daily
Updates:	Daily (stories usually avaliable 24 hours after transmission)
Database Producer:	Asahi Shimbun
Available From:	PROFILE File ANS
	£84 per connect hour
	1p per off-line print (per line)
	Minimum £2 per off-line request

Name: BBC Summary of World Broadcasts
Description: The BBC provides a monitoring and collating service of international
                          information which it accesses through overseas news broadcasts and news
                          agency reports. This service covers 120 countries, and translation is
                          conducted from 50 languages into English. Daily and weekly reports are
                          prepared, and this database contains the full text of these reports.
Source: BBC World Broadcasts reports
Years Covered: 1 Jan 1982 to date
File Size: 250 items added daily
Updates: Daily
Database Producer: BBC
Available From: PROFILE File SWB (current and previous year)
                          File SWBALL (current and previous 6 years)
                          File SWB82, SWB83 etc (for individual years)
                          £84 per connect hour
                          1p per off-line print (per line)
                          Minimum £2 per off-line request

Name: BIS Infomat
Description: BIS Infomat is a newsfile database derived from worldwide sources of daily
                          press articles, journals, broadcasts and institutions. Each item is a concise
                          summary of the original article, which has also been translated from 10
                          languages into English. Topics which can be researched are competitors'
                          activities, new products, new technologies, economic forecasts, key
                          appointments. Sectors covered include automation, biotechnology,
                          computers, electronics, drinks, food, media, packaging and
                          telecommunications. Coverage is 60 per cent UK and Europe, 20 per cent
                          US.
                          Uses include:
                          Market research
                          Newsletter preparation
                          Competitor analysis
                          Economic analysis
Source: International business press in 10 languages
Years Covered: April 1984 to present
File Size: 368 174 records (DIALOG)
Updates: Weekly
                          3000 articles added per update
Database Producer: BIS Infomat Ltd
Available From: MEAD File BIS
                          $20 per hour
                          $11 per search
                          Dialcom Business Direction
                          £120 per connect hour
                          No extra printing charges
                          Data-Star File EBUS
                          £53.88 per connect hour
                          £0.51 per on-line print
                          £0.41 per off-line print
                          SDI profile: £2.86
                          Pergamon Financial File Infomat
                          £70 per connect hour
                          50p per on-line type
                          50p per off-line print
                          SDI profile: £5
                          ESA-IRS File 156
                          £84.40 per connect hour
                          43.4p per on-line type
                          43.4p per off-line print
                          (Special rates apply for subscribers to the printed version)
                          DIALOG File 583

$96 per connect hour
50c per on-line type
60c per off-line print
MEAD-File BIS
BIS Infomat Ltd
Offers services direct which include sending a daily report by post
and monitoring events or competitors according to customer requirements.

(Prices available direct from Infomat)

Name:	Business Dateline
Description:	Business Dateline contains the full text of articles from 110 regional business publications taken throughout the USA and Canada. These articles cover regional business activities and trends as well as information about small companies, new start-ups, family-owned and closely-held firms, their products or services, and the executives who run these companies.
Source:	US and Canadian regional business publications
Years Covered:	1985 to date
File Size:	88 459 records
Updates:	Weekly
Database Producer:	UMI/Data Courier
Available From:	DIALOG File 635
	$114 per connect hour
	$4 per on-line type
	$4.50 per off-line print
	BRS File BDLN
	$60 per connect hour
	$2.90 per on-line type
	$2.85 per off-line print
	SDI profile: $4

Name:	Business Week
Description:	This database contains the full text of the USA international business journal, 'Business Week'. Items are normally available on line on the Friday following the publication date of the previous Monday.
Source:	The American edition of 'Business Week'
Years Covered:	Jan 1985 to date
File Size:	50 items approx added each week
Updates:	Weekly
Database Producer:	Business Week publishers
Available From:	PROFILE File BW
	£84 per connect hour
	1p per off-line print (per line)
	Minimum £2 per off-line request

Name:	Canadian Business and Current Affairs
Description:	Canadian Business and Current Affairs provides indexing to more than 100 000 articles per year appearing in more than 170 Canadian business periodicals and 10 newspapers. From the business perspective, the file provides descriptive annotations on a wide range of company, product, and industry information. From the current affairs perspective, the database covers significant national, provincial, and local news, editorials, selected letters to the editor, government activities, labour news, crime, sports, obituaries, biographies, and reviews.
Source:	Over 170 Canadian business periodicals and 10 newspapers
Years Covered:	July 1980 to date
File Size:	870 074
Updates:	Monthly
Database Producer:	Micromedia Ltd

Available From:	DIALOG File 262
	$72 per connect hour
	20c per off-line print
	SDI profile: $6.95

Name: The Canadian Periodical Index
Description: This database is the on-line version of the reference publication which includes citations from over 350 Canadian, English and French language publications. It also includes over 15 popular American titles. Publications include 'Canadian Business', 'The Financial Post' and 'Maclean's'. InfoGlobe offers a number of other Canadian news and publication databases such as Canadian News-Wire and the Canadian Index of Computer Literature Online from Evans Research.
Source: Canadian and USA periodicals
Years Covered: 1977 to date
File Size: Over 350 publications covered
Updates: Monthly
Database Producer: InfoGlobe
Available From: InfoGlobe
$180 per connect hour

Name: The Daily and Sunday Telegraph
Description: Provides the full text of these two British newspapers, which provide coverage of national and international news, current affairs, politics and business.
Source: As above
Years Covered: From January 1987
File Size: 120 items added daily
Updates: Each issue is normally on line 72 hours after publication
Database Producer:
Available From: PROFILE
£84 per connect hour
1p per off-line print (per line)
Minimum £2 per off-line request

Name: Facts on File
Description: Facts on File provides a weekly record of worldwide news summaries. It covers politics, government, business and the economy, medicine, sports, foreign affairs and the arts.
Source: Worldwide news sources
Years Covered: 1982 to date
File Size: 25372 records
Updates: Weekly
Database Producer: Facts on File Inc
Available From: DIALOG File 264
$60 per connect hour
25c per off-line print
MEAD File FACTS
$5 per on-line search

Name: Financial Times Newspaper Full Text Database
Description: This database provides access to the full text of articles published in the 'Financial Times' newspaper. Information is updated daily and can be accessed around the clock, and around the world. The paper is one of Europe's leading business publications and provides an analysis of UK and international industrial news, current affairs and company information. Advertising and statistical information is not included.
Source: FT International and UK edition
Years Covered: 1986 to date
File Size: 141173 records
Updates: Daily, within 24 hours of publication
Database Producer: Financial Times Business Information Ltd

Available From: PROFILE
£84.00 per connect hour
DIALOG File 622
$96 per connect hour
$1.60 per on-line type
$1.60 per off-line print
MEAD Data Central
$5 per on-line search

Name: Le Monde
Description: Full text of the French daily newspaper, containing news on economics, financial affairs and companies in France plus many other items.
Language: French
Source: 'Le Monde'
Years Covered: Current
File Size: 55 000 records
Updates: Daily
Database Producer:
Available From: G CAM Serveur File MOND
FF 800 per connect hour

Name: National Newspaper Index
Description: National Newspaper Index provides a cover to cover indexing of the three major newspapers in the USA. Items not included are weather charts, stock market tables, horoscopes and crossword puzzles.
Source: 'Christian Science Monitor', 'New York Times' and 'Wall Street Journal'
Years Covered: 1979 to date
File Size: 1 771 500 records
Updates: Monthly
Database Producer: Information Access Corporation
Available From: DIALOG File 111
$90 per connect hour
20c per on-line type
40c per off-line print
SDI profile: £10.95
BRS File NOOZ
$93 per connect hour
20c per on-line type
25c per off-line print

Name: Newsearch
Description: Newsearch is a daily index of more than 2000 news stories, information articles and book reviews from over 1700 of the most important newspapers, magazines and periodicals. The database provides front page to back page indexing of the 'Christian Science Monitor', the 'New York Times', the 'Wall Street Journal', 'Washington Post' and 'Los Angeles Times' as well as indexing of over 370 popular American magazines. The full text of PR Newswire press releases are also included in Newsearch. Every working day the previous day's news stories are indexed and added to the file to provide current information on general news product reviews, executive and corporation news, current events, book, record, theatre reviews, business and trade news and more. At the end of each month the magazine article data is transferred to the Magazine Index database, and the newspaper indexing data is transferred to the National Newspaper Index database.
Source: Over 1700 American publications and PR Newswire
Years Covered: The file covers from the first day of each month to the last day of each month
File Size: The file size varies and may contain from 2 to 6 weeks of data (1200-54 000 records)
Updates: Daily (about 1200 records per day)
Database Producer: Information Access Corporation

Available From:	DIALOG File 211
	$120 per connect hour
	$1 per on-line type
	$2 per off-line print
	SDI profile: Daily (5 prints) $3.95
	Weekly $12.95
	BRS File DALY
	$123 per connect hour
	20c per on-line type
	30c per off-line print
	SDI profile: $4

Name:	Newsline
Description:	Newsline is a Textline Service and comprises a summary of business news stories from UK and continental papers that is available in English on-line by 09.00 hours GMT on the day of publication.
	Newsline provides an efficient awareness service scanning 36 papers in 3 languages for the last 5 days, thus bridging the interval between today and the latest day on Textline. It is, therefore, valuable to anyone whose duties include immediate and constant surveillance of the press and the preparation of daily news summaries.
	Newsline provides facts on companies, industries, economic indicators, public affairs and the EEC.
	Like Textline, it is a menu-driven system, which makes searching very simple. There is the option to select:
	All stories
	Leading stories
	International stories
	Provincial press stories
Source:	29 daily publications
	12 weekly publications (including 'Investors Chronicle' and 'Financial Weekly')
	Publications are from France, Germany and the UK
Years Covered:	Current (latest 5 days)
File Size:	7000 headlines per week
Updates:	220-250 headlines per day
Database Producer:	Reuters
Available From:	Reuters
	£70 per connect hour
	30p per on-line type
	(10p per title; 20p per abstract)
	ESA-IRS File 24
	£94.51 per connect hour
	Print charges are format dependent
	Use ? Charges on line for price list

Name:	Research Index
Description:	This database has international coverage. It provides references to news items and articles of commercial interest taken from over 125 sources including the UK national press, plus trade, economic and business periodicals. Research Index is an extremely cost-effective way of being able to locate specific news items and does away with the usual laborious searching associated with manual methods. It can be used for monitoring news information, as a reference tool for use in large libraries or R & D departments and for use in research projects.
Source:	All national prestige newspapers including 'Scotsman', 'Financial Times', 'Wall Street Journal'. All monthly and weekly trade and financial magazines
Years Covered:	November 1985 to date
File Size:	17 500

Updates:	Every 2 weeks
	4000 new items added per update
Database Producer:	Business Surveys Ltd
Available From:	Pergamon Financial File RIX
	£69 per connect hour
	25p per on-line type
	25p per off-line print
	SDI profile: £5

Name:	Reuters
Description:	Reuters contains the complete text of news releases from the Reuter Financial Report (RFR) and Reuter Library Service (LBY) Newswires. The file provides access to current information on business and international news. Reuter Library Service is one of the most comprehensive sources of world news available. Use of Reuters is restricted to customers in the USA and Canada.
Source:	
Years Covered:	Jan 1987 to date
File Size:	198 800 records
Updates:	Every 15 minutes
Database Producer:	Reuters US Inc, New York
Available From:	DIALOG File 611
	$96 per connect hour
	60c per off-line print
	SDI profile: $3.95

Name:	Tidningsdatabasen
Description:	This database contains full text articles from leading Swedish newspapers and business magazines such as 'Dagens Industri', 'Veckans Affarer', 'Datavarlden', 'Privata Affarer' and the business pages of 'Dagens Nyheter' and 'Svenska Dagbladet'.
	Affarsdata provides another news database called 'Statt' which contains short technical R&D news from around the world. These two databases are offered under Affarsdata's 'A'Jour' service.
Language:	Swedish
Source:	'Dagens Industri', 'Veckans Affarer', 'Datavarlden', 'Privata Affarer', 'Degens Nyheter', 'Svenska Dagbladet' and other publications
Years Covered:	1981, 1982 to date
File Size:	
Updates:	Twice a week:Tidning database
	Monthly: Statt database
Database Producer:	Affarsdata
Available From:	Affarsdata
	SKr 720 per connect hour

Name:	The Times Newspapers
Description:	This database contains the full text of news, features, and business articles of 'The Times' and 'Sunday Times' newspapers. It does not include any other items such as book extracts, tabular information and letters to the editor.
Source:	'The Times' and 'Sunday Times' newspapers
Years Covered:	1 July 1985 to date
File Size:	175 to 200 items added per issue
Updates:	Issues on line within 3/4 days of publication
Database Producer:	The Times Newspapers Ltd
Available From:	PROFILE File TIM
	£84 per connect hour
	1p per off-line print (per line)
	Minimum £2 per off-line request

Name: UPI News
Description: UPI News contains the full text of news stories carried on the United Press
                        International wire. All news currently transmitted by UPI in the categories
                        below is available for searching: Domestic general news
                        Columns and standing features
                        Financial news
                        International news
                        Commentaries
                        Washington DC news
                        Events
                        People or reporters
                        Datelines news category
                        Keywords
                            News and information from within the US and around the world can be
                        reviewed through this database.
Source: United Press International
Years Covered: 1983 to date
File Size: 360 707 in file 260
                        Number of records in file 261 varies
Updates: This database is divided into two files on DIALOG. The current file (261) is
                        updated daily with the full text of news items 48 hours after the story has
                        been transmitted over the UPI wire and contains records from the most
                        recent 3 months (approximate 150 records per update).
                            The backup file (260) is updated monthly with the oldest month of
                        records from the current file and provides information from April 1983
Database Producer: United Press International
Available From: DIALOG
                        File 260 (1983 to current month)
                        $85 per connect hour
                        20c per on-line type
                        25c per off-line print
                        DIALOG
                        File 261 (Current Daily)
                        $85 per connect hour
                        20c per on-line type
                        25c per off-line print

Name: VDIN
Description: VDI Nachrichten (VDIN) is a German full-text newspaper database
                        covering engineering, economics and sciences. It is one of the major
                        German weekly newspapers in the field. Tables, figures and
                        advertisements are not included in the database.
Language: German
Source: Equivalent of the German weekly newspaper 'VDI-Nachrichten'
Years Covered: 1983 to date
File Size: 20 000 records
Updates: Weekly
Database Producer: VDI-Verlag GmbH
Available From: FIZ Technik File VDIN
                        DM 250 per connect hour
                        DM 2 per on-line type
                        DM 2.3 per off-line print
                        SDI profile: DM 10

Name: Washington Post Electronic Edition
Description: The Washington Post Electronic Edition is the electronic version of the
                        morning daily and Sunday Washington Post published in Washington DC.
                        The Post maintains 18 non-US, 5 national and 8 metropolitan news bureaus
                        and contains columns from Pulitzer Prize winning columnists such as
                        David Broder, Ellen Goodman and George F Will. Highlights of Post
                        coverage include its strong national political coverage and in-depth

investigative reporting on government policies and operations in Washington and around the world.

Source:	Equivalent to the daily newspaper 'Washington Post'
Years Covered:	April 1983 to date
File Size:	537 454 records
Updates:	Daily (file 146)
	Monthly (file 147)
Database Producer:	The Washington Post Company
Available From:	DIALOG File 146 (recent 6 months)
	File 147 (April 1983 to date)
	$87 per connect hour
	25c per on-line type
	25c per off-line print

Name:	Washington Presstext
Description:	Washington Presstext provides the complete text of White House and US Department of State news releases, policy statements and background information. Providing comprehensive coverage of all major domestic and international news, actions and events, this database is of particular importance to governmental, legal, journalistic, diplomatic, military, academic, business and financial interests. Of special note are the profiles of over 170 countries, which provide in-depth discussions of these countries, including travel cautions, history, economic conditions and other valuable information.
Source:	White House and US Department of State
Years Covered:	1981 to date
File Size:	36 281 records
Updates:	Daily
Database Producer:	Press Text News Service
Available From:	DIALOG File 145
	$69 per connect hour
	25c per on-line type
	30c per off-line print

Name:	Wirtschaftswoche
Description:	Wirtschaftswoche (WW) is the on-line version of the weekly German business magazine 'Wirtschaftswoche'. It contains news and background reports with full unabridged text. It also provides analyses and forecasts for the following areas:
	Names and news
	Countries
	Economic climate
	Economics and politics
	Money and capital
	Management
	Industry sectors and companies
	Scientific theories
	The Report (the current theme of the week)
	Special features
	Outlook
	Money week
Language:	German
Source:	The weekly edition of 'Wirtschaftswoche'
Years Covered:	June 1984 to date
File Size:	Approx 11 000 articles
Updates:	Weekly
Database Producer:	GWP Gesellschaft fur Wirtschaftspresse mbH
Available From:	GENIOS File WW
	DM 240 per connect hour
	DM 1 per on-line type
	DM 1 per off-line print
	SDI profile: DM 10

Name:	World Affairs Report
Description:	The World Affairs Report database is a digest of worldwide news as seen from Moscow. This file provides subject by subject and country by country analysis of the Soviet attitude toward world events based on both Soviet sources as well as occasional related references from Reuters, 'Le Monde' and major US newspapers and wire services. Each record contains an abstract of a news item that has been translated into English, people who figure prominently in the news, the name of the country that is the subject of the article and references to original sources of the information.
Source:	'Pravda', 'Izvestia', 'Tass', 'Literaturnaya Gazeta', 'Reuters', 'Le Monde', Major US newspapers and wire services.
Years Covered:	1970 to date
File Size:	32377 records
Updates:	Monthly
Database Producer:	California Institute of International Studies
Available From:	DIALOG File 167
	$90 per connect hour
	10c per on-line type
	25c per off-line print

Section VI Overseas Trade Opportunities

Conferences and Trade Fairs

Concursos Publicos
CONF
Conference Papers Index
Fairbase
Ferias y Exposiciones
ma Messe-Kalender
Meeting

Disposals

Accountants Business
Network
BODACC
CAPA

Grants

Acciones de Fomento

AIMS
Euroloc (see EEC Section)
Federal and State Business
Assistance
Finance for New Projects in
the UK
GELD (Money)
STARS

Mergers and Acquisitions

Amdata
BODACC
Mergers
Mergers and Acquisitions
PTS F&S Indexes

Projects and Tender Notices

BOAMP
Business
Business Opportunities-Sell

CHINA COOP
EIS Online
Euroloc (see EEC Section)
FBR
Firmexport (Telexport)
Foreign Traders Index
Oferes (see Company Section)
Pabli (see EEC Section)
Scan-a-Bid-Scan
Sesame (see EEC Section)
TED (see EEC section)
Thomas New Industrial
Products
World Bank International
Business Opportunities
Service

Name:	Acciones de Fomento
Description:	This is a database of grants and other means of financial support for Spanish businesses, including tax relief schemes.
Source:	Official State bulletins (Boletin Oficial de Estado)
	Regional government bulletins, and information provided by financial institutions
Years Covered:	Current
File Size:	1450 documents (600 in operation daily)
Updates:	Daily
Database Producer:	Sistema de Informacion Empresarial
Available From:	Instituto de la Pequena y Mediana Empresa Industrial
	(IMPI) Contact direct for prices

Name: AIMS
Description: AIMS is a computerised information retrieval system which provides
                                information on government financial aid available for business in the UK. It
                                contains three major data files:
                                News file keeps users up to date on the latest changes to government
                                assistance, including changes to existing schemes, announcements of new
                                schemes, expiry of old schemes, deadlines, funding arrangements and EC
                                programme invitations
                                Industrial assistance file covers over 250 financial aid schemes available to
                                industry, commerce and tourism from UK government departments, other
                                sponsoring organisations and from the EC
                                Agricultural assistance file covers over 70 financial aid schemes available to
                                agriculture, horticulture, forestry and fishing businesses
                                    AIMS has advanced retrieval software which enables users to quickly
                                identify schemes relevant to their particular business requirments.
Source: Direct from sponsoring organisations including UK government
                                departments
Years Covered: Current (no historical records)
File Size: Details provided on over 300 assistance schemes
Updates: Daily
Database Producer: European Policies Research Centre, University of Strathclyde
Available From: European Policies Research Centre
                                Annual subscription payable
                                This is discretionary and set to reflect the anticipated use and value of the
                                database to the subscriber
                                Telecom Gold
                                Provides AIMS News on line
                                Contact direct for prices

Name: Amdata
Description: An 'Acquisitions Monthly' and 'Computasoft' comprehensive database on
                                mergers and acquisitions worldwide, including deals since the beginning of
                                1984. This is the first database created in Europe on mergers, acquisitions
                                and buy-outs. Searching can be conducted using any of 86 acquisition data
                                fields, including industry code, bidder name, target name, nationality and
                                bid value.
Source: Press releases; offer documents; banks
                                Plus financial press
Years Covered: 1984 to date
File Size: 11 000
Updates: Weekly (floppy discs sent to customers)
Database Producer: Acquisitions Monthly and Computasoft Ltd
Available From: Acquisition Monthly
                                Contact: Susan Healey
                                £1500 joining fee
                                £15 000 per annum subscription covers both data and specially designed
                                software which allows users to carry out sophisticated analyses

Name: BOAMP
Description: Covers tenders, auctions and announcements of consultations by the
                                French government, local authorites and public bodies.
Source: 'Bulletin Officiel des Annonces Civiles et Commerciales'
Years Covered: Current
File Size:
Updates: As information becomes available
Database Producer: Direction des Journaux Officiels
Available From: Telesystemes-Questel File BOAMP
                                $62 per connect hour
                                31c per on-line type
                                34c per off-line print

Name:	BODACC
Description:	Provides the full text of announcements of French company formations, mergers, reorganisations, acquisitions, delivery of annual returns, and liquidations published in the official gazette, the 'Bulletin Officiel des Annonces Civiles et Commerciales'.
Source:	'Bulletin Officiel des Annonces Civiles et Commerciales'
Years Covered:	Current and previous year
File Size:	Approx 50 000 new announcements per month
Updates:	Daily
Database Producer:	Direction des Journaux Officiels
Available From:	Telesystemes-Questel File BODACC
	$105 per connect hour
	35c per on-line type
	35c per off-line print
	G CAM Serveur File BODA
	FF 700 per connect hour

Name:	Business
Description:	Business is a European database on worldwide trade opportunities and business contacts for manufacturing, marketing, sales, services, representations, cooperations, research and development. The database is sponsored by the German Federal Government. Business includes: Specific import/export opportunities (supply, demand, sales) Representation offered or sought (general, agency, distributorship) Tenders Inward/outward opportunities for cooperation (manufacturing, marketing, joint ventures, investments) Technology offers/demands (know-how, patents, licences) Activity/interest profiles of commercial, industrial and research establishments Trade promotion contacts (agencies, chambers of commerce, industrial associations, etc) Coverage is worldwide and for all industries.
Language:	The main database language is English
Source:	Business opportunities information is taken from a wide range of traditionally published sources including exhibition catalogues and directories. Also included are original company/institute profiles with corporate data and statements of specific business interests. Each record lists a contact address
Years Covered:	October 1983 to date
File Size:	25 000 records
Updates:	Monthly Approx 1000 records added per update
Database Producer:	Business Datenbanken GmbH
Available From:	Data-Star File BUSI
	£67.76 per connect hour
	31p per on-line print
	20p per off-line print
	SDI profile: £4.90
	GENIOS
	DM 210 per connect hour
	DM 0.8 per on-line type
	DM 0.8 per off-line print
	Btx Sudwest Datenbank GmbHf (German Videotex)
	Business GmBH
	Can be contacted direct and instructed to search for contacts and opportunities on your behalf, including SDI searches. Prices obtainable direct from Business GmBH. Business user manual available from above costs DM 80

Name: Business Opportunities – Sell
Description: Sell is a business opportunities database which lists details of products or
                             services on a worldwide basis for which suppliers are currently required.
Source: Company Line UK Ltd
Years Covered: Current
File Size:
Updates: Daily
Database Producer: Company Line UK Ltd, Northampton
Available From: Data-Star
                             Contact direct for prices

Name: CAPA
Description: CAPA provides information from the Belgian official journal ('Le
                             Moniteur') on bankruptcies, judicial arrangements, judicial disabilities and
                             persons placed under guardianship.
                             Subjects covered are:
                             Persons or companies declared bankrupt or who have applied for a deed of
                             judicial arrangement with the creditors
                             Persons deprived of the exercise of certain rights, persons under judicial
                             disability, or placed under guardianship and modifications
                             The closing date of the bankruptcies is mentioned if communicated by the
                             Court.
Language: French and Dutch
Source: Equivalent to the Belgian official journal 'Le Moniteur'
Years Covered: 1976 to date, for bankruptcies
File Size:
Updates: Daily
Database Producer: CREDOC asbl
                             Other services available:
                             online searches
                             off-line prints
                             monthly printed edition
                             1976-83 summary on microfiche
Available From: Belindis
                             BF 3000 per connect hour
                             BF 15 per 10 lines displayed on line
                             BF 15 per off-line print

Name: CHINA COOP
Description: The database CHINA COOP (CHIN) contains proposals for cooperation
                             and descriptions of investment projects, as well as important enquiries and
                             export proposals from the People's Republic of China. The data provides
                             information about the investment and cooperation plans of the Chinese
                             government and their state and economic institutions since 1.1.1984.
                                 CHINA COOP provides information about the activities of economic
                             institutions, foreign trade companies and individual firms and facilitates
                             access to the Chinese market. Information provided is as follows:
                             Town, province
                             Name of project
                             Product (also as SIC-code)
                             Description of the project
                             Cooperation partner(s)
                             Level of investment
                             Form of cooperation
Source: Chinese trade magazines, project lists and catalogues from PR China,
                             articles from the relevant business press, some direct news
Years Covered: Current
File Size: Approx 2600 records
Updates: Monthly
Database Producer: TCH Technologie-Centrum Hannover GmbH und CS China-Service GmbH

Available From: GENIOS File CHIN
                       DM 290 per connect hour
                       DM 15 per on-line type
                       DM 15 per off-line print
                       SDI profile: DM 12

Name: Concursos Publicos
Description: Database of exhibitions organised by the Spanish central government and
                       by regional and local government bodies.
Source: 'Official State Bulletin' and bulletins of the 'Autonomous Regional
                       Government'
Years Covered: Current
File Size: 11 000 annual documents (1000 in operation daily)
Updates: Daily
Database Producer: Sistema de Informacion Empresarial
Available From: Instituto de la Pequena y Mediana Empresa Industrial (IMPI)
                       Contact direct for prices

Name: CONF
Description: CONF contains information on conferences, meetings, workshops,
                       exhibitions held worldwide in the subject areas of energy, physics,
                       computer science, engineering, astronomy and astrophysics, aeronautics,
                       mathematics. Schedules are included as soon as they are announced.
                       Copies of announcements, programmes, etc can be ordered.
Source: Journals, press releases, programmes and announcements
Years Covered: 1976 to date
File Size: 53 000 conference citations
Updates: Weekly
Database Producer: FIZ Karlsruhe
Available From: STN File CONF
                       £64 per connect hour
                       20p per on-line type
                       26p per off-line print

Name: Conference Papers Index
Description: Conference Papers Index provides access to records of more than 100 000
                       scientific and technical papers
                       presented at over 1000 major regional, national and
                       international meetings each year. Conference Papers Index provides a
                       centralised source of information on reports of current research and
                       development from papers presented at conferences and meetings; it
                       provides titles of papers as well as the names and addresses (when
                       available) of the authors of these papers. Also included in this database are
                       announcements of any publications issued from the meetings, available
                       preprints, reprints, abstract booklets, and proceedings volumes, including
                       dates of availability, costs and ordering information. Primary subject areas
                       covered include the life sciences, chemistry, physical sciences, geosciences,
                       and engineering.
Source: American and international meetings and records
Years Covered: 1973 to date
File Size: 1 253 431 records (DIALOG)
                       1 257 000 records (ESA-IRS)
Updates: Monthly
Database Producer: Cambridge Scientific Abstracts
Available From: DIALOG File 77
                       $84 per connect hour
                       40c per on-line type
                       50c per off-line print
                       SDI profile: $7.95

ESA-IRS File 36
£60.20 per connect hour
23.1p per on-line type
31.8p per off-line print
SDI profile: £8.40

Name:	EIS Online
Description:	This database provides access to the British Overseas Trade Board's Export Intelligence Service (EIS). This service is the main source of information provided to UK exporters on export opportunities, market news, and other economic intelligence. The database covers calls for tender, successful bidders, agents seeking principals, trade promotions, trade fairs and economic reports.
Source:	BOTB Export Intelligence notices databank
Years Covered:	8 August 1985 to date
File Size:	Approx 160 items added daily
Updates:	Daily
Database Producer:	BOTB
Available From:	PROFILE File EIS
	£55 monthly standing charge
	£84 per connect hour
	1p per off-line print (per line)
	Minimum £2 per off-line request

Name:	Fairbase
Description:	Fairbase is an international source of information for trade fair visitors and conference participants, exhibitors and organisers, industrial buyers, the hotel industry and travel agencies, etc. It provides announcements on fairs, exhibitions, conferences and seminars with details on the title, date, place and organiser.
Source:	Data is obtained directly from organisers around the world.
Years Covered:	1986-2000
File Size:	17 000 records
Updates:	Monthly
Database Producer:	Fairbase Datenbank GmbH
Available From:	FIZ Technik File FAIRBASE
	DM 250 per connect hour
	DM 1.6 per on-line type
	DM 2.6 per off-line print
	Data-Star File FAIR
	£77.55 per connect hour
	49p per on-line print
	47p per off-line print

Name:	FBR
Description:	The Forschungsberichte Bundesrepublik Deutschland (FBR) covers literature on projects sponsored by the BMFT (The Federal Ministry for Research and Technology). The literature consists mainly of reports, books and serials in German, which are cited centrally, for the first time in the FBR database.
Language:	German
Source:	Research reports
	Books
Years Covered:	1985 to date
File Size:	5200 citations
Updates:	Monthly
Database Producer:	FIZ Karlsruhe
Available From:	STN File FBR
	£58 per connect hour
	20p per on-line type
	26p per off-line print
	SDI profile: £3.00

Name: Federal and State Business Assistance
Description: FSBA is a unique database which offers a guide to federal and state
                    assistance for businesses. Type of assistance includes information,
                    financial, technical procurement leads, management and marketing leads.
                    Each entry provides a summary of the service offered, a telephone number
                    and address, and eligibility requirements (if applicable).
Source: USA Department of Commerce
Years Covered: Current
File Size:
Updates: Every 2 years
Database Producer: Center for the Utilisation of Federal Technology
                    NTIS
                    US Department of Commerce
Available From: BRS File FSBA
                    $50 per connect hour
                    30c per on-line type
                    20c per off-line print

Name: Ferias y Exposiciones
Description: This is a database of major trade fairs and exhibitions held in the EEC
                    countries.
Source: Institutions and organising bodies
Years Covered: Current
File Size: 2000 documents
Updates: Periodically
Database Producer: Sistema de Informacion Empresarial
Available From: Instituto de la Pequena y Mediana Empresa Industrial (IMPI)
                    Contact direct for prices

Name: Finance for New Projects in the UK
Description: This database provides a comprehensive guide to private and public sector
                    initiatives and grants available in the UK. It is designed for businessmen,
                    economic development agencies, business and general libraries, banks,
                    local authorities, chambers of commerce and other financial, legal and
                    business advisers in the UK and overseas.
Source: Government and private sources
Years Covered: Current
File Size:
Updates: Weekly
Database Producer: KPMG Peat Marwick McLintock
Available From: Dialcom Business Direction
                    £84 per connect hour

Name: Firmexport (Telexport)
Description: Covers approximately 36000 French importers and exporters. Information
                    provided includes:
                    Company location
                    Names of owners
                    Products exported or imported
                    Country(s) with which the firm trades
                    Method of transportation
                    Export/import figures
                    Current turnover
                    Companies can be searched for using selected criteria.
Language: French
Source: Chambres de Commerce et d'Industrie
                    Customs documents
Years Covered: Current
File Size: 36000 documents
Updates: Weekly
Database Producer: Chambre de Commerce et d'Industrie de Paris
Available From: G CAM Serveur
                    FF 400 per connect hour

Name: Foreign Traders Index
Description: The Foreign Traders Index is a directory of manufacturers, service
                               organisations, agent representatives, retailers, wholesalers, distributors,
                               and cooperatives, in 130 countries outside the US. Foreign Traders Index is
                               designed to provide information to US businesses or manufacturers by
                               listing those firms which either import goods from the United States or
                               state that they are interested in representing US exporters. Foreign Traders
                               Index can be used for direct marketing or for establishing sales
                               representation in an overseas country. The data provided on each firm
                               includes the nature of its business activity (eg manufacturing, retailing, etc)
                               as well as the product or service it handles. Executive officers, relative size
                               of the firm, number of employees, and date of establishment are also
                               included.
                                   Access to this database is restricted to US users.
Source: US government
Years Covered: Current 4 years
File Size: 72 317 records
Updates: Three reloads per annum
Database Producer: US Dept of Commerce
Available From: DIALOG File 105
                               $54 per connect hour
                               25c per on-line type
                               25c per off-line print

Name: GELD (Money)
Description: This is a German database which covers financial support and subsidies. It
                               provides details of German and international subsidies by subsidy purpose
                               and branch of industry.
                                   The database can be used to get information on support programmes,
                               investment grants and start-up loans.
                                   Areas covered:
                               Possible commitments
                               Warranties
                               Securities
                               Guarantees
                               Counter-securities
                               Counter-guarantees
                               Direct subsidies (extracts from over 1000 support progammes valid in the
                               Federal Republic of Germany)
                               Grants
                               Loans
Language: German
Source: Publications, World Bank, European Community, communiques from
                               federal ministries, federal states (Lander), communes and local bodies
Years Covered: Current
File Size: Over 1500 support programmes
Updates: Continuous throughout the year
Database Producer: ITG Innovationstechnik GmbH & Co KG
                               SDS Subvent Datenbank Systeme
Available From: GENIOS File GELD
                               DM 240 per connect hour
                               DM 6 per on-line type
                               DM 6 per off-line print

Name: m+a Messe-Kalender
Description: The m+a Messe-Kalender Datenbank (trade fair
                               calendar data bank) contains qualitative and quantitative basic data of
                               about 5300 trade fairs and exhibitions in approximately 90 countries.
                               Searches can be conducted by branches of industry, countries, cities and
                               also by dates. The industrial nomenclature includes around 180 terms
                               and/or areas (SIC-code in German translation).
Language: German

Source:	The m+a publishing house, the leading trade publisher for trade fairs and exhibitions, congresses and conferences. M+a obtains information direct from the organisers and/or organisations (approx 1500 worldwide). This information is published in the twice yearly (June and December) 'm+a Kalender – Planer fur Messen und Ausstellungen International' (m+a calendar-planner for international trade fairs and exhibitions)
Years Covered:	Current
File Size:	Approx 5800 trade fairs and exhibitions
Updates:	At least 2 times per annum in May and November. More often if necessary
Database Producer:	ma Verlag fur Messen Ausstellungen und Kongresse GmbH
Available From:	GENIOS File M+A
	DM 240 per connect hour
	DM 1.2 per on-line type
	DM 1.5 per off-line print

Name:	Meeting
Description:	Announcements of congresses, conferences, meetings, workshops, exhibitions and fairs organised around the world. It covers all fields of scientific and technical activity, as well as the social sciences and humanities.
Source:	
Years Covered:	Forthcoming meetings. Most are next year's events, some are announced several years in advance
File Size:	Variable
	Between 7000 and 8000 per year
Updates:	Fortnightly
Database Producer:	Centre d'Études Nucleaires – Saclay Service documentation
Available From:	Telesystemes – Questel
	$86 per connect hour
	43c per on-line type
	46c per off-line print
	SDI: $8 plus print charges

Name:	Mergers
Description:	Mergers is the menu-driven version of M&A Filings DIALOG File 548. It contains detailed abstracts of every original and amended merger and acquisition document released by the Securities and Exchange Commission since early 1985. Copies of the full text of each filing or exhibit reported in the database are available from Charles E Simon & Company. Mergers provides users with detailed M&A transaction information on publicly-traded companies.
Source:	M&A filings released by the SEC
Years Covered:	1985 to date
File Size:	25 000 records
Updates:	Daily
Database Producer:	Charles E Simon & Company
Available From:	DIALOG File Mergers
	$84 per connect hour
	$3 per on-line type
	$3 per off-line print

Name:	Mergers and Acquisitions
Description:	The Mergers and Acquisitions database is a comprehensive source of the most recent information on mergers, acquisitions, divestitures, management Buyouts and partial acquisitions.

The Mergers and Acquisitions database holds over 30 000 US deals and 3000 UK deals and is claimed by its producers to be unique in Europe

Deals can be located using combinations of the following criterion:
Type of deal
Deal status

Date of deal
Industry SIC code
Country
Company name
Whether public or private deals
Size of deal
Adviser's name

Source:	Published and direct sources
Years Covered:	Current
File Size:	Over 33 000 deals
Updates:	As information becomes available
Database Producer:	Infocheck
Available From:	Infocheck
	Contact direct for access and price details

Name:	PTS F&S Indexes
Description:	The F&S Indexes covers both domestic and international company, product, and industry information. It contains information on corporate acquisitions and mergers, new products, technological developments and sociopolitical factors. It summarises analyses of companies by securities firms, contains forecasts of company sales and profits by company officers, and reports on factors influencing future sales and earnings (such as price changes, government antitrust actions, sales and licensing agreements and joint venture agreements).
Source:	Over 2500 worldwide financial and business publications and newspapers, trade journals and government documents
Years Covered:	1972 to date
	1980 to date (Data-Star)
File Size:	3 025 159 records
Updates:	Weekly
Database Producer:	Predicasts Inc
Available From:	DIALOG File 18 1980 to date
	File 98 PTS F&S Indexes 1972-79
	$114 per connect hour
	28c per on-line type
	33c per off-line print
	SDI profile: $7.95
	Data-Star PTIN 1978 to date
	£62.76 per connect hour
	18p per on-line print
	8p per off-line print
	SDI profile: £2.73
	BRS File PTSI
	$90 per connect hour
	37c per on-line type
	32c per off-line print
	SDI profile: $4

Name:	Scan-a-Bid – Scan
Description:	Scan-a-Bid is the computerised version of the magazine 'Development Business' which is published by the United Nations Development Forum and informs on development project opportunities mainly in the Third World.
	The on-line database records details of notices at least 2½ weeks before they appear in print.
Source:	& Procurement Notices from the World Bank, Inter-American Development Bank, Asian Development Bank and the Commission of the European Communities; new projects appearing for the first time in the Monthly Operational Summaries of the World Bank and the Inter-American Development Bank; and other advance project notifications
Years Covered:	November 1984 to date
File Size:	

Updates:	Daily
Database Producer:	Development Business Scan-a-Bid
Available From:	Data-Star
	Contact direct for prices

Scan-a-Bid is available only to subscribers of the Development Business magazine for a fee of US$645 per year unlimited use. A Scan-a-Bid Users Manual for US$15 must be purchased. An application form for using the service can be obtained from the database producer, or from D-S Marketing in London. Those not already using Data-Star must also sign a 'No commitment' contract with Radio Suisse SA

Name:	STARS
Description:	STARS provides over 700 entries on UK government legislation and regulations, services and financial assistance. It contains three major data files:

Legislation file has over 130 entries on company law, taxation, health and safety, employment, planning and environment, importing/exporting, etc

Service file has over 300 sources of advisory, financial and other services, mostly national organisations which offer a specific service to the business community and whose activity is heavily backed by the public sector

Assistance file has over 280 government assistance schemes in the form of grants, soft loans, fiscal concessions and advice offered by the UK government and the EC

Users can search this database using keywords, cross-reference between the three files and group related items.

Source:	UK government and the European Commission
Years Covered:	Current (no historical records)
File Size:	Over 700 entries
	Access to over 1200 addresses
Updates:	Daily
Database Producer:	European Policies Research Centre, University of Strathclyde
Available From:	European Policies Research Centre
	Annual subscription payable

This is discretionary and set to reflect the anticipated use and value of the database to the subscriber

Name:	Thomas New Industrial Products
Description:	Thomas New Industrial Products provides current information on new industrial products and systems. The database is prepared from new product press releases submitted by manufacturers and distributors to 'Industrial Equipment News', a monthly new product magazine published by Thomas Publishing Company. Pertinent information about the product is extracted from each press release for inclusion in the database. The information includes product attributes, performance specifications, product use, trade name and model number and manufacturer or seller name, address and telephone number. The database is designed to meet the product information needs of a variety of users such as market analysts, engineers and purchasing agents.
Source:	'Industrial Equipment News' publication
Years Covered:	1985 to date
File Size:	34 476 records
Updates:	Weekly
Database Producer:	Thomas Publishing Company Inc
Available From:	DIALOG File 536
	$96 per connect hour
	50c per on-line type
	50c per off-line print
	15c per report element
	20c per mailing label (format 10)

Name: World Bank International Business Opportunities Service
Description: This database provides a source of advance information on World Bank
                       project funding and potential contracts. It is relevant to engineers,
                       consultants, contractors and other suppliers of goods and services who will
                       benefit from World Bank project funding in: agriculture, education,
                       $energy, industry, telecommunications and many other sectors. All
                       projects are distinguished by sector and geographical designation.
Source: Equivalent to the printed subscription service
Years Covered:
File Size: 1200 projects
Updates: Monthly ˙
Database Producer: World Bank
Available From: PROFILE
                       £84 per connect hour
                       1p per off-line print (per line)
                       Minimum £2 per off-line request

Section VII Specialist Industry Databases

Service Sectors

Financial Services
American Banker
The Bond Buyer
BusinessWire
Dun's Electronic Yellow Pages Financial (see Company Section)
Euromoney (see Nexis in Marketing Section)
Financial Services Report (see Nexis in Marketing Section)
Financial Times Business Reports (see Marketing Section)
FINIS: Financial Industry Information Service
Insurance Abstracts
International Finance Alert (see Securities Section)
NAARS (see Company Section)
Securities Industry

Law
CAPA (see Overseas Trade Opportunities Section)
Der Betrieb
Disposiciones Legales
Experts in Law
Italian Legal Information System
Lexis
Management Contents (see General Management Section)
Name
Nlex
Orbi
Securities Law Advance

Retail
Economist Intelligence Unit-Retail Business (see Marketing Section)
Industrial Market Location (see Company Section)
Shops

Public Sector
DHSS Data
Encyclopedia of Associations
PAIS International
Polis (UK)
Social Scisearch

Transportation
SAE Global Mobility
Transdoc
TRIS
Volkswagenwerk

Tourism
EIU International Travel and Tourism Reports (see Marketing Section)
EIU Travel and Tourism Analyst (see Marketing Section)
Touristic Information Facts and Abstracts

Publishing
Electronic Publishing Abstracts (see Bibliographic Section)
Publishers, Distributors and Wholesalers

Manufacturing

Information Technology
Artificial Intelligence
Business Software Database
CAD/CAM

Computer Database
Computers and Communications Library (see Nexis in Marketing Section)
Context – Business Microcomputer
Financial Times Business Reports (Fintech, see Marketing Section)
IDB Online
IES-DC (see EEC Section)
IR-Soft (see EEC Section)
ISIS Software Catalogue
Menu – The International Software Database
Microcomputer Index
Microcomputer Software and Hardware Guide
Microsearch
National Computer Index
OTISLINE
PTS New Product Announcements
Robomatix
Spacesoft

Electronics and Engineering
Compendex
EI Engineering Meetings
ELCOM
ISMEC
Merlin-Tech
Who Makes Machinery (see Company Section)
ZDE
ZVEI-Electro/Electronics Buyers Guide (see Company Section)

Defence
DMS Contract Awards
DMS Market Intelligence Reports

PTS Aerospace/Defense
Markets and Technology

Telecommunications
Compustat
Telecommunications (see
Company Section)
Telecommunications
Teledoc

Motor Vehicles/Transportation
Economist Intelligence Unit
(see Marketing Section)
European Automotive News
(see Marketing Section)
SAE Global Mobility

Chemicals
CHEM-INTELL Trade and
Production Statistics (PLST)
Chemical Age Project File
Chemical Business News Base
Chemical Economics
Handbook
Chemical Engineering
Abstracts
Chemical Industry Notes
Chemical Plant Database-Plan
Cscorp
Janssen (see Science and
Technology Section)
VTB

Consumer Products
Association of Home
Appliance Manufacturers
Consumer Reports (see
Marketing Section)
Eurofile (see Marketing
Section)
Euromonitor (see Marketing
Section)
Market Directions (see
Marketing Section)

Packaged Facts (see
Marketing Section)

Food and Drink
Coffeeline
FSTA (see Science and
Technology Section)
Nielsen Market Information
(see Marketing Section)
VITIS-VEA (see Science and
Technology Section)

Rubber and Plastics
Rapra Abstracts
Rapra Tradenames

Textiles
Textile Technology Digest
(see Science and Technology
Section)
Textile-Wirtschaft
Titus (see Science and
Technology Section)
World Textiles

Other Sectors

Construction
BRIX
Ibsedex
ICONDA

Energy and the Environment
APILIT
Canadian Petroleum
Association Statistics
(CPASTATS)
DOE Energy
EABS (see EEC Section)
EDF-DOC
Electric Power Database
Electric Power Industry
Abstracts
ENEL

Energie
Energyline
FTBR Energy File (see
Financial Times Business
Reports, Marketing Section)
INIS
International Petroleum
Report (see AP Dow Jones,
News Section)
Nordic Energy Index
Nuclear Science Abstracts
Oil and Gas Journal Energy
Database
Oil and Gas Journal Energy
Forecasts
P/E News
Sesame (see EEC Section)

Agriculture
Agnews
Agra Europe Online
Agrep
Agribusiness USA
Agricola
Agris International
The Agrochemicals
Handbook (see Science and
Technology Section)
CAB Abstracts
IALINE
Pestdoc (see Science and
Technology Section)

Environment and Pollution
ENREP (see EEC Section)
Forest
Ruralnet (see EEC Section)

Water
AFEE
Water Resources Abstracts

Name: AFEE
Description: The AFEE bibliographic database is the online version of the abstract journal 'Information Eaux', and covers a wide range of subjects relating to fresh water.
Subjects covered:
Hydrogeology – subterranean water
Hydrology – surface water
Sea, coastal areas and shores
Hydrobiology – water quality
Ecotoxicology – water pollution & treatment
Water distribution – agriculture – industry – energy
Health, hygiene and safety
Physical and chemical analysis
Microbiological analysis

	Water policy, planning and economy
	Legislation
	Research & development
Language:	Provides references to documents in English (55 per cent), French (35 per cent) and German and other languages (10 per cent)
Source:	AFEE contains references to mainly journal articles (75 per cent) as well as books, reports, conference papers and proceedings (25 per cent). Patent literature is omitted. Corresponds to monthly publication 'Information Eaux'
Years Covered:	1970 to date
File Size:	Approx 73 000 references
Updates:	Approx 450 references per month
Database Producer:	Association Francaise pour l'Etude des Eaux
Available From:	ESA-IRS File 73
	£49 per connect hour
	13.3p per on-line type
	22p per off-line print
	SDI profile: £7.70

Name:	Agnews
Description:	Agnews is the only electronic news and information service specialising in the Common Agricultural Policy. It contains EEC and world trade news, EEC legislation, exchange rates (updated 3 times daily), daily ECU rates, export refunds and correctives, import levies and premiums. The database is updated constantly throughout the day, direct from Agra Europe's editorial offices in England and Brussels, and by Agra Europe correspondents worldwide. The service is divided into commodity sectors.
Source:	Compiled by Agra Europe staff throughout Europe
Years Covered:	Current
File Size:	
Updates:	Constant updating daily
Database Producer:	Agra Europe (London) Ltd
Available From:	Agra Europe
	Available only on annual subscription

Name:	Agra Europe Online
Description:	Full text database compiled by Agra Europe (London) Ltd.
	Subjects covered include:
	Politics and legislation
	Market reports
	Crop forecasts
	Prices and trends
	Grain and oilseeds review
	Management committees
	EEC and international news
	A recent addition to this service is the East Europe and China database, covering statistics and news on Eastern European and Chinese markets.
Source:	Agra Europe publications
Years Covered:	
File Size:	
Updates:	Weekly (Agra Europe)
	Monthly (East Europe and China)
Database Producer:	Agra Europe (London) Ltd
Available From:	Agra Europe
	Connect hour rates from £60 to £120 per hour
	4p character charge per 512 characters

Name: Agrep

Description: Agrep contains descriptions of ongoing research projects carried out within the EEC and relevant to agriculture in the broader sense, ie including fisheries, forestry, land use and development, food science and technology, agricultural economics. Information retrieved enables users to establish contact directly with the researchers involved. Information is collected on a national basis by the member states under the sponsorship of the Standing Committee of Agricultural Research (SCAR) and under the management of the Commission of the European Communities. Search language is DC-INFO (CCL/BRS)

Source: Project descriptions supplied by the research institutes and collected at national focal points

Years Covered: Average project life is approximately 5 years

File Size: Approximately 24 500 research projects

Updates: Quarterly (about 500 projects added per annum)

Database Producer: The Centre for Veterinary & Agricultural Documentation Royal Veterinary & Agricultural University

Available From: Datacentralen
DK 255 per connect hour
DK 330 per connect hour (for users from countries which are not part of Euronet)
The Centre for Veterinary & Agricultural Documentation offers an information broker service. Contact direct for further details
DIMDI File Agrep
$15.30 to $30.59 per connect hour
5c per off-line print

Name: Agribusiness USA

Description: The Agribusiness USA database provides controlled vocabulary indexing and informative abstracts from approximately 300 industry-related trade journals and government publications. The database provides current access to agricultural business information, which is utilised for strategic planning in many industries. The Agribusiness USA database covers all facets of agribusiness, such as the crop and livestock industries, agricultural chemicals, biotechnology, agricultural finance, farm equipment manufacturing and agricultural marketing. The database is designed to track US and regional agribusiness information including company names, trade names, new product development and government policies.

Source: 300 trade journals and government publications

Years Covered: 1985 to date

File Size: 73 873 records

Updates: Fortnightly

Database Producer: Pioneer Hi-Bred International Inc

Available From: DIALOG File 581
$96 per connect hour
50c per on-line type
60c per off-line print
SDI profile: $6.95

Name: Agricola

Description: Agricola (formerly CAIN) is the database of the National Agricultural Library (NAL). This massive file provides comprehensive coverage of worldwide journal literature and monographs on agriculture and related subjects. Related subjects include: animal studies, botany, chemistry, entomology, fertilisers, forestry, hydrophonics, soils, and more. Both DIALOG files 10 and 110 have a similar format and identical coverage and pricing.

Source: Worldwide journals and monographs

Years Covered: 1970 to 1978 (File 110)
1970 to date (File 10)

File Size: 2 484 832 records

Updates:	Monthly
Database Producer:	US National Agricultural Library
Available From:	DIALOG Files 10, 110
	$39 per connect hour
	10c per on-line type
	20c per off-line print
	SDI profile: $5.95
	BRS File CAIN or CAIB (Backfile)
	$29 per connect hour
	17c per on-line type
	12c per off-line print
	SDI profile: $4
	DIMDI File Agricola
	$20.30 to $35.59 per connect hour
	4c per on-line type
	9c per off-line print
	SDI profile: $3.73

Name:	Agris International
Description:	The Agris International database serves as a comprehensive inventory of worldwide agricultural literature which reflects research results, food production and rural development to help users identify problems involved in all aspects of world food supply. The file corresponds in part to 'AgrIndex', published monthly by the Food and Agriculture Organisation (FAO) of the United Nations. Subject coverage focuses on many topics including: general agriculture; geography and history; education, extension, and advisory work; administration and legislation; economics, development and rural sociology; plant production; protection of plants and stored products; forestry; animal production; aquatic sciences and fisheries; machinery and buildings; natural resources; food science; home economics; human nutrition and pollution.
Source:	Worldwide literature plus the 'AgrIndex' publication
Years Covered:	1975 to date
File Size:	993 291 records (DIALOG)
Updates:	Monthly
Database Producer:	Food and Agriculture Organisation
Available From:	DIALOG File 203
	$50 per connect hour
	10c per on-line type
	25c per off-line print
	ESA-IRS File 29
	£42 per connect hour
	9.8p per off-line print
	SDI profile £2.10
	DIMDI File Agris
	$15.30 to $30.59 per connect hour
	5p per off-line print
	SDI profile: $2.88

Name:	American Banker
Description:	This database corresponds to the printed publication of the same name. It is considered to be the national bible of daily news and information for the banking and financial services industry in the USA, covering local, regional, national and global financial services issues and affairs. Information is full text. It includes news and statistical tables on banking and corporate finance, consumer financial services, automation and payment systems development trends, credit card industry, software, new products plus other areas.
Source:	Various; equivalent to printed publication
Years Covered:	November 1981 to date (varies with host)
File Size:	88 376 records
Updates:	Daily (available each morning of publication)

Database Producer: The Bond Buyer Inc
Available From: DIALOG File 625
(66 000 records. Available on day of issue)
$120 per connect hour
25c per off-line print
SDI Profile: $5.95
Data-Star File Bank
(63 000 records. Available within 7 days of issue)
£45.31 per connect hour
21p per on-line print
15p per off-line print
Textline File Ambkr
(Approximately 5500 records from June 1987 to present. Available within 2 weeks of publication)
Sign on fee £250 (one-off)
£75 per connect hour
10p per headline
20p per abstract
NEXIS File Ambank
(Approximately 106 000 records from 1979 to present. Available on day of publication)
Annual subscription
$5 per individual file search
0.02c print cost per line
NewsNet File FLIO
(Records from 1984 to present. Available on day of publication)
$132 per connect hour (non-validated)
$108 per connect hour (validated)
(includes $120 annual subscription)
No print or record charges

Name: ANAIS
Description: ANAIS is a French economic database. Contains 10 000 annual time series of historic and forecast data for 90 industrial sectors in France. Forecasts cover: domestic consumption, investment demand, industrial production, foreign trade with France, and inter-industry consumption. Industry classes covered include gas, electricity, construction, beverage and alcohol, paper, machinery.
Language: French
Source: National statistics
Years Covered: 1959 to date with 5-year forecasts
File Size: 10 000 annual time series
Updates: Twice per annum
Database Producer: GAMA
University of Paris
Available From: Centre National de la Recherche Scientifique
Contact direct for price and access details

Name: APILIT
Description: APILIT is a bibliographic database, with worldwide coverage of literature relating to the petroleum and energy industries. In addition to the main subject of petroleum, information on broad sections of chemistry, chemical engineering, process control, corrosion, catalysis etc, is also provided.
Subjects covered:
Properties and handling of crude oil and natural gas
Petroleum refining processes
Formulation and properties of fuels, lubricants and other major petroleum products
Special products
Petrochemicals and polymers
Catalysts
Flames and combustion

Corrosion
Process control
Environmental, health and safety matters
Chemicals used in oilfield operations
Pipelines, tankers and other petroleum transport
Storage of petroleum and its products
Synthetic fuels
APILIT is a restricted access database.
Contact ORBIT Search Service or STN for details.

Source:	Over 150 journals in 6 languages, 40 series of recurrent meetings, selected items from 'Chemical Abstracts', 'Petroleum Abstracts', 'Gas Abstracts', 'British Marine Technology Abstracts' and 'Aqualine Abstracts'
Years Covered:	Current
File Size:	1964 to March 1988, 418 000 citations
Updates:	Monthly with approximately 1400 new citations
Database Producer:	American Petroleum Institute
Available From:	STN File Apilit

£62 per connect hour
20p per on-line type
23p per off-line print
SDI profile: £1.84
STN File Apilit2
£91 per connect hour
28p per on-line type
31p per off-line print
ORBIT Search Service File Apilit
Subscribers:
$70 per connect hour
30c per on-line type
35c per off-line print
Non-subscribers:
$110 per connect hour
40c per on-line type
45c per off-line print

Name:	Artificial Intelligence
Description:	Artificial Intelligence is the on-line version of 'Artificial Intelligence and Abstracts', the monthly abstract journal concerned with all aspects of artificial intelligence and related technologies.

Subjects covered:
Business and economics
International news
Human factors
Speciality applications
Automation and robotics
Knowledge-based systems
Computer architecture
Programming and software
Sensors
Human machine interface
Cognitive sciences

Source:	Corresponds to the monthly journal 'Artificial Intelligence Abstracts'. Primary sources are articles, conference papers, books, newsletters, academic, corporate and governmental reports worldwide
Years Covered:	1984 to date
File Size:	Approx 5400 references
Updates:	Approx 100 references per month
Database Producer:	EIC/Intelligence
	Environment Information Center Inc

Available From:	ESA-IRS File 106
	£74.90 per connect hour
	23.1p per on-line type
	35.3p per off-line print
	SDI profile: £10.50

Name:	Association of Home Appliance Manufacturers
Description:	The Association of Home Appliance Manufacturers (AHAM) collects monthly data on home appliance shipments from its members. Forecasts are available for 11 types of home appliances.
	All series are in terms of thousands of units shipped. Seasonally adjusted data are available for each series. The database also includes AHAM's 12-month forecasts of unit shipments for each of the 11 appliances tracked.
Source:	Reports of US manufacturers provided to the Association of Home Appliance Manufacturers
Years Covered:	1960 to date
	12-month forecasts
File Size:	
Updates:	Third week of each month
	12-month forecasts are updated every 6 months
Database Producer:	Haver Analytics Inc/AHAM
Available From:	GE Information Services
	$1.00 per data series

Name:	The Bond Buyer
Description:	'The Bond Buyer' is the daily trade newspaper for the municipal bond market. The database dates back to 1981 and includes the weekly publication 'Credit Markets' on DIALOG. Bond Buyer Full Text contains news and statistical information on the fixed-income markets. The database provides information on municipal bond issues available for negotiated and competitive bidding in each state including the name of the borrowing entity, purpose of issue, issue and maturity dates, amount, interest cost to borrower, and underwriter. It also covers bond sales by state, results of bond elections, proposed bond issues, federal laws and regulations affecting the taxable and tax-exempt bond markets and US Treasury bonds and securities. News and commentary on events, economic trends, and government policies affecting the municipal bond market are included. An excellent index to the paper publication, 'Bond Buyer Full Test', is available online through DIALOG and NEXIS.
	'Credit Markets' is a weekly review newspaper covering the bond industry, available as a sub-file through DIALOG and NewsNet.
Source:	Various; equivalent to printed publication
Years Covered:	1981 to date
File Size:	100041 records
Updates:	Daily
Database Producer:	The Bond Buyer Inc
Available From:	DIALOG File 626
	$120 per connect hour
	25c per off-line print
	SDI profile: $5.95 per update (weekly)
	NEXIS File BNDBYR
	Annual subscription
	$5 per individual file search
	0.02c print cost per line
	NewsNet
	$132 per connect hour (non-validated)
	$108 per connect hour (validated)
	(Includes $120 annual subscription)
	No print charges
	Bond Buyer Full Text and Credit Markets were available from June 1988

Name: BRIX

Description: The BRIX database contains references, with abstracts in many cases, to books, conference proceedings, journal articles and research reports dealing with building research topics. The research reports come from organisations throughout the world. To gather references to journal articles, about 300 journals, many of which are published outside the United Kingdom, are scanned. The database covers the years from 1950 onwards with fairly comprehensive coverage from 1970. All items published by the Building Research Station from 1950 are included.

                The main subject fields are: biodeterioration and preservation of timber, building plant, building problems relevant to developing countries, building processes, building services including acoustics and lighting, construction economics, electric and mechanical engineering, energy conservation, environmental design, environmental pollution, geotechnics and earthquake engineering, materials, structural design, structural engineering, surveying, structural performance, structural properties and uses of timber and board.

Source: Specialist books, journals, conference proceedings, research reports

Years Covered: 1950 to date

File Size: Approx 135000 references

Updates: Approx 10000 references per year

                (7000 of which are current references)

Database Producer: Building Research Station

Available From: ESA-IRS File 77

                £46.20 per connect hour

                10.5p per on-line type

                24.8p per off-line print

                SDI profile: £8.40

Name: Business Software Database

Description: Business Software Database features 10000 records describing business software packages. Each record in the database includes a 150-word description of the package, and name, address and telephone number of the manufacturer. Also covered are: computer languages in which the package is available, computer operating systems with which the package can be used, purchase or lease price (if available), computer hardware that can run the software package, who should use the software and for which industry it was designed, when the package was first available and the number of installations and other services provided by the manufacturer. This software database serves as a locator of software packages for mini and personal computers. The database lists software packages in: accounting/payroll, architecture, banking, communications, consulting, database management, engineering, farming/agriculture, food services, health care, insurance, inventory management, law, manufacturing, property management, real estate, software systems, word processing, etc.

Source: Software manufacturers

Years Covered: 1983 to date

File Size: Approx 10000 records

Updates: Quarterly reloads

Database Producer: Information Sources Inc

Available From: ESA-IRS File 89

                £58.80 per connect hour

                50p per on-line type

                53p per off-line print

                DIALOG File 256

                $90 per connect hour

                90c per on-line type

                90c per off-line print

                Data-Star File SOFT

                £51.73 per connect hour

                35p per on-line print

                25p per off-line print

SDI profile: £1.63
BRS File BSOF
$70 per connect hour
60c per on-line type
55c per off-line print
SDI profile: $4

Name:	BusinessWire
Description:	BusinessWire delivers timely, full text news stories that are simultaneously distributed to over 700 news media and more than 100 institutions and firms in the investment community. Topics covered include finance, business, science, labour, education and entertainment.
Source:	News sources consist of public and investor relations firms, business organisations and associations, government agencies, colleges and universities, trade associations and legal and accounting firms.
Years Covered:	1986 to date
File Size:	75 564 records
Updates:	Daily
Database Producer:	BusinessWire
Available From:	DIALOG File 610

$96 per connect hour
60c per off-line print
SDI profile: $3.95

Name:	CAB Abstracts
Description:	CAB Abstracts is a comprehensive file of agricultural and biological information. It contains records found in the 26 main abstract journals published by the Commonwealth Agricultural Bureaux. Significant papers are abstracted, while less important works are reported with bibliographic details only. The journals included in CAB cover the following subjects: agricultural engineering, animal breeding, animal disease, arid lands, dairy science, forestry, forest products, horticulture, nutrition, veterinary science, entomology, plant breeding, plant pathology, rural recreation and tourism, soils and fertilisers, weeds and world agricultural economics.
Source:	Commonwealth Agricultural Bureaux

Abstract journals
Over 8500 journals in 37 different languages are scanned for inclusion, as well as books, reports, theses, conference proceedings, patents, annual reports, and guides. In some instances, less accessible literature is abstracted by scientists working in other countries

Years Covered:	1972 to date (DIALOG)
	1983 to date (ORBIT)

Approx 130 000 items are indexed each year

File Size:	2 068 179 records (DIALOG)
	1 million records (ORBIT)
Updates:	Monthly
Database Producer:	CAB International
Available From:	DIALOG File 50 (records from 1984 to date)

File 53 (records 1972 to 1983)
$57 per connect hour
30c per on-line type
35c per off-line print
SDI profile: $10.95
BRS File CABA
$54 per connect hour
37c per on-line type
32c per off-line print
Other BRS CAB subfiles:
CAB – Economics, development and education (ECON)
CAB – Human nutrition (NUTR)
CAB – Tourism, leisure and recreation (TOUR)
CAB – Veterinary and medical (VETR)

SDI profile: $4
ESA-IRS File 132
£37.80 per connect hour
21.7p per on-line type
33.9p per off-line print
SDI profile: £3.50
ORBIT Search Service
$100 per connect hour
15c per on-line type
35c per off-line print
SDI profile: $6
DIMDI File CAB Abstracts
$28.30 to $43.59 per connect hour
25c per on-line type
30c per off-line print
SDI profile: $4.88
(10 CAB subfiles offered by DIMDI)

Name:	CAD/CAM
Description:	CAD/CAM is the on-line version of 'CAD/CAM Abstracts' – the monthly journal concerned with all aspects of computer-aided design, test and manufacturing. The file covers the following main subject categories:

Business and economics
International news
Human factors
Graphics and imaging
Computer-aided engineering
Inspection and work monitoring
Product design
Product assembly
Integrated factory systems
Speciality applications
Graphics displays
Human machine interface
Control systems and software
Automation design

Source:	Corresponds to the journal 'CAD/CAM Abstracts'
	Sources are articles, conference papers, patents, academic, corporate and governmental reports worldwide
Years Covered:	1983 to date
File Size:	Approx 5200 references
Updates:	Approx 100 references per month
Database Producer:	EIC/Intelligence
	Environment Information Center Inc
Available From:	ESA-IRS File 107
	£74.90 per connect hour
	23.1p per on-line type
	35.3p per off-line print
	SDI profile: £10.50

Name:	Canadian Petroleum Association Statistics (CPASTATS)
Description:	CPASTATS is a comprehensive database on the Canadian energy industry. The Canadian Petroleum Association, which owns and maintains this database file, has long been recognised for their excellent service in data collection for the industry.

Data cover all aspects of the Canadian petroleum industry: drilling and exploration, production, reserves, refining, stocks, imports and exports, demand and consumption, industry revenues and expenditures, price and transportation. Detail is provided by province or region for many categories.

Source: 'Canadian Petroleum Association Statistical Handbook'
Canadian Dept of Energy, Mines and Resources
'Daily Oil Bulletin'
Plus other sources

Years Covered: Current
Most of the data are monthly, quarterly or annual. A few weekly series
exist

File Size:
Updates: Daily
Database Producer: Haver Analytics Inc
Available From: GE Information Services
$3.00 per data series

Name: CHEM-INTELL Trade and Production Statistics (PLST)
Description: The CHEM-INTELL Trade and Production Statistics database (PLST) holds
annual trade and production figures for over 100 organic and inorganic
chemicals worldwide. These include: petrochemicals, fertilisers, polymers
and rubbers.
Figures are collected for over 100 reporting countries and information from
these is used to deduce figures for additional trading countries.

Source: Computer tapes supplied directly by customs authorities
National and international statistical office publications
Trade associations
Selected periodicals and research reports

Years Covered: PLST Annual Production and Trade totals – 10 years; trade breakdowns (by
major trading partner) – 2 years

File Size:
Updates: Monthly
Database Producer: CHEM-INTELL – Chemical Intelligence Services, UK
Available From: Data-Star
Contact direct for prices

Name: Chemical Age Project File
Description: CAPF contains details of all chemical and related plants completed since
1980. It also covers those currently under construction, planned,
undergoing feasibility study or where construction has been started and
subsequently suspended. This database can be useful for monitoring
competitor activity and locating potential suppliers or customers.

Source: Information obtained direct from companies, journals, newspapers, press
releases, public records, government reports, annual reports

Years Covered: 1980 to date
File Size: 15000
Updates: Weekly
Database Producer: ORBIT Search Service
Available From: Pergamon Financial File CAPF
£72 per connect hour
75p per on-line type
75p per off-line print
SDI profile: £5
ESA-IRS File 148
Gateway Service to Pergamon
£88.91 per connect hour
65.8p per on-line type
65.8p per off-line print

Name: Chemical Business Newsbase
Description: Chemical Business Newsbase (CBNB) includes worldwide chemical news
about chemicals, use and production, with a particular emphasis on
European news. There is significant Japanese and American input. Records
contained in the database summarise items from a wide range of sources
which are appropriate to covering chemical business news. An informative
abstract is present in each record, as well as factual data regarding

	production figures and sales. Bibliographic source information is also provided.
Source:	Journals, European press releases, company reports, advertisements, publishers' lists, and other sources
Years Covered:	October 1984 to date
File Size:	91 560 records
Updates:	Weekly
Database Producer:	Royal Society of Chemistry (UK)
Available From:	DIALOG File 319
	$155 per connect hour
	$1.05 per on-line type
	80c per off-line print
	SDI profile: $14
	Pergamon Financial File CBNB
	£90 per connect hour
	75p per on-line type
	75p per off-line print
	SDI profile: £5
	Data-Star File CBNB
	£90.94 per connect hour
	69p per on-line print
	43p per off-line print
	SDI profile: £3.88

Name:	Chemical Economics Handbook
Description:	Provides annual supply/demand and price data for many of the 1300 major commodity and specialty chemicals, chemical groups, chemical-related industries and US economic indicators covered in the 'Chemical Economics Handbook'. CEH80 and CEH132 information is in tabular form and includes the quarterly and monthly data series currently compiled in the 'Manual of Current Indicators' and other tabulations from the CEH. CEH80 and CEH132 are identical in content, but differ in print formats. CEHINDEX corresponds to the printed CEH Index. It contains index entries and cross- references to CEH80 and CEH132 as well as all tables of contents of reports and product reviews. Online access is limited to CEH subscribers.
Source:	Corresponds to the publication 'Chemical Economics Handbook'
Years Covered:	1955-65 to date
File Size:	Over 10 000 records
Updates:	Monthly
Database Producer:	SRI International
Available From:	ORBIT Search Service
	Files CEH80, CEH132, CEHINDEX
	Major subscribers:
	$80 per connect hour
	Minor subscribers:
	$130 per connect hour
	CEH80 and CEH132:
	Major subscribers:
	$1.0 per on-line type
	75c per off-line print
	Minor subscribers:
	$3.00 per on-line type
	$3.25 per off-line print
	CEHINDEX:
	Major subscribers:
	10c per off-line print
	Minor subscribers:
	5c per on-line type
	15c per off-line print

Name:	Chemical Engineering Abstracts
Description:	Chemical Engineering Abstracts (CEA) is designed to give full coverage of published information required by practising engineers. It includes both practical and theoretical material with a bias towards the practical side. Subjects covered: process design, operation & cost; reaction kinetics & thermodynamics; heat transfer & fluid flow; diffusion & mechanical operations; safety & control; corrosion & prevention; reactors, plant & equipment; material tests & analysis; energy generation, distribution, use; electrical & electronic engineering; computer & applications; mechanical, general & theoretical chemical engineering.
Source:	Corresponds to the 'Chemical Engineering Abstracts Current Awareness Bulletin'. Sources from 80 of the world's primary technical journals. Items selected include full articles, reviews, technical news items and some book reviews
Years Covered:	1970 to date
File Size:	Approx 85 000 references (ESA-IRS) Approx 82 000 references (ORBIT)
Updates:	Approx 3-4000 references per month
Database Producer:	The Royal Society of Chemistry (UK)
Available From:	ESA-IRS File 85 £56.70 per connect hour 32.2p per on-line type 27.6p per off-line print SDI profile: £4.20 ORBIT Search Service File CEA $85 per connect hour 70c per on-line type 40c per off-line print SDI profile: $6.50

Name:	Chemical Industry Notes
Description:	Chemical Industry Notes (CIN) indexes over 80 important worldwide journals, newspapers, and related periodicals which are business oriented and reflect recent events in the chemical industry. Principal coverage of CIN includes: government and society; market data; resources and resource use; people information; products and processes, organisations and institutions; unit cost and price information
Source:	Worldwide journals, periodicals, newspapers
Years Covered:	1974 to present
File Size:	Approx 630 700 records (ORBIT) Approx 685 004 records (DIALOG)
Updates:	Weekly
Database Producer:	Chemical Abstracts Service The American Chemical Society
Available From:	DIALOG File 19 $115 per connect hour 33c per on-line type 50c per off-line print SDI profile: $11.95 ORBIT Search Service File CIN $120 per connect hour 33c per on-line type 45c per off-line print SDI profile: $5.50 Search terms (excluding IRN): 12c per term Extracted prints: 3c per record selected Data-Star File CIND £62.20 per connect hour 18p per on-line print 19p per off-line print SDI profile: £3.29

Name: Chemical Plant Database – Plan
Description: The Chemical Plant Database contains references to some 15 000 plants for
                       over 100 major inorganic and organic chemicals including petrochemicals,
                       fertilisers, polymers, rubbers and synthetic fibres, covering about 4000
                       companies worldwide.
Source: The database producer's editorial staff compile the database by:
                       Direct correspondence with producers, plant contractors and licensors
                       Regular monitoring of a comprehensive range of publications in most
                       European languages
                       Analysis of company reports and press releases
                       Consultation of relevant published market industry surveys
Years Covered: Current
File Size: 15 000 chemical plants
Updates: Monthly
Database Producer: CHEM-INTELL-Chemical Intelligence Services, UK
Available From: Data-Star
                       Contact direct for prices

Name: Coffeeline
Description: The Coffeeline database covers all aspects of the production of coffee from
                       the farming of coffee plants to production, packaging, and marketing. The
                       file includes references selected from a range of 5000 journals from all over
                       the world. It also includes references to books, patents, reports and theses.
                       Coffeeline records are indexed using a controlled vocabulary, and most
                       items added after May 1980 include abstracts.
Source: Over 5000 international journals. Corresponds to the publication
                       'International Coffee Organization, Library Monthly Entries'
Years Covered: 1973 to date
File Size: 19 687 records
Updates: Bimonthly
Database Producer: International Coffee Organisation (ICO)
Available From: DIALOG File 164
                       $65 per connect hour
                       20c per on-line type
                       20c per off-line print

Name: Compendex Plus
Description: Compendex is the on-line version of the Engineering Index
                       (monthly/annually), which provides abstracted information from the
                       world's significant engineering and technological literature.
Source: Over 4500 worldwide journals and selected government reports and books
Years Covered: 1970 to date
                       1976 to date on Data-Star
File Size: 1.9 million records (DIALOG)
                       1.8 million records (ESA-IRS, STN)
                       Over 1.3 million records (ORBIT)
Updates: Monthly
Database Producer: Engineering Information Inc
Available From: DIALOG File 8
                       $108 per connect hour
                       35c per on-line type
                       47c per off-line print
                       SDI profile: $10.95
                       Cedocar File Compendex
                       FF 680 per connect hour
                       FF 2.30 per on-line type
                       FF 2.95 per off-line print
                       BRS File Comp
                       $80 per connect hour
                       46c per on-line type
                       41c per off-line print
                       SDI profile: $4

Data-Star File COMP
£62.76 per connect hour
22p per on-line print
15p per off-line print
SDI profile: £2.87
ESA-IRS File 4
£68.60 per connect hour
21.7p per on-line type
31.8p per off-line print
SDI profile: £4.20
ORBIT Search Service File Compendex
$108 per connect hour
35c per on-line type
47c per off-line print
SDI profile: $6.50
STN File Compendex
£64 per connect hour
23p per on-line type
31p per off-line print
SDI profile: £3

Name:	Computer Database
Description:	The Computer Database is designed to provide information to business and computer professionals, educators, and researchers about hardware, software, applications and services, and to provide information on such rapidly growing high-tech fields as robotics, satellite communications, cable television and videotex as well as electronic systems, instrumentation and measurement. Specialised fields on the database feature company names, product names and prominent people in literature, as well as programming languages, operating systems and published programs. The database includes product evaluations, comparisons, best buys, as well as profiles and financial information on computer, telecommunications and electronic firms.
Source:	USA and international journals, newsletters, business books, courses
Years Covered:	January 1983 to date
File Size:	215771 records
Updates:	Every 2 weeks
Database Producer:	Information Access Company
Available From:	DIALOG File 275

$108 per connect hour
90c per on-line type
95c per off-line print
SDI profile: $11.95
Data-Star File CMPT
£50.08 per connect hour
25p per on-line print
17p per off-line print
SDI profile: £1.63
BRS File CMPT
$90 per connect hour
55c per on-line type
50c per off-line print
SDI profile: $4

Name:	Context – Business Microcomputer Information Service
Description:	This database covers computer market research on all aspects of the computer market in the UK. Market data is provided on PC hardware and software sold through approximately 2000 business microcomputer outlets in the UK. Reports are published 6 times a year and are based on surveys carried out every 2 months. Surveys cover on average a sample consisting of 19 per cent of microcomputer outlets.

Source:	Context (specialist research and consultancy organisation)
Years Covered:	November 1985 to date
File Size:	2000 outlets covered
Updates:	Periodically
Database Producer:	Context
Available From:	MAID
	Annual subscription: £4250 per annum
	(including training, codes, manuals, etc)
	£80 per connect hour

Name:	CSCORP
Description:	CSCORP contains information on suppliers of chemicals. It provides company codes, addresses, departments, subsidiary companies and telephone numbers as well as the classification of the chemical products. The CSCHEM file covers information on the products supplied by companies listed in CSCORP
Source:	Chem Sources – USA
Years Covered:	
File Size:	855 citations
Updates:	Annual
Database Producer:	Directories Publishing Co Inc
Available From:	STN File CSCORP
	£45 per connect hour
	£1.43 per on-line type
	£1.52 per off-line print

Name:	Der Betrieb
Description:	The Der Betrieb (DB) database is the online version of the register of 'Der Betrieb', the biggest German weekly magazine for business economics, taxation law, economic and employment law. It includes as an index the ibz-index register, details of decisions concerning taxation law, and government directives which have been published. It also covers decisions concerning economic, employment and social law and a register of the authors.
Language:	German
Source:	Weekly trade magazine 'Der Betrieb'
Years Covered:	Current
File Size:	105 000 documents
Updates:	Currently twice per annum, monthly updating is planned
Database Producer:	Handelsblatt GmbH, Der Betrieb
Available From:	GENIOS File DB
	DM 240 per connect hour
	DM 1 per on-line type
	DM 1 per off-line print

Name:	DHSS Data
Description:	This is the on-line database of the UK Department of Health and Social Security Library. It is based on the library's long-established database, abstracts, and current awareness bulletins. Many records carry indicative abstracts or annotations. An important feature is the inclusion of full details including sources of supply of official DHSS publications. Subjects covered include Health Service planning and administration, social security and occupational pensions amongst others.
Source:	Books, pamphlets, reports, journal articles, administrative circulars and other official publications
Years Covered:	Late 1983 to date
File Size:	Approximately 12 000 records added per annum
Updates:	Monthly
Database Producer:	Department of Health and Social Security Library (DHSS)

Available From: SCICON
                     £34 per connect hour
                     (exempt users, eg Central Government Departments)
                     £39.10 per connect hour (non-exempt users)

Name: Disposiciones Legales
Description: This is a Spanish database of legal requirements affecting businesses,
                     which has been laid down by regional governments and company law.
Source: Bulletins of regional governments and legal lists
Years Covered: 1980 to date
File Size: 3500 documents
                     Upidates: Daily
Database Producer: Sistema de Informacion Empresarial
Available From: Instituto de la Pequena y Mediana Empresa Industrial
                     (IMPI)
                     Contact direct for prices

Name: DMS Contract Awards
Description: DMS Contract Awards contains detailed information for all government
                     contracts awarded. Coverage includes all contracting actions in excess of
                     $25 000 for research, systems and services in defence, aerospace, energy
                     and transportation markets. Each contract award listing includes: total
                     dollar amount awarded, company receiving the contract, the awarding
                     agency, the defence program involved, date, contract number, place of
                     performance and more. In addition a special trend analysis report is
                     available which allows analysis of contracting trends by fiscal year or
                     quarter. This database can be useful for analysing competitors, tracking
                     aerospace/defence programs, monitoring new technologies and planning
                     business strategies.
                     Also see DMS Defence Newsletter (DIALOG file 587)
Source: US Government
Years Covered: 1981 to date
File Size: 1 771 759 records
Updates: Quarterly
Database Producer: DMS Inc
Available From: DIALOG File 588
                     $84 per connect hour
                     35c per off-line print
                     10c per reports element
                     Crosstab reports available at 2c per record ($25 minimum)

Name: DMS Market Intelligence Reports
Description: DMS Market Intelligence Reports provide the most comprehensive and
                     up-to-date full-text data and analysis for the aerospace and defence
                     industry. Coverage includes virtually all major defence companies,
                     programs, and products. Reports provide detailed and extensive
                     information such as forecasts, major activity, funding, location and military
                     posture. This information is gathered from diverse sources as government
                     documents, defence journals, and field inteviews with key defence people.
                     This database is particularly useful for those involved in market research,
                     business development, and programme management in the
                     aerospace/defence industry. Access is limited to customers approved by
                     DMS.
Source: DMS
Years Covered: Current
File Size: 18 414 records
Updates: Weekly
Database Producer: DMS Inc
Available From: DIALOG File 988
                     $174 per connect hour
                     $6 per off-line print

Name: DOE Energy
Description: DOE Energy, the database of the US Department of Energy, is one of the
                    world's largest sources of literature references on all aspects of energy and
                    related topics. The following energy topics are included: nuclear, wind,
                    fossil, geothermal, tidal and solar. Related topics such as environment,
                    energy policy and conservation are also included.
                        Use of this database is restricted to the United States, the United
                    Kingdom and Northern Ireland, France, the Netherlands, Norway,
                    Finland, Denmark and Sweden.
Source: Journal articles, report literature, conference papers, books, patents,
                    dissertations and translations
Years Covered: DIALOG File 103 (1983 to date)
                    File 104 (1974-82)
File Size: 1 947 871 records
Updates: Twice a week
Database Producer: US Dept of Energy
Available From: DIALOG File 103, 104
                    $84 per connect hour
                    30c per on-line type
                    40c per off-line print
                    SDI profile: $7.95

Name: Dun's Electronic Yellow Pages Financial Services Directory
Description: The Electronic Yellow Pages Financial Services Directory provides on-line
                    yellow page information for banks, savings and loan institutions and credit
                    unions in the United States. A full directory listing is included for each of
                    the financial institutions, both headquarters and branch locations. In
                    addition, Electronic Yellow Pages records include company name and
                    address, modified 4-digit Standard Industrial Classification code,
                    telephone number, county and city population size.
Source: Data is gathered from 4800 US telephone books and is cross-checked and
                    qualified with more than 50 specialised sources
Years Covered: Current
File Size: 375 663 records
Updates: Quarterly reloads
Database Producer: Dun's Marketing Services
Available From: DIALOG File 501
                    $60 per connect hour
                    20c per on-line type
                    20c per off-line print

Name: EDF-DOC
Description: Produced by the French Electricity Board, EDF-DOC is a multidisciplinary
                    file dealing with practical problems related to energy and its technology. It
                    contains original records from various sources including internal reports
                    and conference proceedings.
                        Main subject categories are: energy sources; electric power production,
                    transmission and distribution; domestic and industrial applications of
                    electricity; environment, pollution and biology, nuclear power plants,
                    electric machines; computer systems and applications; applied
                    mathematics.
Language: 45 per cent English, 45 per cent French
Source: Various including internal reports and conference proceedings
Years Covered: 1972 to present
File Size: Approx 378 000 references
Updates: Approx 1500 references per month
                    Database Producer: Electricite de France
                    Service Informatique et Mathematiques appliquees
                    Departement Systemes d'Information et de Documentation

	Thesaurus & List of EDF Source Code available from:
	Electricite de France
	Departement Systemes d'Information et de Documentation
	Division PDGD
Available From:	ESA-IRS File 27
	£44.11 per connect hour
	4.9p per on-line type
	17.8p per off-line print
	Telesystemes-Questel File EDF-DOC
	$75 per on-line connect hour
	31c per on-line type
	31c per off-line print

Name:	EI Engineering Meetings
Description:	EI Engineering Meetings is an index to significant published proceedings of engineering and technical conferences, symposia, meetings, and colloquia from over 40 different countries. Over 2000 publications are covered every year. All areas of engineering including civil, bioengineering, electrical, mechanical, petroleum, automotive and aerospace, are covered. This file has been transferred on DIALOG to Compendex Plus (file 8).
Source:	USA engineering and technical conference publications
Years Covered:	July 1982 to date
File Size:	Approx 500000 records
Updates:	Monthly
Database Producer:	Engineering Information Inc
Available From:	DIALOG See File 8
	ORBIT Search Service File EIMET
	$108 per connect hour
	35c per on-line type
	47c per off-line print
	Datastar File EIEM
	£62.76 per connect hour
	22p per on-line print
	15p per off-line print
	Cedocar File EI Meetings
	FF 680 per connect hour
	FF 2.30 per on-line type
	FF 2.95 per off-line print

Name:	ELCOM
Description:	ELCOM, the international information service in electronics and communications, provides information selected from a wide range of primary journals, government reports, conference proceedings, dissertations and patents.
	The main subject categories are: electronic systems, electronic physics, electronic circuits and devices, communications, theoretical and applied research, business and marketing information.
Source:	Corresponds to the journals 'Electronic and Communications Abstracts' and 'Computer and Information Systems Abstracts'
Years Covered:	1980 to present
File Size:	Approx 108000 references
Updates:	Approx 1600 references are added every 2 months
Database Producer:	Cambridge Scientific Abstracts
Available From:	ESA-IRS File 93
	£60.20 per connect hour
	23.1p per on-line type
	31.8p per off-line print
	SDI profile: £8.40

Name: Electric Power Database
Description: The Electric Power Database covers US and Canadian research on 13 major
                       categories related to issues in electric power including hydroelectric power,
                       fossil fuels, nuclear power, transmission, economics, advanced power
                       systems, and environmental assessment. The records include abstracts of
                       project summaries for past and ongoing research projects. Such projects are
                       conducted largely by companies under contract to EPRI or to other utilities,
                       and by EPRI itself. Research from other corporate and utility sources is also
                       covered.
Source: Corresponds to the publication 'Digest of Research in the Electric Utility
                       Industry'
Years Covered: 1972 to date
File Size: 25 552 records
Updates: Monthly
Database Producer: Electric Power Research Institute (EPRI)
Available From: DIALOG File 241
                       $66 per connect hour
                       35c per on-line type
                       35c per off-line print

Name: Electric Power Industry Abstracts
Description: This database provides access to literature on electric power plants and
                       related facilities. Topics include environmental effects of electric power
                       plants and associated transmission lines, power plant siting
                       methodologies, fuel transportation, storage and use, licensing and permit
                       data, energy resources, monitoring programmes, safety and risk
                       management plans, waste disposal facilities and land-use studies.
Source: Source documents include technical reports and studies prepared by the
                       electric utilities and their consultants
                       Reports from federal and state agencies Siting commissions, and control
                       boards
                       Selected journal articles, conference proceedings, and testimony from
                       Congressional hearings
Years Covered: 1975 to date
File Size: Over 25 000 records
Updates: 5 times per annum
Database Producer: Edison Electric Institute
Available From: ORBIT Search Service File EPIA
                       $86 per connect hour
                       10c per on-line type
                       20c per off-line print

Name: Encyclopedia of Associations
Description: The Encyclopedia of Associations database corresponds to the printed
                       publication of the same name. The file provides detailed information on
                       several thousand trade associations, professional societies, labour unions,
                       fraternal and patriotic organisations, and other types of groups consisting
                       of voluntary members. In addition to the address, phone number and size
                       of organisation, each record provides an abstract giving the scope and
                       purpose of the organisation and lists its publications and the location and
                       date of its annual conference.
Source: Corresponds to the Encyclopedia of Associations' publication
Years Covered: Current edition
File Size: 19 121 records
Updates: Annual reloads
Database Producer: Gale Research Company
Available From: DIALOG File 114
                       $54 per connect hour
                       75c per on-line type
                       75c per off-line print

Name:	ENEL
Description:	The ENEL database is a multidisciplinary file that supplies information on electrical power and related technologies.
	The file contains bibliographic references on conference papers and proceedings written by technical personnel of ENEL and Enel's Research Organisations CESI, CISE, ISMEC and PHOEBUS. It also includes references on ENEL internal technical papers of general interest, as well as citations of the articles of the Italian journals reviewed by 'Bibliografia Elettronica'.
	Subjects covered include: conventional and alternative energy sources; fossil-fired, nuclear, hydro and geothermal power stations; power production, transmission and distribution; domestic and industrial power applications; environmental compatibility of electric plant; materials properties and testing; informatics and related applications; applied mathematics.
Language:	Italian
Source:	Technical papers, conference papers and proceedings
Years Covered:	1980 to date
File Size:	Approx 13000 references
Updates:	Every 2 months
Database Producer:	ENTE Nazionale per l'Energia Elettrica (The Italian Electricity Board)
	Direzione Studi e Ricerche
	Settore Coordinamento e Programmi
	Unita Documentaria
Available From:	ESA-IRS File 60
	£39.90 per connect hour
	15.7p per off-line print
	SDI profile: £4.20

Name:	Energie
Description:	Energie is a bibliographic database covering literature on energy research and technology, particularly those published in German-speaking countries. Special emphasis is given to 'grey' literature.
Language:	English and German
Source:	45 per cent sourced by journals and series
	33 per cent of citations are conference contributions
Years Covered:	1976 to date
File Size:	200000 citations (as at May 1988)
Updates:	Twice per month
Database Producer:	FIZ Karlsruhe
Available From:	STN File Energie
	£58 per connect hour
	20p per on-line type
	26p per off-line print
	SDI profile: £3.00

Name:	Energyline
Description:	Energyline is the on-line version of Energy Information Abstracts and also includes 8000 energy and environment related records dating back to 1971 from the Energy Index. Its data is drawn from various fields such as chemistry or engineering where they relate to energy issues and problems.
Source:	Corresponds to the publication 'Energy Information Abstracts'. Original sources are books, journals, congressional committee prints, conference proceedings, speeches and statistics
Years Covered:	1971 to present
File Size:	62947 records (DIALOG)
	94500 records (ESA-IRS)
	Approx 63500 records (ORBIT)
Updates:	Monthly
Database Producer:	EIC/Intelligence Inc

Available From:	DIALOG File 69
	$120 per connect hour
	45c per on-line type
	45c per off-line print
	SDI profile: $7.95
	ESA-IRS File 19
	£74.90 per connect hour
	23.1p per on-line type
	35.3p per off-line print
	SDI profile: £10.50
	ORBIT Search Service File Energyline
	$116 per connect hour
	45c per on-line type
	45c per off-line print
	SDI profile: $6.95

Name:	European Automotive News Service
Description:	This is a relatively new service available from Pergamon Financial Data Services. The database monitors current events within the vehicle manufacturing industry and the external factors which affect it. PRS scan key daily newspapers from European countries and also extracts material from major industry journals – 'AUTO Industry', 'ADAC Motor Welt', 'Autopista', 'Truck and Bus Builder' etc.
Source:	Newspapers and journals
Years Covered:	Current
File Size:	Over 200 articles input each week
Updates:	Weekly
Database Producer:	PRS Consultancy Group, UK
Available From:	Pergamon Financial
	Contact direct for prices (new file)

Name:	Experts in Law
	Rechtswissenschaftliche Experten und Gutachter
Description:	This database covers the Federal Republic of Germany and West Berlin. It contains references to corporate and individual law experts which include name, address, telephone number and brief professional profile. Langauge:English and German
Source:	Own studies
Years Covered:	Current information
File Size:	2000 citations
Updates:	Quarterly, 200 citations added per annum
Database Producer:	Nomos Datapool
	Nomos Verlagsgesellschaft mbH
Available From:	Edicline File REX
	£60 per connect hour

Name:	FINIS: Financial Industry Information Service
Description:	FINIS: Financial Industry Information Service provides marketing information on organisations in the financial services industry and on products and services offered to corporate and retail customers. FINIS includes items relating to the activities of banks, brokers, credit unions, insurance companies, investment houses, real estate firms, thrift institutions, and related government agencies. Included in the file are abstracts of outstanding student projects from BMA schools, and records representing BMA 'Golden Coin' Award entries.
Source:	Over 200 US journals, books, reports, press releases plus Bank Marketing Association projects
Years Covered:	1982 to date
File Size:	80073 records
Updates:	Fortnightly
Database Producer:	Bank Marketing Association (BMA)

Available From:	DIALOG File 268
	$78 per connect hour
	20c per on-line type
	30c per off-line print
	SDI profile: $9.95
	BRS File FINI
	$65 per connect hour
	48c per on-line type
	40c per off-line print
	SDI profile: $4
	MEAD File FINIS
	$15 per search
	Data-Star
	New file

Name:	Forest
Description:	Forest covers worldwide literature pertinent to the entire wood products industry, from harvesting the standing tree through marketing the final product. Two related areas not covered are chemical pulping and forestry practices (unless they impact directly on product quality).
Source:	Technical journals, government publications, patents, trade journals, abstract bulletins and monographs
Years Covered:	1947 to date
File Size:	Over 20000 records
Updates:	Every 2 months
Database Producer:	Forest Products Research Society
Available From:	ORBIT Search Service File Forest
	$95 per connect hour
	30c per on-line type
	15c per off-line print

Name:	IALINE
Description:	IALINE covers the French agriculture and food industry. Information is provided on the composition, quality and properties of raw materials and ingredients; manufactured products and processing and engineering methods; quality control, regulations, consumption and trade.
Source:	
Years Covered:	Current
File Size:	
Updates:	
Database Producer:	Centre de Documentation des Industries Utilisatrices des Produits Agricoles (CDIUPA)
Available From:	Telesystemes-Questel File IALINE
	$82 per connect hour
	43c per on-line type
	43c per off-line print

Name:	Ibsedex
Description:	Ibsedex contains 50000 references from worldwide literature published since 1960 on all aspects of building services. The database can be classified into three main subject areas: energy, construction and engineering. On any subject, users will find details of books, reports, conference papers, journal articles and standards with, in most cases, a summary of the contents and conclusions. Although the database has international coverage, it has a British bias as the producers – The Building Services Research and Information Association – are primarily serving the UK industry's needs. A companion thesaurus called the Building Services Thesaurus is available to aid searching this database.
Source:	Reports, books, conference papers, journal articles
Years Covered:	Selections go back to 1960 and earlier
File Size:	65000 records (as at Feb 1988)

Updates:	BSRIA updates twice a week
	Other hosts update monthly
Database Producer:	Building Services Research and Information Association
Available From:	BSRIA
	Members:
	£30 per connect hour
	Non-members:
	£40 per connect hour
	Pergamon Financial File Ibsedex
	£54 per connect hour
	17p per on-line type
	18p per off-line print
	SDI profile: £5
	ESA-IRS File 88
	£46.20 per connect hour
	10.5p per on-line type
	24.8p per off-line print
	SDI profile: £8.40

Name:	ICONDA
Description:	This is a bibliographic database covering worldwide literature on all fields of building construction, construction engineering, architecture and town planning. Most citations include abstracts.
Source:	Journals and series, books, conference proceedings, reports and other non-conventional literature
Years Covered:	1976 to date
File Size:	Over 195 000 citations
Updates:	Monthly
	35 000 citations added per update
Database Producer:	International cooperation coordinated by:
	ICONDA Agency
	c/o Information Center for Regional Planning and Building Construction (IRB) of the Fraunhofer Society
Available From:	STN File Iconda
	£72 per connect hour
	23p per on-line type
	33p per off-line print
	SDI profile: £3.95
	ORBIT Search Service File Iconda
	$113 per connect hour
	51c per on-line type
	36c per off-line print
	SDI profile: $8

Name:	IDB Online
Description:	This is the electronic version of the 'Infomatics Daily Bulletin', the daily newspaper on information technology. News items cover new products, new orders and competitor activities. Users can also monitor the activities of manufacturers and third parties. PC News is also available now through IDB Online. This provides a weekly summary of marketing activity in the microcomputer world.
Source:	'Infomatics Daily Bulletin'
	'PC News' (weekly)
Years Covered:	Current
File Size:	
Updates:	
Database Producer:	VNU Business Publications

Available From:	Telecom Gold
	Subscribers to Infomatics Bulletin:
	14.5p per connect minute
	Free Telecom Gold mailbox
	Non-subscribers:
	56p per connect minute
	£40 registration fee for the Telecom Gold mailbox
	(Subscription to the hardcopy version of Infomatics
	Bulletin: £550 per annum)
Name:	INIS
Description:	INIS (International Nuclear Information System) is a file compiled by the IAEA (International Atomic Energy Agency). It contains citations of publications related to the nuclear sciences and their peaceful applications. Almost 60 countries and international bodies participate in this international information system.
	Subjects covered:
	Physical sciences
	General physics, high-energy physics, neutron and nuclear physics
	Chemistry, materials and earth sciences
	Life sciences
	All effects and various aspects of external radiation in biology, radionuclide effects and kinetics health, safety and environment
	Isotopes, isotope and radiation applications
	Engineering and technology
	Peaceful nuclear explosions, nuclear reactors, instrumentation
	Other aspects of nuclear energy
	Economics, nuclear law, safeguards and inspection,
	Nuclear documentation and data handling,
	Mathematical methods and computer codes.
Source:	Articles published in scientific journals, papers and conferences, patent specifications filed, university theses, technical reports from laboratories or institutes, articles distributed through commercial channels, books and other publications
Years Covered:	Jan 1975 to date
File Size:	Over 1.2 million citations
Updates:	Approx 3000 new citations per fortnight
Database Producer:	Studiecentrum voor Kernenergie (SCK)
	Centre d'Etude de l'Energie Nucleaire (CEN)
	Library holds 75 per cent of documents recorded in INIS
Available From:	Belindis File INIS
	BF 1800 per connect hour
	BF 4 per off-line print
	ESA-IRS File 28
	£42 per connect hour
	18.9p per off-line print
	SDI profile: £2.10
	STN File INIS
	£53 per connect hour
	20p per on-line type
	26p per off-line print
	SDI profile: £3
Name:	Insurance Abstracts
Description:	The Insurance Abstracts database covers the specialised literature of life, property and liability insurance. Insurance Abstracts provides comprehensive coverage of over 100 journals. Each record includes a brief abstract and is indexed with a controlled vocabulary. The database corresponds to two printed indexes: 'Life Insurance Index' (1979-84) and 'Property and Liability Index' (1980-81).

Source:	'Life Insurance Index'
	'Property and Liability Index'
	Based on over 100 journals
Years Covered:	1979 to 1984
File Size:	68912 records
Updates:	Closed file
Database Producer:	University Microfilms International
Available From:	DIALOG File 168
	$55 per connect hour
	15c per off-line print

Name:	ISIS
Description:	ISIS (Software Catalogue) consists of four databases containing descriptions of computer programs available in West Germany, Austria and Switzerland. These are equivalent to the ISIS Reports issued by Nomina GmbH, and may be retrieved concurrently or separately.
	ISSR contains over 4000 programs for use with medium to large computer installations.
	ISPC and ISPS contain 3600 programs for use on personal computers.
	ISER contains over 700 programs for use in CAD/CAM, CAE and PPS systems.
Source:	European software houses
Years Covered:	Current
File Size:	8800 records
Updates:	2 times per annum
Database Producer:	Nomina Gesellschaft fur Wirtschafts – und Verwaltungsregister mbH
Available From:	FIZ Technik File ISIS
	DM 250 per connect hour
	DM 3.9 per on-line type
	DM 4.2 per off-line print

Name:	ISMEC
Description:	ISMEC (Information Service in Mechanical Engineering) indexes significant articles in all aspects of mechanical engineering, production engineering, and engineering management from approximately 250 journals published throughout the world. In addition, books, reports and conference proceedings are indexed. The primary emphasis is on comprehensive coverage of leading international journals and conferences on mechanical engineering subjects. The principal areas covered are mechanical, nuclear, electrical, electronic, civil, optical, medical and industrial process engineering; mechanics; production processes; energy and power; transport and handling; and applications of mechanical engineering.
Source:	250 journals worldwide
Years Covered:	1973 to present
File Size:	198691 records (DIALOG)
	205000 records (ESA-IRS)
Updates:	Monthly
Database Producer:	Cambridge Scientific Abstracts
Available From:	DIALOG File 14
	$84 per connect hour
	40c per on-line type
	50c per off-line print
	ESA-IRS File 10
	£60.20 per connect hour
	23.1p per on-line type
	31.8p per off-line print
	SDI profile: £8.40

Name: Italian Legal Information System
Description: The Electronic Documentation Centre of the Italian Supreme Court
                      provides legal data to the Italian legal profession and general public. It uses
                      a legal research and retrieval system called 'Italguire Find', and has been
                      linked to the European network for the transmission of scientific and
                      technical information (Euronet). Twenty legislation, case law and legal
                      literature files are online and cover Italian national and regional legislation.
Source: Italian official legal sources, legal literature
Years Covered: Varies by file
File Size: 20 on-line files
Updates: As information becomes available throughout the year
Database Producer: Electronic Centre for Legal Documentation
                      Italian Supreme Court
Available From: Electronic Centre for Legal Documentation
                      Contact Centre direct for prices and details
                      UK distributors for hard copy version:
                      Sweet & Maxwell

Name: Lexis
Description: Lexis is the world's largest computer-assisted legal research service, used
                      by a majority of leading firms of solicitors in Britain, corporate legal
                      departments, government departments and local authorities. Lexis
                      provides the full text of millions of cases, statutory texts and other legal
                      reference sources. It also includes comprehensive libraries of American and
                      French law. Custom-built equipment is provided to subscribers.
                      Alternatively, Lexis can be used with one of a number of 'approved'
                      personal computers.
Source: As above
Years Covered: Case law from 1945 (tax since 1875)
                      Full text of English, Scots and Irish case law since 1950
                      European case law from the 1954 inception of the European Court of Justice

                      Up-to-date, complete and amended file of English statutory material – in
                      full text
File Size: Each file varies substantially
Updates: Weekly
Database Producer: Mead Data Central
Available From: Butterworth
                      Cost of access to files within Lexis libraries vary according to size of the files
                      as follows:

		From 1.8.88
Small file	£8	£9
Medium file	£9	£10
Large file	£10	£11
Very large file	£11	£12

                      Available worldwide through Mead Data Central

Name: Menu-The International Software Database
Description: Menu-ISD (International Software Database) provides a comprehensive
                      listing of commercially available software for any type of mini or micro
                      computer.
                           Each program record in Menu (ISD) consists of a 100-150 word
                      description of the software package, vendor name, distributor,
                      compatibility requirements, country of currency, date of release, amongst
                      other items. Packages are categorised by specific applications occurring
                      under the headings: commercial, educational, personal, industrial,
                      scientific, professions/industries and systems.
Source: Corresponds with US 'The Software Catalog' distributed by Elsevier
                      Science Publishing Co Inc
Years Covered: Current
File Size: 30 000 records
Updates: Monthly

Database Producer:	International Software Database Corporation
Available From:	DIALOG File 232
	$60 per connect hour
	15c per off-line print

Name:	Merlin-Tech
Description:	The Merlin-Tech database contains bibliographic references from international published literature in electrical and electronic engineering and related sciences.
	Subjects covered:
	Electricity – magnetism
	Electrical engineering
	Electrotechnical devices and equipments
	Power systems
	Energy
	Electronic circuits and instrumentation
	Control systems
	Computer systems and equipments
	Materials
	Testing – reliability – safety
	Interdisciplinary subjects
Language:	French
Source:	International specialist literature
	Corresponds to abstract journal 'Bulletin d'analyse des revues techniques francaise et etrangeres'
Years Covered:	1973 to date
File Size:	Approx 39 000 references
Updates:	Approx 200 references added per update
Database Producer:	Merlin Gerin
	(Service Documentation)
Available From:	ESA-IRS File 65
	£48.31 per connect hour
	15.7p per off-line print
	SDI profile: £2.81

Name:	Microcomputer Index
Description:	Microcomputer Index is a subject index and abstract guide to magazine articles from 50 microcomputer journals. Included are software reviews, descriptions of new microcomputer products. Each record contains a short abstract and complete bibliographic information, plus assigned descriptors.
Source:	Publications indexed include 'Byte', 'Interface Age', 'Personal Computing', 'Infoworld'
Years Covered:	1981 to date
File Size:	72 641
Updates:	Monthly
Database Producer:	Database Services Inc
Available From:	DIALOG File 233
	$60 per connect hour
	25c per on-line type
	25c per off-line print
	SDI profile: $5.95

Name:	Microcomputer Software & Hardware Guide
Description:	The Microcomputer Software & Hardware Guide database contains information on virtually every microcomputer software program and hardware system available or produced in the USA. The database contains three subfiles: (1) bibliographic records for microcomputer software, (2) descriptions of available microcomputers, and (3) descriptions of major microcomputer peripherals. Subfiles 2 and 3 will be added in 1987. Each record includes ordering information, technical specifications, subject classifications, and a brief description.

Source:	Source data is derived from 3500 software publishers and over 1000 hardware manufacturers, as well as industry sources such as press releases, periodicals and books
Years Covered:	Current
File Size:	34 304 records
Updates:	Monthly reloads
Database Producer:	R R Bowker Co
Available From:	DIALOG File 278
	$60 per connect hour
	10c per on-line type
	25c per off-line print

Name:	Microsearch
Description:	Microsearch provides coverage of reviews and instructional articles from microcomputer-related literature. It provides information on availability, applications, compatibility and comparative evaluations of hardware and software products.
Source:	Over 3000 hardware and software manufacturers and over 170 trade journals
Years Covered:	1982 to date
File Size:	Over 45 000 records
Updates:	Monthly
Database Producer:	Information Inc
Available From:	ORBIT Search Service File Microsearch
	$75 per connect hour
	20c per on-line type
	25c per off-line print

Name:	Name
Description:	Name contains the address and other details on legal practitioners (lawyers, counsels, notaries, process servers, jurists, etc) in Belgium.
Language:	French and Dutch
Source:	
Years Covered:	Database started in March 1987
File Size:	Over 12 000 documents (as at March 1987)
Updates:	
Database Producer:	Credoc asbl
Available From:	Belindis File Name
	BF 2000 per connect hour
	BF 10 per 10 lines displayed on line
	BF 10 per off-line print

Name:	National Computer Index
Description:	The National Computer Index is a market intelligence database which identifies the use made of hardware, software and peripherals in 20 000 company sites in the UK. The database is updated monthly on a rolling program so that each company is surveyed every year.
	Using NCI you can target by a wide variety of criteria so that you can present the information in the most useful way. You can, for example, target by geographic location, DP budget, machine type or programming language.
	This database can be useful for:
	Identifying new sales prospects
	Market research projects
	Company profiles
Source:	Company surveys
Years Covered:	Current
File Size:	20 000
Updates:	Monthly
Database Producer:	National Computing Centre

Available From:	Pergamon Financial File NC1
	£75 per connect hour
	£1 per on-line type
	£1 per off-line print
	Statistics: £20
	Labels: 18p

Name:	NLEX
Description:	NLEX contains the integral text of the most important acts, decrees and treaties in force in the Netherlands.
	NLEX users can consult Dutch legislation directly. To select the wanted article(s) one can search on any word used in the gathered Dutch legislation or used in the references adjudged by Koninklijke Vermande.
Language:	Dutch
Source:	Private law
	Penal legislation
	Constitutional and administrative legislation in the Netherlands
Years Covered:	All Dutch legislation to date covered
File Size:	Approx 45 000 documents
Updates:	Monthly
Database Producer:	Koninklijke Vermande bV
Available From:	Belindis
	BF 5000 per connect hour
	BF 7 per off-line print

Name:	Nordic Energy Index
Description:	Nordic Energy Index (NEI) databases are: NEIL, NEIF and NEIX.
	NEIL contains bibliographic references to energy literature published in Nordic countries. It covers scientific and technical literature.
	NEIF contains descriptions of ongoing or newly finished energy research, development and demonstration projects in the Nordic countries.
	NEIX databases cover all energy sources and aspects of the entire energy cycle.
	Search language: DC-Info (CCL/BRS).
Source:	Journals, reports, books, conferences, laws, regulations, dissertations, research projects
Years Covered:	1981 to date
File Size:	16 780 documents (as at January 1987)
Updates:	Monthly
Database Producer:	The Nordic Energy Libraries
Available From:	Datacentralen File NEI
	DK 360 per connect hour
	DK 2 per off-line print

Name:	Nuclear Science Abstracts
Description:	Nuclear Science Abstracts is a comprehensive abstract and index collection of international nuclear science and technology literature. Included in the file are scientific and technical reports of the US Atomic Energy Commission, US Energy Research and Development administrators, associated contractors and other agencies, universities and industrial and research organisations. All aspects of nuclear science and technology are covered.
	Use of DIALOG's File 109 is restricted to users in the USA and the following countries: United Kingdom and Northern Ireland, France, the Netherlands, Norway, Finland, Denmark and Sweden.
Source:	US government agencies, universities, organisations
Years Covered:	1948 to 1976
File Size:	989 523 records
Updates:	8 Closed file
Database Producer:	US Department of Energy

Available From:	DIALOG File 109
	$84 per connect hour
	30c per on-line type
	40c per off-line print

Name:	Oil and Gas Journal Energy Database
Description:	OGJDATA contains a wealth of information on the oil and gas industry. The database is owned and maintained by the 'Oil and Gas Journal'.
	It contains over 35 000 series covering drilling and exploration, reserves, production, demand and consumption, exports and imports, offshore, prices and capital spending. It includes estimates and projections developed by the staff of the 'Oil and Gas Journal' for key data series and detailed information such as rig count by state, well completions by state and type and demand by product category.
Source:	The Department of Energy, the American Petroleum Institute, Hughes Tool Company, and the 'Oil and Gas Journal'
Years Covered:	
File Size:	Over 35 000 data series
Updates:	Updated as soon as figures are released from source
Database Producer:	Haver Analytics Inc/Oil and Gas Journal
Available From:	GE Information Services
	$1 per series weekly data
	$4 per series all other data

Name:	Oil and Gas Journal Energy Forecasts
Description:	FOROGJ is a valuable source for energy industry forecasts. The forecast reports show summarised projections from a variety of industry sources. They are compiled by the Oil and Gas Journal Database staff.
	Forecasts cover nine broad categories: drilling and exploration, US supply and demand, international supply and demand, natural gas, price and capital spending, electric utilities, refining, coal, and Canadian forecasts.
Source:	The Department of Energy, the International Energy Agency, the 'Oil and Gas Journal', oil companies and consulting firms
Years Covered:	Forecast range varies among reports
File Size:	
Updates:	
Database Producer:	Haver Analytics Inc/Oil and Gas Journal
Available From:	GE Information Services
	$10 per forecast report

Name:	ORBI
Description:	ORBI is a bibliographic database on international legal literature. ORBI is the product of a cooperation between CREDOC and the Belgian Ministry of Foreign Affairs. It is simple to use and is designed for general retrieval.
	ORBI contains citations of about 620 publications from about 60 countries. There are two subdivisions:
	Domestic legal systems (in the different countries)
	International law and institutions
	It is possible to search on keywords from the ORBI thesaurus.
	Content of document (keywords):
	Date
	Title
	Author
	Language
	Country
	Reference
	Subject
Language:	Multiple with coded index
Source:	International legal literature
Years Covered:	1960 to date

File Size:	85000 documents
Updates:	
Database Producer:	Credoc asbl
Available From:	Belindis File ORBI
	BF 3960 per connect hour
	BF 5 per off-line print

Name:	OTISLINE
Description:	OTISLINE is produced for the UK Department of Trade and Industry by PERA-OTIS, the official clearing house for material gathered by a network of science and technology counsellors at British Embassies in the major industrial nations. It consists of summaries of current overseas civil, scientific and technological developments and policies. Loans or photocopies of original documents can also be sent upon request. There is a subscription service for both hard copy and online access.
	Uses: This database could be beneficial to senior technical, commercial and R&D personnel, libraries, universities and colleges and others interested in overseas scientific and technical developments.
	Access to the database is available to British citizens only, and the information must be retained within the UK.
Source:	British Embassies overseas
Years Covered:	1985 onwards
File Size:	Approx 1000 records per annum
Updates:	Daily
Database Producer:	PERA-OTIS
Available From:	Science Reference Library
	Online Search Centre
	£15 per search topic plus
	£1.50-£2.00 per minute connect time and print charges
	PERA-OTIS
	£250 subscription fee per annum plus VAT
	(includes access to source documents)

Name:	PAIS International
Description:	PAIS (Public Affairs Information Service) is a bibliographic index to literature in all fields of social science including political science, banking, public administration, international relations, economics, law, public policy, social welfare, sociology, education and social anthropology. Emphasis is put on factual and statistical information and professional publications in fields such as business, finance, law, education and social work.
Source:	The database contains the records from the 'Public Affairs Information Service Bulletin' and the 'Public Affairs Information Service Foreign Language Index'. Over 1200 English language journals and 8000 non-serial publications, including books and government publications, are indexed each year in the 'Bulletin'. The 'Foreign Language Index' provides references in English to records indexed from French, Italian, Portuguese and Spanish publications
Language:	Multilingual
Years Covered:	1972 to date
File Size:	288436 records
Updates:	Monthly
Database Producer:	Public Affairs Information Service Inc
Available From:	DIALOG File 49
	$75 per connect hour
	30c per on-line type
	40c per off-line print
	SDI profile: $8.95
	BRS File PAIS
	$60 per connect hour
	35c per document printed online (maximum)
	35c per document printed offline (maximum)

SDI profile: $4
Data-Star File PAIS
£43.47 per connect hour
13p per on-line print
8p per off-line print
SDI profile: £3.01

Name:	P/E News
Description:	P/E News (Petroleum/Energy Business News Index) covers current political, social and economic information related to the energy industry. Sixteen core publications are indexed cover-to-cover; included in the sixteen are 'Energy Asia', 'International Petroleum Finance', 'Lundberg Letter', 'Middle East Economic Survey', 'National Petroleum News' and others. Approximately 300 business-oriented items per month from journals covered by API Abstract/Literature are also included in P/E News. API Abstracts is a technical information service run by the Central Abstracting and Indexing Service (CAIS).
Source:	16 core US energy industry publications (see above)
Years Covered:	1975 to date
File Size:	440000 records
Updates:	Weekly
Database Producer:	American Petroleum Institute Central Abstracting and Indexing Service
Available From:	DIALOG

Subscribers: File 897
$96 per connect hour
20c per on-line type
25c per off-line print
Non-subscribers: File 257
$96 per connect hour
30c per on-line type
35c per off-line print
SDI profile: $4.95
ORBIT Search Service File P/E News
Subscribers:
$95 per connect hour
20c per on-line type
25c per off-line print
SDI profile: $3.45
Non-subscribers:
$95 per connect hour
30c per on-line type
35c per off-line print
SDI profile: $4.50
Data-Star File PEAB
£43.47 per connect hour
16p per on-line print
9p per off-line print

Name:	Polis (UK)
Description:	Polis is a system of computer based indexing of parliamentary information developed by Scicon Limited for the House of Commons library under a Central Computer and Telecommunications Agency Contract. Access to the service is available to external users approved by the House of Commons. Two main elements of this service are the Thesaurus service and on-line service. The database is categorised into 8 groups which include Parliamentary Questions, EEC Official Publications, UK Official Publications, Parliamentary Papers, etc.
Source:	Parliamentary, EEC and UK official publications
Years Covered:	Current
File Size:	10000 indexing terms
Updates:	Daily

Database Producer: House of Commons Library (UK)
Available From: Scicon
                     Primeshift:
                     £60 per connect hour
                     (exempt users, eg Central Government Departments)
                     £66 per connect hour (non-exempt)
                     Offpeak:
                     £30 per connect hour (exempt)
                     £33 per connect hour (non-exempt)
                     Other services offered, eg permanent search profile storage, training,
                     Thesaurus sales

Name: PTS Aerospace/Defence Markets & Technology
Description: PTS A/DM&T offers abstracting of more than 100 key defence journals and
                     selective abstracting of defence-related articles from over 2000 additional
                     business and trade journals, newspapers and government reports. Press
                     releases and annual reports of companies in the defence industry are also
                     included. All major defence contracts awarded by the US Department of
                     Defence are included in the A/DM&T database, complete with contract
                     number, award date, contractor, agency, type and dollar amount.
                     Subscribers to the print edition of Aerospace/Defence Markets &
                     Technology may contact Predicasts directly for authorisation to search
                     A/DM&T at a reduced rate.
Source: Over 100 US defence journals, plus over 2000 business and trade journals,
                     government reports issued by the US Department of Defence, and
                     company annual reports
Years Covered: 1982 to date
File Size: 157 349 records
Updates: Daily (Predicasts and DIALOG)
                     Monthly (Data-Star)
Database Producer: Predicasts
Available From: DIALOG File 80 980
                     Subscribers: File 980
                     $111 per connect hour
                     58c per on-line type
                     68c per off-line print
                     Non-subscribers: File 80
                     $150 per connect hour
                     68c per on-line type
                     78c per off-line print
                     SDI profile: $5.45
                     Data-Star File PTDT
                     £68.27 per connect hour
                     31p per on-line print
                     22p per off-line print
                     SDI profile: £2.73
                     Cedocar File DMT
                     FF 630 per connect hour
                     FF 1 per on-line type
                     FF 1.5 per off-line print

Name: PTS New Product Announcements Plus (NPA/Plus)
Description: This database contains press releases issued by companies concerning new
                     products which are coming onto the market, new technologies, new
                     licences, joint ventures and other major corporate events such as mergers
                     and acquisitions. The database offers full unedited text of the press
                     releases, well in advance of them appearing in print publicly. Special
                     emphasis is placed on high-tech and emerging industries although over 60
                     industries are covered in total.
                         NPA/Plus is the first database to combine corporate news releases in full
                     text with highly specific PTS indexing.

Source:	Information comes from over 15 000 companies which include private and public companies, manufacturers, distributors and service companies
Years Covered:	1984 to date
File Size:	68 520 records
Updates:	Weekly
Database Producer:	Predicasts Inc
Available From:	DIALOG File 621
	$126 per connect hour
	80c per on-line type
	$1.90 per off-line print
	SDI profile: $7.95
	Data-Star File PTNP
	£62.76 per connect hour
	34p per on-line print
	55p per off-line print
	SDI profile: £2.73

Name:	Publishers, Distributors and Wholesalers
Description:	Publishers, Distributors and Wholesalers includes complete address information for more than 21 000 Books in Print publishers, 15 000 associations, 400 audiocassette publishers, 7000 software producers, 500 microcomputer hardware manufacturers, 1000 microcomputer peripheral manufacturers, 2500 distributors and 1500 wholesalers. In addition to address information, records contain variant names, publisher affiliations, publisher symbols (a key link to Books in Print), discount information, when present, ISBN prefix, and more.
Source:	Books in Print publishers
Years Covered:	Current
File Size:	54 263 records
Updates:	Monthly reloads
Database Producer:	R R Bowker Company
Available From:	DIALOG File 450
	$66 per connect hour
	20c per on-line type
	30c per off-line print

Name:	Rapra Abstracts
Description:	This database provides coverage of the world's primary database on technical and commercial aspects of the rubber and plastics industries.
	This is a unique source of information covering the world's polymer literature including journals, conference proceedings, books, specifications, reports and trade literature. The database enables users to: Find information on the latest processes
	Research new products
	Report on market changes
	Check on health and safety legislation
	Produce quicker reports
	Keep check on company developments
	A new adhesives file has recently been added as a subfile of Rapra Abstract, due to the growing volume of information in this area.
Source:	Over 450 journals, plus conference papers, standards, books, trade literature and directories
Years Covered:	1972 to date
File Size:	Over 265 000 records
Updates:	Every 2 weeks
	20 000 new records added per annum
Database Producer:	Rapra Technology Ltd
Available From:	ORBIT Search Service File Rapra
	$120 per on-line connect hour
	40c per on-line type
	55c per off-line print
	SDI profile: $8.50

Name: Rapra Trade Names
Description: This database covers all aspects of the rubber and plastics industry. It offers access to over 15 000 trade names and trademarks used in the rubber and polymers industries around the world and provides a useful tool for manufacturers, users and buyers.
Source: Trade literature, journals and books worldwide
Years Covered: 1976 to date
File Size: Approx 25 000 records
Updates: Every 2 weeks
Database Producer: Rapra Technology Ltd
Available From: ORBIT Search Sefvice File Raptn
                       $95 per on-line connect hour
                       35c per on-line type
                       45c per off-line print
                       SDI profile: $8.50

Name: Robomatix
Description: Robomatix is the on-line version of 'Robomatix Reporter'- the unique monthly abstract journal concerned with all aspects of robots, their applications and impacts on society.
                       The following subjects are covered:
                       Business, economics
                       Human factors
                       Special applications
                       Computer aided manufacturing (CAM)
                       Inspection & optics, processes
                       Materials handling
                       Product assembly, transport
                       Artificial intelligence (AI) & planning software
                       Sensors, control, locomotion
                       Mechanical design
Source: Articles, conference papers, market studies, government reports worldwide
Years Covered: 1983 to date
File Size: Approx 10 000 references
Updates: Monthly
                       Approx 100 references added per update
Database Producer: EIC/Intelligence
                       Environment Information Center Inc
Available From: ESA-IRS File 84
                       £74.90 per connect hour
                       23.1p per on-line type
                       35.3p per off-line print
                       SDI profile: £10.50

Name: SAE Global Mobility
Description: SAE Global Mobility provides access to technical papers presented at Society of Automotive Engineers (SAE) meetings and conferences. Papers from the International Federation of Automobile Engineering Societies (FISITA) are also covered. Subject coverage is the technology of automobiles and other self-propelled vehicles, such as spacecraft, missiles, military equipment, trucks, tractors, chain saws, and machine equipment. Topics include vehicle safety, materials and structures, testing and instrumentation.
Source: Equivalent to the publication 'SAE Abstracts'
Years Covered: 1965 to date
File Size: Approx 25 000 records
Updates: SAE: quarterly
                       FISITA: bi-annually
Database Producer: Society of Automotive Engineers Inc

Available From: ORBIT Search Service File SAE Global Mobility
                       $100 per connect hour
                       15c per on-line type
                       30c per off-line print
                       SDI profile: $6.50

Name: Securities Industry
Description: The SI database contains quarterly income statements and balance sheet
                       data aggregated for the securities industries and its various sectors. It also
                       contains capital markets data, including NYSE round-lot activity, member
                       trading, market value and number of issues listed on stock exchanges by
                       type of issue.
Source: Securities and exchange commission
Years Covered: 1976 to date
File Size: 4500 series
Updates: Varies by series
Database Producer: Data Resources (DRI)
                       New York Stock Exchange
                       Securities Industries Association
Available From: Data Resources (DRI)

Name: Securities Law Advance
Description: This database provides the full text of 'Securities Regulation and Law
                       Report'. It includes news from major securities organisations:
                       Securities and Exchange Commission
                       Commodities Futures Trading Commission
                       North American Securities Administration Association
                       National Market System
                       Financial Accounting Standards Board
                       Federal and State courts
Source: Equivalent to the publication 'Securities Regulation
                       and Law Report'
Years Covered: Current 6 months
File Size:
Updates: Weekly (Monday 7am Eastern time)
Database Producer: The Bureau of National Affairs Inc (BNA)
                       Database Publishing Unit
Available From: Dialcom

Name: Shops
Description: The busiest shopping areas in Britain, including both high street shops and
                       out-of-town supermarkets, have been surveyed by specialists at SAMI. For
                       every retail outlet the trading name, address, detailed activity and an
                       approximation of square footage has been recorded.
                            This database can be useful for generating mailing lists, identifying
                       prospects for sales staff and monitoring retail outlets of competitors.
Source:
Years Covered: Current
File Size: Over 200 000 retail outlets
Updates: Monthly
Database Producer: SAMI (Sales and Marketing Information Ltd)
Available From: Pergamon Financial File Shops
                       £70 per connect hour
                       50p per on-line type
                       50p per off-line print

Name: Social Scisearch
Description: This is a multidisciplinary database which indexes items from over 1500
                       main social science journals throughout the world and social sciences
                       articles selected from 3000 additional journals in the natural, physical and
                       biomedical sciences. It also includes important monographs. In addition to
                       more conventional retrieval by title words of phrases, source authors,

	journal names, corporate source etc, it is also possible to search by way of the author's cited references.
Source:	Over 1500 international social science journals
Years Covered:	1972 to date
File Size:	2 288 324 records
Updates:	Monthly (DIALOG)
	Monthly and weekly (DIMDI)
Database Producer:	Institute for Scientific Information
Available From:	DIALOG File 7
	Subscribers:
	$63 per connect hour
	Non-subscribers:
	$120 per connect hour
	46c per on-line type
	46c per off-line print
	SDI profile: $11.95
	BRS File SSCZ (Social Scisearch and Backfile merged)
	Subscribers:
	$50 per connect hour
	Non-subscribers:
	$85 per connect hour
	39c per on-line type
	34c per off-line print
	SDI profile: $4
	DIMDI File IN (monthly updates)
	$26.30 to $49.77 per connect hour
	23c per on-line type
	28c per off-line print
	SDI profile: $4.88
	DIMDI File IP (weekly updates)
	Prices as above
	SDI profile: $4.38

Name:	Spacesoft
Description:	The Spacesoft database describes publicly available computer programs of interest to the aerospace industry and other high-technology sectors.
	In addition to computer program packages developed under the auspices of NASA, a limited number of programs developed by other US government agencies, private concerns and universities is found in the Spacesoft inventory.
	Each record contains a detailed description of the computer program and its capabilities including data on program language, program size, distribution format, the price of the program source code and the supporting program documentation. Each program is checked by Cosmic staff before offered publicly and program source codes are checked to ensure that it is complete and can be implemented on the designated computer. Similarly the supporting program documentation is evaluated. Subject fields include programs related to: aeronautics, chemistry, engineering, computer sciences plus other science related areas.
Source:	Corresponds to 'Cosmic International Catalog of Computer 6Programs'
Years Covered:	1983 to date
File Size:	Over 1000 program records
Updates:	Monthly
Database Producer:	The Computer Software Management and Information Centre (USA) and ESTEC, Dept TI
	Contact Mr Peter Hill (Netherlands)
Available From:	ESA-IRS File 69
	£35 per connect hour
	13.6p per off-line print

Name: Telecommunications
Description: Produced by EIC/Intelligence, Telecommunications is the on-line version of
                       'Telecommunications Abstracts' – the monthly abstract journal concerned
                       with all aspects of telecommunications and related technologies for
                       research and applications.
                           The database covers the following main subject categories:
                       Business and economics
                       Policy and regulation
                       Human factors
                       Speciality applications
                       Telephony
                       Radio and video
                       Optics
                       Satellite
                       Computing
                       Mathematics and analysis
                       Physics, electromagnetics and quantum electronics
                       Circuitry and transmission
                       Communications, network and systems theory
                       Acoustics, optics and video
Source: Worldwide journal articles, conference papers, patents, academic and
                       government reports
                       Corresponds to the monthly publication 'Telecommunications Abstracts'
Years Covered: 1983 to date
File Size: Approx 6500 references
Updates: Approx 100 references per month
Database Producer: EIC/Intelligence
                       Environment Information Center Inc
Available From: ESA-IRS File 108
                       £74.90 per connect hour
                       23.1p per on-line type
                       35.3p per off-line print
                       SDI profile: £10.50

Name: Teledoc
Description: This database provides information in the field of telecommunications,
                       electronic and related fields such as electrical engineering, automation,
                       acoustics, optics, physics, mathematics and computer science.
Source:
Years Covered: Current
File Size:
Updates:
Database Producer: Centre National d'Etudes des Telecommunications (CNET)
Available From: Telesystemes-Questel File Teledoc
                       $80 per connect hour
                       28c per on-line type
                       28c per off-line print
                       SDI profile $13.85

Name: Textil-Wirtschaft
Description: The Textil-Wirtschaft database (TW) is the on-line version of the weekly
                       trade newspaper 'Textil-Wirtschaft'. It provides unabridged news and
                       reports from the entire textile and clothing industry and covers:
                       Textile retail trade
                       Textile wholesale trade/textile buying associations
                       Textile and clothing industry
                       Export trade
                       Chemical fibre industry
                       Raw material markets
                       Companies and personnel
Language: German

Source:	Corresponds to the weekly publication 'Textile Industry'
Years Covered:	
File Size:	January 1987 to date
Updates:	Weekly
Database Producer:	Deutscher Fachverlag GmbH
Available From:	GENIOS File TW
	DM 240 per connect hour
	DM 0.8 per on-line type
	DM 0.8 per off-line print

Name:	Touristic-Information Facts and Abstracts
Description:	This database covers German-language trade literature on the worldwide tourism industry. It covers general tourism, aviation, commerce, geography, industry news, notices of industry meetings, history, tourist attractions and annual statistics for each country. Special features include facts on the climate, communications, medical facilities, customs and tourist regulations
	The German title of this database is 'Touristik Information'.
Language:	English and German
Source:	Edicline's own search
	Earning reports and studies
	Plus the full text of Touristic-Info Service
Years Covered:	1984 to date (current information)
File Size:	7000 records
	4000 records added per annum
Updates:	Twice a month
Database Producer:	Edicline (UK)
Available From:	Edicline File TIFA
	£60 per connect hour

Name:	Transdoc
Description:	The Transdoc database records information on literature and current research projects available on transport economics in ECMT members and associated countries (ie Austria, Belgium, Denmark, Finland, France, F R Germany, Greece, Ireland, Italy, Luxembourg, Netherlands, Norway, Portugal, Spain, Sweden, Switzerland, Turkey, United Kingdom, Yugoslavia, Australia, Canada, Japan, USA).
	Subjects covered:
	Transport systems and economics
	Political, planning, sociological and management aspects
	Inland transport and their links with maritime and air transport (ports, airports)
	Urban, domestic and international transport
	Environment and energy issues, land use and planning
Language:	English, French, German
Source:	Abstracted documents include the European and American major journals, books, conference papers, working documents from administrations, studies, theses and reports. More than 400 organisations provide information on current research projects. Corresponds to the annual publication 'Research on Transport Economics'
Years Covered:	1970 to date
File Size:	23000 references
Updates:	200 references monthly
Database Producer:	European Conference of Ministers of Transport/ Conference Europeene des Ministres des Transports
Available From:	ESA-IRS File 74
	£51.10 per connect hour
	4.9p per on-line type
	18.5p per off-line print
	SDI profile: £4.90

Name:	TRIS
Description:	TRIS (Transportation Research Information Service) provides information on air, highway, rail and maritime transport, moss transit and other transportation modes. Subjects covered are: regulations and legislation, energy, environmental and safety concerns, materials, operations and communications. Records can be retrieved as abstracts or resumes of research projects.
Source:	US Department of Transportation Transportation Research Board
Years Covered:	1968 to date
File Size:	255757 records
Updates:	Monthly
Database Producer:	US Department of Transportation
Available From:	DIALOG File 63 $45 per connect hour 5c per on-line type 15c per off-line print SDI profile: $4.95

Name:	Volkswagenwerk
Description:	This is a mainly German sourced database providing information on the automobile and transportation industries including automobile technology. It covers information on technical, technological, economic and business decisions in the transportation industry and subcontractors to automobile technology (eg plastics, electronics). The type of information available has the following coverage: Automobile technology 27 per cent Economy and business 17 per cent Engines 14 per cent Manufacturing 12 per cent Electrics 10 per cent In-house documents 6 per cent
Language:	German abstracts English and German titles
Source:	60 per cent German, 36 per cent English, 4 per cent other. Over 450 journals, conference papers and research reports
Years Covered:	1971 to date
File Size:	96000 records
Updates:	Monthly 5000-6000 citations are added per annum
Database Producer:	Volkswagen AG
Available From:	Data-Star File VWWW £59.59 per connect hour 22p per on-line print 14p per off-line print SDI profile: £3.27 FIZ Technik File Volkswagen DM 250 per connect hour DM 0.8 per on-line type DM 1.1 per off-line print

Name:	VTB
Description:	VTB is a bibliographic database covering worldwide literature on chemical engineering with emphasis on all engineering applications in the chemical and process industry.
Language:	German
Source:	Journals, reports, books, dissertations, publications from industrial companies
Years Covered:	1966 to date
File Size:	156000 citations (as at Feb 1988)
Updates:	4 times per annum

Database Producer:	Bayer AG, Leverkusen and FIZ Chemie
Available From:	STN File VTB
	£56 per connect hour
	20p per on-line type
	28p per off-line print
	SDI profile: £6.60

Name:	Water Resources Abstracts
Description:	Water Resources Abstracts (WRA) is prepared from materials collected by over 50 water research centers and institutes in the United States. The database covers a wide range of water resource topics including water resource economics, ground and surface water hydrology, metropolitan water resources planning and management and water-related aspects of nuclear radiation and safety. The collection is particularly strong in the literature on water planning (demand, economics, cost allocations), water cycle (precipitation, snow, groundwater, lakes, erosion, etc) and water quality (pollution, waste treatment). WRA covers predominantly English-language materials.
Source:	US water research centres and institutes
	Materials collected from monographs, journal articles, reports, patents and conference proceedings
Years Covered:	1968 to date
File Size:	192 544 records
Updates:	Monthly
Database Producer:	US Department of the Interior
Available From:	DIALOG File 117
	$84 per connect hour
	30c per on-line type
	45c per off-line print

Name:	World Textiles
Description:	World Textiles is the on-line version of 'World Textile Abstracts' and indexes world literature on the science and technology of textile and related materials; on the technical economics, production and management of the textile industry; and on the consumption of and international trade in textile materials and products. World Textiles covers a wide range of textile-related subject matter including:
	Synthesis and properties of all important fibre-forming materials, both polymeric and inorganic, and of chemical materials used to coat or treat textile materials
	Applications of fibrous materials in mechanical and civil engineering, medicine, filtration, inflatables Technical management and economics of production processes
	Production, consumption and international trade data
	Information on pollution, safety and health hazards Company financial performance data is not covered.
Source:	Corresponds to the twice-monthly literature survey periodical 'World Textile Abstracts'. Abstracts are taken from approximately 500 international journals; US and British patents; US, UK and international standards, books, pamphlets, technical reports, conference proceedings and statistical publications
Years Covered:	1970 to date
File Size:	154 519 records
Updates:	Monthly
Database Producer:	Shirley Institute

Available From:	DIALOG File 67
	$55 per connect hour
	5c per on-line type
	10c per off-line print
	ESA-IRS File 176
	Gateway Service to Pergamon
	£70.70 per connect hour
	20.3p per on-line type
	23.1p per off-line print

Name:	ZDE
Description:	ZDE contains citations with abstracts to German and international literature on electrical engineering and electronics. It is the largest German-language database in this area.
	The focus is on power engineering, communications, data processing and measurement and control.
Language:	German
Source:	Journals, conference papers, reports, books
Years Covered:	1968 to date
File Size:	888 000 records
Updates:	Monthly
Database Producer:	Fachinformationszentrum Technik eV
Available From:	FIZ Technik File ZDE
	DM 250 per connect hour
	DM 0.8 per on-line type
	DM 1.1 per off-line print

Section VIII Science and Technology

Chemistry

Agrochemicals Handbook (The)
Analytical Abstracts
Chemical Abstracts
Chemical Abstracts Source Index
Chemical Dictionary
Chemical Exposure
Chemquest
Chemzero
ECDIN Databank
Heilbron
Janssen
KKF
Pestdoc
Ringdoc

Food Science

Foods Adlibra
FSTA
VITIS-VEA

Materials Science/Metals

Aluminium
BIIPAM-CTIF
BNF Metals
CETIM
EMIS
Materials Business
Metadex
Packaging Science and Technology Abstracts
Paperchem
SDIM1
SDIM2
Weldasearch
World Aluminium Abstracts

Medical Science

International Pharmaceutical Abstracts
Medrep (see EEC section)
Pharmaceutical News Index

Technology

Asian Geotechnology
Biomass
Current Technology Index
EABS (see EEC Section)
Eurodicautom (see EEC Section)
Federal Research in Progress
FIESTA
Intime-Manufacturing Automation
Japan Technology
JICST
PASCAL
Supertech
TA
Textile Technology Digest
Titus
Transin
WTI

Name: Agrochemicals Handbook (The)
Description: Agrochemicals Handbook provides information on the active components
                         found in agrochemical products used worldwide. This information
                         provides the identity of substances used in crop protection and pest
                         control. For each of the substances found in the Agrochemicals Handbook
                         the following information is given: chemical names, including synonyms
                         and tradenames, CAS Registry number, molecular formula, molecular
                         weight, manufacturers' names, chemical and physical property, toxicity,
                         mode of action, activity, health and safety and more.
Source:
Years Covered: Current
File Size: 567 active ingredients
Updates: Biannually
Database Producer: The Royal Society of Chemistry
Available From: DIALOG File 306
                         $195 per connect hour
                         $1.25 per on-line type
                         95c per off-line print
                         Data-Star File AGRC
                         £100.94 per connect hour
                         79p per on-line print
                         51p per off-line print
                         SDI profile: £3.13

Name: Aluminum
Description: World Aluminum Abstracts, prepared for the Aluminium Association and
                         the European Primary Aluminium Asociation, is a monthly service
                         covering the world's technical literature on aluminium, from ore processing
                         (exclusive of mining) through to end uses such as transportation and
                         building.
                             Broad subject categories are: aluminium industry: ores, alumina
                         production, extraction; melting, casting, foundry; metalworking,
                         fabrication, finishing; physical and mechanical properties; engineering
                         properties and tests; quality control and tests; end uses.
Source: Worldwide technical literature covering over 1600 scientific and technical
                         journals, patents, government reports and conference papers.
                         Corresponds to the abstract journal 'World Aluminum Abstracts'.
                         20 per cent overlap with Metadex.
Years Covered: 1968 to date
File Size: Approx 138000 references
Updates: Approx 630 references per month
Database Producer: American Society for Metals
Available From: ESA-IRS File 9
                         £49.70 per connect hour
                         8.4p per on-line type
                         17.1p per off-line print
                         SDI profile: £2.80

Name: Analytical Abstracts
Description: Analytical Abstracts is devoted to all aspects of analytical chemistry
                         including any general application, inorganic chemistry, organic chemistry,
                         pharmaceutical chemistry and environmental agriculture. The database
                         contains references from approximately 1300 journals, 300 of which are core
                         journals, as well as information gathered from conference papers, books,
                         standards and technical reports. Information found in a record from
                         Analytical Abstracts includes chemical names, including synonyms and/or
                         tradenames, CAS Registry numbers, matrices information.
Source: Journals, conference papers, books, technical reports
Years Covered: 1980 to date
File Size: 96092 records
Updates: Monthly
Database Producer: The Royal Society of Chemistry

Available From:	DIALOG File 305
	$85 per connect hour
	65c per on-line type
	45c per off-line print
	SDI profile: $7.95
	Data-Star File ANAB
	£55.94 per connect hour
	46p per on-line print
	23p per off-line print
	SDI profile: £2.88

Name:	Asian Geotechnology
Description:	This database is a unique source of information for geotechnical engineering research and applications. While covering worldwide literature, the database focuses on publications originating in Asia which are generally not recorded in any other database.
	Subjects covered:
	Soil mechanics
	Rock mechanics
	Foundation engineering
	Engineering geology
	Earthquake engineering
	Related topics include: highway engineering, soil science, groundwater hydrology.
Source:	Worldwide and particularly Asian publications. Corresponds to the abstract journal 'AGE Digest'.
Years Covered:	1973 to present
File Size:	Approx 32 500 references
Updates:	Approx 2400 references per annum
Database Producer:	The Library and Regional Documentation Center of the Asian Institute of Technology
Available From:	ESA-IRS File 70
	£49.70 per connect hour
	9.1p per on-line type
	19.2p per off-line print
	SDI profile: £4.20

Name:	Biomass
Description:	Biomass is the on-line version of Biomass Abstracts. It contains information on scientific and technical data in all areas of energy. The information service is supported by the following countries: Austria, Canada, Federal Republic of Germany, Finland, Republic of Ireland, Italy, Japan, Norway, Portugal, Sweden, Switzerland, UK, USA and the EEC.
Source:	Journals 47 per cent
	Books 26 per cent
	Reports 20 per cent
	Patents 7 per cent
	29 per cent of citations are conference contributions
Years Covered:	
File Size:	1980 to October 1987: 30 000 citations
Updates:	Every 2 months with approximately 600 citations
Database Producer:	International cooperation coordinated by:
	IEA Biomass Conversion Technical Information Service
	Institute for Industrial Research & Standards
	(Republic of Ireland)
	FIZ Karlsruhe
Available From:	STN File Biomass
	£58 per connect hour
	20p per on-line type
	26p per off-line print
	SDI profile: £3

Name:	BIIPAM-CTIF
Description:	The BIIPAM-CTIF bibliographic database contains references to journal articles (85 per cent) and reports, conference papers, standards and books (15 per cent). Patent references are excluded from the file. BIIPAM contains references to documents in French (50 per cent), English (40 per cent) and German (7 per cent) on metallurgical disciplines in particular as well as other fields within the engineering sciences. CTIF is a subfile especially concerned with foundry matters.

Subjects covered:
Metallurgy, foundry working
Corrosion, coating, materials resistance
Pipes, pipelines, fittings
Control, measurements, testing
Mechanics, automation, regulation
Resources, pollution, antipollution
Engineering organisation, management and security Maintenance, handling
Buildings, public works
Plastics
Power engineering, fluid mechanics, hydraulics

Language:	French, English and German
Source:	Corresponds to abstract journals:

'Bulletin DHS (Diffusion Hebdomadaire Systematique)'
(available from Centre de Recherches de Pont a Mousson)
'Bulletin BBF (Bulletin Bibliographique Fonderie)'
(available from CTIF)
These are sourced from journals, reports, conference
papers, standards and books.

Years Covered:	1970 to date
File Size:	Approx 83 000 references
Updates:	Approx 400 references monthly
Database Producer:	Centre de Recherches de Pont a Mousson
	Service Documentation-Diffusion
	CTIF
	Centre Technique des Industries de la Fonderie
Available From:	ESA-IRS File 71
	£49 per connect hour
	13.3p per on-line type
	22p per off-line print
	SDI profile: £7.70

Name:	BNF Metals
Description:	BNF Metals is the machine-readable form of the publication 'BNF Non-Ferrous Metal Abstracts'. The file contains any kind of information required by metallurgists, engineers, technologists and materials scientists.

Subjects covered include properties, processing and uses of non-ferrous metals together with economic and environmental information relating to the non-ferrous metals industry.
Subjects covered:
Extrusion, rolling, melting and casting, metal finishing, corrosion, extraction
Metallurgy
Economics and marketing
Process, control, analysis
Environment

Language:	English, French, German, Italian, Japanese, Russian
Source:	Approximately 400 serials are scanned. Selected British patents, statistical and government publications, new books, technical and conference reports, trade literature standards
Years Covered:	1961 to date
File Size:	Approx 112 500 records
Updates:	Approx 500 records per month

Database Producer: British Non-Ferrous Metals Technology Centre
Available From: ESA-IRS File 34
£49.70 per connect hour
17.1p per off-line print

Name: CETIM
Description: The CETIM database is the machine version of the 'Bulletin de la Construction Mecanique'. It is intended to provide selected information useful to the mechanical industry with emphasis on technology. Main areas covered are the general problems of firms, materials, tests and measurements, control, regulation, automation, metal machining and forming, surface treatments and coatings, thermal treatments, welding, mechanical joints, adhesive bonding, friction, wear, lubrication, machine parts, plastics, equipment, CETIM reports.
Language: French
Source: Corresponds to the monthly publication Bulletin de la Construction Mecanique
Includes CETIM reports
Years Covered: 1975 to date
File Size: Approx 85000 references
Updates: Approx 500 references per month
Database Producer: Centre Technique des Industries Mecaniques
Available From: ESA-IRS File 54
£49 per connect hour
7.7p per on-line type
16.4p per off-line print
SDI profile: £7

Name: Chemical Abstracts
Description: This database provides worldwide coverage of the chemical sciences literature from over 12000 journals, patents from 26 countries, new books, conference proceedings and government research reports. Coverage corresponds to the printed 'Chemical Abstracts Indexes', including 80 main subject sections, such as biochemistry, organic chemistry, macromolecular chemistry, applied chemistry and chemical engineering, and physical and analytical chemistry. There are special searching features from Chemical Abstracts Subject Index Alert, such as Registry Numbers, and molecular formulae.
   See also the companion file, Chemical Dictionary. CASREACT is a new service covering information on reactions of organic substances. This will be available in the second quarter of 1988 via STN and other hosts (to be announced).
Source: Equivalent to the publications:
'Chemical Abstracts, 8th, 9th, 10th, 11th Collective Indexes'
Years Covered: ORBIT Search Service – CAS82: 1982 to date
CAS77: 1977-81
CAS72: 1972-76
CAS67: 1967-71
Other hosts: 1967 to date
File Size: ORBIT Search Service – CAS82: approx 2.3m records
CAS77: approx 2.2m records
CAS72: approx 1.8m records
CAS67: approx 1.3m records
DIALOG: approx 8.1m records
Other hosts: approx 8.0m records
Updates: CAS82: twice a month (ORBIT)
twice a month (other hosts)
Database Producer: 'Chemical Abstracts'
American Chemical Society

Available From:	ORBIT Search Service
	Files CAS82, CAS77, CAS7276, CAS6771
	$102 per connect hour
	33c per on-line type
	44c per off-line print
	SDI profile: $8.50
	Search terms (excluding IRN): 12c per term
	Extracted prints: 3c record selected
	Telesystemes-Questel File CAS
	$105 per on-line connect hour
	38c per on-line type
	50c per off-line print
	10c per search term
	SDI profile: $7 plus print charges
	ESA-IRS File 2
	£67.20 per on-line connect hour
	22.4p per on-line type
	32.5p per off-line print
	SDI profile: £3.50
	Data-Star File CHEM
	£62.20 per connect hour
	18p per on-line print
	19p per off-line print
	SDI profile: £3.29
	BRS CA Search (CHEM) Backfile (CHEB)
	$89 per connect hour
	50c per on-line type
	50c per off-line print
	SDI profile: $4
	DIALOG Files 399, 308, 309, 310, 311, 312
	(CA Search)
	$105 per connect hour
	33c per on-line type
	46c per off-line print
	SDI profile: files 312, 399 $11.95
	STN File CA
	Subscriber:
	£53 per connect hour
	40p per on-line type
	46p per off-line print
	SDI profile: £3.40
	Non-subscriber:
	£60 per connect hour
	59p per on-line type
	65p per off-line print
	SDI profile: £3.97
Name:	Chemical Abstracts Source Index
Description:	This index (CASSI) is a compilation of bibliographic and library holdings information for scientific and technical primary literature relevant to the chemical sciences. The titles listed in CASSI are from several sources: publication and bibliographic information from over 70 years of 'Chemical Abstracts'; about 700 important biological journal titles monitored by the Bio-Sciences Information Services (BIOSIS); several hundred titles published in Beilstein before 1907; and several hundred titles covering pure and theoretical chemical literature from 1830 through 1940 from Chemisches Zentralblatt.
Source:	Equivalent to the printed publications:
	'Chemical Abstracts'
	'Service Source Index'
Years Covered:	1900 to date
File Size:	Over 63 000 records

Updates:	Quarterly
Database Producer:	Chemical Abstracts
	Service of the American Chemical Society
Available From:	ORBIT Search Service File CASSI
	$120 per connect hour
	38c per on-line type
	50c per off-line print
	SDI profile: $9.50
	Search terms (excluding IRN): 12c per term
	Extracted prints 3c per record selected

Name:	Chemical Dictionary
Description:	These are companion files to the Chemical Abstracts databases. They contain all compounds cited in the literature from 1972 to date. Each record contains a Registry Number, the molecular formula, Chemical Abstracts' rigorous nomenclature for a specific compound, and many common synonyms recognised by Chemical Abstracts Service. The Registry Numbers retrieved are then used as search terms in the CAS82, CAS77, CAS72 and CAS67 files.
	Chemical Dictionary (Chemdex) can be searched by chemical name or fragment, molecular formula, molecular formula fragment, or group or row with a periodic chart.
Source:	Equivalent to publications:
	'CA Substance Index'
	'CA Registry Handbook'
	'CA Index Guide'
	'CA Formula Index'
Years Covered:	1972 to date
File Size:	Over 7 million records
Updates:	Quarterly
Database Producer:	Chemical Abstracts
	Service of the American Society
Available From:	ORBIT Search Service
	File Chemdex, Chemdex 2, Chemdex 3, Chemdex 4
	$172 per connect hour
	35c per on-line type
	47c per off-line print

Name:	Chemical Exposure
Description:	Chemical Exposure is a comprehensive database of chemicals that have been identified in both human tissues and body fluids and in feral and food animals. It contains references to selected journal articles, conferences and reports, and spans the range of bodyburden information – information related to human and animal exposure to food, air and water contaminants and pharmaceuticals. Toxic chemicals and other substances can be traced to evaluate their effects. Records from this database include information on chemical properties, synonyms, CAS Registry numbers, formulas, tissue measured, analytical method used, demographics, keywords and more.
Source:	American industry journals, conferences and reports
Years Covered:	1974 to date
File Size:	25607 records
Updates:	Annual
Database Producer:	Science Applications International Corporation
Available From:	DIALOG File 138
	$45 per connect hour
	15c per off-line print

Name:	ChemQuest
Description:	This is a comprehensive, automated catalogue of commercially available research chemicals and where they can be obtained. ChemQuest covers over 60000 commercially important compounds including organics, inorganics, biochemicals, dyes and stains. ChemQuest is an easy-to-use

database that does not require any special chemical and indexing knowledge. Compounds are identified and searched by name, molecular formula and synonyms. Each record gives the source of availability, identification and purity.

Source:	
Years Covered:	Current
File Size:	Over 206 500 catalogue entries referring to over 60 000 substances
Updates:	Periodically
Database Producer:	PergaBase Inc
Available From:	ORBIT Search Service and Pergamon Financial Data Services File ChemQuest
	$115 per connect hour
	35c per on-line type
	50c per off-line print

Name:	Chemzero
Description:	Chemzero is a non-bibliographic, dictionary file containing those chemical substances for which there are no citations in the CA Search files. This enables the chemical searcher to obtain CAS Registry numbers, synonyms and additional information on the many chemical substances registered by the Chemical Abstracts Service but not indexed in the documents covered by CA Search. For each substance listed, the CAS Registry number, molecular formula, CA Substance Index name for the 8th or 9th collective Index Period, and available synonyms are given. In addition, complete ring data are included for each substance. The purpose of the file is to support specific substance searching and substructure searching via nomenclature in the DIALOG chemical files.
Source:	Chemical Abstracts Services (USA)
Years Covered:	1965 to date
File Size:	1 639 514 substances
Updates:	Monthly
Database Producer:	DIALOG Information Services Inc
	Chemical Abstracts Service (USA)
Available From:	DIALOG File 300
	$178 per connect hour
	33c per on-line type
	46c per off-line print

Name:	Current Technology Index
Description:	Current Technology Index (CTI) provides an index to current periodicals from all fields of modern technology. All journals indexed are published in the United Kingdom. The journal articles include aspects of technology on a worldwide basis. Subjects covered include, but are not limited to, the following: acoustic engineering, architecture, aircraft engineering, building, chemical engineering, fishing, mining, food industry, packaging, printing, papermaking, and space science.
Source:	UK technology periodicals
Years Covered:	1981 to date
File Size:	115 662 records
Updates:	Monthly
Database Producer:	Library Association Publishing Ltd
Available From:	DIALOG File 142
	$69 per connect hour
	25c per on-line type
	25c per off-line print

Name:	ECDIN Data Bank
Description:	ECDIN (Environmental Chemicals Data and Information Network) is a chemistry database. It is created in the framework of the Environmental Research Programme of the Joint Research Center of the Commission of the European Communities at the Ispra establishment (Italy). It is designed to be an instrument which will enable people engaged in environmental

management and research to obtain reliable information on chemical products. It contains identifications for over 60 000 compounds. The database is based on the use of the ADABAS database management system.

Source:	Various including research institutes in Europe (plus one in the USA), original publications, DAS, European Customs Union
Years Covered:	Current
File Size:	65 000 compounds – substance identity information
	350 000 chemical names
	50 000 chemical structures
Updates:	
Database Producer:	CEC Joint Research Centre
	Ispra Establishment
Available From:	Datacentralen
	DK 510 per connect hour
	Based on:
	DK 10 per minute for the first 15 minutes
	DK 8 per minute for time beyond the first 15 minutes
	DK 2 per off-line print
	Joint Research Centre
	Ispra Establishment
	Contact direct for prices and access details

Name:	EMIS
Description:	EMIS provides a compilation of the latest published data on the properties of materials important in the fields of microelectronics and solid-state research.

The properties of silicon, gallium arsenide, indium phospide, lithium niobate and quartz are covered in depth, and supplemented by significant data for over 90 other materials.

Each EMIS record contains numeric data and associated text for one property of one material. There are four record types:

Original data

These full-text records contain data contributed by research workers reporting their findings for the first time.

Datareview

These are reviews of the most up-to-date data available specially written for EMIS and referred by leading scientists. These short full-text articles include the bibliographic source details for all the data reviewed.

Literature derived

Compiled from journal articles and published conference papers, these records contain data and associated text describing the material preparation and measurement technique used to obtain the data. More than 3000 serials are regularly scanned for new data.

Handbook type

These records contain data obtained from a variety of published sources.

Source:	Various published sources and research reports
Years Covered:	1982 to date
File Size:	Approx 10 500 records
Updates:	Monthly
Database Producer:	INSPEC (Institution of Electrical Engineers)
	EMIS User Manual contains codes which are essential for searching EMIS. This is available from INSPEC Centres in the UK or USA
Available From:	ESA-IRS File 105
	£56.70 per connect hour
	Use: ?NOTES105 on line for print charge details
	Extra charges are format dependant

Name:	Federal Research in Progress
Description:	The Federal Research in Progress (FEDRIP) database provides access to information about ongoing federally-funded research projects in the fields of physical sciences, engineering and life sciences; research information is provided to NTIS by the sponsoring US government agencies. All records in the database include title, principal investigator, performing organisation and sponsoring organisation. Most records also include a description of the research, although the exact record content varies according to the sponsoring agency.
	DIALOG File 265 (abridged) available worldwide;
	DIALOG File 266 (unabridged – includes US Dept of Energy (DOE) and NASA records not in File 265); available only in the US.
Source:	US government agencies
Years Covered:	Current
File Size:	134 096 records
Updates:	Biannual reloads
Database Producer:	National Technical Information Service (NTIS)
Available From:	DIALOG File 265 266
	$48 per connect hour
	20c per on-line type
	20c per off-line print

Name:	FIESTA
Description:	FIESTA is a bibliographic database which covers the following subjects: aeronautic, arms, electronics, navigation, telecommunications, nuclear science and technology, missile technology plus many other related areas.
Language:	French
Source:	Worldwide literature, reports, theses, serial publications, etc
Years Covered:	1972 to date
File Size:	30 000 references added per annum
Updates:	Every 2 weeks
Database Producer:	Centre de Documentation de l'Armement
Available From:	Cedocar File FIESTA
	FF 140 per connect hour
	FF 1 per on-line type
	FF 1 per off-line print

Name:	Foods Adlibra
Description:	Foods Adlibra contains up-to-date information on the latest developments in food technology and packaging. All new food products introduced since 1974 are covered, and nutritional and toxicology information is also included. Foods Adlibra provides information on every sector of the food industry including retailers, processors, brokers, equipment suppliers, gourmet food importers, as well as general company and food association news. Foods Adlibra provides a resource for information on government guidelines and regulations on the processing and packaging of foods. Marketing and management news, statistics and information on world food economics can also be found in this file.
Source:	Over 250 USA trade periodicals
	Over 500 USA technical research journals
Years Covered:	1974 to date
File Size:	144 391 records
Updates:	Monthly
Database Producer:	General Mills, Foods Adlibra Publications
Available From:	DIALOG File 79
	$63 per connect hour
	10c per on-line type
	15c per off-line print

Name:	FSTA
Description:	Food Science and Technology Abstracts (FSTA) is the online version of the monthly journal with the same name. It contains about 1700 abstracts per issue, taken from an annual coverage of 1800 journals, plus patents, books and reviews in over 40 languages.
	It covers the entire field of food science and technology.
Language:	English. Foreign titles are translated and included in brackets. Original titles are added in the case of German publications or book references
Source:	International sources include patents, books, standards, conference proceedings, reports and reviews
Years Covered:	1969 to date
File Size:	Approx 400 000 records (ORBIT)
	Approx 350 902 records (DIALOG)
Updates:	Monthly
	Approx 1700 references added per month
Database Producer:	International Food Information Service (IFIS GmbH)
Available From:	ORBIT Search Service File FSTA
	$80 per connect hour
	25c per on-line type
	25c per off-line print
	SDI profile: $4.95
	Data-Star File FSTA
	£48.98 per connect hour
	13p per on-line print
	6p per off-line print
	SDI profile: £2.18
	DIALOG File 51
	$81 per connect hour
	30c per on-line type
	30c per off-line print
	SDI profile: $5.95
	DIMDI File FSTA
	$55.30 to $78.77 per connect hour
	15c per on-line type
	20c per off-line print
	SDI profile: $3.88
	ESA-IRS File 251
	£52.50 per connect hour
	14p per on-line type
	19.9p per off-line print
	SDI profile: £4.20
	CISTI
	JICST
	IFIS provides the following services:
	FSTA monthly journal
	IBM magnetic tape
	FSTA Reference Series (Thesauri, manuals, bibliographies)
	Current awareness services
	Retrospective searches
	Photocopy service
Name:	Heilbron
Description:	Heilbron represents the complete text of two major chemical dictionaries from Chapman & Hall Ltd: 'Dictionary of Organic Compounds' (fifth edition) and 'Dictionary of Organometallic Compounds'. Heilbron is a source database of chemical identification, physical-chemical properties, use, hazard, and key reference data to the world's more important chemical substances, as selected by a panel of experts. Heilbron provides chemical substance identification through searching physical and/or chemical properties, compound variants, derivative names, synonyms, CAS Registry numbers, molecular formulae and molecular weight, source

statements, use/importance data, melting point, freezing point, boiling point, solubility, relative density, optical rotation and dissociation constants.

Source:	'Dictionary of Organic Compounds'
	'Dictionary of Organometallic Compounds'
	Plus other source books
Years Covered:	Current
File Size:	196 370 records
Updates:	Twice a year
Database Producer:	Chapman & Hall Ltd
Available From:	DIALOG File 303
	$95 per connect hour
	65c per on-line type
	85c per off-line print

Name:	International Pharmaceutical Abstracts
Description:	International Pharmaceutical Abstracts (IPA) provides information on all phases of the development and use of drugs and on professional pharmaceutical practice. The IPA database is growing at a rate of 7000 citations per year indexed and abstracted from more than 500 pharmaceutical, medical and related journals. In early 1985 coverage was expanded to include state pharmacy journals which deal with state regulations, salaries, guidelines, manpower studies, laws and more. The scope of the database ranges from the clinical, practical, and theoretical to the economic and scientific aspects of the literature. A unique feature of abstracts reporting clinical studies is the inclusion of the study design, number of patients, dosage, dosage forms and dosage schedule.
Source:	Over 500 industry journals
Years Covered:	1970 to present
File Size:	137 993 records (DIALOG)
	142 500 records (ESA-IRS)
Updates:	Monthly
Database Producer:	American Society of Hospital Pharmacists
Available From:	DIALOG File 74
	$69 per connect hour
	27c per on-line type
	38c per off-line print
	SDI profile: $6.95
	BRS File IPAB
	$45 per connect hour
	45c per on-line type
	45c per off-line print
	SDI profile: $4
	ESA-IRS File 102
	£43.40 per connect hour
	11.9p per on-line type
	24.8p per off-line print
	SDI profile: £4.20

Name:	Intime – Manufacturing Automation
Description:	Intime is designed to cover manufacturing processes and applications together with relevant automation aspects. Subjects covered include: manufacturing processes including deburring, grinding, milling, boring, forming, shaping, cutting, welding, finishing processes, industrial robotics, use of computers in manufacturing, cost estimating and management aspects in the manufacturing area.
Source:	Articles from the Society's publications: 'Manufacturing engineering', 'Robotics today'; SME Technical papers; proceedings and transactions of SME conferences; books; videotapes
Years Covered:	1979 to present
File Size:	Approx 11 000 references
Updates:	Approx 250 references per quarter

Database Producer: Society of Manufacturing Engineers
Available From: ESA-IRS File 79
                     Contact direct for price details

Name: Janssen
Description: This is an on-line catalogue of chemical products from Janssen Chimica.
                     Online ordering of products is available.
Source: Janssen Chimica
Years Covered: Current
File Size:
Updates:
Database Producer: Janssen Chimica
Available From: Telesystemes-Questel File Janssen
                     $65 per connect hour
                     30c per on-line type
                     40c per off-line print
                     Janssen
                     $65 per connect hour
                     30c per on-line type
                     40c per off-line print

Name: Japan Technology
Description: Japan Technology corresponds to the printed 'Japanese Technical
                     Abastracts'. It contains abstracts from the major Japanese journals in
                     technology, applied sciences, engineering and business management as
                     well as articles by Japanese authors published in journals outside Japan.
                     Coverage includes journals as well as governmental, commercial, and
                     society research reports. Major subject areas covered include: aerodynamic
                     engineering, automotive engineering, biological sciences, energy and
                     power, chemistry, medicine, physics, metallurgy and transportation.
Source: Approx 600 periodicals and journals
Years Covered: Jan 1986 to date
File Size: 108374 records
Updates: Monthly
Database Producer: University Microfilms International
Available From: DIALOG File 972 (subscribers)
                     File 582 (non-subscribers)
                     Subscribers:
                     $90 per connect hour
                     55c per on-line type
                     75c per off-line print
                     Non-subscribers
                     $120 per connect hour
                     80c per on-line type
                     95c per off-line print
                     SDI profile: $9.95

Name: JICST
Description: The Japan Information Centre for Science and Technology is one of the
                     most comprehensive service centres of scientific and technological
                     information in Japan. It compiles a number of database files. These include:
                     JICST file on science and technology (now available in English)
                     JICST file on medical science in Japan (covers Japanese journals not in
                     Medline)
                     JICST file on current science and technology research in Japan
                     JICST file on government reports
                     These provide comprehensive coverage of Japanese science and technology
                     periodicals available. Other relevant files include NIKKAN KOGYO file,
                     which covers articles from the newspaper 'Nikkan Kogyo Shinbun' on new
                     technological developments and industrial trends.
Source: Specialist periodicals plus the newspaper
                     'Nikkan Kogyo Shinbun'

Years Covered:	1975 to date – Japanese language files
	1983 to date – Government reports file
	1985 to date – JICST (English version)
File Size:	Sourced from over 6000 periodicals
Updates:	Every 2 weeks
Database Producer:	JICST
Available From:	British Library
	Japanese Information Service
	£3.50 per minute connect time plus VAT
	Charge includes a maximum of half an hour linguistic help
	Sales Agents for JICST online service, English language version:
	National Technical Information Service (NTIS) (USA)
	Centre Documentation Scientifique Technique (CDST)
	(France)
	Microinfo Ltd (UK)
	(English language file only available on STN)
	Data Communication Corp (DACOM) (Korea)

Name:	KKF
Description:	KKF (Kunstoffe Kautschuk Fasern) is a plastics and rubber fibres database. It covers German and international scientific and technical literature on the production, processing, applications and technological properties of plastics, and the fundamental physical and chemical properties of polymers. Titles of publications are in German and English. Records added since 1979 include abstracts in German.
Language:	German and English
Source:	96 per cent journals
Years Covered:	1973 to date
File Size:	176 000 citations (May 1988)
Updates:	Monthly
	Approx 1000 citations added per update
Database Producer:	DKI-(Deutsches Kunststoff-Institut), Darmstadt and FIZ Chemie
Available From:	STN File KKF
	£66 per connect hour
	23p per on-line type
	40p per off-line print
	SDI profile: £4.95
	FIZ Technik File DKI
	DM 250 per connect hour
	DM 0.8 per on-line type
	DM 1.1 per off-line print
	SDI profile: DM 10

Name:	Materials Business
Description:	Materials Business File covers technical and commercial developments in iron and steel, non-ferrous metals, composites, plastics, etc. Over 1300 publications including magazines, trade publications, financial reports, dissertations and conference proceedings are reviewed for inclusion. Subjects covered are grouped into 9 categories: (1) Fuel, energy usage, raw materials, recycling; (2) Plant developments and descriptions; (3) Engineering, control and testing, machinery; (4) Environmental issues, waste treatment, health and safety; (5) Product and process development; (6) Applications, competitive materials, substitution; (7) Management, training, regulations, marketing; (8) Economics, statistics, resources, and reserves; and (9) World industry news, company information and general issues.
Source:	Over 1300 specialist publications
Years Covered:	1985 to present
File Size:	29 780 records (DIALOG)
	36 000 records (ESA-IRS)
	Over 33 000 (ORBIT)

Updates:	Monthly
Database Producer:	American Society for Metals (ASM International)
Available From:	DIALOG File 269
	$90 per connect hour
	40c per on-line type
	45c per off-line print
	ESA-IRS File 111
	£53.20 per connect hour
	16.1p per on-line type
	26.2p per off-line print
	SDI profile: £4.20
	ORBIT Search Service File Materials/B
	$90 per connect hour
	40c per on-line type
	45c per off-line print
	SDI profile: $8
	Data-Star File MBUS
	£50.08 per connect hour
	11p per on-line print
	8p per off-line print
	SDI profile: £2.73
	Cedocar File MATBUS
	FF 575 per connect hour
	FF 1.4 per on-line type
	FF 2.0 per off-line print

Name:	METADEX
Description:	The METADEX database, produced by the American Society for Metals (ASM) and The Metals Society (London), provides the most comprehensive coverage of international literature on the science and practice of metallurgy. Included in this database are 'Review of Metal Literature (1966-67)', 'Metals Abstracts (1968 to present)' and 'Alloys Index (1974 to present)'. The 'Steels Supplement to Metals Abstracts' was added in 1983. 'Metals Abstracts' includes about 30 000 citations each year from about 1100 primary journal sources. 'Alloys Index' supplements 'Metals Abstracts' by providing access to the citations through commercial, numerical, ?and compositional alloy designations; specific metallic systems; and intermetallic compounds found within these systems. The 'Steels Supplement' covers information on steel production, fabrication, and use, and development of value to steel-producing and steel-using industries. In addition to specialised topics (including specific alloy designations, intermetallic compounds, and metallurgical systems), 6 basic categories of metallurgy are covered: materials, processes, properties, products, forms, and influencing factors. Sources are international in scope, including the USSR and Eastern European nations among the 43 countries covered.
Source:	International literature covering metallurgy including conference papers, technicals reports, books and reviews
Years Covered:	1966 to present
	Alloys Index 1974 to present
	Steels Supplement 1983 to present
File Size:	Over 721 000 records
Updates:	Monthly
Database Producer:	American Society for Metals (USA)
	The Metals Society (UK)
Available From:	DIALOG File 32
	$90 per connect hour
	40c per on-line type
	45c per off-line print
	SDI profile: $10.95
	ESA-IRS File 3
	£56.70 per connect hour
	15.4p per on-line type

26.2p per off-line print
SDI profile: £4.20
ORBIT Search Service File Metadex
$90 per connect hour
40c per on-line type
45c per off-line print
SDI profile: $8
Cedocar
FF 575 per connect hour
FF 1.4 per on-line type
FF 2.0 per off-line print
STN File Metadex
£55 per connect hour
25p per on-line type
28p per off-line print
SDI profile: £3

Name:	Packaging Science and Technology Abstracts
Description:	Packaging Science and Technology Abstracts (PSTA) provides access to research and development literature in all aspects of packaging science including materials, equipment, packs, transport, storage and testing. PSTA provides indexing to over 400 journals, plus a wide range of sources.
Language:	English and German. All abstracts are in English. German publications have an additional German abstract
Source:	Journals, books, reports, pamphlets, conference proceedings, standards, patents and legislation
Years Covered:	1982 to present
File Size:	Approx 17 059 records (DIALOG) 20 000 records (ESA-IRS) (as of June 1988), including abstracts from International Packaging Abstracts (IPA)
Updates:	Monthly
Database Producer:	International Food Information Service (IFIS GmbH) in cooperation with the Fraunhofer Institut fur Lebensmitteltechnologie und Verpackung (ILV)
Available From:	DIALOG File 252 $81 per connect hour 30c per on-line type 30c per off-line print ESA-IRS File 55 £52.50 per connect hour 14.0p per on-line type 19.9p per off-line print SDI profile: £4.20 DIMDI File PSTA $55.30 to $78.77 per connect hour 15c per on-line type 20c per off-line print SDI profile: $3.88

Name:	Paperchem
Description:	The Paperchem database indexes and abstracts scientific and technical literature dealing with raw materials, principles, processes, technology, and products of the pulp and paper industry. Related subjects such as packaging; graphic arts; forestry and silviculture; the chemistry of carbohydrates, cellulose, hemicelluloses, lignin, and wood extractives; and machinery and equipment are also included. About 50 per cent of Paperchem records are for patent information. Members of the Institute of Paper Chemistry receive a reduced rate when searching Paperchem on DIALOG (File 840).

Source:	US scientific and technical literature
	Corresponds to the publication 'Abstract Bulletin of the Institute of Paper Chemistry'
Years Covered:	July 1967 to date
File Size:	250 090 records
Updates:	Monthly
Database Producer:	Institute of Paper Chemistry
Available From:	DIALOG
	Subscribers: File 840
	$63 per connect hour
	15c per on-line type
	25c per off-line print
	Non-subscribers: File 240
	$87 per connect hour
	25c per on-line type
	35c per off-line print

Name:	PASCAL
Description:	PASCAL is a multidisciplinary database equivalent to the 79 printed Pascal journals. Literature from international sources is indexed and abstracted. Some patents are included in the area of biotechnology. Major subjects covered include: life sciences, biology and medicine; chemistry, applied chemistry and pollution; energy; metallurgy, mechanical and civil engineering; transportation; food and agricultural sciences; earth sciences; physics and space sciences; and computer sciences and engineering. About 50 per cent of the records have abstracts. Records added from 1977 have Spanish keywords.
Language:	French, English and Spanish
Source:	Corresponds to Pascal journals
	International sources include journals, doctoral and masters theses, reports, books and conference proceedings
Years Covered:	1973 to date
File Size:	6 770 000 records
Updates:	Monthly
Database Producer:	Centre de Documetation Scientifique et Technique
	Centre National de la Recherche Scientifique (CNRS)
Available From:	DIALOG File 144
	Prices to be announced
	ESA-IRS File 14
	£40.60 per connect hour
	21.7p per on-line type
	30.4p per off-line print
	SDI profile: £4.90
	Telesystemes-Questel File PASCAL
	$85 per connect hour
	50c per on-line type
	50c per off-line print
	SDI profile: $11.50 plus print charges

Name:	Pestdoc
Description:	Pestdoc covers worldwide literature on pesticides, herbicides and plant protection designed specifically for the information requirements of manufacturers of agricultural chemicals, exclusive of fertilisers. It covers analysis, biochemistry, chemistry, toxicology, insecticides, herbicides, fungicides, molluscicides and rodenticides. On-line access is limited to Pestdoc subscribers.
Source:	Equivalent to the 'Pestdoc Abstract Journal'
	Sources include journal articles, conference proceedings and research reports

Years Covered:	Pestdoc: journal literature 1968-84
	Pestdoc II: conference proceedings, research reports 1975-84
	Pestdoc UDB: all sources, 1985 to date
	Pestdoc II UDB: conference reports, current
File Size:	Over 185 000 records
Updates:	Quarterly
Database Producer:	Derwent Publications Ltd
Available From:	ORBIT Search Service
	Files Pestdoc, Pest2, Pestdoc UDB, Pestdoc II UDB
	Subscribers:
	$50 per connect hour
	20c per off-line print
	SDI profile: $7

Name:	Pharmaceutical News Index
Description:	Pharmaceutical News Index (PNI) is the on-line source of current news about pharmaceuticals, cosmetics, medical devices and related health fields. PNI records are taken from a wide range of American specialist publications. PNI cites and indexes all articles from these publications on drugs; corporation and industry sales, mergers, acquisitions; government legislation, regulations and court actions; and requests for proposals, research grant applications, industry speeches, press releases and other news items.
Source:	US pharmaceutical and medical publications including FDC reports, 'SCRIP World Pharmaceutical News', 'Weekly Pharmacy Reports' and 'Clinical World Medical Device News'
Years Covered:	1974 to date
File Size:	225 736 records
Updates:	Monthly
Database Producer:	UMI/Data Courier
Available From:	DIALOG File 42
	$139 per connect hour
	60c per on-line type
	73c per off-line print
	SDI profile: $11.95

Name:	Ringdoc
Description:	Ringdoc covers worldwide pharmaceutical literature, specifically designed to meet the information needs of pharmaceutical manufacturers. It covers all aspects of drugs, including analysis, biochemistry, chemistry, endocrinology, microbiology, nutrition, pharmacology, side-effects and therapeutics. On-line access is restricted to Ringdoc subscribers. See also companion file: 'Standard Drug File', also available from Pergamon.
Source:	Equivalent to 'Ringdoc Abstract Journal'
	Source materials are primarily journal articles
Years Covered:	Pergamon files:
	RING6475: 1964-75
	RINGDOC: 1976-82
	RINGDOC UDB: 1983 to date
File Size:	Approx 1.2 million records
Updates:	Monthly
Database Producer:	Derwent Publications Ltd
Available From:	ORBIT Search Service Files Ringdoc
	Ringdoc 6475
	Ringdoc UBD
	$50 per connect hour
	20c per off-line print
	SDI profile: $7

Name:	SDIM1
Description:	System for Documentation and Information in Metallurgy, Part 1 (SDIM1) is a database on metallurgy and metallic materials and has the same scope as SDIM2, the follow-up database. The abstracts are available on microfiches.
Language:	German, English and French
Source:	Abstracts from specialist industry journals and documents
Years Covered:	1972 to 1979
File Size:	177000 citations
Updates:	Annual
Database Producer:	Fachinformationszentrum Werkstoffe eV in cooperation with the Commission of the European Communities
Available From:	FIZ Karlsruhe File SDIM1
	DM 195.0 per connect hour
	DM 0.6 per on-line type
	DM 0.8 per off-line print

Name:	SDIM2
Description:	SDIM2 is the continuation to SDIM1 and permits accurate searching for alloys as alloys indexing has become standardised. An alloy can be searched by its alloying elements and also by data on the alloying elements content. Abstracts are available in one of three languages.
Language:	German, English and French
Source:	Over 800 specialist industry journals and series
Years Covered:	1979 to date
File Size:	135700 citations
	36000 items added per annum
Updates:	Annual
Database Producer:	Fachinformationszentrum Werkstoffe eV in cooperation with 'La Centre Nationale de la Recherche Scientifique (CNRS)', Paris
Available From:	FIZ Karlsruhe File SDIM2
	DM 195 per connect hour
	DM 0.75 per on-line type
	DM 0.95 per off-line print
	SDI profile: DM 9.2

Name:	Supertech
Description:	Supertech consists of 5 subfiles with information related to fields of biotechnology, artificial intelligence, computer-aided design/computer-aided manufacturing (CAD/CAM), robotics and telecommunications. References in Supertech are drawn from more than 9000 worldwide sources including trade, scientific, legal and policy journals; professional and technological conferences; university monographs; US government agency reports and white papers; and independent laboratory studies.
Source:	The database corresponds to the monthly abstract journals: 'Telgen Reporter', 'Artificial Intelligence Abstracts', 'CAD/CAM Abstracts', 'Robomatix Reporter' and 'Telecommunications Abstracts'
Years Covered:	1973 to date (robotics and biotechnology)
	1984 to date (artificial intelligence, CAD/CAM and Telecommunications)
File Size:	44935 records
Updates:	Monthly
Database Producer:	EIC/Intelligence Inc
Available From:	DIALOG File 238
	$120 per connect hour
	45c per on-line type
	45c per off-line print
	SDI profile: $7.95

Name: TA
Description: The Technology Assessment database contains information on projects,
                                institutions and publications on technology assessment. It consists of 3
                                files, a project file, an institution file and a publication file. The literature
                                section contains publications of projects plus general literature on TA,
                                which is selected according to importance and currency.
Source: Institutions which carry out the TA projects
Years Covered: Current
File Size: 420 TA project descriptions, 2100 citations
Updates:
Database Producer: Kernforschungszentrum Karlsruhe and FIZ Karlsruhe
Available From: STN File TA
                                £64 per connect hour
                                34p per on-line type
                                40p per off-line print

Name: Textile Technology Digest
Description: Textile Technology Digest provides international coverage of the literature
                                of textiles and related subjects.
                                    Subjects include dyeing, laundering, mill operation, man-made and
                                natural fibres, preservation, home economics, apparel design, marketing
                                and statistics. Virtually every area of the textile industry is covered.
                                Selected articles from current sources summmarise the technology
                                advancements and applications of science and research to the textile
                                industry.
Source: Over 650 journals, plus books, theses, patents, conferences and directories
Years Covered: 1978 to date
File Size: 146 451 records
Updates: Monthly
Database Producer: Institute of Textile Technology
Available From: DIALOG File 119
                                $65 per connect hour
                                5c per on-line type
                                15c per off-line print

Name: Titus
Description: This is a bibliographic database covering literature on textile and
                                textile-related industries. It covers textile engineering processes, products,
                                management and other relevant areas.
                                    The citations with abstracts are in English.
Language: French and English
Source: 61 per cent journals
                                28 per cent patents
Years Covered: 1971 to date
File Size: 155 000 citations (October 1987)
Updates: Monthly
Database Producer: Institut Textile de France (ITF) in cooperation with
                                other partners
                                FIZ Karlsruhe
Available From: STN File Titus
                                £64 per connect hour
                                25p per on-line type
                                31p per off-line print
                                SDI profile: £3
                                FIZ Technik File Titus
                                DM 250 per connect hour
                                DM 0.8 per on-line type
                                DM 1.1 per off-line print
                                SDI profile: DM 10

Name: Transin
Description: Transin provides information on offers and requests for the sale and
                        purchase of industrial techniques and new products. The database has
                        international coverage. Citations of the patent or licence are provided,
                        together with a description of the technology and identification of the
                        contact, ie name and address.
Source: International public and private sources
Years Covered: Current
File Size: Approx 3500
Updates: Monthly
Database Producer: Institut National de la Propriete Industrielle (INPI)
Available From: Telesystemes-Questel File Transin
                        $100 per connect hour
                        $10 per on-line type
                        $10 per off-line print

Name: VITIS-VEA
Description: VITIS-Viticulture and Ecology Abstracts (VITIS-VEA) is produced by the
                        International Food Information Service (IFIS) in cooperation with the
                        Bundesforschungsanstalt fur Rebenzuchtung Geilweilerhof, Siebeldingen.
                        It represents the machine readable version of the documentation section of
                        the scientific journal 'VITIS' from 1969 onwards.
                            The database presents abstracts and bibliographical entries on grape and
                        grapevine science and technology as well as on plant pathology, plant
                        breeding, microbiology, biochemistry, soils, ecology and economic aspects
                        and trade.
Language: Database is published in English. About 10 per cent of entries contain
                        German abstracts, and a few abstracts are included in French
Source: 'VITIS' journal
                        Data gathered worldwide from more than 400 periodicals, books,
                        pamphlets, reports, standards, specifications and legislation
Years Covered: 1969 to date
File Size: Complete file consists of approximately 24 500 items (as at December 1987)
Updates: Quarterly
                        Increase of approximately 400 items per update
Database Producer: International Food Information Service (IFIS GmbH)
Available From: DIMDI File VITIS-VEA
                        $55.30 to $70.59 per connect hour
                        15c per on-line type
                        20c per off-line print
                        SDI profile: $3.88
                        DIALOG Subfile of File 51 (FSTA)
                        $81 per connect hour
                        30c per on-line type
                        30c per off-line print
                        SDI profile: $5.95
                        ESA-IRS Subfile of File 251
                        £52.50 per connect hour
                        14p per on-line type
                        19.9p per off-line print
                        SDI profile: £4.20
                        IFIS
                        Provides the following services:
                        'VITIS-VEA' quarterly journal
                        IBM magnetic tape
                        FSTA Reference Series (Thesauri, manuals, bibliographies)
                        Current awareness services
                        Retrospective searches
                        Photocopy service

Name: Weldasearch
Description: Weldasearch, the database of the Welding Institute, is a comprehensive
                    international database covering all aspects of the joining of metals and
                    plastics. Welded design, welding metallurgy, fatigue and fracture
                    mechanics are included, as well as related areas such as metals spraying
                    and thermal cutting. The file is indexed using the International Welding
                    Thesaurus. There is no corresponding printed index or abstract journal.
                       All aspects of the welding and joining of metals and plastics are included;
                    in particular, the following topics:

Welding	Welding and joining
Brazing	Equipment
Soldering	Corrosion
Thermal cutting	Welded construction
Metal spraying	Quality control
Design of welded	Nondestructive testing
structures	Pipelines
Fatigue of welds	Pressure vessels
Brittle fracture	Offshore structures

Source: Several thousand journals, research reports, books and monographs, new
                    standards, patents (mostly UK), theses, conferences and special
                    publications
Years Covered: 1967 to date
File Size: 95 000 as of January 1987
Updates: Monthly
Database Producer: The Welding Institute
Available From: DIALOG File 99
                    $84 per connect hour
                    20c per on-line type
                    25c per off-line print
                    Weldasearch services savailable from the Welding
                    Institute include:
                    Magnetic tape service
                    'Welding Abstracts' monthly journal
                    Specialist reference lists
                    Current Awareness (SDI) Service

Name: World Aluminium Abstracts
Description: World Aluminum Abstracts provides coverage of the world's technical
                    literature on aluminium, ranging from ore processing (exclusive of mining)
                    through to end uses. All aspects of the aluminium industry, aside from
                    mining, are covered, including the following major subject areas:
                    aluminium industry general, ores, ualumina production and extraction,
                    melting, casting, and foundry, metal-working, fabrications, finishing,
                    physical and mechanical metallurgy, engineering properties and tests,
                    quality control and tests and end uses.
Source: Information is abstracted from approximately 1600 scientific and technical
                    patents, government reports, conference proceedings, dissertations, books
                    and journals
Years Covered: 1968 to date
File Size: 126 697 records (DIALOG)
                    138 000 records (ESA-IRS)
Updates: Monthly
Database Producer: American Society for Metals (ASM International)
Available From: DIALOG File 33
                    $72 per connect hour
                    10c per on-line type
                    20c per off-line print
                    ESA-IRS File 9
                    £49.70 per connect hour
                    8.4p per on-line type
                    17.1p per off-line print
                    SDI profile: £2.80

Name: WTI

Description: The World Transindex database is the machine-readable version of the monthly publication 'World Transindex'. It gathers the translation announcements collected by the International Translation Centre and the Centre National de la Recherche Scientifique. It announces translations of literature relating to all fields of science and technology, from East European and Asiatic languages into Western languages. Translations from Western languages into French, Spanish and Portuguese are also announced.

                        Subject areas cover all fields of science and technology.

Source: Corresponds to the monthly publication 'World Transindex'

Years Covered: 1977 to date

File Size: Approx 262 000 records

Updates: Monthly

                        Approx 2300 records added per month

Database Producer: CIT/ITC

                        (International Translations Centre)

                        Centre National de la Recherche Scientifique

                        (Centre de Documentation Scientifique et Technique)

Available From: ESA-IRS File 33

                        £53.90 per connect hour

                        28p per on-line type

                        36.7p per off-line print

                        SDI profile: £4.90

Section IX
Industry-wide
Databases

Patents and Trademarks

APIPAT
BREV
British Trade Marks
Chinese Patent Abstracts
Claims
Computerpat
ECLATX, EDOC, EPAT, CIB,
FPAT
FMARK
Inpadoc
INSPEC
Japio
Lexpat (See Nexis in
Marketing Section)
PATDPA
Patolis
PATOS European Patents
PATOS German Patent
Applications and Utility

Models
PATOS German Patents
PATOS PCT Applications
TMINT
Transin (see Science and
Technology Section)
US Class
US Patents
US Trademarks
World Patents Index

Standards and Regulations

DIN (The German Standards
and Technical Rules
Database)
DITR (Standards and
Specifications)
GATT
Industry and International
Standards
NODO
NORM
Standards and Specifications
Standards Search

Industry Profiles

CJTRES (see Company
Section)
Exchange (see Nexis in
Marketing section for host
details)
ICC Stockbroker Research
(see Company Section)
Industrial Production (IP)
Industry Data
Industry Performance
Monitor
Jordans Business Surveys
(See Marketing Section)
Keynote Industry Surveys
(See Marketing Section)
Quarterly Financial Report
(see Economics Section)
Quotron 800 (see Securities
Section)

Name: APIPAT

Description: APIPAT is a bibliographic database covering the patents relating to the petroleum and energy industries of most countries that issue patents. Each document consists of the patent number, application and publication dates, patent owner and index terms. The standardised patent dates allow easy cross-reference to other patent databases.

                        APIPAT is a restricted-access database. Access is provided for its 'basic supporters', a group of organisations that share in the cost of producing it.

For other organisations there is restricted access in countries in which a major basic supporter has its headquarters. Contact ORBIT Search Service or STN for details.

Subjects covered:

Handling of crude oil and natural gas

Petroleum refining process

Formulation of fuels, lubricants and other major petroleum products

Special products

Catalysts

Corrosion control

Process control

Environmental, health and safety matters

Chemicals used in oilfield operations

Pipelines, tankers and other petroleum transport

Storage of petroleum and its products

Synthetic fuels

Language:	English
Source:	Patents of the major industrial countries
Years Covered:	1964 to date
File Size:	182 000 citations (as at March 1988)
Updates:	Monthly
	Approx 800 citations added per update
Database Producer:	American Petroleum Institute
Available From:	STN File Apipat
	£62.00 per connect hour
	20p per on-line type
	23p per off-line print
	SDI profile: £1.84
	STN File Apipat2
	£91 per connect hour
	28p per on-line type
	31p per off-line print
	ORBIT Search Service File Apipat
	Subscribers:
	$70 per connect hour
	30c per on-line type
	35c per off-line print
	SDI profile: $3.45
	Non-subscribers:
	$110 per connect hour
	40c per on-line type
	45c per off-line print

Name:	BREV
Description:	The BREV database contains the references to Belgian patents (source: OPRI) and to European patents (including PCT) brought into force in Belgium.
	References comprise the codes of the International Patent Classification and their translation into English. Since 1984 a descriptive text has been added to all references. All sectors of patentable activities are covered.
Source:	European Patent Office
	OPRI (Office de la Propriete Industrielle)
Years Covered:	
File Size:	168 000 patents as at May 1987
Updates:	Monthly
Database Producer:	Ministry of Economic Affairs (Belgium)
	Department of Industrial Property
	(Office de la Propriete Industrielle)
Available From:	Belindis File BREV
	BF 3000 per connect hour
	BF 10 per 10 lines displayed on line
	BF 10 per off-line print

Name:	British Trade Marks
Description:	The British Trade Marks database represents the source of information on all registered trade marks and those for which application for registration has been made.
	The database includes details of live marks regardless of when they were applied for, together with marks which have lapsed.
	Information in the database for every mark includes details of published information in TMJ such as:
	Registered users
	Renewal history
	Assignments
	WHO names
	ISO pesticide names
Source:	UK Trademarks Register
Years Covered:	Current (historic since date of original registrations)
File Size:	500 000 trade marks
Updates:	Continuous
Database Producer:	Compu-Mark's own database of published marks
	Patent Office supply up-published pendings
Available From:	Pergamon Financial
	£77 per connect hour
	30p per on-line type
	30p per off-line print
	Compu-Mark (UK)
	Full automatic search £26 includes 20 minutes free connect time
	Additional status (above 10) 25p
	£1.35 per minute for connect time over the first 20 minutes
	Scan Search – Prefix/Float/Suffix:
	£1.35 per min
	5p per ref
	Search by Regn No or Appln No: £1.50 per status
Name:	Chinese Patent Abstracts
Description:	This database contains English language abstracts covering all patent applications made in China since 1985. It provides a comprehensive record of recent technical developments. This database is owned by the Patent Documentation Service Center of the Patent Office of the People's Republic of China (CENTER) in Beijing, which is represented in Europe by INPADOC in Austria.
Source:	Patent documentation in the Peoples Republic of China
Years Covered:	1985 to date
File Size:	3849 records (DIALOG)
	Approx 6500 records (ORBIT)
Updates:	Biweekly (DIALOG)
	Monthly (ORBIT)
Database Producer:	Patent Documentation Service Center of the People's Republic of China
Available From:	DIALOG File 344
	$120 per connect hour
	40c per on-line type
	40c per off-line print
	ORBIT Search Service File CHINAPATS
	$125 per connect hour
	40c per on-line type
	40c per off-line print
	SDI profile: $8
Name:	Claims
Description:	The Claims, Claims/u, Claims/c databases provide access to over 1.7 million Unites States patents issued by the US Patent and Trademark Office. Chemical patents are covered from 1950 forward; mechanical and electrical patents from 1963 forward.

The Claims database is the base file; Claims/u is the Claims database with Uniterm subject indexing for chemical and chemically related patents; Claims/c is the Claims database with Uniterm indexing plus additional subject indexing and search features for retrieving chemical and chemically related patents.

Subject coverage is anything patentable, encompassing all areas of technology, chemistry, medicine, electronics, engineering and mechanics. The Claims family of databases are the Claims/Citation, Claims/Compound Registry, Claims/Reassignment & Reexamination, Claims/Reference and Claims/US Patent Abstracts files.

Source:	US Patent and Trademark Office
	Patent documents
Years Covered:	1950 to date
File Size:	Over 1.8 million records
Updates:	Weekly
Database Producer:	IFI/Plenum Data Company Inc
Available From:	ORBIT Search Service
	Files Claims, Claims/u, Claims/c
	Claims:
	$105 per connect hour
	25c per on-line type
	25c-50c per off-line print
	Claims/u and Claims/c:
	$300 per connect hour
	25c per on-line type
	15c-50c per off-line print
	SDI profile: $7.50
	DIALOG
	Claims/Comprehensive Files 323, 324, 325, 342
	Claims/Uniterm Files 223, 224, 225, 341
	$300 per connect hour
	25c per on-line type
	50c per off-line print
	Claims/US Patent Abstracts Files 23, 24, 25, 340
	$105 per connect hour
	25c per on-line type
	50c per off-line print
	SDI profile: File 125 $12.95

Name:	Computerpat
Description:	Computerpat covers all United States patents issued for digital data processing systems hardware, since the first was granted in 1942. It includes processors, input/output devices, storage elements, storage management devices, error detection and diagnostic methods, communications systems and applications.
Source:	US patent issuing authorities
Years Covered:	1942 to date
File Size:	Approximately 7500 records
Updates:	Weekly
Database Producer:	Pergamon Financial
Available From:	Pergamon Financial File Computerpat
	£85 per connect hour
	22p per on-line type
	24p per off-line print
	SDI profile: £5
	ESA-IRS File 147
	Gateway Service to Pergamon
	£86.10 per connect hour
	24.5p per on-line type
	26.6p per off-line print

Name:	DIN (The German Standards and Technical Rules Database)
Description:	This database is a comprehensive source of information on all technical rules currently valid in the Federal Republic of Germany, over 43 000 individual documents. Each document is described in some detail, with an English language abstract and references to corresponding International Standards and related German Standards and regulations. Searches for relevant standards can be carried out using English language keywords. DIN has been made fully compatible with the British Standards Institution's BSI Standardline database, already established on Pergamon Financial Data Services, so that retrieval of British and German standards from the same source is possible.
Source:	German Information Centre for Technical Rules (DITR)
Years Covered:	Current
File Size:	43 000 documents
Updates:	
Database Producer:	German Information Centre for Technical Rules (DITR) incorporated within the German Institute for Standardisation (DIN) in Berlin
Available From:	Pergamon Financial Contact direct for prices (new file)

Name:	DITR (Standards and Specifications)
Description:	DITR contains citations mostly with abstracts to current German and international technical rules in the Federal Republic of Germany. It covers standards and draft standards, other technical rules and statutory regulations.
Language:	German with English translations
Source:	Corresponds to the printed 'DIN Catalogue of Technical Rules' issued by DIN Deutsches Institut and sold by Beuth Verlag
Years Covered:	Latest available
File Size:	43 000 records
Updates:	Monthly
Database Producer:	Deutsches Informationszentrum fur Technische Regeln (DITR) Deutsches Institut fur Normung eV (DIN)
Available From:	FIZ Technik File DITR DM 250 per connect hour DM 0.8 per on-line type DM 1.1 per off-line print

Name:	ECLATX (EDOC, EPAT, CIB, FPAT)
Description:	ECLATX: Full text of the internal classification scheme of the European Patent Office. The database file holds approximately 86 700 subdivisions. EDOC: Search documentation of the European Patent Office. It covers published applications and delivered patents issued from over 17 major industrialised countries, as well as European patents, PCT and OAPI. Most important countries covered since the beginning of this century. EPAT: Provides bibliographic and legal status information on all European patents, published applications and Euro-PCT since June 1978. CIB: French version of the International Patent Classification 4th edition. FPAT: Provides bibliographic and legal status information on all patents applied for and published in France since 1969.
Source:	European Patent Office
Years Covered:	As above
File Size:	ECLATX: 86 700 subdivisions EDOC: 15 million documents EPAT: 240 000 documents FPAT: 595 000
Updates:	ECLATX and EDOC: monthly EPAT and FPAT: weekly
Database Producer:	Institut National de la Propriete Industrielle (INPI)

Available From:	Telesystemes Questel
	Files:
	ECLATX: $60 per connect hour
	No off-line prints allowed
	EDOC: $155 per connect hour
	15c per on-line type
	15c per off-line print
	EPAT: $110 per connect hour
	45c per on-line type
	50c per off-line print
	SDI profile: $10 plus print charges
	CIB: $60 per connect hour
	No off-line prints allowed
	FPAT: $110 per connect hour
	45c per on-line type
	50c per off-line print
	SDI profile: $10 plus print charges

Name:	FMARK
Description:	This is a database of trademarks filed and published in France. Information includes bibliographic, administrative and legal information. French trademarks have a validity of 10 years.
Language:	French
Source:	'French Trademark Gazette' and unpublished filed trademarks
Years Covered:	January 1976 to date
File Size:	530000 documents
Updates:	Weekly
Database Producer:	Institut National de la Propriete Industrielle (INPI)
Available From:	Telesystemes-Questel File FMARK
	$120 per on-line connect hour
	50c per on-line type
	60c per off-line print

Name:	GATT
Description:	GATT contains references to Danish standards and technical regulations which provides information on technical barriers to trade, etc.
	GAT 1 contains draft proposals for national standards; GAT 2 contains existing national standards in Denmark; GAT 3 contains current technical regulations which may be considered technical barriers to trade. Each of these 3 databases can be accesed separately.
	Search language: DC INFO (CCL/BRS)
Language:	Danish
Source:	Standards
Years Covered:	Current
File Size:	4350 documents (as at January 1987)
Updates:	6 times per annum
Database Producer:	Dansk Standardiseringsrad (Danish Standards Association)
Available From:	Datacentralen
	DK 360 per connect hour

Name:	Industrial Production (IP)
Description:	IP covers the monthly industrial production data reported by Federal Reserve Board on approximately the 15th of each month. IP provides monthly industrial production indexes for approximately 285 industries, industry groups and market catagories. Data is available in seasonally adjusted and unadjusted format. It corresponds to the Federal Reserve Bulletin G.12.3. Gross value of products are reported in billions of 1982 dollars.
Source:	US Federal Reserve Board
Years Covered:	Current
File Size:	Covers 285 industries
Updates:	Monthly

Database Producer:	Haver Analytics Inc
Available From:	GE Information Services
	$1 per data series
	or subscription options:
	$1500 per annum subscription for unlimited access to all US economic databases
	$2500 per annum subscription to all the USA economic plus international databases

Name:	Industry Data
Description:	Industry Data (Industry) includes annual data profiling USA industries from the Office of Management and Budget and the International Trade Administration. Data provided is published in the 'US Industry Profile' and the 'US Industrial Outlook' and covers industry shipments, product shipments, employment, imports and exports and capital expenditures. Annual data is reported in both current and constant dollars when available. Data is available for about 450 manufacturing industries. Data from the last period of actual history (1985) through to the current year (1988) are projected now.
Source:	Equivalent to the publications 'US Trading Profile' and 'US Industrial Outlook', produced by the US government
Years Covered:	1972 to date
File Size:	Covers 450 industries
Updates:	
Database Producer:	Haver Analytics Inc
Available From:	GE Information Services
	25c per data series
	or subscription options:
	$1500 per annum for unlimited access to all US economic databases
	$2500 per annum subscription for all US economic plus international databases

Name:	Industry and International Standards
Description:	This database provides voluntary engineering standards from private sector societies and organisations in the USA, plus selected foreign national and international standards. Citations include: titles, issue dates and ANSI approval status, IHS classification codes and descriptors.
Source:	IHS Industry & International Standards databases
	NBS Voluntary Engineering Standards databases
Years Covered:	Current
File Size:	Standards for over 400 organisations provided
Updates:	Every other month
Database Producer:	Information Handling Services
Available From:	BRS File STDS
	$55 per connect hour
	16c per on-line type
	21c per off-line print
	SDI profile: $4

Name:	Industry Performance Monitor (IPM)
Description:	Industry Performance Monitor (IPM) provides sales and earnings forecasts for approximately 80 industries as part of their Industry Performance Monitor service. IPM provides annual forecasts of sales and earnings for approximately 80 industries and 9 industry composites. Five-year projections are updated quarterly. Data series are index numbers compatible with S&P stock price indices. The IPM Outlook analyses industry trends over the next 5 years. Industry profiles cover industry conditions, financial status and competitive climate.
Source:	PTC Associates

Years Covered:	1960 to date
	5 year projections updated quarterly
File Size:	Covers 80 industries
Updates:	Quarterly
Database Producer:	Haver Analytics Inc/PTC Associates
Available From:	GE Information Services
	$5 per data series
	$50 per industry profile
	or $2500 per annum subscription charge

Name:	Inpadoc
Description:	Inpadoc lists patents in all areas of technology. The on-line file contains patent data received from the International Patent Documentation Centre, Vienna, Austria. It has developed a bibliographical database consisting of title, inventor and assignee for most patents. This includes over 12 million patent documents from over 50 countries. These are further supplemented by data from the European Patent Office and the International Bureau of WIPO. In addition a further 14.4 million patent documents issued by the major industrialised countries of the world can be accessed through Inpadoc.
Source:	Data processed by Inpadoc are made available by cooperating patent offices in 55 countries, the European Patent Office, and Patent Cooperation Treaty members. Legal status information is provided for AT, CH, DE, DK, EP, FR, GB, NL, US and WO.
Years Covered:	1968 to date (DIALOG)
	Inpadoc: 1968 to date (ORBIT)
	Inpanew: most recent 6-10 weeks of Inpadoc data
	1968 to date (STN)
File Size:	Approx 28 million records (DIALOG)
	Approx 15 million records (ORBIT)
	Approx 15 million records (STN)
Updates:	Weekly (ORBIT)
Database Producer:	International Patent Documentation Centre
Available From:	DIALOG File 345
	$125 per connect hour
	$20 per on-line type
	$20 per off-line print
	DIALOG users can consult online Chronolog File 410
	ORBIT Search Service File Inpadoc
	$120 per connect hour
	20c per on-line type
	40c per off-line print
	SDI profile: $8
	STN File Inpadoc
	£76 per connect hour
	63p per on-line type (BIB plus LS)
	75p per off-line print (BIB plus LS)
	Inpadoc
	Patolis

Name:	INSPEC
Description:	INSPEC is the leading English language abstracting and indexing service covering the fields of physics, electronics and computing. The database covers 4 main subject areas: physics; electrical engineering, electronics, telecommunications; control technology, computing; and information technology. It corresponds to the printed 'Physics Abstracts', 'Electrical and Electronics Abstracts', 'Computer and Control Abstracts' and 'IT Focus'. Journal papers, conference proceedings, technical reports, books, patents and university theses are abstracted and indexed for inclusion in the database. Over 200 journals are abstracted completely.
Source:	Approx 4000 technical journals, 1000 conference proceedings, books and reports

Years Covered:	1969 to date
File Size:	Over 3 million records
Updates:	Monthly
	Approx 3 119 000 records per annum
Database Producer:	The Institution of Electrical Engineers (INSPEC)
Available From:	DIALOG Files 12, 13

File 12: 1969 to 1976
File 13: 1977 to date
$111 per connect hour
54c per on-line type
60c per off-line print
SDI profile: $14.95
BRS Files INSP, INSB (Inspec and Backfile)
$77 per connect hour
55c per on-line type
52c per off-line print
BRS File INSZ (Merged file)
$79 per connect hour
55c per on-line type
52c per off-line print
SDI profile: $4
Data-Star File INSP
£56.14 per connect hour
25p per on-line print
18p per off-line print
SDI profile: £4.30
ESA-IRS File 8
£67.90 per connect hour
25.2p per on-line type
35.3p per off-line print
SDI profile: £4.20
Cedocar File INSPEC
FF 660 per connect hour
FF 2.95 per on-line type
FF 3.25 per off-line print
FIZ Technik File INSPEC
DM 250 per connect hour
DM 0.8 per on-line type
DM 1.1 per off-line print
ORBIT Search Service
File INSPEC: 1977 to date
File INSPEC 6976: 1969 to 1976
$105 per connect hour
48c per on-line type
56c per off-line print
SDI profile: $6.55
STN File INSPEC
£64 per connect hour
35p per on-line type
37p per off-line print
SDI profile: £3
Other hosts:
CAN/OLE National Research Council of Canada
INKA (Federal Republic of Germany)
JICST (Japan)
Tsukuba Daijaku (Japan)
SDC Information Service (USA)
Contact hosts direct for prices

Copies of articles abstracted by INSPEC can be obtained from:
British Library Document Supply Centre
Boston Spa
Wetherby
West Yorkshire LS23 7BQ
Tel: 0937-843434

Name:	Japio
Description:	Japio contains English language abstracts of unexamined Japanese patents.
Source:	Japanese patent documents
Years Covered:	From 1976
File Size:	Over 2.5 million
Updates:	Monthly
Database Producer:	Japio
Available From:	British Library
	Japanese Information Service
	£15 standing charge per search topic
	£3 per connect time plus VAT
	ORBIT Search Service File Japio
	$150 per connect hour
	15-25c per on-line type
	25-45c per off-line print
	SDI profile: $6.50

Name:	NODO
Description:	NODO is a database of Italian customs regulations. It contains:
	The harmonized system nomenclature
	The combined community nomenclature
	The integrated community tariff
	Users can obtain the customs code starting from the description of goods being imported or exported. For each code, users can access details such as tariff and tax regulations, import quotas, refunds on exports, compensatory duties, import embargo regulations.
Language:	Italian
Source:	SINODO Pool formed by Cerved and Sadi (part of the Fiat group)
Years Covered:	Current
File Size:	HS: 5000 items
	CCN: 9500 items
	TARIC: 13 000 items
Updates:	Daily
Database Producer:	Cerved and Sadi (part of the Fiat group)
Available From:	Cerved File NODO
	Lire 122 079 per connect hour (prime time)
	Lire 99 883 per connect hour (non-prime time)

Name:	NORM
Description:	NORM is a bibliographic database with respect to Belgian standards and draft standards. This file contains the reference number, French and Dutch titles, a keyword description and other data on every Belgian standard and draft standard.
Language:	French and Dutch
Source:	Belgian standard documentation from the IBN
Years Covered:	Latest available and historic data
File Size:	3200 (as at January 1986)
Updates:	Monthly
Database Producer:	Institut Belge de Normalisation (IBN)
	Purchase of standards and free consultation of these documents is available
Available From:	Belindis File NORM
	BF 1200 per connect hour
	BF 5 per 10 lines displayed on line
	BF 4 per off-line print

Name: PATDPA
Description: This is a German patent database containing bibliographic data of all kinds
                   of patent documents and utility models published by the Deutsche
                   Patentamt (German Patent Office). The subject coverage is all fields of
                   science and technology.
Language: German
Source: German patent publications
Years Covered: 1968 to date
File Size: 1 746 000 citations
Updates: Weekly
Database Producer: Deutsches Patentamt Munchen and FIZ Karlsruhe
Available From: STN File PATDPA
                   £94 per connect hour
                   34p per on-line type
                   41p per off-line print
                   SDI profile: £1.35

Name: Patolis
Description: This database covers Japanese patents (from 1955), utility models (from
                   1961), designs (from 1965) and trademarks (from 1902) including the latest
                   legal status and latest 2 weeks patents and utility models. It is possible to
                   search on patents and utility models, designs or use keywords. It is
                   possible to access brief bibliographical data, number and class.
                   Alternatively the full abstract is available.
                       Searches are carried out at INPADOC in Vienna, but specialists at the
                   British Library Japanese Information Service are able to assist with the
                   preparation and interpretation of the results which come in a mixture of
                   Japanese and code.
Language: Japanese
Source: Japanese industrial property documents
Years Covered: See above
File Size:
Updates: Monthly
Database Producer: Japan Patent Information Organisation (JAPIO)
Available From: British Library
                   Japanese Information Service
                   £4.00 per connect minute plus VAT
                   (Charges include help in preparing the search, interpreting the results and
                   sending out the results)
                   A search for 1 to 2 patents by filing number would
                   typically take under 8 minutes

Name: PATOS European Patents
Description: This database provides complete bibliographic data (patent and application
                   number, document type, languages, designated states, international patent
                   classification, hybrid classification, title, name and residence of inventor(s),
                   assignee(s) and agent, application and publication dates, examination
                   information, and priority information). The contents are based on the
                   'Auszuegen aus den Europaieschen Patentschriften (EPS)' published by the
                   Wila-Verlag KG, Munich, West Germany.
Language: German; title in German, English and French
Source: European Patent Office
Years Covered: 1978 to date
File Size: Over 90 000 granted European patents
                   Approx 25 000 new documents per year
                   Approx 400-500 new documents per week
Updates: Weekly; the current weekly additions to PATOS-PEPS are also available as
                   part of a separate information source from the update file: PEUU
Database Producer: Bertelsmann InformationsService GmbH and Wila-Verlag KG

Available From:	Bertelsmann File PEPS
	DM 320 royalty per connect hour
	DM 78 per connect hour
	DM 0.5 per on-line citation
	DM 0.5 per off-line citation

Name:	PATOS German Patents
Description:	This database contains approximately 180000 patents including the complete bibliographical data (patent number, document type, international patent classification, title, name and residence of inventor(s), assignee and legal representative, dates of filing, publication and grant, examination information, priority information). The contents are taken from 'Auszuege aus den Patentschriften', published by the Wila-Verlag KG.
Language:	German
Source:	German Patent Office
Years Covered:	1980 to date
File Size:	Approx 180000 German patents
Updates:	Weekly: the current weekly additions to PATOS-PDPS are also available as a separate information source from the update file: PDPU.
Database Producer:	Bertelsmann Informations Service GmbH and Wila-Verlag KG
Available From:	Bertelsmann File PDPS
	DM 320 royalty per connect hour
	DM 78 per connect hour
	DM 0.50 per on-line citation
	DM 0.50 per off-line citation

Name:	PATOS German Patent Applications and Utility Models
Description:	PATO is a German-language patent database for on-line searching of bibliographic data and in the text of the main claims of the first patent applications (Offenlegungsschriften) and utility models (Gebrauchsmuster) published by the German Patent Office.
	Each record includes the complete bibliographic data (patent number, international patent classification, document type, title, name and residence of inventor(s), patent assignee, legal representative, dates of filing and publication, priority information) and the full text of the main claim. 80000 documents published between fall 1981 and spring 1984 also contain the full text of the abstract.
	PATO covers German patent applications for a period of time longer than the legal lifetime of the patents.
	The intended user group includes all patent specialists, attorneys, patent reporters and searchers, research and development engineers in industry, R&D management, patent examiners in patent offices, technical information suppliers, librarians.
	The contents are taken from 'Auszeuge aus den Offenlegungsschriften (OSA)', 'Auszeuge aus den Ausleschriften/Patentschriften (ASA/PSA)', and 'Auszeuge aus den Gebrauchsmustern (GMA)' published by the Wila-Verlag KG.
Language:	German
Source:	German Patent Office
Years Covered:	1968 to date
File Size:	Approx 1.2 million documents
Updates:	Weekly: the current weekly additions to PATOS are also available as a separate information resource from the update files: PATU and PGBU
Database Producer:	Bertlesmann InformationsService GmbH and WILA-Verlag
Available From:	Bertelsmann File PATO
	DM 320 royalty per connect hour
	DM 78 per connect hour
	DM 2.5 per on-line citation
	DM 2.5 per off-line citation

Name:	PATOS PCT Applications
Description:	This database contains approximately 35 000 international patent applications according to the Patent Cooperation Treaty (PCT-Applications) published by the WIPO (World Intellectual Property Organization, Geneva) in the 'PCT Gazette' since 1983. Each record includes the complete bibliographic data (application and publication numbers and dates, international patent classification, title, name and residence of inventor(s), assignee and legal representative, priority information, designated states) and the full text of the abstract. Approximately 8500 new documents are added annually.
Source:	World Intellectual Property Organisation
Years Covered:	1983 to date
File Size:	Approximately 35 000 international patent applications
Updates:	Weekly: the current weekly additions to PATOS-PPCT are also available as a separate information source from the update file: PPCU
Database Producer:	Bertelsmann InformationsService GmbH
Available From:	Bertelsmann File PPCT
	DM 320 royalty per connect hour
	DM 78 per connect hour
	DM 2.5 per on-line citation
	DM 2.5 per off-line citation

Name:	Standards and Specifications
Description:	Standards and Specifications allows standards users and developers to quickly identify sources, status and availability of standards and specifications issued by US governmental bodies and industry on specific terminology, materials, performance testing, products, safety and other requirements and characteristics of interest in a particular field of technology.
	The database provides, for each standard and specification, the standard number, current issue date, issuing organisation, Federal Supply Classification (FSC) and American National Standards Association card number.
	Standards and Specifications contains titles and descriptive information for:
	The US Military (DOD) standards, specifications, military sheet form standards (MSs), Air Force-Navy Aeronautical Standards (ANs), Qualified Product Lists (QPLs), Handbooks, including NATO and related standards The US Federal (GSA) standards, specifications, commercial item descriptions (CIDs) and QPLs
	The US standards developed by many private sector organisations such as the American Society for Testing and Materials, Society of Automotive Engineers, Aerospace Industries Association, American National Standards Institute, Underwriters Laboratories, etc.
Source:	US government bodies, NSA and other standards issuing organisations
Years Covered:	1950 to date
File Size:	Approx 117 000 references
Updates:	
Database Producer:	National Standards Association Inc
Available From:	ESA-IRS File 44
	£42.00 per connect hour
	14.0p per on-line type
	22.7p per off-line print
	DIALOG File 113
	$65 per connect hour
	20c per on-line type
	30c per off-line print

Name: Standards Search
Description: Standards Search covers a diverse range of standards and specifications
                         developed by the Society of Automotive Engineers (SAE) and the American
                         Society for Testing and Materials (ASTM). SAE subject coverage includes
                         engineering standards for the automotive, aerospace and off-highway
                         industry. ASTM covers industry-specific standards, including
                         specifications, test methods, definitions, practices and classifications for
                         materials, products, systems and services.
Source: Equivalent to the following publications:
                         'The Annual Book of ASTM Standards'
                         'The SAE Aerospace Index'
                         'SAE Handbook'
                         'The SAE AMS Index of Aerospace Material' Specifications
Years Covered: Current
File Size: Approx 16 000 records
Updates: Quarterly
Database Producer: Society of Automotive Engineers
                         American Society for Testing and Materials
Available From: ORBIT Search Service File Standards Search
                         $60 per connect hour
                         20c per on-line type
                         25c per off-line print

Name: TMINT
Description: TMINT is a database of international marks registered at the World
                         Intellectual Property Organisation (WIPO). It covers registration, renewals
                         and modifications made to the International Register of Marks published in
                         'Les Marques Internationales'.
Language: French
Source: International publication 'Les Marques Internationales'
Years Covered: January 1966 to date
File Size: Approx 300 000 records
Updates: Monthly
Database Producer: Institut Nationale de la Propriete Industrielle (INPI)
                         and Compu-Mark (Belgium)
Available From: Telesystemes-Questel File TMINT
                         $135 per on-line connect hour
                         50c per on-line type
                         60c per off-line print

Name: US Class
Description: US Class contains all US classifications,
                         cross-reference classifications and unofficial classifications for all patents
                         issued from the first US patent issued in 1790 to date. Searching can be
                         done by classification or by patent number. The total file is updated with
                         any changes in the US classification scheme every 6 months.
Source: Equivalent to the publication 'US Patent Master Classification File'
Years Covered: 1790 to date
File Size: Approx 5 million records
Updates: Every 6 months
Database Producer: Derwent Inc
Available From: ORBIT Search Service File USCLASS
                         $60 per connect hour
                         $2.25 per off-line print (100 citations)

Name: US Patents
Description: US Patents provides complete patent information, including complete
                         front-page information, plus all claims of all US patents issued since 1970.
Source: Equivalent to 'US Patent Master Classification File'
Years Covered: USPA: 1978 to date
                         USPB: 1970-77

File Size:	USPA: 450000 records
	USPB: 785000 records
Updates:	Weekly
Database Producer:	Derwent Inc
Available From:	ORBIT Search Service File USPA
	$100 per connect hour
	15c per on-line type
	50c per off-line print
	SDI profile: $6.50

Name:	US Trademarks
Description:	US Trademarks covers over 1 million trademark registrations and pendings, whether published or unpublished, contained in the US Federal and State Registers. Information can be retrieved on trademarks, owners, numbers and dates of application and registration, class(es) and specification of goods, services and status. A user friendly menu-driven search program is available when accessing the database through Compu-Mark.
Source:	US Federal and State Registers
Years Covered:	
File Size:	1 million
Updates:	Continuous
Database Producer:	Compu-Mark (US)
Available From:	Compu-Mark (US)
	Full automatic search $45
	(free connect time 20 minutes;
	$1.50 per minute after the first 20 minutes)
	State registrations or pending applications only $25
	(free connect time 10 minutes)
	Combined PTO and state $60
	(free connect time 30 minutes)
	Additional status (above 10) 20c
	Scan search prefix/float/suffix:
	$1.50 per minute
	5c per ref
	Search by regs No/Serial no:
	$3 per full text

Name:	World Patents Index
Description:	The World Patents Index (DIALOG WPI, File 350) and World Patents Index Latest (DIALOG WPIL, File 351) files contain data from nearly 3 million inventions represented in more than 6 million patent documents from 30-patent issuing authorities around the world. In addition to bibliographic information, the basic patent record includes the full abstract (for new patents issued from 1981 to the present), informative title, International Patent Classification codes and Derwent subject codes. These files also provide access to equivalent patents, grouped together by patent family in the basic patent record. The use of manual and fragmentation codes is restricted to Derwent subscribers, in accordance with their subscription level.
Source:	Patent issuing authorities worldwide
Years Covered:	1963 to date. Years covered vary depending on the subject area. WPI covers patents up to 1980. WPIL covers patents from 1981 to date
File Size:	Over 4 million records
Updates:	Weekly WPIL (DIALOG File 351)
	Monthly WPI (DIALOG File 350)
Database Producer:	Derwent Publications Ltd

Available From: DIALOG File 350
Subscribers:
$110 per connect hour
15c per on-line type
38c per off-line print
SDI profile: $7.75
File 351
Non-subscribers:
$172 per connect hour
50c per on-line type
82c per off-line print
SDI profile: $7.75
ORBIT Search Service Files WPI, WPIL
Subscribers:
$110 per connect hour
15c per on-line type
38c per off-line print
Non-subcribers:
$172 per connect hour
50c per on-line type
82c per off-line print
Telesystemes-Questel Files WPI, WPIL
Subscribers:
$110 per connect hour
15c per on-line type
38c per off-line print
SDI profile: $7.75 plus print charges
Non-subscribers:
$172 per connect hour
50c per on-line type
(30c when no abstract)
82c per off-line print
SDI profile: $7.75 plus print charges

Section X Securities

International Prices

Australian Stock Exchange
Indices (ASE)
Bridge Information Service
Comtrend
Datastream Valuation
Services
DIALOG Quotes and Trading
Edit
Esprit
Examiner
Exshare
Global Report (see Marketing
Section)
Indes Service
Investors Daily
Marketpulse
Reuter Monitor
Scan
Teledata
TOPIC
Valordata
Valscop-Valeurs
Videcom

International Finance and Credit Checking

Datastream Equity Research
Services
Datastream Investment
Accounting Service
Datastream Valuation
Services
Dunsprint (see Company
Section)
Examiner (see Company
Section)
Global Report (See Marketing
Section)
Investext (see Company
Section)
Moody's Corporate News
(see Company Section)

US Prices

ADP Financial System (USA
and Canada)
Bridge Information Service
DIALOG Quotes and Trading
DRI-SEC (USA and Canada)

Executive Market Follower
Fastock II (USA and Canada)
Ford
Marketscan (USA and
Canada)
Media General Plus (see
Company Section)
MMS Equity Market Analysis
North American Stock Market
(NASTOCK) (USA and
Canada)
Quotron 800
Quotron Symbol Guide (USA
and Canada)
Securities Industry (see
Financial Services Section)
Toronto Stock Exchange 300
Index and Stock Statistics
United States Stock Market
(USSTOCK)
The Unlisted Market Guide
Valport (USA and Canada)
Value-Line Data Base-11 (see
Company Section)

USA Finance and Credit Checking

Corporate and Industry Research Reports Index (CIRR) (see Company Section)
Disclosure (see Company Section)
Global Report (see Marketing Section)
Investdata (see Company Section)
Investors Daily (see Company Section)
Investext (see Company Section)
Moody's Corporate News (see Company Section)
Standard and Poor's News On-Line (see Company Section)

UK Prices

Earnings Guide
Edit
Esprit
Finstat
Over the Counter Information
Prestel Citiservice
Priceplus
Reuter Monitor
TOPIC

UK Finance and Credit Checking

Datastream Equity Research Services
Datastream Investment Accounting Service
Datastream Valuation Services
Dunsprint (see Company Section)
ICC Stockbroker Research (see Company Section)
Infocheck (see Company Section)
Jordanwatch (see Company Section)

Australia

Ausinet Statex (see Company Section)
Australian Financial Markets (ARATE)
Australian Stock Exchange Indices (ASE)

Sydney Stock Exchange
STATEX Service (STATEX)

Europe

France
COTA
Defotel (See Company Section)
Gestion Des Valeurs Mobilieres
Informatitres
Valscop-Valeurs

Luxembourg
Luxembourg Stock Exchange

Norway
Oslo Bors

Spain
Sistema de Informacion Bursatil

Sweden
AktieInformation
Findata (see Company Section)

Switzerland
Valordata

Asia

Hong Kong
Hong Kong Stock Exchange (HKSTOCK)
Hong Kong Stock Exchange Fastprice

Japan
Global Report (see Marketing Section)
Japanese Fastprice
Needs-TS (see Economics Section)
Nikkei Telecom (see Economics Section)

Singapore
Stock Exchange of Singapore (Singstock)

Money Markets

Foreign Exchange
Australian Financial Markets (ARATE)
CCFX
Daily Currency Exchange Rates (Currency)

DRI – FACS
Exshare
Foreign Exchange Database
Foreign Exchange Report (see AP-Dow Jones, News Section)
FT Currency and Share Index
FXBASE
FXPRO
Global Report (See Marketing Section)
International Finance Alert
Investdata System
MMS Currency Market Analysis
Money Market Rates (MRATE)
Prestel Citiservice
Pricedata
Reuter Monitor
Telerate
TOPIC

Bonds
Base de donnees des Obligations Francaises
The Bond Buyer (see Industry Section)
Datastream Fixed Interest Services
DRI FACS
Exbond
Global Report (see Marketing Section)
Middle Tac
Munifacts Plus
Telerate

Commodities, Futures and Options

International
ADP Financial System
AGRA Europe (see Economics Section)
Canadian Stock Options (CDNOPTIONS)
Commodities (Commodity)
Commodity Options (COMOPTIONS)
Commodity News Services
CSI Marstat
Datastream Financial Futures Service
Datastream Traded Option Service
DRI Commodities
Futures Database
Futures – Soft
International Finance Alert
Investdata

Metal and Mineral Prices
(MINPRI)
Metals Week
Prestel Citiservice
Pricedata
Reuter Monitor
Telerate
United Nations Commodity
Trade Statistics
United States Stock Options
(USOPTIONS)
Videcom

USA and Canada

The Bond Buyer (see Industry
Section)
Compact

OTC Listings and Securities

Executive Market Follower
(USA)
Over the Counter Information
(UK)
The Unlisted Market Guide

Name:	ADP Financial System
Description:	ADP Financial System covers securities and commodities in Canada and the US. It provides real-time quotation display capabilites and includes information from regional and national securities, options, OTC and commodities exchanges. It also contains the full text of Futures Focus. Display options include obtaining a full composite quote, a 1-line reference quote, or a listing of last sale prices. There is also a ticker display capability.
Source:	Securities and commodity exchanges in the US and Canada
Years Covered:	Current
File Size:	
Updates:	Continuous (real time)
Database Producer:	ADP Financial Information Services
Available From:	ADP Financial Information Services (only available to US users at present)

Name:	AktieInformation
Description:	AktieInformation provides current stock prices quoted on the Stockholm Stock Exchange. It also provides company information on listed companies. Daily closing prices for major currencies are provided on a separate database called Currencies. Historical closing price and sales volume data is stored for the current year and the previous 2 years.
Source:	Stockholm Stock Exchange
Years Covered:	Current (up to 2 years' historic) Total: 36 months
File Size:	Approx 20 000 records (10 000 records per year)
Updates:	Every 2 minutes (Stock data)
Database Producer:	Affarsdata
Available From:	Affarsdata SKr 720 per connect hour

Name:	Australian Financial Markets (ARATE)
Description:	Australian Financial Markets provides daily interest rate series, exchange rates and commercial bill rates weekly series on Commonwealth government securities and monthly series on semi-government securities.
Source:	
Years Covered:	Certain series from 1976
File Size:	
Updates:	Daily, weekly and monthly (Daily updates occur the morning of the next working day, Melbourne time)
Database Producer:	Commonwealth Trading Bank and Financial Review
Available From:	IP Sharp Access via 39 Magic Contact IP Sharp direct for prices

Name:	Australian Stock Exchange Indices (ASE)
Description:	ASE provides price and accumulation indices for Australian Stock Exchanges. It contains international indices, including the daily Tokyo 225, Hang Seng and Barclay's indices.
Source:	Australian Stock Exchanges Equivalent to 'Australian Stock Exchange Indices Data Base'
Years Covered:	Daily information: 1980 to date Monthly information: 1958 to date
File Size:	
Updates:	Daily and monthly (daily updates by 2100 Sydney time on day of trade)
Database Producer:	Sydney Stock Exchange
Available From:	IP Sharp Access via Pricelink and 39 Magic Contact IP Sharp direct for prices

Name:	Base de Donnees des Obligations Francaises
Description:	BDO provides real time data on French bonds including daily market rates. Also this service allows users to carry out portfolio analyses.
Source:	French Stock Exchanges
Years Covered:	Current
File Size:	2000 bonds
Updates:	Daily
Database Producer:	DAFSA
Available From:	DAFSA

Name:	Bridge Information Service
Description:	This service provides information on over 40000 listed and OTC stocks. It also covers financial USA futures, commodities, foreign securities and all listed options. Much of the information supplied is in real time. Bridge also monitors transactions on the New York and American Stock Exchanges, NASDAQ and commodity exchanges. Information is presented in a variety of formats: real-time automatically updating market monitors, charts and in tabular form. Other services are available including the Dow Jones News/Retrieval.
Source:	American stock and commodity exchanges
Years Covered:	Up to 10 years historic data Data goes back to 1974
File Size:	Approx 40000 securities
Updates:	Continuous (real time)
Database Producer:	Bridge Data Company
Available From:	ADP Data Services Bridge Data Monthly subscription varies according to services required

Name:	Canadian Stock Options (CDNOPTIONS)
Description:	CDNOPTIONS (Canadian Stock Options) covers trading statistics for put and call options traded in Toronto, Montreal and Vancouver. Options in Canada are provided at present for government bonds, indexes, silver and stocks. Time series and static facts are available for each option, including price and trading volume data.
Source:	Canadian exchanges
Years Covered:	Most recent 200 trading days
File Size:	
Updates:	Daily, 2100 Toronto time same day
Database Producer:	Trans Canada Options Inc
Available From:	IP Sharp Access via Pricelink, 55 Retrieve or 39 Magic Contact IP Sharp direct for prices

Name: CCFX
Description: CCFX covers current and historic data on foreign exchange and interest
                     rates. It also covers Eurocurrency rates, US Federal Funds rates, domestic
                     and Treasury bill rates and gold and silver fixings.
Source:
Years Covered: 1976 to date
File Size:
Updates: Daily
Database Producer: Conticurrency Inc
Available From: Computer Sciences Corporation
                     $250 monthly minimum

Name: Commodities (COMMODITY)
Description: Commodities contains historic prices, volume and open interest for all
                     major commodities traded on the London, Paris, New York, Chicago,
                     Kansas City, Winnipeg, Minneapolis, Amsterdam, Singapore, Tokyo,
                     Hong Kong and Toronto/Montreal futures markets. It
                     consists of over 60 000 statistical time series on metals and soft
                     commodities.
                     The database is noted as one of the most extensive services offered by any
                     vendor.
Source: Commodity Systems Inc, Florida
Years Covered: London data: 1973 to date
                     New York and Chicago market data: 1973 to date
                     Toronto and Montreal market data: 1982 to date
                     Paris: 1982 to date
                     Kansas City: 1982 to date
                     Minneapolis: 1982 to date
                     Winnipeg: 1982 to date
                     Tokyo: 1986 to date
                     Hong Kong: 1986 to date
                     Amsterdam: 1985 to date
                     Singapore: 1987 to date
File Size: 60 000 statistical time series
Updates: Daily
Database Producer: IP Sharp
Available From: IP Sharp
                     Access via Pricelink, 55 Retrieve or 39 Magic
                     Contact IP Sharp direct for prices.
                     Interactive Data Corporation (IDC)
                     Analystics charges:
                     $250 per month plus sliding scale per access fee on
                     monthly basis:
                     First 25 000 hits 7c per hit
                     Next 100 000 hits 5c per hit
                     Additional hits 2c per hit
                     Plus 1c per item surcharge

Name: Commodity News Services
Description: This database covers prices and news on commodities traded on US,
                     Winnipeg and London commodity exchanges. Data is divided into 24
                     categories including: livestock, food and fibre, grains, metals, currencies
                     and energy.
Source: US, Winnipeg, London commodity exchanges
Years Covered: Current
File Size:
Updates: Continuous
Database Producer: Commodity News Services Inc
Available From: Agridata Network

Name: Commodity Options (COMOPTIONS)
Description: This database provides historic and statistical information for the analyst via prices, volumes and open interest for all major options and commodities futures traded in the USA. The information is in the form of 'life of contract' series.
Source: USA market sources, commodity exchanges
Years Covered: September 1985 to date
File Size:
Updates: Daily by 2200 Toronto time, same day
Database Producer: IP Sharp
Available From: IP Sharp
Access via Pricelink, 55 Retrieve, or 39 Magic
Contact IP Sharp direct for prices

Name: Compact
Description: This system facilitates the evaluation of futures options, spread selections and market position analyses.
Source:
Years Covered: 1982 to date
File Size:
Updates: Continuous
Database Producer: Chronometrics
Available From: National Computer Network Corporation (NCN)

Name: Comtrend
Description: Comtrend provides real-time price and trading data from the world's major exchanges relevant to dealers and traders. The major innovative feature provided by ADP is its ability to generate real-time charts and graphs from commodity information. There are other useful research facilities such as Comtrend Plus and Trendsetter II which enable users to design their own trading models and construct a personal database using a mixture of 'stored real-time' and research information.
Source: Commodity exchanges worldwide
News on the News Alert Service is taken from 'US Commodity World News'
Years Covered: ADP database goes back to 1969
File Size:
Updates: Real time
Database Producer: ADP Comtrend Ltd (UK)
Available From: ADP Comtrend
Equipment rental:
Comtrend:
£1050 per month for the first terminal
Comtrend plus:
£1220 per month
Trendsetter II:
£430 per month
Alternatively systems can be purchased outright

Name: COTA
Description: COTA provides stock market information on French companies listed on all French stock exchanges. Details include high and low prices, historical prices, quantity of shares sold and the name of brokers. Information is made available 2 hours after the stock markets close.
Source: French Stock Exchanges
Years Covered: Current
File Size: All French stocks
Updates: 6 updates per day
Database Producer: Resaux Commercials Informatiques SA (RCI)
Available From: Resaux Commercials Informatiques SA (RCI)
Monthly subscription or per connect hour rates.
Contact direct for prices.

Name: CSI Marstat
Description: CSI Marstat covers international futures, equities and options data. Each
                   record contains open, high, low and closing prices. Other data includes
                   total volume and open interest.
Source: US Stock Exchanges
Years Covered: 1949 to date
File Size:
Updates: Daily
Database Producer: Commodity Systems Inc
Available From: Commodity Systems Inc
                   $33 monthly minimum

Name: Daily Currency Exchange Rates (CURRENCY)
Description: The Daily Currency Exchange Rates Database provides a total of 715
                   currency exchange rates that are listed on the following markets:
                   Copenhagen, Frankfurt, Helsinki, London, Madrid, Melbourne, New
                   York, Oslo, Paris, Singapore, Toronto, Tokyo, Vienna and Zurich. Rates
                   are reported in terms of the local currency of the reporting country.
                   Information includes daily spot, buying and selling and forward rates.
                   Forward and spot are reported by London, New York, Copenhagen,
                   Melbourne and Toronto.
Source: Data comes primarily from the Federal bank in each country
Years Covered: Varies according to the market. The earliest year that data goes back to is
                   1961
File Size: 715 currency exchange rates
Updates: Daily
Database Producer: IP Sharp
Available From: IP Sharp
                   Access via Infomagic, Pricelink, 39 Magic or 81 Currency
                   Contact IP Sharp direct for prices

Name: Datastream Equity Research Services
Description: These services cover research on market performance (statistics and
                   graphics), company accounts analysis and search facilites. Research data is
                   stored on equities from the UK, USA, Canada, France, Federal Republic of
                   Germany, Switzerland, Netherlands, Hong Kong, Japan, Belgium,
                   Norway, Ireland, Singapore, Malaysia, Spain, Denmark, Austria,
                   Australia, Italy, Sweden and South Africa. Graphics only facilities are
                   available for India, Mexico, Philippines, South Korea, Taiwan and
                   Thailand. Scandinavia and South Africa. Datastream provides access to
                   nearly 6000 stock indices, interest rates, exchange rates and commodities.
                   Most of this data is available daily for at least 10 years.
                      Program 101 is a Universal Equity Research facility, offering basic data for
                   any equity or sector, and company or sector comparisons.
                   Program 1 and 2 covers UK Industrials
                   Program 3 and 4 covers UK Investment Trusts
                   Program 5 and 6 covers UK Financials
                   Program 11 and 12 covers USA Stocks
                   Program 13 and 14 covers Hong Kong Stocks
                   Program 15 and 16 covers Japanese Stocks
                   Program 17 and 18 covers Dutch Stocks
                   Program 19 and 20 covers French Stocks
                   Program 21 and 22 covers German Stocks
                   Program 23 and 24 covers Swiss Stocks
                   Program 110 provides International brokers' forecasts
Source: All major exchanges in Europe, North America and the Far East
Years Covered: 1965 to date (top UK equities)
                   1973 to date (international equities)
File Size: Research data stored on over 20000 international equities
Updates: Real time from UK, Netherlands, France, Belgium,
                   Federal Republic of Germany and Switzerland. Others
                   available after market close

Database Producer:	Datastream
Available From:	Datastream
	Price guide
	Research services:
	£24 000 for first unlimited access
	£18 000 for second access

Name:	Datastream Financial Futures Service
Description:	This is a package of programs and data which offers real-time quotations together with powerful graphics and research facilities. Coverage is UK and international, and includes cashmarket instruments, economic series, stock market indices, financial news services, interest and exchange rates, live coverage of LIFFE prices and USA contracts traded on the IMM and CBOT, and stock index futures from New York and Kansas City.
	Statistics are provided on program 250
	Graphics are provided on program 401
Source:	UK and USA exchanges
Years Covered:	Current
File Size:	
Updates:	Real time
Database Producer:	Datastream
Available From:	Datastream
	Price guide
	Financial futures service:
	£17 000
	Financial futures with full equity research:
	£7250

Name:	Datastream Fixed Interest Services
Description:	Datastream provides statistical and graphics research coverage on a wide range of fixed interest investment instruments. One of the most important features is the portfolio cash flow feature which allows clients to review the estimated income and capital repayments for the fixed-interest part of a portfolio over the next 25 years. It can also be used to review a borrower's repayment schedule. Basic market data is given for all stocks. The search programs give users the facility to identify issues which meet specified criteria.
	Approximately 3700 issues are from the UK
	1750 from the Netherlands
	8500 from the Federal Republic of Germany
	2200 from Switzerland
	450 from the USA
	90 from Canada
	75 from Japan
	350 from Belgium and Luxembourg
	300 from France
	150 from Italy
	1700 from Austria
	105 from Australia
	65 from New Zealand
	There are also over 5000 international bonds including all AIBD Eurobonds.
	Fixed-interest programs are 144, 145 and 940P
Source:	Stock Exchanges
Years Covered:	Current
	File size: Approx 18 000 domestic issues
	Approx 5000 international bonds
Updates:	The majority of stocks are updated every night
Database Producer:	Datastream
	Available from:Datastream
	Price guide
	The databases are available with the Equity Research and the Financial Futures services

Name: Datastream Investment Accounting Service
Description: This is a powerful on-line system designed to meet the specific
                    requirements of the institutional investor. As a fully integrated
                    management information system it provides detailed portfolio accounting
                    and administration, incorporating full multi-currency double entry for
                    security and currency investments, plus printed statutory reports. This
                    service is both comprehensive and flexible, with easy to use data entry
                    facilities. The various components of the service are:
                    The Investment/General Ledger contains all capital accounts necessary for
                    recording security and currency transactions
                    The Income System provides full double entry accounting and reporting
                    facilities for all income transactions
                    The multi-currency Cash Settlement System
                    The Soft Dealing System – portfolio valuations and
                    analysis available
                    See programs 180-189, 284A
Source: Company financial accounts plus sources serving Datastream's portfolio
                    and research services
Years Covered:
File Size: Storage capacity of the Datastream service is virtually unlimited. Clients
                    can load and maintain any number of funds
Updates: Twice a day, once at mid-day for unitised funds and once overnight for all
                    other portfolios
Database Producer: Datastream
Available From: Datastream
                    Price guide: From £7000

Name: Datastream Traded Options Service
Description: This is a package of programs for subscribers who have an interest in
                    options traded on the London Stock Exchange (LSE), the London
                    International Futures Exchange (LIFFE) and the European Options
                    Exchange (EOE). The service includes 'live' and historical trading data,
                    model and market price comparisons, risk/reward and 'what if' analyses.
                    There are a number of special features including exceptional options ie the
                    cheapest, dearest or most highly geared. The service is provided by
                    programs 201A to 201. It can also be accessed by the 401 graphics program.
Source: LSE, LIFFE, EOE
Years Covered: Current and historic
File Size:
Updates: Real time
Database Producer: Datastream
Available From: Datastream
                    Price guide
                    Traded Options service:
                    £9250 per annum for unlimited access or as an add on to the Equity
                    Research service – £4750

Name: Datastream Valuation Services
Description: Datastream is the leading provider of portfolio valuation services in the UK
                    and Europe. Directly or indirectly, Datastream values funds for 250 000
                    private clients, 2500 institutional investors and 1200 unitised funds.
                    Datastream's range of valuation services has been developed to line up
                    with that spectrum of needs, and to form a core part in the complete fund
                    management services Datastream provides.
                    The valuation service meets the business needs of multi-currency
                    portfolios, across any investment complexion, and is supported by price
                    data on 100 000
                    securities. Standard features of all valuations:
                    Access to Datastream's comprehensive worldwide databases
                    Full support and backup services
                    On-line input of bargains
                    Creation/maintenance of unlisted stocks

Portfolio summaries with industrial/geographical/currency breakdowns
Regular printed valuations available from Datastream
On-line or printed valuations can be in any currency
Book costs can be shown in any currency independent of those chosen for market valuations
All services can be fully integrated with investment accounting services with single data entry. An extensive series of checks forms the base line of the Datastream system – ensuring funds are continuously protected from unauthorised access.

Source:	Stock Exchanges in the UK and overseas
	Interface with Datastream Investment Accounting
Years Covered:	Current
File Size:	Over 100 000 securities held on the Datastream system
Updates:	Minimum for most services is daily
Database Producer:	Datastream
Available From:	Datastream
	Price guide:
	From £14 500 if taken as a stand-alone service
	From £1000 with research services

Name:	DIALOG Quotes and Trading
Description:	DIALOG Quotes and Trading is a gateway service. It delivers stock and options quotes, delayed at least 20 minutes, from the New York and American Stock Exchanges, NASDAQ, and the four major options exchanges. In addition to quotes, order entry allows the purchase or sale of any stock or option listed in the 'Wall Street Journal'. Up to 75 portfolios can be set up on DIALOG Quotes and Trading, with the value of the portfolio's securities updated to reflect current market prices as well as the capability to track gains and losses and to project the dividend income of a portfolio. Tax records maintained on the service can include securities, stocks, options, mutual funds and bonds, and reflect all stocks and options sold. This file offers quantitative tools to evaluate stock option transactions.
	This is a gateway service to Trade Plus. Searchers are automatically transferred to the Trade*Plus system after logging on to the file through DIALOG. This service operates with prompted menus.
Source:	New York and American Stock Exchanges, NASDAQ and the four major US options exchanges
Years Covered:	Current
File Size:	System can hold up to 75 portfolios
Updates:	Daily (20-minute delay)
Database Producer:	Trade Plus
Available From:	DIALOG File Quotes
	$36 per connect hour
	Records not available for printing off line

Name:	DRI Commodities
Description:	DRI Commodities covers major commodities traded in the USA, Canadian and London markets including:
	Financials
	Food and feed grains
	Livestock and meat products
	Fibres and wood
	Metals
	Energy futures
	Prices are provided for London futures, opening, high, low and closing prices for USA and Canadian futures.
Source:	Commodity exchanges
Years Covered:	USA: 20 years
	Canada: 10 years
	London: 2 years
File Size:	48 000 series

Updates:	Daily
Database Producer:	Data Resources Inc (DRI)
	Data Products Division HQ
Available From:	Data Resources Inc (DRI)
	Information Plus

Name:	DRI-FACS
Description:	This is a major international financial database covering interest rates, foreign exchange, commercial bank assets and liabilities, and thrift institution activity. Foreign local money markets and Euro-currencies are included.
Source:	
Years Covered:	
File Size:	14000 series
Updates:	Varies with each series
Database Producer:	Data Resources Inc (DRI)
	Data Products Division HQ
Available From:	Data Resources Inc (DRI)
	Information Plus

Name:	DRI-SEC
Description:	DRI-SEC covers USA securites. Data includes daily prices and financial data for debt, equity and government agency security issues. Information is provided from the following exchanges:
	New York
	American
	Over the counter
	USA regional
	Canadian
	Market and industry indicators are also included, plus Merrill Lynch matrix-priced bond yields for corporate debt issues.
Source:	USA and Canadian Stock Exchanges
Years Covered:	1968 to date
File Size:	60000 issues
Updates:	Daily and weekly
Database Producer:	Data Resources Inc (DRI)
	Data Products Division HQ
	Interactive Data Corporation (IDC)
	Securities Products Division
Available From:	Data Resources Inc (DRI)

Name:	Earnings Guide
Description:	Extel Earnings Guide offers the largest database of consensus forecasting estimates available on UK equities. The service presents the combined results of the analysis of over 30 leading stockbrokers with information from Extel Financial's share database (Exshare, which covers over 100000 international equities).
	It presents an efficient method of keeping up to date with City opinion and offers rapid comparison of competing stocks. In addition the service gives the ability to gain 'gateway' access to the actual research material of the contributing brokers (subject to the appropriate password).
	Each forecast presents:
	2-year consensus of forecasts of company earnings
	Spread of forecasts
	2-year consensus projection of EPS
	2-year consensus projection of P/E ratio
	Historic profits, EPS and P/E ratios
	Market capitalisation of the company
	The service is available as a closed user group on TOPIC
Source:	Stockbrokers' analysis
	Extel's Exshare database
Years Covered:	Current

File Size:	500 plus UK listed shares
	Over 100 000 international equities
Updates:	Minimum frequency is weekly
Database Producer:	Extel Financial Ltd
Available From:	Extel Financial Ltd
	Contact Extel direct for prices

Name:	EDIT
Description:	Extel's closed user group on the London Stock Exchange's TOPIC system. The service augments other information available on TOPIC and provides other information relevant to particular types of dealers and investment analysts.

EDIT contains the 'Extel at a glance share guide' which reports on today's expected company news, takeover battles and press comment. This share guide is currently distributed in hard copy to members on the floor of the Exchange before the market actually opens.

Hourly stock market reports cover the changing moods of the market and, coupled with money market, foreign Exchange reports and a number of international market opening and closing reports, provides the user with easily accessible comment on what is currently happening in their market.

The most widely used part of the service is the continuously updated News Headline pages covering important news from the financial, political and sporting worlds.

Source:	Stock market and foreign exchange reports
Years Covered:	Current
File Size:	
Updates:	Continuous
Database Producer:	Extel Financial Ltd
Available From:	Extel Financial
	Contact Extel direct for prices

Name:	ESPRIT
Description:	ESPRIT is the computer system used by Extel Financial to maintain a real-time database of prices and related information to supply both snapshots of the database as intra-day prices and continuous feeds of pricing data.

The Real-Time Feeds service (RTF) provides a digital data feed of real-time information, international Stock Exchange securities, London traded options, major financial indices, LIFFE and foreign exchange rates. The data can be processed by the user for use on in-house computer systems.

The intra-day prices service is presented in the form of periodic 'snapshots' of the ESPRIT database. Although a standard service is available, each 'snapshot' can be tailored precisely to the user's specifications. The coverage is mainly of equities but includes all gilts, USMs, fixed-interest securities, unit trusts and offshore bonds, trade options and foreign exchange.

Source:	International Stock Exchange – HOTLINE, FTSE, TRADELINE, LTOLINE, DATALINE
	18 European Exchanges
	LIFFE
	Unit trust managers – 4500 unit trusts, off-shore
	funds and insurance bonds
	London Commodity Exchange
	London Metal Exchange
	Leading UK Clearing Bank
	Far East equities – closing prices for Pacific Basin stocks
	US – 200 major selected US stocks
Years Covered:	Real-time information
File Size:	
Updates:	RTF – continuous
	Intra-day – 5 times per day

Database Producer: Extel Financial Ltd
Available From: Extel Financial Ltd
                     Contact Extel direct for prices

Name: Examiner
Description: Examiner is an up-to-the minute business and financial news service. Over
                     400 news stories are available for immediate access via a dynamic indexing
                     system. The index logs the Headline of each Examiner news item, together
                     with page numbers where the full text can be found. The index is built up
                     minute by minute as Extel's reporters input information.
                          Data can be presented on printers (the old ticker- tape service) or monitor
                     screens, distributed through local networks, national networks or on a
                     wide range of micros.
                     Data provided:
                     Company news
                     London Stock Market reports – hourly
                     International Stock Market reports – open and close
                     Government information and statistics
                     General news
                     FT indices
                     Foreign exchange and Eurocurrency rates
                     Money market reports
                     Precious metals
                     LIFFE & traded options rates and reports
                     Recent issues service
                     Early and late trading reports
                     Diary of forthcoming events
Source: Various
Years Covered: Current
File Size: Over 400 news stories (equivalent to 2 days of information)
Updates: Daily
Database Producer: Extel Financial Ltd
Available From: Extel Financial Ltd
                     Contact Extel direct for prices

Name: Exbond
Description: Exbond is a database of the terms and conditions of over 13 000
                     international and Eurobonds, and government domestic issues from the
                     major financial centres. Exbond is claimed by its producers to be the most
                     comprehensive and up-to-date database of its type in the world. Exbond
                     contains over 300 items of data for each bond grouped into the following
                     different sections:
                     Description of the bond
                     Bond classification
                     Issue information
                     Guarantor and issuer
                     Coupons, calls, drawing rights
                     FRN data and convertibles
                          Extel's data and computer specialists are available to visit customers to
                     assist when systems are being specified, amended or programmed. A 'hot
                     line' support service is also available.
Source: Information is obtained from the offering telex and prospectus, or from the
                     issuing agent direct
Years Covered: Current
File Size: 300 items of data per bond
Updates: Daily
                     New bonds are added as soon as the offering telex is
                     issued
Database Producer: Extel Financial Ltd
Available From: Extel Financial Ltd
                     Contact Extel direct for prices

Name:	Executive Market Follower
Description:	This database provides stock price quotes and volume data for over 9000 over-the-counter stocks, traded on the NASDAQ and other major USA exchanges.
Source:	Major USA stock exchanges and the NASDAQ Over-the-counter market
Years Covered:	Current
File Size:	9000 stocks
Updates:	Continuously, throughout the day
Database Producer:	Compuserve Inc
Available From:	Compuserve Inc

Name:	Exshare
Description:	Exshare is an international securites database. Data is supplied on a 'snapshot' basis at various times of the day or night by computer-to-computer transmission or on magnetic media (tape, diskette, etc). Coverage includes fixed interest securities, equities and bonds and traded options from all the world's leading markets and most of the minor ones.

More than 500 data items are available for each security including:
Closing prices
Dividends
Capital changes
Redemption
Conversion and take-over data
Industrial and other classifications
Indices
Exchange rates
All of the above are updated daily.

Exshare is principally a 'back office' service, and also includes all unit trusts and offshore fund prices (approximately 4200). These are collected each afternoon by Extel direct from the management companies or their PR companies. The prices are also supplied by Extel to newspapers such as 'The Times' and to specialist service providers such as ICV Citiservice for use on Prestel by intermediaries and private investors.

Source:	Prices obtained direct from stock exchanges or equivalent bodies (eg the Association of International Bond Dealers), or from Reuters who have an agreement with Extel.
Non-prices data is obtained from printed and computer-readable sources worldwide and edited by Extel staff in London
Years Covered:	Current
Historic database of 2½ years of fully adjusted prices is available in Exshare format
File Size:	100 000 plus equities
(coverage is growing continuously)
500 plus data items per security
Updates:	Daily (depending on client requirements)
Database Producer:	Extel Financial
Available From:	Extel Financial
Contact Extel direct for prices
Interactive Data Corporation (IDC)
File International Securities Data Base
$2500 subscription fee per annum, billed quarterly
(for a maximum of 5 space user ids)
Additional $1250 subscription fee per annum for use in DataSheet
Additional $2500 subscription fee to permit downloading
Analystics charges:
$250 per month plus sliding scale per access fee, on monthly basis, 2c to 7c per hit

Name:	Fastock II
Description:	Fastock II covers USA and Canadian securities, from all USA, Toronto and Montreal exchanges. It provides current and historic financial and descriptive data for equity and debt issues, including options and market statistics.
Source:	USA and Canadian Stock Exchanges
Years Covered:	Dividends – 1968 to date
	Security prices – 1971 to date
File Size:	Approximately 105 000 equity and debt issues
	98 000 securities
Updates:	Daily
Database Producer:	ADP Data Services
Available From:	ADP Data Services

Name:	Finstat
Description:	Finstat is an on-line UK prices service offering a daily electronic feed of statistical data from the 'Financial Times'. Each morning users can receive updated key prices on their computer terminal before the printed version of the FT has arrived on their desks. Data is divided into three categories:
	Group 1 Share Information Service
	Group 2 FT Actuaries and FT30 Share Index
	Group 3 FT Unit Trust Information Service
	Different feeds are available via electronic mail on Telecom Gold
Source:	'Financial Times'
Years Covered:	Current
File Size:	Share Information Service provides price and yield for 3000 commonly traded securites and gilts.
Updates:	Data is made available from 6am following the day of trade
Database Producer:	Financial Times Electronic Publishing
Available From:	Financial Times Electronic Publishing
	Share Information Service: £50-£75 per month
	FT Indices: £30
	FT Unit Trust Information: £50
	FT Dividend Information: £50
	3, 6 or 12-month contracts
	Excludes Telecom Gold charge
	Discounts available for FT Indices feed when taken in conjunction with others

Name:	Ford
Description:	Covers USA securites, providing fundamental data on 2000 common stocks, with 76 data items per stock. Included are all major indicators and ratios. Also input is provided by Ford analysts on quality rating, normalised earnings, projected growth rate, plus an investment value based on Ford's dividend discount model and a quarterly earnings trend figure.
	Available weekly, twice a month or monthly on diskette or by direct line to Ford's computer.
	The Ford database contains the data necessary for the investment management of equities.
Source:	Equivalent to the following publications:
	'Ford Value Report'
	'Ford Investment Management Report'
	'Ford Data Base Report'
Years Covered:	Current
	Historic data from 1974 available on request
File Size:	2000 stocks
Updates:	Weekly and monthly
Database Producer:	Ford Investment Services
	Contact: Fran Morse (VP Marketing)

Available From:	Ford Investor Services
	$250 monthly subscription (monthly updates)
	$600 monthly subscription (weekly updates)
	Subscribers:
	$24 per connect hour
	Non-subscribers:
	$96 per connect hour
	Services can be developed to client specifications
	Other hosts:
	FactSet
	FINSTAT
	Lotus Development
	National Investor Data Services
	Randall Helms
	RV Whitehall
	Savant
	Vestek Systems

Name:	Foreign Exchange Data Base
Description:	Contains bid and asked exchange rates for the spot market and for 1-month, 2-month, 3-month, 6-month and 12-month forward rate contracts for 22 major currencies. All exchange rates are expressed in USA dollars per foreign currency unit. It also includes interest rates for 8 Eurocurrencies.
Source:	Collected by IDC; based on quotes from the foreign exchange advisory service of Chase Manhattan bank plus other reputable sources
Years Covered:	December 1977 to date
File Size:	
Updates:	Daily, Monday to Friday
Database Producer:	Interactive Data Corporation (IDC)
Available From:	Interactive Data Corporation (IDC)
	Analytics charges:
	$250 per month, plus sliding scale per access fee, on monthly basis:
	First 25 000 hits 7c per hit
	Next 100 000 hits 5c per hit
	Additional hits 2c per hit

Name:	FT Currency and Share Index Databank
Description:	This database reports on the dealing rates in the foreign exchange, money, gold markets, and on movements in the London Stock Exchange. Information includes the FT30 Share Index, the FTSE 100 Share Index and the FT Actuaries Share Indices. Representative price indices from the major international stock exchanges are also included. There are facilities available to plot and manipulate data for forecasting and analysis.
Source:	London and international exchanges
Years Covered:	Daily from 1979
	Monthly from 1976
File Size:	
Updates:	Daily and monthly
Database Producer:	Financial Times Electronic Publishing
Available From:	Financial Times Electronic Publishing
	(available through Wharton Econometric's host system)
	£3400 per annum subscription service for unlimited access
	£2.25 per series for a pay as you go service

Name:	Futures Database
Description:	The Futures database covers international futures contracts for approximately 90 commodities traded on over 30 major exchanges. Exchanges included are:
	USA
	Canada
	South America
	UK
	Europe
	Asia
	Australia
	Prices provided are daily, open, high, low and settlement; together with cash prices, volumes and open interest.
Source:	Commodity exchanges
Years Covered:	Current
File Size:	200 contracts
Updates:	Daily
Database Producer:	Commodity Systems Inc
Available From:	ADP Data Services

Name:	Futures-Soft
Description:	This service provides the current day's official closing prices for over 500 USA commodity futures.
Source:	
Years Covered:	Current
File Size:	500 futures
Updates:	Daily
Database Producer:	Commodity Information Services Company (CISCO)
Available From:	Commodity Information Services Company (CISCO)

Name:	FXBase – International Interest Rate and Exchange Rate Database
Description:	FXBase provides current and historic data on major Eurocurrency interest rates, domestic interest rates, and foreign exchange rates for the noon London quote. It also provides gold prices and SDR rates. Data is available at 9am (New York time). Current data are available in cross-section format and historical data as time series. Countries covered for domestic interest rates include: Australia, Belgium, Canada, France, Federal Republic of Germany, Italy, Japan, Switzerland, Netherlands, UK and USA.
Source:	Foreign exchange markets
Years Covered:	Daily – 1982 to date
	Weekly – 1980 to date
	Monthly – 1974 to date
File Size:	
Updates:	Daily, weekly, monthly
Database Producer:	Citicorp Database Services
Available From:	Citicorp Database Servces
	$4000 timesharing annual subscription fee
	(Citibank timesharing only)

Name:	FXPRO – Foreign Currency Projections
Description:	FXPRO is a foreign currency forecasting service, covering 31 countries. Country coverage can be expanded on request. The service combines economic assessment with technical analysis and judgmental factors. A textual commentary is provided with each currency projection. Forecasts look 1 year ahead, rolled out for an additional quarter at the end of each 3-month period.
Source:	
Years Covered:	1 year forecasts
File Size:	
Updates:	Monthly
Database Producer:	S J Rundt and Associates Inc

Available From:	IP Sharp
	Acces via Infomagic
	Contact IP Sharp direct for prices

Name:	Gestion des Valeurs Mobilieres
Description:	This is a real-time portfolio management service for transferable securities, and French and foreign stocks and shares. It is mainly geared to the needs of mutual societies, insurance companies and banks.
Source:	French Stock Exchange
Years Covered:	Current
File Size:	
Updates:	Continuous
Database Producer:	DAFSA
Available From:	DAFSA

Name:	The Hong Kong Exchange Fastprice Database
Description:	This database contains daily market information for nearly 400 securities quoted on the Unified Hong Kong Stock Exchange. It covers all stocks, bonds, warrants and funds quoted on the Exchange, as well as the major market indices. It currently has both preliminary closing prices (within about 1 hour of close of trading) and final close of market data (within 3 hours of close). Data items provided on a current day basis, with a choice of pricing times, are High, Volume, Low, Ask/bid where no trade occurred, and close. The HK Stock Exchange's own numbering system is used.
Source:	Prices are made available via the Unified HK Stock Exchange's Electronic Mail Security Information Service (EMSIS) via Cable and Wireless' DIALCOM system, in conjunction with IDC's Hong Kong and London branches
Years Covered:	Current
File Size:	400 securities
Updates:	Delivered via IDC's Global Early File Service shortly after the close of business on the Hong Kong Stock Exchange
Database Producer:	Hong Kong Stock Exchange and IDC
Available From:	Interactive Data Corporation (IDC)

Name:	Hong Kong Stock Exchange (HKSTOCK)
Description:	Daily trading statistics are provided for over 135 stocks listed on the three major Hong Kong Stock Exchanges.
Source:	Far East Stock Exchange
	Hong Kong Stock Exchange
	Kam Ngan Stock Exchange (gold and silver)
Years Covered:	1981 to date
File Size:	135 stocks
Updates:	Daily, 11am (Hong Kong time) the following market day
Database Producer:	IP Sharp, Hong Kong Office
Available From:	IP Sharp
	Access via Infomagic, Pricelink, 39 Magic and 55
	Retrieve
	Contact IP Sharp direct for prices

Name:	Indes Service
Description:	Indes is a new investment decision service developed by Telekurs AG. Information provided includes securities price data, international and national economic news. Facilities exist to enable the user to compile their own list of quotes and have these automatically updated. The 'limits' facility traces quote movements on the market and visual and sound signals warn you when a critical limit has been reached. There is a ticker facility to identify selected quotes. Price selections available include paid, bid and mid price. There are also formula and chart facilities. The service is designed for use on the Mackintosh II computer.
Source:	See Valordata and Investdata
Years Covered:	See Valordata and Investdata

File Size:	See Valordata and Investdata
Updates:	See Valordata and Investdata
Database Producer:	Telekurs AG
Available From:	Telekurs AG
	£15000 per annum for all hardware and feed

Name:	Informatitres
Description:	Informatitres provides information on over 400000 securities made up as follows:
	5600 French quoted
	12000 French unquoted
	19200 foreign quoted
	3200 foreign unquoted
Source:	Paris Stock Exchange
Years Covered:	Current
File Size:	40000 securities
Updates:	
Database Producer:	DAFSA
Available From:	DAFSA

Name:	International Finance Alert
Description:	IFA is a comprehensive financial service covering foreign exchange, commodities and international money markets. It is divided into 3 services which can be offered separately or as a single, integrated package: International Reports providing foreign exchange advice, World Money Market Reports covering trends in interest and exchange rates, and the FT General Commodity and Financial Futures Reports.
Source:	International stock and commodity exchanges
Years Covered:	Current
File Size:	
Updates:	Continuous during the day
Database Producer:	Financial Times Electronic Publishing
Available From:	Financial Times Electronic Publishing
	This service is offered by the following banks to their clients:
	Netherlands: Bank Mees and Hope
	Belgium: Banque Bruxelles Lambert
	Finland: Kansallis Osake Pankki
	USA: Citibank

Name:	Investdata System
Description:	Investdata is a database inquiry system which allows the user to access the Telekurs' database of over 200000 financial instruments trades worldwide. It offers up to 6 complementary programs. Program 1 offers international price data (latest quotations). Program 2 is an international index to securities allocated identification numbers (Valorennummer, etc). Program 3 offers portfolio management data. Program 4 is an economic news service available in the UK and supplied by the AP-Dow Jones FinWire financial news suppliers. Program 5 covers foreign exchange and precious metals. Program 6 offers instant price quotations from international stock exchanges.
Source:	Various including over 80 stock markets throughout the world.
Years Covered:	Current
File Size:	Latest quotations for 78000 securites.
	Portfolio management data for over 130000 securities
Updates:	Real time, daily
Database Producer:	Telekurs AG
Available From:	Telekurs AG
	Using Telekurs hardware:
	1st terminal £600 (per month)
	Program 1 £200 (per month)
	Program 2 £50 (per month)

Program 3 £100 (per month)
Program 4 price on application
Program 5 £100
Program 6 £120
Installation charge £1400
Access charges are based on the number of interrogations made per annum

Name: Investors Daily
Description: This is a bibliographic database with abstracts to 'Investors Daily', a
                       financial newspaper which has features such as NYSE Stocks in the News,
                       Stock Quotes (from all major exchanges), AMEX Stock in the News,
                       Industries in the News, Inside the Market and At the Analysts. Financial
                       graphs from William O'Neil and Co are the highlight of this paper. These
                       are described in the abstract section in the database.
Source: Printed version of 'Investors Daily'
Years Covered: 1986 to present
File Size:
Updates: Monthly
Database Producer: J A Micropublishing Inc
Available From: BRS File IVDA
                       $45 per connect hour
                       $1 per on-line type
                       95c per off-line print
                       SDI profile: $4

Name: Japanese Fastprice Database
Description: This database contains daily close of market pricing information for over
                       2700 securities quoted on the Tokyo Stock Exchange. It offers coverage of
                       all equities quoted on the first and second sections of the Exchange. In
                       addition, prices for approximately 1200 corporate and government bonds
                       are available within 2 hours of close of trading in Tokyo. Data items
                       provided where available are open, high, low, close, volume and
                       ex-dividend marker. The database uses the Japanese Securites Code
                       Council's numbering system.
Source: Jiji Press, Tokyo, in conjunction with IDC's Tokyo and London offices
Years Covered: Current
File Size: 2700 securities
                       1200 bonds
Updates: Delivered via IDC's Global Early File Service shortly
                       after the close of business on the Tokyo Stock Exchange
Database Producer: Jiji Press and IDC
Available From: Interactive Data Corporation (IDC)

Name: The Luxembourg Stock Exchange Database
Description: This database contains daily close of market pricing information for the
                       nearly 6000 securities quoted on the Luxembourg Stock Exchange. It offers
                       complete coverage of all domestic and Eurocurrency equities, bonds and
                       warrants quoted on the Exchange. Data items provided are the closing/last
                       transaction price, ask/bid prices and indicative prices. Both the CEDEL and
                       SEDOL numbering systems are used.
Source: Luxembourg Stock Exchange in conjunction with IDC's Brussels and
                       London offices
Years Covered: Current
File Size: 6000 securities
Updates: Delivered via IDC's Global Early File Service shortly after the close of
                       business on the Stock Exchange
Database Producer: Luxembourg Stock Exchange and IDC
Available From: Interactive Data Corporation (IDC)

Name:	Marketpulse
Description:	Marketpulse provides real-time quotes and trading information from all of the world's major equity, commodity and financial future exchanges on one screen. Marketpulse users can design their own screen displaying the data they want to see. Access to full quote information, Seaq level 2 quotes and news is immediately available along with further facilities linking to internal systems and externally provided research databases.
Source:	Equity, commodity and financial futures exchanges worldwide. Dow Jones, AP-Dow Jones and Extel Examiner news services. Contributors for foreign exchange rates and deposit rates.
Years Covered:	Current
File Size:	
Updates:	Real time
Database Producer:	ADP Comtrend Ltd (UK)
Available From:	ADP Comtrend
	Equipment rental:
	Marketpulse: dependant upon exchanges covered but average of £450 per month per terminal. Hardware IBM PS2s purchased by customer

Name:	Marketscan
Description:	Marketscan provides data on USA and Canadian securities from the following stock exchanges:
	New York
	American
	Montreal
	Toronto
	Alberta
	Vancouver
	Information is provided following the close of markets each day. Historic weekly summaries for up to 250 weeks is available. Canadian mutual fund information is available from January 1986.
Source:	USA and Canadian Stock Exchanges
Years Covered:	Last 250 trading days
File Size:	
Updates:	Daily
Database Producer:	Info Globe
Available From:	Info Globe
	Initial fee $75 (individual database fee)
	$150 per connect hour (prime time)
	$33 per connect hour (non-prime time)
	Other services available include custom searches

Name:	Metal and Mineral Prices (MINPRI)
Description:	This database provides daily time series of prices for aluminium, copper, zinc, lead, tin, gold, silver and nickel.
Source:	'The Australian Financial Review', 'The Metal Bulletin' (London) and the technical press and producers
Years Covered:	1971 to present
File Size:	
Updates:	Weekly
Database Producer:	Australian Bureau of Mineral Resources
Available From:	IP Sharp
	Access via 39 Magic
	Contact IP Sharp direct for prices

Name:	Metals Week
Description:	Metals Week covers international metal prices in the non-ferrous market for:
	Major metals (eg copper, aluminium, copper, lead, etc)
	Precious metals
	Feroalloys
	Light and other metals
	Currency exchange rates
Source:	London Metal Exchange
	New York Commodity Exchange
	Other US regional and international markets
Years Covered:	Varies according to series
File Size:	500 series
Updates:	Varies according to series
Database Producer:	McGraw-Hill Inc
Available From:	Data Resources Inc, Information Plus

Name:	Middle TAC
Description:	Middle TAC can provide 133 items of information depending upon the type of bond. It offers extensive issue, redemption, schedule and coupon details for floating rate notes, convertible bonds, warrants and bullet issues. Data items include Eurobond FRN schedules, Eurobond manager details, Eurobond fees, drawing and conversion schedules, and security details. Each of these items is given an individual record type. For example, the Security details record includes total number of Exchanges where quoted, Moody's and Standard & Poor's rating, etc.
Source:	IDC's own database (US domestic bonds)
	Extel (Eurobonds)
Years Covered:	Current
File Size:	10000 US bonds
	8000 Eurobonds
Updates:	Delivered via IDC's Global Early File Service shortly after the close of business
Database Producer:	IDC, Extel
Available From:	Interactive Data Corporation (IDC)

Name:	MMS Asia/Pacific Market Analysis
Description:	This database provides analysis of the financial and commodity markets from all major financial centres in Asia and Australia. In includes economic and technical analyses of the currency, debt and precious metals markets. It also includes analyses from Europe and the USA, mainly focused on the currency and precious metals markets.
Source:	MMS market analyst reports
Years Covered:	Current
File Size:	
Updates:	Continuous
Database Producer:	Money Market Services (MMS)
Available From:	Telerate
	$195 per month

Name:	MMS Currency Market Analysis
Description:	This database provides coverage of the foreign exchange and international capital markets by MMS economists and analysts in Europe, North America and Asia. It includes analysis of economic and technical factors affecting these markets as well as comprehensive analysis of the major central banks, and a weekly foreign exchange survey.
Source:	MMS economists and financial analysts
Years Covered:	Current and future years
File Size:	Approximately 40 pages
Updates:	Continuous
Database Producer:	Money Market Services (MMS)

Available From: Telerate
                     $275 per month
                     AP-Dow Jones News/Retrieval
                     $120 per connect hour
                     Compuserve
                     Provides the Daily Currency Market Report at $5 per report.

Name: MMS Equity Market Analysis
Description: This database provides analysis of economic factors directly affecting USA
                     equity prices, as well as technical analyses of equity futures and index
                     options. MMS includes fiscal and trade policy analyses, money/liquidity
                     analyses and surveys of quarterly economic forecasts, stock indexes and
                     GNP (Gross National Product) forecasts. In addition, MMS offers 'MMS
                     Gilt Market Analysis' which provides forecasts, analyses and information
                     on all factors affecting the cash or futures market for UK government
                     securities. Comments are written from both an economic and technical
                     standpoint.
Source: MMS survey of quarterly economic forecasts
                     Market analysts
Years Covered: Current
File Size:
Updates: Daily
Database Producer: Money Market Services (MMS)
Available From: Reuters
                     Available on the Reuters Domestic and International Monitor Systems; the
                     Reuters SDS2 'Satellite' System and the Advanced Reuters Terminal (ART)
                     $195 per month (price for equity or gilt market analysis)
                     Bridge Information System
                     $195 per month
                     TOPIC
                     $195 per month
                     AP-Dow Jones News/Retrieval
                     $120 per connect hour
                     Note: MMS also provide hard-copy publications including a free newsletter
                     and bi-weekly briefings. The 'Fedwatch' newsletter covering economics
                     and financial market activity is available direct from MMS or online through
                     Nexis and Compuserve

Name: Money Market Rates (MRATE)
Description: This database provides 246 daily and weekly money market rates for 13
                     countries, including Canada, the USA and many European and Asian
                     countries. The focus is on primary market rates. The aim of the database is
                     to provide investment and securities analysts with a general trend of
                     short-term and fixed-income securities. Information includes USA
                     interest-rate data, dollar swaps and discount rates. Plus Eurocurrency and
                     inter-bank currency rates reported in London, Copenhagen and Singapore.
Source: 'Financial Times': London
                     'The Globe and Mail': Toronto
                     'The Wall Street Journal': New York
                     'The Business Times': Singapore
                     'The Bond and Money Market Letter'
                     Federal Reserve Bank of New York
Years Covered: Current
File Size: 246 rates for 13 countries
Updates: Daily as information is published
Database Producer: IP Sharp
Available From: IP Sharp
                     Access via Pricelink and 39 Magic
                     Contact IP Sharp direct for prices

Name:	Munifacts Plus
Description:	Munifacts covers USA and international municipal and corporate bonds plus US government and Federal Agency market news.
	Four daily wrapups on the money markets include:
	US government and Federal Agency markets
	'Inside' quotes
	Futures activity in T-bills
	Long bonds
	GNMAs
Source:	
Years Covered:	Current
File Size:	2-5000 bonds for sale per day
	Over 400 news items per day
Updates:	Real-time and continuous according to file
Database Producer:	American Banker. The Bond Buyer Inc
Available From:	American Banker. The Bond Buyer Inc
	Contact direct for price and access information

Name:	North American Stock Market (NASTOCK)
Description:	NASTOCK provides current and historic prices and volumes for securities on the following North American and Canadian stock exchanges:
	New York
	American
	Montreal
	Toronto
	Alberta
	Vancouver
	Time series includes volume traded, bid, ask, open, close, high and low dollar value, previous close, dollar value traded and thousand shares outstanding.
Source:	As above
Years Covered:	Toronto: 1979 to date
	Others: 1981 to date
File Size:	
Updates:	Daily, by 2000 Toronto time same day
Database Producer:	IP Sharp
Available From:	IP Sharp
	Access via Infomagic, Priceline, 39 Magic or 55 Retrieve
	Contact IP Sharp for prices

Name:	Oslo Bors Informasjonssystem
Description:	This is the Norwegian Stock Exchange information service. It provides official rates of exchange, bonds, shares rates, historic and current rates.
	There are three databases: First, price information continuously updated from the Stock Exchange (real time in Norway only). Secondly, changes in equity capital are recorded including stock splits and convertibles. Thirdly, there is a company accounts service providing annual and interim reports for all listed companies (over 160) in Norway, except for banks and insurance companies. This service has the same structure as the Findata databases. It includes 150 to 200 variables per company which is most of the items from financial statements and notes to the accounts. This service is updated annually.
Language:	Norwegian
Source:	Norwegian Stock Exchange
	Annual accounts
Years Covered:	1980 to date
File Size:	150-200 variables per company
	160 listed variables Norwegian companies
Updates:	Real time (Norway)
	Daily (Datastream)
Database Producer:	Norwegian Stock Exchange

Available From:	Oslo Bors
	Datastream
	This service is planned to be available via Datastream in the near future.
	Updates will be on a daily basis

Name:	Over the Counter Information
Description:	This database provides share quotes on the UK OTC market, which are continuously updated. It also covers company news and background information.
Source:	London Stock Exchange
Years Covered:	Current
File Size:	Over 500 quotes daily
Updates:	Continuous
Database Producer:	OTC Information Systems plc
Available From:	Prestel
	TOPIC
	£350 per annum extra on normal TOPIC subscription plus other print charges

Name:	Prestel Citiservice
Description:	Citiservice provides access to financial prices, reports and advice.
	Coverage: Commodities and financial futures
	UK and US prices
	News
	Continuously updated 8.30am-10pm
	Unit trust prices
	Latest prices for 6500 unit linked funds
	News
	Performance charts
	Historical database
	Updated daily
	London Stock Exchange
	Citiservice SEAQ covers 3300 shares, gilts, USMs
	Portfolio Manager enables users to create their own personal valuations
	Price ticker
	UK and US stock indices
	Traded options prices
	Continuously updated. Markets often open before 8am.
	Foreign exchange & money markets
	Covers:
	34 currencies
	Spot, forward, deposit rates
	Gilts market, LIFFE, International Monetary Market in Chicago (IMM)
	News – UK and international
	Sourced by Midland Bank, Chase Manhattan, National Westminster, Tullett, Tokyo and Chemical Bank
	Continuously updated
	Bullion:
	Spot, fixed and forward rates
	News
	Provided by Mase Westpac
	Continuously updated 8am-5pm
	News:
	Company announcements
	Financial and business news
	Latest international news
	Share features and statistics
	Continuously updated 8am-5.30pm
	Brokers' Services:
	Market commentary
	Research

	Detailed recommendations
	Continuously updated 8.30-5pm
Source:	Various including banks and stock exchanges
Years Covered:	Current
File Size:	Varies according to service
Updates:	Continuous
Database Producer:	Citiservice
Available From:	Citiservice
	Accessible via a TV with adapter, microcomputer or
	Prestel terminal. Citiservice can organise equipment
	General access charges:
	£18 standing charge per quarter
	(£6.50 for residential customers)
	6p per minute time charge (peak times)
	Non-peak times free
	Citiservice time charge 24p per minute. Discount for
	frequent usage £100 per quarter (off SEAQ Gateway)
	Telephone charges – for UK users at local call rates
	Citiservice SEAQ:
	Initial registration fee £42.00 + VAT
	Non-professional membership fee £42.00 per quarter + VAT
	Professional membership fee £120 per quarter + VAT
	Portfolio Manager:
	No extra charge to Citiservice SEAQ
	subscribers. Other users pay:
	Initial registration fee £15.00 + VAT
	Membership fee £15.00 per quarter + VAT

Name:	Pricedata
Description:	Pricedata contains time series price quotations for the major world commodities and exchange rates of the currencies used in international trade dealings. It also contains the indexes produced by leading economic research and finance bodies on the prices of basic raw materials.
	The commodities cover the following groups: cereals, tea, coffee, sugar and spices, edible oils, textiles, ferrous and non-ferrous metals, precious metals, energy-producing raw materials, etc. The currencies covered are: US dollar, UK sterling, Japanese yen, Dutch florin, Danish crown, Italian lire, French and Swiss francs and the German mark.
	The index series are accompanied by summary tables retrievable as required. Each series bears a title which specifies: trading markets, spot or future prices, trading unit, periodicity and source.
Language:	Multilingual. Retrieval Software ESA-Quest offers the facility to select the language preferred: English, French, German or Italian
Source:	Data of the product and money series are taken directly from the various commodities and exchange markets of London, New York, Chicago, Winnipeg, Paris, Frankfurt, Zurich, Brussels, Amsterdam, Milan, Hong Kong, Singapore, Tokyo, Yokohama and Sydney.
	Index data comes directly from the producers such as Reuter, Confindustria, HWWA, Moody's, Dow Jones, INSEE, UNCTAD and Financial Times
Years Covered:	1973/75 to date
File Size:	800 references
Updates:	Irregular
Database Producer:	SLAMARK International SpA
	Information Systems for Marketing and Planning
Available From:	ESA-IRS File 46

Name: Priceplus
Description: Priceplus is a derivative of the Exshare database. Prices are provided for:
                       UK Gilts
                       Alpha/Beta stocks
                       Gamma/Delta stocks
                       USM/3rd market
                       Traded options
                       Over 1900 international equities
                       Unit trusts
                       Insurance bonds
                       Offshore bonds
                       Indices and exchange rates
                          Priceplus also contains share prices, plus dividend dates and rates, and
                       takeover and capital change markers.
Source: Extel's Exshare database
Years Covered: Current
File Size: N/A
Updates: Daily, via Telecom Gold
                       Weekly or monthly via diskette
Database Producer: Extel Financial Ltd
Available From: Extel Financial Ltd
                       Contact Extel direct for prices

Name: Quotron 800
Description: Quotron is a real-time financial information service covering stocks, bonds,
                       options, commodities, dividends and earnings performance of 26 industry
                       groups plus business and economic news. It also contains a variety of
                       market indicators and statistics.
Source: USA Exchanges
                       'Dow Jones News'
                       Reuters
                       'Commodity World News'
Years Covered: Current
File Size:
Updates: Continuously throughout the day
Database Producer: Quotron Systems Inc
Available From: Quotron Systems Inc

Name: Quotron Symbol Guide
Description: Quotron Symbol Guide provides a listing of ticker symbols and other
                       market symbols used in Quotron 800. It covers the following:
                       USA stocks
                       Canadian stocks
                       New York Stock Exchange
                       American Stock Exchange
                       Mutual funds
                       Bonds
                       Put and call month codes
                       Striking price codes
Source: Equivalent to the publication 'Quotron's Symbol Directory'
Years Covered: Current
File Size:
Updates: Periodically, as data becomes available
Database Producer: Quotron Systems Inc
Available From: Quotron Systems Inc

Name: Reuter Monitor (Service)
Description: Reuter Monitor provides 17 files covering the following major topics:
Money/financial futures
Money markets
Grain/livestock
Metals
Softs
Coins
Energy
Securities
Optional domestic data
Optional international data
Optional securities quotations
Tickers
Contributed information
    Reuters provide over 100 services. Contact direct for further details.
Source: Stock exchanges, stockbroker reports and a wide range of other financial sources
Years Covered: Most recent 24 hours
File Size:
Updates: Continuous
Database Producer: Reuters
Available From: Reuters

Name: Scan
Description: Scan provides current and historical financial data for over 30 000 UK and international securities.
Source: Company financial reports, stock exchanges
Years Covered: Current (historic 1972 to date)
File Size: 30 000 securities
Updates: Daily
Database Producer: Scicon
Available From: Scicon

Name: Sistema de Informacion Bursatil
Description: This database provides current and historic data on share prices quoted on the Madrid Stock Exchange, including data on the volume of transactions. It includes information on earnings and dividends taken from listed companies' annual and quarterly reports, and money market data.
Source: Madrid Stock Exchange
Company financial reports
Years Covered: 1975 to date
File Size:
Updates: Continuously throughout the day
Database Producer: Bolsa Oficial de Comercio de Madrid
Available From: Bolsa Oficial de Comercio de Madrid
Annual subscription required

Name: Stock Exchange of Singapore (SINGSTOCK)
Description: The Stock Exchange of Singapore provides securities data daily for stocks traded on the exchange. It provides indexes for the Singapore and other Asian Exchanges:
Straits Times index
Business Times index
Hong Kong
Taiwan
New Zealand
Tokyo
Manila
Bangkok
Kuala Lumpur

Source:	'Singapore Stock Exchange Daily Journal'
	'Far Eastern Economic Review'
Years Covered:	1982 to date for Singapore and Kuala Lumpur stock data and indexes
	1983 to date for other indexes
File Size:	400 times series for stocks traded on the Singapore Stock Exchange
Updates:	Singapore and Kuala Lumpur – daily
	Others – weekly
Database Producer:	IP Sharp
Available From:	IP Sharp
	Access via Infomagic, Pricelink, 39 Magic or 55 Retrieve
	Contact IP Sharp direct for prices

Name:	Sydney Stock Exchange STATEX Service (STATEX)
Description:	This database contains time series of annual balance sheet information on over 900 companies traded on Australian stock exchanges.
Source:	Sydney Stock Exchange Research Dept
Years Covered:	Annual data for most recent 12 years
File Size:	
Updates:	Daily
Database Producer:	IP Sharp
Available From:	IP Sharp
	Access via Infomagic, 39 Magic
	Contact IP Sharp direct for prices

Name:	Teledata
Description:	The Teledata service (TDS) is designed to provide real-time price data from world markets. It provides latest prices/quotations, ie the day's prices: opening price, closing paid price, closing bid price, closing asked price, middle price, issue price, spot price. Real time prices are available from the London SEAQ, LCE, LME, LIFFE exchanges, 21 USA exchanges, Canadian, German, Dutch, French, Italian, Swiss, Danish, Finnish, Hong Kong, Norwegian, Singapore, Swedish and Japanese (Tokyo) exchanges (real-time).
Source:	69 worldwide exchanges (as above)
Years Covered:	Current
File Size:	
Updates:	Real time
Database Producer:	Telekurs AG
Available From:	Telekurs AG
	Minimum charge £20000 per annum (for approximately 3500 securities) plus £6000 installation and test (one off)
	£4000 per annum feed administration
	Thereafter £3.20 per annum per security, 40p per annum per quote item

Name:	Telerate Financial Information Network
Description:	Telerate covers world markets for commodities, currencies bonds and money market investments. The futures service covers contracts on all major North American exchanges, plus the London Exchange. Items covered include Eurodollar and Eurocurrencies, UK federal funds, certificates of deposit, commercial paper and foreign money market rates.
Source:	North American and London exchanges, banks, brokers and other financial institutions
Years Covered:	Current
	Some data held for 24 hours
File Size:	
Updates:	Continuous
Database Producer:	Telerate Systems Inc
Available From:	Telerate Systems Inc
	Monthly subscription rates:
	£400 UK
	$700 international

Name:	TOPIC (Service)
	Teletext Output of Price Information
Description:	The TOPIC service provides prices for over 2300 equities and gilt-edged securities. The service covers:
	London Traded Options (latest prices from floor of the London Traded Options Market)
	SEAQ real-time market information service
	International service (two-way prices for international securities)
	North American price service
	Foreign exchange
	Overseas prices and indices
	Company announcements
	Money rates and LIFFE
	Commentary and forecasts
	Stock Exchange economic service
	ICC Sharewatch (available to a closed user group)
Source:	Exchanges worldwide
Years Covered:	Current and historic
File Size:	
Updates:	Daily
Database Producer:	The Stock Exchange of the UK and Republic of Ireland
Available From:	The Stock Exchange of the UK and Republic of Ireland
	Charges vary according to service accessed. Contact host direct for details
	PC TOPIC plus other services are available from the above
Name:	Toronto Stock Exchange 300 Index and Stock Statistics (TSE 300)
Description:	IP Sharp hosts the TSE 300 Index and stock statistics providing time series of trading data for the stocks and indexes that make up the 300 Composite Index. The Toronto Stock Exchange provides a variety of products on tape, printed reports and diskette.
Source:	Toronto Stock Exchange
Years Covered:	Current (historic period varies according to individual products)
	Monthly data back to 1956
File Size:	
Updates:	On-line services daily, weekly and monthly
Database Producer:	IP Sharp
Available From:	IP Sharp
	Access via Infomagic, Pricelink, 39 Magic or 55 Retrieve
	Contact IP Sharp direct for prices
	Toronto Stock Exchange
	(1) TSE High Speed Data Feed
	C$500 or US$425
	Billed monthly by the TSE
	Exchange fees:
	Base rate: $22 per interrogation unit (professional)
	$4 per interrogation unit
	(non-professional)
	(2) Consolidated Canadian Market Data Feed
	US vendors US$1300 per month
	C vendors C$1750 per month
	Exchange fees:
	TSE (refer to No 1)
	ME C$15 per bid/ask price
	VSE C$15 per bid/ask price
	Billed by each exchange
	Customers outside Canada:
	Base rate: US$40 per interrogation unit (professional)
	US$3.50 per interrogation unit
	(non-professional)
	(3) SIAC
	CTS Data Feed $1500 per month

CTS and CQS $2500 per month
Plus fees payable to exchanges
(4) NASDAQ
Level 1 Bid/Ask $500 per month
National Market Trading System $500 per month

Name:	United Nations Commodity Trade Statistics Database (SITC)
Description:	SITC provides annual information on commodities, trading partners, imports, exports, re-exports, values (US dollars) and quantity traded for 270 countries and country groupings for over 3000 commodities.
	Active trading nations that report data include: Canada, US, EEC countries, Scandinavia, most ASCAN countries, Saudi Arabia, Korea and Japan (31 countries in total).
Source:	United Nations
Years Covered:	Annually
File Size:	
Updates:	Several times a year, as data is available from the UN
Database Producer:	IP Sharp
Available From:	IP Sharp
	Access via Infomagic or 39 Magic
	Contact IP Sharp direct for prices

Name:	United States Stock (USOPTIONS)
Description:	Options contains daily trading statistics for all put and call options traded on the major USA domestic exchanges. The service contains 136000 time series referring to 14000 stock options, interest rate options, index options and foreign currency options.
Source:	The major exchanges covered include the New York (NYSE), American, Pacific, Philadelphia and Chicago Board Options Exchanges
Years Covered:	
File Size:	136000 time series, 14000 stock options
Updates:	Daily
Database Producer:	IP Sharp
Available From:	IP Sharp
	Access via Infomagic, Pricelink, 39 Magic or 55 Retrieve
	Contact IP Sharp direct for prices

Name:	United States Stock Market (USSTOCK)
Description:	Contains current and historical prices and volumes for securities listed on international exchanges. The US database provides trading statistics for over 15000 common and preferred stocks, warrants, rights and writs for issues traded on the New York, American, Montreal, Midwest, Boston, Pacific, Toronto and Philadelphia Exchanges. Also included are OTC and NASDAQ issues.
Source:	Stock Exchanges in the US and Canada
Years Covered:	1980 to date for NYSE, AMEX, NASDAQ and market indicators
	1982 to date for all others
File Size:	Over 200 market indicators
Updates:	Daily
Database Producer:	IP Sharp
Available From:	IP Sharp
	Access via Infomagic, Pricelink, 39 Magic and 55 Retrieve
	Contact IP Sharp direct for prices

Name:	The Unlisted Market Guide
Description:	This database provides over-the-counter stock market information for over 11000 non-NASDAQ and NASDAQ companies. It covers 3-yearly income statement, 2-yearly balance sheet, and a description of each company's business.
Source:	USA Stock Exchanges
Years Covered:	Current

File Size:	Approx 11 000 companies
Updates:	Weekly
	Approx 50 added each week
Database Producer:	
Available From:	Quotron Systems Inc

Name:	Valordata System
Description:	This is a securities service covering securities worldwide. The principal search parameter for each security is the official Swiss Security Number. Valordata is made up of three distinct services: the Register of Securities Service, the Titelbulletin Service which keeps users informed daily about any changes affecting a security, and the Portfolio Valuation Prices Service. The valuation service provides users with up to date pricing information needed for valuations supplied according to the individual's own requirements.
Source:	Telekurs' own database
Years Covered:	Current
File Size:	
Updates:	Daily
Database Producer:	Telekurs AG
Available From:	Telekurs AG
	Prices available direct from Telekurs
	Portforlio Valuation Service (via Remote Batch Application (RBA))
	Minimum 500 securities at 2p per extraction per annum
	1001-2000 securities 1.6p per annum
	Register of Securities
	Basic charge 80p per annum per security
	Plus £165 per annum for monthly delivery (excluding courier fees, etc)
	Titelbulletin
	£1.10 per annum per security
	Magnetic tape £4000 per annum
	Portfolio Valuation Prices Service
	Monthly delivery £2 per annum per security plus
	£1650 for magnetic tape

Name:	Valport
Description:	This database is part of the Valport portfolio valuation system. It contains data for over 80 000 securities:
	Publicly traded USA and Canadian securities
	Over-the-counter issues
	USA and Canadian exchanges
	USA and Canadian government and agency issues
	Mutual funds
	Unit investment trusts
	Foreign securities traded in the USA
Source:	USA and Canadian exchanges
Years Covered:	Current
	Daily price history – most recent 9 months
File Size:	80 000 securities
Updates:	Daily
Database Producer:	Frederick C Towers & Co
Available From:	Control Data Corporation (USA)

Name:	Valscop-Valeurs
Description:	This database provides French Stock Exchange information including:
	French and foreign stocks
	Shares and securities
	Currencies
	Gold prices
	Trends and records
Source:	French Stock Exchange
Years Covered:	Current

File Size:	8000 debentures and stocks
	22000 foreign securities
	50 currencies
Updates:	Continuous, direct link to the Stock Exchange
Database Producer:	Compagnie des Agents de Changes
Available From:	Valscop Duplex
	FF 240 per connect hour
	Membership fee FF 1250

Name:	Videcom
Description:	Videcom provides real-time price and trading data from 16 financial exchanges in the USA, London and Hong Kong, including Chicago Commodity Exchange, New York Mercantile Exchange, LIFFE, Hong Kong Exchanges and London Metal and Commodity Exchanges. Information can be displayed graphically using a number of forms such as spread/ratio charts and trendline charts. There are also 7 tabular formats which include Boardwatch and Accountswatch, allowing users the flexibility to program pages to display their particular requirements.
Source:	Financial Exchanges in USA, London and Hong Kong
Years Covered:	Data accessible over the last 15 years
File Size:	
Updates:	Real time
Database Producer:	ADP Comtrend Ltd (UK)
Available From:	ADP Comtrend Ltd (UK)
	Equipment rental:
	Videcom £1000 per month for the first terminal
	Plus British Telecom line charges and exchange fees
	Systems can be purchased outright from ADP

Section XI
Accountancy and Tax

Accountants
Accountants Business Network (see Overseas Trade Opportunities)
Business Periodicals Index

Business Review Weekly (Australia) (see Marketing Section)
Datastream Investment Accounting Service (see Securities Section)
ICAA Australian Accounting Database

Management Contents (see General Management Section)
NAARS – Accounting Information (Mead Service) (see Company Section)
Tax Notes Today

Name:	Accountants
Description:	Provides access to worldwide English language literature related to accounting, auditing, taxation, data processing investments, financial management, financial reporting and related legal information. Sources include books, government documents, and journals from the US, Canada, England, Australia, South Africa, Japan and others.
Source:	Equivalent to the 'Accountants' Index' publication. Source documents are 80 per cent journal articles
	and 20 per cent books and pamphlets
Years Covered:	1974 to present
File Size:	Approx 190000 records (as of February 1988)
Updates:	Quarterly
	4000 records added per update
Database Producer:	American Institute of Certified Public Accountants
Available From:	ORBIT Search Service File Accountants
	$85 per connect hour
	20-25c per on-line type
	25-30c per off-line print

Name: Accountants Business Network
Description: ABN provides information on businesses for sale with a value of between
                       £500 000 to £10m. This is a confidential service which is accessible only by
                       the group of 15 large UK accounting firms who organise and administer
                       ABN. It is designed to help those who wish to sell their businesses to find
                       buyers through the extensive client and contact networks of leading
                       accounting firms. Also, member firms can provide introductory details of
                       businesses for sale to those of their clients who are seeking to expand by
                       acquisition.
Source:
Years Covered: Current
File Size: Over 100 companies
Updates: As details become available
Database Producer: Participating firms:
                       Robson Rhodes   Coopers & Lybrand
                       Spicer and Oppenheim   Deloitte Haskins and Sells
                       Stoy Hayward   Ernst and Whinney
                       Touche Ross   Grant Thornton
                       Arthur Anderson   Pannell Kerr Forster
                       Arthur Young   KPMG
                       Binder Hamlyn   Price Waterhouse
                       Clark Whitehill
Available From: ABN forms part of the range of services available from the participating
                       firms of accountants. The cost of using the ABN will form part of the overall
                       fee to be agreed between the client and their advisers.
Note: Clients of Coopers and Lybrand can obtain automatic access to ABN at no
                       extra cost by registering as clients of the Corporate Acquisitions and
                       Disposals Service, whether as buyers or sellers. For further information
                       contact Piers D C Eley at Coopers & Lybrand in London (01-583 5000)

Name: Business Periodicals Index
Description: This is a bibliographic database covering over 304 major international
                       English language periodicals, including trade and business research
                       journals.
                       Major areas covered are:
                       Accounting
                       Advertising and marketing
                       Business and finance
                       Building and construction
                       Computers
                       Economics
                       Labour
                       Engineering
                       International business
                       Real estate
                       Occupational health and safety
Source: International periodicals. Corresponds to 'Business Periodicals Index'
Years Covered: June 1982 to date
File Size: Approximately 304 periodicals
Updates: Twice weekly
Database Producer: The H W Wilson Company
                       UK Marketing Representative
                       Thompson, Henry Ltd
Available From: H W Wilson
                       $300-$2400 annual fee
                       $43-$65 per connect hour
                       No charge for on-line type
                       20c per off-line print (citation)

Name: ICCA Australian Accounting Database
Description: This database covers articles and periodicals relevant to accountancy and
                      related subjects in Australia.
Source: Various including:
                      'Australian Business'
                      'Australian Journal of Management'
                      'Abacus'
                      'Accounting and Finance'
                      'Accounting Forum'
                      'Today's Computer'
                      'Your Business'
                      'Company and Securities Law Journal'
                      'Australian Accountant'
                      'Chartered Accountant in Australia'
Years Covered: 'Chartered Accountant in Australia': 1982 to date
                      All others: 1983 to date
File Size: Over 1500 documents; 250 documents added monthly
Updates: Monthly
Database Producer: Institute of Chartered Accountants in Australia
Available From: ACI Computer Services
                      A$40 per month (fees)
                      A$150 per connect hour
                      25c per off-line print

Name: Tax Notes Today
Description: Tax Notes Today provides analytical summaries together with full text of all
                      important US legislative, regulatory, judicial and policy documents
                      regarding federal taxation.
Source: News stories written by tax attorneys, tax accountants, public finance
                      economists and journalists. Doc materials in TNT are obtained from
                      government agencies and others during the day, processed in the
                      afternoon and evening, to be transmitted to DIALOG each night
Years Covered: Jan 1987 to date
File Size: 31 631 records
Updates: Daily
Database Producer: Tax Analysts (USA)
Available From: DIALOG File 650
                      $96 per connect hour
                      $4 per on-line type
                      $4 per off-line print
                      10c per report element

Section XII
Bibliographic
Databases

Research

Dissertation Abstracts Online
EABS (see EEC Section)
Endoc (see EEC Section)
Euristote (see EEC Section)
Forkat
HADOSS
INFORBW
Institutions for International
Cooperation
IRRD
NTIS
SSIE Current Research
THES

Books and Monographs

BiblioData
Blaise-Line (Service)
Books in Print
British Books in Print
Economic Literature Index
FINP
GPO Monthly Catalog
GPO Publications Reference
File
LC Marc
OCLC Easi Reference
REMARC
SIGLE
Ulrich's Periodicals

Database Directories

Alpha
Cuadra Directory of Online
Databases
Directorio de Bases de Datos
Dundis (see EEC Section)

Information Science

Dundis (See EEC Section)
Electronic Publishing
Abstracts
Infodata
LISA
Online Chronicle
Thesauri (see EEC Section)

User Aids

Brokersguide (see EEC Section)
CCL-Train (see EEC Section)

Cross Directory File
Dialindex
DIALOG Publications
Dianeguide (see EEC Section)
Standard Industrial

Classification
Thesauri (see EEC Section)

Name:	Alpha
Description:	The 'Alpha-Datenbank' (ALPH) is an up-to-date German-language data bank about databanks.
	It provides brief descriptions of the contents of data banks and is particularly suitable for targeting potential data bank facilites.
	As it also contains up-to-date information on prices and other important features, it enables the user to find the data bank which is best value for money for the use intended.
	Information provided:
	Data bank name
	Daba bank owner (host)
	Prices, details about free formats
	Brief data bank descriptions
	Search codes (cross-codes)
	Updating, times
	Quantitative data, tips and other information
Language:	German
Source:	Primary information: original details of the respective producers
Years Covered:	Current
File Size:	Approx 1800 sets of data
Updates:	Monthly. Exception: the position 'No of documents' is updated as least once a year
Database Producer:	Holger Mayer
	Unternehmensberatung fur Informationsverarbeitung
Available From:	GENIOS File ALPH
	DM 190.2 per connect hour
	DM 0.8 per on-line type
	DM 0.8 per off-line print
	SDI profile: DM 10

Name:	BiblioData
Description:	BibioData is the national bibliographic database of the Deutsche Bibliothek in Frankfurt. It contains references to books and serials published in the Federal Republic of Germany on a wide range of subjects. BiblioData also contains references to German books and serials in other countries. BibioData corresponds to the series A, B, C, H and N of 'Deutsche Bibiographie', the national bibliography of the Federal Republic of Germany.
Language:	German
Source:	Equivalent to 'Deutsche Bibliographie' publication
Years Covered:	1966 to date
File Size:	1 752 000 records
Updates:	110 000 annually
Database Producer:	Deutsche Bibliothek
Available From:	STN File Bibliodata
	£64.00 per connect hour
	17p per on-line type
	25p per off-line print
	SDI profile: £3.00

Name:	Blaise-Line (Service)
Description:	Blaise-Line is an on-line bibliographic service run by the British Library. It is a computer-based central resource covering over 6 million records, which include books, worldwide publications, specialist scientific and business publications, grey literature and conference proceedings.

Results of searches can be printed out at the terminal or printed overnight and mailed to the enquirer.

Blaise-Line can be accessed by subscribers on their own local micro or teletype terminal. Alternatively a postal search service caters for those without a terminal or those not Blaise-Line subscribers.

Uses include:

Compiling subject bibliographies

Tracing particular items

Checking availability and price of a book

Checking publishers

Checking whether a book is in stock at the British Library Document Supply Centre

Verifying cataloging decisions

Downloading records

Ordering documents from the British Library Document Supply Centre

Source:	Various
Years Covered:	Varies according to file
File Size:	BNBMARC (British Books Bibliography) 1003759 records
	Whitaker 1020995 records
	LCMARC 2074615 records
	University of London 512908 records
	SIGLE European 'grey literature' 139795 records
	ESTC 18th century catalogue 218382 records
	ISTC 21581 records
	HELPIS audio-visual catalogue 6496 records
	HSS humanities 889039 records
	DSCM monograph listing 318811 records
	SRIS science reference 245139 records
	CONF 237348 records
	AVMARC non-books incl audio visual 9156 records
	(sizes as at 1.6.88)
Updates:	Varies according to file, monthly as a general rule
Database Producer:	British Library
Available From:	Blaise Information Services
	British Library Bibliographical Services
	Subscriptions to Blaise on-line services:
	£55 (UK)
	£65 (Overseas)
	Plus VAT
	£20 per connect hour
	20p per on-line type (per citation)
	25p per off-line print (per page plus 5p per citation)

Name:	Books in Print
Description:	Books in Print is the major source of trade information on books currently published and inprint in the United States. It is a record of forthcoming books, books in print, and books going out of print published or distributed in the US. The database contains listings of books produced by some 12000 US publishers. The records contain basic bibliographic information (author, title, publisher, date) as well as US library headings and classifications, prices and International Standard Book Number (ISBN).
Source:	Equivalent to the publication
Years Covered:	Current
	Books scheduled for publication over the next 6 months
File Size:	1841470
Updates:	Monthly
Database Producer:	RR Bowker

Available From:	DIALOG File 470
	$65 per connect hour
	20c per off-line print
	BRS File BBIP
	$65 per connect hour
	15c per on-line type
	20c per off-line print
	SDI profile: $4

Name:	British Books in Print
Description:	British Books in Print provides comprehensive indexing of books published in the United Kingdom, plus other books published throughout the world which are printed in the English language and which are available within the UK. Only those government publications of wide general interest are included Some maps are also listed in the database.
Source:	Equivalent to the publication 'British Books in Print'
Years Covered:	Current
File Size:	1 256 010 records
Updates:	Monthly
Database Producer:	J Whitaker & Sons Ltd
Available From:	DIALOG File 430
	$60 per connect hour
	15c per off-line print
	Blaise-Line File Whitaker
	£20 per connect hour
	20p per on-line type
	9.55p per off-line print

Name:	Cross Directory File
Description:	The Data-Star Directory file (CROS) allows the user to ascertain the number of documents relating to a particular topic in a selection of, or in all, Data-Star databases.
	Any keyword, operator, truncation, etc may be used in CROS but it is advisable to use the file as a general index. Users can apply their knowledge of the database (subject, coverage, years on line, etc) to analyse the results obtained in CROS and to decide which files to use for the search. The search can then be repeated in the main file(s) using indexing terms, conventions, etc applicable to the database(s) you have chosen.
Source:	N/A
Years Covered:	N/A
File Size:	All Data-Star databases
Updates:	As per individual databases
Database Producer:	Data-Star
Available From:	Data-Star

Name:	Cuadra Directory of Online Databases
Description:	Cuadra provides comprehensive and timely information about on-line databases since 1979. The Directory of Online Databases currently lists 3369 online databases offered through 528 on-line services. It is particularly useful for finding databases to research a particular information question
	Information available includes subject, producer, content, language, time span and frequency of updates.
	Prices are not included.
Source:	Equivalent to the 'Directory of Online Databases'
Years Covered:	Current
File Size:	3700 records
Updates:	Quarterly
Database Producer:	Cuadra/Elsevier

Available From:	ORBIT Search Service File Cuadra
	$75 per connect hour
	75c per on-line type
	85c per off-line print
	Data-Star File CUAD
	£40.71 per connect hour
	35p per on-line type
	28p per off-line print
	Telesystemes-Questel File Cuadra
	$65 per connect hour
	65c per on-line type
	75c per off-line print

Name:	Dialindex
Description:	Dialindex is a collection of the file indexes for all DIALOG databases. Dialindex provides the number of postings for each search statement in each of the specified databases. This database is most useful for determining which file(s) would be most productive for a search statement, in addition for helping to determine how broadly or narrowly to define a search strategy. Pre-prepared subject categories may be used or individual databases may be specified by number.
	Coverage:
	All DIALOG databases
Source:	DIALOG databases
Years Covered:	N/A
File Size:	
Updates:	N/A
Database Producer:	DIALOG Information Services Inc
Available From:	DIALOG File 411
	$45 per connect hour

Name:	DIALOG Publications
Description:	DIALOG Publications is a special feature database which allows you to order all DIALOG publications. After you logon to File 200, you follow normal Dialorder procedures to obtain DIALOG publications. The ordered publication(s) will be sent to your 'mail to' address and your account will be billed. The ease of ordering allows you to place an order on line in less time than manual preparation would require.
Source:	N/A
Years Covered:	Current
File Size:	300 records
Updates:	Monthly
Database Producer:	DIALOG Information Services Inc
Available From:	DIALOG File 200
	$15 per connect hour
	15c per off-line print

Name:	Directorio de Bases de Datos
Description:	Directory of databases accessible from Spain
Source:	Centre for the Development of Industry
Years Covered:	Current
File Size:	669 documents
Updates:	Periodically
Database Producer:	Sistema de Informacion Empresarial
Available From:	Instituto de la Pequena y Mediana Empresa Industrial (IMPI)
	Contact direct for prices

Name:	Dissertation Abstracts Online
Description:	Dissertation Abstracts Online is a definitive subject, title and author guide to virtually every American dissertation accepted at an accredited institution since 1861, when academic doctoral degrees were first granted in the USA. In addition, citations for thousands of Canadian dissertations and an increasing number of papers accepted abroad are included in the database. Professional and honorary degrees are not included. All subject areas are covered. Abstracts are included for a large majority of the degrees granted after January 1980.
Source:	American and Canadian academic institutions
Years Covered:	1861 to date
File Size:	955 147 records
Updates:	Monthly
Database Producer:	University Microfilms International
Available From:	DIALOG File 35
	$72 per connect hour
	25c per on-line type
	25c per off-line print
	SDI profile: $7.95
	BRS File DISS
	$59 per connect hour
	26c per on-line type
	21c per off-line print
	SDI profile: $4

Name:	Economic Literature Index
Description:	The database is an index of articles and book reviews from over 260 major economic journals worldwide and approximately 200 monographs. Each record contains basic bibliographic data plus brief descriptions and descriptor codes. It provides a useful index for literature published since 1969 to date.
Source:	International economic journals
Years Covered:	1969 to date
File Size:	164 429 records
Updates:	Quarterly
Database Producer:	American Economic Association
Available From:	DIALOG File 139
	$75 per connect hour
	15c per off-line print

Name:	Electronic Publishing Abstracts

Description:	Electronic Publishing Abstracts covers scientific, technical and commercial literature in electronic publishing and information technology.
	    Major topics covered include input methods, transmission of data, storage and retrieval of text and images, output methods and electronic alternatives both to the publication of printed documents and the methods of printing published documents.
	    This database is useful to printers, publishers and anyone interested in electronic methods of processing information.

Source:	Equivalent to the 'Electronic Publishing Abstracts' publication
Years Covered:	1975 to date
File Size:	Over 17 500 records
Updates:	Twice a week
Database Producer:	Paper and Board, Printing and Packaging Industries Research Association
Available From:	ORBIT Search Service File EPUBS
	$115 per connect hour
	40c per on-line type
	50c per off-line print
	SDI profile: $8.50

Name: FINP
Description: FINP (Finnish Periodicals Index in Economics and Business) is equivalent
                  to the printed annual bibliography of economic and business journals.
                  Search elements are: keywords, UDC numbers, author's name, broad
                  subject groups, year of publication, language, company name, journal
                  name, and free text searching. Approximately 3000 new references are
                  added per annum.
Language: Mainly Finnish
Source: 600 periodicals scanned
Years Covered: 1975 to date
File Size: Approximately 33 200 citations to articles in 600 journals
Updates: Daily
Database Producer: Helsinki School of Economics
                  Library
Available From: Helsinki School of Economics
                  Annual subscription FiM 1650

Name: Forkat
Description: Forkat is a database of current research projects in science and technology
                  supported by the BMFT (the Federal Ministry for Research and
                  Technology). It is the on-line version of the BMFT support catalogue.
Language: German
Source: Research projects supported by the BMFT in 1986/87
Years Covered: 1986 to date
File Size: 19 000 citations
Updates: Every 3 months
Database Producer: Bundesministerium fur Forschung und Technologie (BMFT)
                  and FIZ Karlsruhe
Available From: STN File Forkat
                  £64 per connect hour
                  33p per on-line type
                  40p per off-line print

Name: GPO Monthly Catalog
Description: The GPO Monthly Catalog contains records of reports, studies, fact sheets,
                  maps, handbooks, conference proceedings, etc, issued by all US Federal
                  government agencies, including the US Congress. Also included in this
                  database are records of all the Senate and House hearings on private and
                  public bills and laws.
                      The GPO Monthly Catalog contains a wealth of information on a wide
                  range of topics including agriculture, economics, energy research, public
                  policy, tax reform, business law, health and many other subjects.
Source: US Federal government publications
                  Equivalent to the publication 'Monthly Catalog of United States
                  Government Publications'
Years Covered: July 1976 to date
File Size: 282 265 records
Updates: Monthly
Database Producer: US Goverment Printing Office
Available From: DIALOG File 66
                  $35 per connect hour
                  10c per off-line print
                  SDI profile: $4.95
                  BRS File GPOM
                  $25 per connect hour
                  15c per on-line type
                  10c per off-line print
                  SDI profile: $4

Name:	GPO Publications Reference File
Description:	The GPO (Government Printing Office) Publications Reference File indexes public documents currently for sale by the Superintendent of Documents, United States Government Printing Office, as well as forthcoming and recently out-of-print publications. These publications are produced by the legislative and executive branches of the US Federal government.
	The GPO Publications Reference File is used to identify, verify or select GPO publications for purchase. Information provided includes: availability, prices and stock numbers.
Source:	US Federal government
Years Covered:	1971 to present
File Size:	20574 records
Updates:	Fortnightly reloads
Database Producer:	US Government Printing Office
Available From:	DIALOG File 166
	$35 per connect hour
	10c per off-line print

Name:	HADOSS
Description:	HWWA-Dossiers (HADOSS) is the on-line version of the world business archives in Hamburg. Business reports can be ordered on line.
Language:	German
Source:	World business archives
Years Covered:	January 1987 to date
File Size:	12000 records
Updates:	6 monthly, 300 records added per update
Database Producer:	Gesellschaft fur Betriebswirtschaftliche Information mbH (GBI)
Available From:	GBI File HADOSS
	DM 120 per connect hour

Name:	Infodata
Description:	Infodata provides facts concerning information science and its practical application.
	Subjects covered: All questions relating to the specialised field of information: information & data methodology; mechanical processing of information; computer languages; information networks; the media; the transmission of information; research into the users of information; research into the classification of information; compendia of information; the efficiency of information and data systems; education in the use of information and data systems; law and politics as they relate to the field of information science.
	It also covers standardisation, terminology, the uses to which information is put, and methods of reproduction (ie photocopying etc).
Language:	German
Source:	Publications, research documents, etc
Years Covered:	1977 to date
File Size:	43000 documents
Updates:	Monthly. Approximately 5000 documents added per annum
Database Producer:	Gesellschaft fur Mathematik und Datenverarbeitung mbH Informationszentrum fur Informationswissenschaft und Praxis (GMD-IZ)
Available From:	Gesellschaft fur Electronische Medien mbH (GEM)
	File Infodata
	DM 180 per connect hour (up to 10 hours)
	DM 150 per connect hour (over 10 hours)
	DM 1 per off-line print

Name:	INFORBW
Description:	This database provides information on research in Baden-Wurttemberg. It covers the names of institutions and the current research projects of the universities of Baden-Wurttemberg.
Language:	German
Source:	Research projects

Years Covered: Current
File Size: 1000 institutions, 5700 projects
Updates: Reloaded periodically
Database Producer: Ministerium fur Wissenschaft und Kunst,
    Baden-Wurttemberg and FIZ Karlsruhe
Available From: STN File Inforbw
    £64 per connect hour
    33p per on-line type
    40p per off-line print

Name: Institutions for International Cooperation
Description: This database covers information on scientific, cultural and educational institutions. It contains information on organisations of the Federal Republic of Germany and West Berlin which are engaged in academic and research exchanges worldwide.
    The German title of this database is Institutionenverze ichnis fuer Internationale Zusammenarbeit
Language: German
Source: Full text of Institutionenverzeichnis fuer Internationale Zusammenarbeit
Years Covered: 1985 to date
File Size: 3500 citations, 100 citations added per annum
Updates: Quarterly
Database Producer: Nomos Datapool
    NOMOS Verlagsgesellschaft mbH
Available From: Edicline File IVIZ
    £60 per connect hour

Name: IRRD
Description: Produced in the framework of the OECD Road Transport Research Programme, the International Road Research Documentation (IRRD) database gathers all literature and information on ongoing research of interest to the road research community worldwide. The main subject categories are: design of roads and related structures; materials, soil and rock mechanics; construction and supervision of construction; earthworks, drainage of soils; pavements, bridges and tunnels; maintenance; traffic and transport; vehicles; accident studies; economics and administration
Source: Approximately 850 journals from 40 countries, announcements of ongoing research projects and applied computer programs.
Years Covered: 1972 to present
File Size: Approx 197000 references
Updates: Approx 1000 references per month
Database Producer: OECD (Organisation de cooperation et de developpement economiques) Programme de Recherche en matiere de routes et de Transport Routiers
Available From: ESA-IRS File 43
    £53.90 per connect hour
    4.9p per on-line type
    19.2p per off-line print
    SDI profile: £4.90

Name: LC Marc
Description: The LC Marc database contains complete bibliographic records for all books cataloged by the US Library of Congress since 1968, beginning with books in English and adding coverage of books in other languages from 1970 through to 1979. The LC Marc database provides online access to a comprehensive, worldwide collection of books that can be searched by author, title, subject, series, publication date and other access points using the same searching capabilities of the DIALOG system that are available for all other databases.
    The LC Marc database also provides a powerful capability to library acquisitions and cataloging departments for bibliographic verification and cataloging.
Source: US Library of Congress Catalog

Years Covered:	1968 to present
File Size:	2 746 138 records
Updates:	Monthly
Database Producer:	US Library of Congress
Available From:	DIALOG File 426 (1980 to date)
	427 (pre-1980)
	$45 per connect hour
	10c per on-line type
	15c per off-line print
	SDI profile: $4.95 (File 426)

Name:	LISA
Description:	LISA (Library and Information Science Abstracts) provides comprehensive coverage of international materials in the field of library and information science. More than 550 journals from 60 countries are screened for inclusion in the file. Since 1980, reports, conference proceedings, theses and monographs have been extensively abstracted. Subject coverage is wide-ranging and includes not only librarianship and library services, but also online information retrieval, videotex, electronic publishing, word processing, teleconferencing, information storage and retrieval, and abstracting and indexing services. Also covered are such related areas as publishing and bookselling, bibliography, archives, non-book materials and associated equipment, education, cultural activities and mass media.
Source:	Over 550 overseas journals from 60 countries, plus reports, theses, monographs
Years Covered:	1969 to present
File Size:	Over 80 000 records
Updates:	Monthly
Database Producer:	Library Association Publishing Ltd
Available From:	DIALOG File 61
	$75 per connect hour
	25c per on-line type
	25c per off-line print
	SDI profile: $7.95
	ORBIT Search Service File LISA
	$75 per connect hour
	25c per on-line type
	25c per off-line print
	SDI profile: $5.95

Name:	NTIS
Description:	The NTIS database consists of government-sponsored research, development and engineering plus analyses prepared by federal agencies, their contractors, or grantees. It is the means through which unclassified, publicly available, unlimited distribution reports are made available for sale from agencies such as NASA, DDC, DOE, HUD, DOT, Department of Commerce, and some 240 other agencies. In addition, some state and local government agencies now contribute their reports to the database.
	This database covers a wide spectrum of subjects including: administration and management, agriculture and food, behaviour and society, building, business and economics, chemistry, civil engineering, energy, health planning, library and information science, materials science, medicine and biology, military science, transportation.
Source:	US Federal government agencies and contractors
Years Covered:	1964 to date
	1970 to date on Data-Star
File Size:	1.3 to over 1.4 million records
Updates:	Twice a week
	Monthly on Data-Star
Database Producer:	National Technical Information Service (NTIS)
	US Department of Commerce

Available From:	DIALOG File 6
	$72 per connect hour
	40c per on-line type
	45c per off-line print
	SDI profile: $8.95
	ORBIT Search Service File NTIS
	$69 per connect hour
	35c per on-line type
	40c per off-line print
	SDI profile: $6.50
	ESA-IRS File 6
	£49 per connect hour
	18.9p per on-line type
	27.6p per off-line print
	SDI profile: £2.10
	Cedocar File NTIS
	FF 450 per connect hour
	FF 1.7 per on-line type
	FF 2 per off-line print
	BRS File NTIS
	$50 per connect hour
	37c per on-line type
	32c per off-line print
	SDI profile: $4
	STN File NTIS
	£42 per connect hour
	17p per on-line type
	23p per off-line print
	SDI profile: £1.80
	Data-Star File NTIS
	£44.02 per connect hour
	19p per on-line print
	13p per off-line print
	SDI profile: £2.10

Name:	OCLC Easi Reference
Description:	The OCLC (Online Union Catalogue) database is a bibliographic database of some 17 million items, 85 per cent of which are books. It is a source of business information in so far as it serves to assist libraries worldwide in locating published material, ordering and offers a range of other services. The OCLC Online System is a large, centralised processing system through which OCLC member libraries and other authorised users perform such tasks as cataloguing and inter-library loans. OCLC participates in a number of international projects and programmes.
Source:	Worldwide literature
Years Covered:	
File Size:	Approx 17 million items
Updates:	
Database Producer:	OCLC
Available From:	OCLC
	Costs vary according to the exact product and service supplied
	Contact OCLC for further details
	BRS File OCLC
	Members:
	$35 per connect hour
	15c per on-line type
	10c per off-line print
	Non-members:
	$65 per connect hour
	23c per on-line type
	18c per off-line print
	SDI profile: $4

Name:	Online Chronicle
Description:	The Online Chronicle is a full-text source for news in the online industry. The Online Chronicle is an expanded version of the News section of 'Online' and 'Database' magazines containing information on major on-line industry events, new databases, computer equipment, search aids and people in the on-line world. Each news item is a textual record that is supplemented by keyword indexing from a controlled vocabulary.
	The Jobline section contains classified ads for available positions in the on-line industry, as well as ads from online professionals who wish to obtain new positions.
Source:	Corresponds to the News section of 'Online' and 'Database' publications
Years Covered:	October 1981 to September 1982
	September 1983 to date
File Size:	5736 records
Updates:	Twice a week
Database Producer:	Online Inc
Available From:	DIALOG File 170
	$35 per connect hour
	15c per on-line type
	30c per off-line print

Name:	REMARC
Description:	The REMARC database represents the cataloged collections of the US Library of Congress from 1879-1980 (English language works prior to 1968 and other languages up to the dates when they entered LC MARC, see LC MARC).
	REMARC provides a valuable means for bibliographic verification and cataloging. It also provides on-line access to a comprehensive, worldwide collection of books and can be searched by author, title, subject, series, publication date and other fields.
Source:	
Years Covered:	DIALOG Files:
	File 421: Pre-1900 and undated
	File 422: 1900-39
	File 423: 1940-59
	File 424: 1960-69
	File 425: 1970-80
File Size:	4252812 records
Updates:	Irregular
Database Producer:	Carrollton Press, Arlington, VA
Available From:	DIALOG Files 421, 422, 423, 424, 425
	$85 per connect hour
	25c per on-line type
	35c per off-line print

Name:	SIGLE
Description:	System for Information on Grey Literature in Europe (SIGLE) is a multi-disciplinary database used for tracing grey literature published within the European Communities and to simplify its delivery. The collection of the bibliographic data, the classification and the specification of the location of the original documents is made by national centres in Belgium, France, the Federal Republic of Germany, Great Britain and the Republic of Ireland. The partner for the Federal Republic of Germany is the Fachinformationszentrum Energie, Physik, Mathematik GmbH, Karlsruhe.
Language:	Mainly French, German and English
Source:	Grey literature in the EEC
Years Covered:	1981 to date
File Size:	83300 citations
Updates:	Every 2 months
	14000 citations added annually
Database Producer:	

Available From:	FIZ Karlsruhe File SIGLE
	DM 175 per connect hour
	DM 0.60 per on-line type
	DM 0.85 per off-line print
	SDI profile: DM 9.2

Name:	SSIE Current Research
Description:	SSIE (Smithsonian Science Information Exchange) Current Research is a database containing reports of both government and privately funded scientific research projects, either in progress or initiated and completed during 1978-82. SSIE Current Research encompasses all fields of basic and applied research in the life, physical, social and engineering sciences. SSIE Current Research covers projects funded from over 1300 federal, state and local government agencies; non-profit associations and foundations; and colleges and universities. Some material is provided from private industry and foreign research organisations; 90 per cent of the information in the database is provided by agencies of the federal government.
	SSIE Current Research is a closed file; updated information on federally-funded research projects may be obtained in DIALOG from files 265 and 266. See 'Federal Research in Progress'.
Source:	Agencies of the US Federal government (90 per cent of the information)
Years Covered:	1978 to February 1982
File Size:	439 265 records
Updates:	Closed file
Database Producer:	National Technical Information Service
Available From:	DIALOG File 65
	$93 per connect hour
	10c per on-line type
	30c per off-line print

Name:	Standard Industrial Classification
Description:	This database helps users to identify appropriate industry sectors or companies within these sectors. Pergamon offers access to both the 1980 UK Standard Industrial Classifications and the US edition. These enable users to identify the correct industry codes and thereby provide a useful key to searching many of the Pergamon InfoLine business databases.
Source:	SIC publications
Years Covered:	Current
File Size:	
Updates:	N/A
Database Producer:	Pergamon
Available From:	Pergamon Financial
	UK File SIC
	USA File USSIC
	£25 per connect hour
	Free on-line type
	15p per off-line print
	ESA-IRS File 171
	(gateway service to Pergamon)
	£35.70 per connect hour
	15.4p per off-line print

Name:	THES
Description:	THES provides references to theses in the field of economics and business in Finland. The database can be searched using keywords, authors, UDC classification, language, year and name of firm.
Source:	University theses
Years Covered:	1983 to date
File Size:	1000 new references added per annum
Updates:	4 times per annum
Database Producer:	Helsinki School of Economics Library
Available From:	Helsinki School of Economics Library
	Annual subscription FiM 1000

Name: Ulrich's Periodicals
Description: This database is a continuously updated source of information on selected periodicals and serials published in the USA and throughout the world. For all currently available issues a complete bibliographic citation is given with buying and ordering information, subject information (over 500 internal headings) and Dewey Decimal Classification Number.

The file contains citations to approximately 123 000 serial publications published regularly as well as annuals, continuations, conference proceedings and other serial publications that are published at least once every 3 years. It also includes approximately 160 000 discontinued publications from 1974 to date.

Regional publications of limited interest, newspapers and government publications are not included.

Source: Over 65 000 periodicals and serials publishers worldwide. Corresponds to the publications: 'Ulrich's International Periodicals Directory', 'Irregular Serials and Annuals', 'Ulrich's Quarterly', 'Sources of Serials'.
Years Covered: Current
File Size: Approx 140 878 records (DIALOG)
                Approx 144 000 references (ESA-IRS) as of June 1988
Updates: Monthly (DIALOG)
                Every 6 weeks (ESA-IRS)
Database Producer: R R Bowker Company
Available From: ESA-IRS File 103
                £60.20 per connect hour
                8.4p per on-line type
                24.8p per off-line print
                BRS File ULRI
                $65 per connect hour
                15c per on-line type
                20c per off-line print
                DIALOG File 480
                $65 per connect hour
                20c per off-line print

Section XIII EEC Databases

Brokersguide (Bibliographic)
C&L Belmont European Community Database
CCL-Train (Bibliographic)
Celex (Law)
Dianeguide (Bibliographic)
Dundis (Bibliographic)
EABS (Science and Technology)

Endoc (Bibliographic)
Enrep (Industry)
Eurodicautom (Science and Technology)
Euristote (Bibliographic)
EUROLOC (Overseas Trade Opportunities)
IES-DC (Industry)
IR-SOFT (Industry)
Medrep
PABLI (Overseas Trade Opportunities)

Ruralnet (Industry)
Sesame (Industry)
Spearhead (Law)
Stars (see Overseas Trade Opportunities)
TED (Overseas Trade Opportunities)
Thesauri (Bibliographic)

Name: Brokersguide
Description: Brokersguide is an on-line directory of information brokers currently active within the EEC member states, ie persons, companies or organisations offering fee-based services, and searching particularly in publicly available databases. A typical Brokersguide record lists hosts and databases in use, outlines the broker's areas of specialisation and succinctly describes their activities and services.
Source: Details supplied by brokers to the European Commission
Years Covered: Database began in January 1987
File Size: 600 brokers
Updates: Monthly

Database Producer:	European Information Market Development Group, Luxembourg
Available From:	ECHO
	Free of charge

Name:	C&L Belmont European Community Database
Description:	This database has been developed by Coopers & Lybrand's European Community Office, C&L Belmont. It is currently accessible to C&L Belmont staff and will become directly available to C&L staff in other offices and countries. C&L Belmont monitors all areas of European Community (EC) developments. The database provides comprehensive and timely coverage of such developments, often ahead of the Commission's own databases. Information items are coded as to source, item date, nature of document, contributor, sector and proof-reading date. Information accessed from the database is used for reports requested by clients of C&L Belmont. C&L Belmont's newsletter 'Monitor' will be available through this online service.
Source:	Over 160 documentary sources. Contacts with EC institutions, trade associations, national ministries, etc. Published material includes official EC publications and sectoral and professional periodicals
Years Covered:	Current
File Size:	Approx 3000 inputs
Updates:	Daily
Database Producer:	C&L Belmont
Available From:	C&L Belmont (Information from this database is available to C&L Belmont clients. A number of accountancy firms, including C&L have set up EC databases for internal and external use in order to provide clients with information in preparation for 1992)

Name:	CCL-Train
Description:	This database is offered by the European Commission's host service Echo to enable users to become familiar with online bibliographic information retrieval services, and the Common Command Language (CCL). Records deal with subjects such as nuclear industry, safety engineering, agriculture and ceramics.
	Unlike a real database, new records will not be added to the Train database, so the user can try any of the examples given in the manual confident that the same results can be obtained.
Language:	French (password TRAINF)
	German (password TRAIND)
	English (password TRAINE)
	Years covered: Current
Source:	Based on a subject of the FABS file
File Size:	1000 records
Updates:	Regular
Database Producer:	European Information Market Development Group, Luxembourg
Available From:	ECHO
	Free of charge
	A free manual is available

Name:	Celex
Description:	Celex contains abstracts of the full text of legislation from the EC Celex database. It includes the legislation pertaining to PROFILE's Spearhead database. It can be searched using full text or special search features.
Source:	EC Celex database
Years Covered:	Up to 1992
File Size:	
Updates:	Monthly
Database Producer:	PROFILE

Available From:	PROFILE
	£60 per connect hour
	1p per off-line print (per line)
	Minimum £2 per off-line request

Name:	Dianeguide
Description:	Dianeguide gives detailed information on database producers, databases and databanks and hosts services available on DIANE (Direct Information Access Network for Europe). The Dianeguide is unique in that it is the only online databank giving users instant access to a directory of hosts, databases and databanks available on DIANE.
Source:	European Commission
Years Covered:	Database set up in 1982
File Size:	Over 800 databases in all subject areas
Updates:	Continuous
Database Producer:	European Information
	Market Development Group, Luxembourg
Available From:	ECHO
	Free of charge
Other Details:	Off-line prints can be ordered on line and are mailed out to users within 24 hours
	A free database manual is available. This manual is used in conjunction with the ECHO GRIPS manual which is also offered to users free of charge
	All manuals are available in English or French. In addition to the manuals, on-line guidance is available

Name:	Dundis
Description:	Dundis is the on-line version of the 'Directory of United Nations Databases and Information Systems'. Dundis will enable users to see which systems, services and databases are currently available within the United Nations network and will inform them as to how to gain access to the hundreds of thousands of documents, technical studies, periodicals and unpublished reports held by the 38UN organisations, specialised agencies and related offices located throughout the world.
	Dundis has a multilingual access point. The field Controlled Terms (CT) contains up to 10 descriptors describing the information system. These descriptors are taken from a trilingual (English, French, Spanish) vocabulary describing the activities of the UN family.
Language:	English, French and Spanish
Source:	Equivalent to the 'Directory of United Nations
	Databases and Information Systems'
Years Covered:	Current
File Size:	Over 600 United Nations Information Services
Updates:	Annual
Database Producer:	United Nations, ACCIS (Advisory Committee for the Coordination of Information Systems)
Available From:	ECHO
	Free of charge
	Off-line prints can be ordered on line and are mailed to users within 24 hours
	A free database manual is available. This manual is used in conjunction with the ECHO GRIPS manual and the trilingual vocabulary which are also offered to Users free of charge
	All manuals are available in English or French. In addition to the manuals, online guidance is available

Name: EABS
Description: The EABS database contains references to the published results of scientific and technical research programmes wholly or party sponsored by the European Commission. It covers a wide range of subject areas including nuclear research, new sources of energy and environmental research. It is a valuable source of information to organisations and individuals wanting to remain informed about the activities of the EC in these fields.
Source: European Commission
Years Covered: 1966 to date
File Size: Over 45000 citations
Updates: Monthly
Database Producer: European Commission
Available From: ECHO
                           Free of charge
                           On-line document ordering available
                           Off-line print ordering available
                           A free manual in English or French is available. Use in conjunction with the ECHO GRIPS manual (also free of charge). On-line guidance is available

Name: Endoc
Description: Endoc is an on-line directory of over 500 Environmental Information and Documentation Centres in the member states of the European Community and the services they provide. These centres are involved in all aspects of environmental research and provide a service useful to those people conducting research on a wide range of projects in this area or to those people generally involved in the environmental field. Endoc is the sister database to ENREP, the only directory of environmental research projects within the EEC. This database is indispensable for every individual or research organisation working in the environmental field and wanting to be informed about the activities of other language organisations.
Language: Endoc uses the unique Multilingual Descriptor System (MDS) for the subject areas covered by the Centres, which allows searches to be conducted in 6 of the official European Community languages: Danish, Dutch, English, French, German and Italian.
Source: European Commission
Years Covered: 1980 to present
File Size: Annual
Updates: Approx 500 Information Centres throughout Europe
Database Producer: European Commission in collaboration with national focal points of member states
Available From: ECHO
                           Free of charge
                           Off-line prints can be ordered on line and are mailed to users within 24 hours
                           Manual available free of charge. Use in conjunction with the ECHO GRIPS manual and the MDS which are also offered to users free of charge. All manuals are available in English or French

Name: Enrep
Description: The Enrep database is an on-line directory of Environmental Research Projects in the member states of European Community collected on a national basis by focal points under the management of the Commission of the European Communities.The research projects cover all aspects of the environmental field and will be of interest to those involved in this area. Enrep is the sister database to Endoc
Language: Enrep uses (for indexing the projects) the unique Multilingual Descriptor System (MDS) which allows searching to be conducted in 6 of the official Community languages: Danish, Dutch, English, French, German and Italian
Source: European Commission
Years Covered: 1980 to date
File Size: Over 30000 research projects from over 5000 organisations

Updates:	Regular
Database Producer:	European Commission in collaboration with national focal points of member states.
Available From:	ECHO
	Free of charge
	Off-line prints can be ordered on line and are mailed out to users within 24 hours
	A free database manual is available. This manual is used in conjunction with the ECHO GRIPS manual and the MDS which are also offered to users free of charge.
	All manuals are available in English or French. In addition to the manuals, on-line guidance is available

Name:	Euristote
Description:	Euristote is an on-line directory of over 10000 theses and studies, both current and completed, which have been conducted since the early 1950s. These theses and studies cover the many aspects of European integration including community politics, competition law, external relations and the European institutions.
	The database also contains information on over 5000 professors and university researchers who are studying the construction of Europe (by university, institute, discipline, specialisation, etc).
	This database is valuable for all those who are interested in European integration or who wish to contact people or organisations who have conducted research in this area.
Language:	This is a multilingual database and studies are entered in their original language. Where the language of a study is not a European Community language, the title is translated into one of the official languages of the European Community
Source:	European Commission. Produced by the Centre for European Studies of the University Catholique de Louvain
Years Covered:	1952 to present
File Size:	Over 10000 theses and studies
Updates:	Quarterly
Database Producer:	European Commission (Directorate General for Information, University Information Division)
Available From:	ECHO
	Free of charge
	Off-line prints can be ordered on line and are mailed to users within 24 hours
	Free manual available. Use in conjunction with the ECHO GRIPS manual

Name:	Eurodicautom
Description:	Eurodicautom is an on-line terminology databank containing scientific and technical terms, contextual phrases and abbreviations in all of the official European Community languages (with the exception of Greek). The databank is invaluable to terminologists looking for translations of particular terms and also to translators needing up-to-date translations of scientific and technical terms which may not yet be available in printed form.
Language:	All official languages of the EEC, except Greek
Source:	European Commission
Years Covered:	Current
File Size:	Over 420000 terms and contextual phrases
	Over 120000 abbreviations
Updates:	Monthly
	Approx 2000 new items added per update
Database Producer:	European Commission

Available From:	ECHO
	Free of charge
	A free manual is available to users The manual is available in English or French. In addition to the manual, on-line guidance is also available

Name:	EUROLOC
Description:	EUROLOC (Locate in Europe Information Retrieval System) contains records of financial assistance schemes available to private sector firms throughout the EEC.
	EUROLOC has 3 main components:
	Industrial assistance – covers some 600 financial assistance schemes available to industry from national governments and from the European Community
	Statistics – holds time series data on statistics of interest to those making international location decisions
	News – highlights recent or likely changes to assistance schemes, as well as general trends in industrial assistance policy.
Source:	National governments and the EC
Years Covered:	Current
	News records for the past 12 months
File Size:	600 scheme records (at October 1986)
Updates:	Daily
Database Producer:	European Policies Research Centre
Available From:	University of Strathclyde
	Annual subscription payable
	This is discretionary and set to reflect the anticipated use and value of the database to the subscriber

Name:	IES – DC
Description:	The aim of IES-DC (Information Exchange System – Data Collections) is to provide useful directory and reference services to the European IT (Information Technology) Community.
	Currently IES-DC covers 3 separate domains of data:
	Publicly funded R&D programmes undertaken in Europe by institutions active in the field of information technology (ESPRIT, RACE, ALVEY, etc)
	Resources and facilities for network services used by institutions active in this domain
	Addresses in the various electronic mail systems of individuals involved in research and management mainly within the ESPRIT programme.
	In order to provide up-to-date information, IES-DC takes stock of existing data collections, already available on a national or a sectoral basis, complements and extends these data into comprehensive and consistent database information with European-wide coverage and access.
Source:	
Years Covered:	Current
File Size:	Over 500 projects
	1000 resources and facilities
	4200 addresses
Updates:	
Database Producer:	Commission of the European Communities, DGXIII
Available From:	ECHO
	Free of charge
	A small IES-DC brochure has been produced to aid searching in the IES-Data Collections. This brochure is available in English only and is free of charge.
	It will be necessary to be a registered customer to access this database later in 1988. Contact ECHO for details

Name: IR-SOFT
Description: IR-SOFT is an inventory of software packages available on the market,
                    which enable the microcomputer user to perform online information
                    retrieval. The inventory lists general-purpose packages as well as packages
                    to be used for specific information services. Information given ranges from
                    the supplier details to the hardware and the operating system required to
                    run the software, plus prices and some general comments on the package.
                    Descriptors are included to assist searching.
Source: Software suppliers
Years Covered: Current
File Size: Over 350 software packages
Updates: Regular
Database Producer: Loughborough University (UK)
Available From: ECHO
                    Free of charge
                    A general description of the database and detailed search hints are available
                    on line with the command: INFO IRSOFT

Name: Medrep
Description: Medrep is the on-line pilot version of the 'Permanent inventory of
                    biomedical and health care research projects in the European
                    Communities'.
                        The main objectives of Medrep are:
                    To visualise trends in (bio)medical research in the EC member states, to
                    draw attention to any gaps and to prevent duplication of research
                    To further scientific contracts between researchers and to arrive at a more
                    efficient planning of research projects by means of a systematic survey of all
                    ongoing projects
                    To provide a basis for coordination and planning of research in the field of
                    the biomedical sciences and health care at national level and to stimulate
                    cooperation between the national bodies and institutions of the EC
                    responsible for this research.
Source: European Commission
Years Covered: 1972 to date
File Size: Over 1200 records
Updates: Regular
Database Producer: European Commission in collaboration with national focal points of the
                    member states.
Available From: ECHO
                    Free of charge

Name: PABLI
Description: PABLI (Pages Bleues Informatisees) is the on-line version of Pages Bleues, a
                    bi-monthly publication produced by the European Commission. The
                    publication's aim is to take stock of the progress made by the EEC's
                    development projects.
                        Development projects can be divided geographically into 3 groups: the
                    ACP states (Convention of Lome), the Mediterranean countries and the
                    non-associated developing countries in Asia and Latin America.
                        For each development project the following information is supplied:
                    Project title
                    Responsible body
                    Estimated cost
                    Brief description of project (works, supplies, technical assistance, etc)
                    How the work is to be carried out
                    Stage of project.
Source: Equivalent to the bi-monthly publication 'Pages Bleues'
Years Covered: Current
File Size:
Updates:
Database Producer: European Commission

Available From:	ECHO
	BF 800 per connect hour
	The Pabli-Telex service enables you to receive a selection of projects of particular interest directly via telex. The selection can be made using a series of keywords corresponding to your exact requirements and will be sent to you automatically
	Telex Costs: EEC countries 70 BF per record
	(non-EEC countries to be decided)

Name:	Ruralnet
Description:	Ruralnet is the on-line version of a directory containing information on local and primarily rural development projects.
	The database enables development specialists such as field workers, community leaders and voluntary development agency officials to share workable and tested project experiences.
	It documents the effective application of studies carried out on a local level, thereby enabling communication between isolated projects.
	The database also provides administrative and policy-making agencies with sufficient background information enabling them to take decisions with regard to the financing and support of more broad-based development operations.
Language:	Multilingual project descriptors available in French, Spanish and German
Source:	Equivalent to the directory 'Ruralnet',
	Published by KG Saur Verlag, Munich
Years Covered:	1960 to date
File Size:	Approx 1000 projects from 55 countries
Updates:	
Database Producer:	ICA Institute of Cultural Affairs International
Available From:	ECHO
	Free of charge
	A special communications gateway will be built up to communicate with the database producer
	A database description and examples are available on line. The user will require a basic knowledge of CCL commands before searching this database

Name:	Sesame
Description:	This is the only on-line source of information on the ever growing number of highly innovative energy projects supported by the European Communities. An up-to-date view of ongoing Community-financed projects is given together with details of all completed projects, carried out under the 'Hydrocarbon Technology and Energy Demonstration' programmes since 1975 and 1978 respectively.
	The Sesame database contains information on projects in the following sectors:
	Demonstration:
	Energy saving
	Renewable sources of energy
	Liquefaction and gasification
	New use of solid fuels, electricity and heat
	Hydrocarbon technology:
	Geophysics and prospecting
	Drilling
	Production systems
	Secondary and enhanced recovery etc
	Details in English cover the technical, funding and operational aspects of each project and in many cases the names and addresses of associated equipment manufacturers are given.
Source:	EEC Directorate for Energy (DG XVII)
Years Covered:	1975 to date (operational since 1983)
File Size:	1200 on-line documents (as of October 1987)
Updates:	Fortnightly

Database Producer:	Directorate General for Energy of the Commission of the European Communities
Available From:	Datacentralen File Sesame
	DK 600 per connect hour
	ECHO (EEC host – videotext service)
	Apply direct to ECHO for prices
	Sectorial catalogues, 'flag brochures' and project final reports are available from the office for Offical Publications of the European Communities

Name:	Spearhead
Description:	Spearhead contains summaries of current European Commission (EC) directives which will affect businesses trading within the European Community.
	It has been produced by PROFILE in conjunction with the UK Department of Trade and Industry. Legislation included may be at three stages 'Adopted', 'Proposed' or 'Projected'. Summaries of 'Proposed' measures contain a contact name and telephone number of the government department dealing with the issue. The file can be searched using freetext, and there are also special search features (also see the Celex database description).
Source:	Variety of EC and government sources, including the 'EC Official Journal'
Years Covered:	Covers measures which have been introduced or planned up to 1992
File Size:	
Updates:	Monthly
Database Producer:	PROFILE
Available From:	PROFILE
	£60 per connect hour
	1p per off-line print (per line)
	Minimum £2 per off-line request

Name:	TED
Description:	TED (Tenders Electronic Daily) is the on-line version of the S Supplement of the 'Official Journal of the European Communities' and contains public calls for tender offered by more than 80 countries. Documents are available on the morning of their publication. Users can save time by being able to go directly to documents relating specifically to their own areas of interest by means of subject and country codes. TED therefore constitutes a valuable source of information on public markets.
Language:	All the official EEC languages with the exception of Greek
Source:	Equivalent to the publication, S Supplement of the 'Official Journal of the European Communities'
Years Covered:	
File Size:	Covers calls for tender offered by over 80 countries
Updates:	Regular
Database Producer:	Office for Official Publications of the European Communities, Luxembourg
Available From:	ECHO
	BF 1000 per connect hour
	The TED-Telex service provides a selection of calls for tender of particular interest to your organisation directly via telex. This selection will be made using a series of keywords corresponding to the requirements of your organisation and will be sent to you automatically according to your instructions
	Price for the TED-Telex service per record received (in Europe):
	short format BF50
	standard format BF100
	full text BF200
	A free manual is available
	4 weeks' free trial on line is on offer or 20 references in the standard format free of charge by telex
	PROFILE File TED
	£84 per connect hour
	1p per off-line print (per line)
	Minimum £2 per off-line request

Name:	Thesauri
Description:	Thesauri is an analytical inventory of all current structured vocabularies which have appeared in at least one of the official languages of the European Community.
	In addition to Thesauri from the EC member states, those from the USA and Canada are well represented.
	The inventory comprises both bibliographical data and details on the structure of the different thesauri available (subject coverage, terms, relationships, display, implementation, etc).
	Thesauri can help you to: choose an appropriate documentation language, avoid duplication of work in the production of new thesauri, and in the standardisation of different thesauri on the same subject field.
Language:	All official languages of the EEC
Source:	
Years Covered:	
File Size:	Over 1000 descriptions of different thesauri
Updates:	
Database Producer:	GID (Gesellschaft fur Information and Dokumentation, Frankfurt) for the European Commission, Luxembourg
Available From:	ECHO
	Free of charge
	Detailed search hints for the database are given on line. If the user wants to have a copy of the manual a copy can be printed out on the terminal

Appendix 1 Publishers of Market Research Reports

Agra Europe
25 Frant Road
Tunbridge Wells
Kent TN2 5JT
UK
Tel: 0892-33813
Fax: 0892-24593
Telex: 95114 AGRATW G

AgriMark Consultants Pty
Ltd
37 Oxford Street
Collingwood
Victoria 3066
Australia
Tel: (010 61) 3-4172533
Fax: (010 61) 3-4191664
Telex: AA 36776

Automotive Industry Data
34 St John Street
Lichfield
Staffordshire WS13 6PB
UK
Tel: 0543-257295
Fax: 0543-256884
Telex: 339279

BEP Data Services
Chiltern House
146 Midland Road
Luton
Beds LU2 OBL
UK
Tel: 0582-421981
Fax: 0582-25473
Telex: 827648 BEPLU G

BSI – Technical Help to
Exporters
Linford Wood
Milton Keynes
MK14 6LE
UK
Tel: 0908-220022
Fax: 0908-320856
Telex: 825777 BSIMK G

Building Societies Association
(The)
3 Savile Row
London W1X 1AF
UK
Tel: 01-437 0655
Fax: 01-734 6416
Telex: 24538 BSA G

Business Communications Co
Inc
25 Van Zant Street
Norwalk
CT 06855-1781
USA
Tel: (010 1) 203-8534266
Fax: (010 1) 203-8530348
Telex: 6502934929

Business Technology
Research Inc
16 Laurel Avenue
PO Box 81219
Wellesley Hills
MA 02181
USA
Tel: (010 1) 671-2373111
Fax: (010 1) 617-4317915

Business Trend Analysts
2171 Jericho Turnpike
Commack
NY 11725
USA
Tel: (010 1) 516-4625454
Telex: 4973973 BTA UI

CRU Consultants Inc
33 West 54th Street
New York
NY 10019
USA
Tel: (010 1) 212-7659600
Fax: (010 1) 212-3150583
Telex: 961054 CRU NYK

Campbell Keegan Ltd
Walham House
Walham Grove
London SW6 1QP
UK
Tel: 01-381 3267
Fax: 01-385 7357

Chem Systems International
Ltd
28 St James's Square
London SW1Y 4JH
UK
Tel: 01-839 4652
Fax: 01-930 1504
Telex: 916636

Chemical Intelligence Service
39A Bowling Green Lane
London
EC1R OBJ
UK
Tel: 01-833 3812
Fax: 01-833 1563
Telex: 28339 CPLCDP G

Commodities Research Unit
Ltd
Consolidated Research
31 Mount Pleasant
London WC1X OAD
UK
Tel: 01-278 0414
Fax: 01-837 0976
Telex: 264008 CRULDN G

Confederation of British
Industry
Centre Point
103 New Oxford Street
London WC1A 1DU
UK
Tel: 01-379 7400
Fax: 01-497 2597
Telex: 21332

Corporate Development
Consultants Ltd
13 High Street
Thornbury
Bristol BS12 2AE
UK
Tel: 0454-419505
Fax: 0454-413421
Telex: 881 3024

Corporate Development
Consultants Ltd
Barry House
20-22 Worple Road
Wimbledon
London SW19 4DH
UK
Tel: 01-947 7411
Fax: 01-879 3363
Telex: 8813024

DRI
11 Broadway
New York
NY 10004
USA
Tel: (010 1) 212-2081200

DRI Europe Ltd
30 Old Queen Street
St James's Park
London SW1H 9HP
UK
Tel: 01-222 9571
Fax: 01-222 6918
Telex: 23363 DRILTD G

Databank Ltd
London House, Old Court
Place
26/40 Kensington High Street
London W8 4PF
UK
Tel: 01-938 1001
Fax: 01-937 0707
Telex: 22861

Databank SA
Velazquez, 92
28006 Madrid
Spain
Tel: (010 34) 1-4359911

Databank SpA
Corso Italia 8
20122 Milan
Italy
Tel: (010 39) 2-8052855
Fax: (010 39) 2-865579
Telex: 324217 DTBK I

Diamond Research Corp
PO Box 128
Oak View
CA 93022
USA
Tel: (010 1) 805-6492209
Fax: (010 1) 805-6491770
Telex: 215006 DRCP UR

Dodwell & Co Ltd
Togin Building
4-2, Marunouchi 1-chome
Chiyoda-ku
Tokyo 100
Japan
Tel: (010 81) 3-2114451
Fax: (010 1) 3-2112154
Telex: J22274

Domicity Ltd
79 Berkeley Street
Toronto
Ontario M5A 2W5
Canada
Tel: (010 1) 416-3665337
Fax: (010 1) 416-3666674
Telex: 06 217622 ACURCOM
TOR

Economist Intelligence Unit
(The)
Business International
1 Dag Hammarskjold Plaza
New York, NY 10017
USA
Tel: (010 1) 212-7506300
Telex: 234767

Economist Intelligence Unit
(The)
c/o MIA, 1 Square Wiser BTE
26
1040 Brussels
Belgium
Tel: (010 32) 2-2306935
Telex: 64805

Economist Intelligence Unit
Ltd (The)
40 Duke Street
London W1A 1DW
UK
Tel: 01-493 6711
Telex: 266353

Economist Publications Ltd
(The)
40 Duke Street
London W1A 1DW
UK
Tel: 01-493 6711
Fax: 01-499 9767
Telex: 266353

Economist Publications Ltd
(The)
10 Rockefeller Plaza (12th
Floor)
New York
NY 10020
USA
Tel: (010 1) 212-5415730
Telex: 148393

Economist Publications Ltd
(The)
Friedrichstrasse 34
6000 Frankfurt am Main 1
West Germany
Tel: (010 49) 69-728141
Telex: 413895

Euromoney Publications plc
Nestor House
Playhouse Yard
London EC4V 5EX
UK
Tel: 01-236 3288
Fax: 01-248 8386
Telex: 8814985/6EUROMON
G

Euromonitor Publications Ltd
87-88 Turnmill Street
London EC1M 5QU
UK
Tel: 01-251 8024
Fax: 01-608 3149
Telex: 21120 MONREF G

Eurostaf Dafsa
16, rue de la Banque
75002 Paris
France
Tel: (010 33) 1-42615124
Telex: 670383

Executive Surveys Ltd
9B Formell Garden
46-8 Blue Pool Road
Hong Kong
Tel: (010 852) 5-741853

Fessel
GFK
1 Franz Josefs Kai 47
1010 Vienna
Austria
Tel: (010 43) 1-53496
Fax: (010 43) 1-53496/194
Telex: 114711

Find/SVP
625 Avenue of the Americas
New York
NY 10011
USA
Tel: (010 1) 212-6454500
Fax: (010 1) 212-6457681
Telex: 148358 FIND/SVP

Food Marketing Institute
1750 K Street, NW
Washington DC 20006
USA
Tel: (010 1) 202-4528444
Fax: (010 1) 202-4294519
Telex: 892722 FMI USA WSH

Freedonia Group Inc (The)
2940 Noble Road
Suite 200
Cleveland
Ohio 44121
USA
Tel: (010 1) 216-3816100
Fax: (010 1) 216-3814296
Telex: 4332054 HQ CLV

Globe Book Services Ltd
Stockton House
1 Melbourne Place
London WC2B 4LF
UK
Tel: 01-379 4687
Fax: 01-379 4980
Telex: 914690

Gordon Simmons Research
Ltd
80 St Martin's Lane
London WC2N 4AA
UK
Tel: 01-240 0256
Fax: 01-379 5670
Telex: 928451

Gorham International Inc
PO Box 8
Gorham
Maine 04038
USA
Tel: (010 1) 207-8922216
Fax: (010 1) 207-8925929
Telex: 94-4479 GORHAMINT

IAL Consultants Ltd
14 Buckingham Palace Road
London SW1W OQP
UK
Tel: 01-828 5036
Fax: 01-828 6349
Telex: 918666 CRECON G

ICC Business Ratios
28/42 Banner Street
London EC1Y 8QE
UK
Tel: 01-253 3906
Fax: 01-250 3084
Telex: 23678

ICC Financial Surveys
28/42 Banner Street
London EC1Y 8QE
UK
Tel: 01-253 9736
Fax: 01-250 3084
Telex: 23678

IMAC Research
Lancaster House
More Lane
Esher, Surrey
UK
Tel: 0372-63121

IMS International
11-13 Melton Street
London NW1 2EH
UK
Tel: 01-387 9880
Fax: 01-388 0036
Telex: 295526

Industrial Market Research
Ltd
Kew Bridge House
Kew Bridge Road
Brentford
Middx TW8 OED
UK
Tel: 01-568 4477
Fax: 01-568 3465
Telex: 917036

Institute of Grocery
Distribution
Grange Lane
Letchmore Heath
Watford
Herts WD2 8DQ
UK
Tel: 092 76-7141
Fax: 092 76-2531
Telex: 8811581

International Planning
Information Inc
465 Convention Way, Suite 1
Redwood City
CA 94063
USA
Tel: (010 1) 415-3649040
Telex: 317-6217

International Resource
Development Inc
21 Locust Avenue No 1C
PO Box 1716
New Canaan
CT 06840
USA
Tel: (010 1) 203-9662525
Telex: 643452

Janet Levin Associates
29 Glebe Road
London SW13 ODZ
UK
Tel: 01-878 1899
Fax: 01-788 2125

John Wiley & Sons Ltd
Baffins Lane
Chichester
West Sussex PO19 IUD
UK
Tel: 0243-784531
Fax: 0234-775878
Telex: 86290

Jordan Information Services
Jordan & Sons Ltd
21 St Thomas Street
Bristol B31 6JS
UK
Tel: 0272-230600
Fax: 0272-230063
Telex: 449119

KAE Development Ltd
7 Arundel Street
London WC2R 3DR
UK
Tel: 01-379 6118
Fax: 01-836 1682
Telex: 21405

Key Note Publications Ltd
28-42 Banner Street
London EC1Y 8QE
UK
Tel: 01-253 300
Fax: 01-250 3084
Telex: 23678

B Klein Publications
PO Box 8503
Coral Springs
Florida 33065
USA
Tel: (010 1) 305-7521708

Kluwer Publishing Ltd
1 Harlequin Avenue
Great West Road
Brentford
Middx TW8 9EW
UK
Tel: 01-568 6441
Fax: 01-847 2610
Telex: 917490 ELEKTR G

Logica Consultancy Ltd
64 Newman Street
London W1A 4SE
UK
Tel: 01-637 9111
Fax: 01-493 7075
Telex: 27200

AF Lewis & Co Inc
79 Madison Avenue
New York
NY 10016
USA
Tel: (010 1) 212-6790770

MSRA Inc
150 Broadway (Room 1606)
New York
NY 10038
USA
Tel: (010 1) 212-4065200
Fax: (010 1) 212-4060088
Telex: 66544

Market Assessment
Publications
2 Duncan Terrace
London N1 8BZ
UK
Tel: 01-278 9517
Fax: 01-278 6246

Market Facts of Canada Ltd
77 Bloor Street West, 12th
Floor
Toronto
Ontario
Canada M5S 3A4
Tel: (010 1) 416-9646262
Fax: (010 1) 416-9645882
Telex: O6 217 698

Market Intelligence Research
Company
2525 Charleston Road
Mountain View
CA 94043
USA
Tel: (010 1) 415-9619000
Fax: (010 1) 415-9615042
Telex: 804294

Market Intelligence Research
Company
55 rue Vandenhoven
1200 Brussels
Belgium
Tel:(010 32) 2-7622781

Marketing Intelligence
Service Ltd
33 Academy Street
Naples
NY 14512
USA
Tel: (010 1) 716-3746326
Fax: (010 1) 716-3745217
Telex: 230469979

Marketing Strategies for
Industry
32 Mill Green Road
Mitcham
Surrey CR4 4HY
UK
Tel: 01-640 6621
Telex: 27950 ref 1153

Martin-Hamblin Research
Mulberry House
36 Smith Square
London SW1P 3HL
UK
Tel: 01-222 8181
Fax: 01-222 3110
Telex: 9419569 MHRES G

Matrix Publishing Group Ltd
Silbury Court
368 Silbury Boulevard
Central Milton Keynes MK9
2AF
UK
Tel: 0908-669388
Fax: 0908-669389
Telex: 826831 MATRIX G

Merlin Ltd
Merlin House
30 North End Road
London W14 0SH
UK
Tel: 01-603 1456
Fax: 01-603 0503
Telex: 269340 MERLIN G

Metal Bulletin Plc
Park House
Park Terrace
Worcester Park
Surrey KT4 7HY
UK
Tel: 01-330 4311
Fax: 01-337 8943
Telex: 21383 METBUL G

Middle East Marketing
Research Bureau Ltd
MEMRB House
21 Academias Avenue, PO
Box 2098
Nicosia 121
Cyprus
Tel: (010 357) 2-311333
Fax: (010 357) 2-311433
Telex: 2488 MEMRB CY

Mintel (Australia)
14 Collins Street
Melbourne 3000
Australia
Tel: (010 61) 3-6561284
Fax: (010 61) 3-6509323
Telex: AA31494

Mintel Publications Ltd
KAE House
7 Arundel Street
London WC2R 3DR
UK
Tel: 01-240 8111
Fax: 01-836 1682
Telex: 21405 KAEMIN G

NOP Market Research Ltd
Tower House
Southampton Street
London WC2E 7HN
UK
Tel: 01-836 1551
Fax: 01-836 2052
Telex: 8953744

National Economic
Development Office
Millbank Tower
Millbank
London SW1P 4QX
UK
Tel: 01-211 3100
Fax: 01-821 1099
Telex: 945059 NEDO G

Northern Business
Information Inc
Attn: Sean White
157 Chambers Street
New York
NY 10007
USA
Tel: (010 1) 212-7320775
Fax: (010 1) 212-2336233
Telex: 499 0412

Ovum Ltd
7 Rathbone Street
London W1P 1AF
UK
Tel: 01-255 2670
Fax: 01-255 1995
Telex: 94012452 (OVUM G)

PJB Publications Ltd
18/20 Hill Rise
Richmond
Surrey TW10 6UA
UK
Tel: 01-948 3262
Fax: 01-948 5598
Telex: 8951042

Packaged Facts
274 Madison Avenue
New York
NY 10016
USA
Tel: (010 1) 212-5325533
Fax: (010 1) 212-6830523

Post News
Stoke-sub-Hamdon
Somerset TA14 6BR
UK
Tel: 0935-88245
Telex: 94013521 (PSTN G)

Probe Research Inc
3 Wing Drive, Suite 240
Cedar Knolls
NJ 07927-1097
USA
Tel: (010 1) 201-2851500
Fax: (010 1) 201-2851519
Telex: 6853420

Prognos AG
Unter Sacheenhausen 37
5000 Cologne 1
Germany, Federal Republic of
Tel: (010 49) 221-16027-0
Fax: (010 49) 221-133822

Prognos AG
Nurnberger Strasse 68/69
1000 Berlin 30
Germany, Federal Republic of
Tel: (010 49) 30-2112099

Prognos AG
3000 Sand Hill Road
Building 1-230
Menlo Park, CA 94025
USA
Tel: (010 1) 415-8549833
Fax: (010 1) 415-8549837

Prognos Ag
Steinengraben 42
4011 Basle
Switzerland
Tel: (010 41) 61-223200
Fax: (010 41) 61-224069
Telex: 963323 PROG CH

RMDP
61-63 Ship Street
Brighton
Sussex BN1 1AE
UK
Tel: (0273) 722687
Fax: 0273 821463
Telex: 87323 FSI G RETAIL

Research Services Ltd
Station House
Harrow Road
Wembley
Middx HA9 6DE
UK
Tel: 01-903 1399
Fax: 01-900 1399
Telex: 923755

Romtec PLC
Hattori House
Vanwall Road
Maidenhead
Berks SL6 4UW
UK
Tel: 0628-770077
Fax: 0628-785433

Roskill Information Services
Ltd
2 Clapham Road
London SW9 0JA
UK
Tel: 01-582 5155
Fax: 01-793 0008
Telex: 917867 ROSKIL G

Scottish Council for
Development and Industry
(The)
23 Chester Street
Edinburgh
Scotland EH3 7ET
UK
Tel: 031-225 7911
ax: 031-220 2116
Telex: 776660

Specialists in Business
Information Inc
3375 Park Avenue, Suite
2000A
Wantagh
NY 11793
USA
Tel: (010 1) 516-7817277
Fax: ((010 1) 516-7814934

Survey Force Ltd
Algarve House
140 Borden Lane
Sittingbourne
Kent ME9 8HW
UK
Tel: 0795-23778
Fax: 0795-27613
Telex: 826717

System Dynamics Ltd
Heronsgate Road
Chorleywood
Rickmansworth
Herts WD3 5BW
UK
Tel: 09278-5466
Fax: 09278-3990
Telex: 94012819 G SYDY G

Taylor Nelson Research Ltd
Taylor Nelson House
44-46 Upper High Street
Epsom
Surrey KT17 4QS
UK
Tel: 03727-29688
Fax: 03727-44100
Telex: 9413815

Technical Insights Inc
PO Box 1304
Fort Lee,
NJ 07024
USA
Tel: (010 1) 201-5684744
Fax: (010 1) 210-5688247
Telex: 230199 SWIFT UR TII

Technomic, Inc
300 S Riverside Plaza
Suite 1940 South
Chicago, IL 60606
USA
Tel: (010 1) 312-8760004
Fax: (010 1) 312-8761158

Telecommunications Industry
Research (TIR)
The Research Centre
4/5 The Square
Barnham, West Sussex PO22
OHB
UK
Tel: 0243-552622
Fax: 0243-553125
Telex: 869449 TIRES G

Theta Corporation
Theta Building
Middlefield
CT 06455
USA
Tel: (010 1) 203-3491054
Telex: 494-5298 THETA

Ulster Marketing Surveys Ltd
115 University Street
Belfast BT7 1HP
Northern Ireland
Tel: 0232-231060/231069
Fax: 0232-243887

Venture Development
Corporation
One Apple Hill
Natick
MA 01760
USA
Tel: (010 1) 617-6539000
Telex: 709190

Venture Economics Canada,
Ltd
240 Richmond Street West
Suite 302
Toronto
Ontario M5V 1W1
Tel: (010 1) 416-9719513
Fax: (010 1) 416-9719529

Venture Economics Inc
PO Box 81348
16 Laurel Avenue
Wellesley Hills MA 02181
USA
Tel: (010 1) 617-4318100
Fax: (010 1) 617-4317915

Venture Economics Ltd
14 Barley Mow Passage
London W4 4PH
UK
Tel: 01-994 8009
Fax: 01-995 0162

Walker Marketing
34 Stonehill Road
Sheen
London SW14 8RW
UK
Tel: 01-878 6218
Fax: 01-891 5567
Telex: 932905 LARCH G

Wharton Information
Systems
First Floor, Regal House
London Road
Twickenham TW1 3QS
UK
Tel: 01-891 6197

USA Office
Tel: (010 1) 312-8760004
Fax: (010 1) 312-8761158

Wilkerson Group, Inc (The)
666 Third Avenue
New York
NY 10017-4011
USA
Tel: (010 1) 212-557 1717
Fax: (010 1) 212-972 1056
Telex: 517629

Yano Research Institute
(USA) Ltd
350 Fifth Avenue
Empire State Building, Suite
8010
New York
NY 10118
USA
Tel: (010 1) 212-9476120
Telex: 225134 YANO UR

Yano Research Institute Ltd
2-10-1 Nihonbashi Hamacho
Nisshin Building
Chuo-ku
Tokyo 103
Japan
Tel: (010 81) 3-6679188
Telex: 2522278 YANO J

Yano Research Institute Ltd
c/o Steeple Hill Consultancy
Services Ltd
83 Bardsley Close
Croydon
Surrey CRO 5PT
UK
Tel: 01-833 1840
Telex: 8952022 – CTYEL G (for
Steeple Hill)

Appendix 2 Database Hosts and Producers

ABC Voor Handel en
Industrie
Koningin Wilhelminalaan 16
2012 JK Haarlem
Netherlands
Tel: (010 31) 23-319031
Telex: 41393 ABCNL

ACI Computer Services
AUSINET
310 Ferntree Gully Road
Clayton
VIC 3168
Australia
Tel: (010 61) 3-5448433
Telex: 33852 ACICSAA

ACT Computer Services Ltd
11735-170 Street
Edmonton
Alberta T5M 3   W7
Canada
Tel: (010 1) 403-451 5555
Telex: 037-2297

ADEPS
Universitee de Bruxelles
Centre d'Analyse des
Donnees
50 Avenue Franklin Roosevelt
1050 Brussels
Belgium
Tel: (010 32) 2-6490030

ADP Comtrend Ltd
Plantation House
31-35 Fenchurch Street
London EC3M 3EP
UK
Tel: 01-623 2261
Telex: 8956192

ADP Data Processing
Network Services Division
175 Jackson Plaza Ann Arbor
MI 48106-2190
USA
Tel: (010 1) 313-7696800

ADP Financial Information
Limited (UK)
62 Cannon Street
London EC4N 6AE
UK
Tel: 01-623 2261
Fax: 01-283 7237

ADP Financial Information
Services (USA)
East Park Drive
Mount Laurel
NJ 08054
USA
Tel: (010 1) 609-2357300

ADP Network Services
2 Pinetrees
Chertsey
Staines
Middx TW18 3DS
UK
Tel: 0784-51355
Fax: 0784-65257

AP-Dow Jones News Services
12 Norwich Street
London EC4A 1BP
UK
Tel: 01-353 2906/7
Telex: 267215

Aarhus School of Economics
Library
Fuglesangsalle 4
8210 Aarhus V
Denmark
Tel: (010 45) 6-153833

Acquisitions Monthly
Lonsdale House
7-9 Lonsdale Gardens
Tunbridge Wells
Kent
UK
Tel: 0892-515454

Affarsdata AB
(Data-Star Agent), Vastra
Hamnagatan 9, Box 2380
40316 Gothenberg
Sweden
Tel: (010 46) 31-178390

Affarsdata i Stockholm AB
Box 3188
10363 Stockholm
Sweden
Tel: (010 46) 8-7364555
Fax: (010 46) 8-200212

Agence France Presse
11-15 Place de la Bourse BP 20
75061 Paris Cedex 02
France
Tel: (010 33) 1-42334466
Telex: 210064 AFPAF

Agra Europe (London) Ltd
25, Frant road
Tunbridge Wells
Kent TN2 5JT
UK
Tel: 0892-33813
Telex: 95114 AGRATW G

Agridata Network
AgriData Resources Inc
330 East Kilbourne Avenue
Milwaukee
WI 53202
USA
Tel: (010 1) 414-2787676

Alberta Bureau of Statistics
(Alberta Treasury)
7th Floor, Sir Frederick W
Haultain Bldg
9811-109 Street
Edmonton
Alberta T5K OC8
Canada
Tel: (010 1) 403-4273058
Telex: 0372137

American Banker Bond Buyer Inc
(Division of Int Thomson Publishing Corp)
1 State Street Plaza
New York
NY 1004
USA
Tel: (010 1) 212-9434830
Telex: 421768 ABKRU1

American Institute of
Certified Public Accountants
Library Services Division
1211 Avenue of the Americas
New York
NY 10036-8775
USA
Tel: (010 1) 212-5756200
Telex: 703396

American Petroleum Institute
Central Abstracting &
Indexing Service
156 William street
New York NY 10038
USA
Tel: (010 1) 212-5879660
Telex: 233405 APIUR

American Society for Metals
Metals Park
Ohio 44073
USA
Tel: (010 1) 216-3385151
Telex: 980619
METALEX-MTPK

American Society for Testing
and Materials
1916 Race street
Philadelphia
PA 19103
USA
Tel: (010 1) 215-2995410
Fax: (010 1) 710-6701037

American Society of Hospital
Pharmacists
4630 Montgomery Avenue
Bethesda
Maryland 20814
USA
Tel: (010 1) 301-6573000

Analyste – Conseil Systeme
Informatique
969 Route de l'Eglise
Ste-Foy Quebec G1V 3V4
Canada
Tel: (010 1) 418-6531456

Arthur D Little Decision
Resources
Cambridge
Massacheusetts
MA 02140
USA
Tel: (010 1) 617-8645770
Telex: 921436

Associated Press
Associated Press House
Third Floor, N Block
12 Norwich Street
London EC4A 1BP
UK
Tel: 01-353 1515
Fax: 01-583 1329
Telex: 262887

Association Francaise pour
l'Etude des Eaux
Place Sophie-Laffitte
Sophia Antipolis
06565 Valbonne Cedex
France
Tel: (010 33) 93-742223

Assolombarda
Sideral Informatica
Via Pantuno 9
20122 Milan
Italy
Tel: (010) 39-288231
Telex: 3106771

Australian Bureau of Statistics
PO Box 10
Belconnen
ACT 2616
Australia
Tel: (010 61) 62-527911
Telex: 62020 ABOSTAA

Australian Financial Review
Information Service
GPO Box 506
Sydney 2000
Australia
Tel: (010 61) 2-2121134

BAR Broadcast Advertisers
Reports Inc
800 Second Ave, Room 803
New York NY 10017
USA
Tel: (010 1) 212-6828500

BRS Information
Technologies
1200 Route 7
Latham
NY 12110
USA
Tel: (010 1) 518-7831161
Telex: 710 444 4965

Bank Marketing Association
(BMA)
309 West Washington
Chicago, IL
USA
Tel: (010 1) 312-7821442
Fax: (010 1) 910-2212897

Banque Francais du
Commerce Exterieur
21 Boulevard Haussmann
75009 Paris
France
Tel: (010 33) 1-42474747

Bayer AG
Bayerwerk
5090 Leverkusen
Germany, Federal Republic of
Tel: (010 49) 214-3071359
Telex: 85103 285 BY D

Belindis
Ministry of Economic Affairs
CTI – Rue J A de Mot 30
1040 Brussels
Belgium
Tel: (010 32) 2-2236111
Telex: 23509 ENERGIE B

Bertelsmann
InformationsService GmbH
Neumarkter Strasse 18
8000 Munich 80
Germany, Federal Republic of
Tel: (010 49) 89-431890
Fax: (010 49) 89-4312837
Telex: 523259 VBMUE

Bolsa de Madrid
Plaza de la Lealtad 1
28014 Madrid
Spain
Tel: (010 34) 1-5214790
Telex: 49184 E

Borsinformation Telecom
Kopenhavns Fondsbors
Nikolaj Plads 6
Post Box 1040
1007 Copenhagen K
Denmark
Tel: (010 45) 1-933366
Telex: 16496 COSTEX DK

R R Bowker Company
205 East 42nd Street
New York
NY 10017
USA
(010 1) 212-9161659
Telex: 127703

Bridge Data Company
6 City Road
London EC1
UK
Tel: 01-256 6234
Fax: 01-256 6910
Telex: 939079

Bridge Data Company Inc
10050 Manchester Road
St Louis
MO 63122
USA
Tel: (010 1) 314-8215660

British Library
Bibliographical Services
2 Sheraton Street
London W1V 4BH
UK
Tel: 01-636 1544 ex242
Telex: 21462 BLREF G

British Non-Ferrous Metals
Technology Centre
Grove Laboratories
Denchworth Road
Wantage OX 12 9BJ
UK
Tel: 023-572992
Telex: 837166 BNFMTC G

British Patent Office
Room 312, State House
66-71 High Holborn
London WC1R 4TP
UK
Tel: 01-831 2525

Btx Sudwest GmbHf
(German Videotex)
Plieninger Str 150
7000 Stuttgart 80
Germany, Federal Republic of
Tel: (010 49) 711-720070

Building Research Station
Bucknalls Lane
Garston
Watford, Herts WD2 7JR
UK
Tel: 0923-674040
Telex: 923220

Building Services Research &
Information Assoc
Old Bracknell Lane West
Bracknell
Berkshire RG12 4AH
UK
Tel: 0344-426511
Telex: 848288 BSRIAC G

Burda GmbH
Abtlg Markt-Service
Postfach 12 30
7600 Offenburg
Germany, Federal Republic of
Tel: (010 49) 781-842883

Bureau of Labor Statistics
US Department of Labor
441 G Street NW, Room 1077
Washington DC 20212
USA
Tel: (010 1) 202-5231364

Bureau of National Affairs Inc
(The)
Database Publishing Unit
1231 25th Street NW
Washington DC 20037
USA
Tel: (010 1) 202-4524132
Telex: 892692

Business Datenbanken GmbH
Poststrasse 42
6900 Heidelberg 1
Germany, Federal Republic of
Tel: (010 49) 6221-166061
Telex: 461782

Business Direction
(British Telecom)
Telephone House
Temple Avenue
London EC4Y OHL
UK
Tel: 01-822 1322
Fax: 01-583 6262
Telex: 261040 PRSTL G

Business Research Corp
(see Technical Data
International)
330 Congress street
Boston
MA 02210
USA
Tel: (010 1) 617-4823341

Business Surveys Ltd
PO Box 21
Dorking
Surrey RH4 2YU
UK
Tel: 0306 712867

Businesswire
44 Montgomery Street
San Fransisco
CA 94104
USA
Tel: (010 1) 415-9864422
TWX: 910 372 6135

Butterworth (Telepublishing)
Limited
61a North Castle Street
Edinburgh EH2 3LJ
UK
Tel: 031-225 7828
Telex: 95678 G

Butterworths
(Telepublishing) Limited
(Distributors of LEXIS service)
4-5 Bell Yard
Temple Bar
London WC2A 2JR
UK
Tel: 01-404 4097
Telex: 95678 LOE No:1023

C&L Belmont
118-128 Avenue de
Cortenbergh-Bte 6
1040 Brussels
Belgium
Tel: (010 32) 2-7359065
Fax: (010 32) 2-7336618
Telex: 64214 BELMNT B

CAB International
Commonwealth Agricultural
Bureaux
Farnham House, Farnham
Royal
Slough SL2 3BN
UK
Tel: 2814-2281
Telex: 847964 COMAGG G

CEC Joint Research Centre
(see Joint Research Centre)

CISI-Wharton
Ebury Gate
23 Lower Belgrave Street
London SW1U ONW
UK

CISI Network Corporation
Uni-Coll Division
3401 Science Center
Philadelphia
PA 19104
USA
Tel: (010 1) 215-3873890

California Institute of
International Studies
766 Santa Ynez
Stanford
CA 94305
USA
Tel: (010 1) 415-3222026

Cambridge Scientific
Abstracts
5161 River Road
Bethesda
Maryland 20816
USA
Tel: (010 1) 301-9511400
Telex: 898452 DISCINC
BHDA

Camerdata SA
Calle Alfonso X1 3
28014 Madrid
Spain
Tel: (010 34) 1-2212984

Canada Systems Group
955 Green Valley Crescent
Ottawa
Ontario K2L 3V4
Canada
Tel: (010 1) 613-7275445

Canadian Petroleum
Association (CPA)
150 6th Avenue SW Suite 3800
Calgary
Alberta T2P 3Y7
Canada
Tel: (010 1) 403-2696721

Carrollton Press
1611 North Kent St Suite 910
Arlington VA 22209
USA
Tel: (010 1) 703-5255940
Telex: 64340

Cedocar
Centre de Documentation de
l'Armement
26 Boulevard Victor
75996 Paris Armees
France
Tel: (010 33) 1-45524504
Telex: CEDOCAR 202778 F

Centaur Publications
(Marketing Week)
50 Poland Street
London W1V 4AX
UK
Tel: 01-439 4222
Fax: 01-439 9669
Telex: 261352 MKT MAG

Center of the Asian Institute
of Technology
The Library & Regional
Documentation
PO Box 2754
Bangkok 10501
Thailand
Telex: 84276 TH

Center for International
Financial Analysis and
Research (CIFAR)
Princeton Professional Park
601 Ewing Street
Princeton
New Jersey
NJ 08540
USA
Tel: (010 1) 609-9210910

Center for the Utilization of
Federal Technology
National Technical
Information Service
5285 Port Royal Road, Room
11R
Springfield
VA 22161
USA
Tel: (010 1) 703-4874838

Central Statistical Office
(CSO)
Government Offices
Gt George Street
London SW1P 3AQ
UK
Tel: 01-270 6363/6364
Fax: 01-270 5828

Centre de Documentation de
L'Armement
26 Boulevard Victor
75996 Paris Armees
France
Tel: (010 33) 1-45524504
Telex: 202778 Cedocar F

Centre de Documentation des
Industries Utilisatrices des
Produits
Agricoles (CDIUPA)
1 avenue des Olympiades
91300 Massy
France
Tel: (010 33) 1-69209738

Centre d'Etude de l'Energie
Nucleaire (CEN)
Boeretang 200
2400 Mol
Belgium
Tel: (010 32) 14-311801
Telex: 31922 SCKCEN MOL

Centre d'Etudes Prospectives
et d'Informations
International (CEPII)
9 rue Georges Pitard
75015 Paris
France
Tel: (010 33) 1-48426422

Centre National d'Etudes des
Telecomm (CNET)
Service de Documentation
Interministeriel
38-40 rue de General Leclerc
92131 Issy les Moulineaux
France
Tel: (010 33) 1-45294444
Telex: 250317 CNETLEC F

Centre National de la
Recherche Scientifique
(CNRS/CDST)
26 Rue Boyer
75971 Paris Cedex 20
France
Tel: (010 33) 1-43583559
Telex: 220880 CNRSDOC F

Centre National de la
Recherche Scientifique
(CNRS)
Institut de la Langue Francais
52 Boulevard Magenta
75010 Paris
France
Tel: (010 33) 1-42450077

Centre de Recherches de Pont
a Mousson
Service
Documentation-Diffusion
BP No 28 Maidieres
54700 Pont a Mousson Cedex
France
Tel: (010 33) 8-3816029
Telex: 961330 CR PAM F

Centre Technique des
Industries de la Fonderie
(CTIF)
Service Documentation
12, Avenue Raphael
75016 Paris
France
Tel: (010 33) 1-5047250
Telex: 611054 CTIF PA F

Centre Technique des
Industries Mecaniques
Boite Postale 67
52 avenue Felix Louat
60304 Senlis
France
Tel: (010 33) 4-4583266
Telex: 140006 CETIM SENLI F

Centre for Veterinary &
Agricultural Documentation
Royal Veterinary &
Agricultural University
Bulowsvej 13
1870 Frederiksberg c
Denmark

Centro Elettronico di
Documentazione Giuridica
Italian Supreme Court
Via Damiano Chiesa 24
00136 Rome
Italy
Tel: (010 39) 6-3308343
Telex: 620461 CEDCAS

Cerved
(EDP Facilities)
Corso Stati Uniti 14
35100 Padova
Italy
Tel: (010 39) 49-849411
Telex: 430433 Cerved

Cerved
(Head Office)
Via Appia Nuova 696
00179 Rome
Italy
Tel: (010 39) 6-793901
Telex: 620061 CERVED

Chambre de Commerce et
d'Industrie de Paris
27 Avenue de Friedland
75382 Paris
France
Tel: (010 33) 1-5619900
Telex: 650100

Chase Econometrics
(see The WEFA Group)

Chemical Abstracts Service
(CAS)
Customer Service
2540 Olentangy River Road
PO Box 3012
Columbus
OH 43210
USA
Tel: (010 1) 614-4213600
Telex: 8104821608

Chronometrics
327 South La Salle, 15th Floor
Chicago
IL 60604
USA
Tel: (010 1) 312-4619434

Citibank NA
Shin-Ohtemachi Bldg
2-1 Ohtemachi 2-Chome
Chiyoda-ku Tokyo 100
Japan
Tel: (010 81) 3-5635621

Citibank NA
One Citicorp Center
153 East 53rd Street
New York, NY 10043
USA
Tel: (010 1) 212-5593419

Citibank NA
Global Electronic Markets
336 Strand
London WC2R 1HB
UK
Tel: 01-438 1596

Citibank NA
Citicorp Center 31/F
18 Whitfield Road
Causeway Bay
Hong Kong

Citicorp Database Services
Citicorp Investment Bank
PO Box 966
New York
NY 10268
USA
Tel: (010 1) 212-9686912

City Data Services Ltd
30, Cursitor Street
London EC4A 1LT
UK
Tel: 01-405 2565

CLIRS Information Services
(FIZ Technik Agent)
55 Lavender Street
AUS-Milsons Point NSW 2061
Australia
Tel: (010 61) 2-9595075
Telex: 74317 AA

Columbia University
Center for International
Business Research
West 116th and Broadway
New York
NY 10027
USA
Tel: (010 1) 212-2808404

Commission of the European
Communities
DG XV11 Sesame
200 rue de la Roi
1049 Brussels
Belgium
Tel: (010 32) 2-2350001
Telex: 21877 COMEU B

Commodity Information
Services Company (CISCO)
327 South LaSalle, No 800
Chicago
IL 60604
USA
Tel: (010 1) 312-9223661

Commodity News Services
Inc
2100 West 89th Street
PO Box 6053
Leawood
KS 66206
USA
Tel: (010 1) 913-6427373
Telex: 42585

Commodity Systems Inc
200 West Palmetto Park Road
Boca Raton
FL 33432-3788
USA
Tel: (010 1) 305-3928663
Telex: 522107

Commonwealth Trading
Bank of Australia
Group Treasury
GPO Box 2719
Sydney
NSW 2001
Australia
Tel: (010 61) 2-2383155
Telex: 20345 COMBANKAA

Compagnie des Agents de
Change
17 Rue Monsigny
75002 Paris
France
Tel: (010 33) 1-42975555

Compu-Mark (UK) Ltd
93 Chancery Lane
London WC2A 1DT
UK
Tel: 01-404 4963
Fax: 01-405 1305
Telex: 25105 COMPUK G

Compu-Mark (US)
1333F Street NW
Washington DC 20004
USA
Tel: (010 1) 202-7377900
Telex: 440388 COMUS

Compu-Mark NV
PO Box 61
2510 Morstel
Belgium
Tel: (010 32) 3-4499840
Telex: 33875 COMPU B

CompuServe Inc
CompuServe Information
Service
5000 Arlington Centre Blvd
Colombus
Ohio 43220
USA
Tel: (010 1) 614-4570802

Computer Software
Management and Information
Center (The)
University of Georgia
Athens
Georgia 30602
USA
Tel: (010 1) 404-5423030

Computersoft Ltd
150 Strand
London WC2R 1JP
UK
Tel: 01-379 5650

Comshare Inc
PO Box 1588
3001 South State Street
Ann Arbor
MI 48106
USA
Tel: (010 1) 313-9944800

Confederation of Information
Communication Industries
(CICI)
19 Bedford Square
London WC1B 3HJ
UK
Tel: 01-580 6321

Conference Board of Canada
25 McArthur road Suite 100
Ottawa Ontario LIL 6R3
Canada
Tel: (010 1) 312-7860800

Conference Europeenne des
Ministres des Transports
19 rue de Franqueville
75775 Paris Cedex 16
France
Tel: (010 33) 1-45248200
Telex: 611040 COMITRANS
PARIS

Confindustria
Viale dell Astronomia 30
Rome
Italy
Tel: (010 39) 6-59031
Telex: 611393 CONFIN I

Congressional Information
Service Inc
4520 East-West Highway
Suite 800
Bethesda
MD 20814
USA
Tel: (010 1) 301-6541550
Telex: 292386

Consorcio d'Informacion y
Documentacio de Cataluna
(CIDC)
Calabria 168
Barcelona 08015
Spain
Tel: (010 34) 3-4252111

Consumers Union
256 Washington street
Mount Vernon
NY 10553
USA
Tel: (010 1) 914-6679400
Telex: 7105620102
CONSUMERS MTV

Context
Business Information Services
26 Kensington High St
London W8
UK
Tel: 01-937 3595
Fax: 01-937 1159

ContiCurrency Inc
1800 Board of Trade Building
Chicago
IL 60604
USA
Tel: (010 1) 312-7860800

Copenhagen Handelsbank
Holmens Kanal 2
1091 Copenhagen
Denmark
Tel: (010 45) 1-128600
Telex: 12186

Copenhagen School of
Economics
Rosenoerns Alle 31
1970 Copenhagen V
Denmark

Corte Suprema di Cassazione
(see Centro Elettronico di
Documentazion)

Cote Desfosses
42, rue Notre-Dame des
Victoires
Paris
France
Tel: (010 33) 1-42332130
Telex: 680326 F

CREDOC asbl
Rue de la Montagne 34, bte 11
1000 Brussels
Belgium
Tel: (010 32) 2-5139213
Telex: 63129 CREDOC B

Crowntek Communications
Inc
650 McNicoll Avenue
Willowdale
Ontario M2H 2E1
Canada
Tel: (010 1) 416-4991012

Cuadra/Elsevier
11835 West Olympic Blvd
Suite 855
Los Angeles
CA 90064
USA
Tel: (010 1) 213-4780066
Telex: 755814 CUADRA SNM

D-S Marketing GmbH
Ostbahnhofstrasse 13,
Postfach 600547
6000 Frankfurt/Main
Germany, Federal Republic of
Tel: (010 49) 69-490643
Telex: 4189459

D-S Marketing Inc
Suite 110
485 Devon Park Drive
Wayne
PA 19087
USA
Tel: (010 1) 215-6876777

D-S Marketing Ltd (Data-Star)
Plaza Suite
114, Jermyn Street
London SW1Y 6HJ
UK
Tel: 01-930 5503
Fax: 01-930 2581
Telex: 94012671
STAR G

DAFSA
125 rue Montmarte
75081 Paris
France
Tel: (010 33) 1-42332123
Telex: 640472 DAF DOC F

DKI – Deutsches Kunststoff –
Institut
Schlossgartenstrasse 6R
6100 Darmstadt
Germany, Federal Republic of
Tel: (010 49) 6151-162106

DMS Inc
100 Northfield street
Greenwich
CT 06830
USA
Tel: (010 1) 203-6617800
Telex: 131526

Daiwa Securities Research
Institute
1-2-1 Kyobashi
Chuo-Ku
Tokyo
Japan
Tel: (010 81) 3-5536014

Danmarks Statistik
Danish National Bureau of
Statistics
The Library
Sejrogade 11
2100 Copenhagen O
Denmark
Tel: (010 45) 1-298222
Telex: 16236 DASTAT DK

Dansk Standardiseringsrad
(Danish Standard
Association)
Aurehojvej 12
2900 Hellerup
Denmark
Tel: (010 45) 1-629315
Telex: 15615 DANSTA DK

Data Communications
Corporation of Korea
(DACOM)
(Dialog Services) The
Business Office
Korea Stock Exchange
Building
1-116 Yeoeido-Dong
Yeongdungpo-ku
Seoul
Korea
Tel: (010 82) 2-7835201
Telex: DACOM K28311

Data Courier Inc
620 South Fifth Street
Louisville
KY 40202
USA
Tel: (010 1) 502-582411
Telex: 204235

Data Resources (DRI) Europe
Inc
Division of Standard & Poor's
FEICO
Via Santa Tecla 2
20121 Milan
Italy
Tel: (010 38) 2-801088

Data Resources (DRI) Europe
Ltd
Division of Standard & Poor's
FEICO
30 Old Queen Street
London SW1H 9HP
UK
Tel: 01-222 9571
Fax: 01-222 6918
Telex: 2363

Data Resources Inc (DRI)
Data Products Division HQ
1750 K Street NW, Suite 1060
Washington DC 20006
USA
Tel: (010 1) 202-86623760
Telex: 440480 DRI WASHDC

Data-Star, Radio-Suisse SA
(FIZ Technik Agent)
Laupenstrasse 18A
3008 Berne
Switzerland
Tel: (010 41) 31-659500

Database Services
2685 Marine Way Suite 1305
Mountain View
Los Altos
CA 94043
USA
Tel: (010 1) 415-9612880

Datacentralen
DC Host Centre
Retortvej 6 – 8
2500 Valby-Copenhagen
Denmark
Tel: (010 45) 1-468122
Telex: 27122 DC DK

Datasolve Ltd
99 Staines Road West
Sunbury-on-Thames
Middx TW16 7AH
UK
Tel: 09327-85566

Datastream International Inc
(Subsidiary of Dun &
Bradstreet)
One World Trade Center
Suite 9069,
New York
NY 10048
USA
Tel: (010 1) 212-9388699
Telex: 420459 DUN UI

Datastream International Ltd
(Subsidiary of Dun &
Bradstreet)
58-64 City Road
London EC1Y 2AL
UK
Tel: 01-250 3000
Fax: 01-253 0171
Telex: 884230

Datastream International Ltd
(Subsidiary of Dun &
Bradstreet)
Hofplein 19
3032 AC Rotterdam
Netherlands
Tel: (010 31) 10-111154
Telex: 26639

Department of Health and
Social Security (DHSS)
Library
Alexander Fleming House
London SE1 6BX
UK
Tel: 01-407 5522 Ext 7233
Telex: 883669 G

Department of Trade and
Industry
Room 392
Ashdown House
123 Victoria Street
London SW1E 6RB
UK
Tel: 01-212 7676

Derwent Inc
6485 Elm St Suite 500
McLean
VA 22101
USA
Tel: (010 1) 703-7900400

Derwent Publications Ltd
Rochdale House
128 Theobalds Road
London WC1 8RP
UK
Tel: 01-242 5823
Telex: 267487 DERPUB G

Deutsche Bibliothek Institut
(DBI)
Zeppelinallee 4-8
6000 Frankfurt/Main 1
Germany, Federal Republic of
Tel: (010 49) 69-75661
Telex: 416643 DEU BID

Deutsche Patentamt
Munchen
Zweibrueckenstrasse 12
8000 Munich 2
Germany, Federal Republic of
Tel: (010 49) 89-21950
Telex: 523534 BPBMD

Deutscher Fachverlag
Schumannstrasse 27
6000 Frankfurt/Main 1
Germany, Federal Republic of
Tel: (010 49) 69-7433380

Deutsches
Informationszentrum fur
Technische
Regeln (DITR)
Burggrafenstrasse 4-10
1000 Berlin 30
Germany, Federal Republic of
Tel: (010 49) 30-2601600
Telex: 185269 DITRD

Dialcom
1109 Spring St Suite 410
Silver Spring
MD 20910
USA
Tel: (010 1) 301-5881572

DIALOG Information
Services (UK)
PO Box 188
Abingdon
Oxfordshire OX1 5AX
UK
Tel: 0865-730275
Telex: 837704 INFORM G

DIALOG Information
Services Inc
3460 Hillview Avenue
Palo Alto
California 94304
USA
Tel: (010 1) 415-8583810
Telex: 334499 (DIALOG)

DIALOG Information
Services, Inc
Tizianweg 2
4010 Hilden
Germany, Federal Republic of
Tel: (010 49) 2103-69904

Die Info Agentur Dr Kurt
Bednar GmbH
(FIZ Technik Agent)
Pfeilgasse 7
1000 Vienna
Austria
Tel: (010 43) 222-486646

Dimensions
The WEFA Group
150 Monument Rd
Bala Clynwd
PA 19004
USA
Tel: (010 1) 215-6676000
Telex: 831609

Direction des Journaux
Officiels
Services des Bulletins
Annexes
26 rue Desaix
75727 Paris Cedex 15
France
Tel: (010 33) 1-45786139
Telex: 201176 DIRJO F

Directorate General for
Energy of the EEC
DG XV11 Sesame
200 Rue de la Loi
1049 Brussels
Belgium

Disclosure Information Group
(USA)
5161 River Road
Bethesda
MD 20816
USA
Tel: (010 1) 301-9511300
Telex: 898452

Dow Jones & Company Inc
PO Box 300
Princeton
NJ 08540
USA
Tel: (010 1) 609-4521511

Drexel Burnham Lambert Inc
60 Broad Street
New York
NY 10004
USA
Tel: (010 1) 212-4806281

Dun and Bradstreet France
Division Marketing
Enterprises
17 avenue de Choisy
75643 Paris Cedex 13
France
Tel: (010 33) 45-841283
Telex: 270086 F

Dun and Bradstreet Ltd
26-32 Clifton Street
London EC2P 2LY
UK
Tel: 01-377 4377
Telex: 886697 DEANBE G

Dun's Marketing Services
49 Old Bloomfield Avenue
Mountain Lakes
NJ 07046
USA
Tel: (010 1) 201-2990181

DUPLEX
Centre Serveur de
Didot-Bottin
28 Rue du Docteur-Finlay
75738 Paris Cedex 15
France
Tel: (010 33) 1-45786166
Telex: 204 286 F

ECHO
European Commission Host
Organisation
177 route d'Esch
1471 Luxembourg
Tel: (010 352) 488041
Telex: 2181 EUROL LU

EIC/Intelligence
Environment Information
Center Inc
48 West 38th Street
New York
NY 10018
USA
Tel: (010 1) 212-9448500
Telex: 668298 EIC

ESA-IRS (European Space
Agency)
ESPRIN, Via Galileo Galilei
00044 Frascati
Rome
Italy
Tel: (010 39) 6-94011
Telex: 610637 ESPRIN 1

ESA-IRS (European Space
Agency)
Mr Ph Lequain
8-10 Rue Mario Nikis
75738 Paris Cedex 15
France
Tel: (010 33) 1-42737203
Telex: 202746

ESA-IRS (European Space
Agency)
CNDST
4 Boulevard de l'Empereur
1000 Brussels
Belgium
Tel: (010 32) 2-5195643
Telex: 21157

ESA-IRS (European Space
Agency)
DTB Library
Anker Engelundsvej 1
2800 Lyngby
Denmark
Tel: (010 45) 2-5195643
Telex: 37148

ESA-IRS (European Space
Agency)
IIRS
Ballymun Road
Dublin 9
Ireland
Tel: (0001) 370101
Telex: 25449

ESA-IRS (European Space
Agency)
COBIDOC
PO Box 16601
1001 RC Amsterdam
Netherlands
Tel: (010 31) 20-223955
Telex: 18766

ESA-IRS (European Space
Agency)
INTA
Torrejon de Ardoz
Madrid
Spain
Tel: (010 34) 1-6755263
Telex: 22026

ESA-IRS (European Space
Agency)
IDC-KTHB
Valhallavagen 81
10044 Stockholm
Sweden
Tel: (010 46) 8-7908970
Telex: 10389

ESA-IRS Agent
CLIRS LTD
Post Office 654
Artamon
NSW 2064
Australia
Tel: (010 61) 2-4398038
Telex: 10715912

ESA-IRS Agent
EUROLINE
PO Box 3121 Station D
Ottawa
Ontario K1P 6H7
Canada
Tel: (010 1) 613-2363434

ESA-IRS Agent
INTERSYS SA
7 Dionissiou Areopagitou
Athens 11742
Greece
Tel: (010 30) 1-9228738
Telex: 216826

ESA-IRS Agent
Information Services
Associates
21 Maynard Court
Los Altos
CA 94022
USA
Tel: (010 1) 415-9482326
Telex: 751914

ESA-IRS Dialtech
(UK Centre) Dept of Trade &
Industry
Room 392, Ashdown House
123 Victoria Street
London SW1E 6RB
UK
Tel: 01-215 6578/6577
Telex: 8813148

ESTC, Dept TI
Postbox 299
2200 AG Nordwijk
Netherlands
Tel: (010 31) 1719-83764
Telex: 39098

Economic Documentation
and Information Centre Ltd
(EDICLINE)
2, Broyle Gate Cottages
Ringmer Nr Lewes
East Sussex BN8 5NA
UK
Tel: 0273-813238

Economist Intelligence Unit
40 Duke Street
London W1A 1DW
UK
Tel: 01-493 6711
Fax: 01-499 9767
Telex: 266353 EIU G

Economist Publications Ltd
(see Economist Intelligence
Unit)
UK

Electric Power Research
Institute (EPRI)
Technical Information Centre
PO Box 10412
Palo Alto
CA 94303
USA
Tel: (010 1) 415-8552411
TWX: 910 373 1163

Electricite de France
Dept Systemes d'Information
et de Documentation
1 Avenue du Generale de
Gaulle
92141 Clamart
France
Tel: (010 33) 7654158
Telex: 270400 EDFERIM F

Electronic Centre for Legal
Documentation
(see Centro Elettronico di
Documentazion)

Electronic Data Systems
Demand Services Division
5615 Fishers Lane
Rockville
MD 20852
USA
Tel: (010 1) 231-6100

Engineering Information Inc
345 East 47th Street
New York
NY 10117
USA
Tel: (010 1) 212-7057600
Telex: 4990438

Ente Nazionale per l'Energie
Elettrica
Direzione Studi e Ricerche
Via Giovanni Battista Martini,
3
00198 Rome
Italy
Tel: (010 39) 6-85092735
Telex: 610518/610528

Entel SA
Paseo de la Castellana 141
28046 Madrid
Spain
Tel: (010 34) 1-4509096

Esselte On-Line
Datastream Representative
Box 1391
Sundbybergsvagen 1
S-171 27 Solna
Sweden
Tel: (010 46) 8-7343400
Telex: 13243 ARKOS

Euromonitor
87-88 Turnmill Street
London EC1M 5QU
UK
Tel: 01-251 8024
Telex: 21120 MONREF
G(2281)

EUROSTAT
Statistical Office of the EEC
Batiment Jean Monnet
BP 1907
1019
Luxembourg
Tel: (010 352) 43011
Telex: 3423 COMMEUR LU

Extel Financial & Business
Services Ltd
Fitzroy House
13-17 Epworth Street
London EC2A 4DL
UK
Tel: 01-251 3333
Fax: 01-251 2725
Telex: 884319

FRI Information Services Ltd
121 Richmond West, Suite 500
Toronto
Ontario M5H 2K1
Canada
Tel: (010 1) 416-8628105

Fachinformationszentrum
Werkstoffe eV
Unter den Eichen 87
1000 Berlin 45
Germany, Federal Republic of
Tel: (010 49) 30-830001-0
Telex: 186387 FIZW D

Facts on File Inc
460 Park Avenue South
New York
NY 10016
USA
Tel: (010 1) 212-6832244
Telex: 238552

Factset Data Systems
369 Lexington Avenue
New York
NY 10017
USA
Tel: (010 1) 212-6872546

Financial Post Information
Service
Financial Post Corporation
Service Group
777 Bay Street, 6th Floor
Toronto
Ontario M5W 1A7
Canada
Tel: (010 1) 416-5965693
Telex: 0219547

Financial Times Electronic
Publishing Ltd
126 Jermyn Street
London SW1Y 4UJ
UK
Tel: 01-925 2323
Fax: 01-925 2125
Telex: London 27347
FTCONF G

FININFO
31 rue du 4 Septembre
75002 Paris
France
Tel: (010 33) 1-42651015

Finstat (Shearson Lehman
Hutton)
Two Broadway 13th Floor
New York
NY 10004
USA
Tel: (010 1) 212-6682272

Fiz Chemie GmbH
PO Box 12 60 50
1000 Berlin 12
Germany, Federal Republic of
Tel: (010 49) 30-319003-0

Fiz Karlsruhe
PO Box 2465
7500 Karlsruhe 1
Germany, Federal Republic of

Fiz-Technik
Postfach 60-05-47
Ostbahnhofstr 13
6000 Frankfurt/Main 60
Germany, Federal Republic of
Tel: (010 49) 69-4308225
Telex: 4189459 FIZT D

Food & Agriculture
Organisation of the UN
AGRIS Coordinating Centre
Via delle Terme di Caracalla
00100 Rome
Italy
Tel: (010 39) 6-57976414
Telex: 610181 FAO 1

Ford Investor Services
11722 Sorrento Valley Road
Suite 1, San Diego
CA 92121
USA
Tel: (010 1) 619-7551327

Forest Products Research
Society
2801 Marshall Court
Madison
WI 53705
USA
Tel: (010 1) 608-2311361

Fraser Williams (Scientific
Systems) Ltd
(Telesystemes Questel Agent)
London House, London Road
South
Poynton
Cheshire SK12 1YP
UK
Tel: 0625-876711

Frederick C Towers & Cò
8033 Herb Farm Drive
Bethesda
MD 20817
USA
Tel: (010 1) 301-4696699

G-CAM Serveur, Division
Banques de Donnes (Data
Star Agent)
Tour Maine-Montparnasse
33 Avenue du Maine
75755 Paris Cedex 15
France
Tel: (010 33) 1-45381535

GE Information Services
114-118 Southampton Row
London WC1B 5AB
UK
Tel: 01-831 8222
Fax: 01-430 0423

GSI (UK) Ltd
Yorktown Industrial Estate
Stanhope Road
Camberley
Surrey GU15 3PS
UK
Tel: 0276-62282

GSI-ECO
25, boulevard de
l'Amiral-Bruix
75782 Paris Cedex 16
France
Tel: (010 33) 1-45021220
Telex: 613163 GSIJOAN F

Gale Research Co
Book Tower
Detroit
MI 48226
USA
Tel: (010 1) 313-9612242
TWX: 810 221 7087

GAMA
Universite de Paris X
2, rue de Rouen
92001 Nanterre
France
Tel: (010 33) 1-47259234

General Electric Information
Services (GEISCO)
401 North Washington Street
Rockville
MD 20850
USA
Tel: (010 1) 301-3404000
Telex: 898431

General Mills
Foods Adlibra Publications
9000 Plymouth Avenue North
Minneapolis
MN 55427
USA
Tel: (010 1) 612-5402720
Telex: 882122 GENMILRES
GOVY

GENIOS
Wirtschaftsdatenbanken
GmbH
Postfach 1102
4000 Dusseldorf 1
Germany, Federal Republic of
Tel: (010 49) 211-8388172
Telex: 17211308 hblverl

Genius Operator
Advertising Databank, Gert
Richter
Bismarckstr 84
1000 Berlin 12
Germany, Federal Republic of
Tel: (010 49) 30-317722

Gesellschaft fur
Betriebwirtschaftliche
Information mbH (GBI
Postfach 80 07 23
Pariserstr 42
8000 Munich 80
Germany, Federal Republic of
Tel: (010 49) 89-4482804

Gesellschaft fur Elektronische
Medien mbH (GEM)
Herriotstrasse 5
6000 Frankfurt/Main 71
Germany, Federal Republic of
Tel: (010 49) 69-66871
Telex: 414351 GIDFM D
(Private company – acquired
GID)

Gesellschaft fur
Informationsmarkt-
Forschung (GIF)
4930 Detmold
Germany, Federal Republic of
Tel: (010 49) 5231-88011

Gesellschaft fur Mathematik
und Datenverarbeitung mbH
z Hd Herrn Dr P Budinger
Herriotstrasse 5
6000 Frankfurt/Main 71
Germany, Federal Republic of
Tel: (010 49) 69-6687360

Gesellschaft fur
Wirtschaftspresse mbH
(GWP)
Kasernenstr 67
4000 Dusseldorf 1
Germany, Federal Republic of
Tel: (010 49) 211-83880

GIANO
Sistema Informatico della
Confindustria
Vialle dell Astronomia 30,
Rome
Italy
Tel: (010 39) 6-59031
Telex: 611393 CONFIN 1

Groupe DPV
24, rue Morere
75014 Paris
France
Tel: (010 33) 1-45415202

Groupe Galande
Chateau de Sens
Rochecorbon
37210 Vouvray
France
Tel: (010 33) 47-525184
Telex: 750034 F

Guardian Business
Information
CCN Systems Ltd
Talbot House, Talbot Street
Nottingham NG1 5HF
UK
Tel: 0602-410888

Handelsblatt GmbH
Kasernenstrasse 67
4000 Dusseldorf 1
Germany, Federal Republic of
Tel: (010 49) 211-8388486
Telex: 17211308 HBL VERL D

Haver Analytics Inc
Contact Maurine Haver
800 Second Avenue, Suite 608
New York
NY 10017
USA
Tel: (010 1) 212-9869300

Helsinki School of Economics
Library
Runeberginkatu 22-24
00100 Helsinki
Finland
Tel: (010 358) 0-43131
Telex: 122220 ECON SF

Holger Mayer,
Unternehmensberatung fur
Informationsverarbeit
Elisabethenstrasse 18
6368 Bad Vilbel 1
Germany, Federal Republic of
Tel: (010 49) 6101-8113

Hoppenstedt
Wirtschaftsdatenbanken
GmbH
Havelstrasse 9
6100 Darmstadt
Germany, Federal Republic of
Tel: (010 49) 6151-3801
Telex: 419258

House of Commons Library
Department of the Library
Westminster
London SW1A 0AA
UK
Tel: 01-219 5714

ICC Canada Ltd
16-26 Banner Street
London EC1Y 8QE
UK
Tel: 01-250 3922
Fax: 01-253 3072
Telex: 23678

ICC Database
16-26 Banner Street
London EC1Y 8QE
UK
Tel: 01-250 3922
Fax: 01-253 3072
Telex: 23678

ICC Information Group
ICC House
81 City Road
London EC1Y 1BD
UK
Tel: 01-250 3922
Fax: 01-251 8776
Telex: 296090

ICONDA Agency
c/o IRB Centre Fraunhofer
Society
Stuttgart
Germany, Federal Republic of

IFI/Plenum Data Company
Inc
302 Swann Avenue
Alexandria
VA 22301
USA
Tel: (010 1) 703-6831085
Telex: 901834

INKA Karlsruhe
(see Fiz Karlsruhe)

INPADOC
Mollwaldplatz 4
1040 Wien
Postfach 163
Austria
Tel: (010 43) 222-658784

INSPEC (USA Center)
IEEE Service Center
445 Hoes Lane
Piscataway
NJ 08854
USA
Tel: (010 1) 201-9810060

INSPEC Institution of Electric
Engineers
Station House
Nightingale Road
Hitchin
Herts SG5 1RJ
UK
Tel: 0462-53331
Telex: 825962 IEE G

IST – Informatheque Inc
(Telesystemes Questel, ICC
Agent)
611 Boulevard Chremazie Est
Montreal
Quebec H2M 2P2
Canada
Tel: (010 1) 514-3831611

ITG Innovationstechnik
GmbH & Co KG
SDS Subvent Datenbank
Systeme
Heinrich-Hertz-Strasse 15
2000 Hamburg 76
Germany, Federal Republic of
Tel: (010 49) 40-2290008

Info Globe
The Globe and Mail
444 Front Street West
Toronto
Ontario MSV 2S9
Canada
Tel: (010 1) 416-5855250
Telex: 06 219629

Infocheck Ltd
28 Scrutton Street
London EC2A 4RQ
UK
Tel: 01-377 8872
Telex: 892530 INFO

Infomat
(Predicasts Subsidiary) VO
TEC Centre
Hambridge Lane
Newbury
Berkshire RG14 5HA
UK
Tel: 0635-34867
Telex: 265451 Ref 87:WQQ363

Information Access Company
A Division of Ziff-Davis Pub
11 Davis Drive
Belmont
CA 940002
USA
Tel: (010 1) 415-5912333
Telex: 1561004 (INFO UT)

Information Handling
Services
PO Box 1154
15 Inverness Way East
Englewood
CO 80150
USA
Tel: (010 1) 303-7900600
TWX: 910 935 0715

Information Intelligence Inc
PO Box 31098
Phoenix
AZ 85046
USA
Tel: (010 1) 602-9962283
Telex: 704787

Information Plus
Data Resources (DRI)
1750 K St NW Suite 1060
Washington DC 20006
USA
Tel: (010 1) 202-8623720
Telex: 440480 DRI WASHDC

Insearch Ltd/DIALOG
(Dialog Services)
PO Box K16
Haymarket
NSW 20000
Australia
Tel: (010 61) 2-2122867
Telex: AA727091 INSRCH

Institut Belge de
Normalisation (IBN)
Avenue de la Brabanconne 29
1040 Brussels
Belgium
Tel: (010 32) 2-7349205
Telex: 23877 BENOR B

Institut National de la
Propriete Industrielle (INPI)
26 bis rue de Leningrad
75800 Paris Cedex 08
France
Tel: (010 33) 1-42945260
Fax: (010 33) 1-42935930
Telex: 290368

Institut National de la
Propriete in Paris Industrielle
(INPI)
29 bis rue de Leningrad
75800 Paris Cedex 08
France
Tel: (010 33) 1-42945260
Telex: 290368 F

Institut National de la
Statistique et des Etudes
Economique (INSEE)
Ministere de l'Economie
18, boulevard
Adolphe-Pinard
75675 Paris Cedex 14
France
Tel: (010 33) 1-45401212
Telex: 204924 INSEE F

Institut Textile de France (ITF)
35 rue des Abondances BP 79
92105 Boulogne Billancourt
Cedex
France
Tel: (010 33) 1-48251890
Telex: 250940 ITEXFRA F

Institute of Chartered
Accountants in Australia
37 York Street
Sydney
NSW 2000
Australia
Tel: (010 61) 2-2901344

Institute for Scientific
Information (ISI)
3501 Market Street
Philadelphia
PA 19104
USA
Tel: (010 1) 215-3860100
Telex: 845305

Institute of Industrial
Research and Standards
(IIRS)
Ballymun Road
Dublin 9
Ireland, Republic of
Tel: (0001) 370101
Telex: 32501 11RSD G

Institute of Paper Chemistry
(The)
PO Box 1039
Appleton
WI 54912
USA
Tel: (010 1) 414-7383241
Telex: 469289

Institute of Textile
Technology
PO Box 391
Charlottesville
VA 22902
USA
Tel: (010 1) 804-2965511

Institution of Electrical
Engineers
Station House
70 Nightingale Road
Hitchin
Herts SG5 1RJ
UK
Tel: 462-53331
Telex: 825962 G

Instituto Espanol de
Comercio Exterior (ICEX)
Paseo de la Castellana 14
28046 Madrid
Spain
Tel: (010 34) 91-4311240
Telex: 44838/44840 IECE

Instituto Nacional de
Estadistica (INE)
Paseo de la Castellana 183
28046 Madrid
Spain
Tel: (010 34) 1-2790162

Instituto Nacional de
Fomento de la Exportacion
(INFE)
Paseo de la Castellana 14
28046 Madrid
Spain
Tel: (010 34) 91-4311240
Telex: 44838/44840 IECE

Instituto de la Pequena y
Mediana Empresa Industrial
(IMPI)
Sistema de Informacion
Empresarial
Paseo de la Castellana 141
2 a planta
28046 Madrid
Spain
Tel: (010 34) 1-4508048

Interactive Data Corporation
(UK)
12-15 Fetter Lane, 6th Floor
London EC4A 1BR
UK
Tel: 01-583 0765
Fax: 01-583 1116
Telex: 8814243 IDCTEL G

Interactive Data Corporation
(USA)
A company of the Dun &
Bradstreet Corp
95 Hayden Avenue
Lexington
MA 02173
USA
Tel: (010 1) 617-8638100

Interactive Data Services Inc
22 Cortland Street
New York
NY 10007
USA
Tel: (010 1) 212-3066627

International Coffee
Organisation (ICO)
22 Berners Street
London W1P 4DD
UK
Tel: 01-580 8591
Telex: 267659 G

International Food
Information Service (IFIS)
GmbH
Herriotstrasse 5
6000 Frankfurt 71
Germany, Federal Republic of
Tel: (010 49) 69-6687338
Telex: 414 351 GIDFM D

International Food
Information Service (IFIS)
Lane End House
Shinfield, Reading
Berkshire RG2 9BB
UK
Tel: 0734-883895
Telex: 847204 (DSIFIS G)

International Labour Office
Central Library and
Documentation Branch
1211 Geneva 22
Switzerland
Tel: (010 41) 22-998676
Telex: 22271 BIT CH

International Labour Office
Social and Labour Bulletin
Section
1211 Geneva 22
Switzerland
Tel: (010 41) 22-996759
Telex: 22271 BIT CH

International Listing Service
Inc
8350 Greensboro Drive Suite
425
McLean
VA 22102
USA
Tel: (010 1) 703-8212456

International Marine Banking
Co Ltd
401 North Washington Street
Rockville
MD 20850
USA
Tel: (010 1) 301-3404000
Telex: 898360

International Monetary Fund
(IMF)
Bureau of Statistics
700 19th Street NW
Washington DC 20431
USA
Tel: (010 1) 202-4737904
Telex: 248331 IMF UR

International Software
Database Corp
1520 South College Avenue
Fort Collins
CO 80524
USA
Tel: (010 1) 303-4825000
Telex: 454590 MENU/ISD

International Translations
Centre (ITC)
101 Doelenstraat
2611 NS Delft
Netherlands
Tel: (010 31) 15-142242
Telex: 38104 ITCNL

Istituto Centrale di Statistica
(ISTAT)
Via Cesare Balbo 16
00100 Rome
Italy
Tel: (010 39) 6-46731
Telex: 610338 1

Janssen Chimica
2340 Beerse
Belgium
Tel: (010 32) 41-602111
Telex: 32540 B

Japan Information Center of
Science and Technology
(JICST)
CPO Box 1478
Tokyo
Japan
Tel: (010 81) 3-5816411
Fax: (010 81) 3-5933375

Japan Patent Information
Organisation (JAPIO)
Bansui Bldg
1-5-16 Toranomon
Minato-ku
Tokyo 105
Japan
Tel: (010 81) 3-5036181
Telex: 2224152 JAPATI J

Japanese Information Service
British Library
25 Southampton Buildings
London WC2A 1AW
UK
Tel: 01-323 7924/5
Fax: 01-323 7495
Telex: 266959

Jay C White
PO Box 1148
Redwood City
CA 94064
USA
Tel: (010 1) 415-5949300

Jiji Press Ltd
International Press Center
76 Shoe Lane
London EC4A 3JB
UK
Tel: 01-353 5417/3902
Telex: LONDON 23413

Jiji Press Ltd
Head Office
1-3 Hibiya Koen
Chiyoda-ku
Tokyo 100
Japan
Tel: (010 81) 3-5911111

John Wiley & Sons Inc
Electronic Publishing Division
605 3rd Avenue
New York NY 10158
USA
Tel: (010 1) 212-8506331

Joint Research Centre (EEC)
Ispra Establishment
21020 Ispra (Varese)
Italy
Tel: (010 39) 332-789111
Telex: 380042/380058 EUR I

Jordan and Sons Ltd
Jordan House
47 Brunswick Place
London N1 6EE
UK
Tel: 01-253 3030
Fax: 01-251 0825
Telex: 261010

Kansallis Osake Pankki
Aleksanterinkatu 42
00100 Helsinki 10
Finland
Tel: (010 358) 1631
Telex: 124412

Kinokuniya Company Ltd
(DIALOG/Questel Agent)
ASK Info Services
Village 101 Bldg
1-7 Sakuragaoka-machi
Shibuya-ku
Tokyo 150
Japan
Tel: (010 81) 3-4634391
Telex: J27655 (KINOASK J)

Kokusai Information Service
Co Ltd
Information Business
Develop (D-S Agent)
Shibuya Sumitomo Sintakie
Bldg
22-3 Jinnan i-chome
Shibuya-ku
Tokyo 150
Japan
Tel: (010 81) 3-4637181
Telex: 2423526 KOKIMF J

Kompass Online
Reed Information Services
Ltd
Windsor Ct, East Grinstead
Hse
East Grinstead
West Sussex RH19 1XA
UK
Tel: 0342-26972
Telex: 95127 INFSER G

KPMG
1 Puddle Dock
Blackfriars
London EC4V 3PD
UK
Tel: 01-236 8000

Kyodo News International Inc
50 Rockerfeller Plaza Suite 816
New York NY 10020
USA
Tel: (010 1) 212-5860152

Learned Information Ltd
Woodside
Hinksey Hill
Oxford OX1 5AU
UK
Tel: 0865-730275
Telex: 837704

Library Association
Publishing Ltd
Library Association
7 Ridgmount Street
London WC1E 7AE
UK
Tel: 01-636 7543
Telex: 21897 LALDN G

Lotus Development
Corporation
(Lynne Wilson Product
Manager for CD-ROM)
One Cambridge Center
Cambridge
Massachusetts 02142
USA
Tel: (010 1) 617-5778500

Lotus Development (UK) Ltd
Consort House
Victoria Street
Windsor
Berkshire SL4 1EX
UK
Tel: 0753-840281
Telex: 846110

M+a Verlag fur Messen,
Ausstellungen und
Kongresse GmbH
Grosse Eschenheimer Str 16
6000 Frankfurt/Main
Germany, Federal Republic of
Tel: (010 49) 69-281030
Telex: 411699 CMF D

Maid Systems Ltd
Maid House
26 Baker Street
London W1M 1DF
UK
Tel: 01-935 6460
Fax: 01-487 3768

Market Data Retrieval Inc
Ketchum Place
Westport
CT 06880
USA
Tel: (010 1) 203-2268941

Market Location Ltd
17 Waterloo Place
Warwick Street
Leamington Spa
Warwickshire CV32 5LA
UK
Tel: 0926-34235

Maruzen Company
(Telesystemes Questel Agent)
Masis Centre
PO Box 5335
Tokyo 100-31
Japan
Tel: (010 81) 3-2716068

McCarthy Information Ltd
Ash Walk
Warminster
Wiltshire BA12 8BY
UK
Tel: 0985-215151
Fax: 0985 217479

McGraw-Hill Inc
1221 Avenue of the Americas
New York
NY 10020
USA
Tel: (010 1) 212-5122823
Telex: 127960
TWX: 7105814879

Mead Data Central Inc
9393 Springboro Pike, PO Box 933
Dayton
OH 45401
USA
Tel: (010 1) 513-8657936
Fax: (010 1) 513-8656909

Mead Data Central
International
International House
1 St Katherine's Way
London E1 9UN
UK
Tel: 01-488 9187
Fax: 01-480 7228

Mead Data Central
International
Sun Life Centre
200 King Street W, Suite 1901
Toronto
Ontario M5H 3T4
Canada
Tel: (010 1) 800-3879042
Telefax 416 591 8492

Media General Financial
Services Inc
(Division of Media General)
PO Box C 32333
Richmond
VA 23293 0001
USA
Tel: (010 1) 804-6496946

Merlin Gerin
Service Documentation
38050 Grenoble Cedex
France
Tel: (010 33) 76-579460
Telex: 320842 MERGER

Merrill Lynch
Economics Inc
1 Liberty Plaza
165 Broadway
New York
NY 10080
USA
Tel: (010 1) 804-6496946

Metals Society (The)
1 Carlton House Terrace
London SW1Y 5DB
UK
Tel: 01-839 4071
Telex: 8814813

Micromedia Ltd
144 Front Street West
Toronto
Ontario MJ5 2L7
Canada
Tel: (010 1) 416-5935211
Telex: 06524668

Micromedia Ltd/DIALOG
(Dialog Service)
158 Pearl Street
Toronto
Ontario M5H 1L3
Canada
Tel: (010 1) 800-3872689
Telex: 06524668

J A Micropublishing Inc
271 Main Street
Box 218, Eastchester
NY 10707
USA
Tel: (010 1) 914-7932130
TWX: 710 562 0119

Ministere du Developpement
Industriel et Scientifique
110 rue de Grenelle
75700 Paris
France
Tel: (010 33) 1-45563636

Ministerio de Industria y
Energia
Paseo de la Castellana 141-2
28046 Madrid
Spain
Tel: (010 34) 1-2507817
Telex: 42204 MISC

Ministry of Economic Affairs
Department of Industrial
Property
Rue JA De Mot 24-26
1040 Brussels
Belgium
Tel: (010 32) 2-2336044

Ministry of Economic Affairs
Fonds Quetelet Library
Rue de l'Industrie, 6
1040 Brussels
Belgium
Tel: (010 32) 2-5127950

Ministry of Foreign Affairs
Central Library
Rue Quatre-Bras, 2
1000 Brussels
Belgium
Tel: (010 32) 2-5168111

Mitsui & Co (USA) Inc
Pan American Building
200 Park Avenue
New York
NY 10166 0130
USA
Tel: (010 1) 212-8784000
Telex: 012056

Mitsui & Co Ltd
Temple Court
11 Queen Victoria Street
London EC4N 4SB
UK
Tel: 01-822 0321

Money Market Services
(MMS International)
275 Shoreline Drive
Redwood City
CA 94065
USA
Tel: (010 1) 415-5950610

Money Market Services
(MMS International)
2204 Alexander House
16-20 Chater Road
Hong Kong
Tel: (010 852) 5-213206

Money Market Services Ltd
49 Park Lane
London W1Y 3LB
UK
Tel: 01-408 0025
Fax: 01-409 1506

Moody's Investors Service Inc
(D & B subsidiary)
99 Church Street
New York
NY 10007
USA
Tel: (010 1) 212-5530857
Telex: 521889

National Computer Network
Corp (NCN)
1929 North Harlem Avenue
Chicago
IL 60635
USA
Tel: (010 1) 312-6226666

National Computing Centre
Oxford Road
Manchester
UK
Tel: 061-228 6333

National Register Publishing
Company (NRPC)
MacMillan Directory Division
3002 Glenview Road
Wilmette
IL 60091
USA
Tel: (010 1) 312-4412373

National Standards
Associations, Inc
5161 River Road
Bethesda
MD 20816
USA
Tel: (010 1) 301-9511389
Telex: 89 8452 DISCINC
BHDA

National Technical
Information Service (NTIS)
US Department of Commerce
5285 Port Royal Road
Springfield
Virginia 22161
USA
Tel: (010 1) 703-4874600
Telex: 899405

Netherlands Foreign Trade
Agency
Bezuidenhautseweg 151
2594 AG The Hague
Netherlands
Tel: (010 31) 70-797221
Telex: 31099 ECOZA NL

New York Stock Exchange
11 Wall Street
New York
NY 10005
USA
Tel: (010 1) 212-6563800
Telex: 7105815464

NewsNet Inc
945 Haverford Road
Bryn Mawr
PA 19010
USA
Tel: (010 1) 215-5278030

AC Nielsen
Nielsen Plaza
Northbrook
IL 60062
USA
Tel: (010 1) 312-4986300
Telex: 206466

AC Nielsen Co Ltd
Nielsen House
London Road
Headington
Oxford OX3 9RX
UK
Tel: 0865-742742

Nihon Keizai Shimbun
(Nikkei)
1-9-5, Otemachi
Chiyoda-Ku
Tokyo 100
Japan
Tel: (010 81) 3-2700251
Telex: 22308 NIKKEI J

Nippon Telegraph &
Telephone
1-6-6, Uchisaiwai Cho
Chiyoda-ku
Tokyo
Japan
Tel: (010 81) 3-5095111
Telex: 2225300 J

Nomina Gesellschaft fur
Wirtschafts-und
Verwaltungsregister
Landsberger Strasse 338
8 Munich 21
Germany, Federal Republic of
Tel: (010 49) 89-5600461
Telex: 5212689 INF D

Nomos Datapool
Nomos Verlagsgesellschaft
mbH
Waldsee Strasse 3-5, Postfach
610
7570 Baden-Baden
Germany, Federal Republic of
Tel: (010 49) 7221-210425

Nomura Research Institute
Edobashi Building
1-11-1 Nihonbashi
Chuo-ku
Tokyo 103
Japan
Tel: (010 81) 3-2764762
Telex: 27586 NRITKY J

Nordic Energy Library
Riso Bibliotek
Forskningscenter Riso
4000 Roskilde
Denmark
Tel: (010 45) 2-371212
Telex: 43116 RISOE DK

NORDICOM
State & University Library
Universitetsparken
8000 Aarhus C
Denmark
Tel: (010 45) 6-122022

Norwegian School of
Economics
Library
Hellevien 30
5035 Bergen Sandviken
Norway

OCLC Europe
Lloyds Bank Chambers
75 Edmund Street
Birmingham B3 3HA
UK
Tel: 021-236 3224
Telex: 336520 TFSTRS G

OR Telematique
7 rue de Sens
Rochecorbon
37210 Vouvray
France
Tel: (010 33) 47-525184
Telex: 750034

OTC Information Systems plc
39 Upper Brook Street
London W1Y 3FB
UK
Tel: 01-493 0112
Fax: 01-491 1178

Oil and Gas Journal
PO Box 1260
Tulsa
OK 74101
USA
Tel: (010 1) 918-8329346
Telex: 203604

Online GmbH
Poststrasse 42
6900 Heidelberg
Germany, Federal Republic of
Tel: (010 49) 6221-21536
Telex: 461782

Online Inc
11 Tannery Lane
Weston
CT 06883
USA
Tel: (010 1) 203-2278466

Orbit Search Service
(Division of Pergamon Orbit
Infoline Ltd)
8000 Westpark Drive
McLean, VA 22102
USA
Tel: (010 1) 703-4420900

Orbit Search Service
(Division of Pergamon Orbit
Infoline Ltd)
Archilles House
Western Avenue
London W3 0UA
UK
Tel: 01-992 3456
Fax: 01-993 7335
Telex: 8814614

Organisation for Economic
Cooperation & Development
(OECD)
Data Dissemination &
Reception
2 rue Andre Pascal
75775 Paris Cedex 16
France
Tel: (010 33) 1-45248200
Telex: 620160 OCDE PARIS

Oslo Bors
Tollbugt 2
0152 Oslo 1
Norway
Tel: (010 47) 2-423880

Osterreichisches Statistiches
Zentralamt
Technisch-Methodische
Abteilung
Hintere Zollamtsstrasse 2B
1033 Vienna
Austria
Tel: (010 43) 222-6628-0

PTC Associates
180 Wilson Street
Fairfield
CT 06432
USA
Tel: (010 1) 203-3726307

Paper and Board Packaging
Industries Research Assoc
(PIRA)
Randalls Road
Leatherhead
Surrey KT22 7RU
UK
Tel: 0372-376161
Telex: 929810

Paris Chamber of Commerce
and Industry
Economic Documentation
Centre
27 Avenue de Friedland
75382 Paris Cedex 08
France
Tel: (010 33) 1-42897270
Telex: 650100 CCI PARIS F

Pera-Otis
Melton Mowbray
Leicestershire LE13 OPB
UK
Tel: 0664-501501

PergaBase Inc
8000 Westpark Drive Suite 400
McLean
VA 22102
USA
Tel: (010 1) 703-4420900
Telex: 901811

Pergamon Financial Data
Services
(Division of Pergamon Orbit
Infoline)
Achilles House
Western Avenue
London W3 0UA
UK
Tel: 01-992 3456
Telex: 8814614

Pergamon Infoline
(Division of Pergamon Orbit
Infoline)
12 Vandy Street
London EC2A 2DE
UK
Tel: 01-377 4650
Telex: 8814614

Pergamon Orbit
PO Box 544
Potts Point
NSW 2011
Australia
Tel: (010 61) 2-3602691
Telex: AA27458

Pergamon Orbit
USACO Corporation
13-12 Shimbashi 1-Chome
Minato-ku
Tokyo 105
Japan
Tel: (010 81) 3-5026471
Telex: J26274 USACO
TOKYO

Pergamon Orbit Infoline
Registered Office:
Headington Hill Hall
Oxford OX3 0BW
UK

Petroconsultants (CES) Ltd
Burleigh House
13 Newmarket Street
Cambridge CB5 8EG
UK
Tel: 0223-315933

Pioneer Hi-Bred International
Inc
PO Box 183
5608 Merle Hay Road
Johnston
IA 50131
USA
Tel: (010 1) 515-2703926

Predicasts Inc
11001 Cedar Avenue
Cleveland
Ohio 44106
USA
Tel: (010 1) 216-7953000
Telex: 985604

Presstext News Service
818 18th Street NW Suite 470
Washington DC 20006
USA
Tel: (010 1) 202-2238444

Prestel Citiservice
City Office:
Colechurch House
1 London Bridge Walk
London SE1 2SX
UK
Tel: 01-407 2878

Prestel Citiservice
Woodsted house
72 Chertsey Road
Woking
Surrey GU21 5BJ
UK
Tel: 04862-27431
Telex: 859737 ICV G

PROFILE Information
Sunbury House
79 Staines Road West
Sunbury-on-Thames
Middx TW16 7AH
UK
Tel: 0932-761444

Public Affairs Information
Service Inc
11 West 40th Street
New York
NY 10018
USA
Tel: (010 1) 212-7366629

Questel Inc
(Telesystemes Questel
subsidiary)
5201 Leesburg Pike Suite
Falls Church
VA 22041
USA
Tel: (010 1) 703-8451133

Quotron Systems Inc
5454 Beethoven Street
PO Box 66914
Los Angeles
CA 90066
USA
Tel: (010 1) 213-8274600

Rapra Technology Ltd
Shawbury
Shrewsbury
Shropshire SY4 4NR
UK
Tel: 0939-250383
Telex: 35134

Resaux Commerciales
Informatiques (RCI) SA
Calvacom Service
87 Boulevard de Grenelle
75705 Paris
France
Tel: (010 33) 1-7832030

Reuters Holdings
85 Fleet Street
London EC4 4AJ
UK
Tel: 01-250 1122
Telex: 23222

Royal Institute of Technology
Library
(FIZ Technik Agent)
Info and Documentation
Center
IDC-KTHB Valhallavagen 81
10044 Stockholm
Sweden
Tel: (010 46) 8-7878969

Royal Society of Chemistry
(STN Representative)
Nottingham University
Nottingham NG7 2RD
UK
Tel: 0602-507411
TWX 37488

S J Rundt and Associates Inc
130 East 63rd Street
New York
NY 10021
USA
Tel: (010 1) 212-8380141

SCB Statistics Sweden
100 Karlvagen
11581 Stockholm
Sweden
Tel: (010 46) 8-7834000
Telex: 15261 SWESTAT S

SDC Information Service
2525 Colarado Avenue
Santa Monica
CA 90406
USA

SRI International
333 Ravenswood Avenue
Menio Park
CA 94025
USA
Tel: (010 1) 415-8596300
Telex: 334486

STN (INKADATA)
Information System
Karlsruhe
7514 Eggenstein
Leopoldshafen 2
Germany, Federal Republic of
Tel: (010 49) 7247-824600
Telex: 17724110 FIZE D

STN International
Head Office
PO Box 2465
7500 Karlsruhe 1
Germany, Federal Republic of
Tel: (010 49) 7247-824566
Telex: 17724710

STN International
(Service Center)
2540 Olentangy River Road
PO Box 02228
Columbus
OH 43202
USA
Tel: (010 1) 614-4213600
Telex: 6842086 CHMAB

STN International
(Service Center c/o JICST)
5-2 Nagata-cho, 2 Chome
Chiyoda-ku
Tokyo 100
Japan
Tel: (010 81) 3-5816411
Telex: JICSTECH TOKYO

Sales and Marketing
Information Ltd (SAMI)
17 Waterloo Place
Warwick Street
Leamington Spa
Warwickshire CV32 5LA
UK
Tel: 0926-831221

Salomon Brothers
1 New York Plaza
New York
NY 10004
USA
Tel: (010 1) 212-7477947

SARIN SpA
SS Pontina km 29.100
00040 Pomezia
Rome
Italy
Tel: (010 39) 6-911971
Telex: 616436 SARIN I

Scicon Ltd
Brick Close
Kiln Farm
Milton Keynes MK11 3EJ
UK
Tel: 0908-565656
Telex: 826693 SCICON G

Science Applications
International Corporation
PO Box 2501
Oak Ridge
TN 37831
USA
Tel: (010 1) 615-4829031

SEAT SpA
Viale del Policinico 147
00161 Rome
Italy
Tel: (010 39) 6-84941
Telex: 2122481

Securities Industries
Association
120 Broadway 35th Floor
New York
NY 10271
USA
Tel: (010 1) 212-6081500

I P Sharp Associates
Hong Kong Office
Suite 606, Tower 1
Admiralty Centre
Hong Kong
Tel: (010 852) 5-294341

I P Sharp Associates Inc
International Headquarters
1200 First Federal Plaza
Rochester
New York 14614
USA
Tel: (010 1) 716-5467270

I P Sharp Associates Ltd
European Headquarters
Heron House
10 Dean Farrar St
London SW1H ODX
UK
Tel: 01-222 7033
Fax: 01-799 1827
Telex: 265037 ALB G

I P Sharp Associates Ltd
Suite 1900, Exchange Tower
2 First Canadian Place
Toronto, Ontario M5X 1E3
Canada
Tel: (010 1) 416-3645361

I P Sharp Associates (S) Pte
Ltd
Far East Headquarters
SIA Building, 77 Robinson
Road
No 14-00
0106
Singapore
Tel: (010 65) 2230211

I P Sharp Associates Pty Ltd
8th Floor, Carlton Centre
55 Elizabeth Street
Sydney NSW 2000
Australia
Tel: (010 61) 2-2326366

Shaw Data Services
122 East 42nd Street
New York
NY 10168
USA
Tel: (010 1) 212-6828877

Shirley Institute
Didsbury
Manchester M20 8RX
UK
Tel: 061-445 8141
Telex: 668417 SHIRLY G

Sirio
Via Orazio 2
Milan
Italy
Tel: (010 39) 2-88231

Sistema Informatico della
Confindustria
Viale dell Astronomia 30
Rome
Italy

Slamark International SpA
Information Systems for
Marketing & Plan
Via G Trevis 88 – 00147
00147 Rome
Italy
Tel: (010 39) 6-5710649
Telex: 613408

Societa Nazionale di
Informatica delle Camere di
Commercio
Direzione Generale
Via Appia Nuova n696
Rome 00179
Italy

Societe D'Etudes Pour le
Developpement Economique
et Social (SEDES)
15 Rue Bleue
75009 Paris
France
Tel: (010 33) 1-47706161

Societe Generale de Banque
Centre d'Information
Montagne du Parc 3
1000 Brussels
Belgium
Tel: (010 32) 2-5163350

Society of Manufacturing
Engineers
One SME Drive
PO Box 930
Dearborn
Michigan 48121
USA
Tel: (010 1) 313-2711500
Telex: 297742 SMEUR

Standard & Poor's
Corporation
Media Relations Department
25 Broadway
New York
NY 10004
USA
Tel: (010 1) 212- 2088622

Standard & Poor's
Corporation
Financial Systems & Trading
Services
11 Broadway
New York
NY 10004
USA
Tel: (010 1) 212-4120335

Statistical Office of the
European Communities
(see EUROSTAT)

Statistics Canada (CANSIM)
Ottawa
Ontario K1A OT6
Canada
Tel: (010 1) 613-9908203

Statistisk Sentralbyra (Central
Statistical Office)
The Library
Postbox 8131 Dep
0033 Oslo 1
Norway
Tel: (010 47) 2-413820

Stichting Economische
Publikaties
Bezuidenhoutseweg 151
2594 AG The Hague
Netherlands
Tel: (010 31) 70-798933
Telex: 31099

Stock Exchange of the UK and
Republic of Ireland
Marketing Department
Old Broad Street
London EC2N 1HP
UK
Tel: 01-588 2355

Stockholm School of
Economics
Library
PO Box 6501
11383 Stockholm
Sweden
Tel: (010 46) 8-7360120

Sweet & Maxwell
11 New Fetter Lane
London EC4P 4EE
UK
Tel: 01-583 9855

Sydney Stock Exchange
Research Department
20 Bond Street, 20th Floor
Sydney
NSW 2000
Australia
Tel: (010 61) 2-2310066
Telex: 20630 AA

TCH Technologie-Centrum
Hannover GmbH
und CS China-Service
Vahrenwalder Str 7
3000 Hannover 1
Germany, Federal Republic of
Tel: (010 49) 511-48202

Tele Consulte
Distributors of LEXIS service
in France
(Contact Mead Data Central
for details)

Telecom Gold Ltd
60-68 St Thomas Street
London SE1 3QU
UK
Tel: 01-403 6777
Fax: 01-403 7065
Telex: 894001

Telekurs (Deutschland)
GmbH
(Subsidiary of Telekurs AG)
Niedenau 13-19
6000 Frankfurt 1
Germany, Federal Republic of
Tel: (010 49) 69-717000
Telex: 0414189841

Telekurs (France) Sarl
(Subsidiary of Telekurs AG)
9 Boulevard de Italiens
75002 Paris
France
Tel: (010 33) 14-2617555
Fax: (010 33) 14-7039773

Telekurs (Nederland) BV
(Subsidiary of Telekurs AG)
Rokinplaza
Papenbroekssteeg 2
1012 NW Amsterdam
Netherlands
Tel: (010 31) 20-253038
Fax: (010 31) 20-239295

Telekurs (North America) Inc
(Subsidiary of Telekurs AG)
3 River Bend Center
Stamford
Connecticut
USA
Tel: (010 1) 203-3538100

Telekurs (UK) Ltd
(Subsidiary of Telekurs AG)
5/7 St Helen's Place
London EC3A 6BH
UK
Tel: 01-256 5298
Fax: 01-588 7123

Telekurs AG
Neue Hard 11
8005 Zurich
Switzerland
Tel: (010 41) 1-2752111
Fax: (010 41) 1-428010

Telerate Systems Inc (USA)
1 World Trade Center
104th Floor
New York
NY 10048
USA
Tel: (010 1) 212-9385200

Telesystemes Questel
83-85 Boulevard
Vincent-Auriol
75013 Paris
France
Tel: (010 33) 1-45826464
Telex: 204594 F

Thomas Publishing Company
Inc
One Penn Plaza
New York
NY 10001
USA
Tel: (010 1) 212-2907291

Thompson Henry Ltd
London Road
Sunningdale
Berkshire SL5 0EP
UK
Tel: 0990-291072

Tilastokeskus (Central
Statistical
Office of Finland)
The Library
PB 504
00101 Helsinki 10
Finland
Tel: (010 358) 0-17341

Toronto Stock Exchange
The Exchange Tower
2 First Canadian Place
Toronto
Ontario M5X 1J2
Canada
Tel: (010 1) 416-9474700
Telex: 06217759

Trade*Plus Inc
480 California Avenue
Suite 303
Palo Alto
CA 94306
USA
Tel: (010 1) 415-3244554

Trans Canada Options Inc
2 First Canadian Place
Exchange Tower, 3rd Floor
Toronto
Ontario M5X 1J2
Canada
Tel: (010 1) 416-9474700

Trinet Inc
9 Campus Drive
Parsippany
NJ 07054
USA
Tel: (010 1) 201-2673600
Telex: 703636

Tsukuba Daijaku
Tsukuba JICST Library
293 Oaza Sakamaru
Tsukuba-shi 300-26
Japan
Tel: (010 81) 29247-5311

US Bureau of the Census
Washington DC 20233
USA
Tel: (010 1) 301-7637273

US Department of Commerce
14th Street between
Constitution Avenue &
E St NW
Washington DC 20230
USA
Tel: (010 1) 202-5230777

US Department of Energy
1000 Independance Ave SW
Washington DC 20585
USA
Tel: (010 1) 202-2522363

US Department of the Interior
425 National Center
Reston
VA 22092
USA
Tel: (010 1) 703-6486820

US Department of
Transportation and
Transportation Research
Data Administration Division
Washington DC 20590
USA
Tel: (010 1) 202-3664844

US Government Printing
Office
Superintendant of
Documents
Washington DC 20401
USA
Tel: (010 1) 202-2753299
TWX: 7108229413

US Library of Commerce
Washington DC 20540
USA
Tel: (010 1) 202-2875108

US National Agricultural
Library
US Dept of Agriculture
Beltsville
MD 20705
USA
Tel: (010 1) 301-3443846

Union Francaise d'Annuaire
Professionnels (UFAP)
13 Avenue Vladimir Komarov
78190 Trappes
France
Tel: (010 33) 1-30506148

United Nations
Secretariat
Palais des Nations
1211 Geneva 10
Switzerland
Telex: 289696 CH

United Press International
220 East 42nd Street
New York
NY 10017
USA
Tel: (010 1) 212-8508600

University Microfilms
International
300 North Zeeb Road
Ann Arbor
MI 48106
USA
Tel: (010 1) 313-7614700
Telex: 0235569

University of California
Dept of Economics
D-008 La Jolla
CA 92093
USA

University of Strathclyde
European Policies Research
Centre
26 Richmond Street
Glasgow G1 1XH
UK
Tel: 041-552 4400 Ext 3908
Fax: 041-552 0775
Telex: 77472

Value Line Inc
711 Third Avenue
New York NY 10017
USA
Tel: (010 1) 212-6873965

VDI Verlag GmbH
Graf-Recke-Strasse 84
4000 Dusseldorf 1
Germany, Federal Republic of
Tel: (010 49) 211-62141
Telex: 08586525 D

Verband der Vereine
Creditreform eV
Hellersberger Strasse 12
4040 Neuss 1
Germany, Federal Republic of
Tel: (010 49) 2101-1080

Verlag Hoppenstedt & Co
Havelstrasse 9
6100 Darmstadt 1
Germany, Federal Republic of
Tel: (010 49) 6151-380272

Verlag W Sachon GmbH & Co
Schloss Mindelberg
8948 Mindelheim
Germany, Federal Republic of
Tel: (010 49) 8261-99971

Vestek Systems
353 Sacramento Street Suite
2100
San Fransisco
CA 94111
USA
Tel: (010 1) 415-3986340

Vickers Stock Research
Corporation
226 New York Avenue
Huntington
NY 11743
USA
Tel: (010 1) 516-4237710

Volkswagen AG
FE-Dokumentation
3180 Wolfsburg 1
Germany, Federal Republic of
Tel: (010 49) 5361-924639
Telex: 95860 VWW D

VNU Business Publications
VNU House
32-34 Broadwick Street
London W1A 2HG
UK
Tel: 01-439 4242

Washington Post Company
(The)
1150 15th Street NW
Washington DC 20071
USA
Tel: (010 1) 202-3346016
Telex: 89522 WSHA
WASHPOST

WEFA Group (The)
150 Monument Road
Bala Cynwyd
PA 19004
USA
Tel: (010 1) 215-6676000
Telex: 831609

WEFA Ltd
Wharton Economic and
Financial Informatio
Ebury Gate
23 Lower Belgrave Street
London SW1W ONW
Tel: 01-730 8171
Telex: 916635 SIAGTE G

Welding Institute (The)
Abington Hall
Abington
Cambridge CB1 6AL
UK
0223 891162
81183 WELDEX G

J Whitaker & Sons Ltd
12 Dyott Street
London WC1A 1DF
UK
Tel: 01-836-8911

WILA-Verlag fur
Wirtschaftswerbung
Wilhem Lampl KG
Landsberger Strasse 191 A
8000 Munich 21
Germany, Federal Republic of
Tel: (010 49) 89-5795283

Wilshire Associates
1299 Ocean Avenue
Santa Monica
CA 90401
USA
Tel: (010 1) 213-4513051

WILSONLINE
The HW Wilson Company
950 University Avenue
Bronx
NY 10452
USA
Tel: (010 1) 212-5888400

WILSONLINE
UK Marketing Rep
Thompson, Henry Ltd
London Road
Sunningdale
Berks SL5 OEP
UK
Tel: 24615-22639

Wood Gundy Inc
Royal Trust Tower
PO Box 274 T-D Center
Toronto
Ontario M5K 1M7
Canada
Tel: (010 1) 416-8698100

World Bank
1818 H Street NW
Washington DC 20433
USA
Tel: (010 1) 202-477123
Cable: INTBAFRAD

Wright Investors' Services
Park City Plaza
10 Middle Street
Bridgeport
CT 06604
USA
Tel: (010 1) 203-3336666

Zachs Investment Research
Inc
2 North Riverside Plaza Room
1900
Chicago
IL 60606
USA
Tel: (010 1) 312-5599405

Appendix 3 Database Country Coverage and Subject Area Summary Chart

Alphabetical listing/page numbers

Name	Country	Subject	
ABC	Germany	Company	
ABC Europe	Europe	Company	
ABI Inform	International	General management	Market and industry news
Absatzwirtschaft	Germany	Market and industry news	
Abstracts of Working Papers in Economics	International	Economics	Research
Acciones de Fomento	Spain	Grants	
Accountants	International	Accountancy	Financial services
Accountants Business Network	UK	Acquisitions/ disposals	
Accountancy Adelin	France	Company	
ADP Financial System	USA	Stocks	Commodities
Advertising Age	USA	Advertising	
AFEE	International	Water	
Agnews	Europe	Agriculture	
Agora Economique	International	News	Economics
Agra Europe Online	Europe	Agriculture	
Agrep	Europe	Agriculture	Food science
Agribusiness USA	USA	Agriculture	
Agricola	International	Agriculture	
Agris International	International	Agriculture	Food science
Agrochemicals Handbook (The)	International	Chemistry	Agriculture
AIMS	UK	Grants	
AktieInformation	Sweden	Stocks	Company
Alberta Statistical Information System	Canada	Economics	
Alpha	Germany	Databases	
Aluminium	International	Material science	Metals
Amdata	International	Mergers	
American Banker	USA	Financial services	Market and industry news
Analytical Abstracts	International	Chemistry	
AP News	USA	News	
AP-Dow Jones News Services	International	News	Financial services
Apilit	International	Energy	Petrol
APIPAT	International	Patents	Energy
Arthur D Little/Online	International	Market directories	Industry profiles
Artificial Intelligence	International	IT	Technology
Asahi News Service	Japan	News	Company
ASI	USA	Economics	
Asian Geotechnology	Asia	Technology	
Association of Home Appliance Manufacturers	USA	Consumer products	
Ausinet Statex	Australia	Company	Stocks
Australian Bureau of Statistics (ABS)	Australia	Economics	

Alphabetical listing/page numbers

Name	Country	Subject	
Australian Financial Markets (ARATE)	International	Finance	Interest rates
Australian Stock Exchange Indices (ASE)	International	Stocks	
Austria Economic Outlook (OEKON)	Austria	Economics	
Balance of Payments	International	Economics	
Banque de Donnees Locales Macroeconomique	France	Economics	
Base de Datos Estadisticos Municipales	Spain	Economics	
Base de Donnees des Obligations Francaises	France	Bonds	
BBC Summary of World Broadcasts	International	News	Economics
BD-INE	Spain	Economics	
BDI-German Industry	Germany	Company	
Biblio Data	Germany	Books	
Bibliographic for Public Management and Admin.	Germany	General management	
BIIPAM-CTIF	Europe	Material science	
Biomass	International	Technology	Energy
BIS Infomat	International	Market and industry news	News
Blaise-Line	International	Books	
BLISS	Germany	General management	
BNF Metals	International	Material science	Metals
BOAMP	France	Projects	
BODACC	France	Mergers	Disposals
Bond Buyer (The)	USA	Financial services	Bonds
Books in Print	USA	Books	
Bottin des Enterprises	France	Company	
BREV	Belgium	Patents	
Bridge Information Service	USA	Stocks	Commodities
British Books in Print	International	Books	
British Trade Marks	UK	Trademark	
BRIX	International	Construction	
Brokersguide	Europe	EEC	User aids
Burda-MarketingInfo-System	Germany	Advertising	
Business	International	Projects	Projects
Business Dateline	USA	News	Company directory
Business Opportunities-Sell	International	Projects	
Business Periodicals Index	International	Accountancy	Market and industry news
Business Review Weekly	Australia	Market and industry news	Accountancy
Business Science Experts	Germany	Who's who	
Business Software Database	USA	IT	
Business Trend Analysts	USA	Market reports	Consumer products
Business Week	USA	News	Market and industry news
BusinessWire	USA	Financial services	News
C&L Belmont Database	Europe	EEC	Law
CAB Abstracts	International	Agriculture	Environment
CAD/CAM	USA	IT	Electronics
Camerdata	Spain	Company	
Canadian Business and Current Affairs	International	News	Market and industry news

Alphabetical listing/page numbers

Name	Country	Subject	
Canadian Financial Database	International	Company	Finance
Canadian Periodical Index	Canada	News	
Canadian Petroleum Association Statistics (CPASTATS)	Canada	Energy	
Canadian Stock Options (CDNOPTIONS)	Canada	Options	
CANSIM	Canada	Economics	
CAPA	Belgium	Disposals	Law
CCFX	International	Foreign exchange	Interest rates
CCL-Train	Europe	EEC	User aids
Celex	Europe	EEC	Law
Cendata	USA	Economics	
Centrale des Portefeuilles	France	Company	
Centrally Planned Economies	Eastern Bloc	Economics	
CETIM	France	Technology	
CHEM-INTELL Trade and Production Statistics	International	Chemicals	
Chemical Abstracts		Chemistry	
Chemical Abstracts Source Index		Chemistry	
Chemical Age Project File	UK	Chemicals	
Chemical Business Newsbase	International	Chemicals	
Chemical Dictionary		Chemistry	
Chemical Economics Handbook	USA	Chemicals	Chemistry
Chemical Engineering Abstracts	International	Chemicals	
Chemical Exposure		Chemistry	
Chemical Industry Notes	International	Chemicals	
Chemical Plant Database-Plan	International	Chemicals	
Chemquest		Chemistry	
Chemzero		Chemistry	
CHINA-COOP	China	Projects	
Chinese Patent Abstracts	China	Patents	
Citibase Weekly	USA	Economics	
Citicorp Citibase US Economic Data	USA	Economics	
CJIND	France	Economics	
CJTRES	France	Company	Industry profiles
Claims	USA	Patents	Chemicals
Coffeeline	International	Food	
Commodities (Commodity)	International	Commodities	
Commodity News Services	International	Commodities	
Commodity Options (COMOPTIONS)	USA	Options	
Compact	USA	Futures	Options
Company Facts and Addresses	Germany	Company	
Compendex Plus	International	Electronics	Technology
Compustat	USA	Public company	Telecomms
Computer Database	USA	IT	Telecomms
Computerpat	USA	Patents	IT
Comtrend	International	Stocks	
Concursos Publicos	Spain	Conferences	
CONF	International	Conferences	IT

Alphabetical listing/page numbers

Alphabetical listing/page numbers

Name	Country	Subject	
Delphes	France	Company	
Der Betrieb	Germany	Law	Accountancy
Deutsche Bundesbank Data (Bundesbank)	Germany	Economics	
DHSS Data	UK	Public sector	Social science
Dialindex		User aids	
DIALOG Publications		User aids	
DIALOG Quotes and Trading	USA	Stocks	Options
Dianeguide	Europe	EEC	User aids
DIN (German Standards and Technical Rules)	Germany	Standards	
Direction of Trade Statistics	International	Economics	
Directorio de Bases de Datos	Spain	Databases	
Directorio de Empresas Industriales	Spain	Company	
Directory of American Research and Technology	USA	Who's who	Research
Disclosure	USA	Who's Who	Public company
Disclosure/Spectrum Ownership	USA	Public company	
Disposiciones Legales	Spain	Law	
Dissertation Abstracts Online	USA	Research	
DITR (Standards and Specifications)	Germany	Standards	
DMS Contract Awards	USA	Defence	
DMS Market Intelligence Reports	USA	Defence	
DOE Energy	USA	Energy	Environment
DRI – Cost Forecasting	International	Economics	
DRI Commodities	USA	Commodities	Futures
DRI Europe	Europe	Economics	
DRI-Facs	USA	Foreign exchange	Bonds
DRI-SEC	USA	Stocks	
Dun's Electronic Yellow Pages Construction	USA	Company directory	Construction
Dun's Electronic Yellow Pages Financial	USA	Company directory	Finance
Dun's Electronic Yellow Pages Manufacturers	USA	Company directory	
Dun's Electronic Yellow Pages Professionals	USA	Company directory	Finance
Dun's Electronic Yellow Pages Retailers	USA	Company directory	Retail
Dun's Electronic Yellow Pages Services	USA	Company directory	Finance
Dun's Electronic Yellow Pages Wholesalers	USA	Company directory	Retail
Dun's Market Identifiers	UK	Company	
Dundis	Europe	EEC	Information science
Dunsdata	International	Company	
Dunsprint (Online Service)	International	Company	
EABS	Europe	EEC	Technology
EAE	France	Company	
Earnings Guide	UK	Stocks	
Eastern Bloc Countries Economic Statistics	Eastern bloc	Economics	
ECDIN Databank		Chemistry	

Alphabetical listing/page numbers

Name	Country	Subject	
Eclatx	Europe	Patents	
ECOCAT	Spain	Economics	
Econ base: Timeseries & Forecasts	International	Economics	
Economics Abstracts International	International	Economics	
Economic Literature Index	International	Books	Economics
Economist (The)	International	Market and industry news	Economics
Economist Intelligence Unit	International	Market reports	Motor
EDF-DOC	France	Energy	
EDIT	International	Stocks	Market and industry News
EI Engineering Meetings	USA	Electronics	
Einkaufs-1x1	Germany	Company	
EIS Online	International	Projects	
EIU International Travel & Tourism Reports	International	Market reports	Tourism
EIU Travel & Tourism Analyst	International	Market reports	Tourism
Economist Intelligence Unit Retail Business	UK	Market reports	Retail
ELCOM	International	Electronics	
Electric Power Database	USA	Energy	Environment
Electric Power Industry Abstracts	International	Energy	Environment
Electronic Publishing Abstracts	UK	Information science	Publishing
EMIS	International	Material science	Electronics
Empresas	Spain	Company	
Encyclopedia of Associations	USA	Public sector	
ENDOC	Europe	EEC	Research
ENEL	Italy	Energy	Technology
Energie	Europe	Energy	
Energyline	USA	Energy	
ENREP	Europe	EEC	Research
ESPAN	Spain	Economics	
Esprit	International	Stocks	
Essor	France	Company	
Estacom	Spain	Economics	
Euristote	Europe	EEC	Research
Eurodicautom	Europe	EEC	Technology
Eurofacts	Europe	Economics	Industry profiles
Eurofile	Europe	Market reports	Consumer products
EUROLOC	Europe	EEC	Grants
Euromonitor	Europe	Market reports	Consumer products
European Automotive News Service	Europe	Motor	Market reports
European Kompass Online (EKOL)	Europe	Company	
Examiner	International	Stocks	Market and industry news
Exbond	International	Bonds	
Exchange	International	Company	Industry profiles
Executive Market Follower	USA	Stocks	
Experts in Law	Germany	Law	
Exshare	International	Stocks	Foreign exchange
Exstat	UK	Company	
Facts on File	USA	News	

Alphabetical listing/page numbers

Name	Country	Subject	
Fairbase	International	Conferences	
Fali	Belgium	Economics	
Fastock 11	USA	Stocks	
FBR	Germany	Projects	
Federal and State Business Assistance	USA	Grants	
Federal Republic of Germany Statistical Data	Germany	Economics	
Federal Research in Progress	USA	Technology	Research
Ferias y Exposiciones	Spain	Conferences	
FIESTA	International	Technology	Telecomms
Finance for New Projects in the UK	UK	Grants	
Financial Post Canadian Corporate Database	Canada	Company	
Financial Times Business Reports	International	Market and industry	News
Financial Times Company Abstracts	International	Company	
Financial Times Newspaper Fulltext	UK	News	
Find/SVP	International	Market reports	Consumer products
Findata	Sweden	Company	Economics
FINDEX	International	Market directories	
FINF-Numeric	Germany	Company	
FINF-Text	Germany	Company	
FINIS: Financial Industry Information Service	USA	Financial services	
FINP	Finland	Books	Economics
Finstat	UK	Stocks	
Firmen-info-Bank	Germany	Company	
Firmexport (Telexport)	France	Projects	
Flow of Funds	USA	Economics	
FMARK	France	Trade mark	
Fonds Quetelet	France	Economics	
Foods Adlibra	USA	Food science	Food
Ford	USA	Stocks	
Foreign Exchange Database	International	Foreign exchange	
Foreign Trade and Economic Abstracts	International	Economics	
Foreign Traders Index	International	Projects	
Forest	International	Environment	Material science
Forkat	Germany	Research	Technology
Frost and Sullivan Market Research	International	Market reports	Market forecasts
Frost and Sullivan Political Risk	International	Economics	
FSTA	International	Food science	
FT Currency & Share Index	International	Foreign exchange	Stocks
Futures Database	International	Commodities	Futures
Futures-Soft	USA	Commodities	Futures
FXBASE	International	Foreign exchange	
FXPRO	International	Foreign exchange	
GATT	Denmark	Standards	
GELD (Money)	Germany	Grants	
General Electric Company (GECAST)	USA	Economics	
Genius Operator	Germany	Advertising	

Alphabetical listing/page numbers

Name	Country	Subject	
Gestion des Valeurs Mobilieres	France	Stocks	
Global Perspective (TM) Country Outlooks	International	Economics	
Global Report	International	Market and industry news	Finance
GLOBE	International	Economics	
Globe and Mail Online (The)	Canada	Market and industry news	Company
GPO Monthly Catalog	USA	Books	Public sector
GPO Publications Reference File	USA	Books	Public sector
HADOSS	Germany	Research	
Handelsblatt	Germany	Market and industry news	Company
Harvard Business Review	International	General management	
Heilbron		Chemistry	
Henley Centre for Forecasting	UK	Market reports	Economics
Hong Kong Stock Exchange (HKSTOCK)	Hong Kong	Stocks	
Hong Kong Stock Exchange Fastprice	Hong Kong	Stocks	
Hoppendstedt Austria	Austria	Company	
Hoppendstedt Netherlands	Netherlands	Company	
Hoppenstedt Directory of German Companies	Germany	Company	
IALINE	France	Agriculture	Food
Ibsedex	International	Construction	
ICC British Company Directory	UK	Company	Accountancy
ICC Canadian Corporations	Canada	Company	
ICC British Company Financial Datasheets	UK	Company	
ICC Full Text Company Accounts	UK	Company	Market reports
ICC Industrial Averages	UK	Company	Industry profiles
ICC International Business Research	UK	Market reports	Company
ICC Sharewatch	UK	Company	
ICC Stockbroker Research	UK	Company	Industry profiles
ICC Viewdata Service	UK	Company	Industry profiles
ICCA Australian Accounting Database	Australia	Accountancy	Financial services
ICONDA	International	Construction	
IDB Online	UK	IT	
IES-DC	Europe	EEC	IT
IMF International Financial Statistics	International	Economics	
INDES Service	International	Stocks	
Industrial Market Location	UK	Company	Industry profiles
Industrial Production (IP)	USA	Industry profiles	Economics
Industry and International Standards	USA	Standards	Electronics
Industry Data	USA	Industry profiles	Economics
Industry Data Sources	International	Market directories	
Industry Performance Monitor	USA	Industry profiles	Economics
Infocheck	UK	Company	Finance
Infodata	Germany	Information science	

Alphabetical listing/page numbers

Name	Country	Subject		
INFORBW	Germany	Research		
Information Service-Exchange	International	General management		
Informatitres	France	Stocks		
INIS	International	Energy	Technology	
Inpadoc	International	Patents	Technology	
INPI STE 3	France	Company		
INSPEC	International	Patents	Electronics	
Institute of International Finance	International	Economics		
Institutions for International Cooperation	International	Research		
Insurance Abstracts	USA	Financial services		
International Comparisons (INTCOMP)	International	Economics		
International Economic Indicators	International	Economics		
International Finance Alert	International	Foreign exchange	Financial services	
International Pharmaceutical Abstracts	International	Medical		
International Risk Data	International	Economics	News	
Intime – Manufacturing Automation	International	Technology	IT	
Investdata System	International	Foreign exchange	Stocks	
Investext	International	Company	Finance	
Investors Daily	International	Stocks	Stocks	
IR-SOFT	Europe	EEC	IT	
Irish Company Profiles	Ireland	Company		
IRRD	International	research	Environment	
ISCO	Italy	Economics		
ISET	Italy	Economics	Industry profiles	
ISIS	International	General management	Market and industry News	
ISIS	Austria	Economics		
ISIS Software Catalogue	Europe	IT		
ISMEC	International	Electronics		
Italian Legal Information System	Italy	Law		
Janssen	France	Chemistry	Chemicals	
Japan Economic Newswire Plus	Japan	Economics	News	
Japan Technology	Japan	Technology		
Japanese Fastprice	Japan	Stocks		
JAPIO	Japan	Patents		
JICST	Japan	Technology		
Jordans Business Surveys	UK	Market reports	Industry profiles	
Jordans Direct	UK	Company		
JordanWatch	UK	Company	Finance	
Key British Enterprises	UK	Company		
Keynote Industry Surveys	UK	Market reports	Industry profiles	
KKF	International	Chemistry	Chemicals	
Kompass Online	UK	Company	Who's who	
Kompass Online Scandinavia	Sweden	Company		
Labor	USA	Economics	Industry profiles	
Labordoc	International	Economics		
Laborinfo	International	Economics		
LC Marc	International	Books		
Le Monde	France	News	Company	

Alphabetical listing/page numbers

Name	Country	Subject	
Leading Edge Reports	USA	Market reports	IT
Les Administrateurs	France	Who's who	
Lexis	Europe	Law	
Liens Financiers	France	Company	
LISA	International	Information science	
List Stat	Scandinavia	Economics	
Luxembourg Stock Exchange	Luxembourg	Stocks	
M+a Messe Kalender	International	Conferences	
Magazine ASAP	USA	Market and industry news	
Magazine Index	USA	Market and industry news	
Management and Marketing Abstracts	International	General management	Market and industry news
Management Contents	USA	General management	Accountancy
Management Experten-Nachweis	Europe	Who's who	
Market Directions	Europe	Market reports	Consumer products
Market Facts Inc	USA	Market reports	Financial services
Marketing Surveys Index	International	Market directories	
Marketing Week	UK	Market and industry	News
Marketpulse	International	Stocks	
Marketscan	USA	Stocks	
Marquis Who's Who	USA	Who's Who	
Materials Business	International	Metals	Environment
McCarthy Online Company Fact Sheets	International	Company	
McCarthy Online Press Cutting Service	UK	Company	
McGraw-Hill Publications Online	USA	Market and industry	News
Meal Quarterly Digest	UK	Advertising	Consumer products
Media General Plus	USA	Public Company	Stocks
Medrep	Europe	EEC	Medical
Meeting	Germany	Conferences	
Menu-The International Software Database	USA	IT	
Mercatis	France	Market reports	Retail
Mergers	USA	Mergers	
Mergers and Acquisitions	UK	Mergers	
MERL-ECO	France	Economics	Industry profiles
Merlin-Tech	International	Electronics	Technology
Metadex	International	Metals	Material science
Metal and Mineral Prices (MINPRI)	International	Commodities	Futures
Metals Week	International	Commodities	
Microcomputer Index	USA	IT	
Microcomputer Software and Hardware Guide	USA	IT	
Microexstat	UK	Company	Industry profiles
Microsearch	USA	IT	
Middle Tac	International	Bonds	
Mideast	Middle East	Economics	News
Mintel Reports	UK	Market reports	
MMS Asia/Pacific Market Analysis	Asia	Commodities	Economics

Alphabetical listing/page numbers

Name	Country	Subject	
MMS Currency Market Analysis	International	Foreign exchange	
MMS Debt Market Analysis	International	Economics	Bonds
MMS Equity Market Analysis	USA	Stocks	Futures
Money Market Rates (MRATE)	International	Foreign exchange	Interest rates
Moody's Corporate News - International	International	Company	Finance
Moody's Corporate News - US	USA	Public company	Finance
Moody's Corporate Profiles	USA	Public company	
MSI Market Reports	UK	Market reports	
Multi Media Service	USA	Advertising	Consumer products
Munifacts Plus	USA	Bonds	
Munzinger Landerarchiv	International	Economics	
NAARS	USA	Public company	Accountancy
NAME	Belgium	Law	
National Computer Index	UK	IT	
National Development Plans	International	Economics	
National Newspaper Index	USA	News	
NCOM	Scandinavia	Advertising	
Needs-TS	Japan	Economics	Stocks
Newsearch	USA	News	
Newsline	Europe	News	
NEXIS	International	Market and industry news	
Nielsen Market Information	UK	Market reports	Consumer products
Nikkei Telecomm	Japan	Economics	Company
NLEX	Netherlands	Law	
NODO	Italy	Standards	
Nomura Research Institute (NRI/E)	Japan	Economics	
Nordic Energy Index	Scandinavia	Energy	Technology
NORM	Belgium	Standards	
North American Stock Market (NASTOCK)	USA	Stocks	
NTIS	USA	Research	Public sector
Nuclear Science Abstracts	USA	Energy	Technology
OCLC Easi-Reference	International	Books	
OECD Data	International	Economics	
OECD Main Economic Indicators	International	Economics	
Oferes	Spain	Company	Projects
Oil and Gas Journal Energy Database	USA	Energy	
Oil and Gas Journal Energy Forecasts	International	Energy	
Online Chronicle	USA	Information science	Databases
ORBI	International	Law	
Oslo Bors	Norway	Stocks	
OTISLINE	International	IT	Technology
Over the Counter Information	UK	Stocks	Company
P/E News	International	Energy	
PABLI	Europe	EEC	Projects
Packaged Facts	USA	Market reports	Consumer products

Alphabetical listing/page numbers

Name	Country	Subject	
Packaging Science and Technology Abstracts	International	Material science	Technology
PAIS International	International	Public sector	Social science
Paperchem	USA	Material science	Technology
PASCAL	International	Technology	Electronics
PATDPA	Germany	Patents	
PATOS PCT Applications	International	Patents	
Patolis	Japan	Patents	
PATOS European Patents	Europe	Patents	
PATOS German Patent Applicats.	Germany	Patents	
PATOS German Patents	Germany	Patents	
Pestdoc	International	Chemistry	Agriculture
Pharmaceutical News Index	International	Medical	
Polis (UK)	UK	Public sector	EEC
Prestel Citiservice	International	Stocks	
Prezzi	Italy	Economics	
Pricedata	International	Foreign exchange	Commodities
Priceplus	UK	Stocks	Bonds
Producer Price Indexes	USA	Economics	
PROGNO	Germany	Economics	News
PTS Aerospace/Defense Markets & Technology	USA	Defence	
PTS Annual Reports Abstracts	USA	Public company	
PTS F & S Indexes	International	Company	Mergers
PTS International Forecasts	International	Economics	Industry profiles
PTS Marketing & Advertising Reference Service	USA	Advertising	Consumer products
PTS New Product Announcements	USA	IT	Company
PTS Promt	International	Company	Industry profiles
PTS US Forecasts	USA	Economics	Industry profiles
PTS US Time Series	USA	Economics	Industry profiles
Publishers, Distributors & Wholesalers	USA	Publishing	
Quarterly Financial Report	USA	Economics	Company
Qui Decide en France	France	Company	Who's who
Quotron 800	International	Stocks	Industry profiles
Quotron Symbol Guide	USA	Stocks	Bonds
Rapra Abstracts	International	Rubber	
Rapra Trade Names	International	Rubber	
Refernce Book of Corporate Management	USA	Who's who	
Registro de Establecimientos Industriales	Spain	Company	
REMARC	International	Books	
Report on Business Corporate Database	Canada	Company	
Research Index	International	News	Market and industry news
Reserve Bank of Australia Bulletin (RBA)	Australia	Economics	
Retribuzioni Operai e Apprendisti	Italy	Economics	
Reuter Monitor	International	Stocks	Futures
Reuters	International	News	
Reuter's Country Reports	International	Economics	
Ringdoc	International	Chemistry	Medical

Alphabetical listing/page numbers

Name	Country	Subject	
Robomatix	USA	IT	Technology
Ruralnet	Europe	EEC	Environment
Saatchi and Saatchi Compton Media	International	Advertising	
SAE Global Mobility	International	Transport	Motor
SANI	Italy	Company	
SANP	Italy	Company	Finance
SCAN	International	Stocks	
Scan-a-Bid-Scan	International	Projects	
SCANP	Scandinavia	General management	Economics
SCIMP	Europe	General management	
SDIM1	Europe	Material science	
SDIM2	Europe	Material science	
SDOE	Italy	Company	
SEC 1 National Accounts	Europe	Economics	EEC
Securities Industry	USA	Financial services	Stocks
Securities Law Advance	USA	Law	Financial services
Sesame	Europe	EEC	Energy
Shops	UK	Retail	Market reports
Sibil	Italy	Company	
SIGLE	Europe	Books	
Sirene	France	Company	
Sistema de Informacion Bursatil	Spain	Stocks	Finance
Sistema de Informacion de Emprasarial	Spain	Company	
Social Scisearch	International	Public sector	Social science
Societe Generale de Banque	Belgium	Economics	Company
Soliditet Online Service (SOS)	Denmark	Company	
Spacesoft	USA	IT	Transport
Spearhead	Europe	EEC	Law
Sphinx	France	Economics	
SSIE Current Research	USA	Research	Technology
Standard & Poor's (S&P) Marketscope	USA	Public company	Stocks
Standard & Poor's Corporate Descriptions	USA	Public company	
Standard & Poor's News	USA	Public company	Finance
Standard & Poor's Register - Biographical	USA	Who's who	
Standard & Poor's Register Corporate	USA	Company directory	
Standard Industrial Classification	UK	User aids	
Standards and Specifications	USA	Standards	Transport
Standards Search	USA	Standards	Transport
Stars	UK	Grants	EEC
Statistiche del Commercio Estero dell' Italia	Italy	Economics	
Statistiche Economiche	Italy	Economics	
Statistics Sweden	Sweden	Economics	
Stock Exchange of Singapore (SINGSTOCK)	Singapore	Stocks	
Stor-Tele	Sweden	Company	
Superstat	Italy	Economics	
Supertech	International	Technology	Telecomms

Alphabetical listing/page numbers

Name	Country	Subject	
Survey of United States Forecasts	USA	Economics	
Sveriges Handelskalander	Sweden	Company	
SYCE	Spain	Company	
Sydney Stock Exchange STATEX Service (STATEX)	Australia	Stocks	Company
TA	Germany	Technology	Projects
Tax Notes Today	USA	Accountancy	
TED	Europe	EEC	Projects
Tele Inform	France	Company	
Teleborsen	Denmark	Market and industry news	Company
Telecom	Denmark	Company	Stocks
Telecommunications	International	Telecomms	
Teledata	International	Stocks	
Teledoc	France	Telecomms	
Telefirm	France	Company	
Telerate	UK	Commodities	Bonds
TEND	France	Economics	
Textile Technology Digest	International	Technology	Textiles
Textile-Wirtschaft	Germany	Textiles	
Textline	International	Company	News
THES	Finland	Research	
Thesauri	Europe	EEC	User aids
Thomas New Industrial Products	USA	Projects	New products
Thomas Regional Industrial Suppliers	USA	Company directory	Trade opportunities
Thomas Register Online	USA	Company directory	
Tidningsdatabasen	Sweden	News	Market and industry news
Times Newspapers (The)	UK	News	Market and industry news
Titus	Europe	Technology	Textiles
TMINT	International	Trademark	
TOPIC	International	Stocks	Options
Toronto Stock Exchange 300 Index & Stock Stat	Canada	Stocks	
Touristic-Information Facts and Abstracts	International	Tourism	
Trade and Industry asap	USA	Market and industry	News
Trade and Industry Index	USA	Market and industry	News
Trade Statistics	International	Economics	Trade opportunities
Transdoc	International	Transport	Energy
Transin	International	Technology	New products
Trinet Company Database	USA	Company directory	
Trinet Establishment Database	USA	Company directory	
TRIS	USA	Transport	Environment
UK Company Profile	UK	Company	
Ulrich's Periodicals	International	Books	
United Nations Commodity Trade Statistics	International	Commodities	Economics
United Nations Industrial Statistics	International	Economics	Industry profiles

Alphabetical listing/page numbers

Name	Country	Subject	
United Nations National Accounts	International	Economics	
United Nations Population Statistics	International	Economics	
United States Economic Statistics	USA	Economics	
United States National Accounts	USA	Economics	
United States Stock Market (USSTOCK)	USA	Stocks	
United States Stock Options (USOPTIONS)	USA	Options	
Unlisted Market Guide (The)	USA	Stocks	OTC
UPI News	USA	News	
US Class	USA	Patents	
US Patents	USA	Patents	
US Trademarks	USA	Trademark	
USA Monitor	USA	Market reports	Consumer products
Vademecum	Germany	Who's Who	Research
Valordata	International	Stocks	
Valport	USA	Stocks	
Valscop-Valeurs	France	Stocks	
Value Line Data Base-11	USA	Public company	Financial services
VDIN	Germany	News	Market and industry news
Verband der Vereine Creditreform eV	Germany	Company	Finance
Videcom	International	Stocks	Commodities
VITIS-VEA	International	Food science	Technology
Volkswagenwerk	Germany	Transport	Motor
VTB	International	Chemicals	
Washington Post Electronic Edition	USA	News	
Washington Presstext	USA	News	Public sector
Water Resources Abstracts	USA	Water	Environment
Weldasearch	International	Metals	
Wharton Econometric World Forecasts	International	Economics	
Who Inform	Germany	Whos Who	General management
Who Makes Machinery	Germany	Company	Electronics
Who Owns Whom	International	Company	
Who Supplies What	Germany	Company	
Wirtschaftswoche	Germany	News	Market and industry news
World Affairs Report	USSR	News	
World Aluminium Abstracts	International	Metals	Technology
World Bank Debt Tables (WDEBT)	International	Economics	
World Bank International Business Opps Service	International	Projects	
World Patents Index	International	Patents	
World Textiles	International	Textiles	
Worldscope	International	Company	Accountancy
WTI	International	Technology	Research
ZDE	Germany	Electronics	
ZVEI Electro-Buying Guide	Germany	Company	Electronics

Appendix 4 International Telephone Codes and Time Difference

Country	Intl Country Code	Time Difference in hours from GMT
Afghanistan	00*	+4½
Albania	00*	+1
Algeria	213	+1
Andorra	33 628	+1
Angola	244	+1
Anguilla	1 809 497	−4
Antarctica Aust. Territory	00*	+4/10½
Antigua	1 809 46	−4
Antilles (Netherlands)	599	−4
Argentina	54	−3
Aruba	297 8	−4
Ascension Islands	247	0
Australia	61	+8-10
Austria	43	+1
Azores	351	0
Bahamas	1 809	−5
Bahrain	973	+3
Bangladesh	880	+6
Barbados	1 809	−4
Belgium	32	+1
Belize	501	−6
Benin	229	+1
Bequia	00*	−4
Bermuda	1 809 29	−4
Bhutan	00*	+5½
Bolivia	591	−4
Bophuthatswana (South Africa)	27	+2
Botswana	267	+2
Brazil	55	−2 & 3
Brunei	673	+8
Bulgaria	359	+2
Burkina Faso	226 0	
Burma	95	+6½
Burundi	00*	+2
Cameroon	237	+1
Canada	1	−3-9
Canary Islands	34	0
Cape Verde Islands	00*	−2
Cayman Islands	1 809 94	−5
Central African Republic	00*	+1
Chad	00*	+1
Chile	56	−4
China, People's Republic of	86	+8
Christmas Island	00*	+7
Cocos Islands	00*	+6
Colombia	57	−5
Comoro Islands	00*	+3
Congo	00*	+1
Cook Islands (Hervy)	682	−10

Country	Intl Country Code	Time Difference in hours from GMT
Costa Rica	506	−6
Cote d'Ivoire	225	0
Cuba	53	−5
Cyprus	357	+2
Czechoslovakia	42	+1
Denmark	45	+1
Djibouti	253	+3
Dominica	1 809 449	−4
Dominican Republic	1 809	−4
Ecuador	593	−5
Egypt	20	+2
El Salvador	503	−6
Equatorial Guinea	00*	0
Ethiopia	251	+3
Falkland Islands	00*	−3
Faroe Islands	298	0
Fiji	679	+12
Finland	358	+2
France	33	+1
French Guiana	594	−4
French Polynesia (Tahiti)	689	−10
Gabon	241	+1
Gambia	220	0
Germany, East	37	+1
Germany, West	49	+1
Ghana	233	0
Gibraltar	350	+1
Greece	30	+2
Greenland	299	−3
Grenada	1 809 444	−4
Guadaloupe	590	−4
Guam	671	+10
Guatemala	502	−6
Guinea	00*	0
Guinea-Bissau	00*	0
Guyana	592	−3
Haiti	509	−5
Honduras	504	−6
Hong Kong	852	+8
Hungary	36	+1
Iceland	354	0
India	91	+5½
Indonesia	62	+7-9
Iran	98	+3½
Iraq	964	+3
Ireland, Republic of	0001 (Dublin City)	0
Ireland, Republic of	353 (Rest of Republic)	0
Ireland, Northern	44	0
Israel	972	+2
Italy	39	+1
Ivory Coast	225	0
Jamaica	1 809	−5
Japan	81	+9
Jordan	962	+2
Kampuchea	00*	+7
Kenya	254	+3
Kiribati	00*	+12
Korea, North	00*	+9
Korea, South	82	+9

Country	Intl Country Code	Time Difference in hours from GMT
Kuwait	965	+3
Laos	00*	+7
Lebanon	961	+2
Lesotho	266	+2
Liberia	231	0
Libya	218	+2
Liechtenstein	41 75	+1
Luxembourg	352	+1
Macau	853	+8
Madagascar	261	+3
Madeira	351 91	0
Malawi	265	+2
Malaysia	60	+8
Maldive Islands	960	+5
Mali	00*	0
Malta	356	+1
Marshall Islands	00*	+12
Martinique	596	−4
Mauritania	00*	0
Mauritius	230	+4
Mexico	52	−6
Micronesia	00*	+9-12
Midway Island	00*	−11
Monaco	33 93	+1
Mongolia	00*	+7
Montserrat	1 809 491	−4
Morocco	212	0
Mozambique	258	+2
Namibia	264	+2
Nauru Islands	674	+12
Nepal	977	+5½
Netherlands	31	+1
Netherlands Antilles	599	−4
New Caledonia	687	+11
New Zealand	64	+12
Nicaragua	505	−6
Niger	227	0
Nigeria	234	+1
Niue Island	00*	−11
Norfolk Island	672 3	+11½
Norway	47	+1
Oman	968	+4
Pakistan	92	+5
Palau	00*	+9-11
Panama	507	−5
Papua New Guinea	675	+10
Paraguay	595	−3
Peru	51	−5
Philippines	63	+8
Pitcairn Island	00*	−8½
Poland	48	+1
Portugal	351	0
Puerto Rico	1 809	−4
Qatar	974	+3
Reunion	262	+4
Rodriguez Island	00*	+4
Romania	40	+2
Rwanda	00*	+2
Saipan (North Mariana Islands)	00*	+10

Country	Intl Country Code	Time Difference in hours from GMT
Samoa (US)	684	−11
Samoa (Western)	685	−11
San Marino	39 541	+1
Sao Tome & Principe Islands	00*	0
Saudi Arabia	966	+3
Senegal	221	0
Seychelles	248	+4
Sierra Leone	232	0
Singapore	65	+8
Solomon Islands	677	+11
Somalia	252	+3
South Africa	27	+2
Spain	34	+1
Sri Lanka	94	+5½
St Helena	00*	0
St Kitts & Nevis	1 809 465	−4
St Lucia	1 809 45	−4
St Pierre & Miquelon	508	−3
St Vincent & the Grenadines	1 809 45	−4
Sudan	249	+2
Surinam	597	−3
Swaziland	268	+2
Sweden	46	+1
Switzerland	41	+1
Syria	963	+2
Tahiti (French Polynesia)	689	−10
Taiwan	886	+8
Tanzania	255	+3
Thailand	66	+7
Togo	228	0
Tonga	676	+13
Transkei (South Africa)	27	+2
Trinidad & Tobago	1 809	−4
Tristan da Cunha	00*	0
Tunisia	216	+1
Turkey	90	+2
Turks & Caicos Islands	1 809 946	−5
Tuvalu	00*	+12
Uganda	256	+3
United Arab Emirates**	971	+4
United Kingdom	44	0
Uruguay	598	−3
USA	1	−5-11
USSR	7	+3-12
Vanuatu	678	+11
Vatican City	39 66982	+1
Venezuela	58	−4
Vietnam	00*	+7
Virgin Islands (British)	1 809 49	−4
Virgin Islands (US)	1 809	−4
Wake Island	00*	+12
Yemen Arab Republic, North	967	+3
Yemen, South	00*	+3
Yugoslavia	38	+1
Zaire	243	+1
Zambia	260	+2
Zimbabwe	263	+2

* 00 indicates international operator service only
** The United Arab Emirates is composed of seven Emirates: Abu Dhabi, Ajman, Dubai, Fujeirah, Ras al Khaimah, Sharjah and Umm al Qaiwain.